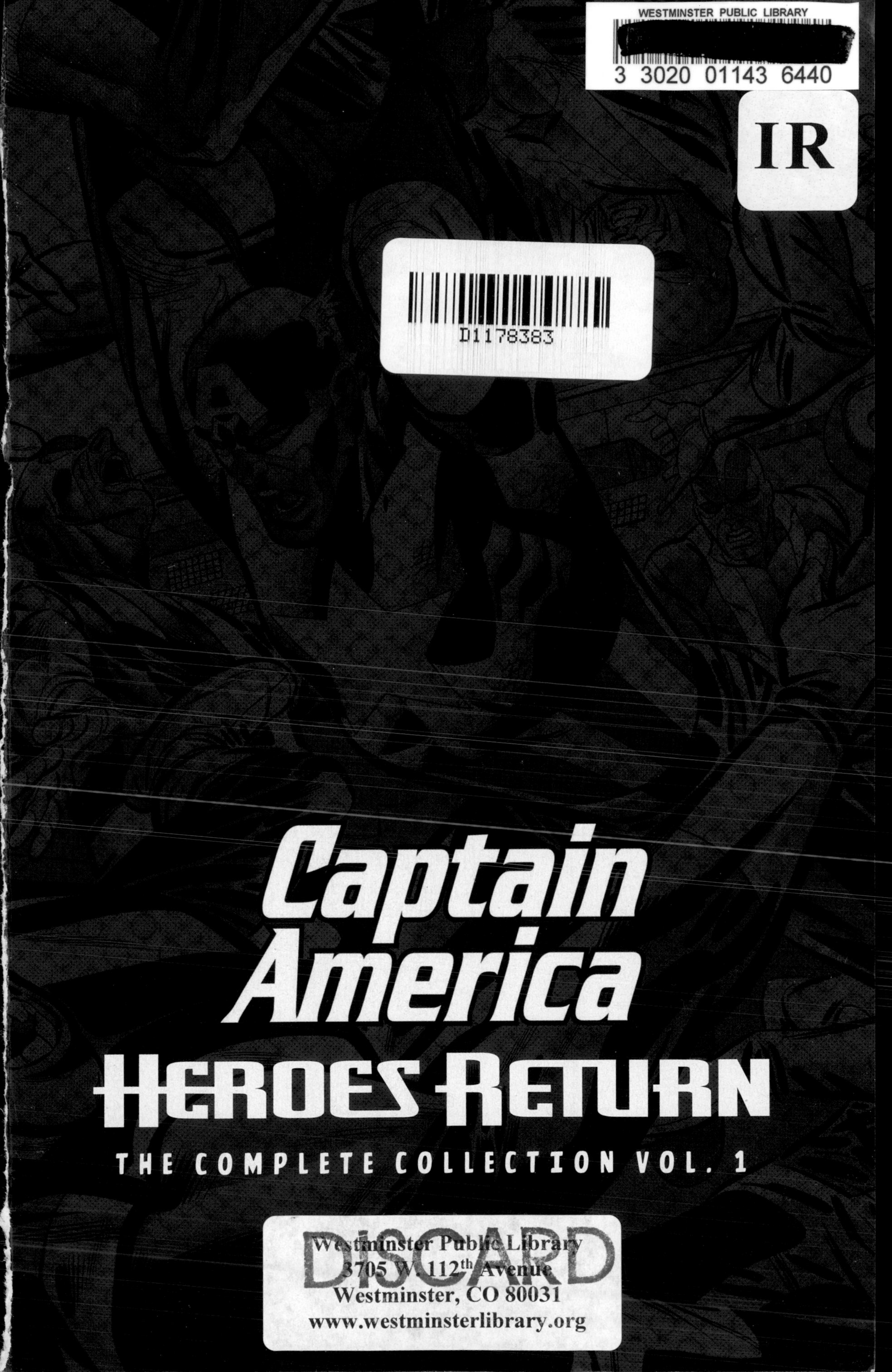

Captain America
Heroes Return

THE COMPLETE COLLECTION VOL. 1

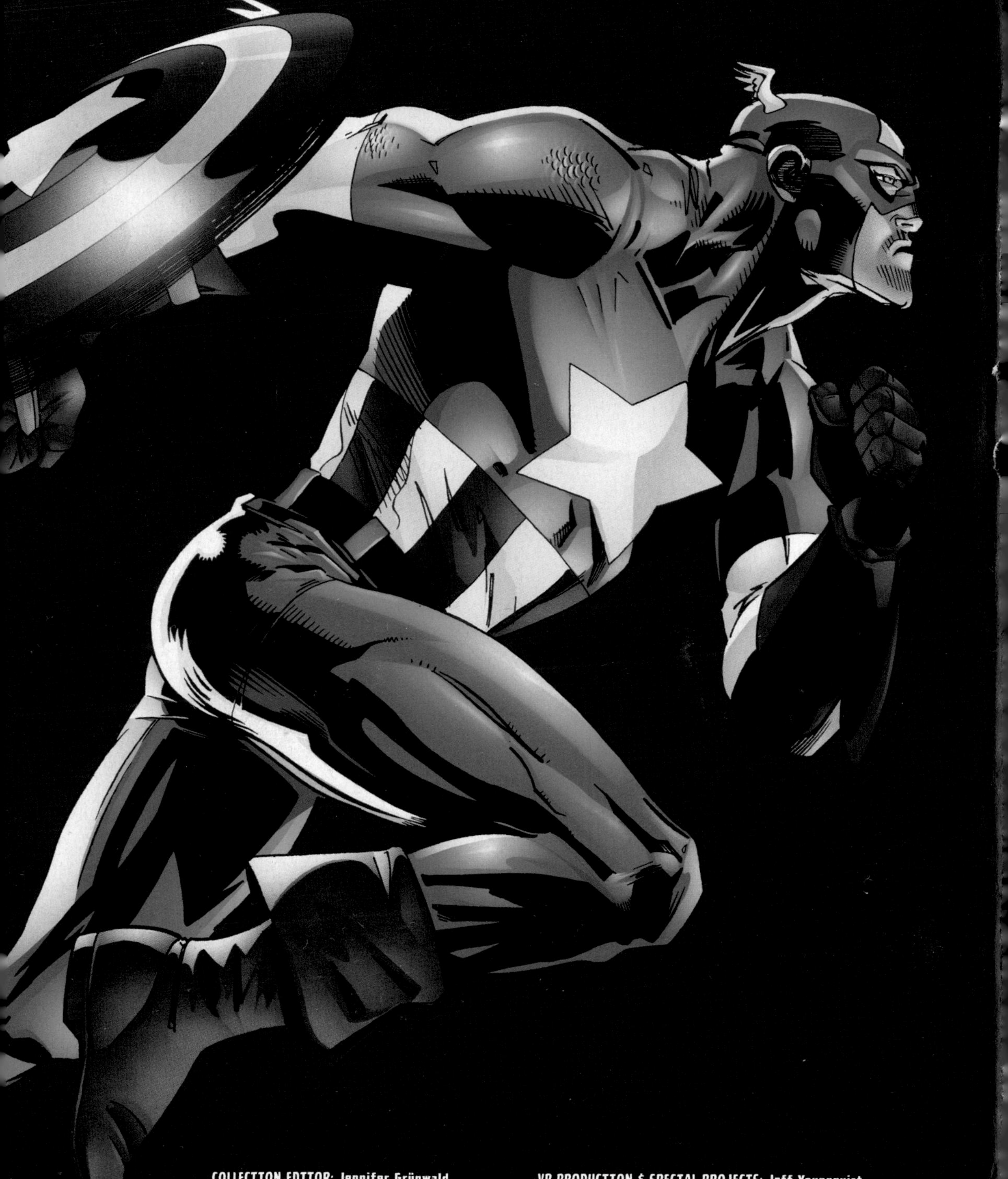

COLLECTION EDITOR: Jennifer Grünwald
ASSISTANT EDITOR: Daniel Kirchhoffer
ASSISTANT MANAGING EDITOR: Maia Loy
ASSISTANT MANAGING EDITOR: Lisa Montalbano
ASSOCIATE MANAGER, DIGITAL ASSETS: Joe Hochstein
VP PRODUCTION & SPECIAL PROJECTS: Jeff Youngquist
PRODUCTION: Ryan Devall & Joe Frontirre
BOOK DESIGNER: Salena Mahina & Adam Del Re
SVP PRINT, SALES & MARKETING: David Gabriel
EDITOR IN CHIEF: C.B. Cebulski

CAPTAIN AMERICA: HEROES RETURN — THE COMPLETE COLLECTION VOL. 1. Contains material originally published in magazine form as CAPTAIN AMERICA (1998) #1-12, IRON MAN/CAPTAIN AMERICA ANNUAL '98 and CAPTAIN AMERICA/CITIZEN V ANNUAL '98. First printing 2020. ISBN 978-1-302-92324-2. Published by MARVEL WORLDWIDE, INC., a subsidiary of MARVEL ENTERTAINMENT, LLC. OFFICE OF PUBLICATION: 1290 Avenue of the Americas, New York, NY 10104. **Printed in the U.S.A.** KEVIN FEIGE, Chief Creative Officer; DAN BUCKLEY, President, Marvel Entertainment; JOE QUESADA, EVP & Creative Director; DAVID BOGART, Associate Publisher & SVP of Talent Affairs; TOM BREVOORT, VP, Executive Editor; NICK LOWE, Executive Editor, VP of Content, Digital Publishing; DAVID GABRIEL, VP of Print & Digital Publishing; JEFF YOUNGQUIST, VP of Production & Special Projects; ALEX MORALES, Director of Publishing Operations; DAN EDINGTON, Managing Editor; RICKEY PURDIN, Director of Talent Relations; JENNIFER GRÜNWALD, Senior Editor, Special Projects; SUSAN CRESPI, Production Manager; STAN LEE, Chairman Emeritus. For information regarding advertising in Marvel Comics or on Marvel.com, please contact Vit DeBellis, Custom Solutions & Integrated Advertising Manager, at vdebellis@marvel.com. For Marvel subscription inquiries, please call 888-511-5480. **Manufactured between 12/25/2020 and 1/26/2021 by FRY COMMUNICATIONS, MECHANICSBURG, PA, USA.**

10 9 8 7 6 5 4 3 2 1

Captain America
HEROES RETURN
THE COMPLETE COLLECTION VOL. 1

WRITERS
Mark Waid & Kurt Busiek with Roger Stern,
Karl Kesel & Barbara Kesel

PENCILERS
Ron Garney, Dale Eaglesham, Andy Kubert,
Patch Zircher & Mark Bagley

INKERS
Bob Wiacek, Scott Koblish, Jesse Delperdang &
Randy Emberlin with John Beatty, Andy Smith,
Greg Adams & Scott Hanna

COLORISTS
Joe Rosas, Jason Wright, Chris Sotomayor,
Tom Smith & Digital Chameleon

LETTERERS
John Costanza, Todd Klein and Richard Starkings &
Comicraft's Emerson Miranda & co.

ASSISTANT EDITORS
Paul Tutrone & Gregg Schigiel

EDITORS
Matt Idelson & Tom Brevoort

FRONT COVER ARTISTS
Ron Garney & Bob Wiacek

BACK COVER ARTISTS
Mark Bagley, Karl Kesel and Tanya Horie & Richard Horie

Captain America created by Joe Simon & Jack Kirby

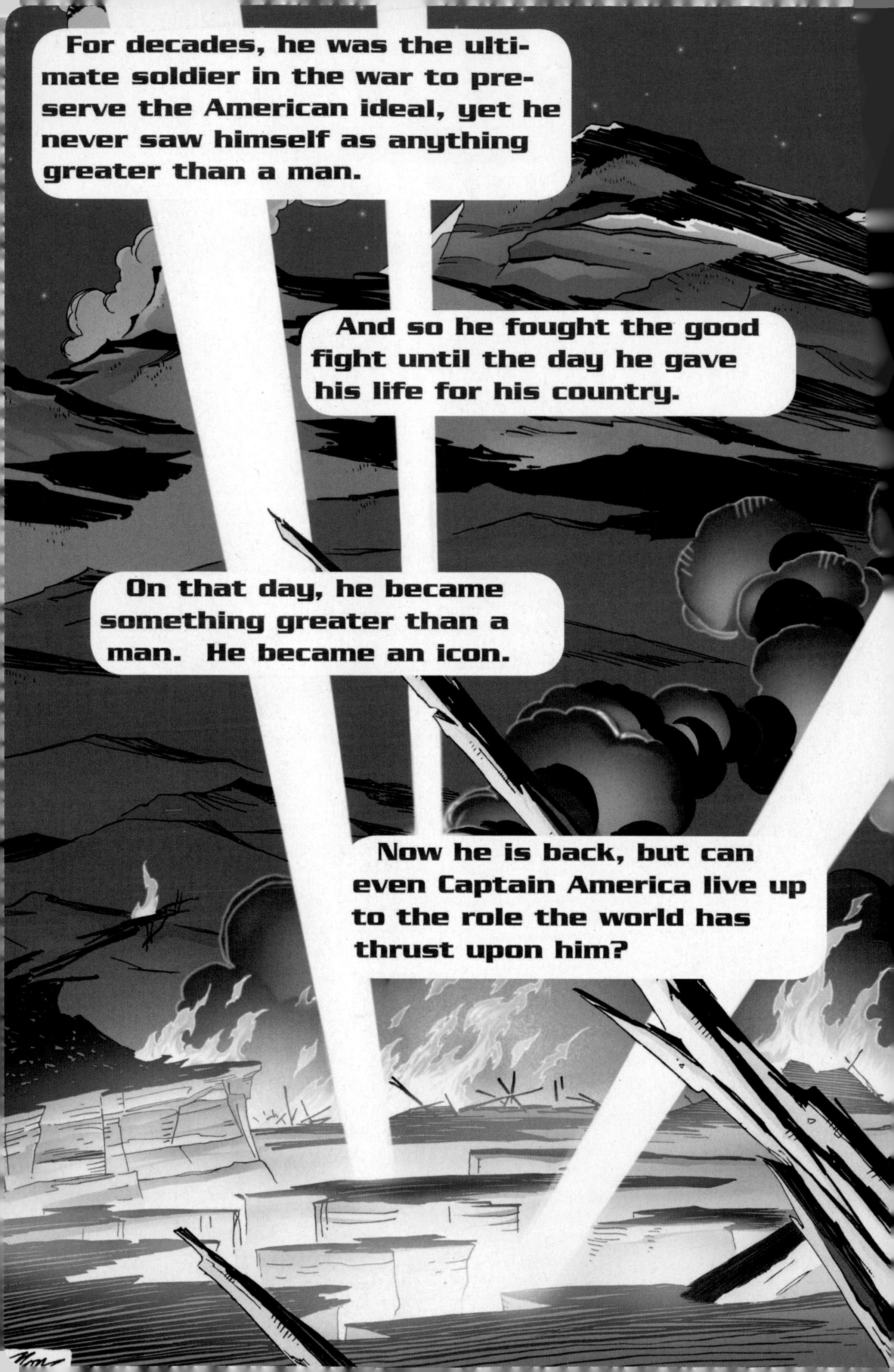
For decades, he was the ultimate soldier in the war to preserve the American ideal, yet he never saw himself as anything greater than a man.
And so he fought the good fight until the day he gave his life for his country.
On that day, he became something greater than a man. He became an icon.
Now he is back, but can even Captain America live up to the role the world has thrust upon him?

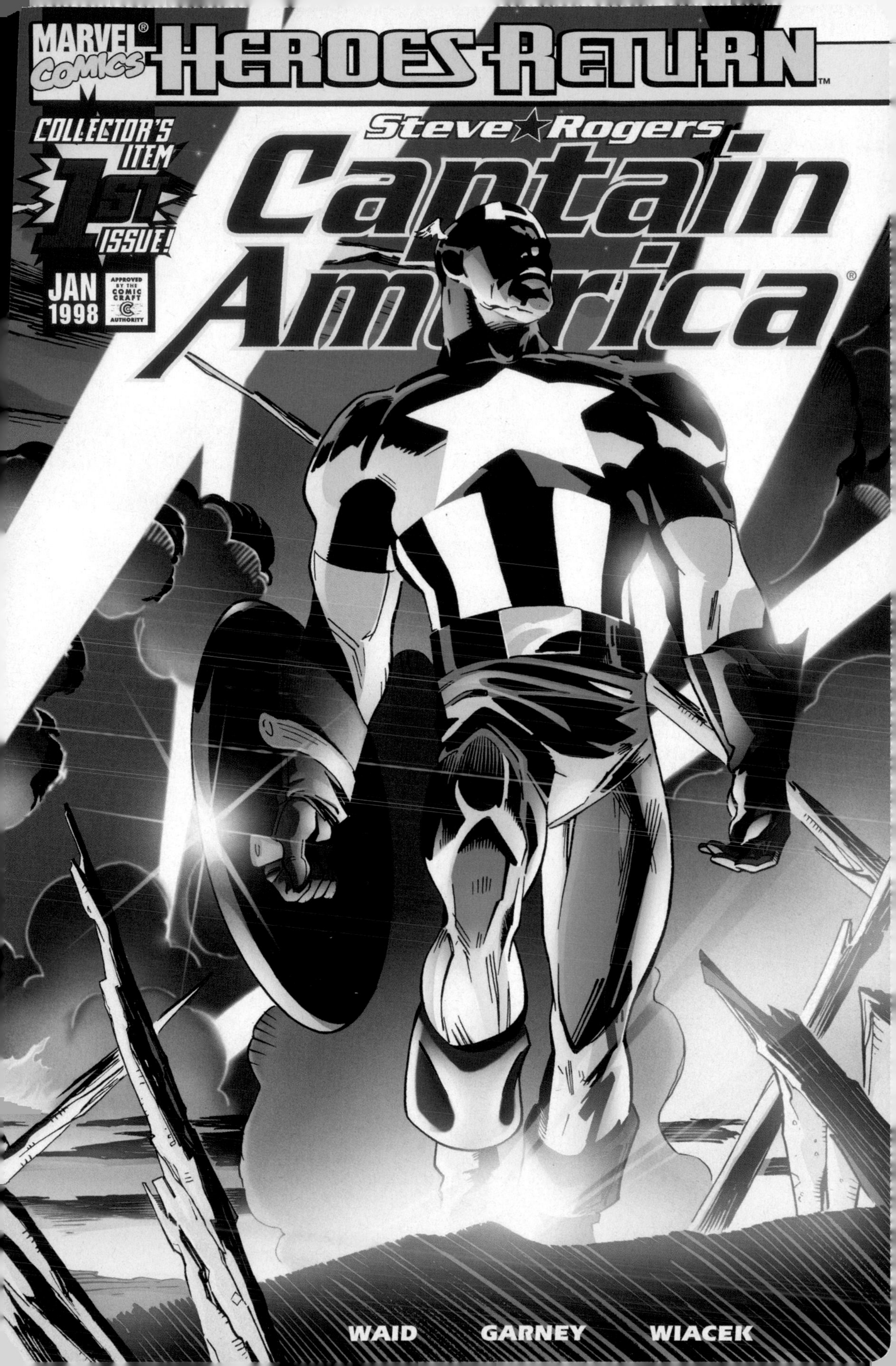
MARVEL® COMICS
HEROES RETURN™
COLLECTOR'S ITEM 1ST ISSUE!
JAN 1998
APPROVED BY THE COMICS CODE AUTHORITY
Steve Rogers
Captain America®
WAID GARNEY WIACEK

STAN LEE Presents

THE RETURN OF

Steve ★ *Rogers*

Captain America

MARK WAID	RON GARNEY	BOB WIACEK
writer	penciler	inker
JOE ROSAS	DIGITAL CHAMELEON	
colorist	separations	BOB HARRAS
JOHN COSTANZA	MATT IDELSON	editor in chief
letterer	editor	

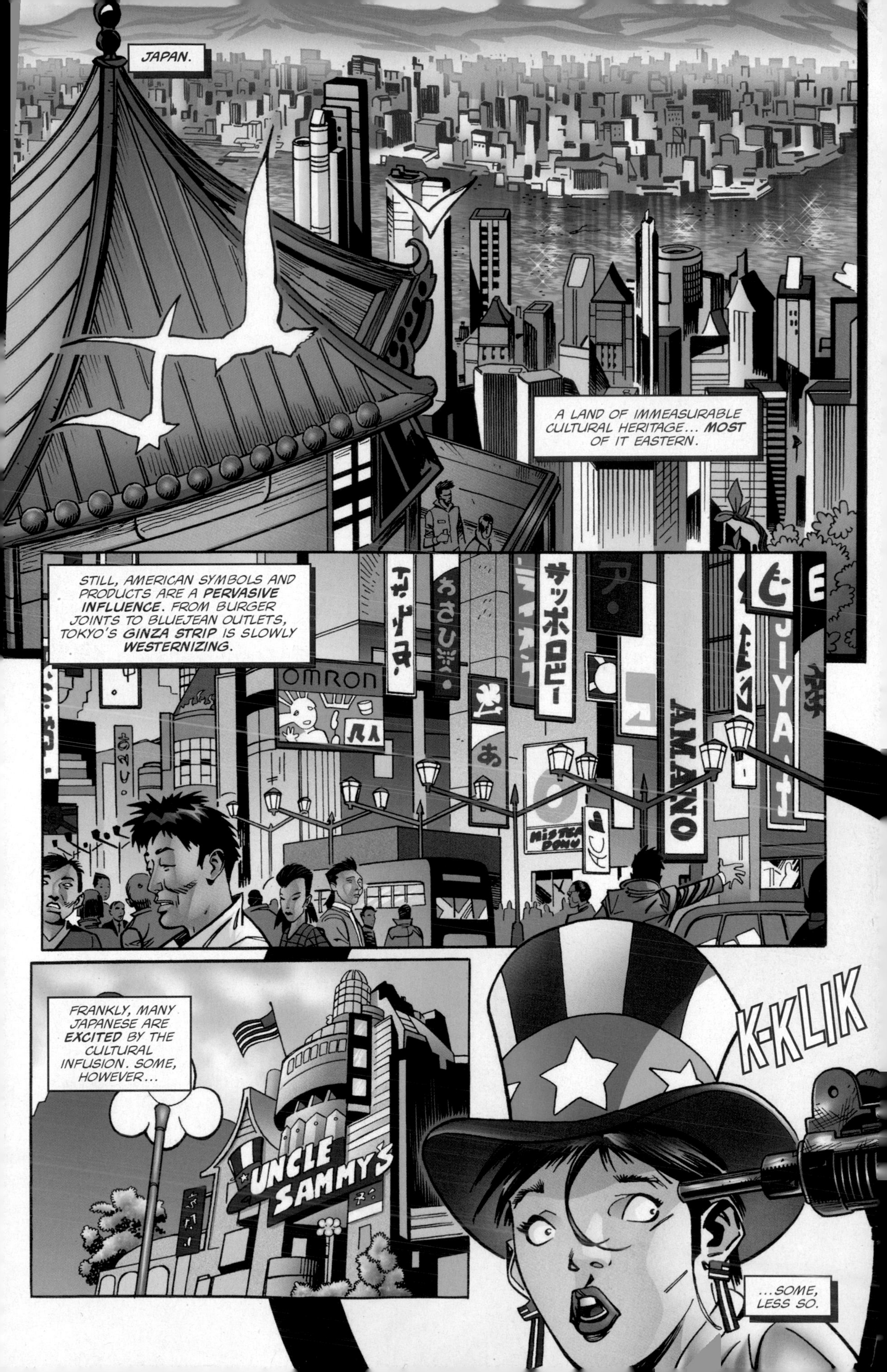
JAPAN.
A LAND OF IMMEASURABLE CULTURAL HERITAGE... MOST OF IT EASTERN.
STILL, AMERICAN SYMBOLS AND PRODUCTS ARE A PERVASIVE INFLUENCE. FROM BURGER JOINTS TO BLUEJEAN OUTLETS, TOKYO'S GINZA STRIP IS SLOWLY WESTERNIZING.
OMRON
サッポロビー
AMANO
FRANKLY, MANY JAPANESE ARE EXCITED BY THE CULTURAL INFUSION. SOME, HOWEVER...
UNCLE SAMMY'S
K-KLIK
...SOME, LESS SO.

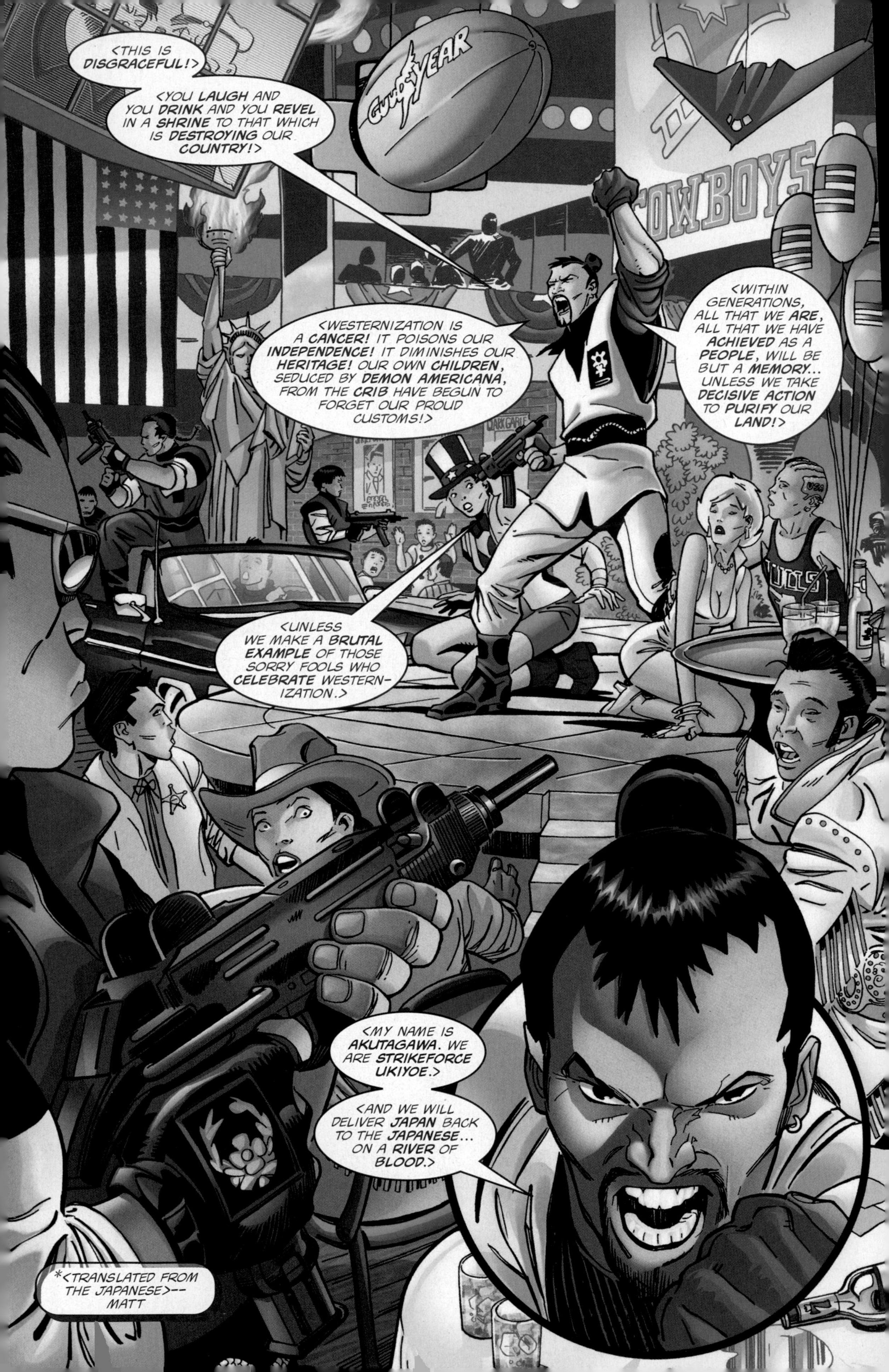

<THIS IS DISGRACEFUL!>
<YOU LAUGH AND YOU DRINK AND YOU REVEL IN A SHRINE TO THAT WHICH IS DESTROYING OUR COUNTRY!>
<WESTERNIZATION IS A CANCER! IT POISONS OUR INDEPENDENCE! IT DIMINISHES OUR HERITAGE! OUR OWN CHILDREN, SEDUCED BY DEMON AMERICANA, FROM THE CRIB HAVE BEGUN TO FORGET OUR PROUD CUSTOMS!>
<WITHIN GENERATIONS, ALL THAT WE ARE, ALL THAT WE HAVE ACHIEVED AS A PEOPLE, WILL BE BUT A MEMORY... UNLESS WE TAKE DECISIVE ACTION TO PURIFY OUR LAND!>
<UNLESS WE MAKE A BRUTAL EXAMPLE OF THOSE SORRY FOOLS WHO CELEBRATE WESTERN-IZATION.>
<MY NAME IS AKUTAGAWA. WE ARE STRIKEFORCE UKIYOE.>
<AND WE WILL DELIVER JAPAN BACK TO THE JAPANESE... ON A RIVER OF BLOOD.>
*<TRANSLATED FROM THE JAPANESE>-- MATT

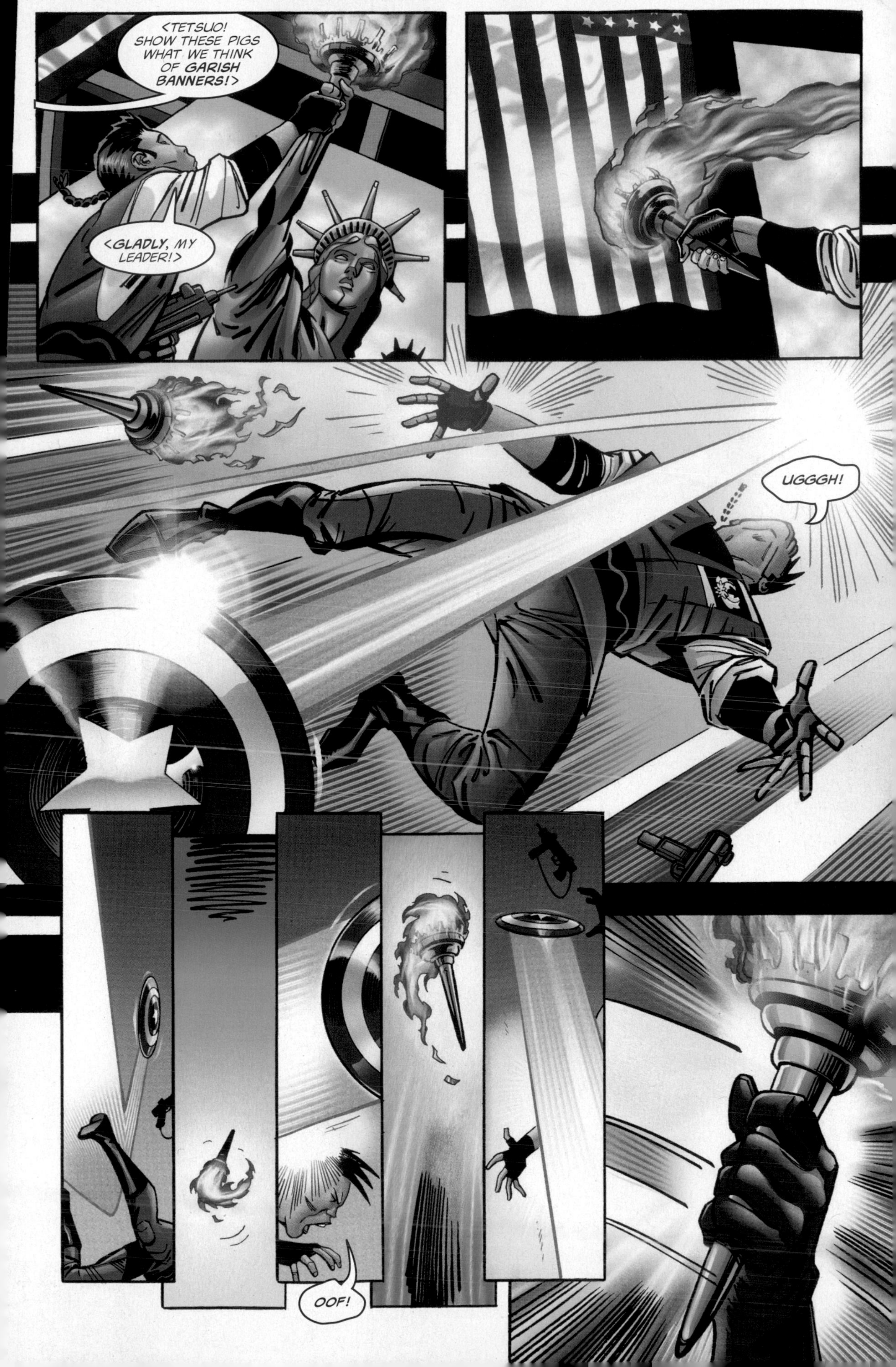

<TETSUO! SHOW THESE PIGS WHAT WE THINK OF GARISH BANNERS!>
<GLADLY, MY LEADER!>
UGGGH!
OOF!

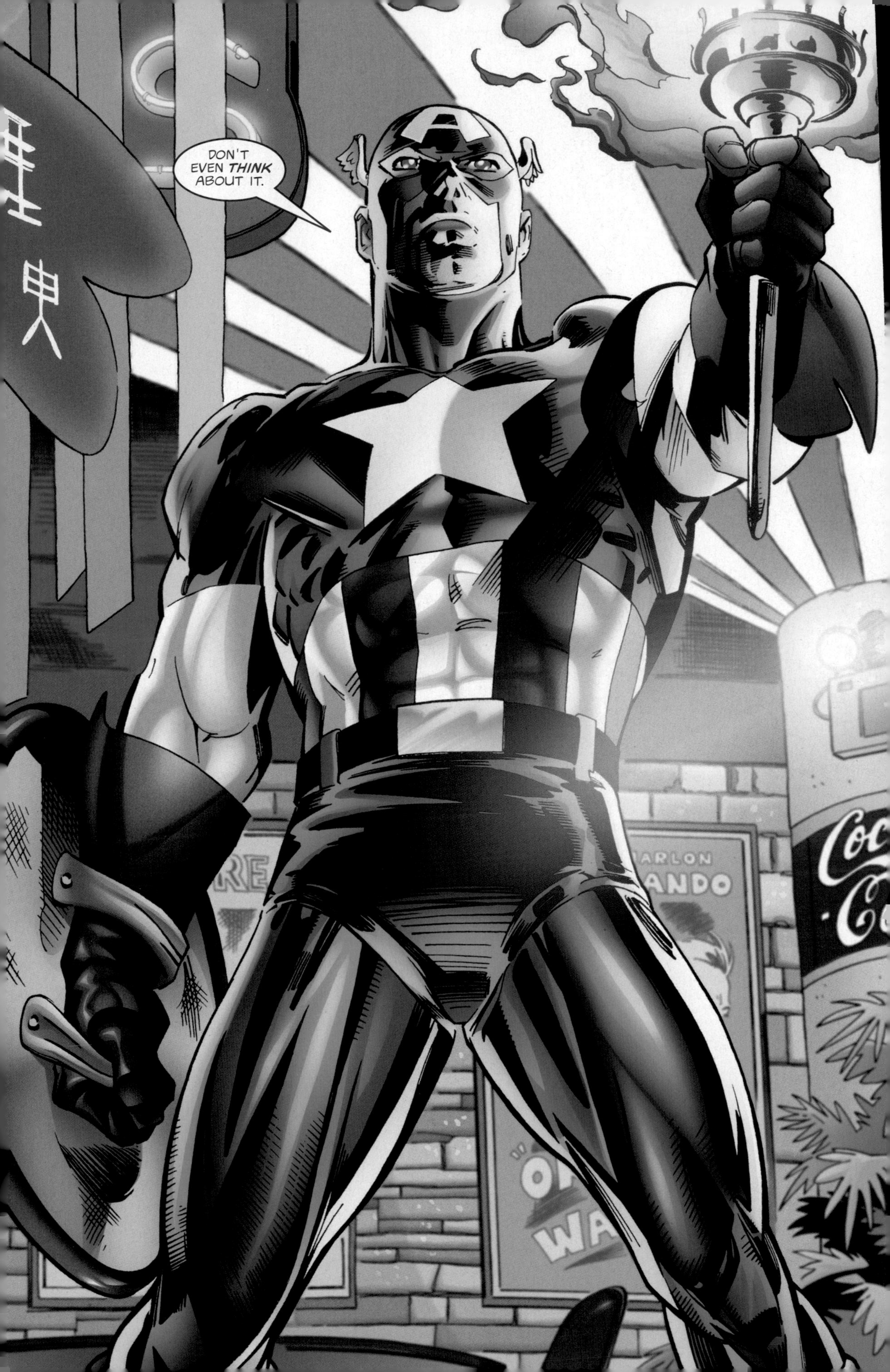
DON'T EVEN *THINK* ABOUT IT.

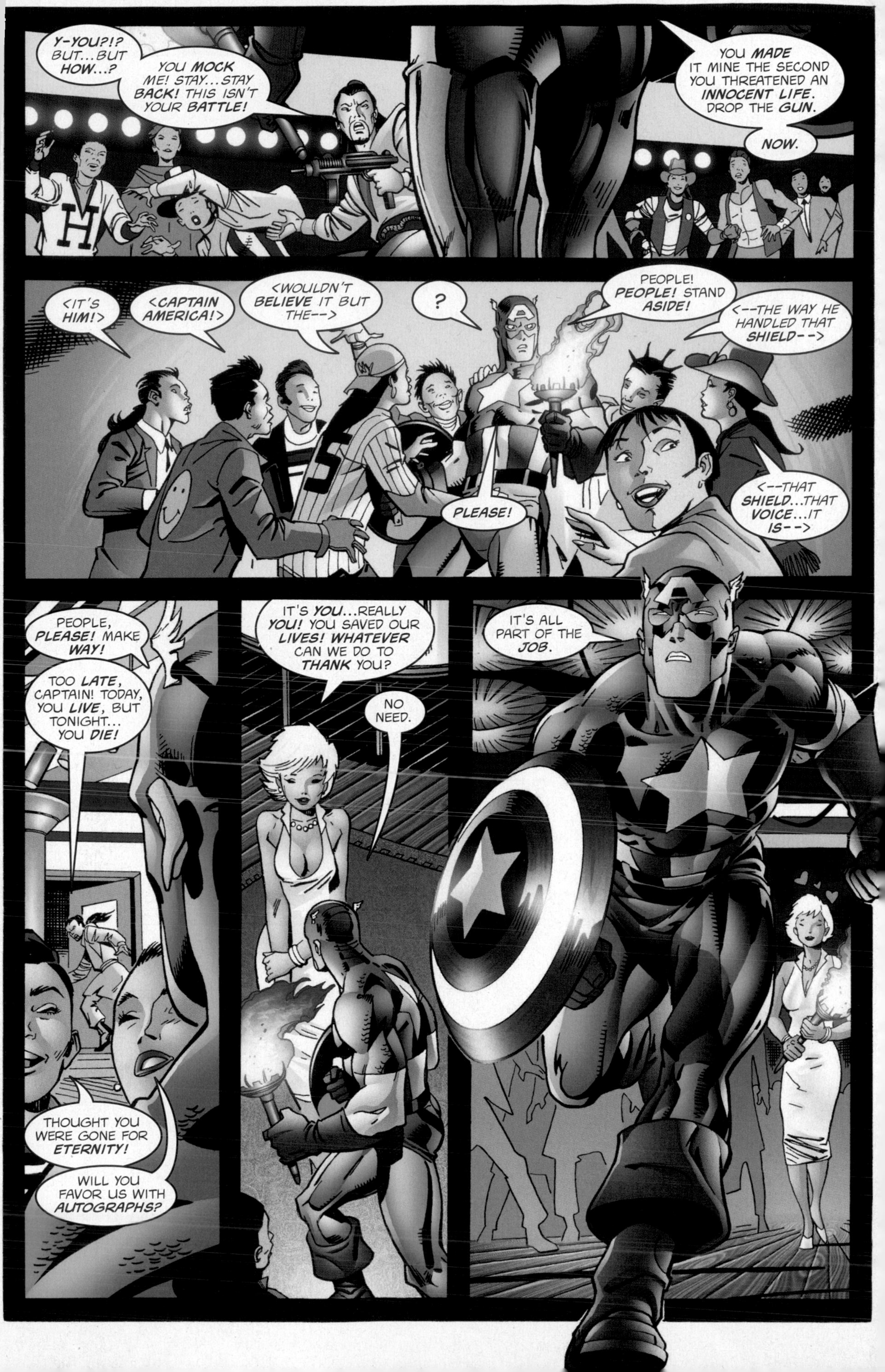
Y-YOU?!? BUT...BUT HOW...?
YOU MOCK ME! STAY...STAY BACK! THIS ISN'T YOUR BATTLE!
YOU MADE IT MINE THE SECOND YOU THREATENED AN INNOCENT LIFE. DROP THE GUN.
NOW.
<IT'S HIM!>
<CAPTAIN AMERICA!>
<WOULDN'T BELIEVE IT BUT THE-->
?
PEOPLE! PEOPLE! STAND ASIDE!
<--THE WAY HE HANDLED THAT SHIELD-->
PLEASE!
<--THAT SHIELD...THAT VOICE...IT IS-->
PEOPLE, PLEASE! MAKE WAY!
TOO LATE, CAPTAIN! TODAY, YOU LIVE, BUT TONIGHT... YOU DIE!
THOUGHT YOU WERE GONE FOR ETERNITY!
WILL YOU FAVOR US WITH AUTOGRAPHS?
IT'S YOU...REALLY YOU! YOU SAVED OUR LIVES! WHATEVER CAN WE DO TO THANK YOU?
NO NEED.
IT'S ALL PART OF THE JOB.

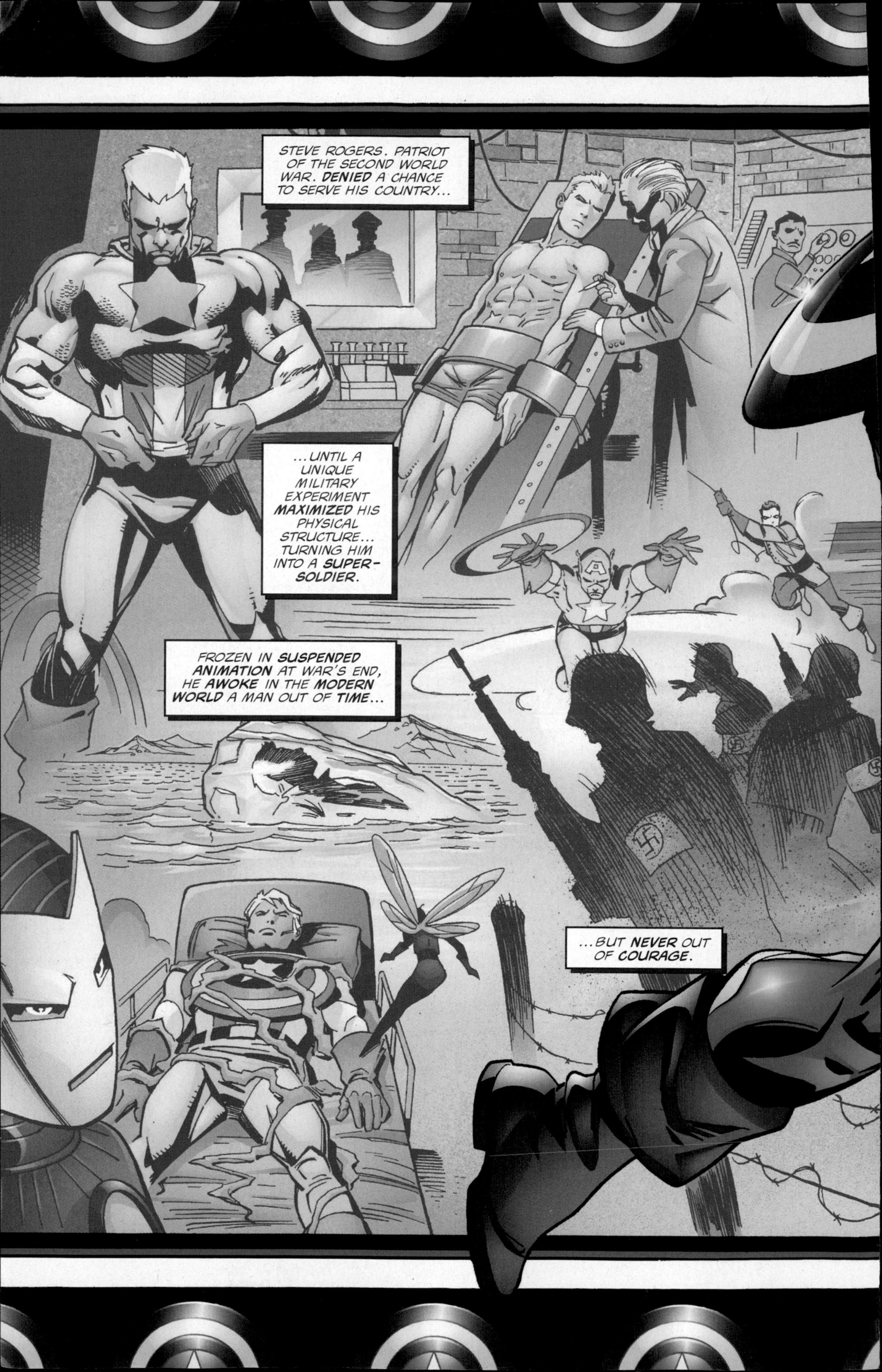
STEVE ROGERS. PATRIOT OF THE SECOND WORLD WAR. DENIED A CHANCE TO SERVE HIS COUNTRY...
...UNTIL A UNIQUE MILITARY EXPERIMENT MAXIMIZED HIS PHYSICAL STRUCTURE... TURNING HIM INTO A SUPER-SOLDIER.
FROZEN IN SUSPENDED ANIMATION AT WAR'S END, HE AWOKE IN THE MODERN WORLD A MAN OUT OF TIME...
...BUT NEVER OUT OF COURAGE.

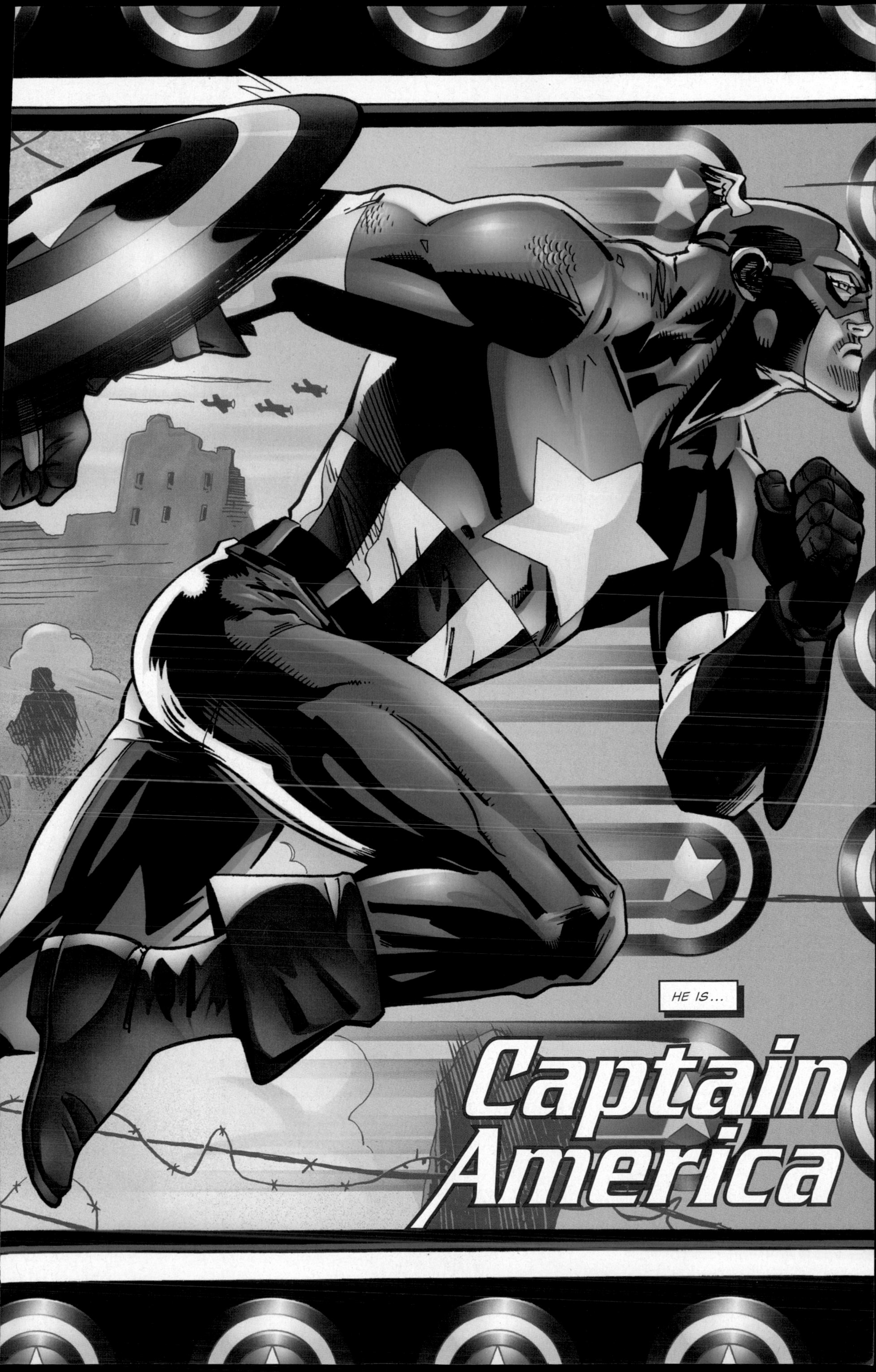
HE IS...
Captain America

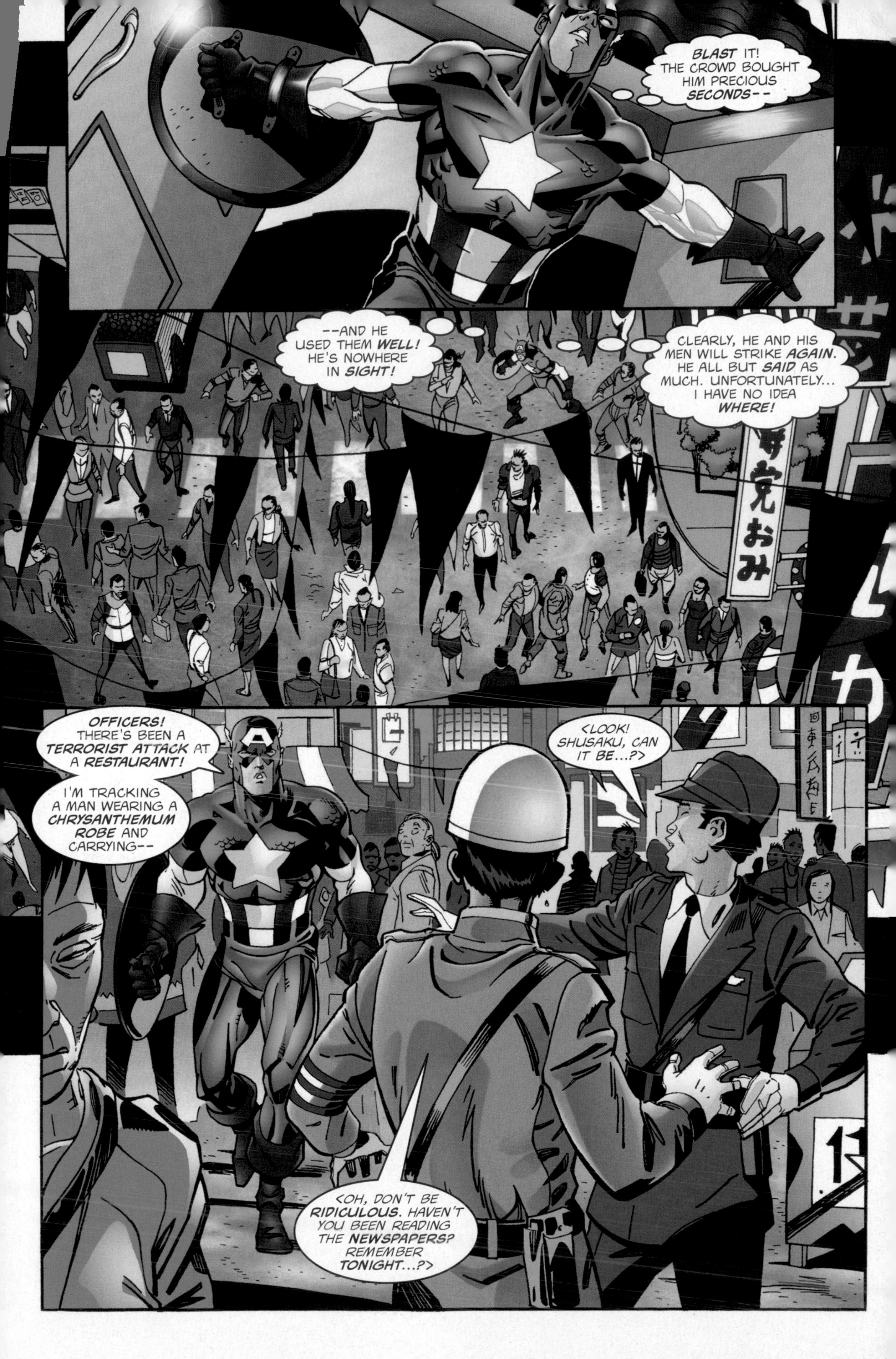
BLAST IT! THE CROWD BOUGHT HIM PRECIOUS SECONDS--
--AND HE USED THEM WELL! HE'S NOWHERE IN SIGHT!
CLEARLY, HE AND HIS MEN WILL STRIKE AGAIN. HE ALL BUT SAID AS MUCH. UNFORTUNATELY... I HAVE NO IDEA WHERE!
OFFICERS! THERE'S BEEN A TERRORIST ATTACK AT A RESTAURANT!
I'M TRACKING A MAN WEARING A CHRYSANTHEMUM ROBE AND CARRYING--
<LOOK! SHUSAKU, CAN IT BE...?>
<OH, DON'T BE RIDICULOUS. HAVEN'T YOU BEEN READING THE NEWSPAPERS? REMEMBER TONIGHT...?>

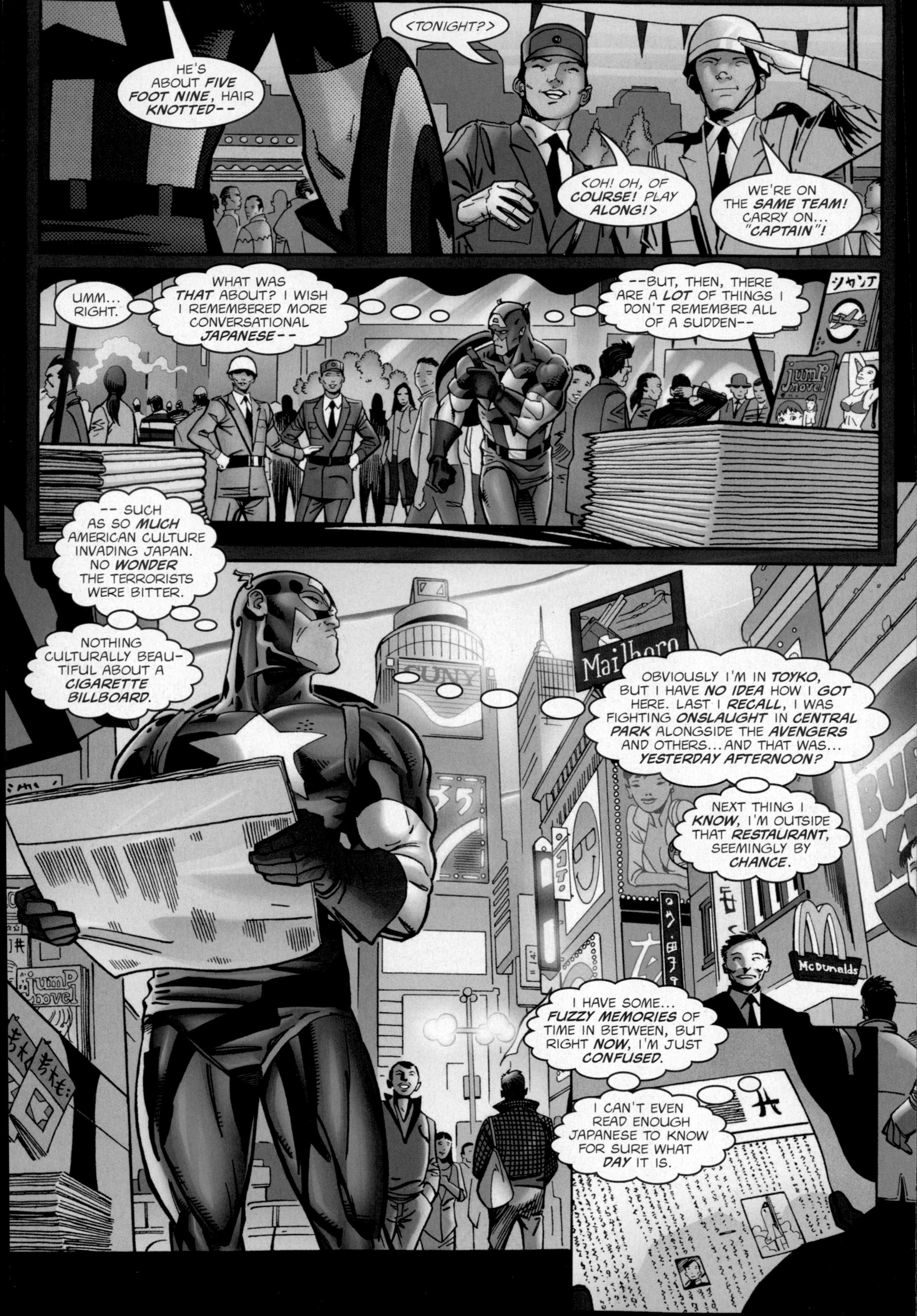
HE'S ABOUT FIVE FOOT NINE, HAIR KNOTTED--
<TONIGHT?>
<OH! OH, OF COURSE! PLAY ALONG!>
WE'RE ON THE SAME TEAM! CARRY ON... "CAPTAIN"!
UMM... RIGHT.
WHAT WAS THAT ABOUT? I WISH I REMEMBERED MORE CONVERSATIONAL JAPANESE--
--BUT, THEN, THERE ARE A LOT OF THINGS I DON'T REMEMBER ALL OF A SUDDEN--
-- SUCH AS SO MUCH AMERICAN CULTURE INVADING JAPAN. NO WONDER THE TERRORISTS WERE BITTER.
NOTHING CULTURALLY BEAUTIFUL ABOUT A CIGARETTE BILLBOARD.
Mailboro
SUNY
OBVIOUSLY I'M IN TOYKO, BUT I HAVE NO IDEA HOW I GOT HERE. LAST I RECALL, I WAS FIGHTING ONSLAUGHT IN CENTRAL PARK ALONGSIDE THE AVENGERS AND OTHERS...AND THAT WAS... YESTERDAY AFTERNOON?
NEXT THING I KNOW, I'M OUTSIDE THAT RESTAURANT, SEEMINGLY BY CHANCE.
McDunalds
I HAVE SOME... FUZZY MEMORIES OF TIME IN BETWEEN, BUT RIGHT NOW, I'M JUST CONFUSED.
I CAN'T EVEN READ ENOUGH JAPANESE TO KNOW FOR SURE WHAT DAY IT IS.

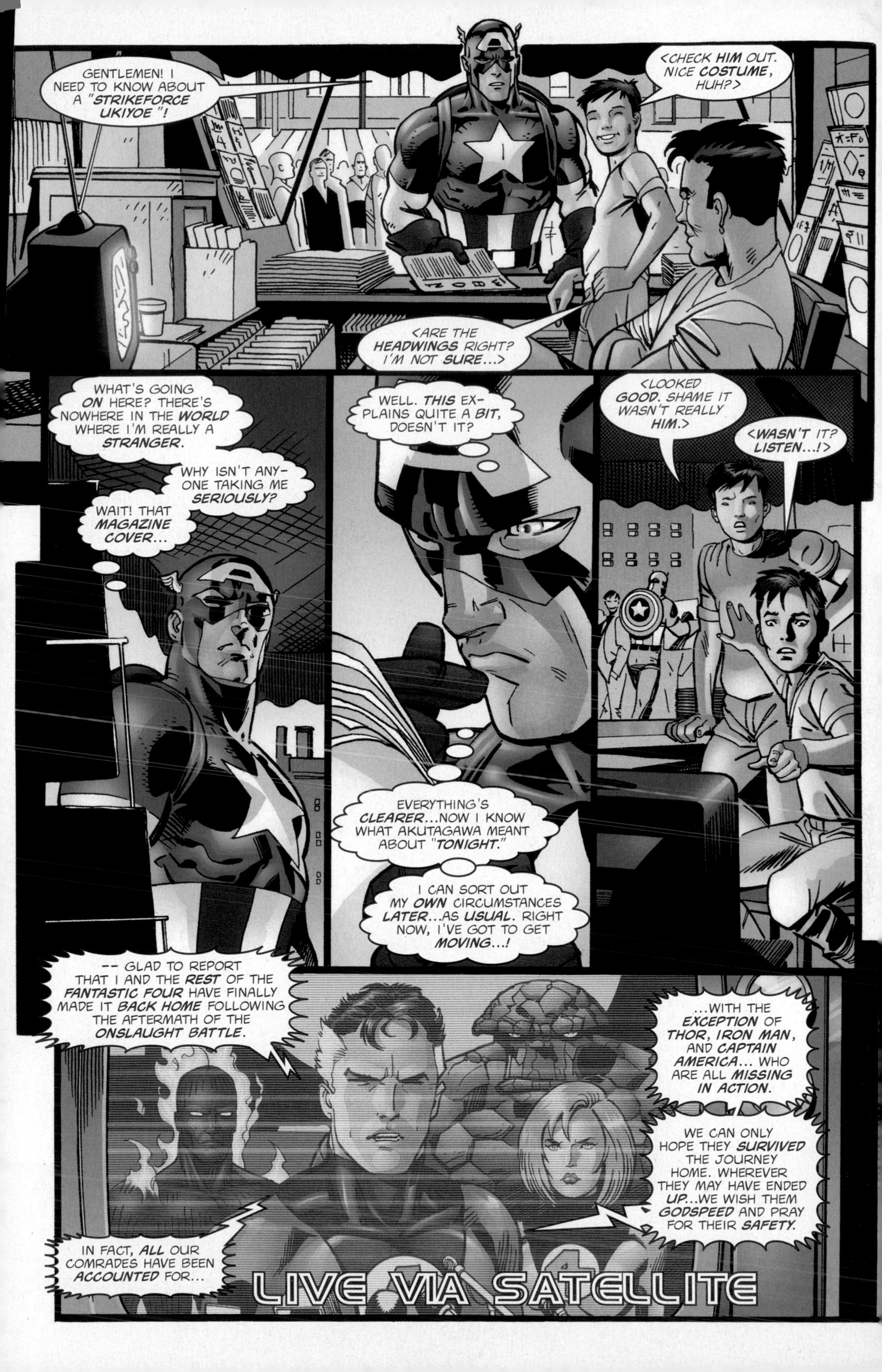
GENTLEMEN! I NEED TO KNOW ABOUT A "STRIKEFORCE UKIYOE"!
<CHECK HIM OUT. NICE COSTUME, HUH?>
<ARE THE HEADWINGS RIGHT? I'M NOT SURE...>
WHAT'S GOING ON HERE? THERE'S NOWHERE IN THE WORLD WHERE I'M REALLY A STRANGER.
WHY ISN'T ANYONE TAKING ME SERIOUSLY?
WAIT! THAT MAGAZINE COVER...
WELL. THIS EXPLAINS QUITE A BIT, DOESN'T IT?
EVERYTHING'S CLEARER...NOW I KNOW WHAT AKUTAGAWA MEANT ABOUT "TONIGHT."
I CAN SORT OUT MY OWN CIRCUMSTANCES LATER...AS USUAL. RIGHT NOW, I'VE GOT TO GET MOVING...!
<LOOKED GOOD. SHAME IT WASN'T REALLY HIM.>
<WASN'T IT? LISTEN...!>
-- GLAD TO REPORT THAT I AND THE REST OF THE FANTASTIC FOUR HAVE FINALLY MADE IT BACK HOME FOLLOWING THE AFTERMATH OF THE ONSLAUGHT BATTLE.
...WITH THE EXCEPTION OF THOR, IRON MAN, AND CAPTAIN AMERICA... WHO ARE ALL MISSING IN ACTION.
WE CAN ONLY HOPE THEY SURVIVED THE JOURNEY HOME. WHEREVER THEY MAY HAVE ENDED UP...WE WISH THEM GODSPEED AND PRAY FOR THEIR SAFETY.
IN FACT, ALL OUR COMRADES HAVE BEEN ACCOUNTED FOR...
LIVE VIA SATELLITE

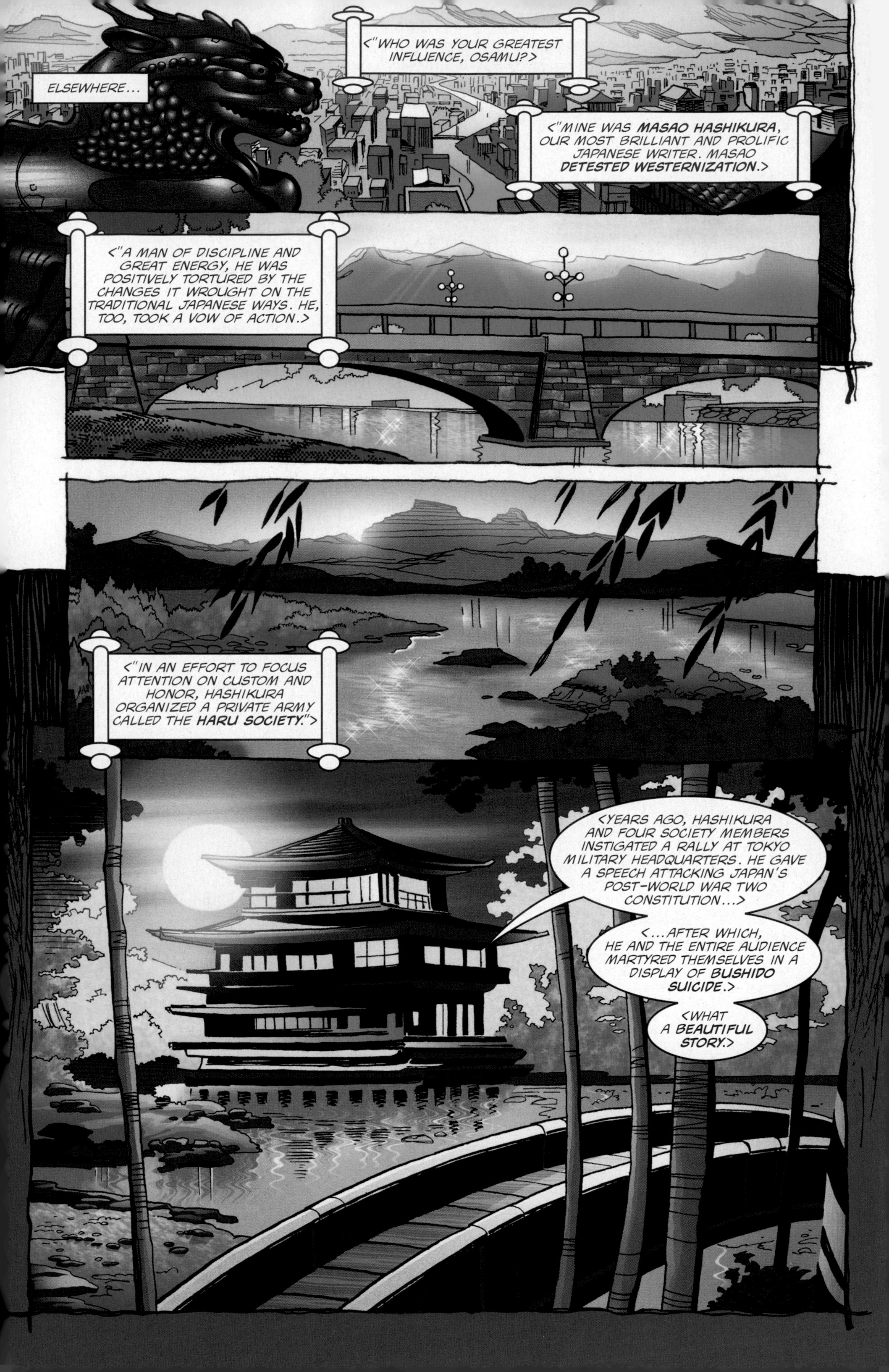
ELSEWHERE...
<"WHO WAS YOUR GREATEST INFLUENCE, OSAMU?>
<"MINE WAS MASAO HASHIKURA, OUR MOST BRILLIANT AND PROLIFIC JAPANESE WRITER. MASAO DETESTED WESTERNIZATION.>
<"A MAN OF DISCIPLINE AND GREAT ENERGY, HE WAS POSITIVELY TORTURED BY THE CHANGES IT WROUGHT ON THE TRADITIONAL JAPANESE WAYS. HE, TOO, TOOK A VOW OF ACTION.>
<"IN AN EFFORT TO FOCUS ATTENTION ON CUSTOM AND HONOR, HASHIKURA ORGANIZED A PRIVATE ARMY CALLED THE HARU SOCIETY.">
<YEARS AGO, HASHIKURA AND FOUR SOCIETY MEMBERS INSTIGATED A RALLY AT TOKYO MILITARY HEADQUARTERS. HE GAVE A SPEECH ATTACKING JAPAN'S POST-WORLD WAR TWO CONSTITUTION...>
<...AFTER WHICH, HE AND THE ENTIRE AUDIENCE MARTYRED THEMSELVES IN A DISPLAY OF BUSHIDO SUICIDE.>
<WHAT A BEAUTIFUL STORY.>

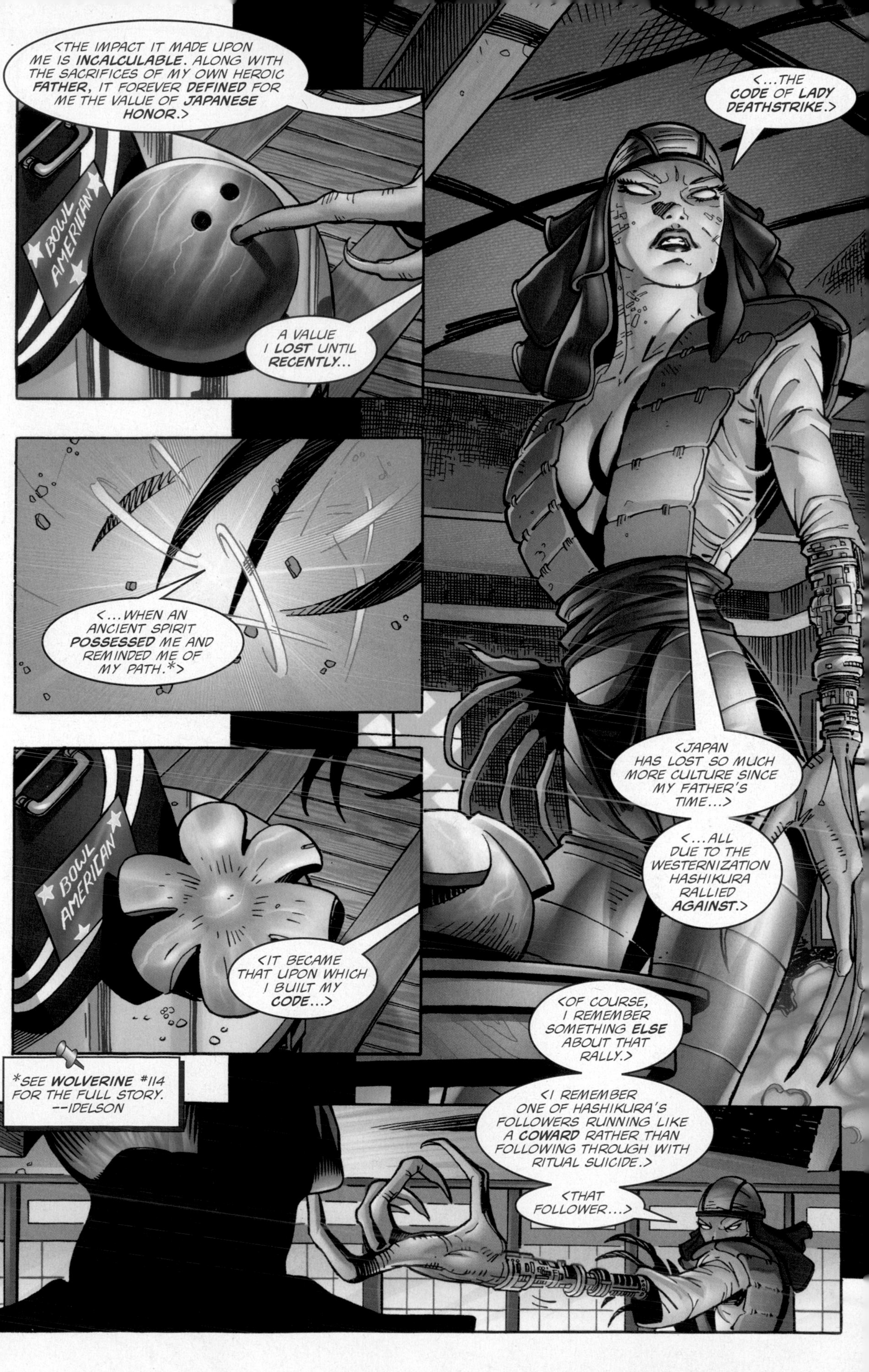

<THE IMPACT IT MADE UPON ME IS INCALCULABLE. ALONG WITH THE SACRIFICES OF MY OWN HEROIC FATHER, IT FOREVER DEFINED FOR ME THE VALUE OF JAPANESE HONOR.>
BOWL AMERICAN
A VALUE I LOST UNTIL RECENTLY...
<...THE CODE OF LADY DEATHSTRIKE.>
<...WHEN AN ANCIENT SPIRIT POSSESSED ME AND REMINDED ME OF MY PATH.*>
BOWL AMERICAN
<IT BECAME THAT UPON WHICH I BUILT MY CODE...>
<JAPAN HAS LOST SO MUCH MORE CULTURE SINCE MY FATHER'S TIME...>
<...ALL DUE TO THE WESTERNIZATION HASHIKURA RALLIED AGAINST.>
*SEE WOLVERINE #114 FOR THE FULL STORY. --IDELSON
<OF COURSE, I REMEMBER SOMETHING ELSE ABOUT THAT RALLY.>
<I REMEMBER ONE OF HASHIKURA'S FOLLOWERS RUNNING LIKE A COWARD RATHER THAN FOLLOWING THROUGH WITH RITUAL SUICIDE.>
<THAT FOLLOWER...>

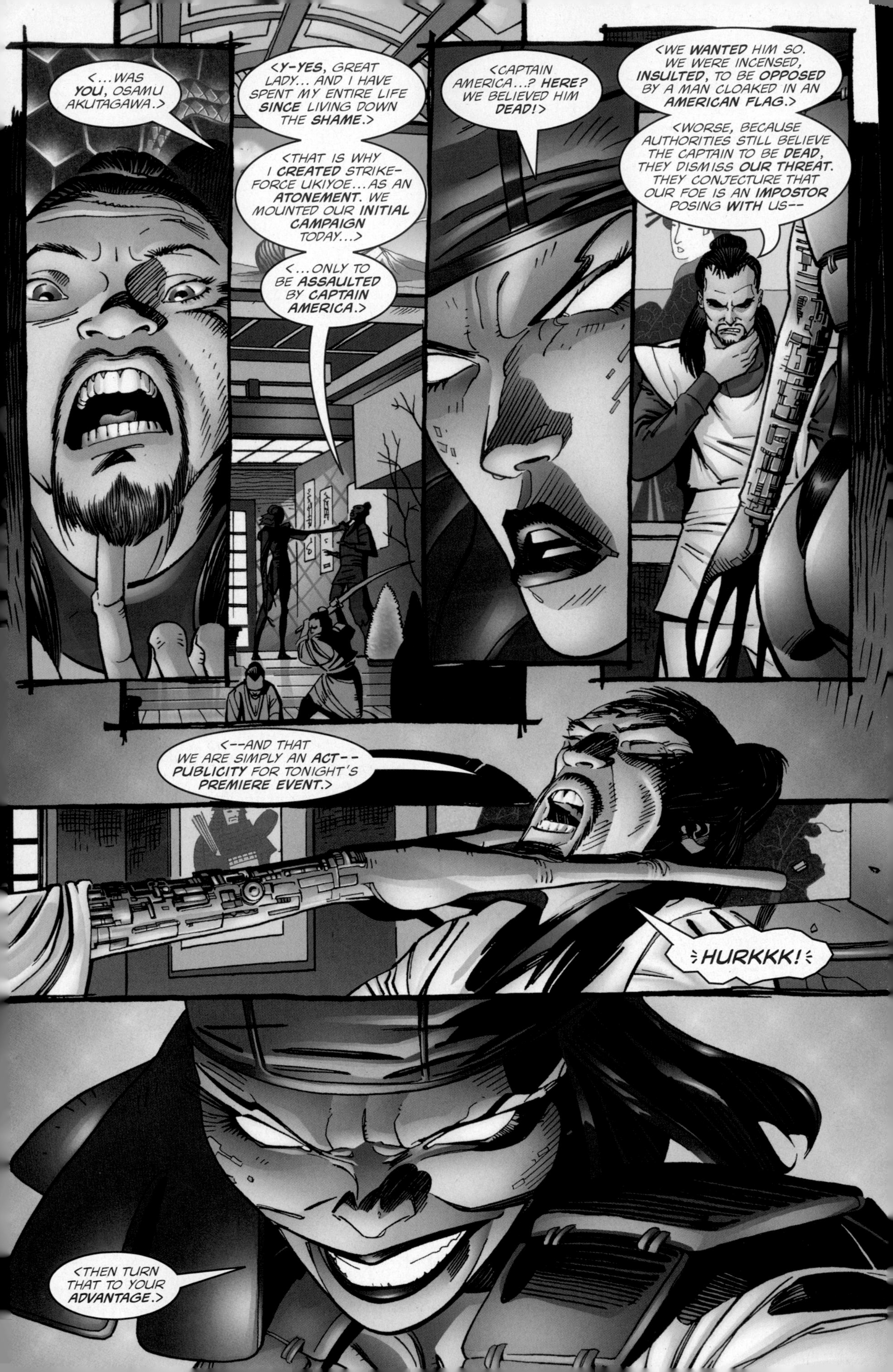
<...WAS YOU, OSAMU AKUTAGAWA.>
<Y-YES, GREAT LADY... AND I HAVE SPENT MY ENTIRE LIFE SINCE LIVING DOWN THE SHAME.>
<THAT IS WHY I CREATED STRIKE-FORCE UKIYOE...AS AN ATONEMENT. WE MOUNTED OUR INITIAL CAMPAIGN TODAY...>
<...ONLY TO BE ASSAULTED BY CAPTAIN AMERICA.>
<CAPTAIN AMERICA...? HERE? WE BELIEVED HIM DEAD!>
<WE WANTED HIM SO. WE WERE INCENSED, INSULTED, TO BE OPPOSED BY A MAN CLOAKED IN AN AMERICAN FLAG.>
<WORSE, BECAUSE AUTHORITIES STILL BELIEVE THE CAPTAIN TO BE DEAD, THEY DISMISS OUR THREAT. THEY CONJECTURE THAT OUR FOE IS AN IMPOSTOR POSING WITH US--
<--AND THAT WE ARE SIMPLY AN ACT--PUBLICITY FOR TONIGHT'S PREMIERE EVENT.>
HURKKK!
<THEN TURN THAT TO YOUR ADVANTAGE.>

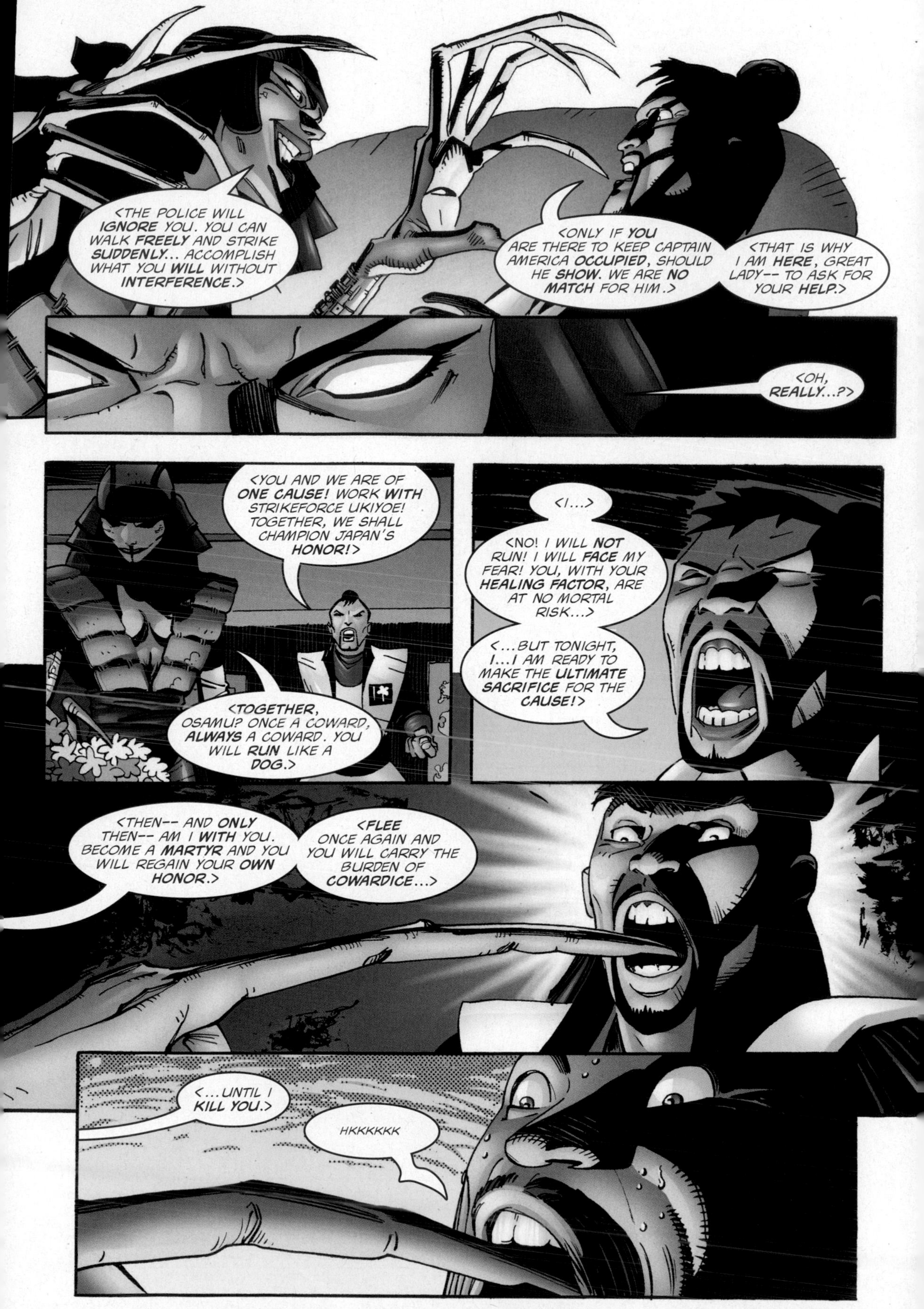
<THE POLICE WILL IGNORE YOU. YOU CAN WALK FREELY AND STRIKE SUDDENLY... ACCOMPLISH WHAT YOU WILL WITHOUT INTERFERENCE.>
<ONLY IF YOU ARE THERE TO KEEP CAPTAIN AMERICA OCCUPIED, SHOULD HE SHOW. WE ARE NO MATCH FOR HIM.>
<THAT IS WHY I AM HERE, GREAT LADY-- TO ASK FOR YOUR HELP.>
<OH, REALLY...?>
<YOU AND WE ARE OF ONE CAUSE! WORK WITH STRIKEFORCE UKIYOE! TOGETHER, WE SHALL CHAMPION JAPAN'S HONOR!>
<TOGETHER, OSAMU? ONCE A COWARD, ALWAYS A COWARD. YOU WILL RUN LIKE A DOG.>
<I...>
<NO! I WILL NOT RUN! I WILL FACE MY FEAR! YOU, WITH YOUR HEALING FACTOR, ARE AT NO MORTAL RISK...>
<...BUT TONIGHT, I...I AM READY TO MAKE THE ULTIMATE SACRIFICE FOR THE CAUSE!>
<THEN-- AND ONLY THEN-- AM I WITH YOU. BECOME A MARTYR AND YOU WILL REGAIN YOUR OWN HONOR.>
<FLEE ONCE AGAIN AND YOU WILL CARRY THE BURDEN OF COWARDICE...>
<...UNTIL I KILL YOU.>
HKKKKKK

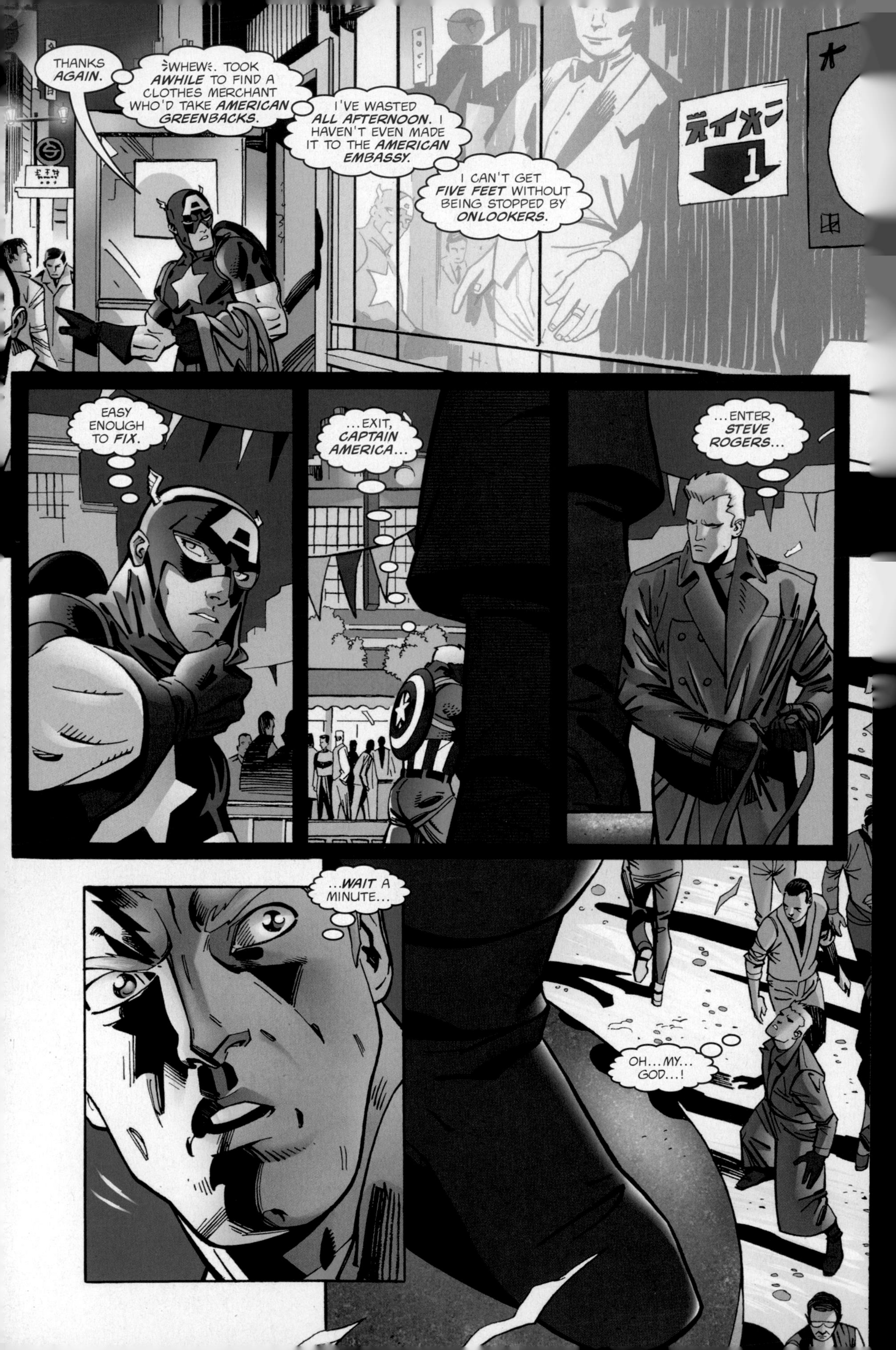
THANKS AGAIN.
WHEW. TOOK AWHILE TO FIND A CLOTHES MERCHANT WHO'D TAKE AMERICAN GREENBACKS.
I'VE WASTED ALL AFTERNOON. I HAVEN'T EVEN MADE IT TO THE AMERICAN EMBASSY.
I CAN'T GET FIVE FEET WITHOUT BEING STOPPED BY ONLOOKERS.
ディオン
1
EASY ENOUGH TO FIX.
...EXIT, CAPTAIN AMERICA...
...ENTER, STEVE ROGERS...
...WAIT A MINUTE...
OH...MY... GOD...!

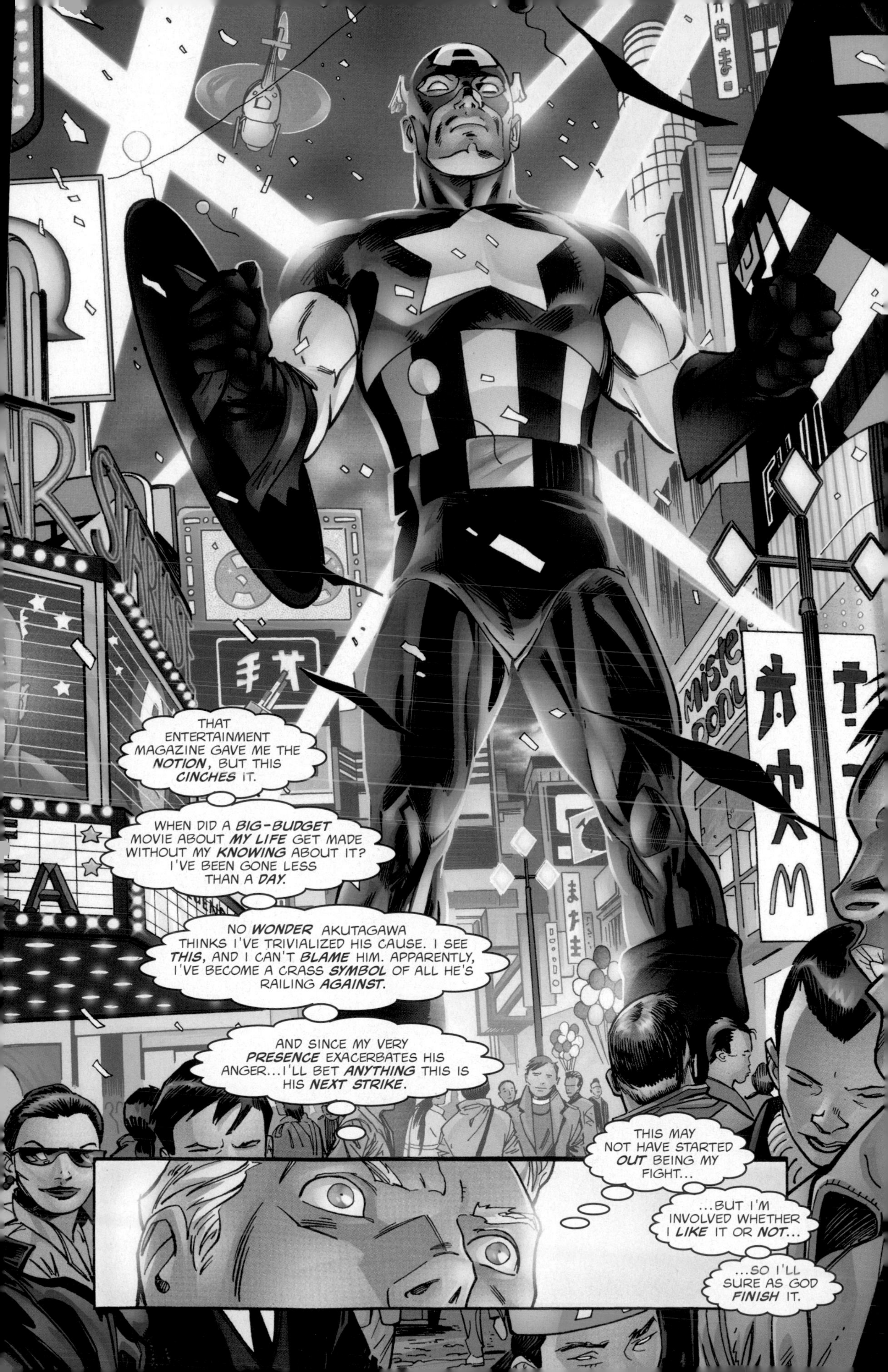

THAT ENTERTAINMENT MAGAZINE GAVE ME THE NOTION, BUT THIS CINCHES IT.
WHEN DID A BIG-BUDGET MOVIE ABOUT MY LIFE GET MADE WITHOUT MY KNOWING ABOUT IT? I'VE BEEN GONE LESS THAN A DAY.
NO WONDER AKUTAGAWA THINKS I'VE TRIVIALIZED HIS CAUSE. I SEE THIS, AND I CAN'T BLAME HIM. APPARENTLY, I'VE BECOME A CRASS SYMBOL OF ALL HE'S RAILING AGAINST.
AND SINCE MY VERY PRESENCE EXACERBATES HIS ANGER...I'LL BET ANYTHING THIS IS HIS NEXT STRIKE.
THIS MAY NOT HAVE STARTED OUT BEING MY FIGHT...
...BUT I'M INVOLVED WHETHER I LIKE IT OR NOT...
...SO I'LL SURE AS GOD FINISH IT.

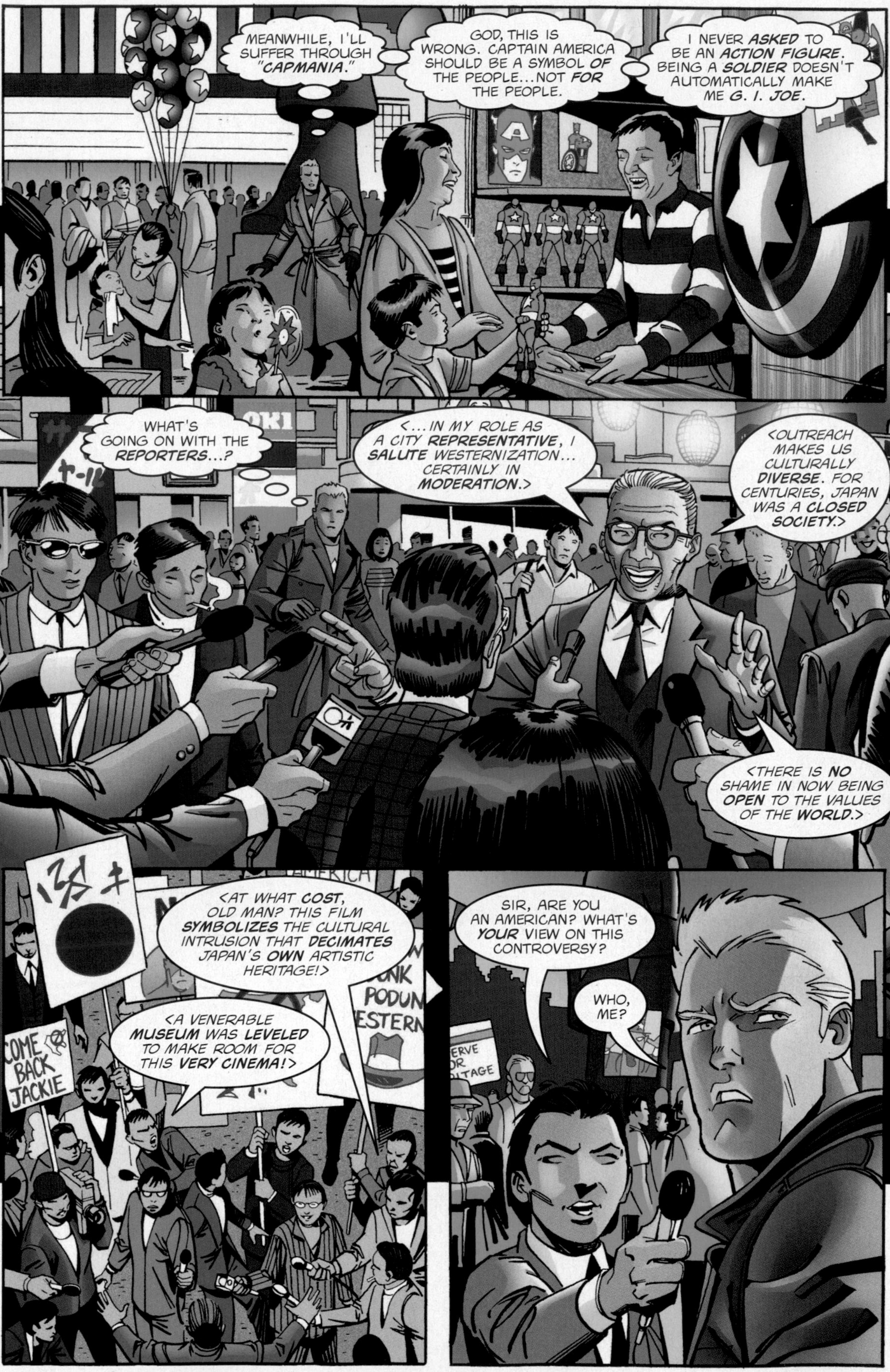
MEANWHILE, I'LL SUFFER THROUGH "CAPMANIA."
GOD, THIS IS WRONG. CAPTAIN AMERICA SHOULD BE A SYMBOL OF THE PEOPLE...NOT FOR THE PEOPLE.
I NEVER ASKED TO BE AN ACTION FIGURE. BEING A SOLDIER DOESN'T AUTOMATICALLY MAKE ME G. I. JOE.
OKI
WHAT'S GOING ON WITH THE REPORTERS...?
<...IN MY ROLE AS A CITY REPRESENTATIVE, I SALUTE WESTERNIZATION... CERTAINLY IN MODERATION.>
<OUTREACH MAKES US CULTURALLY DIVERSE. FOR CENTURIES, JAPAN WAS A CLOSED SOCIETY.>
<THERE IS NO SHAME IN NOW BEING OPEN TO THE VALUES OF THE WORLD.>
<AT WHAT COST, OLD MAN? THIS FILM SYMBOLIZES THE CULTURAL INTRUSION THAT DECIMATES JAPAN'S OWN ARTISTIC HERITAGE!>
<A VENERABLE MUSEUM WAS LEVELED TO MAKE ROOM FOR THIS VERY CINEMA!>
COME BACK JACKIE
SIR, ARE YOU AN AMERICAN? WHAT'S YOUR VIEW ON THIS CONTROVERSY?
WHO, ME?

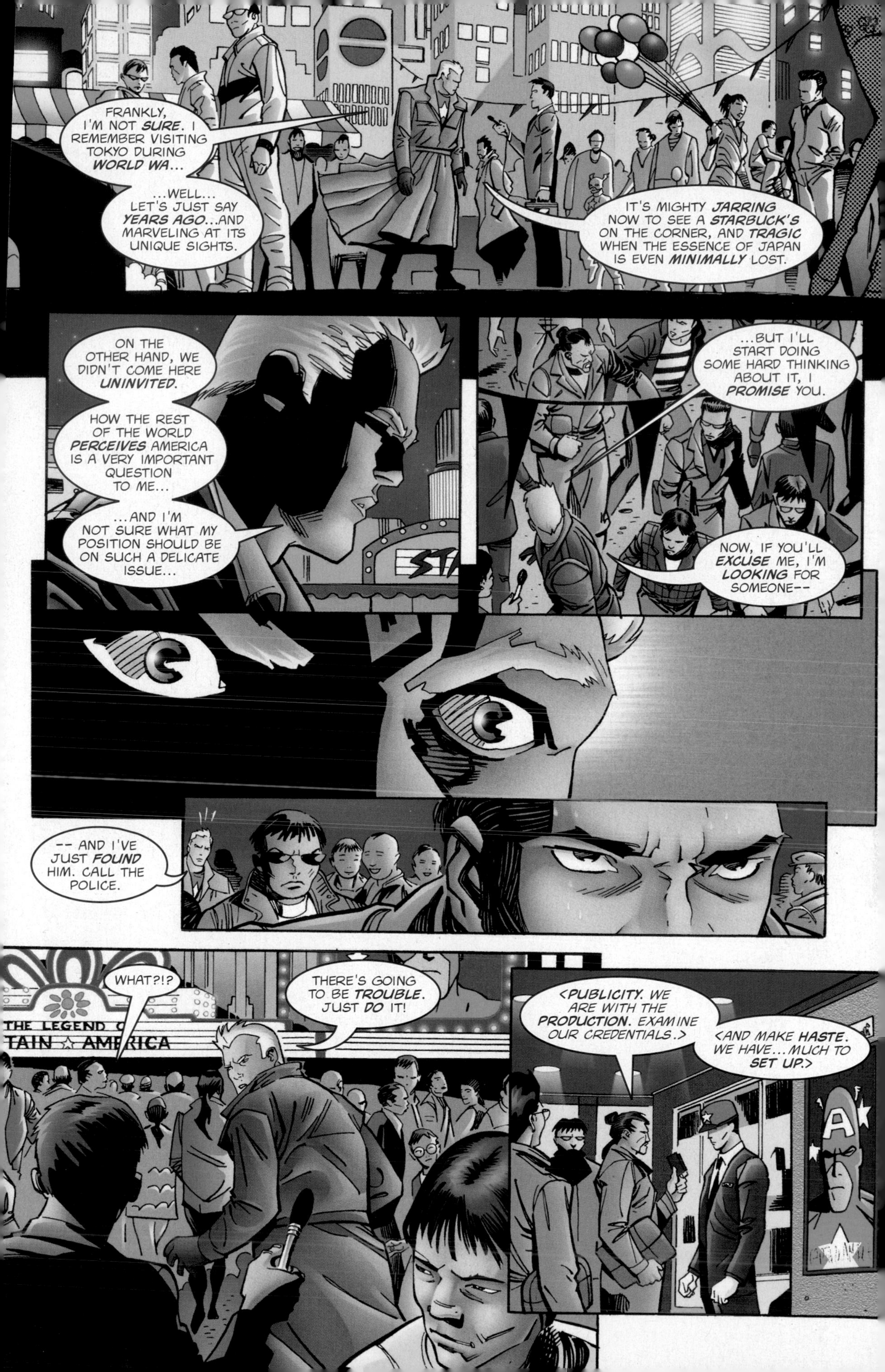

FRANKLY, I'M NOT SURE. I REMEMBER VISITING TOKYO DURING WORLD WA...
...WELL... LET'S JUST SAY YEARS AGO...AND MARVELING AT ITS UNIQUE SIGHTS.
IT'S MIGHTY JARRING NOW TO SEE A STARBUCK'S ON THE CORNER, AND TRAGIC WHEN THE ESSENCE OF JAPAN IS EVEN MINIMALLY LOST.
ON THE OTHER HAND, WE DIDN'T COME HERE UNINVITED.
HOW THE REST OF THE WORLD PERCEIVES AMERICA IS A VERY IMPORTANT QUESTION TO ME...
...AND I'M NOT SURE WHAT MY POSITION SHOULD BE ON SUCH A DELICATE ISSUE...
...BUT I'LL START DOING SOME HARD THINKING ABOUT IT, I PROMISE YOU.
NOW, IF YOU'LL EXCUSE ME, I'M LOOKING FOR SOMEONE--
-- AND I'VE JUST FOUND HIM. CALL THE POLICE.
WHAT?!?
THE LEGEND O
TAIN ☆ AMERICA
THERE'S GOING TO BE TROUBLE. JUST DO IT!
<PUBLICITY. WE ARE WITH THE PRODUCTION. EXAMINE OUR CREDENTIALS.>
<AND MAKE HASTE. WE HAVE...MUCH TO SET UP.>

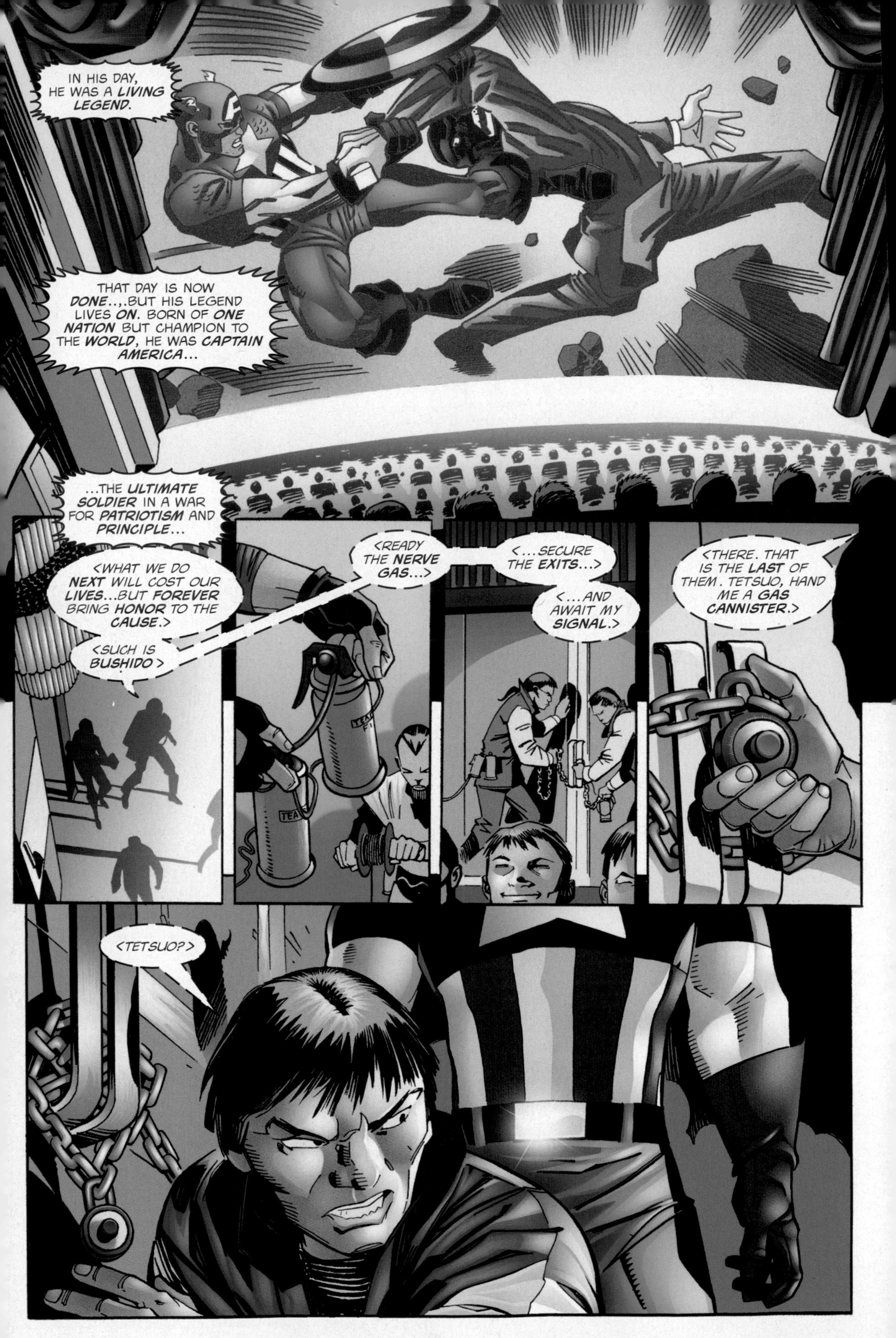

IN HIS DAY, HE WAS A LIVING LEGEND.
THAT DAY IS NOW DONE...,.BUT HIS LEGEND LIVES ON. BORN OF ONE NATION BUT CHAMPION TO THE WORLD, HE WAS CAPTAIN AMERICA...
...THE ULTIMATE SOLDIER IN A WAR FOR PATRIOTISM AND PRINCIPLE...
<WHAT WE DO NEXT WILL COST OUR LIVES...BUT FOREVER BRING HONOR TO THE CAUSE.>
<SUCH IS BUSHIDO>
<READY THE NERVE GAS...>
<...SECURE THE EXITS...>
<...AND AWAIT MY SIGNAL.>
<THERE. THAT IS THE LAST OF THEM. TETSUO, HAND ME A GAS CANNISTER.>
<TETSUO?>

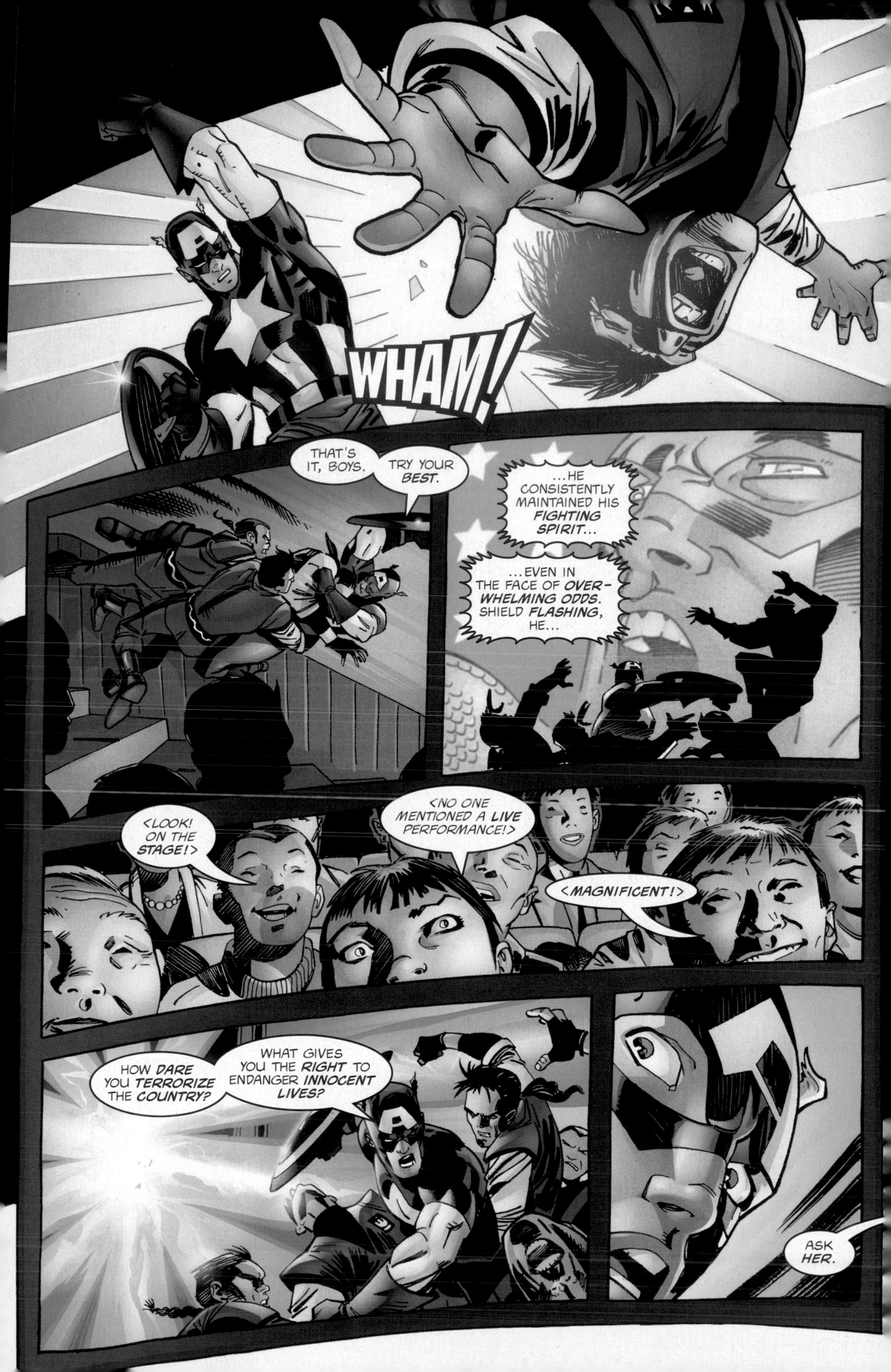

WHAM!
THAT'S IT, BOYS.
TRY YOUR BEST.
...HE CONSISTENTLY MAINTAINED HIS FIGHTING SPIRIT...
...EVEN IN THE FACE OF OVER-WHELMING ODDS. SHIELD FLASHING, HE...
<LOOK! ON THE STAGE!>
<NO ONE MENTIONED A LIVE PERFORMANCE!>
<MAGNIFICENT!>
HOW DARE YOU TERRORIZE THE COUNTRY?
WHAT GIVES YOU THE RIGHT TO ENDANGER INNOCENT LIVES?
ASK HER.

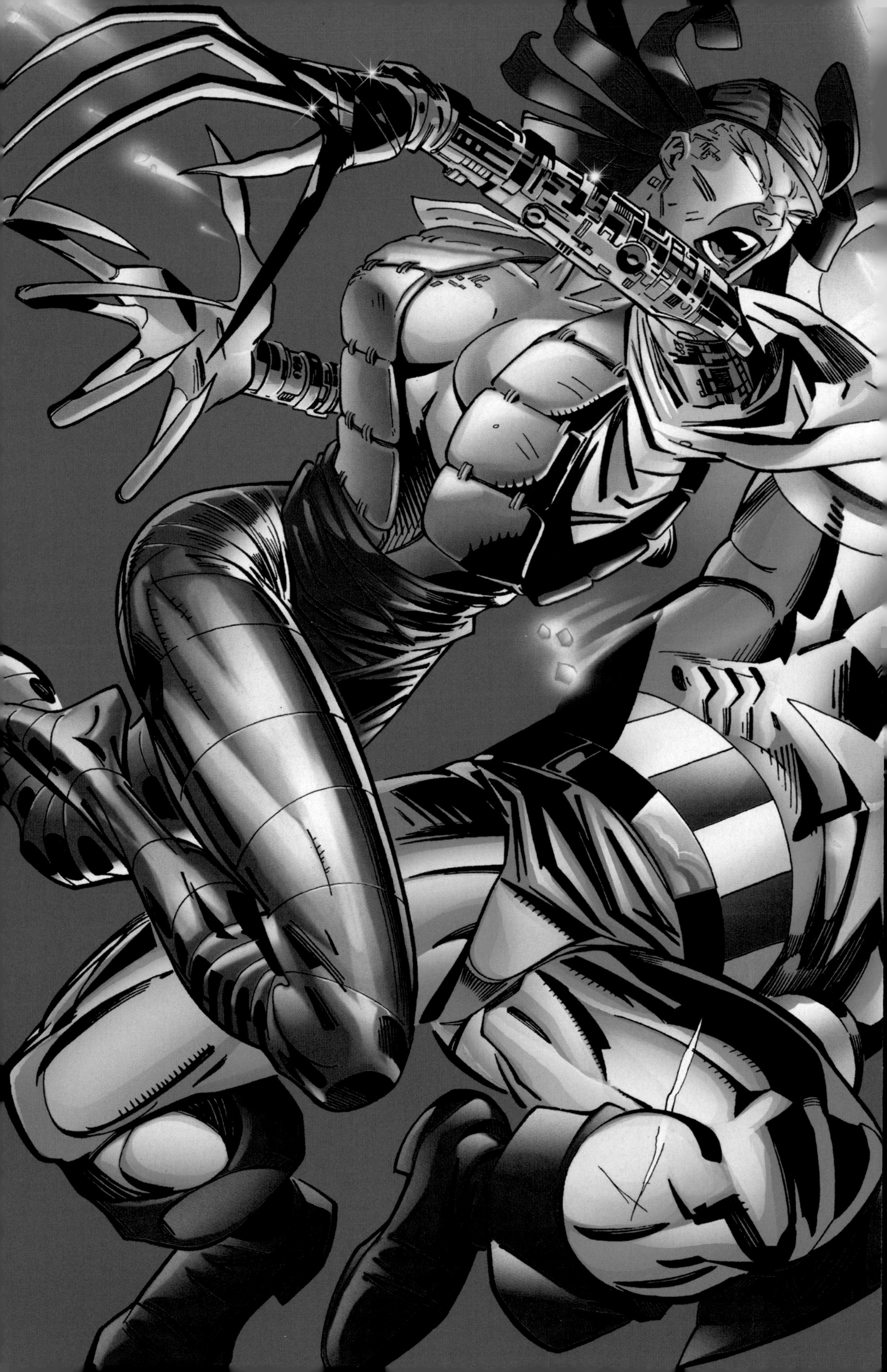

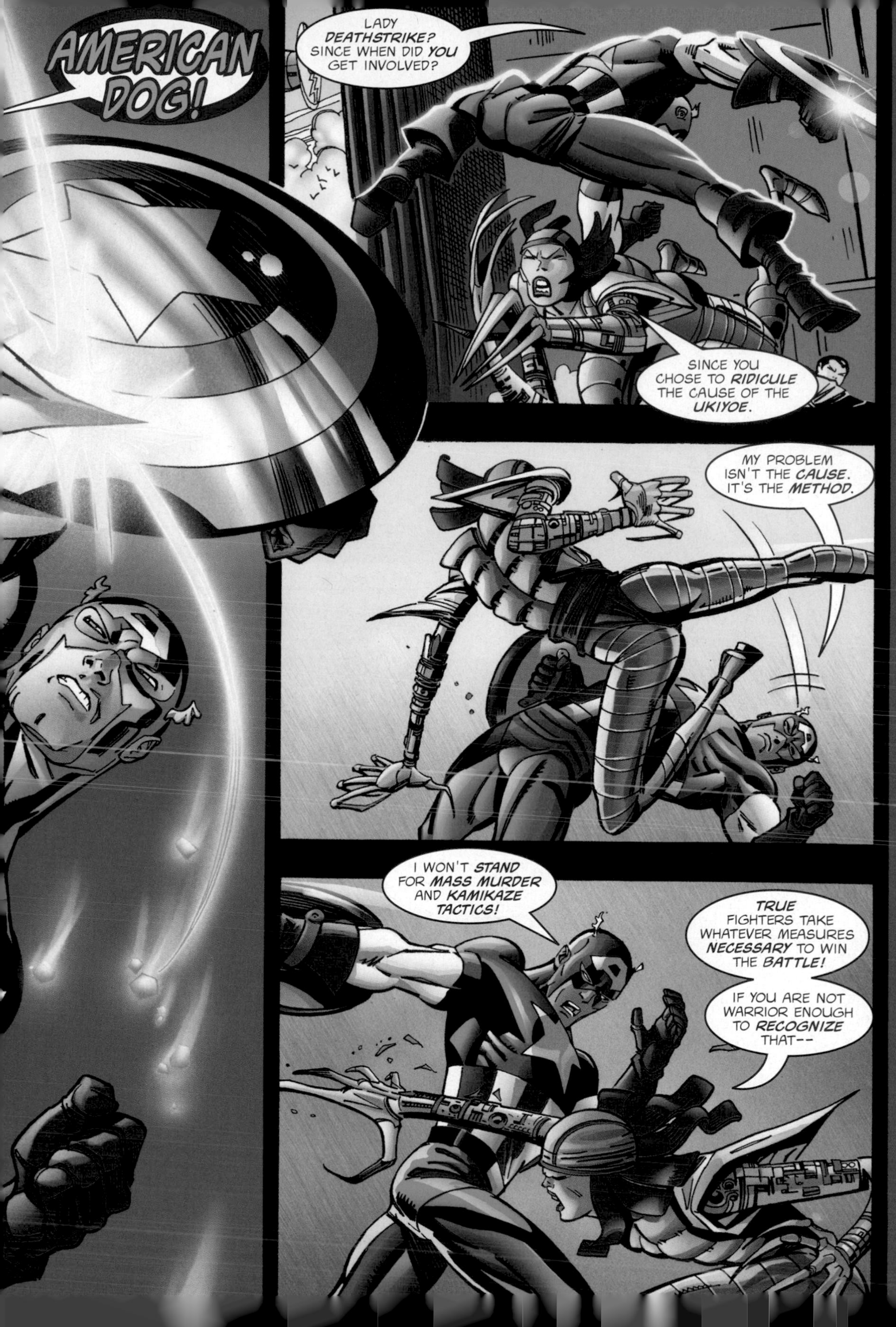
AMERICAN DOG!
LADY DEATHSTRIKE? SINCE WHEN DID YOU GET INVOLVED?
SINCE YOU CHOSE TO RIDICULE THE CAUSE OF THE UKIYOE.
MY PROBLEM ISN'T THE CAUSE. IT'S THE METHOD.
I WON'T STAND FOR MASS MURDER AND KAMIKAZE TACTICS!
TRUE FIGHTERS TAKE WHATEVER MEASURES NECESSARY TO WIN THE BATTLE!
IF YOU ARE NOT WARRIOR ENOUGH TO RECOGNIZE THAT--

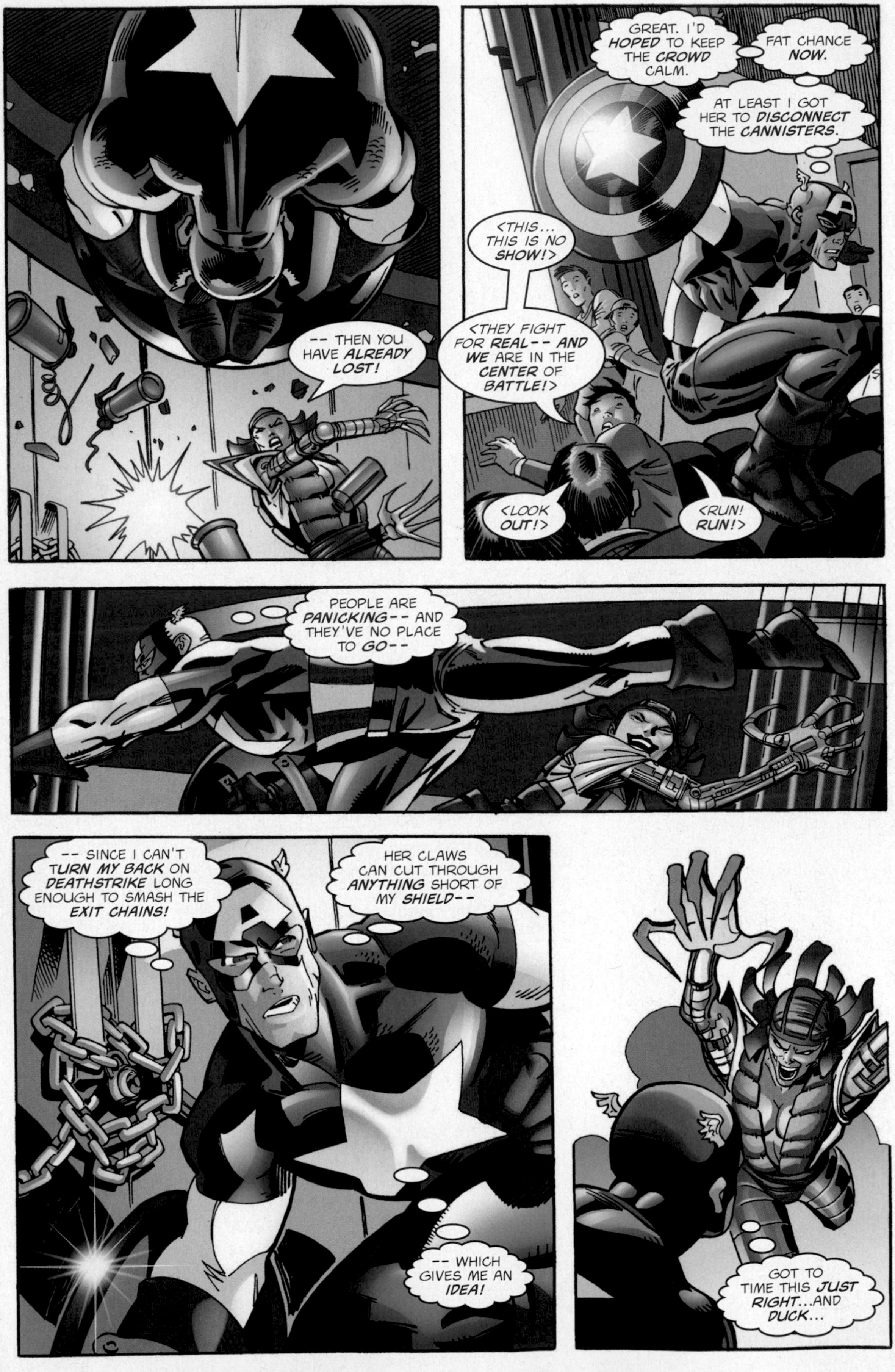
-- THEN YOU HAVE ALREADY LOST!
GREAT. I'D HOPED TO KEEP THE CROWD CALM.
FAT CHANCE NOW.
AT LEAST I GOT HER TO DISCONNECT THE CANNISTERS.
<THIS... THIS IS NO SHOW!>
<THEY FIGHT FOR REAL-- AND WE ARE IN THE CENTER OF BATTLE!>
<LOOK OUT!>
<RUN! RUN!>
PEOPLE ARE PANICKING-- AND THEY'VE NO PLACE TO GO--
-- SINCE I CAN'T TURN MY BACK ON DEATHSTRIKE LONG ENOUGH TO SMASH THE EXIT CHAINS!
HER CLAWS CAN CUT THROUGH ANYTHING SHORT OF MY SHIELD--
-- WHICH GIVES ME AN IDEA!
GOT TO TIME THIS JUST RIGHT...AND DUCK...

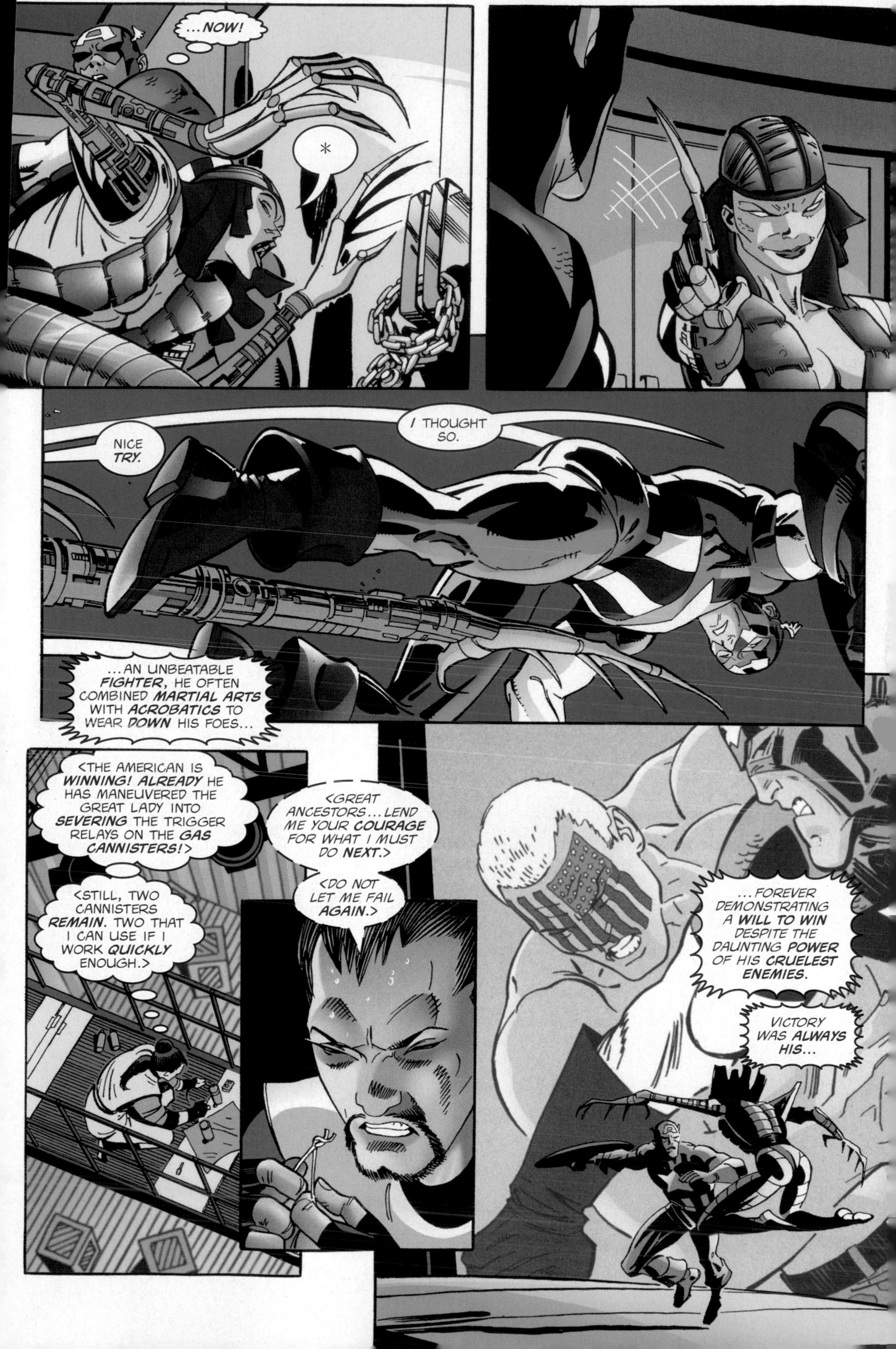
...NOW!
*
NICE TRY.
I THOUGHT SO.
...AN UNBEATABLE FIGHTER, HE OFTEN COMBINED MARTIAL ARTS WITH ACROBATICS TO WEAR DOWN HIS FOES...
<THE AMERICAN IS WINNING! ALREADY HE HAS MANEUVERED THE GREAT LADY INTO SEVERING THE TRIGGER RELAYS ON THE GAS CANNISTERS!>
<STILL, TWO CANNISTERS REMAIN. TWO THAT I CAN USE IF I WORK QUICKLY ENOUGH.>
<GREAT ANCESTORS...LEND ME YOUR COURAGE FOR WHAT I MUST DO NEXT.>
<DO NOT LET ME FAIL AGAIN.>
...FOREVER DEMONSTRATING A WILL TO WIN DESPITE THE DAUNTING POWER OF HIS CRUELEST ENEMIES.
VICTORY WAS ALWAYS HIS...

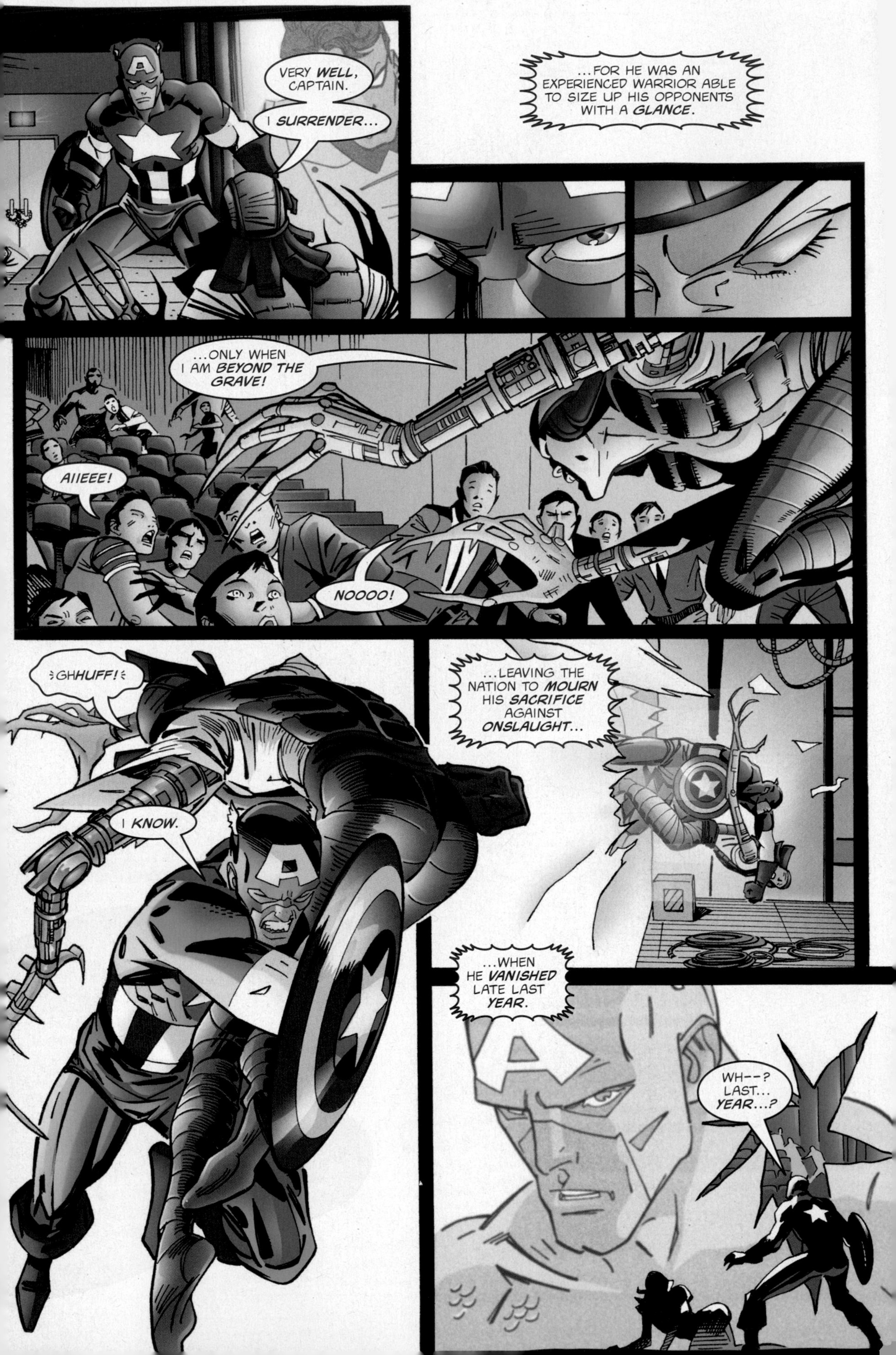
VERY WELL, CAPTAIN.
I SURRENDER...
...FOR HE WAS AN EXPERIENCED WARRIOR ABLE TO SIZE UP HIS OPPONENTS WITH A GLANCE.
...ONLY WHEN I AM BEYOND THE GRAVE!
AIIEEE!
NOOOO!
GHHUFF!
I KNOW.
...LEAVING THE NATION TO MOURN HIS SACRIFICE AGAINST ONSLAUGHT...
...WHEN HE VANISHED LATE LAST YEAR.
WH--? LAST... YEAR...?

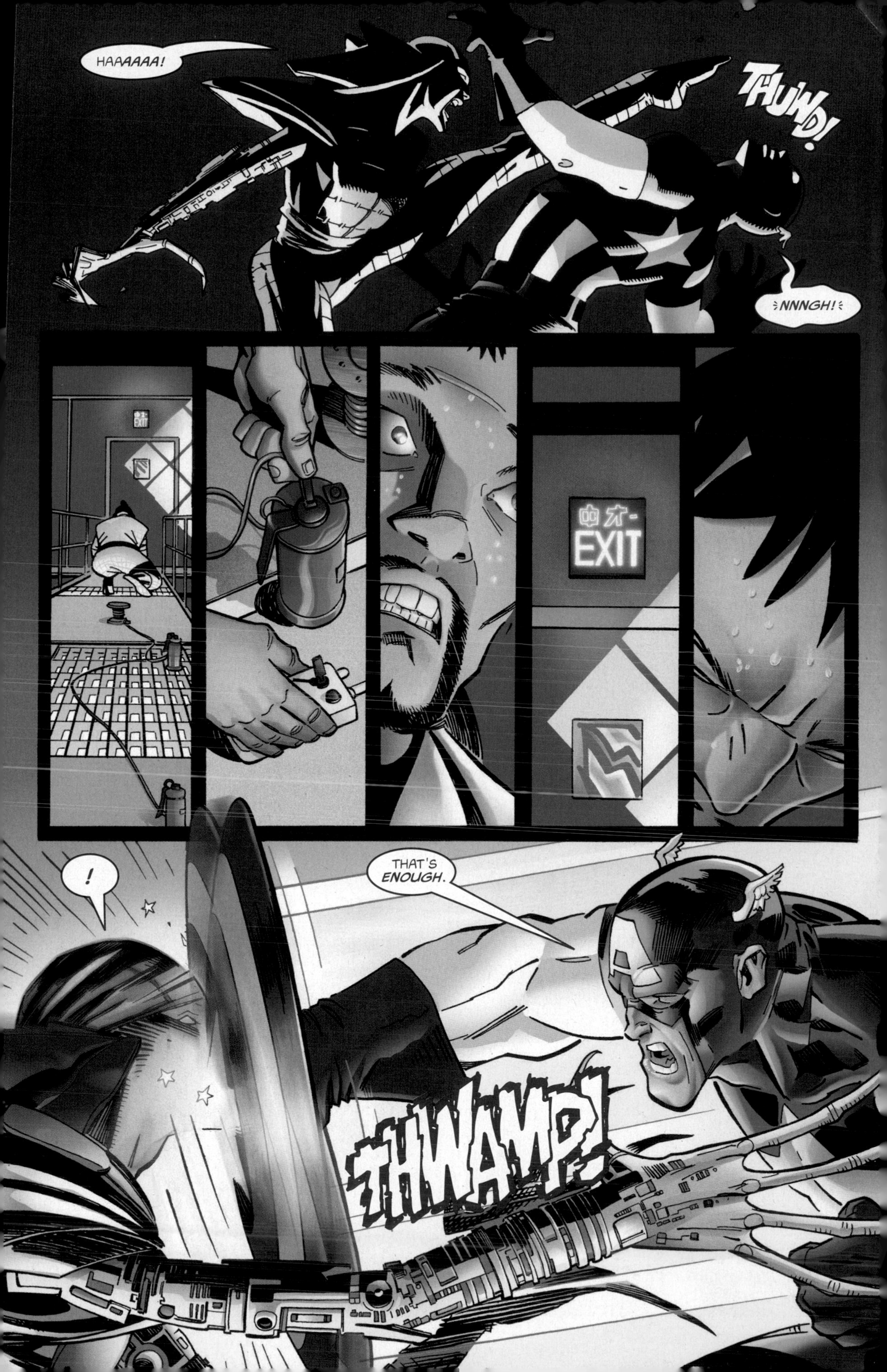
HAAAAAA!
THUND!
NNNGH!
中オー
EXIT
!
THAT'S ENOUGH.
THWAMP!

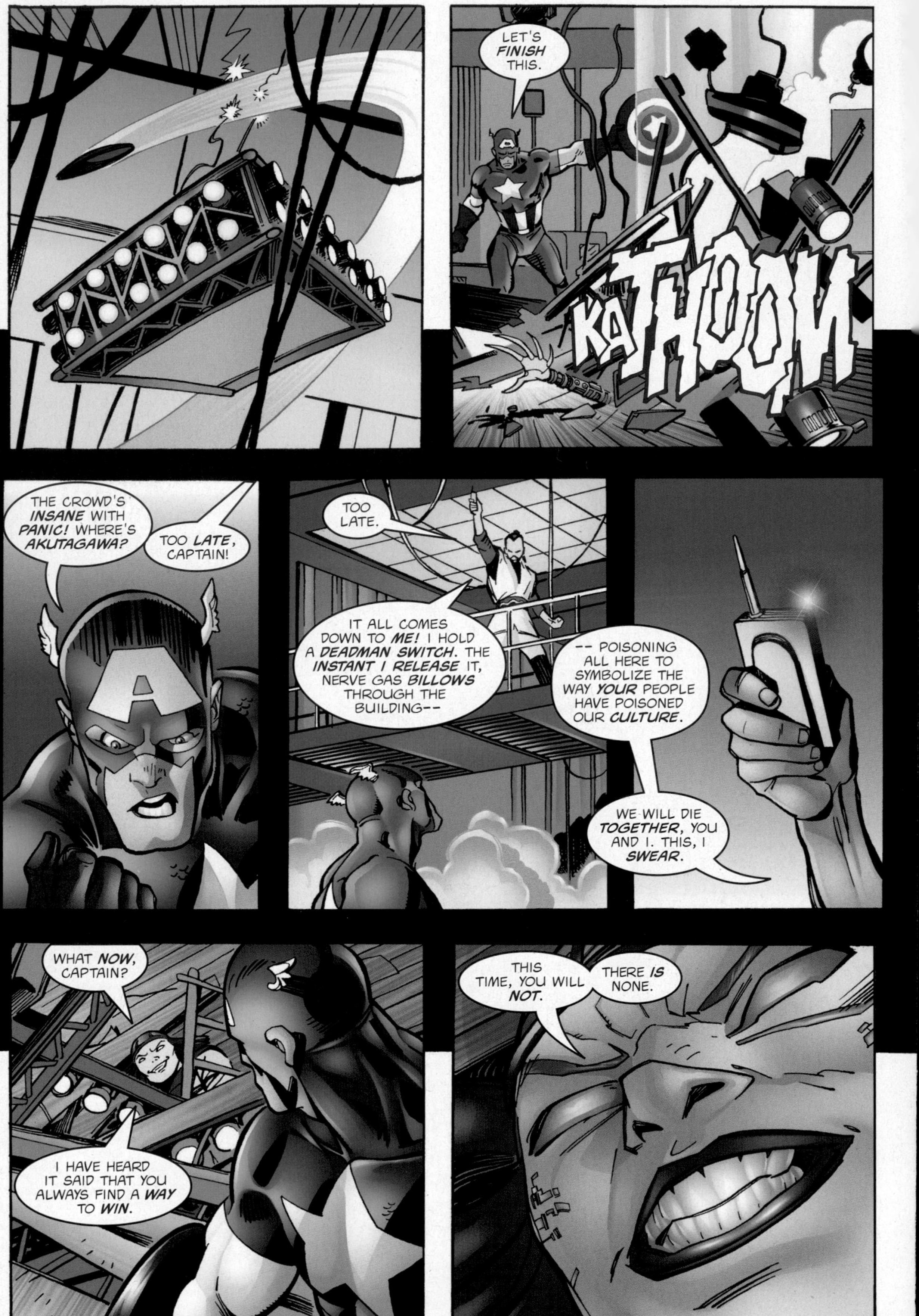
LET'S FINISH THIS.
KATHOOM
THE CROWD'S INSANE WITH PANIC! WHERE'S AKUTAGAWA?
TOO LATE, CAPTAIN!
TOO LATE.
IT ALL COMES DOWN TO ME! I HOLD A DEADMAN SWITCH. THE INSTANT I RELEASE IT, NERVE GAS BILLOWS THROUGH THE BUILDING--
-- POISONING ALL HERE TO SYMBOLIZE THE WAY YOUR PEOPLE HAVE POISONED OUR CULTURE.
WE WILL DIE TOGETHER, YOU AND I. THIS, I SWEAR.
WHAT NOW, CAPTAIN?
I HAVE HEARD IT SAID THAT YOU ALWAYS FIND A WAY TO WIN.
THIS TIME, YOU WILL NOT.
THERE IS NONE.

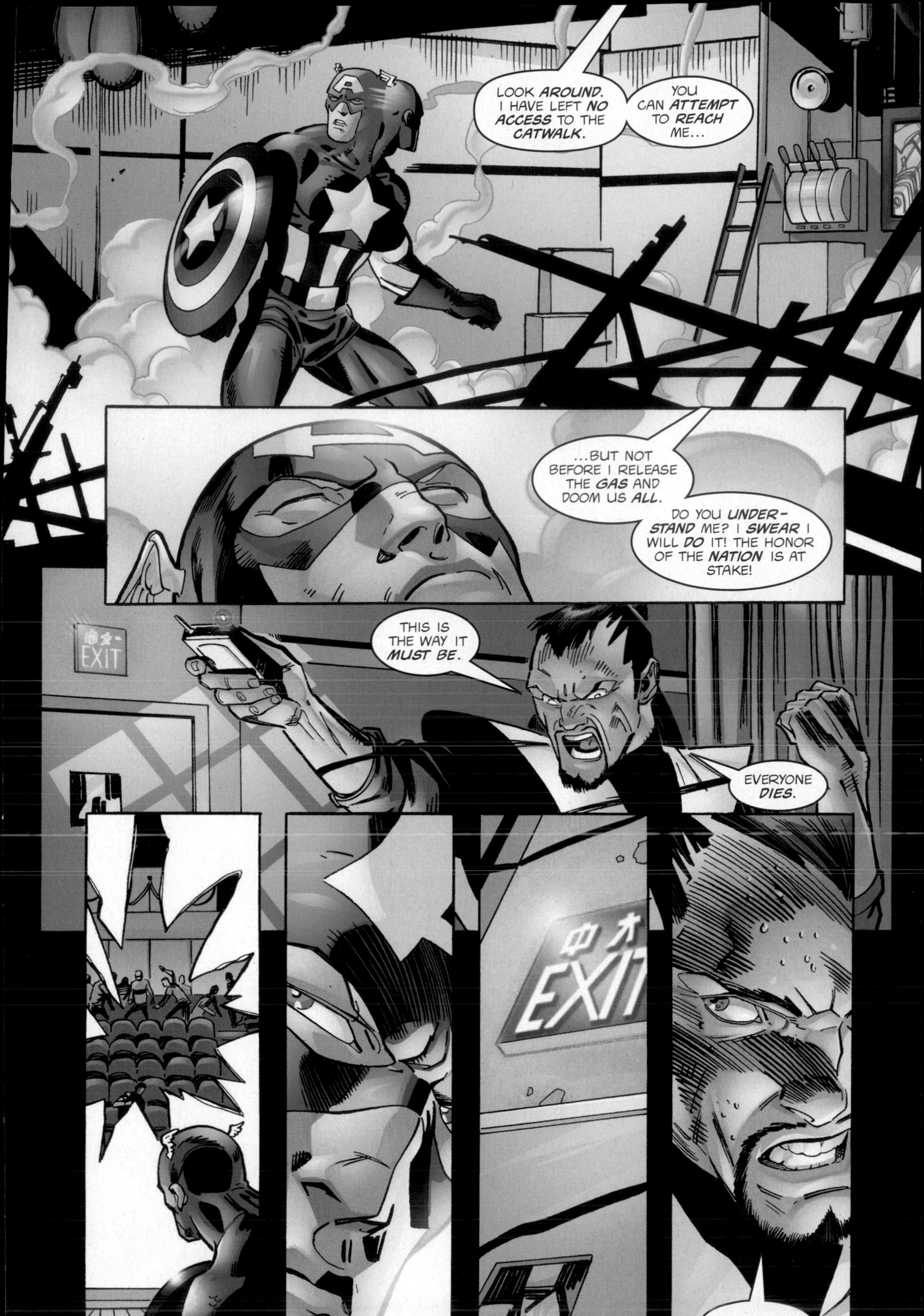
LOOK AROUND. I HAVE LEFT NO ACCESS TO THE CATWALK.
YOU CAN ATTEMPT TO REACH ME...
...BUT NOT BEFORE I RELEASE THE GAS AND DOOM US ALL.
DO YOU UNDER-STAND ME? I SWEAR I WILL DO IT! THE HONOR OF THE NATION IS AT STAKE!
EXIT
THIS IS THE WAY IT MUST BE.
EVERYONE DIES.
EXIT
EVERYONE.

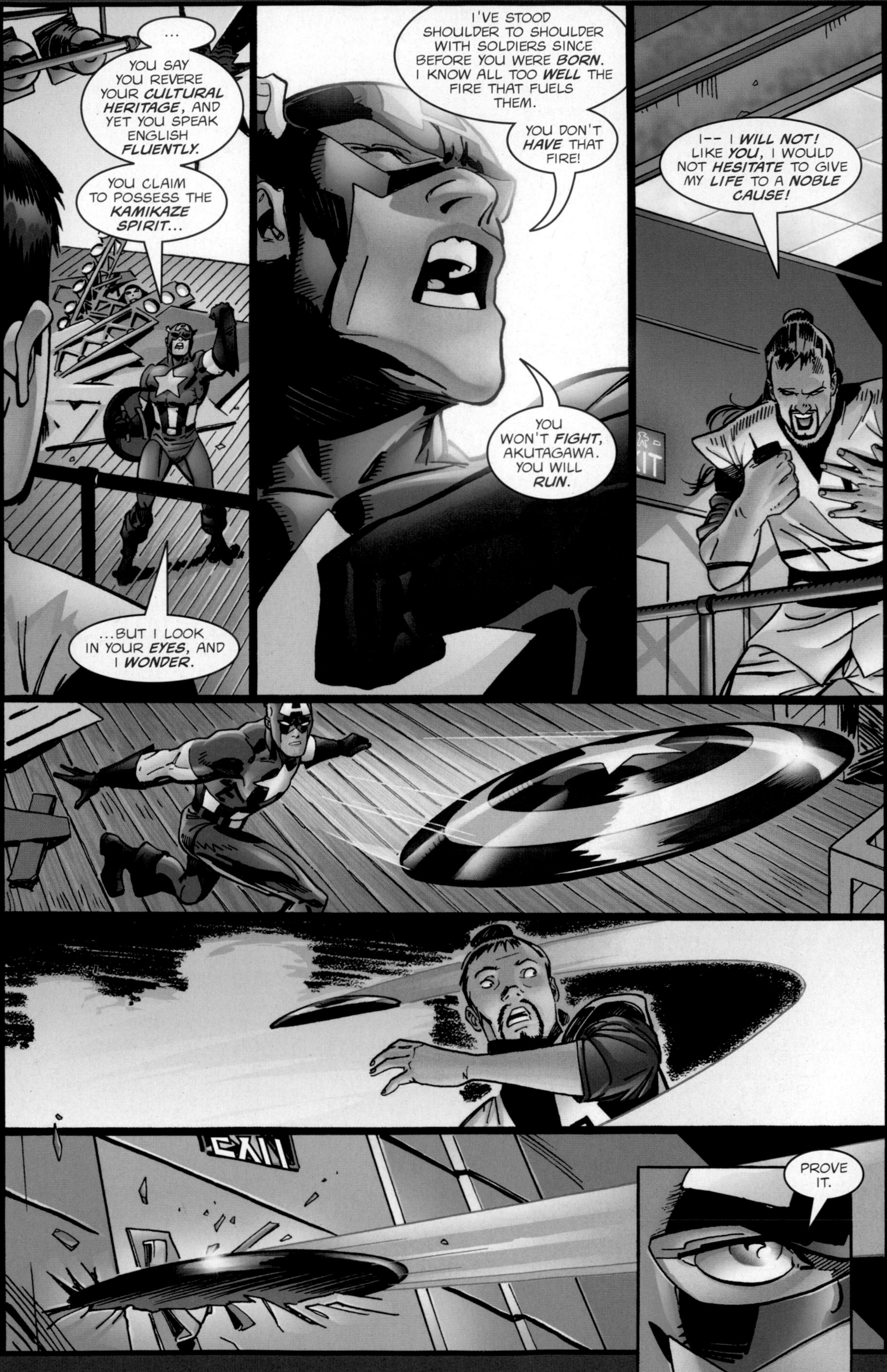
...
YOU SAY YOU REVERE YOUR CULTURAL HERITAGE, AND YET YOU SPEAK ENGLISH FLUENTLY.
YOU CLAIM TO POSSESS THE KAMIKAZE SPIRIT...
...BUT I LOOK IN YOUR EYES, AND I WONDER.
I'VE STOOD SHOULDER TO SHOULDER WITH SOLDIERS SINCE BEFORE YOU WERE BORN. I KNOW ALL TOO WELL THE FIRE THAT FUELS THEM.
YOU DON'T HAVE THAT FIRE!
YOU WON'T FIGHT, AKUTAGAWA. YOU WILL RUN.
I-- I WILL NOT! LIKE YOU, I WOULD NOT HESITATE TO GIVE MY LIFE TO A NOBLE CAUSE!
EXIT
PROVE IT.

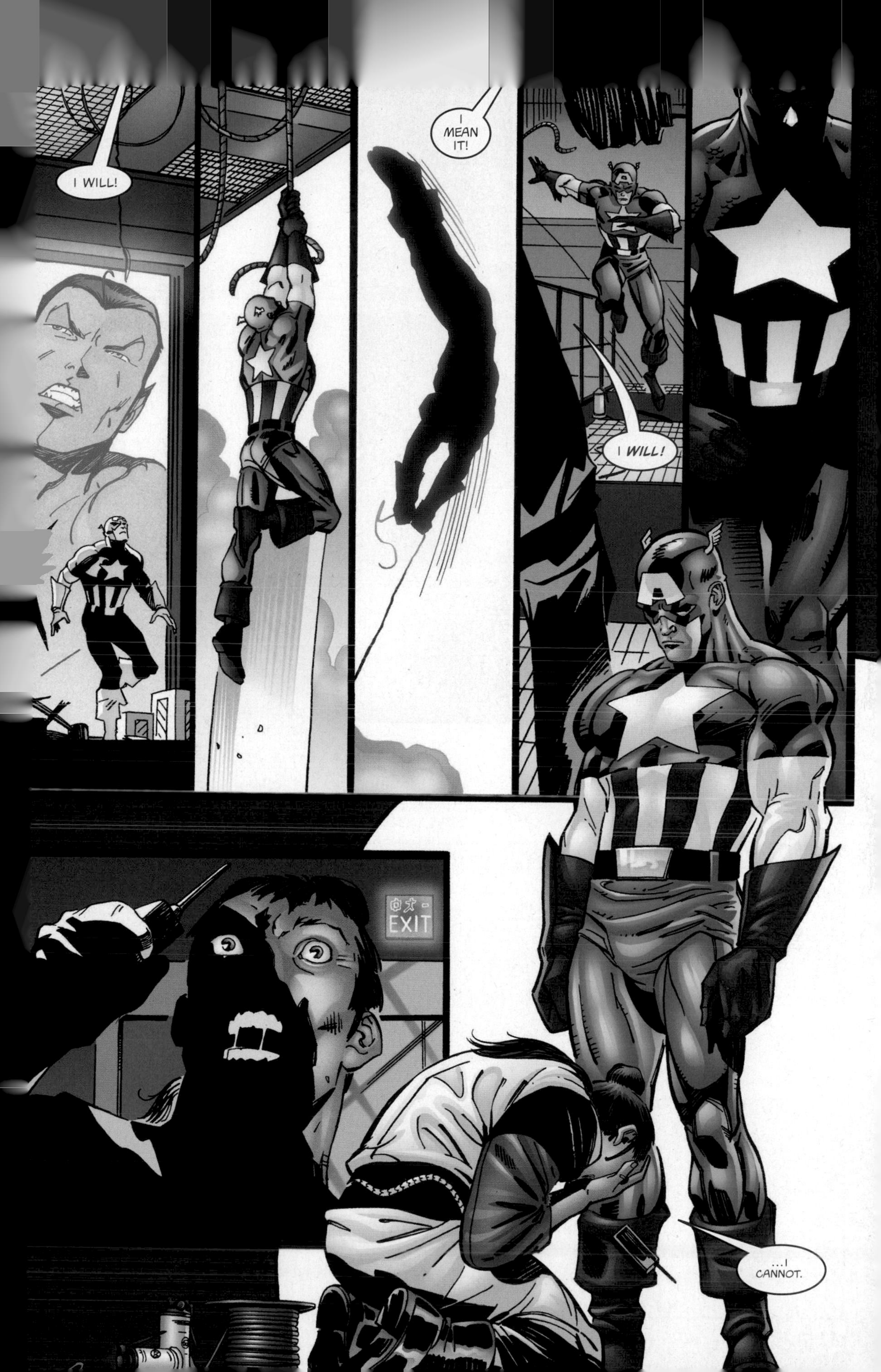
I WILL!
I MEAN IT!
I WILL!
EXIT
...I CANNOT.

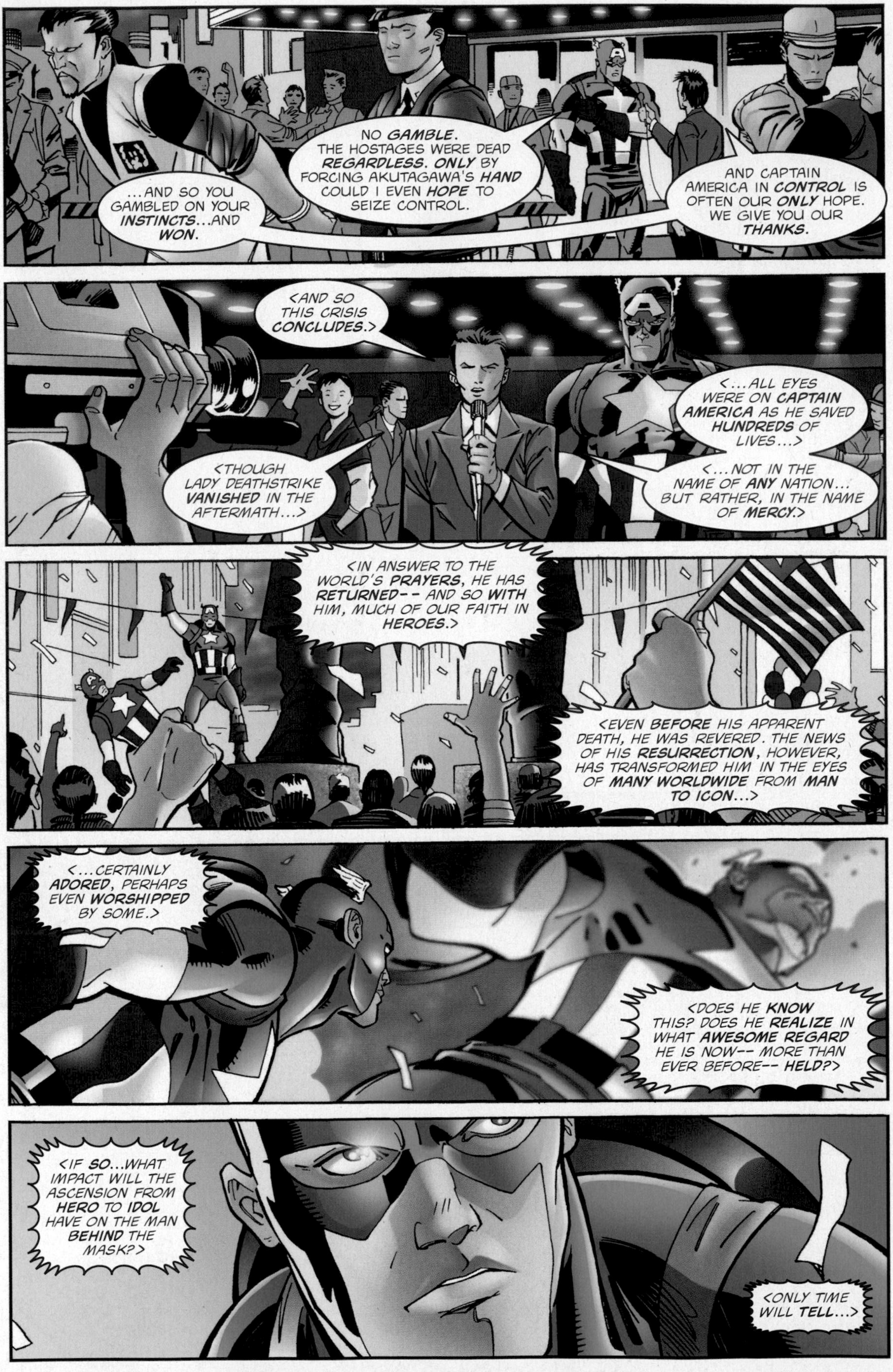

...AND SO YOU GAMBLED ON YOUR INSTINCTS...AND WON.
NO GAMBLE. THE HOSTAGES WERE DEAD REGARDLESS. ONLY BY FORCING AKUTAGAWA'S HAND COULD I EVEN HOPE TO SEIZE CONTROL.
AND CAPTAIN AMERICA IN CONTROL IS OFTEN OUR ONLY HOPE. WE GIVE YOU OUR THANKS.
<AND SO THIS CRISIS CONCLUDES.>
<THOUGH LADY DEATHSTRIKE VANISHED IN THE AFTERMATH...>
<...ALL EYES WERE ON CAPTAIN AMERICA AS HE SAVED HUNDREDS OF LIVES...>
<...NOT IN THE NAME OF ANY NATION... BUT RATHER, IN THE NAME OF MERCY.>
<IN ANSWER TO THE WORLD'S PRAYERS, HE HAS RETURNED-- AND SO WITH HIM, MUCH OF OUR FAITH IN HEROES.>
<EVEN BEFORE HIS APPARENT DEATH, HE WAS REVERED. THE NEWS OF HIS RESURRECTION, HOWEVER, HAS TRANSFORMED HIM IN THE EYES OF MANY WORLDWIDE FROM MAN TO ICON...>
<...CERTAINLY ADORED, PERHAPS EVEN WORSHIPPED BY SOME.>
<DOES HE KNOW THIS? DOES HE REALIZE IN WHAT AWESOME REGARD HE IS NOW-- MORE THAN EVER BEFORE-- HELD?>
<IF SO...WHAT IMPACT WILL THE ASCENSION FROM HERO TO IDOL HAVE ON THE MAN BEHIND THE MASK?>
<ONLY TIME WILL TELL...>

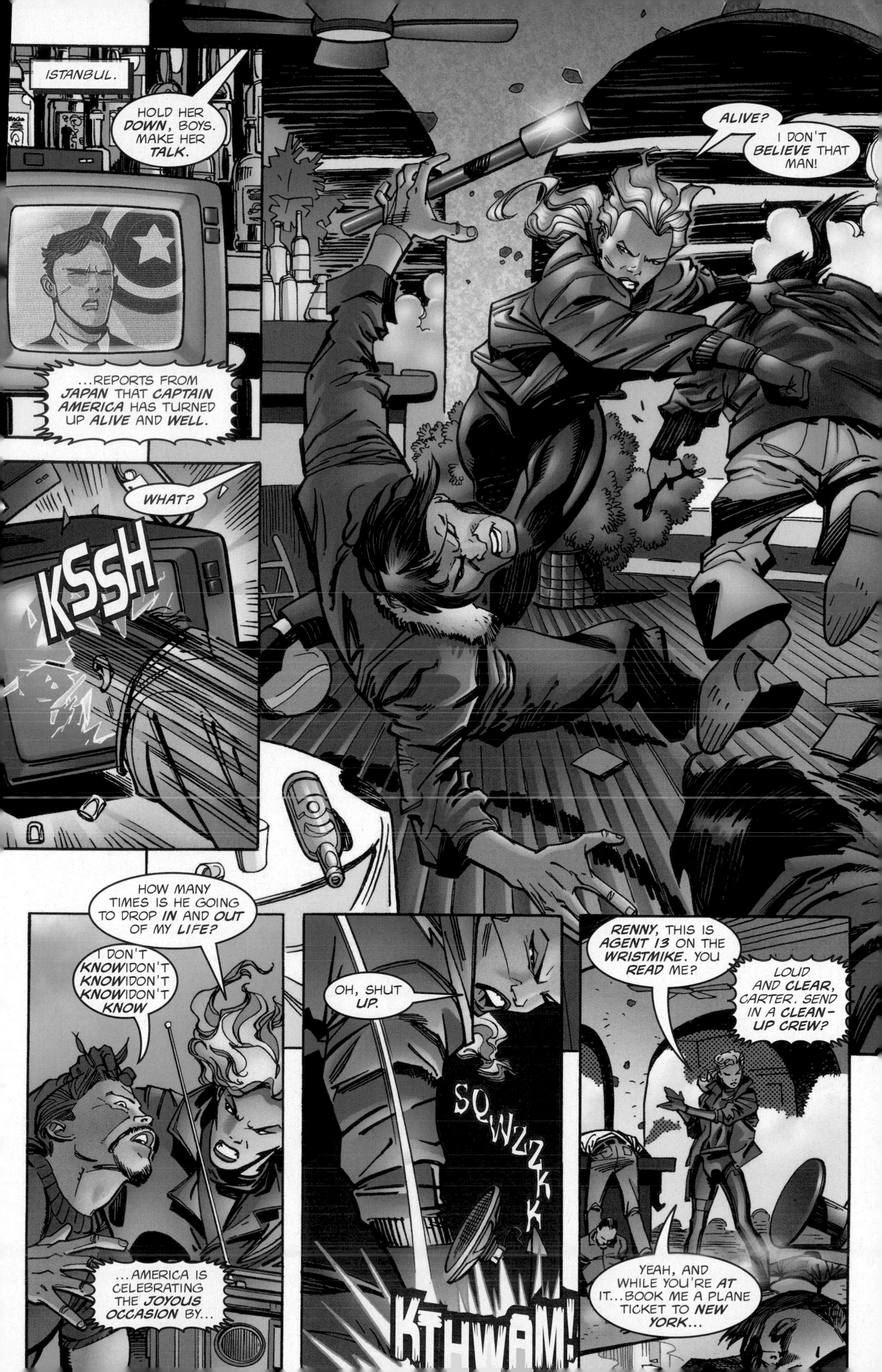
ISTANBUL.
HOLD HER DOWN, BOYS. MAKE HER TALK.
...REPORTS FROM JAPAN THAT CAPTAIN AMERICA HAS TURNED UP ALIVE AND WELL.
ALIVE?
I DON'T BELIEVE THAT MAN!
WHAT?
KSSH
HOW MANY TIMES IS HE GOING TO DROP IN AND OUT OF MY LIFE?
I DON'T KNOWIDON'T KNOWIDON'T KNOWIDON'T KNOW
...AMERICA IS CELEBRATING THE JOYOUS OCCASION BY...
OH, SHUT UP.
SQWZZKK
KTHWAM!
RENNY, THIS IS AGENT 13 ON THE WRISTMIKE. YOU READ ME?
LOUD AND CLEAR, CARTER. SEND IN A CLEAN-UP CREW?
YEAH, AND WHILE YOU'RE AT IT...BOOK ME A PLANE TICKET TO NEW YORK...

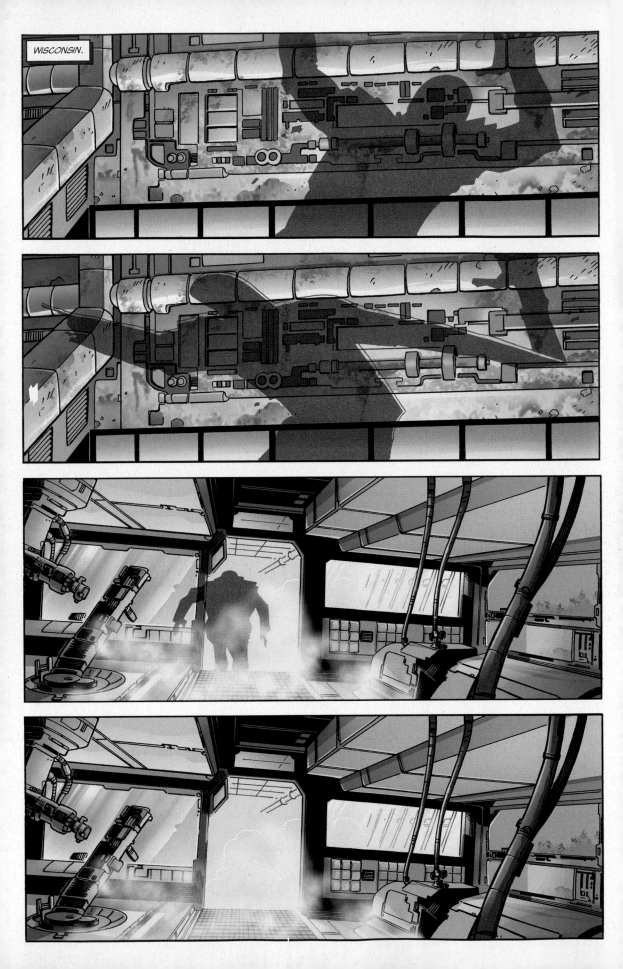

WISCONSIN.

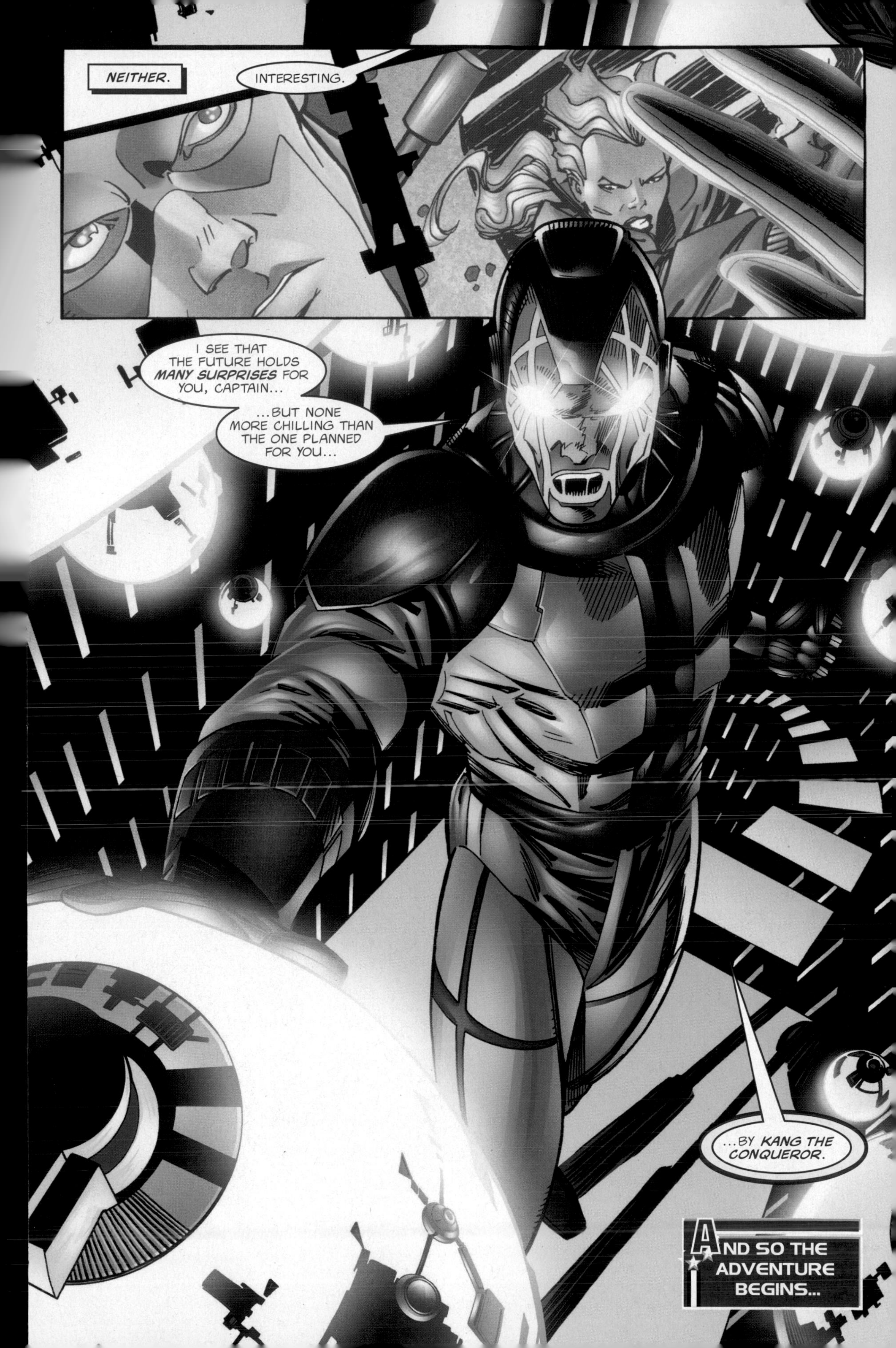

NEITHER.
INTERESTING.
I SEE THAT THE FUTURE HOLDS MANY SURPRISES FOR YOU, CAPTAIN...
...BUT NONE MORE CHILLING THAN THE ONE PLANNED FOR YOU...
...BY KANG THE CONQUEROR.
AND SO THE ADVENTURE BEGINS...

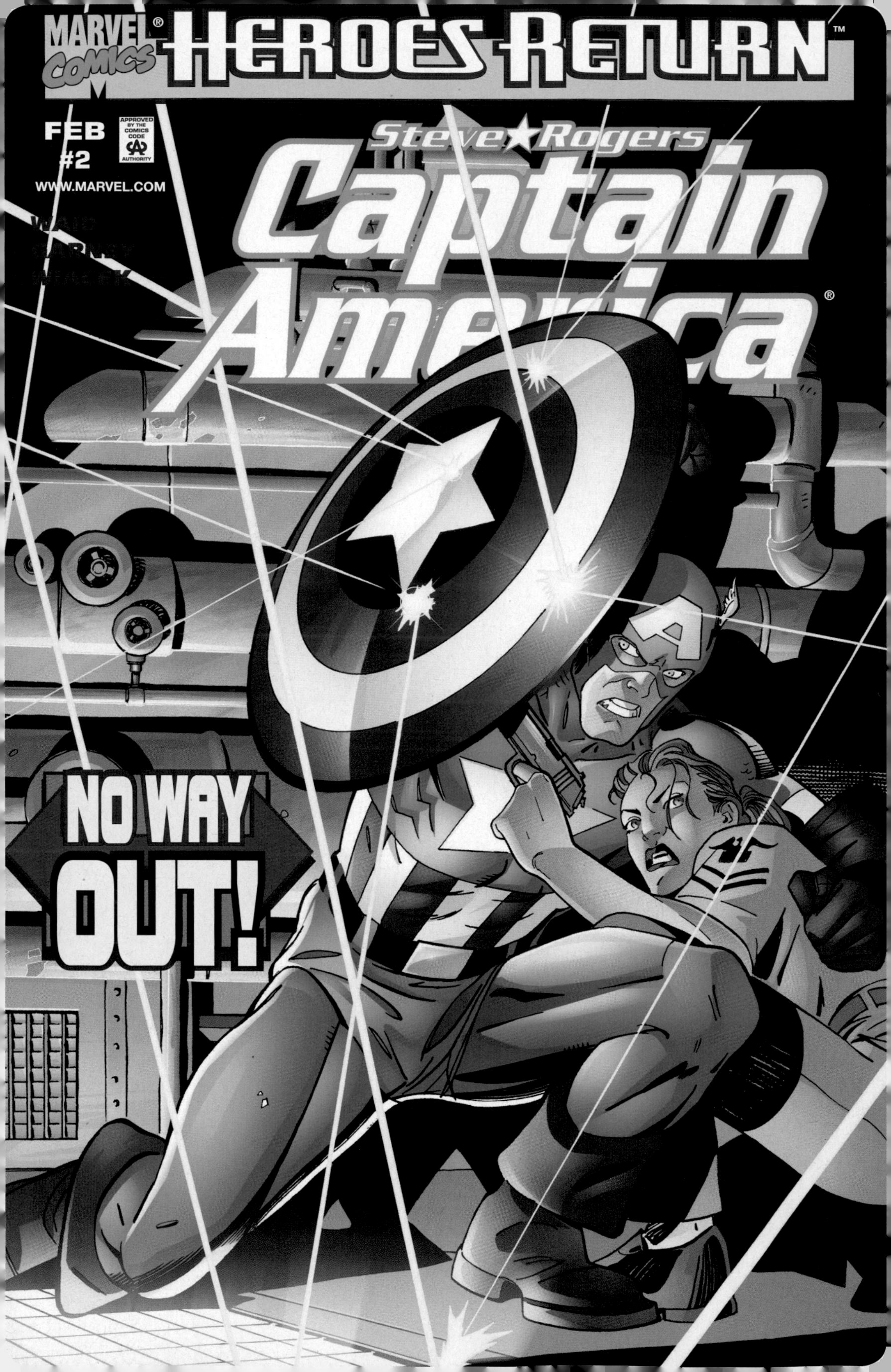
MARVEL COMICS
HEROES RETURN
FEB
#2
APPROVED BY THE COMICS CODE AUTHORITY
WWW.MARVEL.COM
Steve★Rogers
Captain America
NO WAY OUT!

Stan Lee Presents

CAPTAIN AMERICA

in:

To SERVE And PROTECT

by

MARK WAID & RON GARNEY

BOB WIACEK – JOHN COSTANZA

JOE ROSAS – DIGITAL CHAMELEON

MATT IDELSON – BOB HARRAS

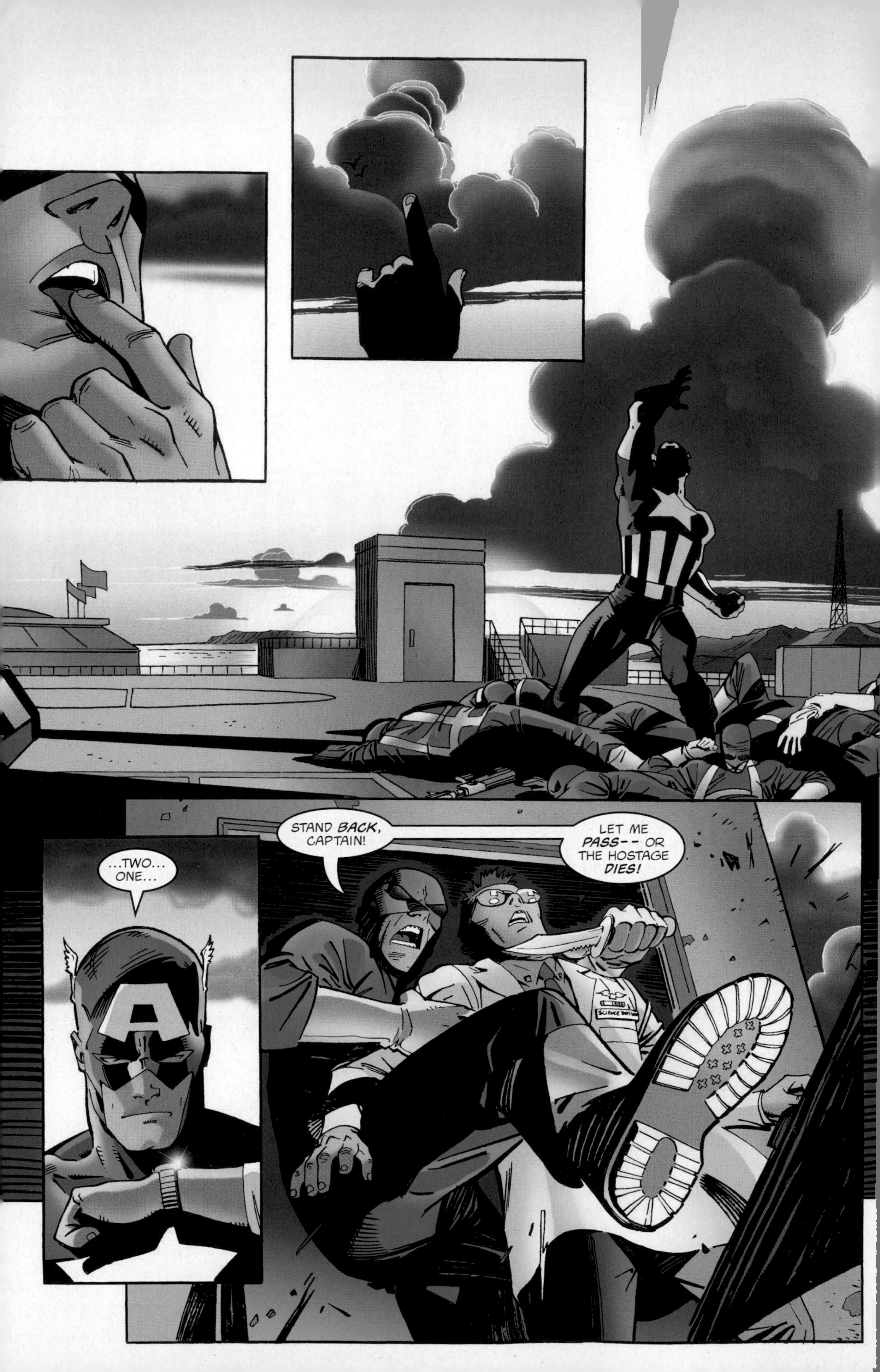
...TWO... ONE...
STAND BACK, CAPTAIN!
LET ME PASS-- OR THE HOSTAGE DIES!

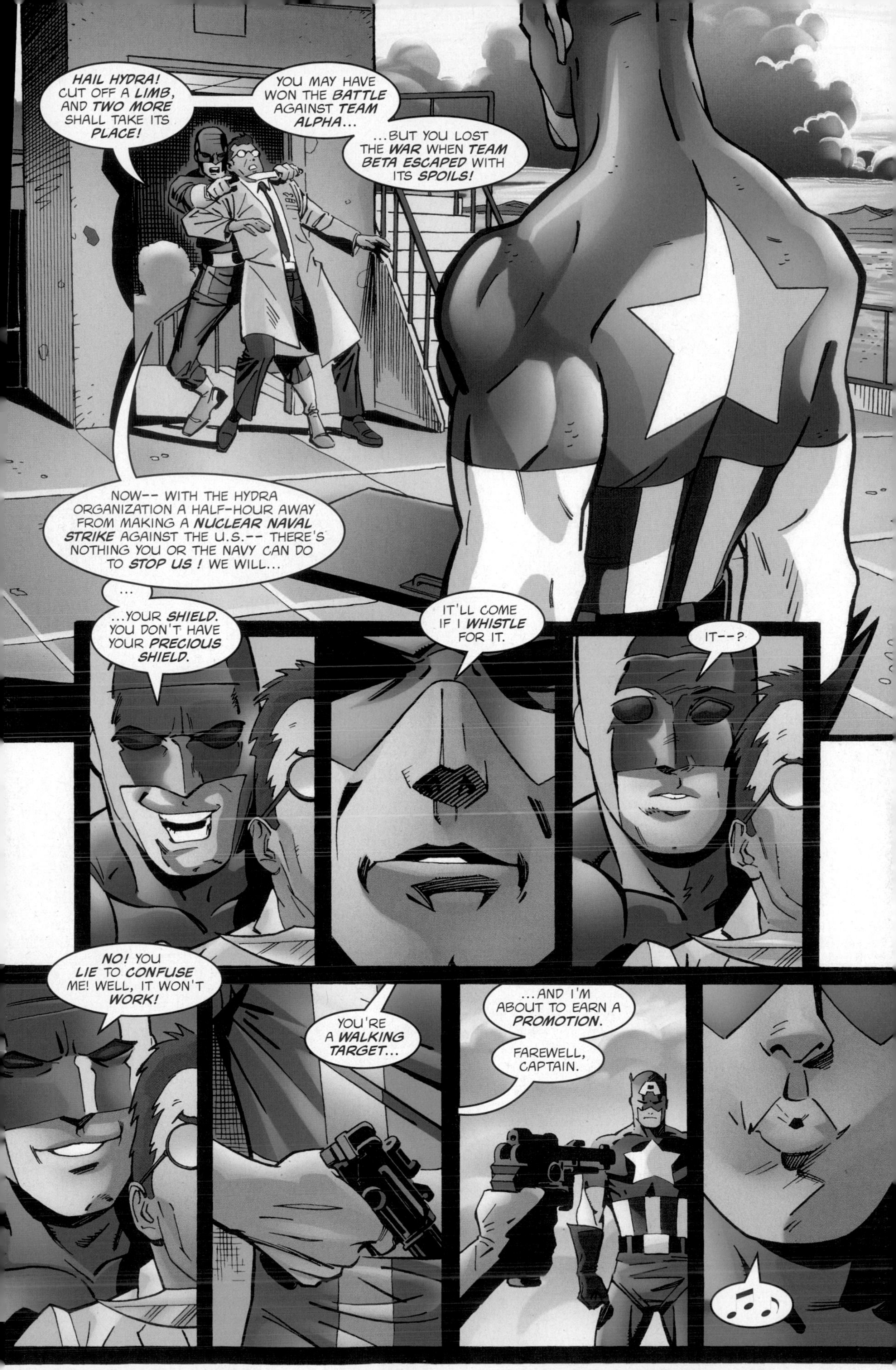
HAIL HYDRA! CUT OFF A LIMB, AND TWO MORE SHALL TAKE ITS PLACE!
YOU MAY HAVE WON THE BATTLE AGAINST TEAM ALPHA...
...BUT YOU LOST THE WAR WHEN TEAM BETA ESCAPED WITH ITS SPOILS!
NOW-- WITH THE HYDRA ORGANIZATION A HALF-HOUR AWAY FROM MAKING A NUCLEAR NAVAL STRIKE AGAINST THE U.S.-- THERE'S NOTHING YOU OR THE NAVY CAN DO TO STOP US ! WE WILL...
...
...YOUR SHIELD. YOU DON'T HAVE YOUR PRECIOUS SHIELD.
IT'LL COME IF I WHISTLE FOR IT.
IT--?
NO! YOU LIE TO CONFUSE ME! WELL, IT WON'T WORK!
YOU'RE A WALKING TARGET...
...AND I'M ABOUT TO EARN A PROMOTION.
FAREWELL, CAPTAIN.

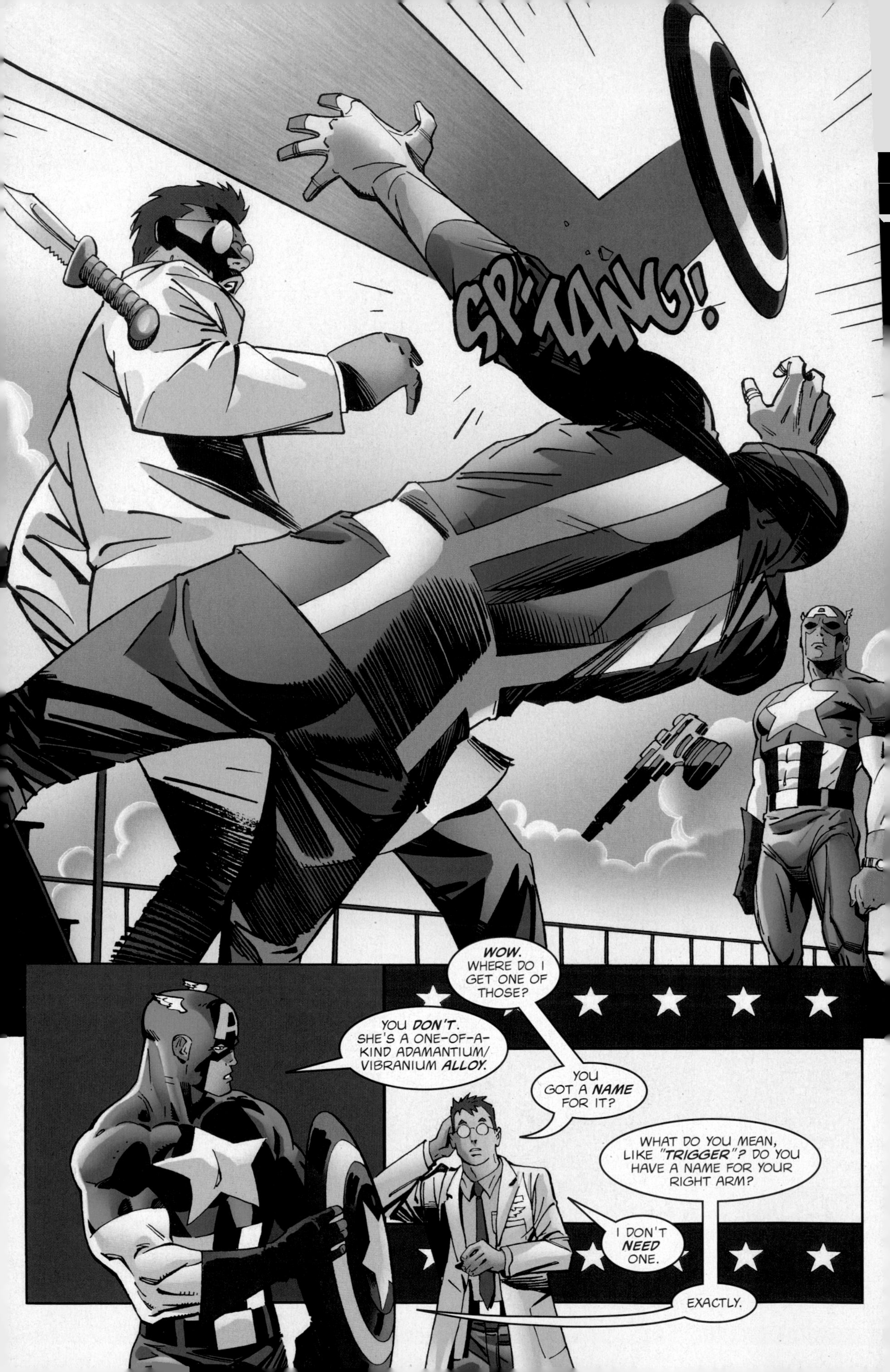

SP'TANG!
WOW. WHERE DO I GET ONE OF THOSE?
YOU DON'T. SHE'S A ONE-OF-A-KIND ADAMANTIUM/VIBRANIUM ALLOY.
YOU GOT A NAME FOR IT?
WHAT DO YOU MEAN, LIKE "TRIGGER"? DO YOU HAVE A NAME FOR YOUR RIGHT ARM?
I DON'T NEED ONE.
EXACTLY.

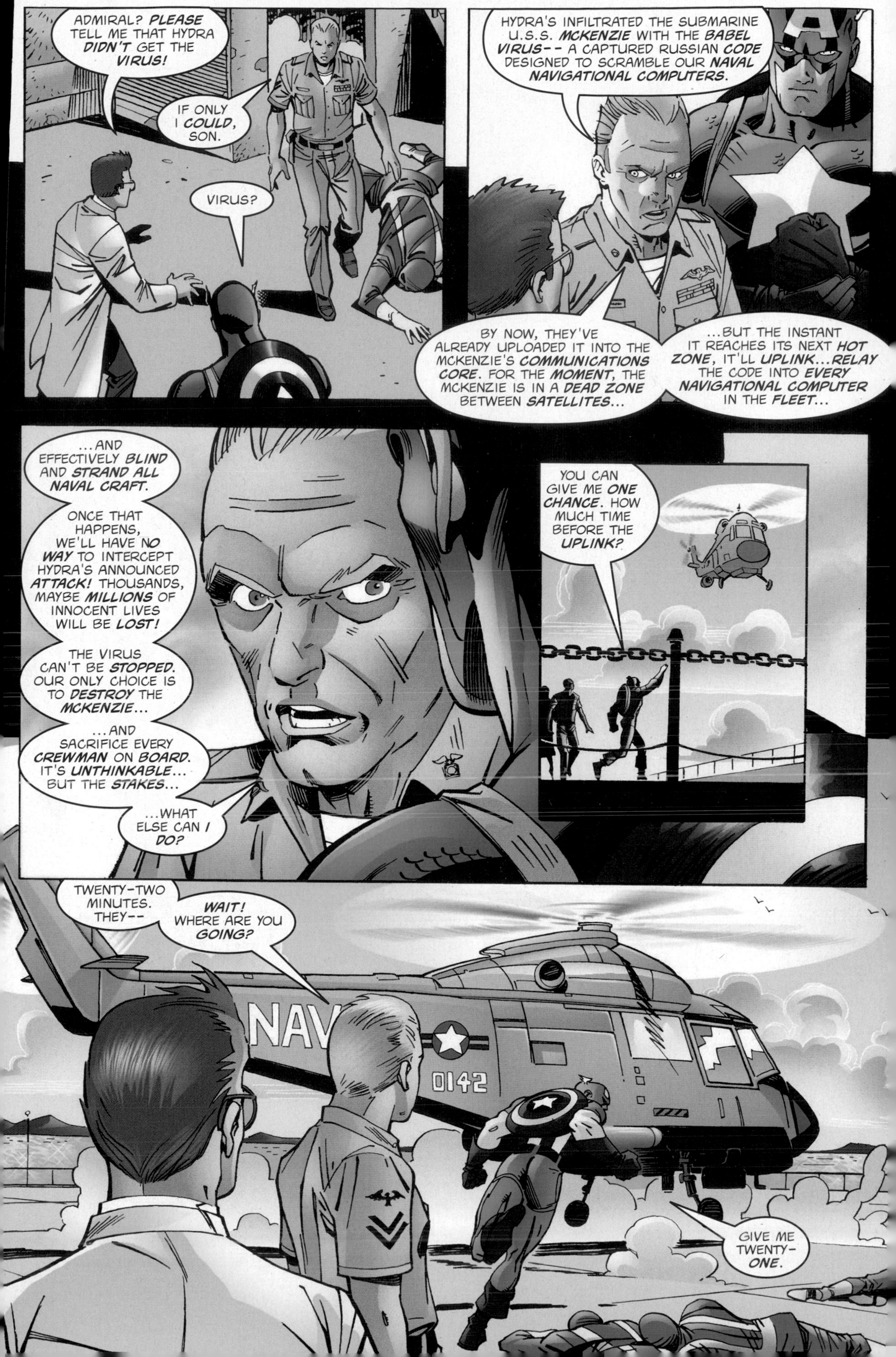
ADMIRAL? PLEASE TELL ME THAT HYDRA DIDN'T GET THE VIRUS!
IF ONLY I COULD, SON.
VIRUS?
HYDRA'S INFILTRATED THE SUBMARINE U.S.S. MCKENZIE WITH THE BABEL VIRUS-- A CAPTURED RUSSIAN CODE DESIGNED TO SCRAMBLE OUR NAVAL NAVIGATIONAL COMPUTERS.
BY NOW, THEY'VE ALREADY UPLOADED IT INTO THE MCKENZIE'S COMMUNICATIONS CORE. FOR THE MOMENT, THE MCKENZIE IS IN A DEAD ZONE BETWEEN SATELLITES...
...BUT THE INSTANT IT REACHES ITS NEXT HOT ZONE, IT'LL UPLINK...RELAY THE CODE INTO EVERY NAVIGATIONAL COMPUTER IN THE FLEET...
...AND EFFECTIVELY BLIND AND STRAND ALL NAVAL CRAFT.
ONCE THAT HAPPENS, WE'LL HAVE NO WAY TO INTERCEPT HYDRA'S ANNOUNCED ATTACK! THOUSANDS, MAYBE MILLIONS OF INNOCENT LIVES WILL BE LOST!
THE VIRUS CAN'T BE STOPPED. OUR ONLY CHOICE IS TO DESTROY THE MCKENZIE...
...AND SACRIFICE EVERY CREWMAN ON BOARD. IT'S UNTHINKABLE... BUT THE STAKES...
...WHAT ELSE CAN I DO?
YOU CAN GIVE ME ONE CHANCE. HOW MUCH TIME BEFORE THE UPLINK?
TWENTY-TWO MINUTES. THEY--
WAIT! WHERE ARE YOU GOING?
NAV
0142
GIVE ME TWENTY-ONE.

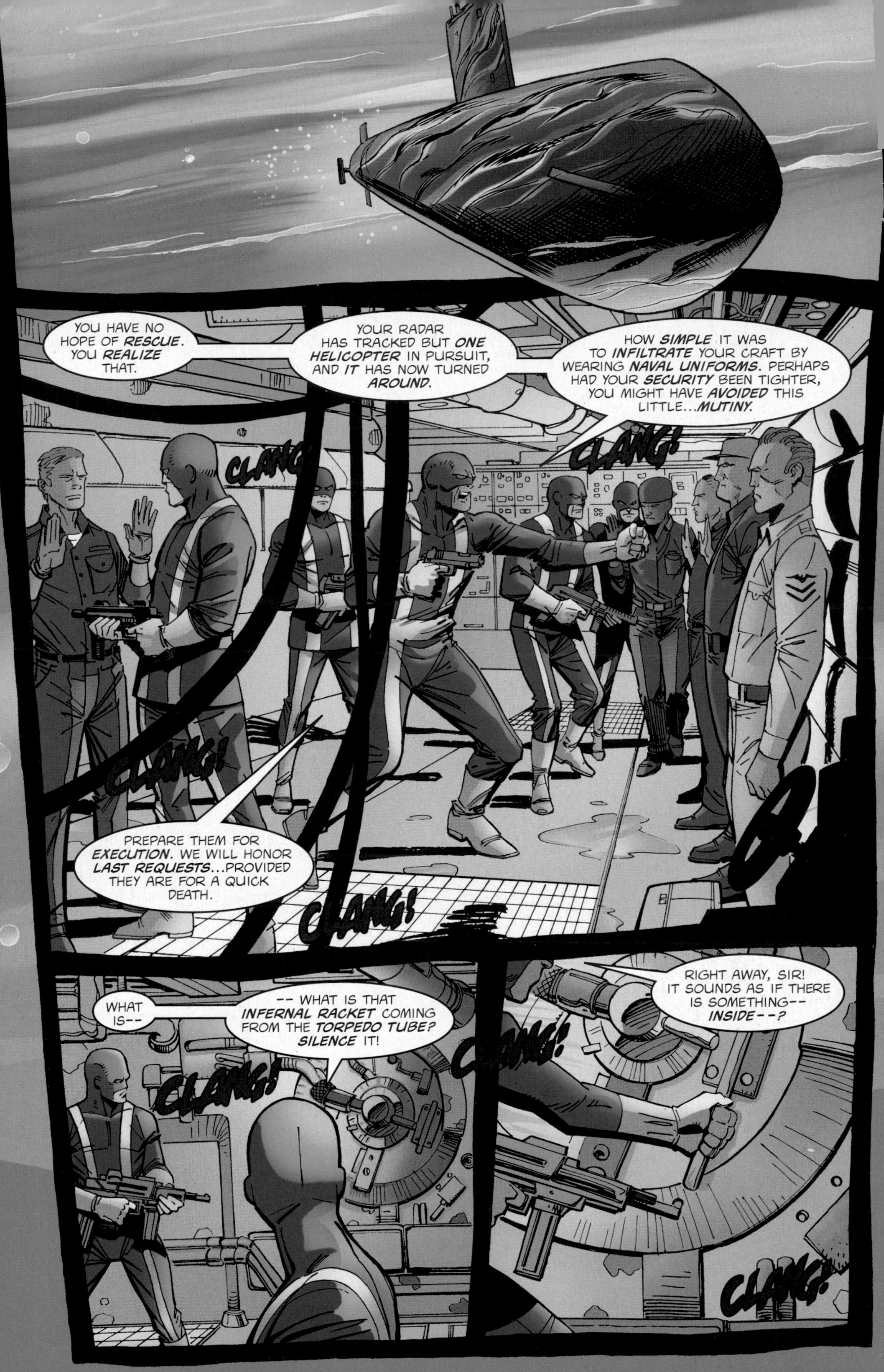
YOU HAVE NO HOPE OF RESCUE. YOU REALIZE THAT.
YOUR RADAR HAS TRACKED BUT ONE HELICOPTER IN PURSUIT, AND IT HAS NOW TURNED AROUND.
HOW SIMPLE IT WAS TO INFILTRATE YOUR CRAFT BY WEARING NAVAL UNIFORMS. PERHAPS HAD YOUR SECURITY BEEN TIGHTER, YOU MIGHT HAVE AVOIDED THIS LITTLE...MUTINY.
CLANG!
CLANG!
CLANG!
PREPARE THEM FOR EXECUTION. WE WILL HONOR LAST REQUESTS...PROVIDED THEY ARE FOR A QUICK DEATH.
CLANG!
WHAT IS--
-- WHAT IS THAT INFERNAL RACKET COMING FROM THE TORPEDO TUBE? SILENCE IT!
CLANG!
RIGHT AWAY, SIR! IT SOUNDS AS IF THERE IS SOMETHING-- INSIDE--?
CLANG!
CLANG!

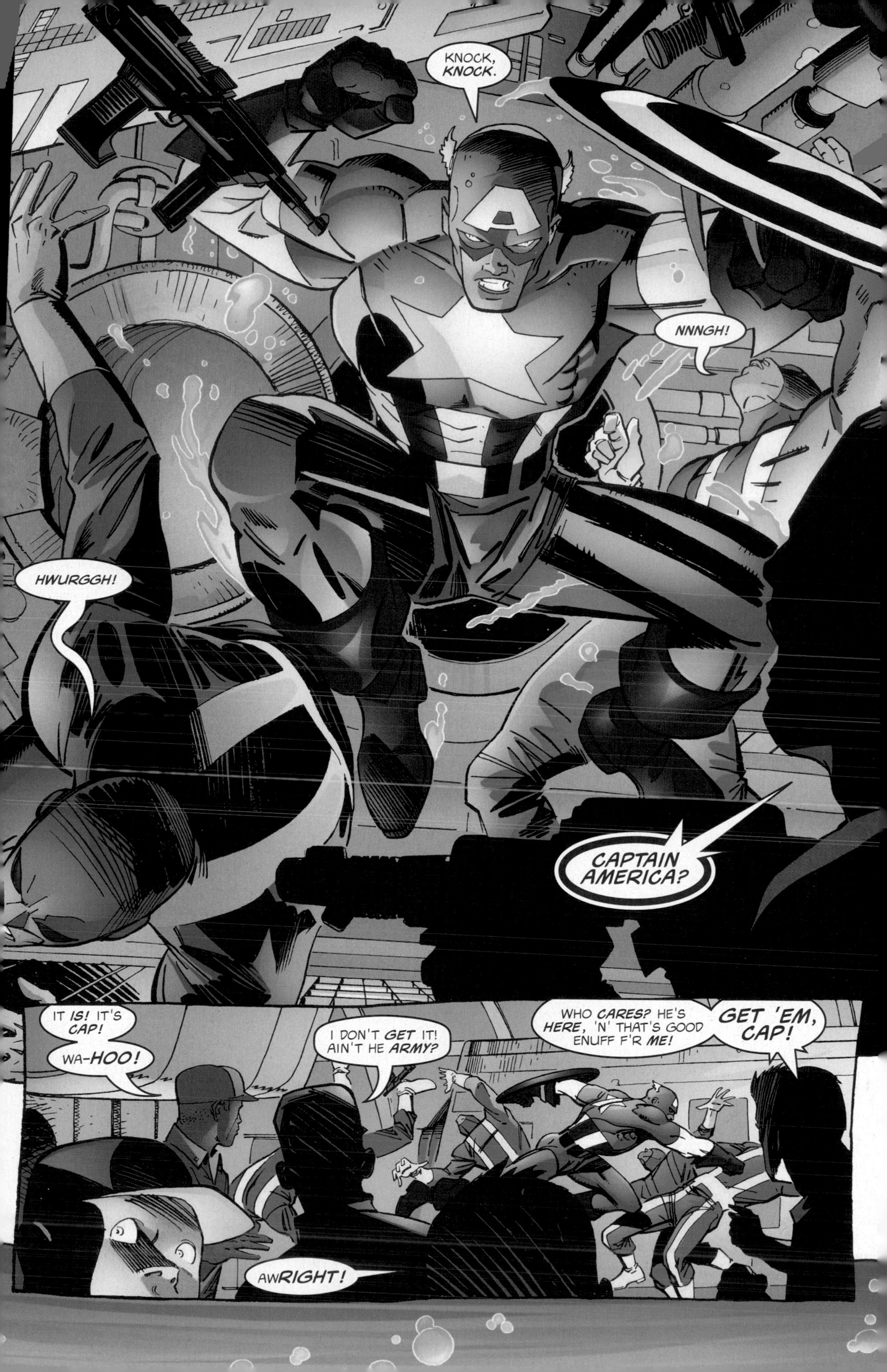
KNOCK, KNOCK.
NNNGH!
HWURGGH!
CAPTAIN AMERICA?
IT IS! IT'S CAP!
WA-HOO!
I DON'T GET IT! AIN'T HE ARMY?
WHO CARES? HE'S HERE, 'N' THAT'S GOOD ENUFF F'R ME!
GET 'EM, CAP!
AWRIGHT!

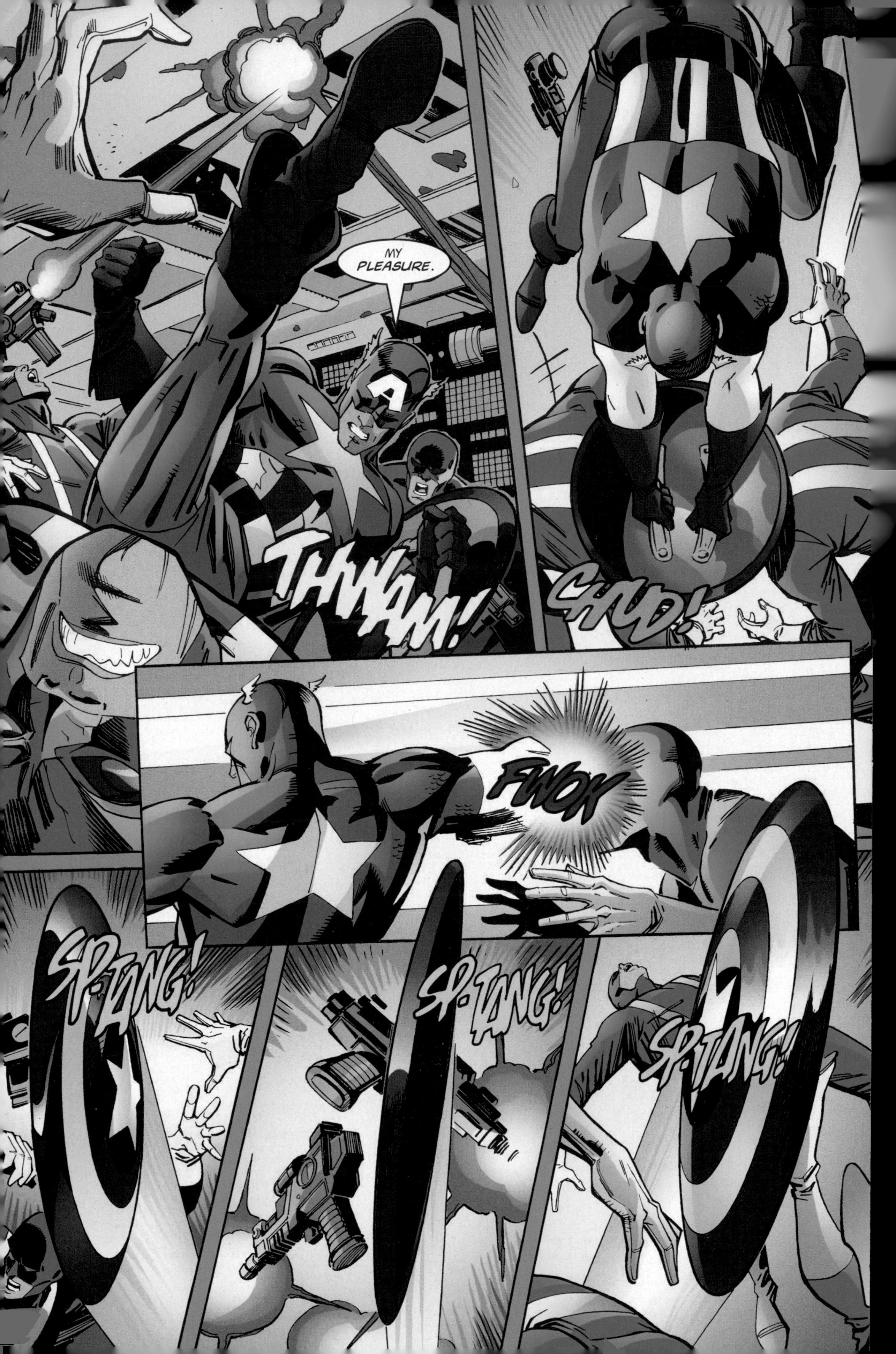
MY PLEASURE.
THWAM!
CHUD!
FWOK
SP-TANG!
SP-TANG!
SP-TANG!

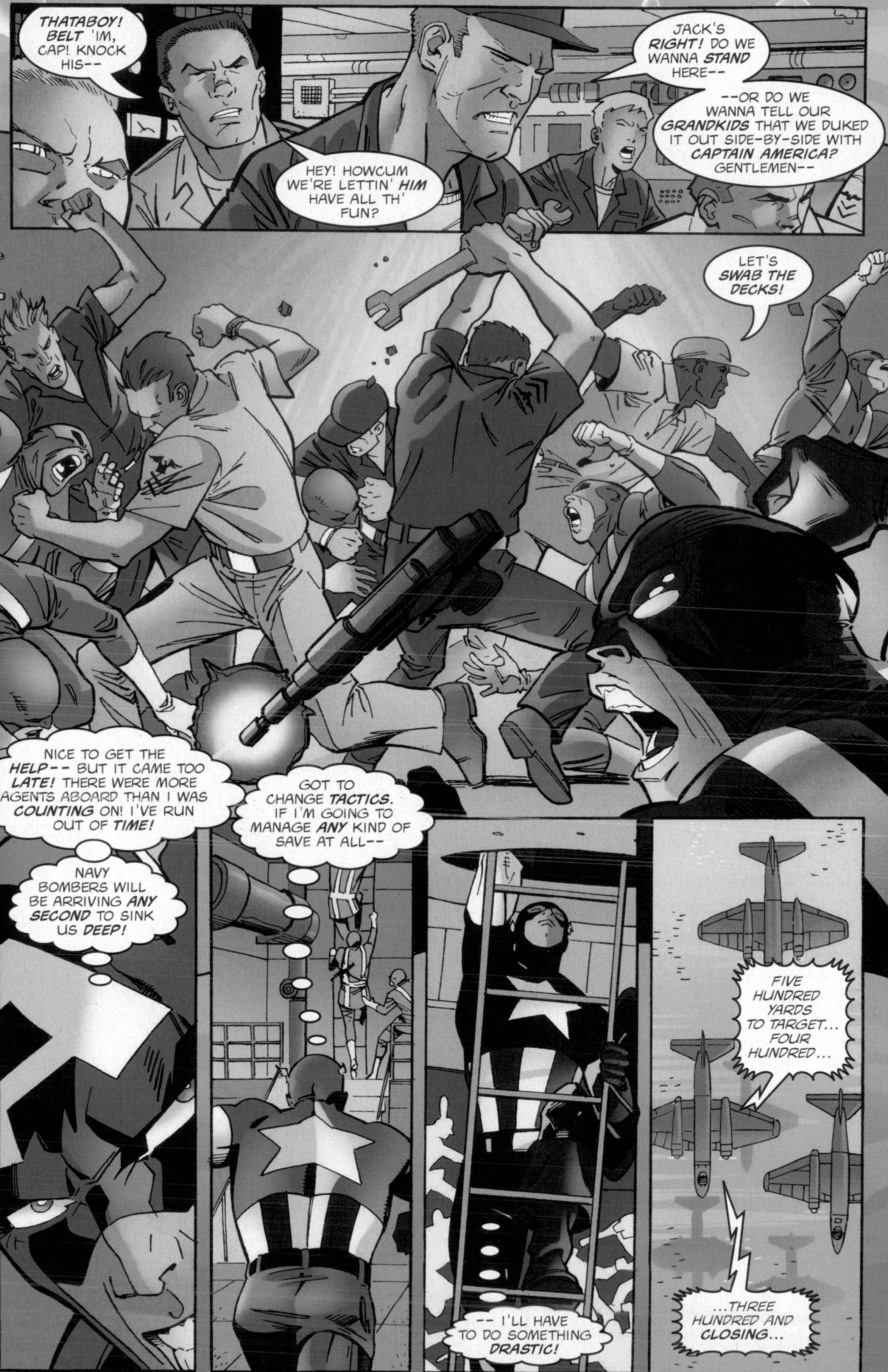
THATABOY! BELT 'IM, CAP! KNOCK HIS--
HEY! HOWCUM WE'RE LETTIN' HIM HAVE ALL TH' FUN?
JACK'S RIGHT! DO WE WANNA STAND HERE--
--OR DO WE WANNA TELL OUR GRANDKIDS THAT WE DUKED IT OUT SIDE-BY-SIDE WITH CAPTAIN AMERICA? GENTLEMEN--
LET'S SWAB THE DECKS!
NICE TO GET THE HELP-- BUT IT CAME TOO LATE! THERE WERE MORE AGENTS ABOARD THAN I WAS COUNTING ON! I'VE RUN OUT OF TIME!
NAVY BOMBERS WILL BE ARRIVING ANY SECOND TO SINK US DEEP!
GOT TO CHANGE TACTICS. IF I'M GOING TO MANAGE ANY KIND OF SAVE AT ALL--
-- I'LL HAVE TO DO SOMETHING DRASTIC!
FIVE HUNDRED YARDS TO TARGET... FOUR HUNDRED...
...THREE HUNDRED AND CLOSING...

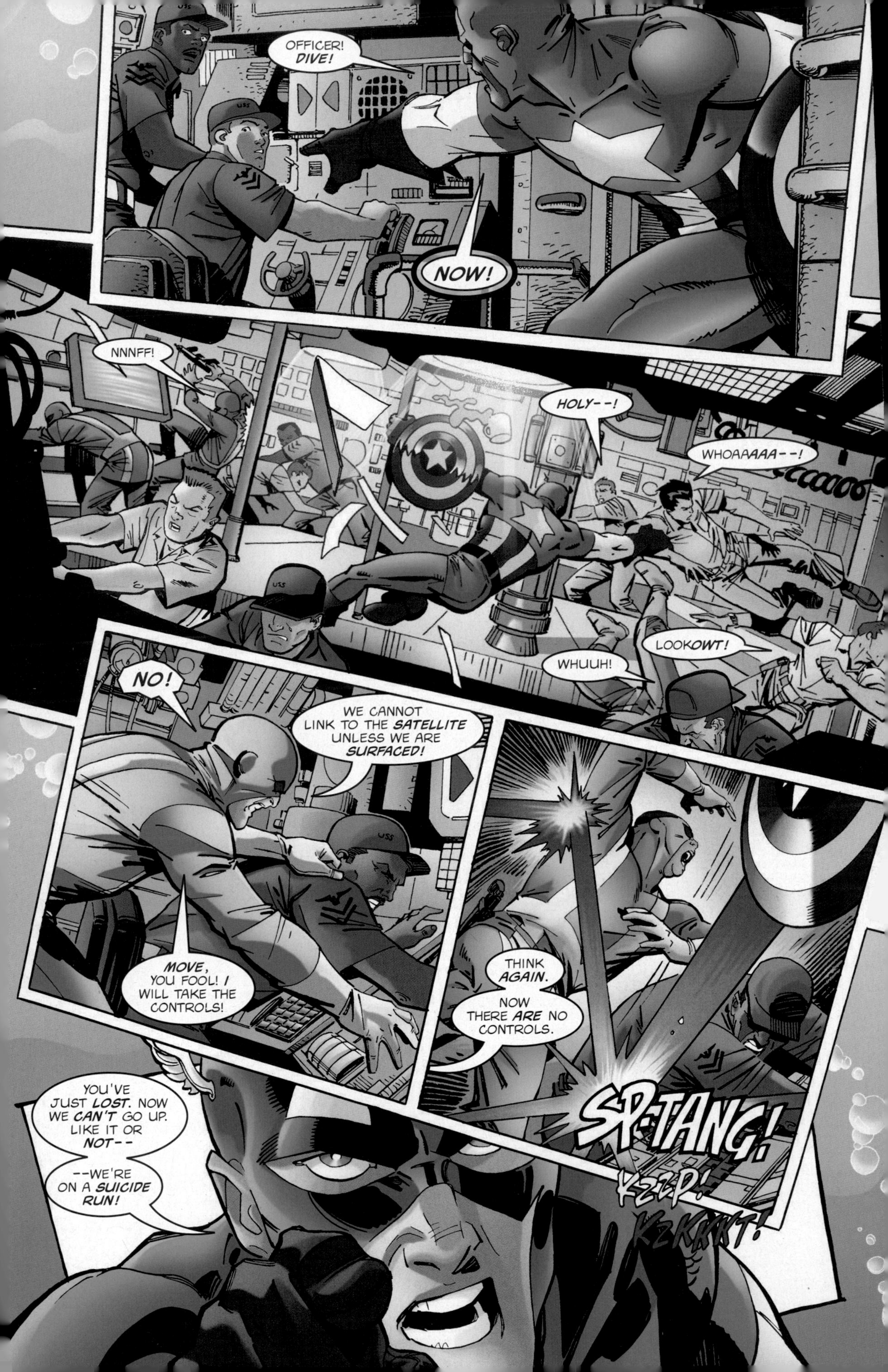
OFFICER! DIVE!
NOW!
NNNFF!
HOLY--!
WHOAAAAA--!
LOOKOWT!
WHUUH!
NO!
WE CANNOT LINK TO THE SATELLITE UNLESS WE ARE SURFACED!
MOVE, YOU FOOL! I WILL TAKE THE CONTROLS!
THINK AGAIN.
NOW THERE ARE NO CONTROLS.
SP-TANG!
KZZP!
KZKKKT!
YOU'VE JUST LOST. NOW WE CAN'T GO UP. LIKE IT OR NOT--
--WE'RE ON A SUICIDE RUN!

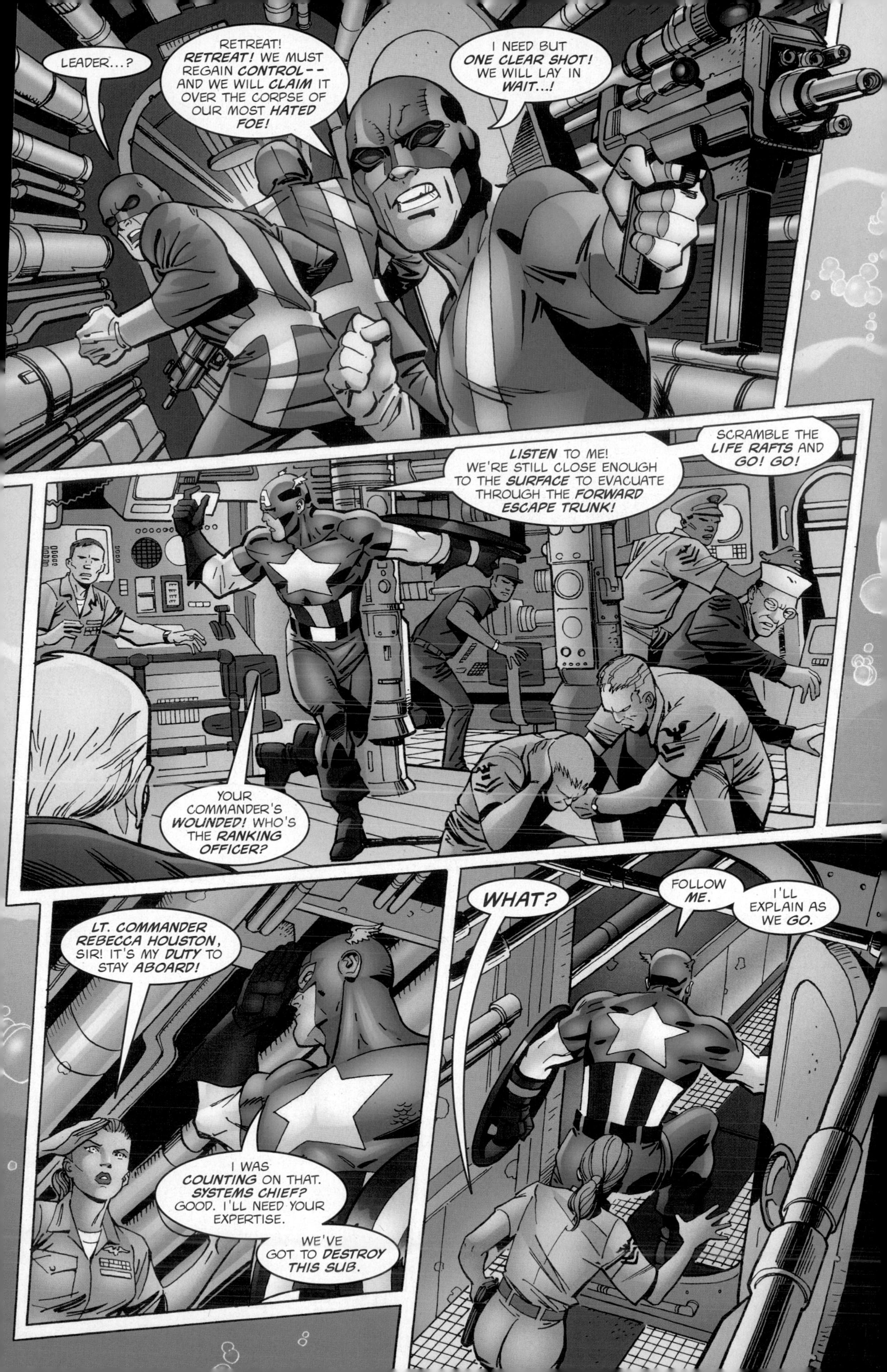
LEADER...?
RETREAT! RETREAT! WE MUST REGAIN CONTROL-- AND WE WILL CLAIM IT OVER THE CORPSE OF OUR MOST HATED FOE!
I NEED BUT ONE CLEAR SHOT! WE WILL LAY IN WAIT...!
LISTEN TO ME! WE'RE STILL CLOSE ENOUGH TO THE SURFACE TO EVACUATE THROUGH THE FORWARD ESCAPE TRUNK!
SCRAMBLE THE LIFE RAFTS AND GO! GO!
YOUR COMMANDER'S WOUNDED! WHO'S THE RANKING OFFICER?
LT. COMMANDER REBECCA HOUSTON, SIR! IT'S MY DUTY TO STAY ABOARD!
I WAS COUNTING ON THAT. SYSTEMS CHIEF? GOOD. I'LL NEED YOUR EXPERTISE.
WE'VE GOT TO DESTROY THIS SUB.
WHAT?
FOLLOW ME.
I'LL EXPLAIN AS WE GO.

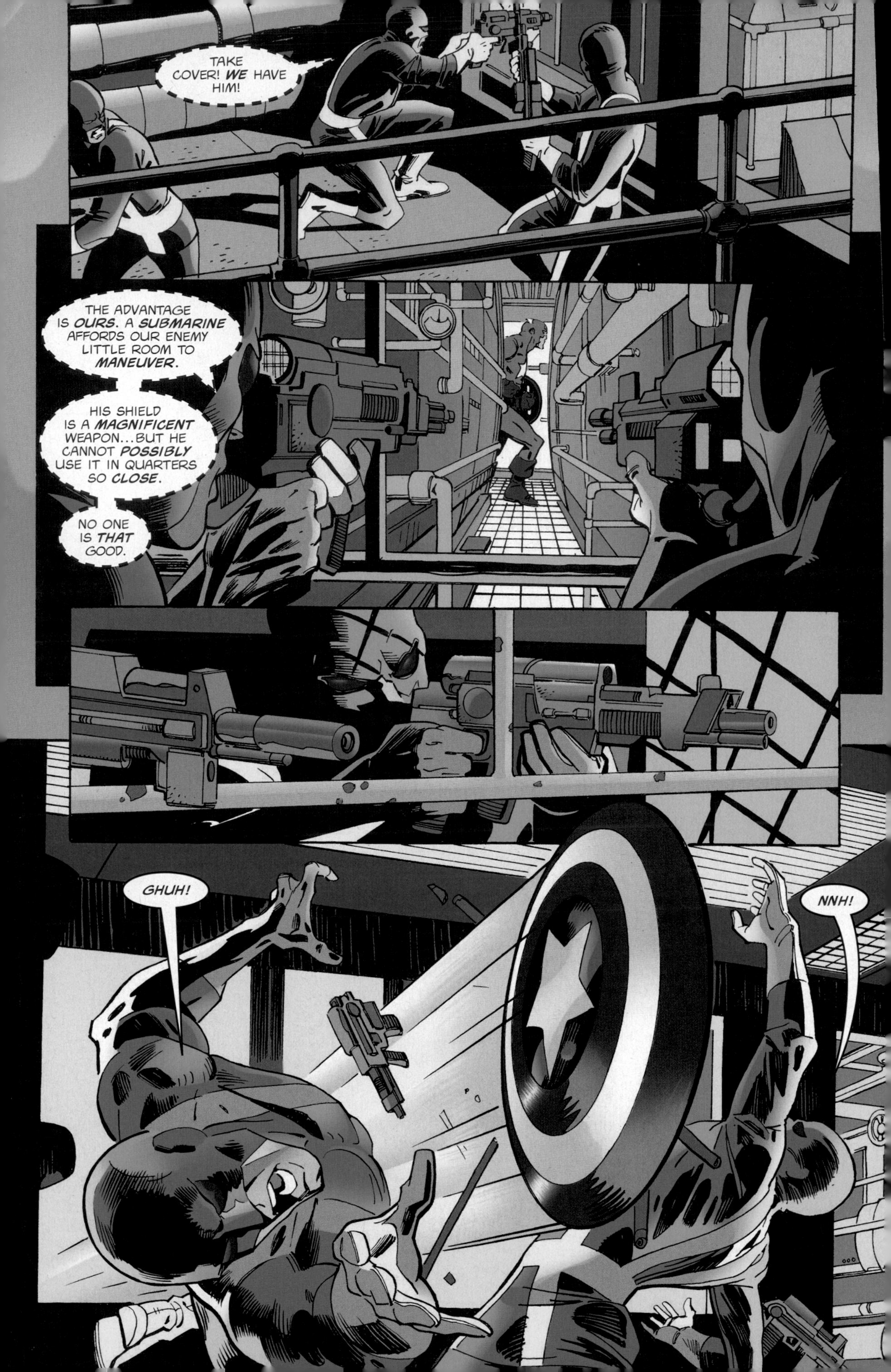
TAKE COVER! WE HAVE HIM!
THE ADVANTAGE IS OURS. A SUBMARINE AFFORDS OUR ENEMY LITTLE ROOM TO MANEUVER.
HIS SHIELD IS A MAGNIFICENT WEAPON...BUT HE CANNOT POSSIBLY USE IT IN QUARTERS SO CLOSE.
NO ONE IS THAT GOOD.
GHUH!
NNH!

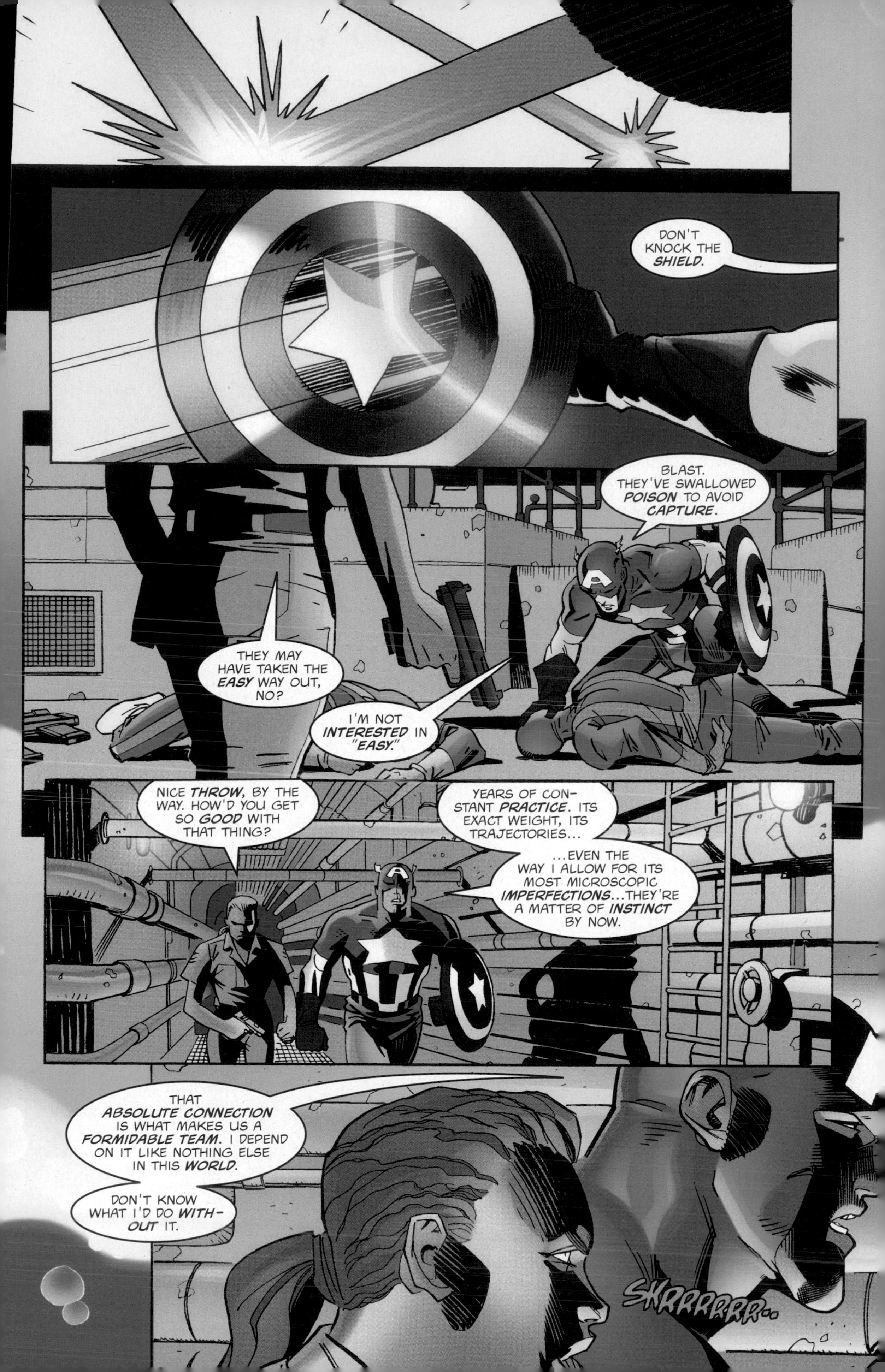
DON'T KNOCK THE SHIELD.
BLAST. THEY'VE SWALLOWED POISON TO AVOID CAPTURE.
THEY MAY HAVE TAKEN THE EASY WAY OUT, NO?
I'M NOT INTERESTED IN "EASY."
NICE THROW, BY THE WAY. HOW'D YOU GET SO GOOD WITH THAT THING?
YEARS OF CON-STANT PRACTICE. ITS EXACT WEIGHT, ITS TRAJECTORIES...
...EVEN THE WAY I ALLOW FOR ITS MOST MICROSCOPIC IMPERFECTIONS...THEY'RE A MATTER OF INSTINCT BY NOW.
THAT ABSOLUTE CONNECTION IS WHAT MAKES US A FORMIDABLE TEAM. I DEPEND ON IT LIKE NOTHING ELSE IN THIS WORLD.
DON'T KNOW WHAT I'D DO WITH-OUT IT.
SKRRRRRRR..

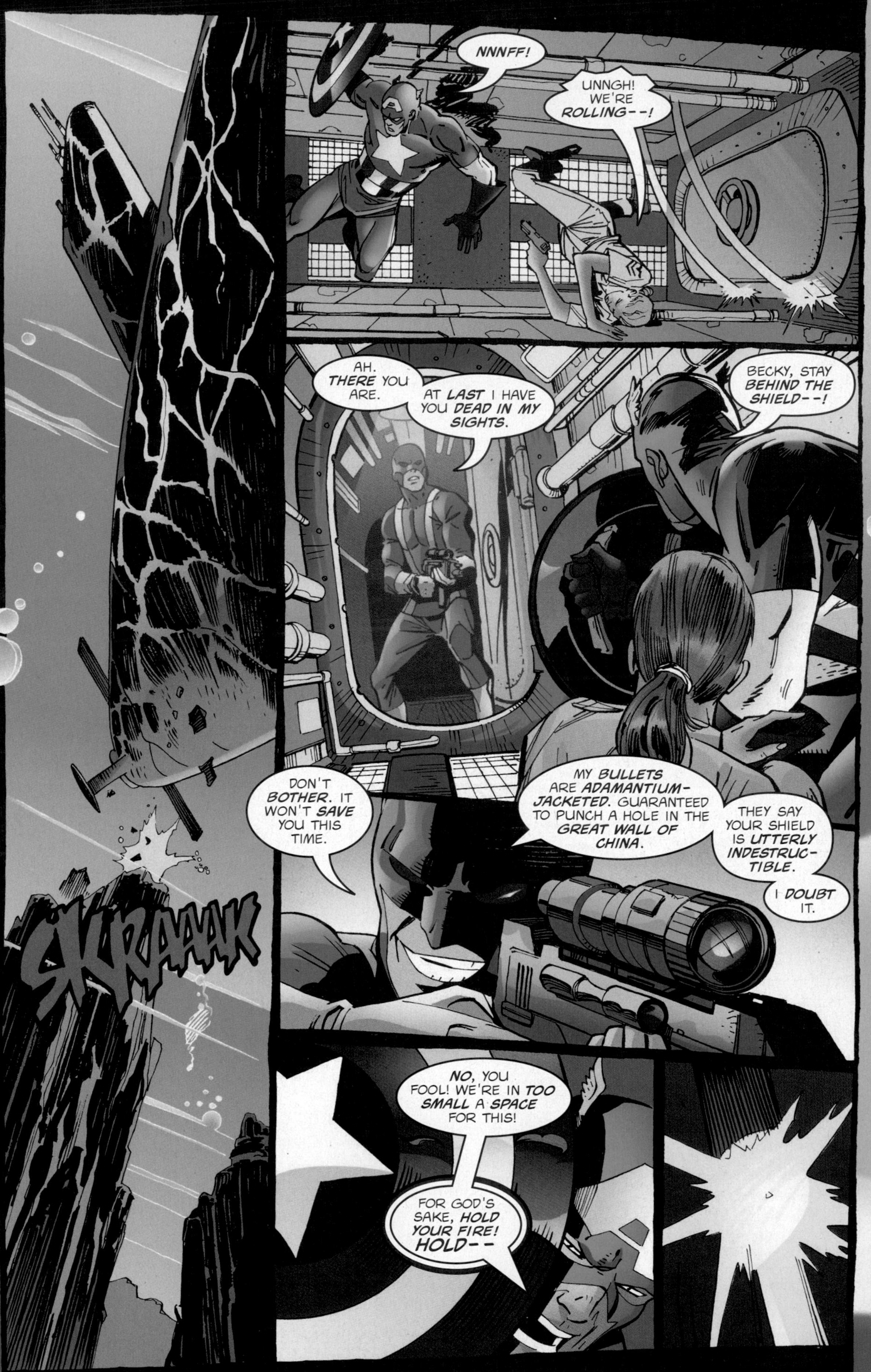
SKRAAAK
NNNFF!
UNNGH! WE'RE ROLLING--!
AH. THERE YOU ARE.
AT LAST I HAVE YOU DEAD IN MY SIGHTS.
BECKY, STAY BEHIND THE SHIELD--!
DON'T BOTHER. IT WON'T SAVE YOU THIS TIME.
MY BULLETS ARE ADAMANTIUM-JACKETED. GUARANTEED TO PUNCH A HOLE IN THE GREAT WALL OF CHINA.
THEY SAY YOUR SHIELD IS UTTERLY INDESTRUC-TIBLE.
I DOUBT IT.
NO, YOU FOOL! WE'RE IN TOO SMALL A SPACE FOR THIS!
FOR GOD'S SAKE, HOLD YOUR FIRE! HOLD--

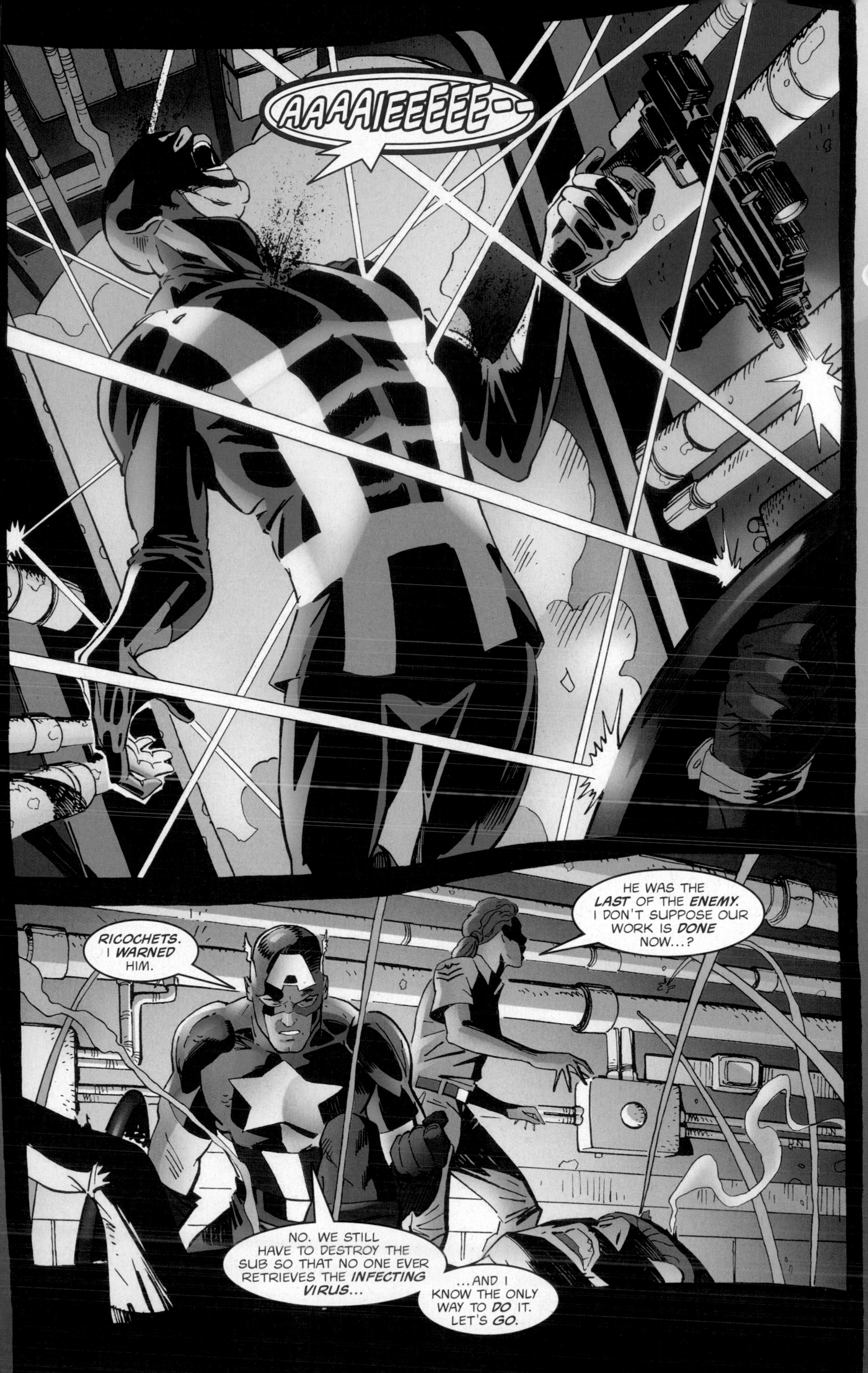
AAAAIEEEEEE--
RICOCHETS. I WARNED HIM.
HE WAS THE LAST OF THE ENEMY. I DON'T SUPPOSE OUR WORK IS DONE NOW...?
NO. WE STILL HAVE TO DESTROY THE SUB SO THAT NO ONE EVER RETRIEVES THE INFECTING VIRUS...
...AND I KNOW THE ONLY WAY TO DO IT. LET'S GO.

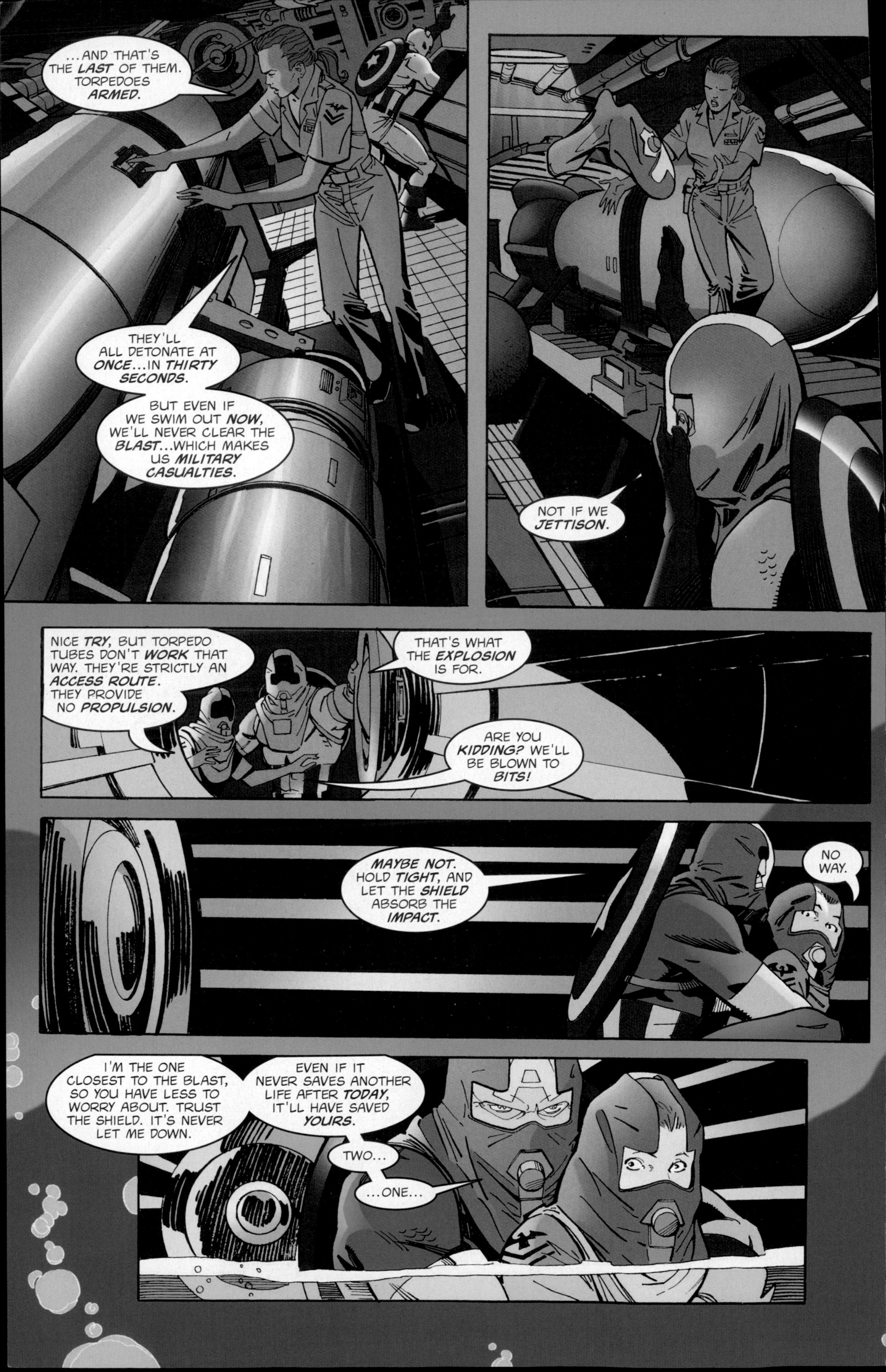
...AND THAT'S THE LAST OF THEM. TORPEDOES ARMED.
THEY'LL ALL DETONATE AT ONCE...IN THIRTY SECONDS.
BUT EVEN IF WE SWIM OUT NOW, WE'LL NEVER CLEAR THE BLAST...WHICH MAKES US MILITARY CASUALTIES.
NOT IF WE JETTISON.
NICE TRY, BUT TORPEDO TUBES DON'T WORK THAT WAY. THEY'RE STRICTLY AN ACCESS ROUTE. THEY PROVIDE NO PROPULSION.
THAT'S WHAT THE EXPLOSION IS FOR.
ARE YOU KIDDING? WE'LL BE BLOWN TO BITS!
MAYBE NOT. HOLD TIGHT, AND LET THE SHIELD ABSORB THE IMPACT.
NO WAY.
I'M THE ONE CLOSEST TO THE BLAST, SO YOU HAVE LESS TO WORRY ABOUT. TRUST THE SHIELD. IT'S NEVER LET ME DOWN.
EVEN IF IT NEVER SAVES ANOTHER LIFE AFTER TODAY, IT'LL HAVE SAVED YOURS.
TWO...
...ONE...

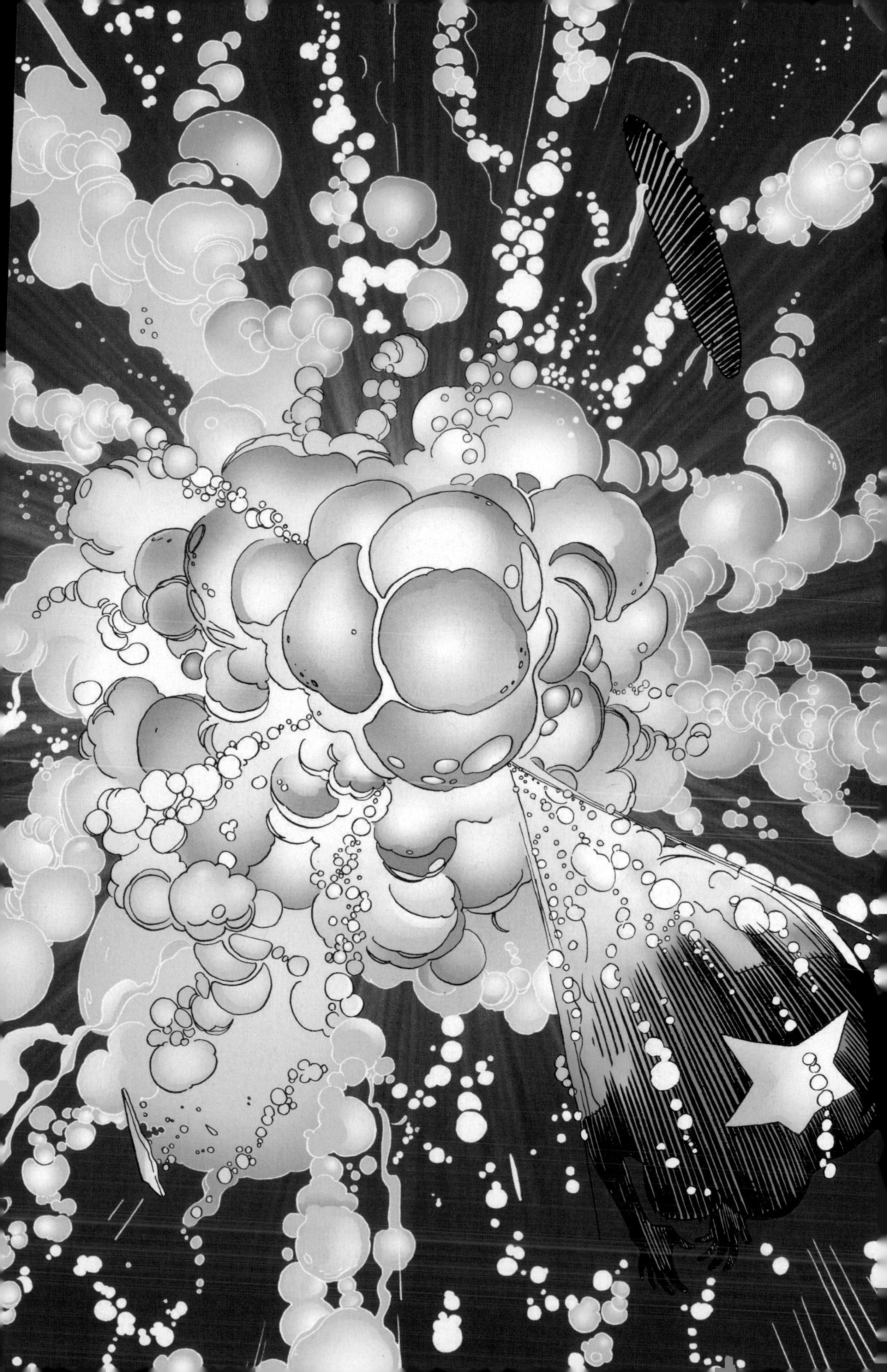

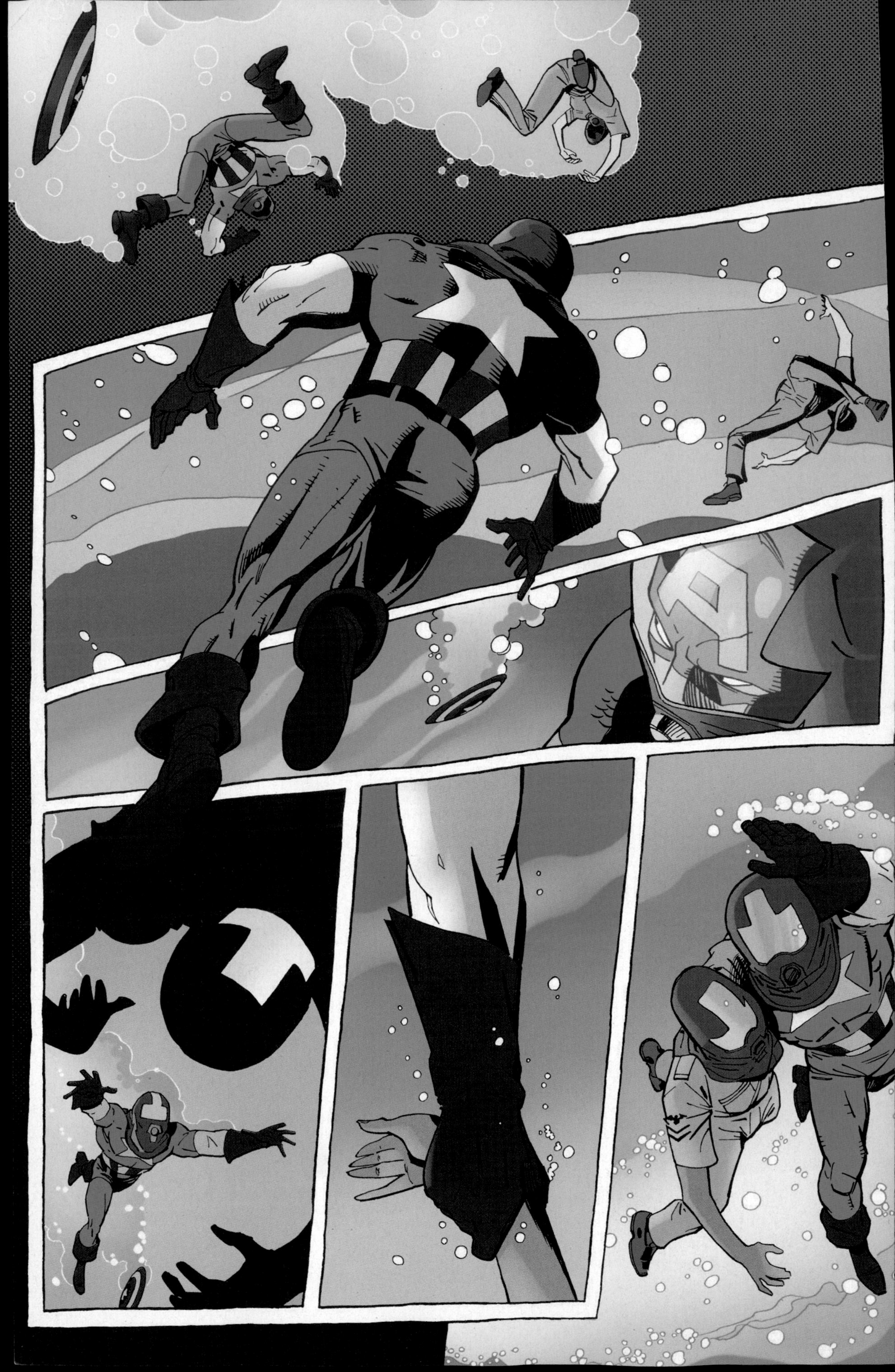

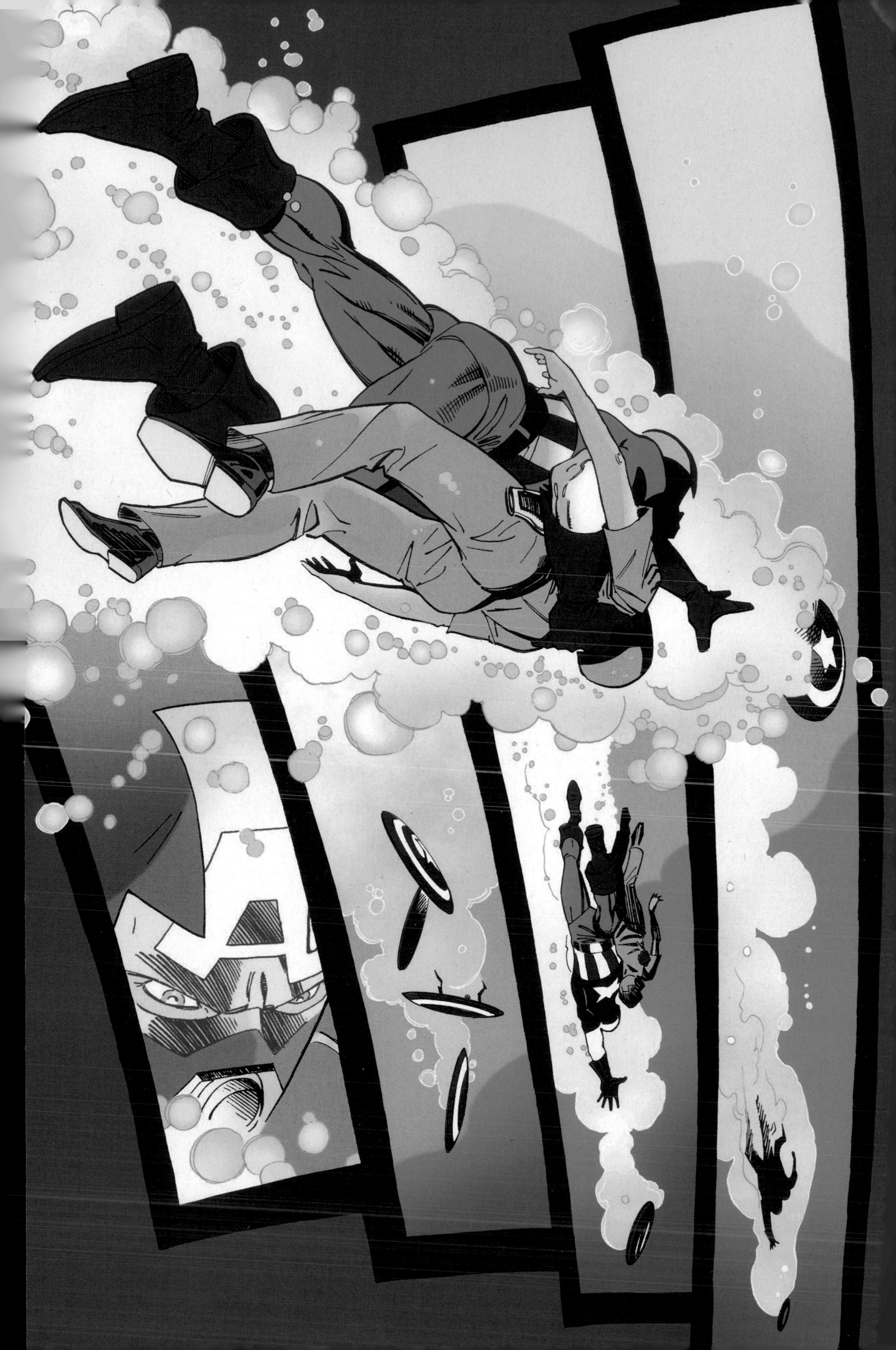

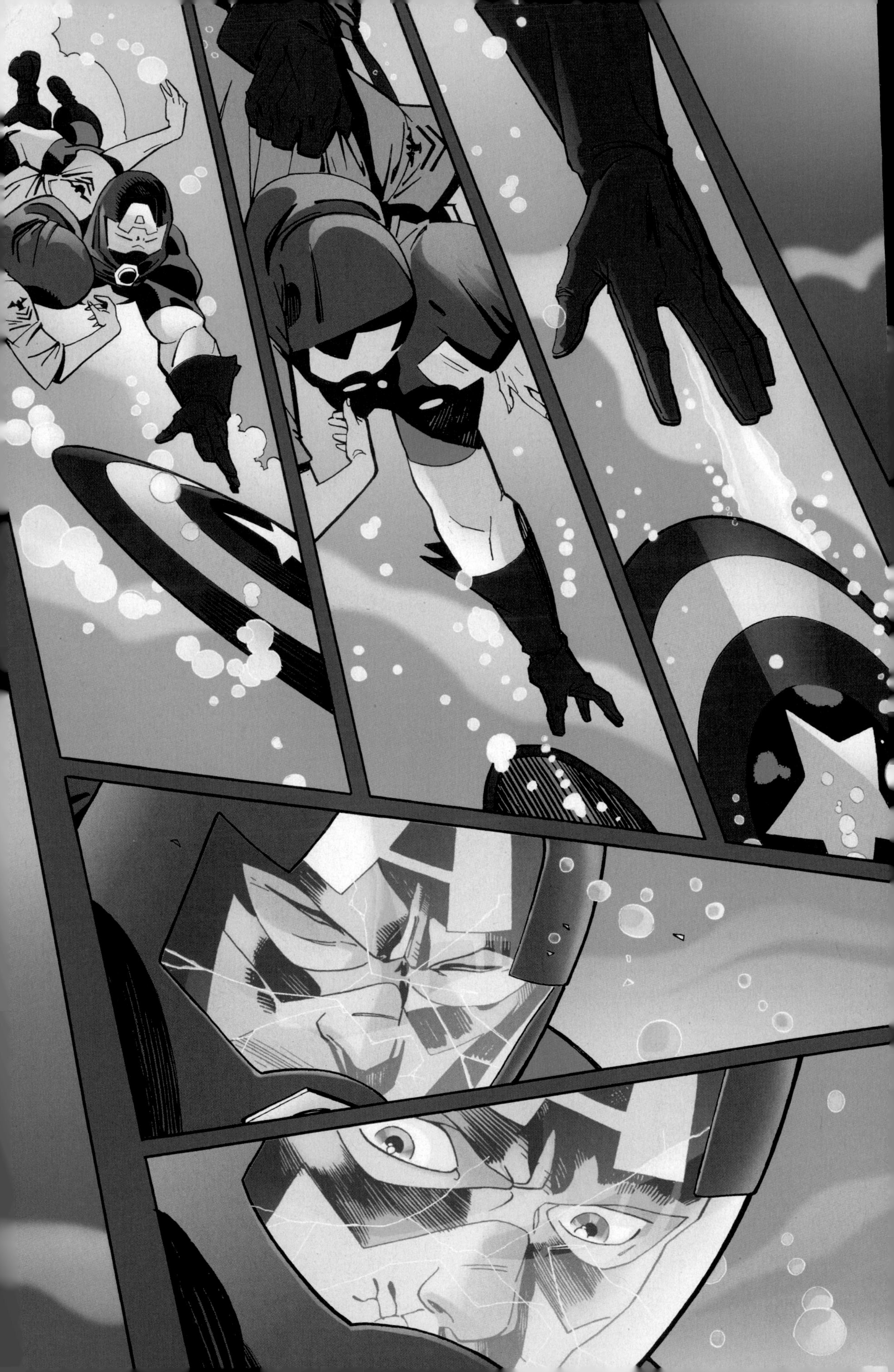

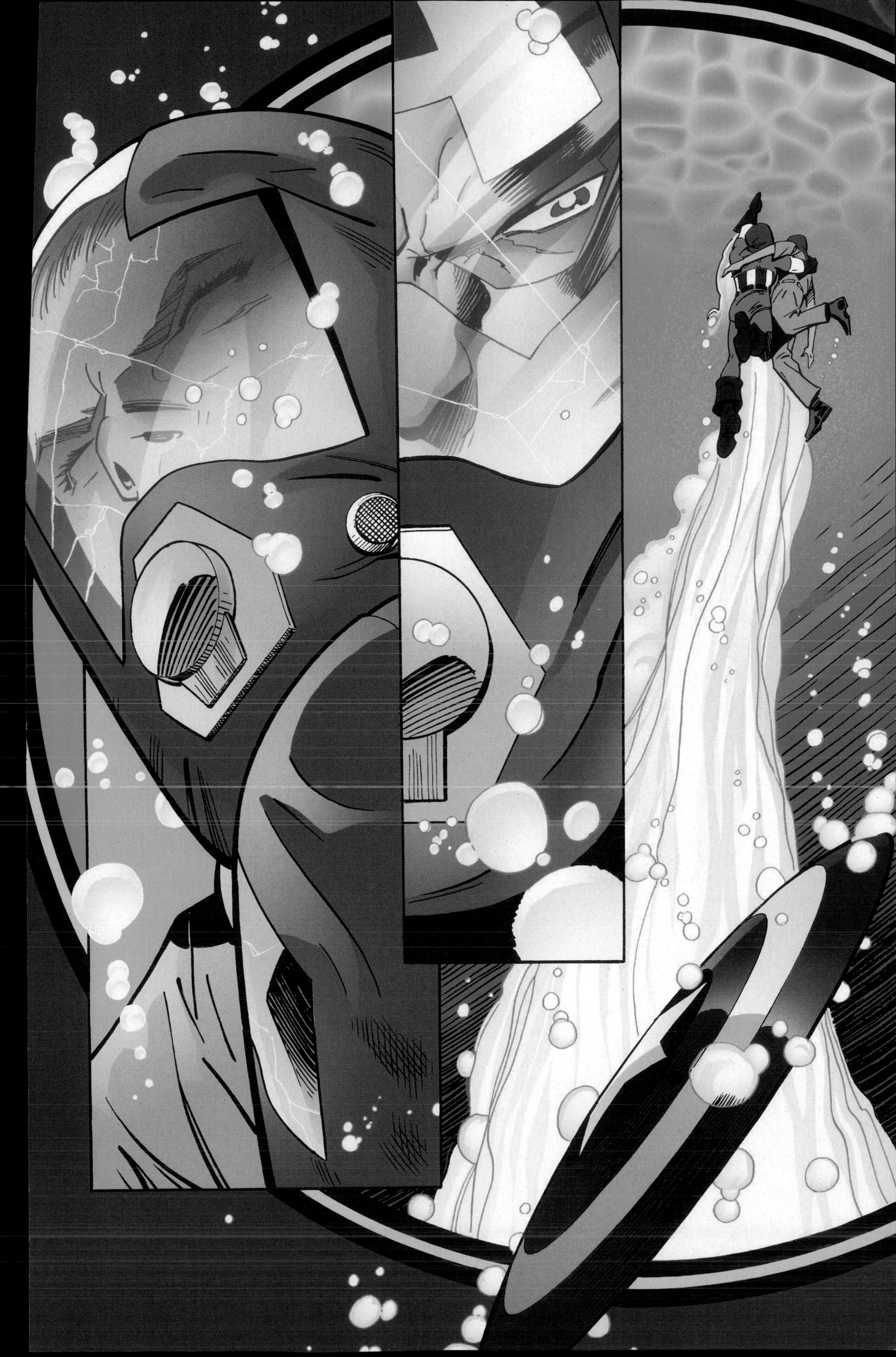

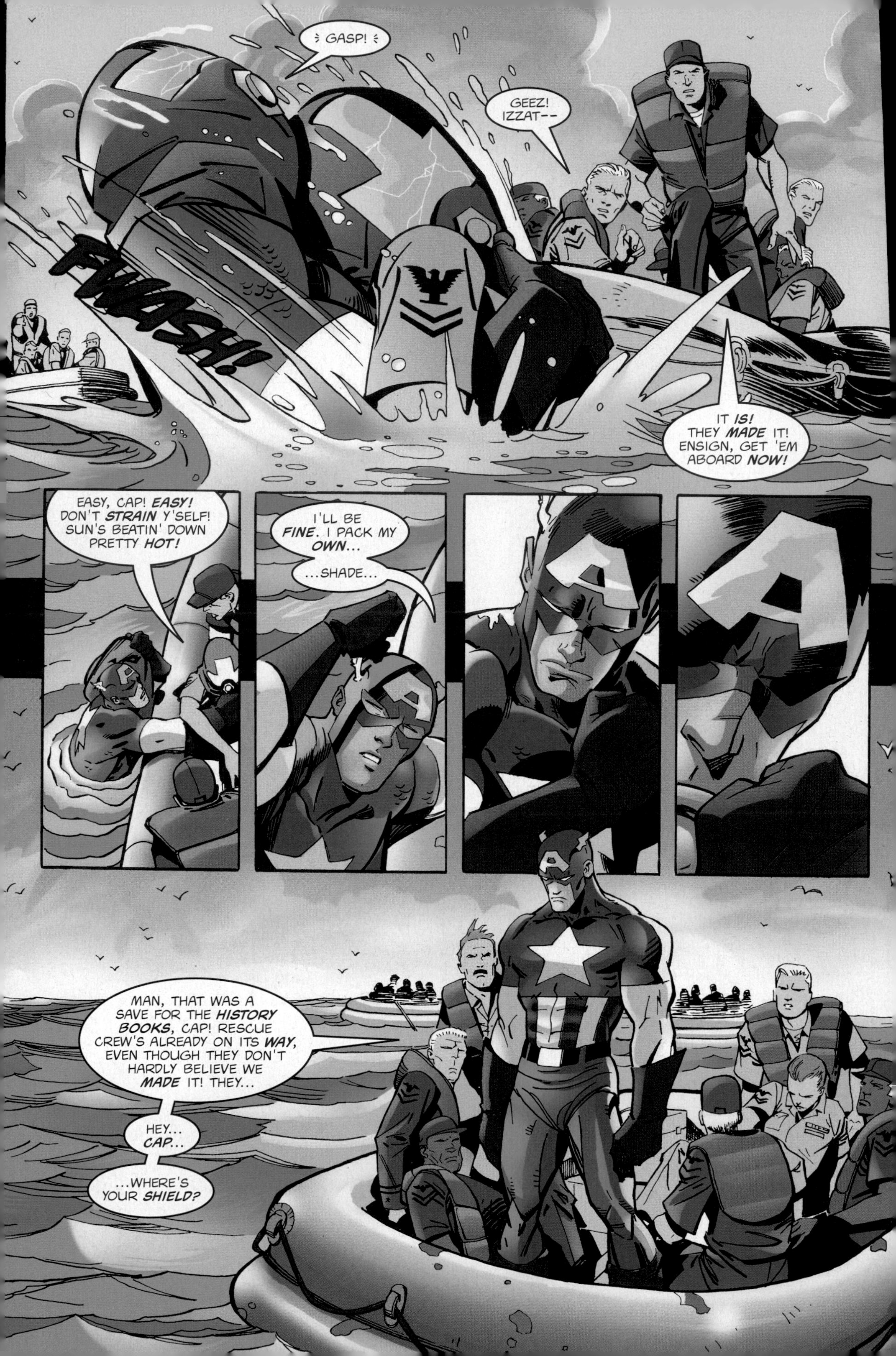
GASP!
GEEZ! IZZAT--
FWASH!
IT IS! THEY MADE IT! ENSIGN, GET 'EM ABOARD NOW!
EASY, CAP! EASY! DON'T STRAIN Y'SELF! SUN'S BEATIN' DOWN PRETTY HOT!
I'LL BE FINE. I PACK MY OWN...
...SHADE...
MAN, THAT WAS A SAVE FOR THE HISTORY BOOKS, CAP! RESCUE CREW'S ALREADY ON ITS WAY, EVEN THOUGH THEY DON'T HARDLY BELIEVE WE MADE IT! THEY...
HEY... CAP...
...WHERE'S YOUR SHIELD?

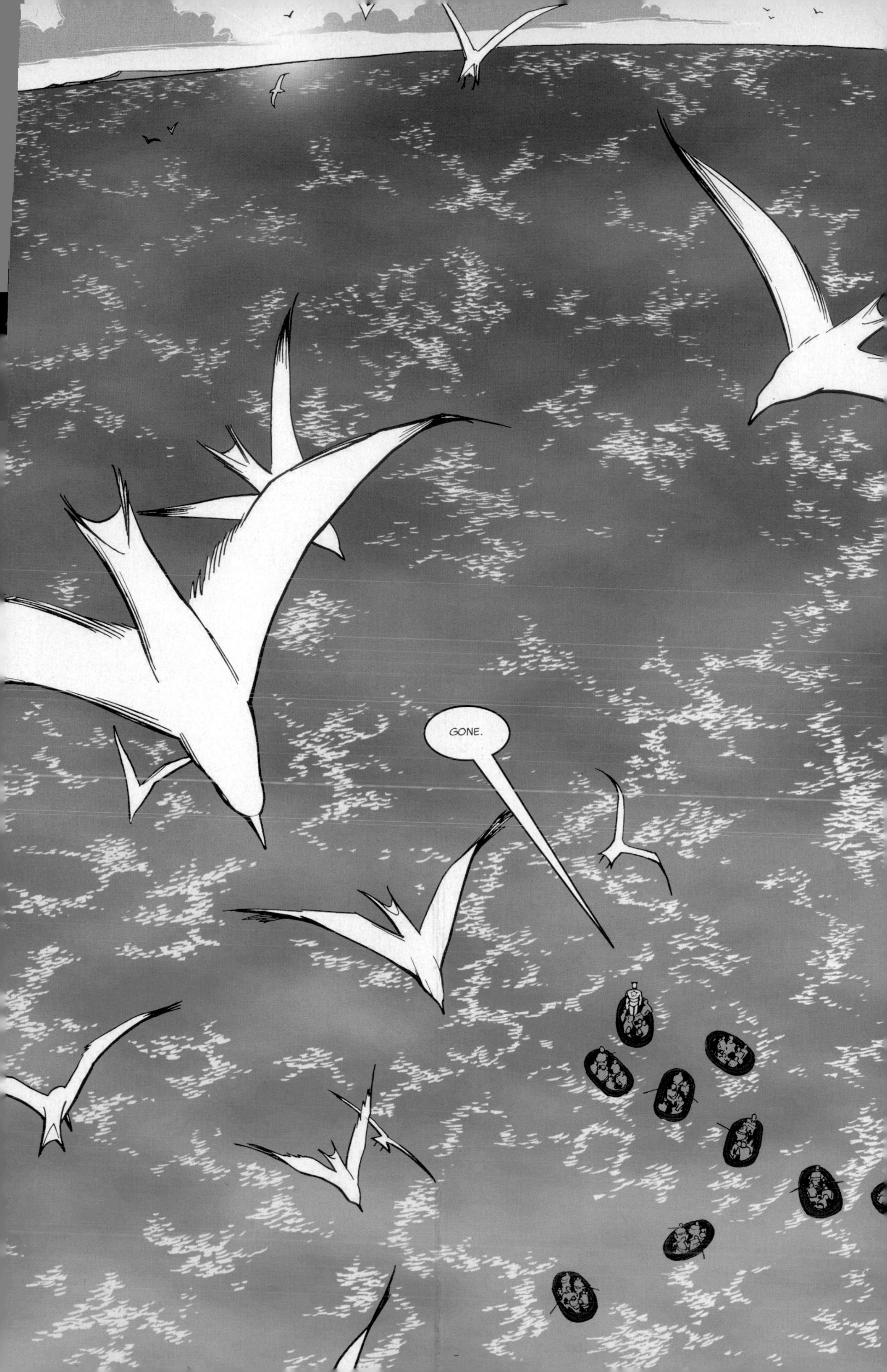
GONE.

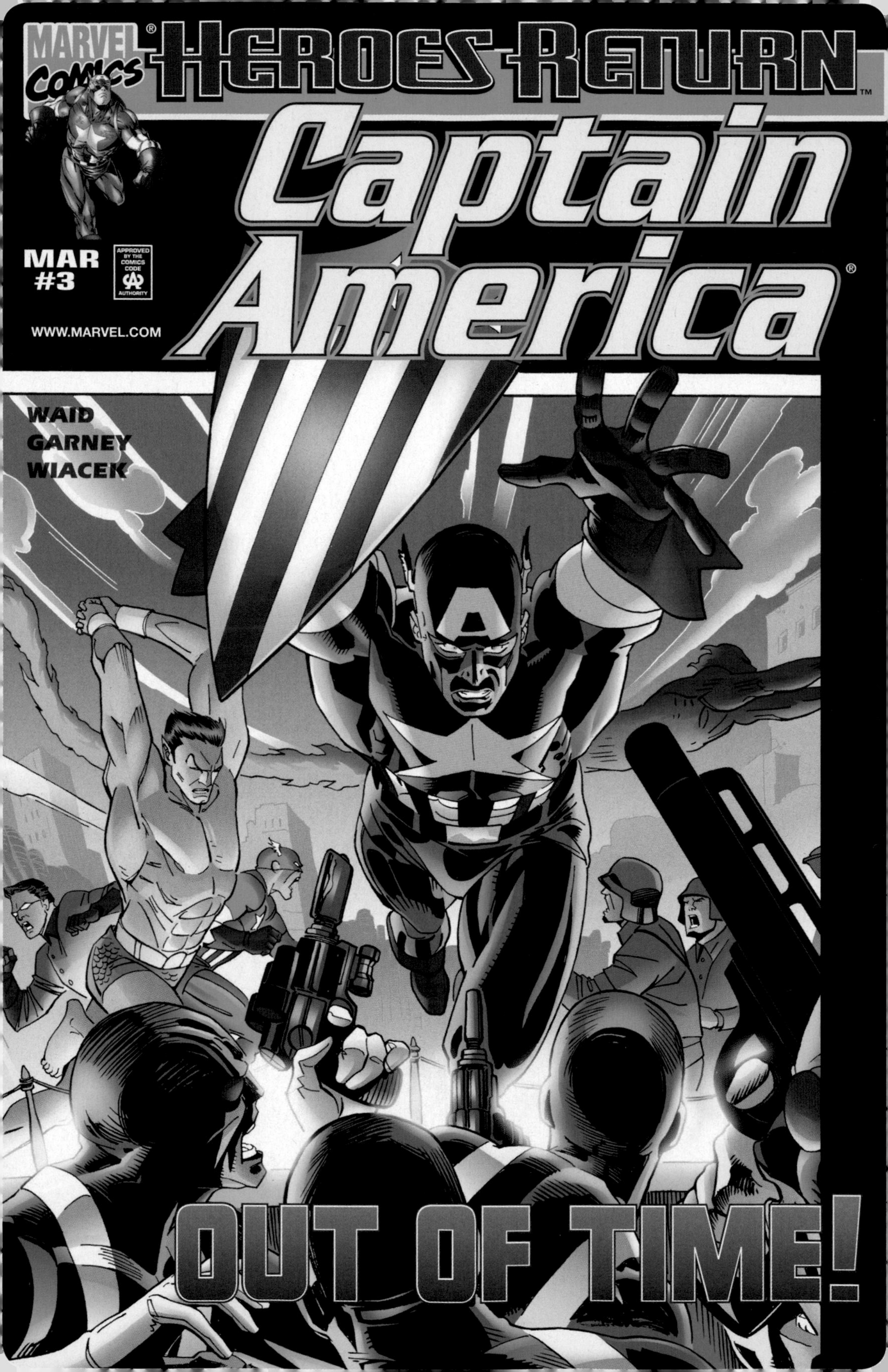
MARVEL COMICS
HEROES RETURN
Captain America
MAR #3
APPROVED BY THE COMICS CODE AUTHORITY
WWW.MARVEL.COM
WAID
GARNEY
WIACEK
OUT OF TIME!

Stan Lee presents Captain America

MUSEUM PIECE

editor in chief MARK WAID AND RON GARNEY•storytellers BOB WIACEK•inker JOE ROSAS•colorist DIGITAL CHAMELEON•separations JOHN COSTANZA•letterer MATT IDELSON•editor BOB HARRAS•

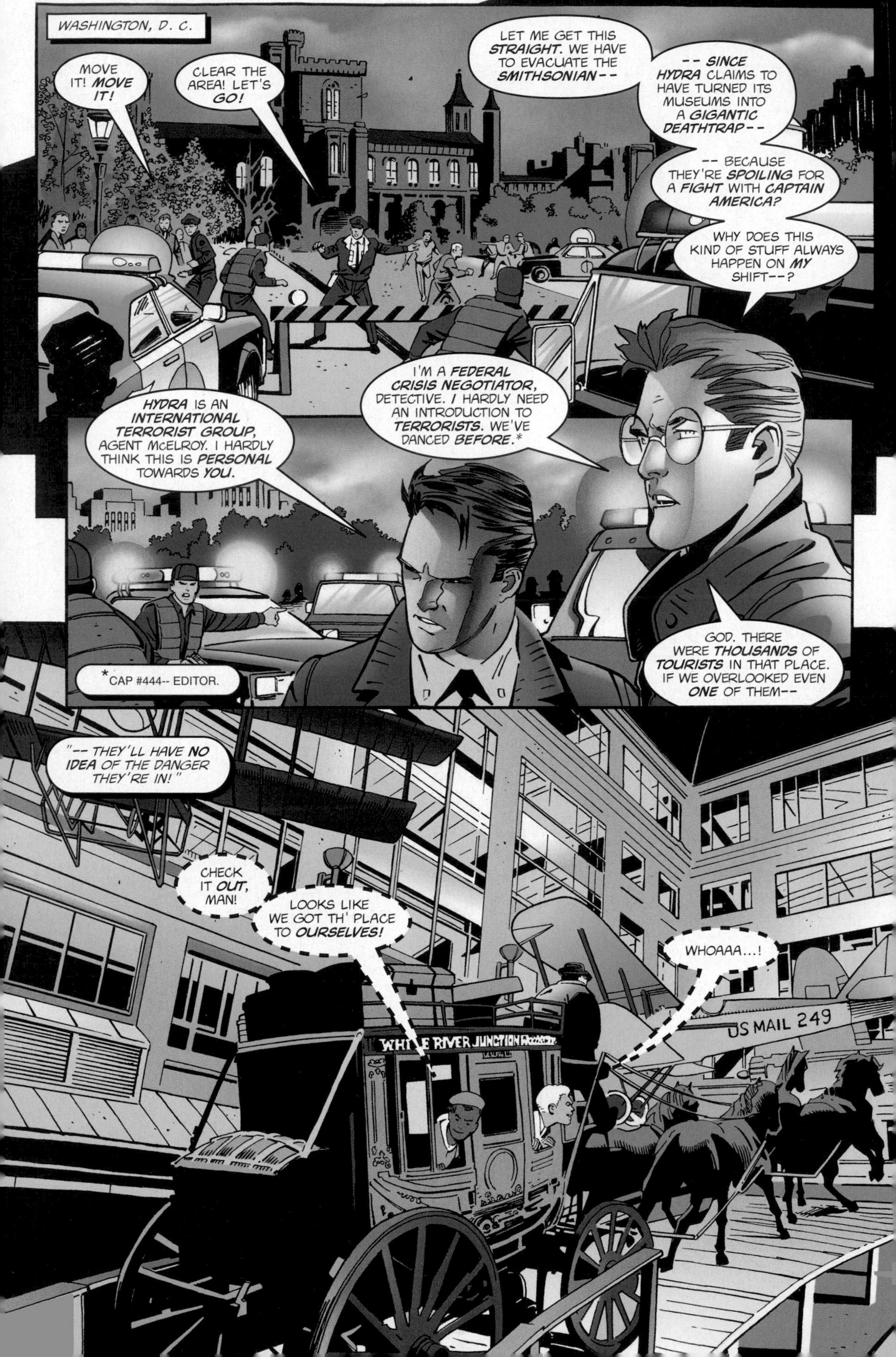
WASHINGTON, D. C.
MOVE IT! MOVE IT!
CLEAR THE AREA! LET'S GO!
LET ME GET THIS STRAIGHT. WE HAVE TO EVACUATE THE SMITHSONIAN--
-- SINCE HYDRA CLAIMS TO HAVE TURNED ITS MUSEUMS INTO A GIGANTIC DEATHTRAP--
-- BECAUSE THEY'RE SPOILING FOR A FIGHT WITH CAPTAIN AMERICA?
WHY DOES THIS KIND OF STUFF ALWAYS HAPPEN ON MY SHIFT--?
HYDRA IS AN INTERNATIONAL TERRORIST GROUP, AGENT McELROY. I HARDLY THINK THIS IS PERSONAL TOWARDS YOU.
I'M A FEDERAL CRISIS NEGOTIATOR, DETECTIVE. I HARDLY NEED AN INTRODUCTION TO TERRORISTS. WE'VE DANCED BEFORE.*
*CAP #444-- EDITOR.
GOD. THERE WERE THOUSANDS OF TOURISTS IN THAT PLACE. IF WE OVERLOOKED EVEN ONE OF THEM--
"-- THEY'LL HAVE NO IDEA OF THE DANGER THEY'RE IN!"
CHECK IT OUT, MAN!
LOOKS LIKE WE GOT TH' PLACE TO OURSELVES!
WHOAAA...!
US MAIL 249

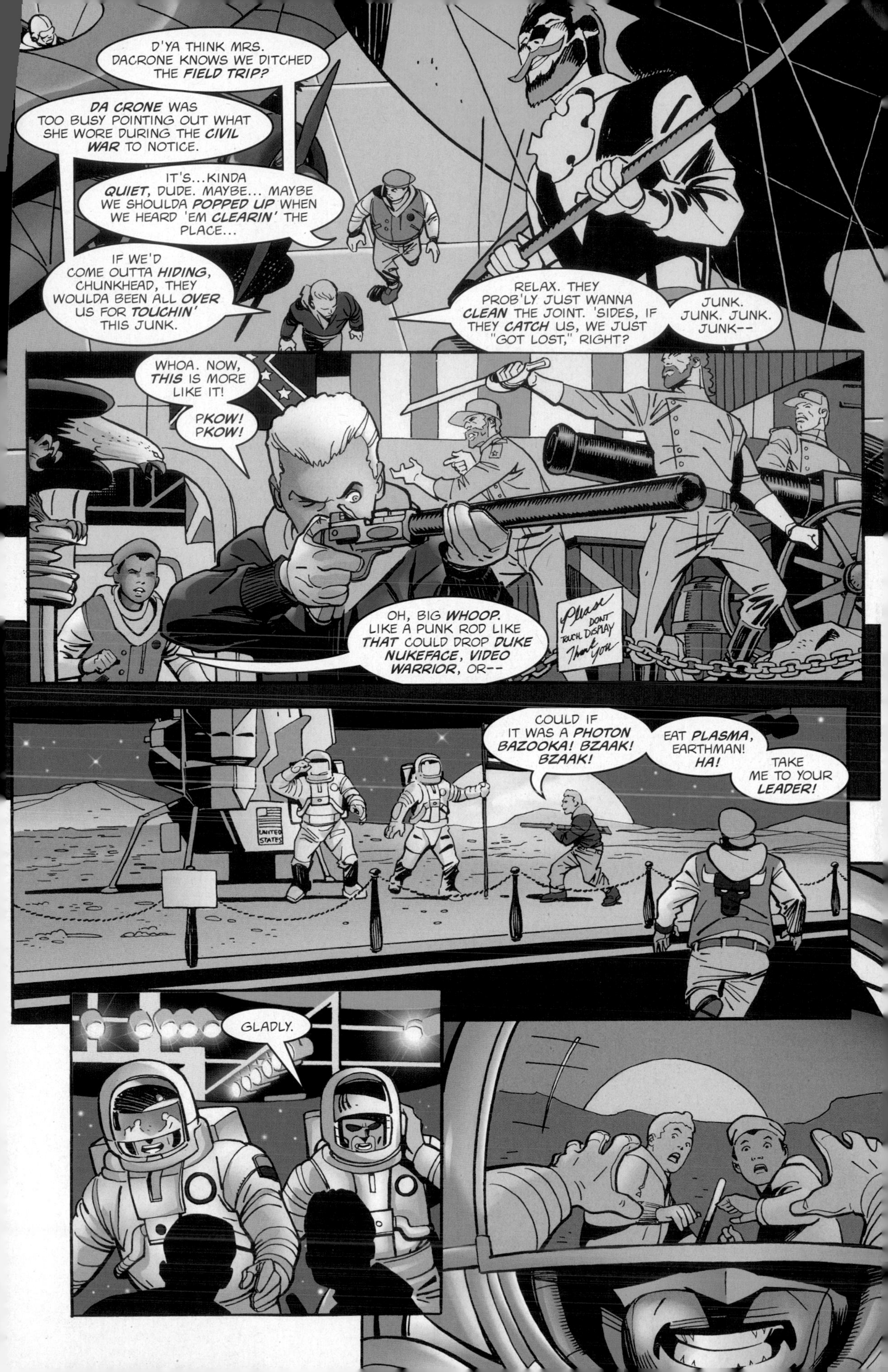
D'YA THINK MRS. DACRONE KNOWS WE DITCHED THE FIELD TRIP?
DA CRONE WAS TOO BUSY POINTING OUT WHAT SHE WORE DURING THE CIVIL WAR TO NOTICE.
IT'S...KINDA QUIET, DUDE. MAYBE... MAYBE WE SHOULDA POPPED UP WHEN WE HEARD 'EM CLEARIN' THE PLACE...
IF WE'D COME OUTTA HIDING, CHUNKHEAD, THEY WOULDA BEEN ALL OVER US FOR TOUCHIN' THIS JUNK.
RELAX. THEY PROB'LY JUST WANNA CLEAN THE JOINT. 'SIDES, IF THEY CATCH US, WE JUST "GOT LOST," RIGHT?
JUNK. JUNK. JUNK. JUNK--
WHOA. NOW, THIS IS MORE LIKE IT!
PKOW! PKOW!
OH, BIG WHOOP. LIKE A PUNK ROD LIKE THAT COULD DROP DUKE NUKEFACE, VIDEO WARRIOR, OR--
Please DONT TOUCH DISPLAY Thank You
COULD IF IT WAS A PHOTON BAZOOKA! BZAAK! BZAAK!
EAT PLASMA, EARTHMAN! HA!
TAKE ME TO YOUR LEADER!
UNITED STATES
GLADLY.

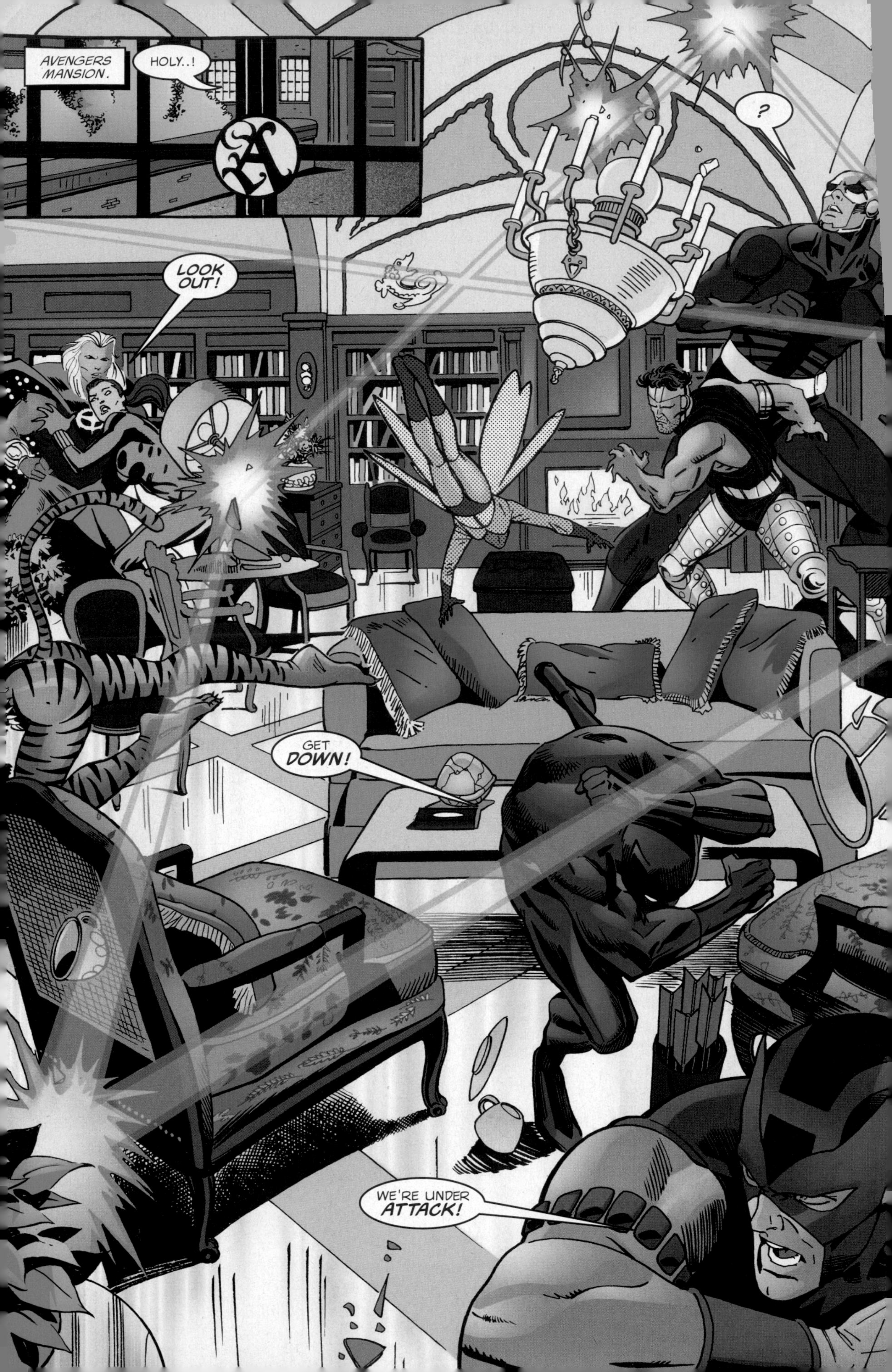
AVENGERS MANSION.
HOLY..!
?
LOOK OUT!
GET DOWN!
WE'RE UNDER ATTACK!

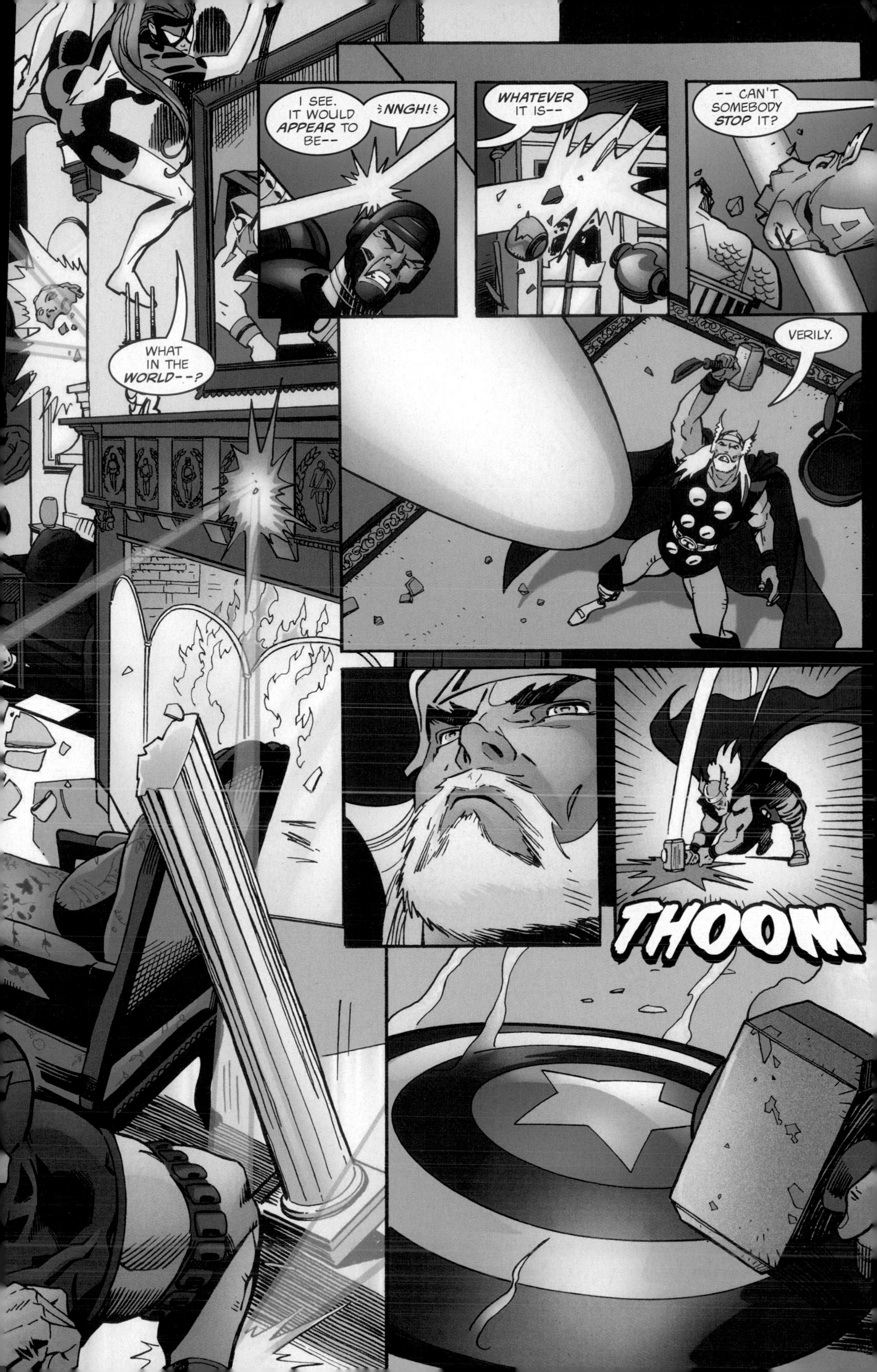
I SEE. IT WOULD APPEAR TO BE--
NNGH!
WHATEVER IT IS--
-- CAN'T SOMEBODY STOP IT?
WHAT IN THE WORLD--?
VERILY.
THOOM

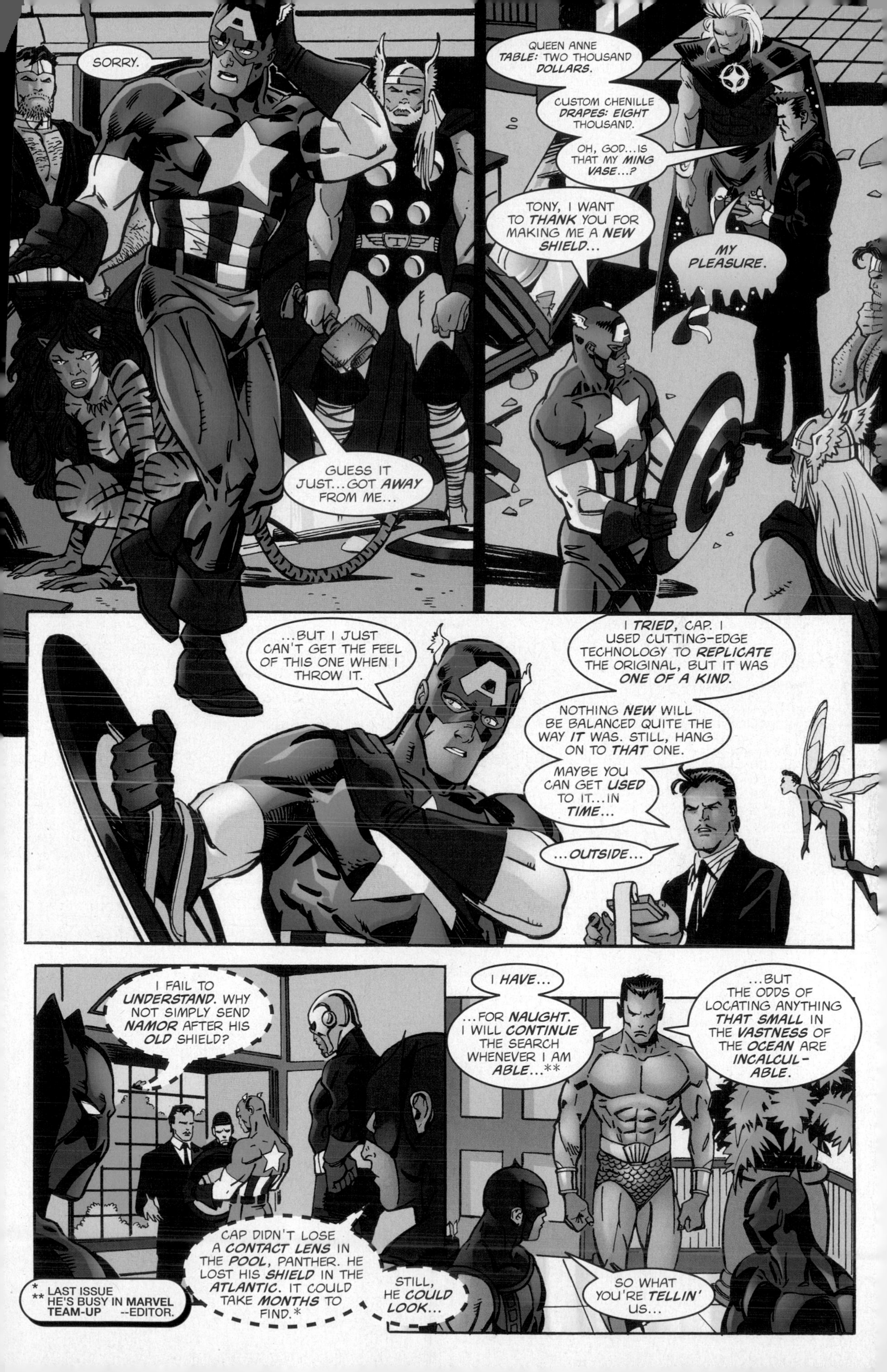
SORRY.
GUESS IT JUST...GOT AWAY FROM ME...
QUEEN ANNE TABLE: TWO THOUSAND DOLLARS.
CUSTOM CHENILLE DRAPES: EIGHT THOUSAND.
OH, GOD...IS THAT MY MING VASE...?
TONY, I WANT TO THANK YOU FOR MAKING ME A NEW SHIELD...
MY PLEASURE.
...BUT I JUST CAN'T GET THE FEEL OF THIS ONE WHEN I THROW IT.
I TRIED, CAP. I USED CUTTING-EDGE TECHNOLOGY TO REPLICATE THE ORIGINAL, BUT IT WAS ONE OF A KIND.
NOTHING NEW WILL BE BALANCED QUITE THE WAY IT WAS. STILL, HANG ON TO THAT ONE.
MAYBE YOU CAN GET USED TO IT...IN TIME...
...OUTSIDE...
I FAIL TO UNDERSTAND. WHY NOT SIMPLY SEND NAMOR AFTER HIS OLD SHIELD?
CAP DIDN'T LOSE A CONTACT LENS IN THE POOL, PANTHER. HE LOST HIS SHIELD IN THE ATLANTIC. IT COULD TAKE MONTHS TO FIND.*
STILL, HE COULD LOOK...
I HAVE...
...FOR NAUGHT. I WILL CONTINUE THE SEARCH WHENEVER I AM ABLE...**
...BUT THE ODDS OF LOCATING ANYTHING THAT SMALL IN THE VASTNESS OF THE OCEAN ARE INCALCULABLE.
SO WHAT YOU'RE TELLIN' US...
* LAST ISSUE
** HE'S BUSY IN MARVEL TEAM-UP --EDITOR.

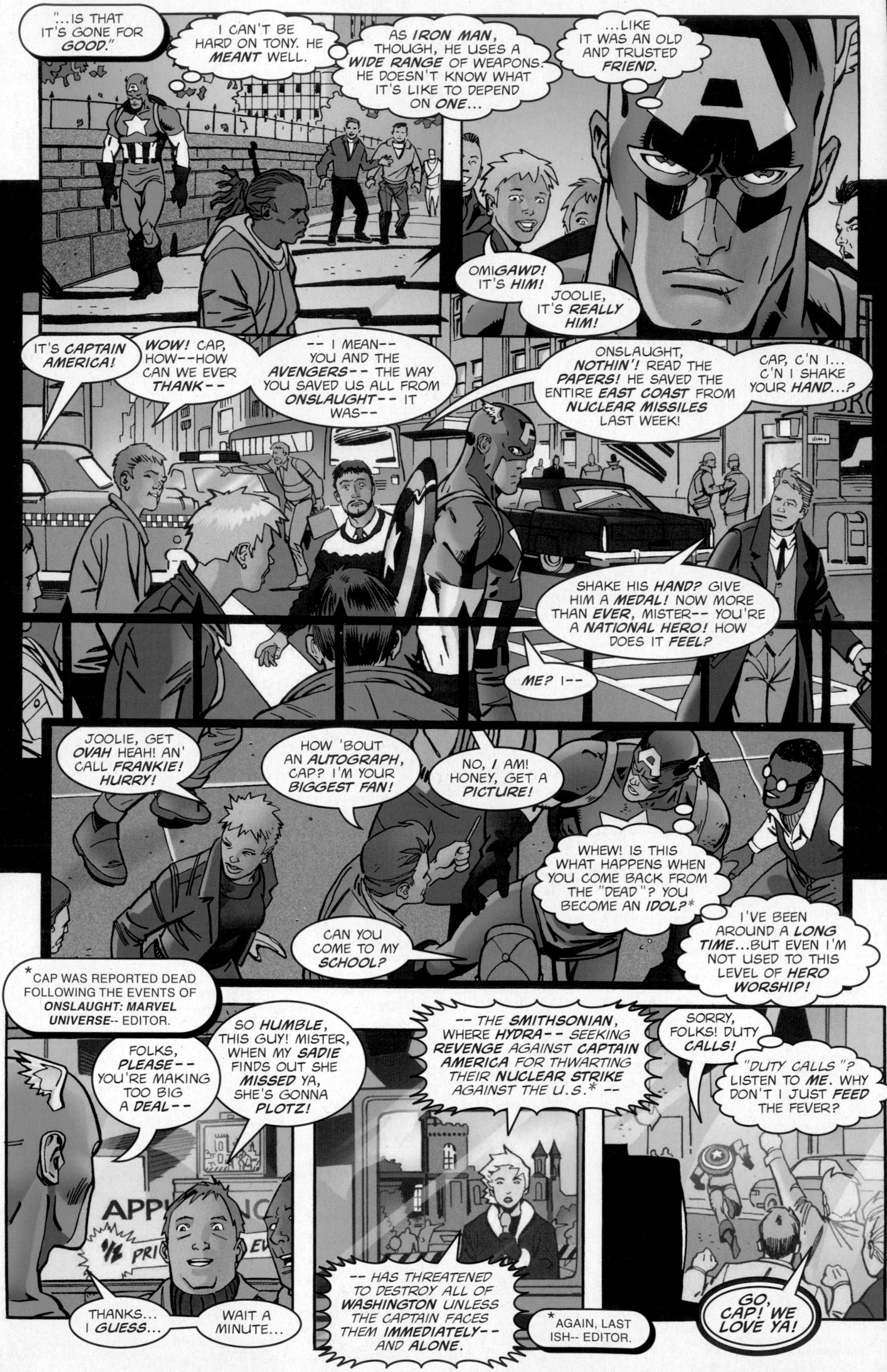
"...IS THAT IT'S GONE FOR GOOD."
I CAN'T BE HARD ON TONY. HE MEANT WELL.
AS IRON MAN, THOUGH, HE USES A WIDE RANGE OF WEAPONS. HE DOESN'T KNOW WHAT IT'S LIKE TO DEPEND ON ONE...
...LIKE IT WAS AN OLD AND TRUSTED FRIEND.
OMIGAWD! IT'S HIM!
JOOLIE, IT'S REALLY HIM!
IT'S CAPTAIN AMERICA!
WOW! CAP, HOW--HOW CAN WE EVER THANK--
-- I MEAN-- YOU AND THE AVENGERS-- THE WAY YOU SAVED US ALL FROM ONSLAUGHT-- IT WAS--
ONSLAUGHT, NOTHIN'! READ THE PAPERS! HE SAVED THE ENTIRE EAST COAST FROM NUCLEAR MISSILES LAST WEEK!
CAP, C'N I... C'N I SHAKE YOUR HAND...?
SHAKE HIS HAND? GIVE HIM A MEDAL! NOW MORE THAN EVER, MISTER-- YOU'RE A NATIONAL HERO! HOW DOES IT FEEL?
ME? I--
JOOLIE, GET OVAH HEAH! AN' CALL FRANKIE! HURRY!
HOW 'BOUT AN AUTOGRAPH, CAP? I'M YOUR BIGGEST FAN!
NO, I AM! HONEY, GET A PICTURE!
WHEW! IS THIS WHAT HAPPENS WHEN YOU COME BACK FROM THE "DEAD"? YOU BECOME AN IDOL?*
CAN YOU COME TO MY SCHOOL?
I'VE BEEN AROUND A LONG TIME...BUT EVEN I'M NOT USED TO THIS LEVEL OF HERO WORSHIP!
*CAP WAS REPORTED DEAD FOLLOWING THE EVENTS OF ONSLAUGHT: MARVEL UNIVERSE-- EDITOR.
FOLKS, PLEASE-- YOU'RE MAKING TOO BIG A DEAL--
SO HUMBLE, THIS GUY! MISTER, WHEN MY SADIE FINDS OUT SHE MISSED YA, SHE'S GONNA PLOTZ!
APPL
1/2 PRI
THANKS... I GUESS...
WAIT A MINUTE...
-- THE SMITHSONIAN, WHERE HYDRA-- SEEKING REVENGE AGAINST CAPTAIN AMERICA FOR THWARTING THEIR NUCLEAR STRIKE AGAINST THE U.S.* --
-- HAS THREATENED TO DESTROY ALL OF WASHINGTON UNLESS THE CAPTAIN FACES THEM IMMEDIATELY-- AND ALONE.
*AGAIN, LAST ISH-- EDITOR.
SORRY, FOLKS! DUTY CALLS!
"DUTY CALLS"? LISTEN TO ME. WHY DON'T I JUST FEED THE FEVER?
GO, CAP! WE LOVE YA!

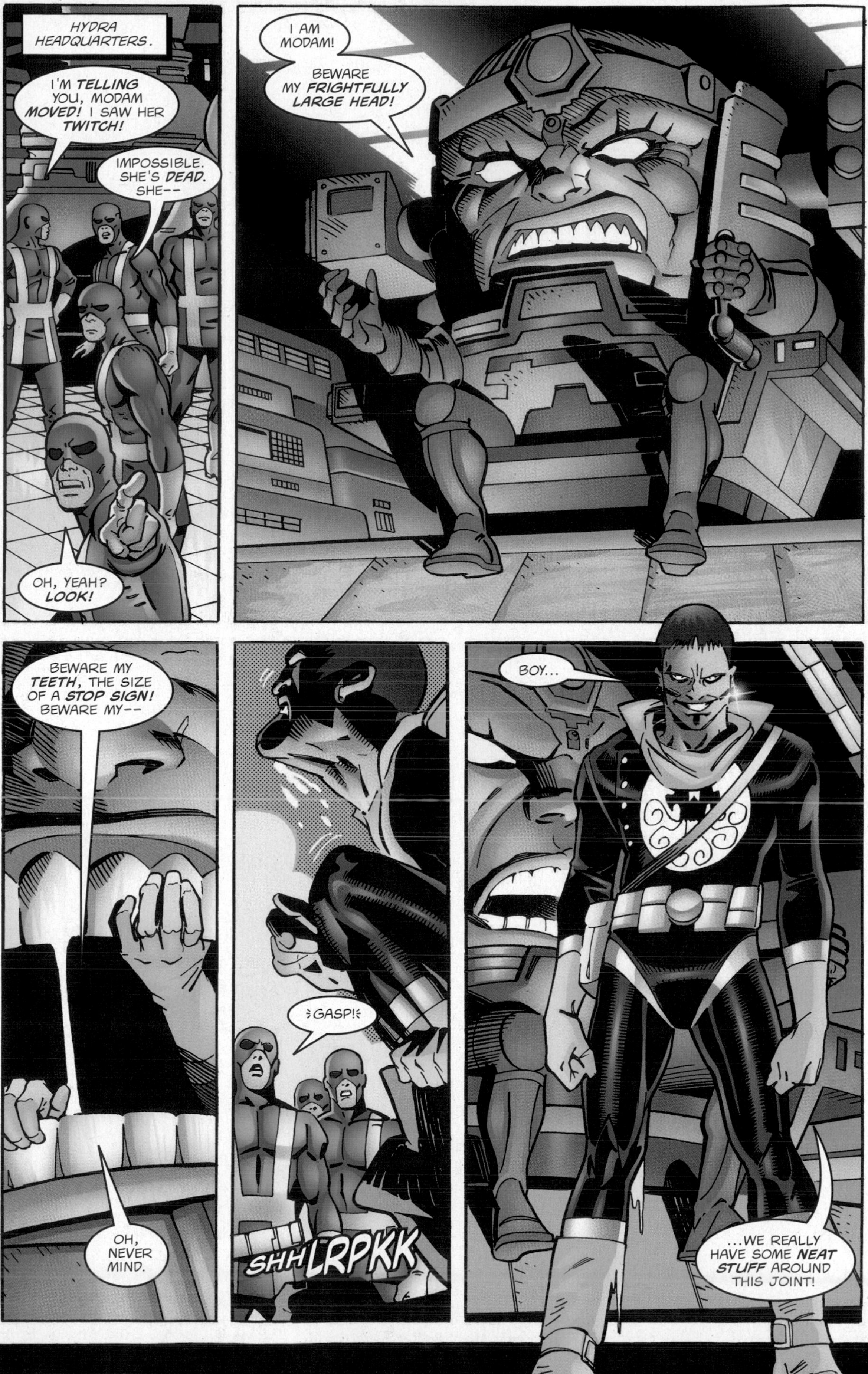
HYDRA HEADQUARTERS.
I'M TELLING YOU, MODAM MOVED! I SAW HER TWITCH!
IMPOSSIBLE. SHE'S DEAD. SHE--
OH, YEAH? LOOK!
I AM MODAM!
BEWARE MY FRIGHTFULLY LARGE HEAD!
BEWARE MY TEETH, THE SIZE OF A STOP SIGN! BEWARE MY--
OH, NEVER MIND.
GASP!
SHHLRPKK
BOY...
...WE REALLY HAVE SOME NEAT STUFF AROUND THIS JOINT!

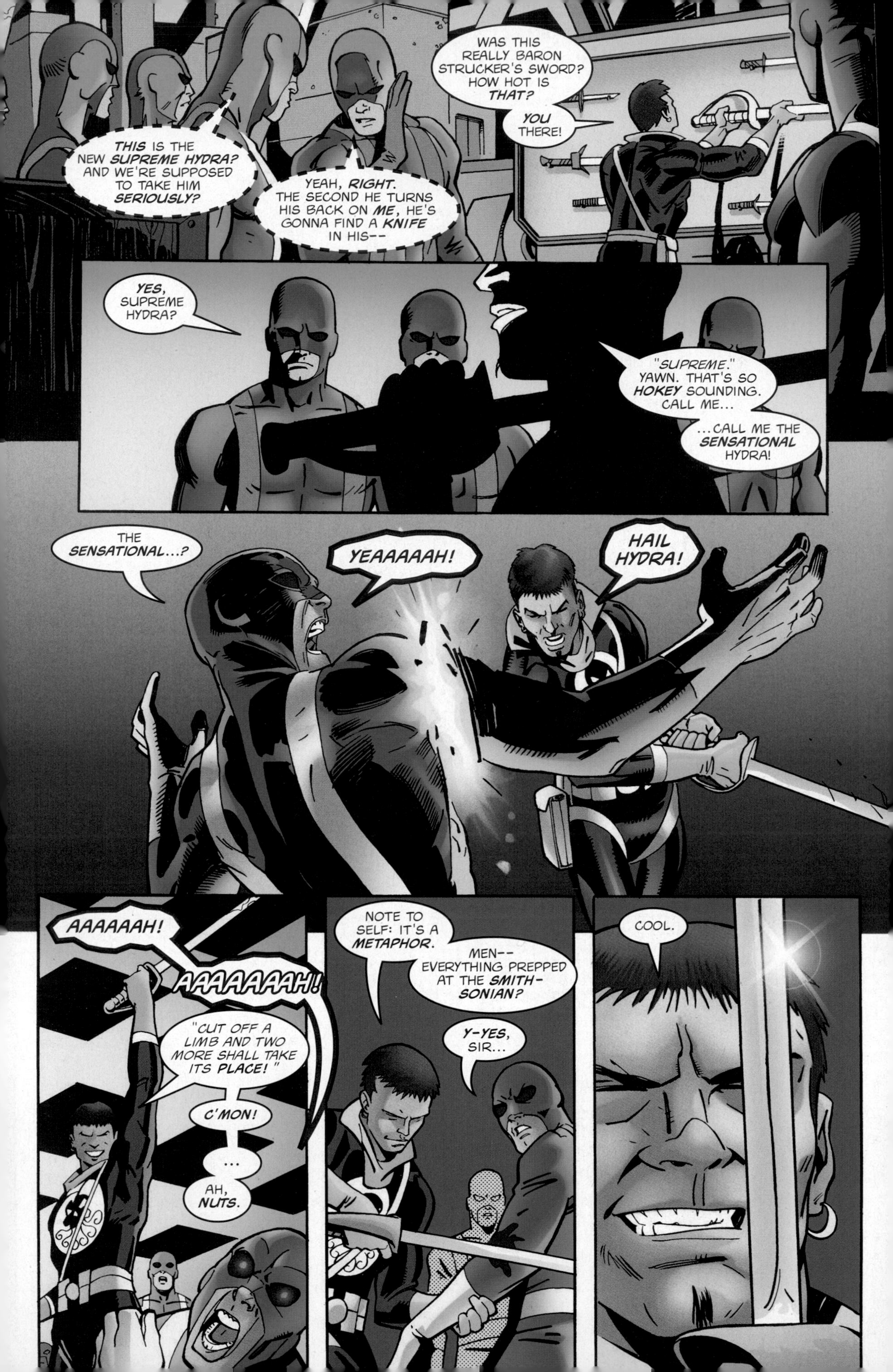
THIS IS THE NEW SUPREME HYDRA? AND WE'RE SUPPOSED TO TAKE HIM SERIOUSLY?
YEAH, RIGHT. THE SECOND HE TURNS HIS BACK ON ME, HE'S GONNA FIND A KNIFE IN HIS--
WAS THIS REALLY BARON STRUCKER'S SWORD? HOW HOT IS THAT?
YOU THERE!
YES, SUPREME HYDRA?
"SUPREME." YAWN. THAT'S SO HOKEY SOUNDING. CALL ME...
...CALL ME THE SENSATIONAL HYDRA!
THE SENSATIONAL...?
YEAAAAAH!
HAIL HYDRA!
AAAAAAH!
AAAAAAAAH!
"CUT OFF A LIMB AND TWO MORE SHALL TAKE ITS PLACE!"
C'MON!
...
AH, NUTS.
NOTE TO SELF: IT'S A METAPHOR.
MEN-- EVERYTHING PREPPED AT THE SMITH-SONIAN?
Y-YES, SIR...
COOL.

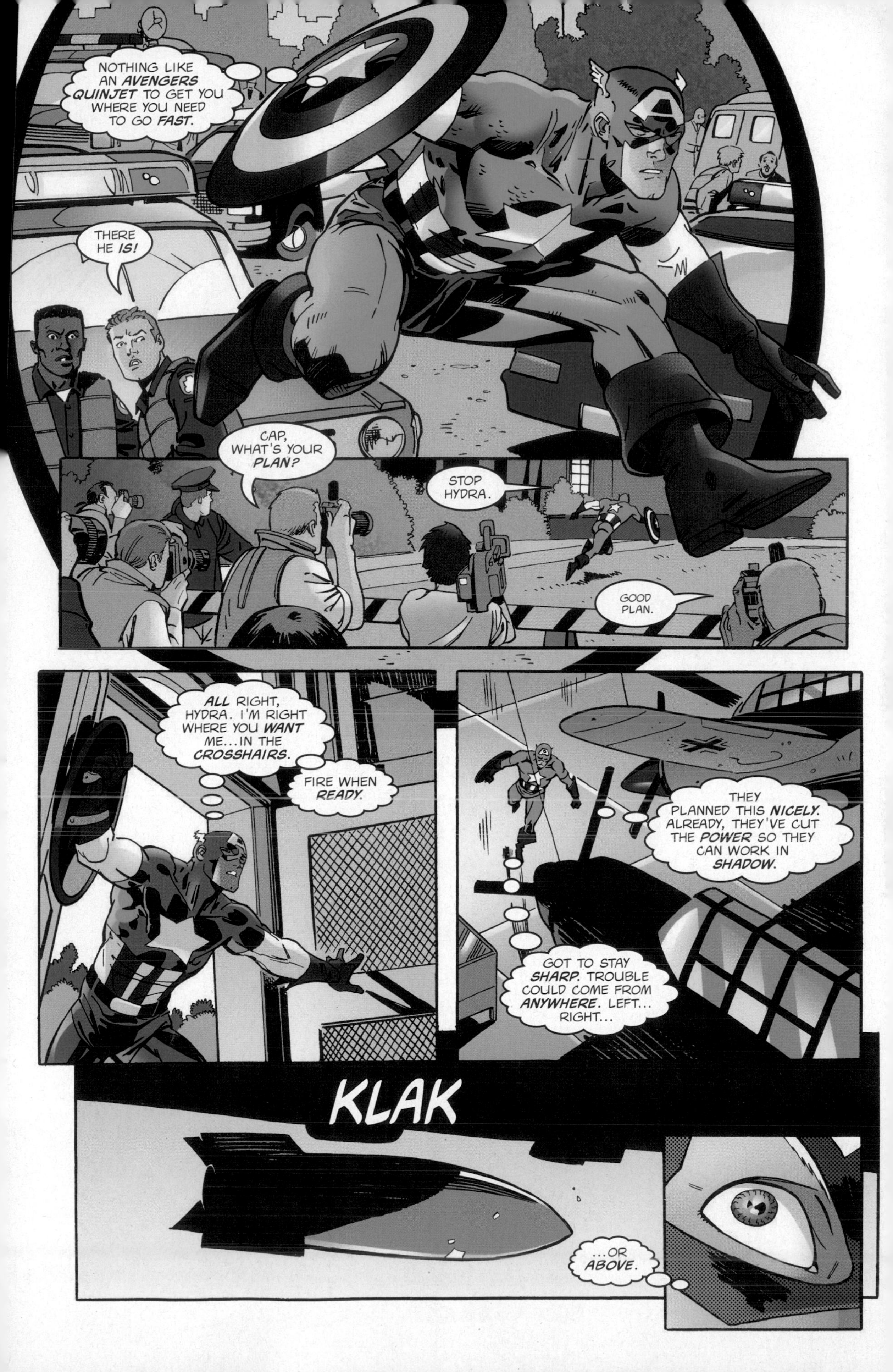

NOTHING LIKE AN AVENGERS QUINJET TO GET YOU WHERE YOU NEED TO GO FAST.
THERE HE IS!
CAP, WHAT'S YOUR PLAN?
STOP HYDRA.
GOOD PLAN.
ALL RIGHT, HYDRA. I'M RIGHT WHERE YOU WANT ME...IN THE CROSSHAIRS.
FIRE WHEN READY.
THEY PLANNED THIS NICELY. ALREADY, THEY'VE CUT THE POWER SO THEY CAN WORK IN SHADOW.
GOT TO STAY SHARP. TROUBLE COULD COME FROM ANYWHERE. LEFT... RIGHT...
KLAK
...OR ABOVE.

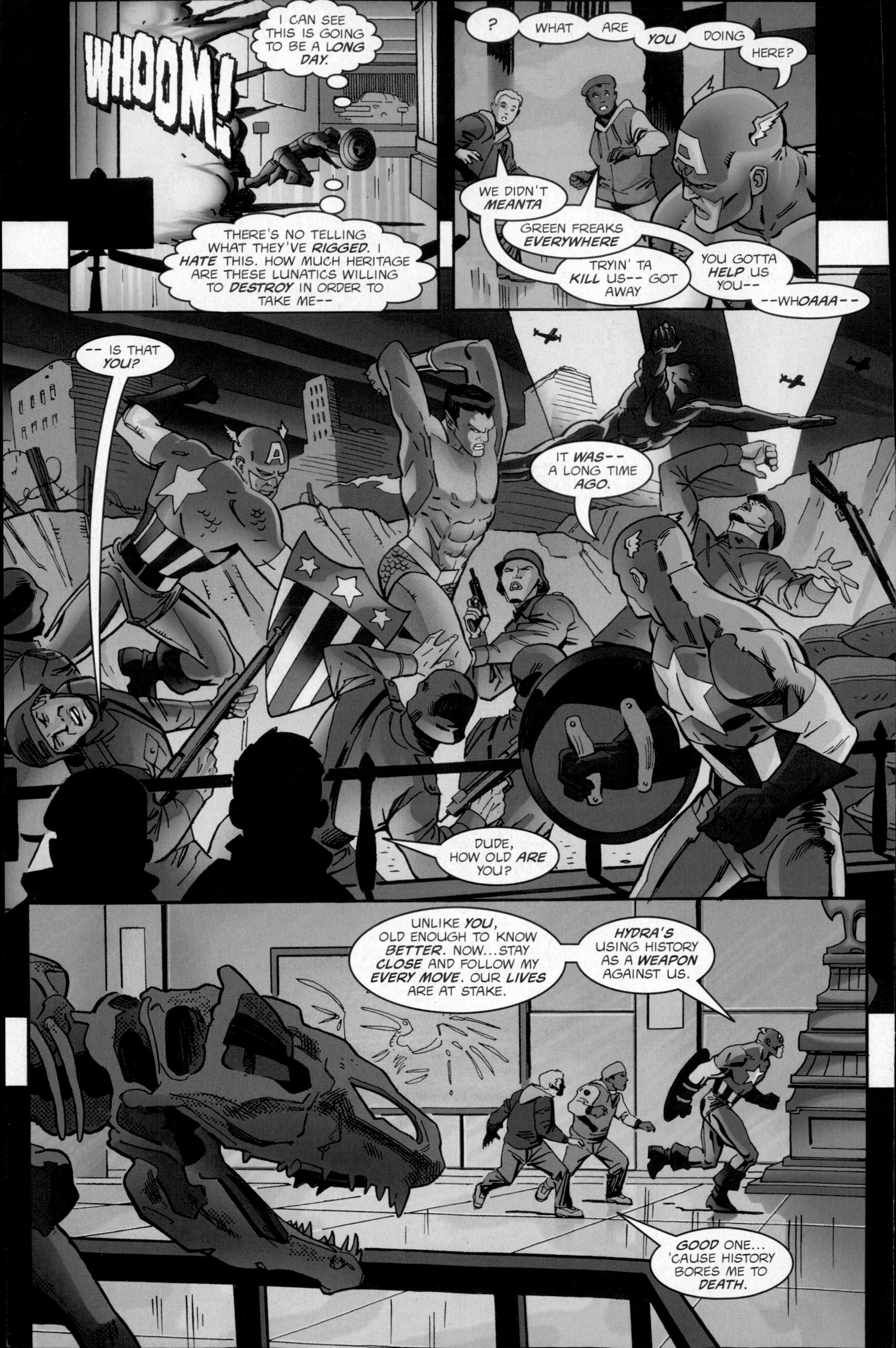
WHOOM!
I CAN SEE THIS IS GOING TO BE A LONG DAY.
THERE'S NO TELLING WHAT THEY'VE RIGGED. I HATE THIS. HOW MUCH HERITAGE ARE THESE LUNATICS WILLING TO DESTROY IN ORDER TO TAKE ME--
? WHAT ARE YOU DOING HERE?
WE DIDN'T MEANTA
GREEN FREAKS EVERYWHERE
TRYIN' TA KILL US-- GOT AWAY
YOU GOTTA HELP US YOU--
--WHOAAA--
-- IS THAT YOU?
IT WAS-- A LONG TIME AGO.
DUDE, HOW OLD ARE YOU?
UNLIKE YOU, OLD ENOUGH TO KNOW BETTER. NOW...STAY CLOSE AND FOLLOW MY EVERY MOVE. OUR LIVES ARE AT STAKE.
HYDRA'S USING HISTORY AS A WEAPON AGAINST US.
GOOD ONE... 'CAUSE HISTORY BORES ME TO DEATH.

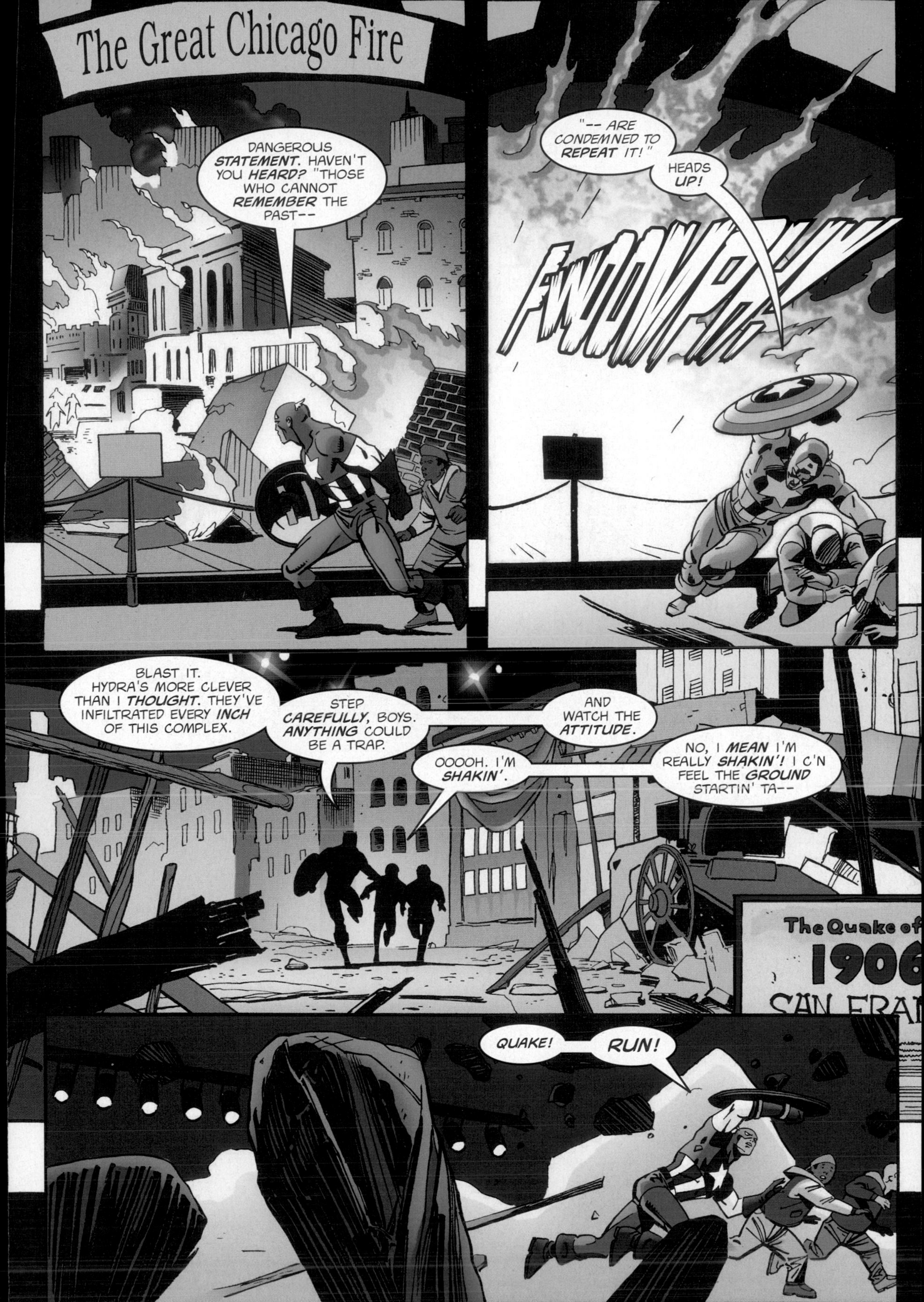
The Great Chicago Fire
DANGEROUS STATEMENT. HAVEN'T YOU HEARD? "THOSE WHO CANNOT REMEMBER THE PAST--
"-- ARE CONDEMNED TO REPEAT IT!"
HEADS UP!
FWOOMPH
BLAST IT. HYDRA'S MORE CLEVER THAN I THOUGHT. THEY'VE INFILTRATED EVERY INCH OF THIS COMPLEX.
STEP CAREFULLY, BOYS. ANYTHING COULD BE A TRAP.
AND WATCH THE ATTITUDE.
OOOOH. I'M SHAKIN'.
NO, I MEAN I'M REALLY SHAKIN'! I C'N FEEL THE GROUND STARTIN' TA--
The Quake of
QUAKE!
RUN!

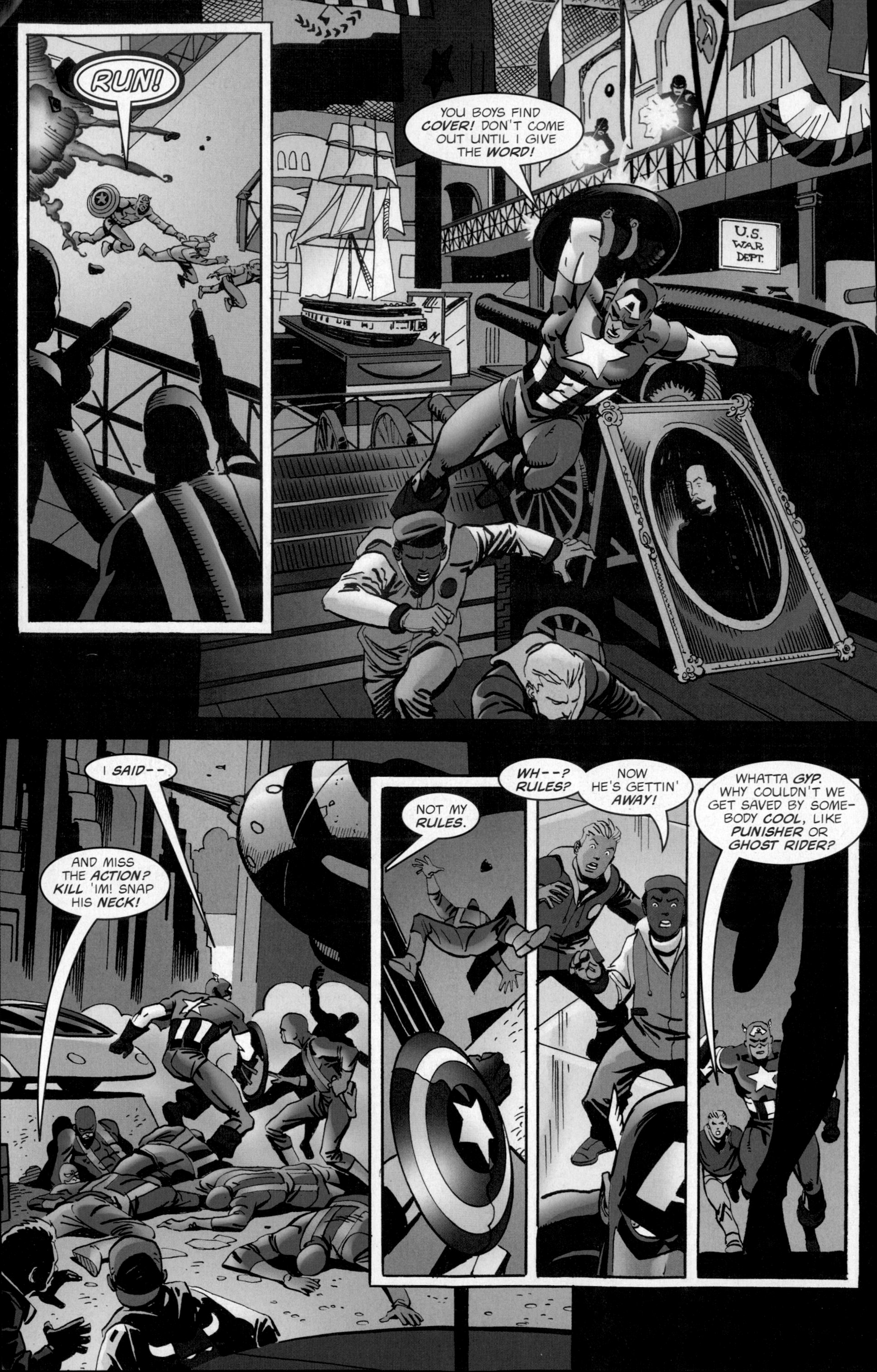
RUN!
YOU BOYS FIND COVER! DON'T COME OUT UNTIL I GIVE THE WORD!
U.S. WAR DEPT.
I SAID--
AND MISS THE ACTION? KILL 'IM! SNAP HIS NECK!
NOT MY RULES.
WH--? RULES?
NOW HE'S GETTIN' AWAY!
WHATTA GYP. WHY COULDN'T WE GET SAVED BY SOMEBODY COOL, LIKE PUNISHER OR GHOST RIDER?

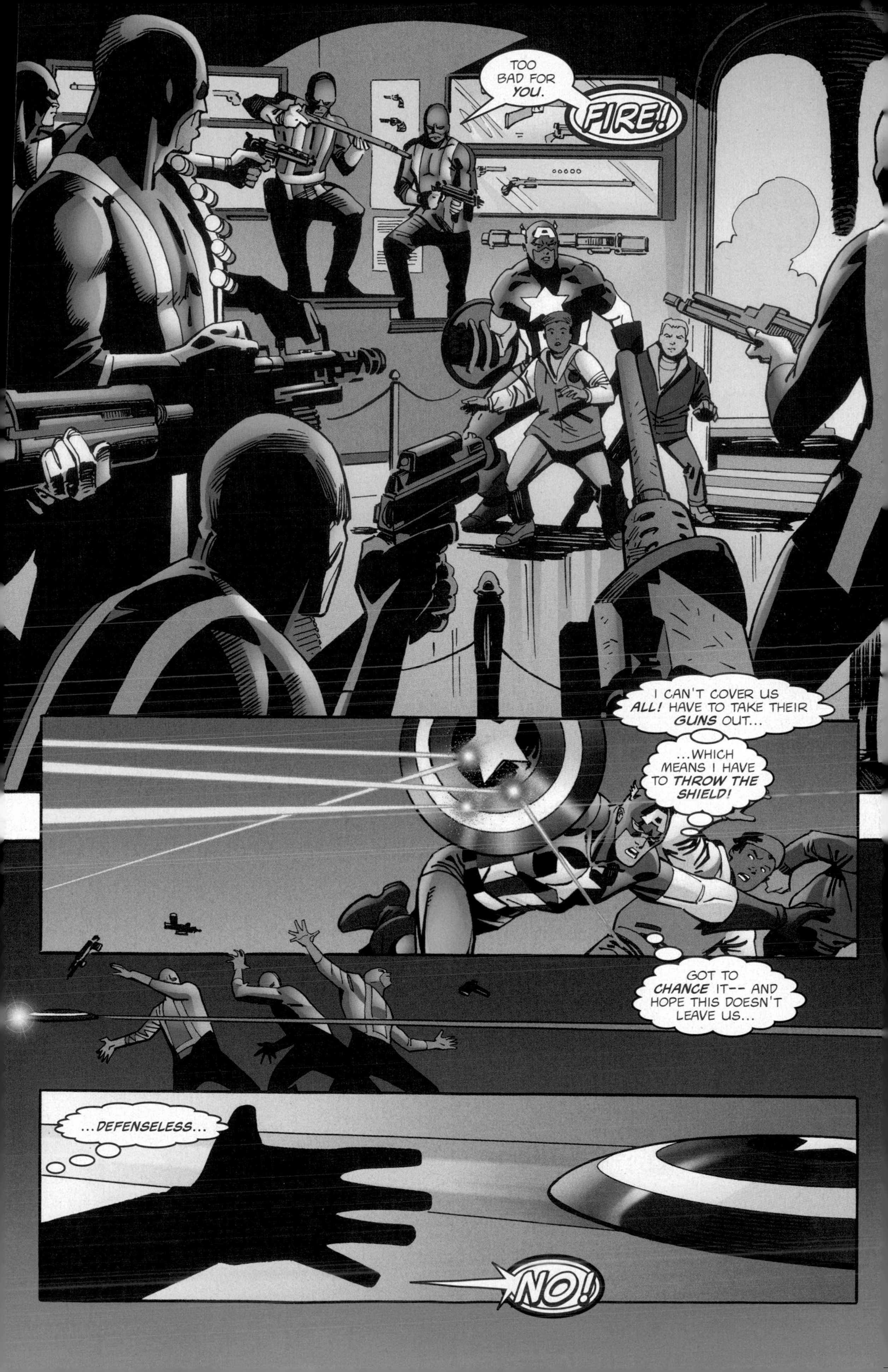
TOO BAD FOR YOU.
FIRE!
I CAN'T COVER US ALL! HAVE TO TAKE THEIR GUNS OUT...
...WHICH MEANS I HAVE TO THROW THE SHIELD!
GOT TO CHANCE IT-- AND HOPE THIS DOESN'T LEAVE US...
...DEFENSELESS...
NO!

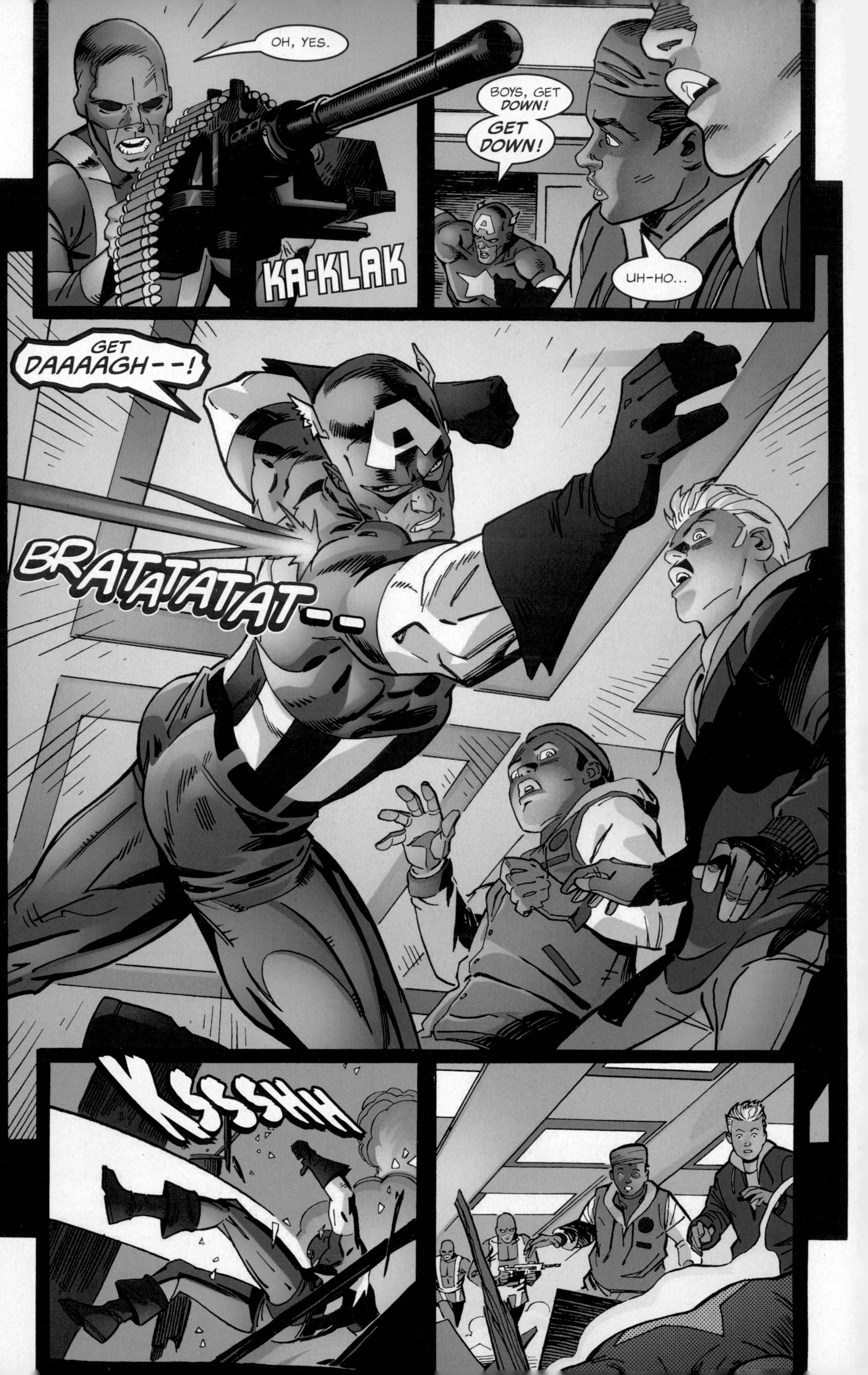
OH, YES.
KA-KLAK
BOYS, GET DOWN!
GET DOWN!
UH-HO...
GET DAAAAGH--!
BRATATATATAT--
KSSSHH

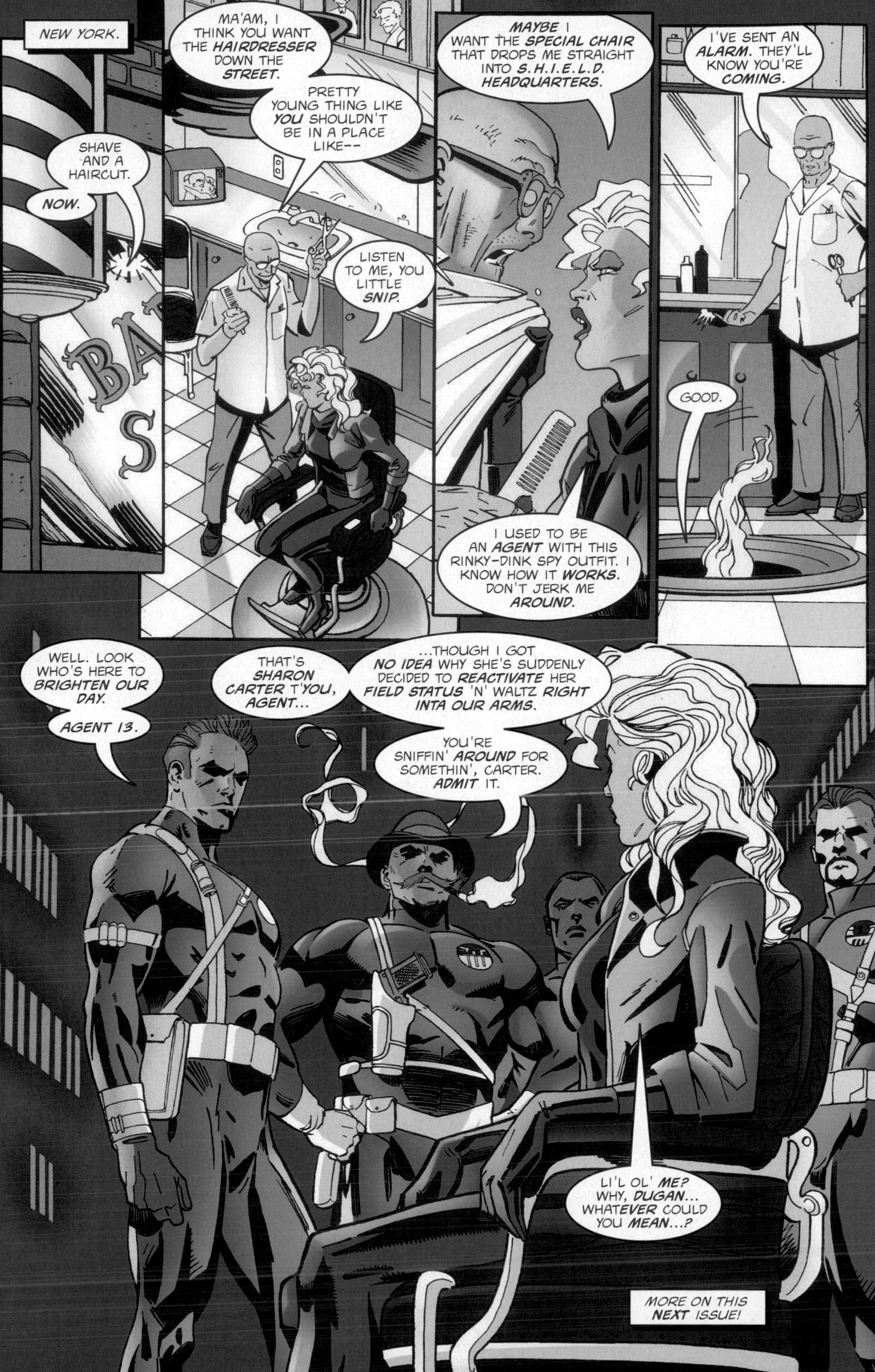
NEW YORK.
SHAVE AND A HAIRCUT.
NOW.
MA'AM, I THINK YOU WANT THE HAIRDRESSER DOWN THE STREET.
PRETTY YOUNG THING LIKE YOU SHOULDN'T BE IN A PLACE LIKE--
LISTEN TO ME, YOU LITTLE SNIP.
MAYBE I WANT THE SPECIAL CHAIR THAT DROPS ME STRAIGHT INTO S.H.I.E.L.D. HEADQUARTERS.
I USED TO BE AN AGENT WITH THIS RINKY-DINK SPY OUTFIT. I KNOW HOW IT WORKS. DON'T JERK ME AROUND.
I'VE SENT AN ALARM. THEY'LL KNOW YOU'RE COMING.
GOOD.
WELL. LOOK WHO'S HERE TO BRIGHTEN OUR DAY.
AGENT 13.
THAT'S SHARON CARTER T'YOU, AGENT...
...THOUGH I GOT NO IDEA WHY SHE'S SUDDENLY DECIDED TO REACTIVATE HER FIELD STATUS 'N' WALTZ RIGHT INTA OUR ARMS.
YOU'RE SNIFFIN' AROUND FOR SOMETHIN', CARTER. ADMIT IT.
LI'L OL' ME? WHY, DUGAN... WHATEVER COULD YOU MEAN...?
MORE ON THIS NEXT ISSUE!

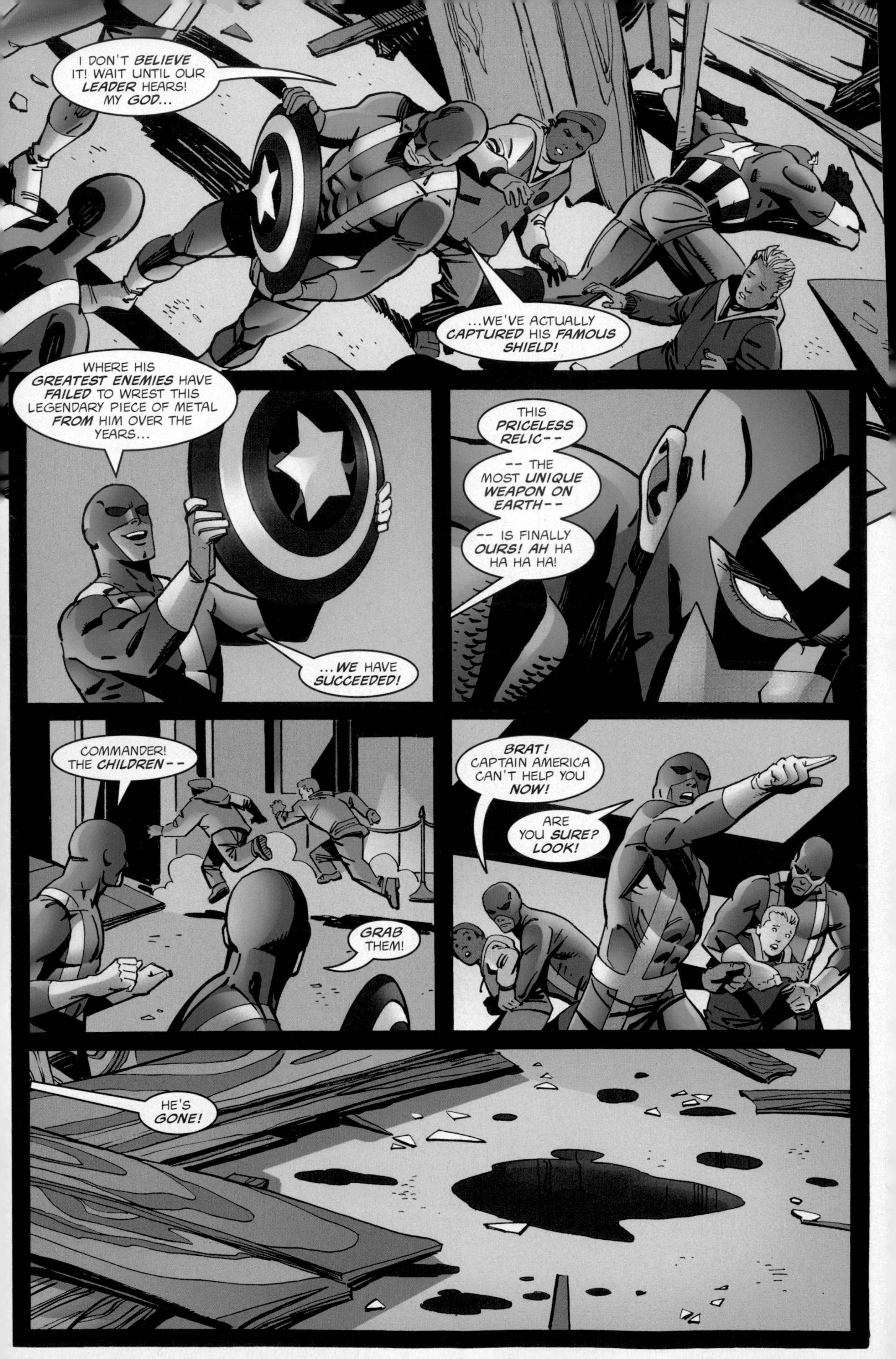
I DON'T BELIEVE IT! WAIT UNTIL OUR LEADER HEARS! MY GOD...
...WE'VE ACTUALLY CAPTURED HIS FAMOUS SHIELD!
WHERE HIS GREATEST ENEMIES HAVE FAILED TO WREST THIS LEGENDARY PIECE OF METAL FROM HIM OVER THE YEARS...
...WE HAVE SUCCEEDED!
THIS PRICELESS RELIC--
-- THE MOST UNIQUE WEAPON ON EARTH--
-- IS FINALLY OURS! AH HA HA HA HA!
COMMANDER! THE CHILDREN--
GRAB THEM!
BRAT! CAPTAIN AMERICA CAN'T HELP YOU NOW!
ARE YOU SURE? LOOK!
HE'S GONE!

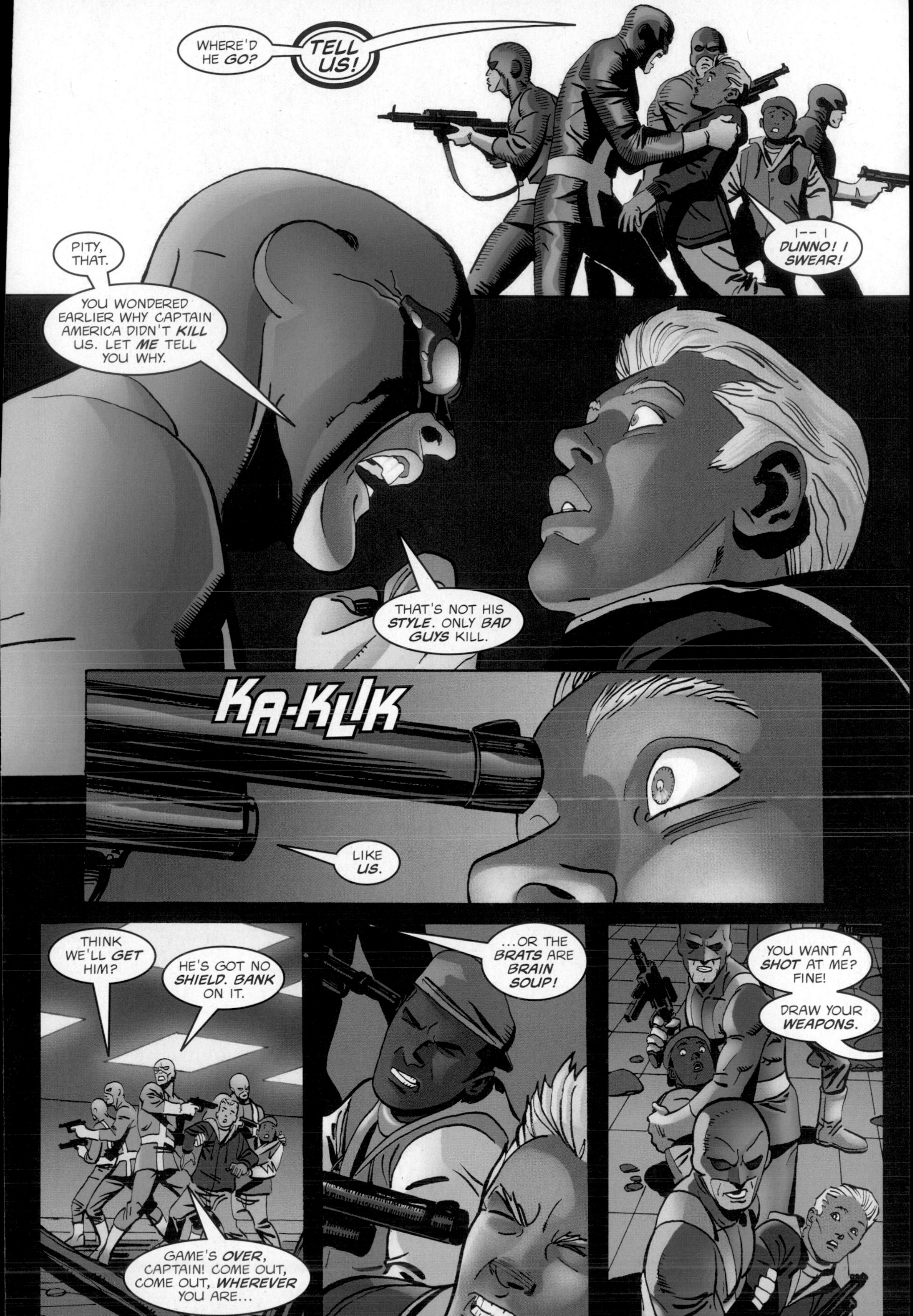
WHERE'D HE GO?
TELL US!
I-- I DUNNO! I SWEAR!
PITY, THAT.
YOU WONDERED EARLIER WHY CAPTAIN AMERICA DIDN'T KILL US. LET ME TELL YOU WHY.
THAT'S NOT HIS STYLE. ONLY BAD GUYS KILL.
KA-KLIK
LIKE US.
THINK WE'LL GET HIM?
HE'S GOT NO SHIELD. BANK ON IT.
GAME'S OVER, CAPTAIN! COME OUT, COME OUT, WHEREVER YOU ARE...
...OR THE BRATS ARE BRAIN SOUP!
YOU WANT A SHOT AT ME? FINE!
DRAW YOUR WEAPONS.

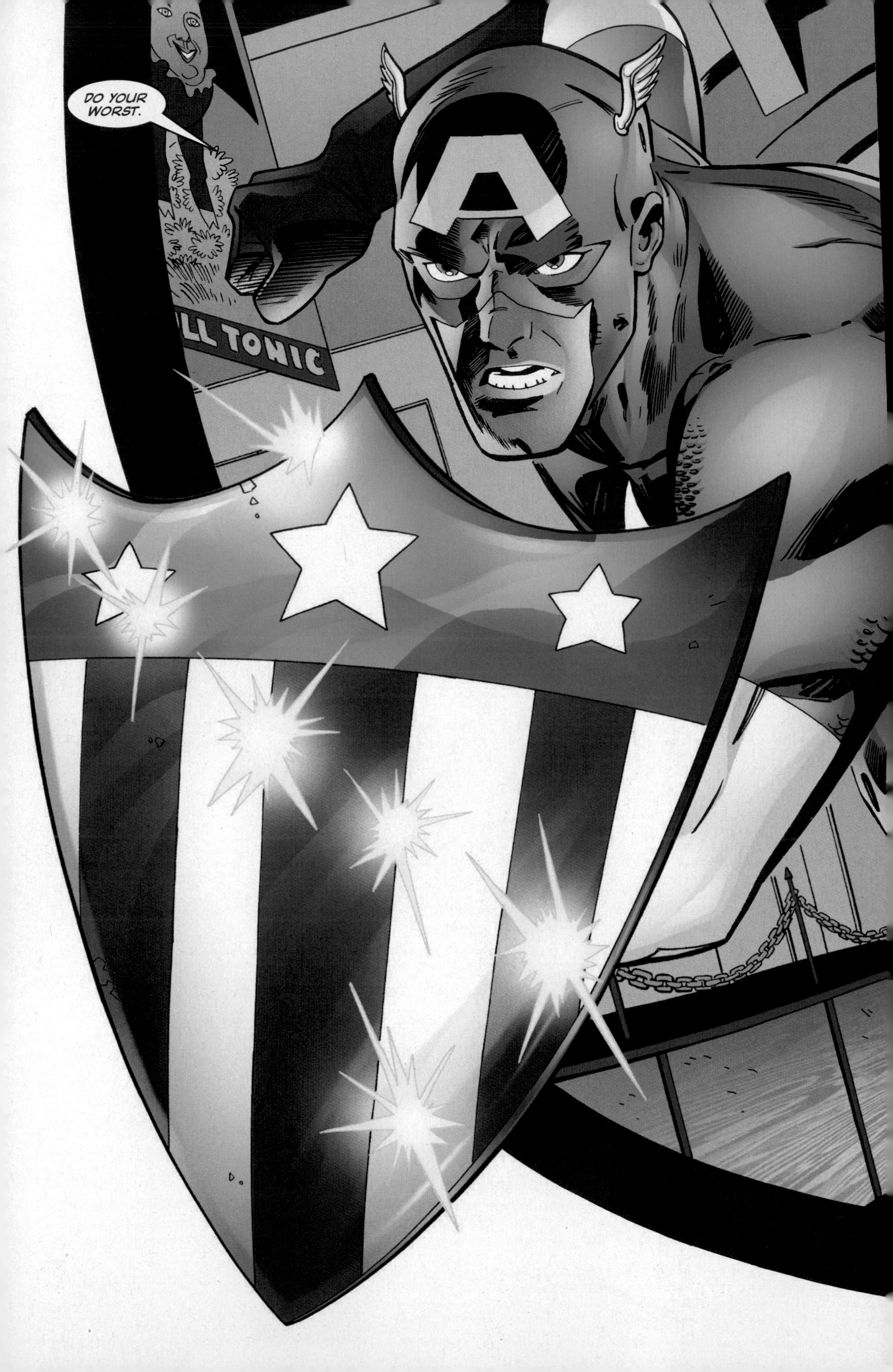
DO YOUR WORST.
LL TONIC

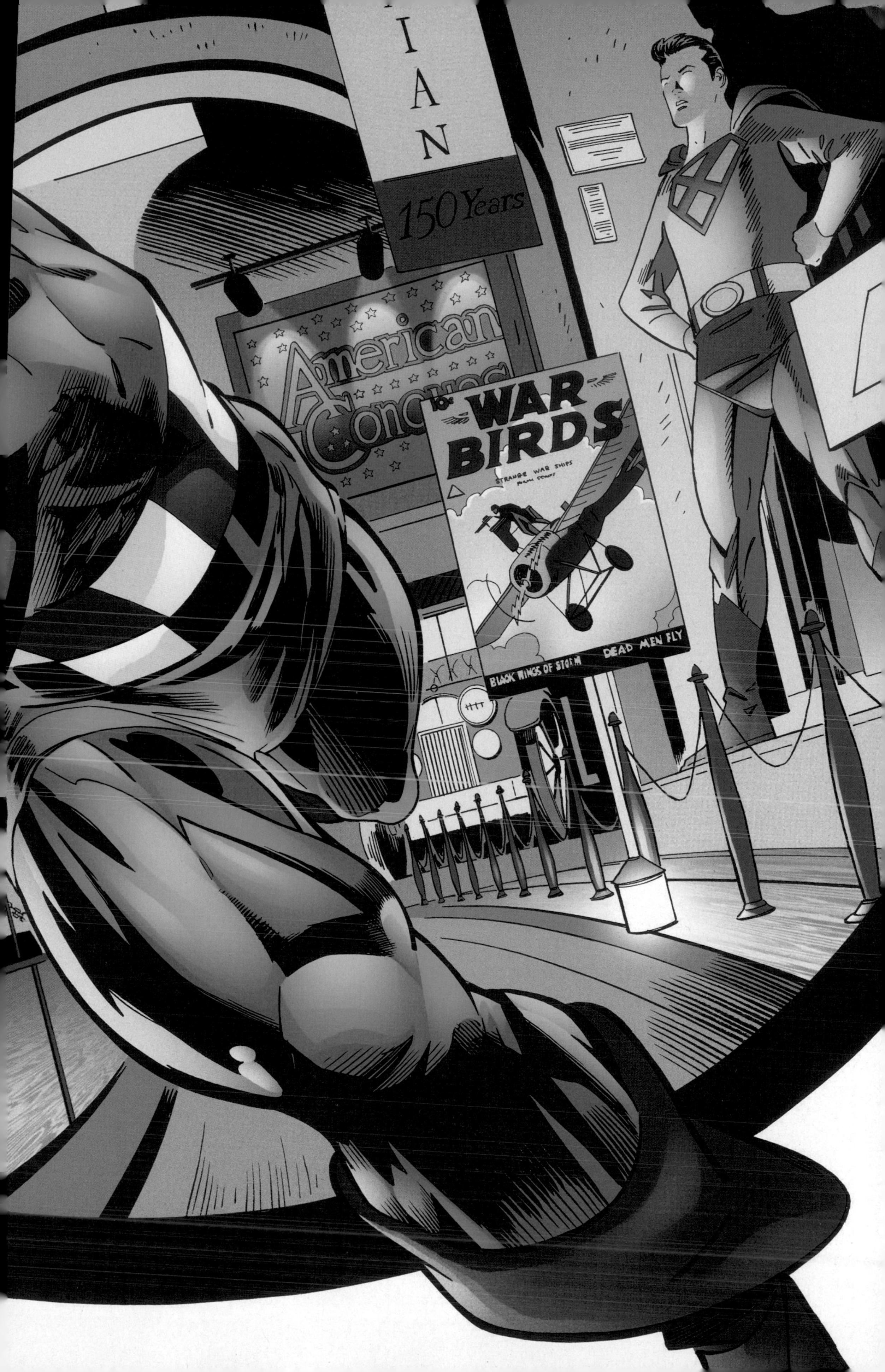
IAN
150 Years
American
10¢
WAR BIRDS
STRANGE WAR SHIPS
BLACK WINGS OF STORM
DEAD MEN FLY

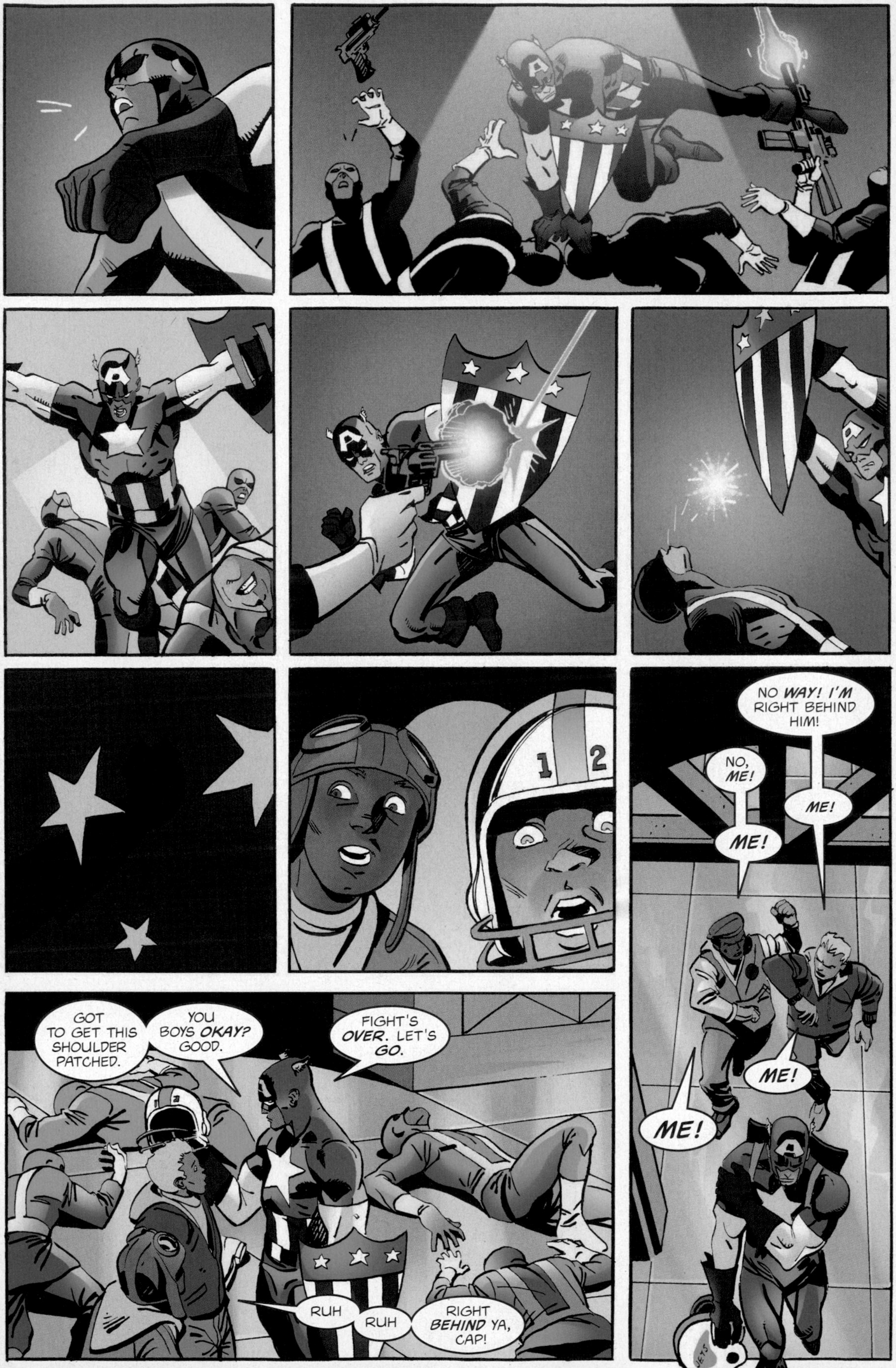

NO WAY! I'M RIGHT BEHIND HIM!
NO, ME!
ME!
ME!
ME!
ME!
GOT TO GET THIS SHOULDER PATCHED.
YOU BOYS OKAY? GOOD.
FIGHT'S OVER. LET'S GO.
RUH
RUH
RIGHT BEHIND YA, CAP!

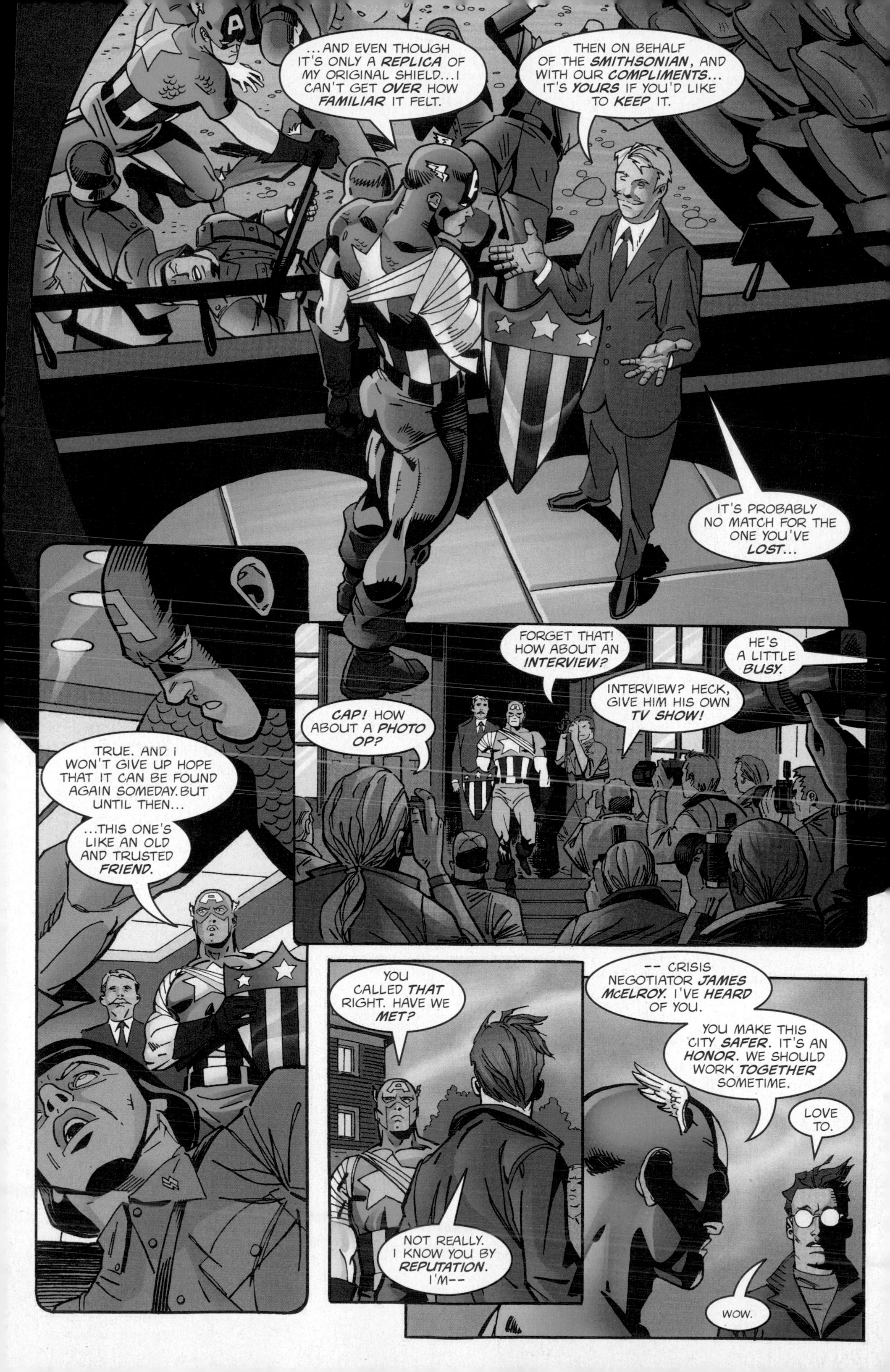
...AND EVEN THOUGH IT'S ONLY A REPLICA OF MY ORIGINAL SHIELD...I CAN'T GET OVER HOW FAMILIAR IT FELT.
THEN ON BEHALF OF THE SMITHSONIAN, AND WITH OUR COMPLIMENTS... IT'S YOURS IF YOU'D LIKE TO KEEP IT.
IT'S PROBABLY NO MATCH FOR THE ONE YOU'VE LOST...
TRUE. AND I WON'T GIVE UP HOPE THAT IT CAN BE FOUND AGAIN SOMEDAY. BUT UNTIL THEN...
...THIS ONE'S LIKE AN OLD AND TRUSTED FRIEND.
CAP! HOW ABOUT A PHOTO OP?
FORGET THAT! HOW ABOUT AN INTERVIEW?
INTERVIEW? HECK, GIVE HIM HIS OWN TV SHOW!
HE'S A LITTLE BUSY.
YOU CALLED THAT RIGHT. HAVE WE MET?
NOT REALLY. I KNOW YOU BY REPUTATION. I'M--
-- CRISIS NEGOTIATOR JAMES McELROY. I'VE HEARD OF YOU.
YOU MAKE THIS CITY SAFER. IT'S AN HONOR. WE SHOULD WORK TOGETHER SOMETIME.
LOVE TO.
WOW.

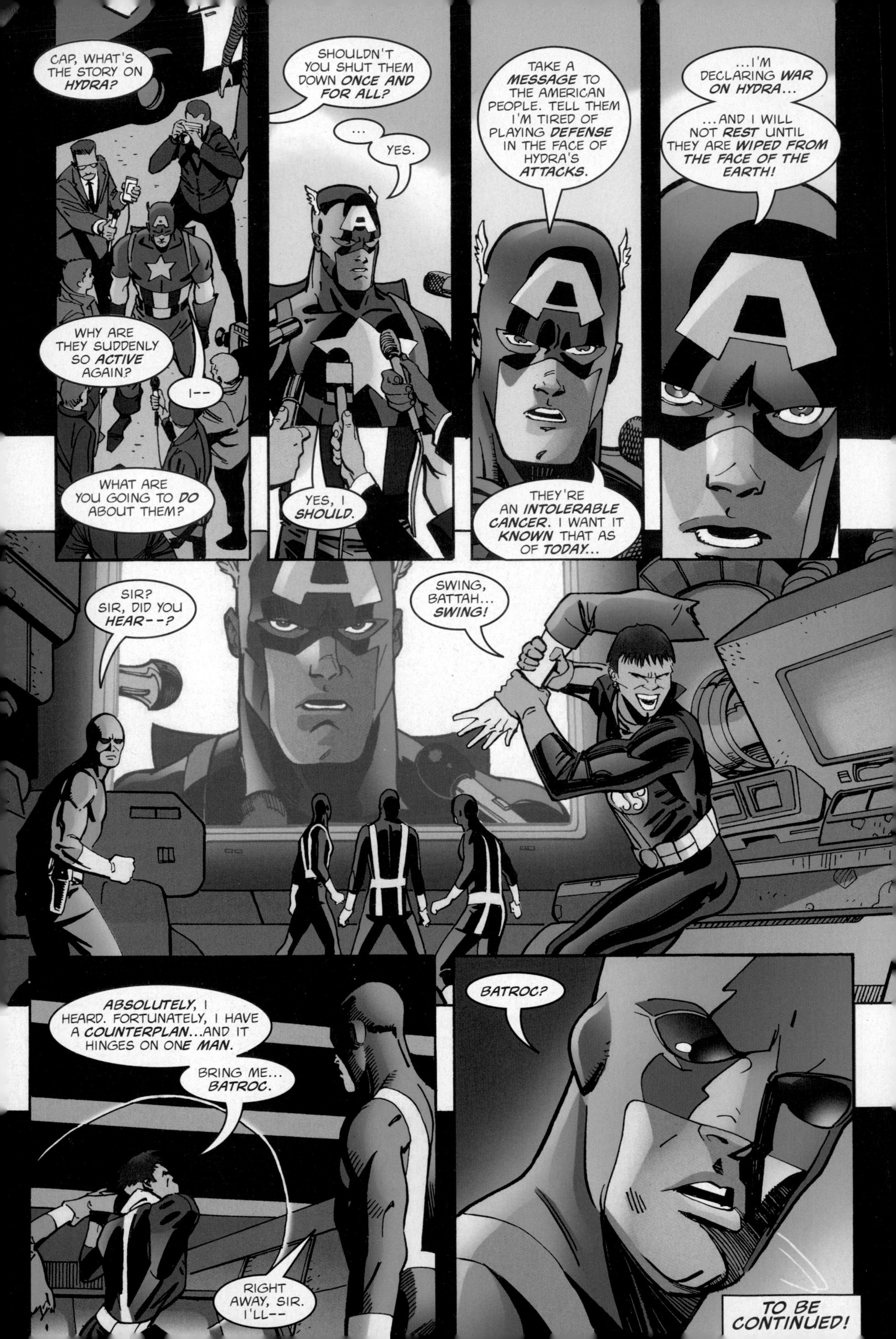
CAP, WHAT'S THE STORY ON HYDRA?
WHY ARE THEY SUDDENLY SO ACTIVE AGAIN?
I--
WHAT ARE YOU GOING TO DO ABOUT THEM?
SHOULDN'T YOU SHUT THEM DOWN ONCE AND FOR ALL?
...
YES.
YES, I SHOULD.
TAKE A MESSAGE TO THE AMERICAN PEOPLE. TELL THEM I'M TIRED OF PLAYING DEFENSE IN THE FACE OF HYDRA'S ATTACKS.
THEY'RE AN INTOLERABLE CANCER. I WANT IT KNOWN THAT AS OF TODAY...
...I'M DECLARING WAR ON HYDRA...
...AND I WILL NOT REST UNTIL THEY ARE WIPED FROM THE FACE OF THE EARTH!
SIR? SIR, DID YOU HEAR--?
SWING, BATTAH... SWING!
ABSOLUTELY, I HEARD. FORTUNATELY, I HAVE A COUNTERPLAN...AND IT HINGES ON ONE MAN.
BRING ME... BATROC.
RIGHT AWAY, SIR. I'LL--
BATROC?
TO BE CONTINUED!

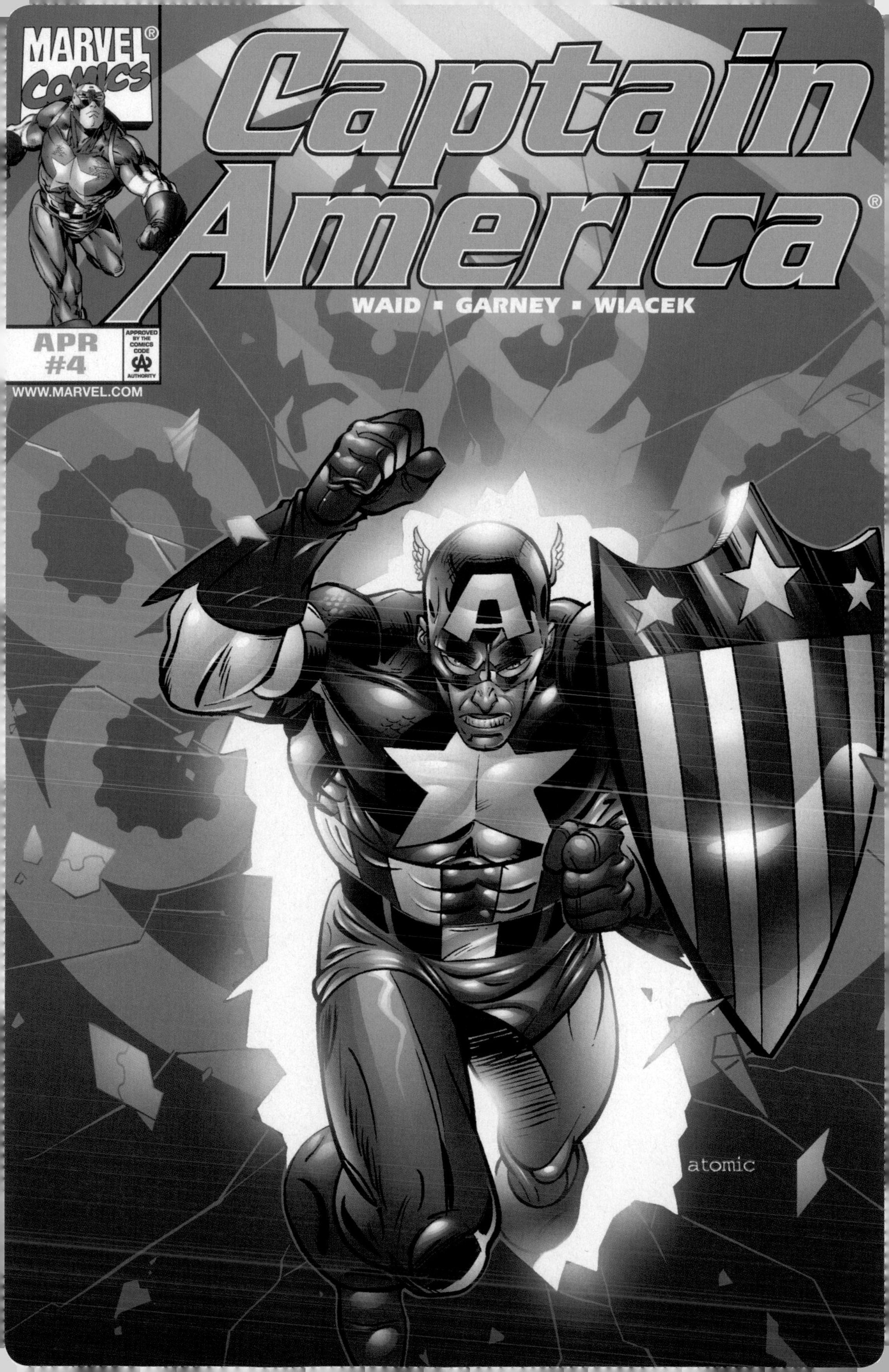

MARVEL® COMICS
Captain America®
WAID • GARNEY • WIACEK
APR #4
APPROVED BY THE COMICS CODE AUTHORITY
WWW.MARVEL.COM
atomic

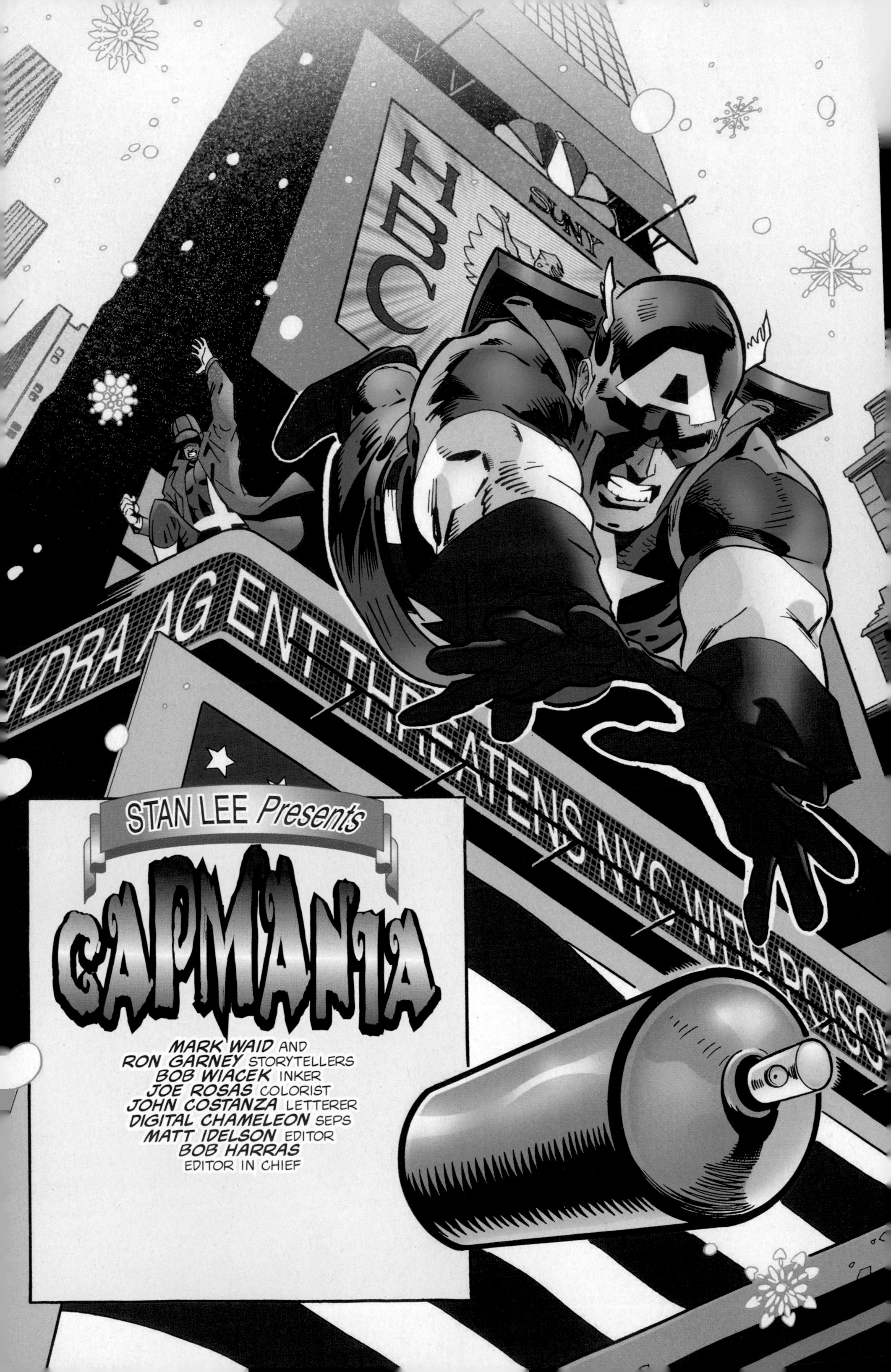

HBC
SUNY
YDRA AG ENT THREATENS NYC WITH POISON
STAN LEE Presents
CAPMANIA
MARK WAID AND
RON GARNEY STORYTELLERS
BOB WIACEK INKER
JOE ROSAS COLORIST
JOHN COSTANZA LETTERER
DIGITAL CHAMELEON SEPS
MATT IDELSON EDITOR
BOB HARRAS
EDITOR IN CHIEF

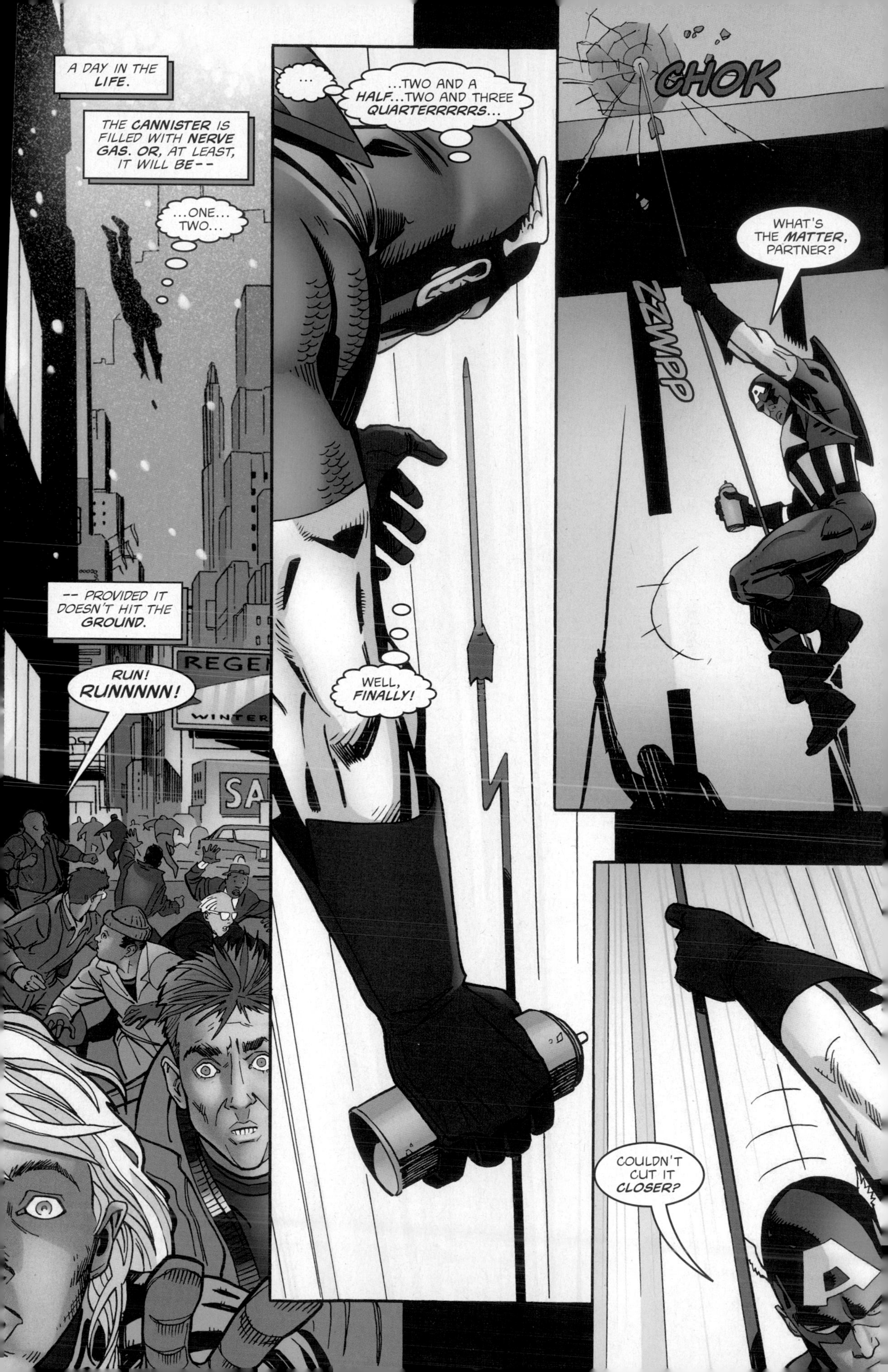

A DAY IN THE LIFE.
THE CANNISTER IS FILLED WITH NERVE GAS. OR, AT LEAST, IT WILL BE--
...ONE... TWO...
-- PROVIDED IT DOESN'T HIT THE GROUND.
REGEN
WINTER
RUN! RUNNNNN!
...
...TWO AND A HALF...TWO AND THREE QUARTERRRRRS...
WELL, FINALLY!
CHOK
ZZWPP
WHAT'S THE MATTER, PARTNER?
COULDN'T CUT IT CLOSER?

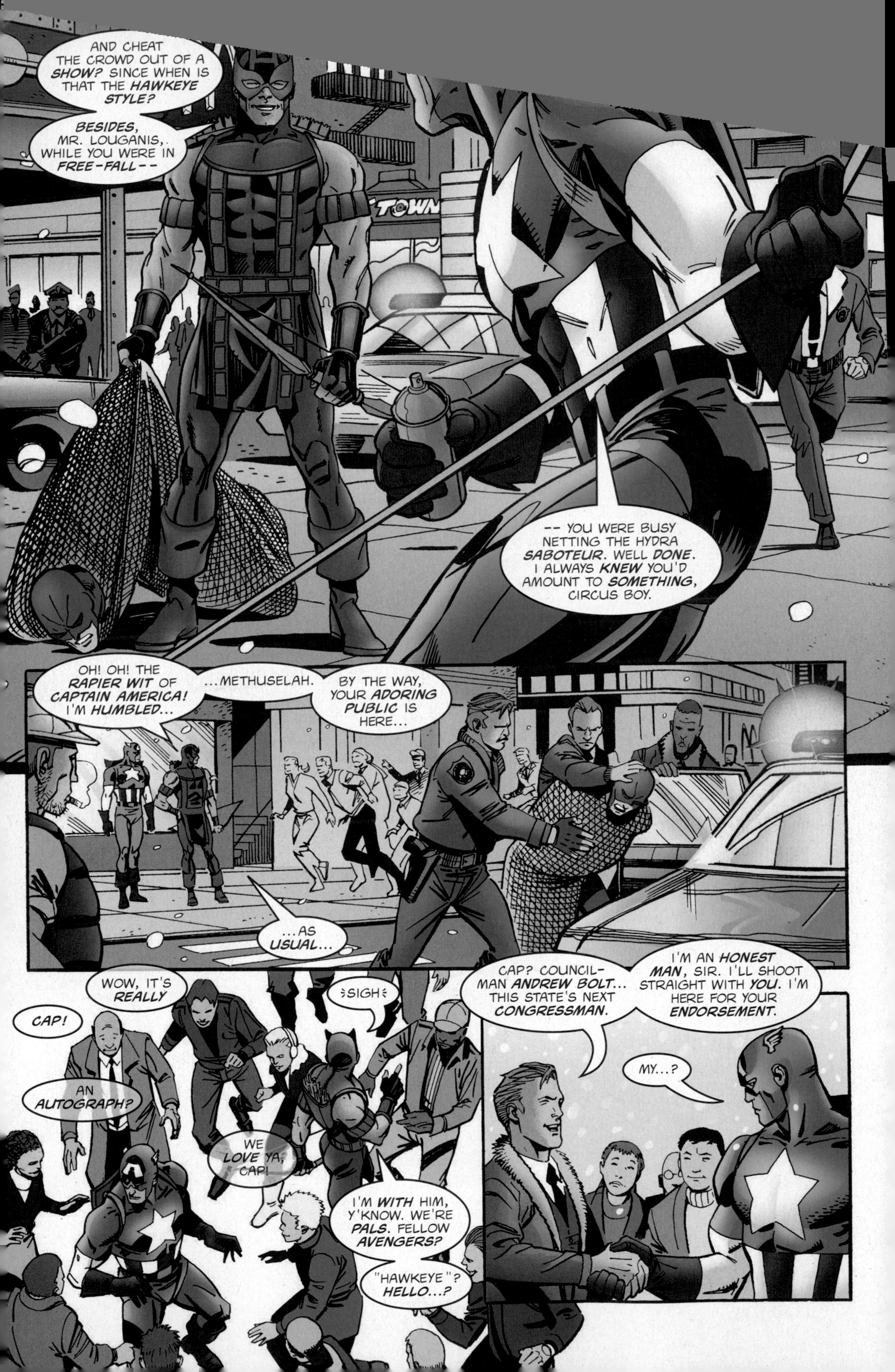
AND CHEAT THE CROWD OUT OF A SHOW? SINCE WHEN IS THAT THE HAWKEYE STYLE?
BESIDES, MR. LOUGANIS,. WHILE YOU WERE IN FREE-FALL--
-- YOU WERE BUSY NETTING THE HYDRA SABOTEUR. WELL DONE. I ALWAYS KNEW YOU'D AMOUNT TO SOMETHING, CIRCUS BOY.
TOWN
OH! OH! THE RAPIER WIT OF CAPTAIN AMERICA! I'M HUMBLED...
...METHUSELAH.
BY THE WAY, YOUR ADORING PUBLIC IS HERE...
...AS USUAL...
WOW, IT'S REALLY
CAP!
AN AUTOGRAPH?
WE LOVE YA, CAP!
SIGH
I'M WITH HIM, Y'KNOW. WE'RE PALS. FELLOW AVENGERS?
"HAWKEYE"? HELLO...?
CAP? COUNCIL-MAN ANDREW BOLT... THIS STATE'S NEXT CONGRESSMAN.
I'M AN HONEST MAN, SIR. I'LL SHOOT STRAIGHT WITH YOU. I'M HERE FOR YOUR ENDORSEMENT.
MY...?

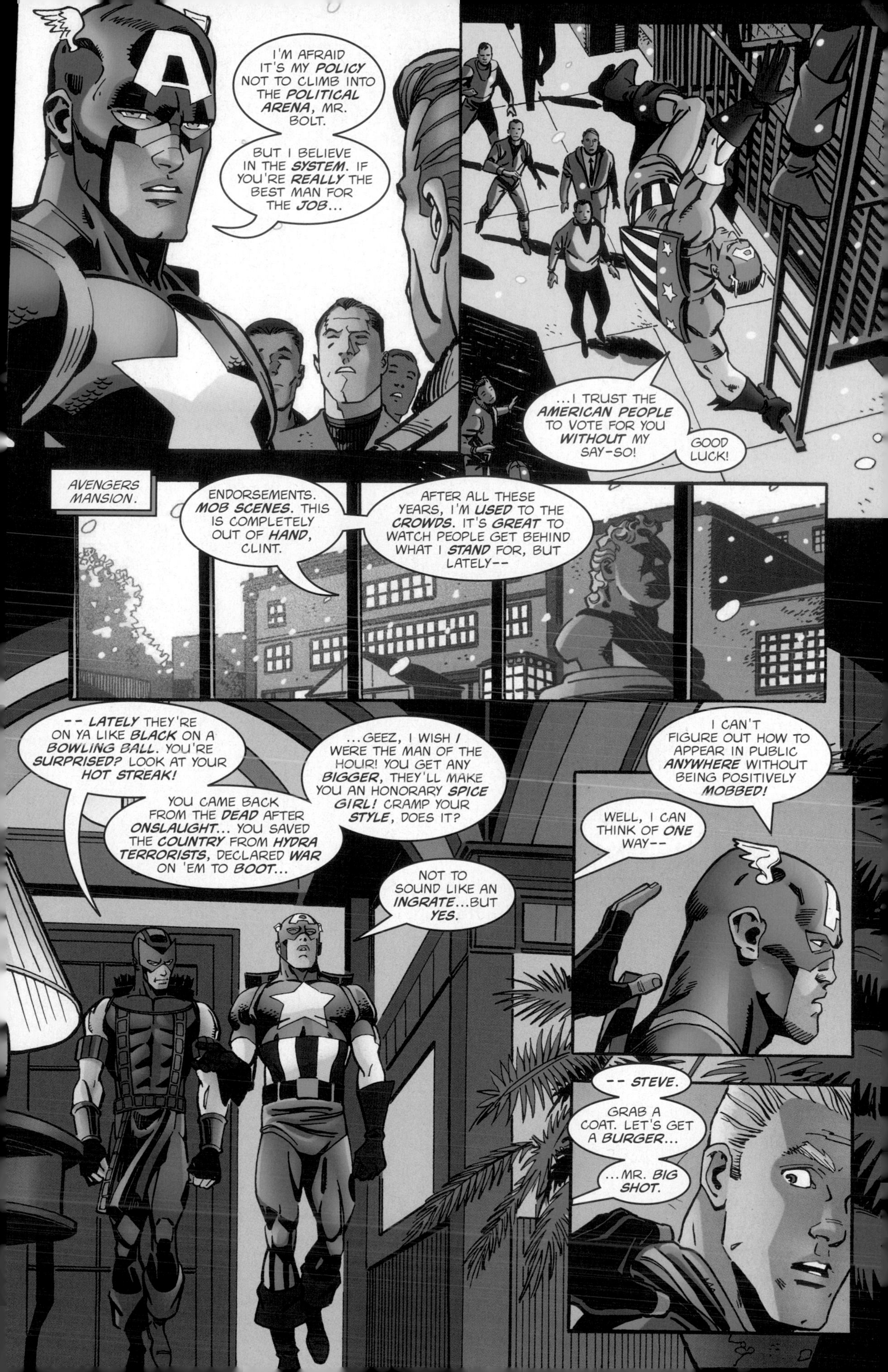

I'M AFRAID IT'S MY POLICY NOT TO CLIMB INTO THE POLITICAL ARENA, MR. BOLT.
BUT I BELIEVE IN THE SYSTEM. IF YOU'RE REALLY THE BEST MAN FOR THE JOB...
...I TRUST THE AMERICAN PEOPLE TO VOTE FOR YOU WITHOUT MY SAY-SO!
GOOD LUCK!
AVENGERS MANSION.
ENDORSEMENTS. MOB SCENES. THIS IS COMPLETELY OUT OF HAND, CLINT.
AFTER ALL THESE YEARS, I'M USED TO THE CROWDS. IT'S GREAT TO WATCH PEOPLE GET BEHIND WHAT I STAND FOR, BUT LATELY--
-- LATELY THEY'RE ON YA LIKE BLACK ON A BOWLING BALL. YOU'RE SURPRISED? LOOK AT YOUR HOT STREAK!
YOU CAME BACK FROM THE DEAD AFTER ONSLAUGHT... YOU SAVED THE COUNTRY FROM HYDRA TERRORISTS, DECLARED WAR ON 'EM TO BOOT...
...GEEZ, I WISH I WERE THE MAN OF THE HOUR! YOU GET ANY BIGGER, THEY'LL MAKE YOU AN HONORARY SPICE GIRL! CRAMP YOUR STYLE, DOES IT?
NOT TO SOUND LIKE AN INGRATE...BUT YES.
I CAN'T FIGURE OUT HOW TO APPEAR IN PUBLIC ANYWHERE WITHOUT BEING POSITIVELY MOBBED!
WELL, I CAN THINK OF ONE WAY--
-- STEVE.
GRAB A COAT. LET'S GET A BURGER...
...MR. BIG SHOT.

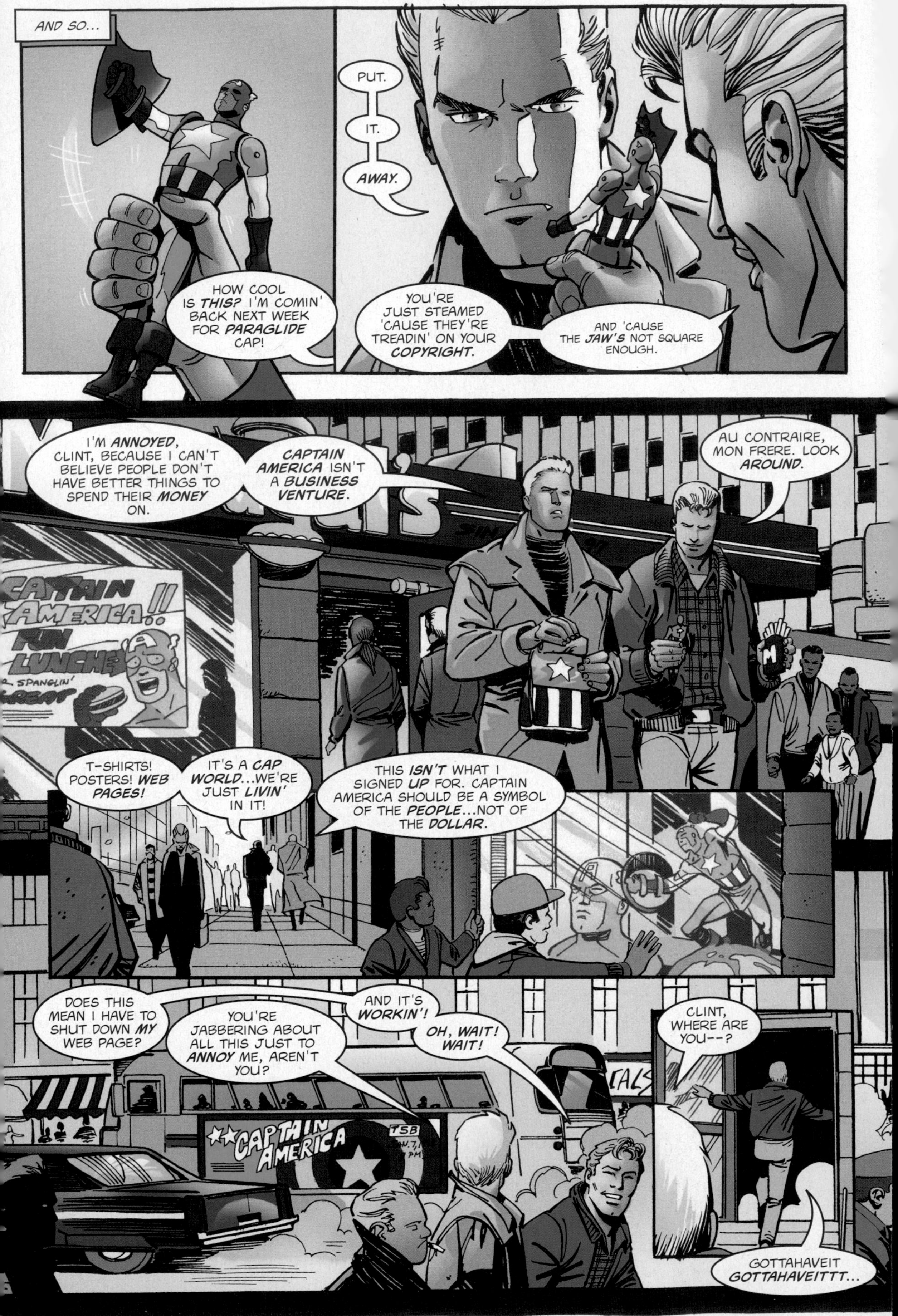
AND SO...
PUT. IT. AWAY.
HOW COOL IS THIS? I'M COMIN' BACK NEXT WEEK FOR PARAGLIDE CAP!
YOU'RE JUST STEAMED 'CAUSE THEY'RE TREADIN' ON YOUR COPYRIGHT.
AND 'CAUSE THE JAW'S NOT SQUARE ENOUGH.
I'M ANNOYED, CLINT, BECAUSE I CAN'T BELIEVE PEOPLE DON'T HAVE BETTER THINGS TO SPEND THEIR MONEY ON.
CAPTAIN AMERICA ISN'T A BUSINESS VENTURE.
AU CONTRAIRE, MON FRERE. LOOK AROUND.
CAPTAIN AMERICA!! FUN LUNCHES
T-SHIRTS! POSTERS! WEB PAGES!
IT'S A CAP WORLD...WE'RE JUST LIVIN' IN IT!
THIS ISN'T WHAT I SIGNED UP FOR. CAPTAIN AMERICA SHOULD BE A SYMBOL OF THE PEOPLE...NOT OF THE DOLLAR.
DOES THIS MEAN I HAVE TO SHUT DOWN MY WEB PAGE?
YOU'RE JABBERING ABOUT ALL THIS JUST TO ANNOY ME, AREN'T YOU?
AND IT'S WORKIN'!
OH, WAIT! WAIT!
CLINT, WHERE ARE YOU--?
CAPTAIN AMERICA
TSB
GOTTAHAVEIT GOTTAHAVEITTT...

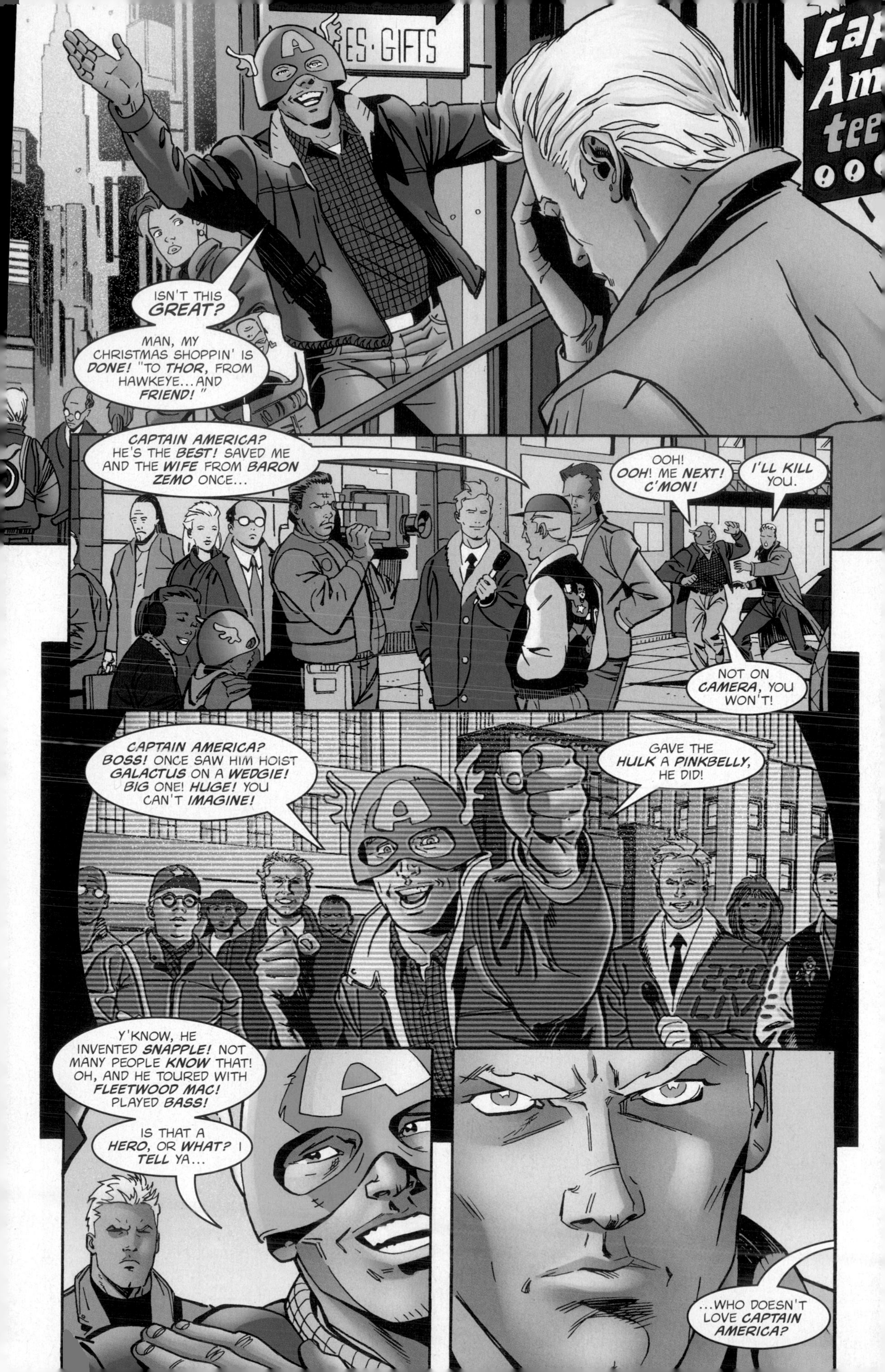

...ES · GIFTS
ISN'T THIS GREAT?
MAN, MY CHRISTMAS SHOPPIN' IS DONE! "TO THOR, FROM HAWKEYE...AND FRIEND!"
CAPTAIN AMERICA? HE'S THE BEST! SAVED ME AND THE WIFE FROM BARON ZEMO ONCE...
OOH! OOH! ME NEXT! C'MON!
I'LL KILL YOU.
NOT ON CAMERA, YOU WON'T!
CAPTAIN AMERICA? BOSS! ONCE SAW HIM HOIST GALACTUS ON A WEDGIE! BIG ONE! HUGE! YOU CAN'T IMAGINE!
GAVE THE HULK A PINKBELLY, HE DID!
Y'KNOW, HE INVENTED SNAPPLE! NOT MANY PEOPLE KNOW THAT! OH, AND HE TOURED WITH FLEETWOOD MAC! PLAYED BASS!
IS THAT A HERO, OR WHAT? I TELL YA...
...WHO DOESN'T LOVE CAPTAIN AMERICA?

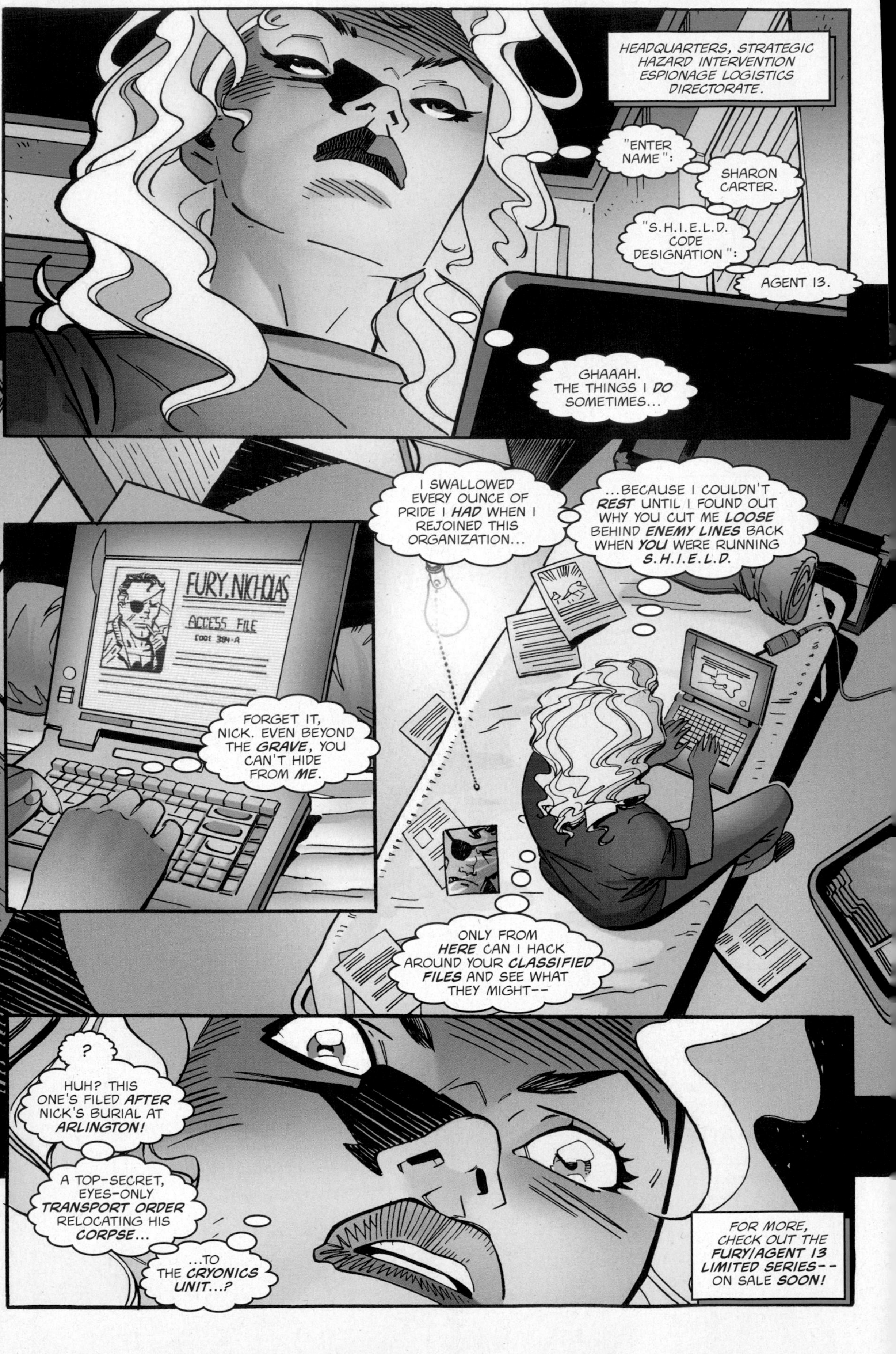
HEADQUARTERS, STRATEGIC HAZARD INTERVENTION ESPIONAGE LOGISTICS DIRECTORATE.
"ENTER NAME":
SHARON CARTER.
"S.H.I.E.L.D. CODE DESIGNATION":
AGENT 13.
GHAAAH. THE THINGS I DO SOMETIMES...
I SWALLOWED EVERY OUNCE OF PRIDE I HAD WHEN I REJOINED THIS ORGANIZATION...
...BECAUSE I COULDN'T REST UNTIL I FOUND OUT WHY YOU CUT ME LOOSE BEHIND ENEMY LINES BACK WHEN YOU WERE RUNNING S.H.I.E.L.D.
FURY, NICHOLAS
ACCESS FILE
FORGET IT, NICK. EVEN BEYOND THE GRAVE, YOU CAN'T HIDE FROM ME.
ONLY FROM HERE CAN I HACK AROUND YOUR CLASSIFIED FILES AND SEE WHAT THEY MIGHT--
?
HUH? THIS ONE'S FILED AFTER NICK'S BURIAL AT ARLINGTON!
A TOP-SECRET, EYES-ONLY TRANSPORT ORDER RELOCATING HIS CORPSE...
...TO THE CRYONICS UNIT...?
FOR MORE, CHECK OUT THE FURY/AGENT 13 LIMITED SERIES--ON SALE SOON!

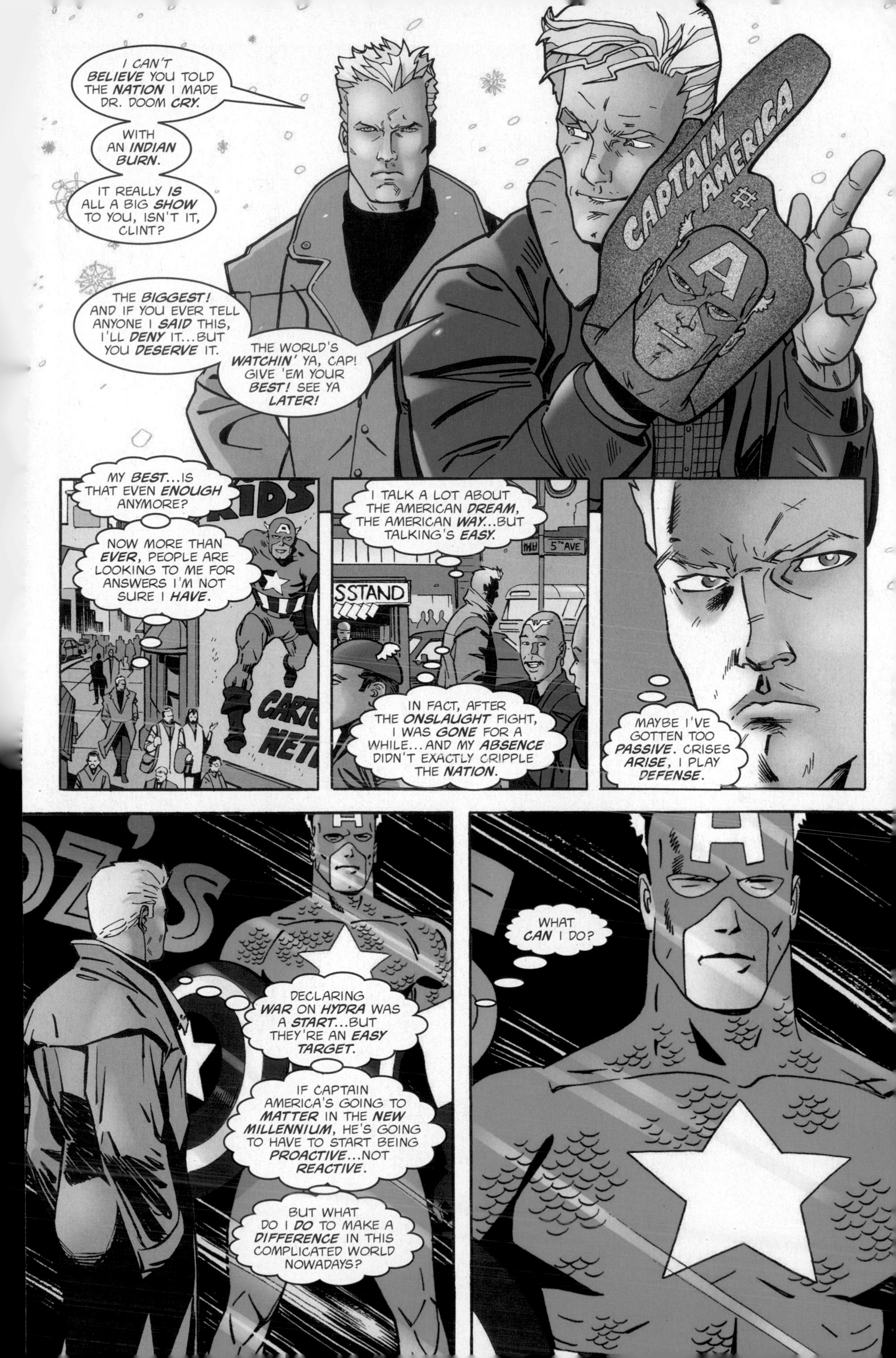

I CAN'T BELIEVE YOU TOLD THE NATION I MADE DR. DOOM CRY.
WITH AN INDIAN BURN.
IT REALLY IS ALL A BIG SHOW TO YOU, ISN'T IT, CLINT?
THE BIGGEST! AND IF YOU EVER TELL ANYONE I SAID THIS, I'LL DENY IT...BUT YOU DESERVE IT.
THE WORLD'S WATCHIN' YA, CAP! GIVE 'EM YOUR BEST! SEE YA LATER!
CAPTAIN AMERICA #1
A
MY BEST...IS THAT EVEN ENOUGH ANYMORE?
NOW MORE THAN EVER, PEOPLE ARE LOOKING TO ME FOR ANSWERS I'M NOT SURE I HAVE.
I TALK A LOT ABOUT THE AMERICAN DREAM, THE AMERICAN WAY...BUT TALKING'S EASY.
5TH AVE
SSTAND
IN FACT, AFTER THE ONSLAUGHT FIGHT, I WAS GONE FOR A WHILE...AND MY ABSENCE DIDN'T EXACTLY CRIPPLE THE NATION.
MAYBE I'VE GOTTEN TOO PASSIVE. CRISES ARISE, I PLAY DEFENSE.
DECLARING WAR ON HYDRA WAS A START...BUT THEY'RE AN EASY TARGET.
IF CAPTAIN AMERICA'S GOING TO MATTER IN THE NEW MILLENNIUM, HE'S GOING TO HAVE TO START BEING PROACTIVE...NOT REACTIVE.
BUT WHAT DO I DO TO MAKE A DIFFERENCE IN THIS COMPLICATED WORLD NOWADAYS?
WHAT CAN I DO?

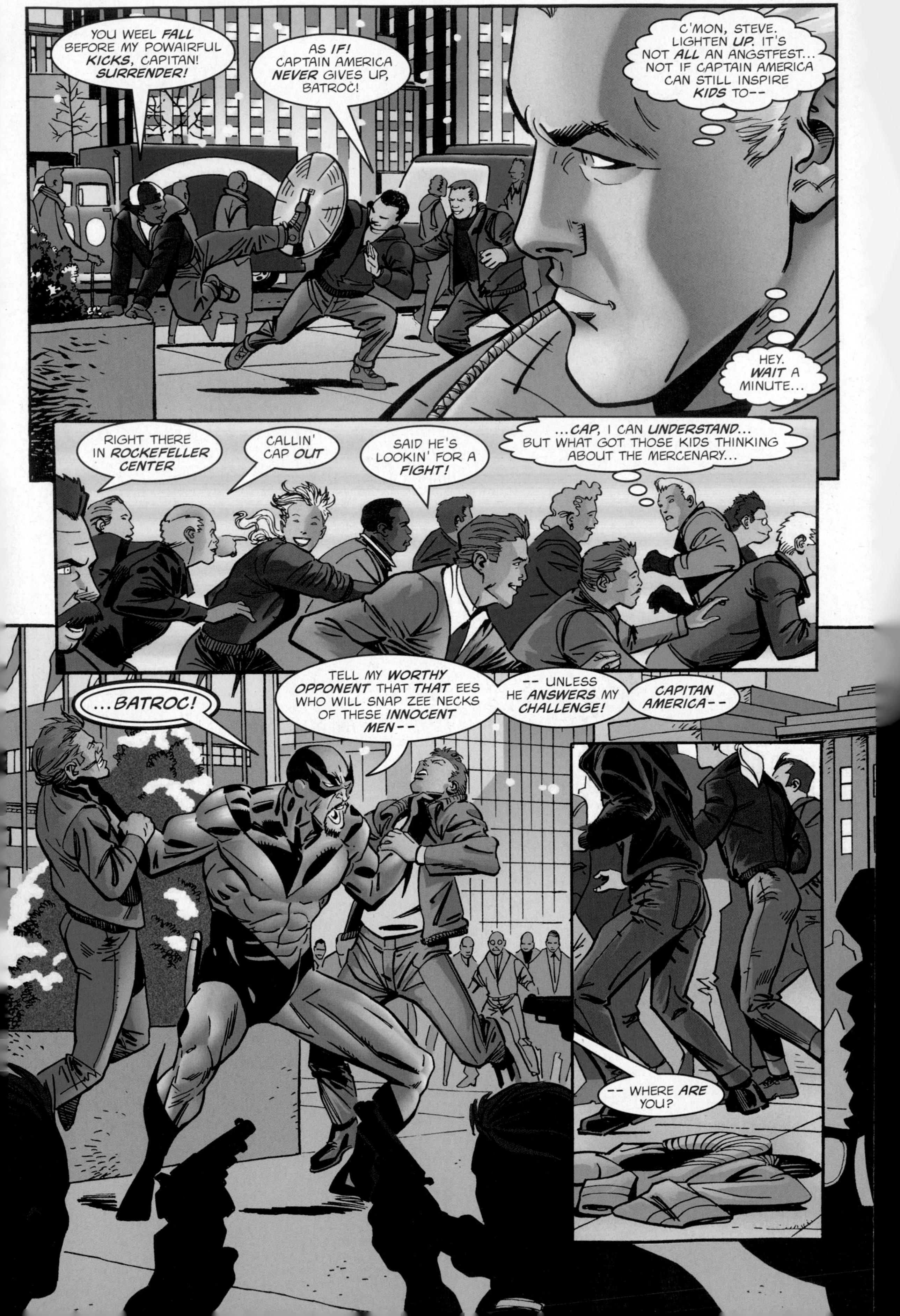
YOU WEEL FALL BEFORE MY POWAIRFUL KICKS, CAPITAN! SURRENDER!
AS IF! CAPTAIN AMERICA NEVER GIVES UP, BATROC!
C'MON, STEVE. LIGHTEN UP. IT'S NOT ALL AN ANGSTFEST... NOT IF CAPTAIN AMERICA CAN STILL INSPIRE KIDS TO--
HEY. WAIT A MINUTE...
RIGHT THERE IN ROCKEFELLER CENTER
CALLIN' CAP OUT
SAID HE'S LOOKIN' FOR A FIGHT!
...CAP, I CAN UNDERSTAND... BUT WHAT GOT THOSE KIDS THINKING ABOUT THE MERCENARY...
...BATROC!
TELL MY WORTHY OPPONENT THAT THAT EES WHO WILL SNAP ZEE NECKS OF THESE INNOCENT MEN--
-- UNLESS HE ANSWERS MY CHALLENGE!
CAPITAN AMERICA--
-- WHERE ARE YOU?

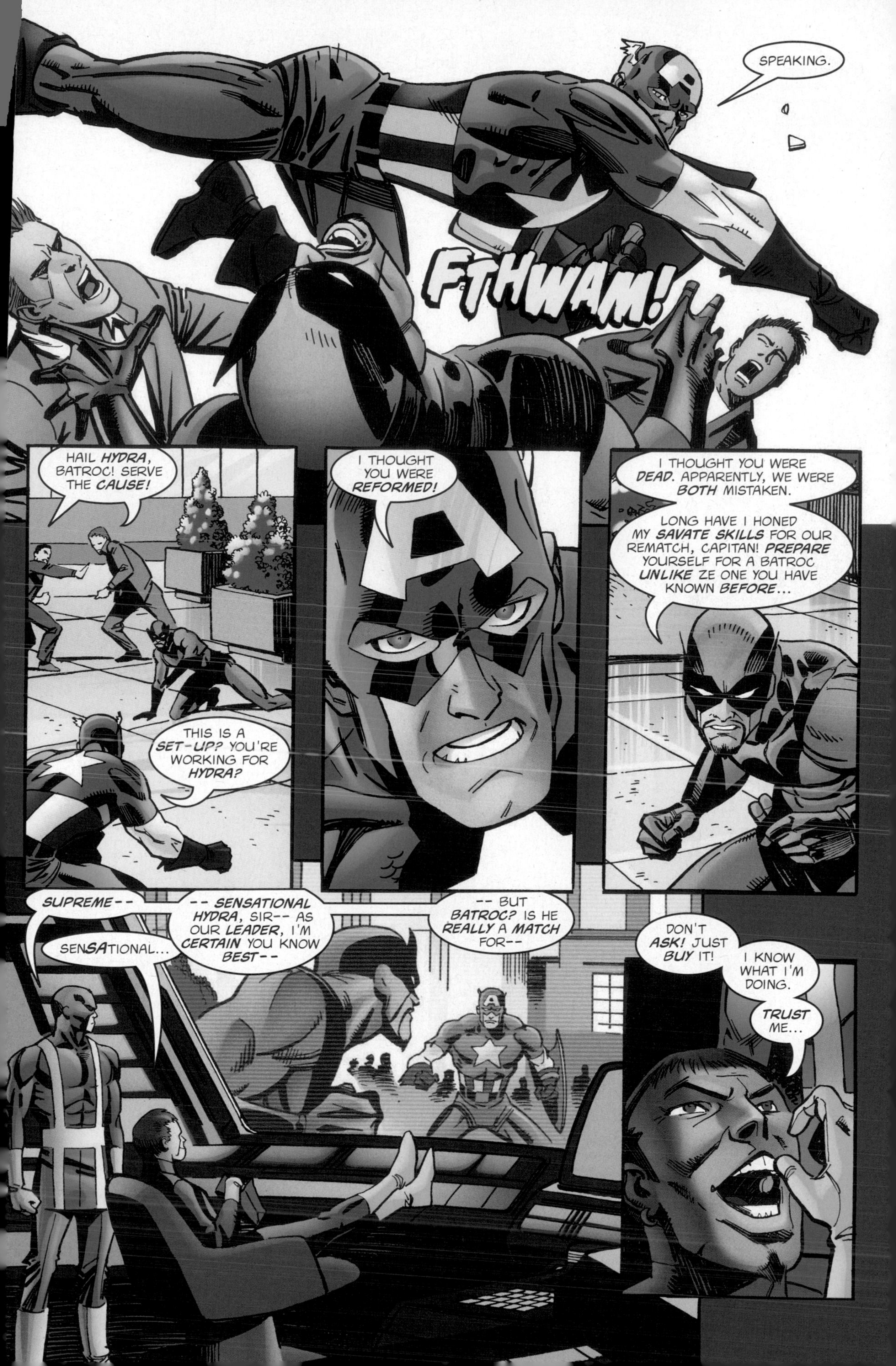
SPEAKING.
FTHWAM!
HAIL HYDRA, BATROC! SERVE THE CAUSE!
THIS IS A SET-UP? YOU'RE WORKING FOR HYDRA?
I THOUGHT YOU WERE REFORMED!
I THOUGHT YOU WERE DEAD. APPARENTLY, WE WERE BOTH MISTAKEN.
LONG HAVE I HONED MY SAVATE SKILLS FOR OUR REMATCH, CAPITAN! PREPARE YOURSELF FOR A BATROC UNLIKE ZE ONE YOU HAVE KNOWN BEFORE...
SUPREME--
SENSATIONAL...
-- SENSATIONAL HYDRA, SIR-- AS OUR LEADER, I'M CERTAIN YOU KNOW BEST--
-- BUT BATROC? IS HE REALLY A MATCH FOR--
DON'T ASK! JUST BUY IT!
I KNOW WHAT I'M DOING.
TRUST ME...

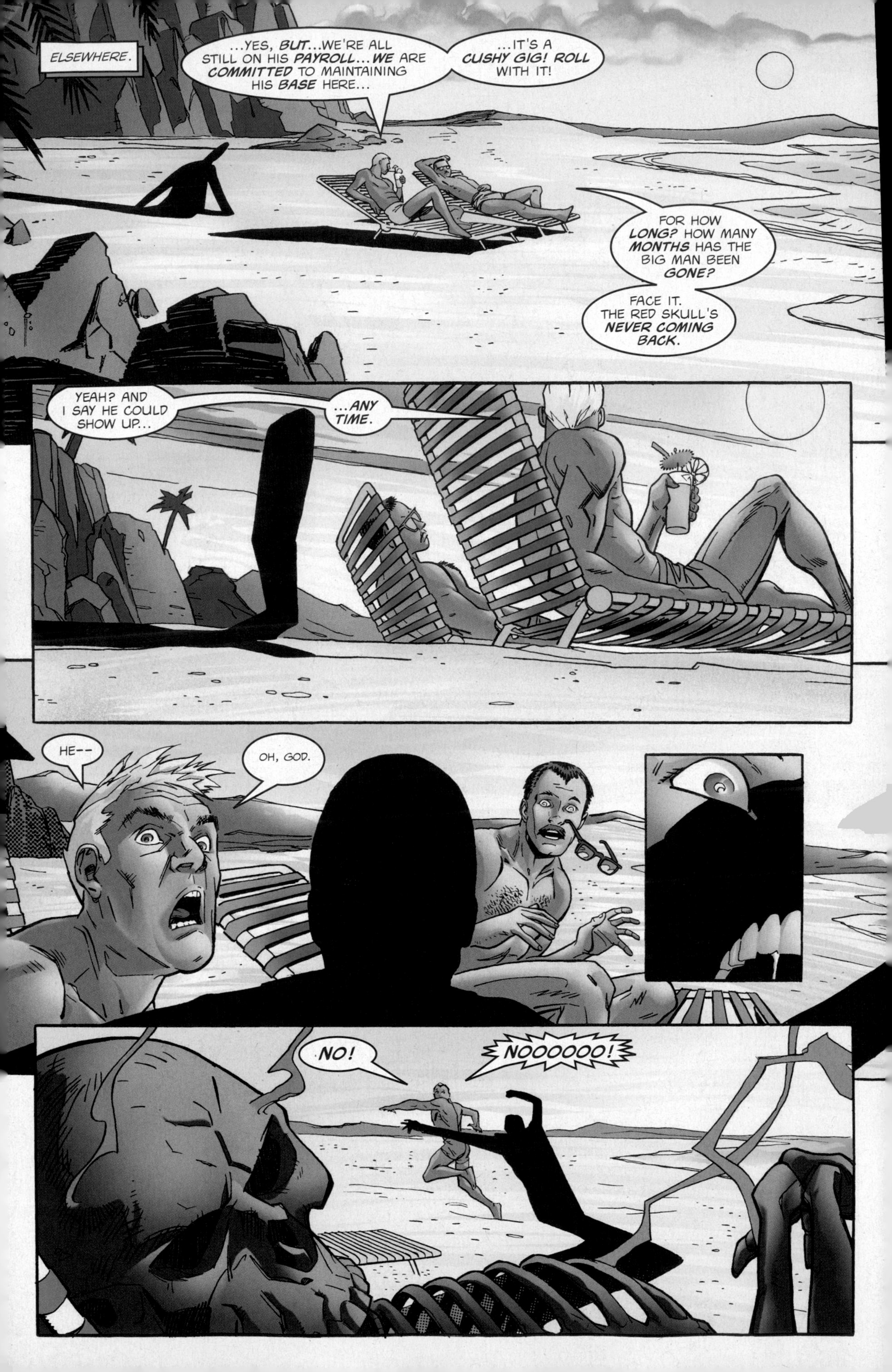
ELSEWHERE.
...YES, BUT...WE'RE ALL STILL ON HIS PAYROLL...WE ARE COMMITTED TO MAINTAINING HIS BASE HERE...
...IT'S A CUSHY GIG! ROLL WITH IT!
FOR HOW LONG? HOW MANY MONTHS HAS THE BIG MAN BEEN GONE?
FACE IT. THE RED SKULL'S NEVER COMING BACK.
YEAH? AND I SAY HE COULD SHOW UP...
...ANY TIME.
HE--
OH, GOD.
NO!
NOOOOOO!

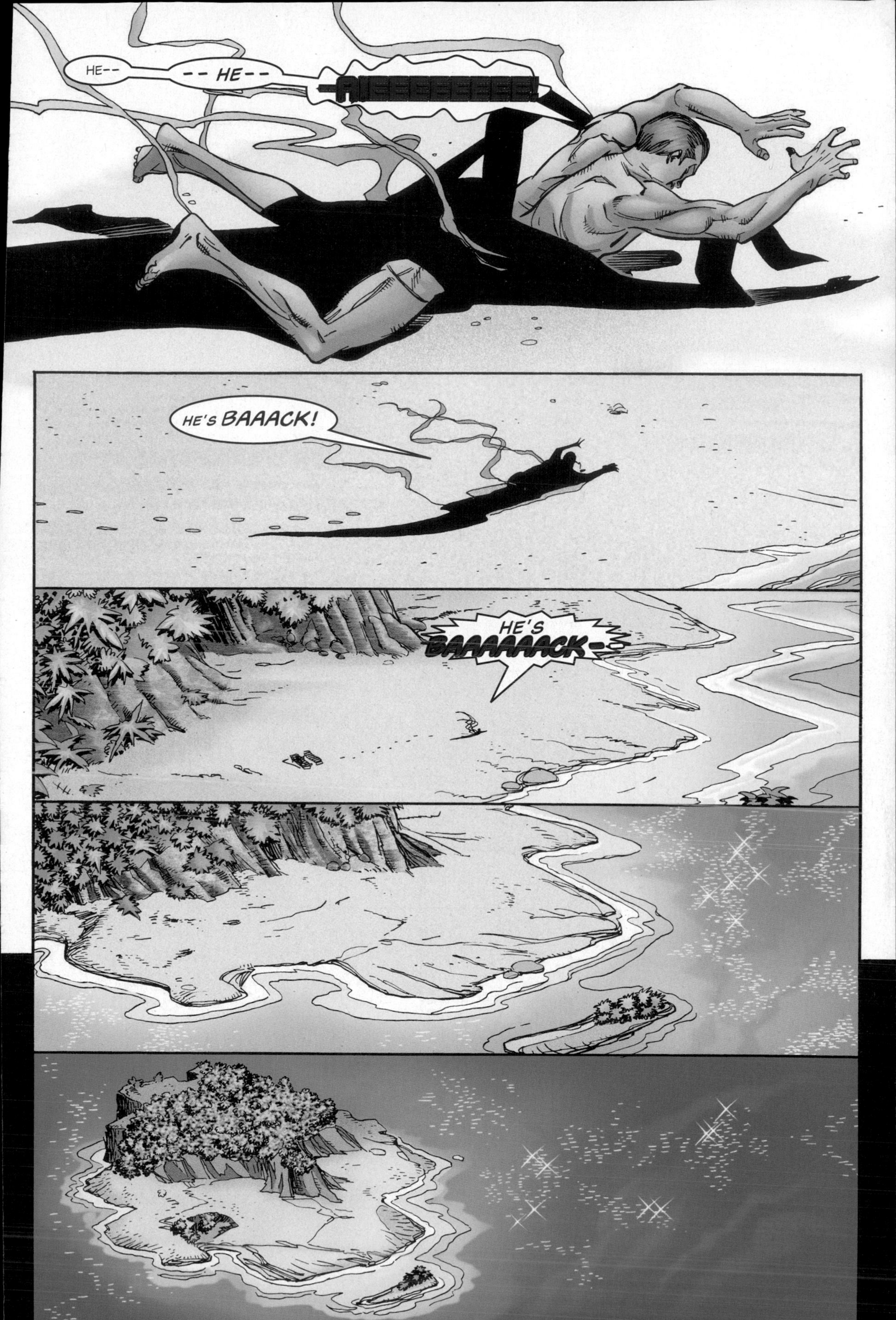
HE--
-- HE--
-AIEEEEEEEE!
HE's BAAACK!
HE'S BAAAAAACK-

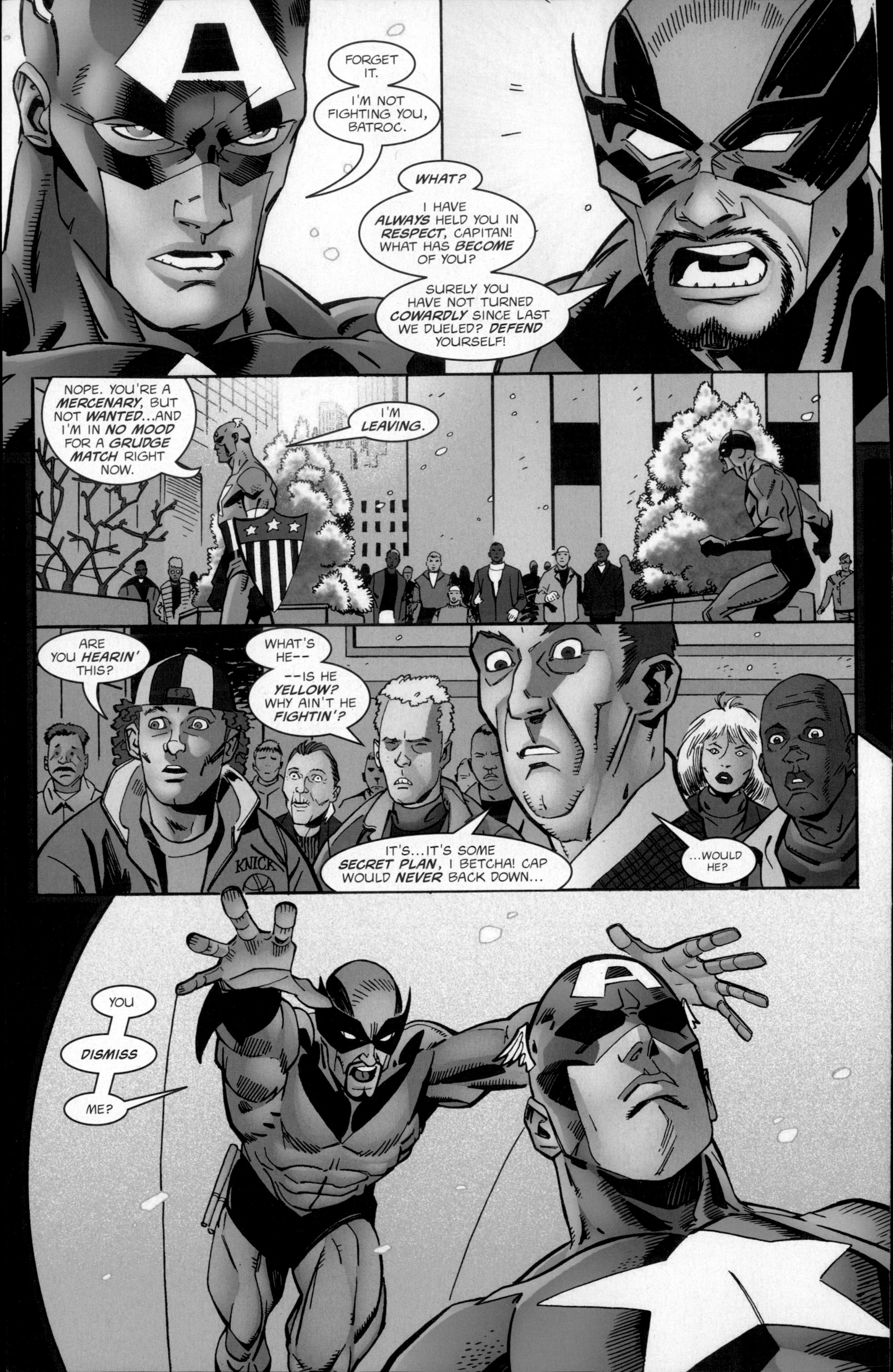
FORGET IT.
I'M NOT FIGHTING YOU, BATROC.
WHAT?
I HAVE ALWAYS HELD YOU IN RESPECT, CAPITAN! WHAT HAS BECOME OF YOU?
SURELY YOU HAVE NOT TURNED COWARDLY SINCE LAST WE DUELED? DEFEND YOURSELF!
NOPE. YOU'RE A MERCENARY, BUT NOT WANTED...AND I'M IN NO MOOD FOR A GRUDGE MATCH RIGHT NOW.
I'M LEAVING.
ARE YOU HEARIN' THIS?
WHAT'S HE--
--IS HE YELLOW? WHY AIN'T HE FIGHTIN'?
IT'S...IT'S SOME SECRET PLAN, I BETCHA! CAP WOULD NEVER BACK DOWN...
...WOULD HE?
KNICK
YOU
DISMISS
ME?

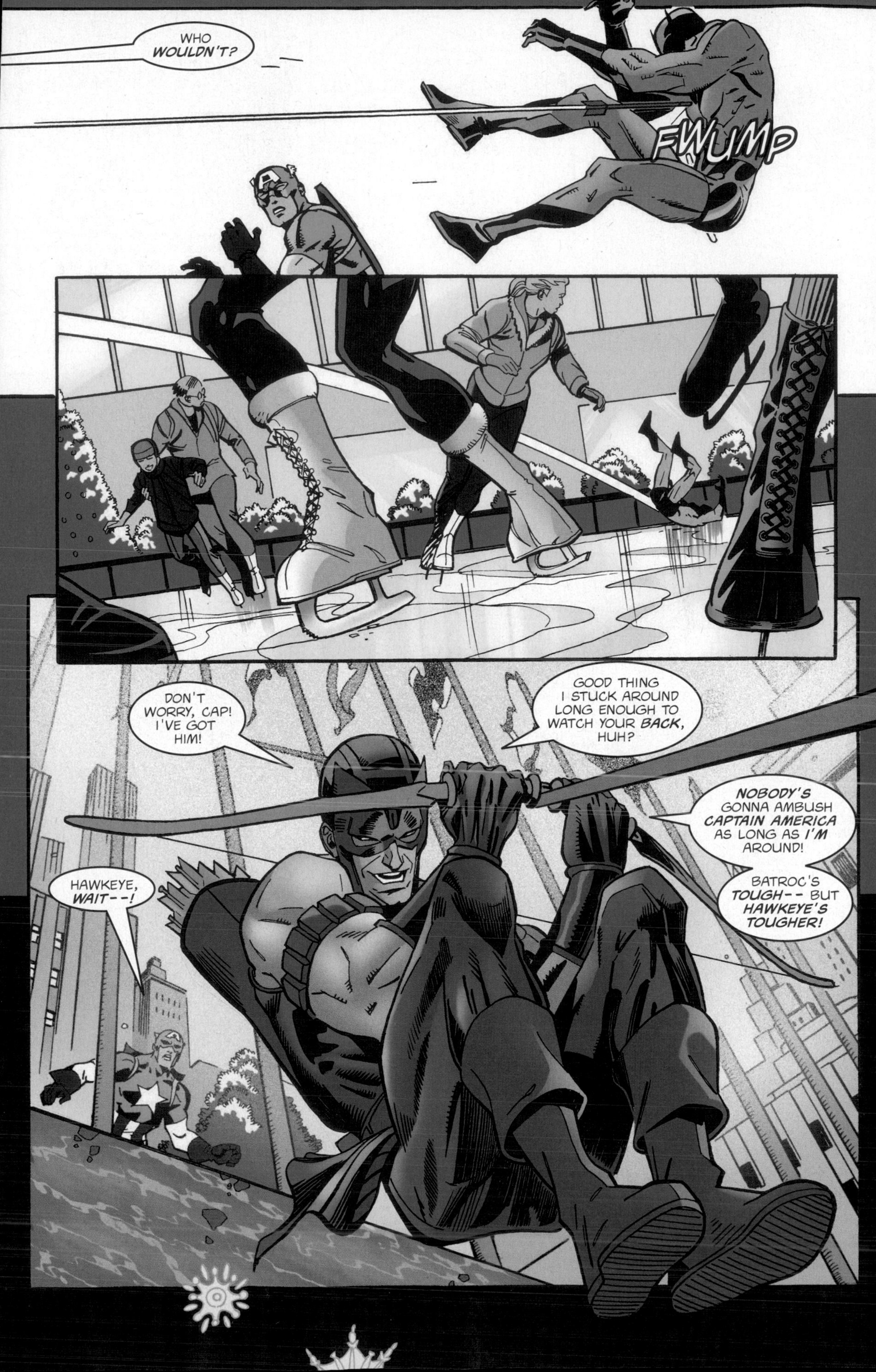

WHO WOULDN'T?
FWUMP
DON'T WORRY, CAP! I'VE GOT HIM!
GOOD THING I STUCK AROUND LONG ENOUGH TO WATCH YOUR BACK, HUH?
NOBODY'S GONNA AMBUSH CAPTAIN AMERICA AS LONG AS I'M AROUND!
BATROC'S TOUGH-- BUT HAWKEYE'S TOUGHER!
HAWKEYE, WAIT--!

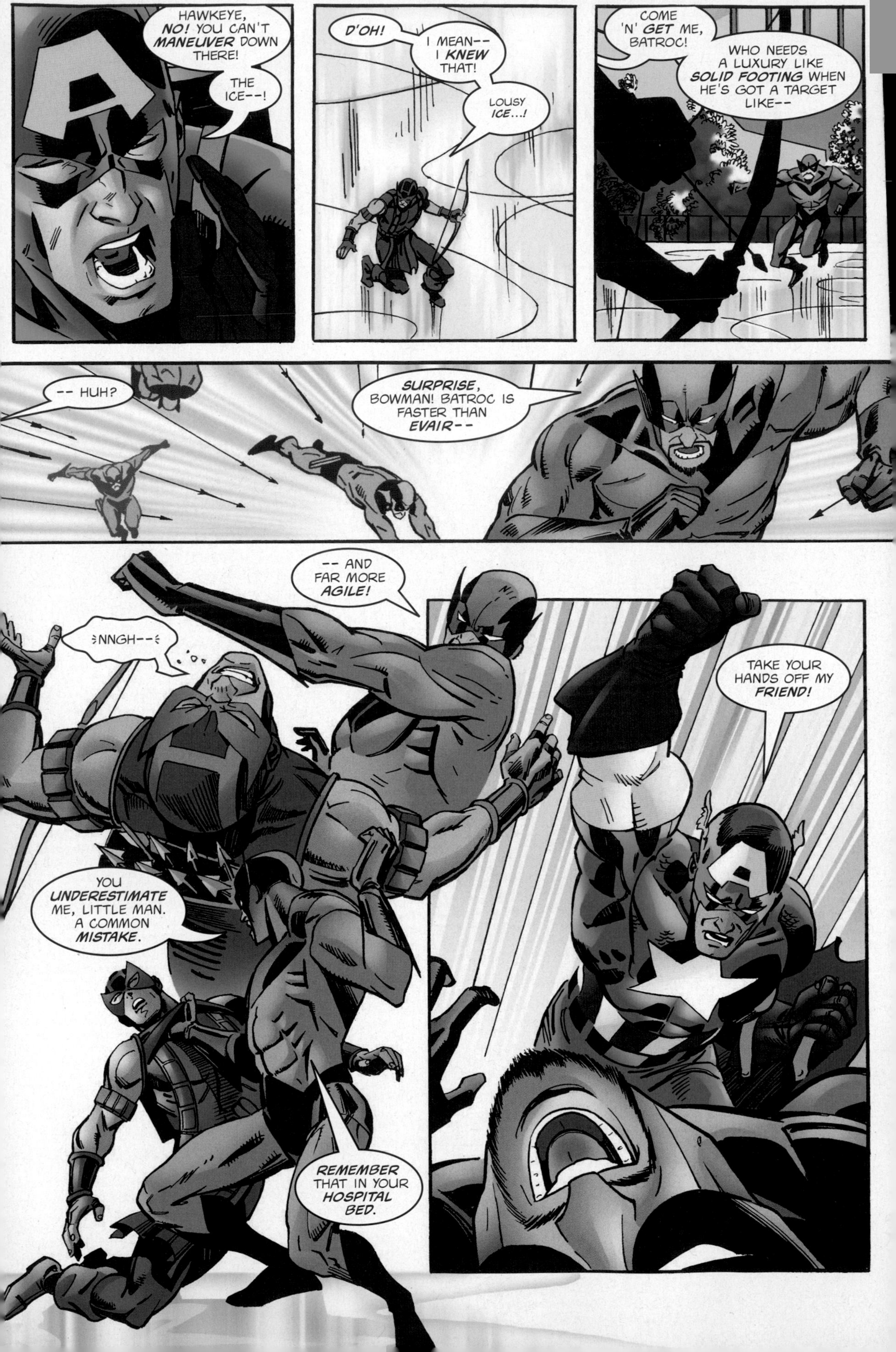
HAWKEYE, NO! YOU CAN'T MANEUVER DOWN THERE!
THE ICE--!
D'OH!
I MEAN-- I KNEW THAT!
LOUSY ICE...!
COME 'N' GET ME, BATROC!
WHO NEEDS A LUXURY LIKE SOLID FOOTING WHEN HE'S GOT A TARGET LIKE--
-- HUH?
SURPRISE, BOWMAN! BATROC IS FASTER THAN EVAIR--
-- AND FAR MORE AGILE!
NNGH--
YOU UNDERESTIMATE ME, LITTLE MAN. A COMMON MISTAKE.
REMEMBER THAT IN YOUR HOSPITAL BED.
TAKE YOUR HANDS OFF MY FRIEND!

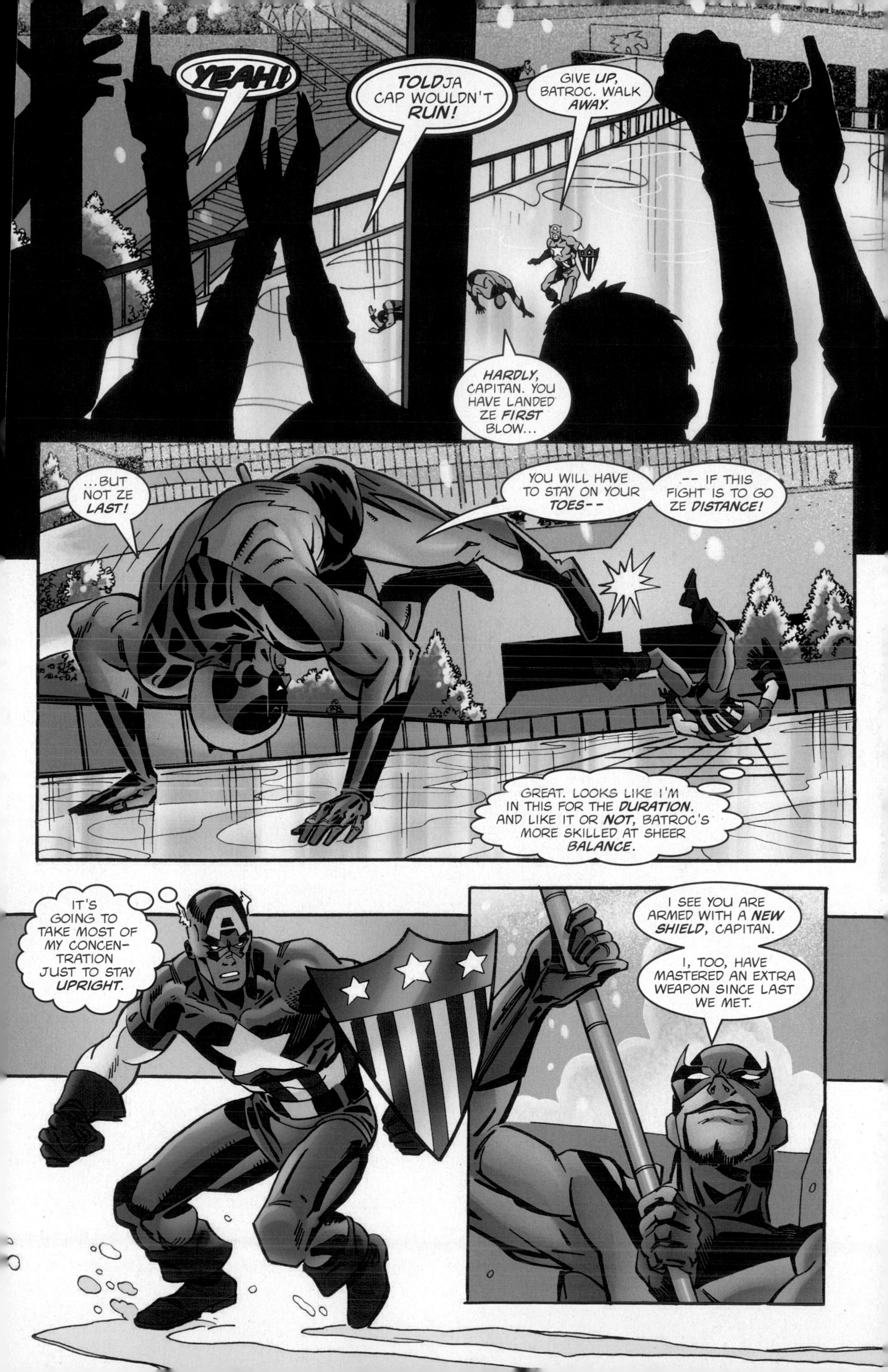
YEAH!
TOLDJA CAP WOULDN'T RUN!
GIVE UP, BATROC. WALK AWAY.
HARDLY, CAPITAN. YOU HAVE LANDED ZE FIRST BLOW...
...BUT NOT ZE LAST!
YOU WILL HAVE TO STAY ON YOUR TOES--
-- IF THIS FIGHT IS TO GO ZE DISTANCE!
GREAT. LOOKS LIKE I'M IN THIS FOR THE DURATION. AND LIKE IT OR NOT, BATROC'S MORE SKILLED AT SHEER BALANCE.
IT'S GOING TO TAKE MOST OF MY CONCEN-TRATION JUST TO STAY UPRIGHT.
I SEE YOU ARE ARMED WITH A NEW SHIELD, CAPITAN.
I, TOO, HAVE MASTERED AN EXTRA WEAPON SINCE LAST WE MET.

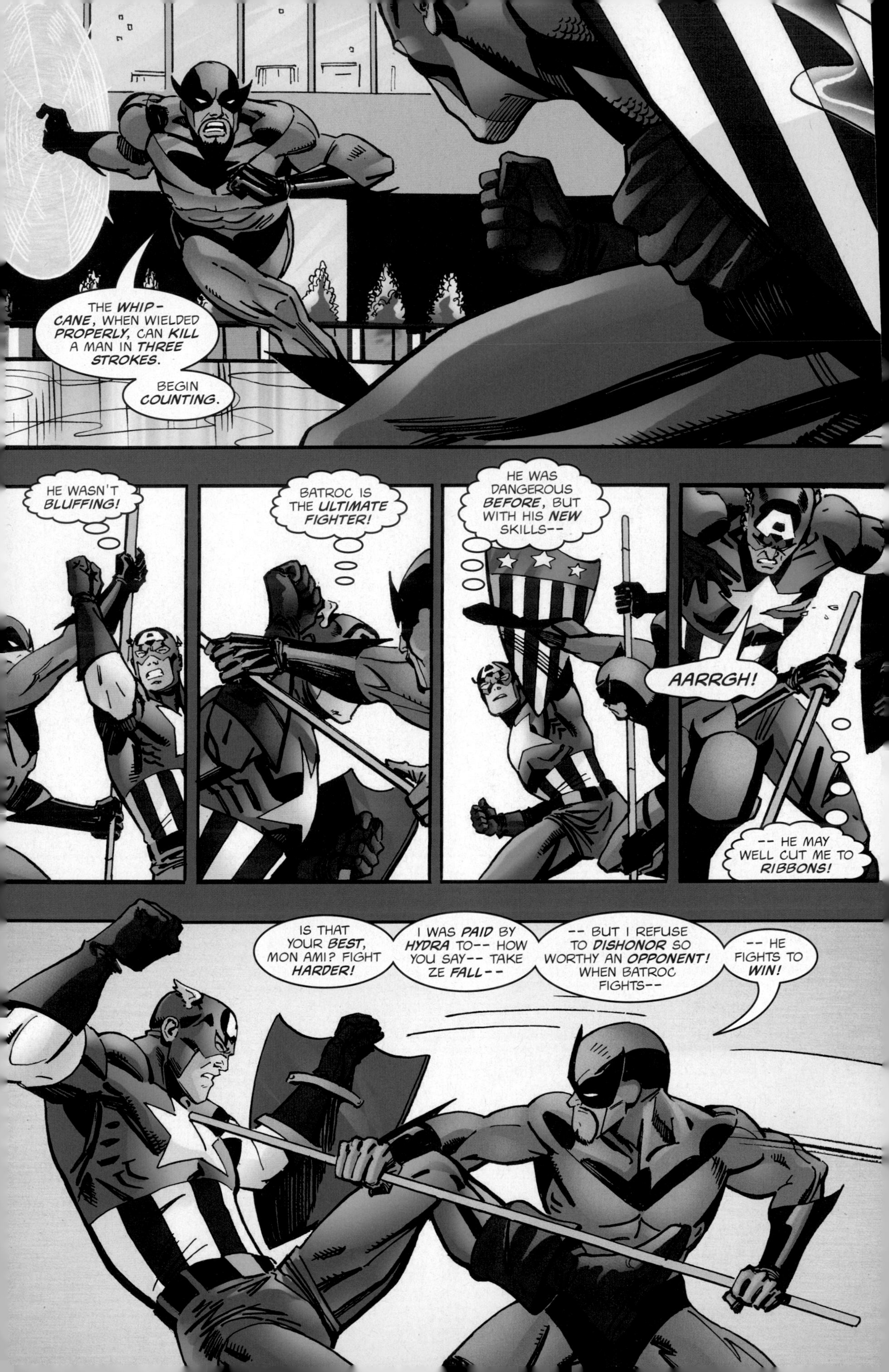
THE WHIP-CANE, WHEN WIELDED PROPERLY, CAN KILL A MAN IN THREE STROKES.
BEGIN COUNTING.
HE WASN'T BLUFFING!
BATROC IS THE ULTIMATE FIGHTER!
HE WAS DANGEROUS BEFORE, BUT WITH HIS NEW SKILLS--
AARRGH!
-- HE MAY WELL CUT ME TO RIBBONS!
IS THAT YOUR BEST, MON AMI? FIGHT HARDER!
I WAS PAID BY HYDRA TO-- HOW YOU SAY-- TAKE ZE FALL--
-- BUT I REFUSE TO DISHONOR SO WORTHY AN OPPONENT! WHEN BATROC FIGHTS--
-- HE FIGHTS TO WIN!

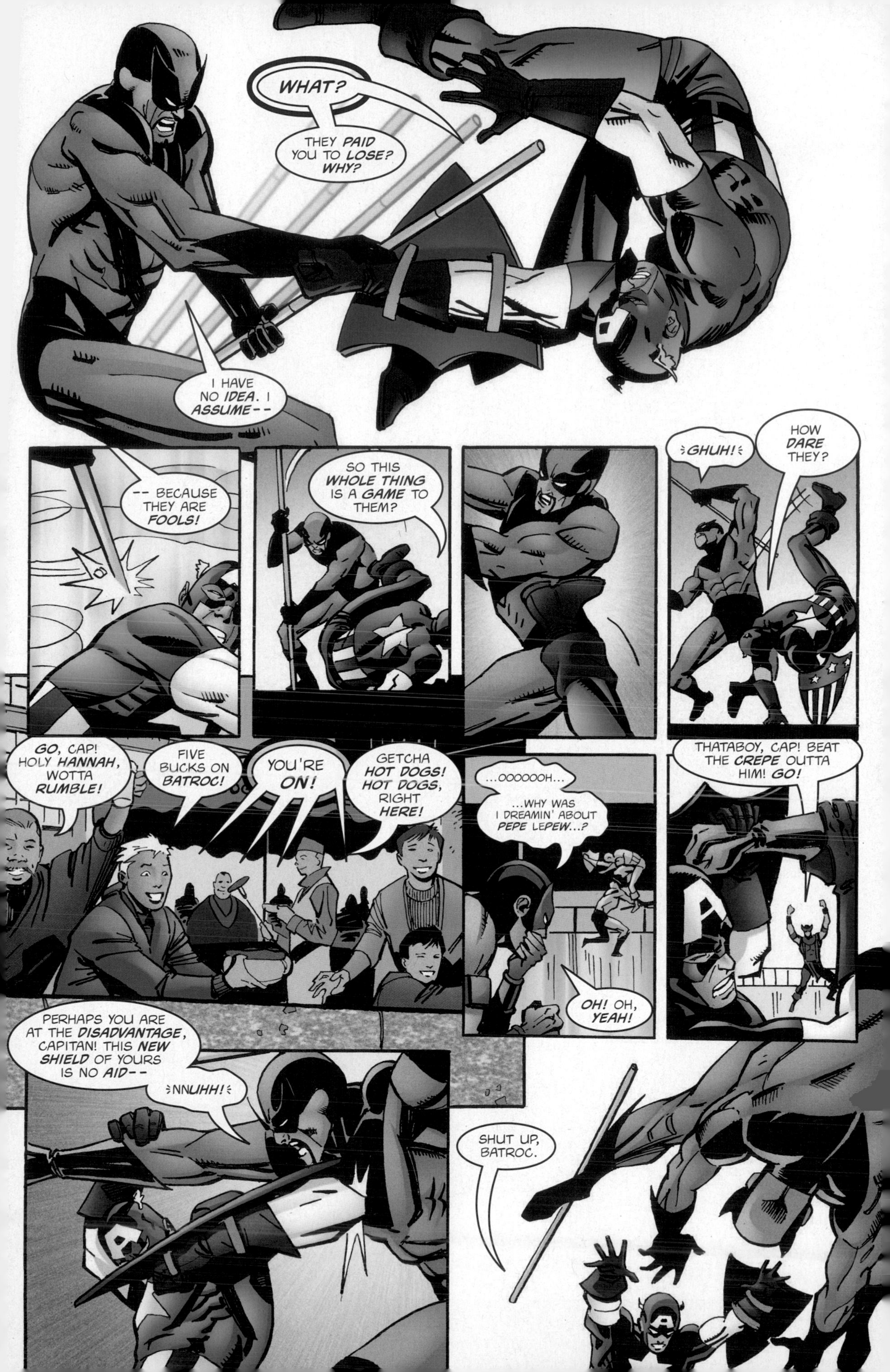
WHAT?
THEY PAID YOU TO LOSE? WHY?
I HAVE NO IDEA. I ASSUME--
-- BECAUSE THEY ARE FOOLS!
SO THIS WHOLE THING IS A GAME TO THEM?
GHUH!
HOW DARE THEY?
GO, CAP! HOLY HANNAH, WOTTA RUMBLE!
FIVE BUCKS ON BATROC!
YOU'RE ON!
GETCHA HOT DOGS! HOT DOGS, RIGHT HERE!
...OOOOOOH...
...WHY WAS I DREAMIN' ABOUT PEPE LEPEW...?
OH! OH, YEAH!
THATABOY, CAP! BEAT THE CREPE OUTTA HIM! GO!
PERHAPS YOU ARE AT THE DISADVANTAGE, CAPITAN! THIS NEW SHIELD OF YOURS IS NO AID--
NNUHH!
SHUT UP, BATROC.

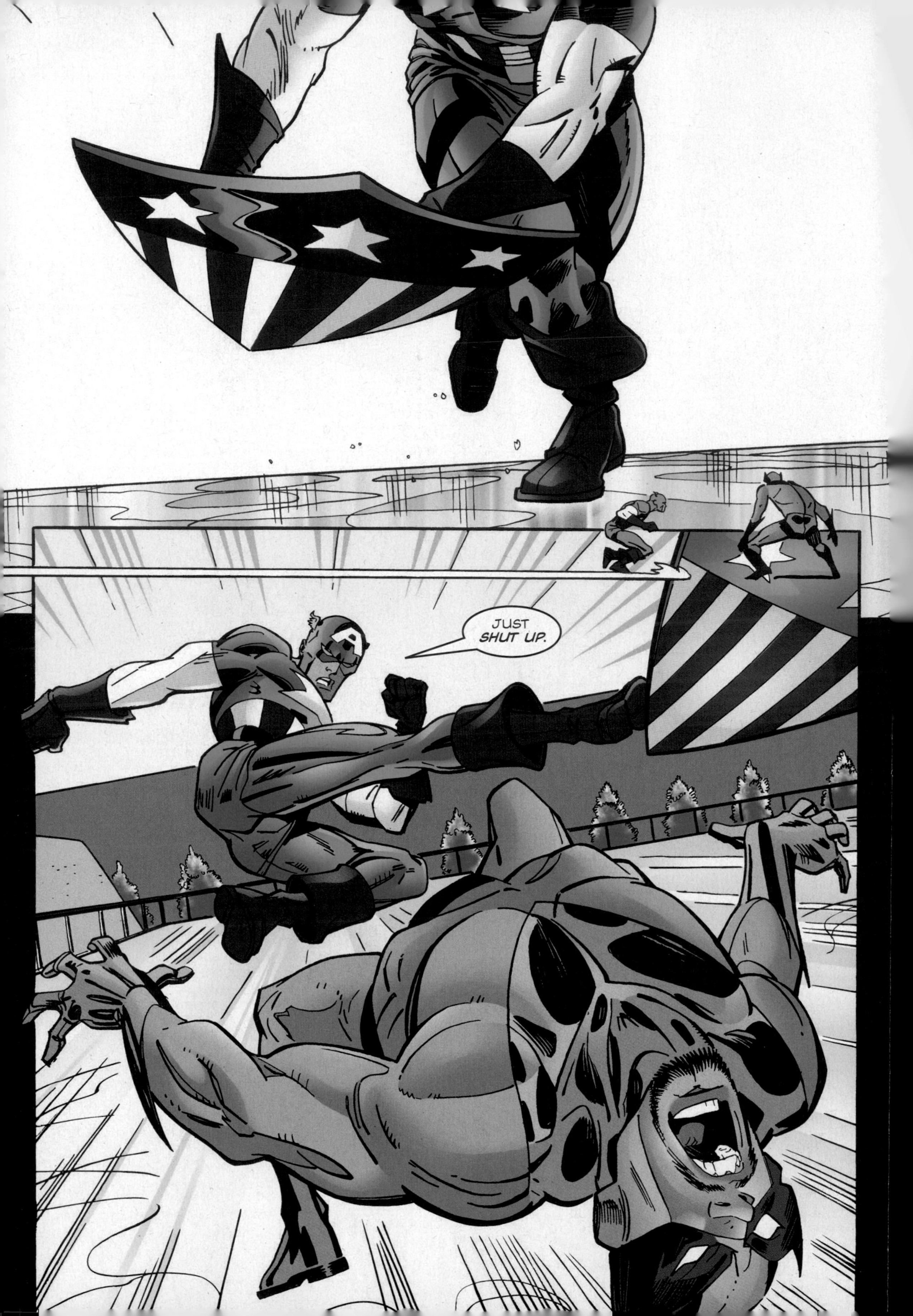
JUST SHUT UP.

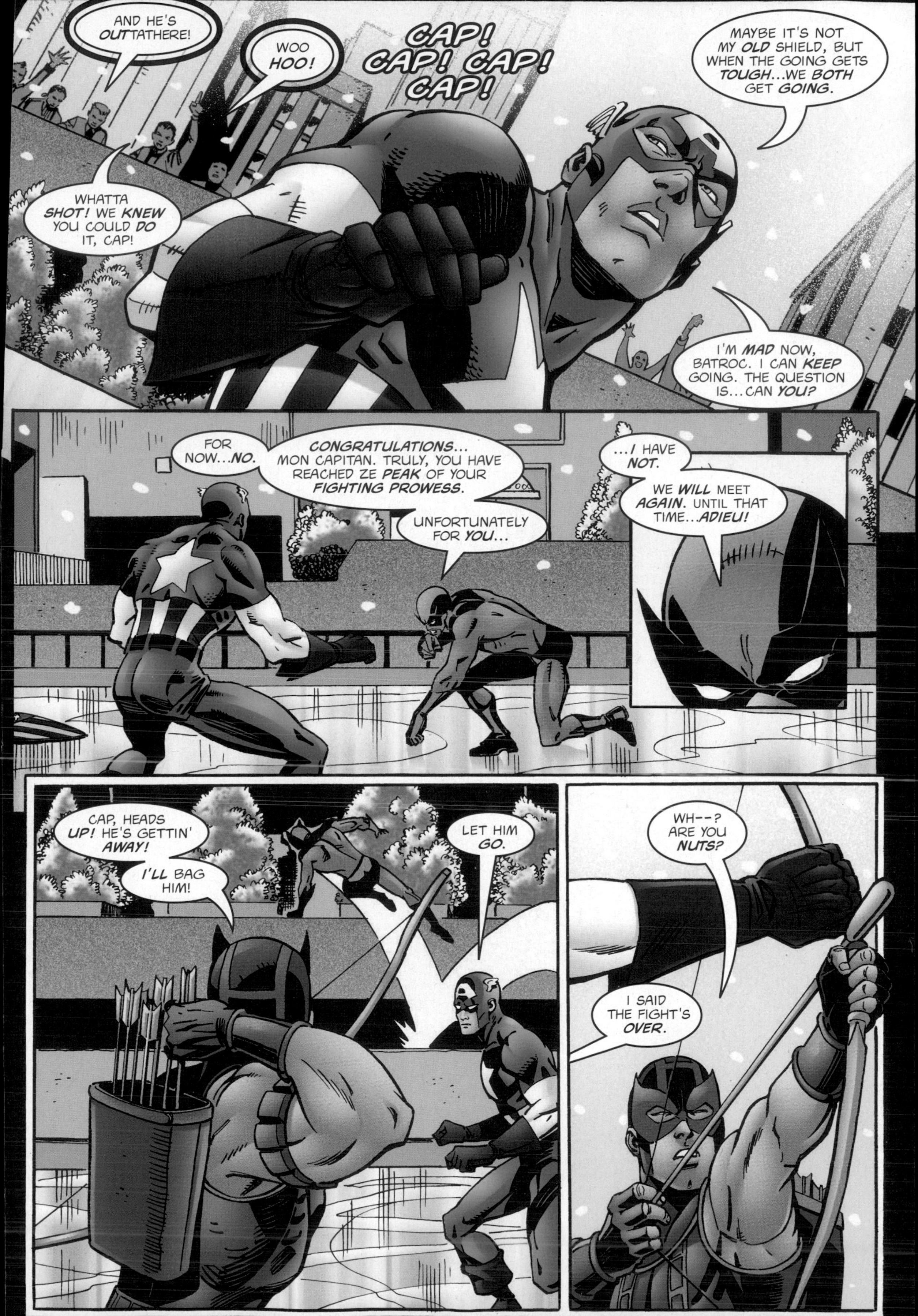
AND HE'S OUTTATHERE!
WOO HOO!
CAP! CAP! CAP! CAP!
WHATTA SHOT! WE KNEW YOU COULD DO IT, CAP!
MAYBE IT'S NOT MY OLD SHIELD, BUT WHEN THE GOING GETS TOUGH...WE BOTH GET GOING.
I'M MAD NOW, BATROC. I CAN KEEP GOING. THE QUESTION IS...CAN YOU?
FOR NOW...NO.
CONGRATULATIONS... MON CAPITAN. TRULY, YOU HAVE REACHED ZE PEAK OF YOUR FIGHTING PROWESS.
UNFORTUNATELY FOR YOU...
...I HAVE NOT.
WE WILL MEET AGAIN. UNTIL THAT TIME...ADIEU!
CAP, HEADS UP! HE'S GETTIN' AWAY!
I'LL BAG HIM!
LET HIM GO.
WH--? ARE YOU NUTS?
I SAID THE FIGHT'S OVER.

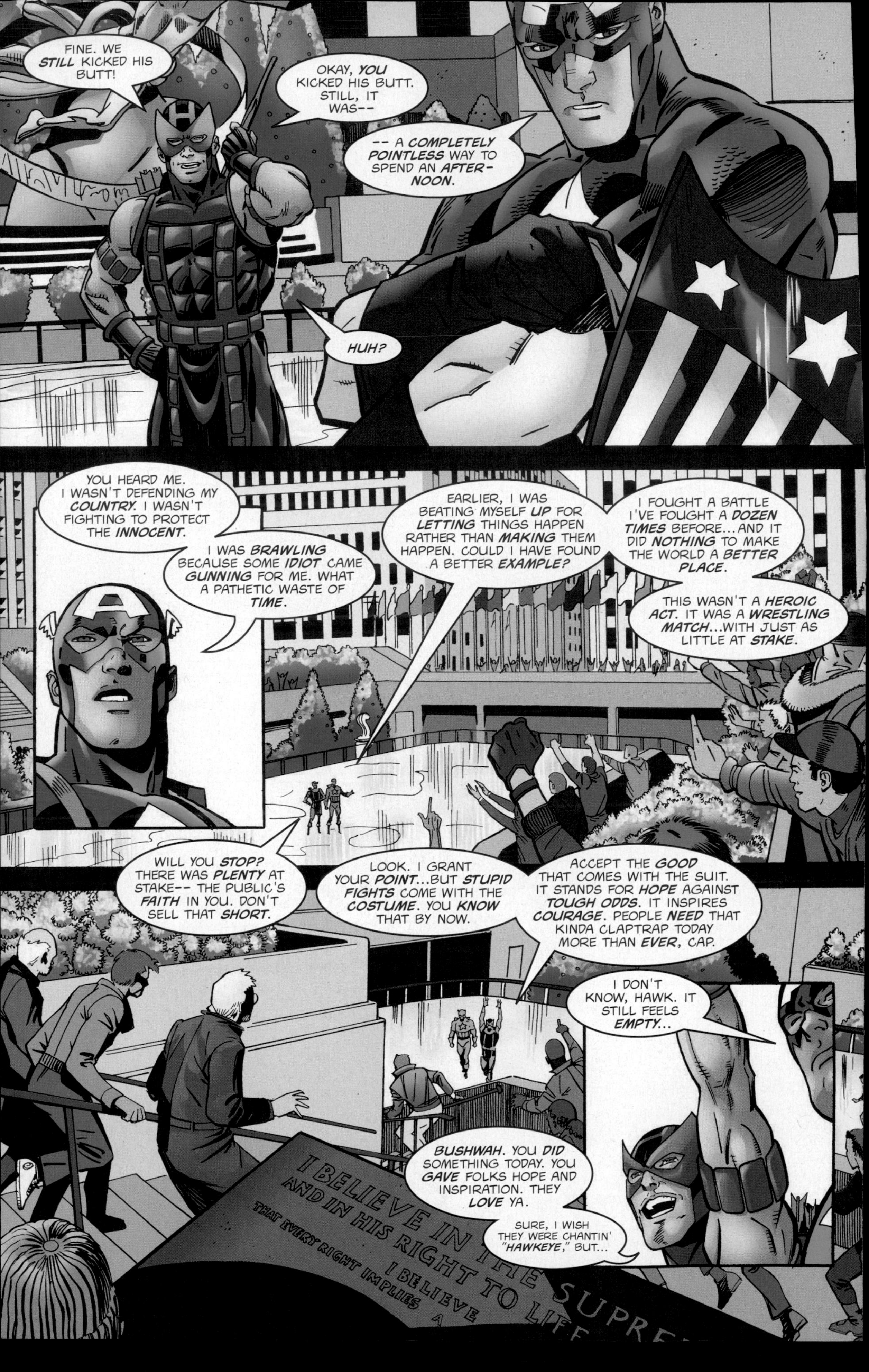
FINE. WE STILL KICKED HIS BUTT!
OKAY, YOU KICKED HIS BUTT. STILL, IT WAS--
-- A COMPLETELY POINTLESS WAY TO SPEND AN AFTERNOON.
HUH?
YOU HEARD ME. I WASN'T DEFENDING MY COUNTRY. I WASN'T FIGHTING TO PROTECT THE INNOCENT.
I WAS BRAWLING BECAUSE SOME IDIOT CAME GUNNING FOR ME. WHAT A PATHETIC WASTE OF TIME.
EARLIER, I WAS BEATING MYSELF UP FOR LETTING THINGS HAPPEN RATHER THAN MAKING THEM HAPPEN. COULD I HAVE FOUND A BETTER EXAMPLE?
I FOUGHT A BATTLE I'VE FOUGHT A DOZEN TIMES BEFORE...AND IT DID NOTHING TO MAKE THE WORLD A BETTER PLACE.
THIS WASN'T A HEROIC ACT. IT WAS A WRESTLING MATCH...WITH JUST AS LITTLE AT STAKE.
WILL YOU STOP? THERE WAS PLENTY AT STAKE-- THE PUBLIC'S FAITH IN YOU. DON'T SELL THAT SHORT.
LOOK. I GRANT YOUR POINT...BUT STUPID FIGHTS COME WITH THE COSTUME. YOU KNOW THAT BY NOW.
ACCEPT THE GOOD THAT COMES WITH THE SUIT. IT STANDS FOR HOPE AGAINST TOUGH ODDS. IT INSPIRES COURAGE. PEOPLE NEED THAT KINDA CLAPTRAP TODAY MORE THAN EVER, CAP.
I DON'T KNOW, HAWK. IT STILL FEELS EMPTY...
BUSHWAH. YOU DID SOMETHING TODAY. YOU GAVE FOLKS HOPE AND INSPIRATION. THEY LOVE YA.
SURE, I WISH THEY WERE CHANTIN' "HAWKEYE," BUT...
I BELIEVE IN THE SUPRE
AND IN HIS RIGHT TO LIFE
I BELIEVE
THAT EVERY RIGHT IMPLIES A

CAP! CAP! CAP! CAP! CAP! CAP! CAP! CAP!

GIMME AN "H!"

CAP! CAP! CAP! CAP!

CAP! CAP! CAP! CAP!

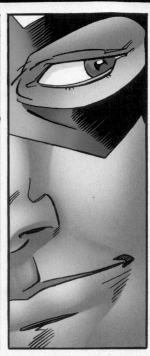

FORGIVE ME, SENSATIONAL HYDRA...BUT I'M CONFUSED.

YOU *SENT* BATROC TO FAIL? IF YOU *KNEW* THAT CAPTAIN AMERICA COULD *WIN* THIS FIGHT...WHY SEND BATROC AT *ALL?*

WHY *ESCALATE* THE FRENZY OVER CAPTAIN AMERICA?

ARE YOU *KIDDING* ME? *WORK* WITH ME HERE. TRY TO KEEP *UP.*

I WANT THE WHOLE *WORLD* TO *WORSHIP* CAPTAIN AMERICA. AFTER ALL, THE BIGGER THEY *ARE...*

...THE HARDER THEY *FALL.*

NEXT: **POWER** *and* **GLORY!**

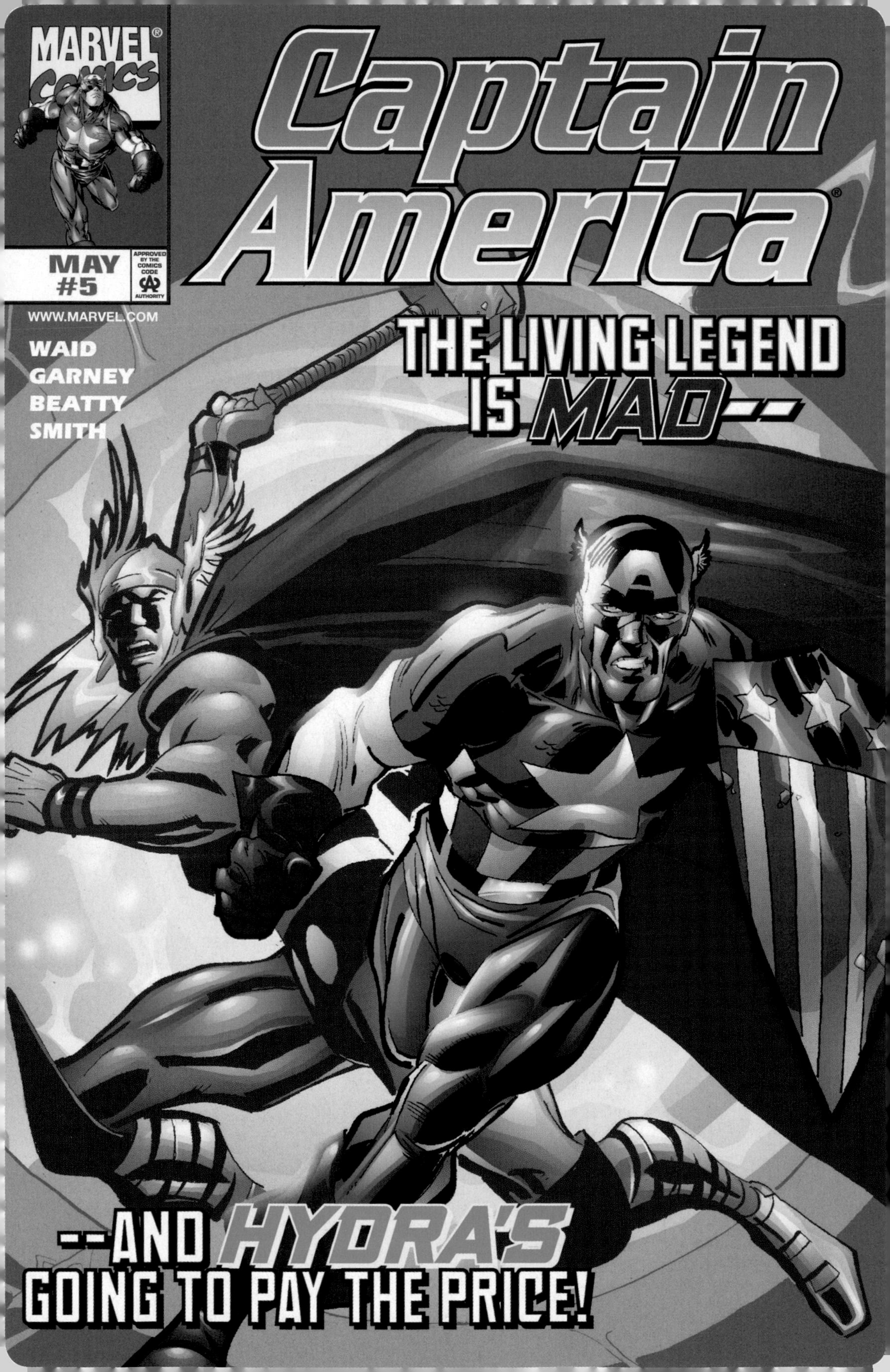
MARVEL COMICS
Captain America
MAY #5
APPROVED BY THE COMICS CODE AUTHORITY
WWW.MARVEL.COM
WAID
GARNEY
BEATTY
SMITH
THE LIVING LEGEND IS MAD--
--AND HYDRA'S GOING TO PAY THE PRICE!

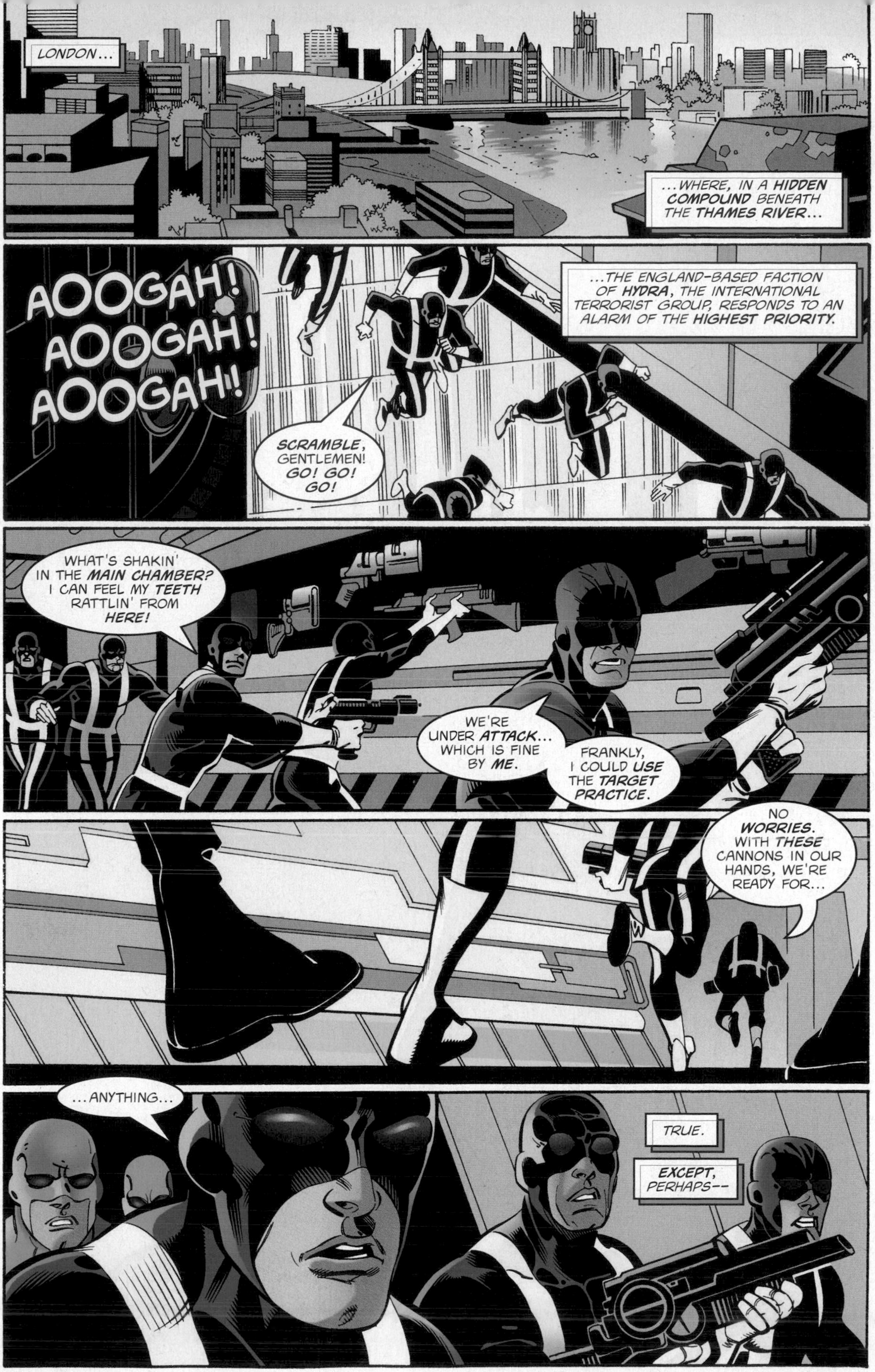
LONDON...
...WHERE, IN A HIDDEN COMPOUND BENEATH THE THAMES RIVER...
AOOGAH! AOOGAH! AOOGAH!
...THE ENGLAND-BASED FACTION OF HYDRA, THE INTERNATIONAL TERRORIST GROUP, RESPONDS TO AN ALARM OF THE HIGHEST PRIORITY.
SCRAMBLE, GENTLEMEN! GO! GO! GO!
WHAT'S SHAKIN' IN THE MAIN CHAMBER? I CAN FEEL MY TEETH RATTLIN' FROM HERE!
WE'RE UNDER ATTACK... WHICH IS FINE BY ME.
FRANKLY, I COULD USE THE TARGET PRACTICE.
NO WORRIES. WITH THESE CANNONS IN OUR HANDS, WE'RE READY FOR...
...ANYTHING...
TRUE.
EXCEPT, PERHAPS--

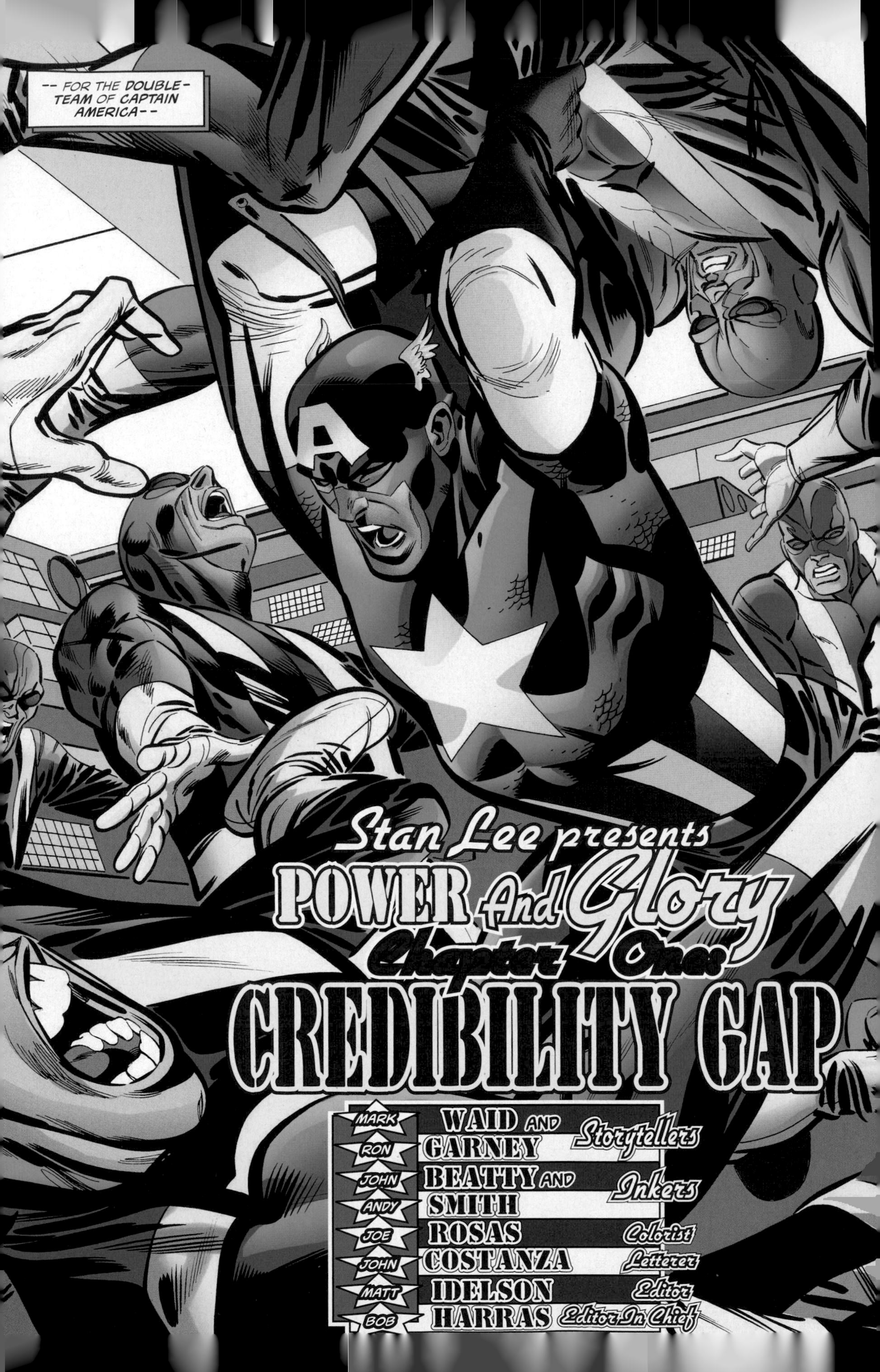
-- FOR THE DOUBLE-TEAM OF CAPTAIN AMERICA--
Stan Lee presents
POWER And Glory
Chapter One:
CREDIBILITY GAP
MARK WAID AND RON GARNEY Storytellers
JOHN BEATTY AND ANDY SMITH Inkers
JOE ROSAS Colorist
JOHN COSTANZA Letterer
MATT IDELSON Editor
BOB HARRAS Editor In Chief

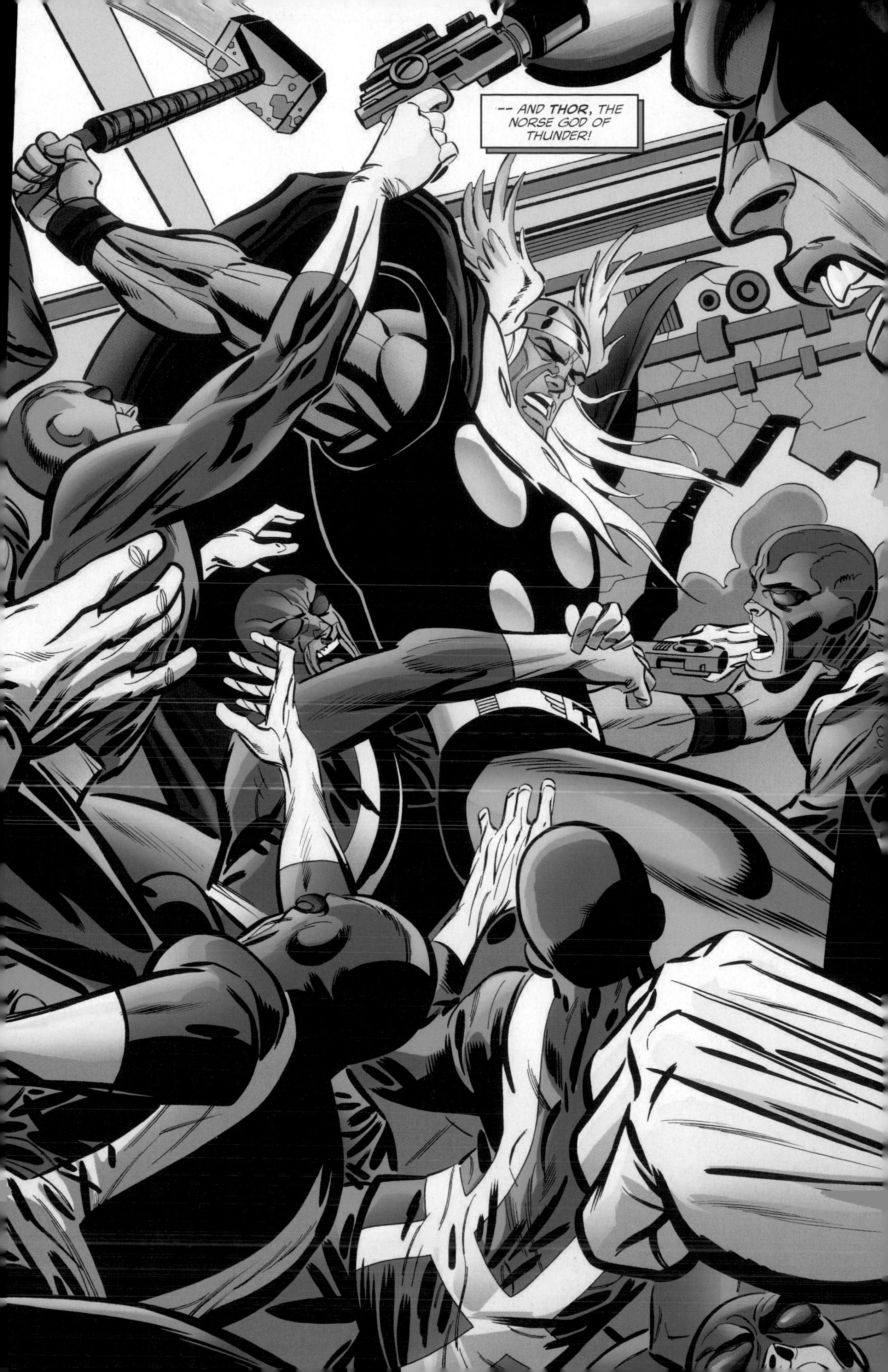
-- AND THOR, THE NORSE GOD OF THUNDER!

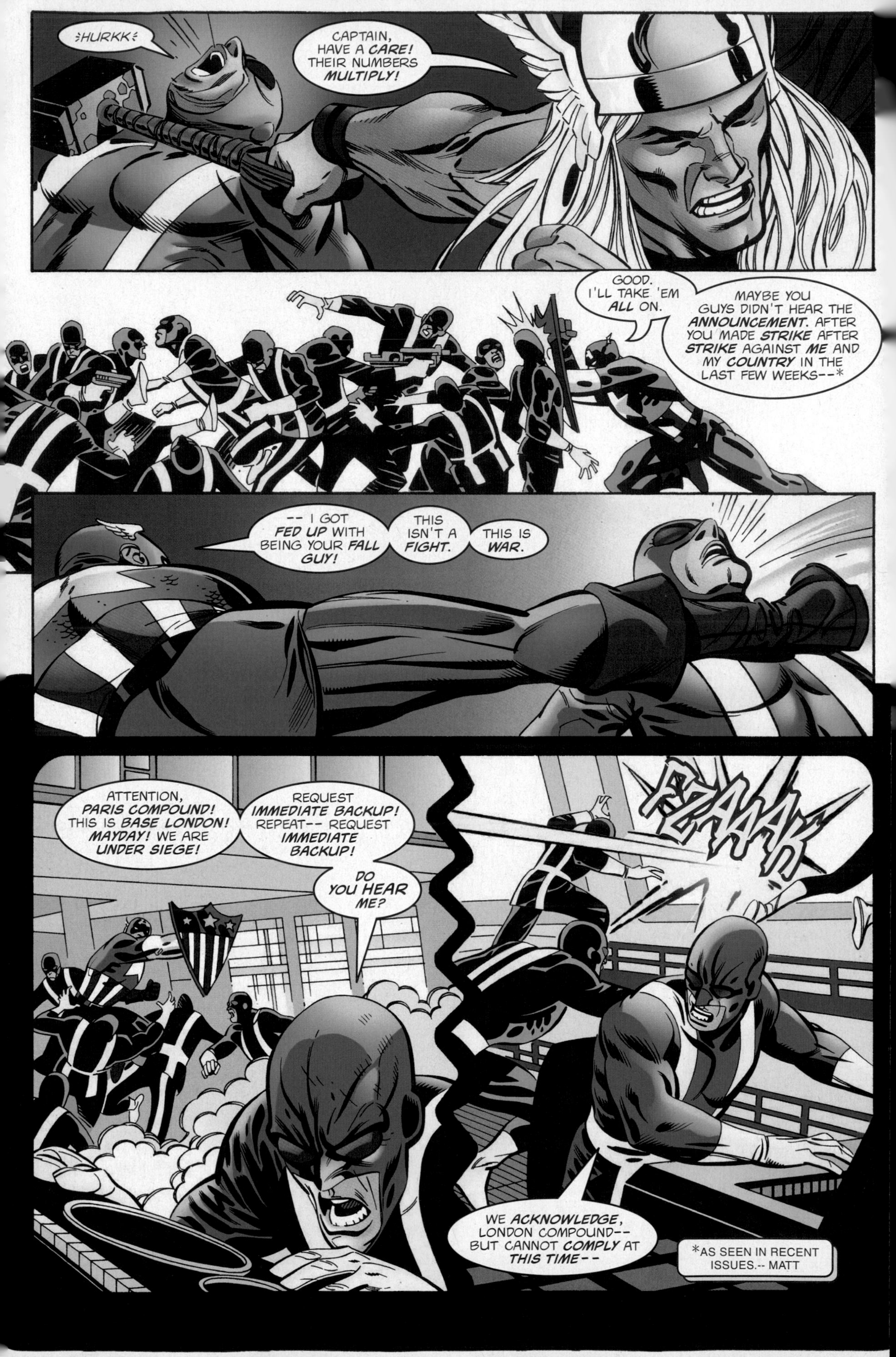
HURKK
CAPTAIN, HAVE A CARE! THEIR NUMBERS MULTIPLY!
GOOD. I'LL TAKE 'EM ALL ON.
MAYBE YOU GUYS DIDN'T HEAR THE ANNOUNCEMENT. AFTER YOU MADE STRIKE AFTER STRIKE AGAINST ME AND MY COUNTRY IN THE LAST FEW WEEKS--*
-- I GOT FED UP WITH BEING YOUR FALL GUY!
THIS ISN'T A FIGHT.
THIS IS WAR.
ATTENTION, PARIS COMPOUND! THIS IS BASE LONDON! MAYDAY! WE ARE UNDER SIEGE!
REQUEST IMMEDIATE BACKUP! REPEAT-- REQUEST IMMEDIATE BACKUP!
DO YOU HEAR ME?
FZAAAK
WE ACKNOWLEDGE, LONDON COMPOUND-- BUT CANNOT COMPLY AT THIS TIME--
*AS SEEN IN RECENT ISSUES.-- MATT

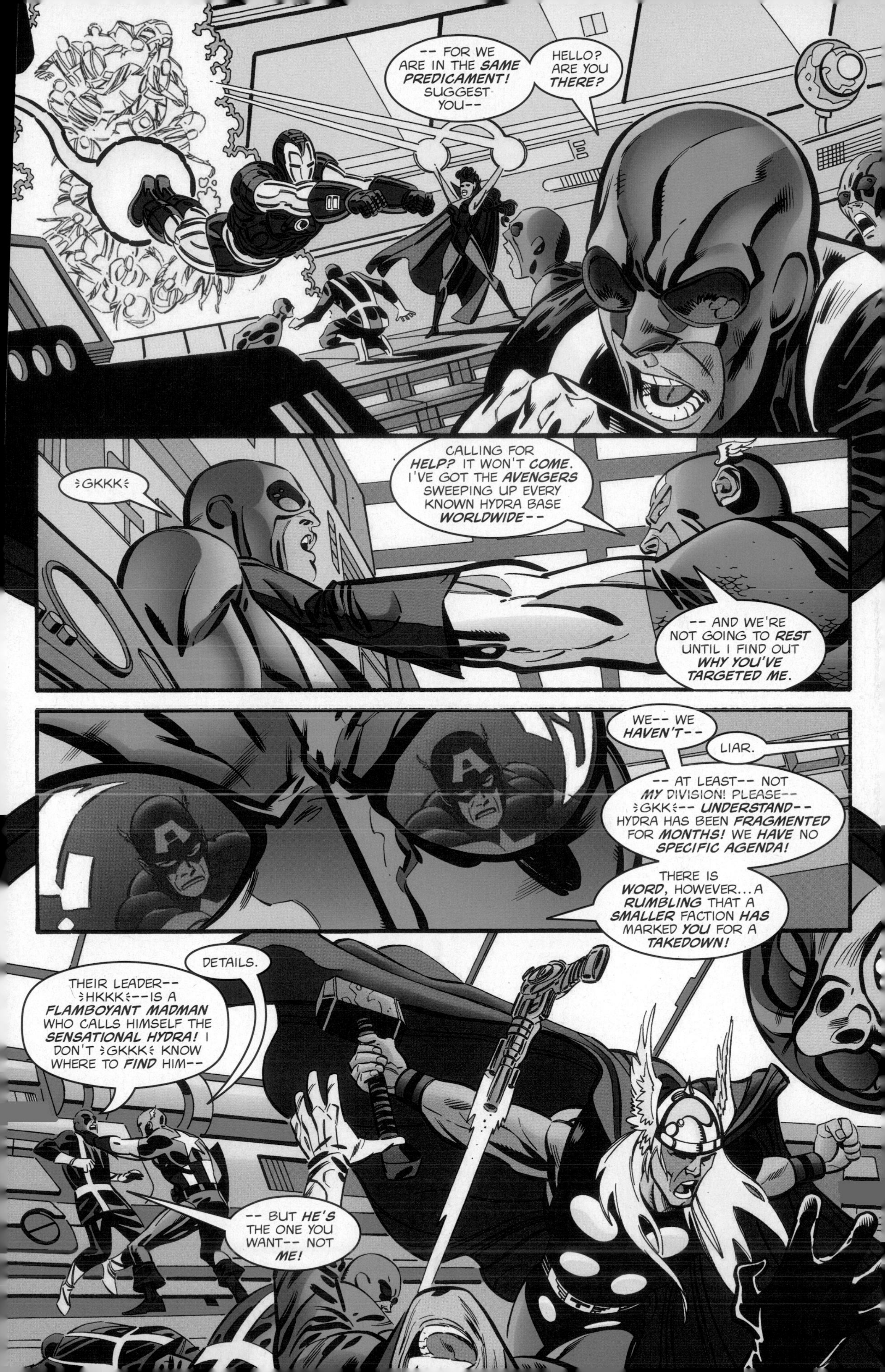

-- FOR WE ARE IN THE SAME PREDICAMENT! SUGGEST YOU--
HELLO? ARE YOU THERE?
⁑GKKK⁑
CALLING FOR HELP? IT WON'T COME. I'VE GOT THE AVENGERS SWEEPING UP EVERY KNOWN HYDRA BASE WORLDWIDE--
-- AND WE'RE NOT GOING TO REST UNTIL I FIND OUT WHY YOU'VE TARGETED ME.
WE-- WE HAVEN'T--
LIAR.
-- AT LEAST-- NOT MY DIVISION! PLEASE-- ⁑GKK⁑-- UNDERSTAND-- HYDRA HAS BEEN FRAGMENTED FOR MONTHS! WE HAVE NO SPECIFIC AGENDA!
THERE IS WORD, HOWEVER... A RUMBLING THAT A SMALLER FACTION HAS MARKED YOU FOR A TAKEDOWN!
DETAILS.
THEIR LEADER-- ⁑HKKK⁑--IS A FLAMBOYANT MADMAN WHO CALLS HIMSELF THE SENSATIONAL HYDRA! I DON'T ⁑GKKK⁑ KNOW WHERE TO FIND HIM--
-- BUT HE'S THE ONE YOU WANT-- NOT ME!

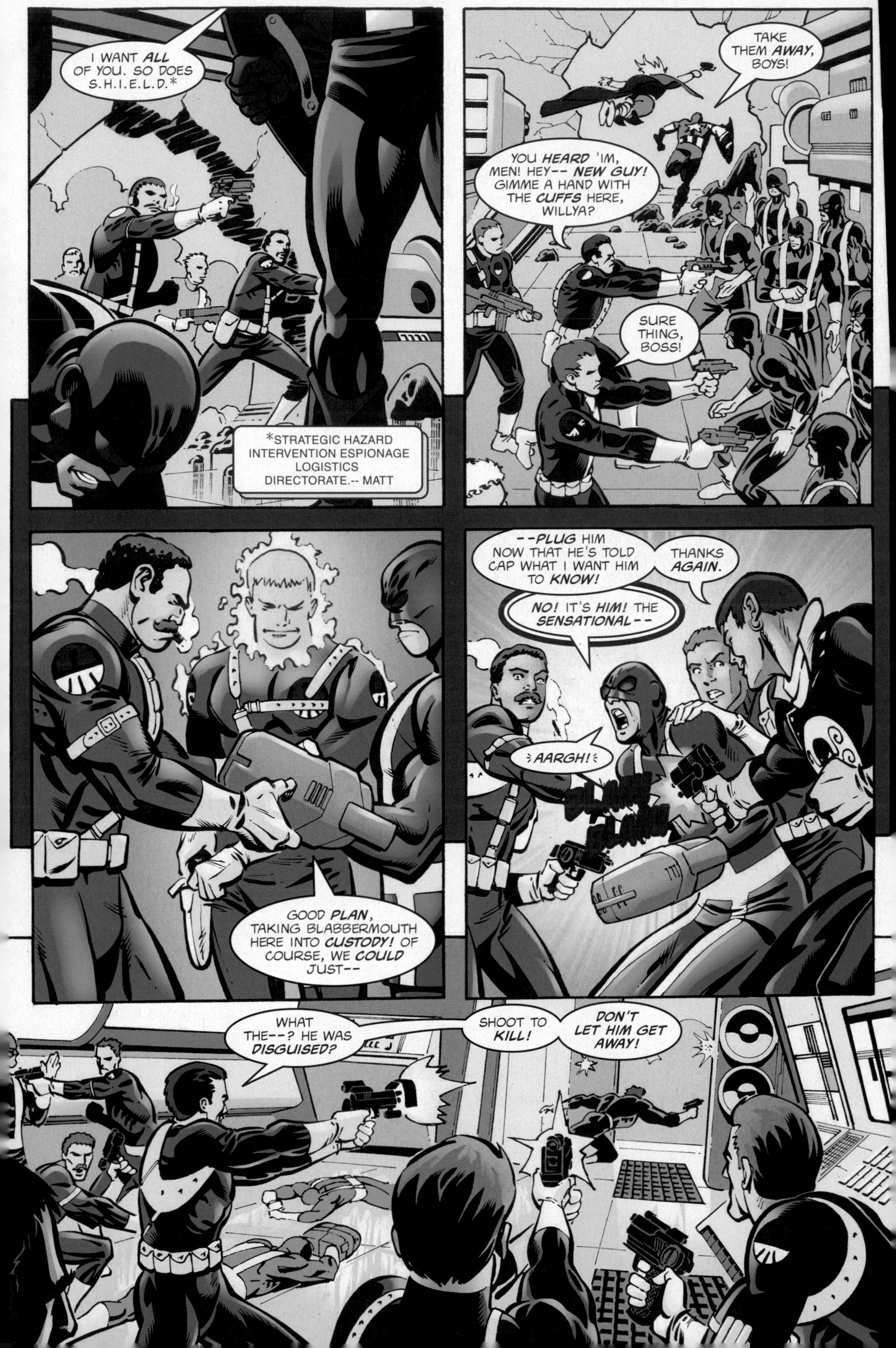

I WANT ALL OF YOU. SO DOES S.H.I.E.L.D.*
*STRATEGIC HAZARD INTERVENTION ESPIONAGE LOGISTICS DIRECTORATE.-- MATT
TAKE THEM AWAY, BOYS!
YOU HEARD 'IM, MEN! HEY-- NEW GUY! GIMME A HAND WITH THE CUFFS HERE, WILLYA?
SURE THING, BOSS!
GOOD PLAN, TAKING BLABBERMOUTH HERE INTO CUSTODY! OF COURSE, WE COULD JUST--
--PLUG HIM NOW THAT HE'S TOLD CAP WHAT I WANT HIM TO KNOW!
THANKS AGAIN.
NO! IT'S HIM! THE SENSATIONAL--
AARGH!
WHAT THE--? HE WAS DISGUISED?
SHOOT TO KILL!
DON'T LET HIM GET AWAY!

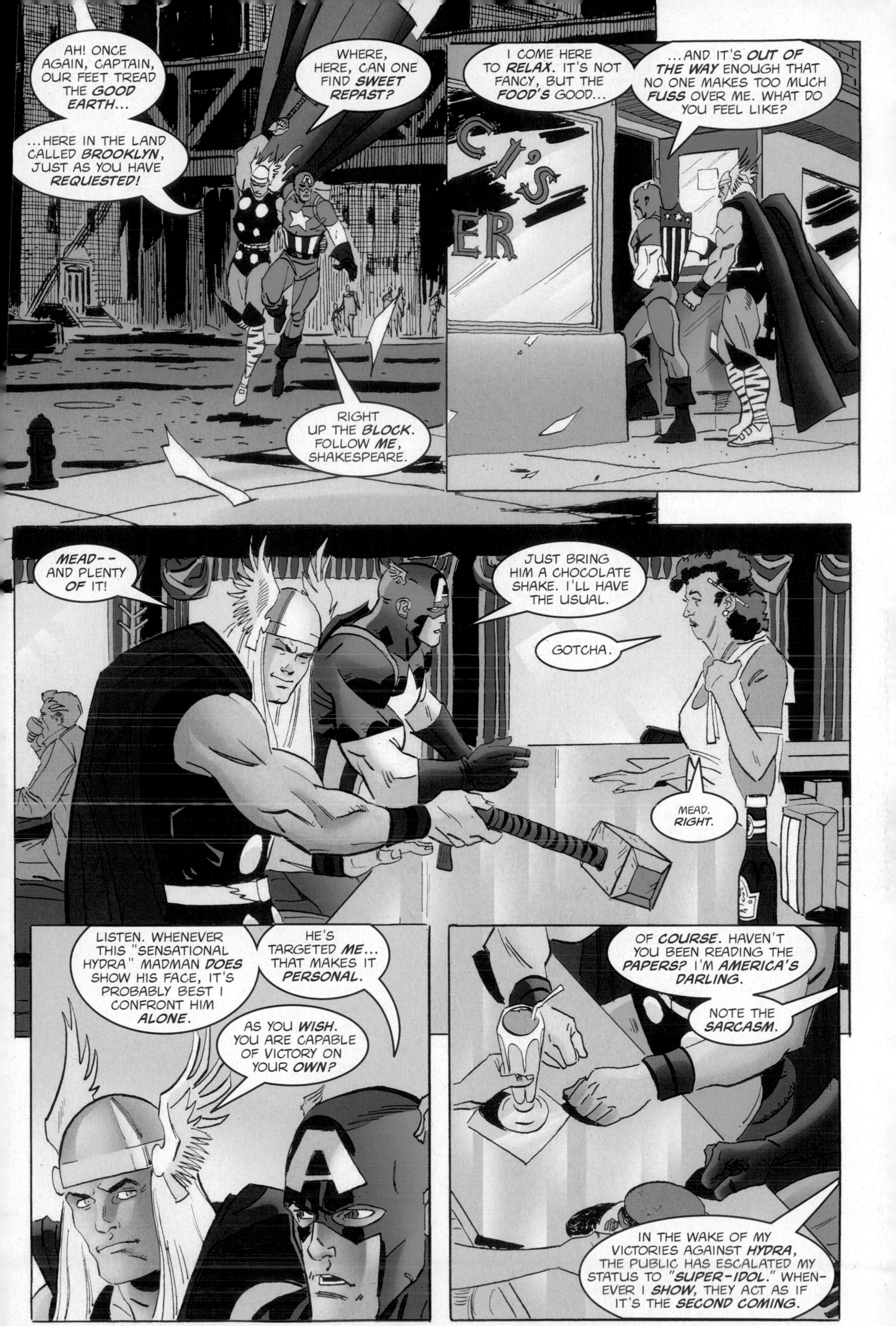
AH! ONCE AGAIN, CAPTAIN, OUR FEET TREAD THE GOOD EARTH...
...HERE IN THE LAND CALLED BROOKLYN, JUST AS YOU HAVE REQUESTED!
WHERE, HERE, CAN ONE FIND SWEET REPAST?
RIGHT UP THE BLOCK. FOLLOW ME, SHAKESPEARE.
I COME HERE TO RELAX. IT'S NOT FANCY, BUT THE FOOD'S GOOD...
...AND IT'S OUT OF THE WAY ENOUGH THAT NO ONE MAKES TOO MUCH FUSS OVER ME. WHAT DO YOU FEEL LIKE?
CI'S
ER
MEAD-- AND PLENTY OF IT!
JUST BRING HIM A CHOCOLATE SHAKE. I'LL HAVE THE USUAL.
GOTCHA.
MEAD. RIGHT.
LISTEN. WHENEVER THIS "SENSATIONAL HYDRA" MADMAN DOES SHOW HIS FACE, IT'S PROBABLY BEST I CONFRONT HIM ALONE.
HE'S TARGETED ME... THAT MAKES IT PERSONAL.
AS YOU WISH. YOU ARE CAPABLE OF VICTORY ON YOUR OWN?
OF COURSE. HAVEN'T YOU BEEN READING THE PAPERS? I'M AMERICA'S DARLING.
NOTE THE SARCASM.
IN THE WAKE OF MY VICTORIES AGAINST HYDRA, THE PUBLIC HAS ESCALATED MY STATUS TO "SUPER-IDOL." WHEN-EVER I SHOW, THEY ACT AS IF IT'S THE SECOND COMING.

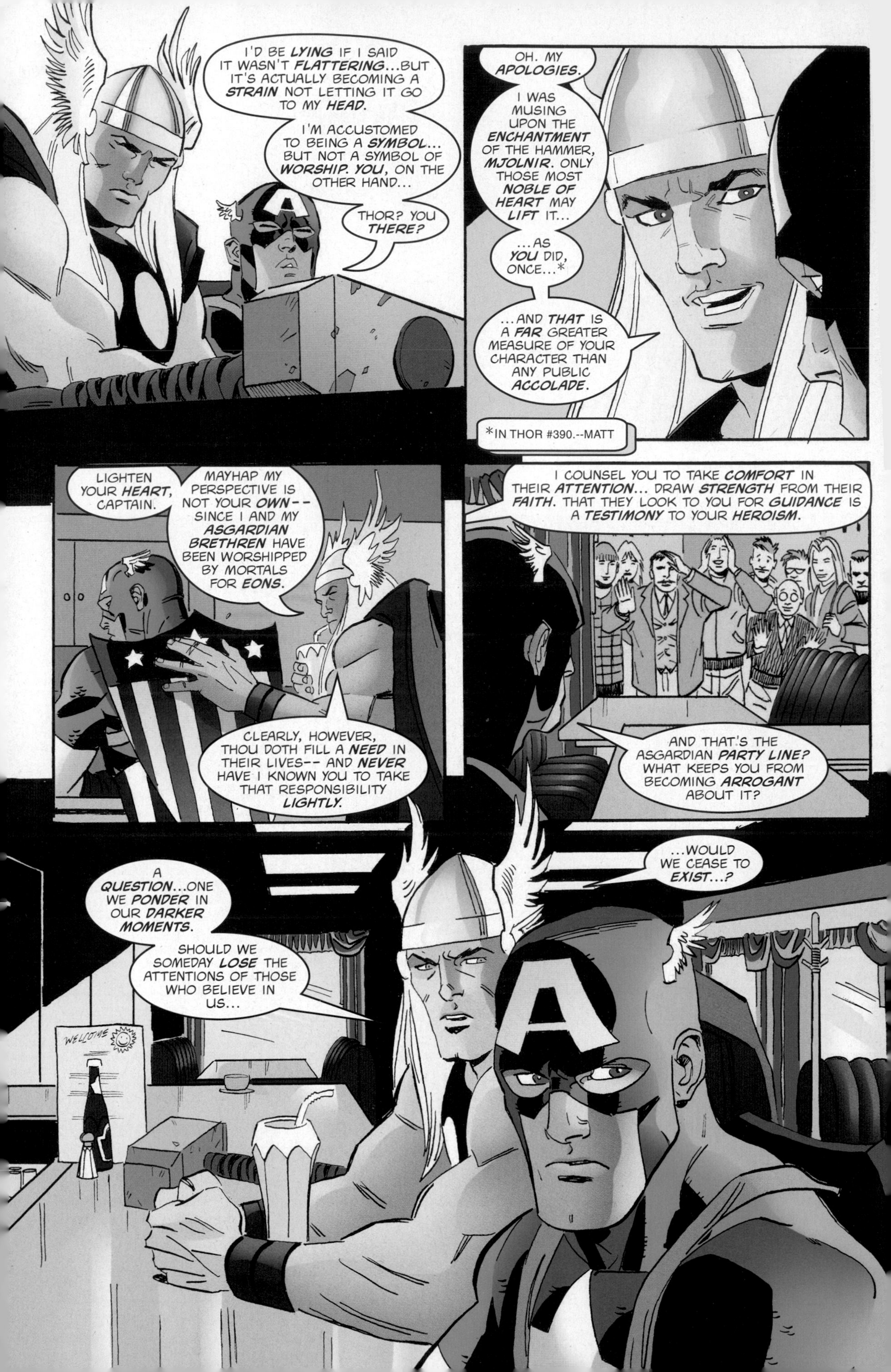
I'D BE LYING IF I SAID IT WASN'T FLATTERING...BUT IT'S ACTUALLY BECOMING A STRAIN NOT LETTING IT GO TO MY HEAD.
I'M ACCUSTOMED TO BEING A SYMBOL... BUT NOT A SYMBOL OF WORSHIP. YOU, ON THE OTHER HAND...
THOR? YOU THERE?
OH. MY APOLOGIES.
I WAS MUSING UPON THE ENCHANTMENT OF THE HAMMER, MJOLNIR. ONLY THOSE MOST NOBLE OF HEART MAY LIFT IT...
...AS YOU DID, ONCE...*
...AND THAT IS A FAR GREATER MEASURE OF YOUR CHARACTER THAN ANY PUBLIC ACCOLADE.
*IN THOR #390.--MATT
LIGHTEN YOUR HEART, CAPTAIN.
MAYHAP MY PERSPECTIVE IS NOT YOUR OWN-- SINCE I AND MY ASGARDIAN BRETHREN HAVE BEEN WORSHIPPED BY MORTALS FOR EONS.
CLEARLY, HOWEVER, THOU DOTH FILL A NEED IN THEIR LIVES-- AND NEVER HAVE I KNOWN YOU TO TAKE THAT RESPONSIBILITY LIGHTLY.
I COUNSEL YOU TO TAKE COMFORT IN THEIR ATTENTION... DRAW STRENGTH FROM THEIR FAITH. THAT THEY LOOK TO YOU FOR GUIDANCE IS A TESTIMONY TO YOUR HEROISM.
AND THAT'S THE ASGARDIAN PARTY LINE? WHAT KEEPS YOU FROM BECOMING ARROGANT ABOUT IT?
A QUESTION...ONE WE PONDER IN OUR DARKER MOMENTS.
SHOULD WE SOMEDAY LOSE THE ATTENTIONS OF THOSE WHO BELIEVE IN US...
...WOULD WE CEASE TO EXIST...?
WELCOME

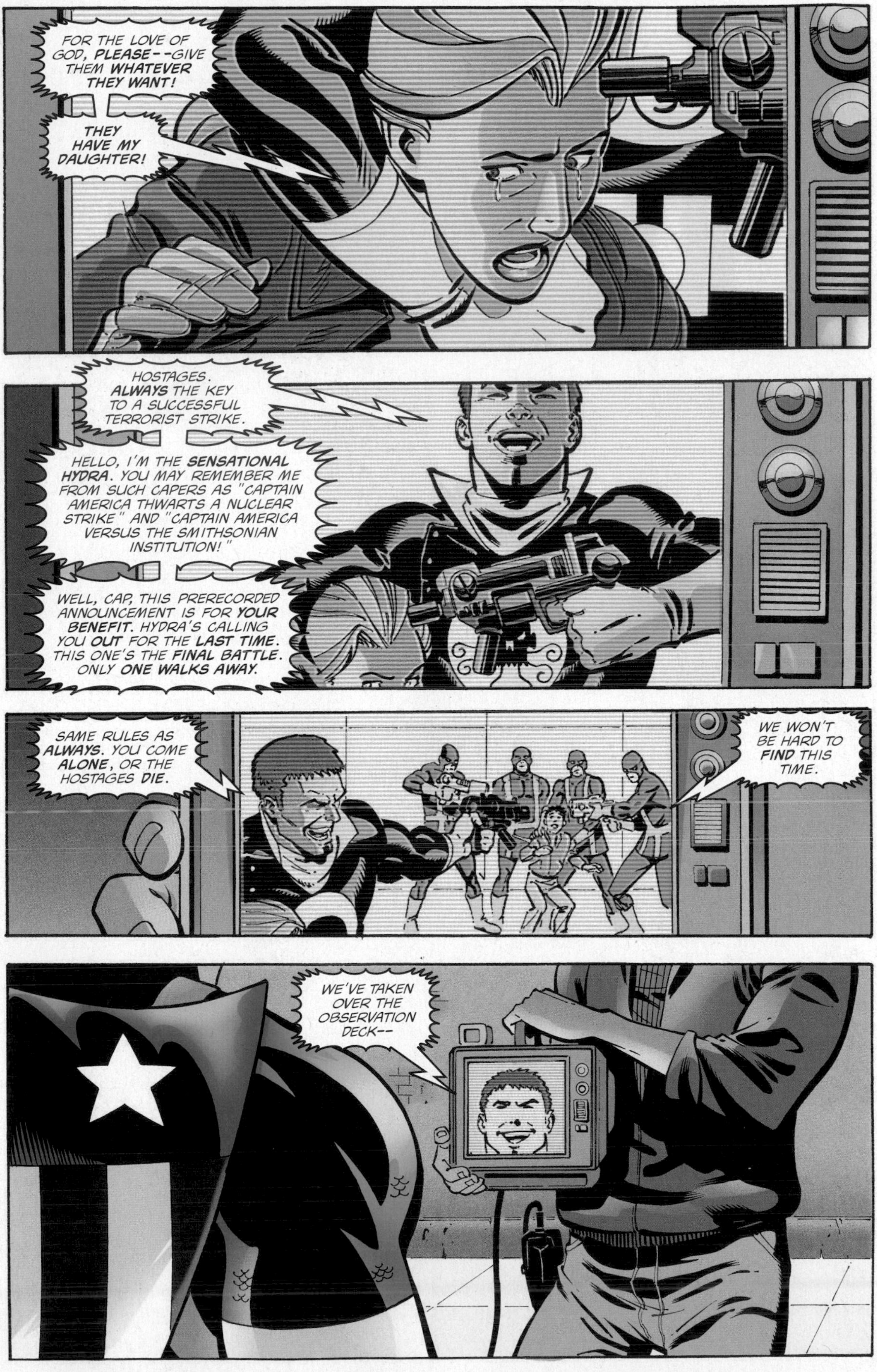
FOR THE LOVE OF GOD, PLEASE--GIVE THEM WHATEVER THEY WANT!
THEY HAVE MY DAUGHTER!
HOSTAGES. ALWAYS THE KEY TO A SUCCESSFUL TERRORIST STRIKE.
HELLO, I'M THE SENSATIONAL HYDRA. YOU MAY REMEMBER ME FROM SUCH CAPERS AS "CAPTAIN AMERICA THWARTS A NUCLEAR STRIKE" AND "CAPTAIN AMERICA VERSUS THE SMITHSONIAN INSTITUTION!"
WELL, CAP, THIS PRERECORDED ANNOUNCEMENT IS FOR YOUR BENEFIT. HYDRA'S CALLING YOU OUT FOR THE LAST TIME. THIS ONE'S THE FINAL BATTLE. ONLY ONE WALKS AWAY.
SAME RULES AS ALWAYS. YOU COME ALONE, OR THE HOSTAGES DIE.
WE WON'T BE HARD TO FIND THIS TIME.
WE'VE TAKEN OVER THE OBSERVATION DECK--

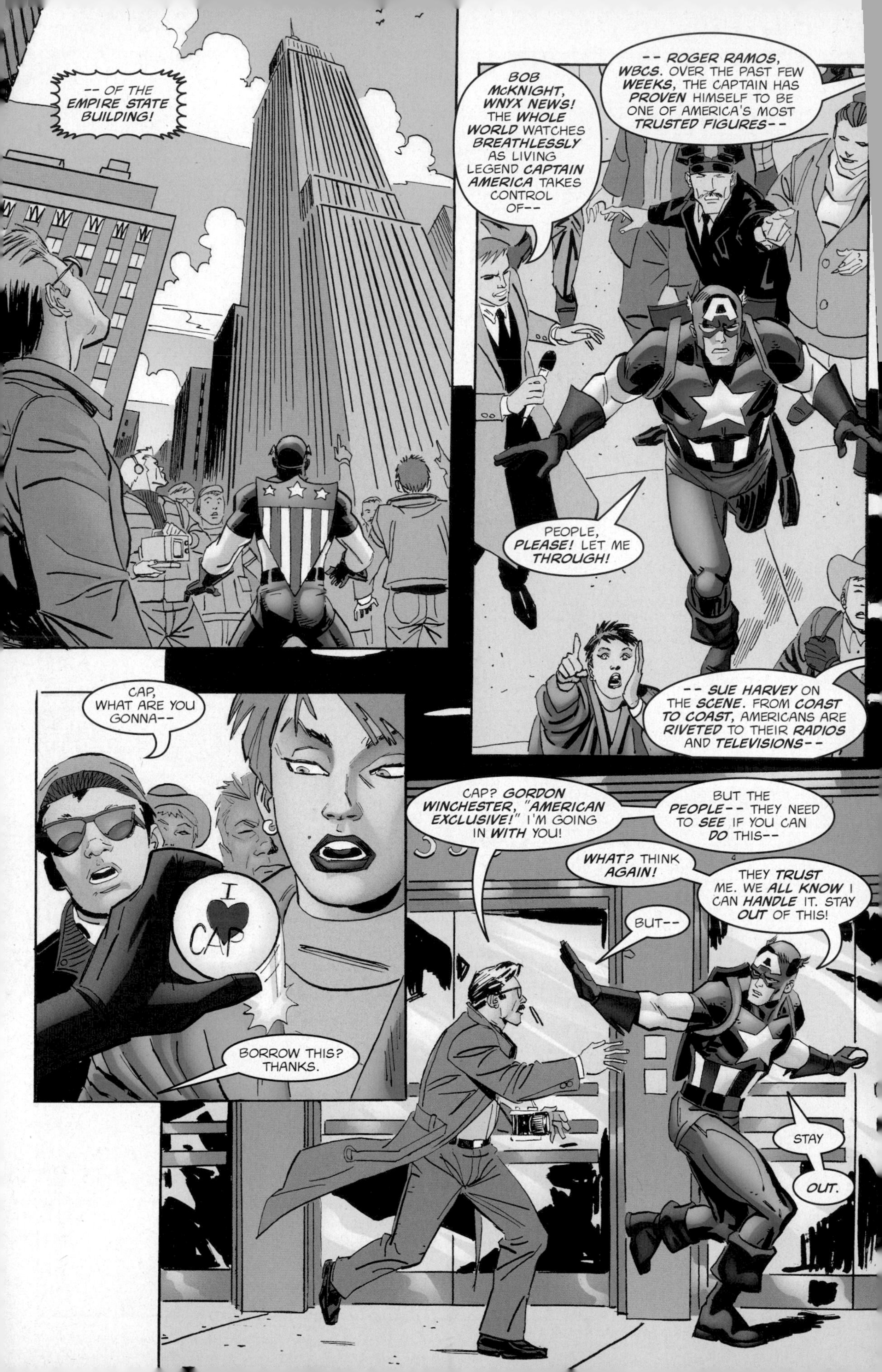
-- OF THE EMPIRE STATE BUILDING!
BOB McKNIGHT, WNYX NEWS! THE WHOLE WORLD WATCHES BREATHLESSLY AS LIVING LEGEND CAPTAIN AMERICA TAKES CONTROL OF--
-- ROGER RAMOS, WBCS. OVER THE PAST FEW WEEKS, THE CAPTAIN HAS PROVEN HIMSELF TO BE ONE OF AMERICA'S MOST TRUSTED FIGURES--
PEOPLE, PLEASE! LET ME THROUGH!
-- SUE HARVEY ON THE SCENE. FROM COAST TO COAST, AMERICANS ARE RIVETED TO THEIR RADIOS AND TELEVISIONS--
CAP, WHAT ARE YOU GONNA--
I ♥ CAP
BORROW THIS? THANKS.
CAP? GORDON WINCHESTER, "AMERICAN EXCLUSIVE!" I'M GOING IN WITH YOU!
WHAT? THINK AGAIN!
BUT THE PEOPLE-- THEY NEED TO SEE IF YOU CAN DO THIS--
THEY TRUST ME. WE ALL KNOW I CAN HANDLE IT. STAY OUT OF THIS!
BUT--
STAY
OUT.

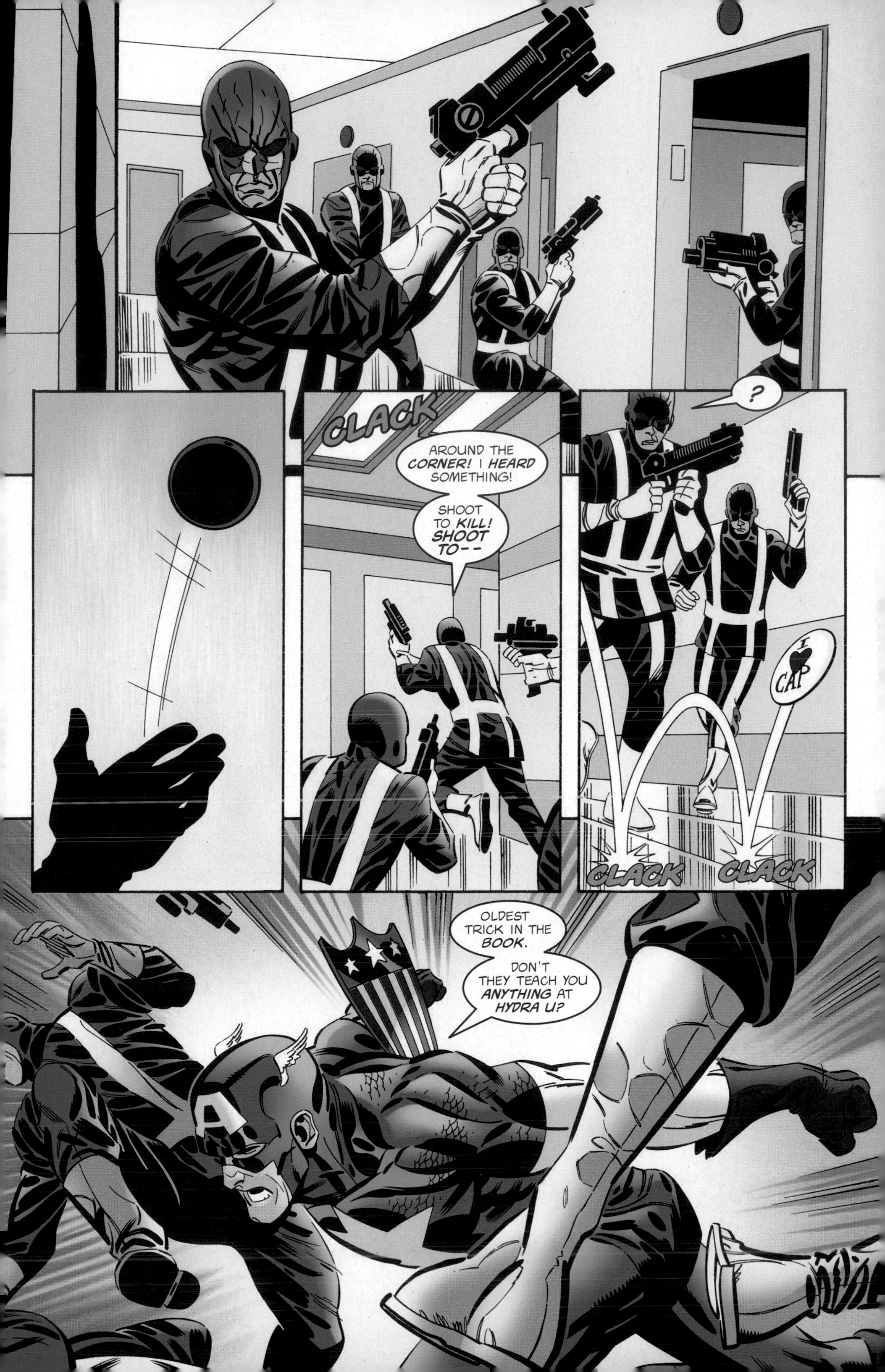
CLACK
AROUND THE CORNER! I HEARD SOMETHING!
SHOOT TO KILL! SHOOT TO--
?
I ♥ CAP
CLACK
CLACK
OLDEST TRICK IN THE BOOK.
DON'T THEY TEACH YOU ANYTHING AT HYDRA U?

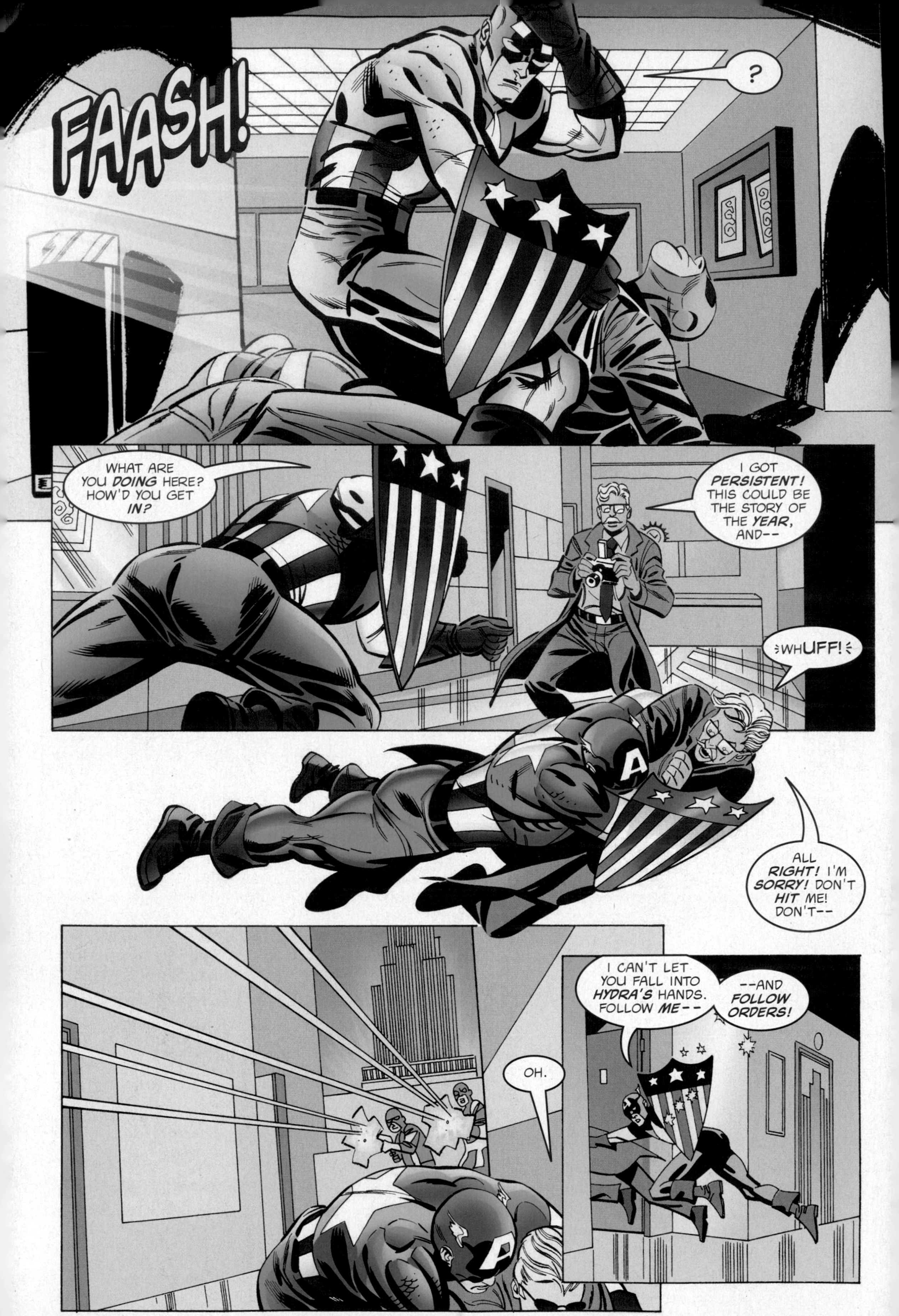
FAASH!
?
WHAT ARE YOU DOING HERE? HOW'D YOU GET IN?
I GOT PERSISTENT! THIS COULD BE THE STORY OF THE YEAR, AND--
WHUFF!
ALL RIGHT! I'M SORRY! DON'T HIT ME! DON'T--
OH.
I CAN'T LET YOU FALL INTO HYDRA'S HANDS. FOLLOW ME--
--AND FOLLOW ORDERS!

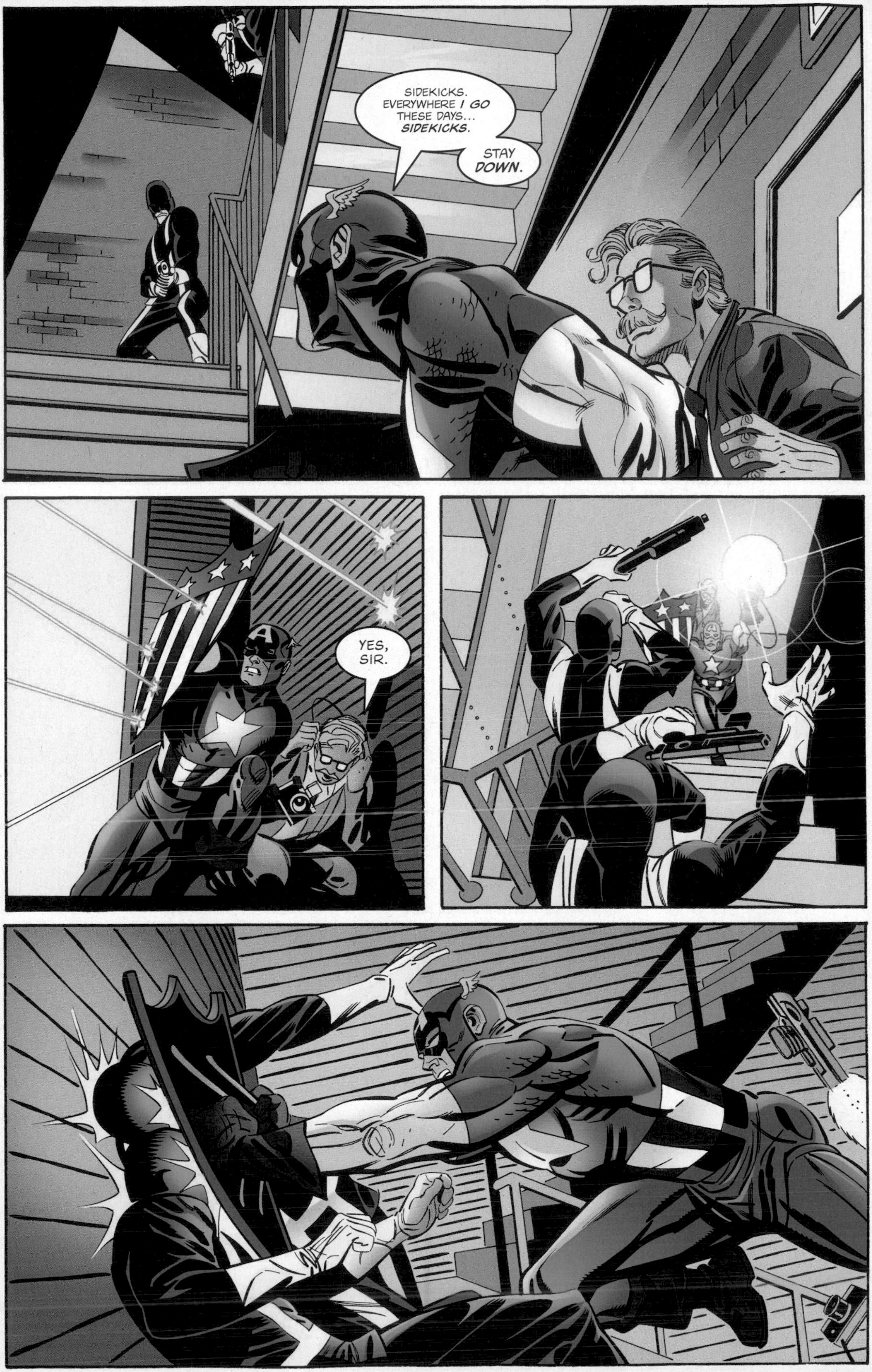
SIDEKICKS. EVERYWHERE I GO THESE DAYS... SIDEKICKS.
STAY DOWN.
YES, SIR.

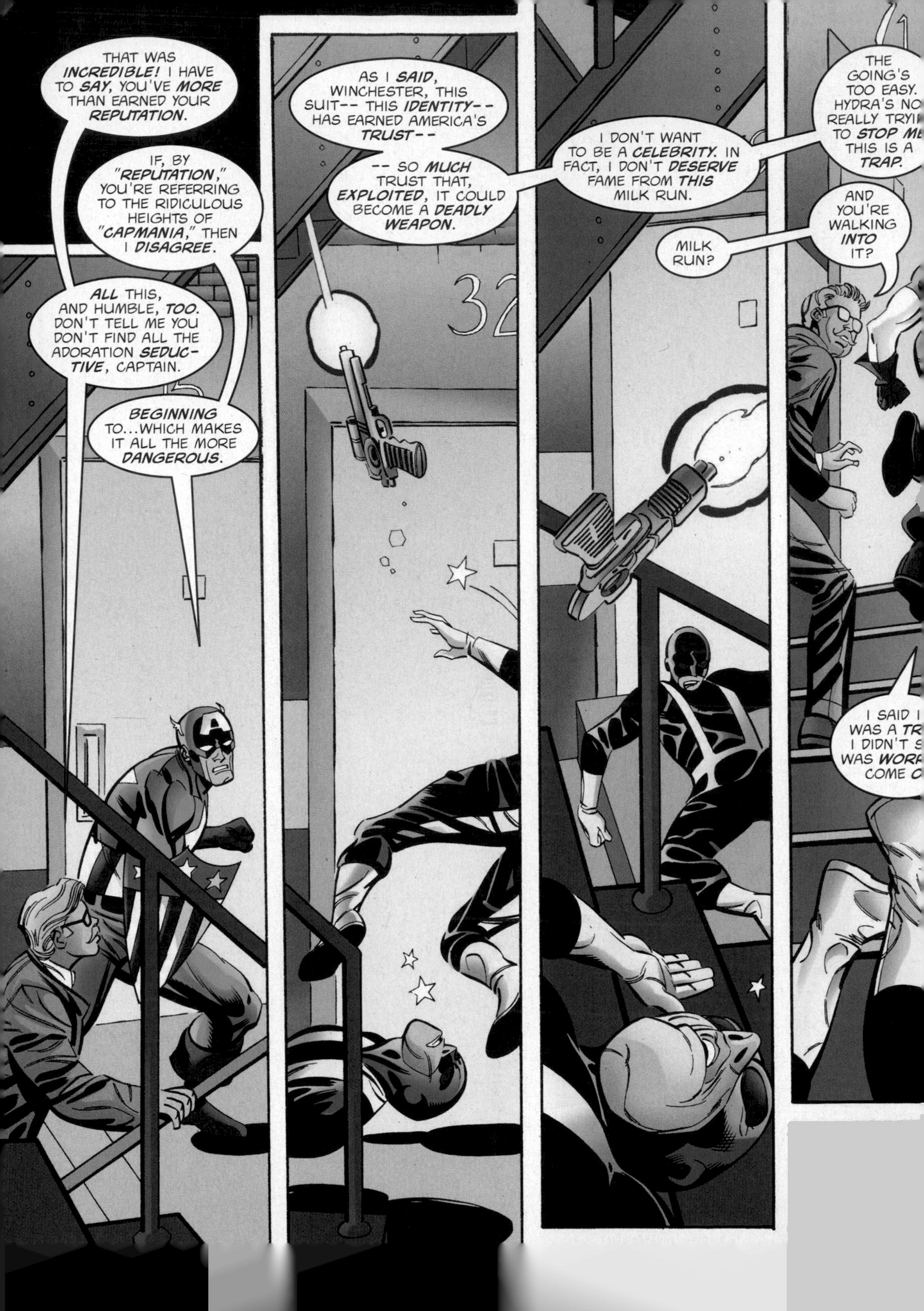

THAT WAS INCREDIBLE! I HAVE TO SAY, YOU'VE MORE THAN EARNED YOUR REPUTATION.
IF, BY "REPUTATION," YOU'RE REFERRING TO THE RIDICULOUS HEIGHTS OF "CAPMANIA," THEN I DISAGREE.
ALL THIS, AND HUMBLE, TOO. DON'T TELL ME YOU DON'T FIND ALL THE ADORATION SEDUC-TIVE, CAPTAIN.
BEGINNING TO...WHICH MAKES IT ALL THE MORE DANGEROUS.
AS I SAID, WINCHESTER, THIS SUIT-- THIS IDENTITY-- HAS EARNED AMERICA'S TRUST--
-- SO MUCH TRUST THAT, EXPLOITED, IT COULD BECOME A DEADLY WEAPON.
32
I DON'T WANT TO BE A CELEBRITY. IN FACT, I DON'T DESERVE FAME FROM THIS MILK RUN.
MILK RUN?

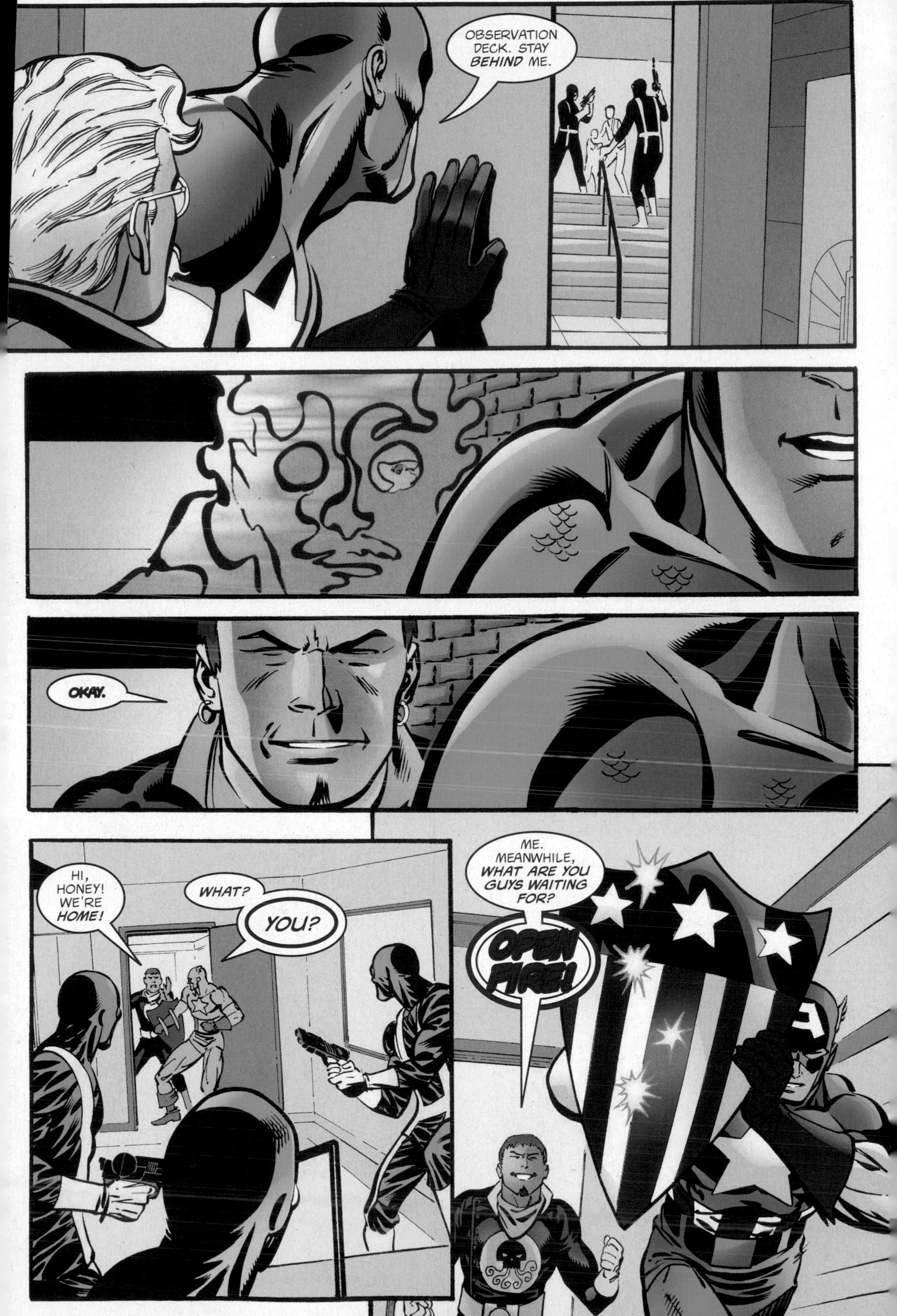

OBSERVATION DECK. STAY BEHIND ME.
OKAY.
HI, HONEY! WE'RE HOME!
WHAT?
YOU?
ME. MEANWHILE, WHAT ARE YOU GUYS WAITING FOR?
OPEN FIRE!

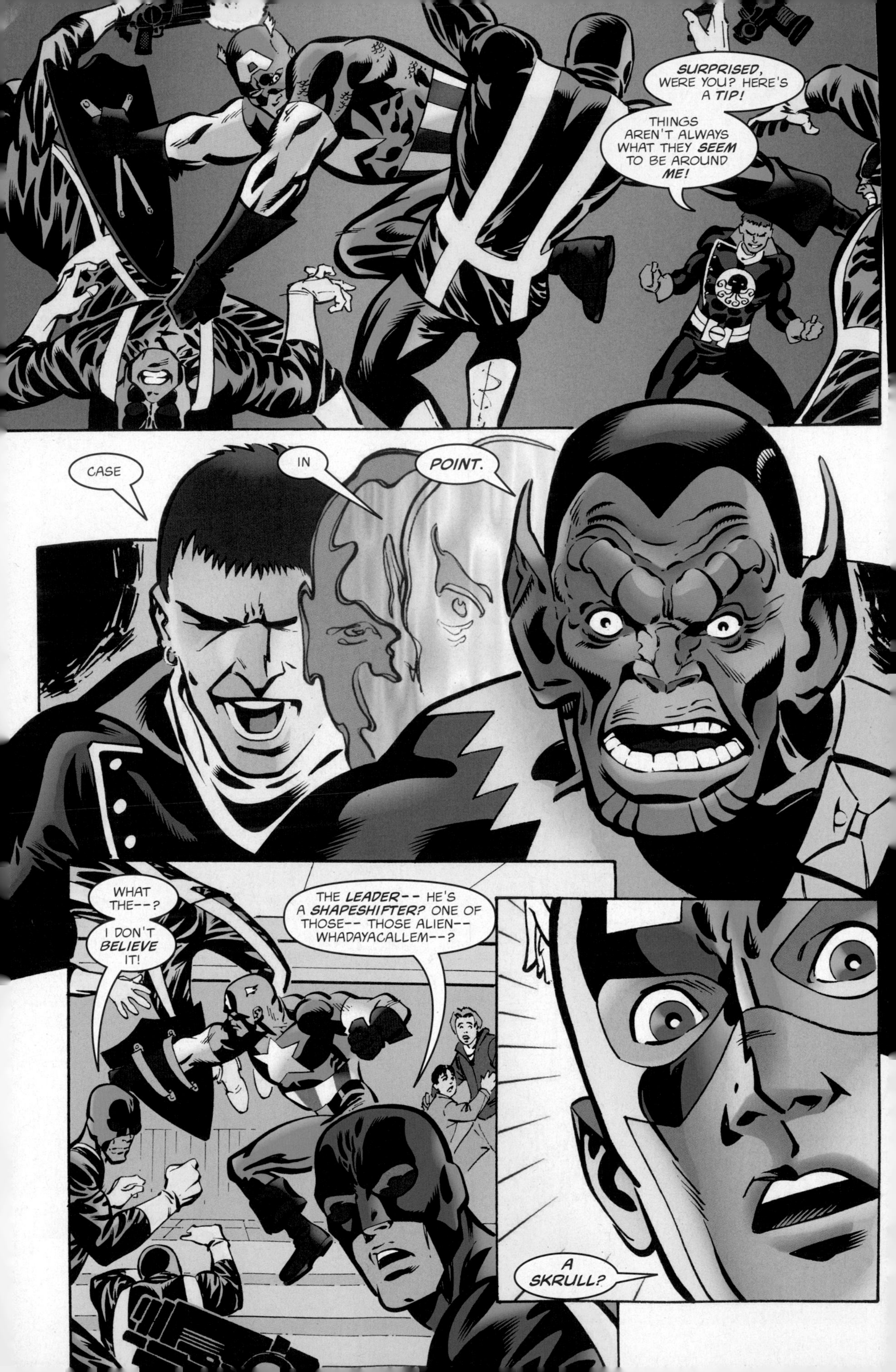
SURPRISED, WERE YOU? HERE'S A TIP!
THINGS AREN'T ALWAYS WHAT THEY SEEM TO BE AROUND ME!
CASE
IN
POINT.
WHAT THE--?
I DON'T BELIEVE IT!
THE LEADER-- HE'S A SHAPESHIFTER? ONE OF THOSE-- THOSE ALIEN-- WHADAYACALLEM--?
A SKRULL?

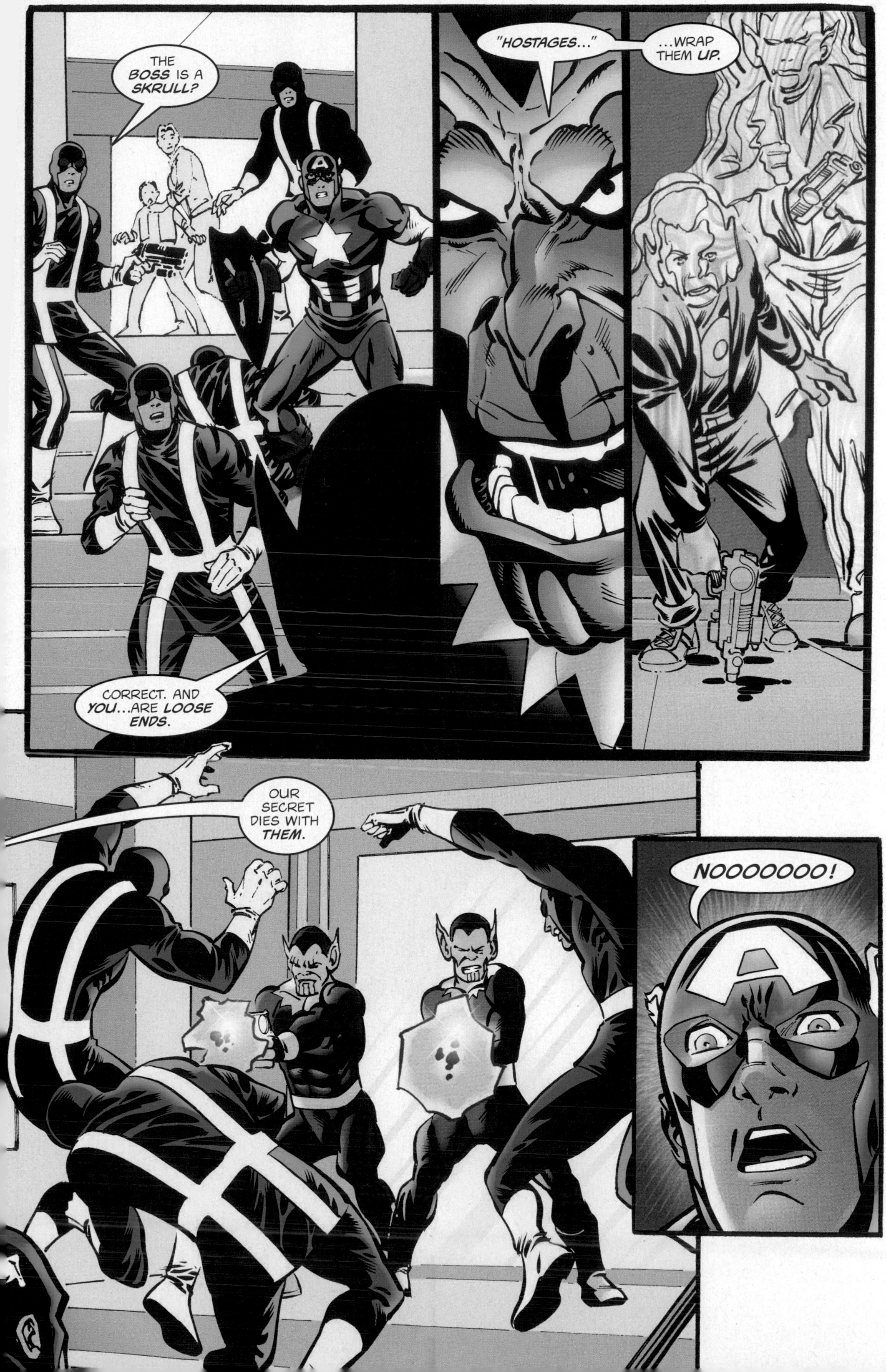
THE BOSS IS A SKRULL?
CORRECT. AND YOU...ARE LOOSE ENDS.
"HOSTAGES..."
...WRAP THEM UP.
OUR SECRET DIES WITH THEM.
NOOOOOOO!

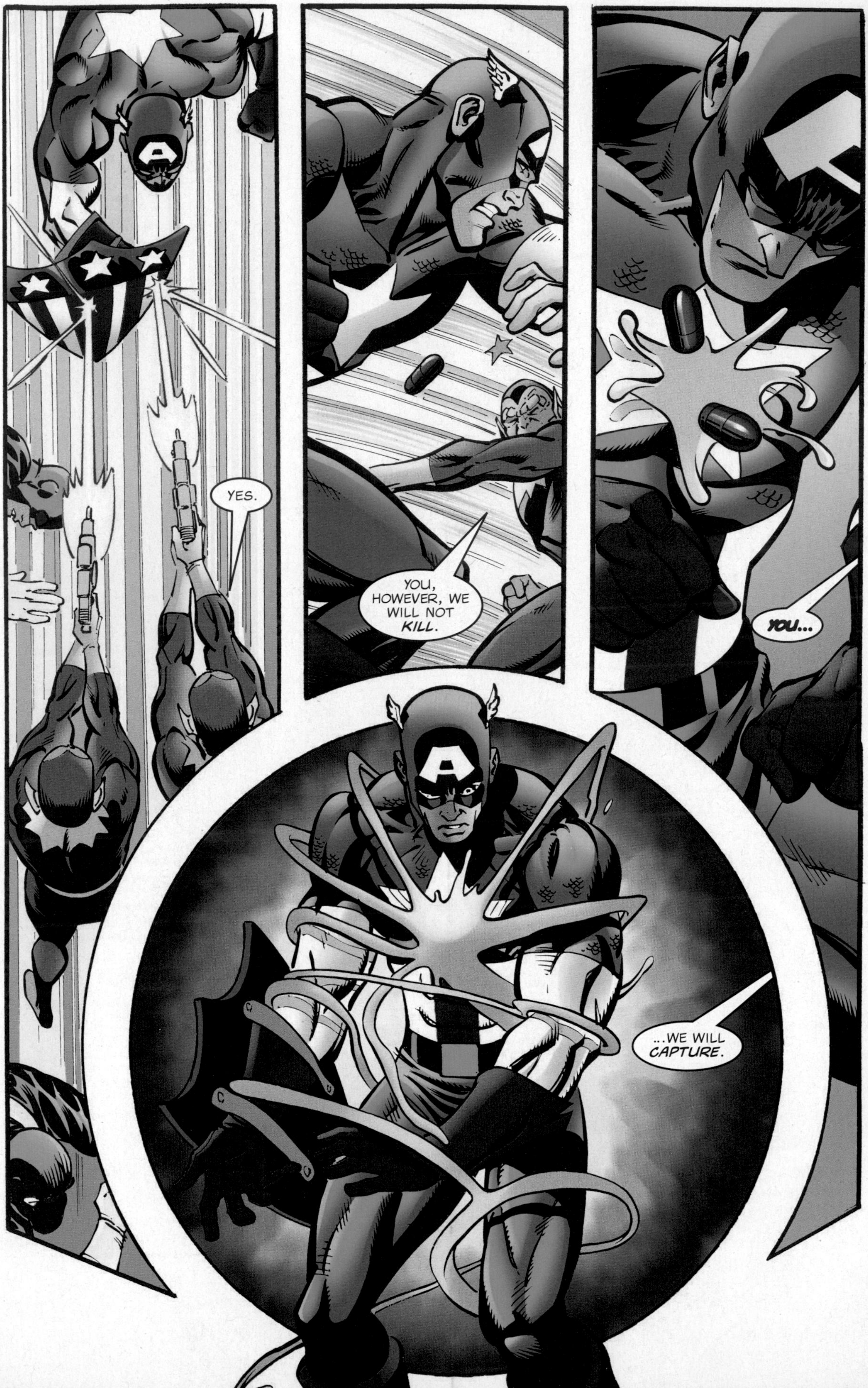
YES.
YOU, HOWEVER, WE WILL NOT KILL.
YOU...
...WE WILL CAPTURE.

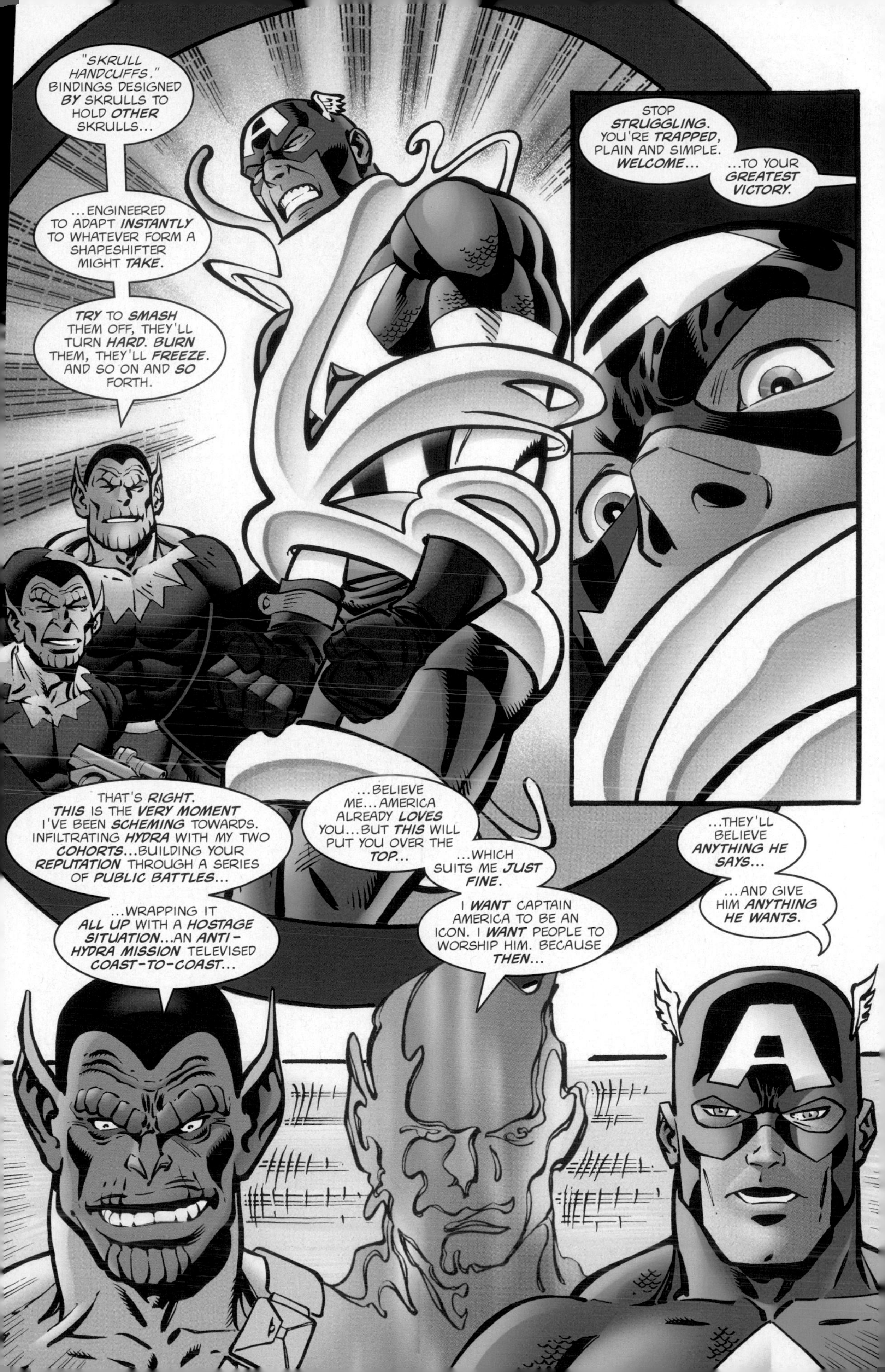
"SKRULL HANDCUFFS." BINDINGS DESIGNED BY SKRULLS TO HOLD OTHER SKRULLS...
...ENGINEERED TO ADAPT INSTANTLY TO WHATEVER FORM A SHAPESHIFTER MIGHT TAKE.
TRY TO SMASH THEM OFF, THEY'LL TURN HARD. BURN THEM, THEY'LL FREEZE. AND SO ON AND SO FORTH.
STOP STRUGGLING. YOU'RE TRAPPED, PLAIN AND SIMPLE. WELCOME...
...TO YOUR GREATEST VICTORY.
THAT'S RIGHT. THIS IS THE VERY MOMENT I'VE BEEN SCHEMING TOWARDS. INFILTRATING HYDRA WITH MY TWO COHORTS...BUILDING YOUR REPUTATION THROUGH A SERIES OF PUBLIC BATTLES...
...WRAPPING IT ALL UP WITH A HOSTAGE SITUATION...AN ANTI-HYDRA MISSION TELEVISED COAST-TO-COAST...
...BELIEVE ME...AMERICA ALREADY LOVES YOU...BUT THIS WILL PUT YOU OVER THE TOP...
...WHICH SUITS ME JUST FINE.
I WANT CAPTAIN AMERICA TO BE AN ICON. I WANT PEOPLE TO WORSHIP HIM. BECAUSE THEN...
...THEY'LL BELIEVE ANYTHING HE SAYS...
...AND GIVE HIM ANYTHING HE WANTS.

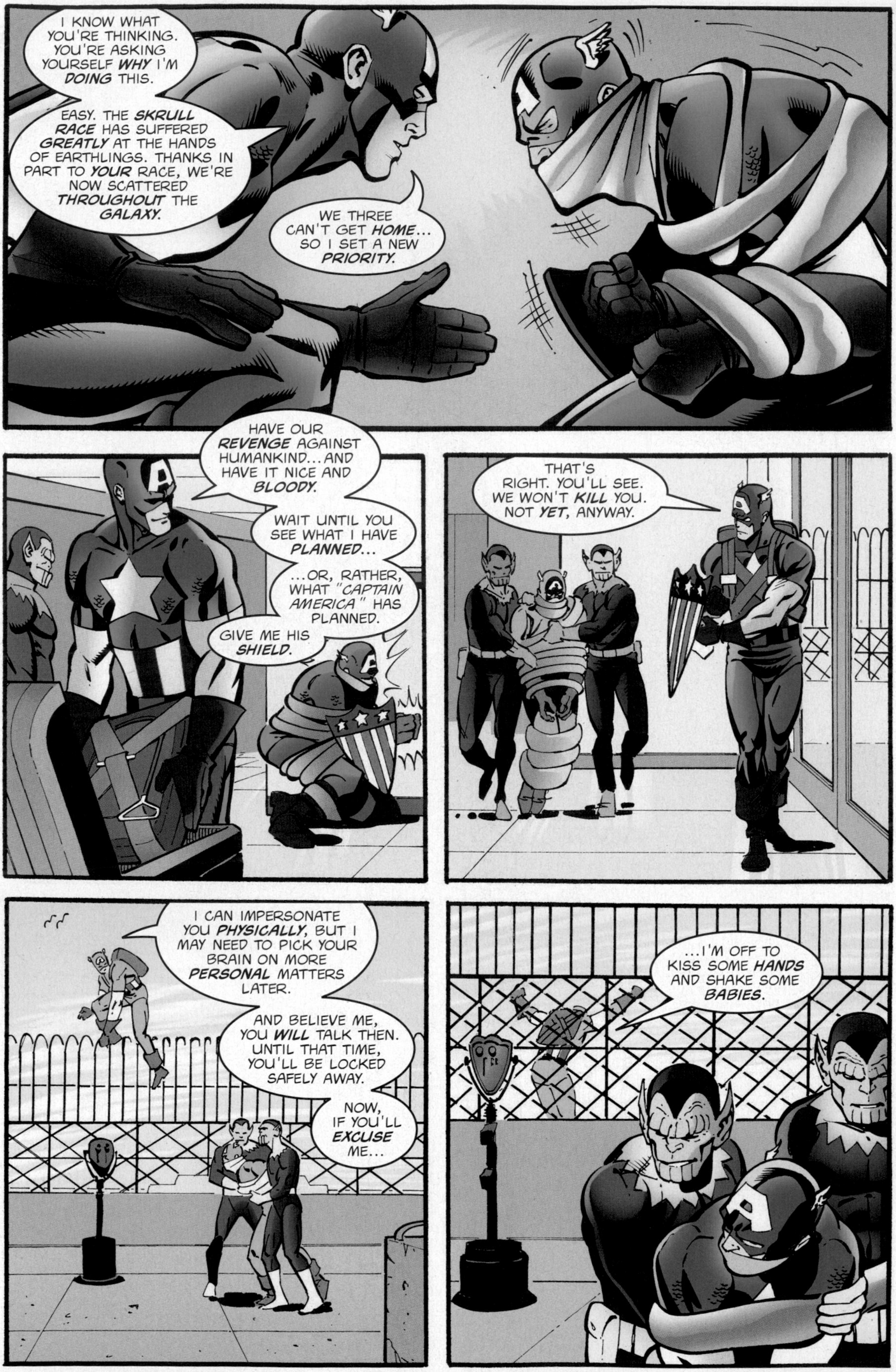

I KNOW WHAT YOU'RE THINKING. YOU'RE ASKING YOURSELF WHY I'M DOING THIS.
EASY. THE SKRULL RACE HAS SUFFERED GREATLY AT THE HANDS OF EARTHLINGS. THANKS IN PART TO YOUR RACE, WE'RE NOW SCATTERED THROUGHOUT THE GALAXY.
WE THREE CAN'T GET HOME... SO I SET A NEW PRIORITY.
HAVE OUR REVENGE AGAINST HUMANKIND... AND HAVE IT NICE AND BLOODY.
WAIT UNTIL YOU SEE WHAT I HAVE PLANNED...
...OR, RATHER, WHAT "CAPTAIN AMERICA" HAS PLANNED.
GIVE ME HIS SHIELD.
THAT'S RIGHT. YOU'LL SEE. WE WON'T KILL YOU. NOT YET, ANYWAY.
I CAN IMPERSONATE YOU PHYSICALLY, BUT I MAY NEED TO PICK YOUR BRAIN ON MORE PERSONAL MATTERS LATER.
AND BELIEVE ME, YOU WILL TALK THEN. UNTIL THAT TIME, YOU'LL BE LOCKED SAFELY AWAY.
NOW, IF YOU'LL EXCUSE ME...
...I'M OFF TO KISS SOME HANDS AND SHAKE SOME BABIES.

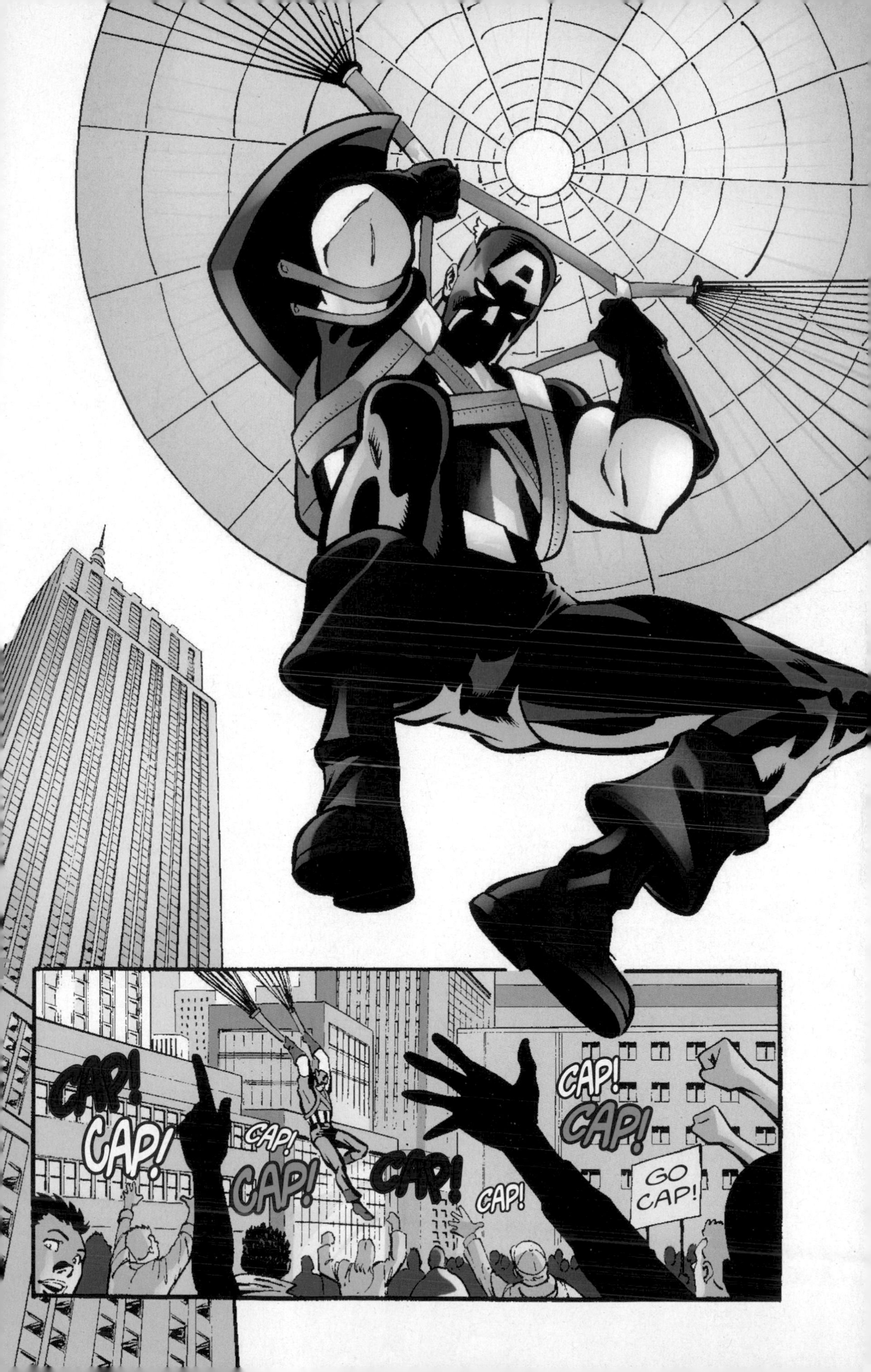
CAP!
CAP!
CAP!
CAP!
CAP!
CAP!
CAP!
CAP!
GO CAP!

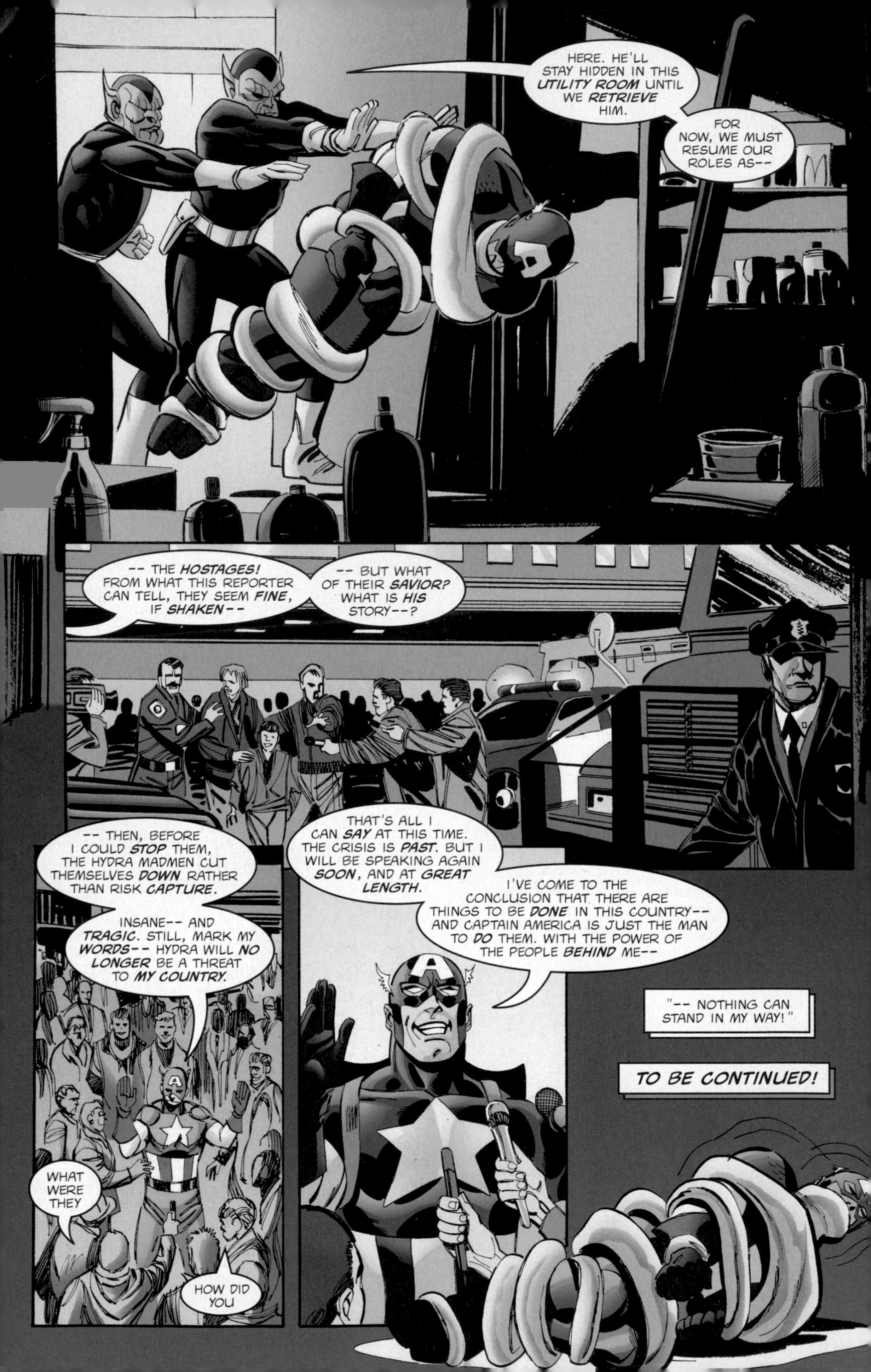
HERE. HE'LL STAY HIDDEN IN THIS UTILITY ROOM UNTIL WE RETRIEVE HIM.
FOR NOW, WE MUST RESUME OUR ROLES AS--
-- THE HOSTAGES! FROM WHAT THIS REPORTER CAN TELL, THEY SEEM FINE, IF SHAKEN--
-- BUT WHAT OF THEIR SAVIOR? WHAT IS HIS STORY--?
-- THEN, BEFORE I COULD STOP THEM, THE HYDRA MADMEN CUT THEMSELVES DOWN RATHER THAN RISK CAPTURE.
INSANE-- AND TRAGIC. STILL, MARK MY WORDS-- HYDRA WILL NO LONGER BE A THREAT TO MY COUNTRY.
WHAT WERE THEY
HOW DID YOU
THAT'S ALL I CAN SAY AT THIS TIME. THE CRISIS IS PAST. BUT I WILL BE SPEAKING AGAIN SOON, AND AT GREAT LENGTH.
I'VE COME TO THE CONCLUSION THAT THERE ARE THINGS TO BE DONE IN THIS COUNTRY-- AND CAPTAIN AMERICA IS JUST THE MAN TO DO THEM. WITH THE POWER OF THE PEOPLE BEHIND ME--
"-- NOTHING CAN STAND IN MY WAY!"
TO BE CONTINUED!

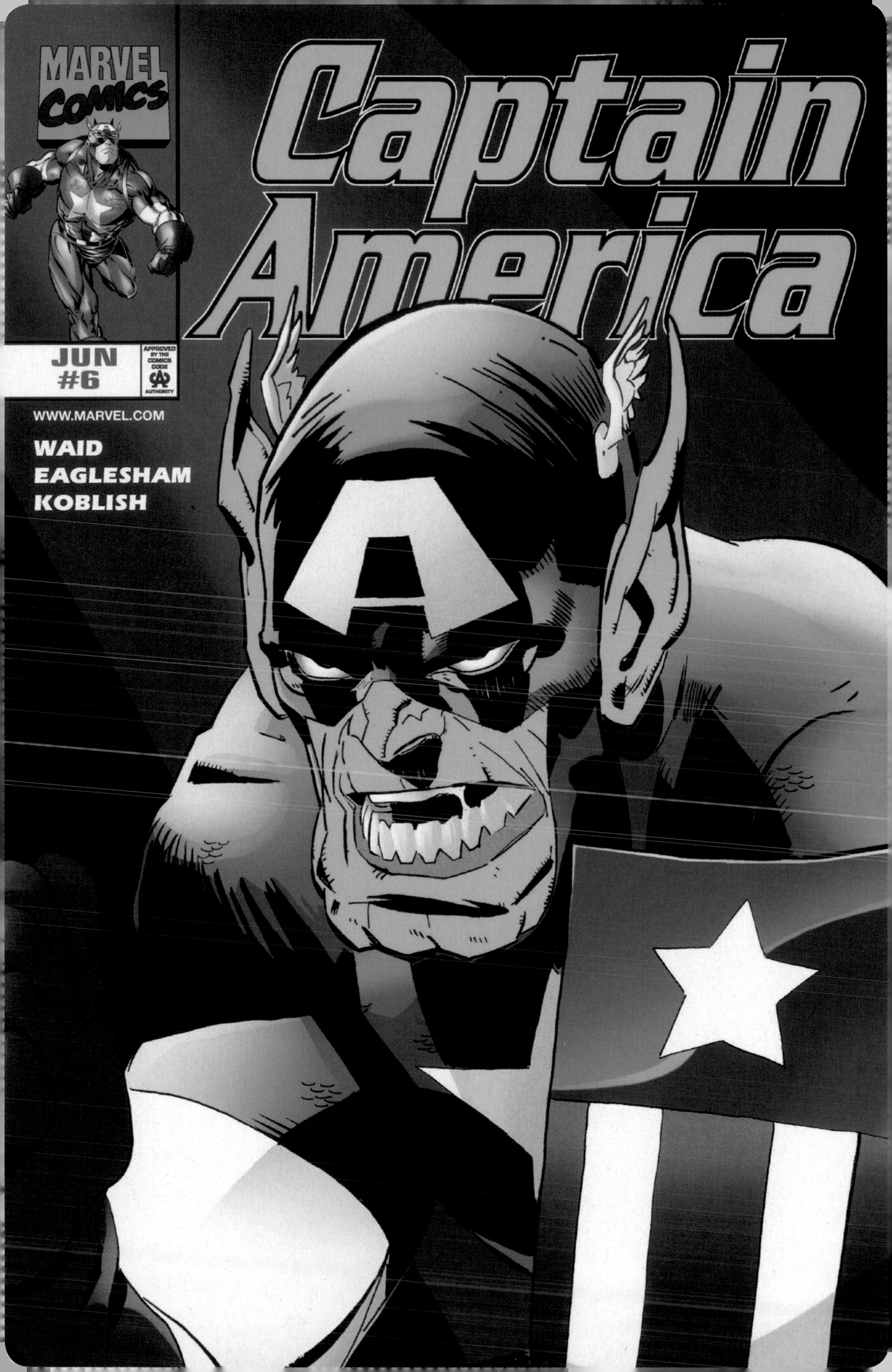
MARVEL COMICS
Captain America
JUN #6
APPROVED BY THE COMICS CODE AUTHORITY
WWW.MARVEL.COM
WAID
EAGLESHAM
KOBLISH

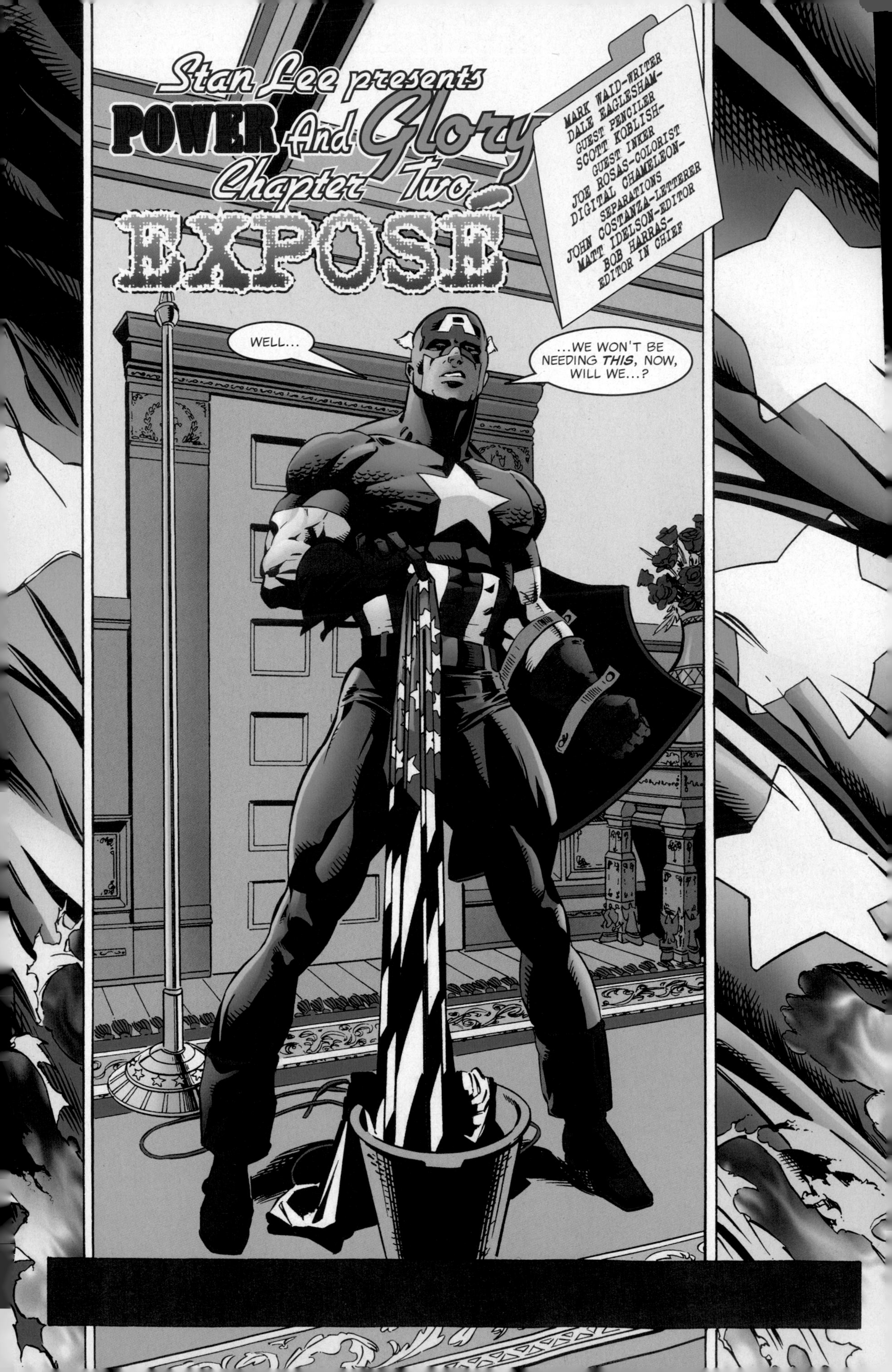
Stan Lee presents
POWER And Glory
Chapter Two:
EXPOSÉ
MARK WAID-WRITER
DALE EAGLESHAM-GUEST PENCILER
SCOTT KOBLISH-GUEST INKER
JOE ROSAS-COLORIST
CHAMELEON-DIGITAL CHAMELEON SEPARATIONS
JOHN COSTANZA-LETTERER
MATT IDELSON-EDITOR
BOB HARRAS-EDITOR IN CHIEF
WELL...
...WE WON'T BE NEEDING THIS, NOW, WILL WE...?
[redacted]

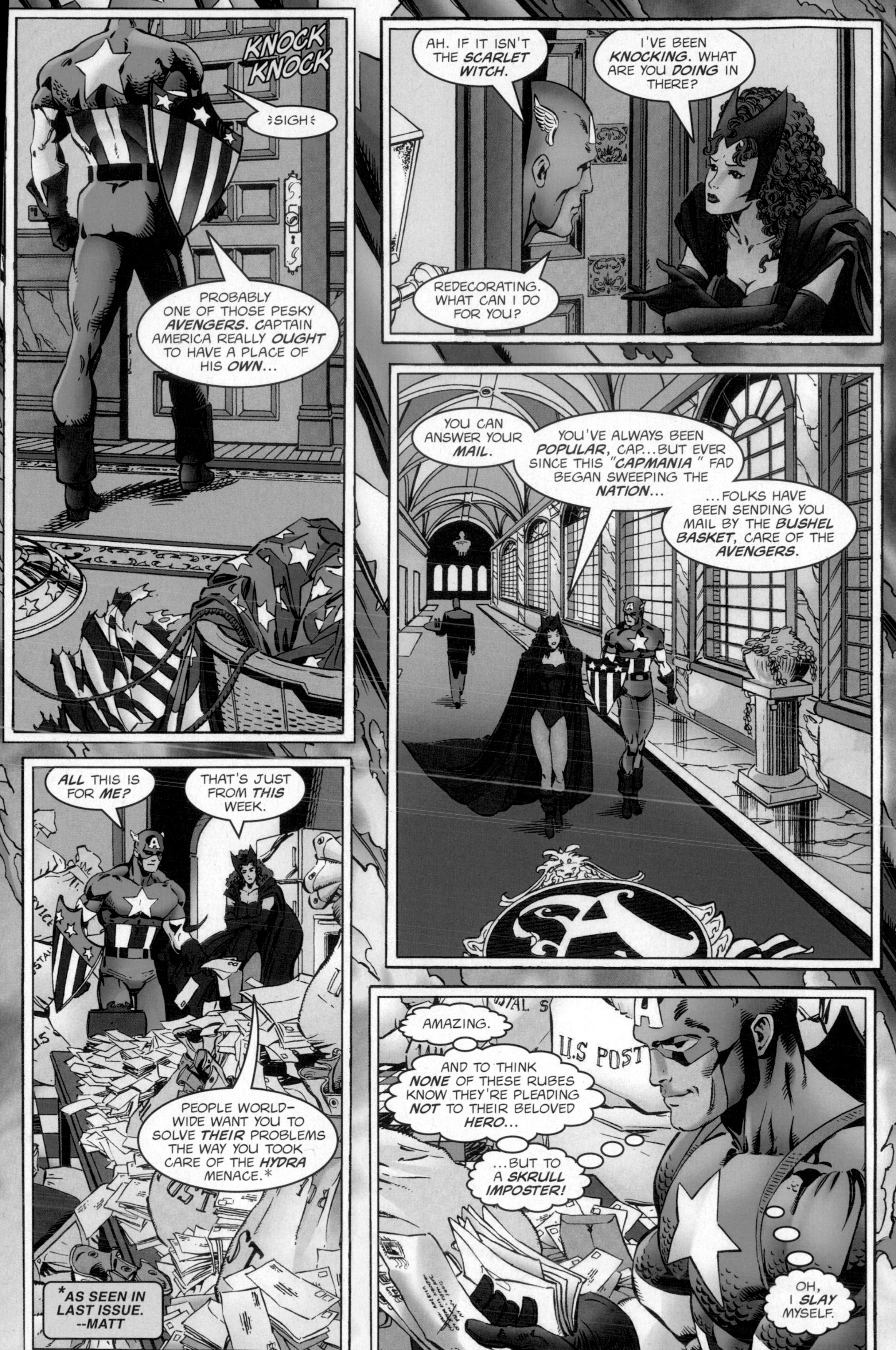
KNOCK KNOCK
SIGH
PROBABLY ONE OF THOSE PESKY AVENGERS. CAPTAIN AMERICA REALLY OUGHT TO HAVE A PLACE OF HIS OWN...
AH. IF IT ISN'T THE SCARLET WITCH.
I'VE BEEN KNOCKING. WHAT ARE YOU DOING IN THERE?
REDECORATING. WHAT CAN I DO FOR YOU?
YOU CAN ANSWER YOUR MAIL.
YOU'VE ALWAYS BEEN POPULAR, CAP...BUT EVER SINCE THIS "CAPMANIA" FAD BEGAN SWEEPING THE NATION...
...FOLKS HAVE BEEN SENDING YOU MAIL BY THE BUSHEL BASKET, CARE OF THE AVENGERS.
ALL THIS IS FOR ME?
THAT'S JUST FROM THIS WEEK.
PEOPLE WORLD-WIDE WANT YOU TO SOLVE THEIR PROBLEMS THE WAY YOU TOOK CARE OF THE HYDRA MENACE.*
*AS SEEN IN LAST ISSUE. --MATT
U.S POST
AMAZING.
AND TO THINK NONE OF THESE RUBES KNOW THEY'RE PLEADING NOT TO THEIR BELOVED HERO...
...BUT TO A SKRULL IMPOSTER!
OH, I SLAY MYSELF.

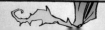

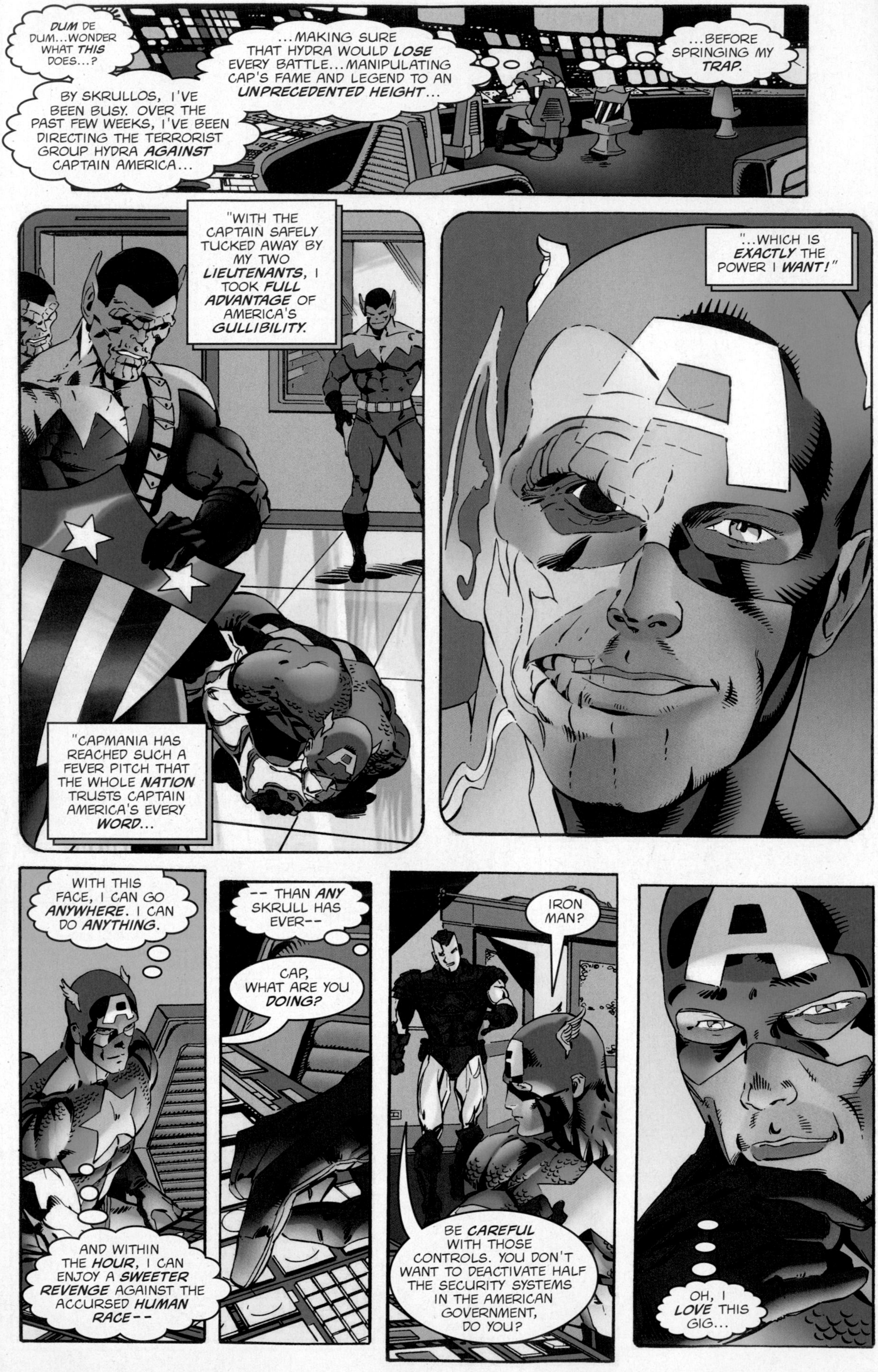
DUM DE DUM...WONDER WHAT THIS DOES...?
BY SKRULLOS, I'VE BEEN BUSY. OVER THE PAST FEW WEEKS, I'VE BEEN DIRECTING THE TERRORIST GROUP HYDRA AGAINST CAPTAIN AMERICA...
...MAKING SURE THAT HYDRA WOULD LOSE EVERY BATTLE...MANIPULATING CAP'S FAME AND LEGEND TO AN UNPRECEDENTED HEIGHT...
...BEFORE SPRINGING MY TRAP.
"WITH THE CAPTAIN SAFELY TUCKED AWAY BY MY TWO LIEUTENANTS, I TOOK FULL ADVANTAGE OF AMERICA'S GULLIBILITY.
"CAPMANIA HAS REACHED SUCH A FEVER PITCH THAT THE WHOLE NATION TRUSTS CAPTAIN AMERICA'S EVERY WORD...
"...WHICH IS EXACTLY THE POWER I WANT!"
WITH THIS FACE, I CAN GO ANYWHERE. I CAN DO ANYTHING.
AND WITHIN THE HOUR, I CAN ENJOY A SWEETER REVENGE AGAINST THE ACCURSED HUMAN RACE--
-- THAN ANY SKRULL HAS EVER--
CAP, WHAT ARE YOU DOING?
IRON MAN?
BE CAREFUL WITH THOSE CONTROLS. YOU DON'T WANT TO DEACTIVATE HALF THE SECURITY SYSTEMS IN THE AMERICAN GOVERNMENT, DO YOU?
OH, I LOVE THIS GIG...

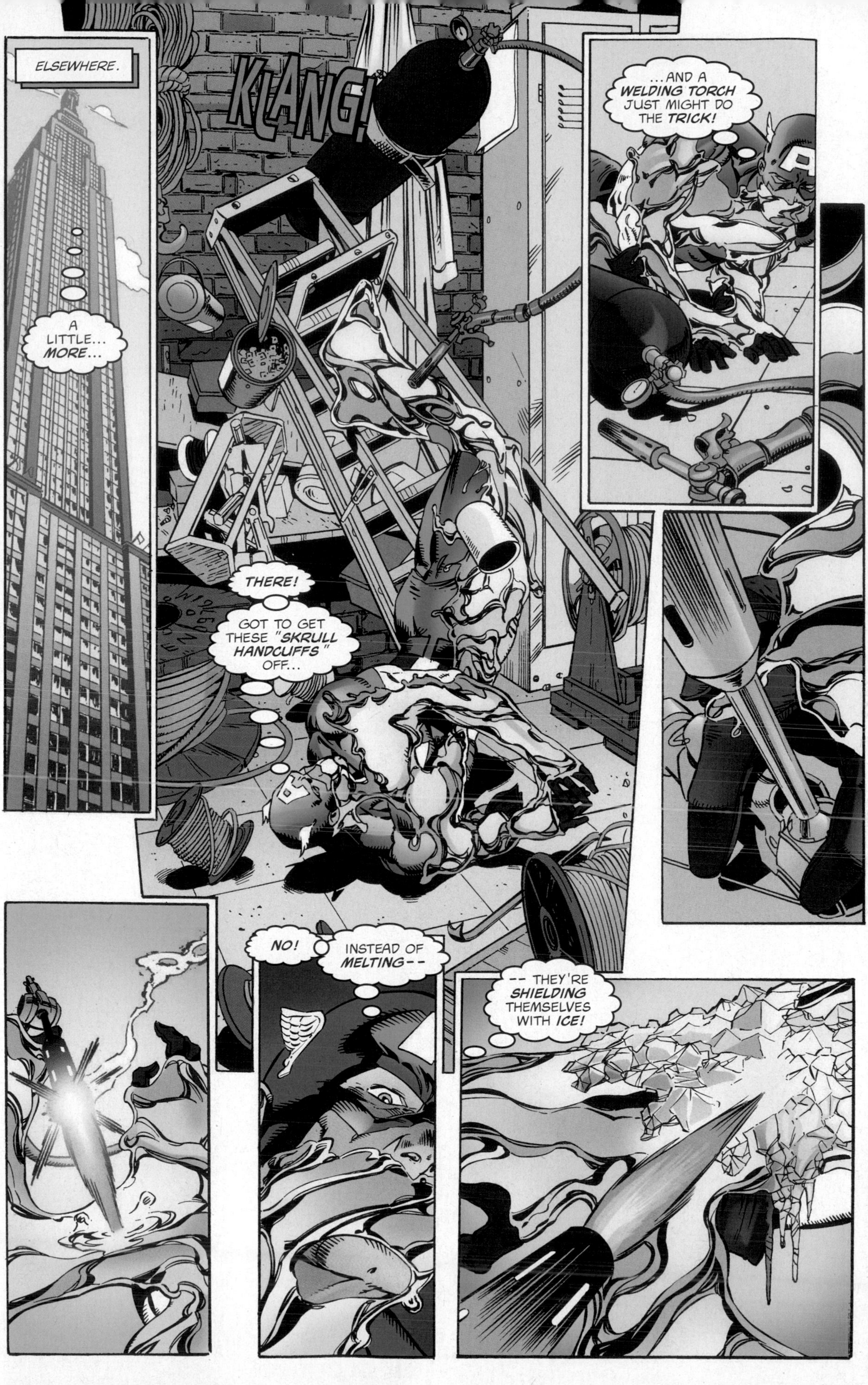
ELSEWHERE.
A LITTLE... MORE...
KLANG!
THERE!
GOT TO GET THESE "SKRULL HANDCUFFS" OFF...
...AND A WELDING TORCH JUST MIGHT DO THE TRICK!
NO!
INSTEAD OF MELTING--
-- THEY'RE SHIELDING THEMSELVES WITH ICE!

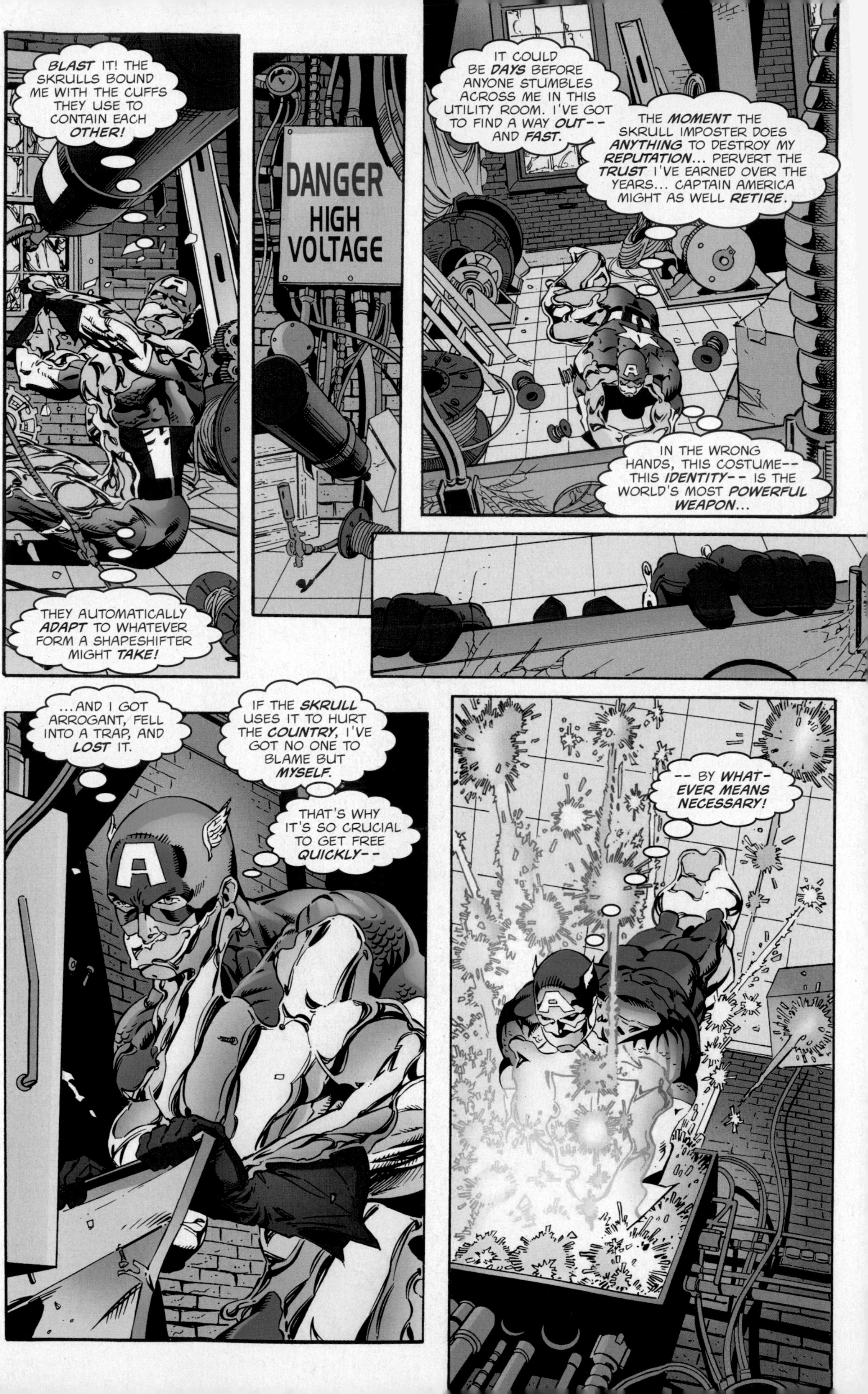
BLAST IT! THE SKRULLS BOUND ME WITH THE CUFFS THEY USE TO CONTAIN EACH OTHER!
THEY AUTOMATICALLY ADAPT TO WHATEVER FORM A SHAPESHIFTER MIGHT TAKE!
DANGER
HIGH VOLTAGE
IT COULD BE DAYS BEFORE ANYONE STUMBLES ACROSS ME IN THIS UTILITY ROOM. I'VE GOT TO FIND A WAY OUT-- AND FAST.
THE MOMENT THE SKRULL IMPOSTER DOES ANYTHING TO DESTROY MY REPUTATION... PERVERT THE TRUST I'VE EARNED OVER THE YEARS... CAPTAIN AMERICA MIGHT AS WELL RETIRE.
IN THE WRONG HANDS, THIS COSTUME-- THIS IDENTITY-- IS THE WORLD'S MOST POWERFUL WEAPON...
...AND I GOT ARROGANT, FELL INTO A TRAP, AND LOST IT.
IF THE SKRULL USES IT TO HURT THE COUNTRY, I'VE GOT NO ONE TO BLAME BUT MYSELF.
THAT'S WHY IT'S SO CRUCIAL TO GET FREE QUICKLY--
-- BY WHAT-EVER MEANS NECESSARY!

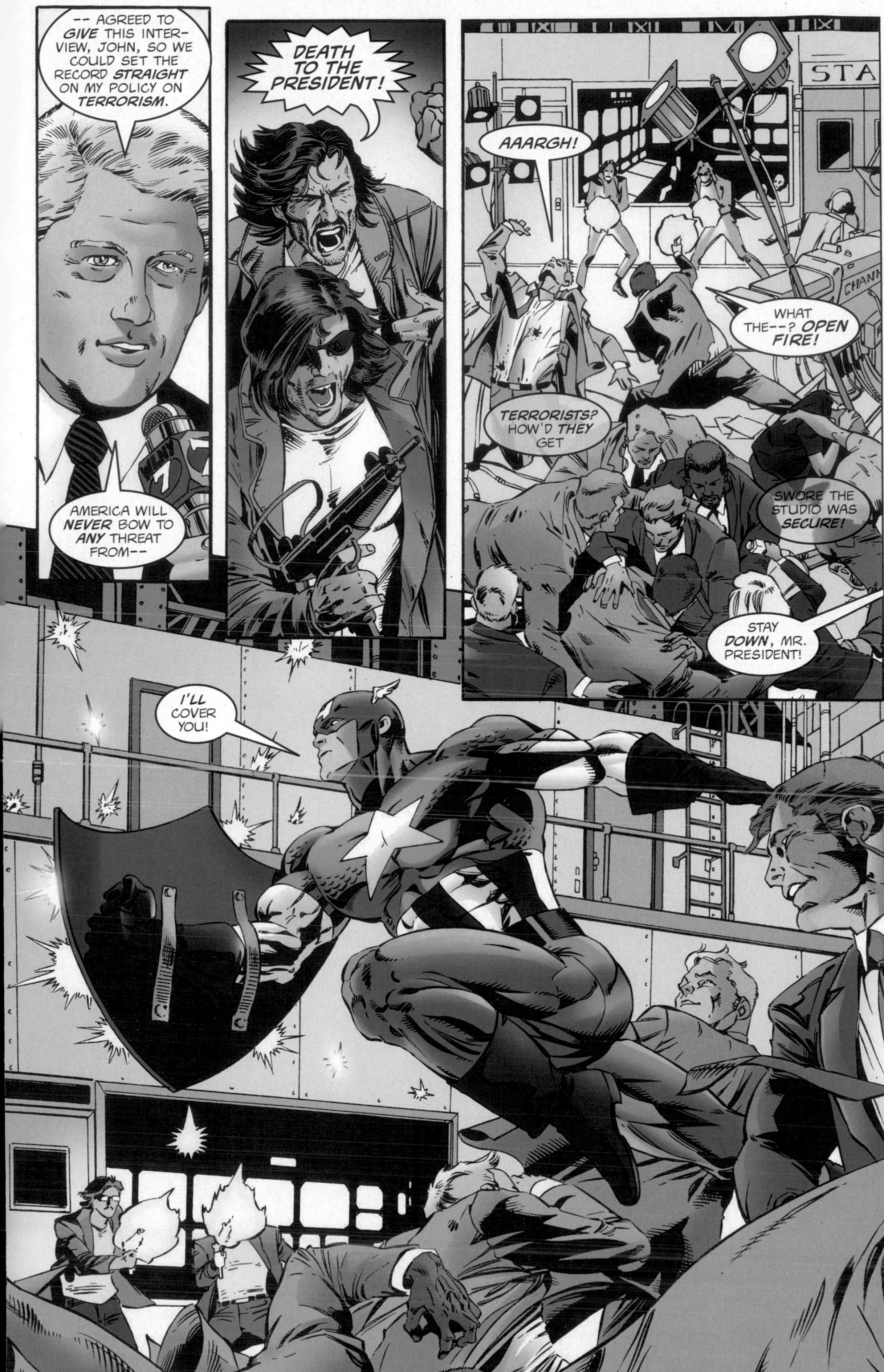
-- AGREED TO GIVE THIS INTERVIEW, JOHN, SO WE COULD SET THE RECORD STRAIGHT ON MY POLICY ON TERRORISM.
AMERICA WILL NEVER BOW TO ANY THREAT FROM--
DEATH TO THE PRESIDENT!
AAARGH!
WHAT THE--? OPEN FIRE!
TERRORISTS? HOW'D THEY GET
SWORE THE STUDIO WAS SECURE!
STAY DOWN, MR. PRESIDENT!
I'LL COVER YOU!

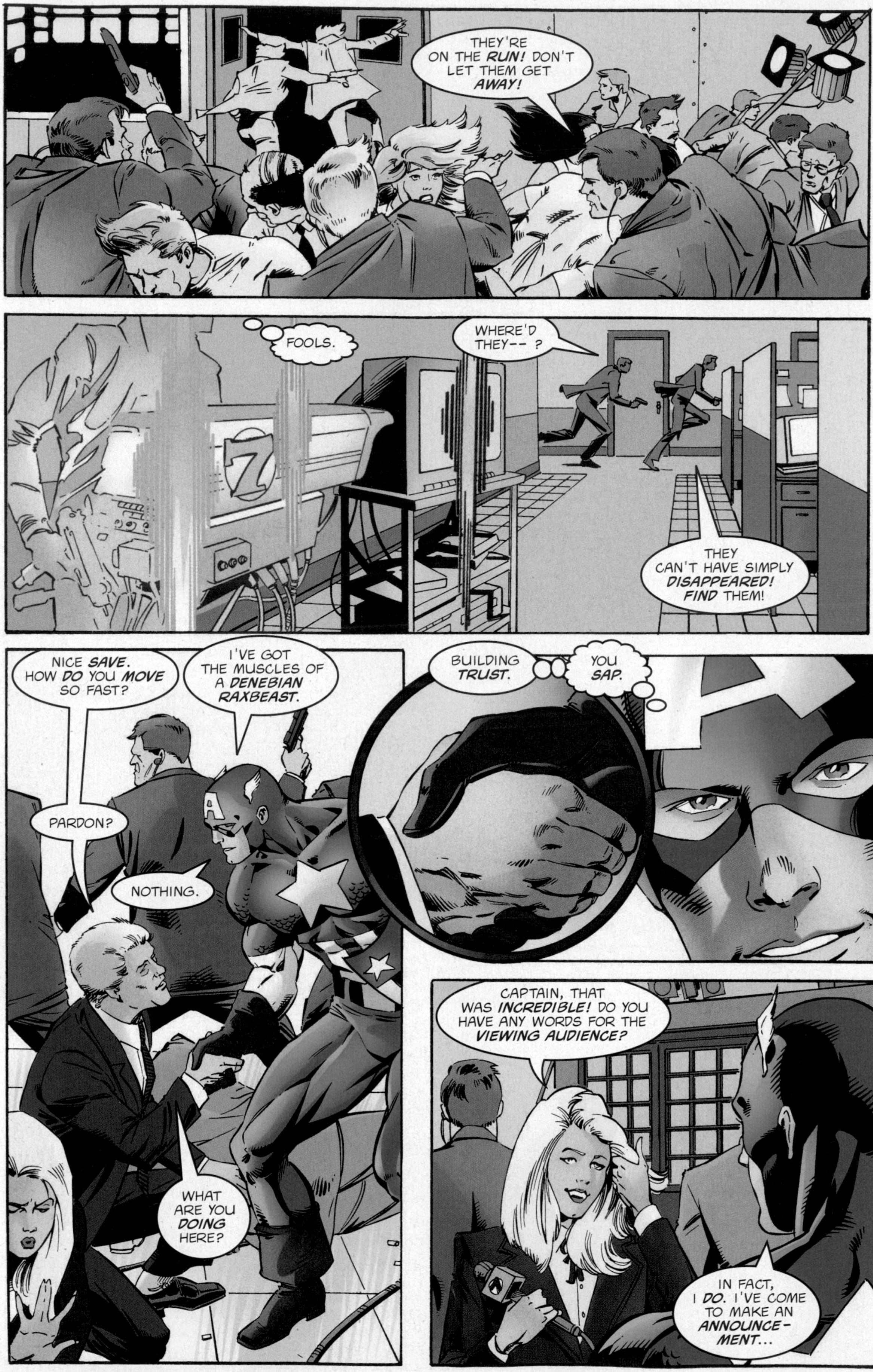
THEY'RE ON THE RUN! DON'T LET THEM GET AWAY!
FOOLS.
WHERE'D THEY-- ?
THEY CAN'T HAVE SIMPLY DISAPPEARED! FIND THEM!
NICE SAVE. HOW DO YOU MOVE SO FAST?
I'VE GOT THE MUSCLES OF A DENEBIAN RAXBEAST.
PARDON?
NOTHING.
WHAT ARE YOU DOING HERE?
BUILDING TRUST.
YOU SAP.
CAPTAIN, THAT WAS INCREDIBLE! DO YOU HAVE ANY WORDS FOR THE VIEWING AUDIENCE?
IN FACT, I DO. I'VE COME TO MAKE AN ANNOUNCE-MENT...

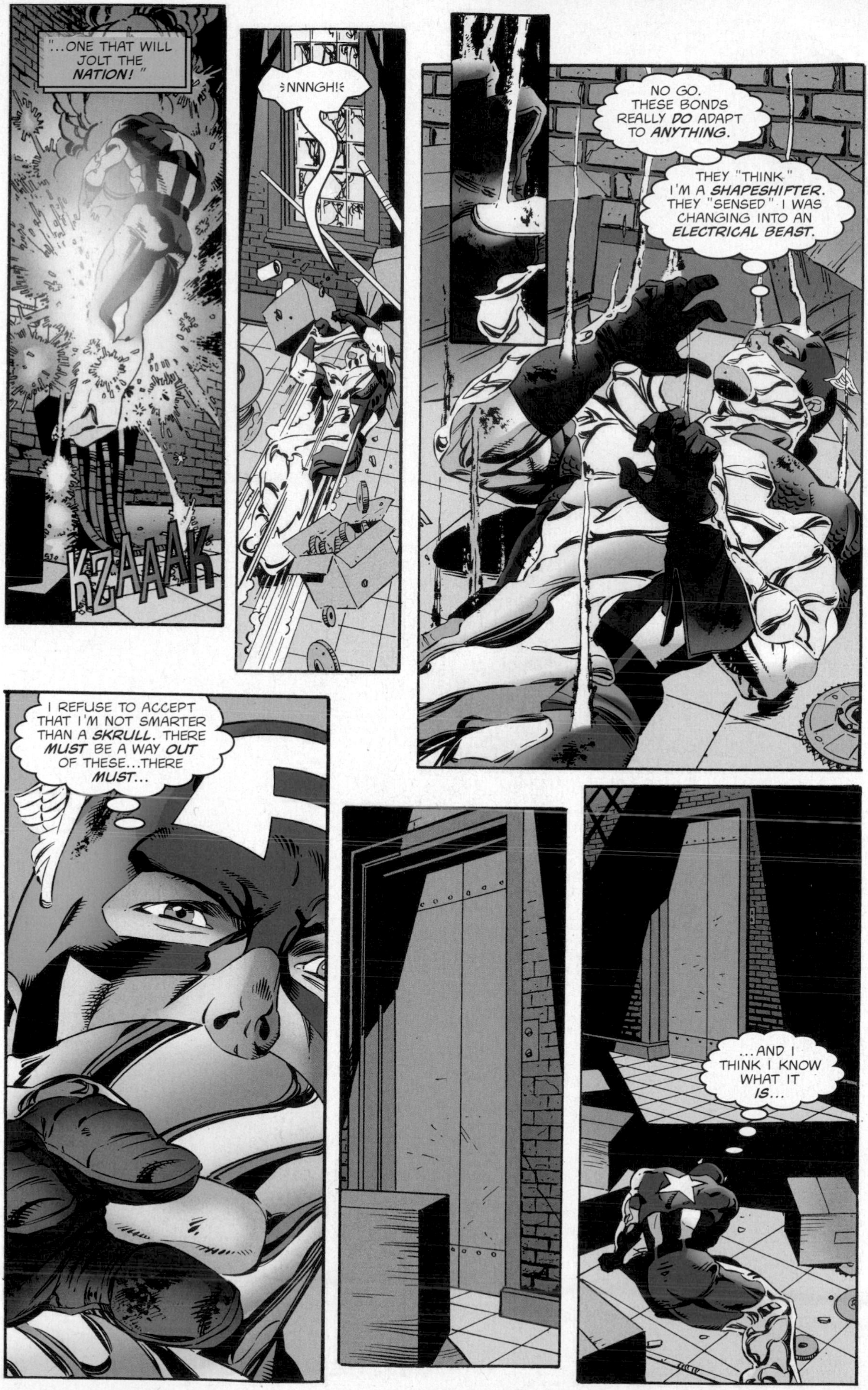
"...ONE THAT WILL JOLT THE NATION!"
KZAAAK
NNNGH!
NO GO. THESE BONDS REALLY DO ADAPT TO ANYTHING.
THEY "THINK" I'M A SHAPESHIFTER. THEY "SENSED" I WAS CHANGING INTO AN ELECTRICAL BEAST.
I REFUSE TO ACCEPT THAT I'M NOT SMARTER THAN A SKRULL. THERE MUST BE A WAY OUT OF THESE...THERE MUST...
...AND I THINK I KNOW WHAT IT IS...

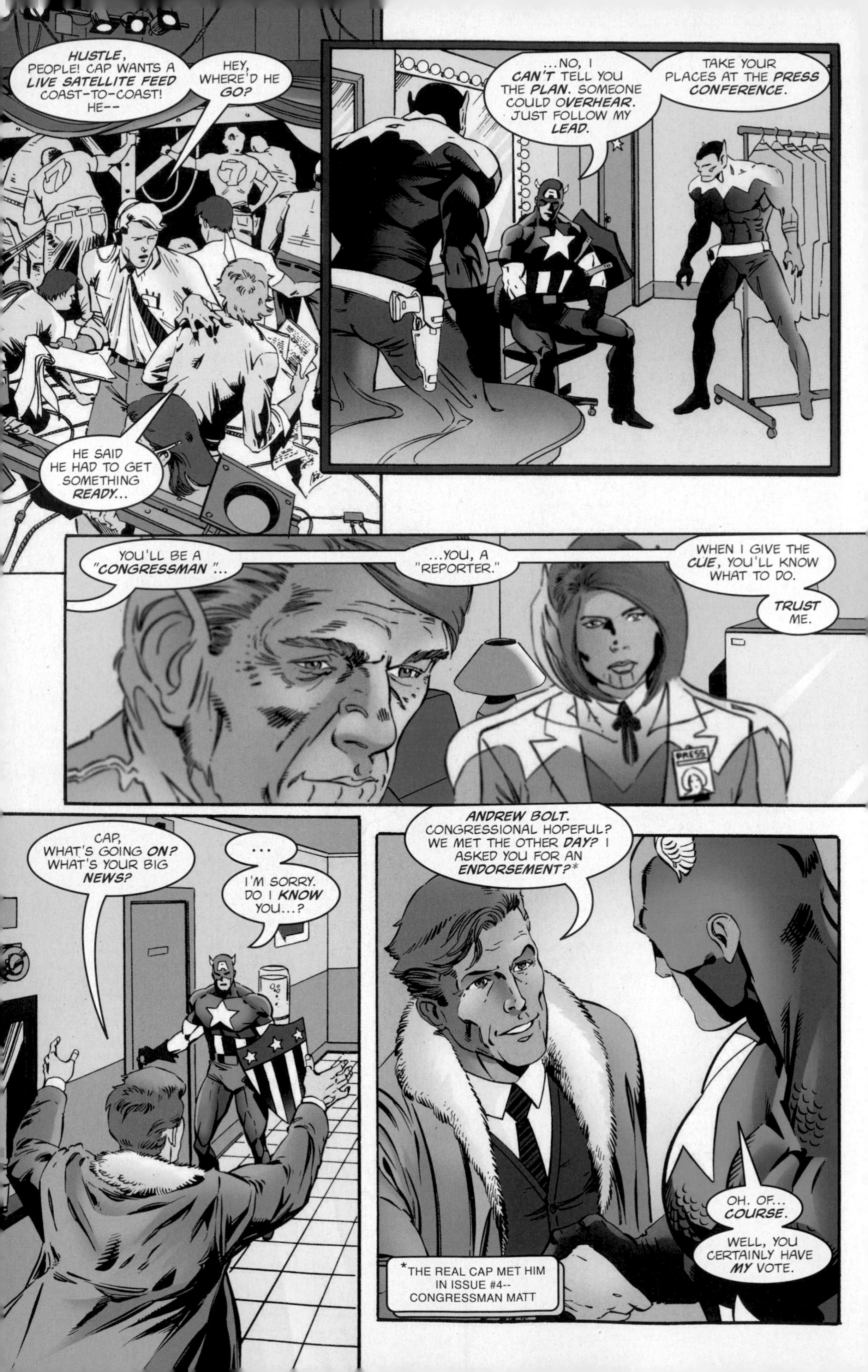

HUSTLE, PEOPLE! CAP WANTS A LIVE SATELLITE FEED COAST-TO-COAST! HE--
HEY, WHERE'D HE GO?
HE SAID HE HAD TO GET SOMETHING READY...
...NO, I CAN'T TELL YOU THE PLAN. SOMEONE COULD OVERHEAR. JUST FOLLOW MY LEAD.
TAKE YOUR PLACES AT THE PRESS CONFERENCE.
YOU'LL BE A "CONGRESSMAN"...
...YOU, A "REPORTER."
WHEN I GIVE THE CUE, YOU'LL KNOW WHAT TO DO.
TRUST ME.
PRESS
CAP, WHAT'S GOING ON? WHAT'S YOUR BIG NEWS?
...
I'M SORRY. DO I KNOW YOU...?
ANDREW BOLT. CONGRESSIONAL HOPEFUL? WE MET THE OTHER DAY? I ASKED YOU FOR AN ENDORSEMENT?*
OH. OF... COURSE.
WELL, YOU CERTAINLY HAVE MY VOTE.
*THE REAL CAP MET HIM IN ISSUE #4-- CONGRESSMAN MATT

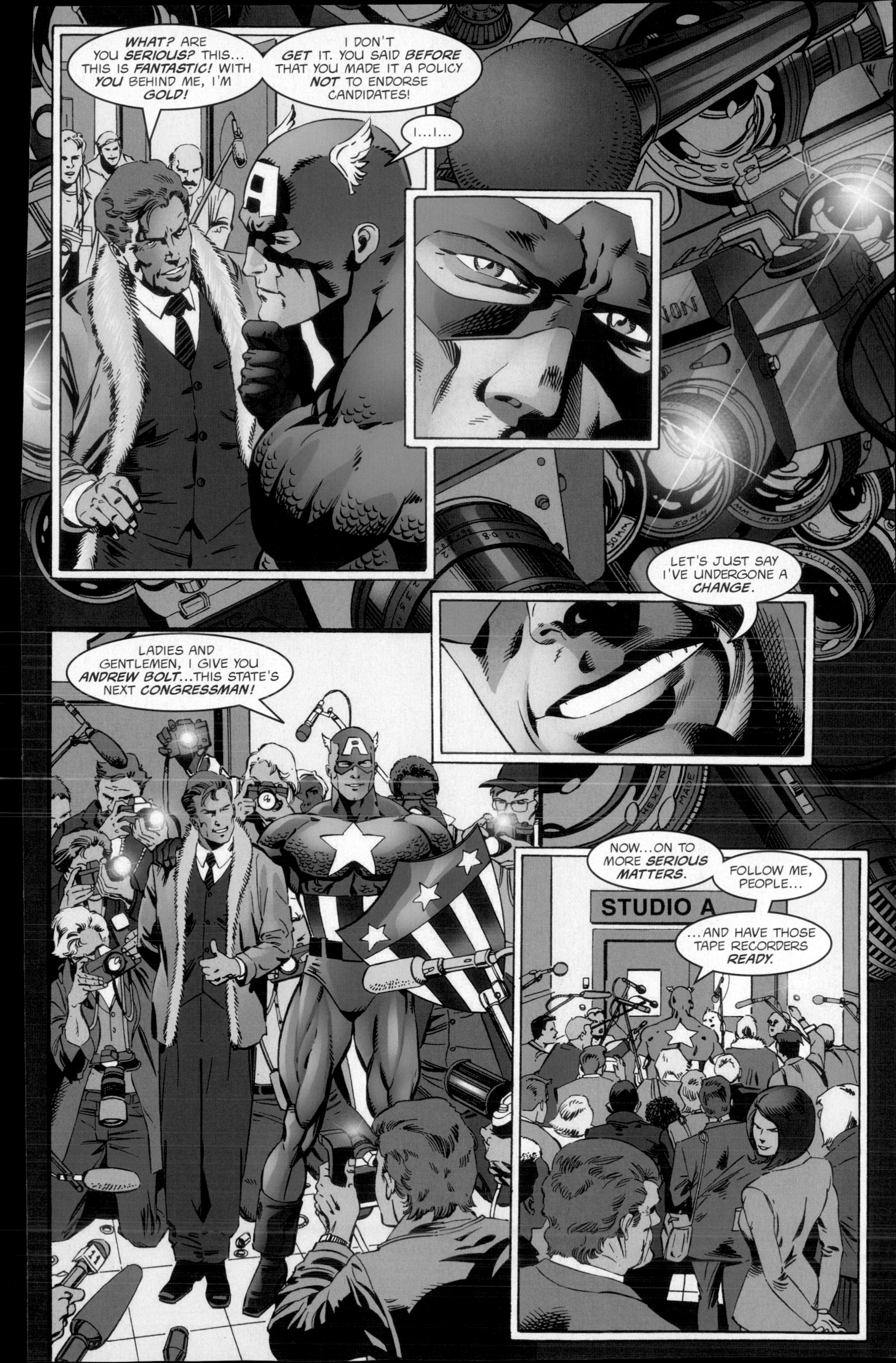
WHAT? ARE YOU SERIOUS? THIS... THIS IS FANTASTIC! WITH YOU BEHIND ME, I'M GOLD!
I DON'T GET IT. YOU SAID BEFORE THAT YOU MADE IT A POLICY NOT TO ENDORSE CANDIDATES!
I...I...
LET'S JUST SAY I'VE UNDERGONE A CHANGE.
LADIES AND GENTLEMEN, I GIVE YOU ANDREW BOLT...THIS STATE'S NEXT CONGRESSMAN!
NOW...ON TO MORE SERIOUS MATTERS.
FOLLOW ME, PEOPLE...
STUDIO A
...AND HAVE THOSE TAPE RECORDERS READY.

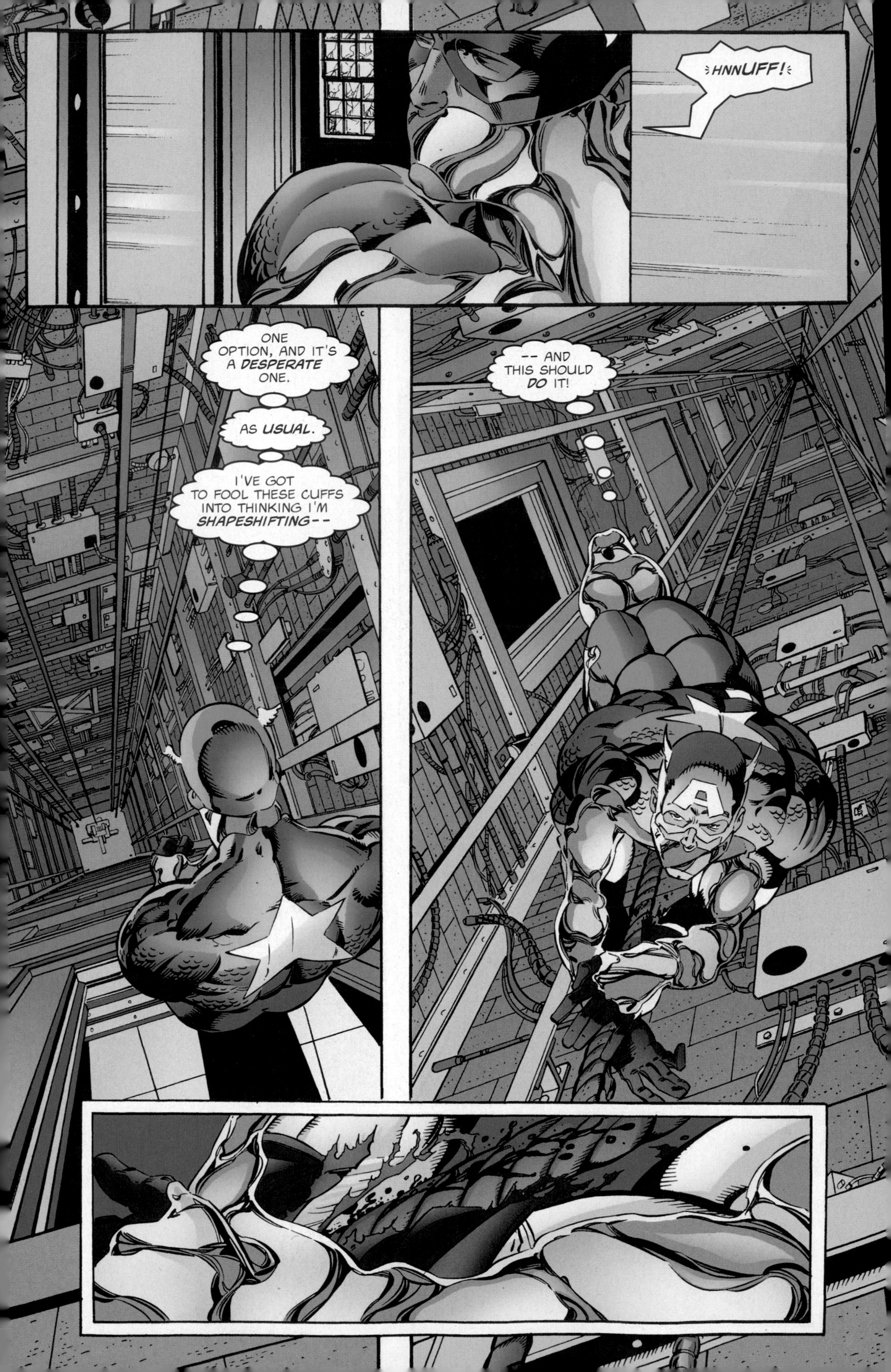
HNNUFF!
ONE OPTION, AND IT'S A DESPERATE ONE.
AS USUAL.
I'VE GOT TO FOOL THESE CUFFS INTO THINKING I'M SHAPESHIFTING--
-- AND THIS SHOULD DO IT!

MMMRRGHH!
COME ON...
...COME ON...
...YES!

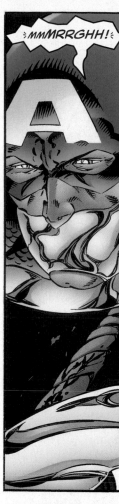

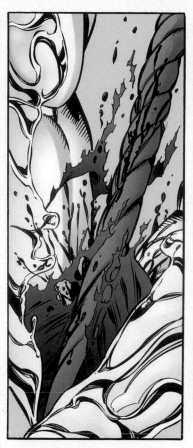

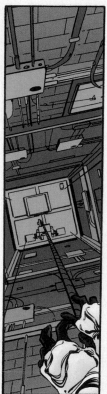

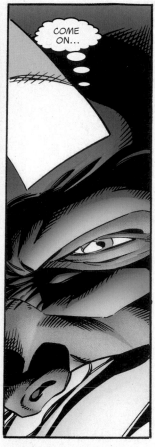

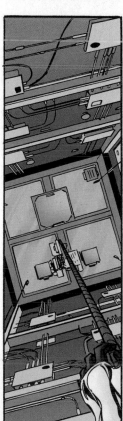

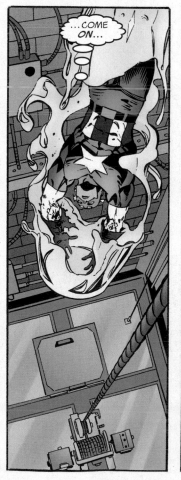

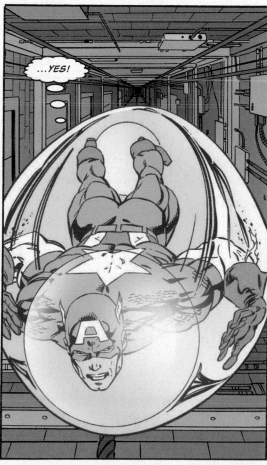

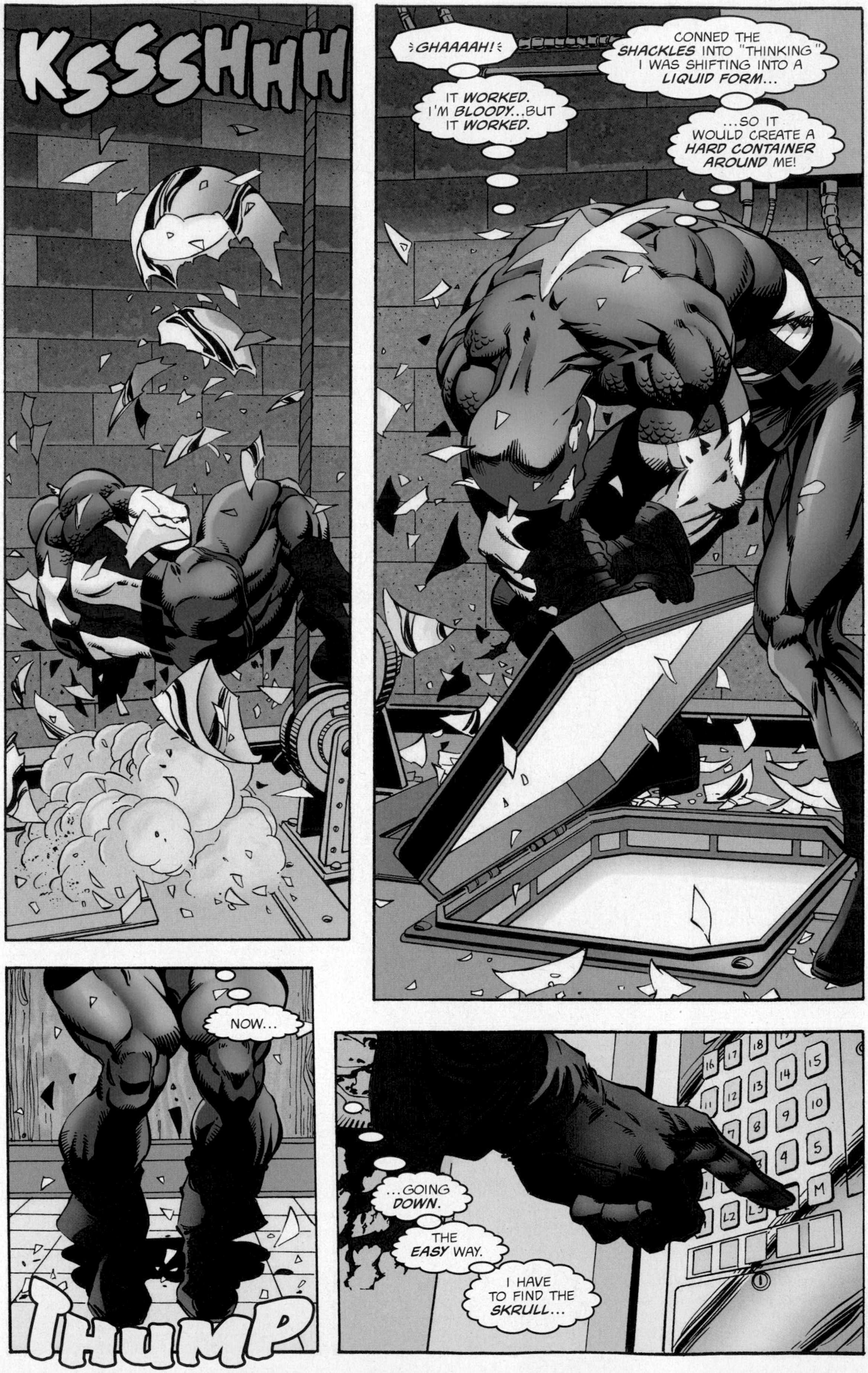
KSSSHHH
GHAAAAH!
IT WORKED. I'M BLOODY...BUT IT WORKED.
CONNED THE SHACKLES INTO "THINKING" I WAS SHIFTING INTO A LIQUID FORM...
...SO IT WOULD CREATE A HARD CONTAINER AROUND ME!
NOW...
THUMP
...GOING DOWN.
THE EASY WAY.
I HAVE TO FIND THE SKRULL...

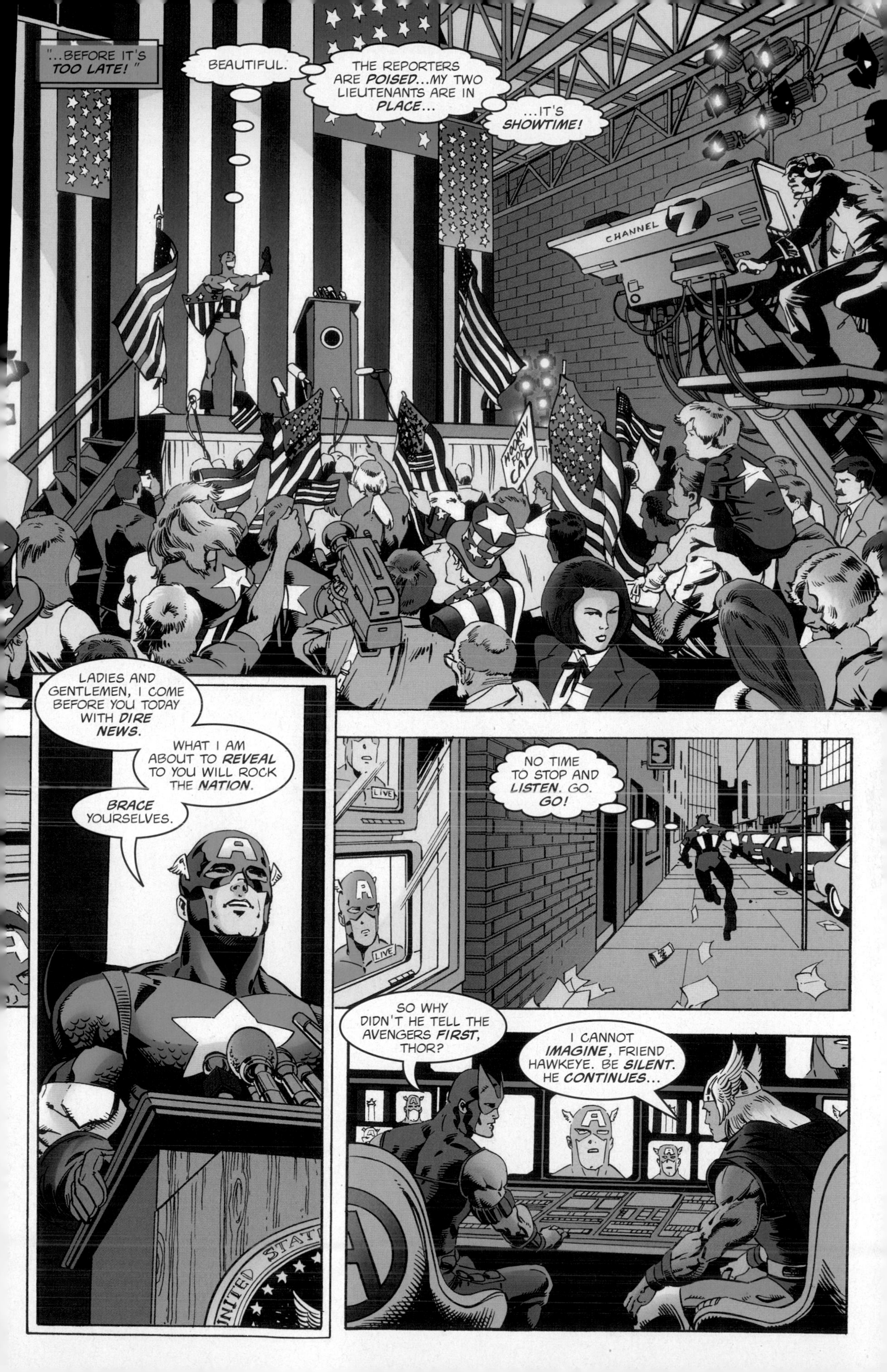

"...BEFORE IT'S TOO LATE!"
BEAUTIFUL.
THE REPORTERS ARE POISED...MY TWO LIEUTENANTS ARE IN PLACE...
...IT'S SHOWTIME!
CHANNEL 7
HOORAY FOR CAP
LADIES AND GENTLEMEN, I COME BEFORE YOU TODAY WITH DIRE NEWS.
WHAT I AM ABOUT TO REVEAL TO YOU WILL ROCK THE NATION.
BRACE YOURSELVES.
LIVE
LIVE
5
NO TIME TO STOP AND LISTEN. GO. GO!
SO WHY DIDN'T HE TELL THE AVENGERS FIRST, THOR?
I CANNOT IMAGINE, FRIEND HAWKEYE. BE SILENT. HE CONTINUES...
UNITED STAT

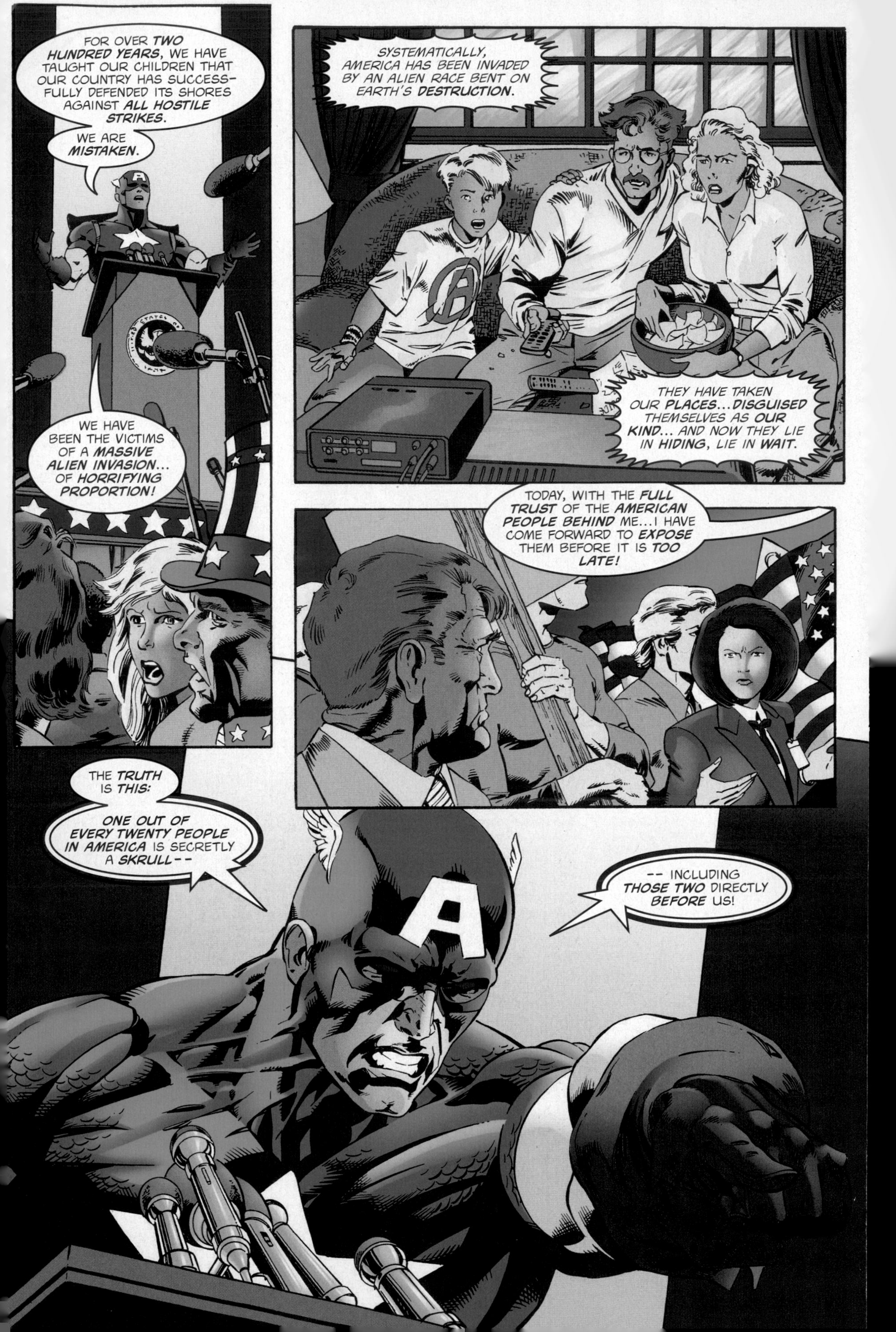
FOR OVER TWO HUNDRED YEARS, WE HAVE TAUGHT OUR CHILDREN THAT OUR COUNTRY HAS SUCCESSFULLY DEFENDED ITS SHORES AGAINST ALL HOSTILE STRIKES.
WE ARE MISTAKEN.
SYSTEMATICALLY, AMERICA HAS BEEN INVADED BY AN ALIEN RACE BENT ON EARTH'S DESTRUCTION.
THEY HAVE TAKEN OUR PLACES...DISGUISED THEMSELVES AS OUR KIND... AND NOW THEY LIE IN HIDING, LIE IN WAIT.
WE HAVE BEEN THE VICTIMS OF A MASSIVE ALIEN INVASION... OF HORRIFYING PROPORTION!
TODAY, WITH THE FULL TRUST OF THE AMERICAN PEOPLE BEHIND ME...I HAVE COME FORWARD TO EXPOSE THEM BEFORE IT IS TOO LATE!
THE TRUTH IS THIS:
ONE OUT OF EVERY TWENTY PEOPLE IN AMERICA IS SECRETLY A SKRULL--
-- INCLUDING THOSE TWO DIRECTLY BEFORE US!

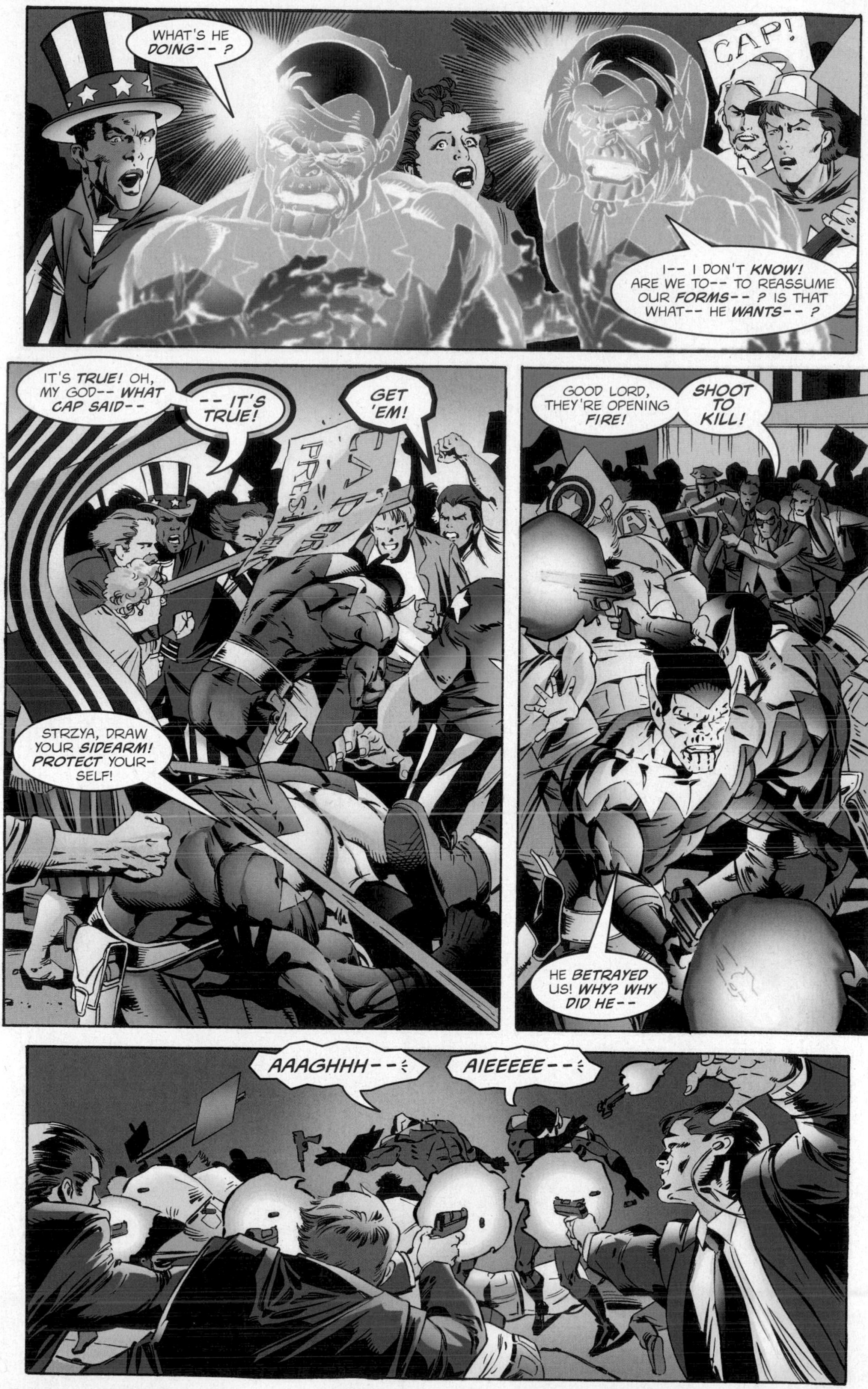
WHAT'S HE DOING-- ?
CAP!
I-- I DON'T KNOW! ARE WE TO-- TO REASSUME OUR FORMS-- ? IS THAT WHAT-- HE WANTS-- ?
IT'S TRUE! OH, MY GOD-- WHAT CAP SAID--
--IT'S TRUE!
GET 'EM!
CAP FOR PRESIDENT
STRZYA, DRAW YOUR SIDEARM! PROTECT YOURSELF!
GOOD LORD, THEY'RE OPENING FIRE!
SHOOT TO KILL!
HE BETRAYED US! WHY? WHY DID HE--
AAAGHHH--
AIEEEEE--

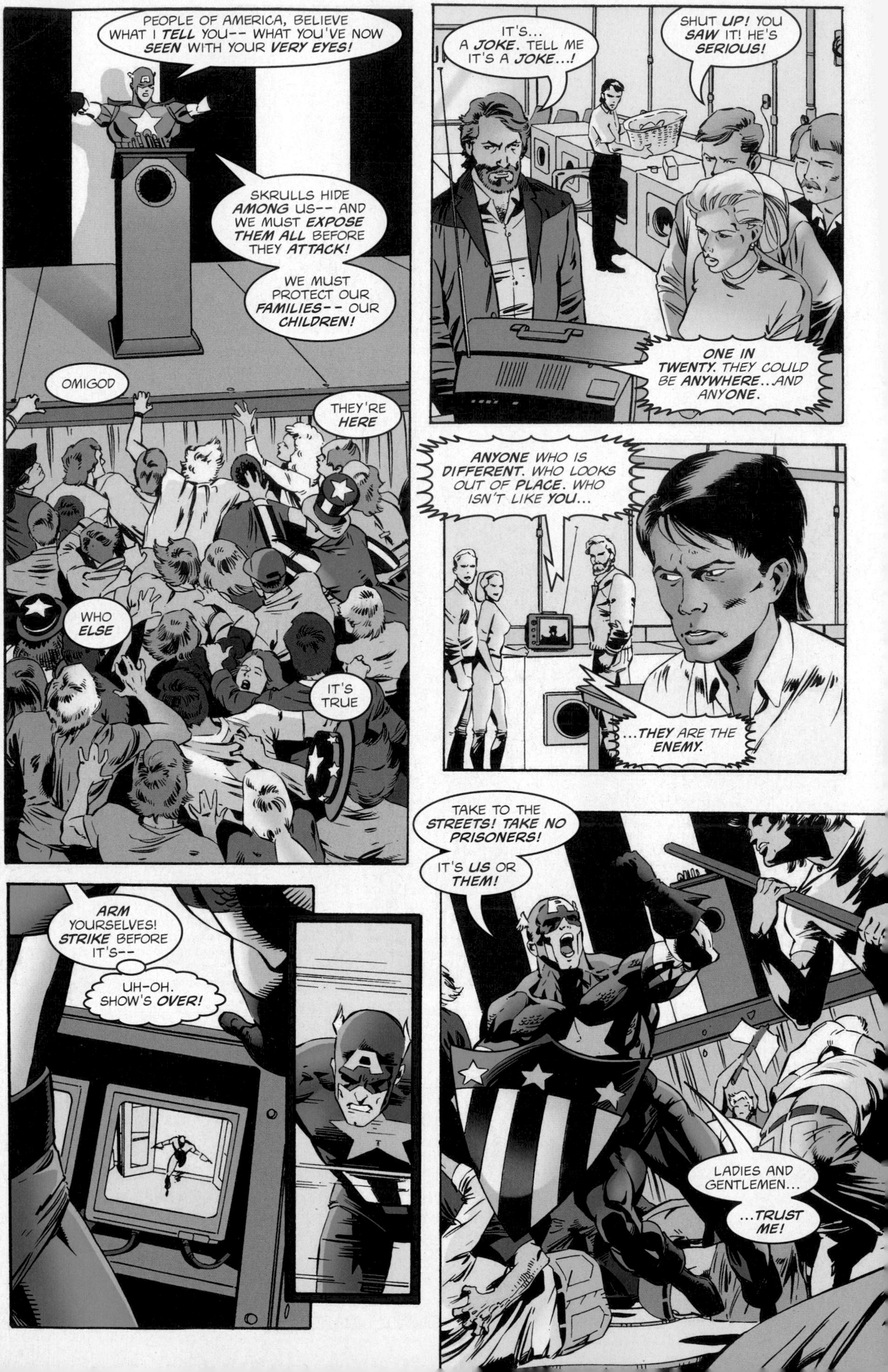

PEOPLE OF AMERICA, BELIEVE WHAT I TELL YOU-- WHAT YOU'VE NOW SEEN WITH YOUR VERY EYES!
SKRULLS HIDE AMONG US-- AND WE MUST EXPOSE THEM ALL BEFORE THEY ATTACK!
WE MUST PROTECT OUR FAMILIES-- OUR CHILDREN!
OMIGOD
THEY'RE HERE
WHO ELSE
IT'S TRUE
IT'S... A JOKE. TELL ME IT'S A JOKE...!
SHUT UP! YOU SAW IT! HE'S SERIOUS!
ONE IN TWENTY. THEY COULD BE ANYWHERE...AND ANYONE.
ANYONE WHO IS DIFFERENT. WHO LOOKS OUT OF PLACE. WHO ISN'T LIKE YOU...
...THEY ARE THE ENEMY.
ARM YOURSELVES! STRIKE BEFORE IT'S--
UH-OH. SHOW'S OVER!
TAKE TO THE STREETS! TAKE NO PRISONERS!
IT'S US OR THEM!
LADIES AND GENTLEMEN...
...TRUST ME!

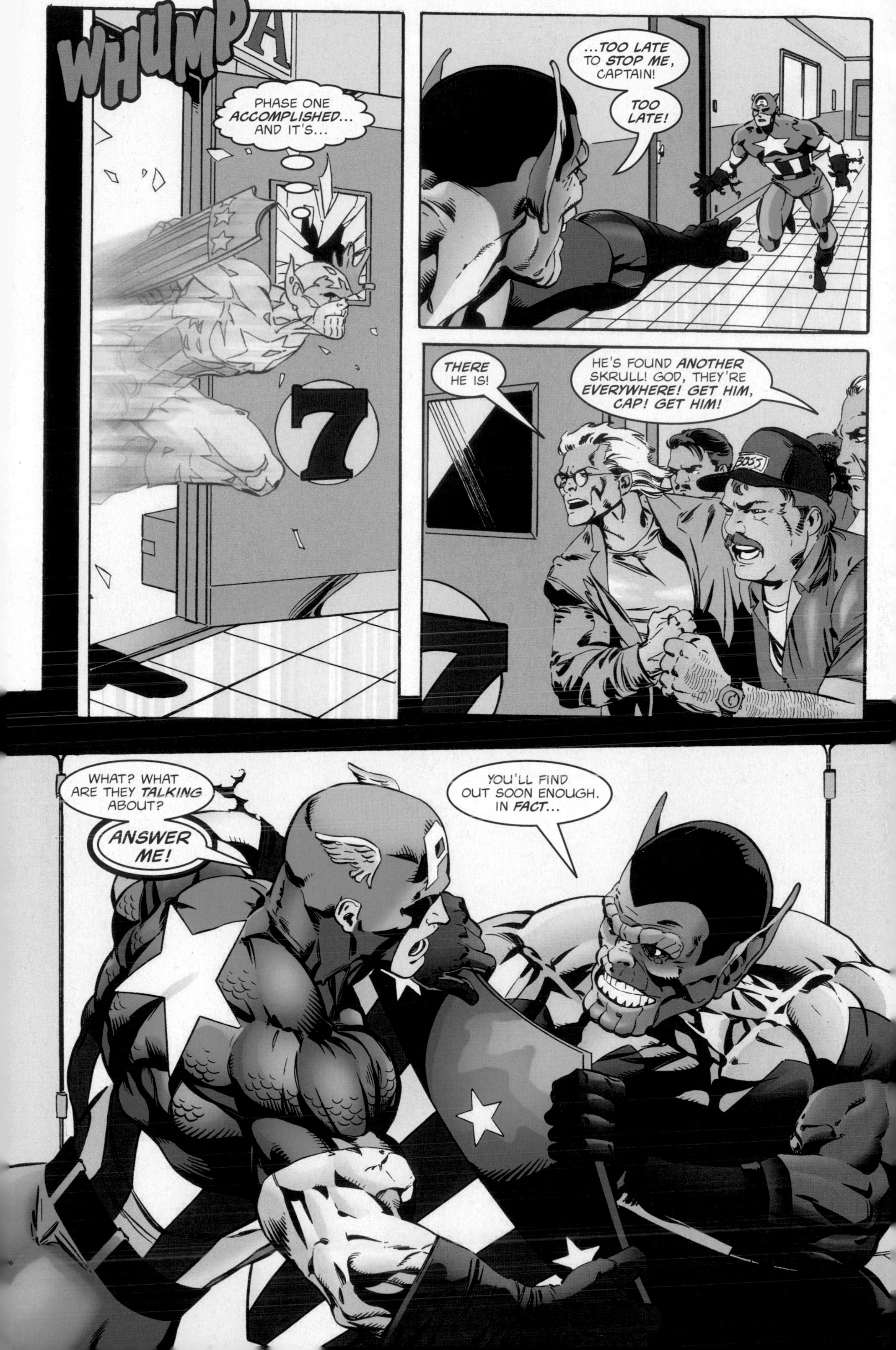
WHUMPA
PHASE ONE ACCOMPLISHED... AND IT'S...
...TOO LATE TO STOP ME, CAPTAIN!
TOO LATE!
THERE HE IS!
HE'S FOUND ANOTHER SKRULL! GOD, THEY'RE EVERYWHERE! GET HIM, CAP! GET HIM!
BOSS
WHAT? WHAT ARE THEY TALKING ABOUT?
ANSWER ME!
YOU'LL FIND OUT SOON ENOUGH. IN FACT...

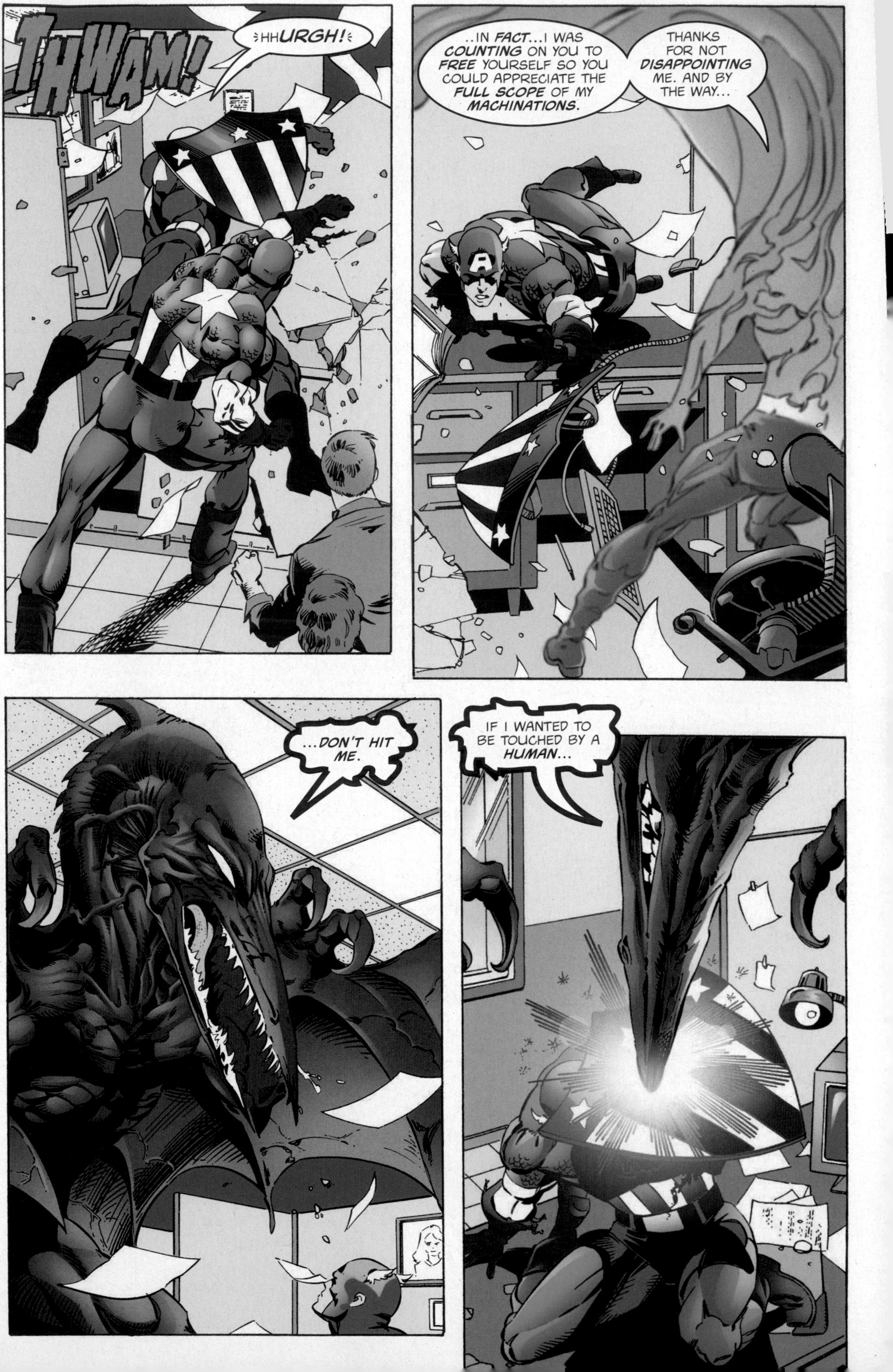
THWAM!
HHURGH!
...IN FACT...I WAS COUNTING ON YOU TO FREE YOURSELF SO YOU COULD APPRECIATE THE FULL SCOPE OF MY MACHINATIONS.
THANKS FOR NOT DISAPPOINTING ME. AND BY THE WAY...
...DON'T HIT ME.
IF I WANTED TO BE TOUCHED BY A HUMAN...

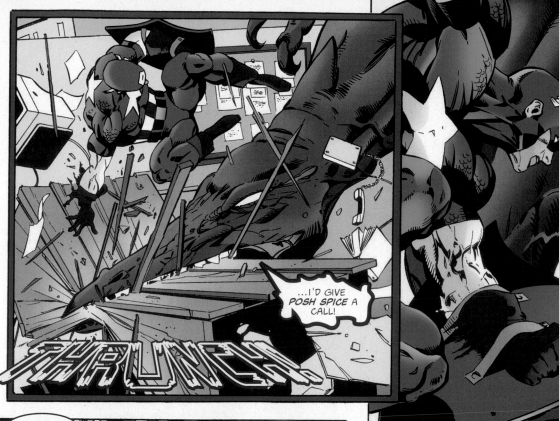

...I'D GIVE POSH SPICE A CALL!

KRRUNCH

I GOT HIM, CAP!

YOU IDIOT! PUT THAT DOWN!

YOU ALMOST HIT CAP!

I WAS AIMING FOR A SKRULL! CAP'S COUNTING ON US TO TAKE THEM OUT!

OF COURSE, IF YOU'RE SO ANXIOUS TO STOP ME--

-- MAYBE YOU GUYS ARE SKRULLS, TOO--!

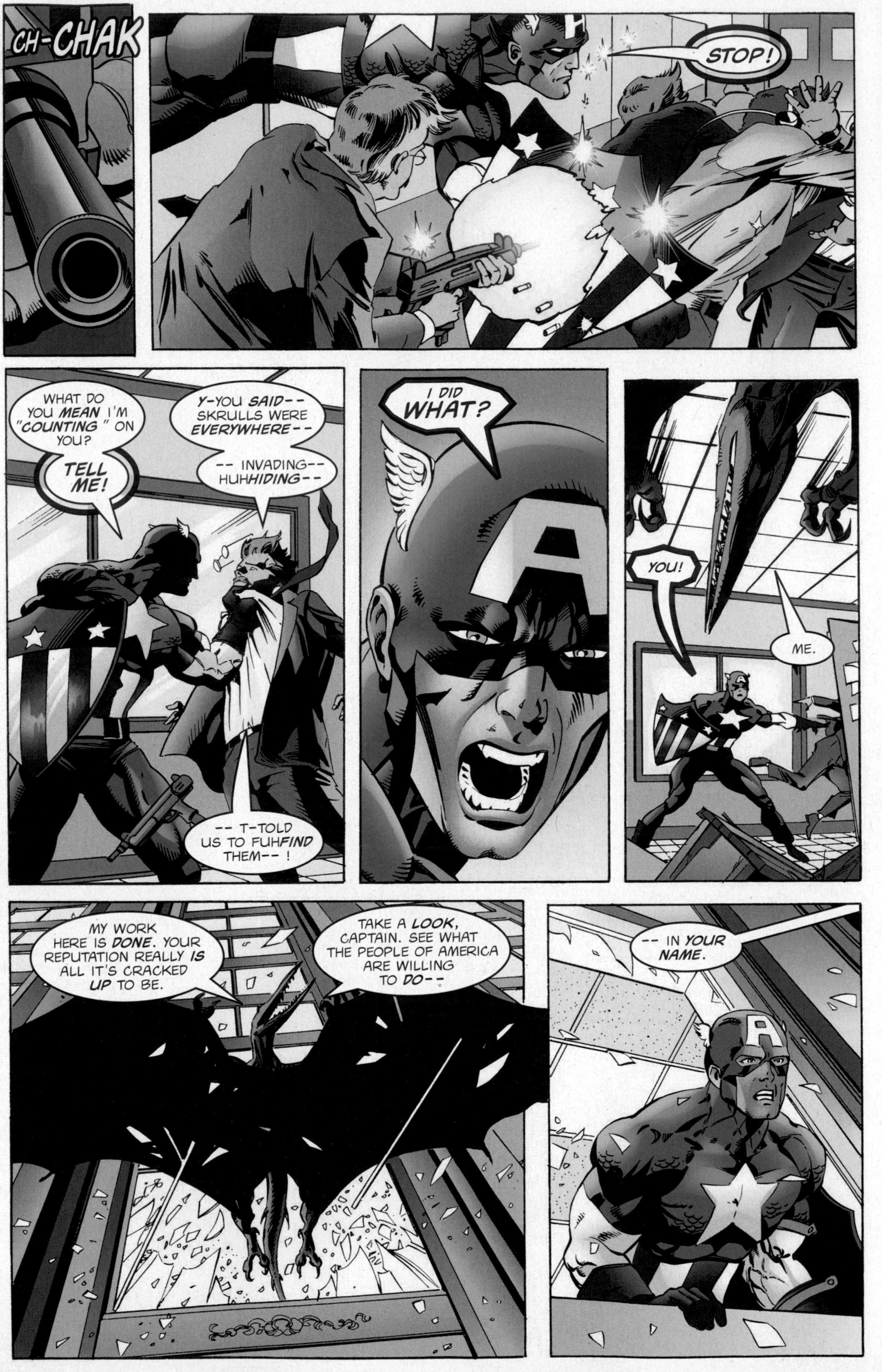
CH-CHAK
STOP!
WHAT DO YOU MEAN I'M "COUNTING" ON YOU?
TELL ME!
Y-YOU SAID-- SKRULLS WERE EVERYWHERE--
-- INVADING-- HUHHIDING--
-- T-TOLD US TO FUHFIND THEM-- !
I DID WHAT?
YOU!
ME.
MY WORK HERE IS DONE. YOUR REPUTATION REALLY IS ALL IT'S CRACKED UP TO BE.
TAKE A LOOK, CAPTAIN. SEE WHAT THE PEOPLE OF AMERICA ARE WILLING TO DO--
-- IN YOUR NAME.

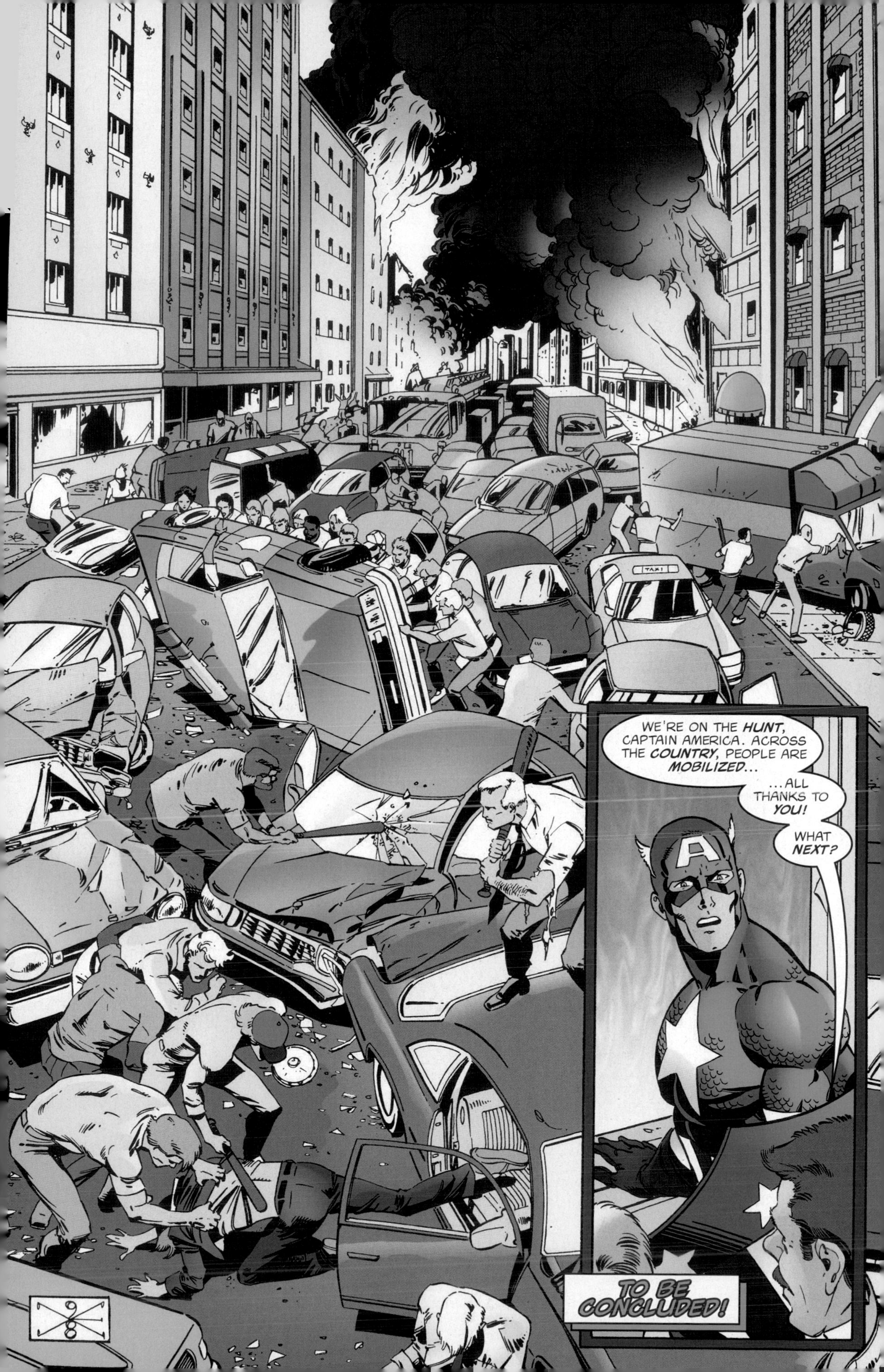
WE'RE ON THE HUNT, CAPTAIN AMERICA. ACROSS THE COUNTRY, PEOPLE ARE MOBILIZED...
...ALL THANKS TO YOU!
WHAT NEXT?
TO BE CONCLUDED!
TAXI

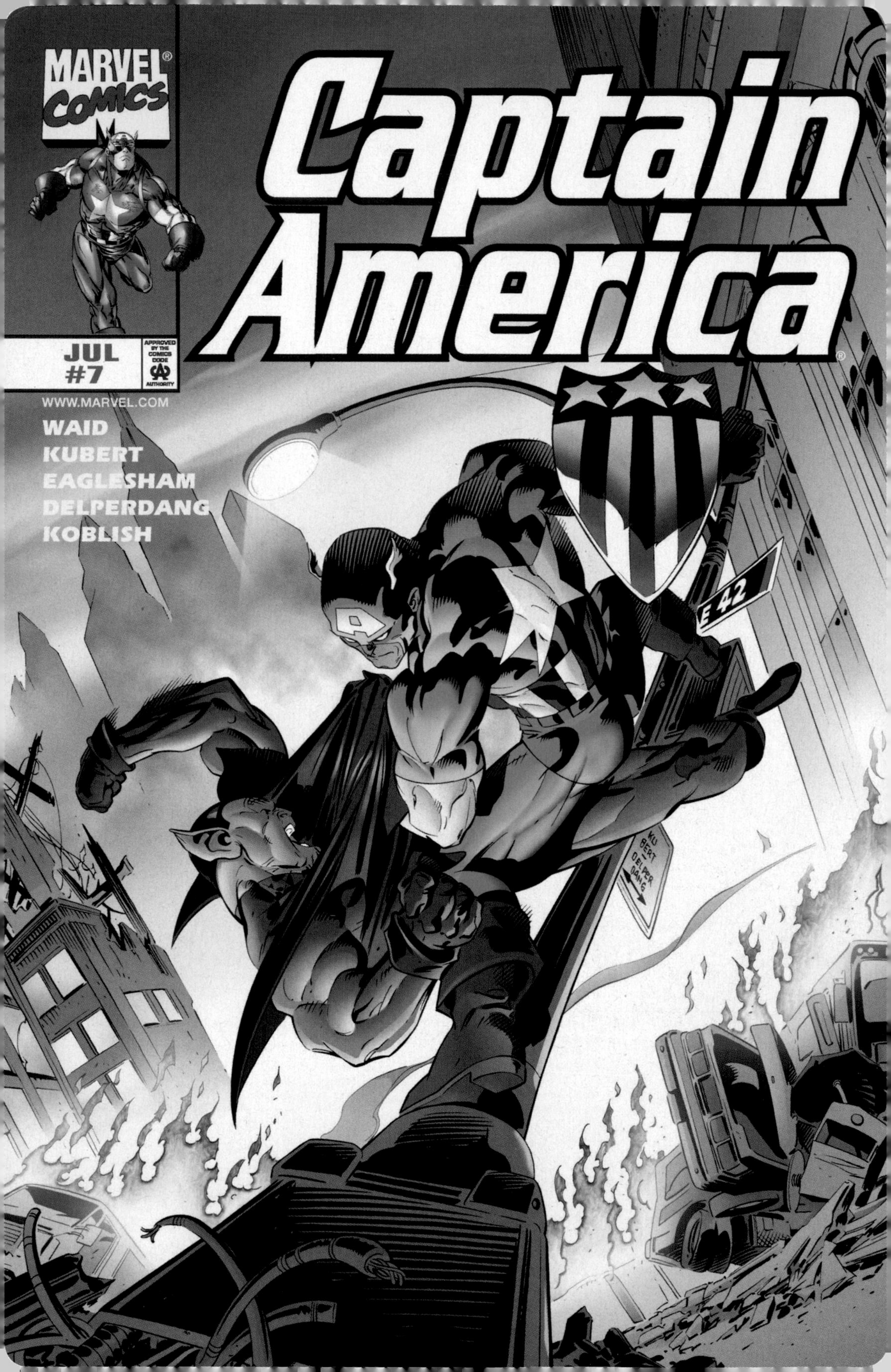
MARVEL COMICS
Captain America
JUL
#7
APPROVED BY THE COMICS CODE AUTHORITY
WWW.MARVEL.COM
WAID
KUBERT
EAGLESHAM
DELPERDANG
KOBLISH
E 42
KU BERT DELPER DANG

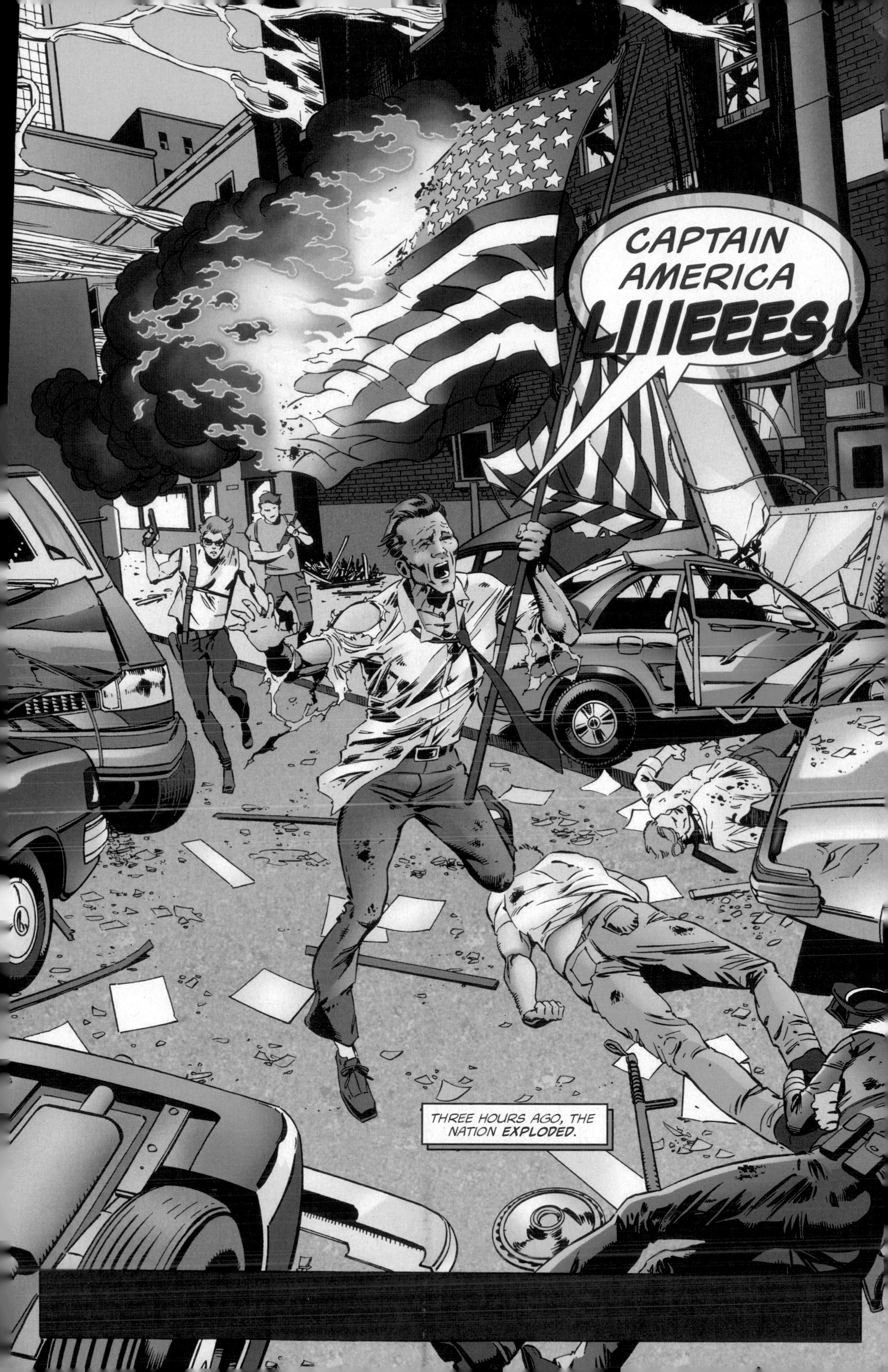
CAPTAIN AMERICA LIIIEEES!
THREE HOURS AGO, THE NATION EXPLODED.

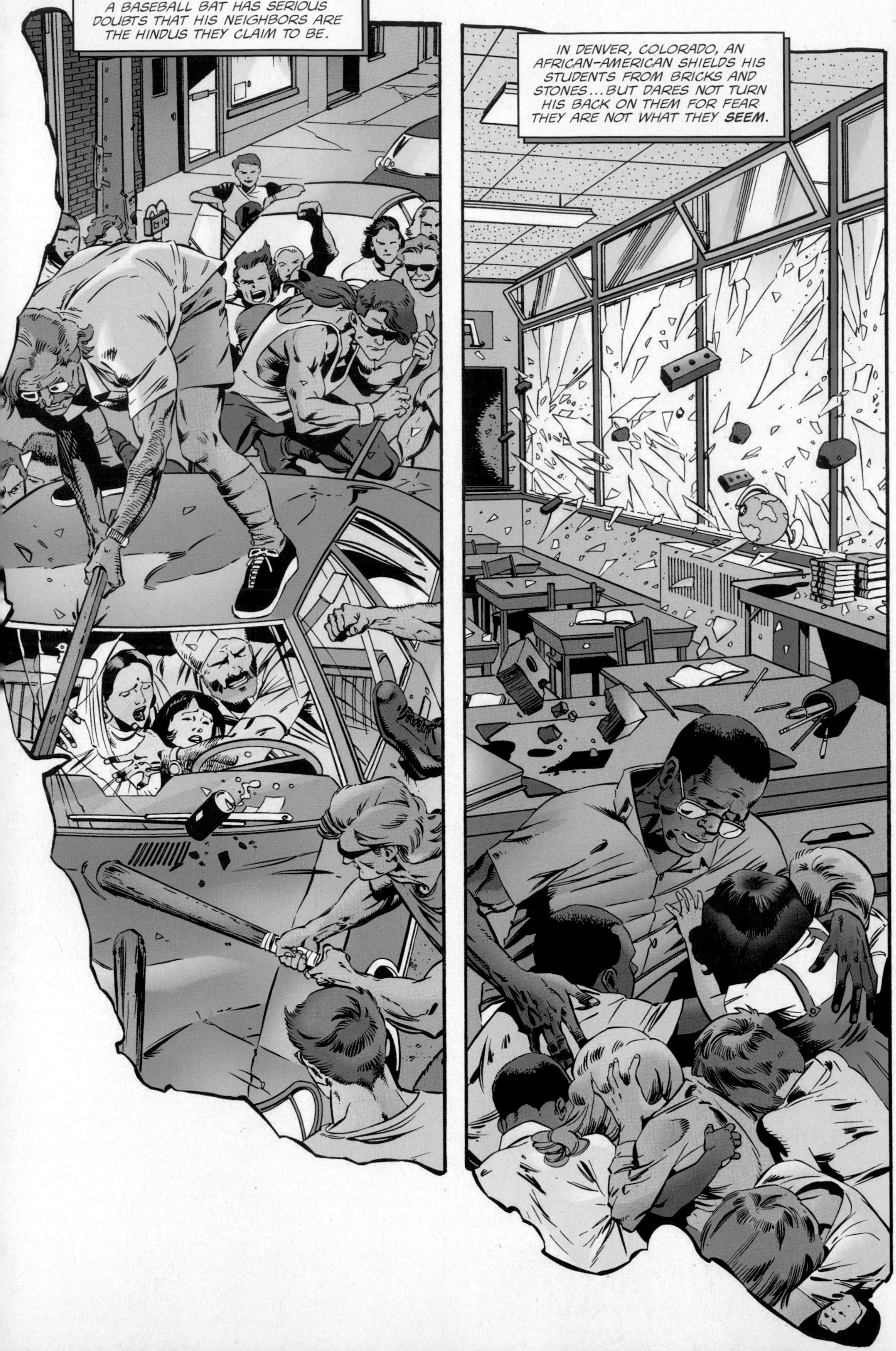
NOW, IN LOS ANGELES, A MAN WITH A BASEBALL BAT HAS SERIOUS DOUBTS THAT HIS NEIGHBORS ARE THE HINDUS THEY CLAIM TO BE.
IN DENVER, COLORADO, AN AFRICAN-AMERICAN SHIELDS HIS STUDENTS FROM BRICKS AND STONES...BUT DARES NOT TURN HIS BACK ON THEM FOR FEAR THEY ARE NOT WHAT THEY **SEEM**.

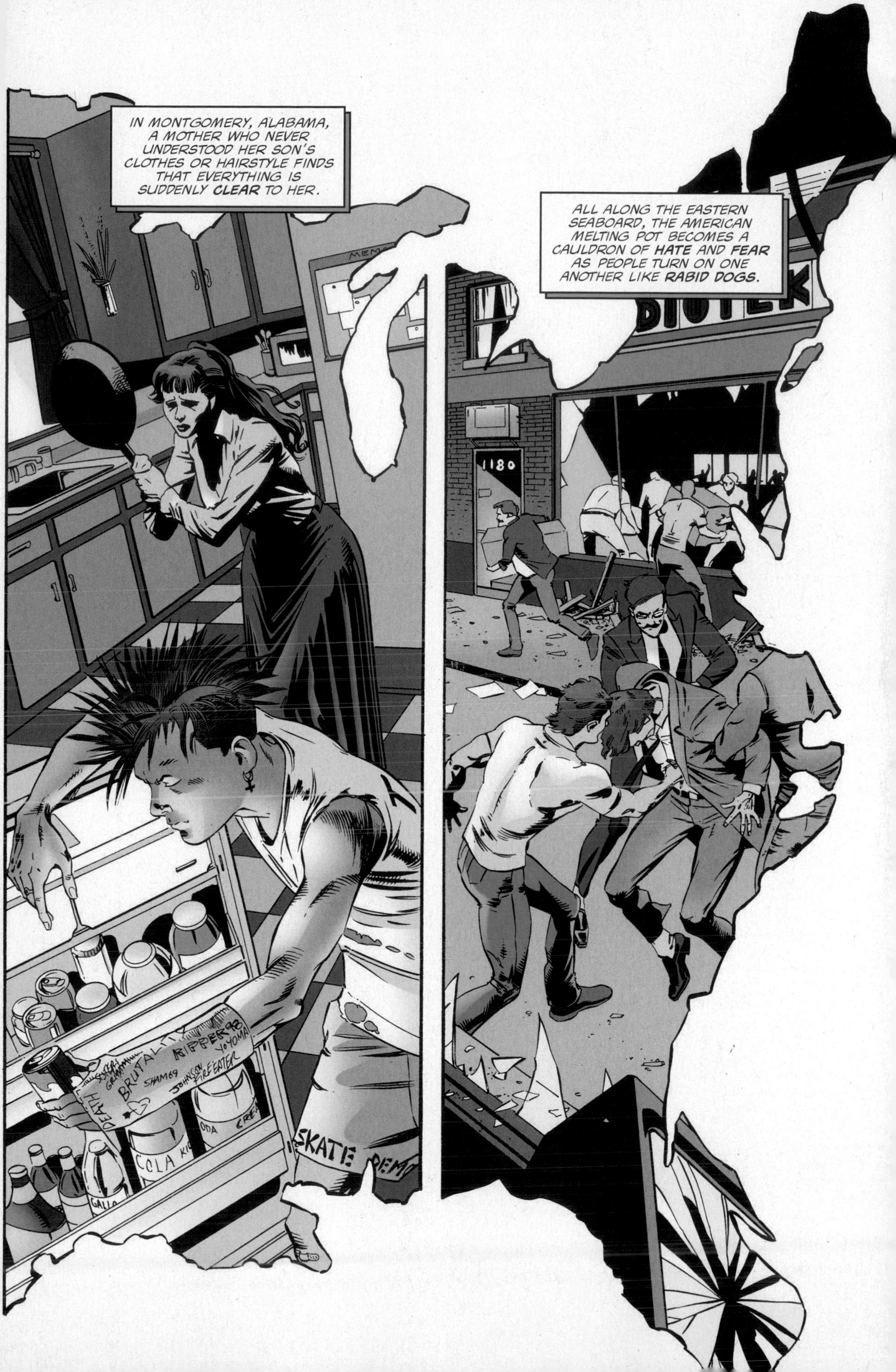
IN MONTGOMERY, ALABAMA, A MOTHER WHO NEVER UNDERSTOOD HER SON'S CLOTHES OR HAIRSTYLE FINDS THAT EVERYTHING IS SUDDENLY **CLEAR** TO HER.
ALL ALONG THE EASTERN SEABOARD, THE AMERICAN MELTING POT BECOMES A CAULDRON OF **HATE** AND **FEAR** AS PEOPLE TURN ON ONE ANOTHER LIKE **RABID DOGS**.
1180
BRUTALITY
DEATH
SKATE
COLA

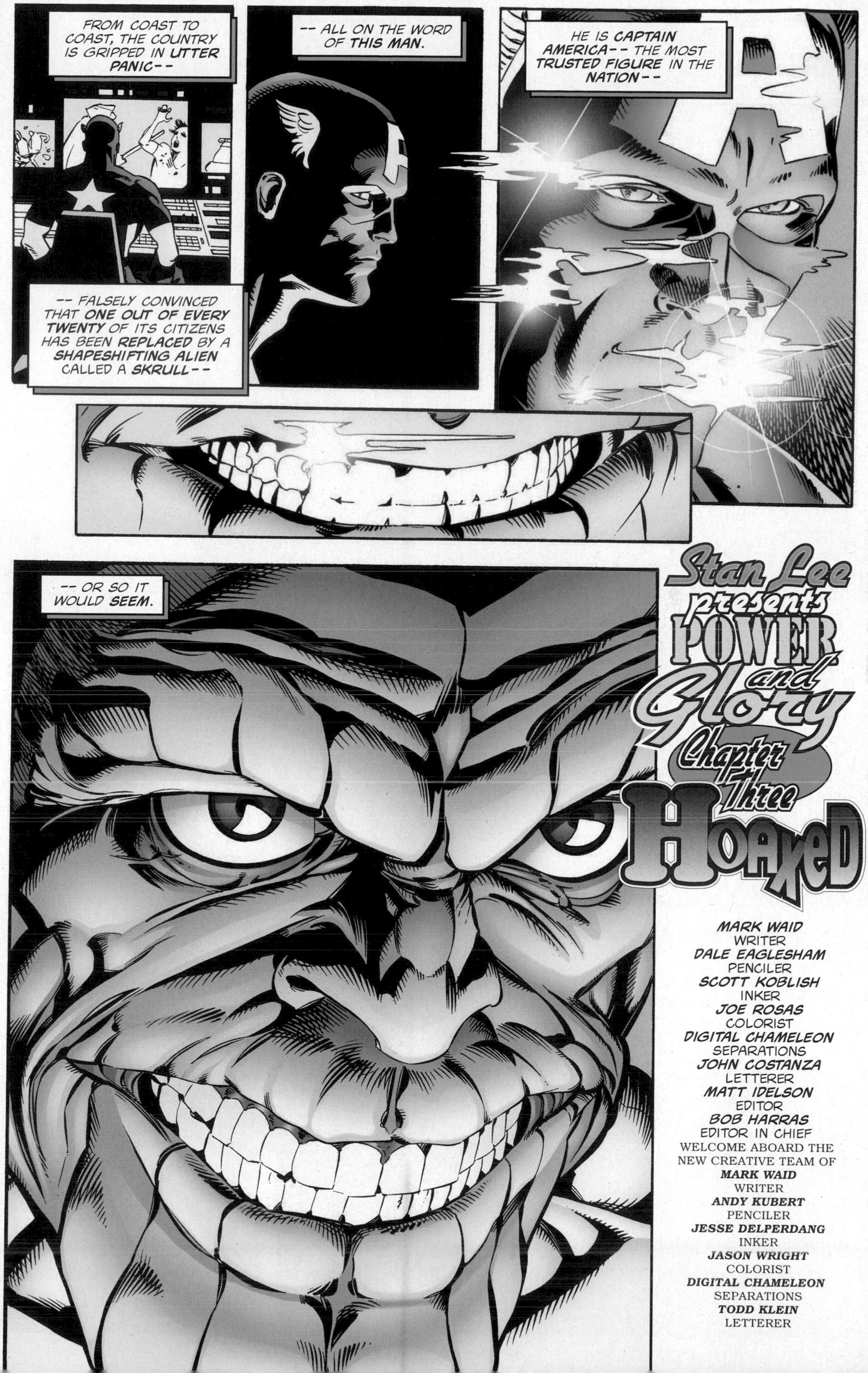
FROM COAST TO COAST, THE COUNTRY IS GRIPPED IN UTTER PANIC--
-- FALSELY CONVINCED THAT ONE OUT OF EVERY TWENTY OF ITS CITIZENS HAS BEEN REPLACED BY A SHAPESHIFTING ALIEN CALLED A SKRULL--
-- ALL ON THE WORD OF THIS MAN.
HE IS CAPTAIN AMERICA-- THE MOST TRUSTED FIGURE IN THE NATION--
-- OR SO IT WOULD SEEM.
Stan Lee presents POWER and Glory
Chapter Three
HOAXED
MARK WAID
WRITER
DALE EAGLESHAM
PENCILER
SCOTT KOBLISH
INKER
JOE ROSAS
COLORIST
DIGITAL CHAMELEON
SEPARATIONS
JOHN COSTANZA
LETTERER
MATT IDELSON
EDITOR
BOB HARRAS
EDITOR IN CHIEF
WELCOME ABOARD THE NEW CREATIVE TEAM OF
MARK WAID
WRITER
ANDY KUBERT
PENCILER
JESSE DELPERDANG
INKER
JASON WRIGHT
COLORIST
DIGITAL CHAMELEON
SEPARATIONS
TODD KLEIN
LETTERER

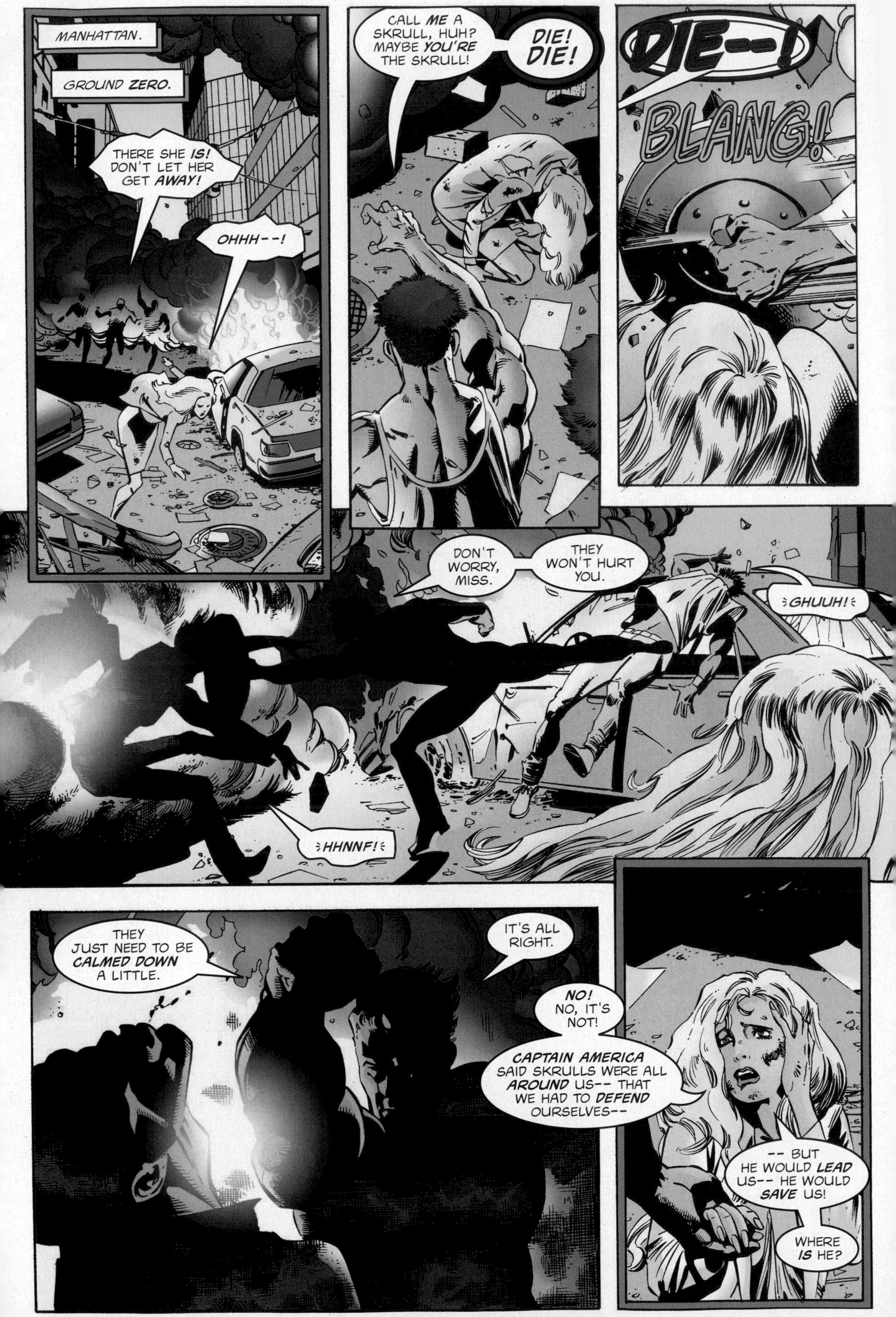
MANHATTAN.
GROUND ZERO.
THERE SHE IS! DON'T LET HER GET AWAY!
OHHH--!
CALL ME A SKRULL, HUH? MAYBE YOU'RE THE SKRULL!
DIE! DIE!
DIE--!
BLANG!
DON'T WORRY, MISS.
THEY WON'T HURT YOU.
GHUUH!
HHNNF!
THEY JUST NEED TO BE CALMED DOWN A LITTLE.
IT'S ALL RIGHT.
NO! NO, IT'S NOT!
CAPTAIN AMERICA SAID SKRULLS WERE ALL AROUND US-- THAT WE HAD TO DEFEND OURSELVES--
-- BUT HE WOULD LEAD US-- HE WOULD SAVE US!
WHERE IS HE?

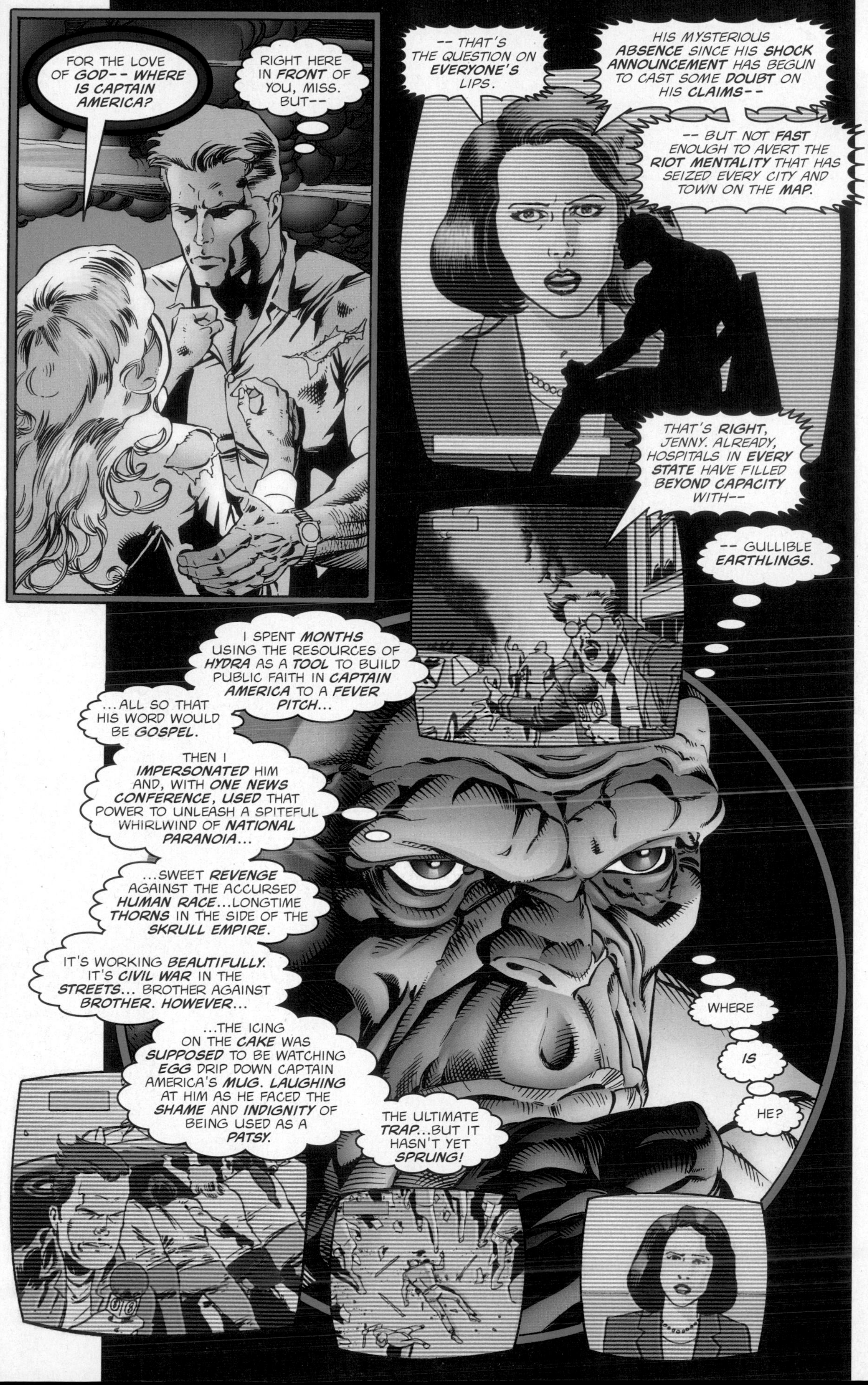
FOR THE LOVE OF GOD-- WHERE IS CAPTAIN AMERICA?
RIGHT HERE IN FRONT OF YOU, MISS. BUT--
-- THAT'S THE QUESTION ON EVERYONE'S LIPS.
HIS MYSTERIOUS ABSENCE SINCE HIS SHOCK ANNOUNCEMENT HAS BEGUN TO CAST SOME DOUBT ON HIS CLAIMS--
-- BUT NOT FAST ENOUGH TO AVERT THE RIOT MENTALITY THAT HAS SEIZED EVERY CITY AND TOWN ON THE MAP.
THAT'S RIGHT, JENNY. ALREADY, HOSPITALS IN EVERY STATE HAVE FILLED BEYOND CAPACITY WITH--
-- GULLIBLE EARTHLINGS.
I SPENT MONTHS USING THE RESOURCES OF HYDRA AS A TOOL TO BUILD PUBLIC FAITH IN CAPTAIN AMERICA TO A FEVER PITCH...
...ALL SO THAT HIS WORD WOULD BE GOSPEL.
THEN I IMPERSONATED HIM AND, WITH ONE NEWS CONFERENCE, USED THAT POWER TO UNLEASH A SPITEFUL WHIRLWIND OF NATIONAL PARANOIA...
...SWEET REVENGE AGAINST THE ACCURSED HUMAN RACE...LONGTIME THORNS IN THE SIDE OF THE SKRULL EMPIRE.
IT'S WORKING BEAUTIFULLY. IT'S CIVIL WAR IN THE STREETS... BROTHER AGAINST BROTHER. HOWEVER...
...THE ICING ON THE CAKE WAS SUPPOSED TO BE WATCHING EGG DRIP DOWN CAPTAIN AMERICA'S MUG. LAUGHING AT HIM AS HE FACED THE SHAME AND INDIGNITY OF BEING USED AS A PATSY.
WHERE
IS
HE?
THE ULTIMATE TRAP...BUT IT HASN'T YET SPRUNG!

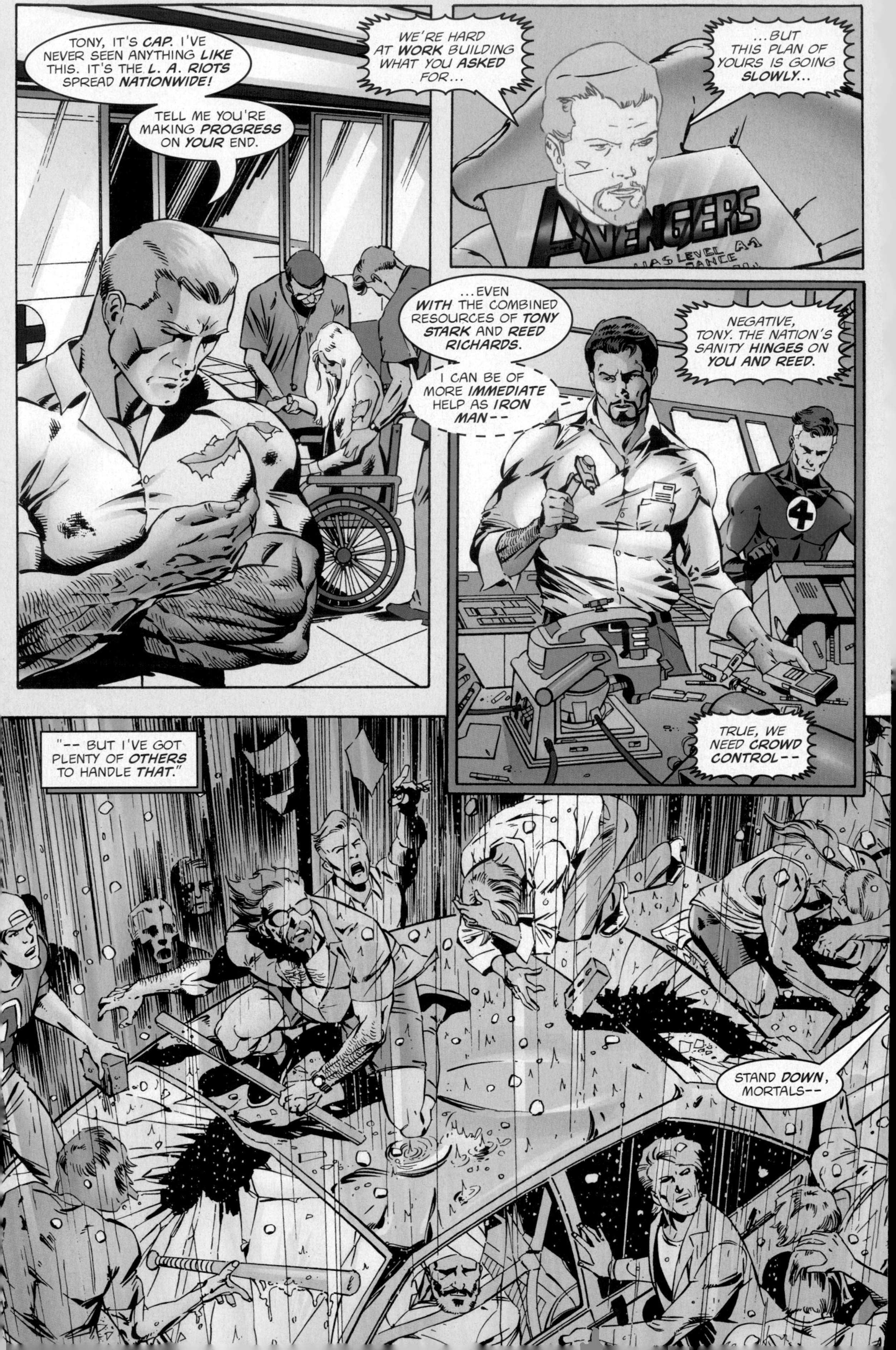

TONY, IT'S CAP. I'VE NEVER SEEN ANYTHING LIKE THIS. IT'S THE L. A. RIOTS SPREAD NATIONWIDE!
TELL ME YOU'RE MAKING PROGRESS ON YOUR END.
WE'RE HARD AT WORK BUILDING WHAT YOU ASKED FOR...
...BUT THIS PLAN OF YOURS IS GOING SLOWLY...
AVENGERS
...EVEN WITH THE COMBINED RESOURCES OF TONY STARK AND REED RICHARDS.
I CAN BE OF MORE IMMEDIATE HELP AS IRON MAN--
NEGATIVE, TONY. THE NATION'S SANITY HINGES ON YOU AND REED.
TRUE, WE NEED CROWD CONTROL--
"-- BUT I'VE GOT PLENTY OF OTHERS TO HANDLE THAT."
STAND DOWN, MORTALS--

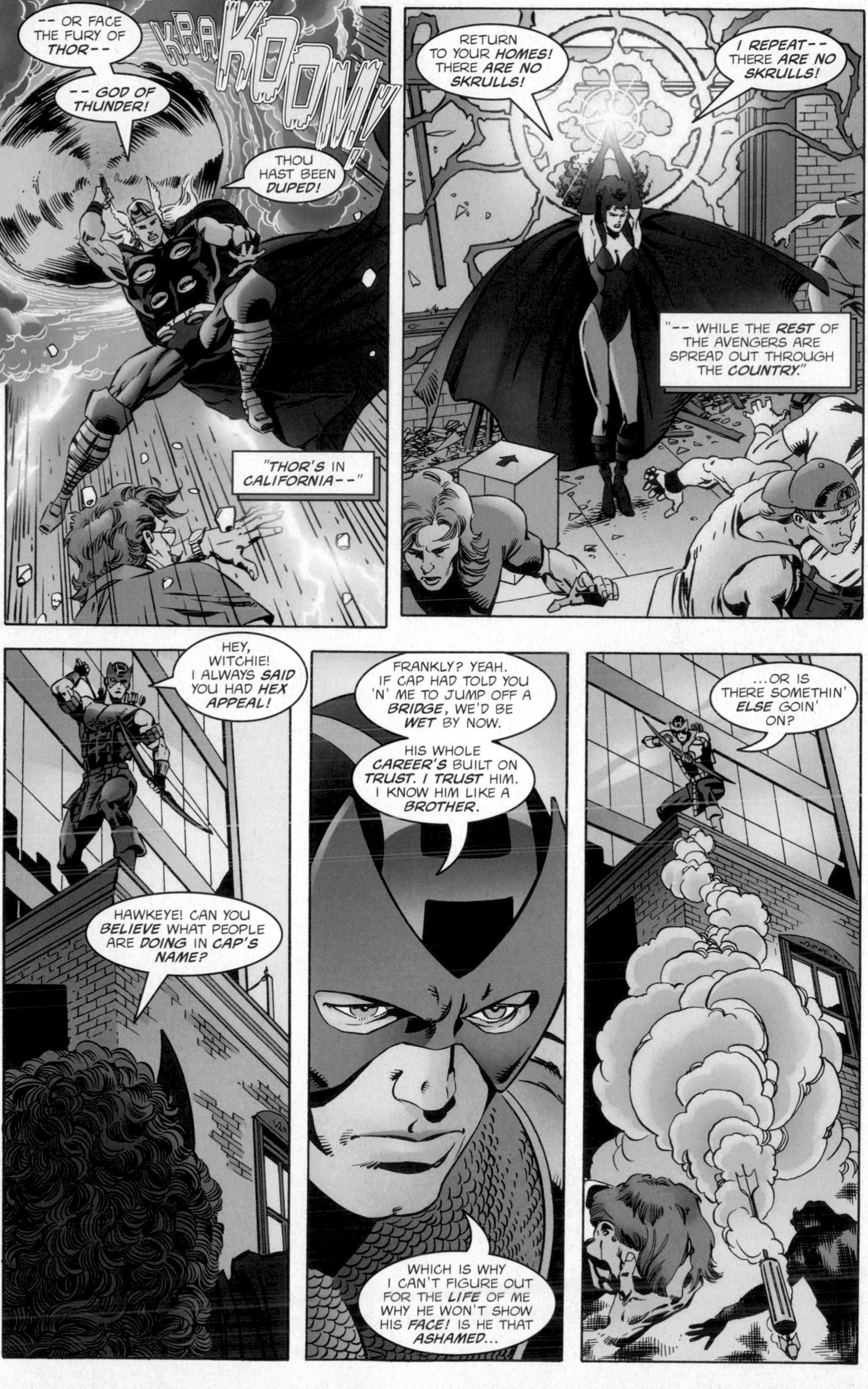
-- OR FACE THE FURY OF THOR--
-- GOD OF THUNDER!
KRAKOOM!
THOU HAST BEEN DUPED!
"THOR'S IN CALIFORNIA--"
RETURN TO YOUR HOMES! THERE ARE NO SKRULLS!
I REPEAT-- THERE ARE NO SKRULLS!
"-- WHILE THE REST OF THE AVENGERS ARE SPREAD OUT THROUGH THE COUNTRY."
HEY, WITCHIE! I ALWAYS SAID YOU HAD HEX APPEAL!
HAWKEYE! CAN YOU BELIEVE WHAT PEOPLE ARE DOING IN CAP'S NAME?
FRANKLY? YEAH. IF CAP HAD TOLD YOU 'N' ME TO JUMP OFF A BRIDGE, WE'D BE WET BY NOW.
HIS WHOLE CAREER'S BUILT ON TRUST. I TRUST HIM. I KNOW HIM LIKE A BROTHER.
WHICH IS WHY I CAN'T FIGURE OUT FOR THE LIFE OF ME WHY HE WON'T SHOW HIS FACE! IS HE THAT ASHAMED...
...OR IS THERE SOMETHIN' ELSE GOIN' ON?

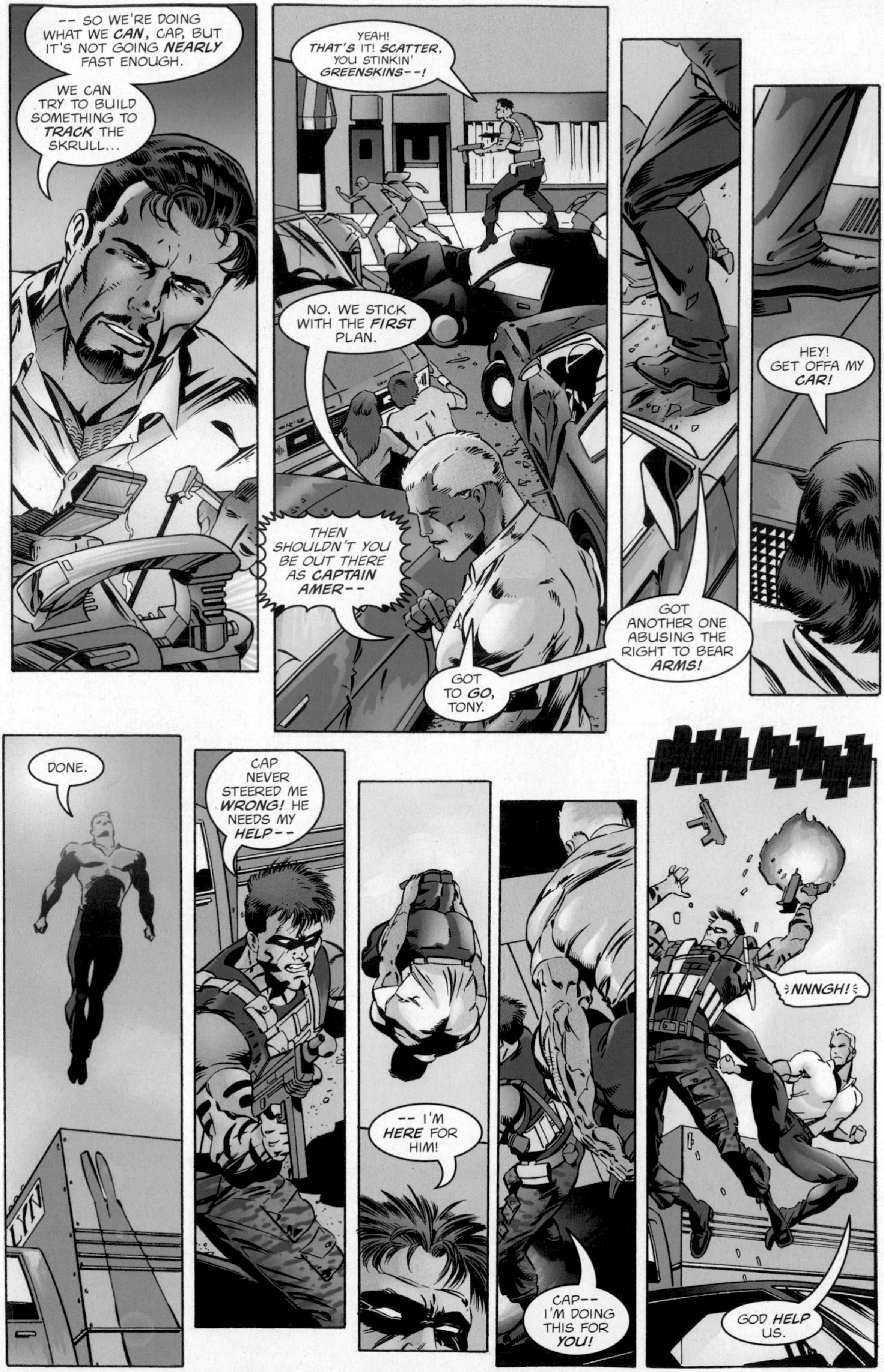
-- SO WE'RE DOING WHAT WE CAN, CAP, BUT IT'S NOT GOING NEARLY FAST ENOUGH.
WE CAN TRY TO BUILD SOMETHING TO TRACK THE SKRULL...
YEAH! THAT'S IT! SCATTER, YOU STINKIN' GREENSKINS--!
NO. WE STICK WITH THE FIRST PLAN.
THEN SHOULDN'T YOU BE OUT THERE AS CAPTAIN AMER--
GOT TO GO, TONY.
GOT ANOTHER ONE ABUSING THE RIGHT TO BEAR ARMS!
HEY! GET OFFA MY CAR!
DONE.
CAP NEVER STEERED ME WRONG! HE NEEDS MY HELP--
-- I'M HERE FOR HIM!
CAP-- I'M DOING THIS FOR YOU!
NNNGH!
GOD HELP US.

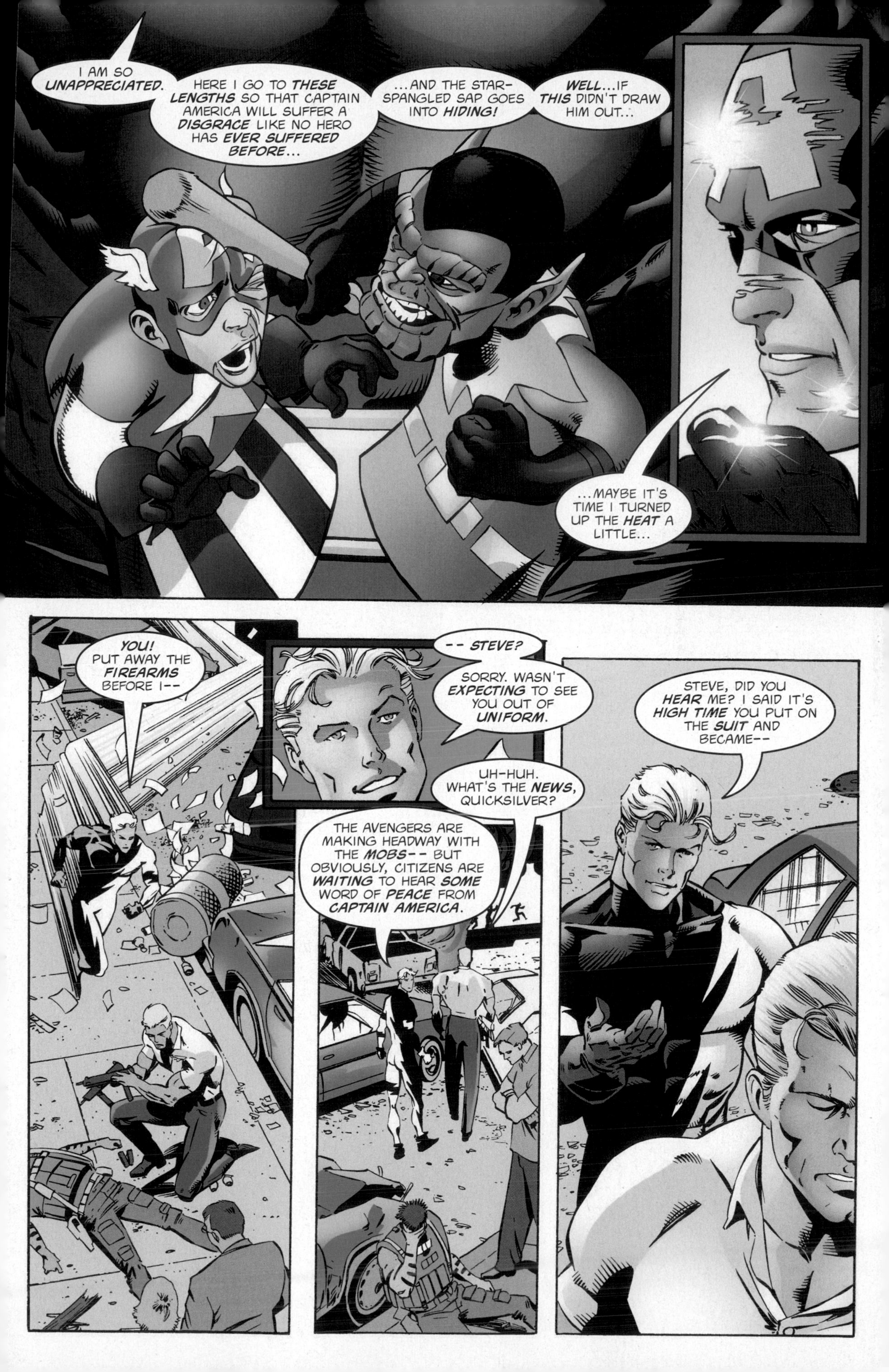
I AM SO UNAPPRECIATED.
HERE I GO TO THESE LENGTHS SO THAT CAPTAIN AMERICA WILL SUFFER A DISGRACE LIKE NO HERO HAS EVER SUFFERED BEFORE...
...AND THE STAR-SPANGLED SAP GOES INTO HIDING!
WELL...IF THIS DIDN'T DRAW HIM OUT...
...MAYBE IT'S TIME I TURNED UP THE HEAT A LITTLE...
YOU! PUT AWAY THE FIREARMS BEFORE I--
-- STEVE?
SORRY. WASN'T EXPECTING TO SEE YOU OUT OF UNIFORM.
UH-HUH. WHAT'S THE NEWS, QUICKSILVER?
THE AVENGERS ARE MAKING HEADWAY WITH THE MOBS-- BUT OBVIOUSLY, CITIZENS ARE WAITING TO HEAR SOME WORD OF PEACE FROM CAPTAIN AMERICA.
STEVE, DID YOU HEAR ME? I SAID IT'S HIGH TIME YOU PUT ON THE SUIT AND BECAME--

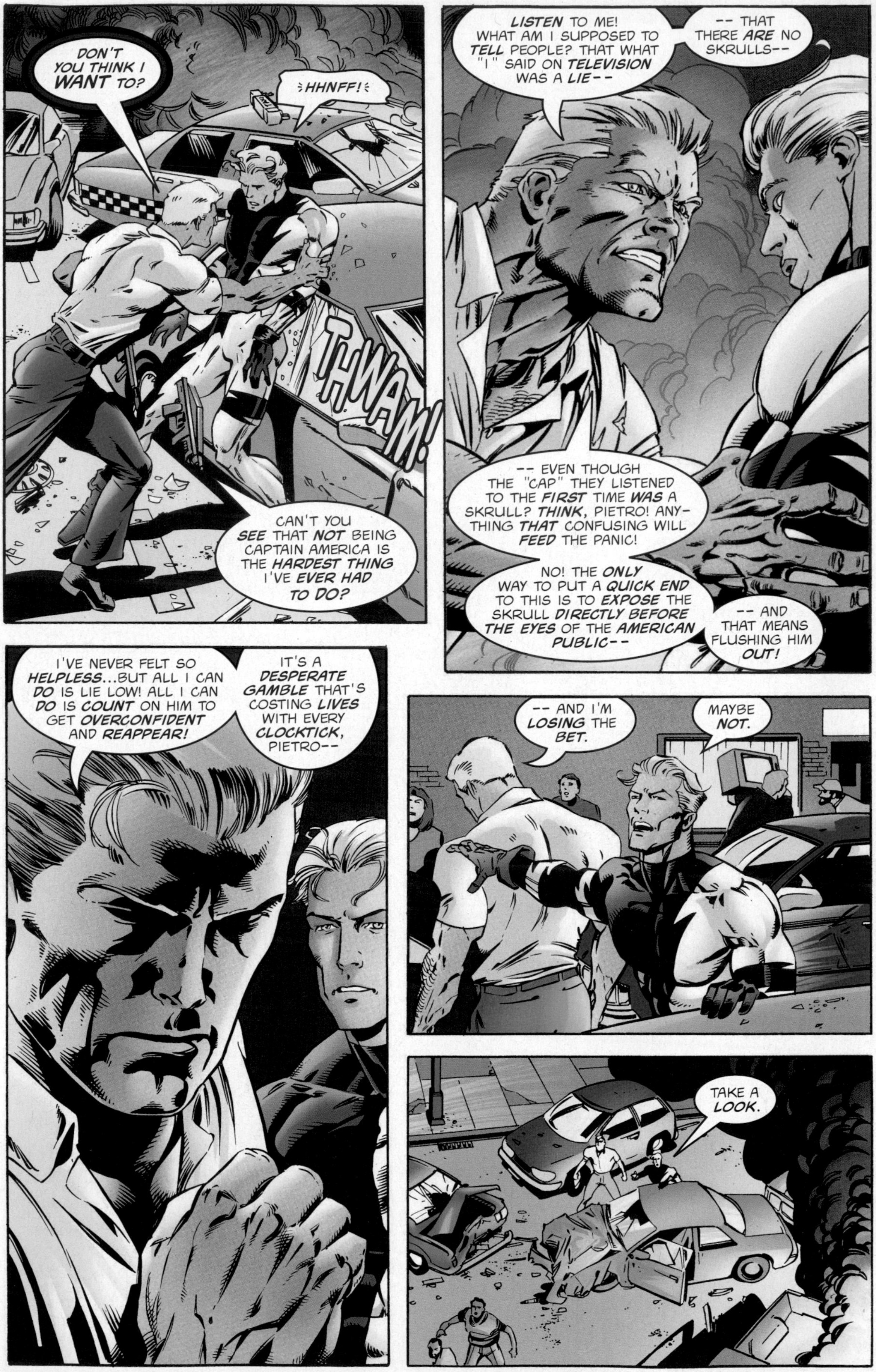

DON'T YOU THINK I WANT TO?
HHNFF!
THWAM!
CAN'T YOU SEE THAT NOT BEING CAPTAIN AMERICA IS THE HARDEST THING I'VE EVER HAD TO DO?
LISTEN TO ME! WHAT AM I SUPPOSED TO TELL PEOPLE? THAT WHAT "I" SAID ON TELEVISION WAS A LIE--
-- THAT THERE ARE NO SKRULLS--
-- EVEN THOUGH THE "CAP" THEY LISTENED TO THE FIRST TIME WAS A SKRULL? THINK, PIETRO! ANY-THING THAT CONFUSING WILL FEED THE PANIC!
NO! THE ONLY WAY TO PUT A QUICK END TO THIS IS TO EXPOSE THE SKRULL DIRECTLY BEFORE THE EYES OF THE AMERICAN PUBLIC--
-- AND THAT MEANS FLUSHING HIM OUT!
I'VE NEVER FELT SO HELPLESS...BUT ALL I CAN DO IS LIE LOW! ALL I CAN DO IS COUNT ON HIM TO GET OVERCONFIDENT AND REAPPEAR!
IT'S A DESPERATE GAMBLE THAT'S COSTING LIVES WITH EVERY CLOCKTICK, PIETRO--
-- AND I'M LOSING THE BET.
MAYBE NOT.
TAKE A LOOK.

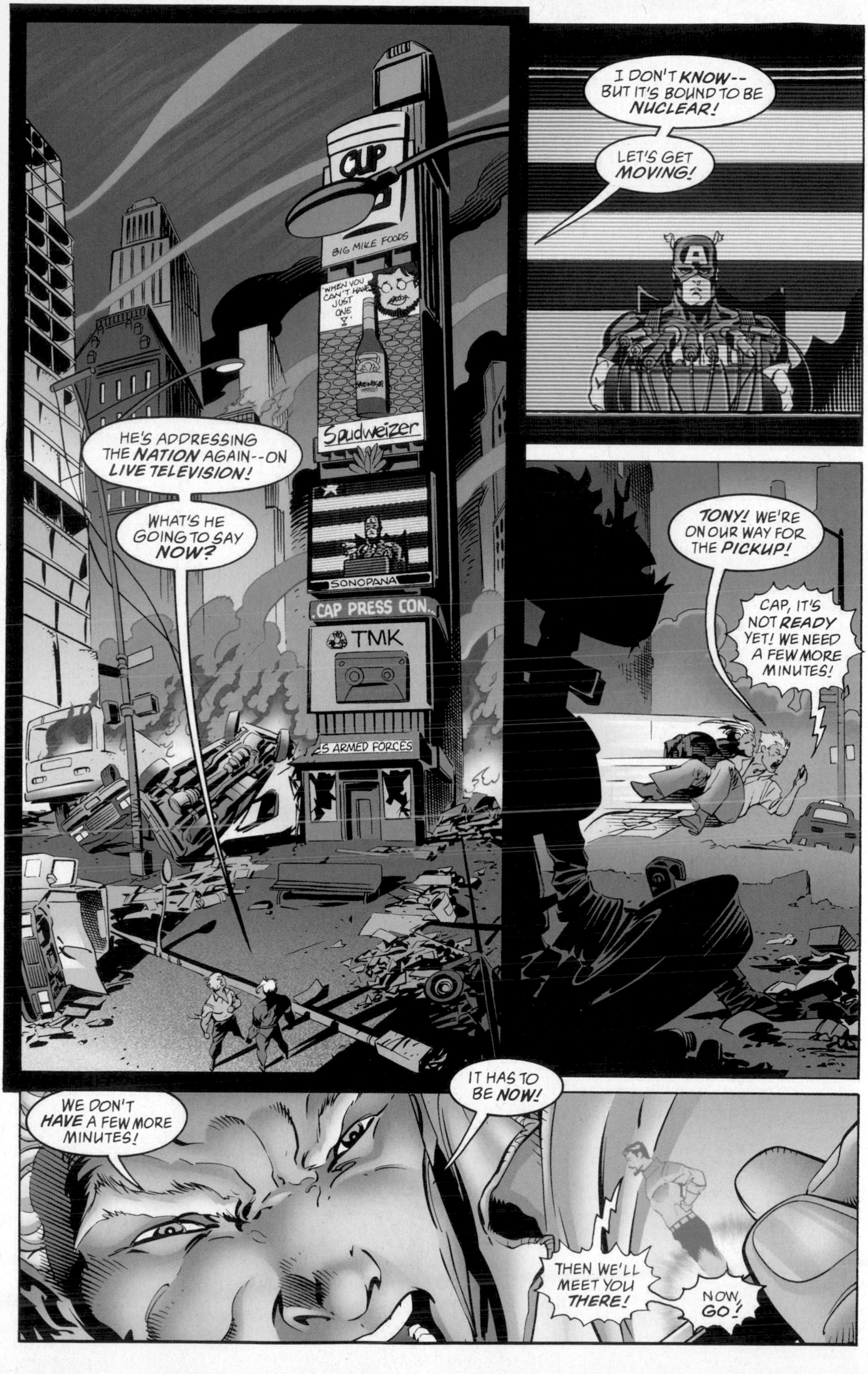
CUP
BIG MIKE FOODS
'WHEN YOU CAN'T HAVE JUST ONE'
Spudweizer
SONOPANA
.CAP PRESS CON..
TMK
S ARMED FORCES
HE'S ADDRESSING THE NATION AGAIN--ON LIVE TELEVISION!
WHAT'S HE GOING TO SAY NOW?
I DON'T KNOW-- BUT IT'S BOUND TO BE NUCLEAR!
LET'S GET MOVING!
TONY! WE'RE ON OUR WAY FOR THE PICKUP!
CAP, IT'S NOT READY YET! WE NEED A FEW MORE MINUTES!
WE DON'T HAVE A FEW MORE MINUTES!
IT HAS TO BE NOW!
THEN WE'LL MEET YOU THERE!
NOW, GO!

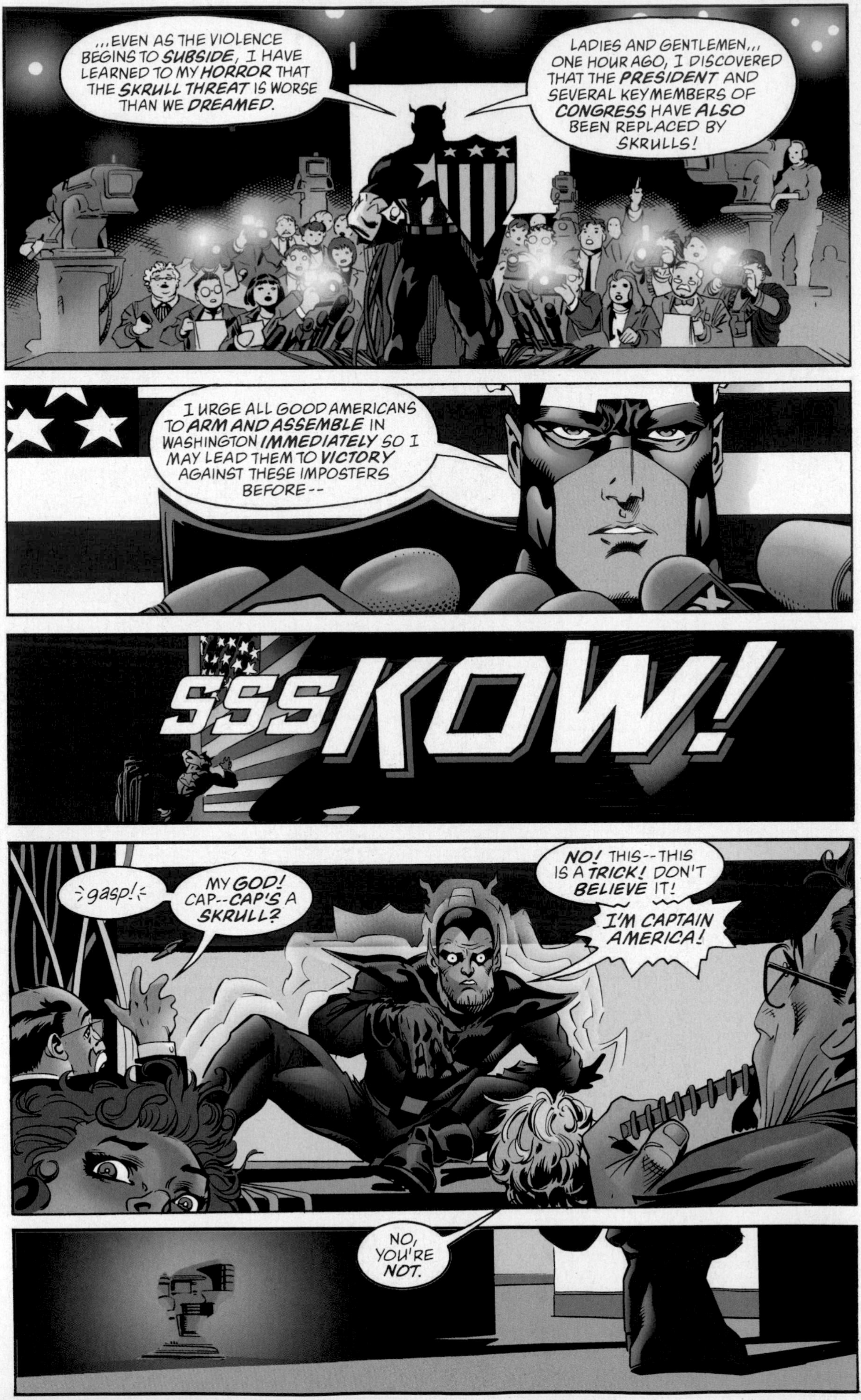
...EVEN AS THE VIOLENCE BEGINS TO SUBSIDE, I HAVE LEARNED TO MY HORROR THAT THE SKRULL THREAT IS WORSE THAN WE DREAMED.
LADIES AND GENTLEMEN... ONE HOUR AGO, I DISCOVERED THAT THE PRESIDENT AND SEVERAL KEY MEMBERS OF CONGRESS HAVE ALSO BEEN REPLACED BY SKRULLS!
I URGE ALL GOOD AMERICANS TO ARM AND ASSEMBLE IN WASHINGTON IMMEDIATELY SO I MAY LEAD THEM TO VICTORY AGAINST THESE IMPOSTERS BEFORE--
SSSKOW!
gasp!
MY GOD! CAP--CAP'S A SKRULL?
NO! THIS--THIS IS A TRICK! DON'T BELIEVE IT!
I'M CAPTAIN AMERICA!
NO, YOU'RE NOT.

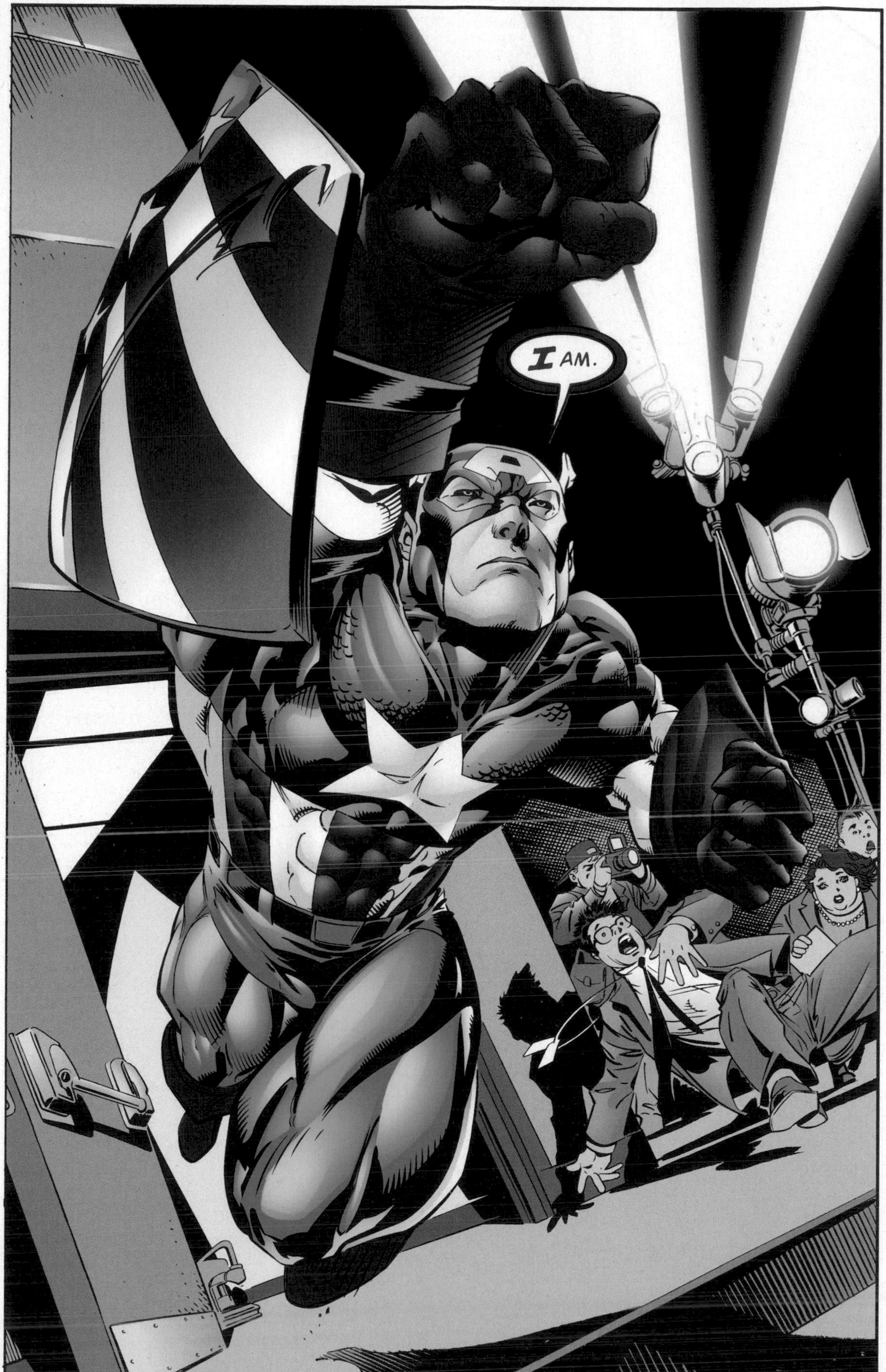
I AM.

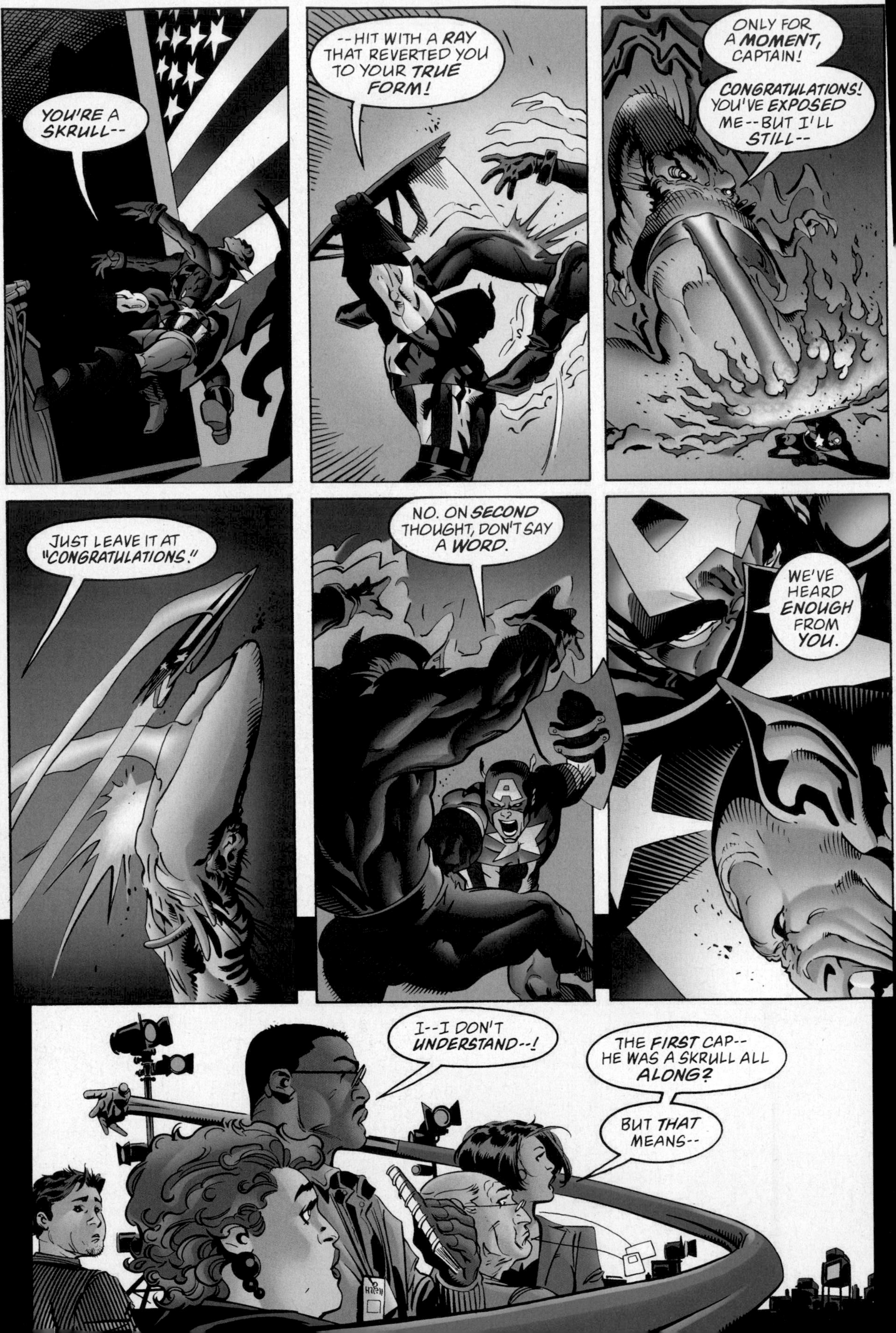
YOU'RE A SKRULL--
--HIT WITH A RAY THAT REVERTED YOU TO YOUR TRUE FORM!
ONLY FOR A MOMENT, CAPTAIN!
CONGRATULATIONS! YOU'VE EXPOSED ME--BUT I'LL STILL--
JUST LEAVE IT AT "CONGRATULATIONS."
NO. ON SECOND THOUGHT, DON'T SAY A WORD.
WE'VE HEARD ENOUGH FROM YOU.
I--I DON'T UNDERSTAND--!
THE FIRST CAP--HE WAS A SKRULL ALL ALONG?
BUT THAT MEANS--

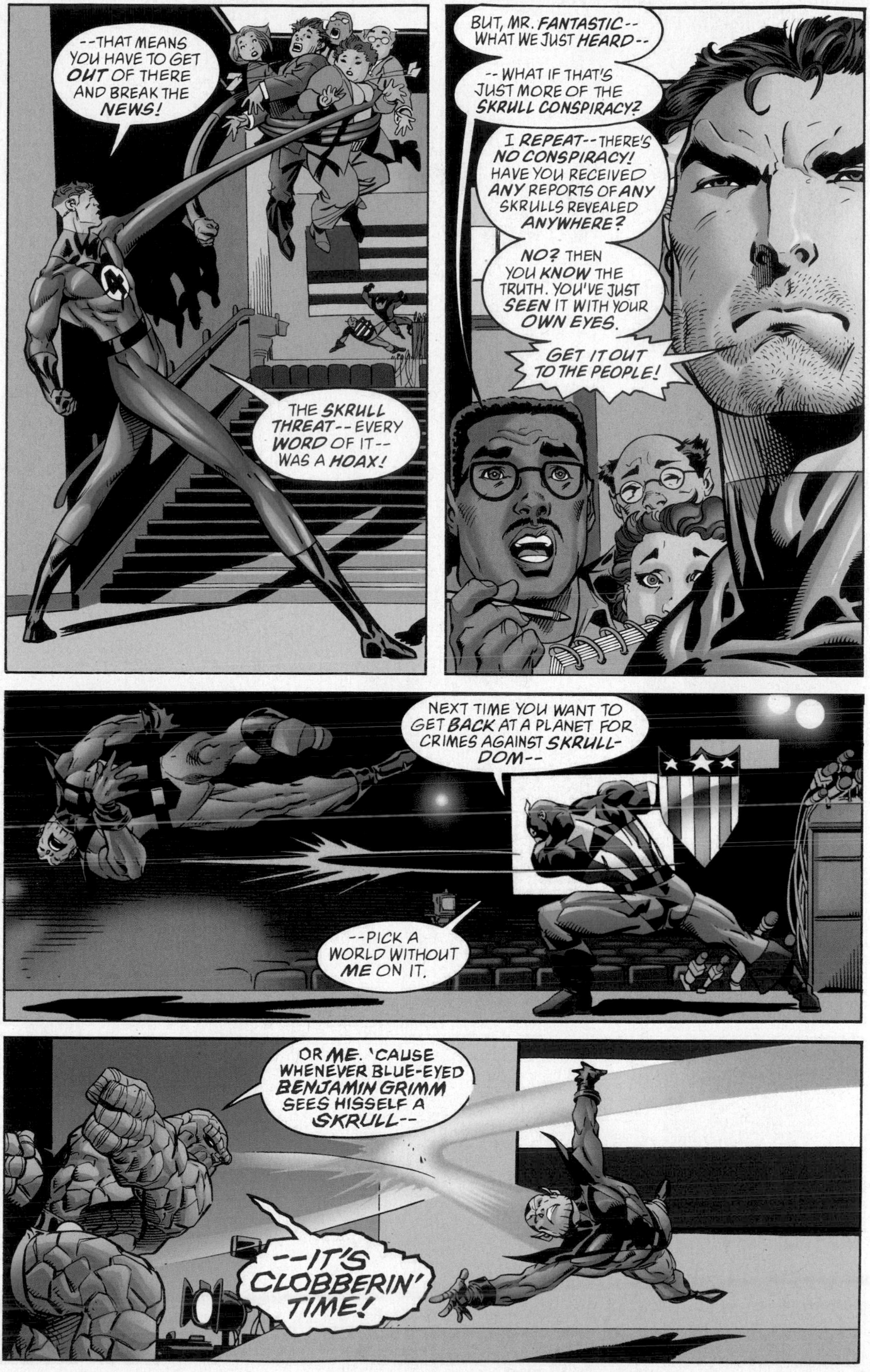
--THAT MEANS YOU HAVE TO GET OUT OF THERE AND BREAK THE NEWS!
THE SKRULL THREAT--EVERY WORD OF IT--WAS A HOAX!
BUT, MR. FANTASTIC--WHAT WE JUST HEARD--
--WHAT IF THAT'S JUST MORE OF THE SKRULL CONSPIRACY?
I REPEAT--THERE'S NO CONSPIRACY! HAVE YOU RECEIVED ANY REPORTS OF ANY SKRULLS REVEALED ANYWHERE?
NO? THEN YOU KNOW THE TRUTH. YOU'VE JUST SEEN IT WITH YOUR OWN EYES.
GET IT OUT TO THE PEOPLE!
NEXT TIME YOU WANT TO GET BACK AT A PLANET FOR CRIMES AGAINST SKRULL-DOM--
--PICK A WORLD WITHOUT ME ON IT.
OR ME. 'CAUSE WHENEVER BLUE-EYED BENJAMIN GRIMM SEES HISSELF A SKRULL--
--IT'S CLOBBERIN' TIME!

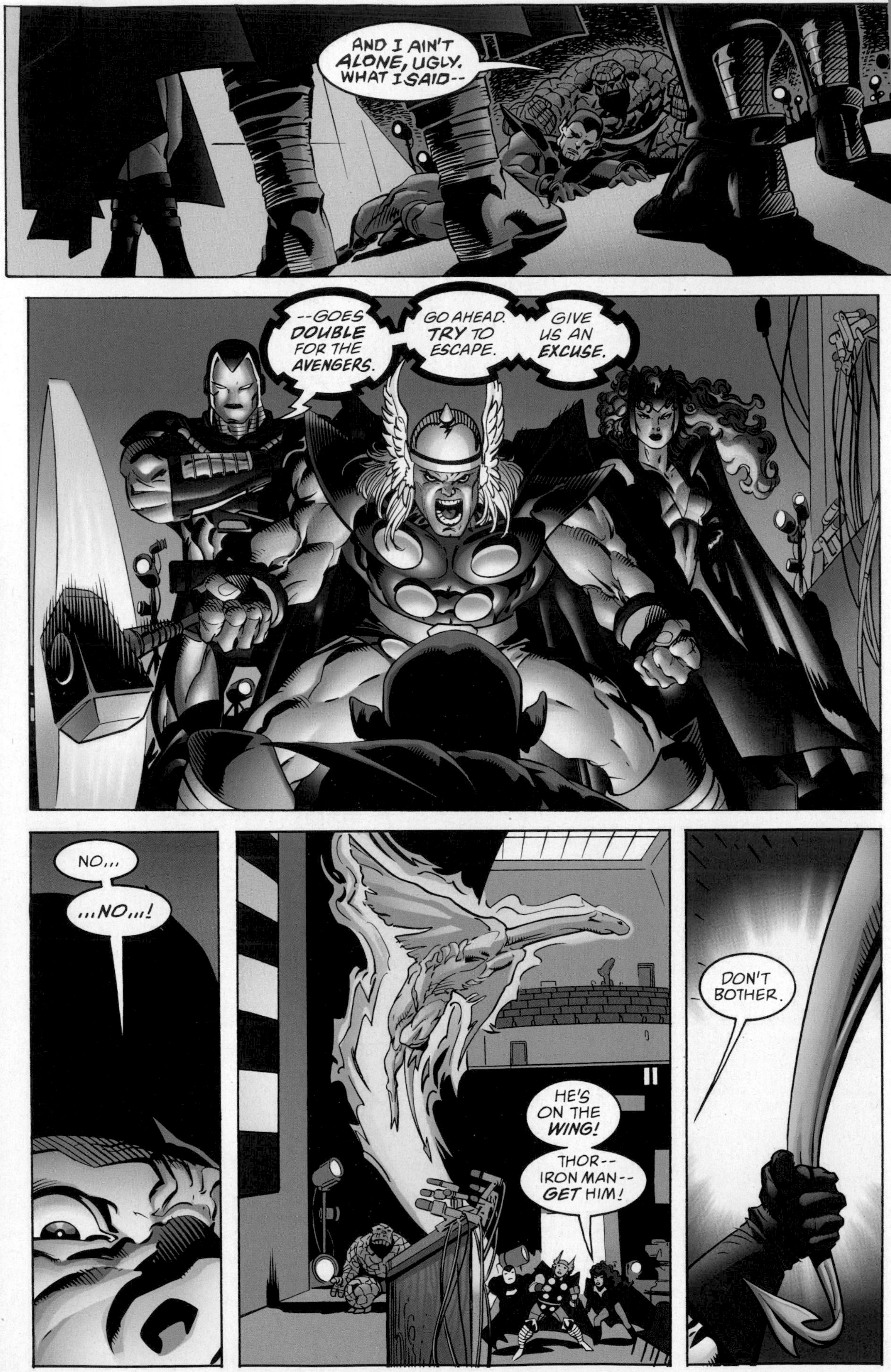
AND I AIN'T ALONE, UGLY. WHAT I SAID--
--GOES DOUBLE FOR THE AVENGERS.
GO AHEAD. TRY TO ESCAPE.
GIVE US AN EXCUSE.
NO...
...NO...!
HE'S ON THE WING!
THOR-- IRON MAN-- GET HIM!
DON'T BOTHER.

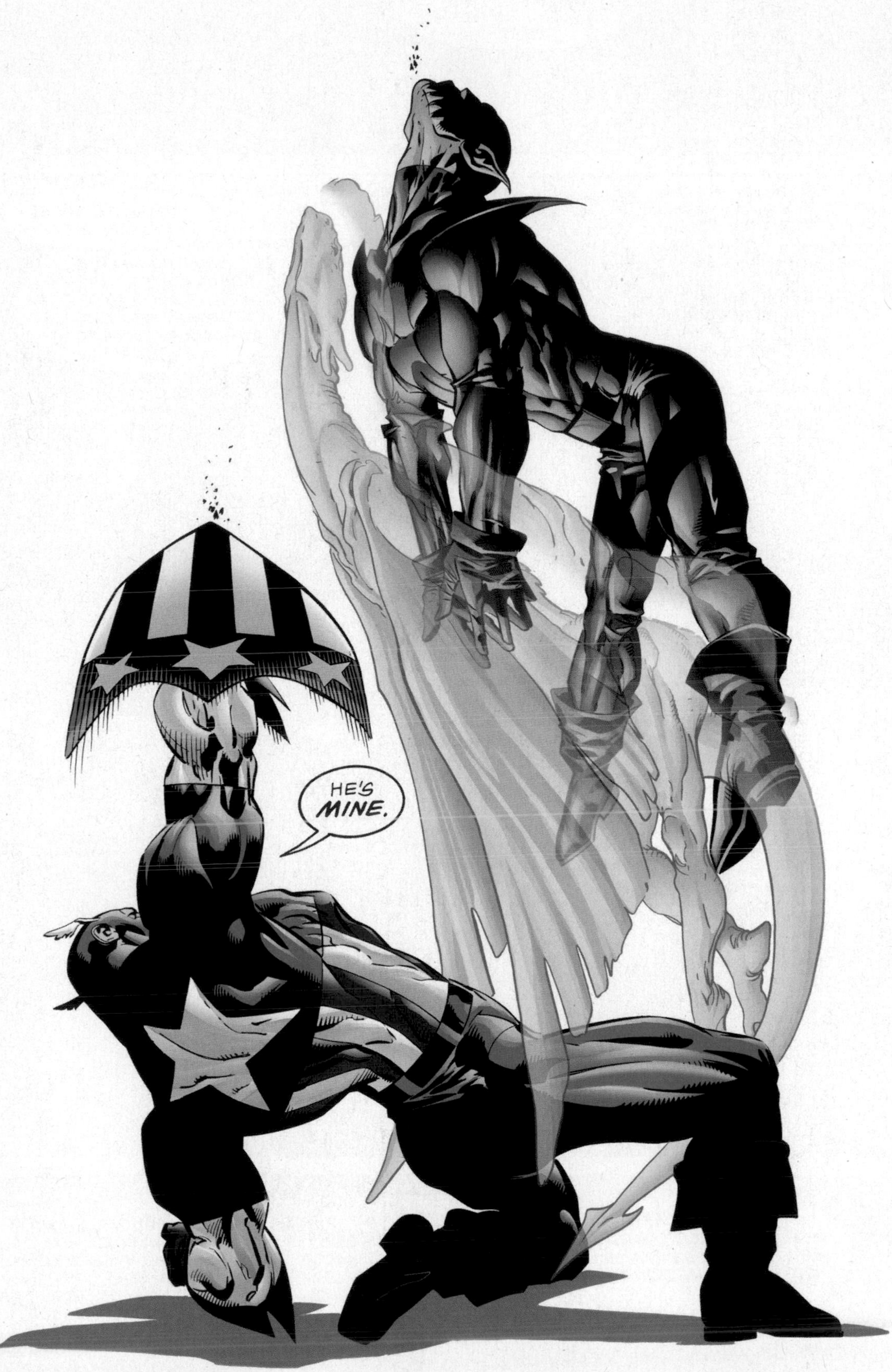
HE'S MINE.

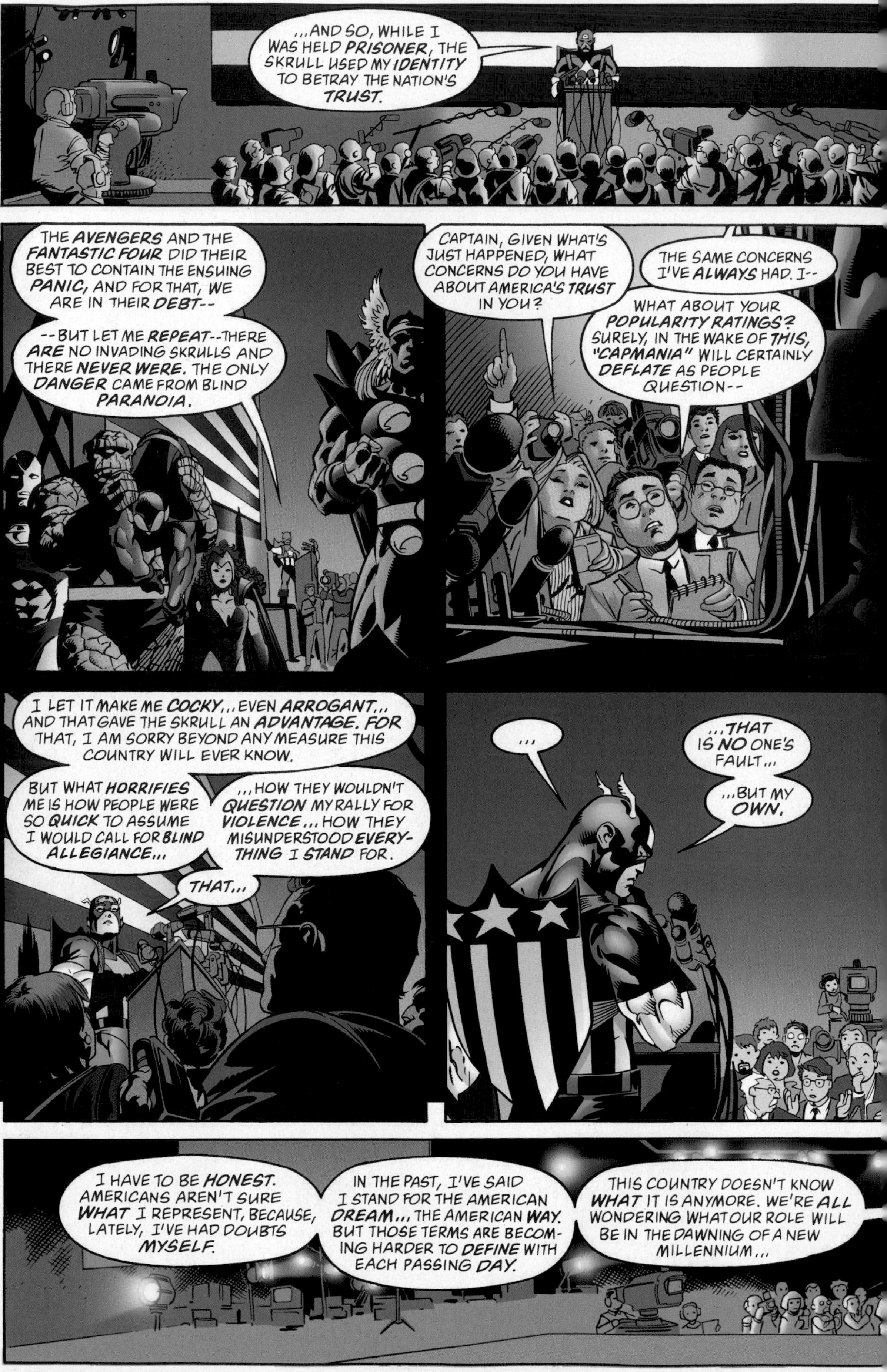
...AND SO, WHILE I WAS HELD PRISONER, THE SKRULL USED MY IDENTITY TO BETRAY THE NATION'S TRUST.
THE AVENGERS AND THE FANTASTIC FOUR DID THEIR BEST TO CONTAIN THE ENSUING PANIC, AND FOR THAT, WE ARE IN THEIR DEBT--
--BUT LET ME REPEAT--THERE ARE NO INVADING SKRULLS AND THERE NEVER WERE. THE ONLY DANGER CAME FROM BLIND PARANOIA.
CAPTAIN, GIVEN WHAT'S JUST HAPPENED, WHAT CONCERNS DO YOU HAVE ABOUT AMERICA'S TRUST IN YOU?
THE SAME CONCERNS I'VE ALWAYS HAD. I--
WHAT ABOUT YOUR POPULARITY RATINGS? SURELY, IN THE WAKE OF THIS, "CAPMANIA" WILL CERTAINLY DEFLATE AS PEOPLE QUESTION--
I LET IT MAKE ME COCKY... EVEN ARROGANT... AND THAT GAVE THE SKRULL AN ADVANTAGE. FOR THAT, I AM SORRY BEYOND ANY MEASURE THIS COUNTRY WILL EVER KNOW.
BUT WHAT HORRIFIES ME IS HOW PEOPLE WERE SO QUICK TO ASSUME I WOULD CALL FOR BLIND ALLEGIANCE...
...HOW THEY WOULDN'T QUESTION MY RALLY FOR VIOLENCE... HOW THEY MISUNDERSTOOD EVERYTHING I STAND FOR.
THAT...
...
...THAT IS NO ONE'S FAULT...
...BUT MY OWN.
I HAVE TO BE HONEST. AMERICANS AREN'T SURE WHAT I REPRESENT, BECAUSE, LATELY, I'VE HAD DOUBTS MYSELF.
IN THE PAST, I'VE SAID I STAND FOR THE AMERICAN DREAM... THE AMERICAN WAY. BUT THOSE TERMS ARE BECOMING HARDER TO DEFINE WITH EACH PASSING DAY.
THIS COUNTRY DOESN'T KNOW WHAT IT IS ANYMORE. WE'RE ALL WONDERING WHAT OUR ROLE WILL BE IN THE DAWNING OF A NEW MILLENNIUM...

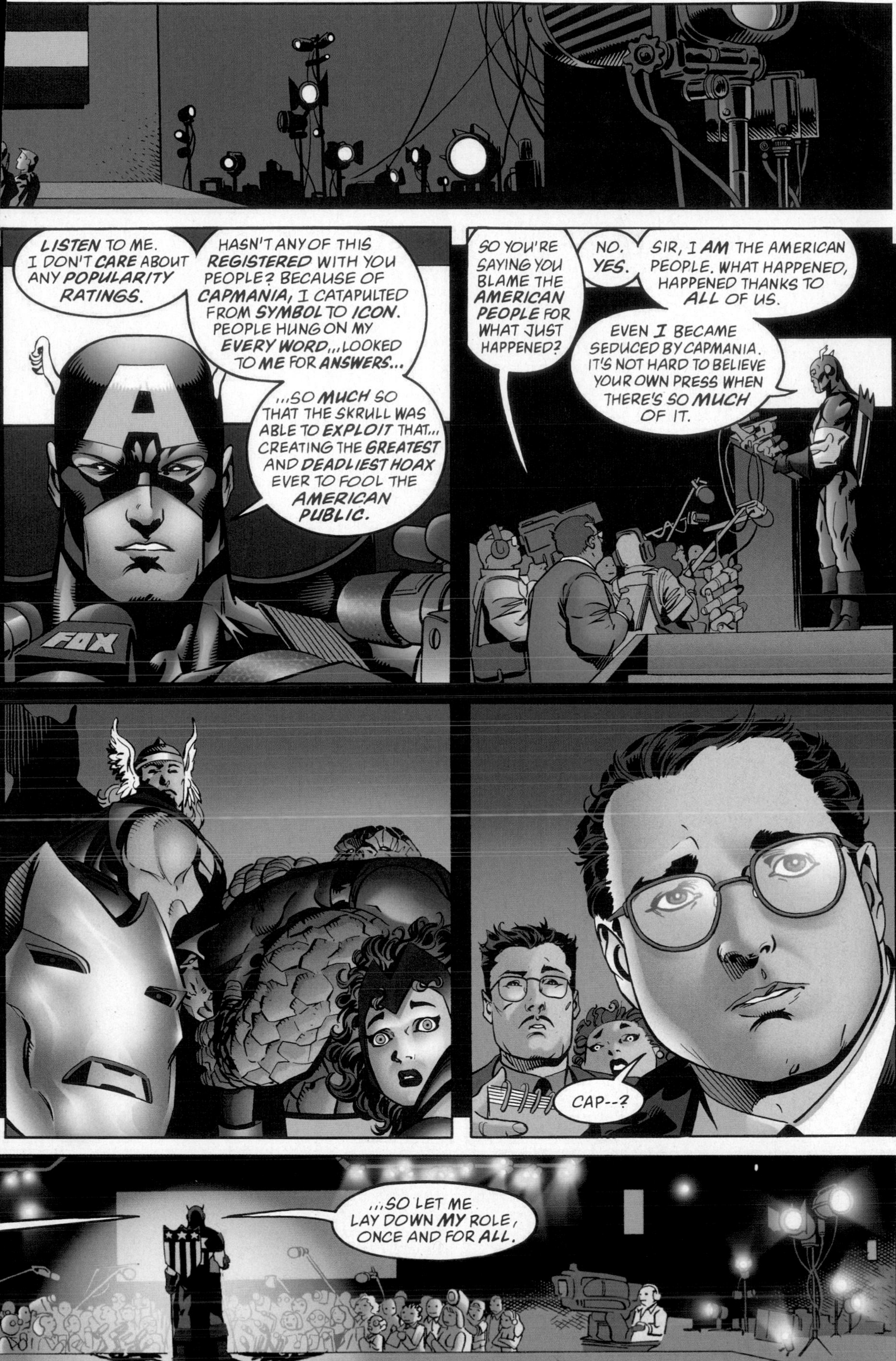
LISTEN TO ME. I DON'T CARE ABOUT ANY POPULARITY RATINGS.
HASN'T ANY OF THIS REGISTERED WITH YOU PEOPLE? BECAUSE OF CAPMANIA, I CATAPULTED FROM SYMBOL TO ICON. PEOPLE HUNG ON MY EVERY WORD...LOOKED TO ME FOR ANSWERS...
...SO MUCH SO THAT THE SKRULL WAS ABLE TO EXPLOIT THAT... CREATING THE GREATEST AND DEADLIEST HOAX EVER TO FOOL THE AMERICAN PUBLIC.
FOX
SO YOU'RE SAYING YOU BLAME THE AMERICAN PEOPLE FOR WHAT JUST HAPPENED?
NO. YES.
SIR, I AM THE AMERICAN PEOPLE. WHAT HAPPENED, HAPPENED THANKS TO ALL OF US.
EVEN I BECAME SEDUCED BY CAPMANIA. IT'S NOT HARD TO BELIEVE YOUR OWN PRESS WHEN THERE'S SO MUCH OF IT.
CAP--?
...SO LET ME LAY DOWN MY ROLE, ONCE AND FOR ALL.

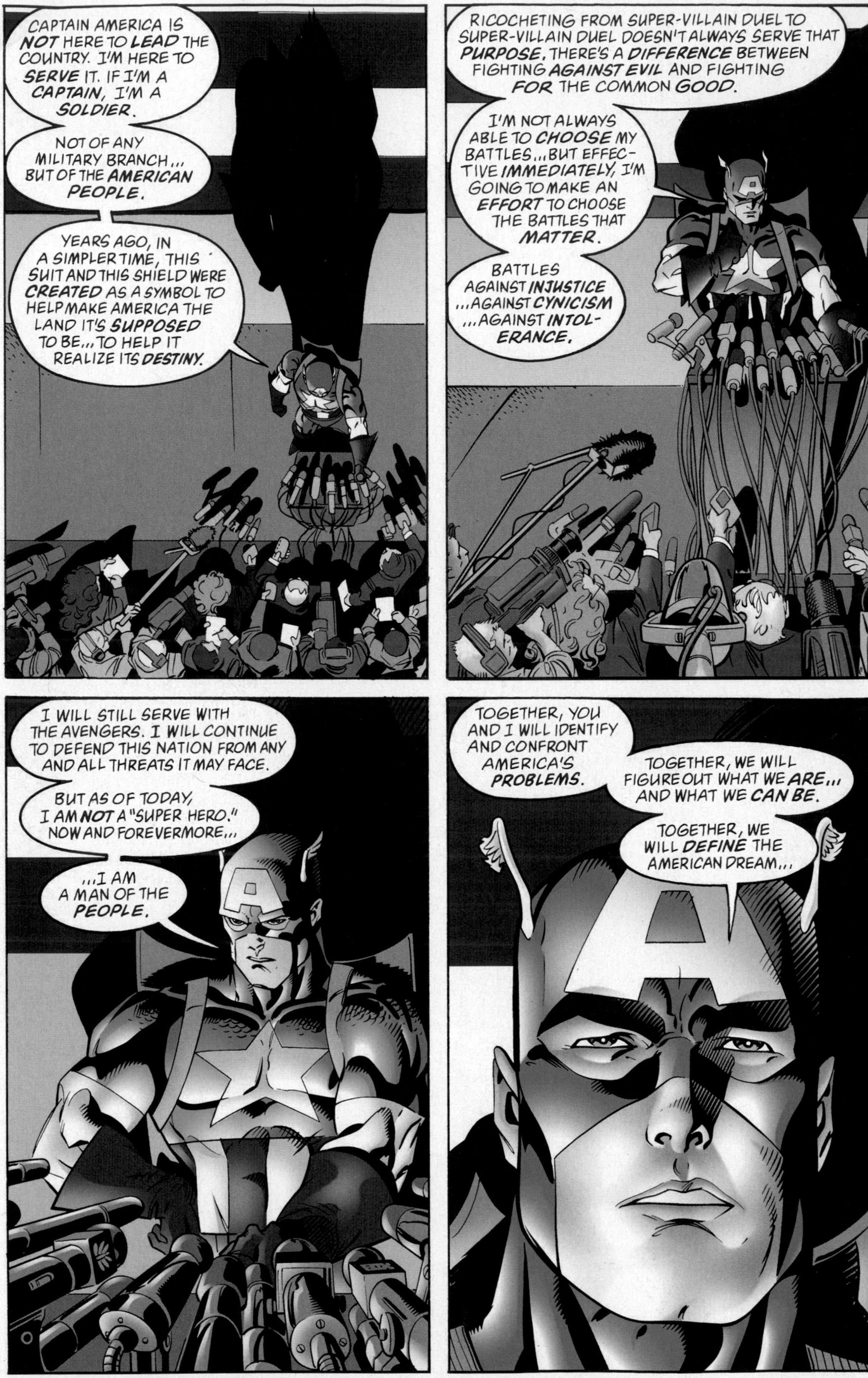
CAPTAIN AMERICA IS NOT HERE TO LEAD THE COUNTRY. I'M HERE TO SERVE IT. IF I'M A CAPTAIN, I'M A SOLDIER.
NOT OF ANY MILITARY BRANCH... BUT OF THE AMERICAN PEOPLE.
YEARS AGO, IN A SIMPLER TIME, THIS SUIT AND THIS SHIELD WERE CREATED AS A SYMBOL TO HELP MAKE AMERICA THE LAND IT'S SUPPOSED TO BE... TO HELP IT REALIZE ITS DESTINY.
RICOCHETING FROM SUPER-VILLAIN DUEL TO SUPER-VILLAIN DUEL DOESN'T ALWAYS SERVE THAT PURPOSE. THERE'S A DIFFERENCE BETWEEN FIGHTING AGAINST EVIL AND FIGHTING FOR THE COMMON GOOD.
I'M NOT ALWAYS ABLE TO CHOOSE MY BATTLES... BUT EFFECTIVE IMMEDIATELY, I'M GOING TO MAKE AN EFFORT TO CHOOSE THE BATTLES THAT MATTER.
BATTLES AGAINST INJUSTICE ...AGAINST CYNICISM ...AGAINST INTOLERANCE.
I WILL STILL SERVE WITH THE AVENGERS. I WILL CONTINUE TO DEFEND THIS NATION FROM ANY AND ALL THREATS IT MAY FACE.
BUT AS OF TODAY, I AM NOT A "SUPER HERO." NOW AND FOREVERMORE...
...I AM A MAN OF THE PEOPLE.
TOGETHER, YOU AND I WILL IDENTIFY AND CONFRONT AMERICA'S PROBLEMS.
TOGETHER, WE WILL FIGURE OUT WHAT WE ARE... AND WHAT WE CAN BE.
TOGETHER, WE WILL DEFINE THE AMERICAN DREAM...

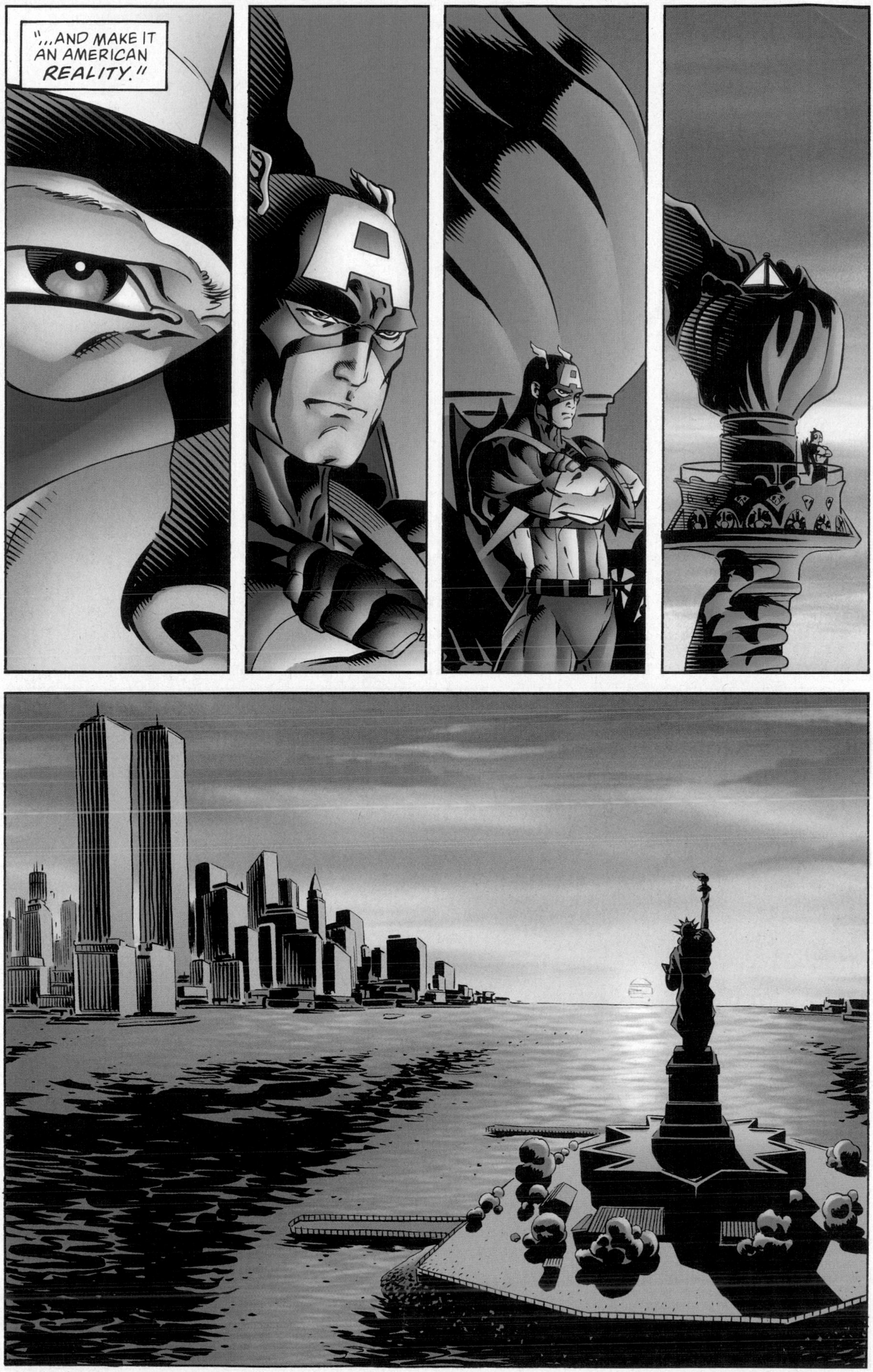
"...AND MAKE IT AN AMERICAN REALITY."

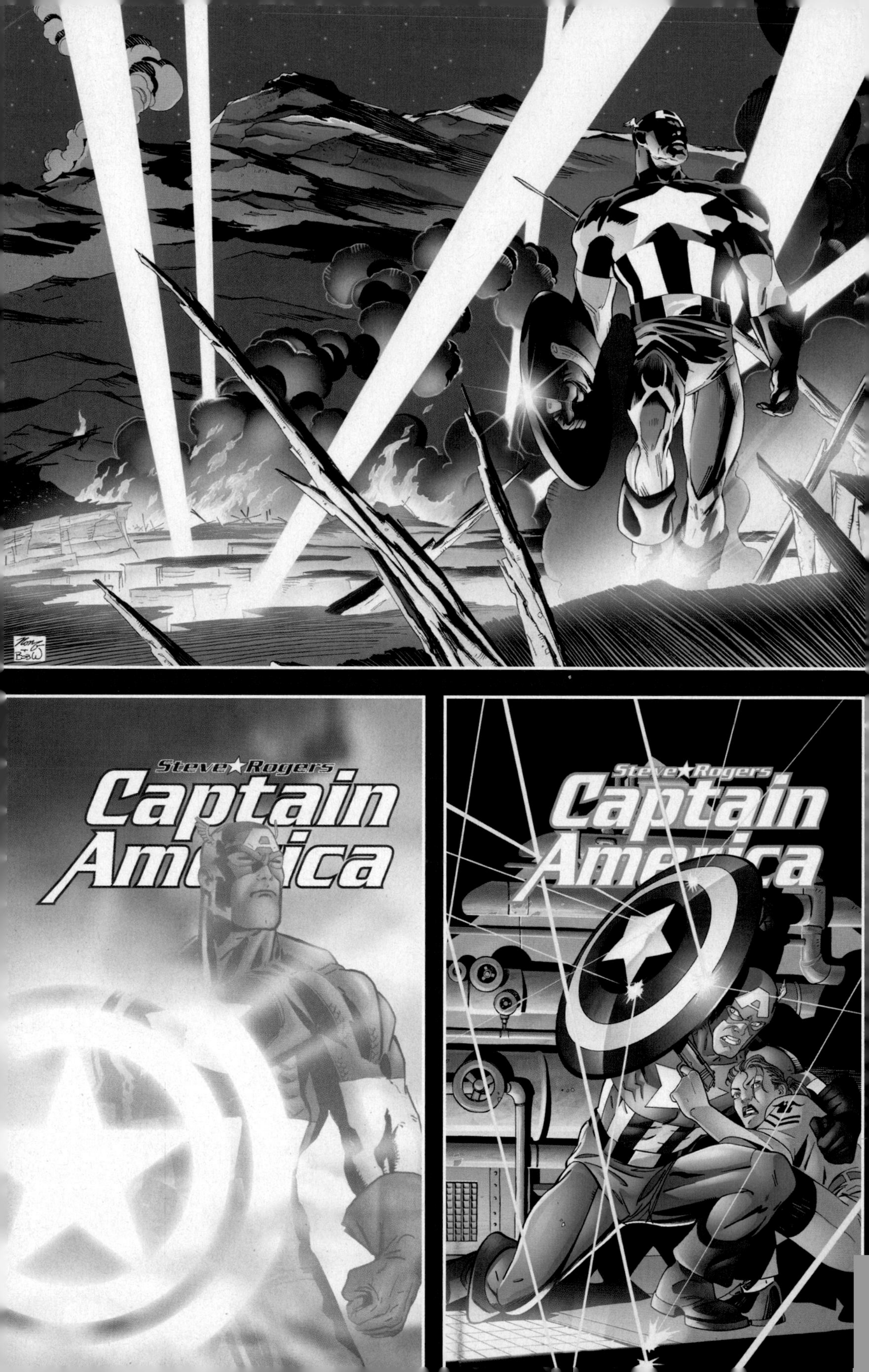
Steve★Rogers
Captain America
Steve★Rogers
Captain America

PREVIOUSLY IN

"LIVE KREE OR DIE!"

PART 1: IRON MAN #7

The Kree Lunatic Legion brought the Supreme Intelligence, synthetic ruler of their people, to their base on Earth's moon. The Legion planned to strike at Earth as retribution for the Avengers' near-fatal attack on the Intelligence months before — but the Intelligence secretly wanted them to fail. Meanwhile, Cap's fellow Avenger Warbird recently lost much of her power and turned to alcohol for solace. Iron Man confronted her, but, drunk, she attacked him. Luckily, the attack flushed out the Legion, who were building a powerful energy generator nearby. The Kree fled, and Warbird pursued…

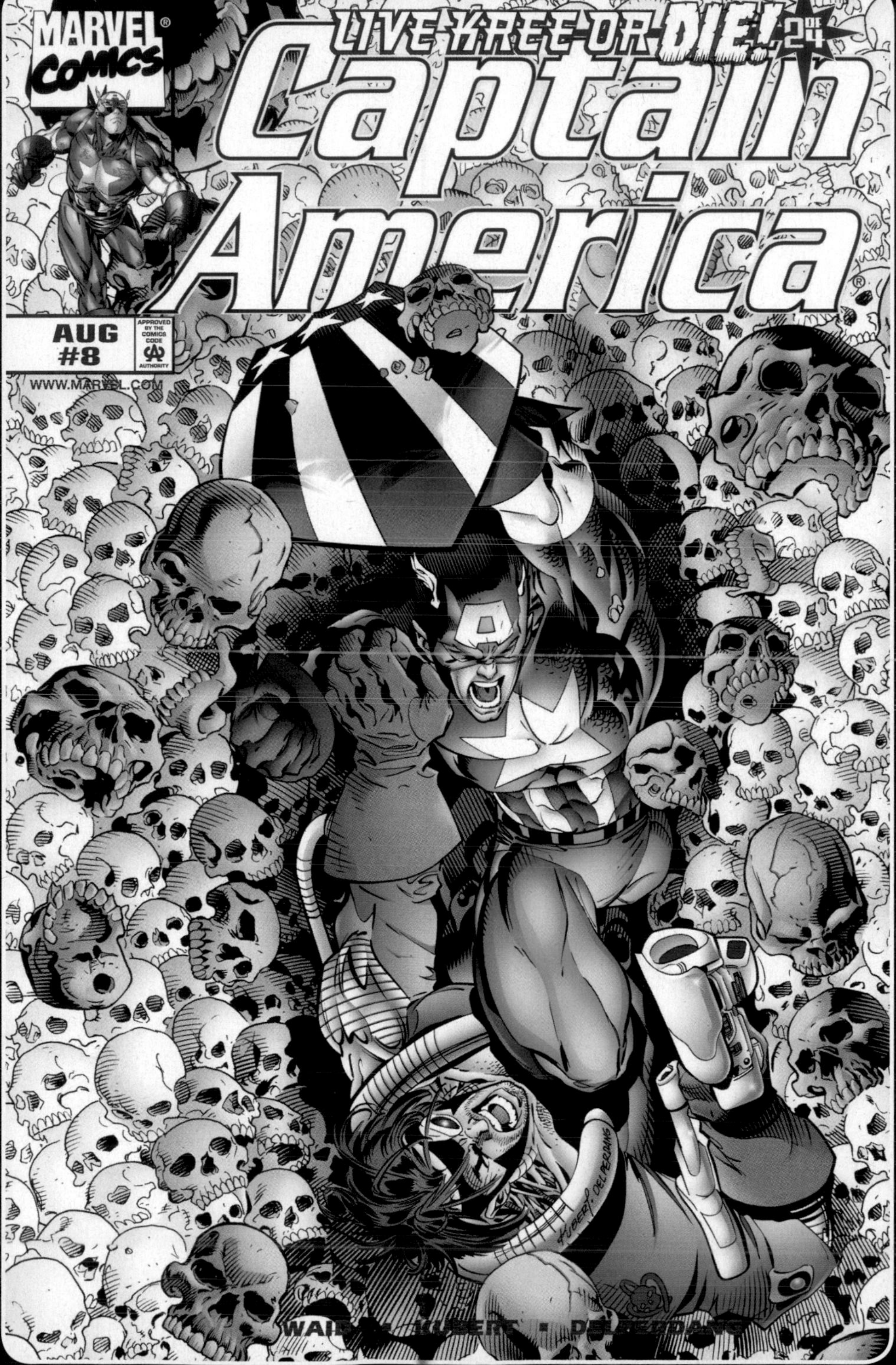
MARVEL COMICS
LIVE KREE OR DIE! 2 OF 4
Captain America
AUG #8
APPROVED BY THE COMICS CODE AUTHORITY
WWW.MARVEL.COM

THERE IS NO *HOPE* HERE.

DURING *WORLD WAR TWO,* THE NAZIS BROUGHT UNLUCKY INNOCENTS TO PRISON CAMPS FOR EXPERIMENTATION.

THE PRISONERS WERE BRUTALIZED...TREATED LIKE ANIMALS...

...AND, EVENTUALLY, HERDED INTO SEALED CHAMBERS...

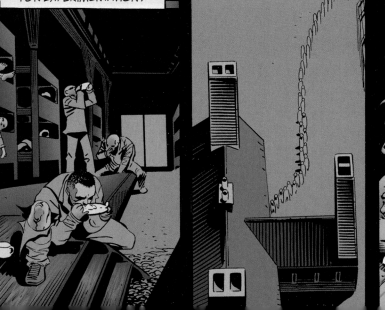

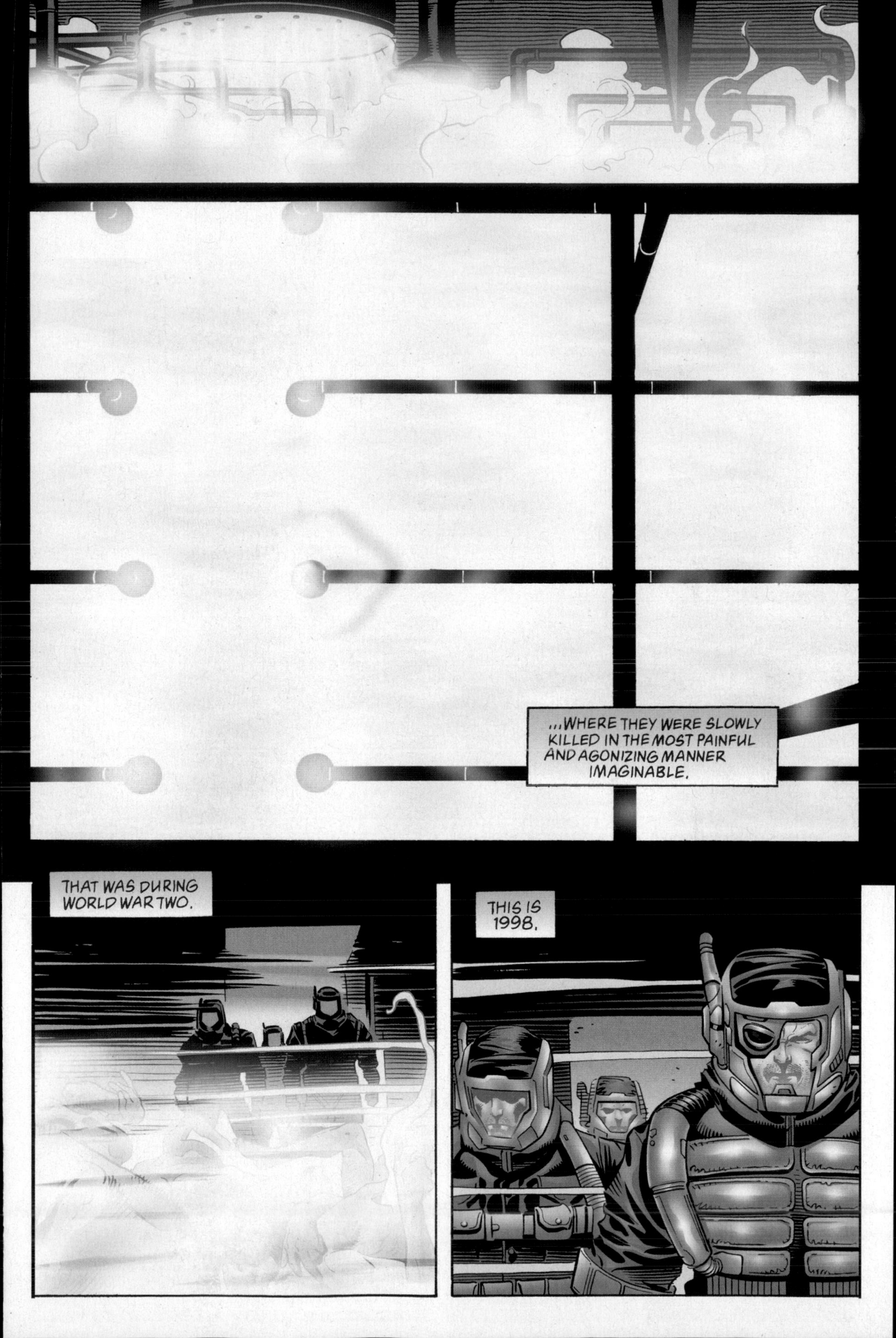
...WHERE THEY WERE SLOWLY KILLED IN THE MOST PAINFUL AND AGONIZING MANNER IMAGINABLE.
THAT WAS DURING WORLD WAR TWO.
THIS IS 1998.

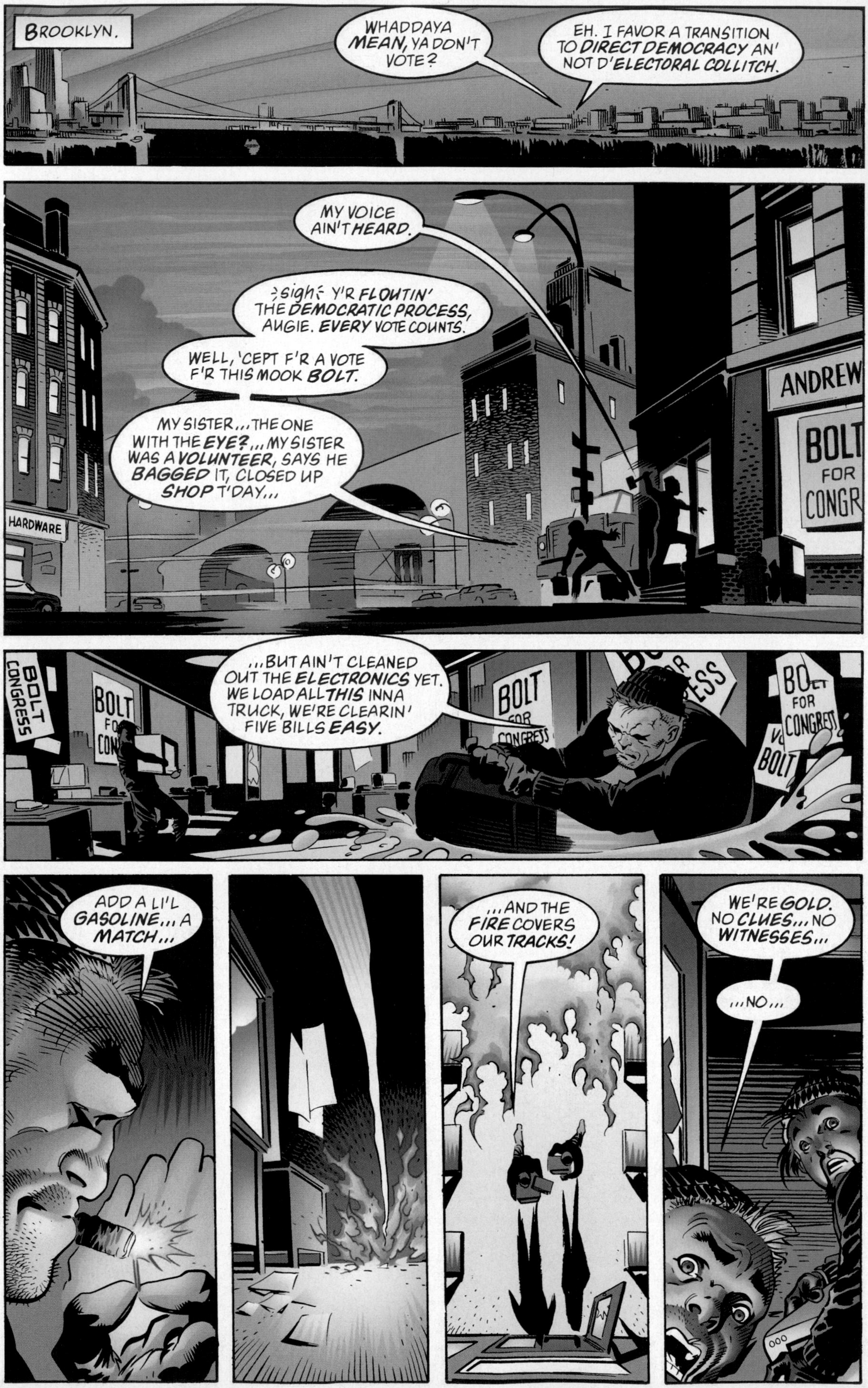
BROOKLYN.
WHADDAYA MEAN, YA DON'T VOTE?
EH. I FAVOR A TRANSITION TO DIRECT DEMOCRACY AN' NOT D'ELECTORAL COLLITCH.
MY VOICE AIN'T HEARD.
sigh Y'R FLOUTIN' THE DEMOCRATIC PROCESS, AUGIE. EVERY VOTE COUNTS.
WELL, 'CEPT F'R A VOTE F'R THIS MOOK BOLT.
MY SISTER... THE ONE WITH THE EYE?... MY SISTER WAS A VOLUNTEER, SAYS HE BAGGED IT, CLOSED UP SHOP T'DAY...
HARDWARE
ANDREW
BOLT FOR CONGR
...BUT AIN'T CLEANED OUT THE ELECTRONICS YET. WE LOAD ALL THIS INNA TRUCK, WE'RE CLEARIN' FIVE BILLS EASY.
BOLT CONGRESS
BOLT FOR CONGRESS
ADD A LI'L GASOLINE... A MATCH...
...AND THE FIRE COVERS OUR TRACKS!
WE'RE GOLD. NO CLUES... NO WITNESSES...
...NO...

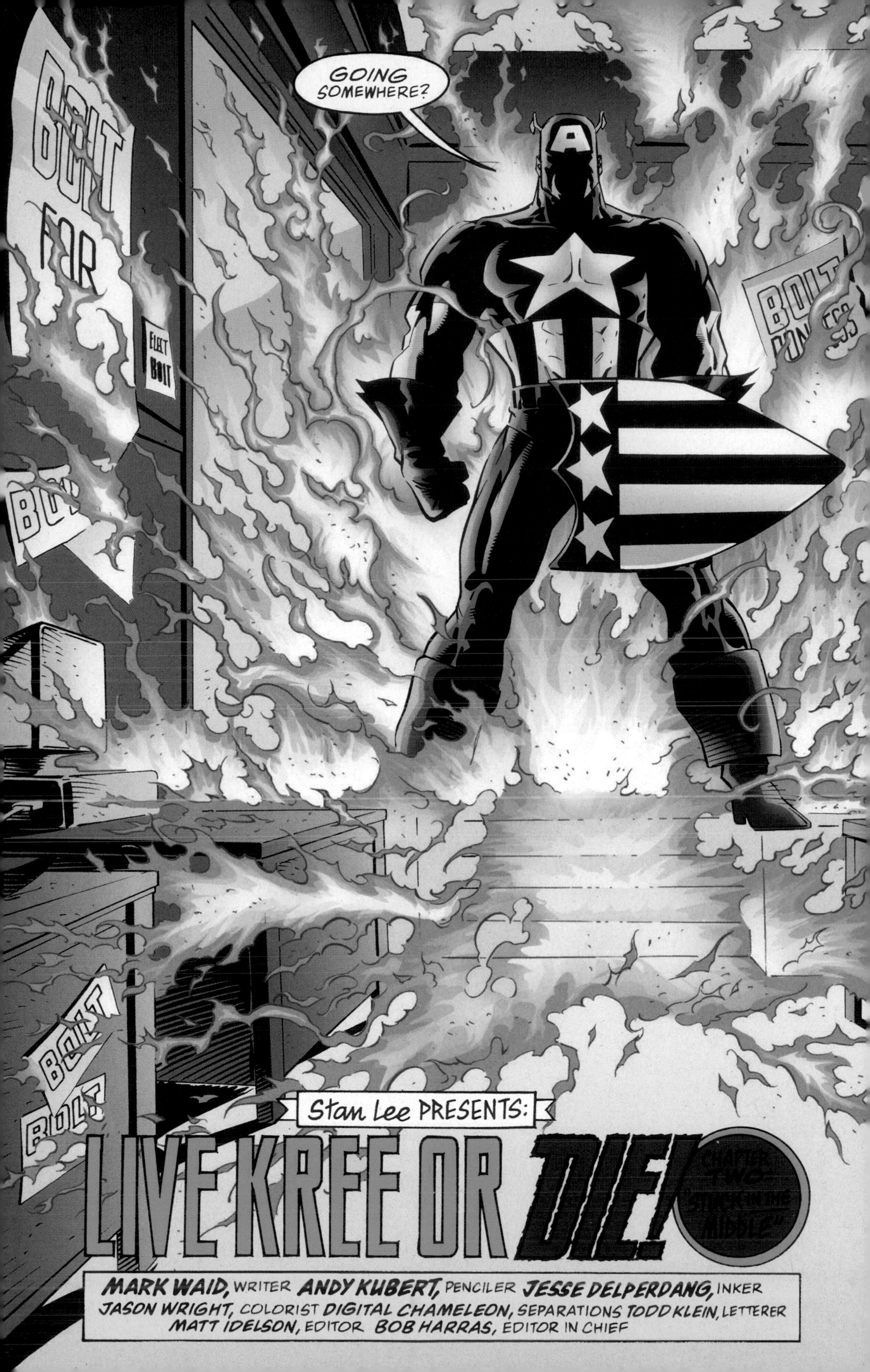
GOING SOMEWHERE?
Stan Lee PRESENTS:
LIVE KREE OR DIE!
CHAPTER TWO— "STUCK IN THE MIDDLE"
MARK WAID, WRITER ANDY KUBERT, PENCILER JESSE DELPERDANG, INKER
JASON WRIGHT, COLORIST DIGITAL CHAMELEON, SEPARATIONS TODD KLEIN, LETTERER
MATT IDELSON, EDITOR BOB HARRAS, EDITOR IN CHIEF

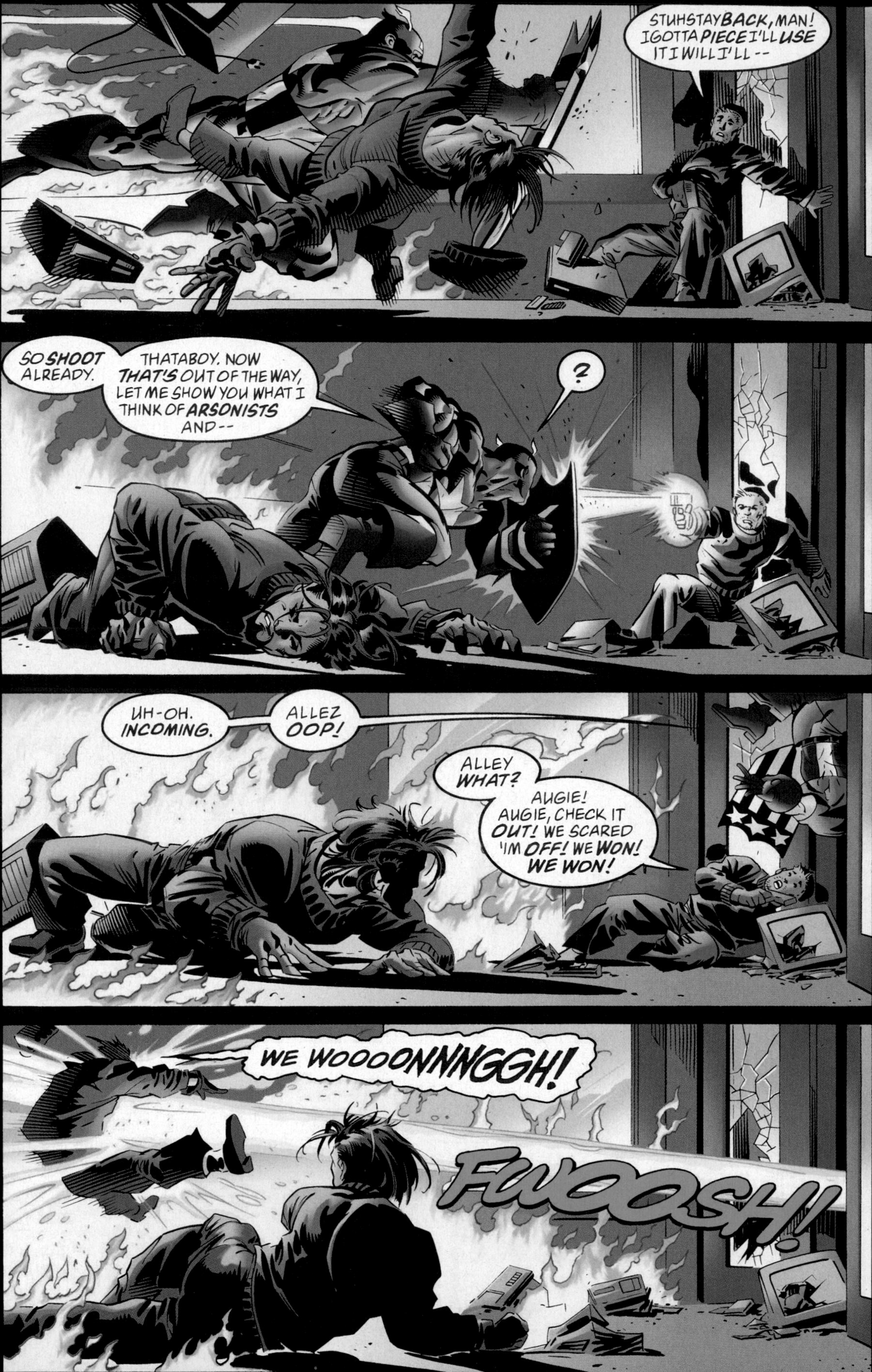
STUHSTAY BACK, MAN! IGOTTA PIECE I'LL USE IT I WILL I'LL --
SO SHOOT ALREADY.
THATABOY. NOW THAT'S OUT OF THE WAY, LET ME SHOW YOU WHAT I THINK OF ARSONISTS AND --
?
UH-OH. INCOMING.
ALLEZ OOP!
ALLEY WHAT?
AUGIE! AUGIE, CHECK IT OUT! WE SCARED 'IM OFF! WE WON! WE WON!
WE WOOOONNNGGH!
FWOOSH!!

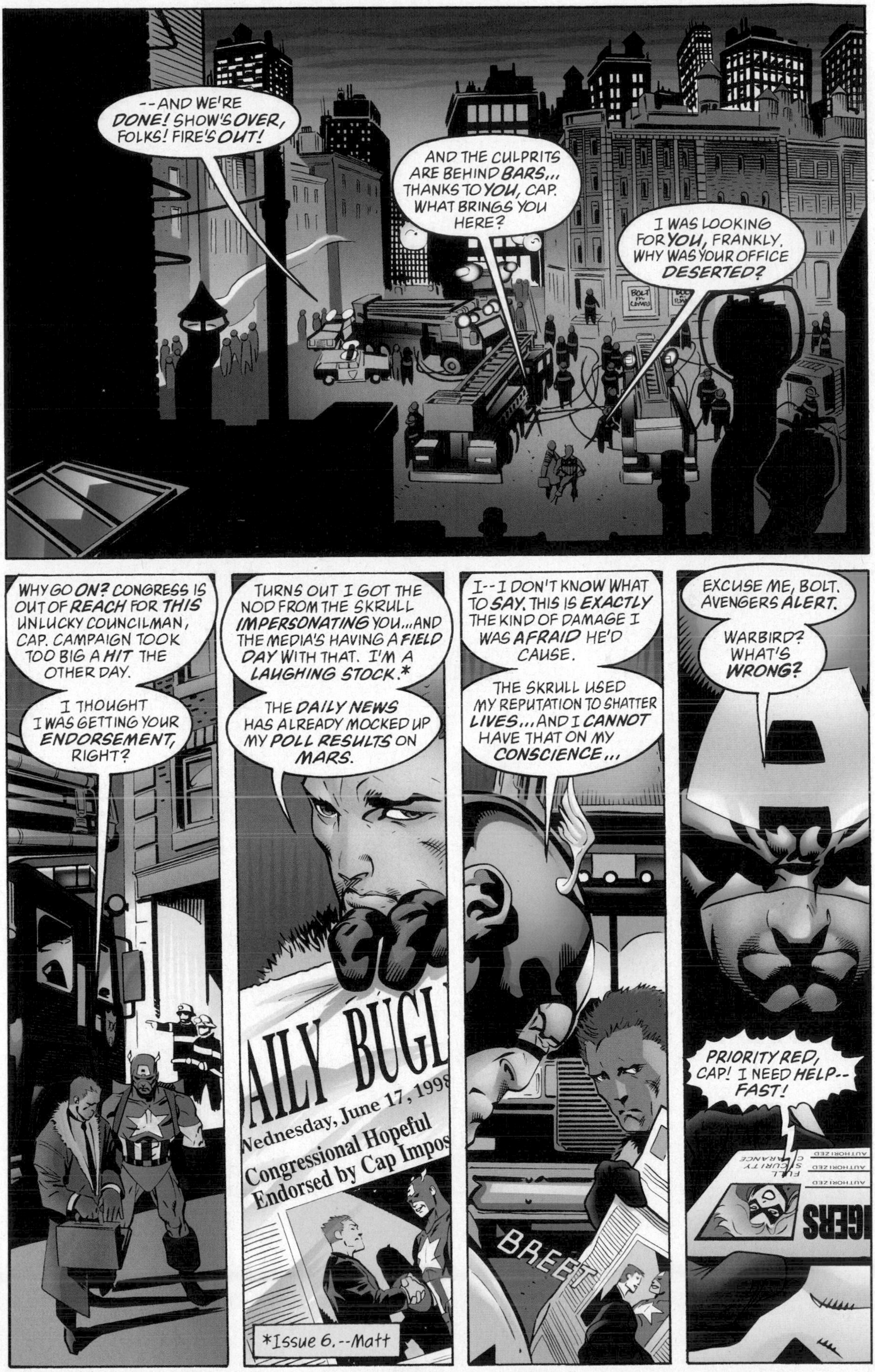
--AND WE'RE DONE! SHOW'S OVER, FOLKS! FIRE'S OUT!
AND THE CULPRITS ARE BEHIND BARS... THANKS TO YOU, CAP. WHAT BRINGS YOU HERE?
I WAS LOOKING FOR YOU, FRANKLY. WHY WAS YOUR OFFICE DESERTED?
WHY GO ON? CONGRESS IS OUT OF REACH FOR THIS UNLUCKY COUNCILMAN, CAP. CAMPAIGN TOOK TOO BIG A HIT THE OTHER DAY.
I THOUGHT I WAS GETTING YOUR ENDORSEMENT, RIGHT?
TURNS OUT I GOT THE NOD FROM THE SKRULL IMPERSONATING YOU...AND THE MEDIA'S HAVING A FIELD DAY WITH THAT. I'M A LAUGHING STOCK.*
THE DAILY NEWS HAS ALREADY MOCKED UP MY POLL RESULTS ON MARS.
AILY BUGL
Congressional Hopeful Endorsed by Cap Impos
*Issue 6.--Matt
I--I DON'T KNOW WHAT TO SAY. THIS IS EXACTLY THE KIND OF DAMAGE I WAS AFRAID HE'D CAUSE.
THE SKRULL USED MY REPUTATION TO SHATTER LIVES...AND I CANNOT HAVE THAT ON MY CONSCIENCE...
BREEET
EXCUSE ME, BOLT. AVENGERS ALERT.
WARBIRD? WHAT'S WRONG?
PRIORITY RED, CAP! I NEED HELP--FAST!

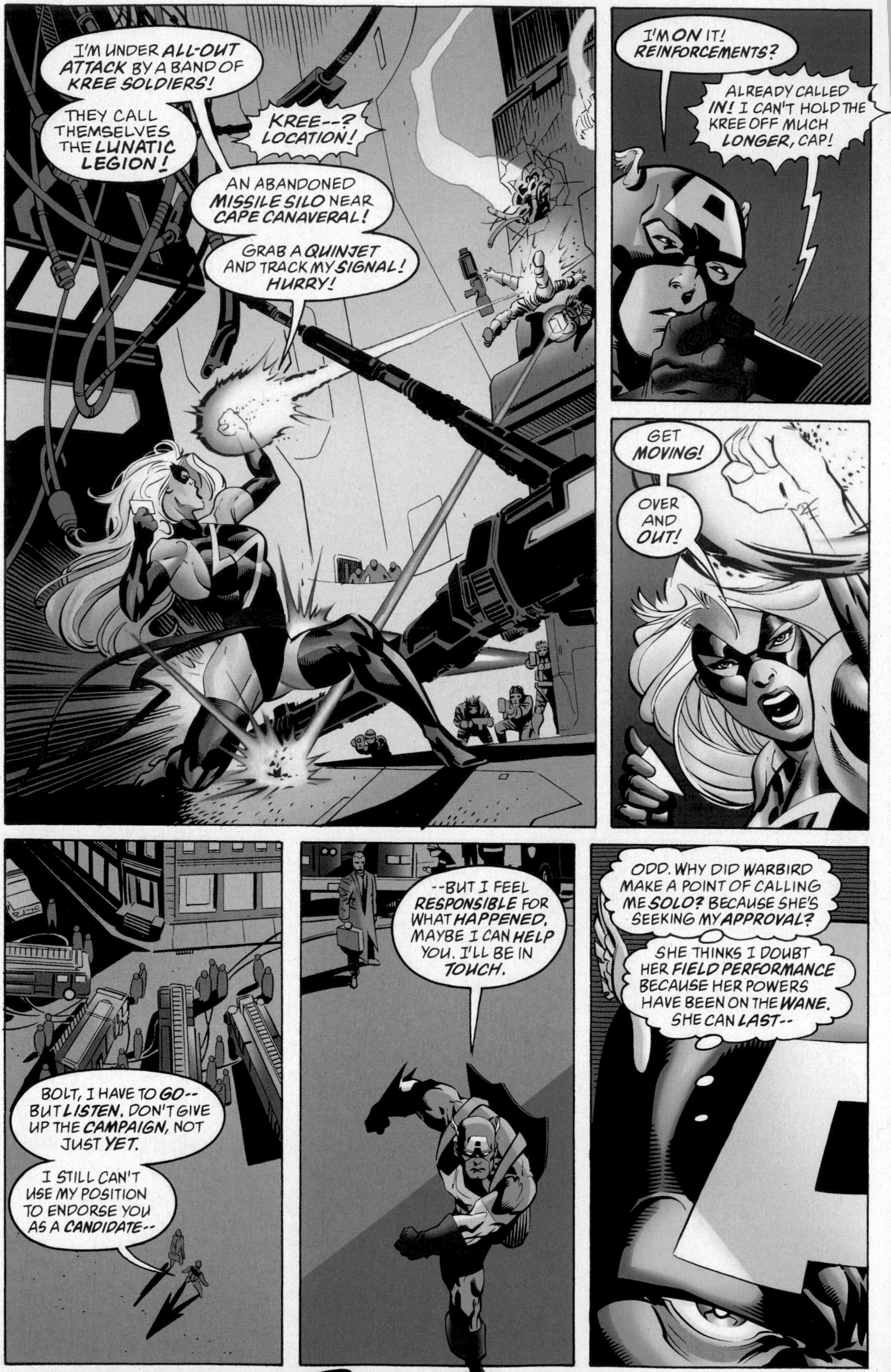
I'M UNDER ALL-OUT ATTACK BY A BAND OF KREE SOLDIERS!
THEY CALL THEMSELVES THE LUNATIC LEGION!
KREE--? LOCATION!
AN ABANDONED MISSILE SILO NEAR CAPE CANAVERAL!
GRAB A QUINJET AND TRACK MY SIGNAL! HURRY!
I'M ON IT! REINFORCEMENTS?
ALREADY CALLED IN! I CAN'T HOLD THE KREE OFF MUCH LONGER, CAP!
GET MOVING!
OVER AND OUT!
BOLT, I HAVE TO GO-- BUT LISTEN. DON'T GIVE UP THE CAMPAIGN, NOT JUST YET.
I STILL CAN'T USE MY POSITION TO ENDORSE YOU AS A CANDIDATE--
--BUT I FEEL RESPONSIBLE FOR WHAT HAPPENED. MAYBE I CAN HELP YOU. I'LL BE IN TOUCH.
ODD. WHY DID WARBIRD MAKE A POINT OF CALLING ME SOLO? BECAUSE SHE'S SEEKING MY APPROVAL?
SHE THINKS I DOUBT HER FIELD PERFORMANCE BECAUSE HER POWERS HAVE BEEN ON THE WANE. SHE CAN LAST--

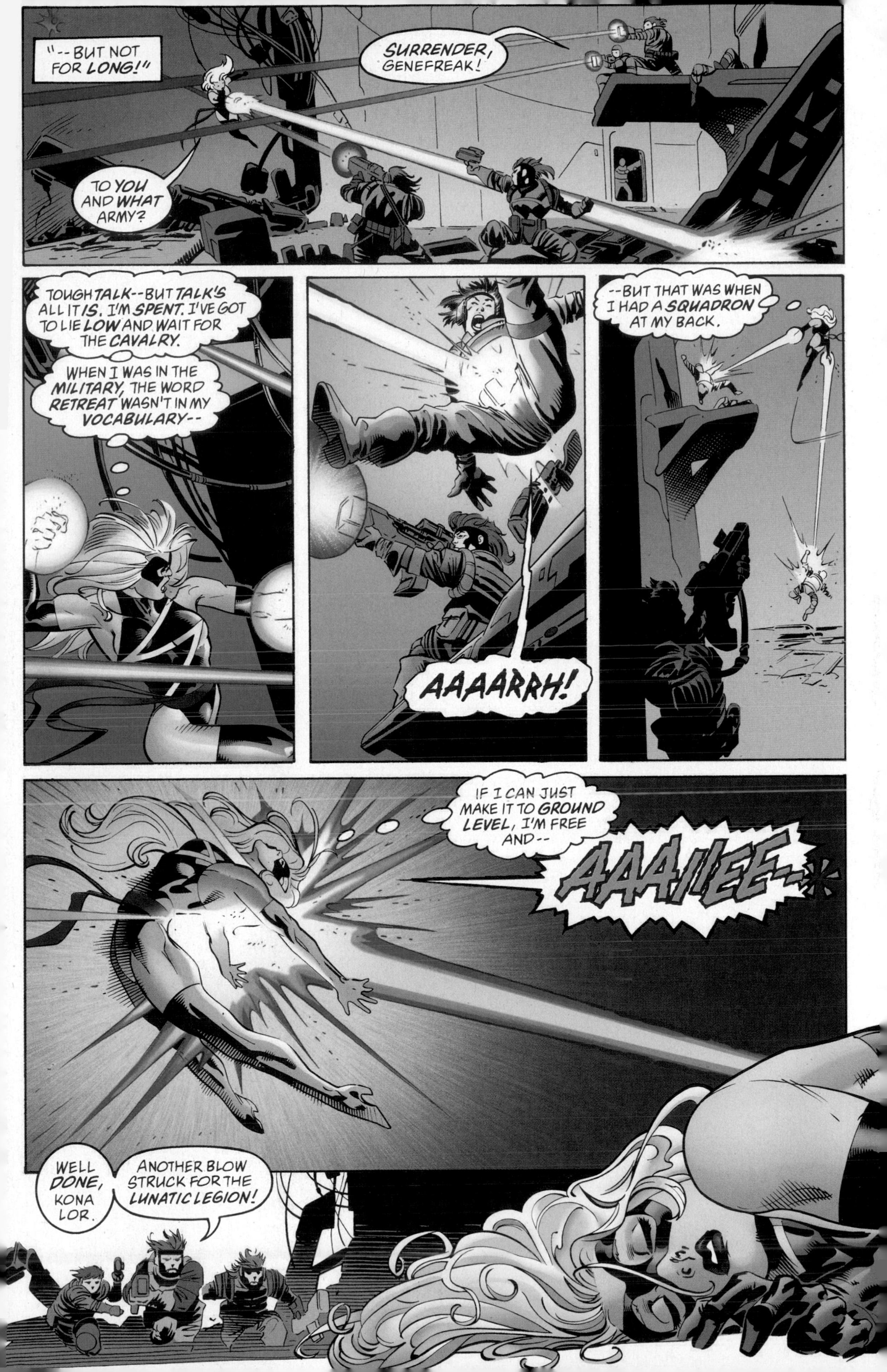
"--BUT NOT FOR LONG!"
SURRENDER, GENEFREAK!
TO YOU AND WHAT ARMY?
TOUGH TALK--BUT TALK'S ALL IT IS. I'M SPENT. I'VE GOT TO LIE LOW AND WAIT FOR THE CAVALRY.
WHEN I WAS IN THE MILITARY, THE WORD RETREAT WASN'T IN MY VOCABULARY--
AAAARRH!
--BUT THAT WAS WHEN I HAD A SQUADRON AT MY BACK.
IF I CAN JUST MAKE IT TO GROUND LEVEL, I'M FREE AND--
AAAIIEE--
WELL DONE, KONA LOR.
ANOTHER BLOW STRUCK FOR THE LUNATIC LEGION!

I SAY WE INCINERATE HER WHERE SHE *FELL*.

THE SOONER OUR ENEMIES ARE *VANQUISHED*, THE SOONER THIS PITIABLE MUDBALL WILL BE GROUND TO DUST BY THE *KREE EMPIRE*.

HAVE A *CARE*, KONA. YOUR TEMPER *AGAIN* THREATENS TO BETRAY THE *GREATER GOOD*.

REMEMBER, DUE TO AN ACCIDENT OF *SCIENCE*, THIS GENEFREAK'S UNIQUE MOLECULAR STRUCTURE IS HALF *HUMAN*, HALF *KREE*.

AS *SUCH*, SHE MAY BE A *MEANS* TO OUR *END*. IN THE *MEANTIME*, LET US... *USE* HER.

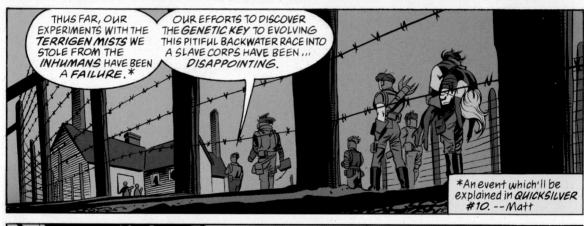

THUS FAR, OUR EXPERIMENTS WITH THE *TERRIGEN MISTS* WE STOLE FROM THE *INHUMANS* HAVE BEEN A *FAILURE*.*

OUR EFFORTS TO DISCOVER THE *GENETIC KEY* TO EVOLVING THIS PITIFUL BACKWATER RACE INTO A SLAVE CORPS HAVE BEEN... *DISAPPOINTING*.

*An event which'll be explained in *QUICKSILVER* #10. --Matt

PERHAPS THIS *"WARBIRD'S"* PHYSIOLOGY WILL PROVIDE THE NECESSARY *CATALYST* FOR THE MUTATION WE SEEK.

OR *NOT*.

AH, WELL, REGARDLESS OF *WHAT* HAPPENS...

...IT WILL BE FUN TO *WATCH*...

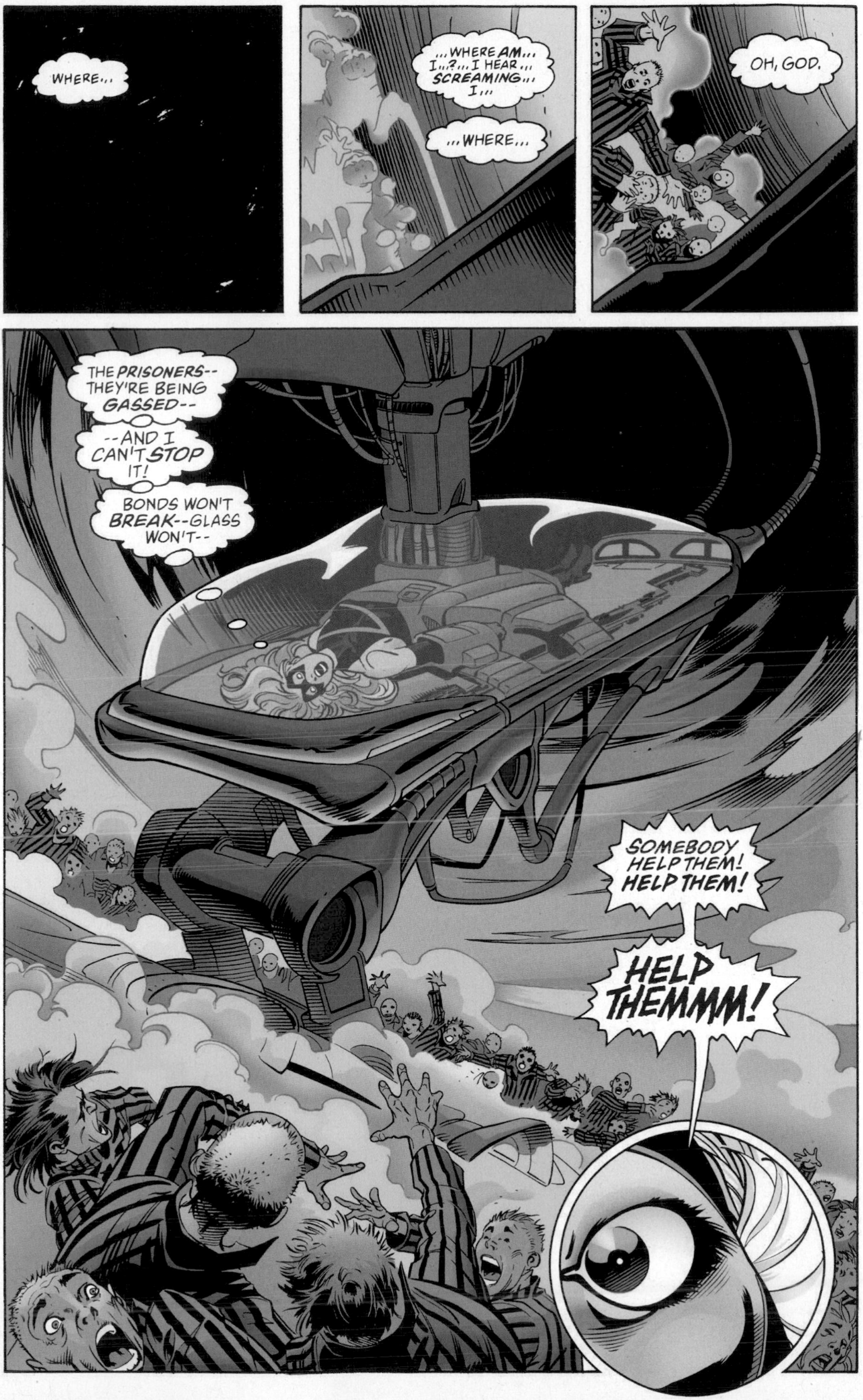
WHERE...
...WHERE AM I...?...I HEAR... SCREAMING... I...
...WHERE...
OH, GOD.
THE PRISONERS-- THEY'RE BEING GASSED--
--AND I CAN'T STOP IT!
BONDS WON'T BREAK--GLASS WON'T--
SOMEBODY HELP THEM! HELP THEM!
HELP THEMMM!

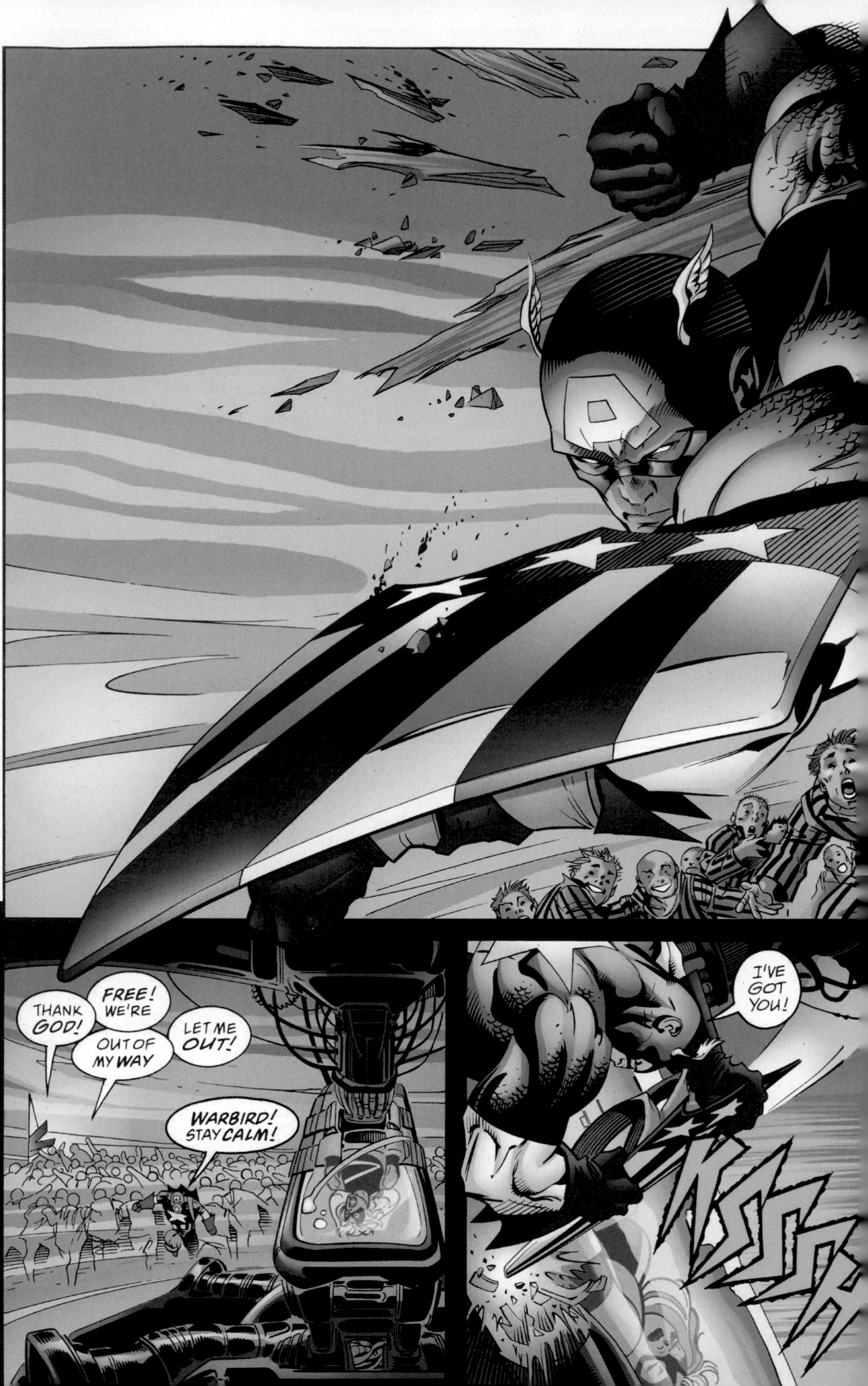

THANK GOD!
FREE! WE'RE
OUT OF MY WAY
LET ME OUT!
WARBIRD! STAY CALM!
I'VE GOT YOU!
KSSSK

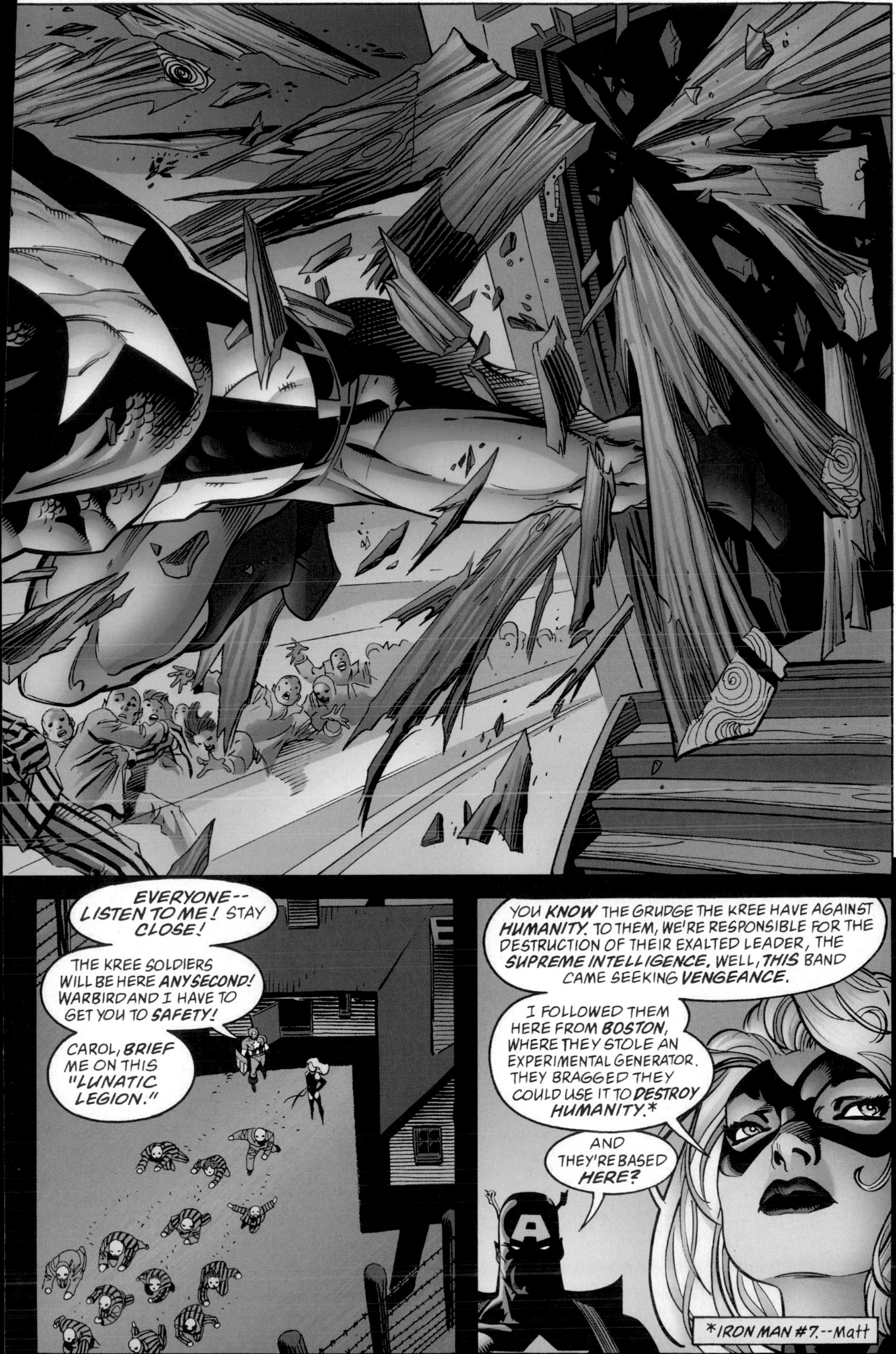
EVERYONE-- LISTEN TO ME! STAY CLOSE!
THE KREE SOLDIERS WILL BE HERE ANY SECOND! WARBIRD AND I HAVE TO GET YOU TO SAFETY!
CAROL, BRIEF ME ON THIS "LUNATIC LEGION."
YOU KNOW THE GRUDGE THE KREE HAVE AGAINST HUMANITY. TO THEM, WE'RE RESPONSIBLE FOR THE DESTRUCTION OF THEIR EXALTED LEADER, THE SUPREME INTELLIGENCE. WELL, THIS BAND CAME SEEKING VENGEANCE.
I FOLLOWED THEM HERE FROM BOSTON, WHERE THEY STOLE AN EXPERIMENTAL GENERATOR. THEY BRAGGED THEY COULD USE IT TO DESTROY HUMANITY.*
AND THEY'RE BASED HERE?
*IRON MAN #7.--Matt

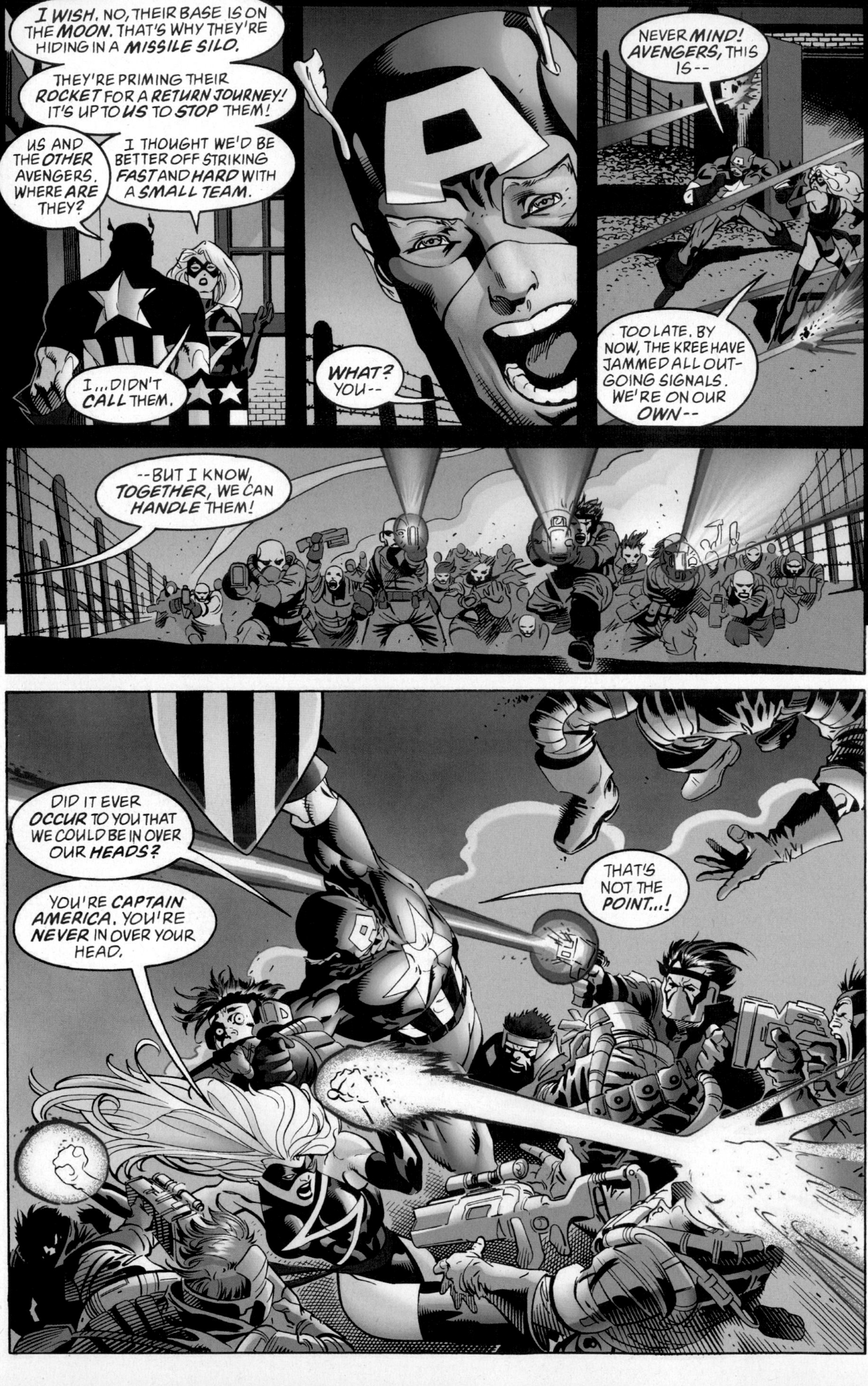
I WISH. NO, THEIR BASE IS ON THE MOON. THAT'S WHY THEY'RE HIDING IN A MISSILE SILO.
THEY'RE PRIMING THEIR ROCKET FOR A RETURN JOURNEY! IT'S UP TO US TO STOP THEM!
US AND THE OTHER AVENGERS. WHERE ARE THEY?
I THOUGHT WE'D BE BETTER OFF STRIKING FAST AND HARD WITH A SMALL TEAM.
I...DIDN'T CALL THEM.
WHAT? YOU--
NEVER MIND! AVENGERS, THIS IS--
TOO LATE. BY NOW, THE KREE HAVE JAMMED ALL OUT-GOING SIGNALS. WE'RE ON OUR OWN--
--BUT I KNOW, TOGETHER, WE CAN HANDLE THEM!
DID IT EVER OCCUR TO YOU THAT WE COULD BE IN OVER OUR HEADS?
YOU'RE CAPTAIN AMERICA. YOU'RE NEVER IN OVER YOUR HEAD.
THAT'S NOT THE POINT...!

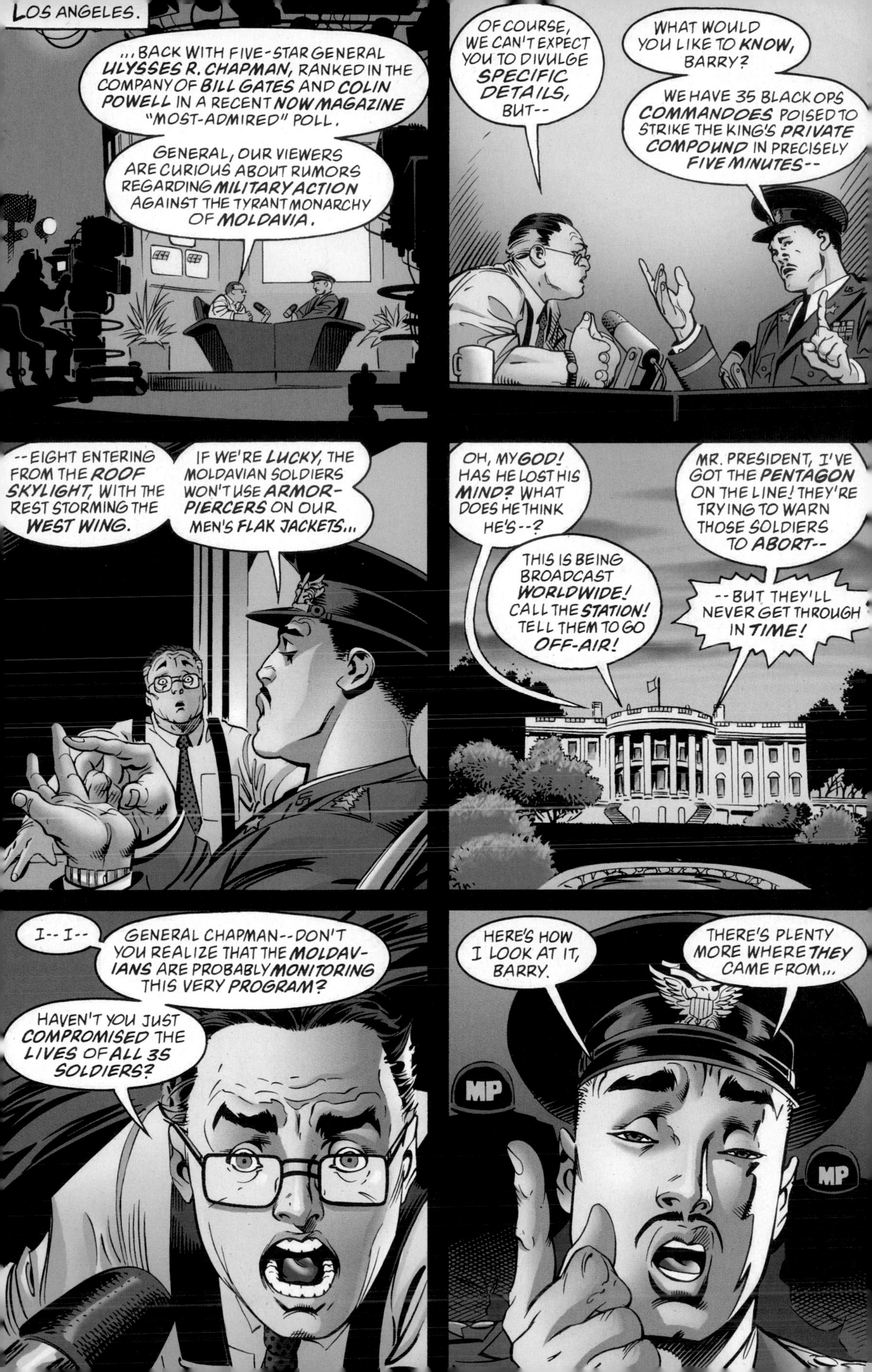
LOS ANGELES.
...BACK WITH FIVE-STAR GENERAL ULYSSES R. CHAPMAN, RANKED IN THE COMPANY OF BILL GATES AND COLIN POWELL IN A RECENT NOW MAGAZINE "MOST-ADMIRED" POLL.
GENERAL, OUR VIEWERS ARE CURIOUS ABOUT RUMORS REGARDING MILITARY ACTION AGAINST THE TYRANT MONARCHY OF MOLDAVIA.
OF COURSE, WE CAN'T EXPECT YOU TO DIVULGE SPECIFIC DETAILS, BUT--
WHAT WOULD YOU LIKE TO KNOW, BARRY?
WE HAVE 35 BLACK OPS COMMANDOES POISED TO STRIKE THE KING'S PRIVATE COMPOUND IN PRECISELY FIVE MINUTES--
--EIGHT ENTERING FROM THE ROOF SKYLIGHT, WITH THE REST STORMING THE WEST WING.
IF WE'RE LUCKY, THE MOLDAVIAN SOLDIERS WON'T USE ARMOR-PIERCERS ON OUR MEN'S FLAK JACKETS...
OH, MY GOD! HAS HE LOST HIS MIND? WHAT DOES HE THINK HE'S--?
THIS IS BEING BROADCAST WORLDWIDE! CALL THE STATION! TELL THEM TO GO OFF-AIR!
MR. PRESIDENT, I'VE GOT THE PENTAGON ON THE LINE! THEY'RE TRYING TO WARN THOSE SOLDIERS TO ABORT--
--BUT THEY'LL NEVER GET THROUGH IN TIME!
I-- I--
GENERAL CHAPMAN--DON'T YOU REALIZE THAT THE MOLDAVIANS ARE PROBABLY MONITORING THIS VERY PROGRAM?
HAVEN'T YOU JUST COMPROMISED THE LIVES OF ALL 35 SOLDIERS?
HERE'S HOW I LOOK AT IT, BARRY.
THERE'S PLENTY MORE WHERE THEY CAME FROM...
MP
MP

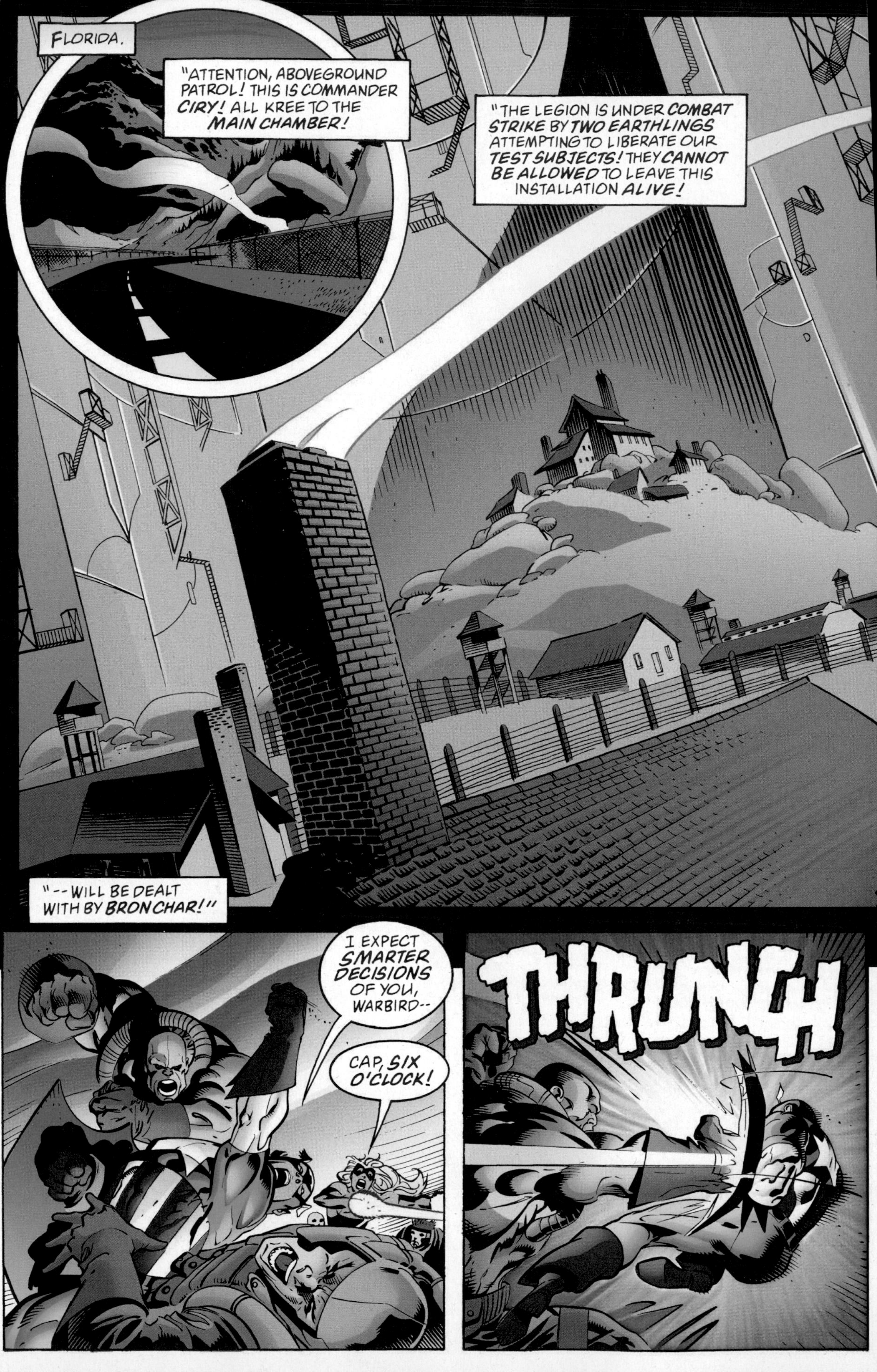
FLORIDA.
"ATTENTION, ABOVEGROUND PATROL! THIS IS COMMANDER CIRY! ALL KREE TO THE MAIN CHAMBER!
"THE LEGION IS UNDER COMBAT STRIKE BY TWO EARTHLINGS ATTEMPTING TO LIBERATE OUR TEST SUBJECTS! THEY CANNOT BE ALLOWED TO LEAVE THIS INSTALLATION ALIVE!
"--WILL BE DEALT WITH BY BRONCHAR!"
I EXPECT SMARTER DECISIONS OF YOU, WARBIRD--
CAP, SIX O'CLOCK!
THRUNCH

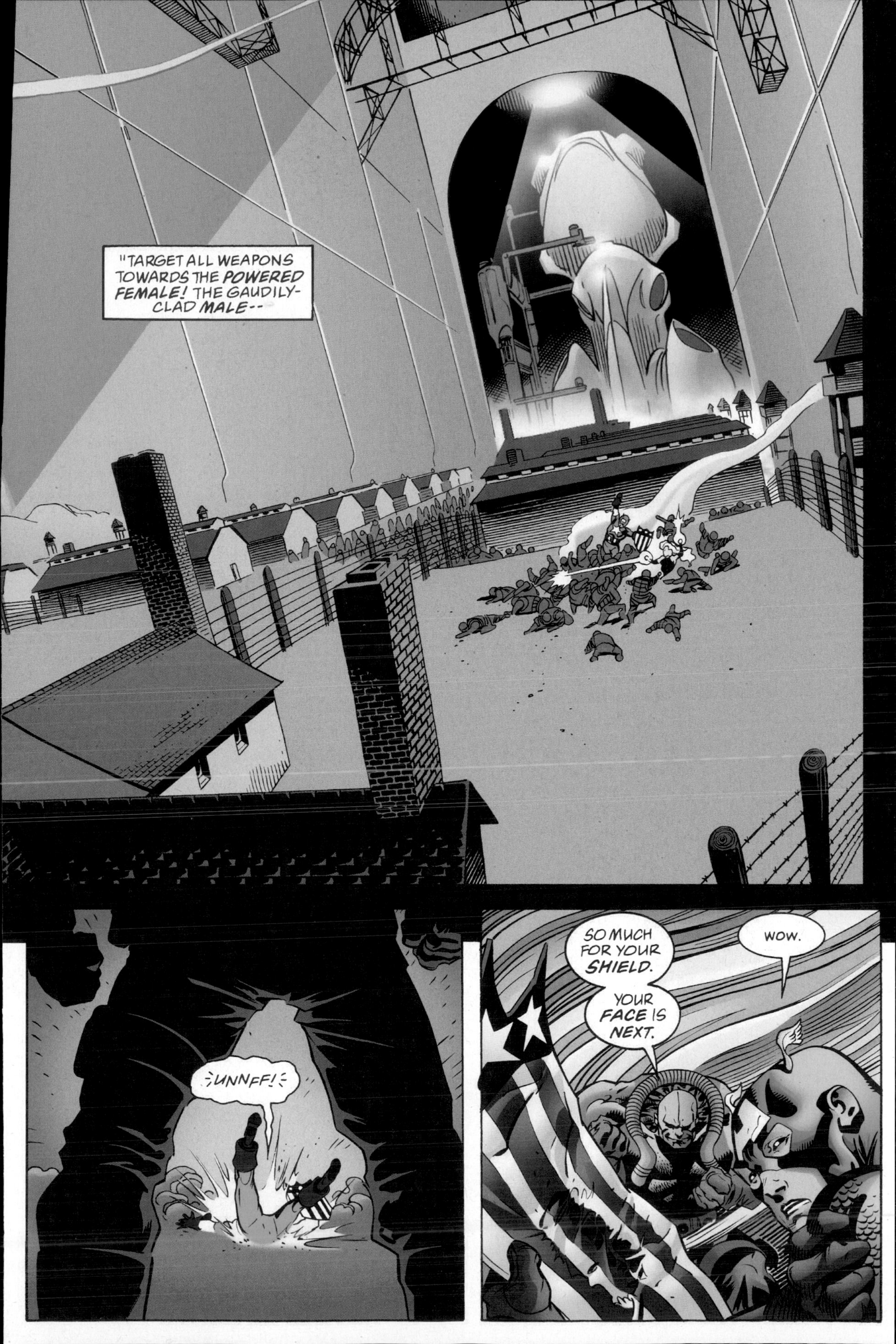
"TARGET ALL WEAPONS TOWARDS THE POWERED FEMALE! THE GAUDILY-CLAD MALE--
UNNFF!
SO MUCH FOR YOUR SHIELD.
YOUR FACE IS NEXT.
WOW.

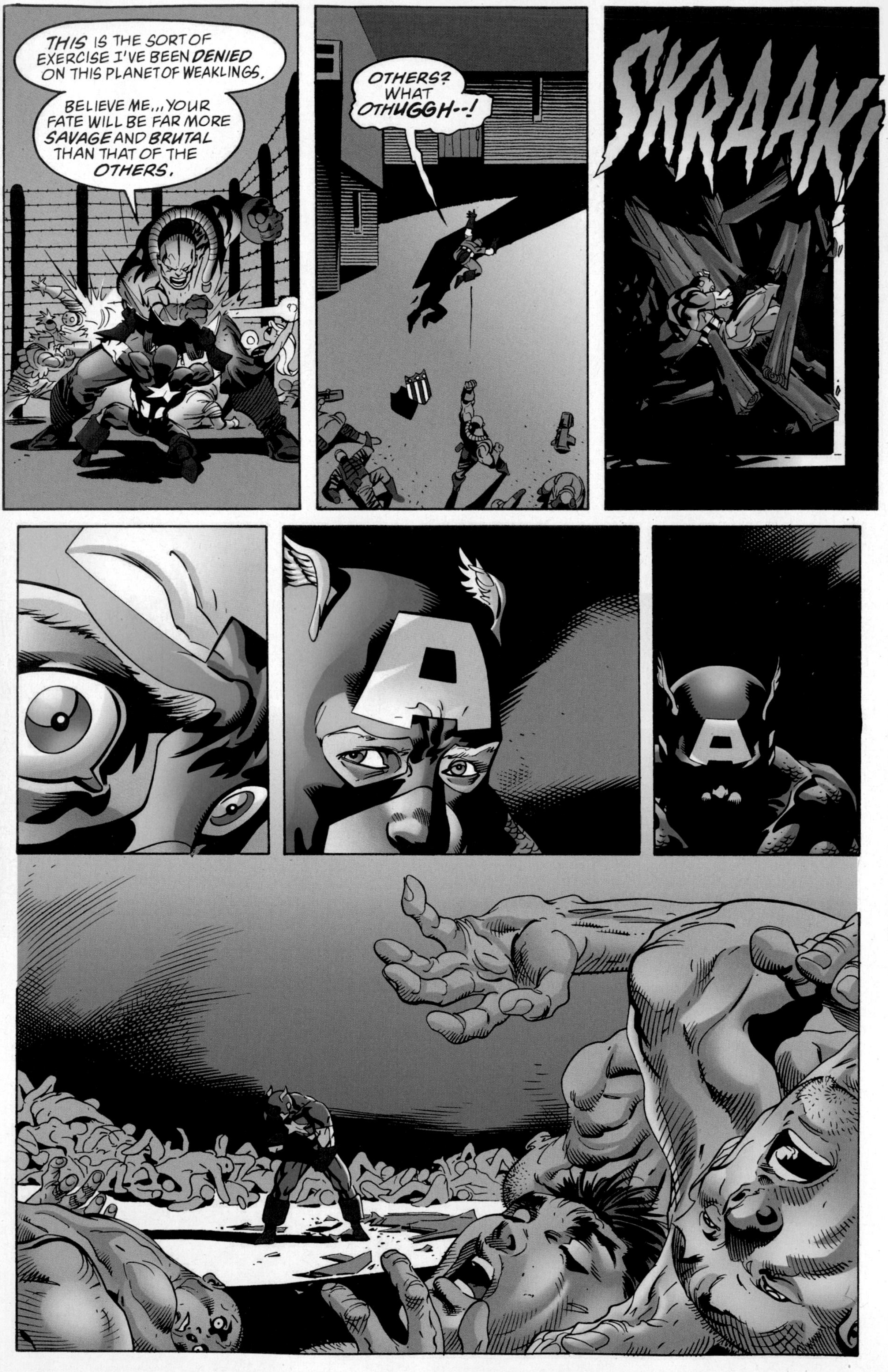
THIS IS THE SORT OF EXERCISE I'VE BEEN DENIED ON THIS PLANET OF WEAKLINGS.
BELIEVE ME... YOUR FATE WILL BE FAR MORE SAVAGE AND BRUTAL THAN THAT OF THE OTHERS.
OTHERS? WHAT OTHUGGH--!
SKRAAK!

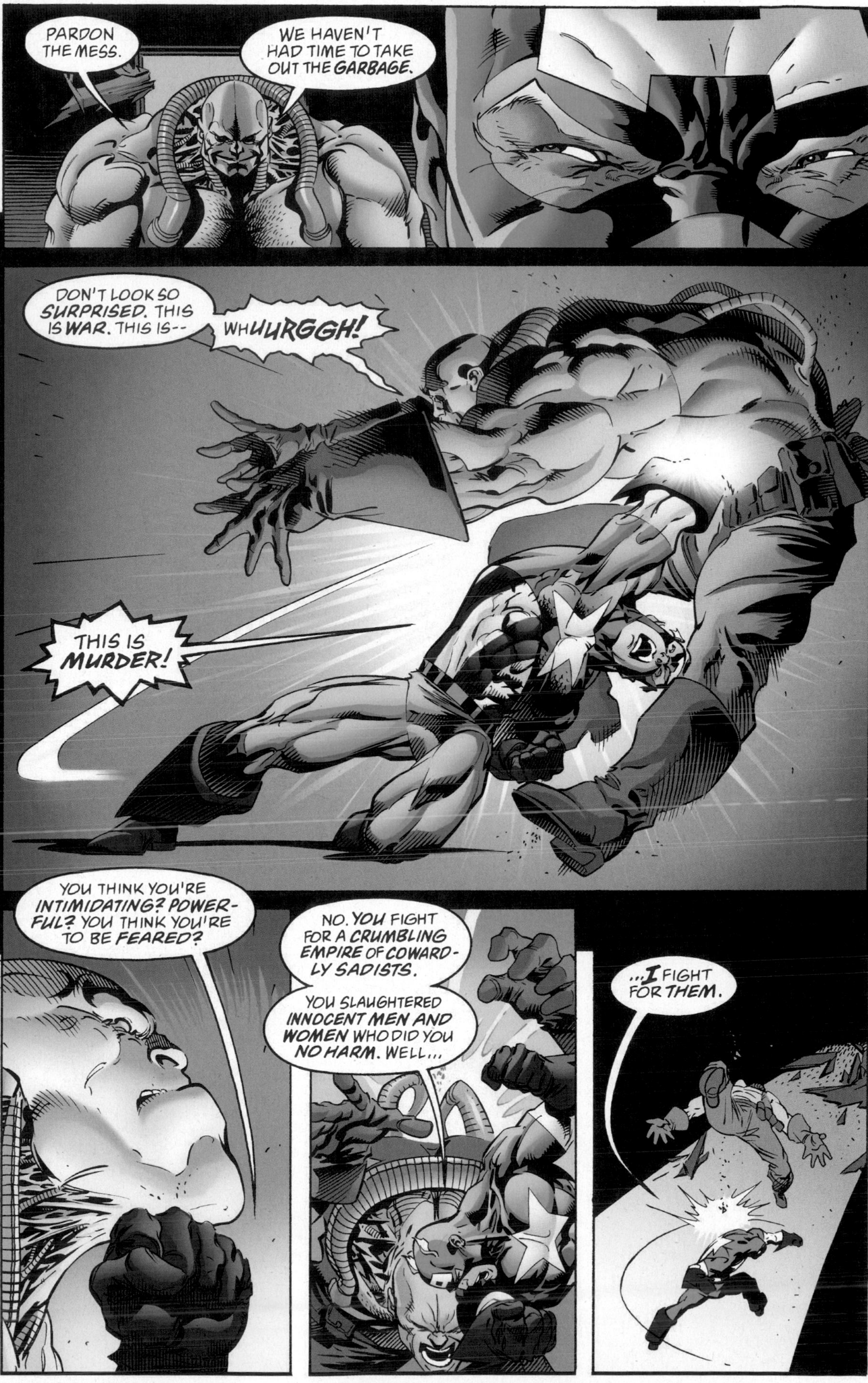
PARDON THE MESS.
WE HAVEN'T HAD TIME TO TAKE OUT THE GARBAGE.
DON'T LOOK SO SURPRISED. THIS IS WAR. THIS IS--
WHUURGGH!
THIS IS MURDER!
YOU THINK YOU'RE INTIMIDATING? POWERFUL? YOU THINK YOU'RE TO BE FEARED?
NO. YOU FIGHT FOR A CRUMBLING EMPIRE OF COWARDLY SADISTS.
YOU SLAUGHTERED INNOCENT MEN AND WOMEN WHO DID YOU NO HARM. WELL...
...I FIGHT FOR THEM.

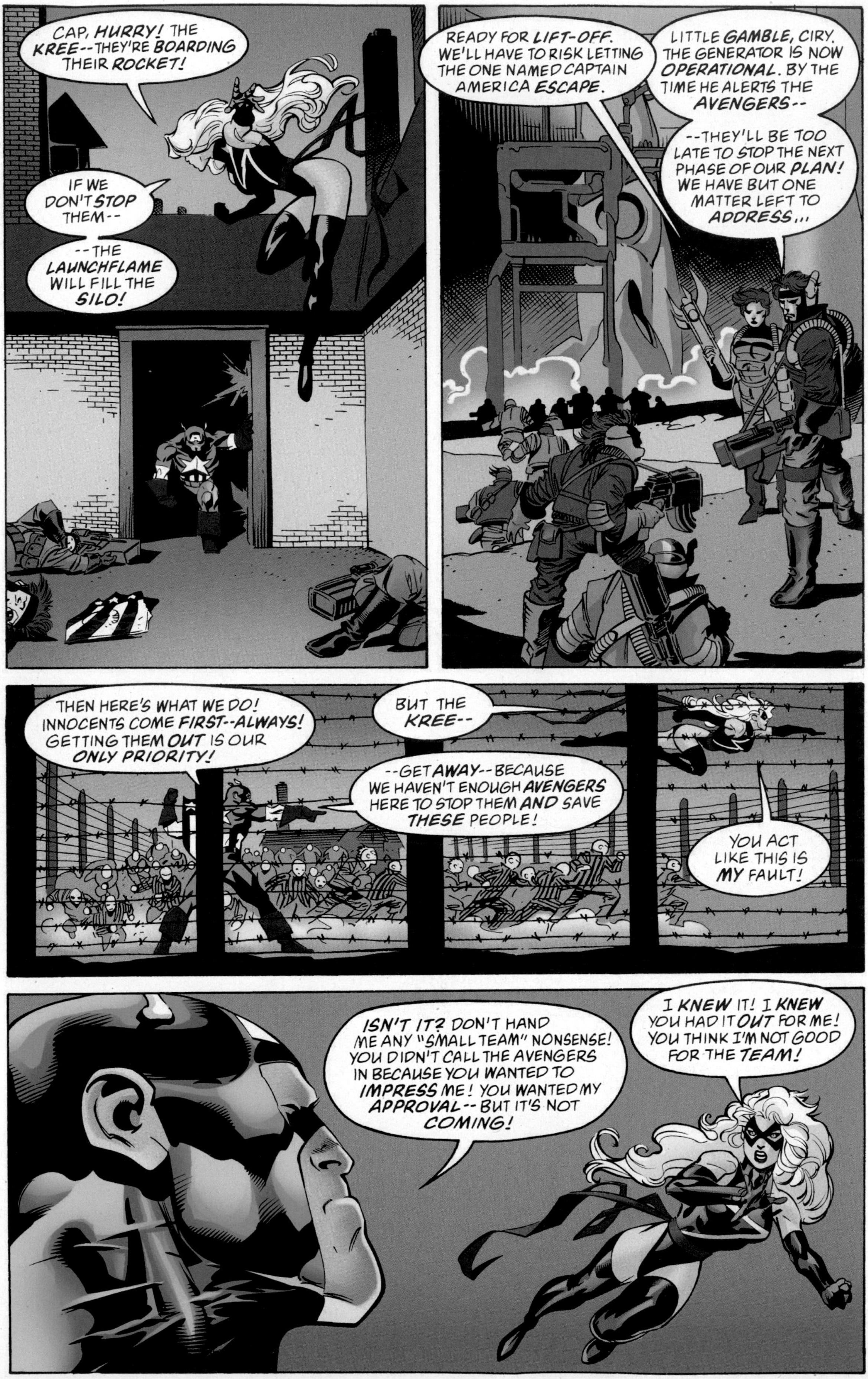
CAP, HURRY! THE KREE--THEY'RE BOARDING THEIR ROCKET!
IF WE DON'T STOP THEM--
--THE LAUNCHFLAME WILL FILL THE SILO!
READY FOR LIFT-OFF. WE'LL HAVE TO RISK LETTING THE ONE NAMED CAPTAIN AMERICA ESCAPE.
LITTLE GAMBLE, CIRY. THE GENERATOR IS NOW OPERATIONAL. BY THE TIME HE ALERTS THE AVENGERS--
--THEY'LL BE TOO LATE TO STOP THE NEXT PHASE OF OUR PLAN! WE HAVE BUT ONE MATTER LEFT TO ADDRESS...
THEN HERE'S WHAT WE DO! INNOCENTS COME FIRST--ALWAYS! GETTING THEM OUT IS OUR ONLY PRIORITY!
BUT THE KREE--
--GET AWAY--BECAUSE WE HAVEN'T ENOUGH AVENGERS HERE TO STOP THEM AND SAVE THESE PEOPLE!
YOU ACT LIKE THIS IS MY FAULT!
ISN'T IT? DON'T HAND ME ANY "SMALL TEAM" NONSENSE! YOU DIDN'T CALL THE AVENGERS IN BECAUSE YOU WANTED TO IMPRESS ME! YOU WANTED MY APPROVAL--BUT IT'S NOT COMING!
I KNEW IT! I KNEW YOU HAD IT OUT FOR ME! YOU THINK I'M NOT GOOD FOR THE TEAM!

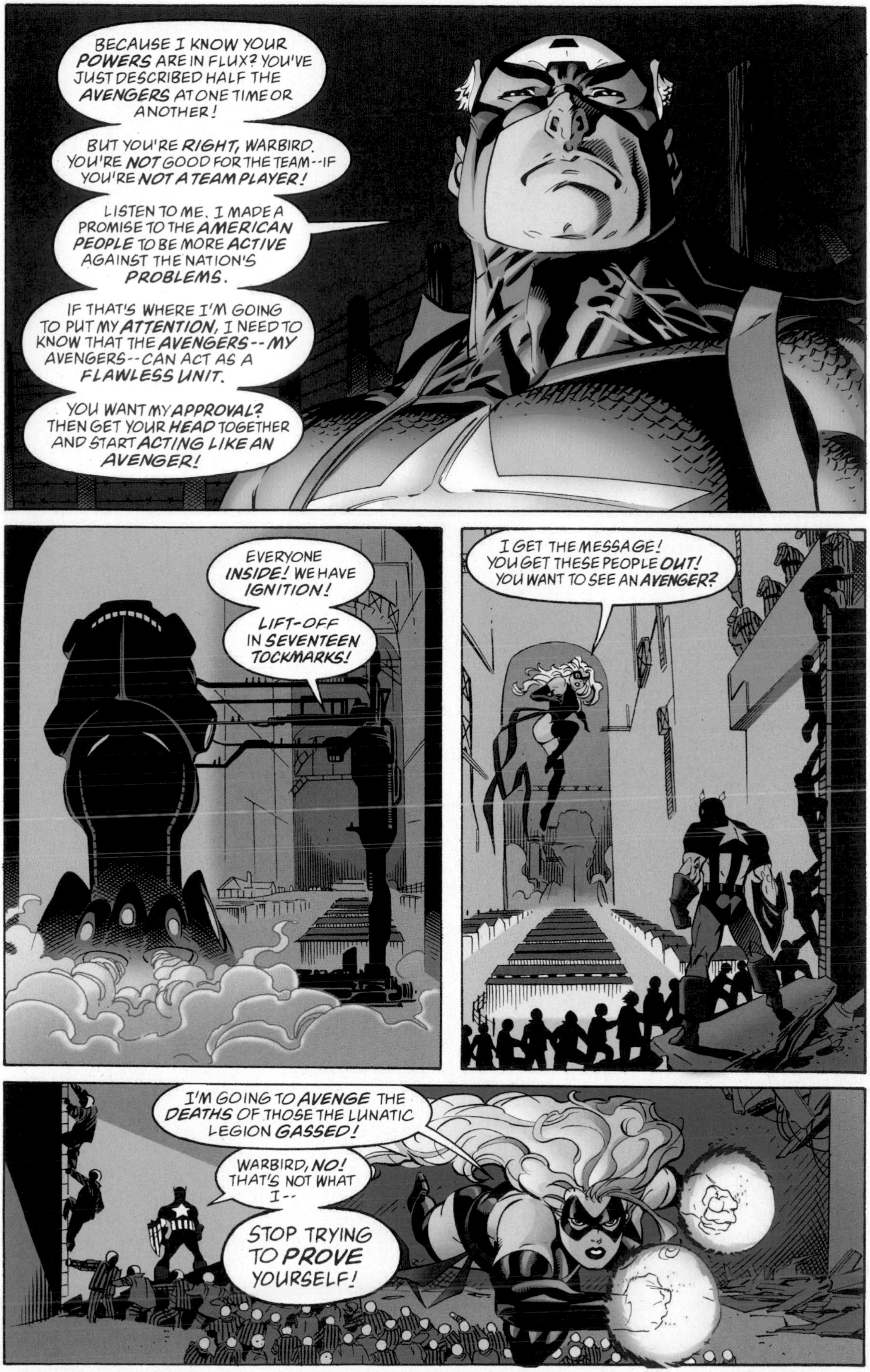
BECAUSE I KNOW YOUR POWERS ARE IN FLUX? YOU'VE JUST DESCRIBED HALF THE AVENGERS AT ONE TIME OR ANOTHER!
BUT YOU'RE RIGHT, WARBIRD. YOU'RE NOT GOOD FOR THE TEAM--IF YOU'RE NOT A TEAM PLAYER!
LISTEN TO ME. I MADE A PROMISE TO THE AMERICAN PEOPLE TO BE MORE ACTIVE AGAINST THE NATION'S PROBLEMS.
IF THAT'S WHERE I'M GOING TO PUT MY ATTENTION, I NEED TO KNOW THAT THE AVENGERS--MY AVENGERS--CAN ACT AS A FLAWLESS UNIT.
YOU WANT MY APPROVAL? THEN GET YOUR HEAD TOGETHER AND START ACTING LIKE AN AVENGER!
EVERYONE INSIDE! WE HAVE IGNITION!
LIFT-OFF IN SEVENTEEN TOCKMARKS!
I GET THE MESSAGE! YOU GET THESE PEOPLE OUT! YOU WANT TO SEE AN AVENGER?
I'M GOING TO AVENGE THE DEATHS OF THOSE THE LUNATIC LEGION GASSED!
WARBIRD, NO! THAT'S NOT WHAT I--
STOP TRYING TO PROVE YOURSELF!

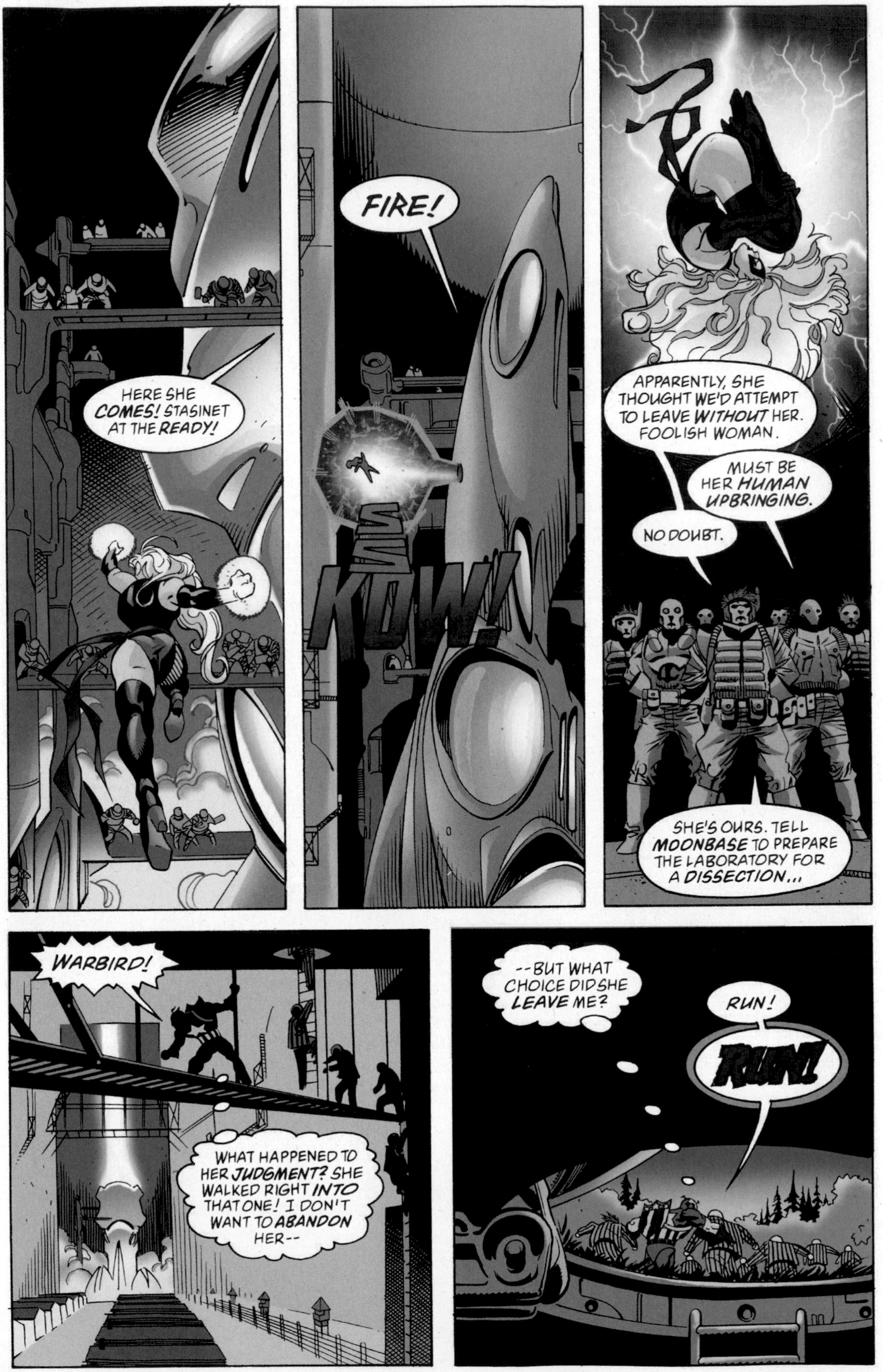
HERE SHE COMES! STASINET AT THE READY!
FIRE!
SSKOW!
APPARENTLY, SHE THOUGHT WE'D ATTEMPT TO LEAVE WITHOUT HER. FOOLISH WOMAN.
MUST BE HER HUMAN UPBRINGING.
NO DOUBT.
SHE'S OURS. TELL MOONBASE TO PREPARE THE LABORATORY FOR A DISSECTION...
WARBIRD!
WHAT HAPPENED TO HER JUDGMENT? SHE WALKED RIGHT INTO THAT ONE! I DON'T WANT TO ABANDON HER--
--BUT WHAT CHOICE DID SHE LEAVE ME?
RUN!
RUN!

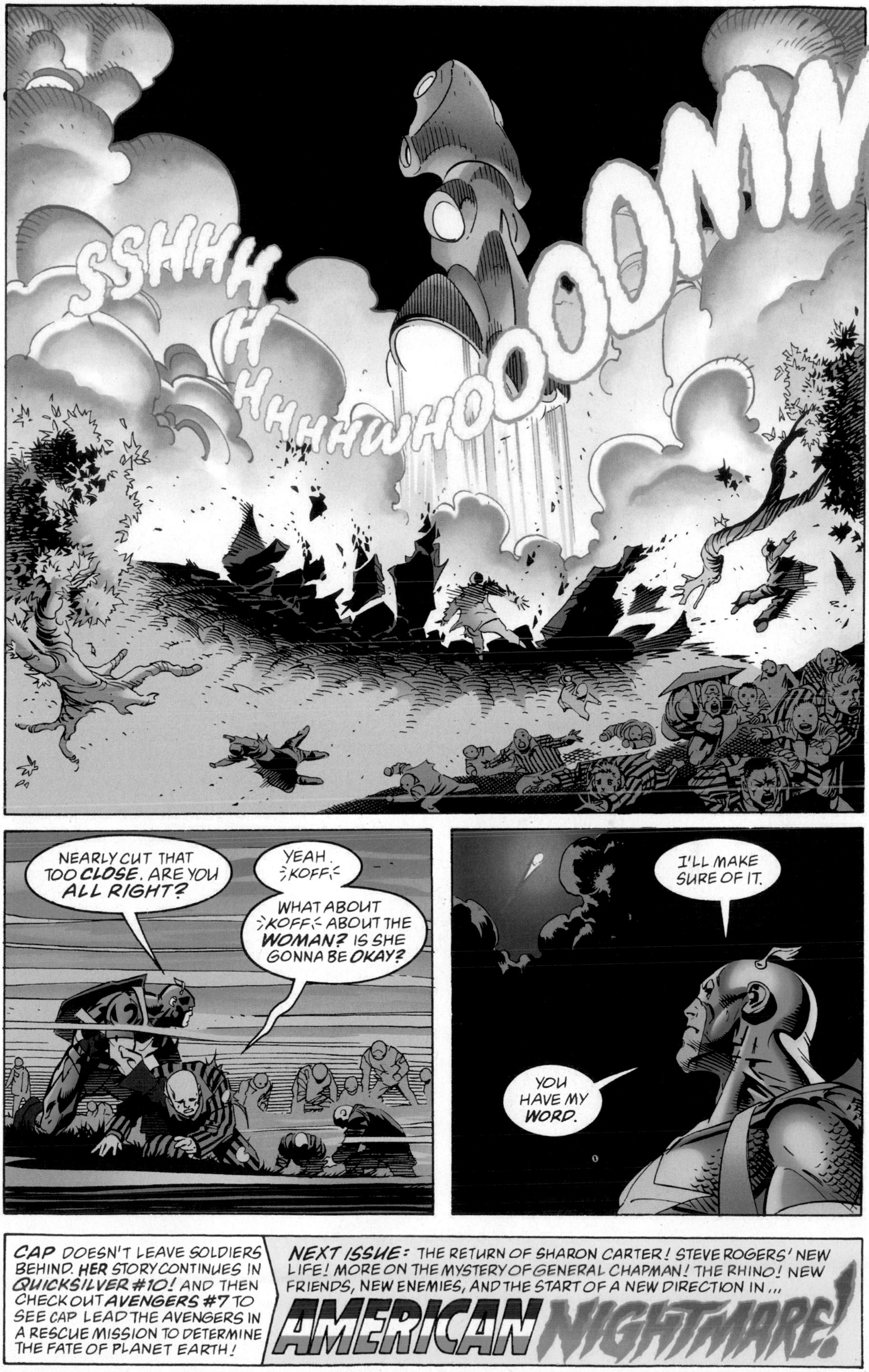
SSHHHHHHHHHHWHOOOOOOMMM
NEARLY CUT THAT TOO CLOSE. ARE YOU ALL RIGHT?
YEAH. KOFF
WHAT ABOUT KOFF ABOUT THE WOMAN? IS SHE GONNA BE OKAY?
I'LL MAKE SURE OF IT.
YOU HAVE MY WORD.
CAP DOESN'T LEAVE SOLDIERS BEHIND. HER STORY CONTINUES IN QUICKSILVER #10! AND THEN CHECK OUT AVENGERS #7 TO SEE CAP LEAD THE AVENGERS IN A RESCUE MISSION TO DETERMINE THE FATE OF PLANET EARTH!
NEXT ISSUE: THE RETURN OF SHARON CARTER! STEVE ROGERS' NEW LIFE! MORE ON THE MYSTERY OF GENERAL CHAPMAN! THE RHINO! NEW FRIENDS, NEW ENEMIES, AND THE START OF A NEW DIRECTION IN...
AMERICAN NIGHTMARE!

"LIVE KREE OR DIE!" PARTS 3–4

QUICKSILVER #10 • AVENGERS #7

The Legion revealed that they had stolen some of the Inhumans' mutagenic Terrigen Mists. Studying Warbird's half-Kree biology, they finalized their plan to use the generator to power a Kree Omni-Wave Projector, filtering its beam through the Mists and causing all human life to either transform into genetic duplicates of the Kree — or die horribly. Hawkeye, Quicksilver and the Scarlet Witch used the Inhuman dog Lockjaw to teleport to the moon, where the Supreme Intelligence revealed the Legion's entire plan. Quicksilver freed Warbird, but, suffering from withdrawal, she desperately drank some Kree liquor. Inebriated, she destroyed the power generator but also injured Lockjaw, who was barely able to teleport the Avengers back to Earth.

The Avengers prepared to court-martial Warbird, but they were interrupted by a distress call from the moon, warning that the Legion had decided to power the Projector with their own life energy. As the rest of the Avengers headed for the moon, Warbird angrily quit the team. The Avengers battled the Legion, but the villains transformed into energy and fueled the Projector. Unable to shut the device off, Thor opened a dimensional portal, and the Avengers pushed the Projector through with only seconds to spare. Captain America confronted the Intelligence, suspecting that he had sent the distress call to undermine the Legion — but left unaware that the Intelligence had also mentally controlled the Skrull who recently took Cap's place...

GET THE WHOLE STORY IN

AVENGERS: LIVE KREE OR DIE TPB!

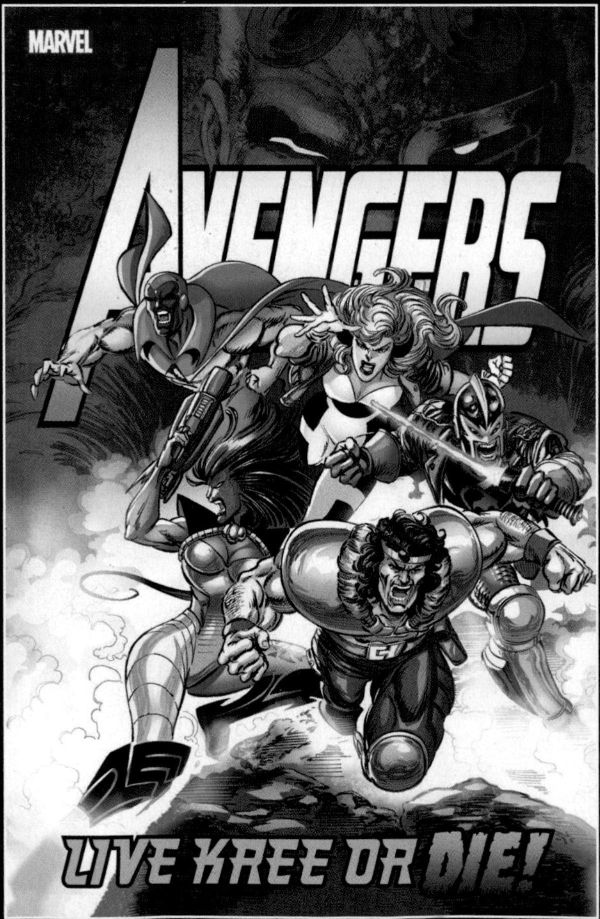
MARVEL
AVENGERS
LIVE KREE OR DIE!

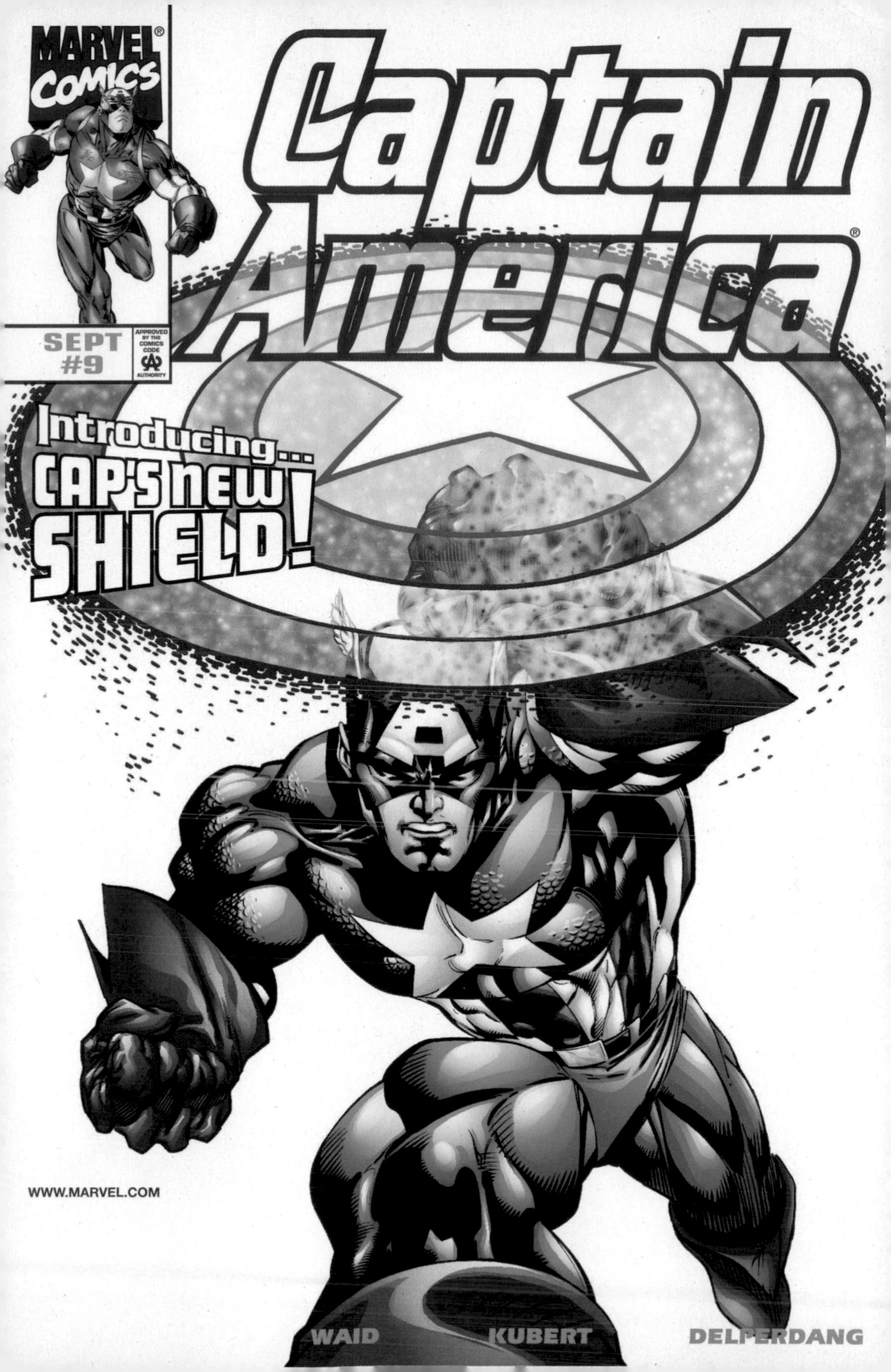

MARVEL COMICS
Captain America
SEPT #9
APPROVED BY THE COMICS CODE AUTHORITY
Introducing... CAP'S NEW SHIELD!
WWW.MARVEL.COM
WAID
KUBERT
DELPERDANG

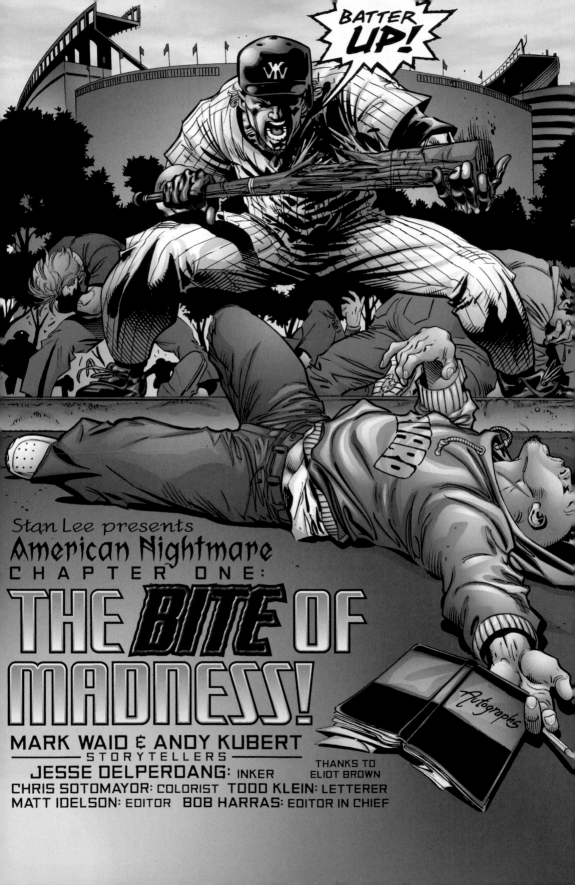

BATTER UP!

Stan Lee presents
American Nightmare
CHAPTER ONE:
THE BITE OF MADNESS!

MARK WAID & ANDY KUBERT
—— STORYTELLERS ——
JESSE DELPERDANG: INKER
THANKS TO
ELIOT BROWN
CHRIS SOTOMAYOR: COLORIST   TODD KLEIN: LETTERER
MATT IDELSON: EDITOR   BOB HARRAS: EDITOR IN CHIEF

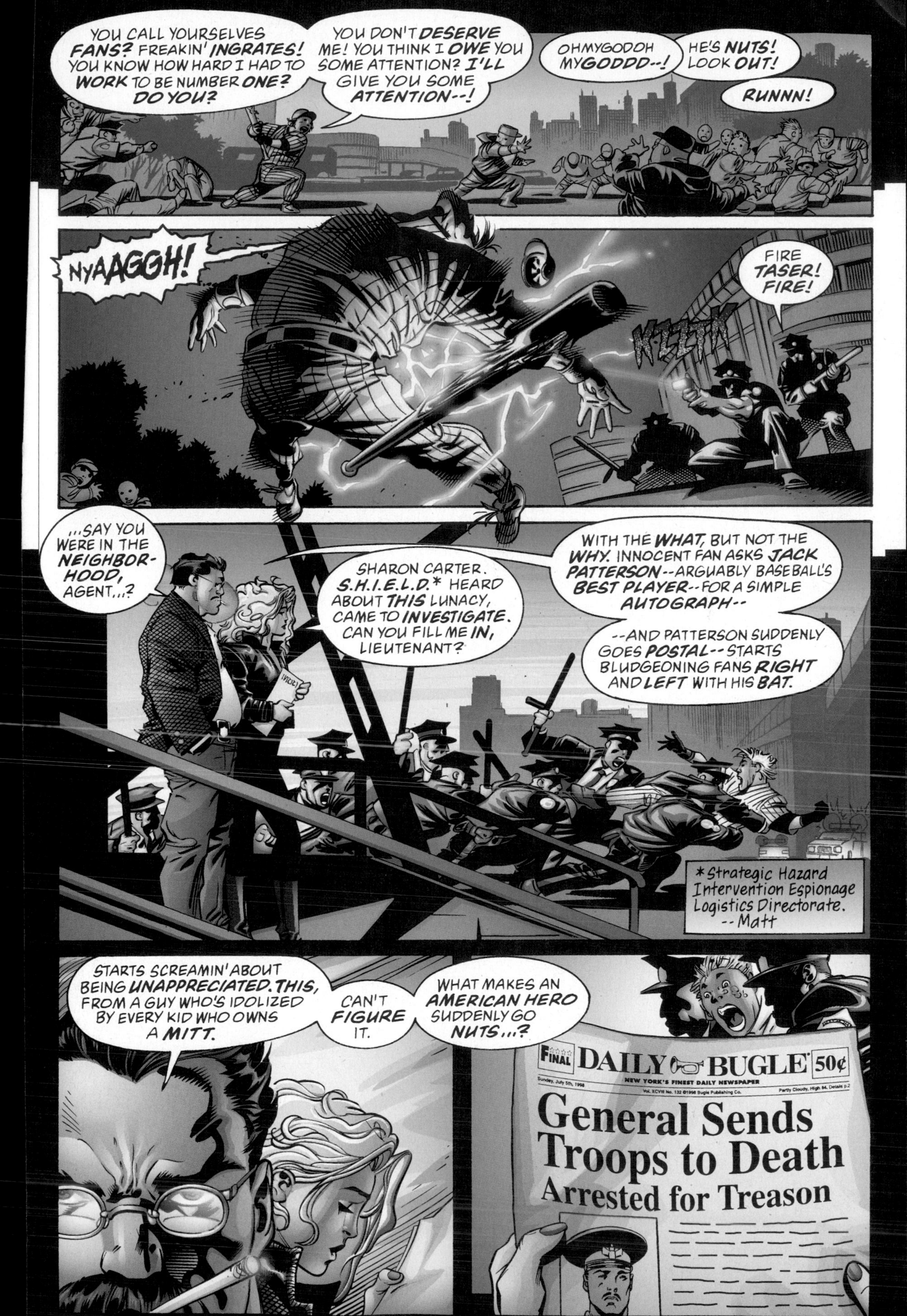
YOU CALL YOURSELVES FANS? FREAKIN' INGRATES! YOU KNOW HOW HARD I HAD TO WORK TO BE NUMBER ONE? DO YOU?
YOU DON'T DESERVE ME! YOU THINK I OWE YOU SOME ATTENTION? I'LL GIVE YOU SOME ATTENTION--!
OHMYGODOH MYGODDD--!
HE'S NUTS! LOOK OUT!
RUNNN!
NyAAGGH!
FIRE TASER! FIRE!
K'ZZTK
...SAY YOU WERE IN THE NEIGHBOR-HOOD, AGENT...?
SHARON CARTER. S.H.I.E.L.D.* HEARD ABOUT THIS LUNACY, CAME TO INVESTIGATE. CAN YOU FILL ME IN, LIEUTENANT?
WITH THE WHAT, BUT NOT THE WHY. INNOCENT FAN ASKS JACK PATTERSON--ARGUABLY BASEBALL'S BEST PLAYER--FOR A SIMPLE AUTOGRAPH--
--AND PATTERSON SUDDENLY GOES POSTAL--STARTS BLUDGEONING FANS RIGHT AND LEFT WITH HIS BAT.
*Strategic Hazard Intervention Espionage Logistics Directorate. --Matt
STARTS SCREAMIN' ABOUT BEING UNAPPRECIATED. THIS, FROM A GUY WHO'S IDOLIZED BY EVERY KID WHO OWNS A MITT.
CAN'T FIGURE IT.
WHAT MAKES AN AMERICAN HERO SUDDENLY GO NUTS...?
FINAL DAILY BUGLE 50¢
NEW YORK'S FINEST DAILY NEWSPAPER
Sunday, July 5th, 1998
Vol. XCVIII No. 132 ©1998 Bugle Publishing Co.
Partly Cloudy, High 84. Details p.2
General Sends Troops to Death
Arrested for Treason

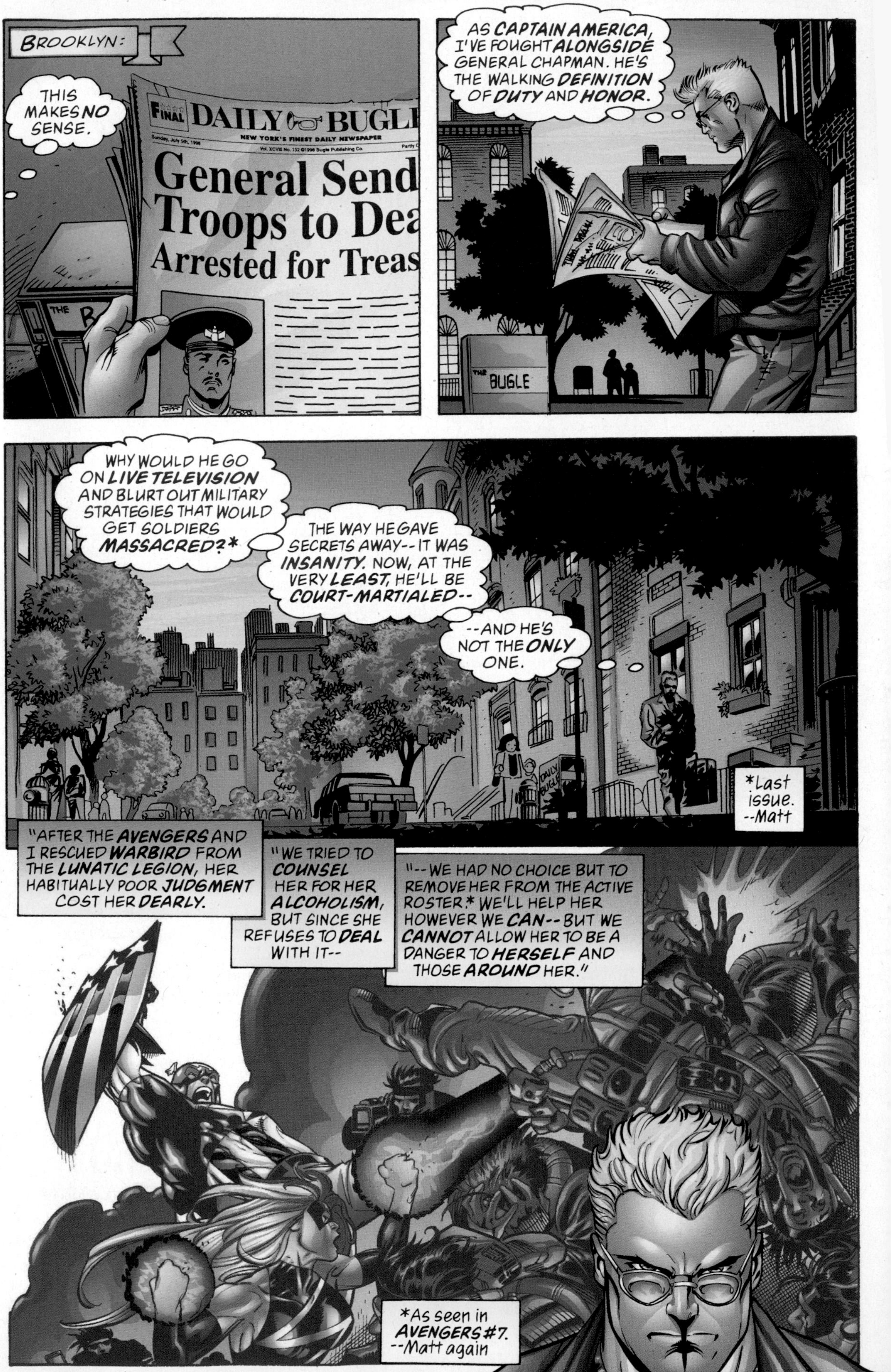
BROOKLYN:
THIS MAKES NO SENSE.
FINAL DAILY BUGLE
NEW YORK'S FINEST DAILY NEWSPAPER
General Send
Troops to Dea
Arrested for Treas
AS CAPTAIN AMERICA, I'VE FOUGHT ALONGSIDE GENERAL CHAPMAN. HE'S THE WALKING DEFINITION OF DUTY AND HONOR.
THE BUGLE
WHY WOULD HE GO ON LIVE TELEVISION AND BLURT OUT MILITARY STRATEGIES THAT WOULD GET SOLDIERS MASSACRED?*
THE WAY HE GAVE SECRETS AWAY-- IT WAS INSANITY. NOW, AT THE VERY LEAST, HE'LL BE COURT-MARTIALED--
--AND HE'S NOT THE ONLY ONE.
DAILY BUGLE
*Last issue. --Matt
"AFTER THE AVENGERS AND I RESCUED WARBIRD FROM THE LUNATIC LEGION, HER HABITUALLY POOR JUDGMENT COST HER DEARLY.
"WE TRIED TO COUNSEL HER FOR HER ALCOHOLISM, BUT SINCE SHE REFUSES TO DEAL WITH IT--
"--WE HAD NO CHOICE BUT TO REMOVE HER FROM THE ACTIVE ROSTER.* WE'LL HELP HER HOWEVER WE CAN-- BUT WE CANNOT ALLOW HER TO BE A DANGER TO HERSELF AND THOSE AROUND HER."
*As seen in AVENGERS #7. --Matt again

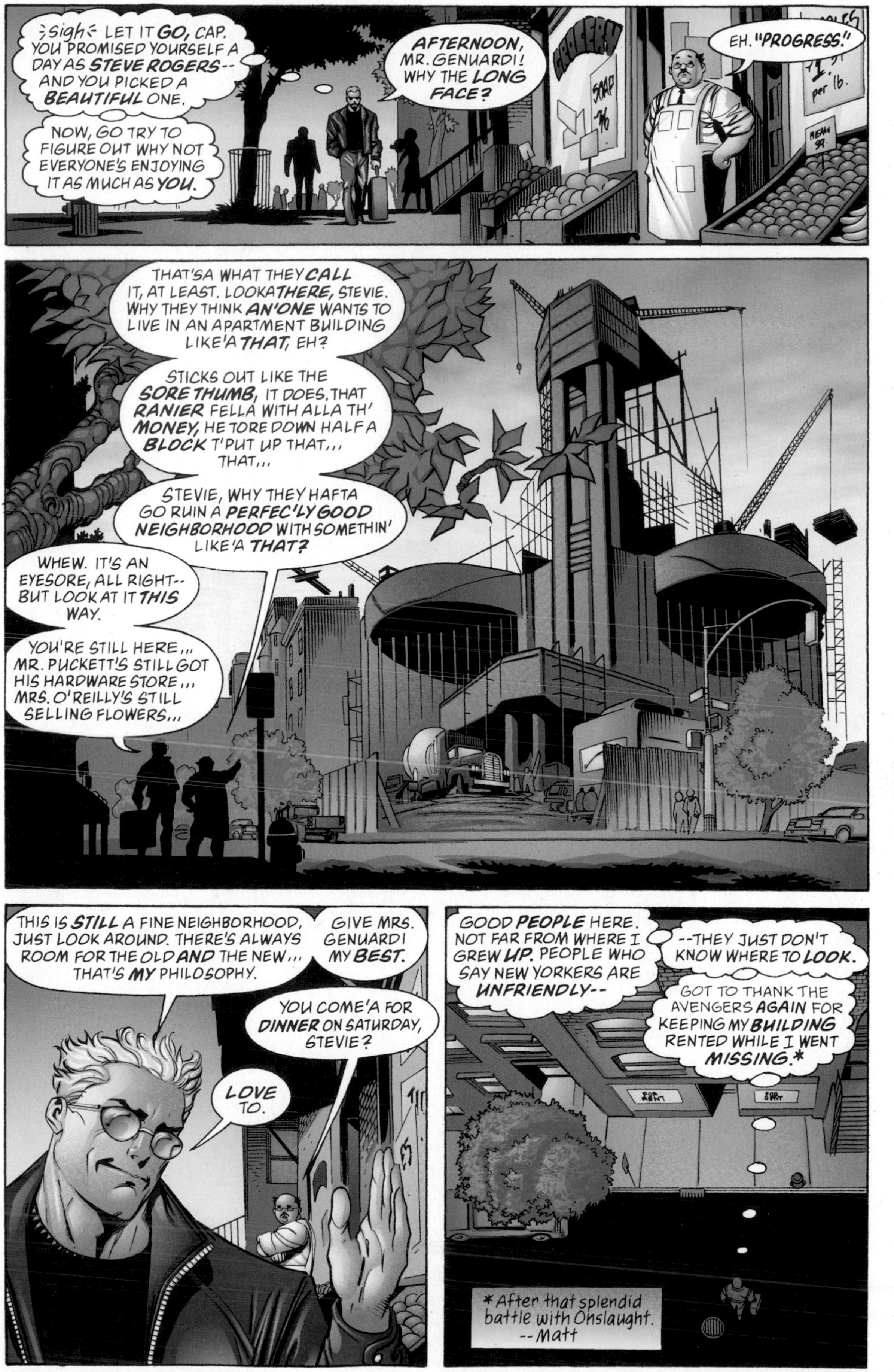

;sigh; LET IT GO, CAP. YOU PROMISED YOURSELF A DAY AS STEVE ROGERS--AND YOU PICKED A BEAUTIFUL ONE.
NOW, GO TRY TO FIGURE OUT WHY NOT EVERYONE'S ENJOYING IT AS MUCH AS YOU.
AFTERNOON, MR. GENUARDI! WHY THE LONG FACE?
EH. "PROGRESS."
THAT'SA WHAT THEY CALL IT, AT LEAST. LOOKA THERE, STEVIE. WHY THEY THINK AN'ONE WANTS TO LIVE IN AN APARTMENT BUILDING LIKE'A THAT, EH?
STICKS OUT LIKE THE SORE THUMB, IT DOES. THAT RANIER FELLA WITH ALLA TH' MONEY, HE TORE DOWN HALF A BLOCK T'PUT UP THAT... THAT...
STEVIE, WHY THEY HAFTA GO RUIN A PERFEC'LY GOOD NEIGHBORHOOD WITH SOMETHIN' LIKE'A THAT?
WHEW. IT'S AN EYESORE, ALL RIGHT--BUT LOOK AT IT THIS WAY.
YOU'RE STILL HERE... MR. PUCKETT'S STILL GOT HIS HARDWARE STORE... MRS. O'REILLY'S STILL SELLING FLOWERS...
THIS IS STILL A FINE NEIGHBORHOOD. JUST LOOK AROUND. THERE'S ALWAYS ROOM FOR THE OLD AND THE NEW... THAT'S MY PHILOSOPHY.
GIVE MRS. GENUARDI MY BEST.
YOU COME'A FOR DINNER ON SATURDAY, STEVIE?
LOVE TO.
GOOD PEOPLE HERE. NOT FAR FROM WHERE I GREW UP. PEOPLE WHO SAY NEW YORKERS ARE UNFRIENDLY--
--THEY JUST DON'T KNOW WHERE TO LOOK.
GOT TO THANK THE AVENGERS AGAIN FOR KEEPING MY BUILDING RENTED WHILE I WENT MISSING.*
*After that splendid battle with Onslaught. --Matt

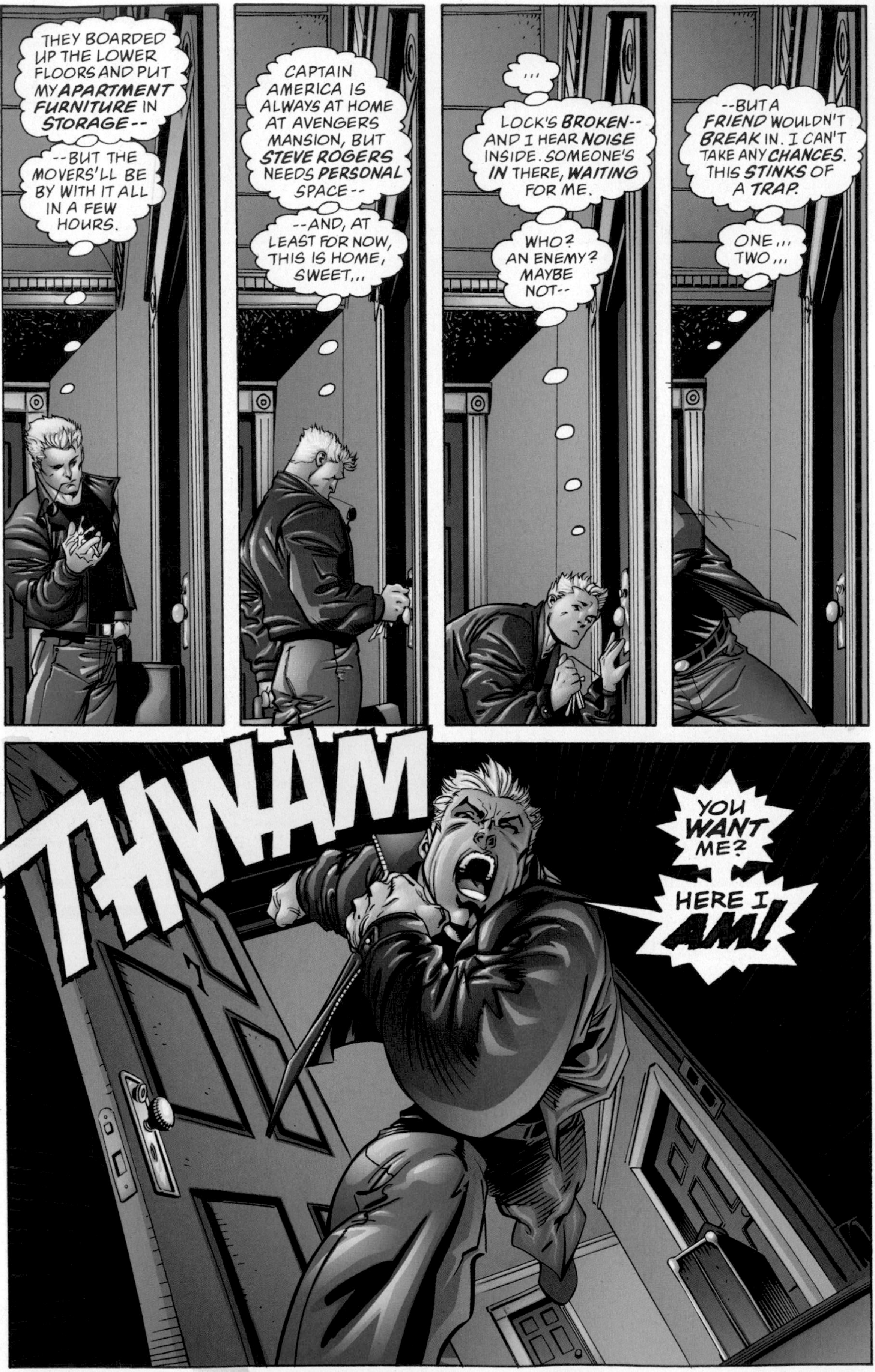
THEY BOARDED UP THE LOWER FLOORS AND PUT MY APARTMENT FURNITURE IN STORAGE--
--BUT THE MOVERS'LL BE BY WITH IT ALL IN A FEW HOURS.
CAPTAIN AMERICA IS ALWAYS AT HOME AT AVENGERS MANSION, BUT STEVE ROGERS NEEDS PERSONAL SPACE--
--AND, AT LEAST FOR NOW, THIS IS HOME, SWEET...
...
LOCK'S BROKEN-- AND I HEAR NOISE INSIDE. SOMEONE'S IN THERE, WAITING FOR ME.
WHO? AN ENEMY? MAYBE NOT--
--BUT A FRIEND WOULDN'T BREAK IN. I CAN'T TAKE ANY CHANCES. THIS STINKS OF A TRAP.
ONE... TWO...
THWAM
YOU WANT ME?
HERE I AM!

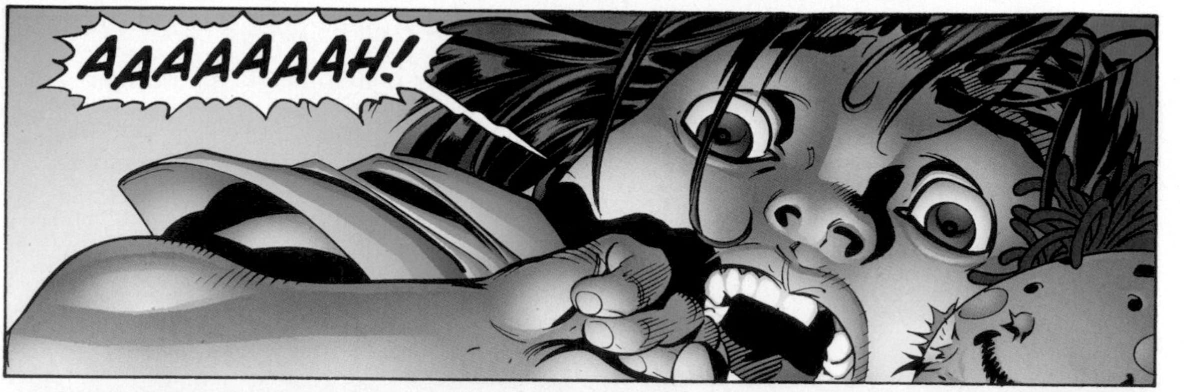
AAAAAAAH!

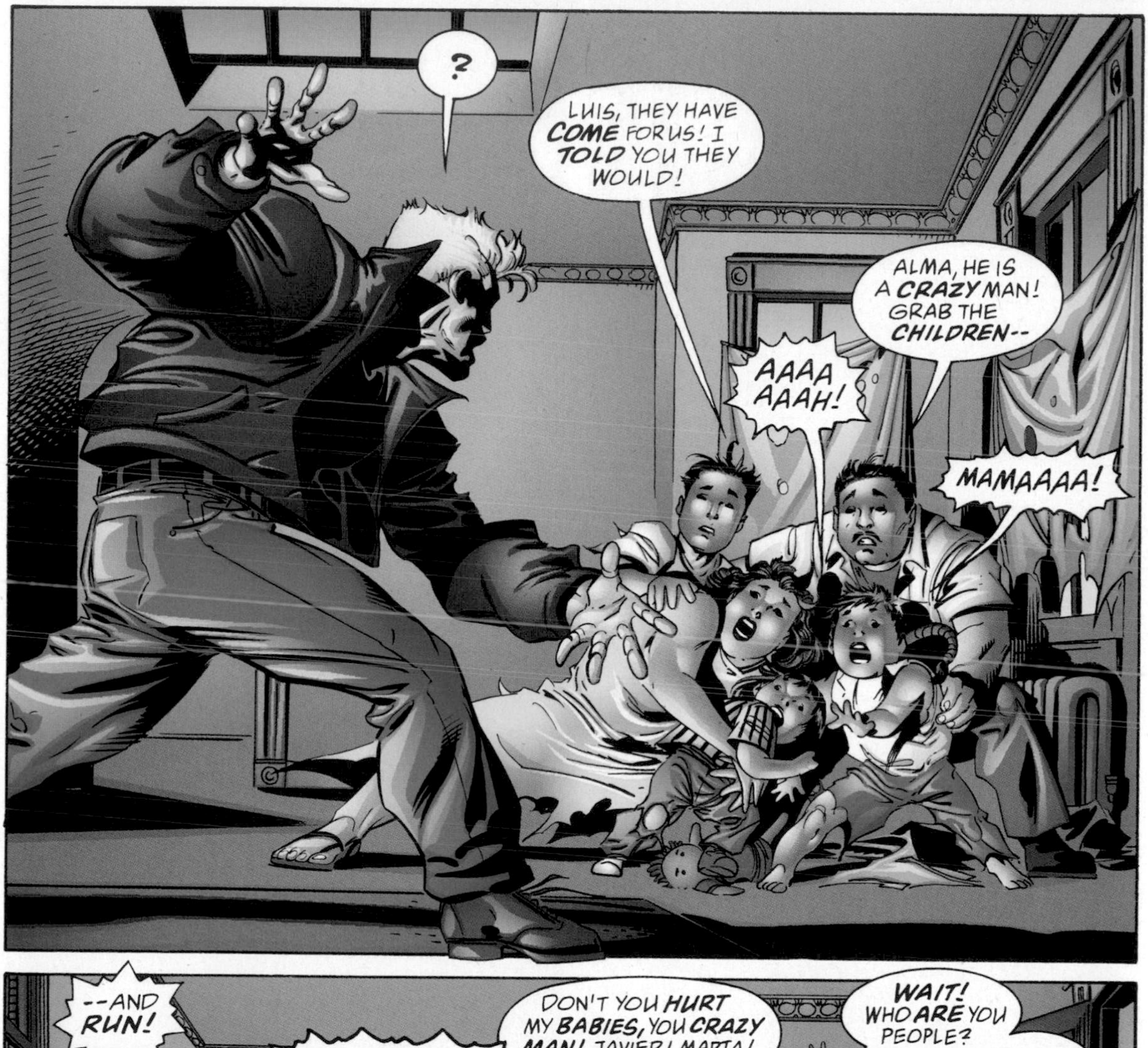
?
LUIS, THEY HAVE COME FOR US! I TOLD YOU THEY WOULD!
ALMA, HE IS A CRAZY MAN! GRAB THE CHILDREN--
AAAA AAAH!
MAMAAAA!

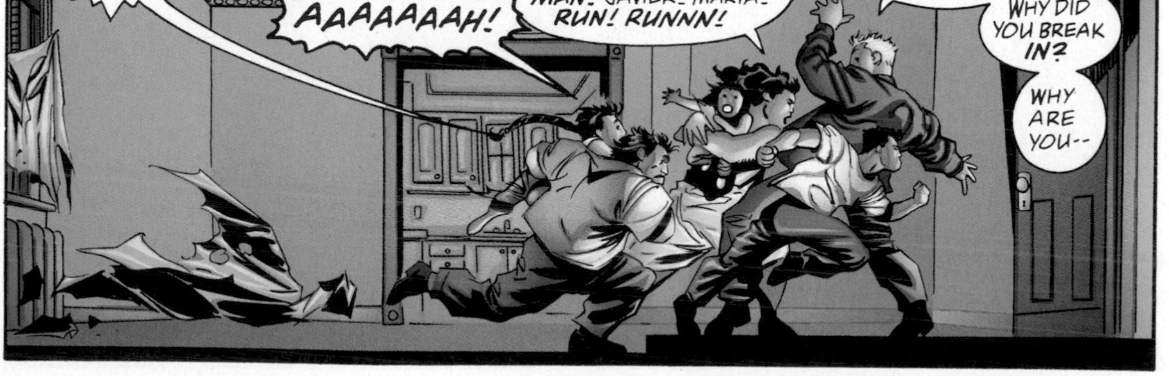
--AND RUN!
AAAAAAAH!
DON'T YOU HURT MY BABIES, YOU CRAZY MAN! JAVIER! MARTA! RUN! RUNNN!
WAIT! WHO ARE YOU PEOPLE?
WHY DID YOU BREAK IN?
WHY ARE YOU--

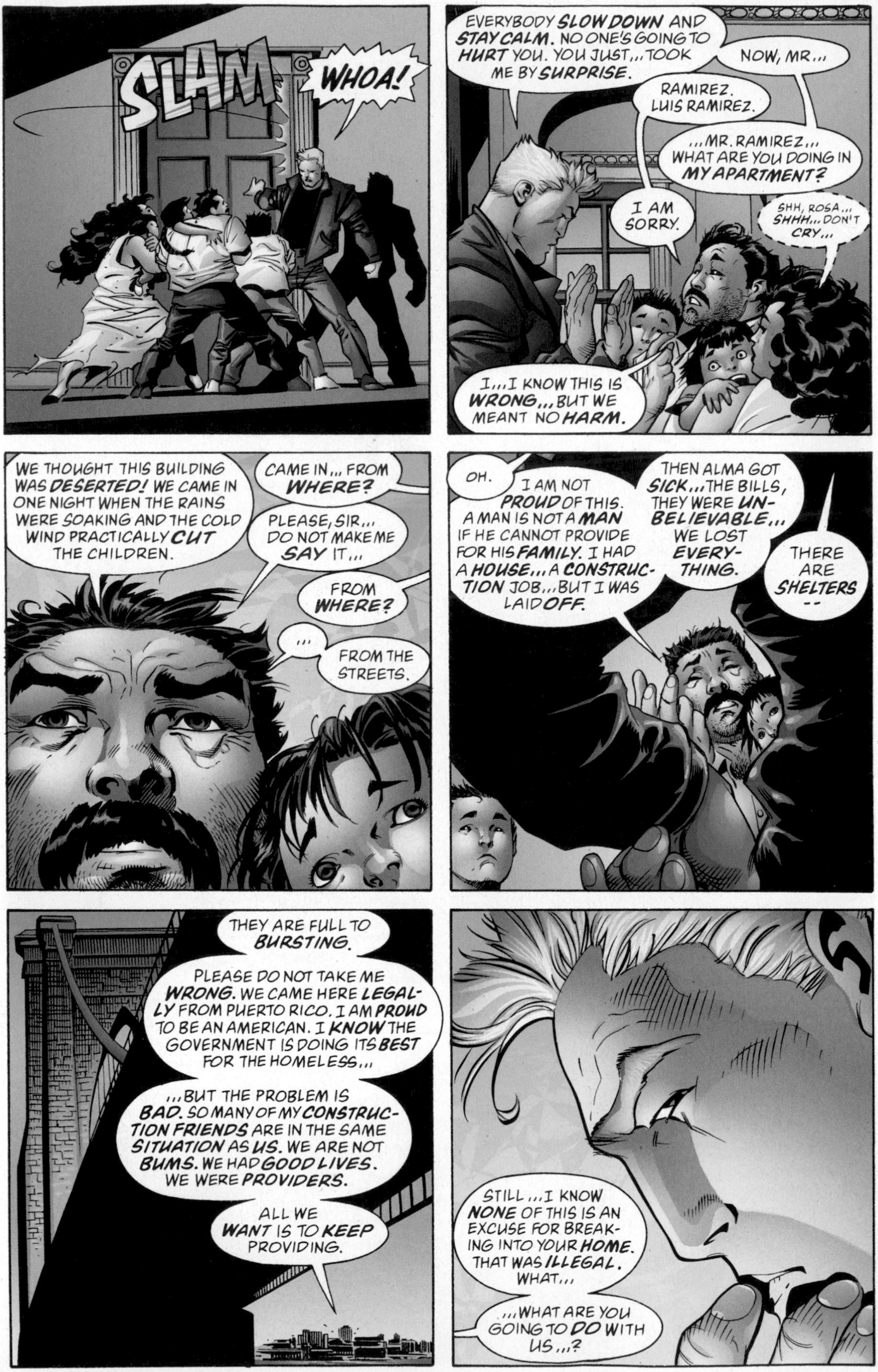
SLAM
WHOA!
EVERYBODY SLOW DOWN AND STAY CALM. NO ONE'S GOING TO HURT YOU. YOU JUST,,, TOOK ME BY SURPRISE.
NOW, MR,,,
RAMIREZ. LUIS RAMIREZ.
,,,MR. RAMIREZ,,, WHAT ARE YOU DOING IN MY APARTMENT?
I AM SORRY.
SHH, ROSA,,, SHHH,,, DON'T CRY,,,
I,,, I KNOW THIS IS WRONG,,, BUT WE MEANT NO HARM.
WE THOUGHT THIS BUILDING WAS DESERTED! WE CAME IN ONE NIGHT WHEN THE RAINS WERE SOAKING AND THE COLD WIND PRACTICALLY CUT THE CHILDREN.
CAME IN,,, FROM WHERE?
PLEASE, SIR,,, DO NOT MAKE ME SAY IT,,,
FROM WHERE?
,,,
FROM THE STREETS.
OH.
I AM NOT PROUD OF THIS. A MAN IS NOT A MAN IF HE CANNOT PROVIDE FOR HIS FAMILY. I HAD A HOUSE,,, A CONSTRUCTION JOB,,, BUT I WAS LAID OFF.
THEN ALMA GOT SICK,,, THE BILLS, THEY WERE UNBELIEVABLE,,, WE LOST EVERYTHING.
THERE ARE SHELTERS --
THEY ARE FULL TO BURSTING.
PLEASE DO NOT TAKE ME WRONG. WE CAME HERE LEGALLY FROM PUERTO RICO. I AM PROUD TO BE AN AMERICAN. I KNOW THE GOVERNMENT IS DOING ITS BEST FOR THE HOMELESS,,,
,,,BUT THE PROBLEM IS BAD. SO MANY OF MY CONSTRUCTION FRIENDS ARE IN THE SAME SITUATION AS US. WE ARE NOT BUMS. WE HAD GOOD LIVES. WE WERE PROVIDERS.
ALL WE WANT IS TO KEEP PROVIDING.
STILL,,, I KNOW NONE OF THIS IS AN EXCUSE FOR BREAKING INTO YOUR HOME. THAT WAS ILLEGAL. WHAT,,,
,,,WHAT ARE YOU GOING TO DO WITH US,,,?

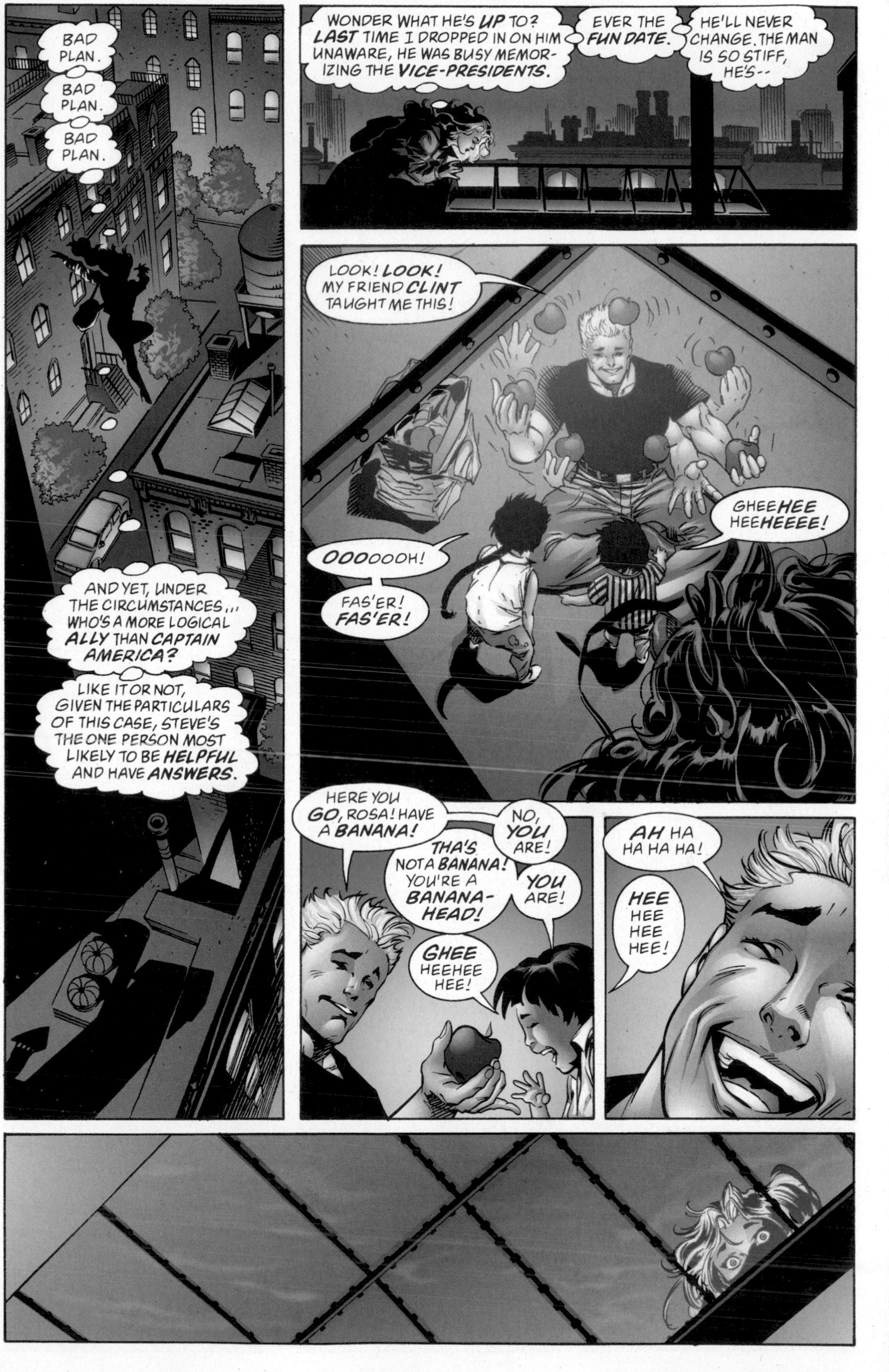
BAD PLAN.
BAD PLAN.
BAD PLAN.
AND YET, UNDER THE CIRCUMSTANCES... WHO'S A MORE LOGICAL ALLY THAN CAPTAIN AMERICA?
LIKE IT OR NOT, GIVEN THE PARTICULARS OF THIS CASE, STEVE'S THE ONE PERSON MOST LIKELY TO BE HELPFUL AND HAVE ANSWERS.
WONDER WHAT HE'S UP TO? LAST TIME I DROPPED IN ON HIM UNAWARE, HE WAS BUSY MEMORIZING THE VICE-PRESIDENTS.
EVER THE FUN DATE.
HE'LL NEVER CHANGE. THE MAN IS SO STIFF, HE'S--
LOOK! LOOK! MY FRIEND CLINT TAUGHT ME THIS!
GHEEHEE HEEHEEEE!
OOOOOOH!
FAS'ER! FAS'ER!
HERE YOU GO, ROSA! HAVE A BANANA!
THA'S NOT A BANANA! YOU'RE A BANANA-HEAD!
NO, YOU ARE!
YOU ARE!
GHEE HEEHEE HEE!
AH HA HA HA HA!
HEE HEE HEE HEE!

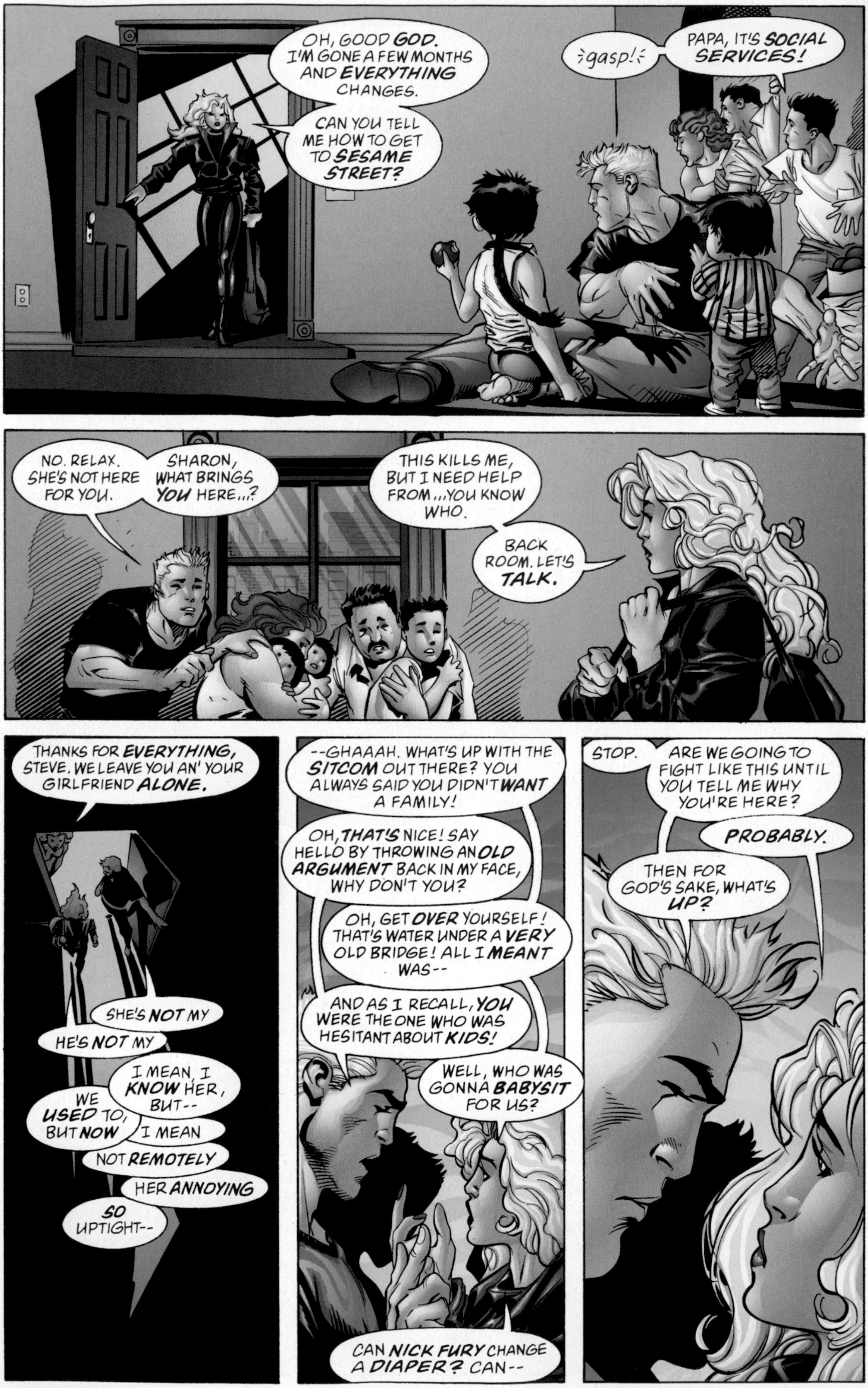
OH, GOOD GOD. I'M GONE A FEW MONTHS AND EVERYTHING CHANGES.
CAN YOU TELL ME HOW TO GET TO SESAME STREET?
gasp!
PAPA, IT'S SOCIAL SERVICES!
NO. RELAX. SHE'S NOT HERE FOR YOU.
SHARON, WHAT BRINGS YOU HERE...?
THIS KILLS ME, BUT I NEED HELP FROM...YOU KNOW WHO.
BACK ROOM. LET'S TALK.
THANKS FOR EVERYTHING, STEVE. WE LEAVE YOU AN' YOUR GIRLFRIEND ALONE.
SHE'S NOT MY
HE'S NOT MY
I MEAN, I KNOW HER, BUT--
WE USED TO, BUT NOW
I MEAN
NOT REMOTELY
HER ANNOYING
SO UPTIGHT--
--GHAAAH. WHAT'S UP WITH THE SITCOM OUT THERE? YOU ALWAYS SAID YOU DIDN'T WANT A FAMILY!
OH, THAT'S NICE! SAY HELLO BY THROWING AN OLD ARGUMENT BACK IN MY FACE, WHY DON'T YOU?
OH, GET OVER YOURSELF! THAT'S WATER UNDER A VERY OLD BRIDGE! ALL I MEANT WAS--
AND AS I RECALL, YOU WERE THE ONE WHO WAS HESITANT ABOUT KIDS!
WELL, WHO WAS GONNA BABYSIT FOR US?
CAN NICK FURY CHANGE A DIAPER? CAN--
STOP.
ARE WE GOING TO FIGHT LIKE THIS UNTIL YOU TELL ME WHY YOU'RE HERE?
PROBABLY.
THEN FOR GOD'S SAKE, WHAT'S UP?

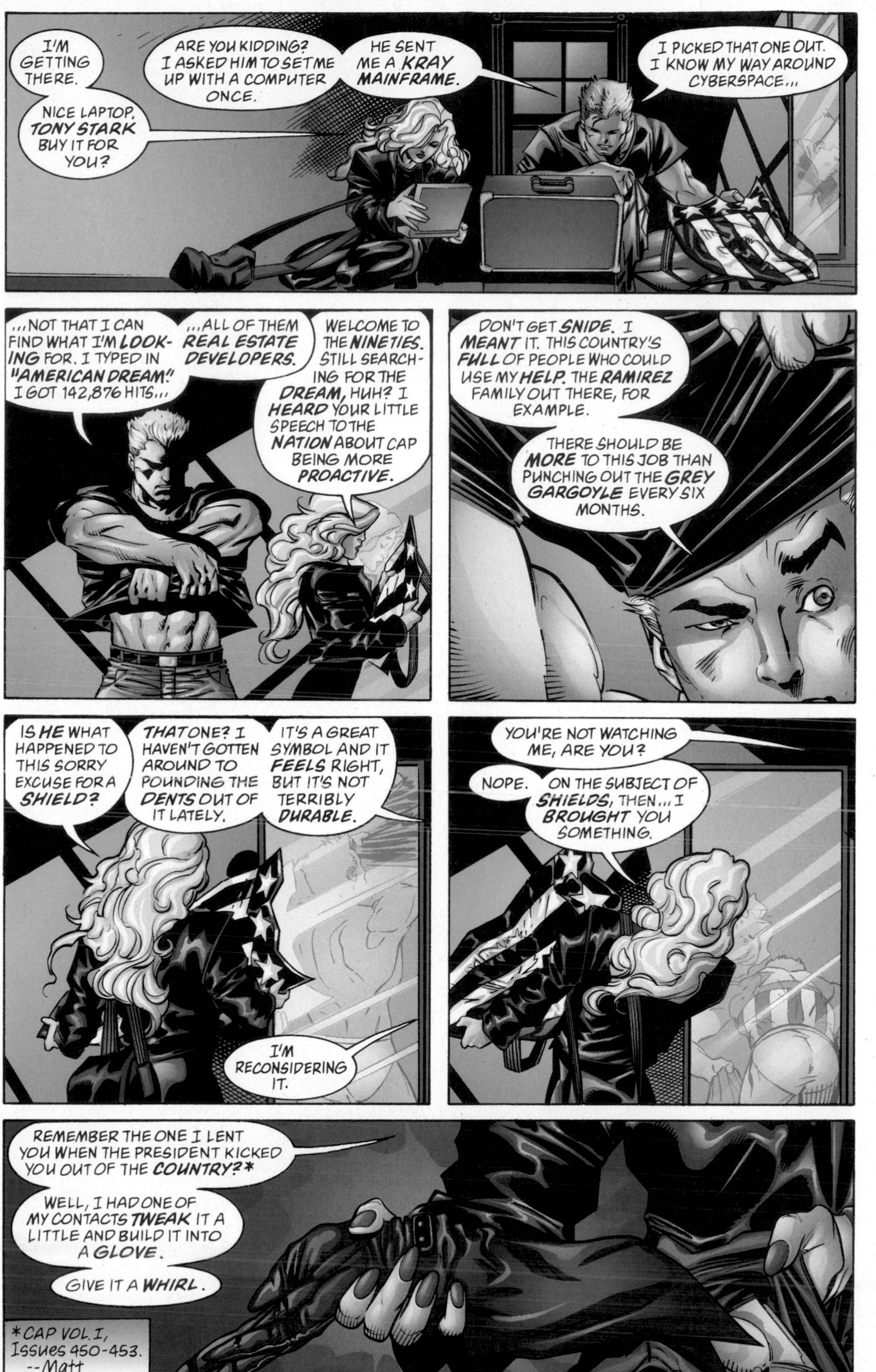
I'M GETTING THERE.
NICE LAPTOP. TONY STARK BUY IT FOR YOU?
ARE YOU KIDDING? I ASKED HIM TO SET ME UP WITH A COMPUTER ONCE.
HE SENT ME A KRAY MAINFRAME.
I PICKED THAT ONE OUT. I KNOW MY WAY AROUND CYBERSPACE...
...NOT THAT I CAN FIND WHAT I'M LOOKING FOR. I TYPED IN "AMERICAN DREAM." I GOT 142,876 HITS...
...ALL OF THEM REAL ESTATE DEVELOPERS.
WELCOME TO THE NINETIES. STILL SEARCHING FOR THE DREAM, HUH? I HEARD YOUR LITTLE SPEECH TO THE NATION ABOUT CAP BEING MORE PROACTIVE.
DON'T GET SNIDE. I MEANT IT. THIS COUNTRY'S FULL OF PEOPLE WHO COULD USE MY HELP. THE RAMIREZ FAMILY OUT THERE, FOR EXAMPLE.
THERE SHOULD BE MORE TO THIS JOB THAN PUNCHING OUT THE GREY GARGOYLE EVERY SIX MONTHS.
IS HE WHAT HAPPENED TO THIS SORRY EXCUSE FOR A SHIELD?
THAT ONE? I HAVEN'T GOTTEN AROUND TO POUNDING THE DENTS OUT OF IT LATELY.
IT'S A GREAT SYMBOL AND IT FEELS RIGHT, BUT IT'S NOT TERRIBLY DURABLE.
I'M RECONSIDERING IT.
YOU'RE NOT WATCHING ME, ARE YOU?
NOPE.
ON THE SUBJECT OF SHIELDS, THEN... I BROUGHT YOU SOMETHING.
REMEMBER THE ONE I LENT YOU WHEN THE PRESIDENT KICKED YOU OUT OF THE COUNTRY?*
WELL, I HAD ONE OF MY CONTACTS TWEAK IT A LITTLE AND BUILD IT INTO A GLOVE.
GIVE IT A WHIRL.
*CAP VOL. I, Issues 450-453. --Matt

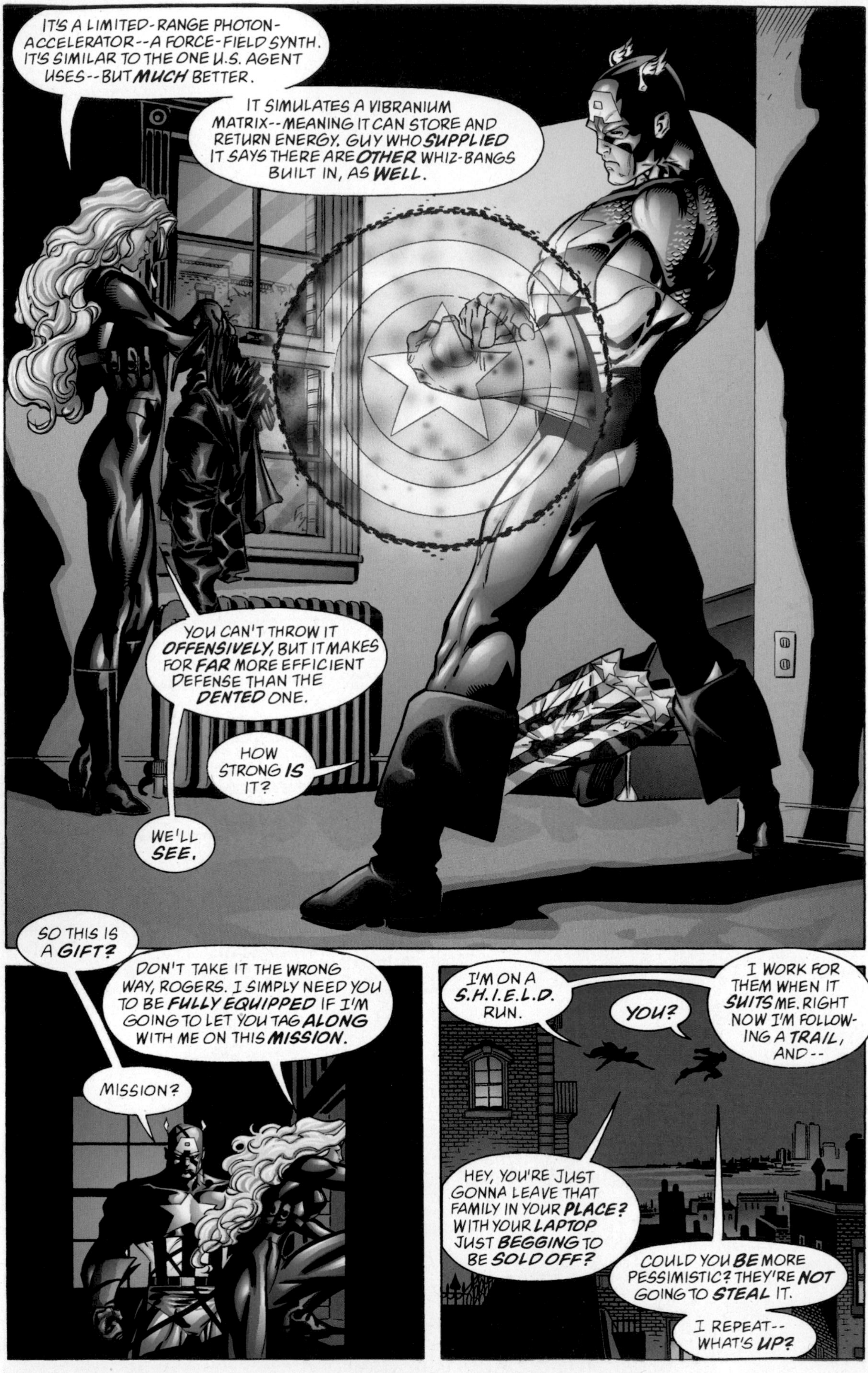
IT'S A LIMITED-RANGE PHOTON-ACCELERATOR--A FORCE-FIELD SYNTH. IT'S SIMILAR TO THE ONE U.S. AGENT USES--BUT MUCH BETTER.
IT SIMULATES A VIBRANIUM MATRIX--MEANING IT CAN STORE AND RETURN ENERGY. GUY WHO SUPPLIED IT SAYS THERE ARE OTHER WHIZ-BANGS BUILT IN, AS WELL.
YOU CAN'T THROW IT OFFENSIVELY, BUT IT MAKES FOR FAR MORE EFFICIENT DEFENSE THAN THE DENTED ONE.
HOW STRONG IS IT?
WE'LL SEE.
SO THIS IS A GIFT?
DON'T TAKE IT THE WRONG WAY, ROGERS. I SIMPLY NEED YOU TO BE FULLY EQUIPPED IF I'M GOING TO LET YOU TAG ALONG WITH ME ON THIS MISSION.
MISSION?
I'M ON A S.H.I.E.L.D. RUN.
YOU?
I WORK FOR THEM WHEN IT SUITS ME. RIGHT NOW I'M FOLLOWING A TRAIL, AND--
HEY, YOU'RE JUST GONNA LEAVE THAT FAMILY IN YOUR PLACE? WITH YOUR LAPTOP JUST BEGGING TO BE SOLD OFF?
COULD YOU BE MORE PESSIMISTIC? THEY'RE NOT GOING TO STEAL IT.
I REPEAT--WHAT'S UP?

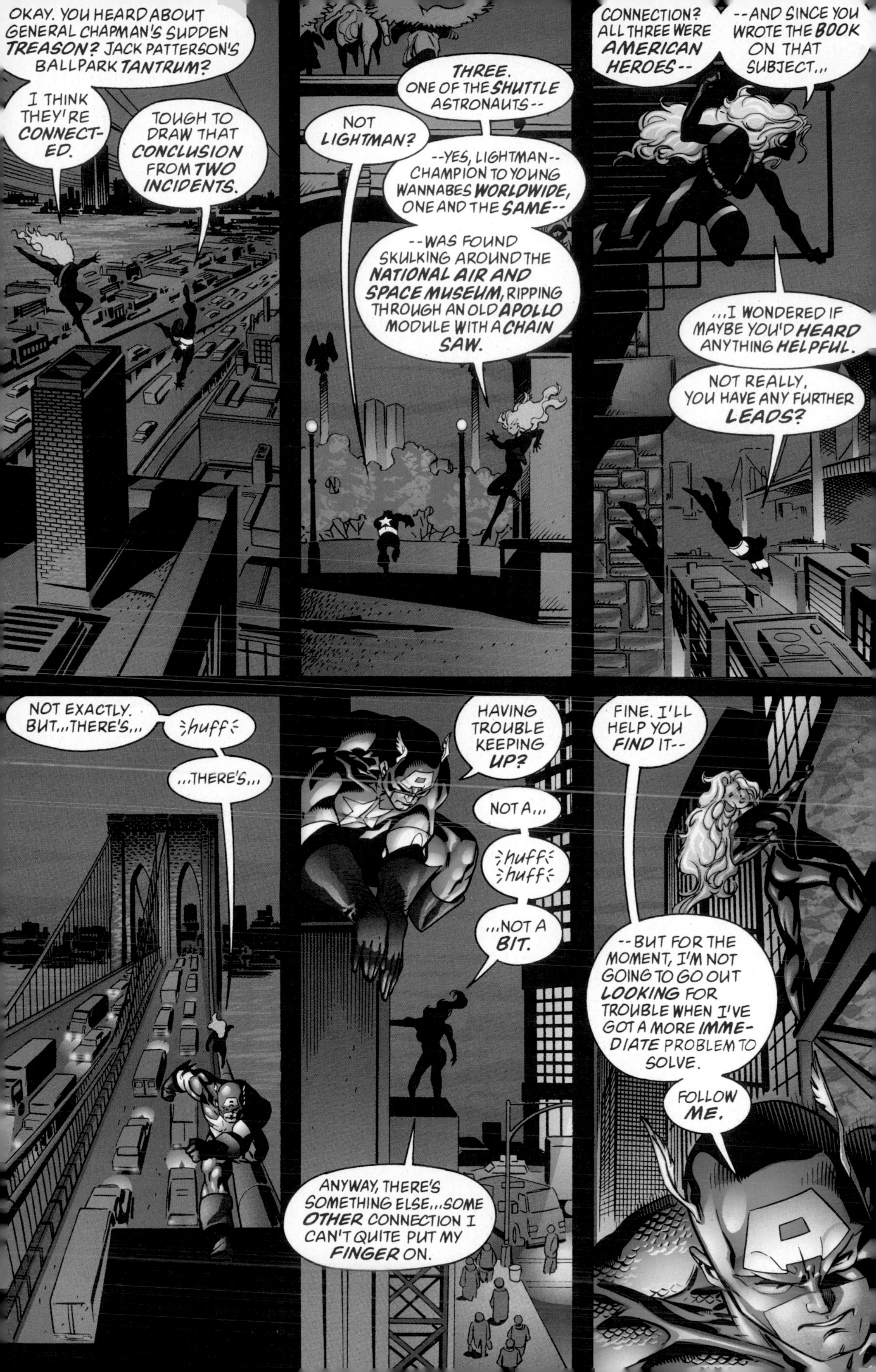
OKAY. YOU HEARD ABOUT GENERAL CHAPMAN'S SUDDEN TREASON? JACK PATTERSON'S BALLPARK TANTRUM?
I THINK THEY'RE CONNECT-ED.
TOUGH TO DRAW THAT CONCLUSION FROM TWO INCIDENTS.
THREE. ONE OF THE SHUTTLE ASTRONAUTS--
NOT LIGHTMAN?
--YES, LIGHTMAN--CHAMPION TO YOUNG WANNABES WORLDWIDE, ONE AND THE SAME--
--WAS FOUND SKULKING AROUND THE NATIONAL AIR AND SPACE MUSEUM, RIPPING THROUGH AN OLD APOLLO MODULE WITH A CHAIN SAW.
CONNECTION? ALL THREE WERE AMERICAN HEROES--
--AND SINCE YOU WROTE THE BOOK ON THAT SUBJECT...
...I WONDERED IF MAYBE YOU'D HEARD ANYTHING HELPFUL.
NOT REALLY. YOU HAVE ANY FURTHER LEADS?
NOT EXACTLY. BUT...THERE'S...
huff
...THERE'S...
HAVING TROUBLE KEEPING UP?
NOT A...
huff huff
...NOT A BIT.
ANYWAY, THERE'S SOMETHING ELSE...SOME OTHER CONNECTION I CAN'T QUITE PUT MY FINGER ON.
FINE. I'LL HELP YOU FIND IT--
--BUT FOR THE MOMENT, I'M NOT GOING TO GO OUT LOOKING FOR TROUBLE WHEN I'VE GOT A MORE IMME-DIATE PROBLEM TO SOLVE.
FOLLOW ME.

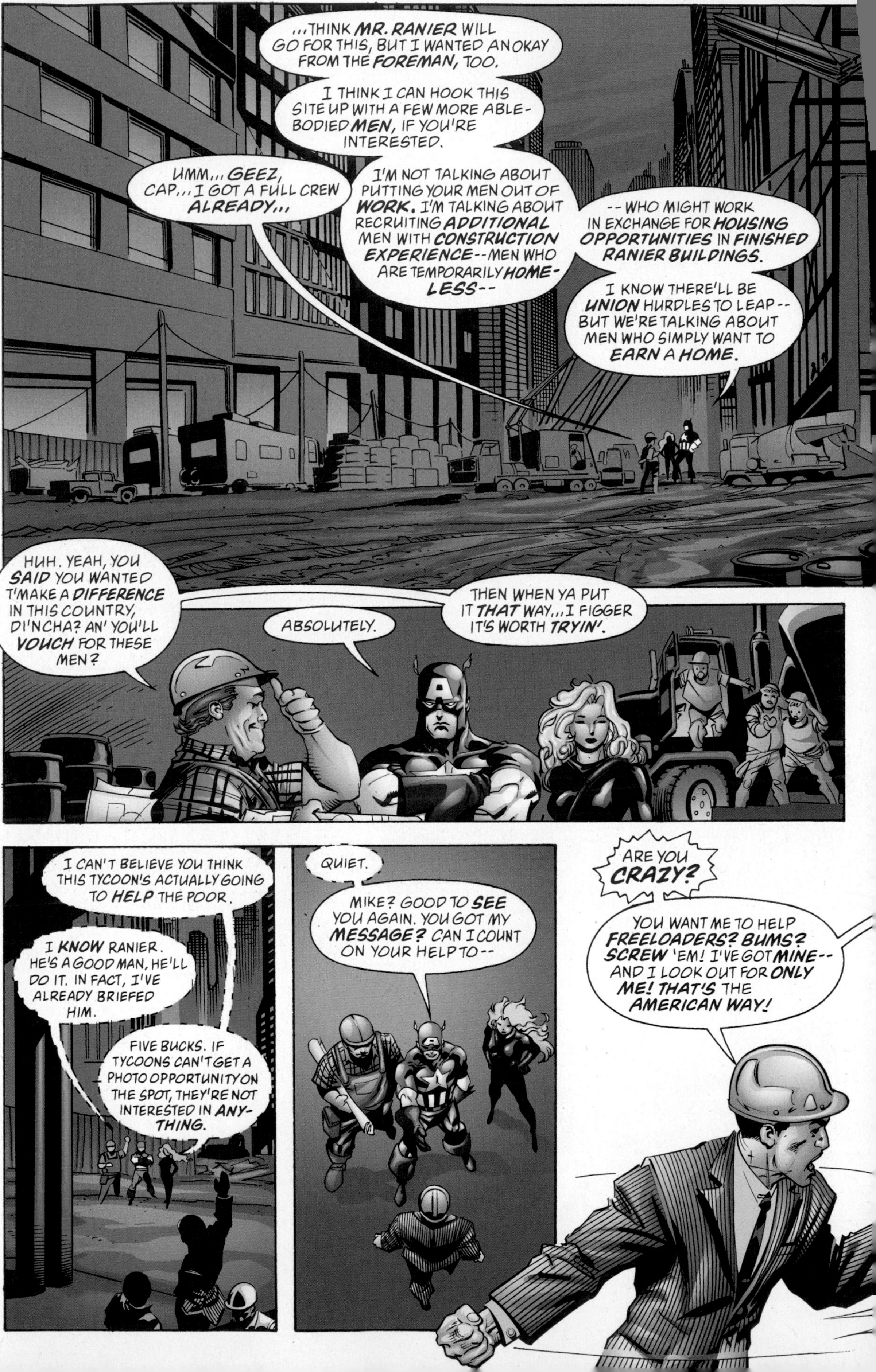
...THINK MR. RANIER WILL GO FOR THIS, BUT I WANTED AN OKAY FROM THE FOREMAN, TOO.
I THINK I CAN HOOK THIS SITE UP WITH A FEW MORE ABLE-BODIED MEN, IF YOU'RE INTERESTED.
UMM... GEEZ, CAP... I GOT A FULL CREW ALREADY...
I'M NOT TALKING ABOUT PUTTING YOUR MEN OUT OF WORK. I'M TALKING ABOUT RECRUITING ADDITIONAL MEN WITH CONSTRUCTION EXPERIENCE--MEN WHO ARE TEMPORARILY HOME-LESS--
--WHO MIGHT WORK IN EXCHANGE FOR HOUSING OPPORTUNITIES IN FINISHED RANIER BUILDINGS.
I KNOW THERE'LL BE UNION HURDLES TO LEAP--BUT WE'RE TALKING ABOUT MEN WHO SIMPLY WANT TO EARN A HOME.
HUH. YEAH, YOU SAID YOU WANTED T'MAKE A DIFFERENCE IN THIS COUNTRY, DI'NCHA? AN' YOU'LL VOUCH FOR THESE MEN?
ABSOLUTELY.
THEN WHEN YA PUT IT THAT WAY... I FIGGER IT'S WORTH TRYIN'.
I CAN'T BELIEVE YOU THINK THIS TYCOON'S ACTUALLY GOING TO HELP THE POOR.
I KNOW RANIER. HE'S A GOOD MAN, HE'LL DO IT. IN FACT, I'VE ALREADY BRIEFED HIM.
FIVE BUCKS. IF TYCOONS CAN'T GET A PHOTO OPPORTUNITY ON THE SPOT, THEY'RE NOT INTERESTED IN ANY-THING.
QUIET.
MIKE? GOOD TO SEE YOU AGAIN. YOU GOT MY MESSAGE? CAN I COUNT ON YOUR HELP TO--
ARE YOU CRAZY?
YOU WANT ME TO HELP FREELOADERS? BUMS? SCREW 'EM! I'VE GOT MINE--AND I LOOK OUT FOR ONLY ME! THAT'S THE AMERICAN WAY!

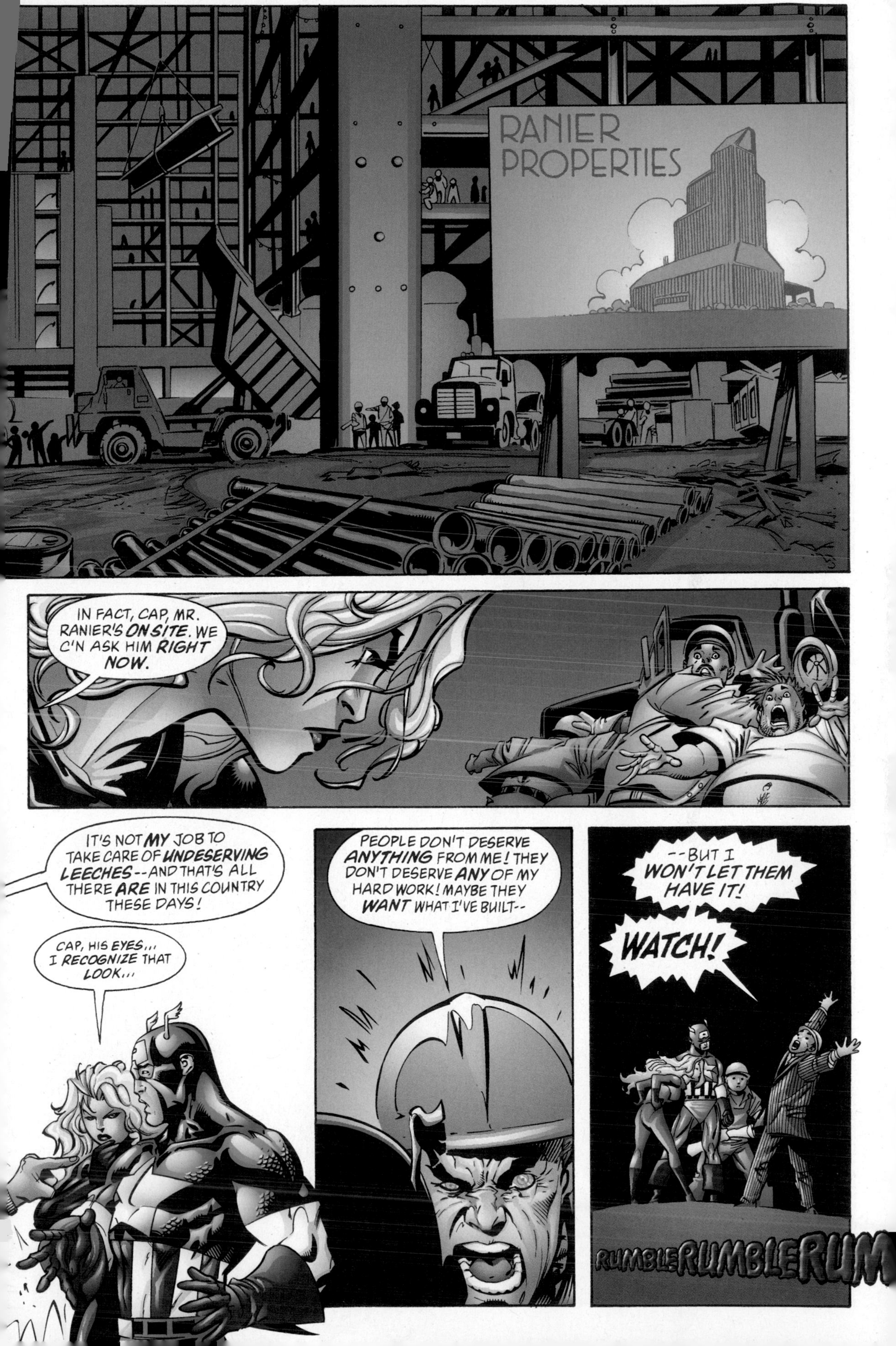
RANIER PROPERTIES
IN FACT, CAP, MR. RANIER'S ON SITE. WE C'N ASK HIM RIGHT NOW.
IT'S NOT MY JOB TO TAKE CARE OF UNDESERVING LEECHES--AND THAT'S ALL THERE ARE IN THIS COUNTRY THESE DAYS!
CAP, HIS EYES... I RECOGNIZE THAT LOOK...
PEOPLE DON'T DESERVE ANYTHING FROM ME! THEY DON'T DESERVE ANY OF MY HARD WORK! MAYBE THEY WANT WHAT I'VE BUILT--
--BUT I WON'T LET THEM HAVE IT!
WATCH!
RUMBLE RUMBLE RUM

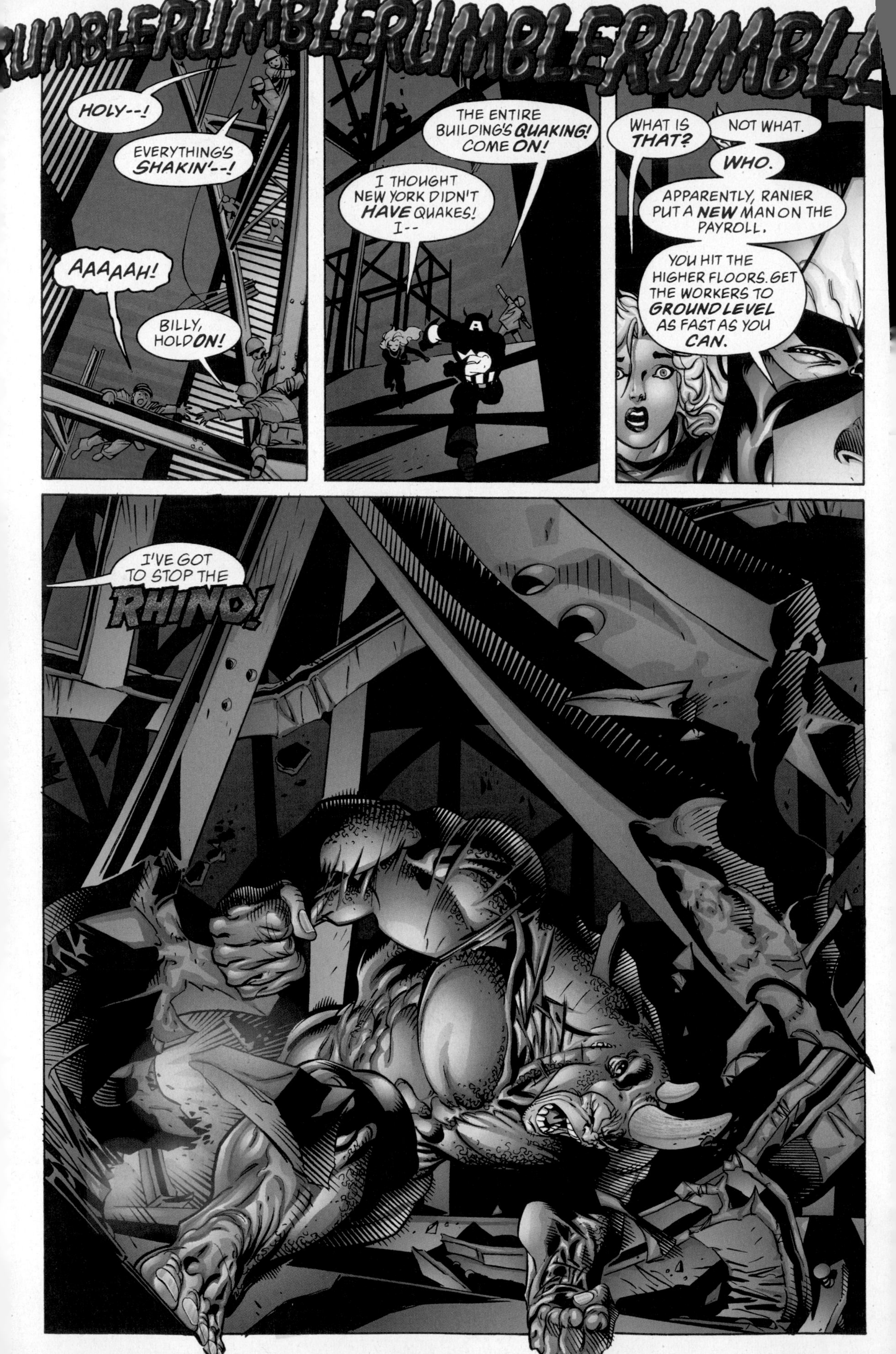
RUMBLERUMBLERUMBLERUMBL
HOLY--!
EVERYTHING'S SHAKIN'--!
AAAAAH!
BILLY, HOLD ON!
THE ENTIRE BUILDING'S QUAKING! COME ON!
I THOUGHT NEW YORK DIDN'T HAVE QUAKES! I--
WHAT IS THAT?
NOT WHAT.
WHO.
APPARENTLY, RANIER PUT A NEW MAN ON THE PAYROLL.
YOU HIT THE HIGHER FLOORS. GET THE WORKERS TO GROUND LEVEL AS FAST AS YOU CAN.
I'VE GOT TO STOP THE RHINO!

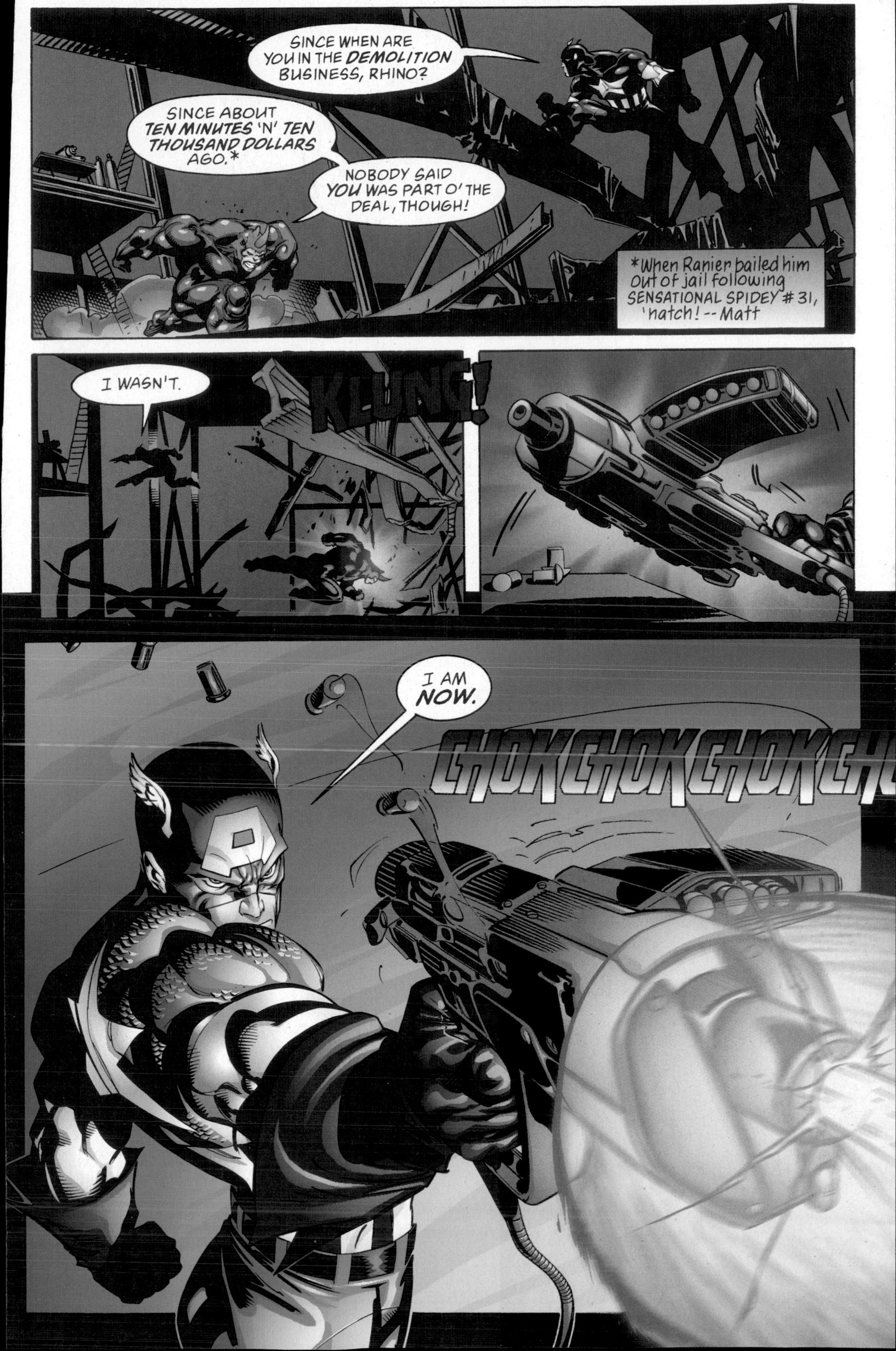
SINCE WHEN ARE YOU IN THE DEMOLITION BUSINESS, RHINO?
SINCE ABOUT TEN MINUTES 'N' TEN THOUSAND DOLLARS AGO.*
NOBODY SAID YOU WAS PART O' THE DEAL, THOUGH!
*When Ranier bailed him out of jail following SENSATIONAL SPIDEY #31, 'natch! -- Matt
I WASN'T.
KLUNG!
I AM NOW.
CHOKCHOKCHOKCHO

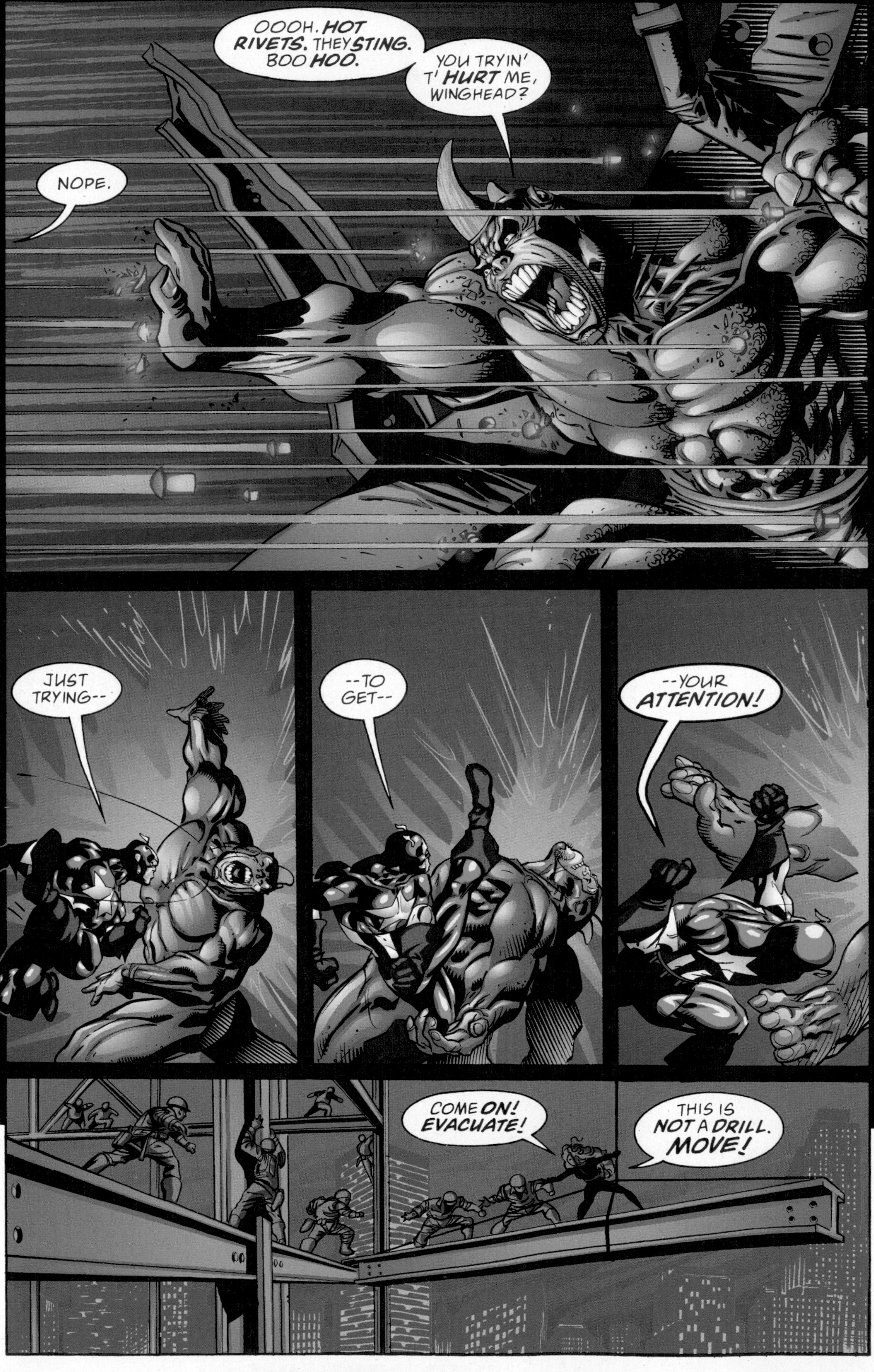
OOOH. HOT RIVETS. THEY STING. BOO HOO.
YOU TRYIN' T' HURT ME, WINGHEAD?
NOPE.
JUST TRYING--
--TO GET--
--YOUR ATTENTION!
COME ON! EVACUATE!
THIS IS NOT A DRILL. MOVE!

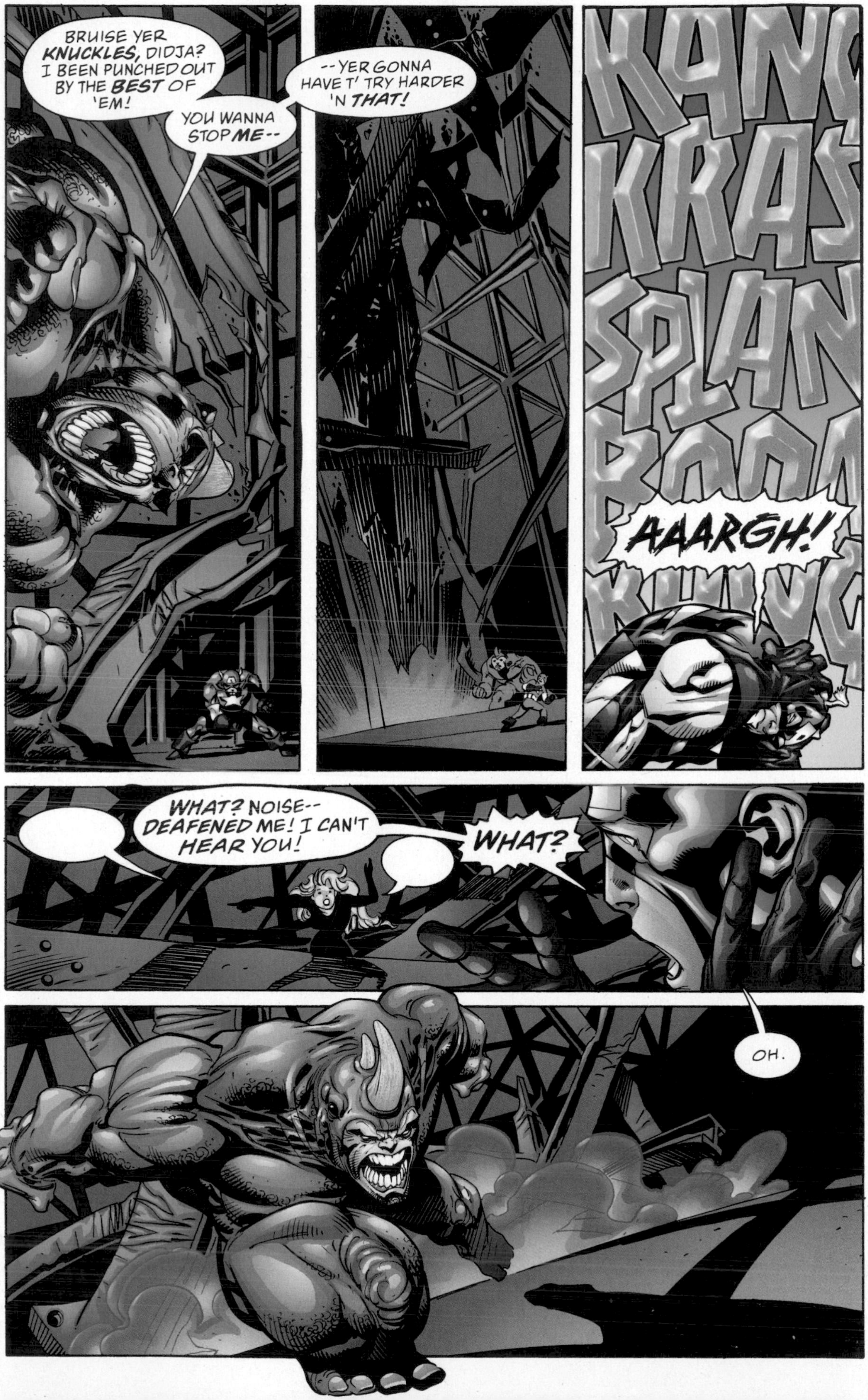
BRUISE YER KNUCKLES, DIDJA? I BEEN PUNCHED OUT BY THE BEST OF 'EM!
YOU WANNA STOP ME--
--YER GONNA HAVE T' TRY HARDER 'N THAT!
AAARGH!
WHAT? NOISE-- DEAFENED ME! I CAN'T HEAR YOU!
WHAT?
OH.

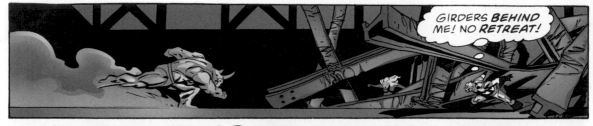

GIRDERS *BEHIND* ME! NO *RETREAT!*

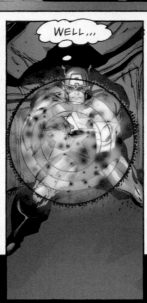

WELL...

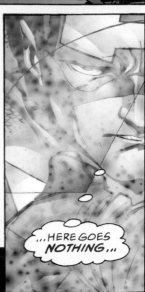

...HERE GOES *NOTHING*...

SPANG

ANGANGANG

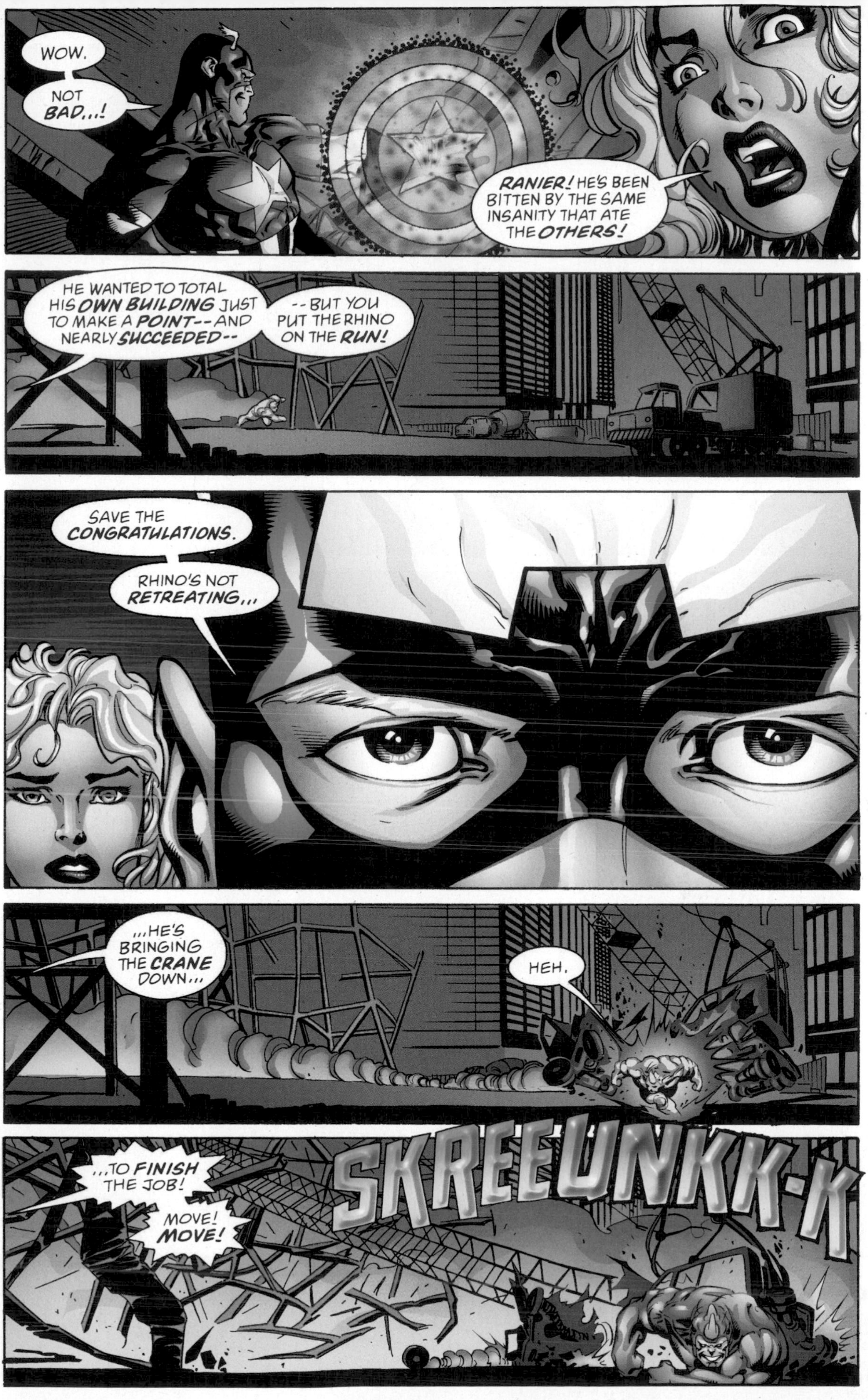
WOW.
NOT BAD...!
RANIER! HE'S BEEN BITTEN BY THE SAME INSANITY THAT ATE THE OTHERS!
HE WANTED TO TOTAL HIS OWN BUILDING JUST TO MAKE A POINT-- AND NEARLY SUCCEEDED--
--BUT YOU PUT THE RHINO ON THE RUN!
SAVE THE CONGRATULATIONS.
RHINO'S NOT RETREATING...
...HE'S BRINGING THE CRANE DOWN...
HEH.
...TO FINISH THE JOB!
MOVE! MOVE!
SKREEUNKK-K

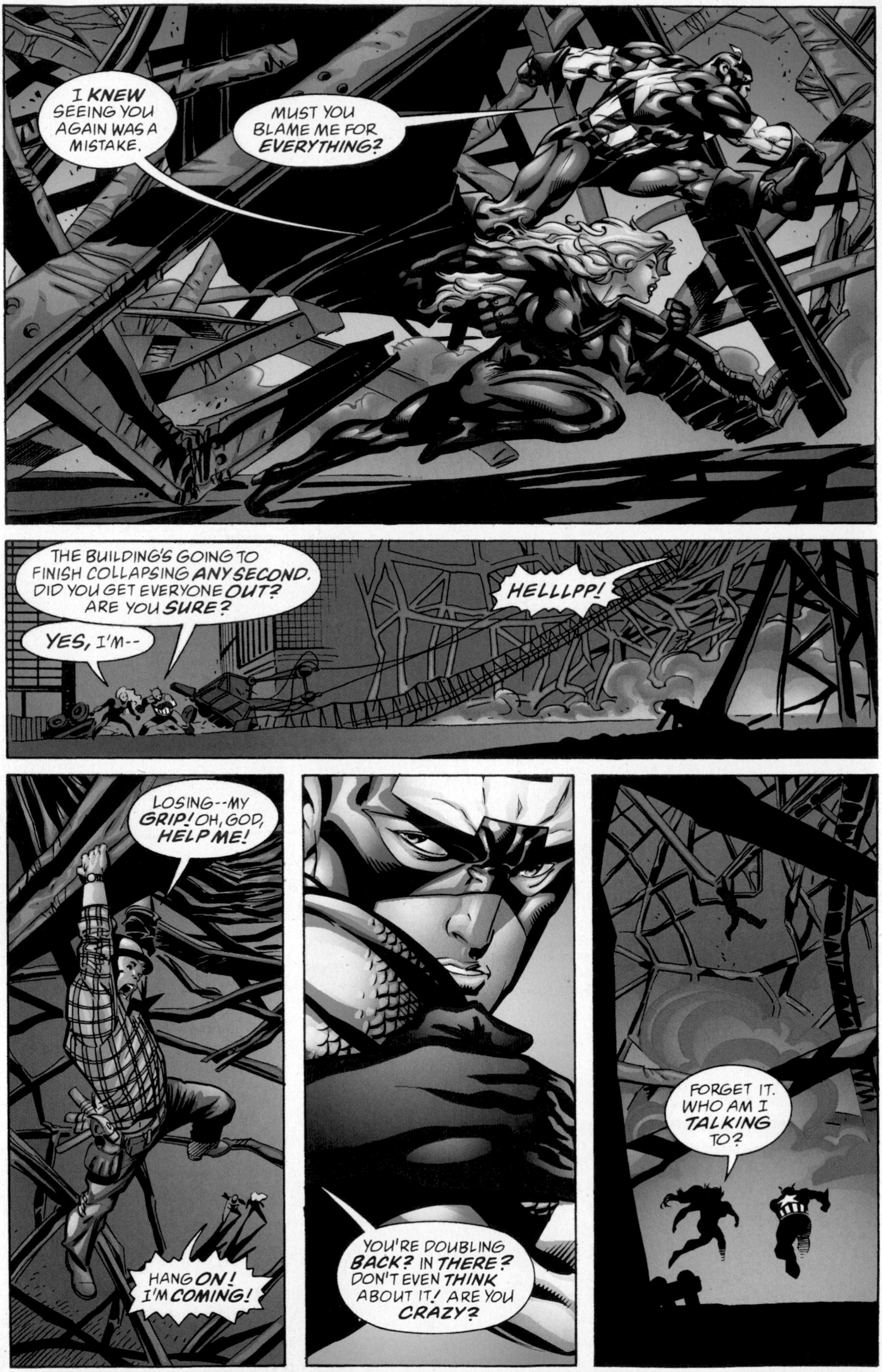
I KNEW SEEING YOU AGAIN WAS A MISTAKE.
MUST YOU BLAME ME FOR EVERYTHING?
THE BUILDING'S GOING TO FINISH COLLAPSING ANY SECOND. DID YOU GET EVERYONE OUT? ARE YOU SURE?
YES, I'M--
HELLLPP!
LOSING--MY GRIP! OH, GOD, HELP ME!
HANG ON! I'M COMING!
YOU'RE DOUBLING BACK? IN THERE? DON'T EVEN THINK ABOUT IT! ARE YOU CRAZY?
FORGET IT. WHO AM I TALKING TO?

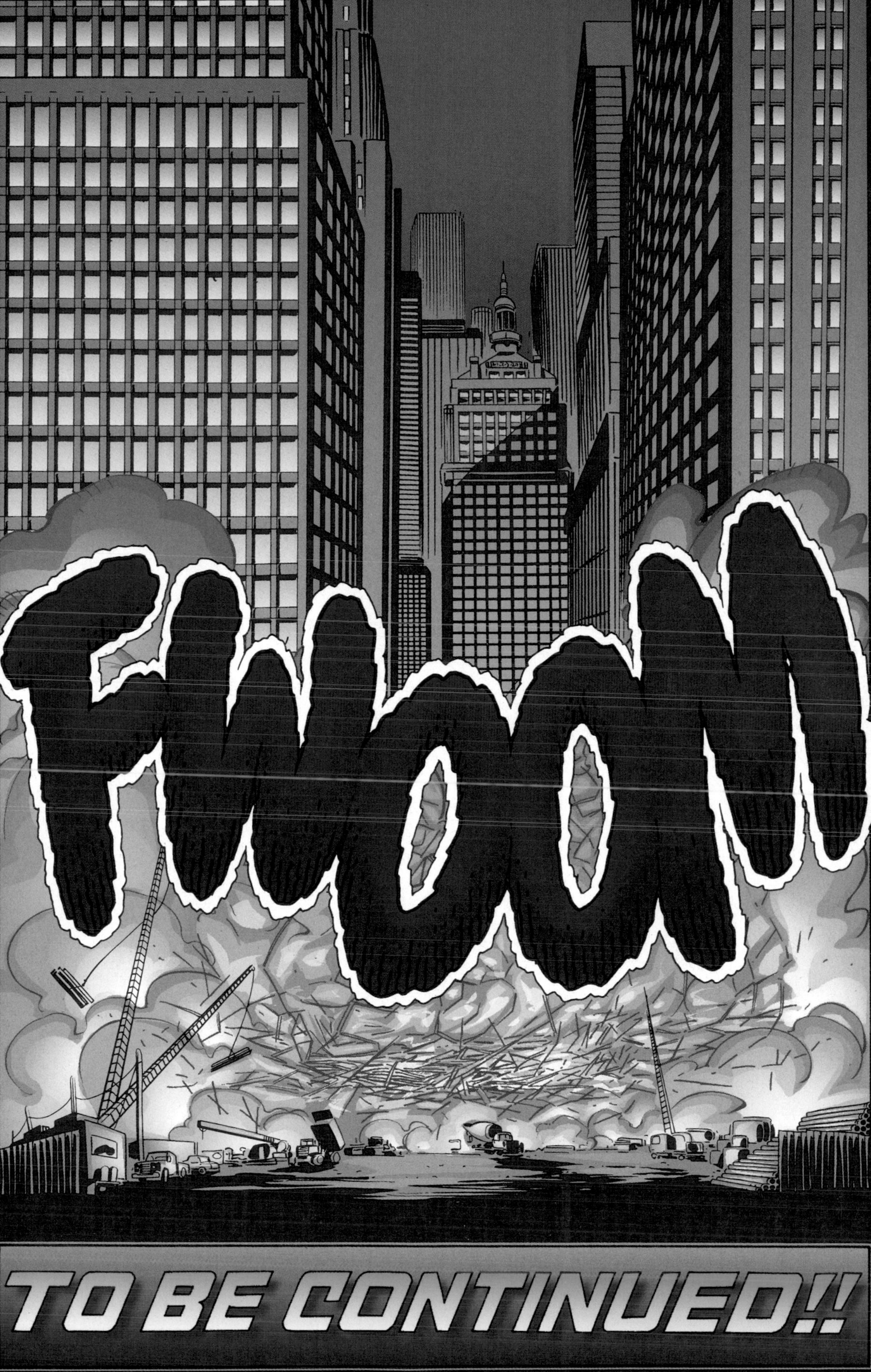
FWOOM
TO BE CONTINUED!!

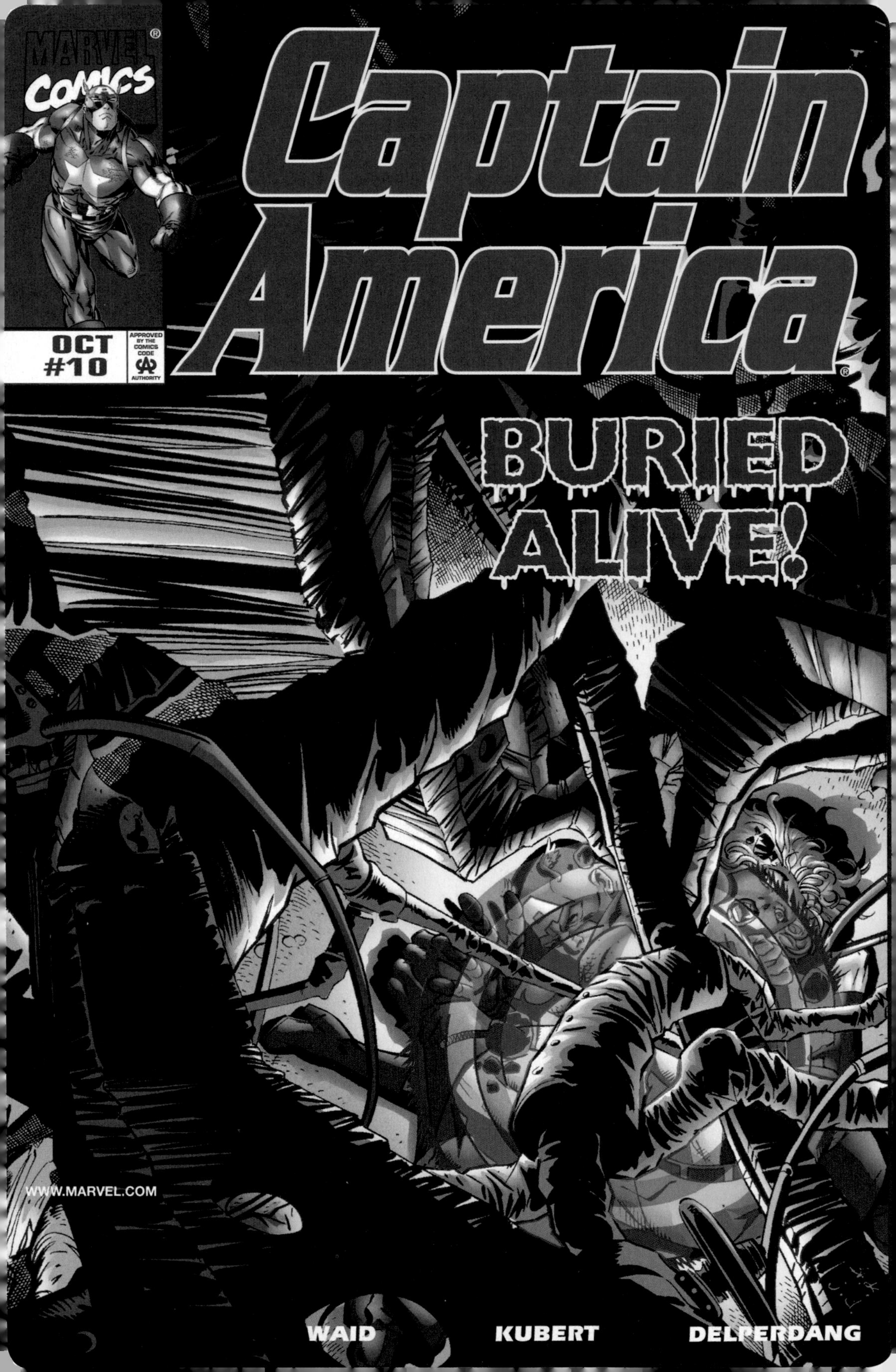

MARVEL COMICS
Captain America
OCT #10
APPROVED BY THE COMICS CODE AUTHORITY
BURIED ALIVE!
WWW.MARVEL.COM
WAID
KUBERT
DELPERDANG

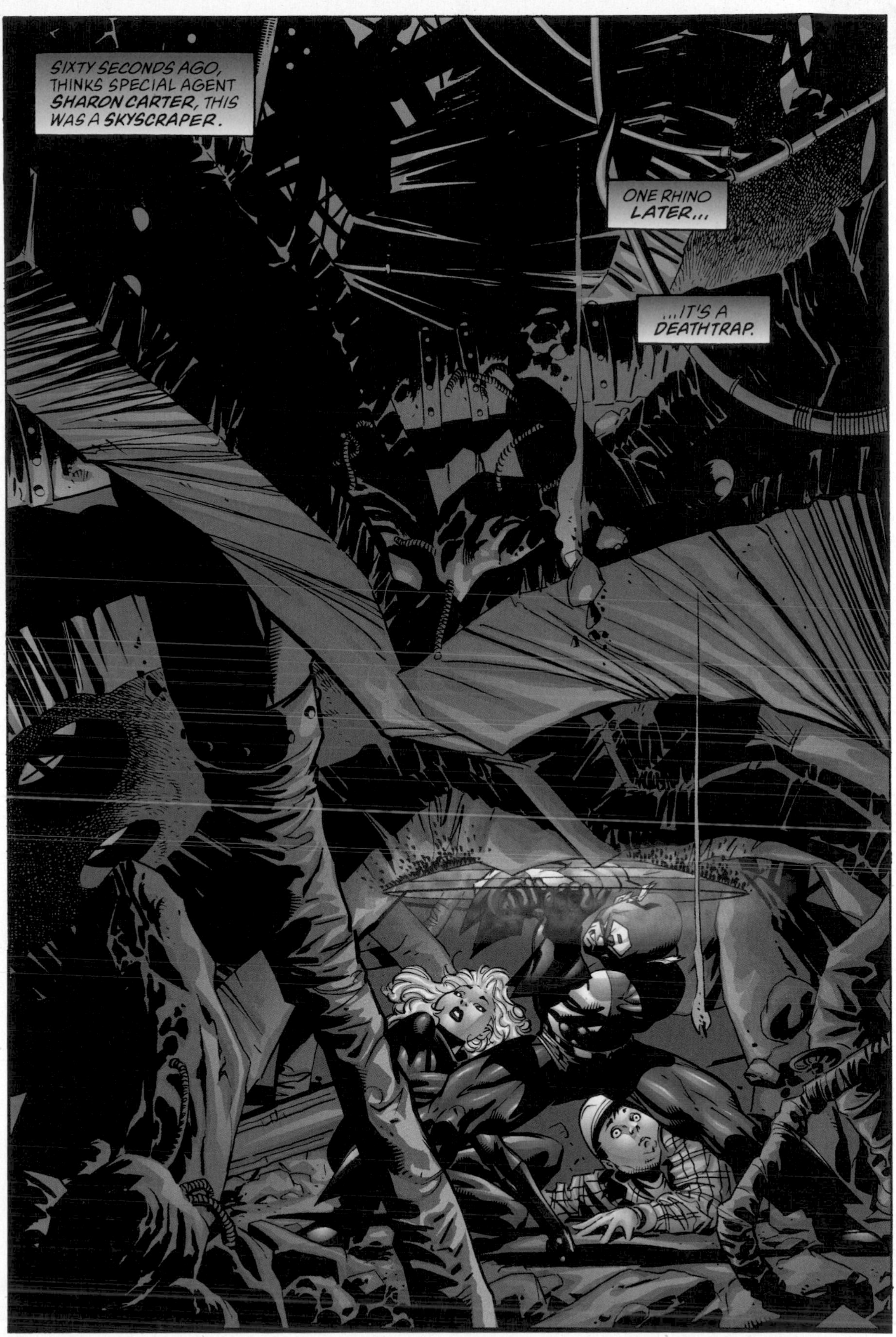
SIXTY SECONDS AGO, THINKS SPECIAL AGENT SHARON CARTER, THIS WAS A SKYSCRAPER.
ONE RHINO LATER...
...IT'S A DEATHTRAP.

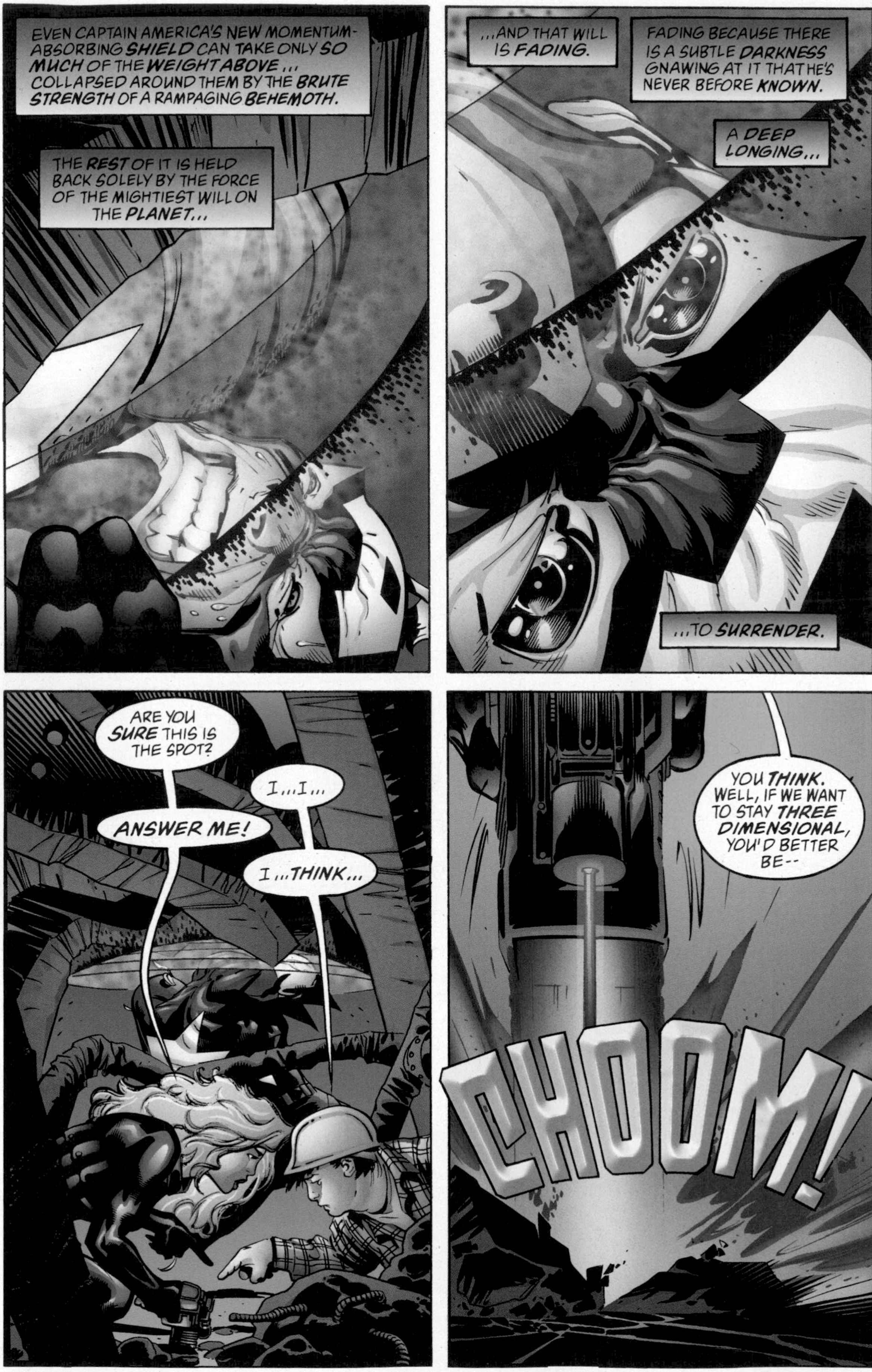
EVEN CAPTAIN AMERICA'S NEW MOMENTUM-ABSORBING SHIELD CAN TAKE ONLY SO MUCH OF THE WEIGHT ABOVE... COLLAPSED AROUND THEM BY THE BRUTE STRENGTH OF A RAMPAGING BEHEMOTH.
THE REST OF IT IS HELD BACK SOLELY BY THE FORCE OF THE MIGHTIEST WILL ON THE PLANET...
...AND THAT WILL IS FADING.
FADING BECAUSE THERE IS A SUBTLE DARKNESS GNAWING AT IT THAT HE'S NEVER BEFORE KNOWN.
A DEEP LONGING...
...TO SURRENDER.
ARE YOU SURE THIS IS THE SPOT?
I...I...
ANSWER ME!
I...THINK...
YOU THINK. WELL, IF WE WANT TO STAY THREE DIMENSIONAL, YOU'D BETTER BE--
CHOOOM!

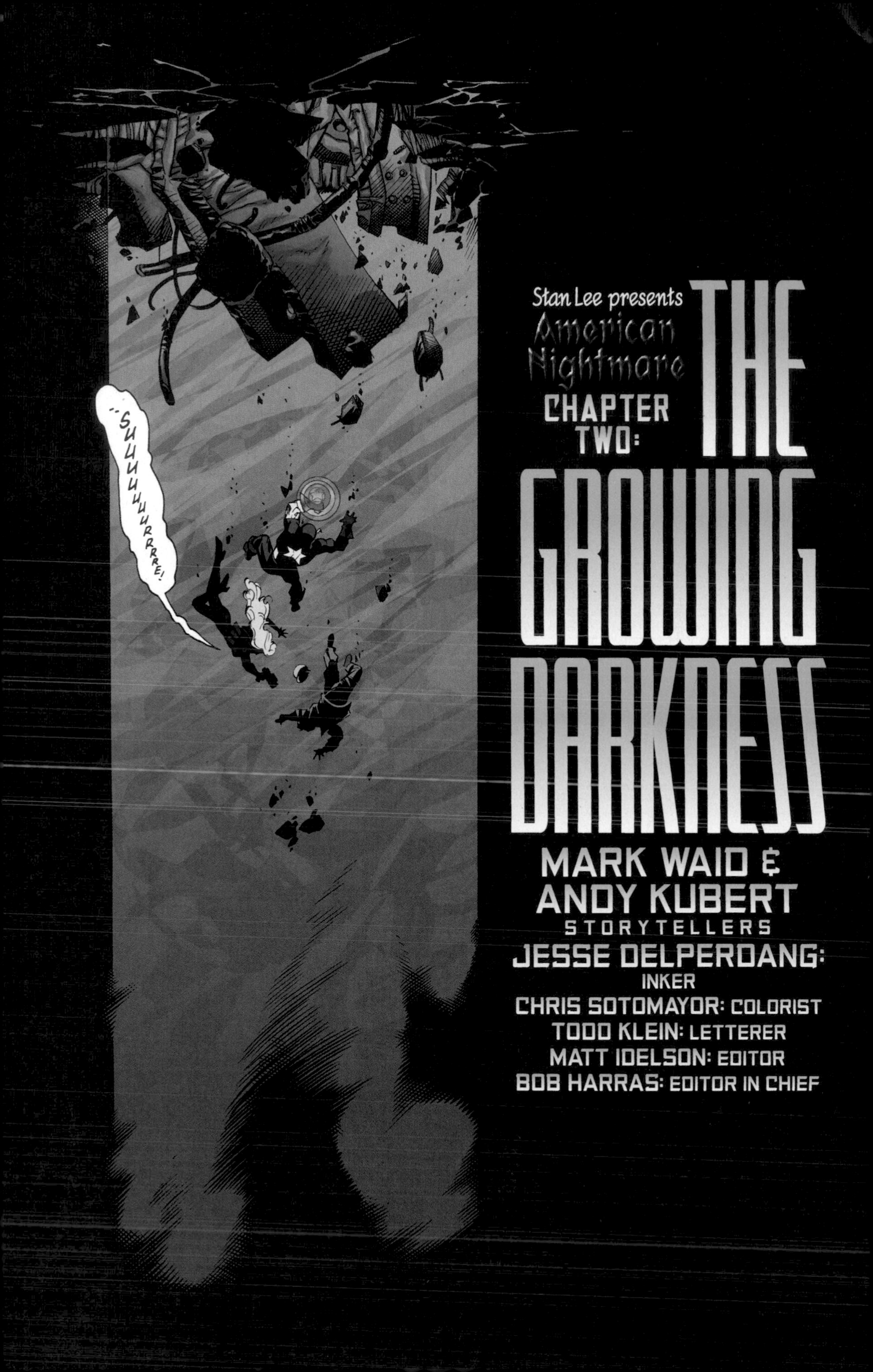
..SUUUUUURRRRE!
Stan Lee presents
American Nightmare
CHAPTER TWO:
THE GROWING DARKNESS
MARK WAID & ANDY KUBERT
STORYTELLERS
JESSE DELPERDANG:
INKER
CHRIS SOTOMAYOR: COLORIST
TODD KLEIN: LETTERER
MATT IDELSON: EDITOR
BOB HARRAS: EDITOR IN CHIEF

whew! SAFE!
HOW DO YOU FIGURE?
?
I MADE A HOLE IN THE FLOOR!
THEN IN ALL LIKELIHOOD--
CHANG KLANGANGANGANGANGANG
--WE'RE NOT THE ONLY THING COMING THROUGH IT!
RUN!
THAT WAS JUST A PRELUDE. WHEN THE RHINO DEMOLISHED THE BUILDING, WE WERE SMART ENOUGH TO SCRAMBLE TOWARDS BASEMENT ACCESS--
--BUT THE CEILING ABOVE US WON'T HOLD FOR LONG. WE HAVE TO GET OUT OF HERE BEFORE WE'RE CRUSHED.
YOU OKAY, SIR?
EEP.
SURE, EASY ENOUGH. I MEAN, WE'VE ONLY GOT AN ENTIRE SKYSCRAPER ON TOP OF US AND ALL.
AND, I MIGHT ADD, A VERY LIMITED SUPPLY OF AIR.
THEN DON'T WASTE IT BY COMPLAINING. WE HAVE TO--
SKRIIIITCH
HELLO?
SEE? SOMEONE'S ALREADY BEEN SENT DOWN TO LOOK FOR US.
WHOEVER YOU ARE--THANKS FOR THE SAVE!

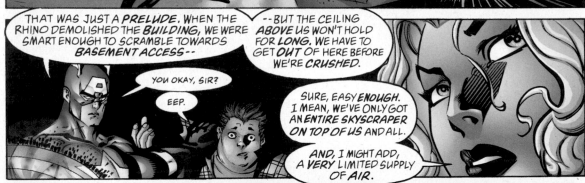

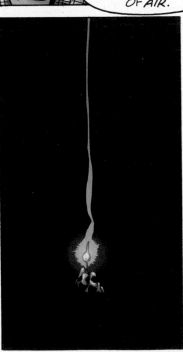

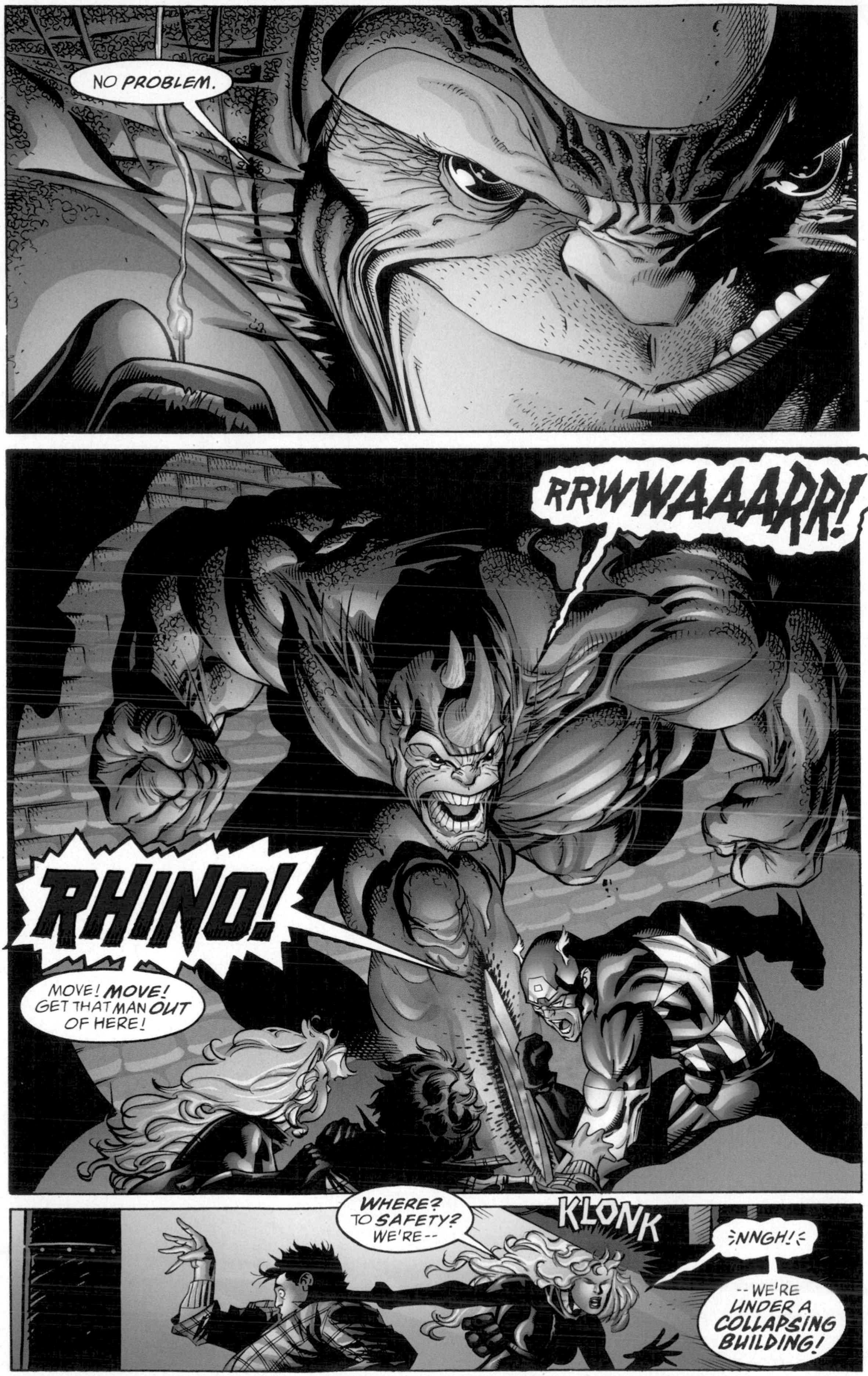
NO PROBLEM.
RRWWAAARR!
RHINO!
MOVE! MOVE! GET THAT MAN OUT OF HERE!
WHERE? TO SAFETY? WE'RE--
KLONK
NNGH!
--WE'RE UNDER A COLLAPSING BUILDING!

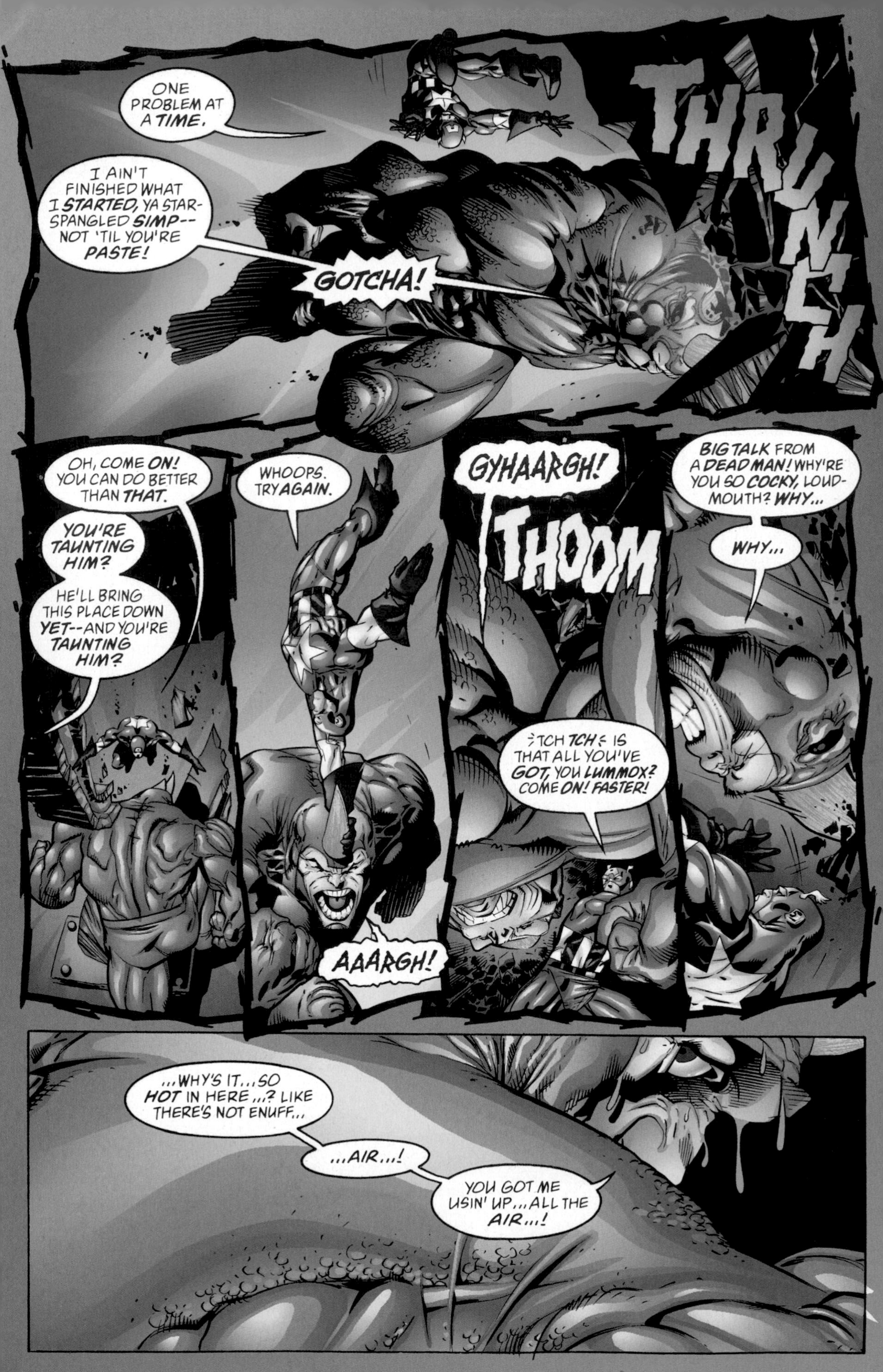

ONE PROBLEM AT A TIME.
THRUNCH
I AIN'T FINISHED WHAT I STARTED, YA STAR-SPANGLED SIMP-- NOT 'TIL YOU'RE PASTE!
GOTCHA!
OH, COME ON! YOU CAN DO BETTER THAN THAT.
YOU'RE TAUNTING HIM?
HE'LL BRING THIS PLACE DOWN YET--AND YOU'RE TAUNTING HIM?
WHOOPS. TRY AGAIN.
AAARGH!
GYHAARGH!
THOOM
TCH TCH IS THAT ALL YOU'VE GOT, YOU LUMMOX? COME ON! FASTER!
BIG TALK FROM A DEAD MAN! WHY'RE YOU SO COCKY, LOUD-MOUTH? WHY...
WHY...
...WHY'S IT...SO HOT IN HERE...? LIKE THERE'S NOT ENUFF...
...AIR...!
YOU GOT ME USIN' UP...ALL THE AIR...!

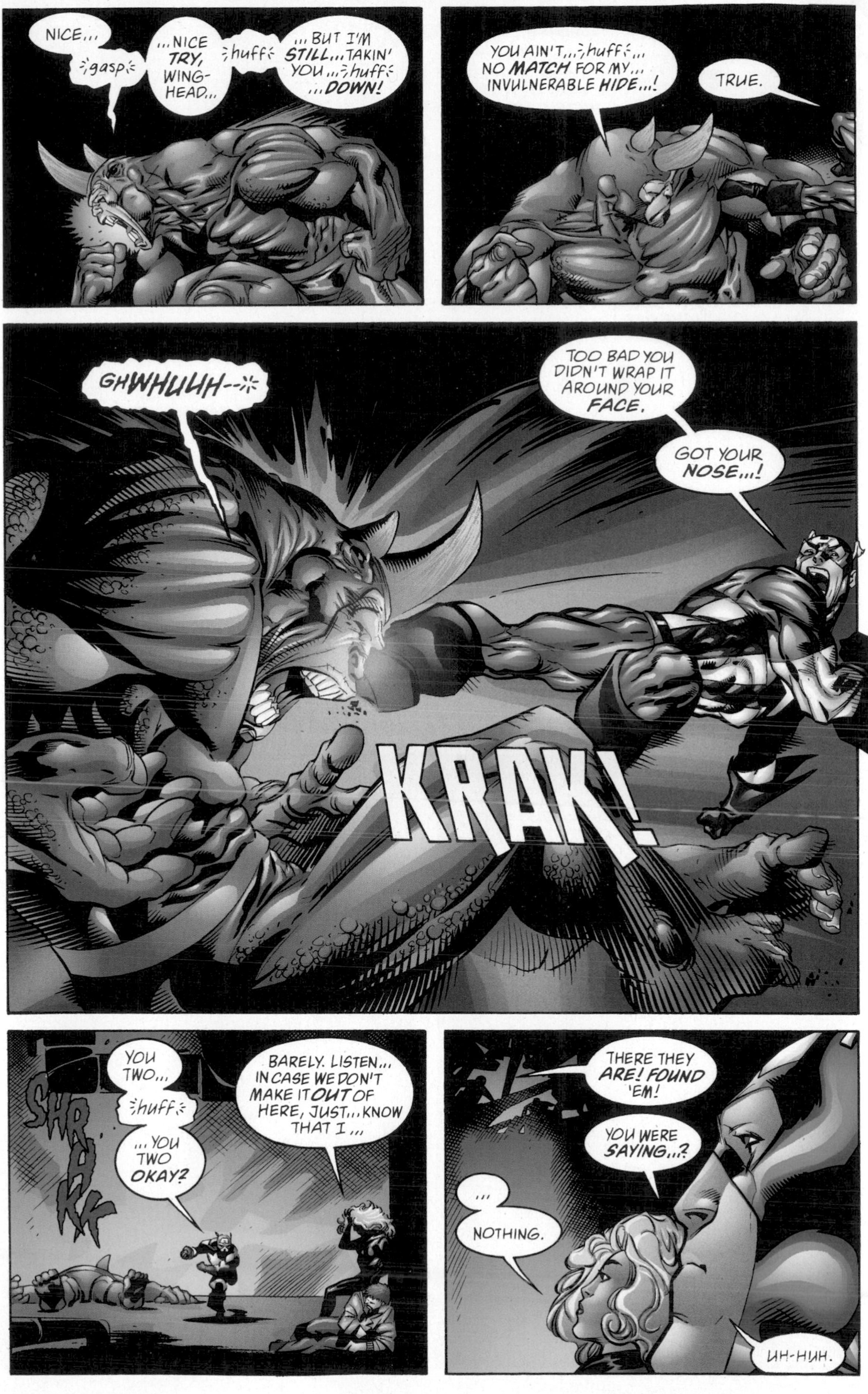
NICE...
gasp
...NICE TRY, WING-HEAD...
huff
...BUT I'M STILL...TAKIN' YOU... huff ...DOWN!
YOU AIN'T... huff ... NO MATCH FOR MY... INVULNERABLE HIDE...!
TRUE.
GHWHUUH--
TOO BAD YOU DIDN'T WRAP IT AROUND YOUR FACE.
GOT YOUR NOSE...!
KRAK!
SHRAKK
YOU TWO...
huff
...YOU TWO OKAY?
BARELY. LISTEN... IN CASE WE DON'T MAKE IT OUT OF HERE, JUST... KNOW THAT I...
THERE THEY ARE! FOUND 'EM!
YOU WERE SAYING...?
...
NOTHING.
UH-HUH.

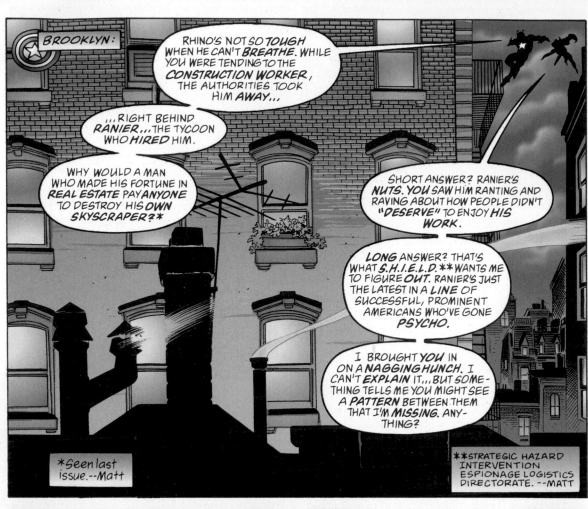

BROOKLYN:

RHINO'S NOT SO TOUGH WHEN HE CAN'T BREATHE. WHILE YOU WERE TENDING TO THE CONSTRUCTION WORKER, THE AUTHORITIES TOOK HIM AWAY...

...RIGHT BEHIND RANIER...THE TYCOON WHO HIRED HIM.

WHY WOULD A MAN WHO MADE HIS FORTUNE IN REAL ESTATE PAY ANYONE TO DESTROY HIS OWN SKYSCRAPER?*

SHORT ANSWER? RANIER'S NUTS. YOU SAW HIM RANTING AND RAVING ABOUT HOW PEOPLE DIDN'T "DESERVE" TO ENJOY HIS WORK.

LONG ANSWER? THAT'S WHAT S.H.I.E.L.D.** WANTS ME TO FIGURE OUT. RANIER'S JUST THE LATEST IN A LINE OF SUCCESSFUL, PROMINENT AMERICANS WHO'VE GONE PSYCHO.

I BROUGHT YOU IN ON A NAGGING HUNCH. I CAN'T EXPLAIN IT...BUT SOMETHING TELLS ME YOU MIGHT SEE A PATTERN BETWEEN THEM THAT I'M MISSING. ANYTHING?

*Seen last issue.--Matt

**STRATEGIC HAZARD INTERVENTION ESPIONAGE LOGISTICS DIRECTORATE. --MATT

FRANKLY, THAT'S NOT WHERE MY THOUGHTS ARE THIS SECOND. I'M DISAPPOINTED RANIER WAS A DEAD END TO ME.

I'D HOPED TO USE HIS CONNECTIONS TO FIND A HOME FOR THE RAMIREZ FAMILY. NOW I'VE LET THEM DOWN.

THE RAMIREZES? THE FAMILY IN YOUR APARTMENT?

ROGERS, THAT'S A BIG HEART YOU'VE GOT...BUT THEY'RE SQUATTERS!

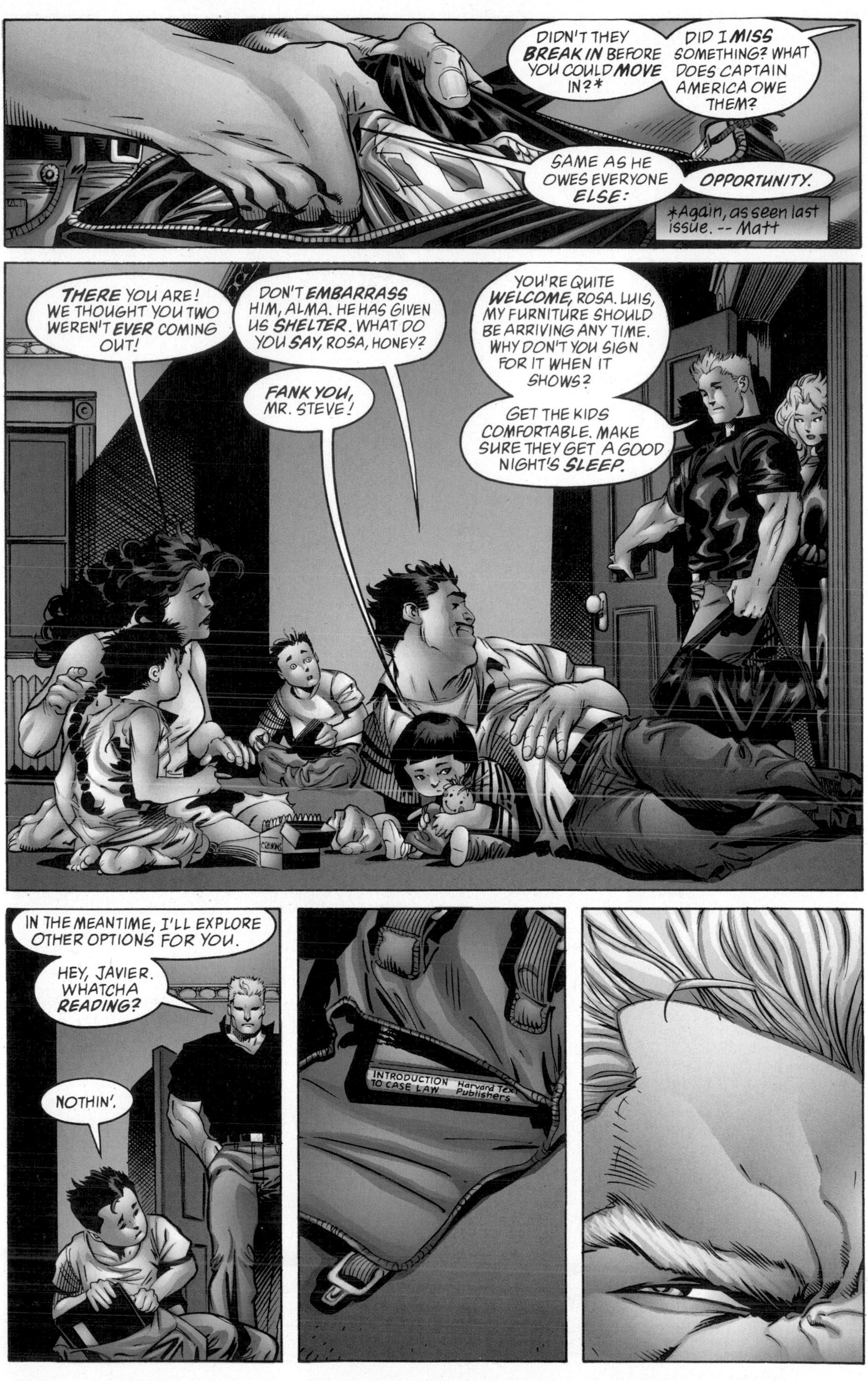

DIDN'T THEY BREAK IN BEFORE YOU COULD MOVE IN?*
DID I MISS SOMETHING? WHAT DOES CAPTAIN AMERICA OWE THEM?
SAME AS HE OWES EVERYONE ELSE:
OPPORTUNITY.
*Again, as seen last issue. -- Matt
THERE YOU ARE! WE THOUGHT YOU TWO WEREN'T EVER COMING OUT!
DON'T EMBARRASS HIM, ALMA. HE HAS GIVEN US SHELTER. WHAT DO YOU SAY, ROSA, HONEY?
FANK YOU, MR. STEVE!
YOU'RE QUITE WELCOME, ROSA. LUIS, MY FURNITURE SHOULD BE ARRIVING ANY TIME. WHY DON'T YOU SIGN FOR IT WHEN IT SHOWS?
GET THE KIDS COMFORTABLE. MAKE SURE THEY GET A GOOD NIGHT'S SLEEP.
IN THE MEANTIME, I'LL EXPLORE OTHER OPTIONS FOR YOU.
HEY, JAVIER. WHATCHA READING?
NOTHIN'.
INTRODUCTION TO CASE LAW
Harvard Tex Publishers

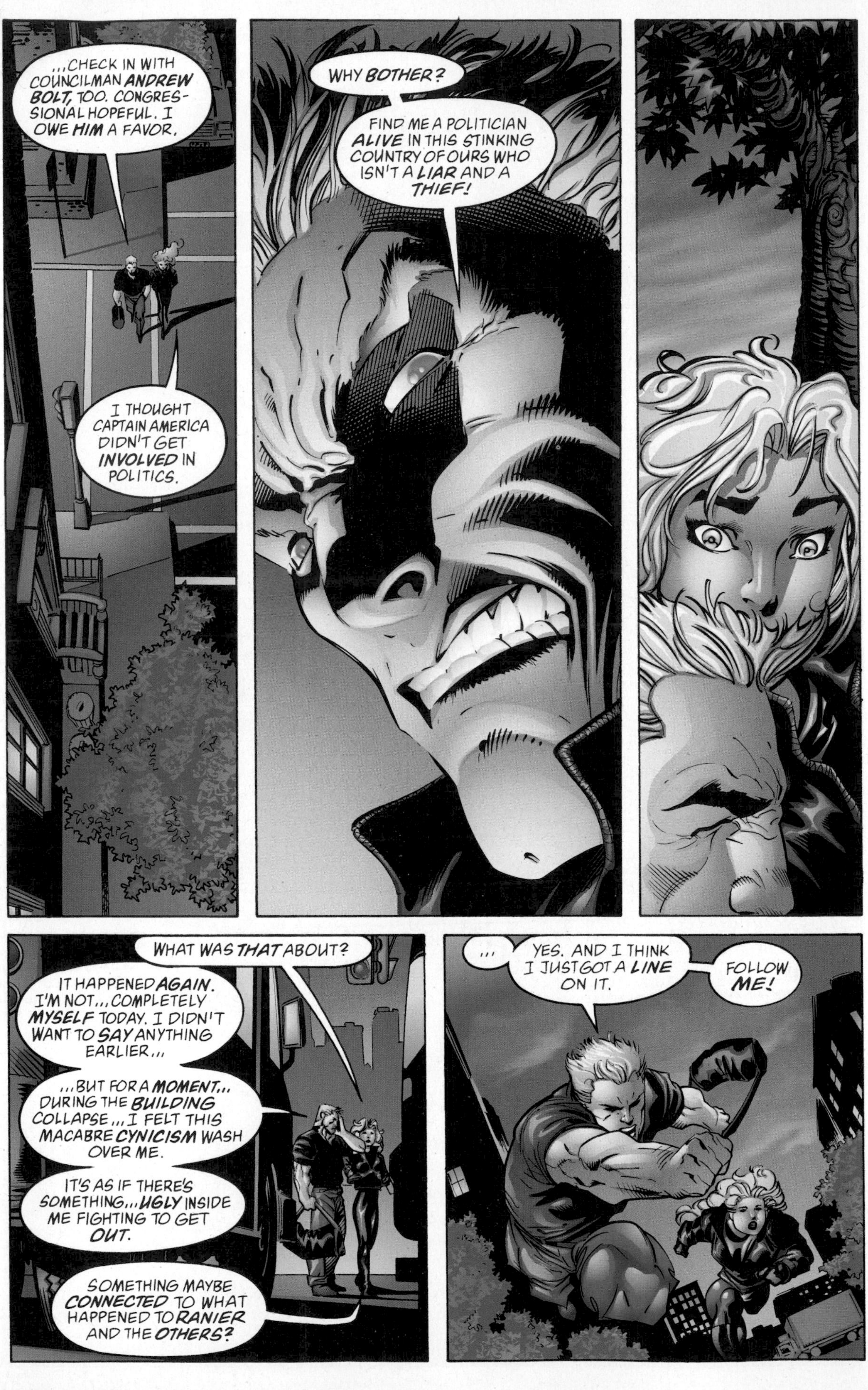
...CHECK IN WITH COUNCILMAN ANDREW BOLT, TOO. CONGRES-SIONAL HOPEFUL. I OWE HIM A FAVOR.
I THOUGHT CAPTAIN AMERICA DIDN'T GET INVOLVED IN POLITICS.
WHY BOTHER?
FIND ME A POLITICIAN ALIVE IN THIS STINKING COUNTRY OF OURS WHO ISN'T A LIAR AND A THIEF!
WHAT WAS THAT ABOUT?
IT HAPPENED AGAIN. I'M NOT... COMPLETELY MYSELF TODAY. I DIDN'T WANT TO SAY ANYTHING EARLIER...
...BUT FOR A MOMENT... DURING THE BUILDING COLLAPSE... I FELT THIS MACABRE CYNICISM WASH OVER ME.
IT'S AS IF THERE'S SOMETHING... UGLY INSIDE ME FIGHTING TO GET OUT.
SOMETHING MAYBE CONNECTED TO WHAT HAPPENED TO RANIER AND THE OTHERS?
...
YES. AND I THINK I JUST GOT A LINE ON IT.
FOLLOW ME!

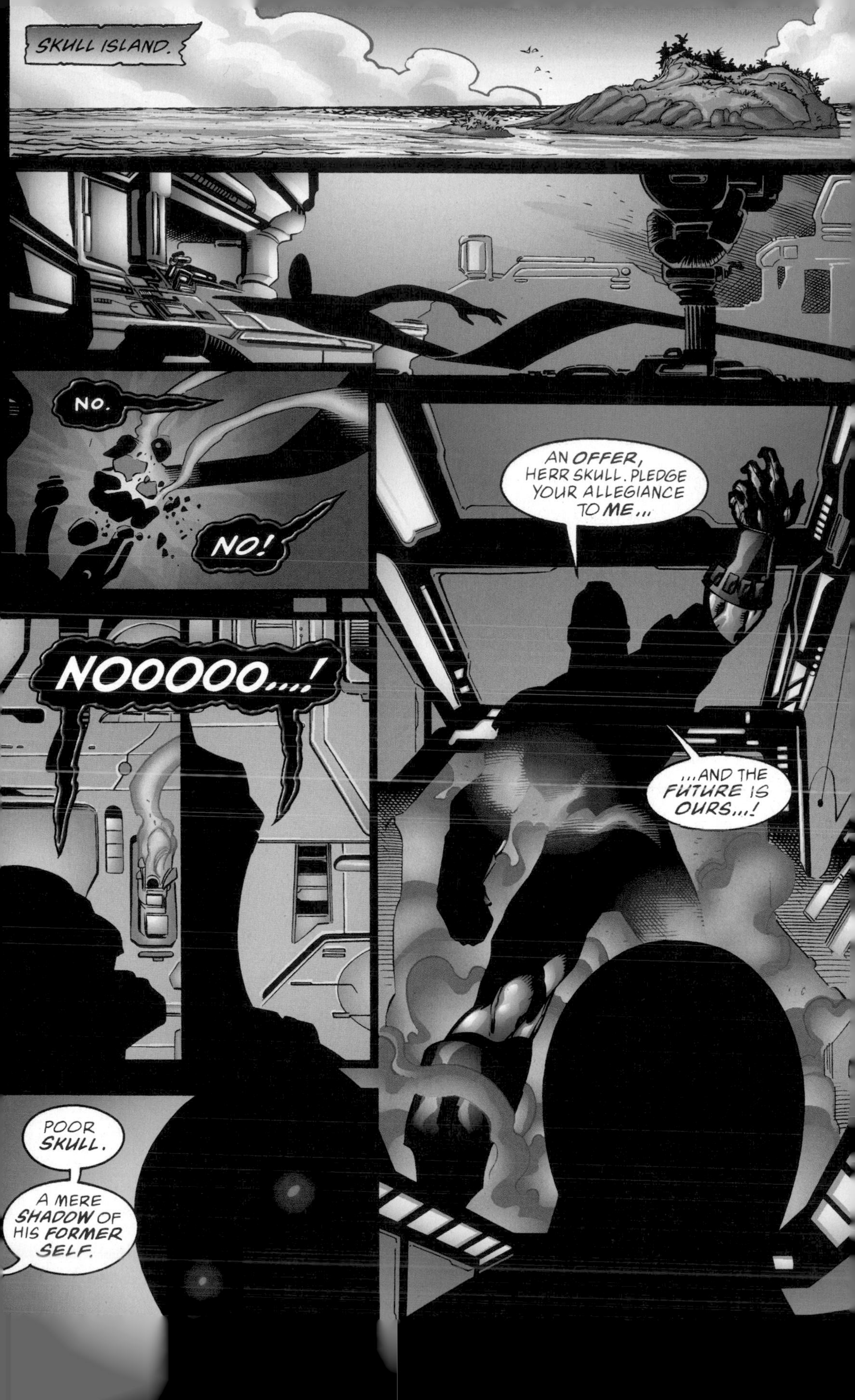
SKULL ISLAND.
NO.
NO!
AN OFFER, HERR SKULL. PLEDGE YOUR ALLEGIANCE TO ME...
NOOOOO...!
...AND THE FUTURE IS OURS...!
POOR SKULL.
A MERE SHADOW OF HIS FORMER SELF.

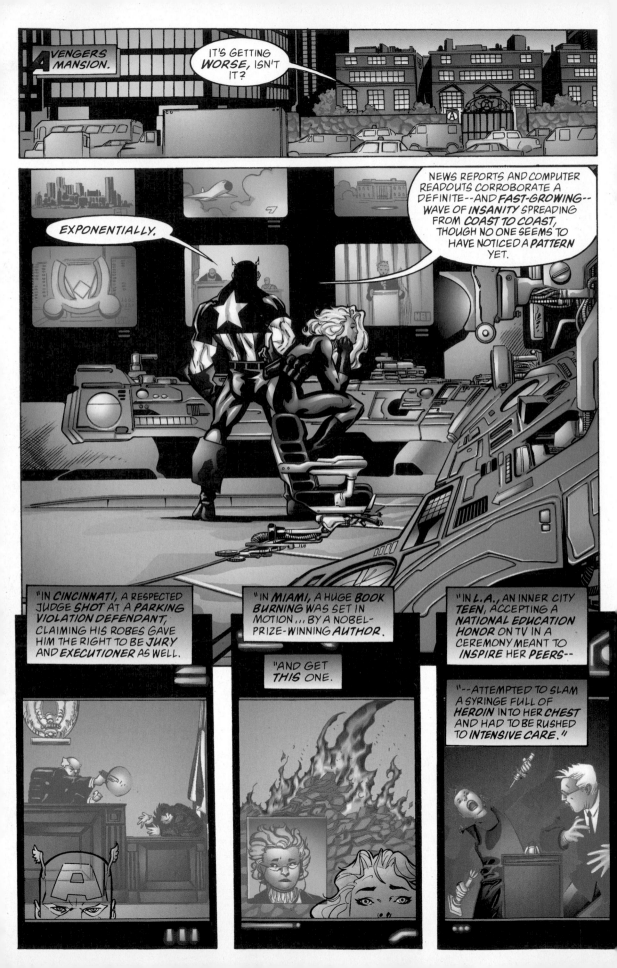

AVENGERS MANSION.

IT'S GETTING *WORSE*, ISN'T IT?

EXPONENTIALLY.

NEWS REPORTS AND COMPUTER READOUTS CORROBORATE A DEFINITE--AND *FAST-GROWING*--WAVE OF *INSANITY* SPREADING FROM *COAST TO COAST*, THOUGH NO ONE SEEMS TO HAVE NOTICED A *PATTERN* YET.

"IN *CINCINNATI*, A RESPECTED JUDGE *SHOT* AT A *PARKING VIOLATION* DEFENDANT, CLAIMING HIS ROBES GAVE HIM THE RIGHT TO BE *JURY* AND *EXECUTIONER* AS WELL.

"IN *MIAMI*, A HUGE *BOOK BURNING* WAS SET IN MOTION... BY A *NOBEL-PRIZE-WINNING AUTHOR.*

"AND GET *THIS* ONE.

"IN *L.A.*, AN INNER CITY *TEEN*, ACCEPTING A *NATIONAL EDUCATION HONOR* ON TV IN A CEREMONY MEANT TO *INSPIRE* HER *PEERS*--

"--ATTEMPTED TO SLAM A SYRINGE FULL OF *HEROIN* INTO HER *CHEST* AND HAD TO BE RUSHED TO *INTENSIVE CARE.*"

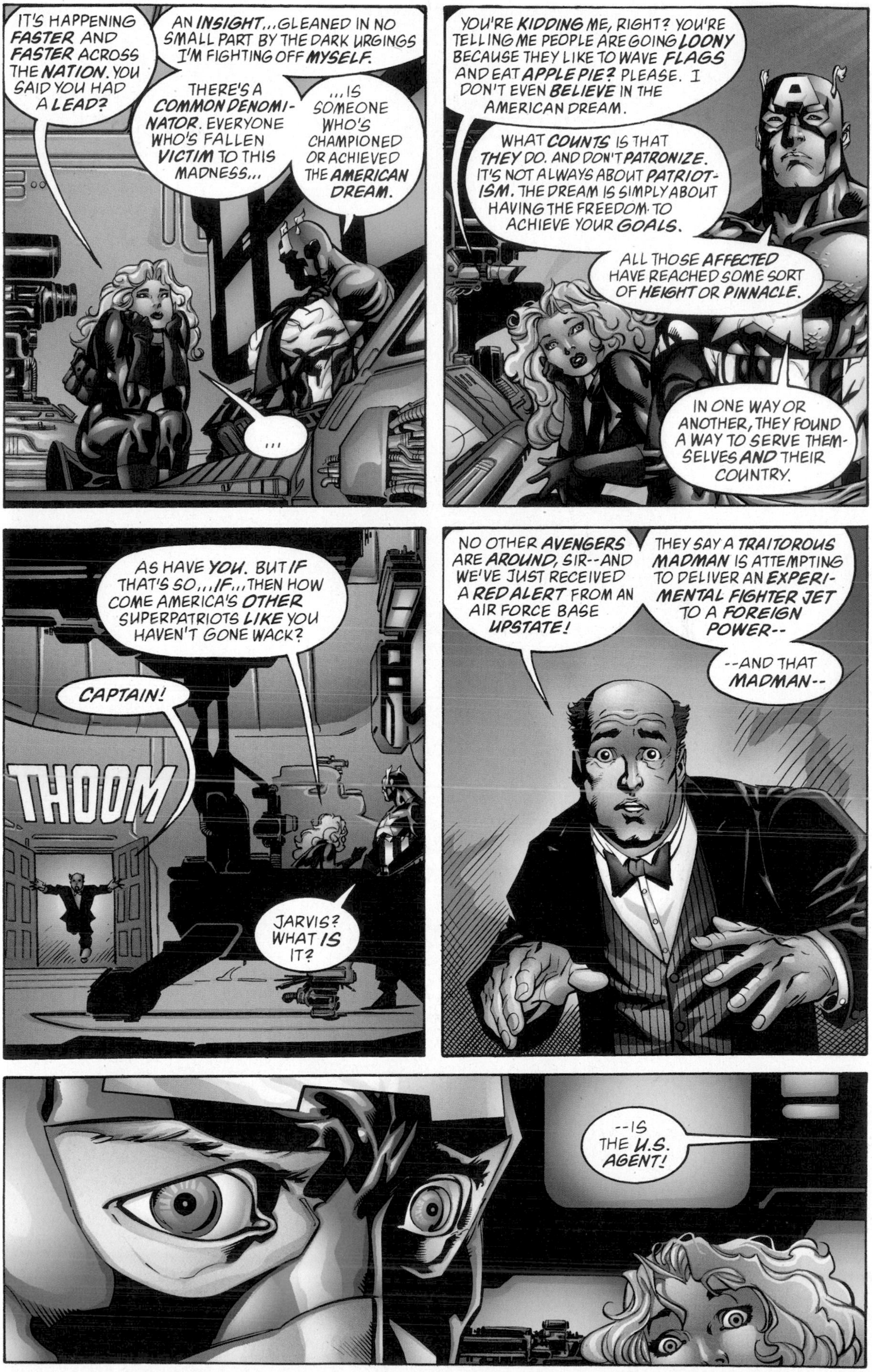
IT'S HAPPENING FASTER AND FASTER ACROSS THE NATION. YOU SAID YOU HAD A LEAD?
AN INSIGHT... GLEANED IN NO SMALL PART BY THE DARK URGINGS I'M FIGHTING OFF MYSELF.
THERE'S A COMMON DENOMINATOR. EVERYONE WHO'S FALLEN VICTIM TO THIS MADNESS...
...IS SOMEONE WHO'S CHAMPIONED OR ACHIEVED THE AMERICAN DREAM.
...
YOU'RE KIDDING ME, RIGHT? YOU'RE TELLING ME PEOPLE ARE GOING LOONY BECAUSE THEY LIKE TO WAVE FLAGS AND EAT APPLE PIE? PLEASE. I DON'T EVEN BELIEVE IN THE AMERICAN DREAM.
WHAT COUNTS IS THAT THEY DO. AND DON'T PATRONIZE. IT'S NOT ALWAYS ABOUT PATRIOTISM. THE DREAM IS SIMPLY ABOUT HAVING THE FREEDOM TO ACHIEVE YOUR GOALS.
ALL THOSE AFFECTED HAVE REACHED SOME SORT OF HEIGHT OR PINNACLE.
IN ONE WAY OR ANOTHER, THEY FOUND A WAY TO SERVE THEMSELVES AND THEIR COUNTRY.
AS HAVE YOU. BUT IF THAT'S SO... IF... THEN HOW COME AMERICA'S OTHER SUPERPATRIOTS LIKE YOU HAVEN'T GONE WACK?
CAPTAIN!
THOOM
JARVIS? WHAT IS IT?
NO OTHER AVENGERS ARE AROUND, SIR--AND WE'VE JUST RECEIVED A RED ALERT FROM AN AIR FORCE BASE UPSTATE!
THEY SAY A TRAITOROUS MADMAN IS ATTEMPTING TO DELIVER AN EXPERIMENTAL FIGHTER JET TO A FOREIGN POWER--
--AND THAT MADMAN--
--IS THE U.S. AGENT!

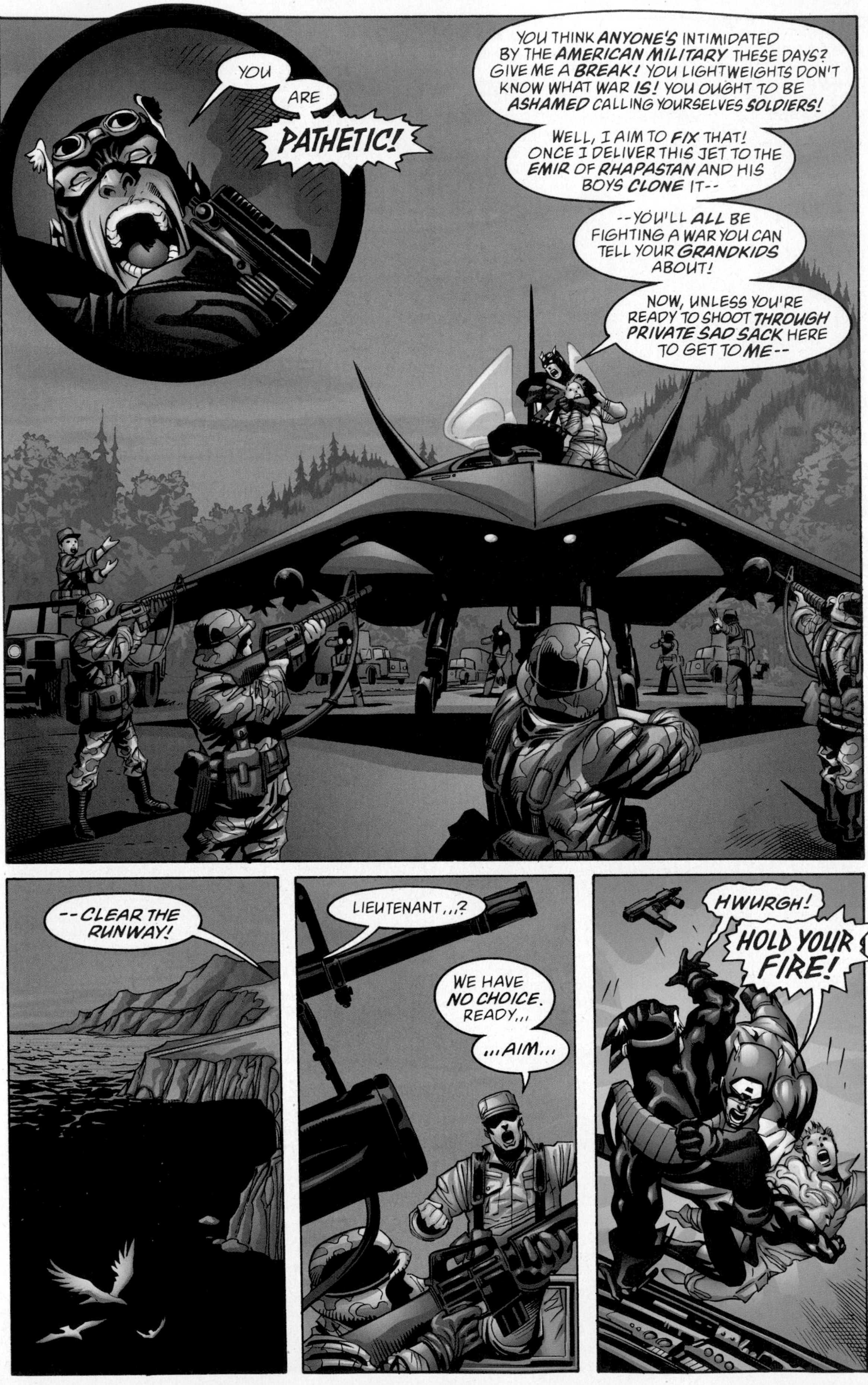
YOU
ARE
PATHETIC!
YOU THINK ANYONE'S INTIMIDATED BY THE AMERICAN MILITARY THESE DAYS? GIVE ME A BREAK! YOU LIGHTWEIGHTS DON'T KNOW WHAT WAR IS! YOU OUGHT TO BE ASHAMED CALLING YOURSELVES SOLDIERS!
WELL, I AIM TO FIX THAT! ONCE I DELIVER THIS JET TO THE EMIR OF RHAPASTAN AND HIS BOYS CLONE IT--
--YOU'LL ALL BE FIGHTING A WAR YOU CAN TELL YOUR GRANDKIDS ABOUT!
NOW, UNLESS YOU'RE READY TO SHOOT THROUGH PRIVATE SAD SACK HERE TO GET TO ME--
--CLEAR THE RUNWAY!
LIEUTENANT...?
WE HAVE NO CHOICE. READY...
...AIM...
HWURGH!
HOLD YOUR FIRE!

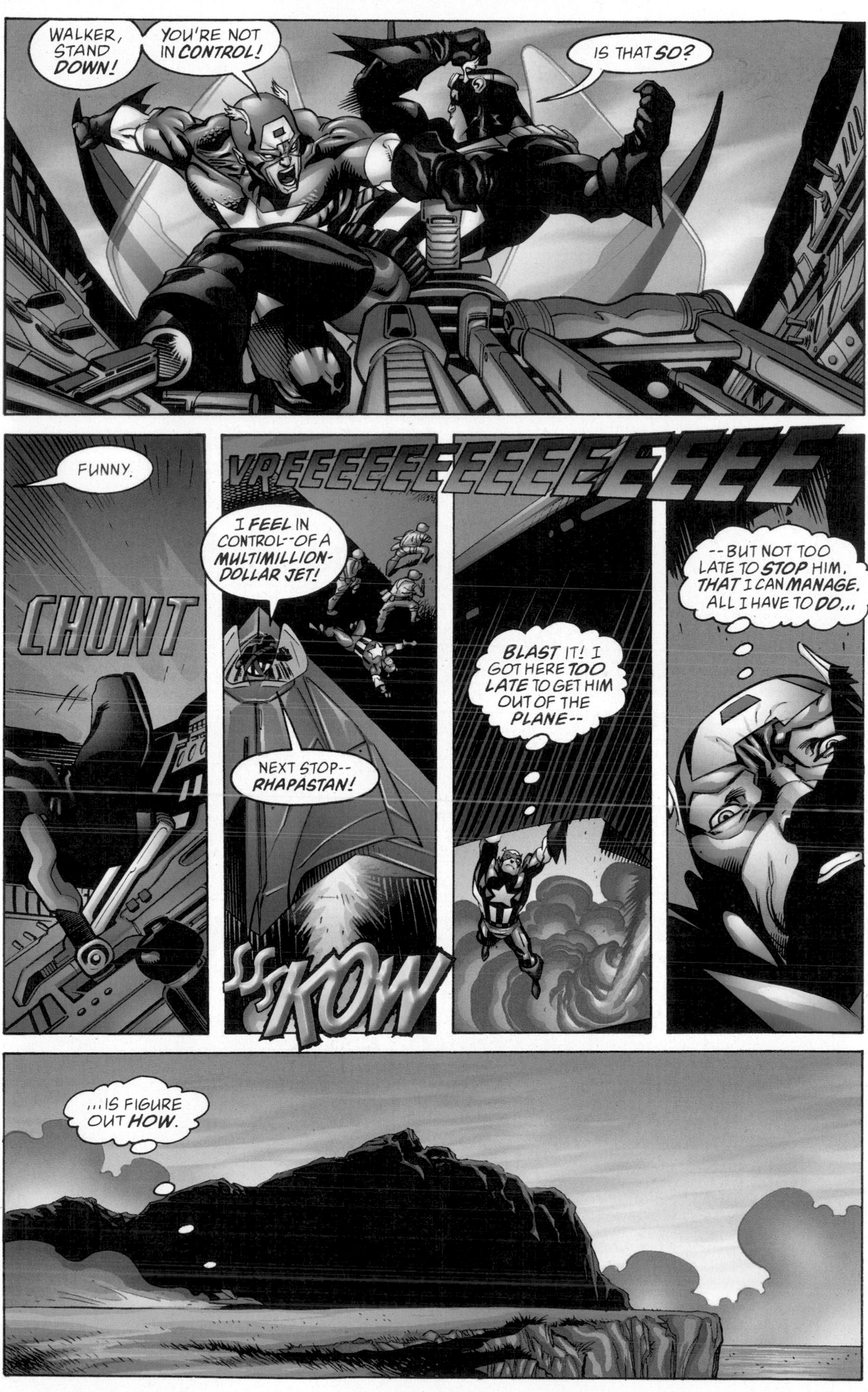
WALKER, STAND DOWN!
YOU'RE NOT IN CONTROL!
IS THAT SO?
FUNNY.
CHUNT
VREEEEEEEEEEEEEEEE
I FEEL IN CONTROL--OF A MULTIMILLION-DOLLAR JET!
NEXT STOP--RHAPASTAN!
KOW
BLAST IT! I GOT HERE TOO LATE TO GET HIM OUT OF THE PLANE--
--BUT NOT TOO LATE TO STOP HIM. THAT I CAN MANAGE. ALL I HAVE TO DO...
...IS FIGURE OUT HOW.

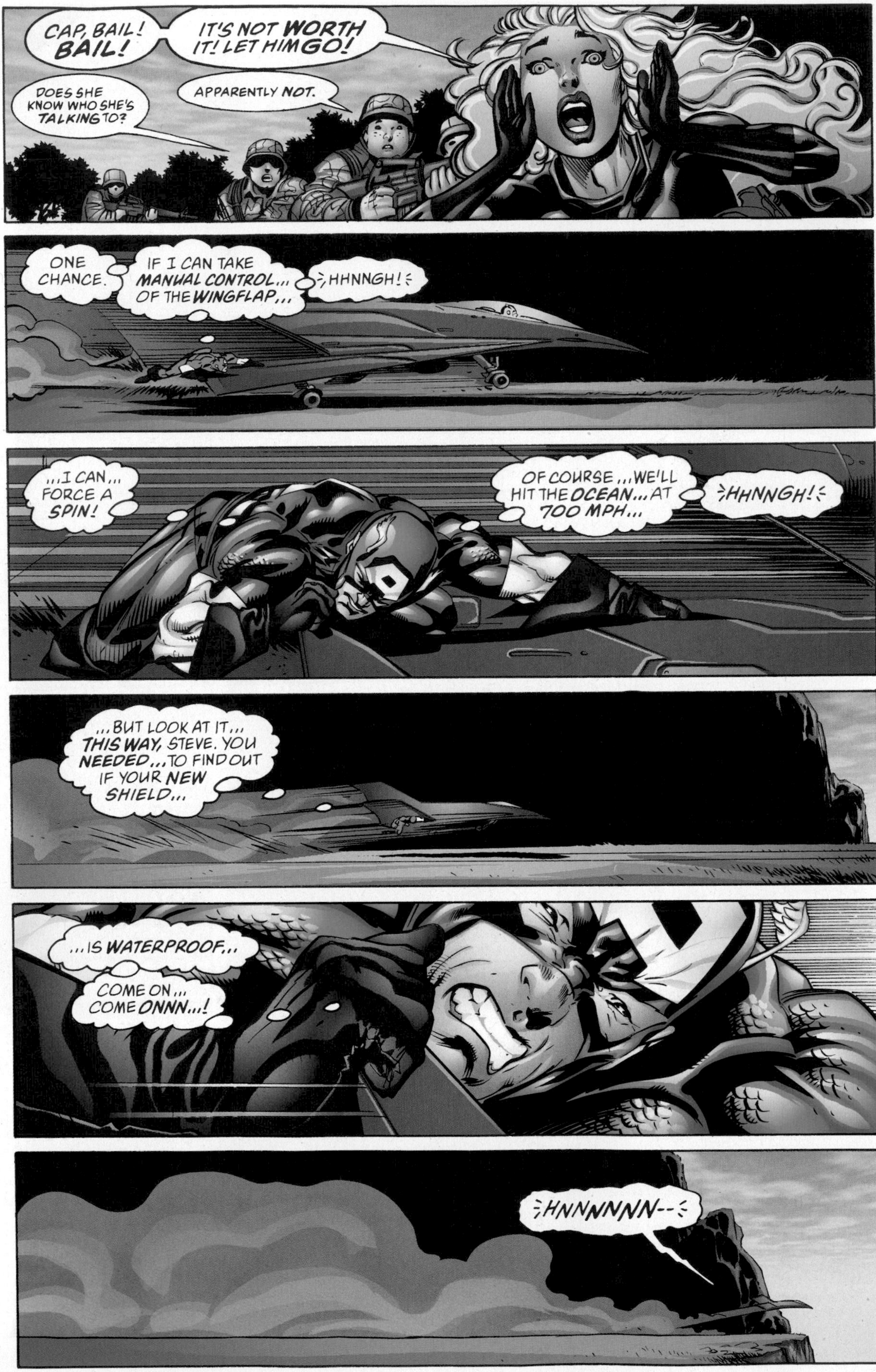
CAP, BAIL! BAIL!
IT'S NOT WORTH IT! LET HIM GO!
DOES SHE KNOW WHO SHE'S TALKING TO?
APPARENTLY NOT.
ONE CHANCE.
IF I CAN TAKE MANUAL CONTROL... OF THE WINGFLAP...
HHNNGH!
...I CAN... FORCE A SPIN!
OF COURSE... WE'LL HIT THE OCEAN... AT 700 MPH...
HHNNGH!
...BUT LOOK AT IT... THIS WAY, STEVE. YOU NEEDED... TO FIND OUT IF YOUR NEW SHIELD...
...IS WATERPROOF...
COME ON... COME ONNN...!
HNNNNNN--

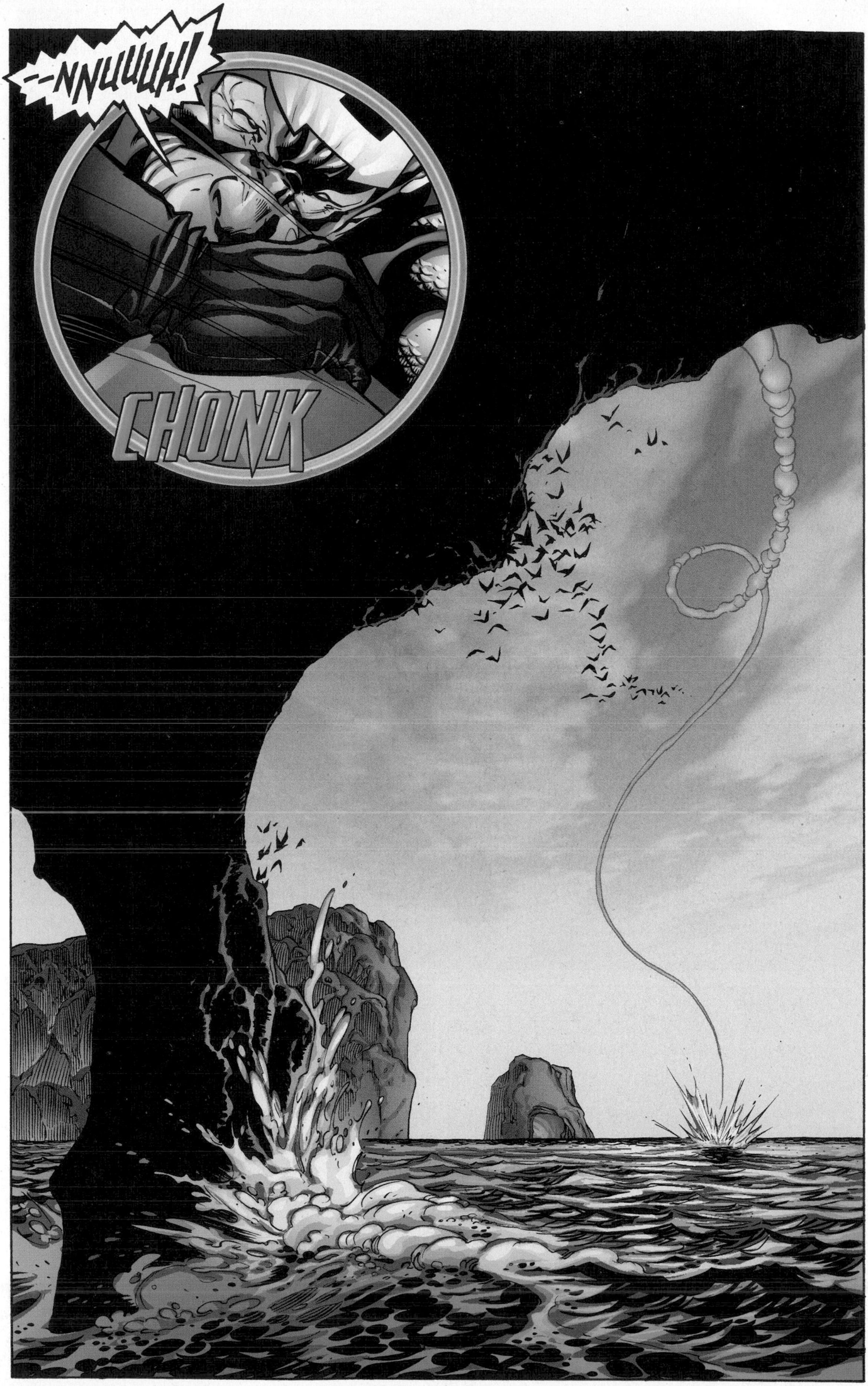
--NNUUUH!
CHONK

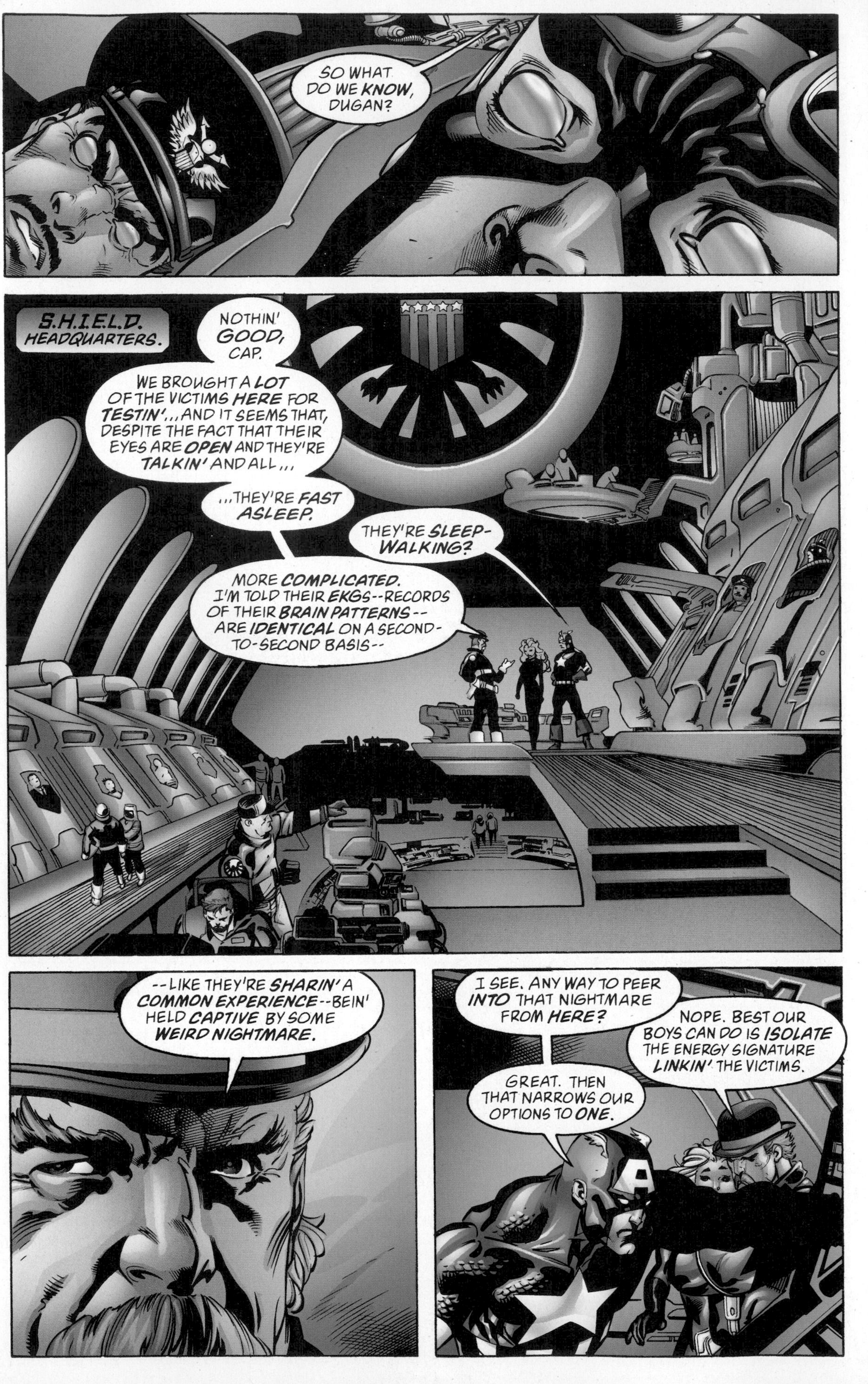
SO WHAT DO WE KNOW, DUGAN?
S.H.I.E.L.D. HEADQUARTERS.
NOTHIN' GOOD, CAP.
WE BROUGHT A LOT OF THE VICTIMS HERE FOR TESTIN'... AND IT SEEMS THAT, DESPITE THE FACT THAT THEIR EYES ARE OPEN AND THEY'RE TALKIN' AND ALL...
...THEY'RE FAST ASLEEP.
THEY'RE SLEEP-WALKING?
MORE COMPLICATED. I'M TOLD THEIR EKGS--RECORDS OF THEIR BRAIN PATTERNS--ARE IDENTICAL ON A SECOND-TO-SECOND BASIS--
--LIKE THEY'RE SHARIN' A COMMON EXPERIENCE--BEIN' HELD CAPTIVE BY SOME WEIRD NIGHTMARE.
I SEE. ANY WAY TO PEER INTO THAT NIGHTMARE FROM HERE?
NOPE. BEST OUR BOYS CAN DO IS ISOLATE THE ENERGY SIGNATURE LINKIN' THE VICTIMS.
GREAT. THEN THAT NARROWS OUR OPTIONS TO ONE.

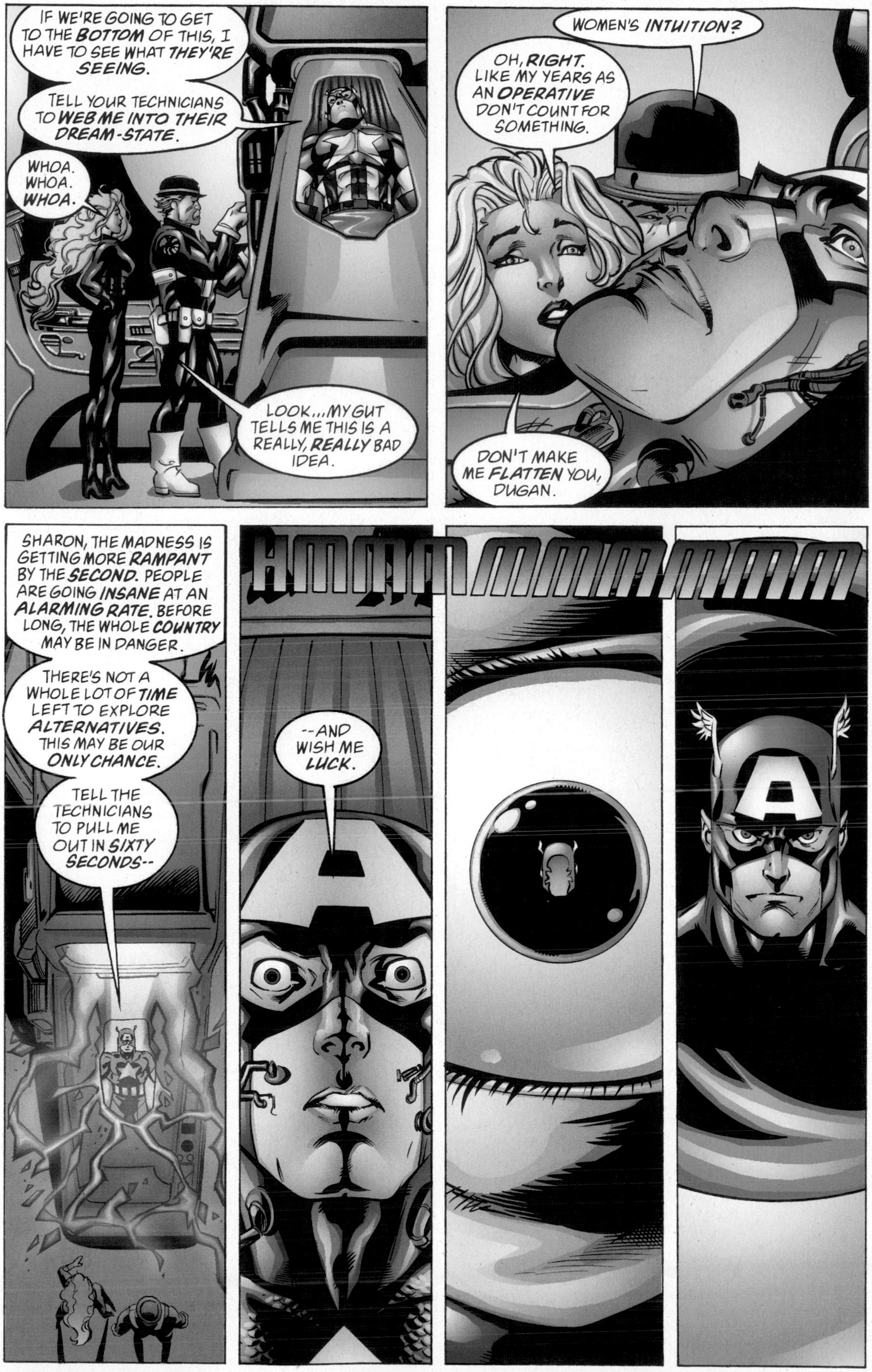

IF WE'RE GOING TO GET TO THE BOTTOM OF THIS, I HAVE TO SEE WHAT THEY'RE SEEING.
TELL YOUR TECHNICIANS TO WEB ME INTO THEIR DREAM-STATE.
WHOA. WHOA. WHOA.
LOOK...MY GUT TELLS ME THIS IS A REALLY, REALLY BAD IDEA.
WOMEN'S INTUITION?
OH, RIGHT. LIKE MY YEARS AS AN OPERATIVE DON'T COUNT FOR SOMETHING.
DON'T MAKE ME FLATTEN YOU, DUGAN.
SHARON, THE MADNESS IS GETTING MORE RAMPANT BY THE SECOND. PEOPLE ARE GOING INSANE AT AN ALARMING RATE. BEFORE LONG, THE WHOLE COUNTRY MAY BE IN DANGER.
THERE'S NOT A WHOLE LOT OF TIME LEFT TO EXPLORE ALTERNATIVES. THIS MAY BE OUR ONLY CHANCE.
TELL THE TECHNICIANS TO PULL ME OUT IN SIXTY SECONDS--
HMMMMMMMMMMMM
--AND WISH ME LUCK.

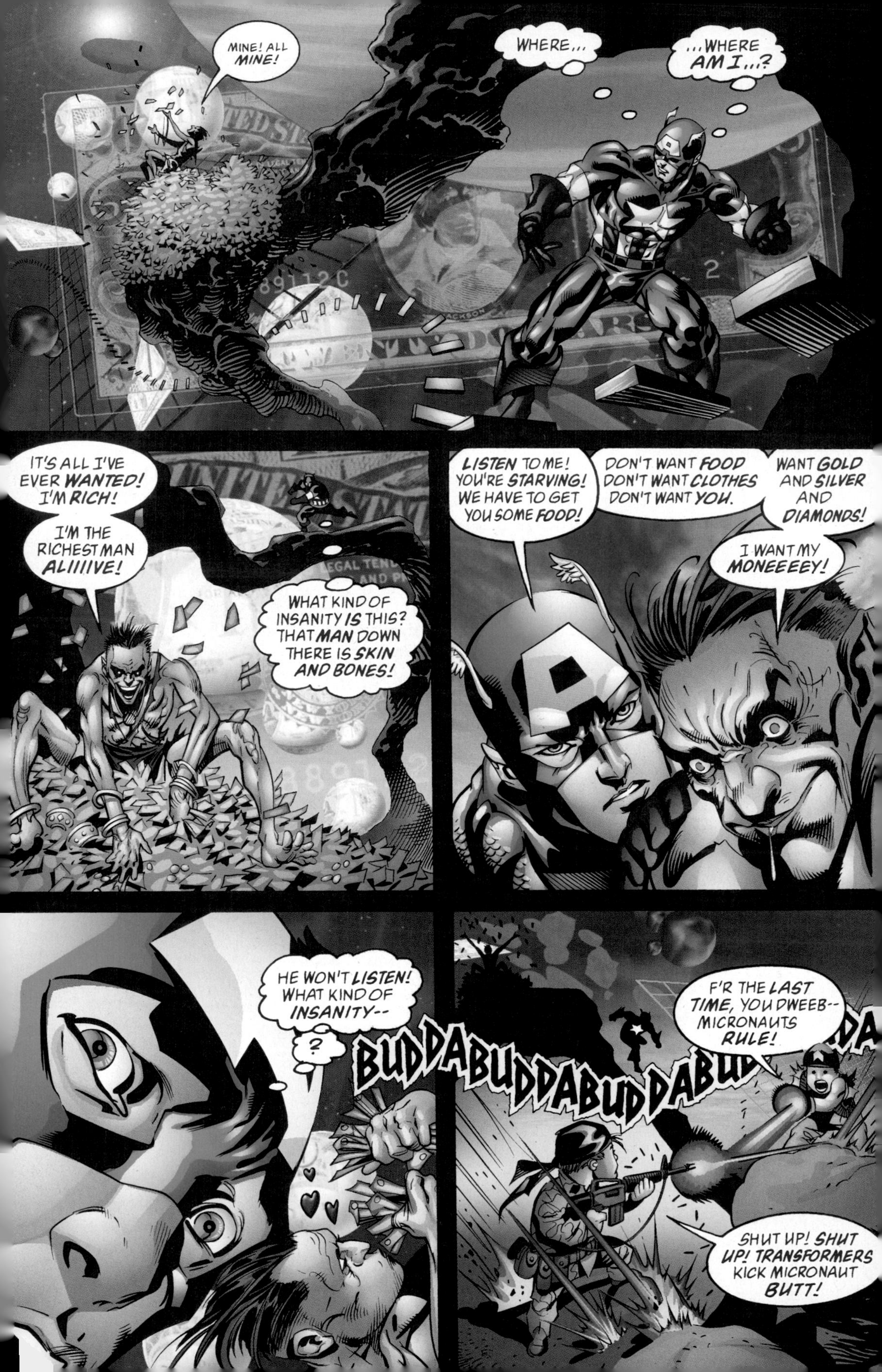
MINE! ALL MINE!
WHERE...
...WHERE AM I...?
IT'S ALL I'VE EVER WANTED! I'M RICH!
I'M THE RICHEST MAN ALIIIIIVE!
WHAT KIND OF INSANITY IS THIS? THAT MAN DOWN THERE IS SKIN AND BONES!
LISTEN TO ME! YOU'RE STARVING! WE HAVE TO GET YOU SOME FOOD!
DON'T WANT FOOD DON'T WANT CLOTHES DON'T WANT YOU.
WANT GOLD AND SILVER AND DIAMONDS!
I WANT MY MONEEEEY!
HE WON'T LISTEN! WHAT KIND OF INSANITY--
?
BUDDABUDDABUDDABUDDA
F'R THE LAST TIME, YOU DWEEB--MICRONAUTS RULE!
SHUT UP! SHUT UP! TRANSFORMERS KICK MICRONAUT BUTT!

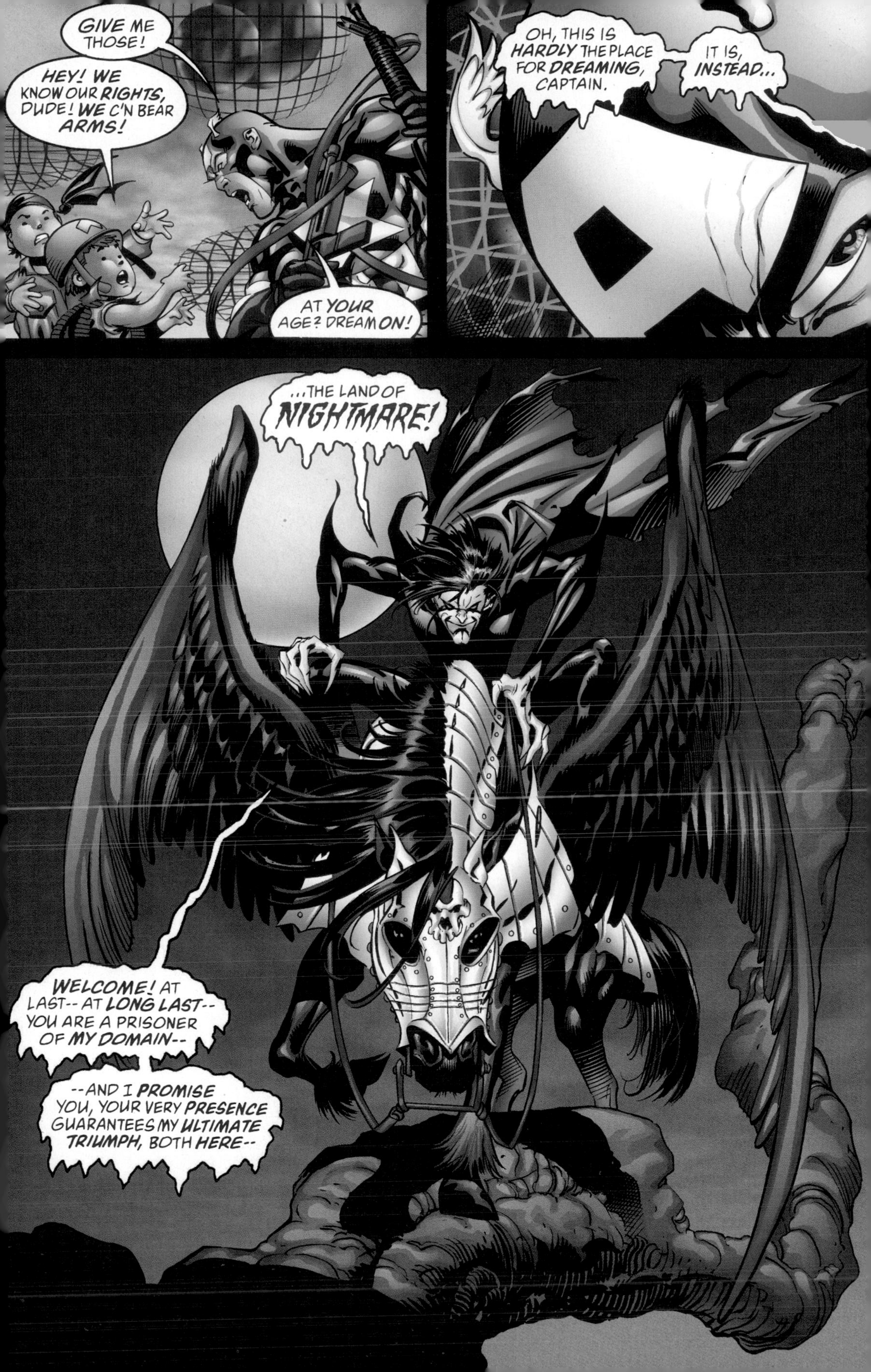
GIVE ME THOSE!
HEY! WE KNOW OUR RIGHTS, DUDE! WE C'N BEAR ARMS!
AT YOUR AGE? DREAM ON!
OH, THIS IS HARDLY THE PLACE FOR DREAMING, CAPTAIN.
IT IS, INSTEAD...
...THE LAND OF NIGHTMARE!
WELCOME! AT LAST-- AT LONG LAST-- YOU ARE A PRISONER OF MY DOMAIN--
--AND I PROMISE YOU, YOUR VERY PRESENCE GUARANTEES MY ULTIMATE TRIUMPH, BOTH HERE--

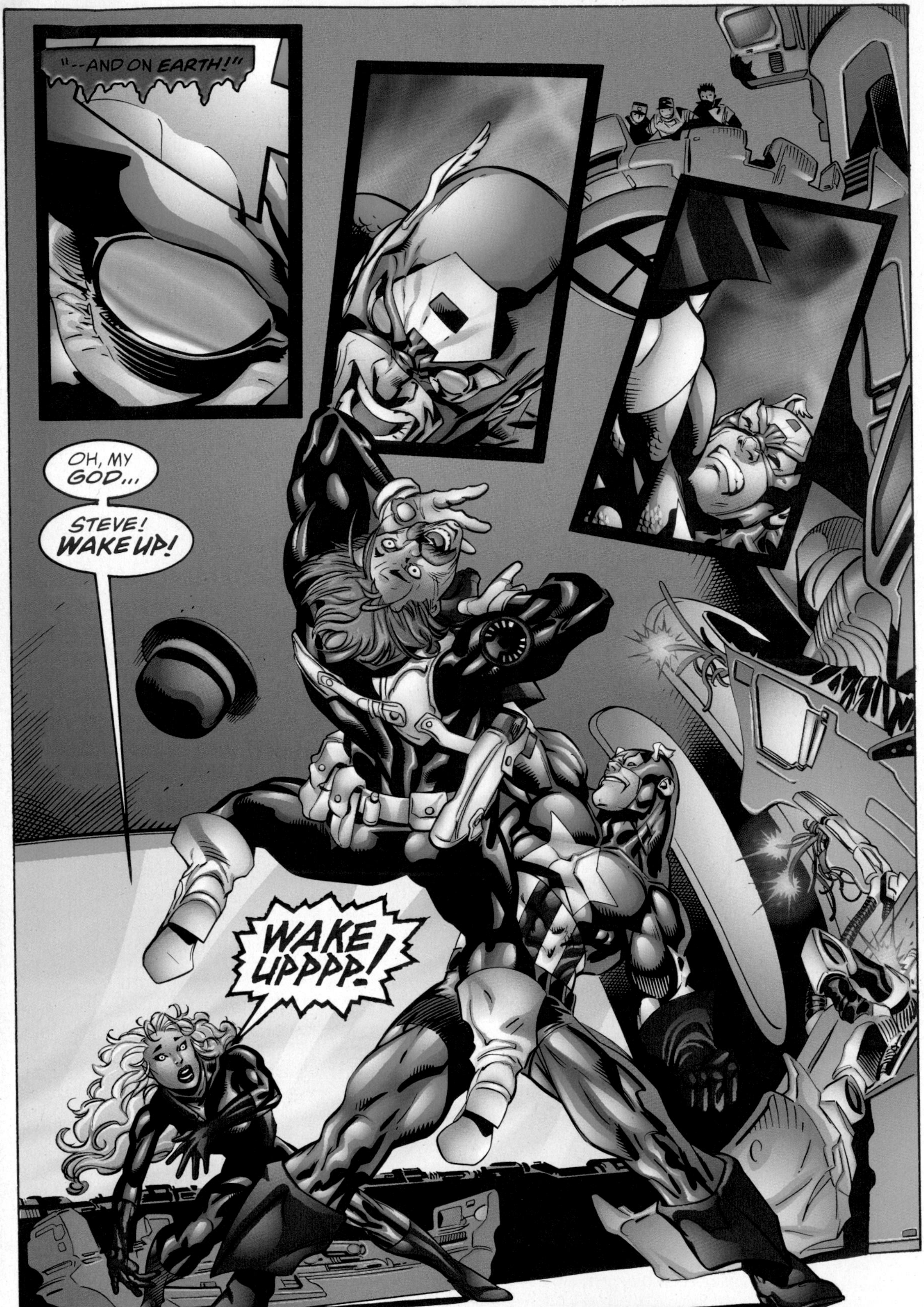
"--AND ON EARTH!"
OH, MY GOD...
STEVE! WAKE UP!
WAKE UPPPP!

TO BE CONTINUED!

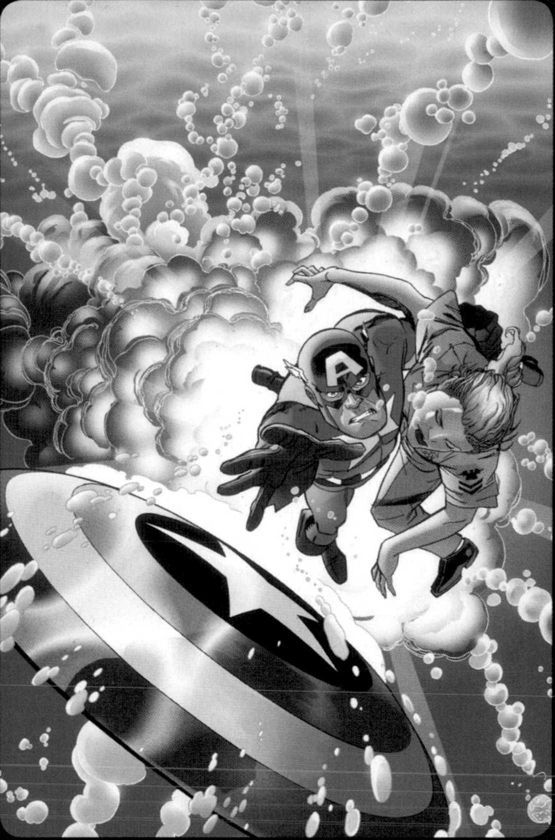

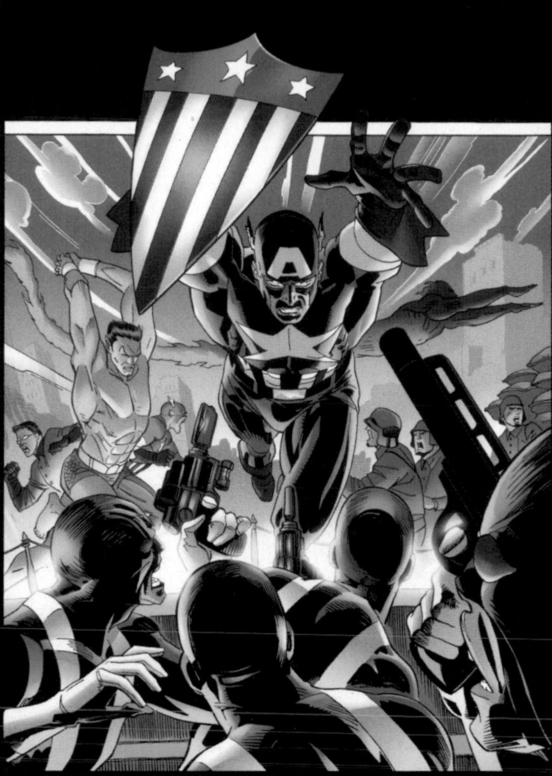

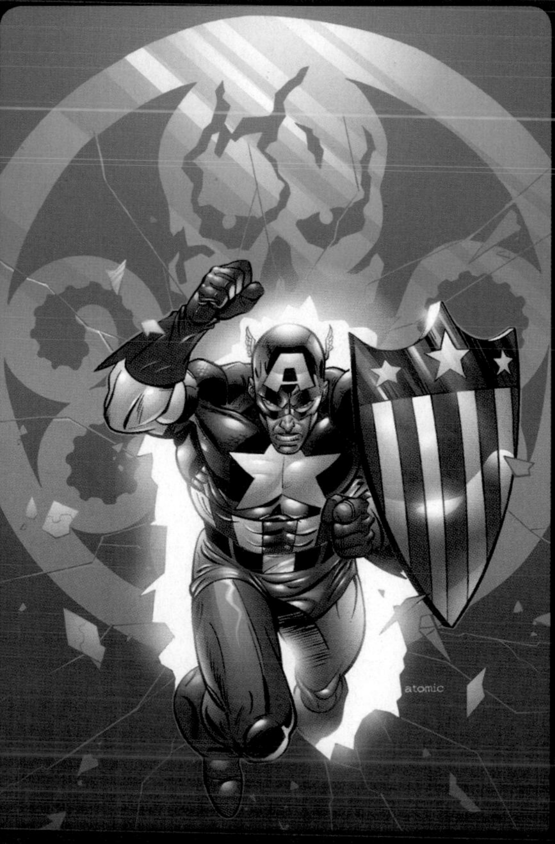
atomic

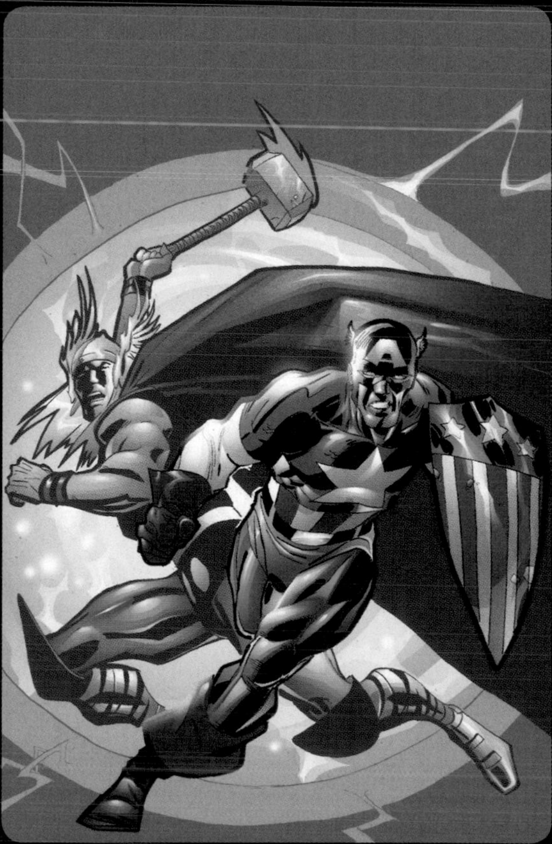

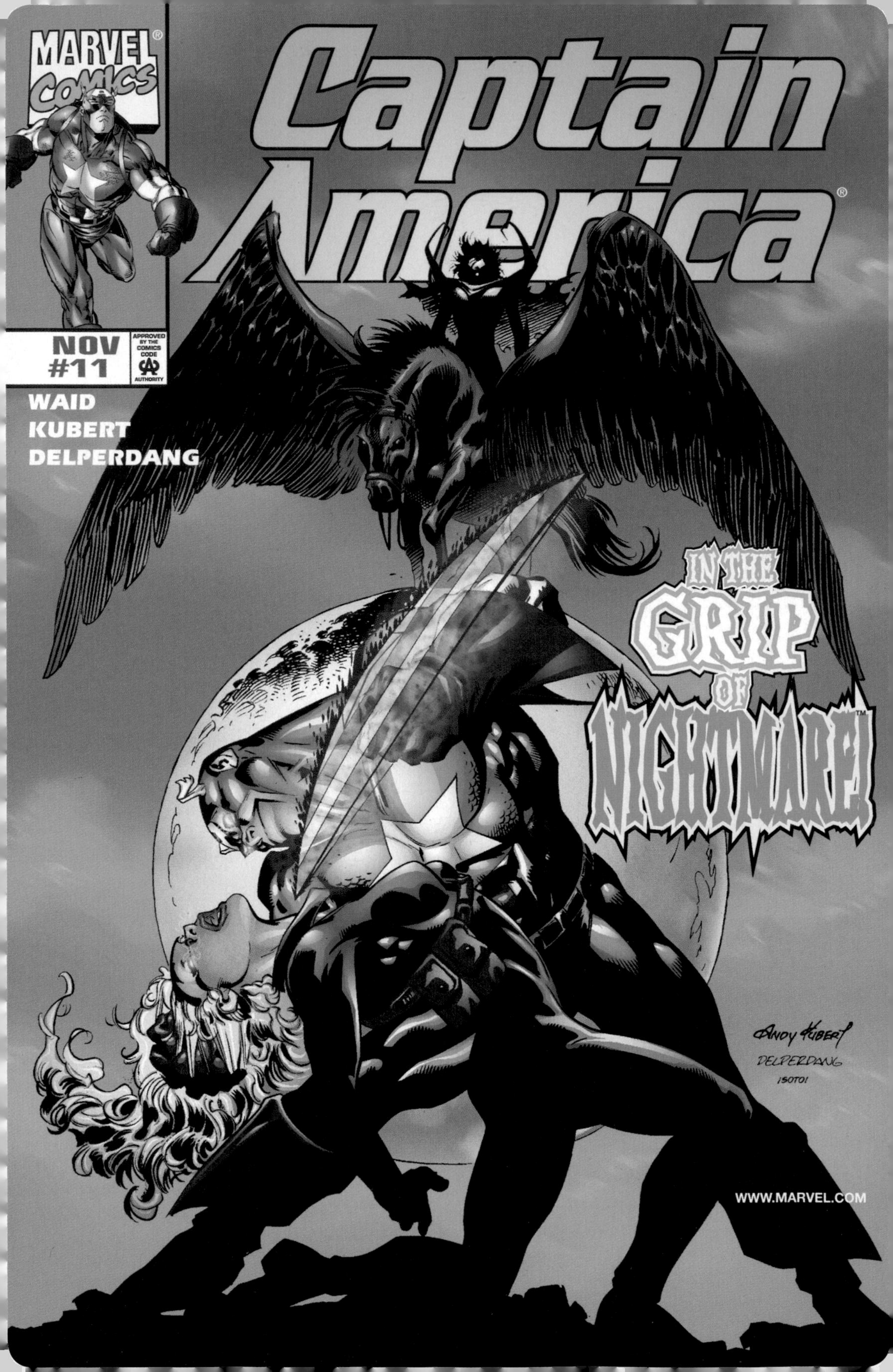
MARVEL COMICS
Captain America
NOV
#11
APPROVED BY THE COMICS CODE AUTHORITY
WAID
KUBERT
DELPERDANG
IN THE GRIP OF NIGHTMARE!
ANDY KUBERT
DELPERDANG
ISOTO!
WWW.MARVEL.COM

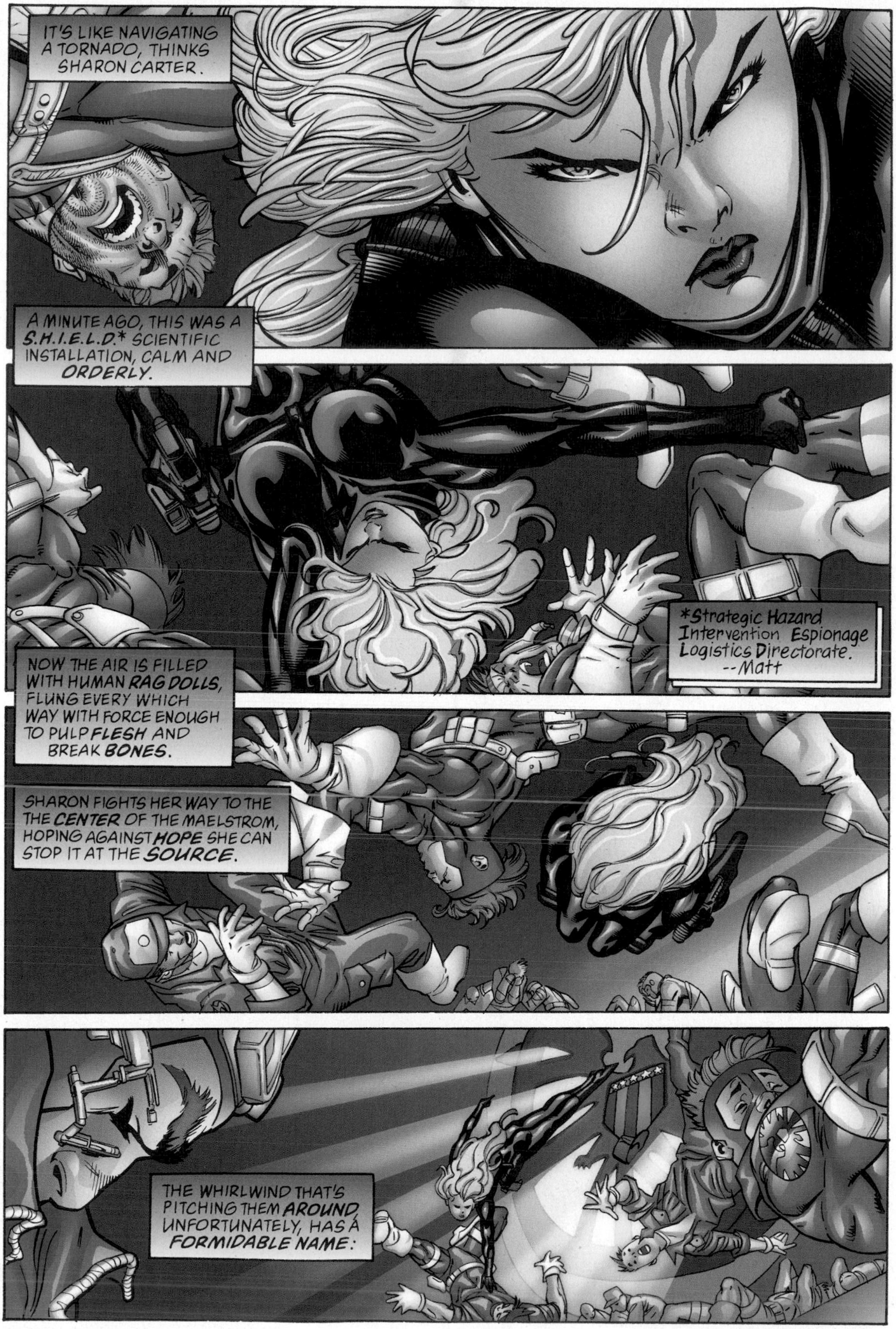
IT'S LIKE NAVIGATING A TORNADO, THINKS SHARON CARTER.
A MINUTE AGO, THIS WAS A S.H.I.E.L.D.* SCIENTIFIC INSTALLATION, CALM AND ORDERLY.
*Strategic Hazard Intervention Espionage Logistics Directorate. --Matt
NOW THE AIR IS FILLED WITH HUMAN RAG DOLLS, FLUNG EVERY WHICH WAY WITH FORCE ENOUGH TO PULP FLESH AND BREAK BONES.
SHARON FIGHTS HER WAY TO THE THE CENTER OF THE MAELSTROM, HOPING AGAINST HOPE SHE CAN STOP IT AT THE SOURCE.
THE WHIRLWIND THAT'S PITCHING THEM AROUND, UNFORTUNATELY, HAS A FORMIDABLE NAME:

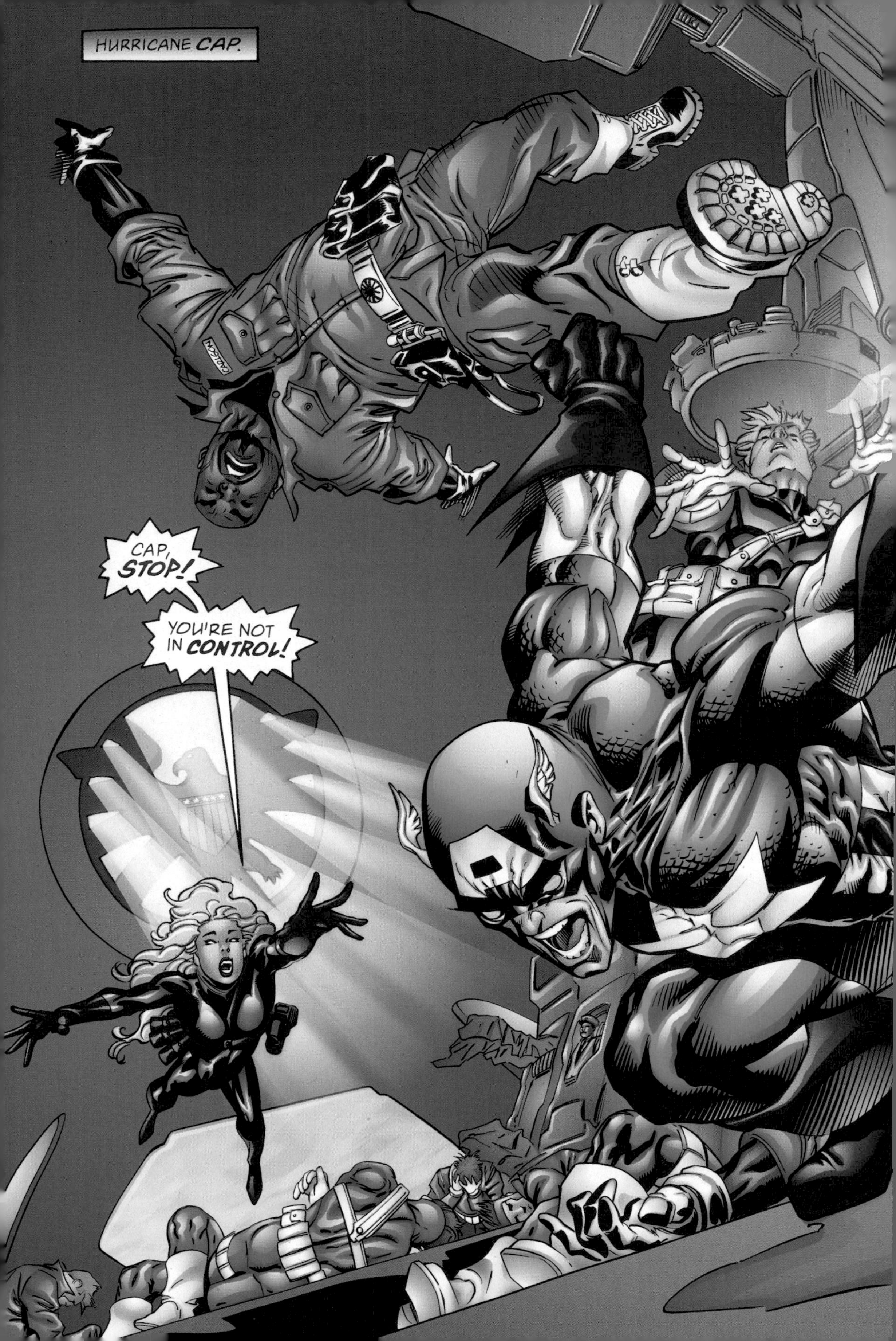
HURRICANE CAP.
CAP, STOP!
YOU'RE NOT IN CONTROL!

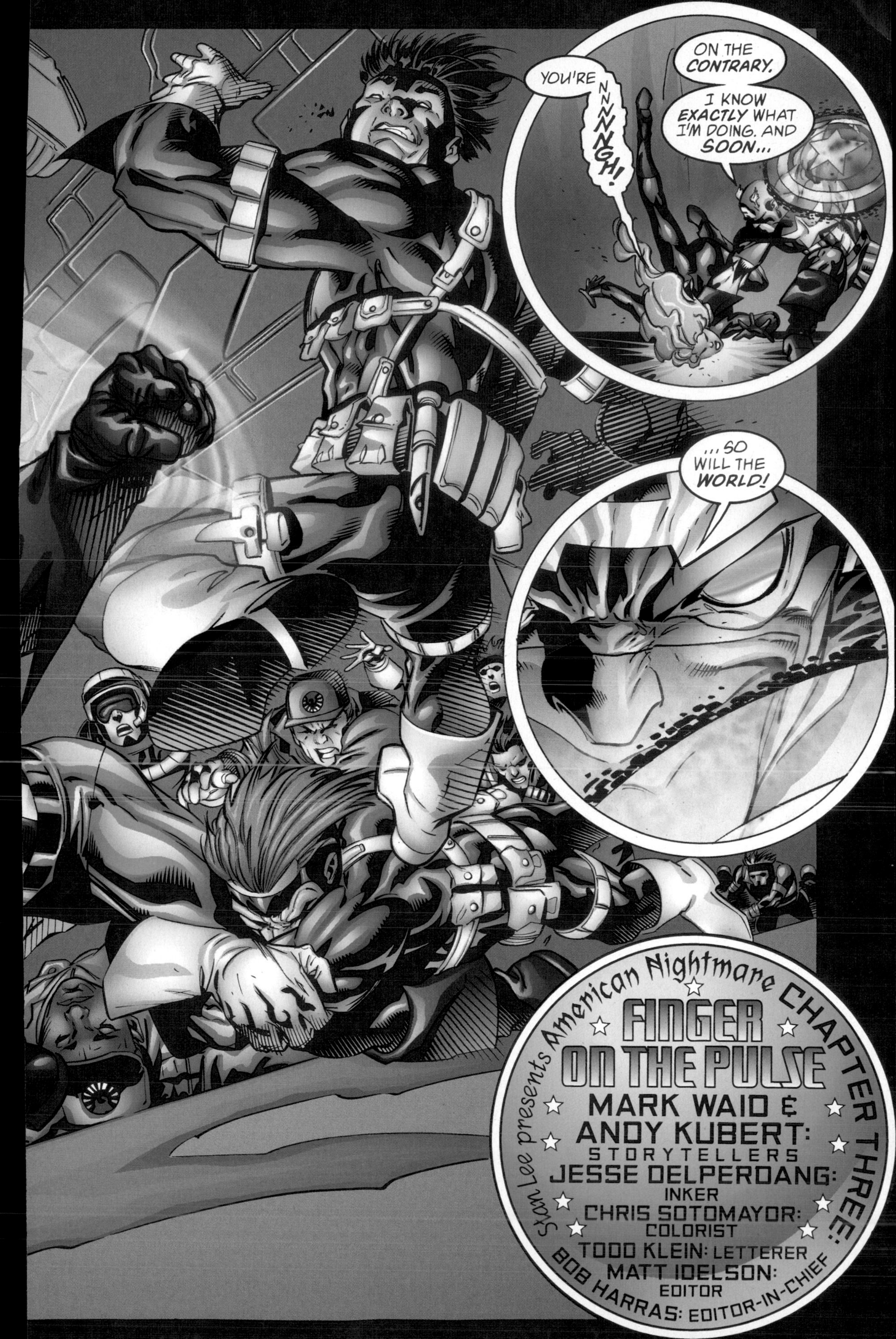
YOU'RE NNNNNNGH!
ON THE CONTRARY.
I KNOW EXACTLY WHAT I'M DOING. AND SOON...
...SO WILL THE WORLD!
Stan Lee presents American Nightmare CHAPTER THREE:
FINGER ON THE PULSE
MARK WAID & ANDY KUBERT: STORYTELLERS
JESSE DELPERDANG: INKER
CHRIS SOTOMAYOR: COLORIST
TODD KLEIN: LETTERER
MATT IDELSON: EDITOR
BOB HARRAS: EDITOR-IN-CHIEF

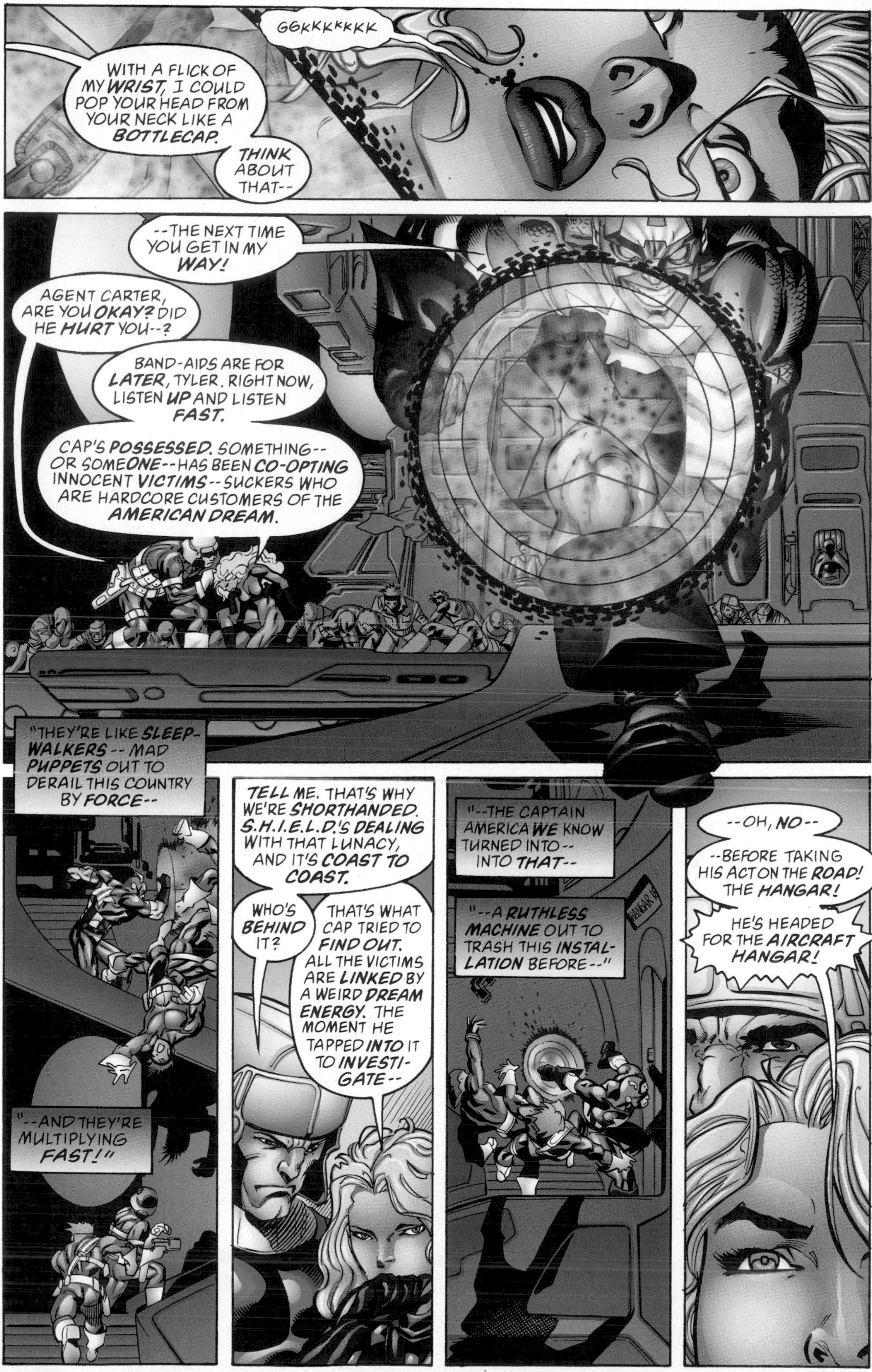

GGKKKKKKK
WITH A FLICK OF MY WRIST, I COULD POP YOUR HEAD FROM YOUR NECK LIKE A BOTTLECAP.
THINK ABOUT THAT--
--THE NEXT TIME YOU GET IN MY WAY!
AGENT CARTER, ARE YOU OKAY? DID HE HURT YOU--?
BAND-AIDS ARE FOR LATER, TYLER. RIGHT NOW, LISTEN UP AND LISTEN FAST.
CAP'S POSSESSED. SOMETHING--OR SOMEONE--HAS BEEN CO-OPTING INNOCENT VICTIMS--SUCKERS WHO ARE HARDCORE CUSTOMERS OF THE AMERICAN DREAM.
"THEY'RE LIKE SLEEP-WALKERS--MAD PUPPETS OUT TO DERAIL THIS COUNTRY BY FORCE--
"--AND THEY'RE MULTIPLYING FAST!"
TELL ME. THAT'S WHY WE'RE SHORTHANDED. S.H.I.E.L.D.'S DEALING WITH THAT LUNACY, AND IT'S COAST TO COAST.
WHO'S BEHIND IT?
THAT'S WHAT CAP TRIED TO FIND OUT. ALL THE VICTIMS ARE LINKED BY A WEIRD DREAM ENERGY. THE MOMENT HE TAPPED INTO IT TO INVESTI-GATE--
"--THE CAPTAIN AMERICA WE KNOW TURNED INTO--INTO THAT--
"--A RUTHLESS MACHINE OUT TO TRASH THIS INSTAL-LATION BEFORE--"
--OH, NO--
--BEFORE TAKING HIS ACT ON THE ROAD! THE HANGAR!
HE'S HEADED FOR THE AIRCRAFT HANGAR!

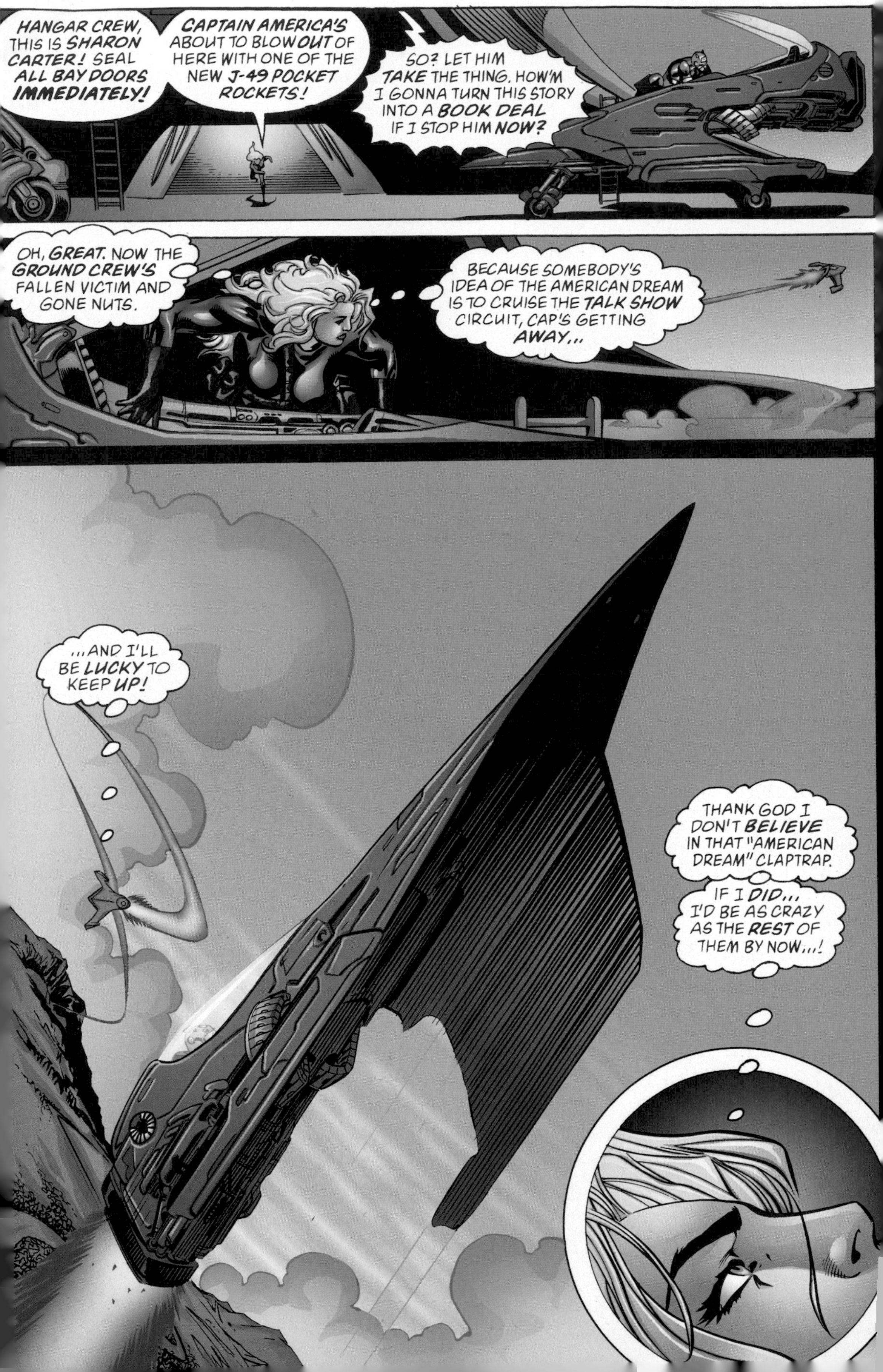
HANGAR CREW, THIS IS SHARON CARTER! SEAL ALL BAY DOORS IMMEDIATELY!
CAPTAIN AMERICA'S ABOUT TO BLOW OUT OF HERE WITH ONE OF THE NEW J-49 POCKET ROCKETS!
SO? LET HIM TAKE THE THING. HOW'M I GONNA TURN THIS STORY INTO A BOOK DEAL IF I STOP HIM NOW?
OH, GREAT. NOW THE GROUND CREW'S FALLEN VICTIM AND GONE NUTS.
BECAUSE SOMEBODY'S IDEA OF THE AMERICAN DREAM IS TO CRUISE THE TALK SHOW CIRCUIT, CAP'S GETTING AWAY...
...AND I'LL BE LUCKY TO KEEP UP!
THANK GOD I DON'T BELIEVE IN THAT "AMERICAN DREAM" CLAPTRAP.
IF I DID... I'D BE AS CRAZY AS THE REST OF THEM BY NOW...!

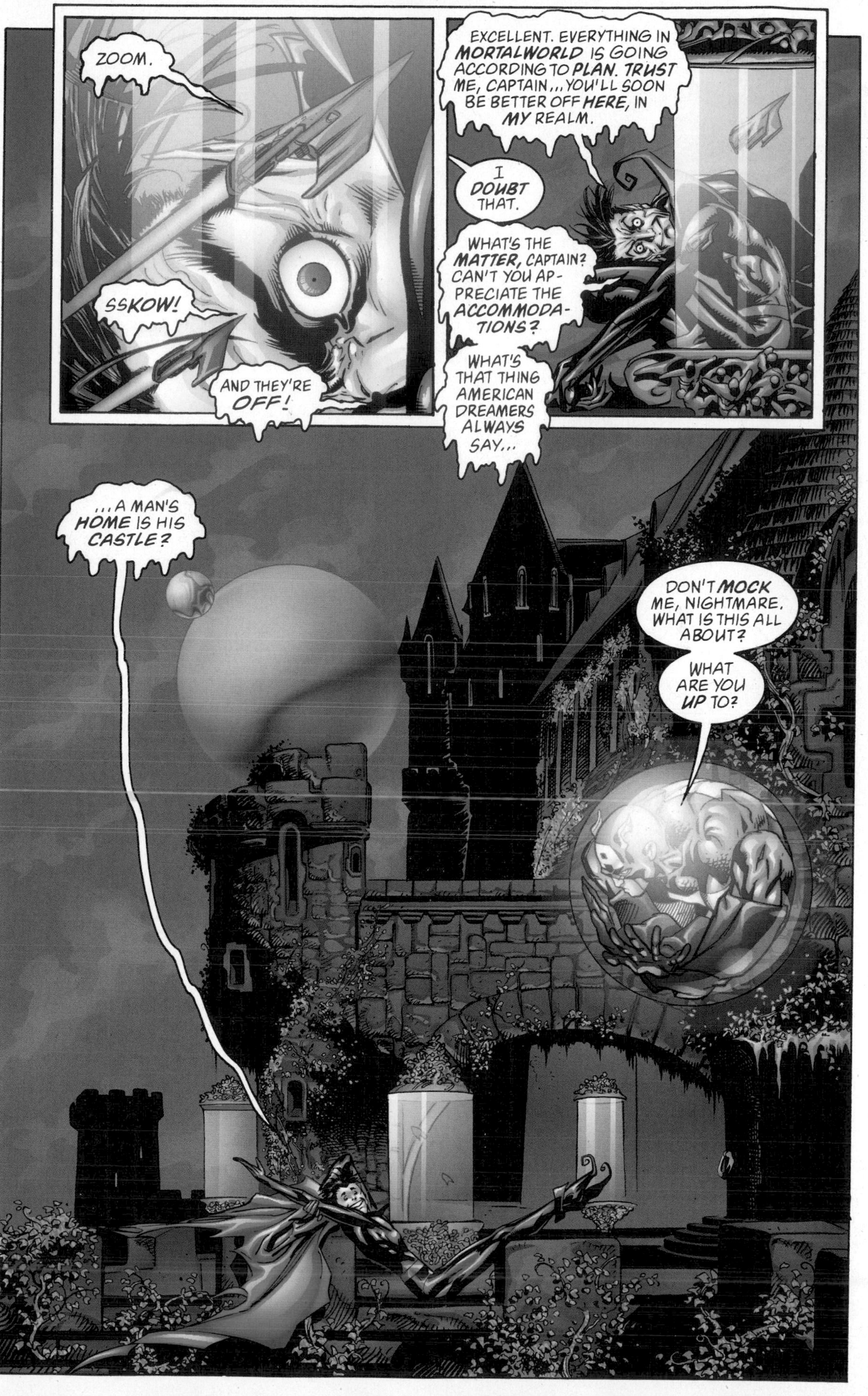
ZOOM.
SSKOW!
AND THEY'RE OFF!
EXCELLENT. EVERYTHING IN MORTALWORLD IS GOING ACCORDING TO PLAN. TRUST ME, CAPTAIN... YOU'LL SOON BE BETTER OFF HERE, IN MY REALM.
I DOUBT THAT.
WHAT'S THE MATTER, CAPTAIN? CAN'T YOU APPRECIATE THE ACCOMMODATIONS?
WHAT'S THAT THING AMERICAN DREAMERS ALWAYS SAY...
...A MAN'S HOME IS HIS CASTLE?
DON'T MOCK ME, NIGHTMARE. WHAT IS THIS ALL ABOUT?
WHAT ARE YOU UP TO?

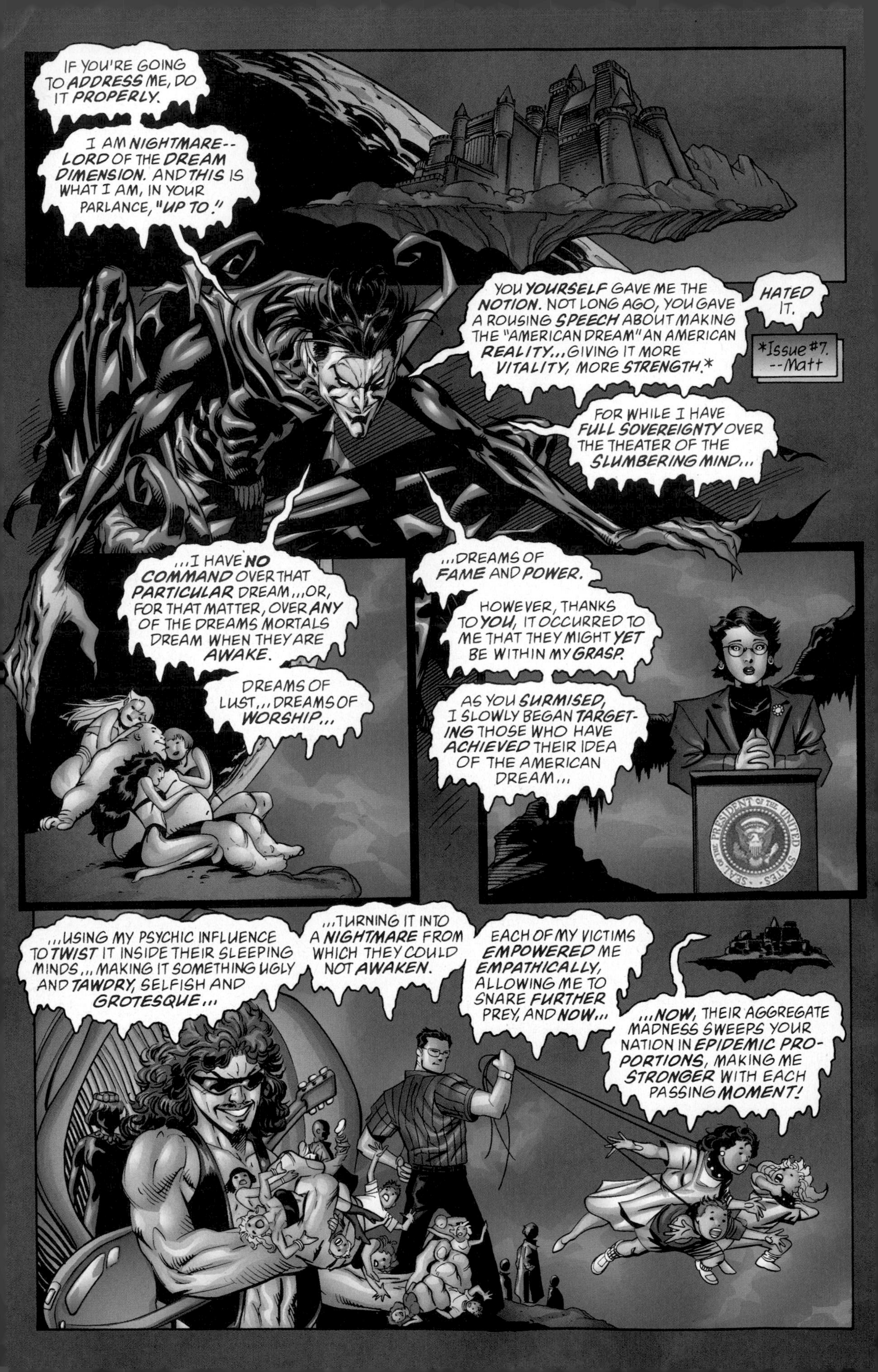
IF YOU'RE GOING TO ADDRESS ME, DO IT PROPERLY.
I AM NIGHTMARE--LORD OF THE DREAM DIMENSION. AND THIS IS WHAT I AM, IN YOUR PARLANCE, "UP TO."
YOU YOURSELF GAVE ME THE NOTION. NOT LONG AGO, YOU GAVE A ROUSING SPEECH ABOUT MAKING THE "AMERICAN DREAM" AN AMERICAN REALITY... GIVING IT MORE VITALITY, MORE STRENGTH.*
HATED IT.
*Issue #7. --Matt
FOR WHILE I HAVE FULL SOVEREIGNTY OVER THE THEATER OF THE SLUMBERING MIND...
...I HAVE NO COMMAND OVER THAT PARTICULAR DREAM... OR, FOR THAT MATTER, OVER ANY OF THE DREAMS MORTALS DREAM WHEN THEY ARE AWAKE.
DREAMS OF LUST... DREAMS OF WORSHIP...
...DREAMS OF FAME AND POWER.
HOWEVER, THANKS TO YOU, IT OCCURRED TO ME THAT THEY MIGHT YET BE WITHIN MY GRASP.
AS YOU SURMISED, I SLOWLY BEGAN TARGETING THOSE WHO HAVE ACHIEVED THEIR IDEA OF THE AMERICAN DREAM...
SEAL OF THE PRESIDENT OF THE UNITED STATES
...USING MY PSYCHIC INFLUENCE TO TWIST IT INSIDE THEIR SLEEPING MINDS... MAKING IT SOMETHING UGLY AND TAWDRY, SELFISH AND GROTESQUE...
...TURNING IT INTO A NIGHTMARE FROM WHICH THEY COULD NOT AWAKEN.
EACH OF MY VICTIMS EMPOWERED ME EMPATHICALLY, ALLOWING ME TO SNARE FURTHER PREY, AND NOW...
...NOW, THEIR AGGREGATE MADNESS SWEEPS YOUR NATION IN EPIDEMIC PROPORTIONS, MAKING ME STRONGER WITH EACH PASSING MOMENT!

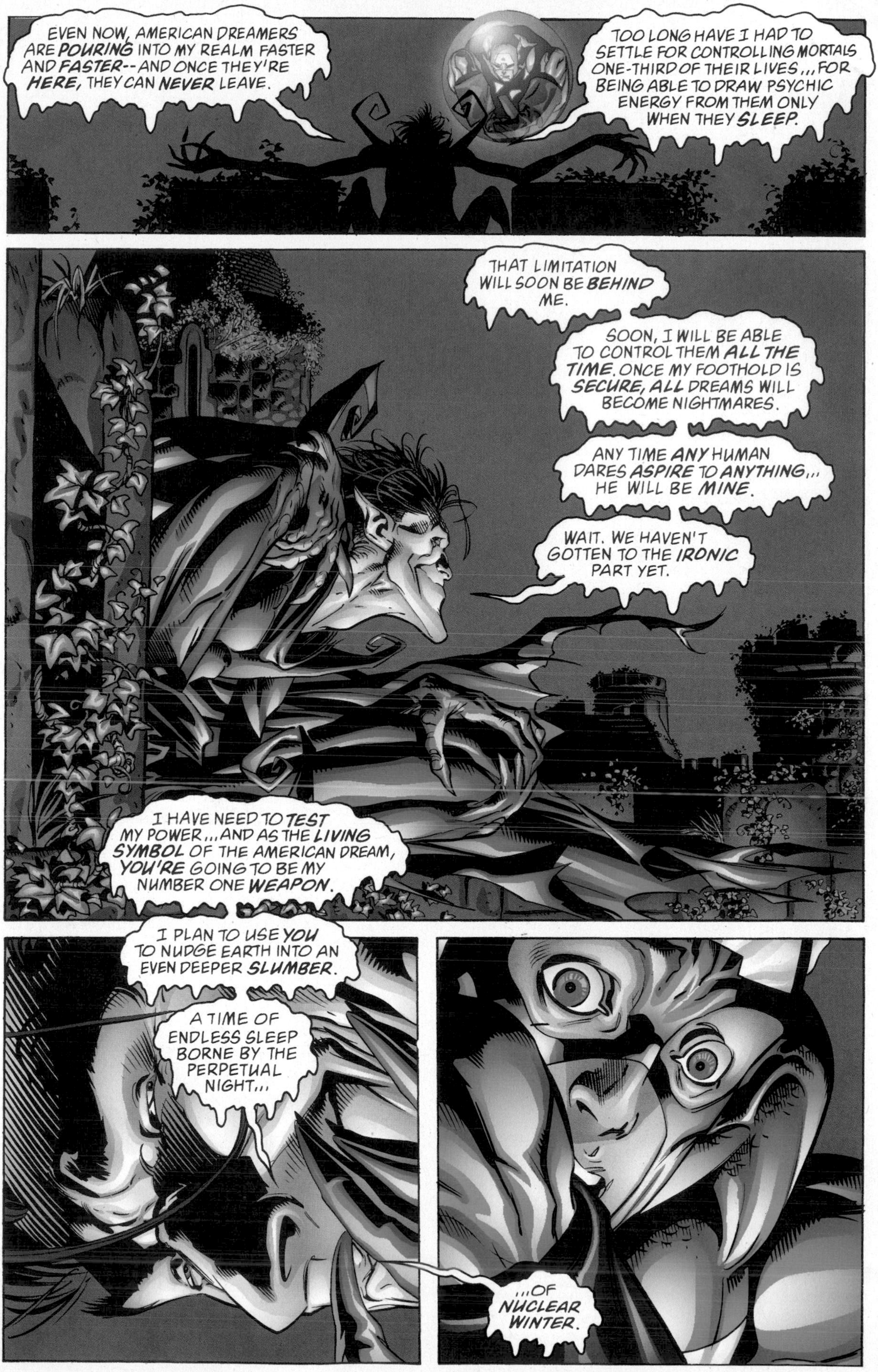
EVEN NOW, AMERICAN DREAMERS ARE POURING INTO MY REALM FASTER AND FASTER--AND ONCE THEY'RE HERE, THEY CAN NEVER LEAVE.
TOO LONG HAVE I HAD TO SETTLE FOR CONTROLLING MORTALS ONE-THIRD OF THEIR LIVES... FOR BEING ABLE TO DRAW PSYCHIC ENERGY FROM THEM ONLY WHEN THEY SLEEP.
THAT LIMITATION WILL SOON BE BEHIND ME.
SOON, I WILL BE ABLE TO CONTROL THEM ALL THE TIME. ONCE MY FOOTHOLD IS SECURE, ALL DREAMS WILL BECOME NIGHTMARES.
ANY TIME ANY HUMAN DARES ASPIRE TO ANYTHING... HE WILL BE MINE.
WAIT. WE HAVEN'T GOTTEN TO THE IRONIC PART YET.
I HAVE NEED TO TEST MY POWER... AND AS THE LIVING SYMBOL OF THE AMERICAN DREAM, YOU'RE GOING TO BE MY NUMBER ONE WEAPON.
I PLAN TO USE YOU TO NUDGE EARTH INTO AN EVEN DEEPER SLUMBER.
A TIME OF ENDLESS SLEEP BORNE BY THE PERPETUAL NIGHT...
...OF NUCLEAR WINTER.

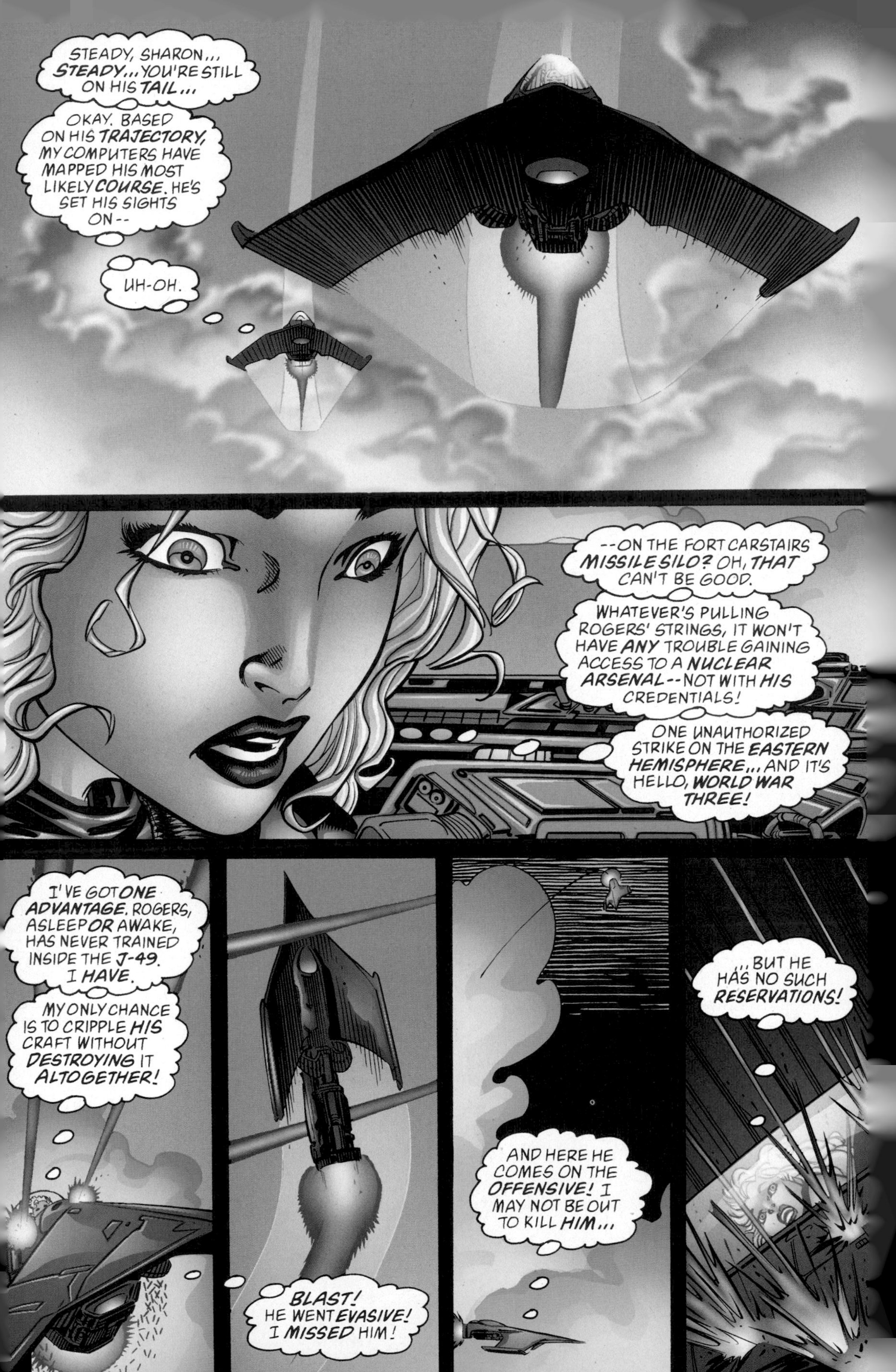

STEADY, SHARON... STEADY... YOU'RE STILL ON HIS TAIL...
OKAY. BASED ON HIS TRAJECTORY, MY COMPUTERS HAVE MAPPED HIS MOST LIKELY COURSE. HE'S SET HIS SIGHTS ON--
UH-OH.
--ON THE FORT CARSTAIRS MISSILE SILO? OH, THAT CAN'T BE GOOD.
WHATEVER'S PULLING ROGERS' STRINGS, IT WON'T HAVE ANY TROUBLE GAINING ACCESS TO A NUCLEAR ARSENAL--NOT WITH HIS CREDENTIALS!
ONE UNAUTHORIZED STRIKE ON THE EASTERN HEMISPHERE... AND IT'S HELLO, WORLD WAR THREE!
I'VE GOT ONE ADVANTAGE. ROGERS, ASLEEP OR AWAKE, HAS NEVER TRAINED INSIDE THE J-49. I HAVE.
MY ONLY CHANCE IS TO CRIPPLE HIS CRAFT WITHOUT DESTROYING IT ALTOGETHER!
BLAST! HE WENT EVASIVE! I MISSED HIM!
AND HERE HE COMES ON THE OFFENSIVE! I MAY NOT BE OUT TO KILL HIM...
...BUT HE HAS NO SUCH RESERVATIONS!

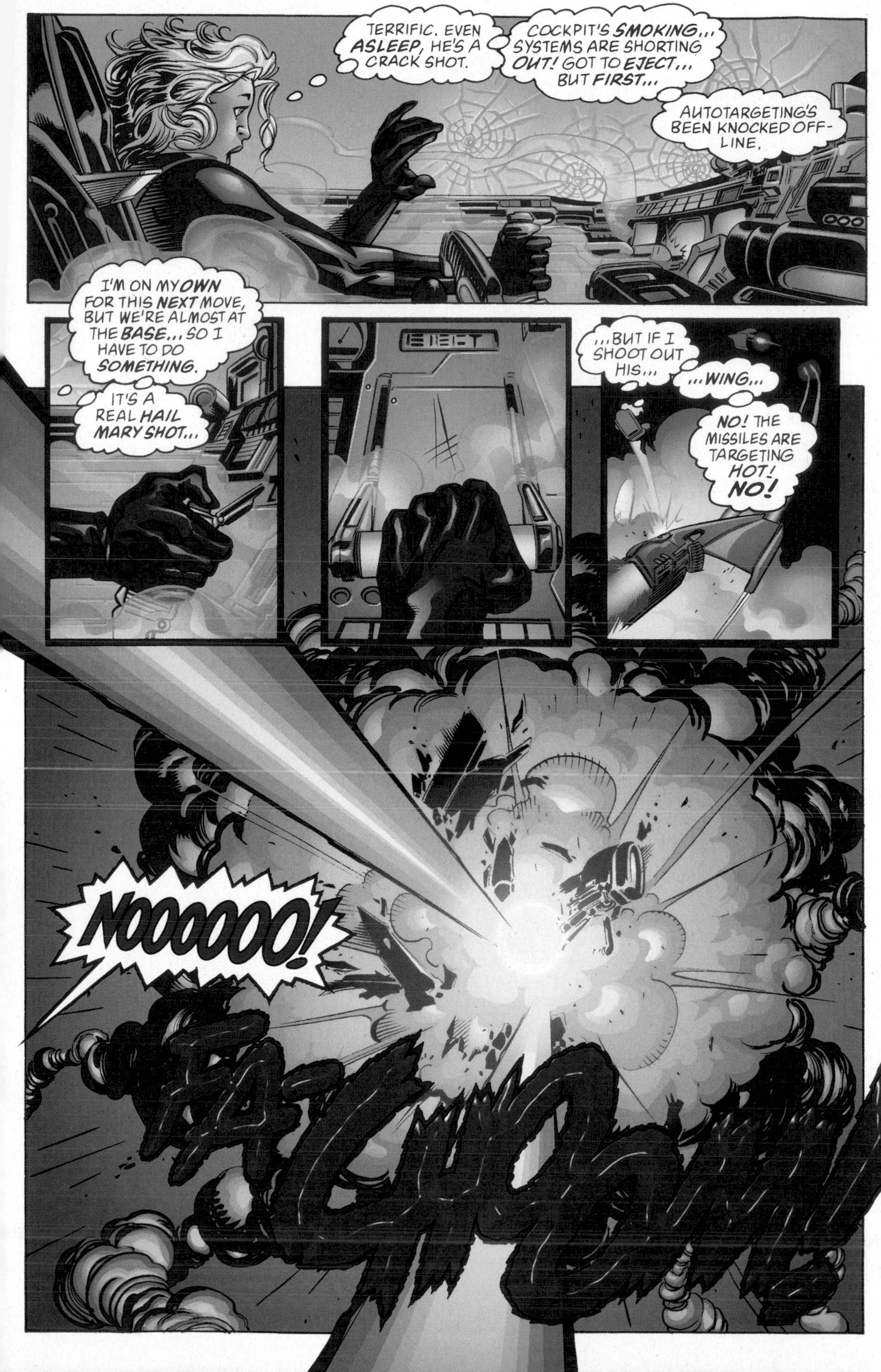

TERRIFIC. EVEN ASLEEP, HE'S A CRACK SHOT.
COCKPIT'S SMOKING... SYSTEMS ARE SHORTING OUT! GOT TO EJECT... BUT FIRST...
AUTOTARGETING'S BEEN KNOCKED OFF-LINE.
I'M ON MY OWN FOR THIS NEXT MOVE, BUT WE'RE ALMOST AT THE BASE... SO I HAVE TO DO SOMETHING.
IT'S A REAL HAIL MARY SHOT...
EJECT
...BUT IF I SHOOT OUT HIS...
...WING...
NO! THE MISSILES ARE TARGETING HOT! NO!
NOOOOOO!

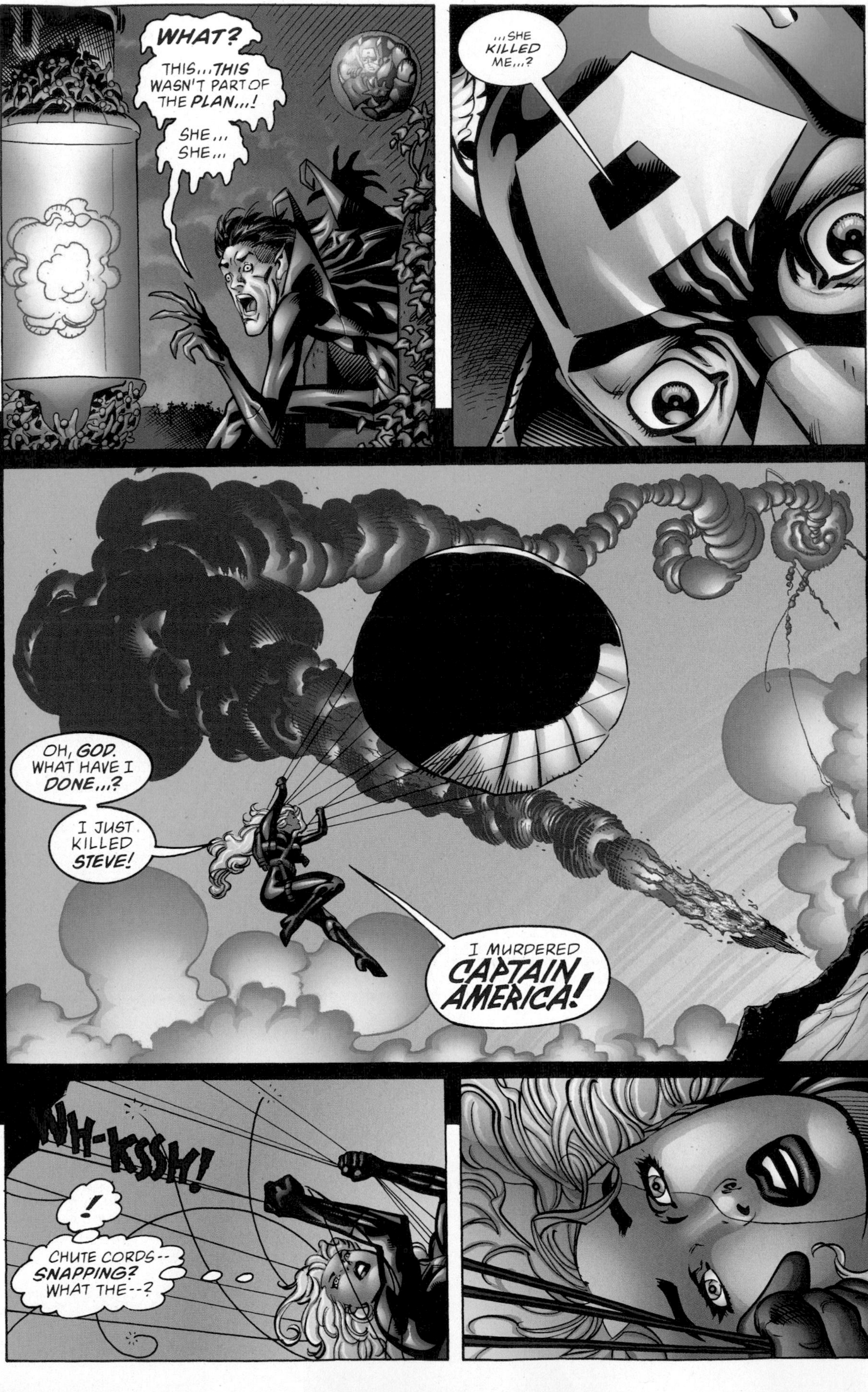
WHAT?
THIS...THIS WASN'T PART OF THE PLAN...!
SHE... SHE...
...SHE KILLED ME...?
OH, GOD. WHAT HAVE I DONE...?
I JUST KILLED STEVE!
I MURDERED CAPTAIN AMERICA!
NH-KSSH!
!
CHUTE CORDS-- SNAPPING? WHAT THE--?

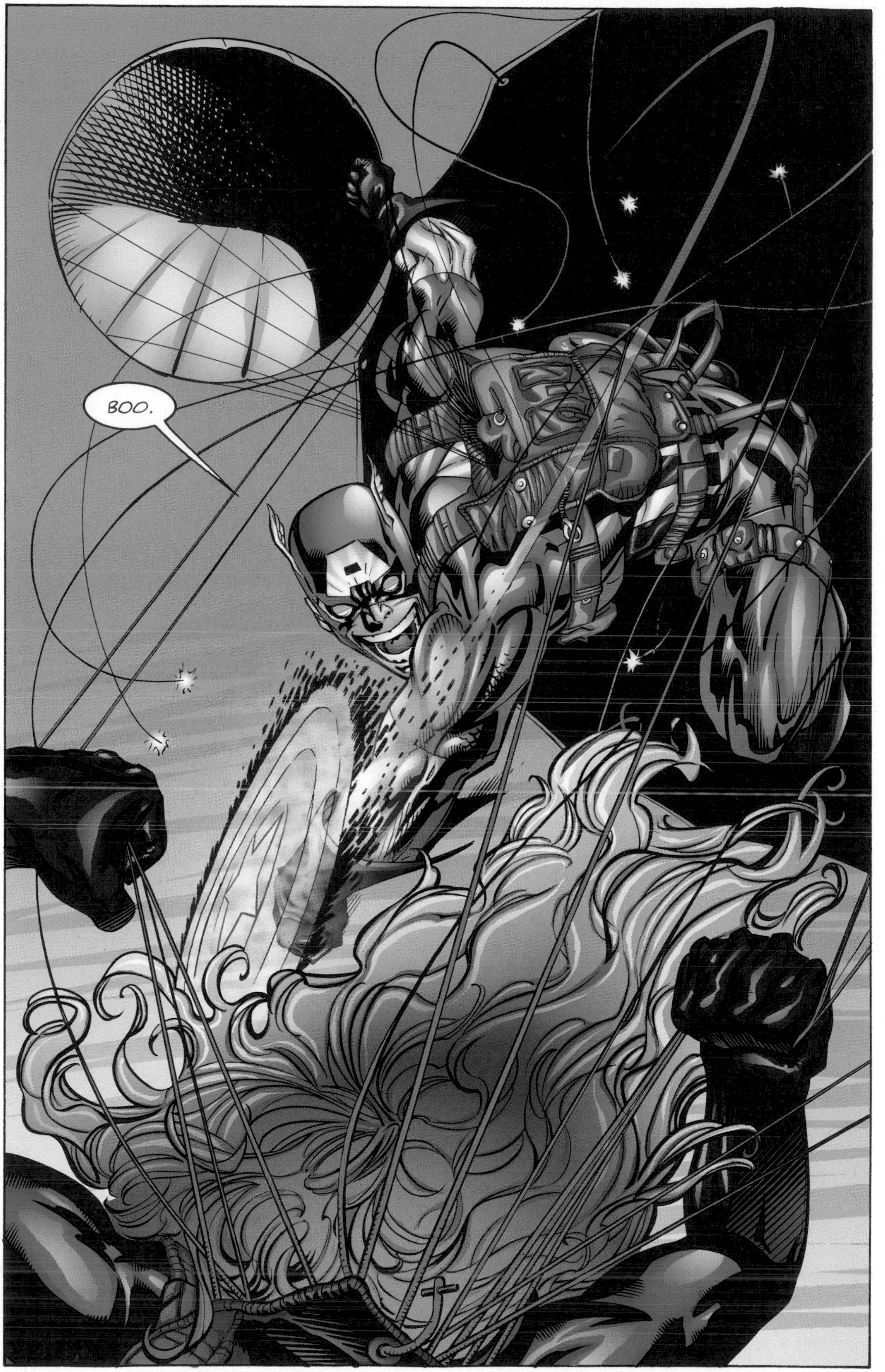
BOO.

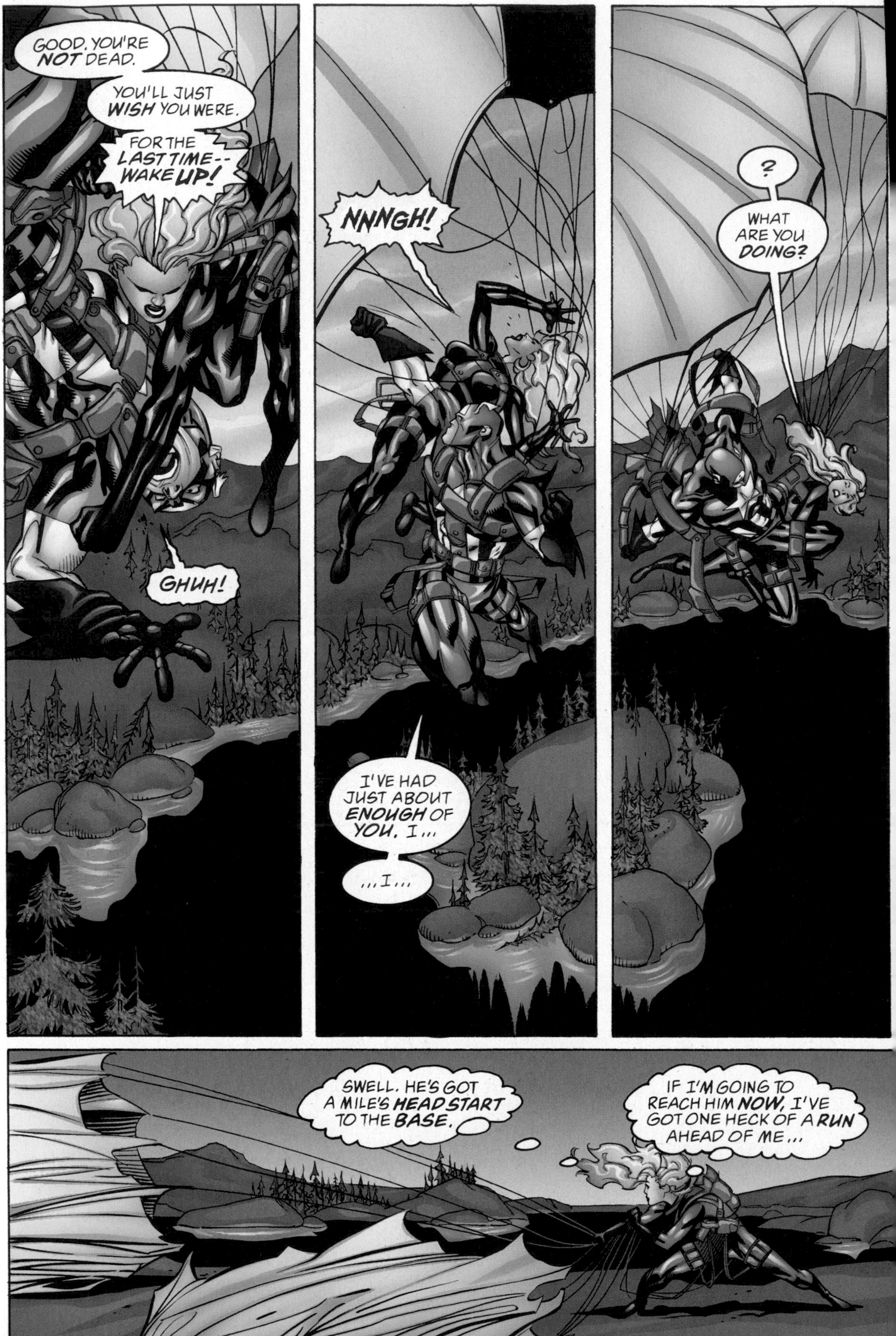
GOOD. YOU'RE NOT DEAD.
YOU'LL JUST WISH YOU WERE.
FOR THE LAST TIME-- WAKE UP!
GHUH!
NNNGH!
I'VE HAD JUST ABOUT ENOUGH OF YOU. I...
...I...
?
WHAT ARE YOU DOING?
SWELL. HE'S GOT A MILE'S HEAD START TO THE BASE.
IF I'M GOING TO REACH HIM NOW, I'VE GOT ONE HECK OF A RUN AHEAD OF ME...

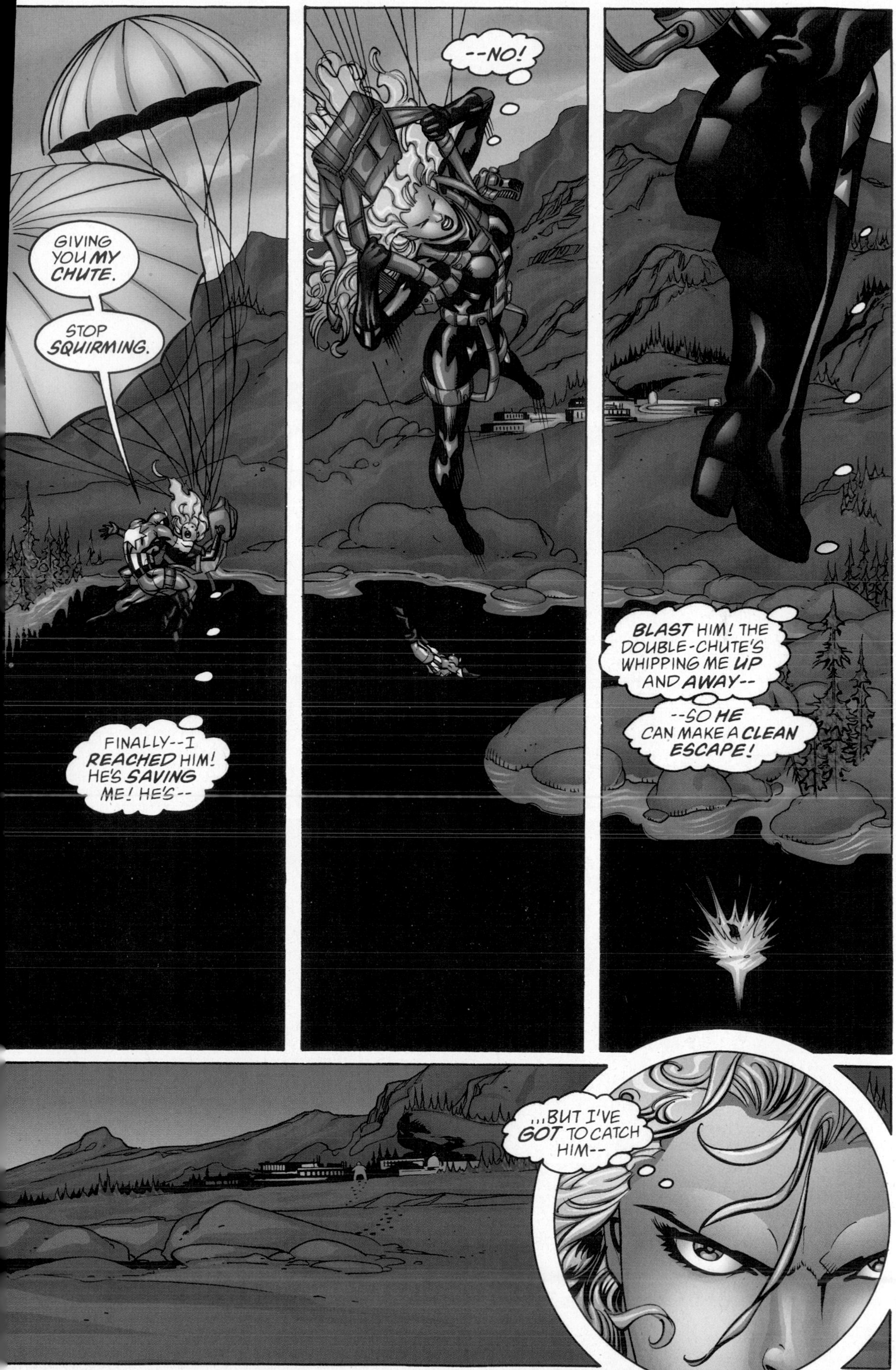

GIVING YOU MY CHUTE.
STOP SQUIRMING.
FINALLY--I REACHED HIM! HE'S SAVING ME! HE'S--
--NO!
BLAST HIM! THE DOUBLE-CHUTE'S WHIPPING ME UP AND AWAY--
--SO HE CAN MAKE A CLEAN ESCAPE!
...BUT I'VE GOT TO CATCH HIM--

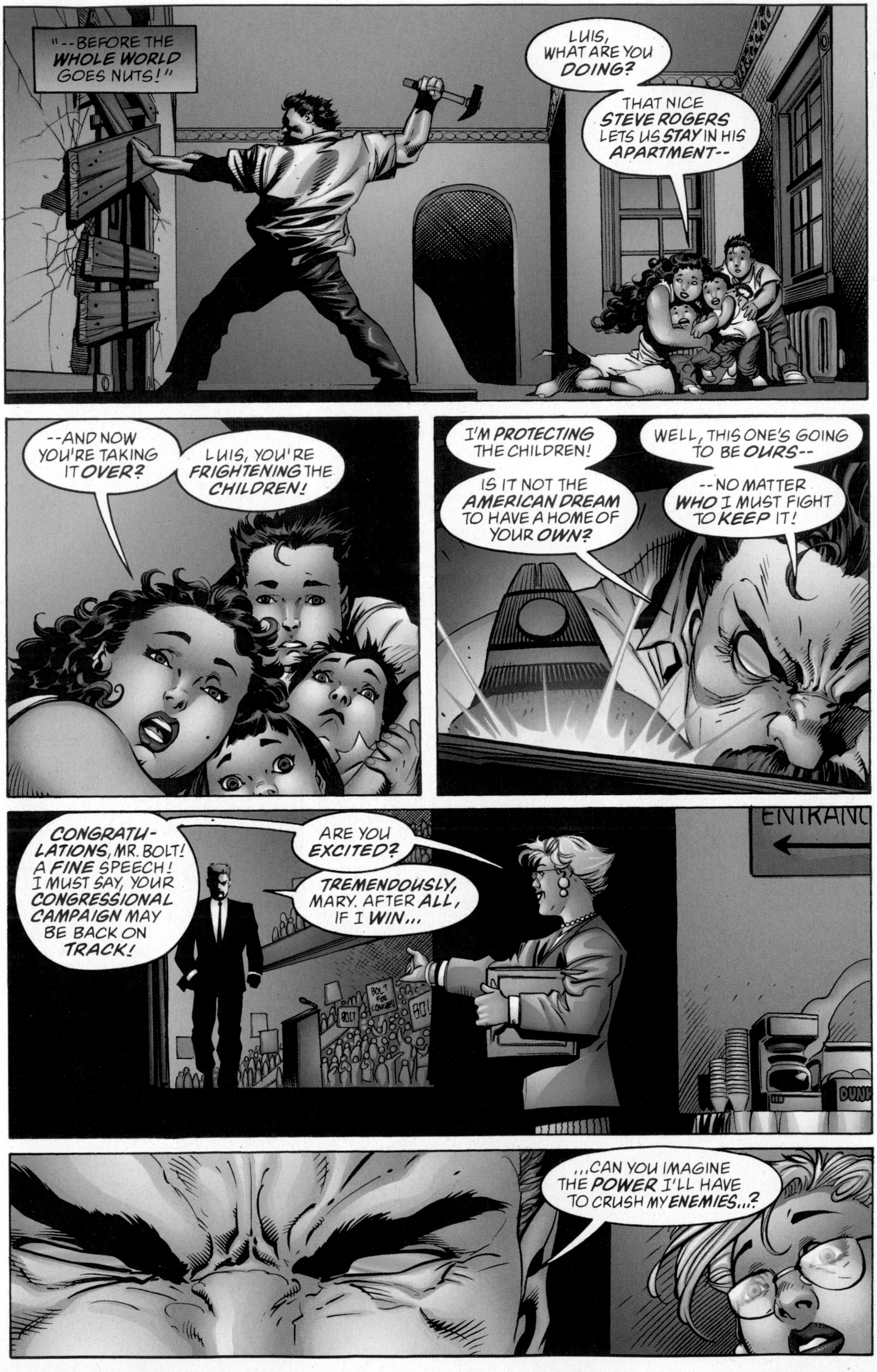
"--BEFORE THE WHOLE WORLD GOES NUTS!"
LUIS, WHAT ARE YOU DOING?
THAT NICE STEVE ROGERS LETS US STAY IN HIS APARTMENT--
--AND NOW YOU'RE TAKING IT OVER?
LUIS, YOU'RE FRIGHTENING THE CHILDREN!
I'M PROTECTING THE CHILDREN!
IS IT NOT THE AMERICAN DREAM TO HAVE A HOME OF YOUR OWN?
WELL, THIS ONE'S GOING TO BE OURS--
--NO MATTER WHO I MUST FIGHT TO KEEP IT!
CONGRATULATIONS, MR. BOLT! A FINE SPEECH! I MUST SAY, YOUR CONGRESSIONAL CAMPAIGN MAY BE BACK ON TRACK!
ARE YOU EXCITED?
TREMENDOUSLY, MARY. AFTER ALL, IF I WIN...
ENTRANC
BOLT FOR CONGRESS
BOLT
...CAN YOU IMAGINE THE POWER I'LL HAVE TO CRUSH MY ENEMIES...?

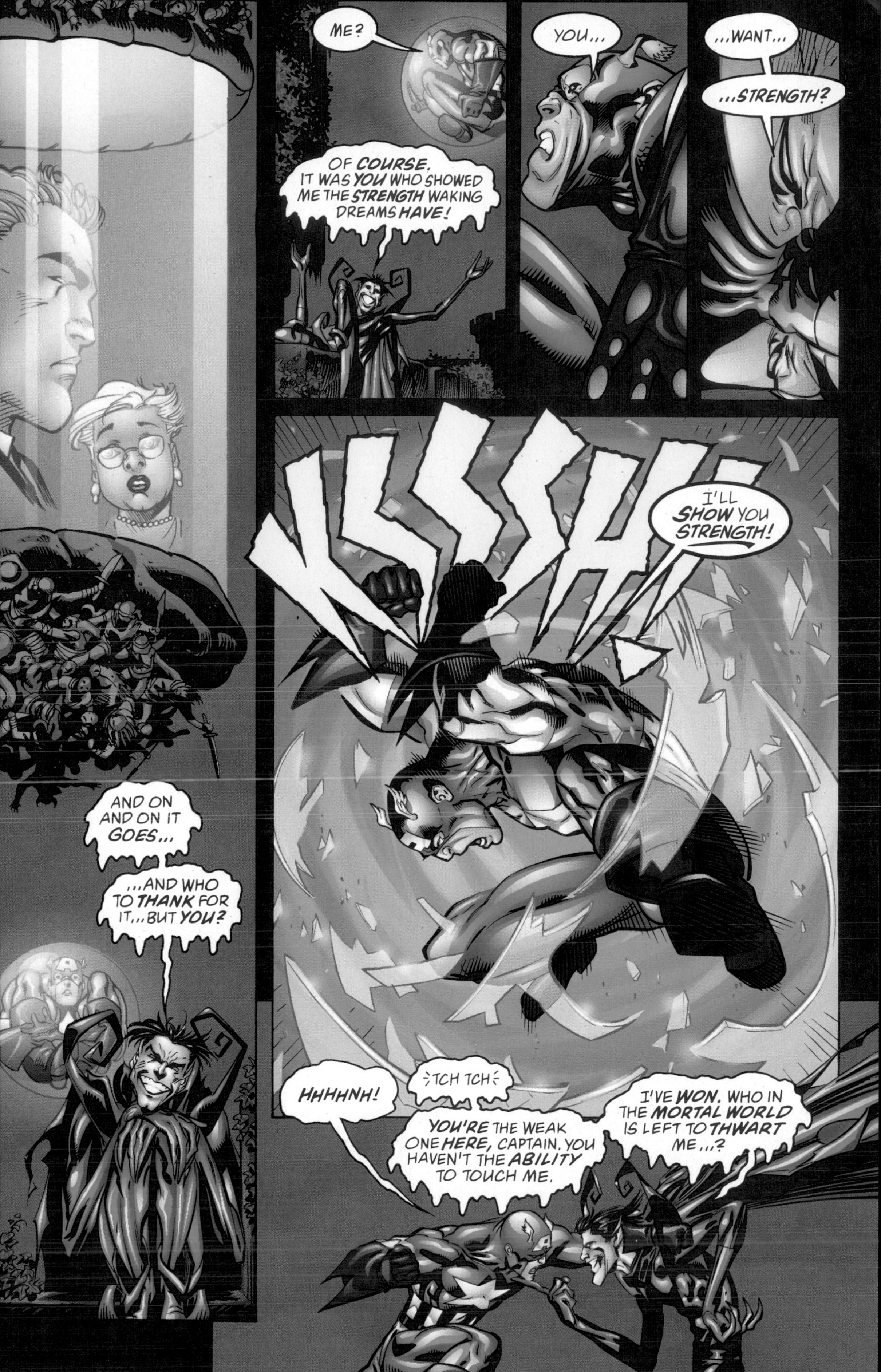
ME?
OF COURSE. IT WAS YOU WHO SHOWED ME THE STRENGTH WAKING DREAMS HAVE!
YOU...
...WANT...
...STRENGTH?
AND ON AND ON IT GOES...
...AND WHO TO THANK FOR IT... BUT YOU?
KSSSH!
I'LL SHOW YOU STRENGTH!
HHHHNH!
TCH TCH
YOU'RE THE WEAK ONE HERE, CAPTAIN. YOU HAVEN'T THE ABILITY TO TOUCH ME.
I'VE WON. WHO IN THE MORTAL WORLD IS LEFT TO THWART ME...?

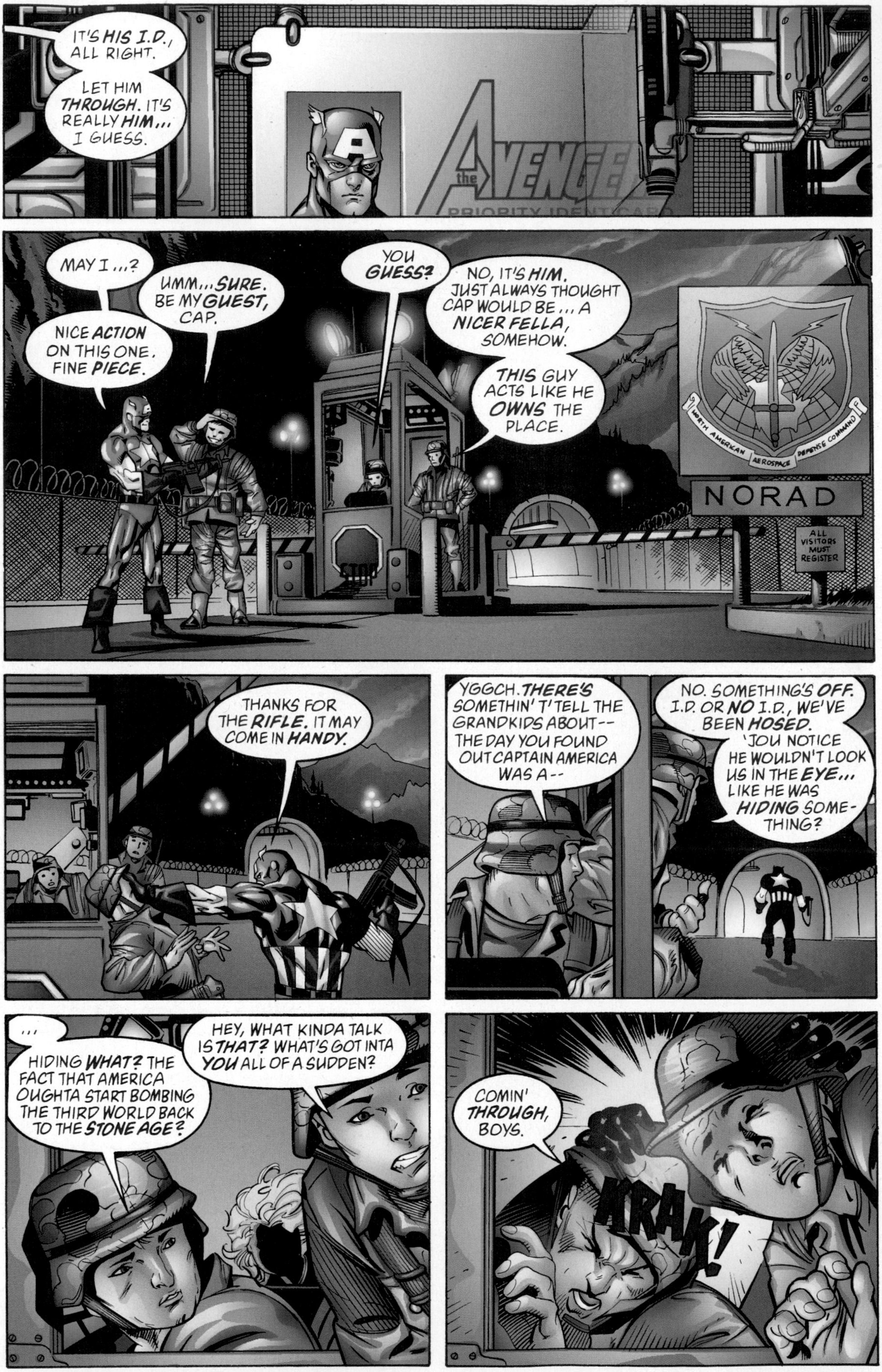

IT'S HIS I.D., ALL RIGHT.
LET HIM THROUGH. IT'S REALLY HIM... I GUESS.
AVENGERS
MAY I...?
NICE ACTION ON THIS ONE. FINE PIECE.
UMM... SURE. BE MY GUEST, CAP.
YOU GUESS?
NO, IT'S HIM. JUST ALWAYS THOUGHT CAP WOULD BE... A NICER FELLA, SOMEHOW.
THIS GUY ACTS LIKE HE OWNS THE PLACE.
NORTH AMERICAN AEROSPACE DEFENSE COMMAND
NORAD
ALL VISITORS MUST REGISTER
THANKS FOR THE RIFLE. IT MAY COME IN HANDY.
YGGCH. THERE'S SOMETHIN' T'TELL THE GRANDKIDS ABOUT-- THE DAY YOU FOUND OUT CAPTAIN AMERICA WAS A--
NO. SOMETHING'S OFF. I.D. OR NO I.D., WE'VE BEEN HOSED. 'JOU NOTICE HE WOULDN'T LOOK US IN THE EYE... LIKE HE WAS HIDING SOME-THING?
...
HIDING WHAT? THE FACT THAT AMERICA OUGHTA START BOMBING THE THIRD WORLD BACK TO THE STONE AGE?
HEY, WHAT KINDA TALK IS THAT? WHAT'S GOT INTA YOU ALL OF A SUDDEN?
COMIN' THROUGH, BOYS.
KRAK!

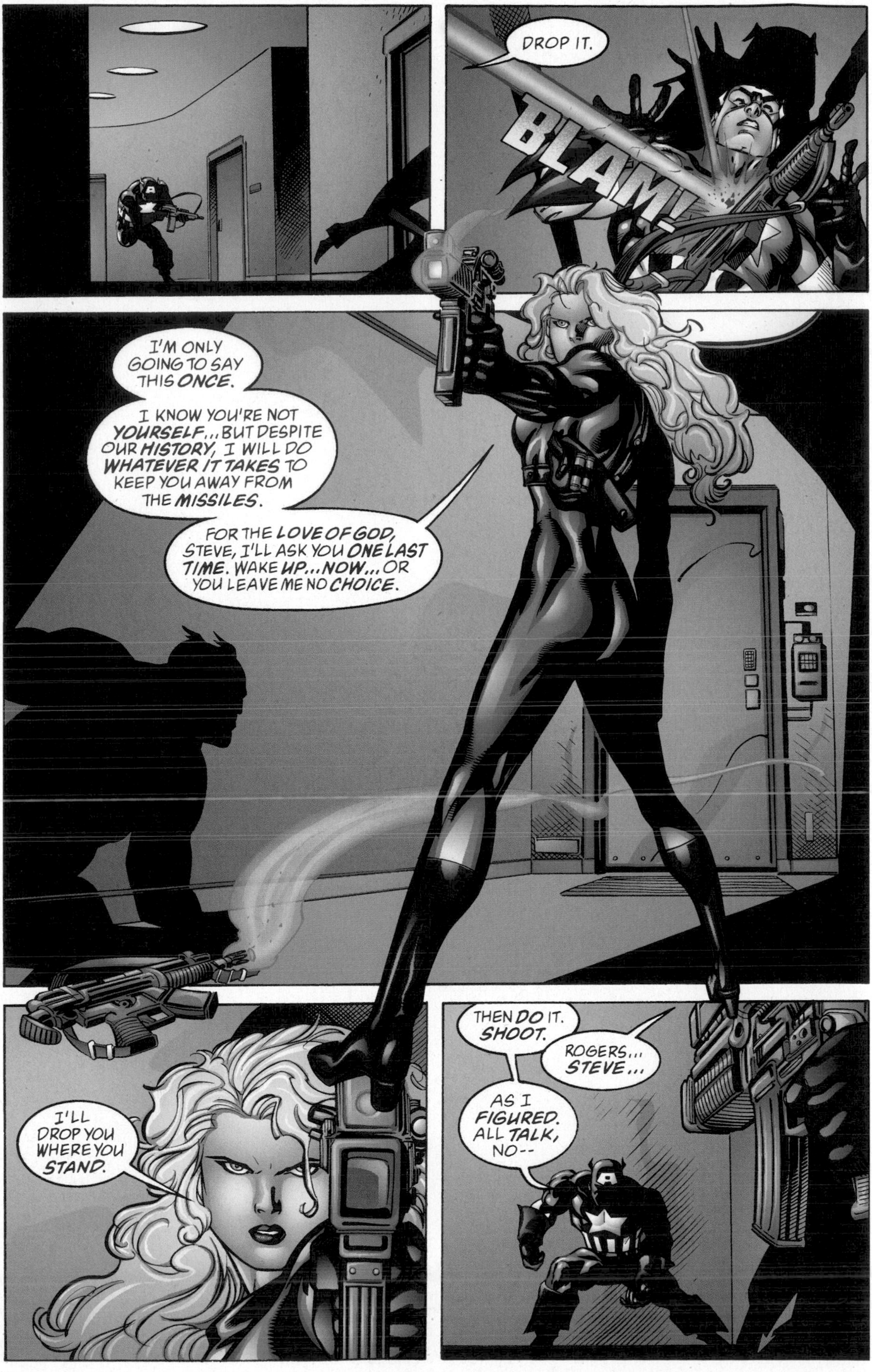
DROP IT.
BLAM!
I'M ONLY GOING TO SAY THIS ONCE.
I KNOW YOU'RE NOT YOURSELF... BUT DESPITE OUR HISTORY, I WILL DO WHATEVER IT TAKES TO KEEP YOU AWAY FROM THE MISSILES.
FOR THE LOVE OF GOD, STEVE, I'LL ASK YOU ONE LAST TIME. WAKE UP... NOW... OR YOU LEAVE ME NO CHOICE.
I'LL DROP YOU WHERE YOU STAND.
THEN DO IT. SHOOT.
ROGERS... STEVE...
AS I FIGURED. ALL TALK, NO--

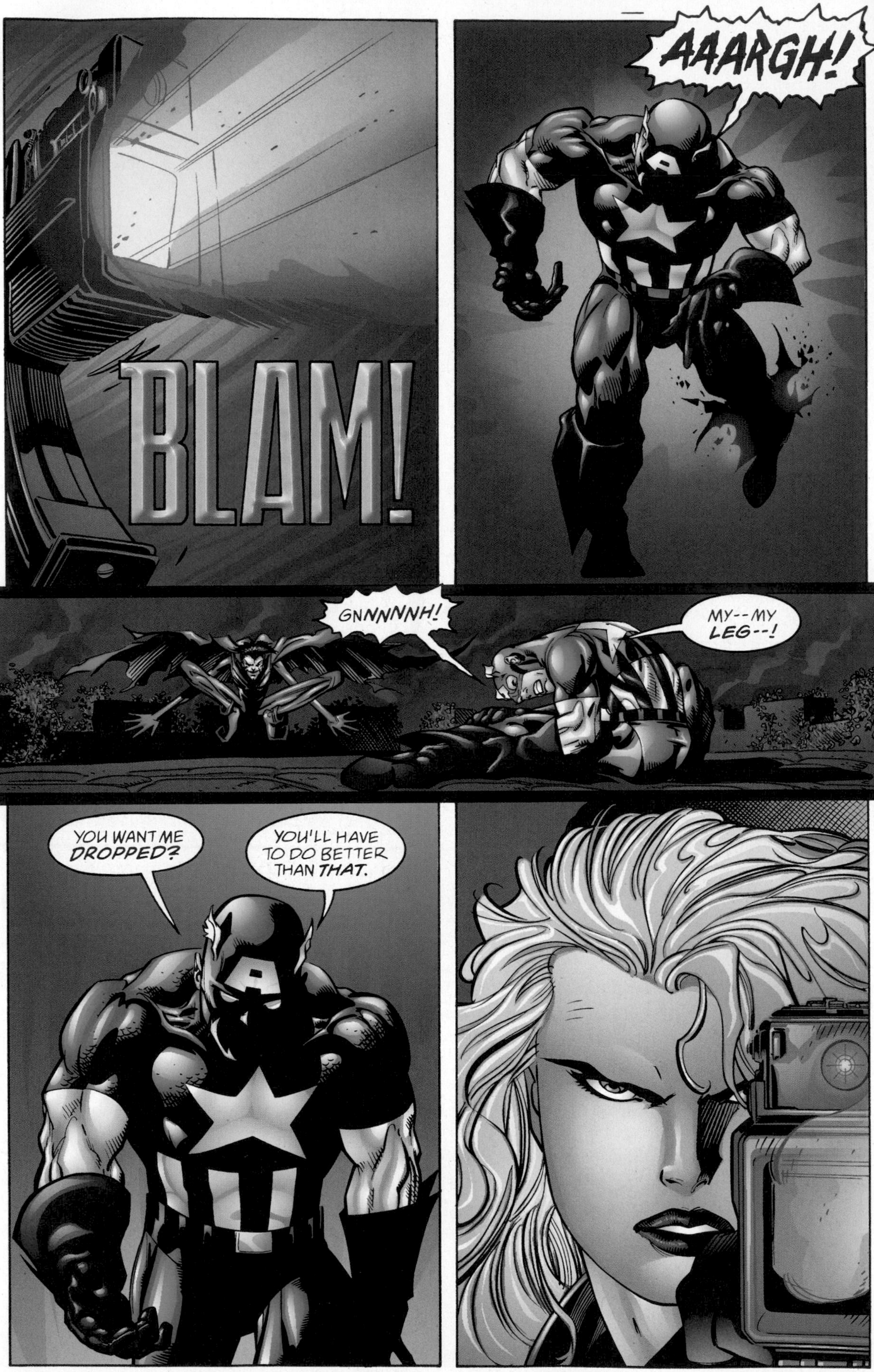
BLAM!
AAARGH!
GNNNNNH!
MY--MY LEG--!
YOU WANT ME DROPPED?
YOU'LL HAVE TO DO BETTER THAN THAT.

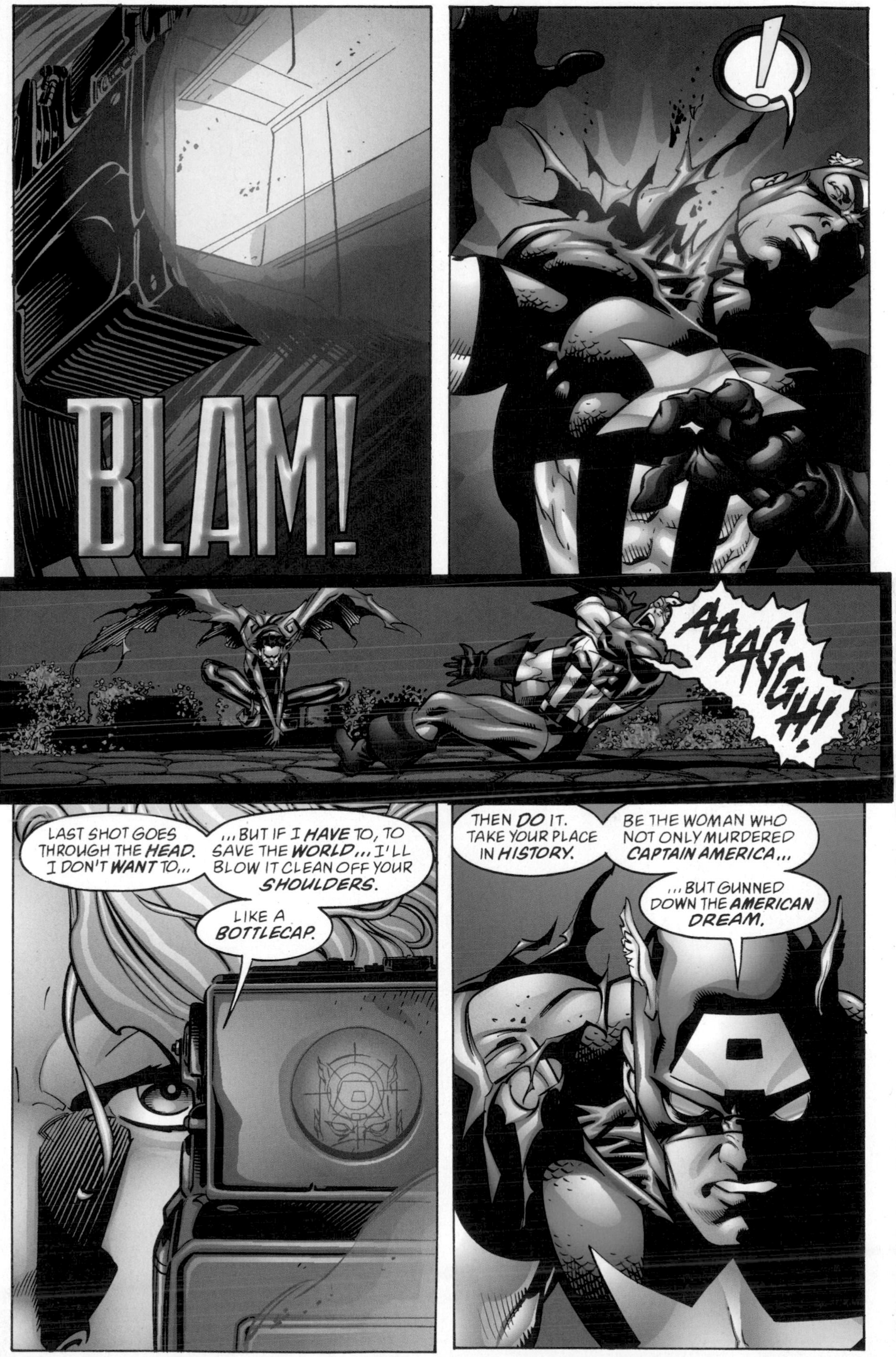
BLAM!
!
AAAGGH!
LAST SHOT GOES THROUGH THE HEAD. I DON'T WANT TO...
...BUT IF I HAVE TO, TO SAVE THE WORLD... I'LL BLOW IT CLEAN OFF YOUR SHOULDERS.
LIKE A BOTTLECAP.
THEN DO IT. TAKE YOUR PLACE IN HISTORY.
BE THE WOMAN WHO NOT ONLY MURDERED CAPTAIN AMERICA...
...BUT GUNNED DOWN THE AMERICAN DREAM.

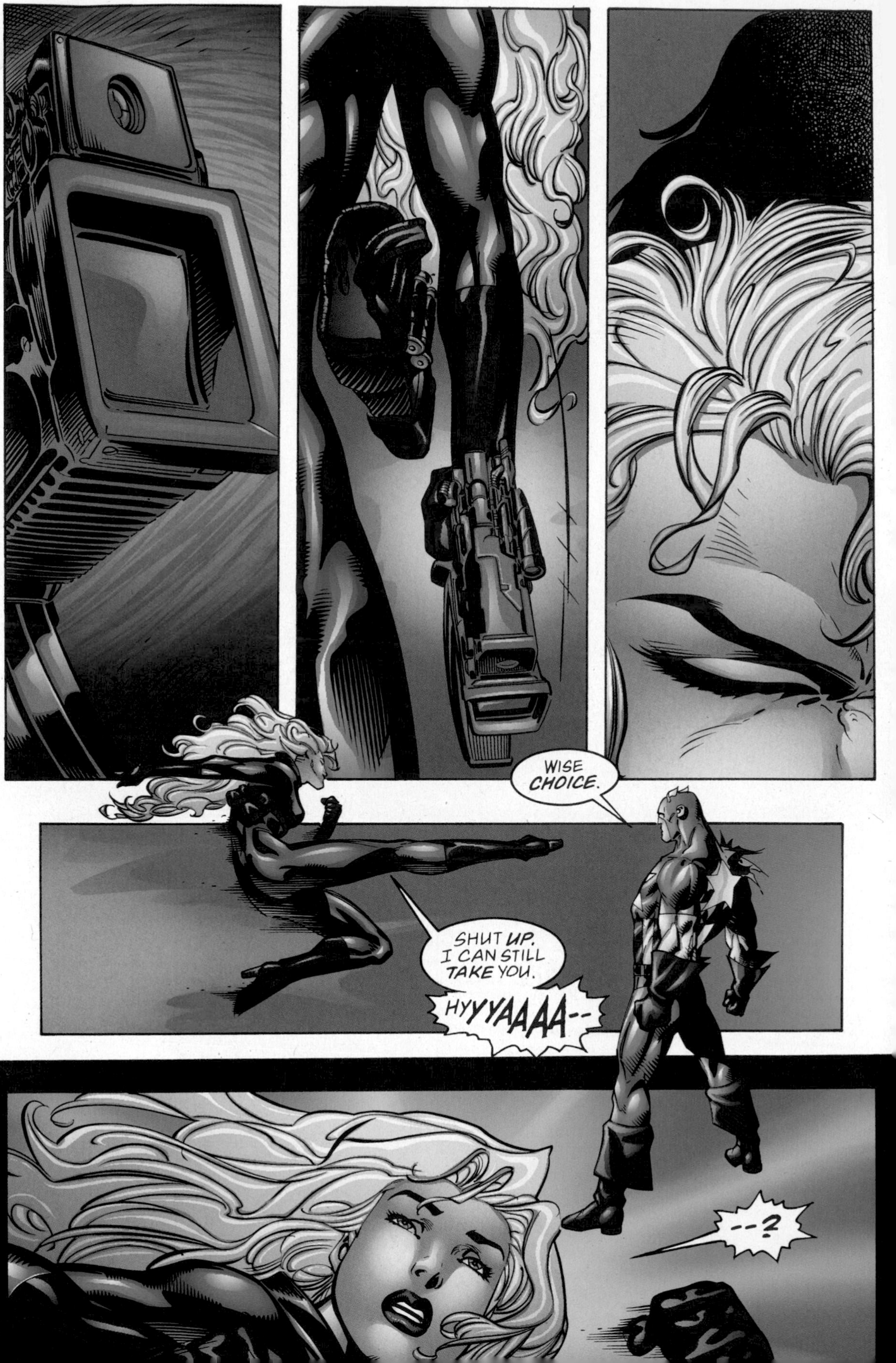
WISE CHOICE.
SHUT UP. I CAN STILL TAKE YOU.
HYYYAAAA--
--?

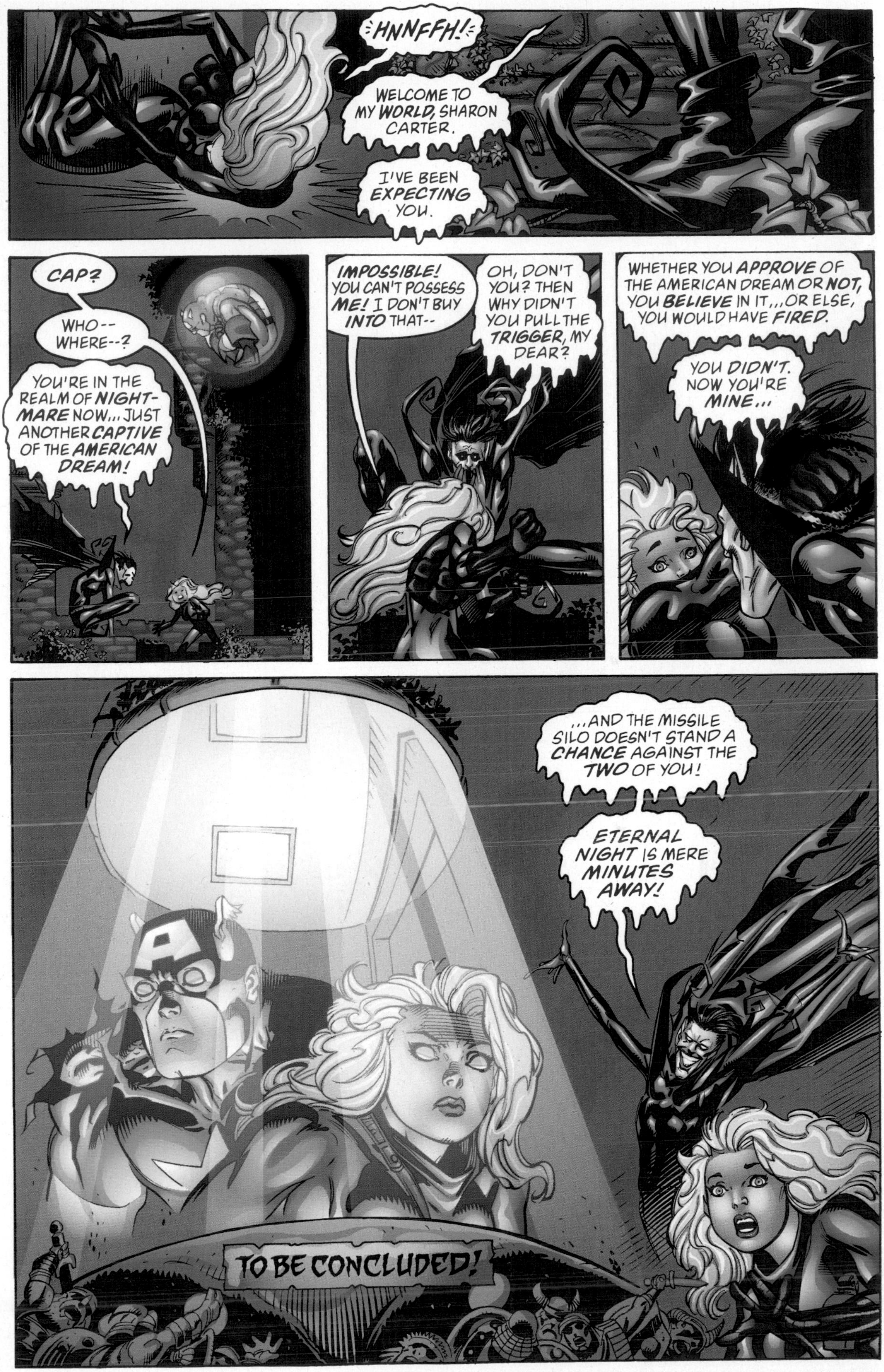
HNNFFH!
WELCOME TO MY WORLD, SHARON CARTER.
I'VE BEEN EXPECTING YOU.
CAP?
WHO-- WHERE--?
YOU'RE IN THE REALM OF NIGHT-MARE NOW... JUST ANOTHER CAPTIVE OF THE AMERICAN DREAM!
IMPOSSIBLE! YOU CAN'T POSSESS ME! I DON'T BUY INTO THAT--
OH, DON'T YOU? THEN WHY DIDN'T YOU PULL THE TRIGGER, MY DEAR?
WHETHER YOU APPROVE OF THE AMERICAN DREAM OR NOT, YOU BELIEVE IN IT,,,OR ELSE, YOU WOULD HAVE FIRED.
YOU DIDN'T. NOW YOU'RE MINE...
...AND THE MISSILE SILO DOESN'T STAND A CHANCE AGAINST THE TWO OF YOU!
ETERNAL NIGHT IS MERE MINUTES AWAY!
TO BE CONCLUDED!

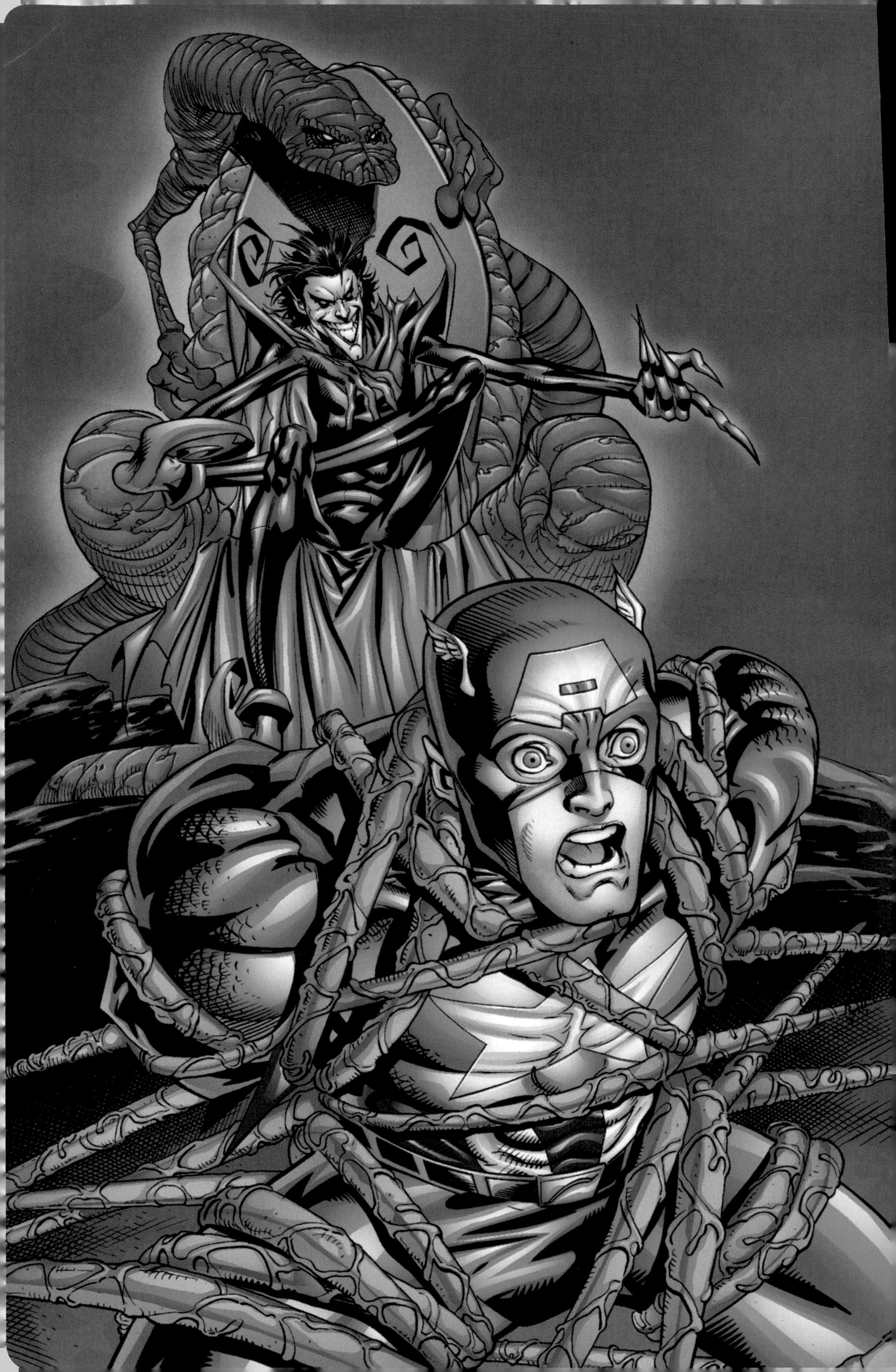

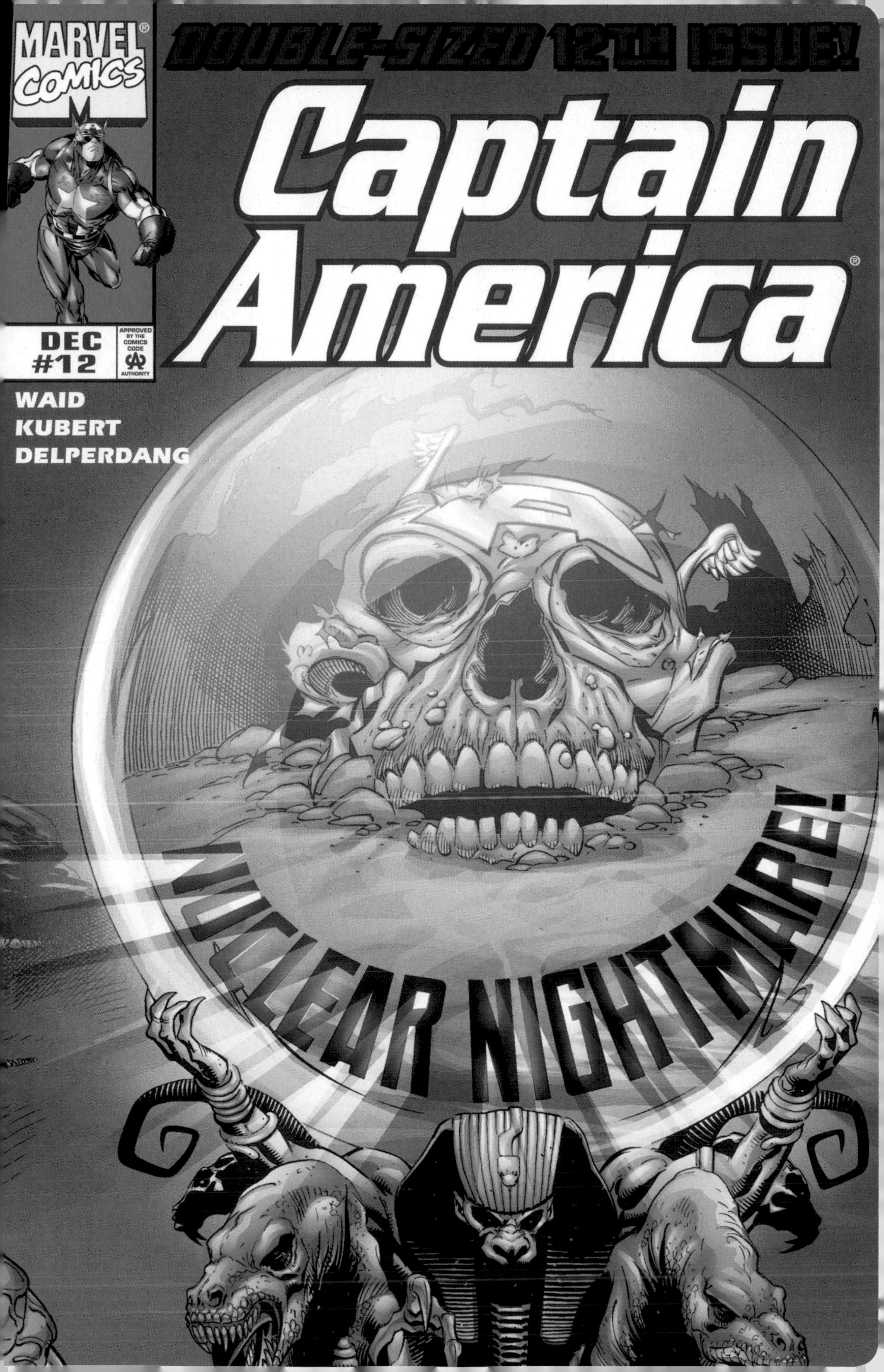

MARVEL COMICS
DOUBLE-SIZED 12TH ISSUE!
Captain America
DEC #12
APPROVED BY THE COMICS CODE AUTHORITY
WAID
KUBERT
DELPERDANG
NUCLEAR NIGHTMARE!

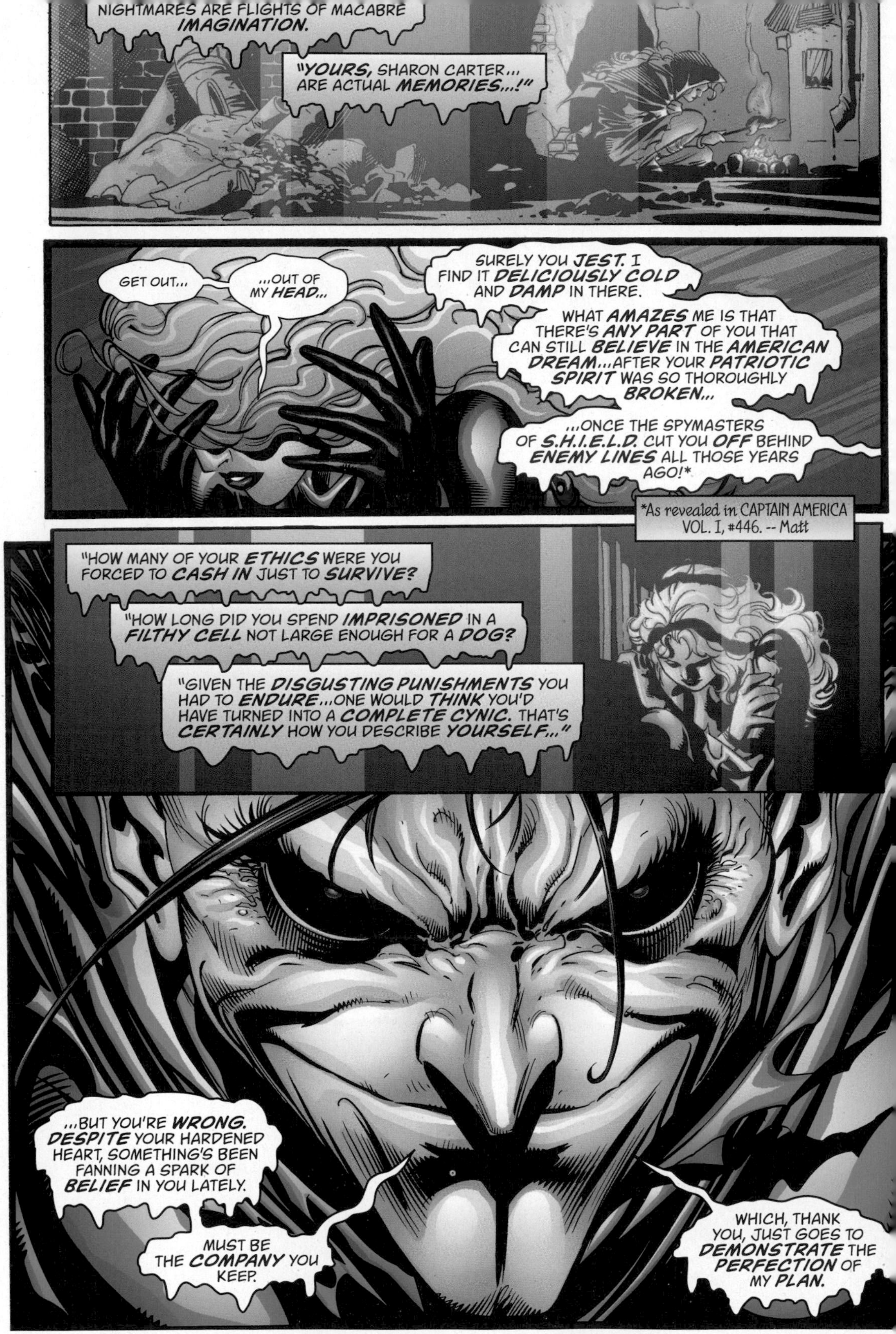
NIGHTMARES ARE FLIGHTS OF MACABRE IMAGINATION.
"YOURS, SHARON CARTER... ARE ACTUAL MEMORIES...!"
GET OUT...
...OUT OF MY HEAD...
SURELY YOU JEST. I FIND IT DELICIOUSLY COLD AND DAMP IN THERE.
WHAT AMAZES ME IS THAT THERE'S ANY PART OF YOU THAT CAN STILL BELIEVE IN THE AMERICAN DREAM...AFTER YOUR PATRIOTIC SPIRIT WAS SO THOROUGHLY BROKEN...
...ONCE THE SPYMASTERS OF S.H.I.E.L.D. CUT YOU OFF BEHIND ENEMY LINES ALL THOSE YEARS AGO!*
*As revealed in CAPTAIN AMERICA VOL. I, #446. -- Matt
"HOW MANY OF YOUR ETHICS WERE YOU FORCED TO CASH IN JUST TO SURVIVE?
"HOW LONG DID YOU SPEND IMPRISONED IN A FILTHY CELL NOT LARGE ENOUGH FOR A DOG?
"GIVEN THE DISGUSTING PUNISHMENTS YOU HAD TO ENDURE...ONE WOULD THINK YOU'D HAVE TURNED INTO A COMPLETE CYNIC. THAT'S CERTAINLY HOW YOU DESCRIBE YOURSELF..."
...BUT YOU'RE WRONG. DESPITE YOUR HARDENED HEART, SOMETHING'S BEEN FANNING A SPARK OF BELIEF IN YOU LATELY.
MUST BE THE COMPANY YOU KEEP.
WHICH, THANK YOU, JUST GOES TO DEMONSTRATE THE PERFECTION OF MY PLAN.

I AM *NIGHTMARE*. AS *LORD* OF MY *REALM*, I DRAW MY *PSYCHIC POWER* FROM THE DREAMS OF *SLEEPING MORTALS*. UNKNOWINGLY, THEY *FEED* ME FULLY *ONE-THIRD* OF THEIR *LIVES*.

I CRAVE *MORE*.

I DESIRE COMMAND OVER THEIR *WAKING* DREAMS AS WELL...THEIR ASPIRA-TIONS OF *WEALTH*, OF *POWER*, OF ALL THINGS *COVETED* BY THE HUMAN *SPIRIT*.

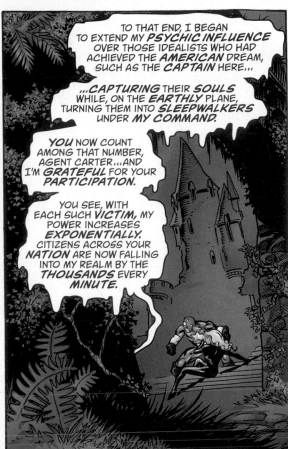

TO THAT END, I BEGAN TO EXTEND MY *PSYCHIC INFLUENCE* OVER THOSE IDEALISTS WHO HAD ACHIEVED THE *AMERICAN DREAM*, SUCH AS THE *CAPTAIN* HERE...

...*CAPTURING* THEIR *SOULS* WHILE, ON THE *EARTHLY* PLANE, TURNING THEM INTO *SLEEPWALKERS* UNDER *MY COMMAND*.

YOU NOW COUNT AMONG THAT NUMBER, AGENT CARTER...AND I'M *GRATEFUL* FOR YOUR *PARTICIPATION*.

YOU SEE, WITH EACH SUCH *VICTIM*, MY POWER INCREASES *EXPONENTIALLY*. CITIZENS ACROSS YOUR *NATION* ARE NOW FALLING INTO MY REALM BY THE *THOUSANDS* EVERY *MINUTE*.

SOON, I WILL OWN *ALL* OF THEM. *ALL* DREAMS, ALL *YEARNINGS*, WILL BECOME *UGLY NIGHTMARES*, *MINE* TO *CONTROL*.

NOW, TO *TEST* MY POWER, I HAVE CO-OPTED *YOU*, CAPTAIN...*LIVING SYMBOL* OF THE AMERICAN DREAM... TO SHOW YOUR PEOPLE JUST HOW DARK THAT DREAM CAN *BE*.

FOR WHAT *IS* DARKNESS BUT A ROAD TO *SLUMBER*?

AND WHAT *GREATER* DARKNESS...

...THAN THE LONG NIGHT OF *NUCLEAR WINTER*?

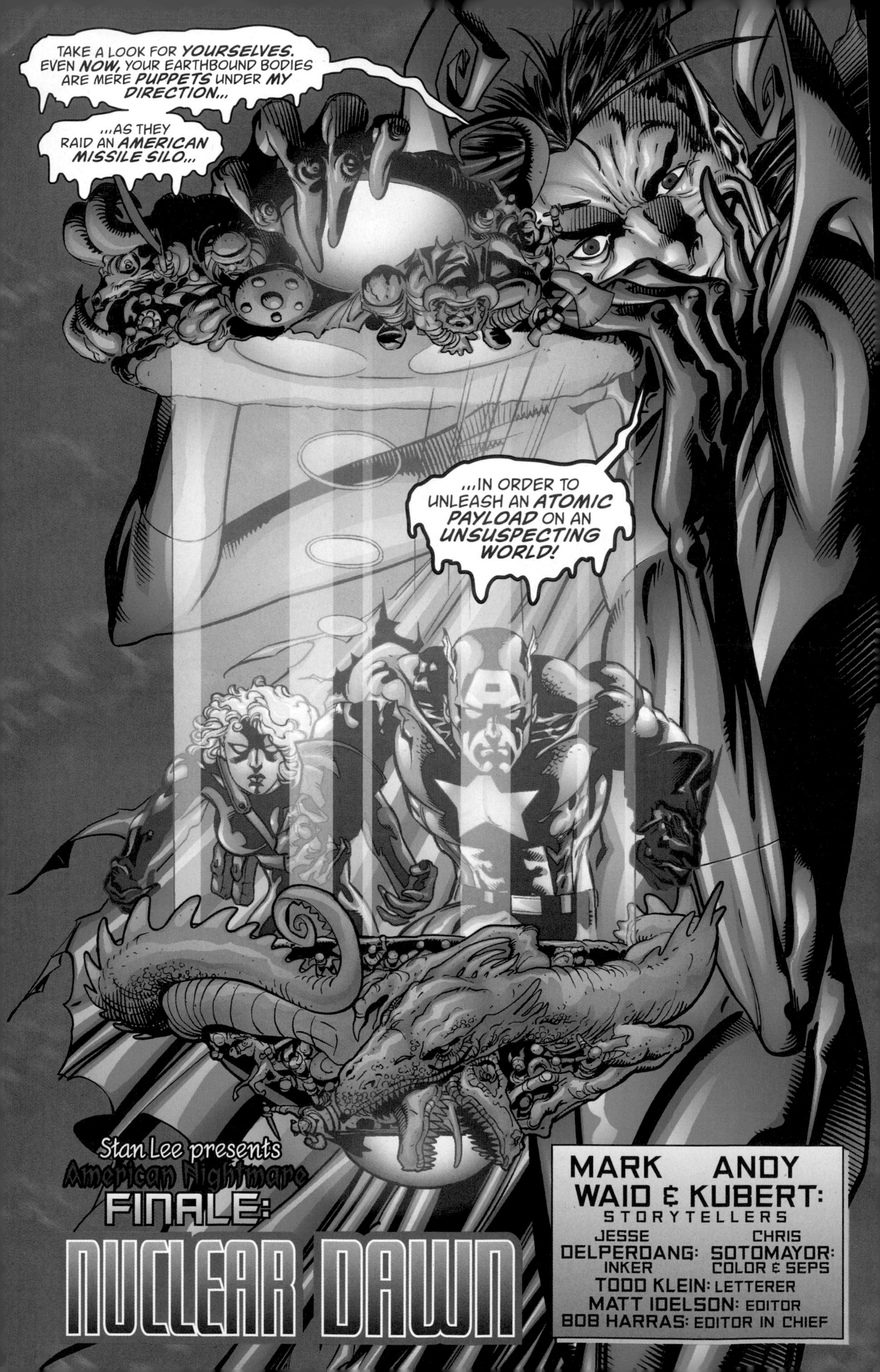
TAKE A LOOK FOR YOURSELVES. EVEN NOW, YOUR EARTHBOUND BODIES ARE MERE PUPPETS UNDER MY DIRECTION...
...AS THEY RAID AN AMERICAN MISSILE SILO...
...IN ORDER TO UNLEASH AN ATOMIC PAYLOAD ON AN UNSUSPECTING WORLD!
Stan Lee presents
American Nightmare
FINALE:
NUCLEAR DAWN
MARK WAID & ANDY KUBERT: STORYTELLERS
JESSE DELPERDANG: INKER
CHRIS SOTOMAYOR: COLOR & SEPS
TODD KLEIN: LETTERER
MATT IDELSON: EDITOR
BOB HARRAS: EDITOR IN CHIEF

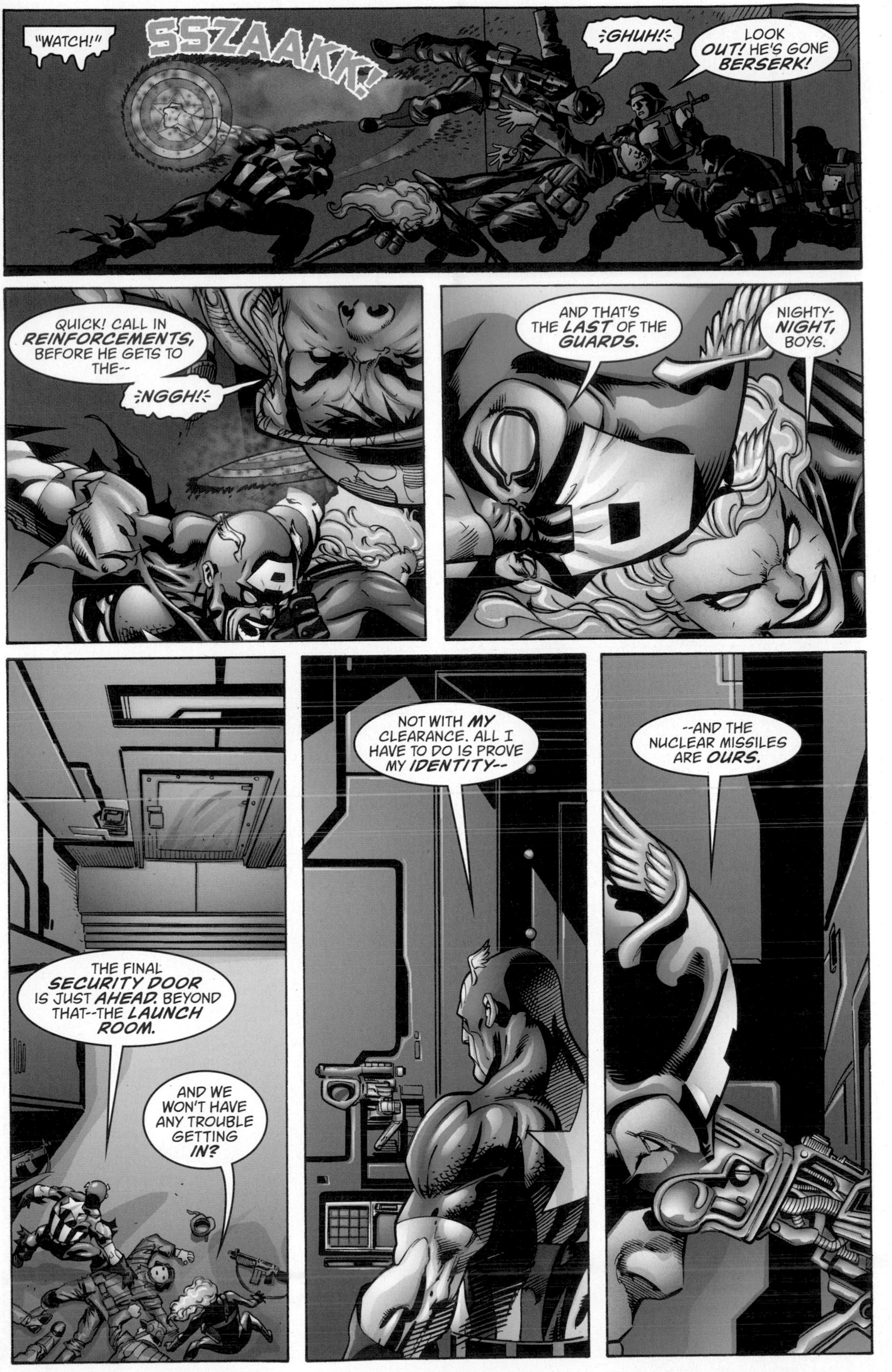
"WATCH!"
SSZAAKK!
GHUH!
LOOK OUT! HE'S GONE BERSERK!
QUICK! CALL IN REINFORCEMENTS, BEFORE HE GETS TO THE--
NGGH!
AND THAT'S THE LAST OF THE GUARDS.
NIGHTY-NIGHT, BOYS.
THE FINAL SECURITY DOOR IS JUST AHEAD. BEYOND THAT--THE LAUNCH ROOM.
AND WE WON'T HAVE ANY TROUBLE GETTING IN?
NOT WITH MY CLEARANCE. ALL I HAVE TO DO IS PROVE MY IDENTITY--
--AND THE NUCLEAR MISSILES ARE OURS.

Access request /
CAPTAIN AMERICA

Retinal scan
engaged...

›BRRZT‹

Match?
INCOMPATIBLE
Access
DENIED

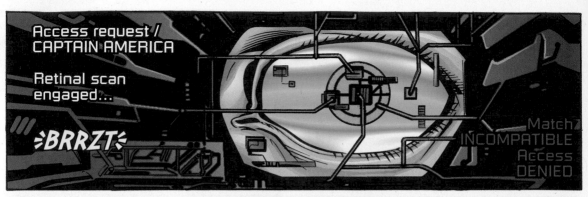

NO!

I HADN'T **COUNTED** ON THAT! THE ONLY PHYSIO-LOGICAL **CHANGE** TO MY **SLEEPWALKERS** IS IN THE **EYES!**

NO MATTER! THAT MAY HAVE BOUGHT YOUR WORLD A **MINUTE** OR TWO, BUT NO **MORE!** HE'LL FIND A WAY INTO THAT ROOM, AND THEN--

--AH.

I SEE I'M RANTING TO **MYSELF.** MY CAPTIVES HAVE **FLED!**

FLY **FORTH,** WINGED ONES! BRING HIM **BACK!**

BRING **CAPTAIN AMERICA** TO ME--

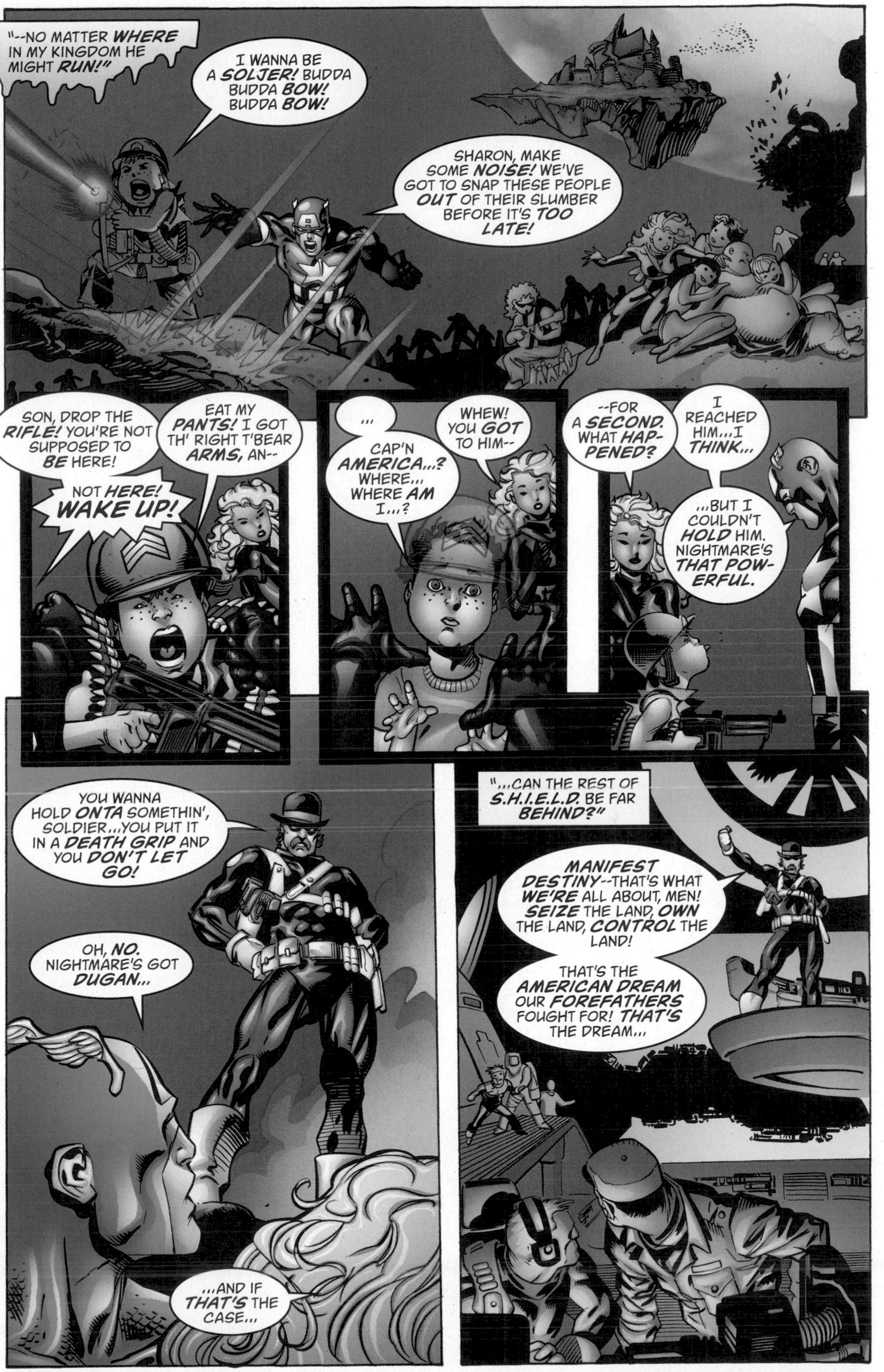
"--NO MATTER WHERE IN MY KINGDOM HE MIGHT RUN!"
I WANNA BE A SOLJER! BUDDA BUDDA BOW! BUDDA BOW!
SHARON, MAKE SOME NOISE! WE'VE GOT TO SNAP THESE PEOPLE OUT OF THEIR SLUMBER BEFORE IT'S TOO LATE!
SON, DROP THE RIFLE! YOU'RE NOT SUPPOSED TO BE HERE!
EAT MY PANTS! I GOT TH' RIGHT T'BEAR ARMS, AN--
NOT HERE! WAKE UP!
...
CAP'N AMERICA...? WHERE... WHERE AM I...?
WHEW! YOU GOT TO HIM--
--FOR A SECOND. WHAT HAPPENED?
I REACHED HIM...I THINK...
...BUT I COULDN'T HOLD HIM. NIGHTMARE'S THAT POWERFUL.
YOU WANNA HOLD ONTA SOMETHIN', SOLDIER...YOU PUT IT IN A DEATH GRIP AND YOU DON'T LET GO!
OH, NO. NIGHTMARE'S GOT DUGAN...
...AND IF THAT'S THE CASE...
"...CAN THE REST OF S.H.I.E.L.D. BE FAR BEHIND?"
MANIFEST DESTINY--THAT'S WHAT WE'RE ALL ABOUT, MEN! SEIZE THE LAND, OWN THE LAND, CONTROL THE LAND!
THAT'S THE AMERICAN DREAM OUR FOREFATHERS FOUGHT FOR! THAT'S THE DREAM...

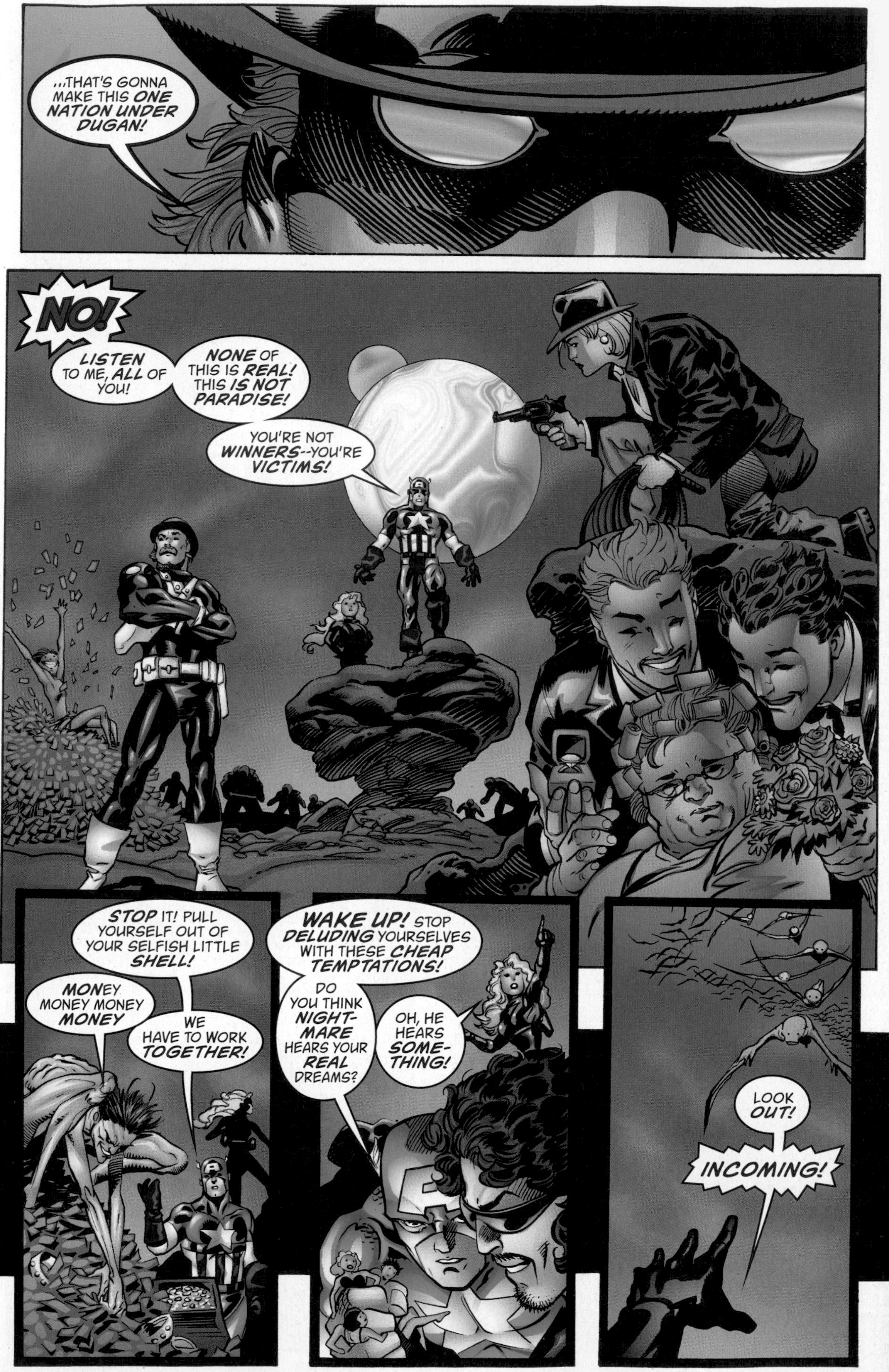
...THAT'S GONNA MAKE THIS ONE NATION UNDER DUGAN!
NO!
LISTEN TO ME, ALL OF YOU!
NONE OF THIS IS REAL! THIS IS NOT PARADISE!
YOU'RE NOT WINNERS--YOU'RE VICTIMS!
STOP IT! PULL YOURSELF OUT OF YOUR SELFISH LITTLE SHELL!
MONEY MONEY MONEY MONEY
WE HAVE TO WORK TOGETHER!
WAKE UP! STOP DELUDING YOURSELVES WITH THESE CHEAP TEMPTATIONS!
DO YOU THINK NIGHT-MARE HEARS YOUR REAL DREAMS?
OH, HE HEARS SOME-THING!
LOOK OUT!
INCOMING!

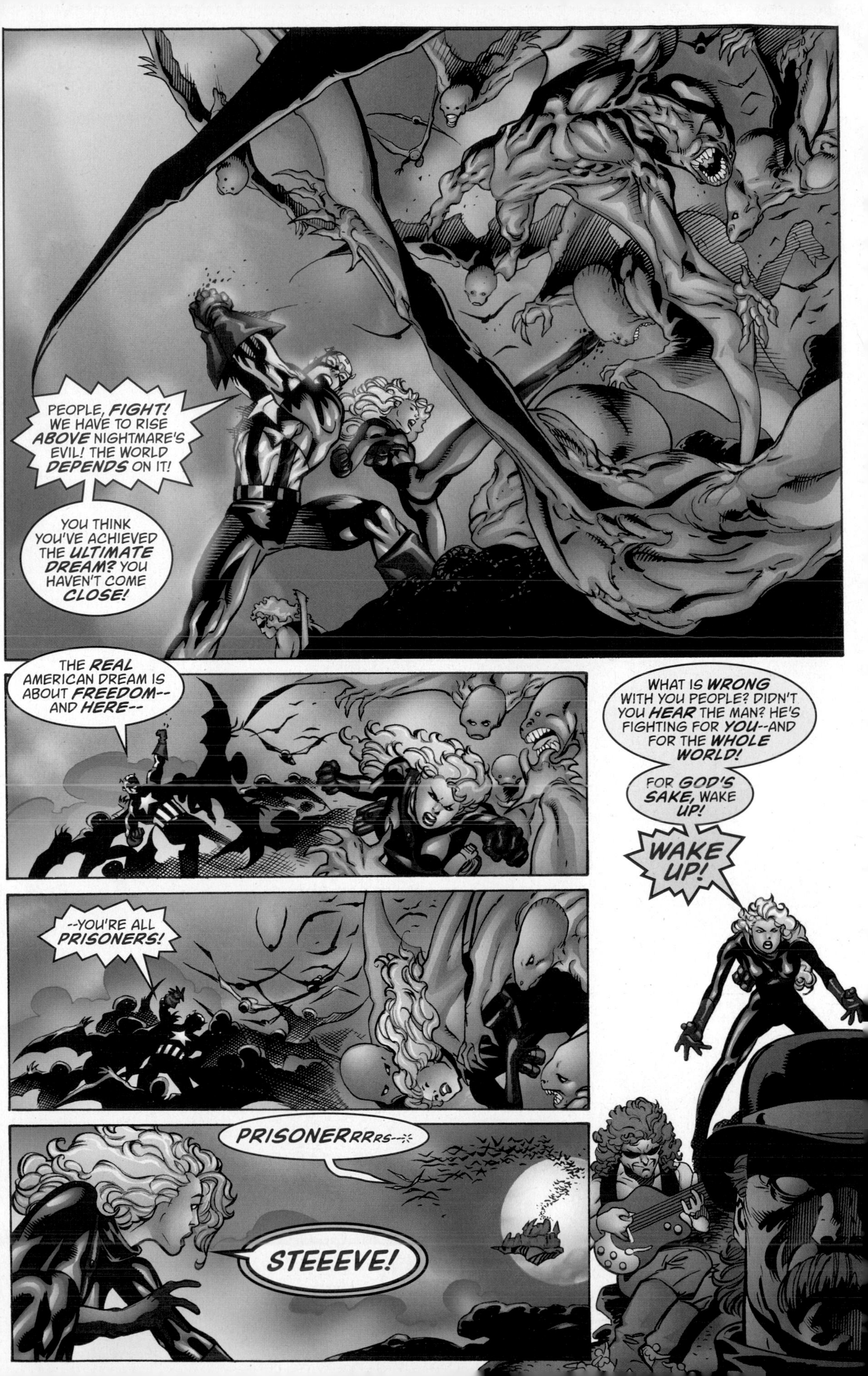
PEOPLE, FIGHT! WE HAVE TO RISE ABOVE NIGHTMARE'S EVIL! THE WORLD DEPENDS ON IT!
YOU THINK YOU'VE ACHIEVED THE ULTIMATE DREAM? YOU HAVEN'T COME CLOSE!
THE REAL AMERICAN DREAM IS ABOUT FREEDOM-- AND HERE--
--YOU'RE ALL PRISONERS!
PRISONERRRRS--
WHAT IS WRONG WITH YOU PEOPLE? DIDN'T YOU HEAR THE MAN? HE'S FIGHTING FOR YOU--AND FOR THE WHOLE WORLD!
FOR GOD'S SAKE, WAKE UP!
WAKE UP!
STEEEVE!

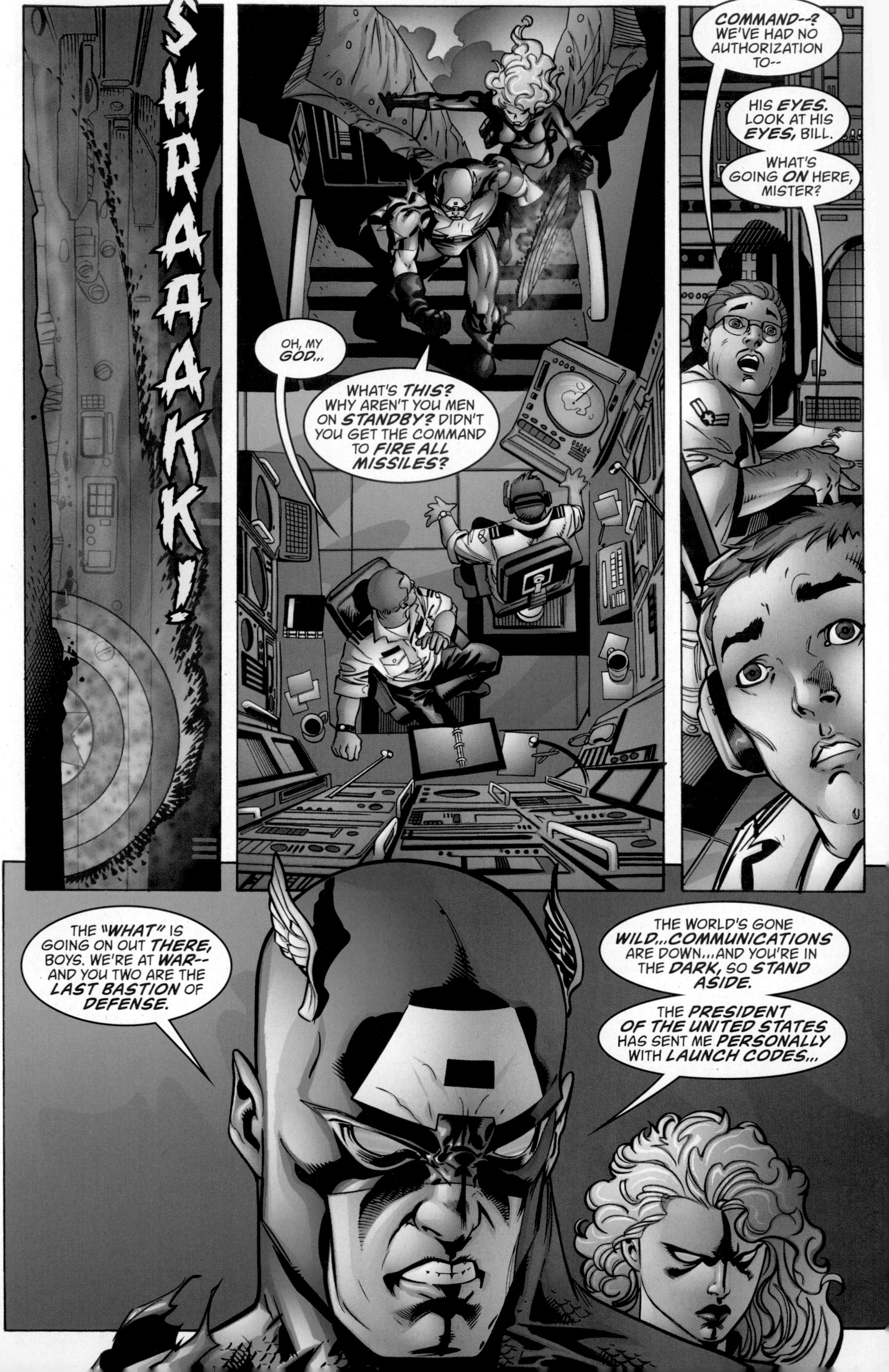
SHRAAAKK!
OH, MY GOD...
WHAT'S THIS? WHY AREN'T YOU MEN ON STANDBY? DIDN'T YOU GET THE COMMAND TO FIRE ALL MISSILES?
COMMAND--? WE'VE HAD NO AUTHORIZATION TO--
HIS EYES. LOOK AT HIS EYES, BILL.
WHAT'S GOING ON HERE, MISTER?
THE "WHAT" IS GOING ON OUT THERE, BOYS. WE'RE AT WAR-- AND YOU TWO ARE THE LAST BASTION OF DEFENSE.
THE WORLD'S GONE WILD...COMMUNICATIONS ARE DOWN...AND YOU'RE IN THE DARK, SO STAND ASIDE.
THE PRESIDENT OF THE UNITED STATES HAS SENT ME PERSONALLY WITH LAUNCH CODES...

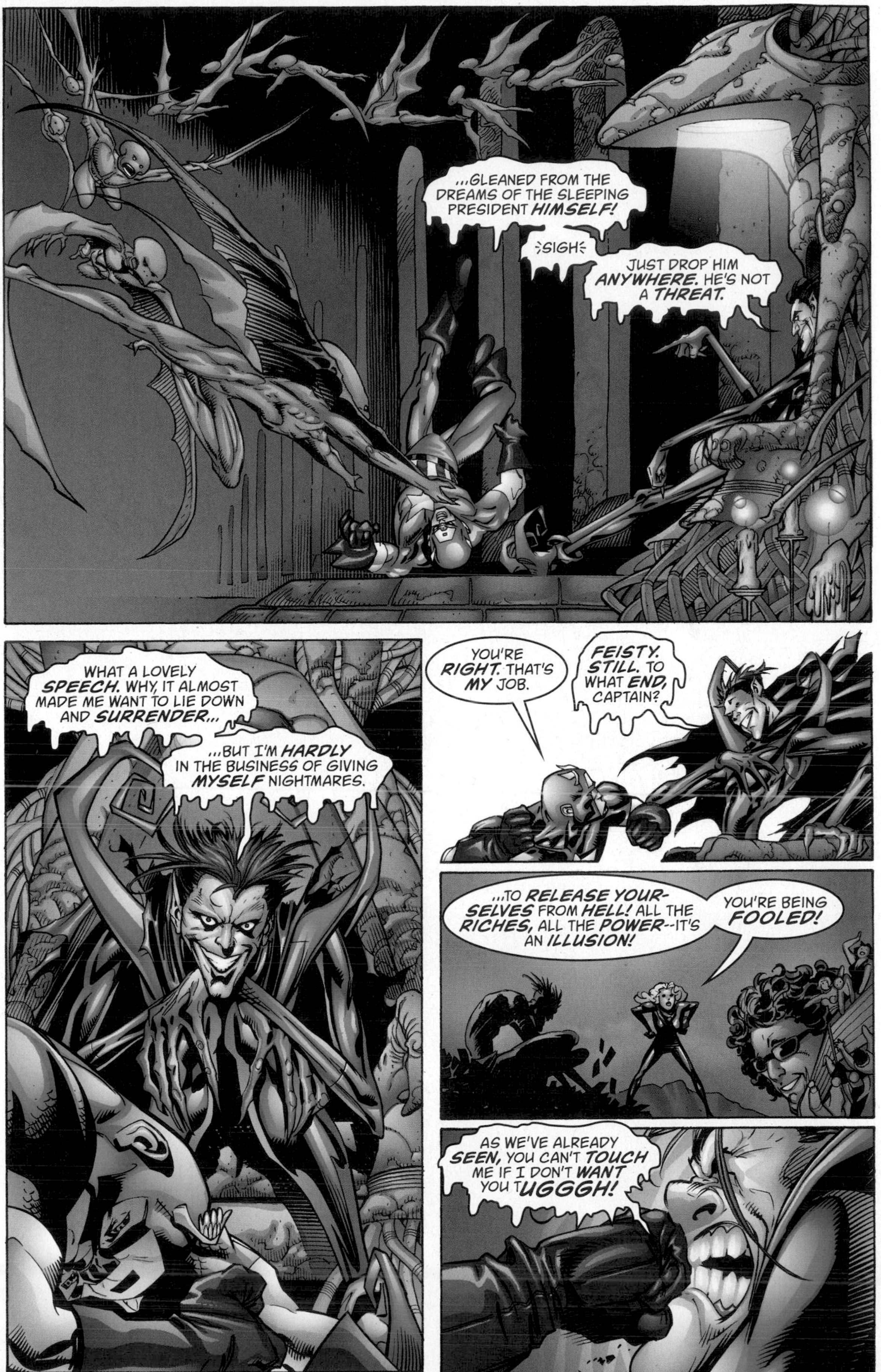
...GLEANED FROM THE DREAMS OF THE SLEEPING PRESIDENT HIMSELF!
SIGH
JUST DROP HIM ANYWHERE. HE'S NOT A THREAT.
WHAT A LOVELY SPEECH. WHY, IT ALMOST MADE ME WANT TO LIE DOWN AND SURRENDER...
...BUT I'M HARDLY IN THE BUSINESS OF GIVING MYSELF NIGHTMARES.
YOU'RE RIGHT. THAT'S MY JOB.
FEISTY. STILL. TO WHAT END, CAPTAIN?
...TO RELEASE YOURSELVES FROM HELL! ALL THE RICHES, ALL THE POWER--IT'S AN ILLUSION!
YOU'RE BEING FOOLED!
AS WE'VE ALREADY SEEN, YOU CAN'T TOUCH ME IF I DON'T WANT YOU TUGGGH!

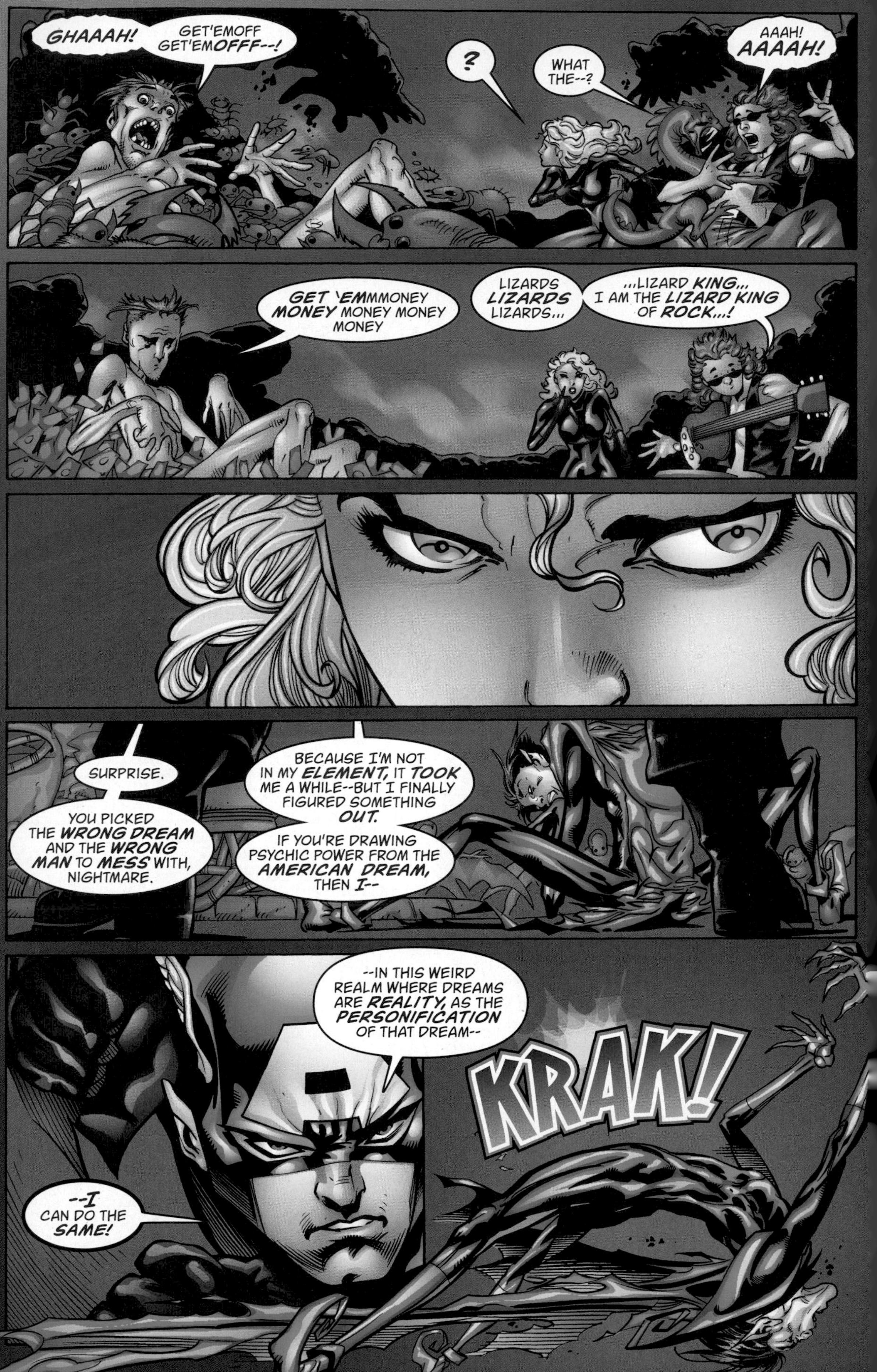
GHAAAH!
GET'EMOFF GET'EMOFFF--!
?
WHAT THE--?
AAAH! AAAAH!
GET 'EMMMONEY MONEY MONEY MONEY MONEY
LIZARDS LIZARDS LIZARDS...
...LIZARD KING... I AM THE LIZARD KING OF ROCK...!
SURPRISE.
YOU PICKED THE WRONG DREAM AND THE WRONG MAN TO MESS WITH, NIGHTMARE.
BECAUSE I'M NOT IN MY ELEMENT, IT TOOK ME A WHILE--BUT I FINALLY FIGURED SOMETHING OUT.
IF YOU'RE DRAWING PSYCHIC POWER FROM THE AMERICAN DREAM, THEN I--
--IN THIS WEIRD REALM WHERE DREAMS ARE REALITY, AS THE PERSONIFICATION OF THAT DREAM--
KRAK!
--I CAN DO THE SAME!

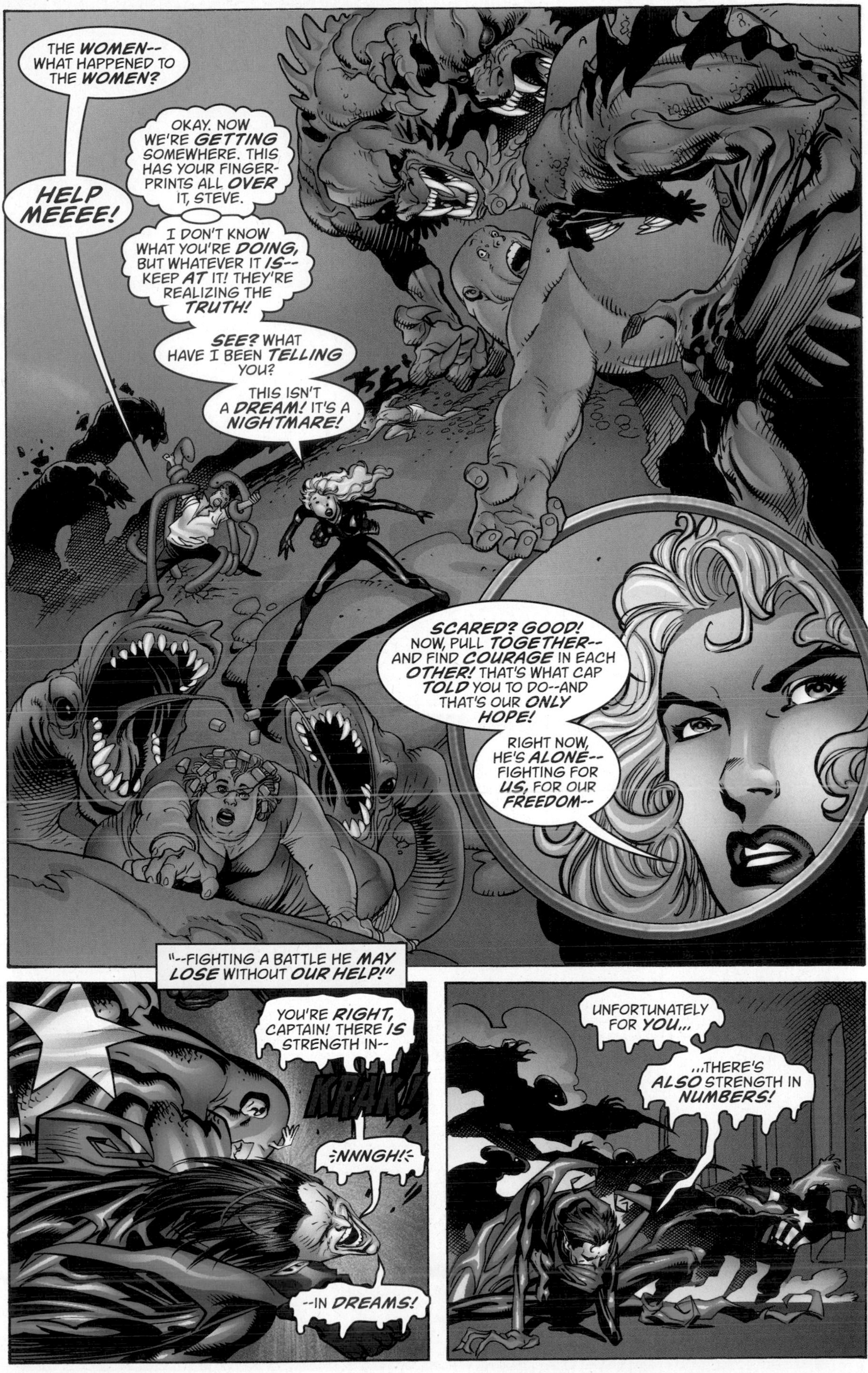
THE WOMEN-- WHAT HAPPENED TO THE WOMEN?
HELP MEEEE!
OKAY. NOW WE'RE GETTING SOMEWHERE. THIS HAS YOUR FINGER-PRINTS ALL OVER IT, STEVE.
I DON'T KNOW WHAT YOU'RE DOING, BUT WHATEVER IT IS-- KEEP AT IT! THEY'RE REALIZING THE TRUTH!
SEE? WHAT HAVE I BEEN TELLING YOU?
THIS ISN'T A DREAM! IT'S A NIGHTMARE!
SCARED? GOOD! NOW, PULL TOGETHER-- AND FIND COURAGE IN EACH OTHER! THAT'S WHAT CAP TOLD YOU TO DO--AND THAT'S OUR ONLY HOPE!
RIGHT NOW, HE'S ALONE-- FIGHTING FOR US, FOR OUR FREEDOM--
"--FIGHTING A BATTLE HE MAY LOSE WITHOUT OUR HELP!"
YOU'RE RIGHT, CAPTAIN! THERE IS STRENGTH IN--
KRAK!
NNNGH!
--IN DREAMS!
UNFORTUNATELY FOR YOU...
...THERE'S ALSO STRENGTH IN NUMBERS!

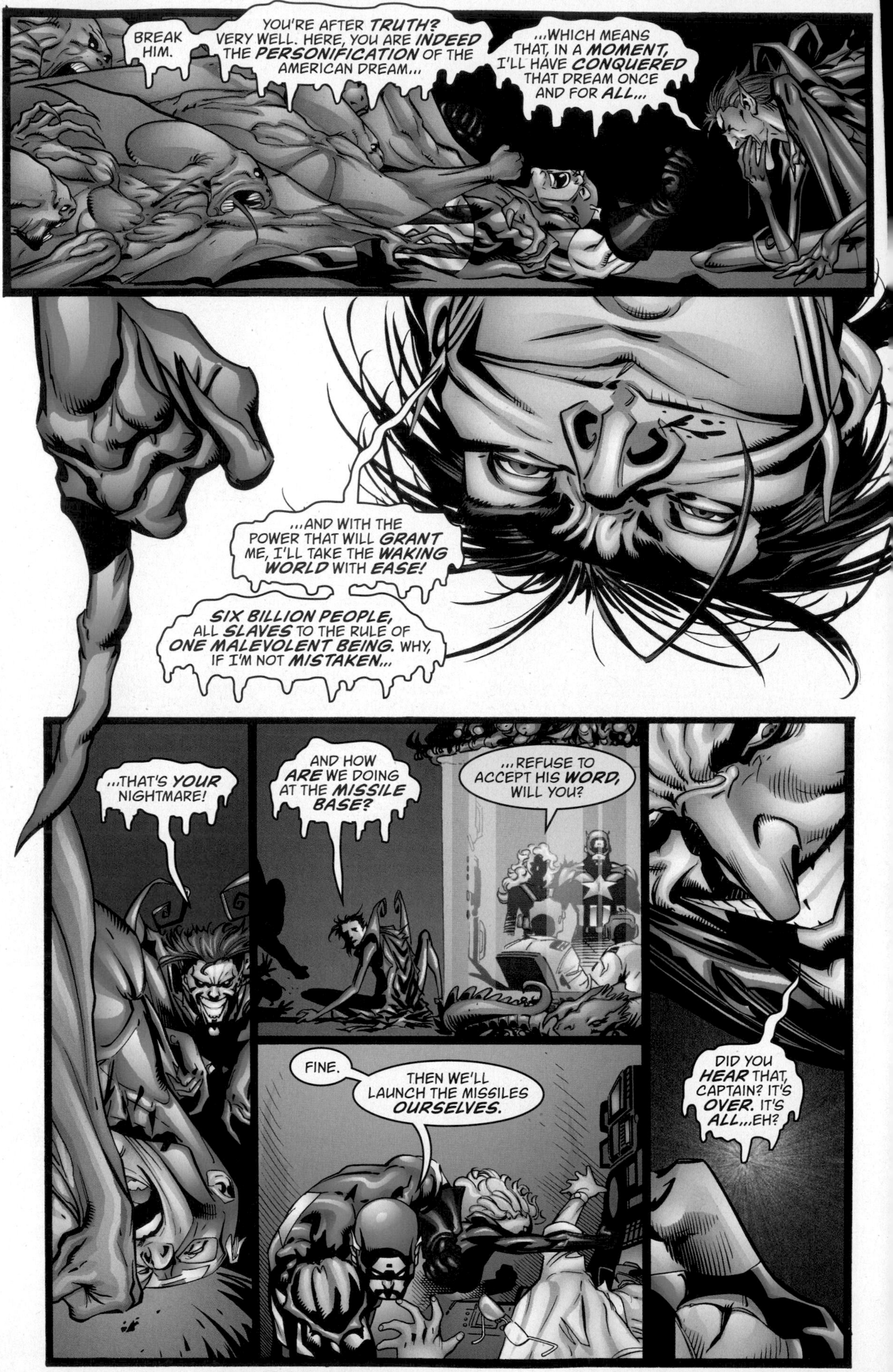
BREAK HIM.
YOU'RE AFTER TRUTH? VERY WELL. HERE, YOU ARE INDEED THE PERSONIFICATION OF THE AMERICAN DREAM...
...WHICH MEANS THAT, IN A MOMENT, I'LL HAVE CONQUERED THAT DREAM ONCE AND FOR ALL...
...AND WITH THE POWER THAT WILL GRANT ME, I'LL TAKE THE WAKING WORLD WITH EASE!
SIX BILLION PEOPLE, ALL SLAVES TO THE RULE OF ONE MALEVOLENT BEING. WHY, IF I'M NOT MISTAKEN...
...THAT'S YOUR NIGHTMARE!
AND HOW ARE WE DOING AT THE MISSILE BASE?
...REFUSE TO ACCEPT HIS WORD, WILL YOU?
FINE.
THEN WE'LL LAUNCH THE MISSILES OURSELVES.
DID YOU HEAR THAT, CAPTAIN? IT'S OVER. IT'S ALL...EH?

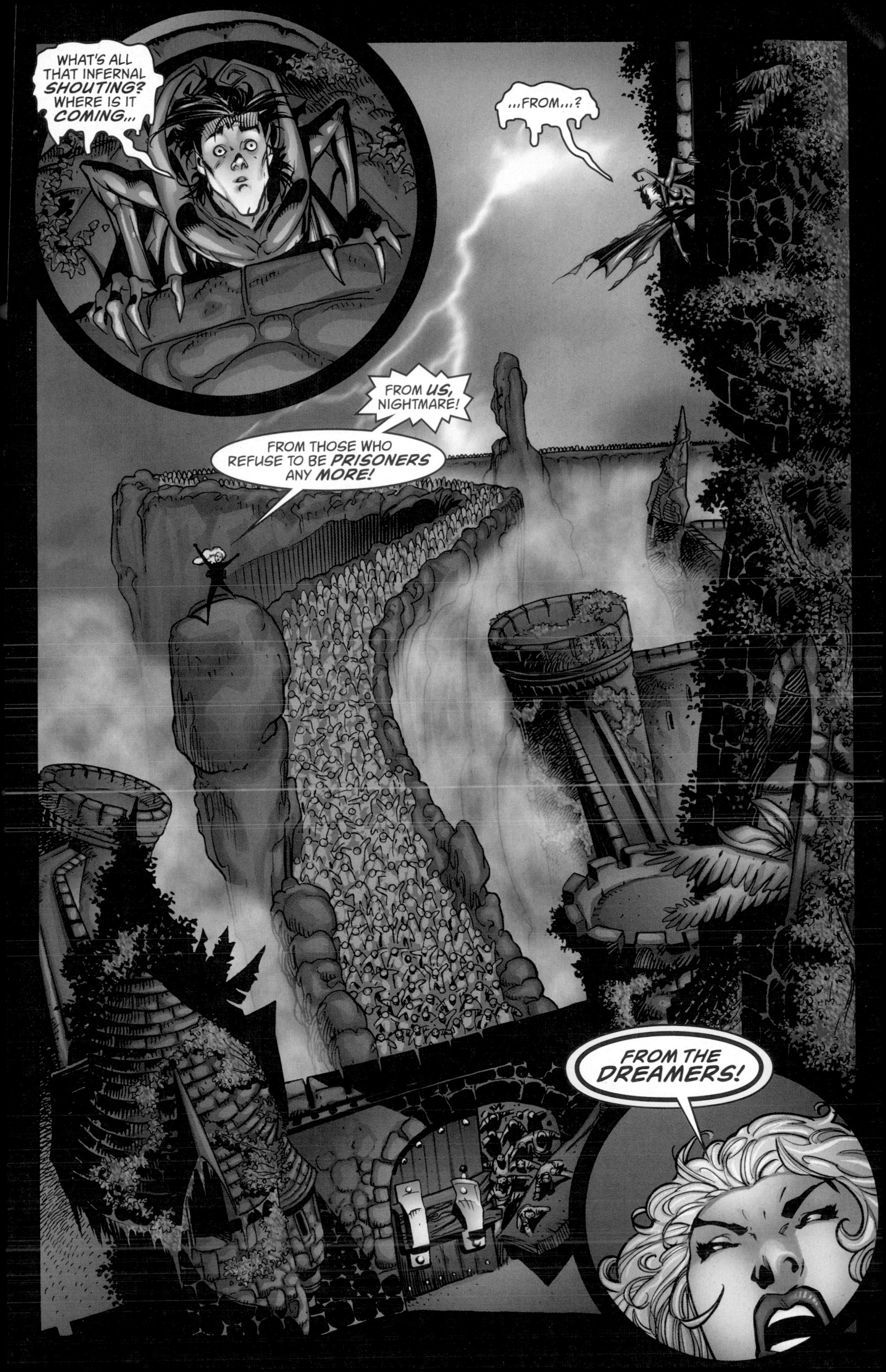
WHAT'S ALL THAT INFERNAL SHOUTING? WHERE IS IT COMING...
...FROM...?
FROM US, NIGHTMARE!
FROM THOSE WHO REFUSE TO BE PRISONERS ANY MORE!
FROM THE DREAMERS!

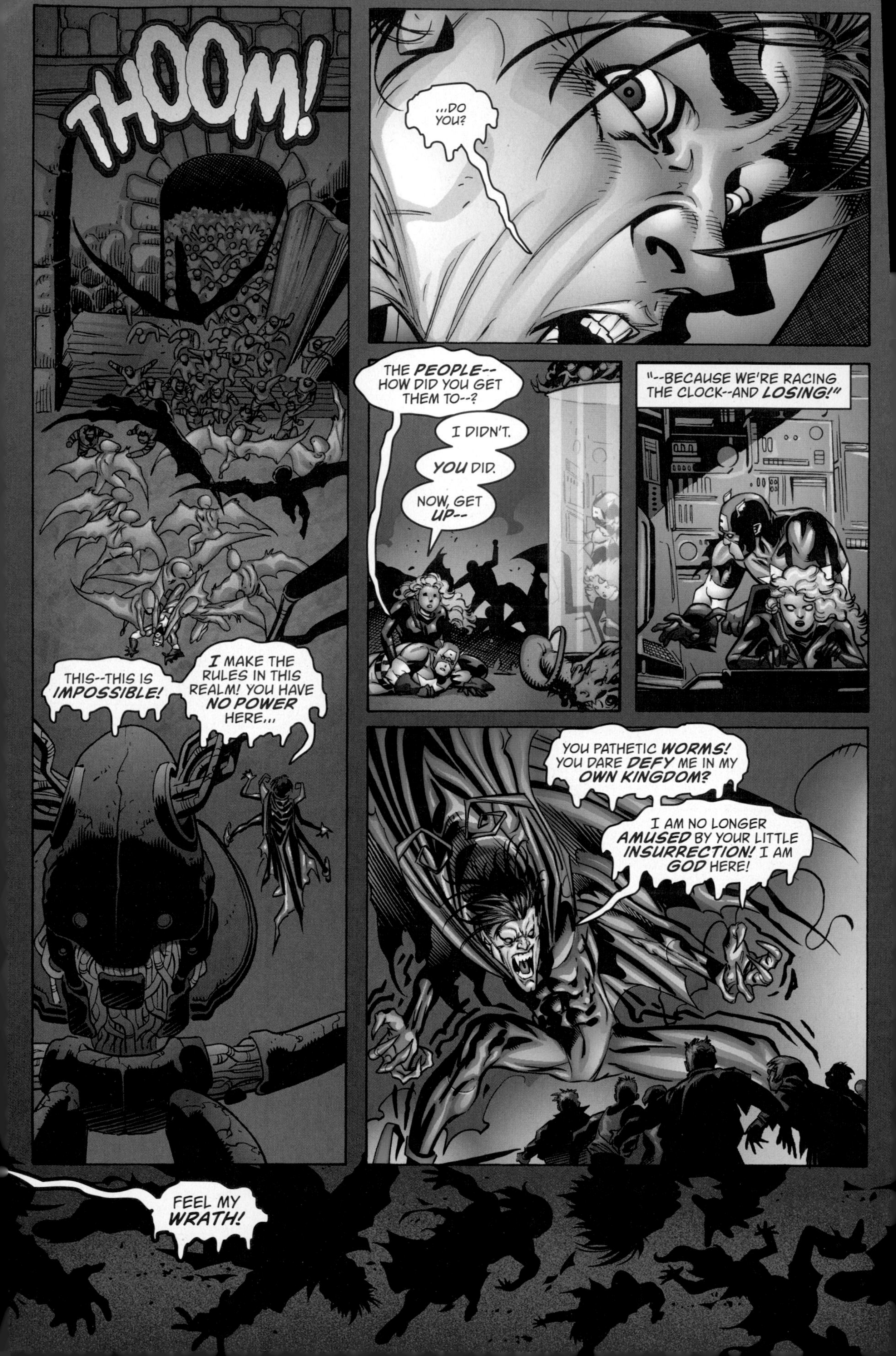
THOOM!
...DO YOU?
THE PEOPLE-- HOW DID YOU GET THEM TO--?
I DIDN'T.
YOU DID.
NOW, GET UP--
"--BECAUSE WE'RE RACING THE CLOCK--AND LOSING!"
THIS--THIS IS IMPOSSIBLE!
I MAKE THE RULES IN THIS REALM! YOU HAVE NO POWER HERE...
YOU PATHETIC WORMS! YOU DARE DEFY ME IN MY OWN KINGDOM?
I AM NO LONGER AMUSED BY YOUR LITTLE INSURRECTION! I AM GOD HERE!
FEEL MY WRATH!

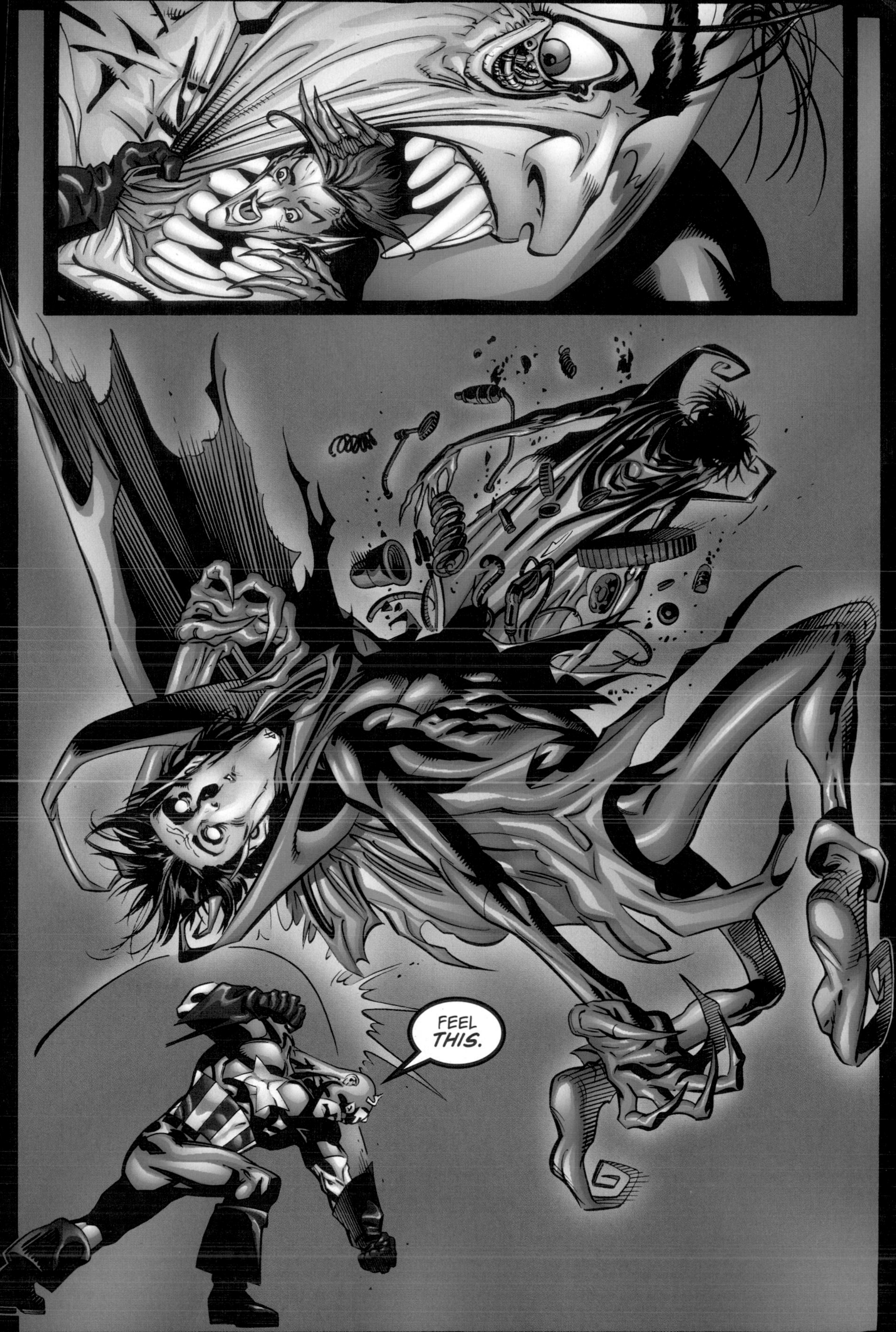
FEEL THIS.

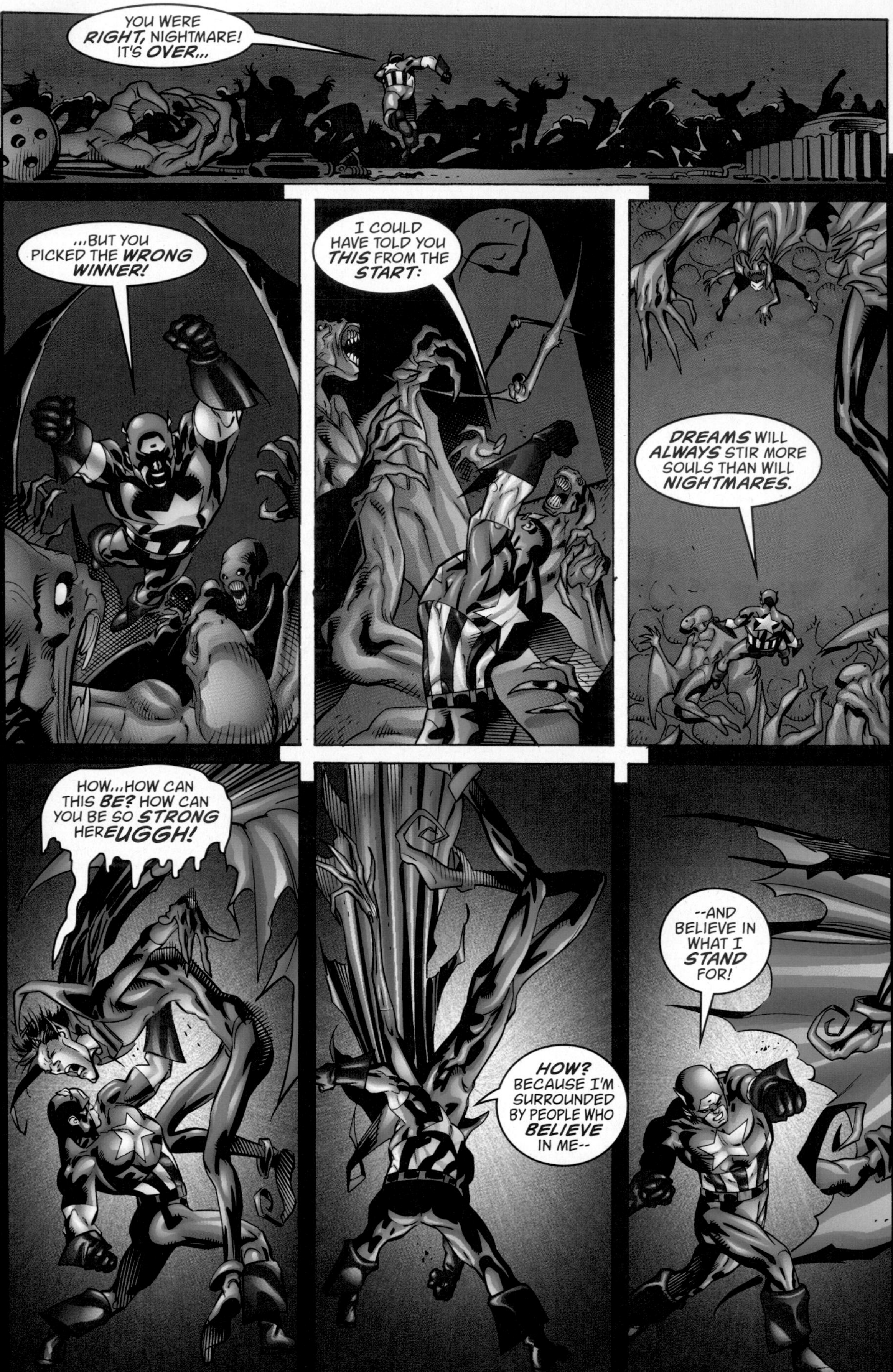
YOU WERE RIGHT, NIGHTMARE! IT'S OVER...
...BUT YOU PICKED THE WRONG WINNER!
I COULD HAVE TOLD YOU THIS FROM THE START:
DREAMS WILL ALWAYS STIR MORE SOULS THAN WILL NIGHTMARES.
HOW...HOW CAN THIS BE? HOW CAN YOU BE SO STRONG HEREEUGGH!
HOW? BECAUSE I'M SURROUNDED BY PEOPLE WHO BELIEVE IN ME--
--AND BELIEVE IN WHAT I STAND FOR!

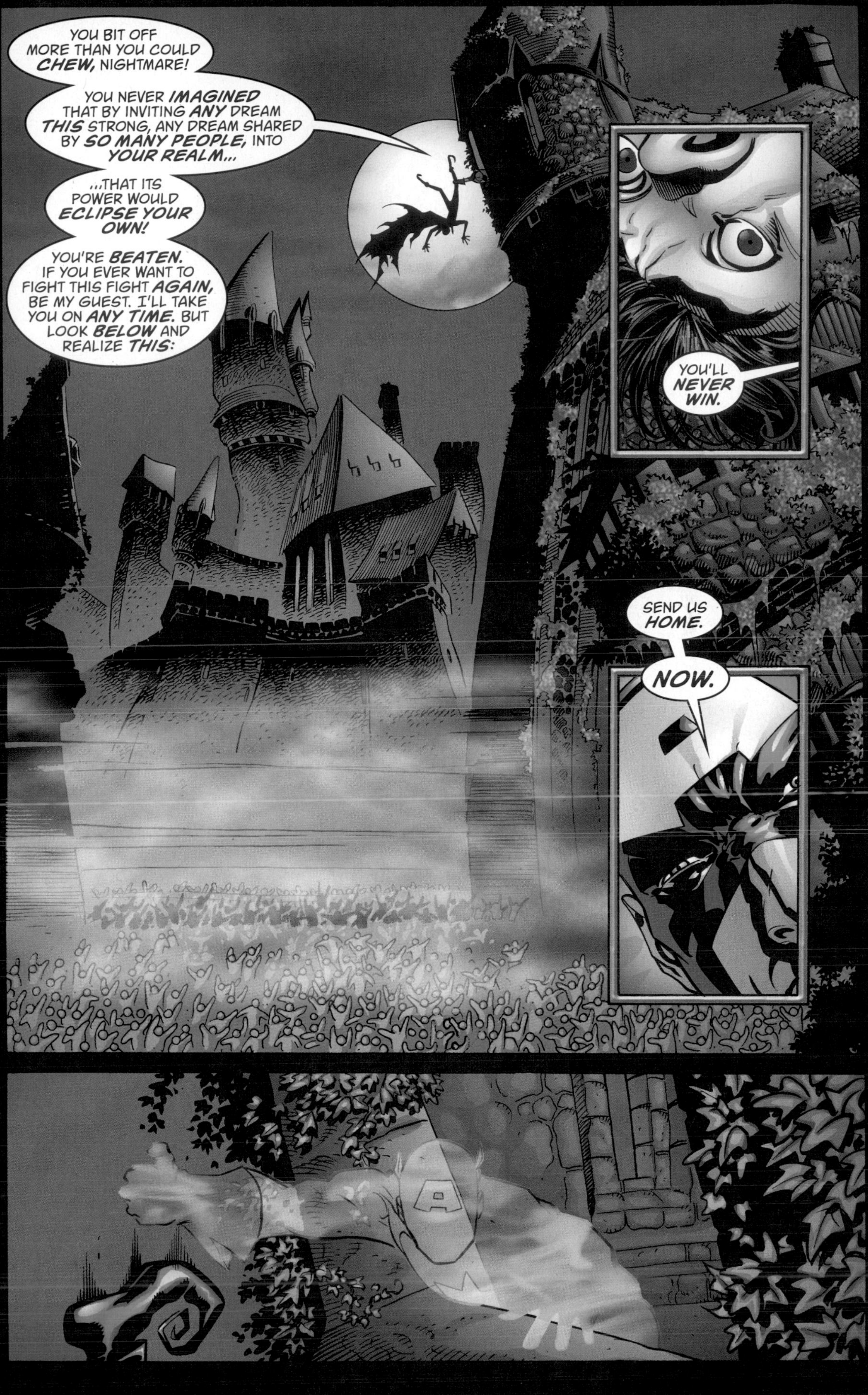
YOU BIT OFF MORE THAN YOU COULD CHEW, NIGHTMARE!
YOU NEVER IMAGINED THAT BY INVITING ANY DREAM THIS STRONG, ANY DREAM SHARED BY SO MANY PEOPLE, INTO YOUR REALM...
...THAT ITS POWER WOULD ECLIPSE YOUR OWN!
YOU'RE BEATEN. IF YOU EVER WANT TO FIGHT THIS FIGHT AGAIN, BE MY GUEST. I'LL TAKE YOU ON ANY TIME. BUT LOOK BELOW AND REALIZE THIS:
YOU'LL NEVER WIN.
SEND US HOME.
NOW.

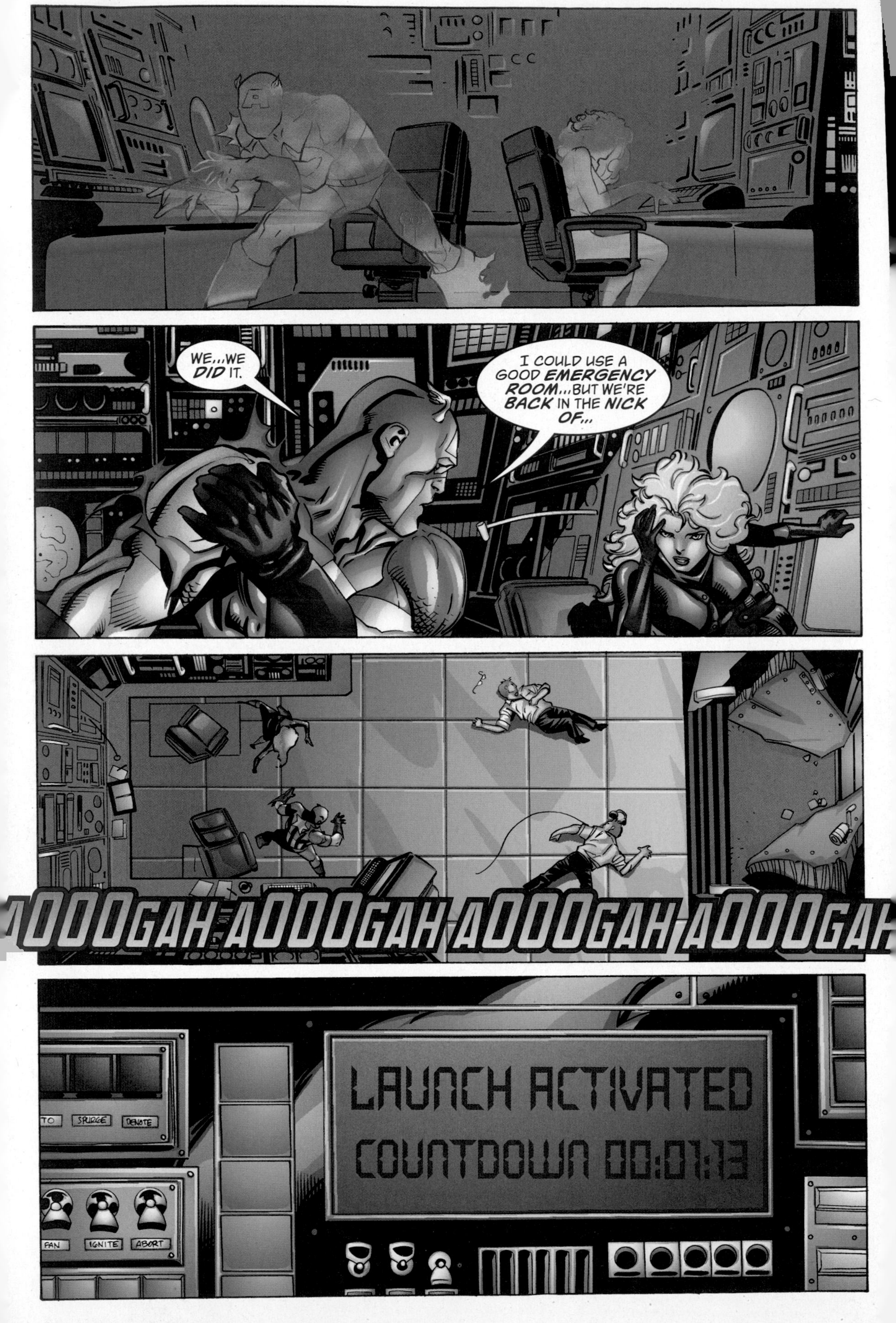
WE...WE DID IT.
I COULD USE A GOOD EMERGENCY ROOM...BUT WE'RE BACK IN THE NICK OF...
AOOOGAH AOOOGAH AOOOGAH AOOOGAH
LAUNCH ACTIVATED
COUNTDOWN 00:01:13
FAN
IGNITE
ABORT

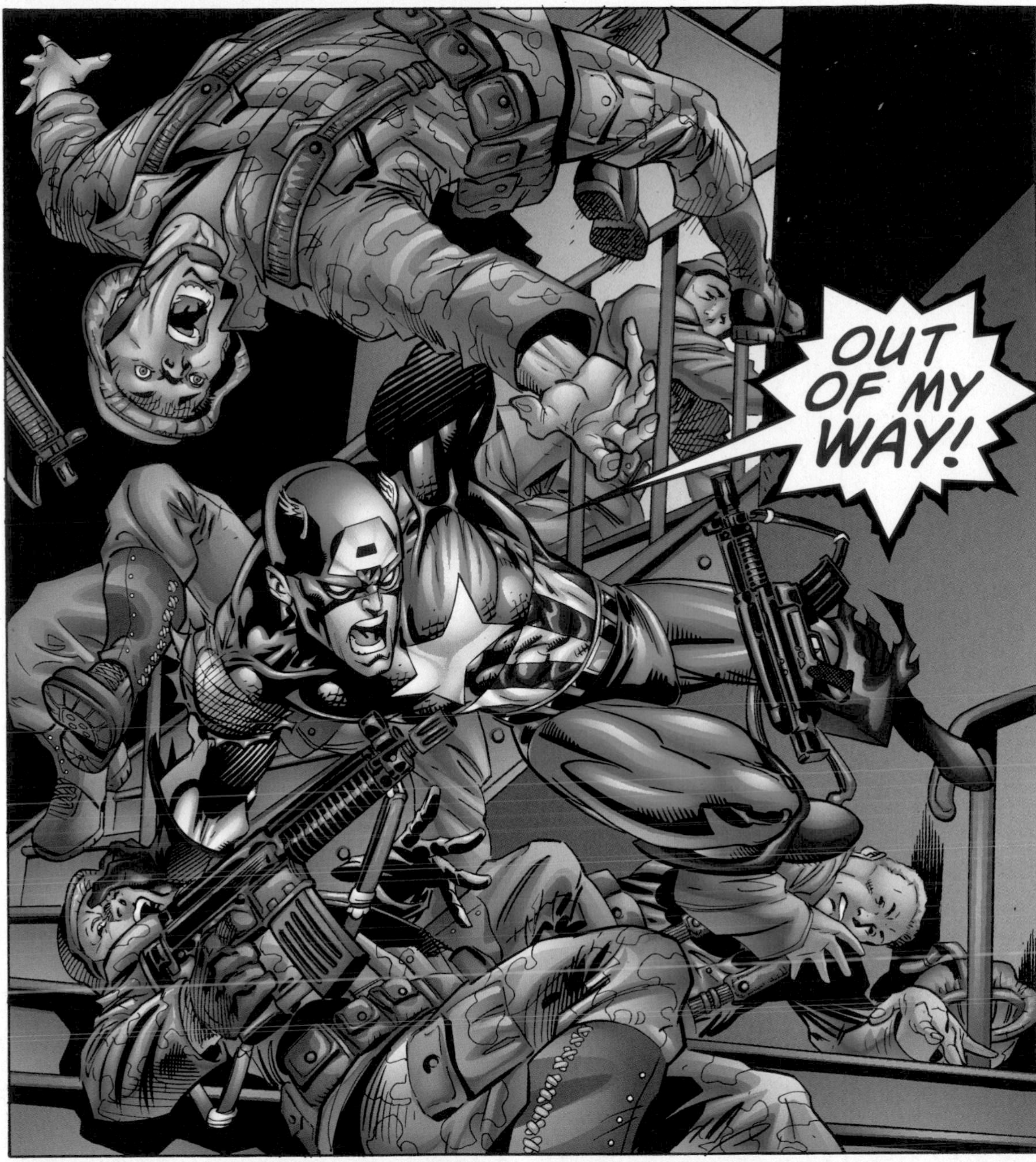
OUT OF MY WAY!
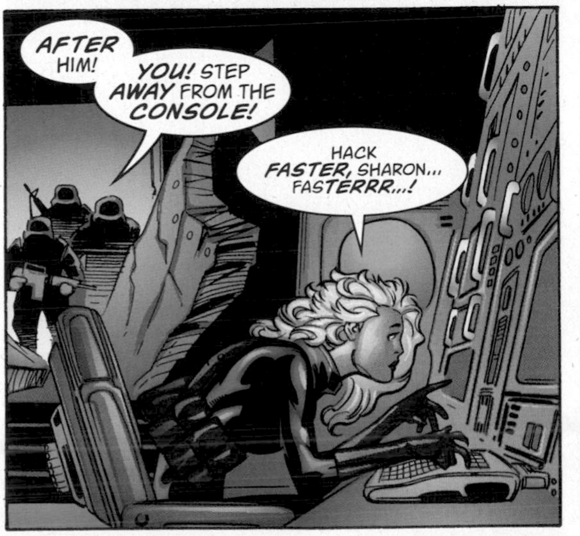
AFTER HIM!
YOU! STEP AWAY FROM THE CONSOLE!
HACK FASTER, SHARON... FASTERRR...!
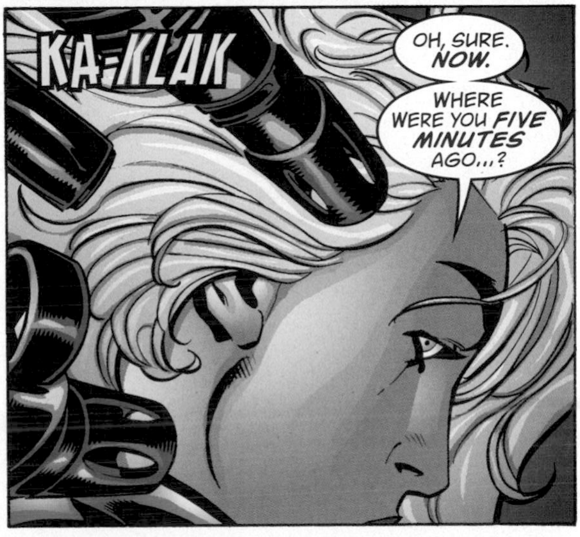
KA-KLAK
OH, SURE. NOW.
WHERE WERE YOU FIVE MINUTES AGO...?

LIFTOFF IN T-MINUS THIRTY-FIVE...

...SILO DOORS UNLOCKED...

...AND OPENING...

...T-MINUS THIRTY...

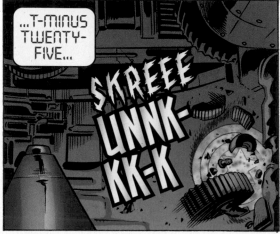

...T-MINUS TWENTY-FIVE...

SKREEE UNNK-KK-K

BLAST IT! I'M TOO LATE!

THOUGHT I COULD JAM THE SILO GEARS IN TIME--BUT NO! THE DOOR'S STILL HALF-OPEN!

ALL I CAN DO NOW...

NNNNNNFF!

...IS CLOSE IT BY HAND!

...T-MINUS TWENTY...

...T-MINUS FIFTEEN...

IT'S *TOO LATE* TO ABORT *TAKEOFF*--

--BUT NUKES NEED TO REACH A *SPECIFIED ALTITUDE* TO BE *ATOMICALLY ARMED!*

NNNGH! COME *ON*...

...T-MINUS TEN...

IF I CAN *SEAL* THE *TITANIUM DOORS,* THE MISSILE WILL STILL *LAUNCH*--

--BUT IT'LL *CRIPPLE* ITSELF AND *SELF-ABORT* WHEN IT CRASHES *THROUGH!*

COME *ONNN*...

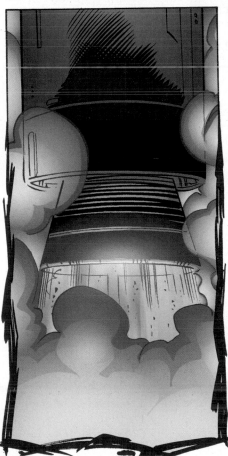

...T-MINUS NINE ...EIGHT...

COME *ON!*

CHOOM!

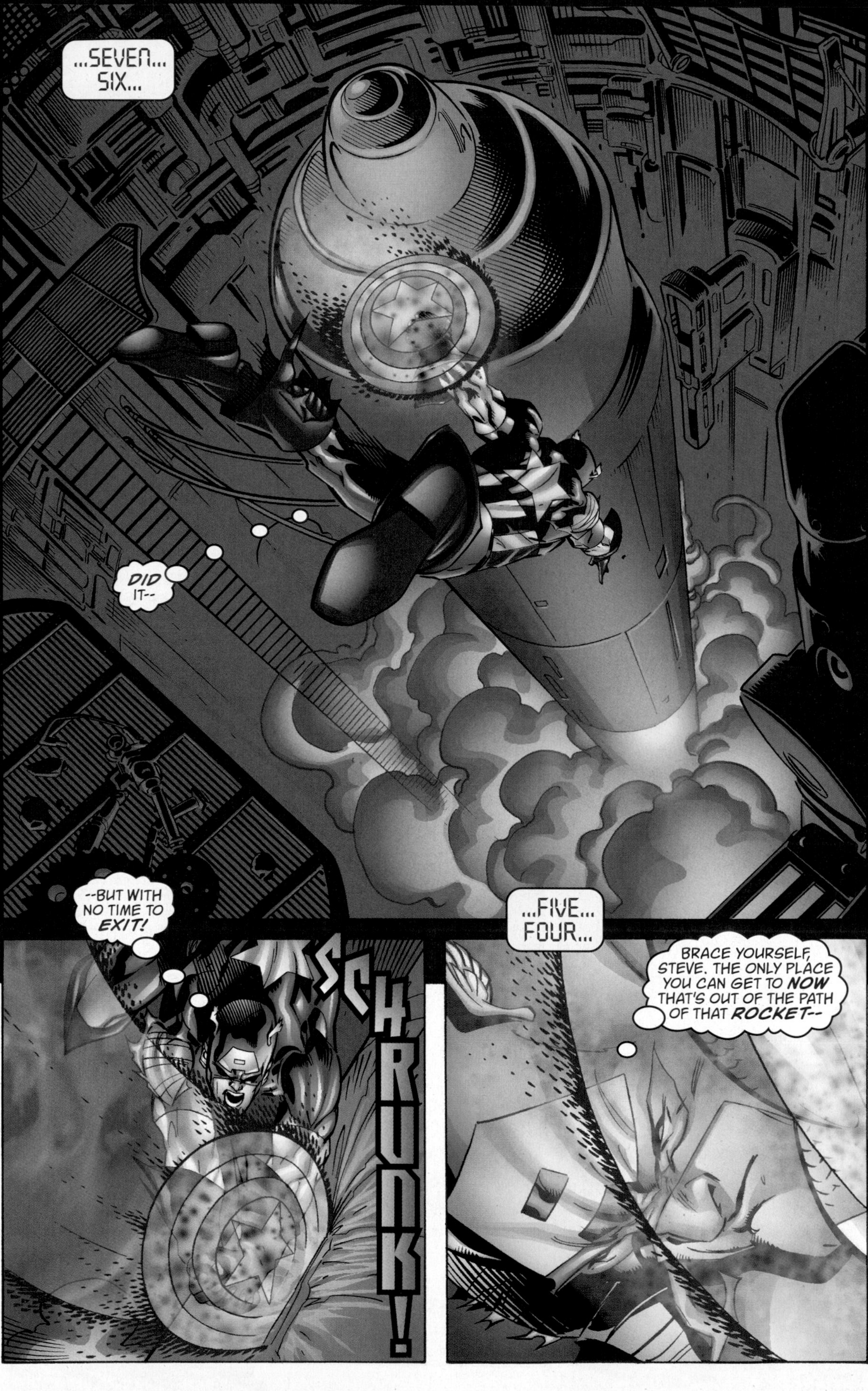
...SEVEN... SIX...
DID IT--
--BUT WITH NO TIME TO EXIT!
SCHRUNK!
...FIVE... FOUR...
BRACE YOURSELF, STEVE. THE ONLY PLACE YOU CAN GET TO NOW THAT'S OUT OF THE PATH OF THAT ROCKET--

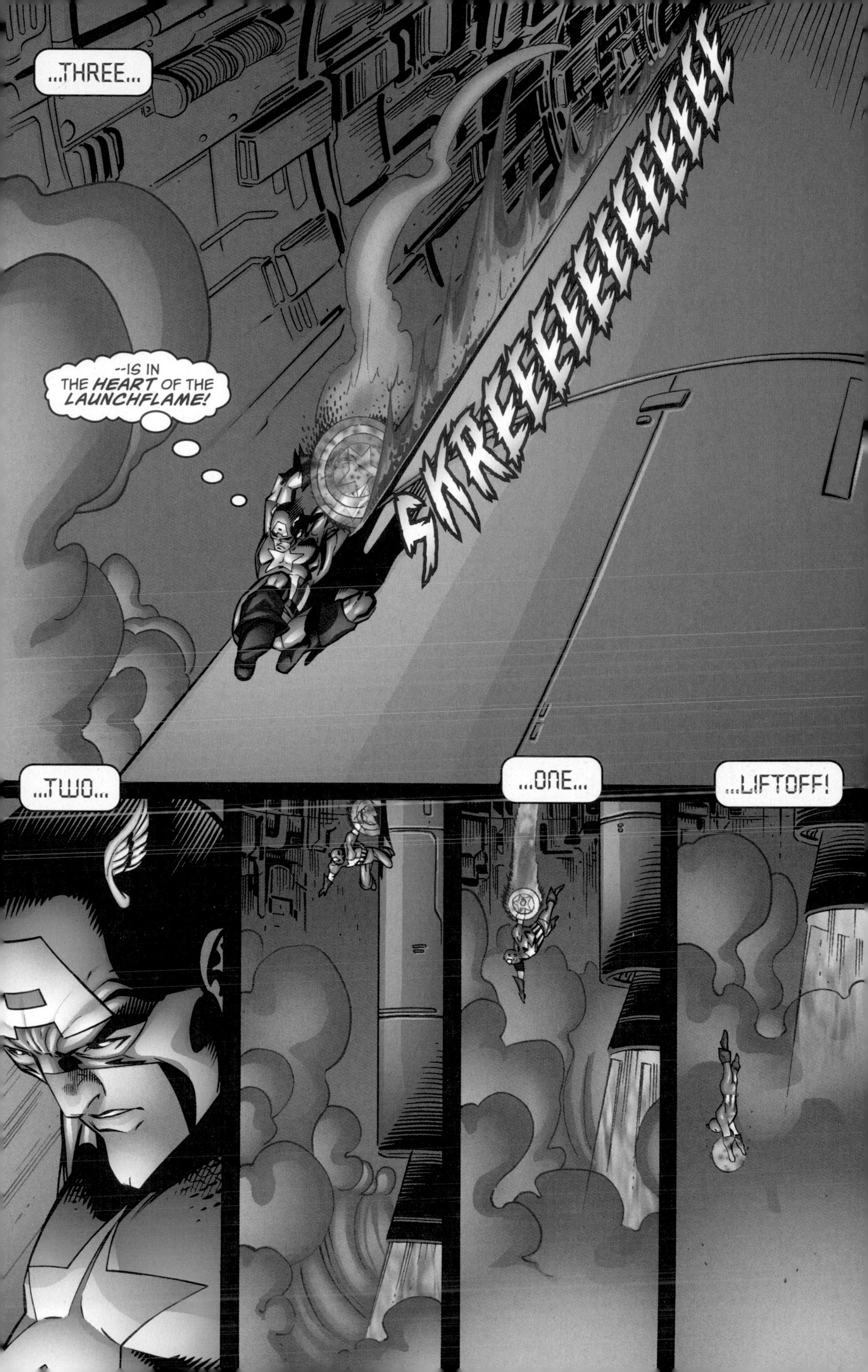
...THREE...
--IS IN THE HEART OF THE LAUNCHFLAME!
SKREEEEEEEEEE
...TWO...
...ONE...
...LIFTOFF!

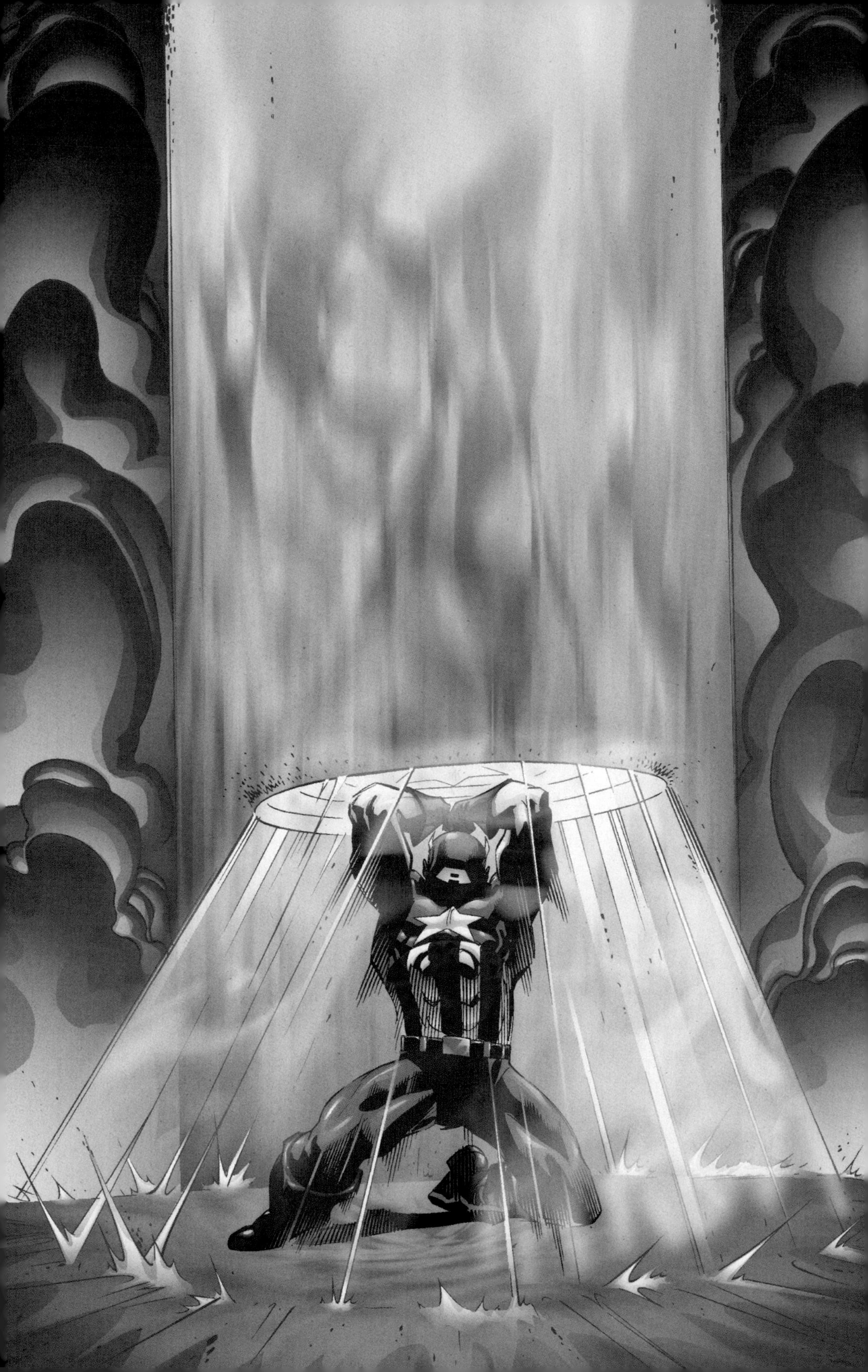

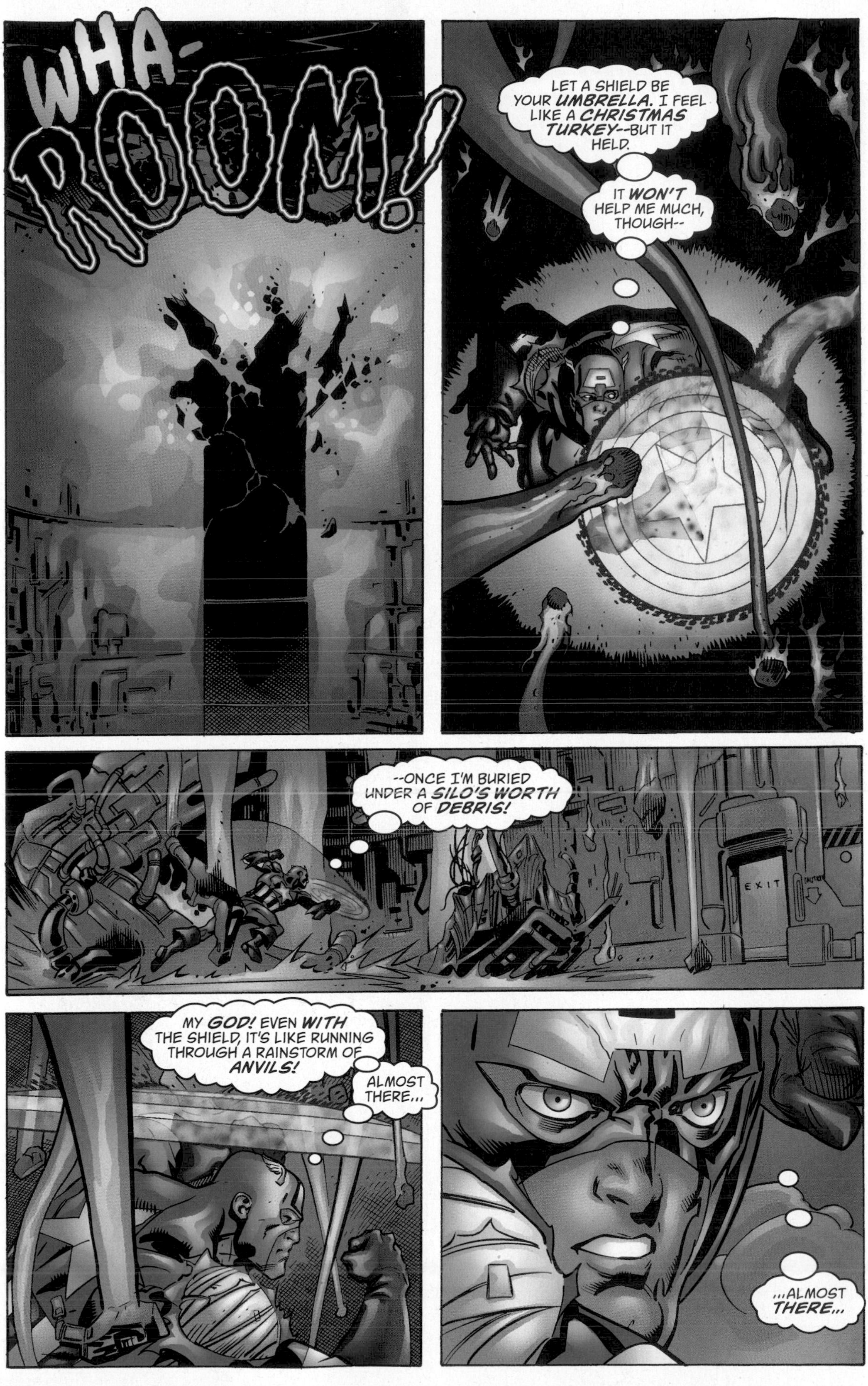
WHA-ROOM!
LET A SHIELD BE YOUR UMBRELLA. I FEEL LIKE A CHRISTMAS TURKEY--BUT IT HELD.
IT WON'T HELP ME MUCH, THOUGH--
--ONCE I'M BURIED UNDER A SILO'S WORTH OF DEBRIS!
EXIT
MY GOD! EVEN WITH THE SHIELD, IT'S LIKE RUNNING THROUGH A RAINSTORM OF ANVILS!
ALMOST THERE...
...ALMOST THERE...

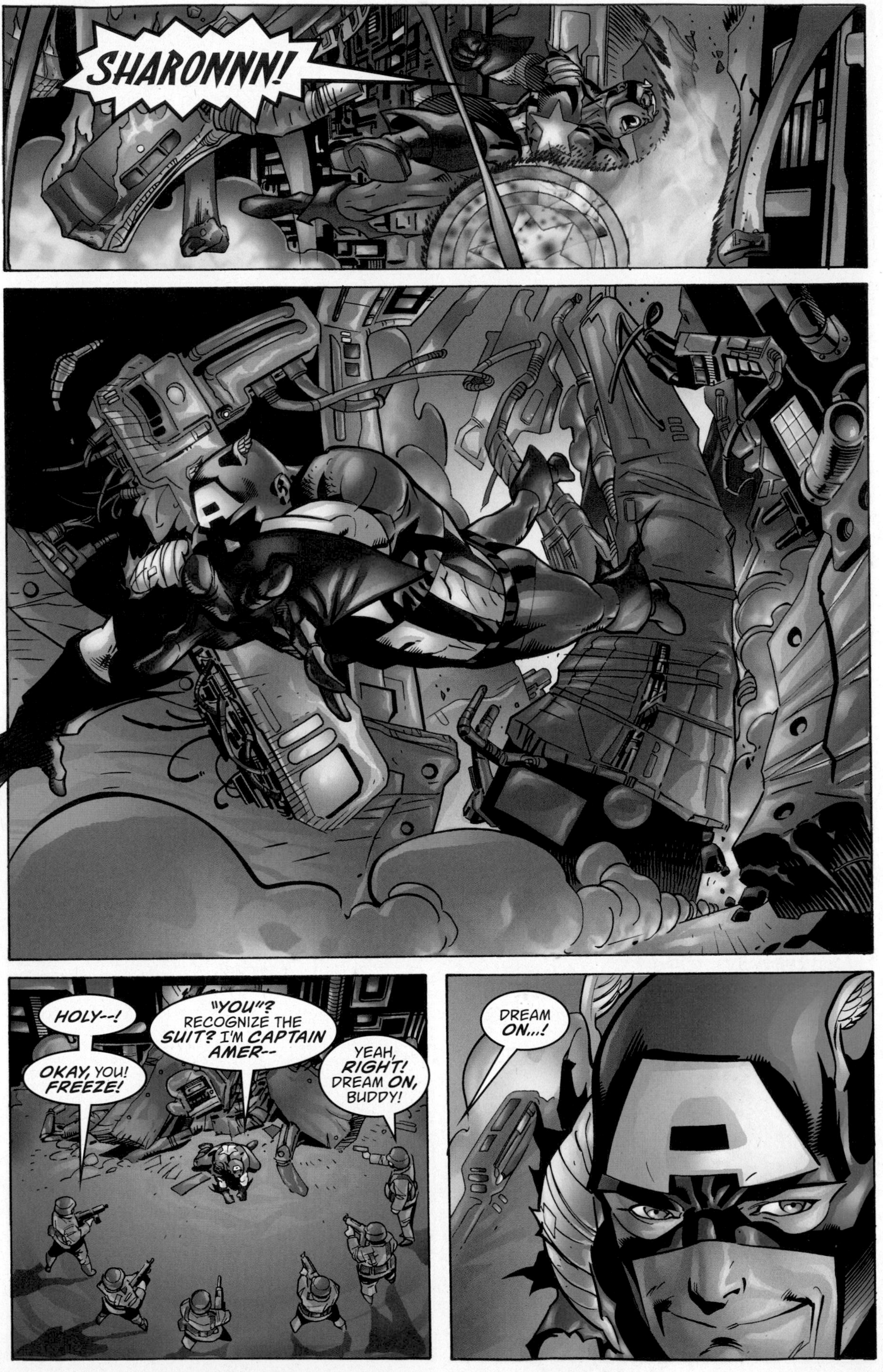
SHARONNN!
HOLY--!
OKAY, YOU! FREEZE!
"YOU"? RECOGNIZE THE SUIT? I'M CAPTAIN AMER--
YEAH, RIGHT! DREAM ON, BUDDY!
DREAM ON...!

...AND NIGHTMARE'S VICTIMS--HERE 'N' ALL OVER TH' *COUNTRY*--ARE COMIN' *AROUND*, CAP.

TO MOST OF 'EM, THE WHOLE EXPERIENCE WAS JUST A *BAD DREAM*. HOW 'BOUT FOR *YOU* TWO?

I'LL LIVE.

ME, *TOO*--AND *OUTSIDE* OF MILITARY CUSTODY. THANKS FOR SQUARING THINGS WITH THE *ARMY*, DUGAN.

EXECUTIVE ORDER, CAP. *S.H.I.E.L.D.'s* CLEARIN' *ALL* THE SLEEPWALKERS OF THEIR CRIMINAL ACTIONS. WE'LL COME UP WITH SOME *PLAUSIBLE* EXPLANATION FOR 'EM.

BELIEVE ME...WE'VE SEEN *WEIRDER* STUFF.

WHAT? WHAT'S WRONG? DAY *SAVED*, RIGHT? TELL THE GOVERN-MENT TO TAKE THE SILO OUT OF YOUR *PAYCHECK*.

IT'S NOT THAT. IT'S HOW DUGAN TALKED ABOUT NIGHTMARE'S SCHEMES AS IF SUPERNATURAL FORCES WERE THE MOST NATURAL THING IN THE *WORLD*.

"AS IF I SHOULD *EXPECT* TO ENCOUNTER THEM AGAIN... IF NOT *NOW*,...

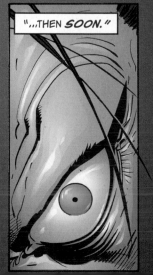

"...THEN *SOON*."

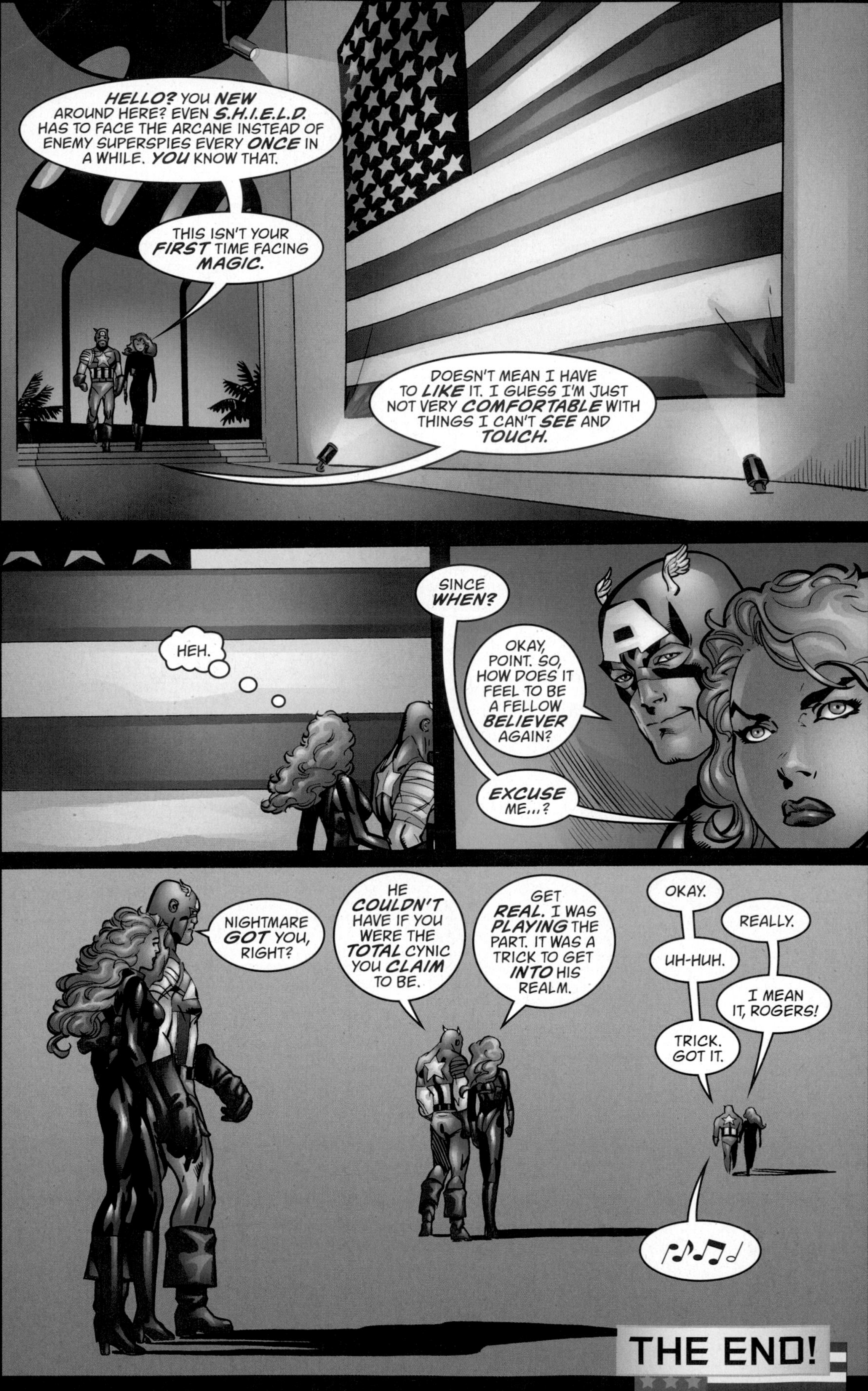
HELLO? YOU NEW AROUND HERE? EVEN S.H.I.E.L.D. HAS TO FACE THE ARCANE INSTEAD OF ENEMY SUPERSPIES EVERY ONCE IN A WHILE. YOU KNOW THAT.
THIS ISN'T YOUR FIRST TIME FACING MAGIC.
DOESN'T MEAN I HAVE TO LIKE IT. I GUESS I'M JUST NOT VERY COMFORTABLE WITH THINGS I CAN'T SEE AND TOUCH.
HEH.
SINCE WHEN?
OKAY, POINT. SO, HOW DOES IT FEEL TO BE A FELLOW BELIEVER AGAIN?
EXCUSE ME...?
NIGHTMARE GOT YOU, RIGHT?
HE COULDN'T HAVE IF YOU WERE THE TOTAL CYNIC YOU CLAIM TO BE.
GET REAL. I WAS PLAYING THE PART. IT WAS A TRICK TO GET INTO HIS REALM.
OKAY.
REALLY.
UH-HUH.
I MEAN IT, ROGERS!
TRICK. GOT IT.
♪♪♫♩
THE END!

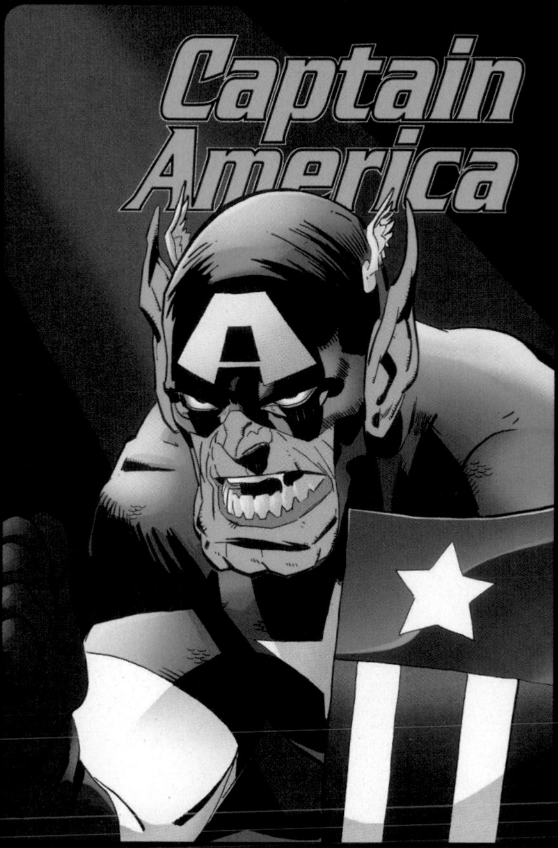
Captain
America

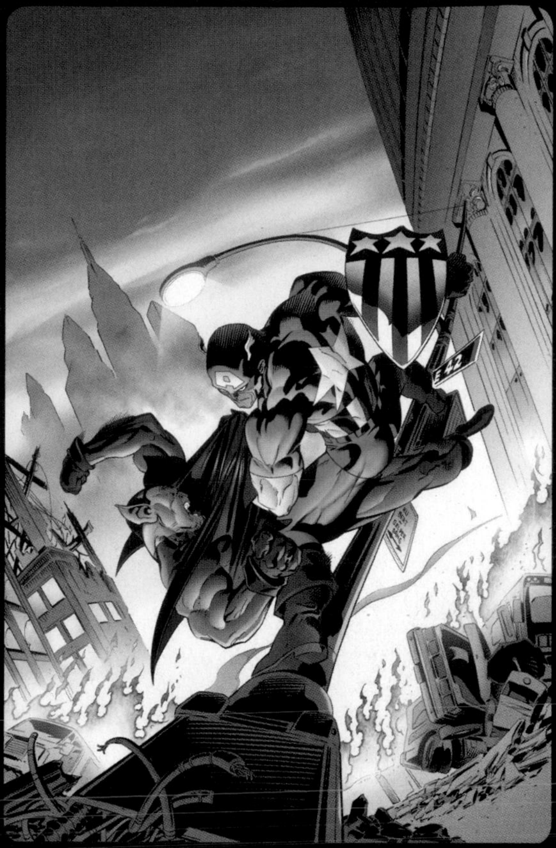

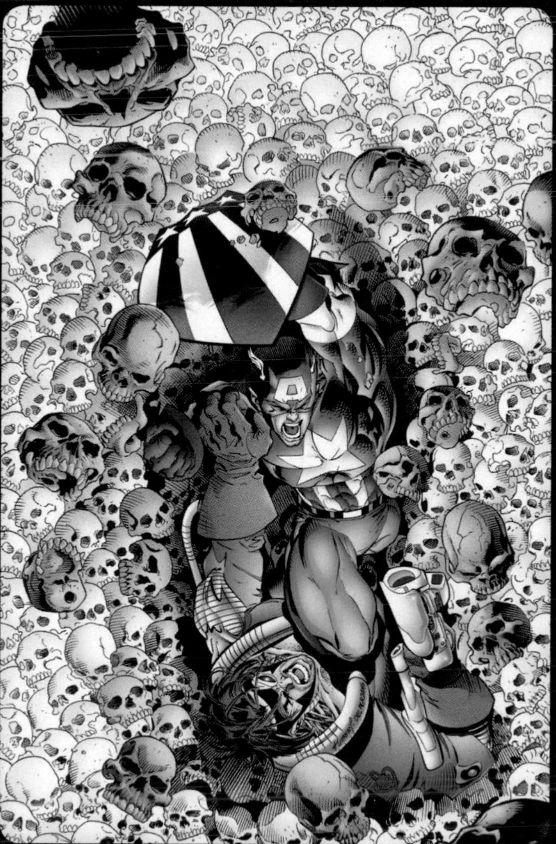

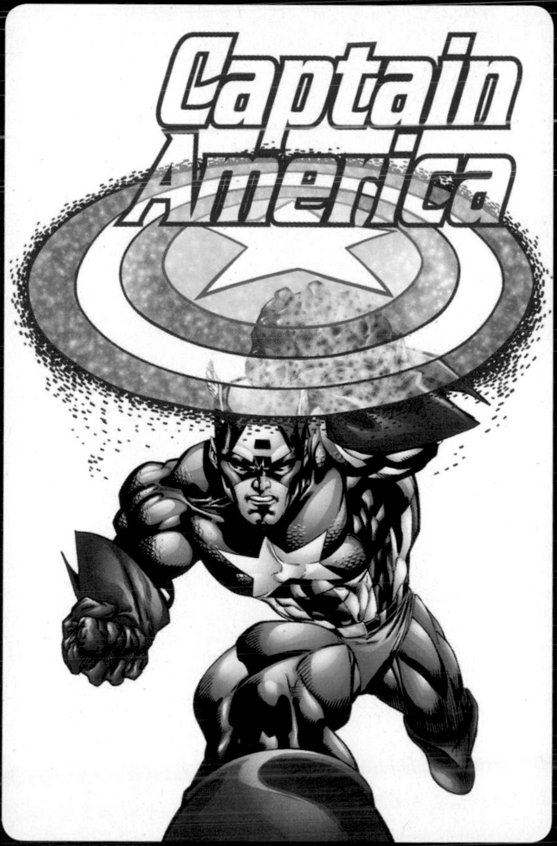
Captain
America

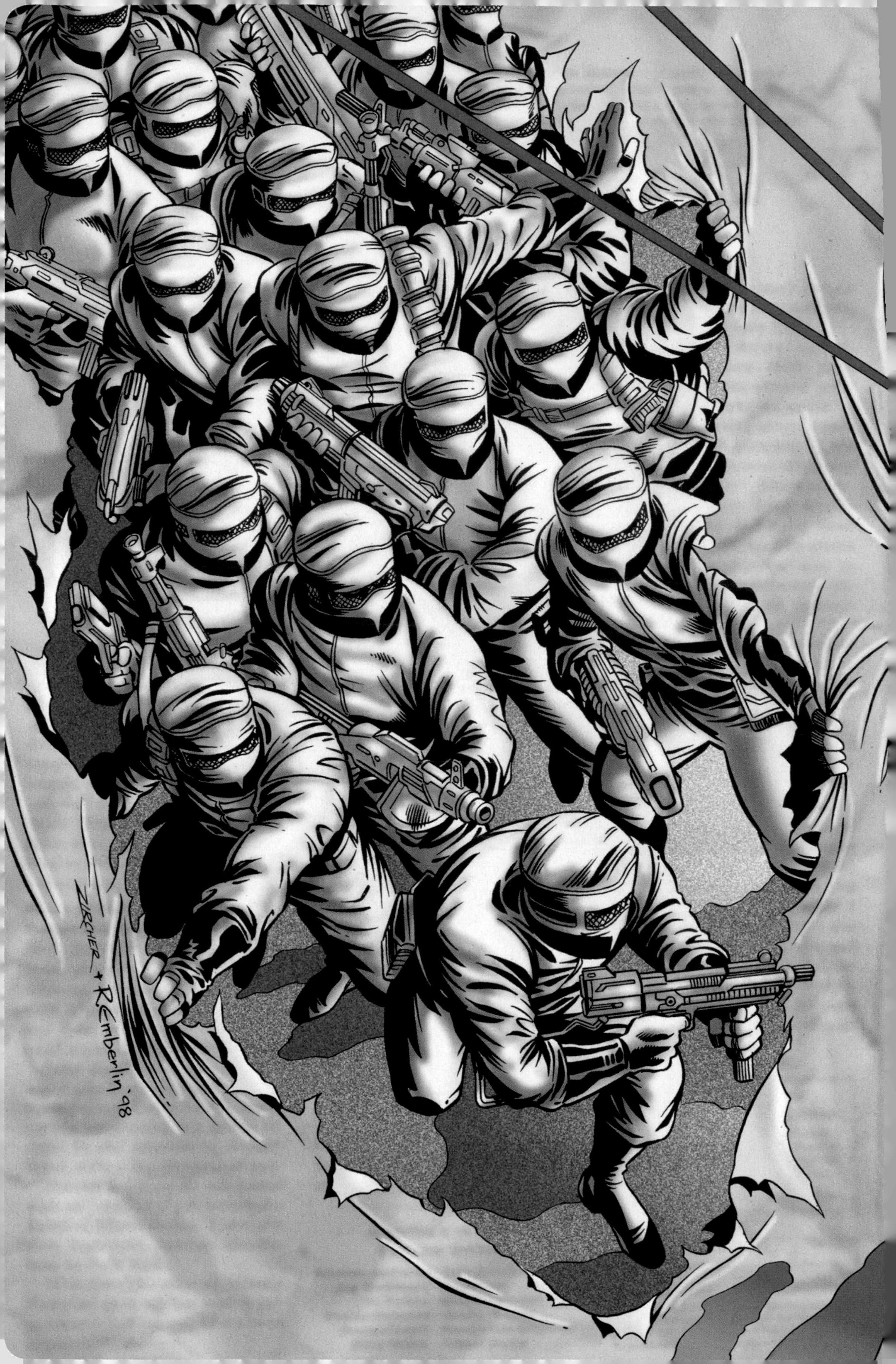
ZIRCHER + REmberlin '98

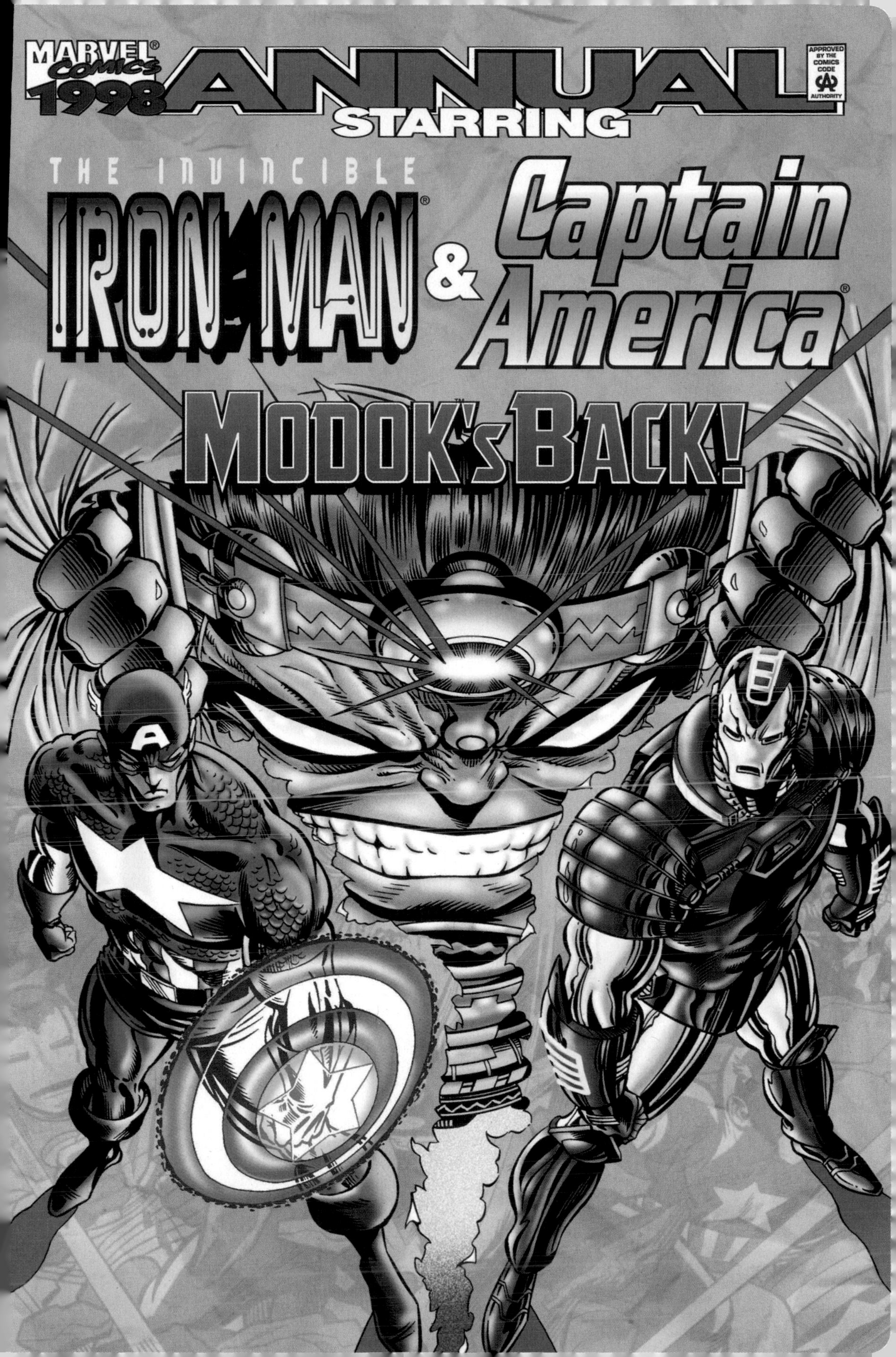
MARVEL COMICS
1998
ANNUAL
STARRING
APPROVED BY THE COMICS CODE AUTHORITY
THE INVINCIBLE
IRON MAN
&
Captain America
MODOK's BACK!

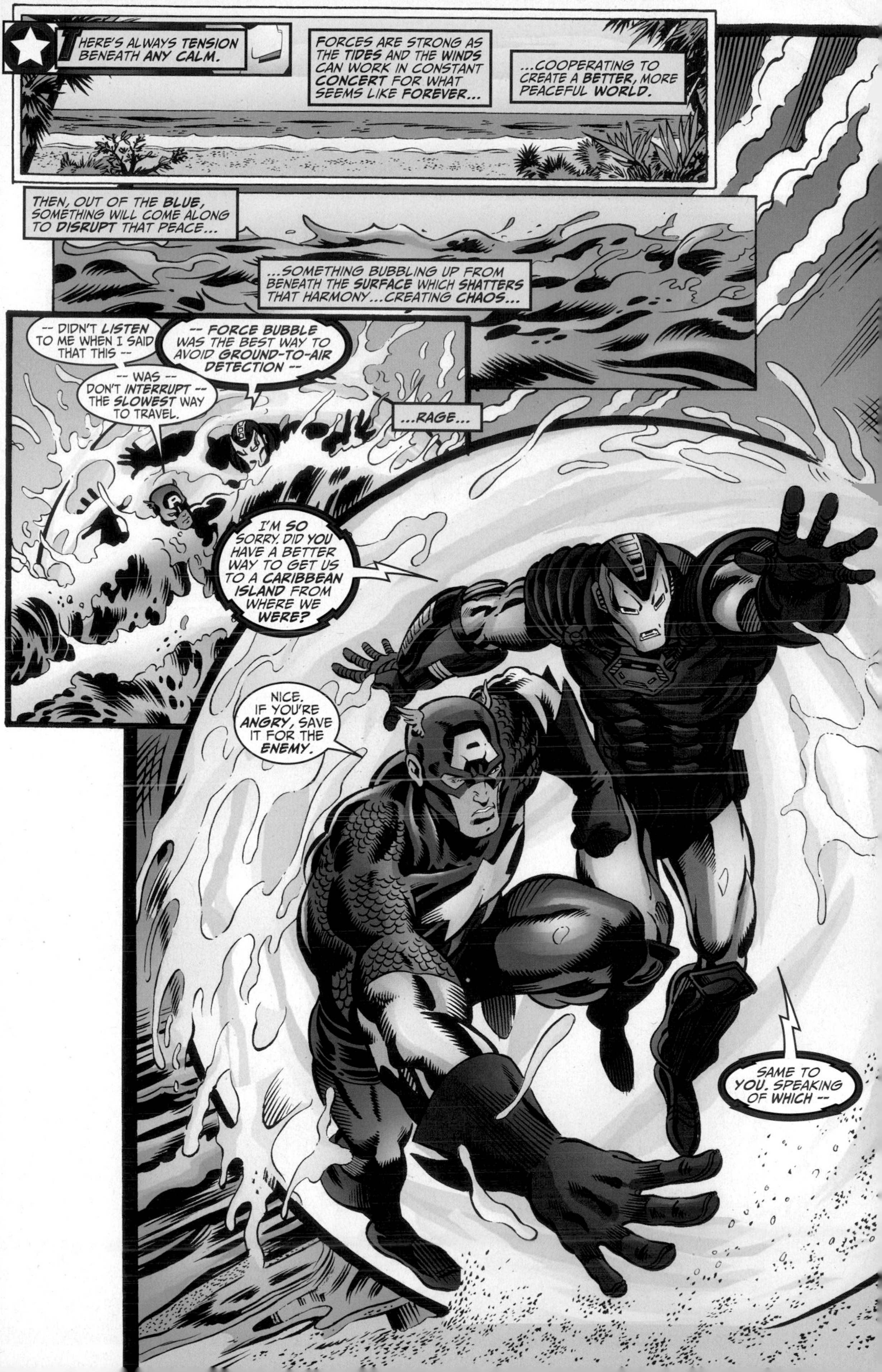
THERE'S ALWAYS TENSION BENEATH ANY CALM.
FORCES ARE STRONG AS THE TIDES AND THE WINDS CAN WORK IN CONSTANT CONCERT FOR WHAT SEEMS LIKE FOREVER...
...COOPERATING TO CREATE A BETTER, MORE PEACEFUL WORLD.
THEN, OUT OF THE BLUE, SOMETHING WILL COME ALONG TO DISRUPT THAT PEACE...
...SOMETHING BUBBLING UP FROM BENEATH THE SURFACE WHICH SHATTERS THAT HARMONY...CREATING CHAOS...
-- DIDN'T LISTEN TO ME WHEN I SAID THAT THIS --
-- FORCE BUBBLE WAS THE BEST WAY TO AVOID GROUND-TO-AIR DETECTION --
-- WAS -- DON'T INTERRUPT -- THE SLOWEST WAY TO TRAVEL.
...RAGE...
I'M SO SORRY. DID YOU HAVE A BETTER WAY TO GET US TO A CARIBBEAN ISLAND FROM WHERE WE WERE?
NICE. IF YOU'RE ANGRY, SAVE IT FOR THE ENEMY.
SAME TO YOU. SPEAKING OF WHICH --

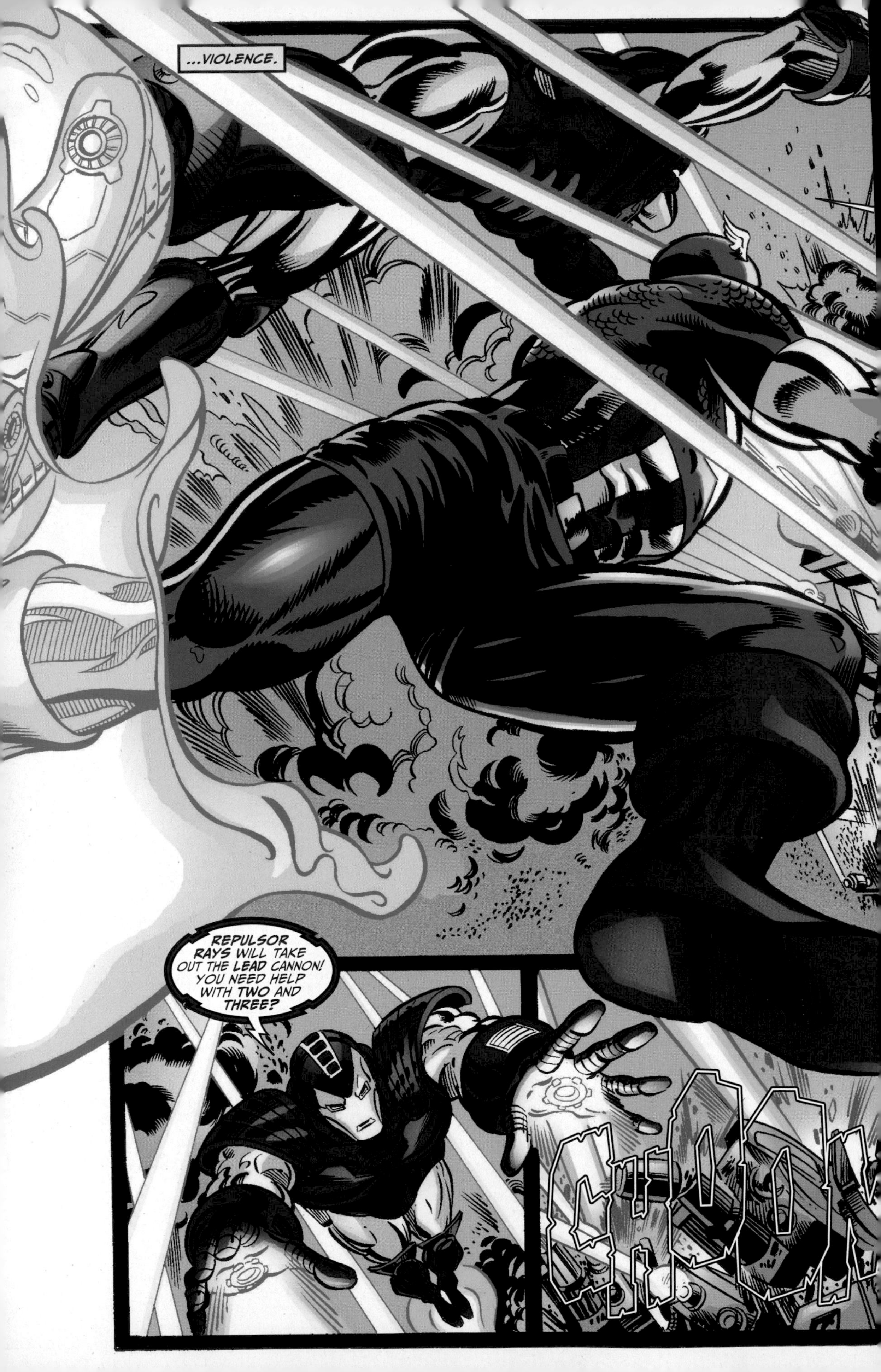
...VIOLENCE.
REPULSOR RAYS WILL TAKE OUT THE LEAD CANNON! YOU NEED HELP WITH TWO AND THREE?

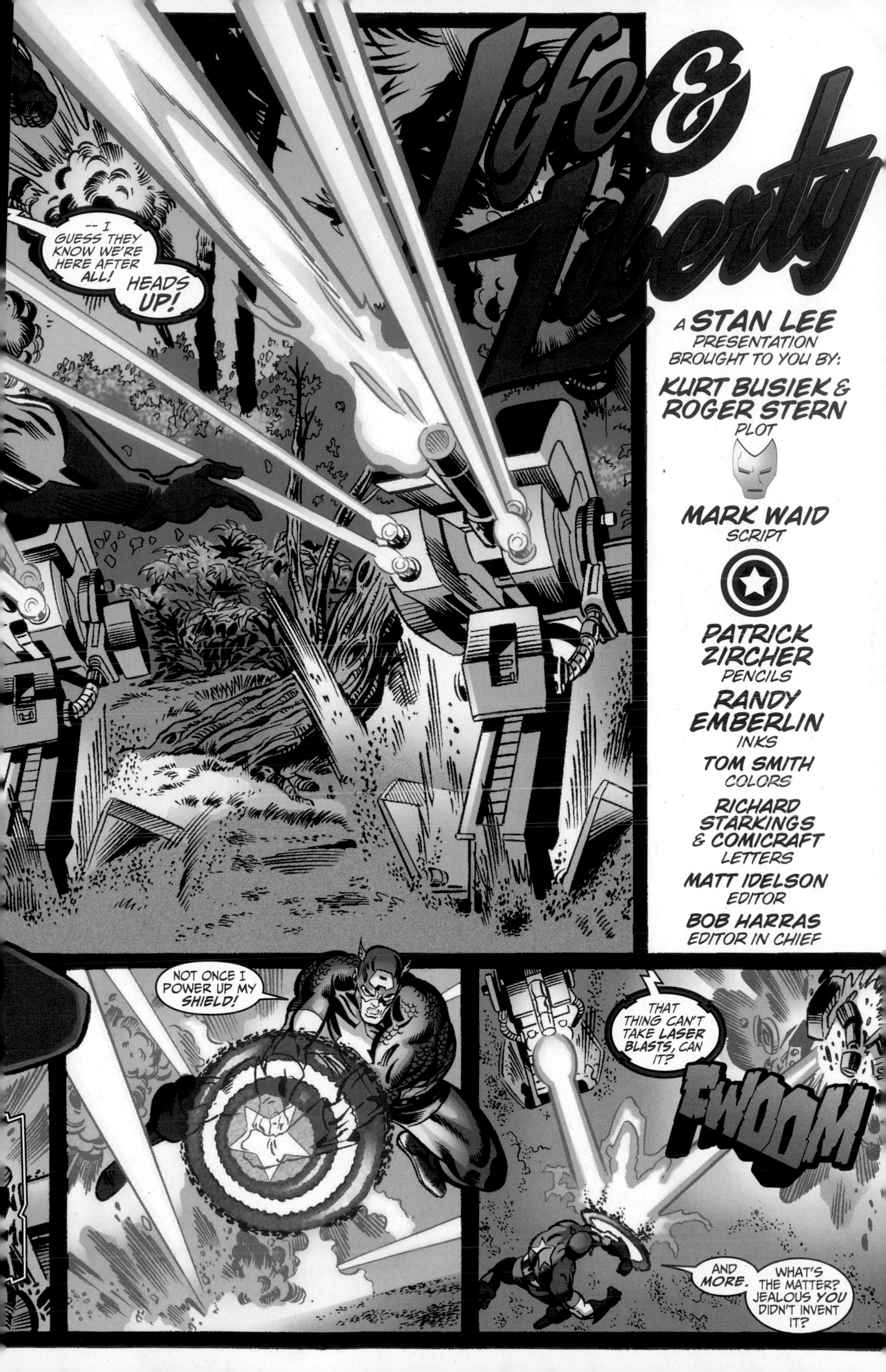
-- I GUESS THEY KNOW WE'RE HERE AFTER ALL!
HEADS UP!
Life & Liberty
A STAN LEE PRESENTATION BROUGHT TO YOU BY:
KURT BUSIEK & ROGER STERN
PLOT
MARK WAID
SCRIPT
PATRICK ZIRCHER
PENCILS
RANDY EMBERLIN
INKS
TOM SMITH
COLORS
RICHARD STARKINGS & COMICRAFT
LETTERS
MATT IDELSON
EDITOR
BOB HARRAS
EDITOR IN CHIEF
NOT ONCE I POWER UP MY SHIELD!
THAT THING CAN'T TAKE LASER BLASTS, CAN IT?
FWOOM
AND MORE.
WHAT'S THE MATTER? JEALOUS YOU DIDN'T INVENT IT?

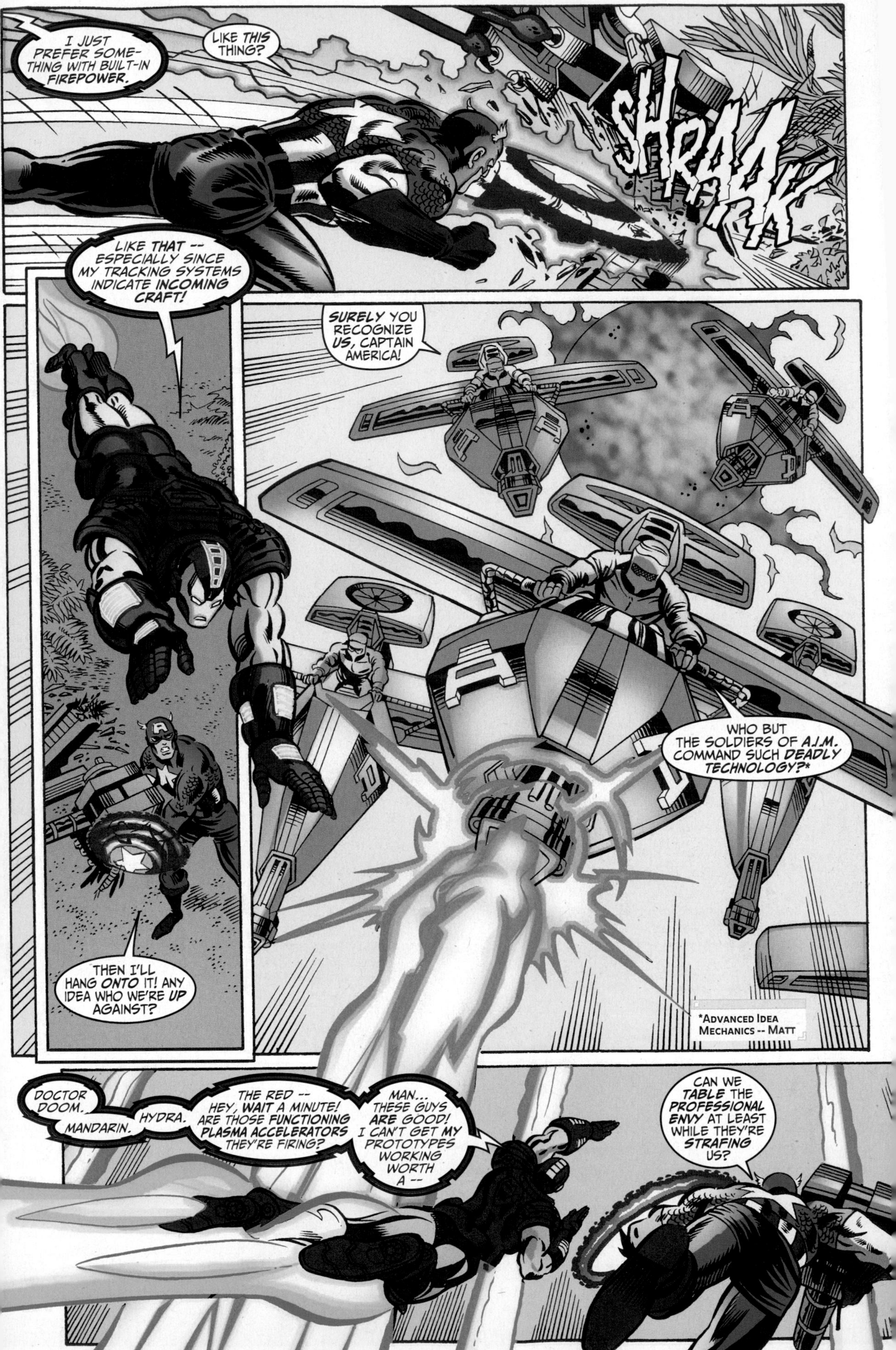

I JUST PREFER SOME-THING WITH BUILT-IN FIREPOWER.
LIKE THIS THING?
SHRAAKK
LIKE THAT -- ESPECIALLY SINCE MY TRACKING SYSTEMS INDICATE INCOMING CRAFT!
THEN I'LL HANG ONTO IT! ANY IDEA WHO WE'RE UP AGAINST?
SURELY YOU RECOGNIZE US, CAPTAIN AMERICA!
WHO BUT THE SOLDIERS OF A.I.M. COMMAND SUCH DEADLY TECHNOLOGY?*
*ADVANCED IDEA MECHANICS -- MATT
DOCTOR DOOM.
MANDARIN.
HYDRA.
THE RED -- HEY, WAIT A MINUTE! ARE THOSE FUNCTIONING PLASMA ACCELERATORS THEY'RE FIRING?
MAN... THESE GUYS ARE GOOD! I CAN'T GET MY PROTOTYPES WORKING WORTH A --
CAN WE TABLE THE PROFESSIONAL ENVY AT LEAST WHILE THEY'RE STRAFING US?

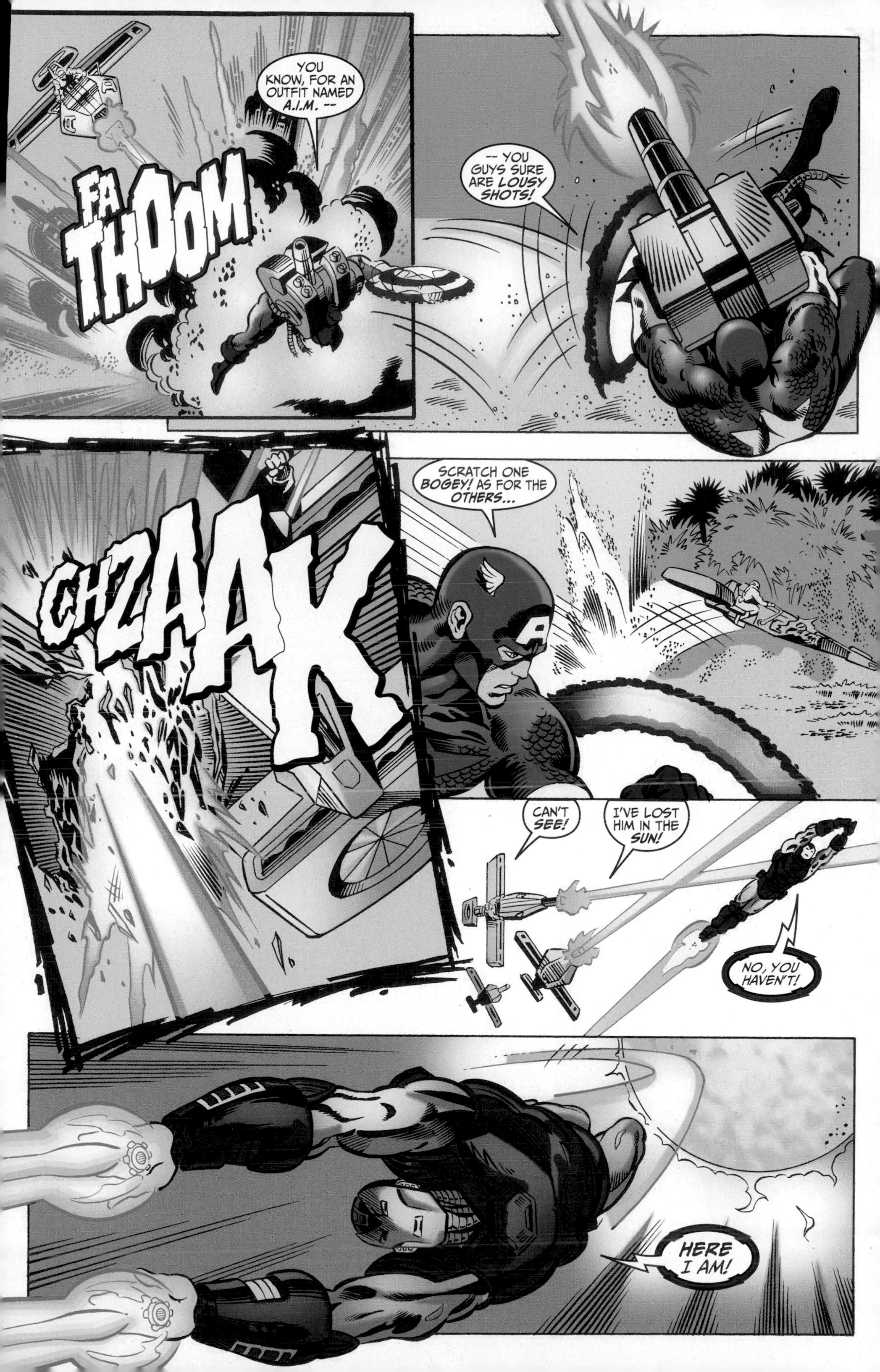
YOU KNOW, FOR AN OUTFIT NAMED A.I.M. --
FA THOOM
-- YOU GUYS SURE ARE LOUSY SHOTS!
CHZAAK
SCRATCH ONE BOGEY! AS FOR THE OTHERS...
CAN'T SEE!
I'VE LOST HIM IN THE SUN!
NO, YOU HAVEN'T!
HERE I AM!

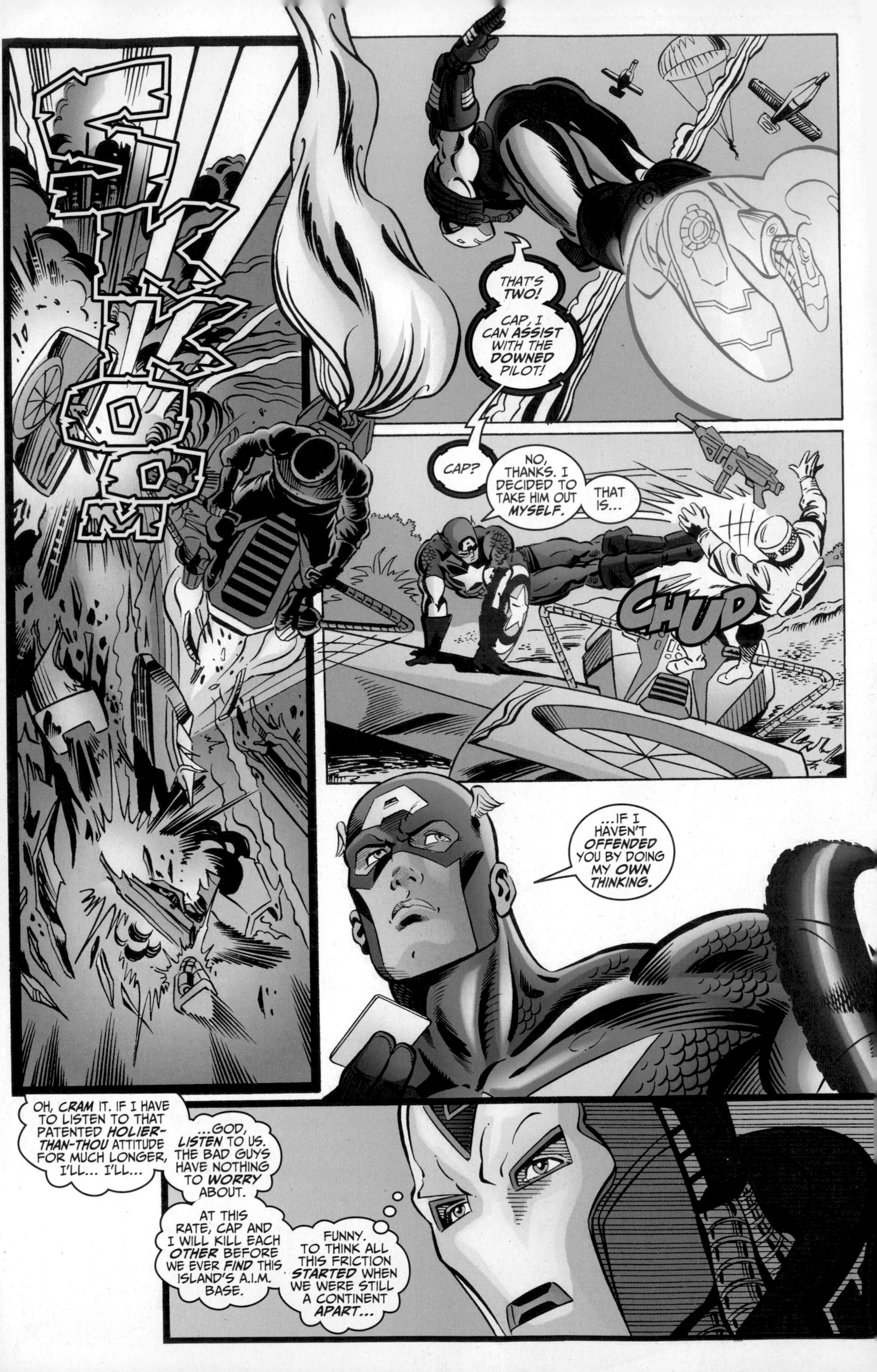
THOOOM
THAT'S TWO! CAP, I CAN ASSIST WITH THE DOWNED PILOT!
CAP?
NO, THANKS. I DECIDED TO TAKE HIM OUT MYSELF.
THAT IS...
CHUD
...IF I HAVEN'T OFFENDED YOU BY DOING MY OWN THINKING.
OH, CRAM IT. IF I HAVE TO LISTEN TO THAT PATENTED HOLIER-THAN-THOU ATTITUDE FOR MUCH LONGER, I'LL... I'LL...
...GOD, LISTEN TO US. THE BAD GUYS HAVE NOTHING TO WORRY ABOUT.
AT THIS RATE, CAP AND I WILL KILL EACH OTHER BEFORE WE EVER FIND THIS ISLAND'S A.I.M. BASE.
FUNNY. TO THINK ALL THIS FRICTION STARTED WHEN WE WERE STILL A CONTINENT APART...

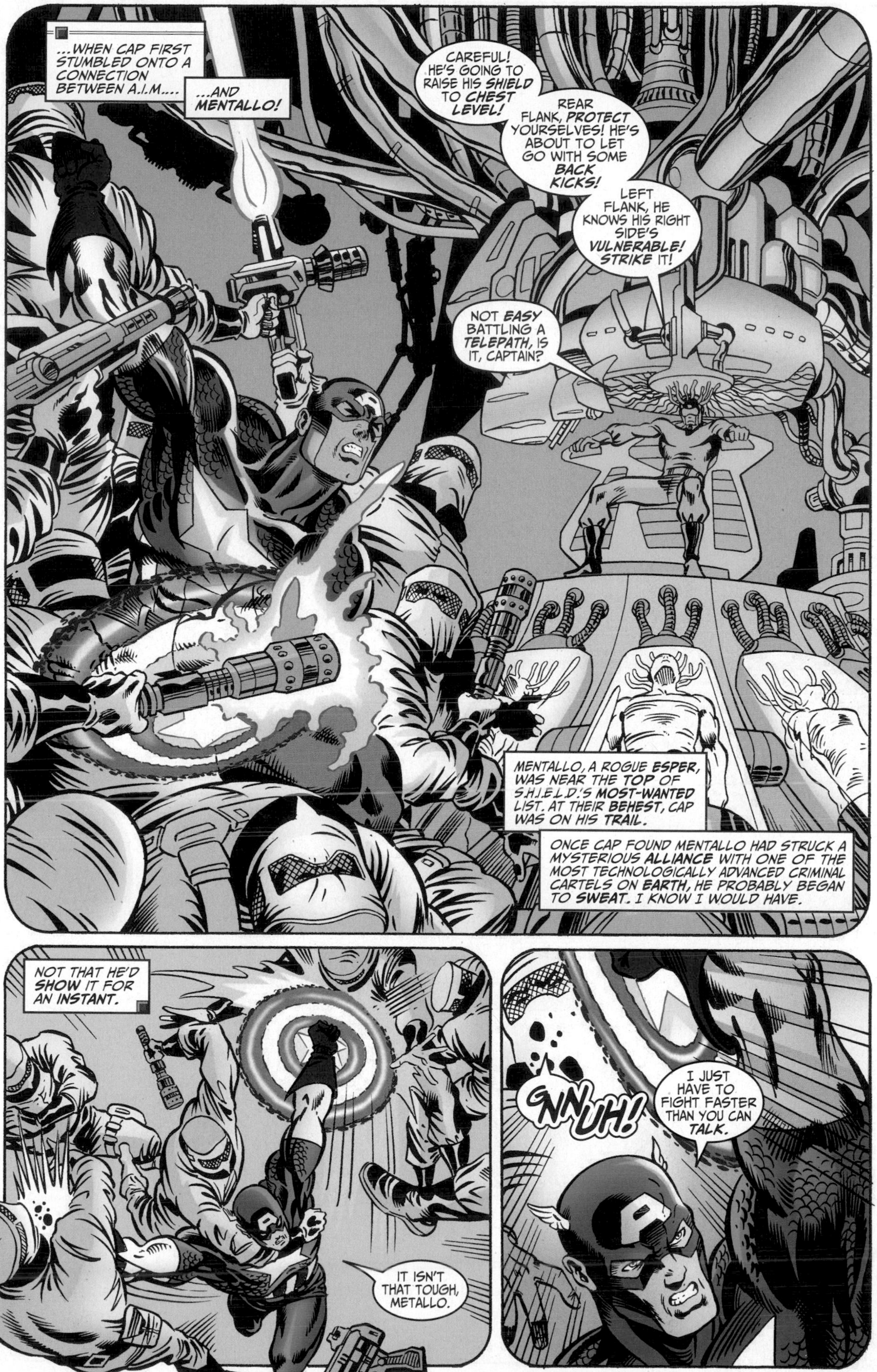
...WHEN CAP FIRST STUMBLED ONTO A CONNECTION BETWEEN A.I.M....
...AND MENTALLO!
CAREFUL! HE'S GOING TO RAISE HIS SHIELD TO CHEST LEVEL!
REAR FLANK, PROTECT YOURSELVES! HE'S ABOUT TO LET GO WITH SOME BACK KICKS!
LEFT FLANK, HE KNOWS HIS RIGHT SIDE'S VULNERABLE! STRIKE IT!
NOT EASY BATTLING A TELEPATH, IS IT, CAPTAIN?
MENTALLO, A ROGUE ESPER, WAS NEAR THE TOP OF S.H.I.E.L.D.'S MOST-WANTED LIST. AT THEIR BEHEST, CAP WAS ON HIS TRAIL.
ONCE CAP FOUND MENTALLO HAD STRUCK A MYSTERIOUS ALLIANCE WITH ONE OF THE MOST TECHNOLOGICALLY ADVANCED CRIMINAL CARTELS ON EARTH, HE PROBABLY BEGAN TO SWEAT. I KNOW I WOULD HAVE.
NOT THAT HE'D SHOW IT FOR AN INSTANT.
IT ISN'T THAT TOUGH, METALLO.
GNNUH!
I JUST HAVE TO FIGHT FASTER THAN YOU CAN TALK.

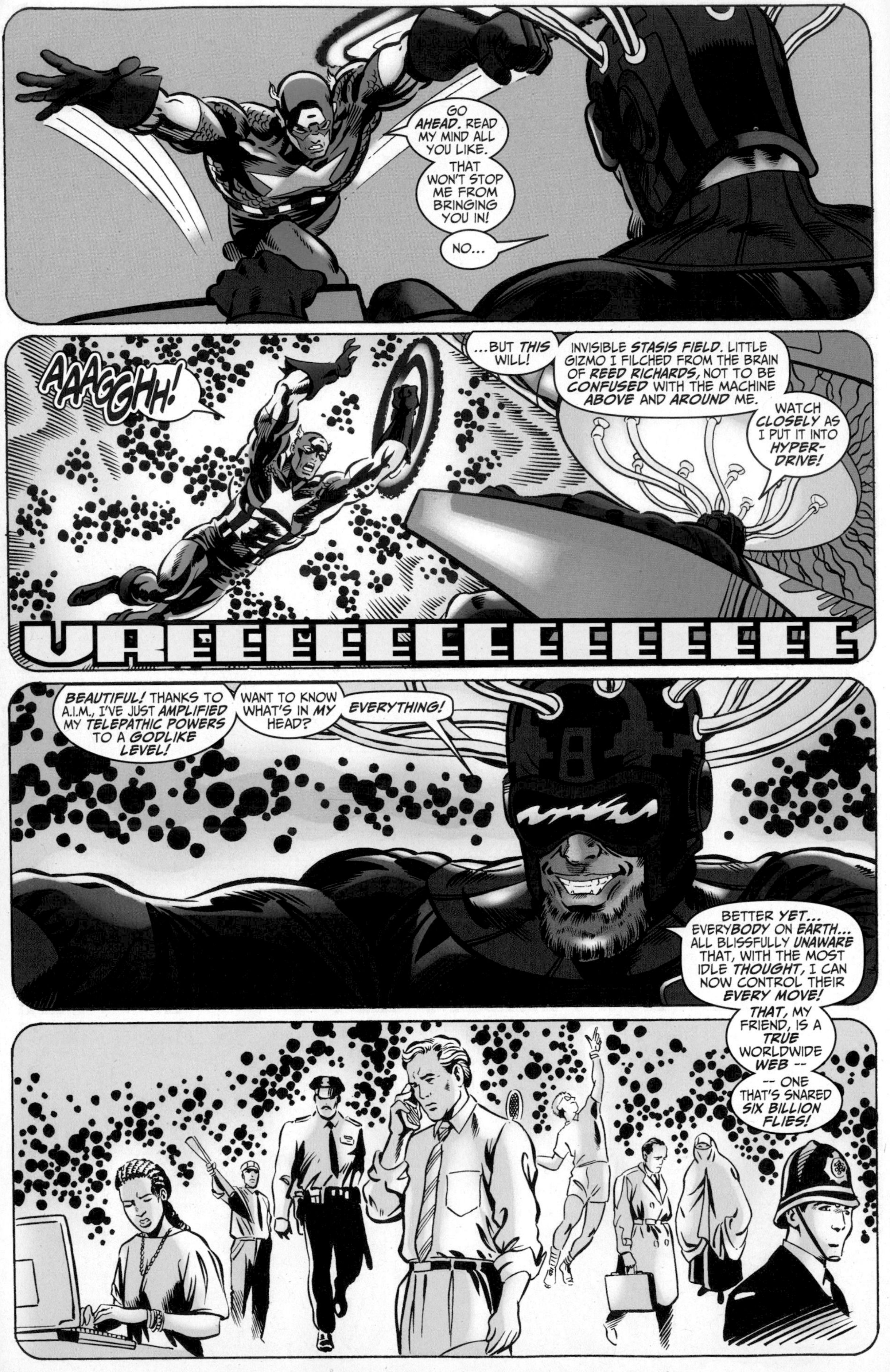
GO AHEAD. READ MY MIND ALL YOU LIKE.
THAT WON'T STOP ME FROM BRINGING YOU IN!
NO...
AAAGGHH!
...BUT THIS WILL!
INVISIBLE STASIS FIELD. LITTLE GIZMO I FILCHED FROM THE BRAIN OF REED RICHARDS, NOT TO BE CONFUSED WITH THE MACHINE ABOVE AND AROUND ME.
WATCH CLOSELY AS I PUT IT INTO HYPER-DRIVE!
VREEEEEEEEEEEEEE
BEAUTIFUL! THANKS TO A.I.M., I'VE JUST AMPLIFIED MY TELEPATHIC POWERS TO A GODLIKE LEVEL!
WANT TO KNOW WHAT'S IN MY HEAD?
EVERYTHING!
BETTER YET... EVERYBODY ON EARTH... ALL BLISSFULLY UNAWARE THAT, WITH THE MOST IDLE THOUGHT, I CAN NOW CONTROL THEIR EVERY MOVE!
THAT, MY FRIEND, IS A TRUE WORLDWIDE WEB --
-- ONE THAT'S SNARED SIX BILLION FLIES!

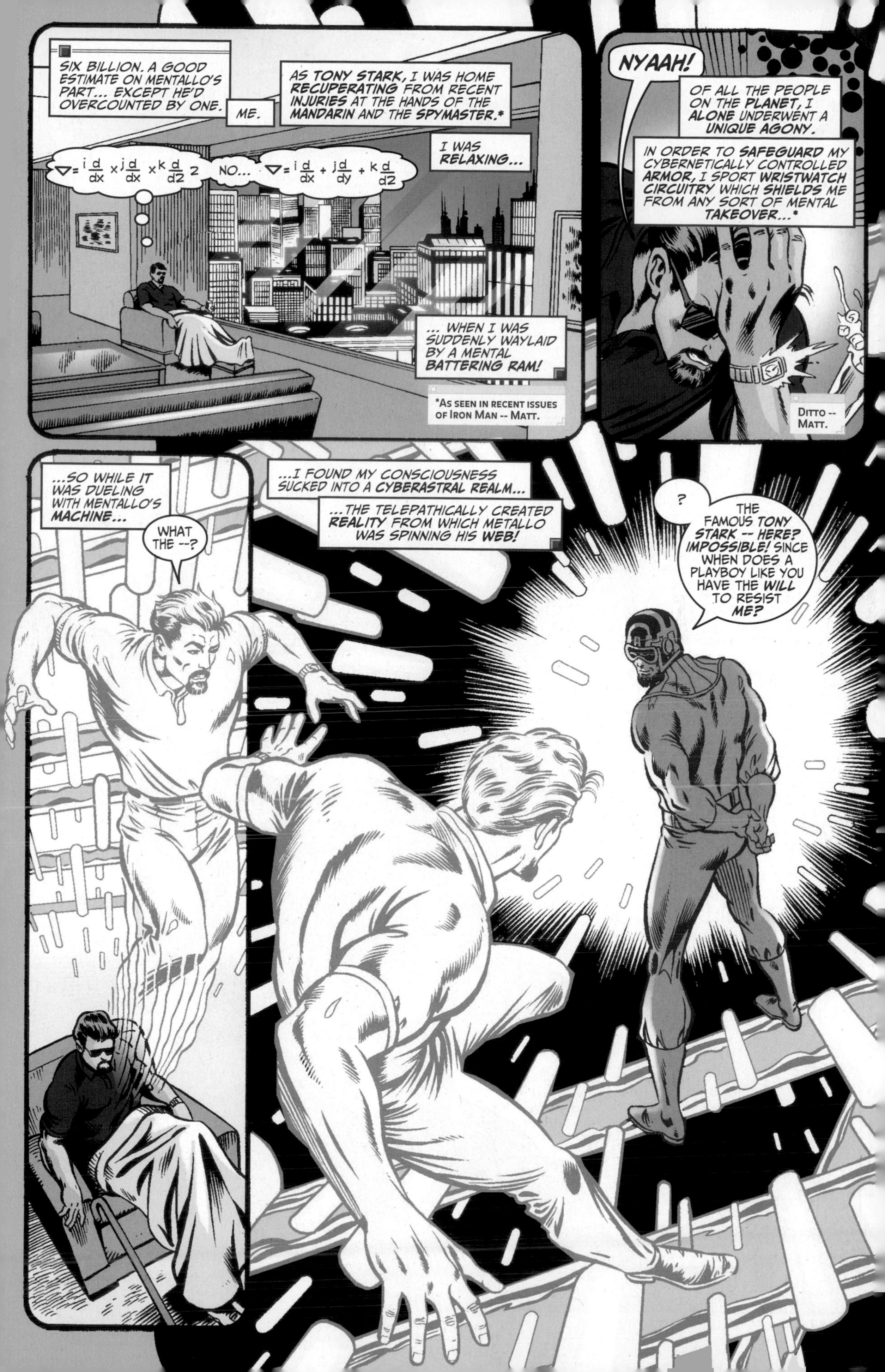

SIX BILLION. A GOOD ESTIMATE ON MENTALLO'S PART... EXCEPT HE'D OVERCOUNTED BY ONE.
ME.
AS TONY STARK, I WAS HOME RECUPERATING FROM RECENT INJURIES AT THE HANDS OF THE MANDARIN AND THE SPYMASTER.*
I WAS RELAXING...
NO...
...WHEN I WAS SUDDENLY WAYLAID BY A MENTAL BATTERING RAM!
*As seen in recent issues of Iron Man -- Matt.
NYAAH!
OF ALL THE PEOPLE ON THE PLANET, I ALONE UNDERWENT A UNIQUE AGONY.
IN ORDER TO SAFEGUARD MY CYBERNETICALLY CONTROLLED ARMOR, I SPORT WRISTWATCH CIRCUITRY WHICH SHIELDS ME FROM ANY SORT OF MENTAL TAKEOVER...*
Ditto -- Matt.
...SO WHILE IT WAS DUELING WITH MENTALLO'S MACHINE...
...I FOUND MY CONSCIOUSNESS SUCKED INTO A CYBERASTRAL REALM...
...THE TELEPATHICALLY CREATED REALITY FROM WHICH METALLO WAS SPINNING HIS WEB!
WHAT THE --?
?
THE FAMOUS TONY STARK -- HERE? IMPOSSIBLE! SINCE WHEN DOES A PLAYBOY LIKE YOU HAVE THE WILL TO RESIST ME?

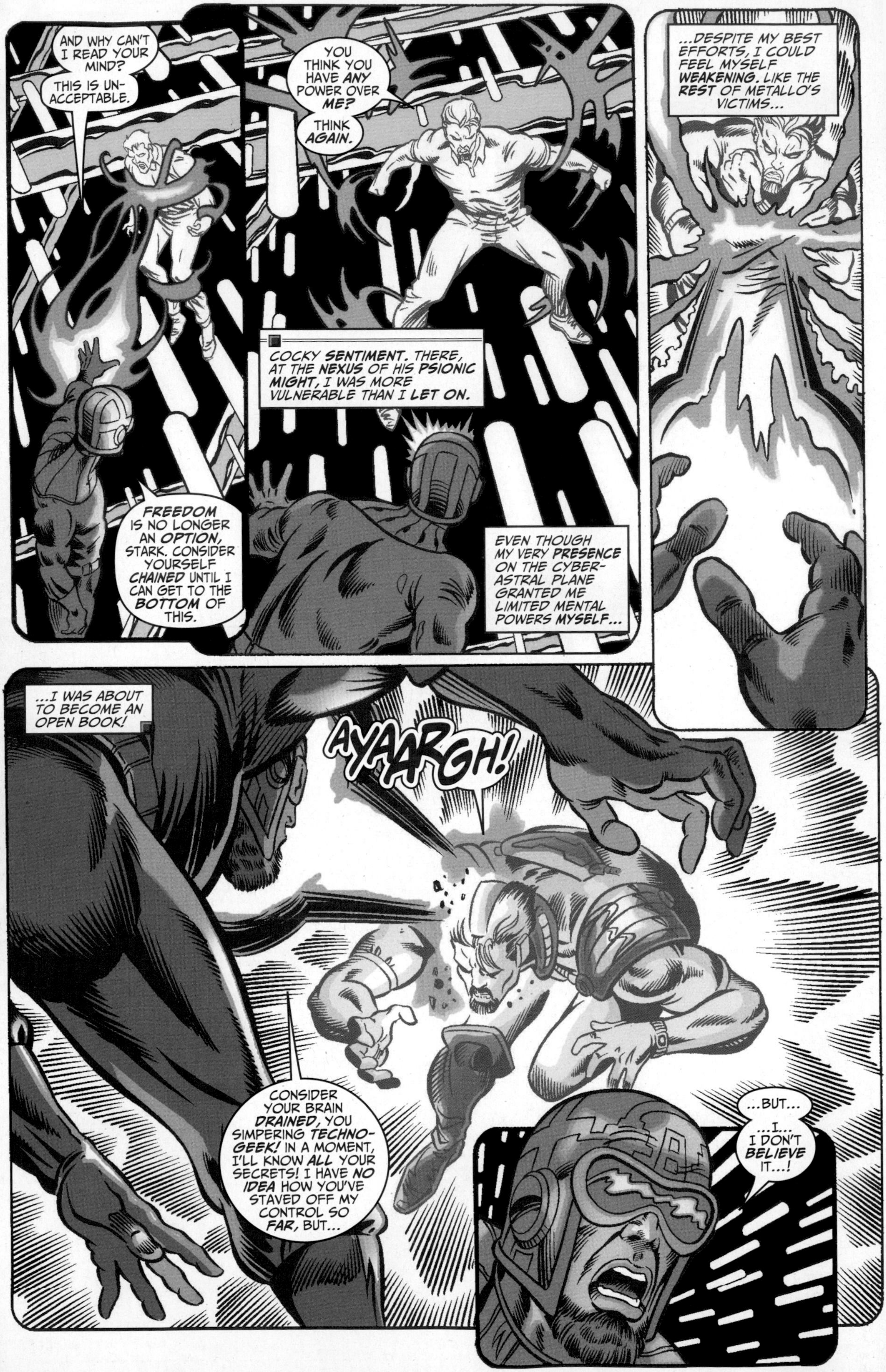
AND WHY CAN'T I READ YOUR MIND?
THIS IS UN-ACCEPTABLE.
FREEDOM IS NO LONGER AN OPTION, STARK. CONSIDER YOURSELF CHAINED UNTIL I CAN GET TO THE BOTTOM OF THIS.
YOU THINK YOU HAVE ANY POWER OVER ME?
THINK AGAIN.
COCKY SENTIMENT. THERE, AT THE NEXUS OF HIS PSIONIC MIGHT, I WAS MORE VULNERABLE THAN I LET ON.
EVEN THOUGH MY VERY PRESENCE ON THE CYBER-ASTRAL PLANE GRANTED ME LIMITED MENTAL POWERS MYSELF...
...DESPITE MY BEST EFFORTS, I COULD FEEL MYSELF WEAKENING. LIKE THE REST OF METALLO'S VICTIMS...
...I WAS ABOUT TO BECOME AN OPEN BOOK!
AYAARGH!
CONSIDER YOUR BRAIN DRAINED, YOU SIMPERING TECHNO-GEEK! IN A MOMENT, I'LL KNOW ALL YOUR SECRETS! I HAVE NO IDEA HOW YOU'VE STAVED OFF MY CONTROL SO FAR, BUT...
...BUT...
...I... I DON'T BELIEVE IT...!

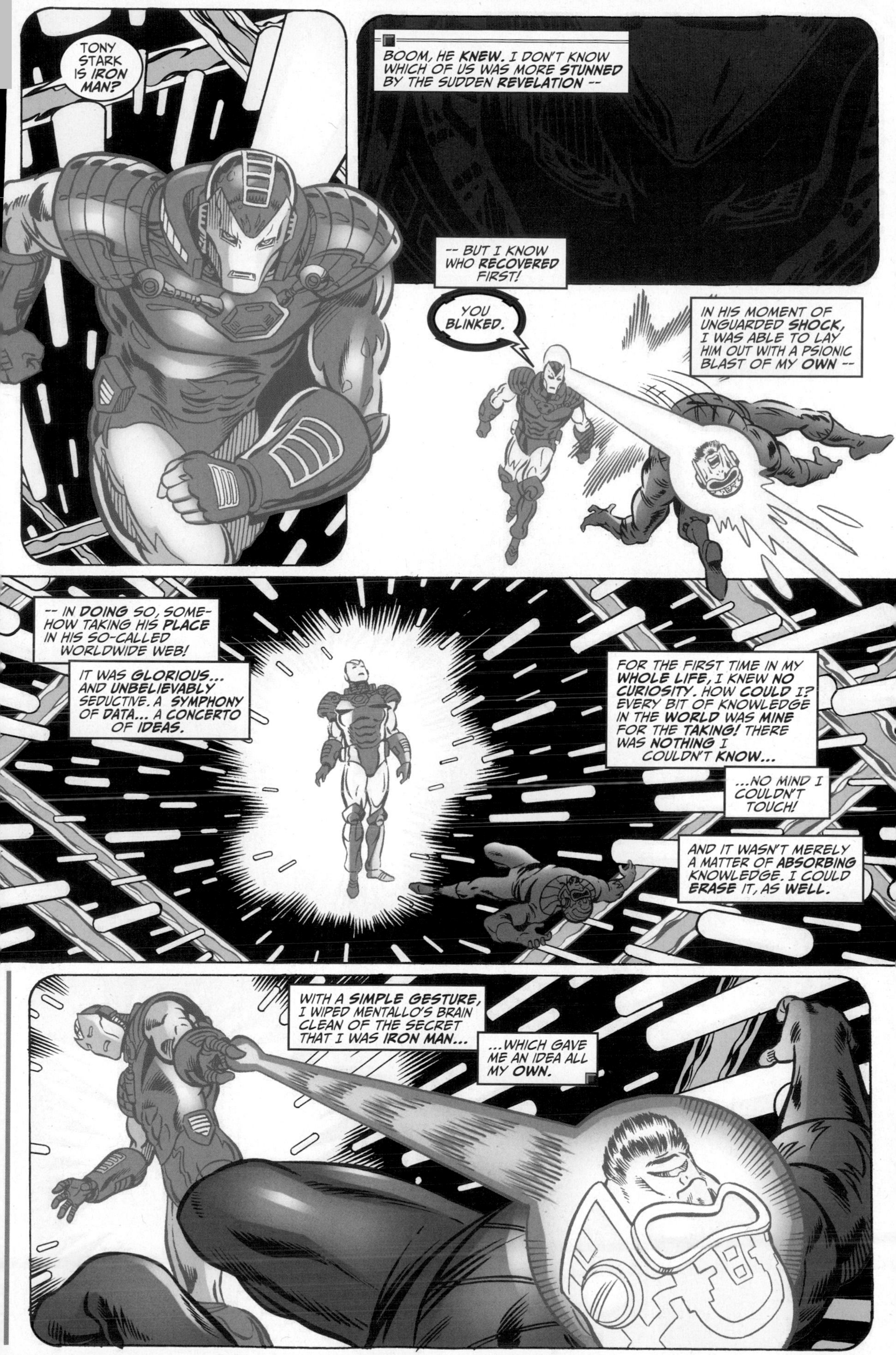
TONY STARK IS IRON MAN?
BOOM, HE KNEW. I DON'T KNOW WHICH OF US WAS MORE STUNNED BY THE SUDDEN REVELATION --
-- BUT I KNOW WHO RECOVERED FIRST!
YOU BLINKED.
IN HIS MOMENT OF UNGUARDED SHOCK, I WAS ABLE TO LAY HIM OUT WITH A PSIONIC BLAST OF MY OWN --
-- IN DOING SO, SOMEHOW TAKING HIS PLACE IN HIS SO-CALLED WORLDWIDE WEB!
IT WAS GLORIOUS... AND UNBELIEVABLY SEDUCTIVE. A SYMPHONY OF DATA... A CONCERTO OF IDEAS.
FOR THE FIRST TIME IN MY WHOLE LIFE, I KNEW NO CURIOSITY. HOW COULD I? EVERY BIT OF KNOWLEDGE IN THE WORLD WAS MINE FOR THE TAKING! THERE WAS NOTHING I COULDN'T KNOW...
...NO MIND I COULDN'T TOUCH!
AND IT WASN'T MERELY A MATTER OF ABSORBING KNOWLEDGE. I COULD ERASE IT, AS WELL.
WITH A SIMPLE GESTURE, I WIPED MENTALLO'S BRAIN CLEAN OF THE SECRET THAT I WAS IRON MAN...
...WHICH GAVE ME AN IDEA ALL MY OWN.

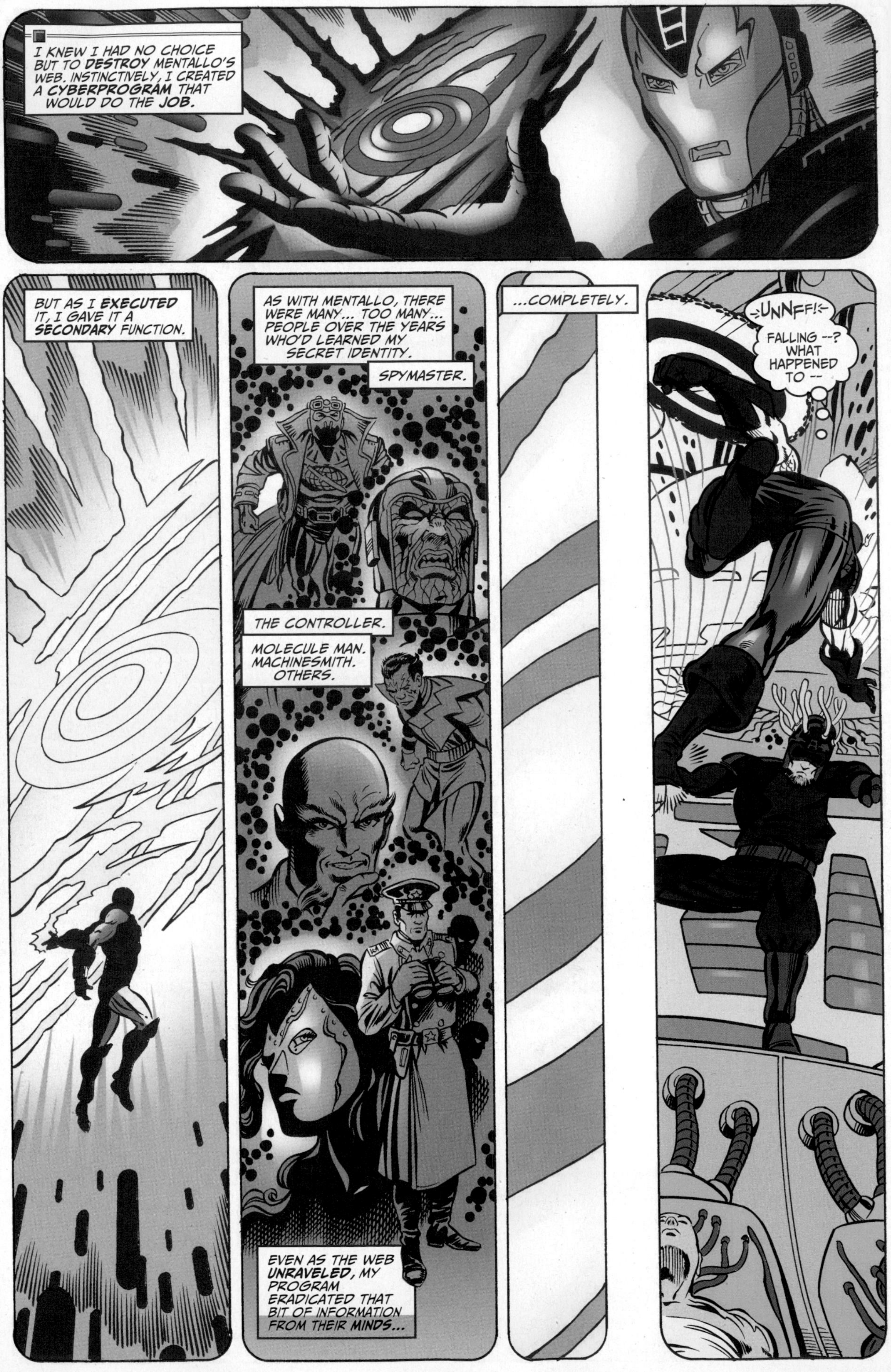
I KNEW I HAD NO CHOICE BUT TO DESTROY MENTALLO'S WEB. INSTINCTIVELY, I CREATED A CYBERPROGRAM THAT WOULD DO THE JOB.
BUT AS I EXECUTED IT, I GAVE IT A SECONDARY FUNCTION.
AS WITH MENTALLO, THERE WERE MANY... TOO MANY... PEOPLE OVER THE YEARS WHO'D LEARNED MY SECRET IDENTITY.
SPYMASTER.
THE CONTROLLER.
MOLECULE MAN. MACHINESMITH. OTHERS.
EVEN AS THE WEB UNRAVELED, MY PROGRAM ERADICATED THAT BIT OF INFORMATION FROM THEIR MINDS...
...COMPLETELY.
UNNFF!
FALLING --? WHAT HAPPENED TO --

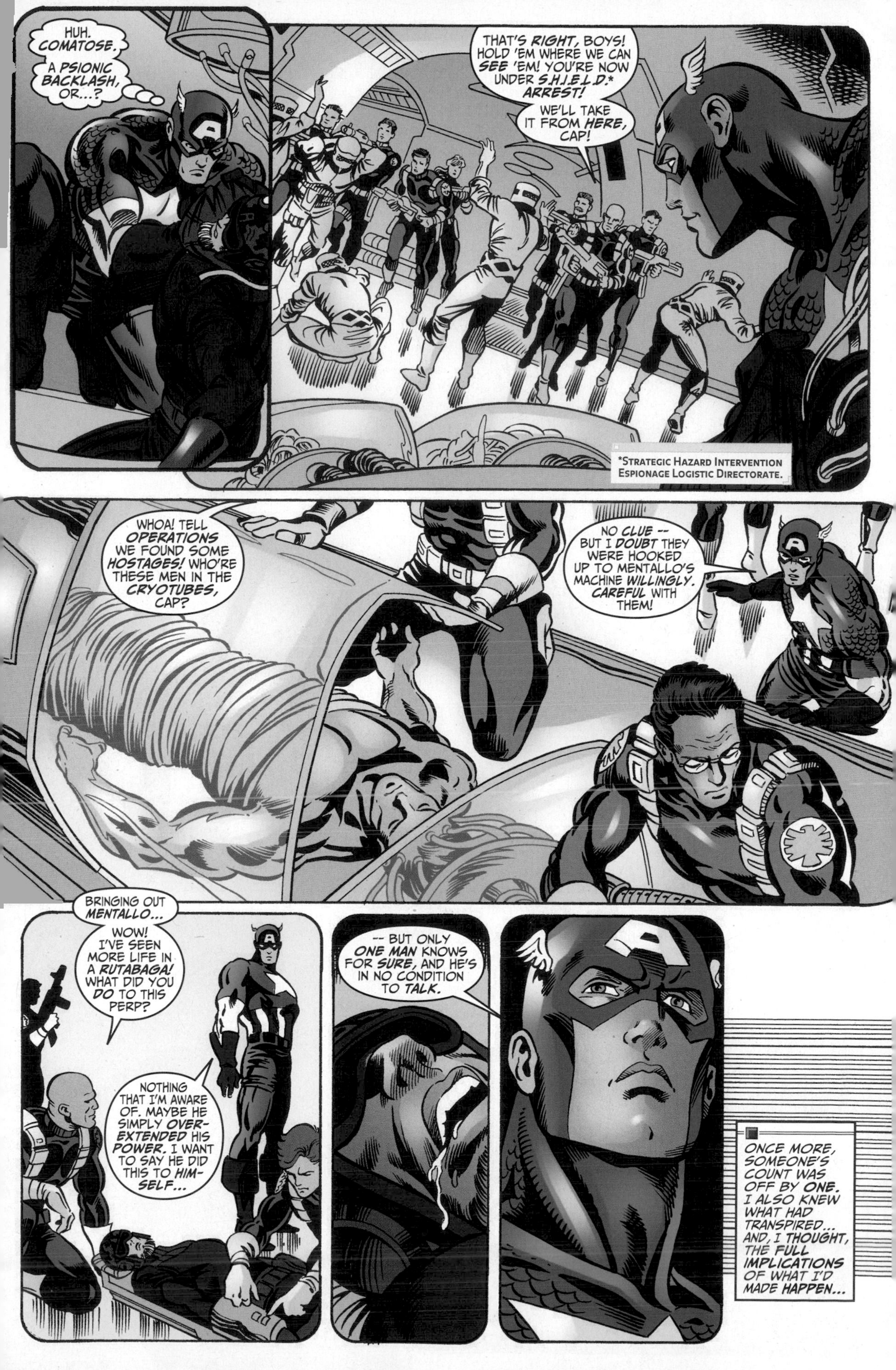
HUH. COMATOSE. A PSIONIC BACKLASH, OR...?
THAT'S RIGHT, BOYS! HOLD 'EM WHERE WE CAN SEE 'EM! YOU'RE NOW UNDER S.H.I.E.L.D.* ARREST!
WE'LL TAKE IT FROM HERE, CAP!
*STRATEGIC HAZARD INTERVENTION ESPIONAGE LOGISTIC DIRECTORATE.
WHOA! TELL OPERATIONS WE FOUND SOME HOSTAGES! WHO'RE THESE MEN IN THE CRYOTUBES, CAP?
NO CLUE -- BUT I DOUBT THEY WERE HOOKED UP TO MENTALLO'S MACHINE WILLINGLY. CAREFUL WITH THEM!
BRINGING OUT MENTALLO...
WOW! I'VE SEEN MORE LIFE IN A RUTABAGA! WHAT DID YOU DO TO THIS PERP?
NOTHING THAT I'M AWARE OF. MAYBE HE SIMPLY OVER-EXTENDED HIS POWER. I WANT TO SAY HE DID THIS TO HIM-SELF...
-- BUT ONLY ONE MAN KNOWS FOR SURE, AND HE'S IN NO CONDITION TO TALK.
ONCE MORE, SOMEONE'S COUNT WAS OFF BY ONE. I ALSO KNEW WHAT HAD TRANSPIRED... AND, I THOUGHT, THE FULL IMPLICATIONS OF WHAT I'D MADE HAPPEN...

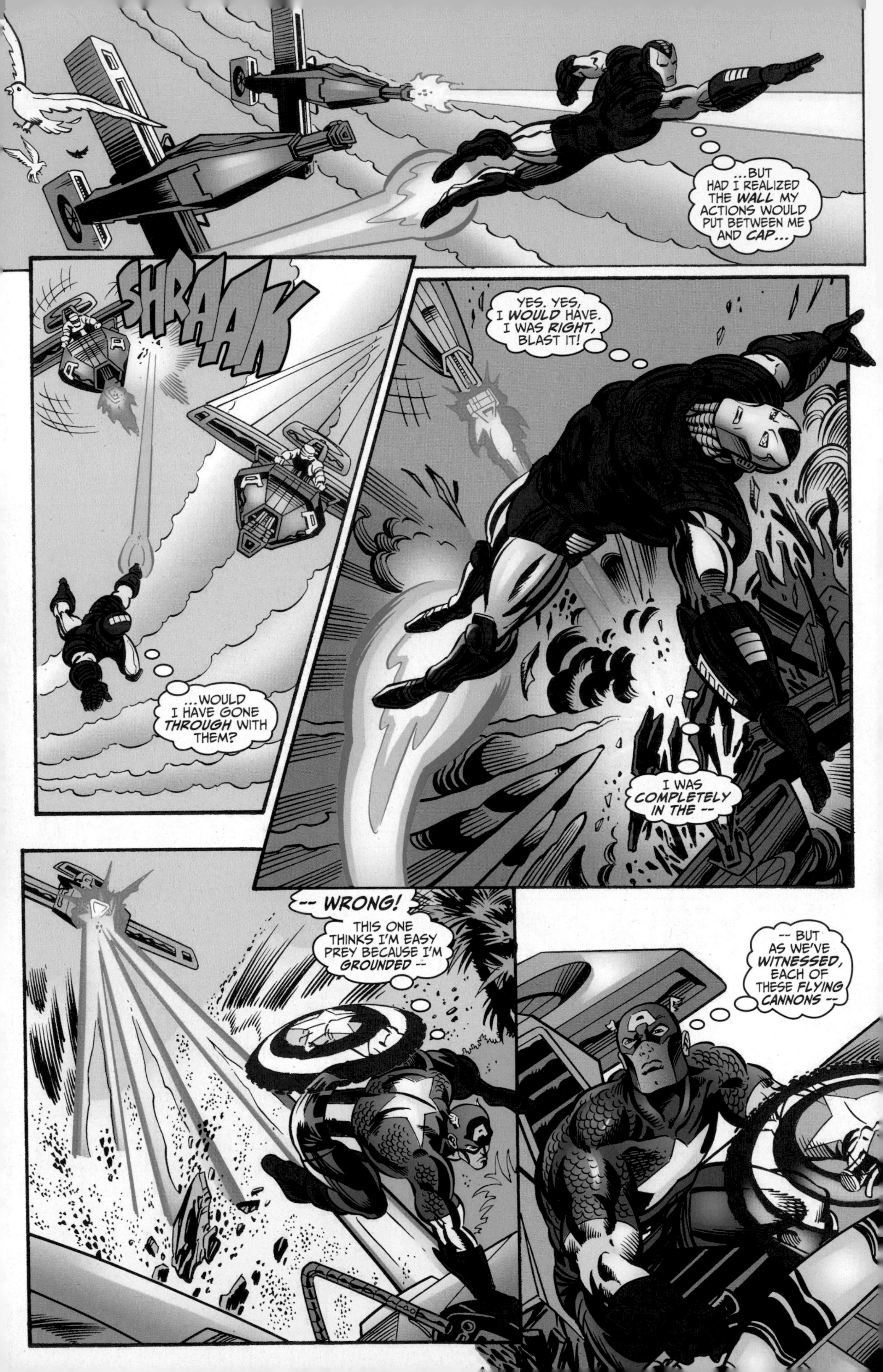
...BUT HAD I REALIZED THE WALL MY ACTIONS WOULD PUT BETWEEN ME AND CAP...
SHRAAK
...WOULD I HAVE GONE THROUGH WITH THEM?
YES. YES, I WOULD HAVE. I WAS RIGHT, BLAST IT!
I WAS COMPLETELY IN THE --
-- WRONG!
THIS ONE THINKS I'M EASY PREY BECAUSE I'M GROUNDED --
-- BUT AS WE'VE WITNESSED, EACH OF THESE FLYING CANNONS --

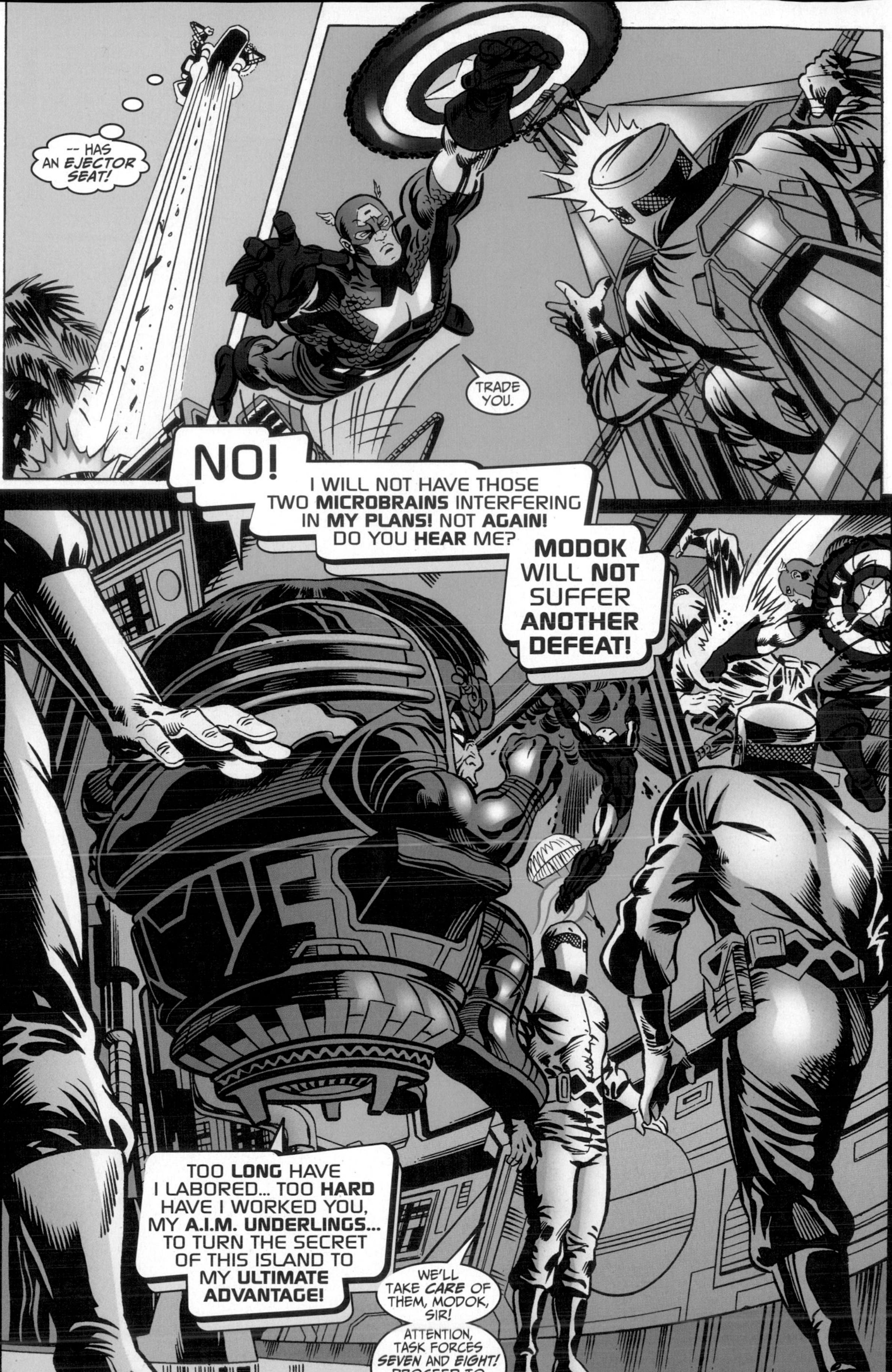
-- HAS AN EJECTOR SEAT!
TRADE YOU.
NO!
I WILL NOT HAVE THOSE TWO MICROBRAINS INTERFERING IN MY PLANS! NOT AGAIN! DO YOU HEAR ME?
MODOK WILL NOT SUFFER ANOTHER DEFEAT!
TOO LONG HAVE I LABORED... TOO HARD HAVE I WORKED YOU, MY A.I.M. UNDERLINGS... TO TURN THE SECRET OF THIS ISLAND TO MY ULTIMATE ADVANTAGE!
WE'LL TAKE CARE OF THEM, MODOK, SIR!
ATTENTION, TASK FORCES SEVEN AND EIGHT! PROCEED TO BATTLEZONE ALPHA --

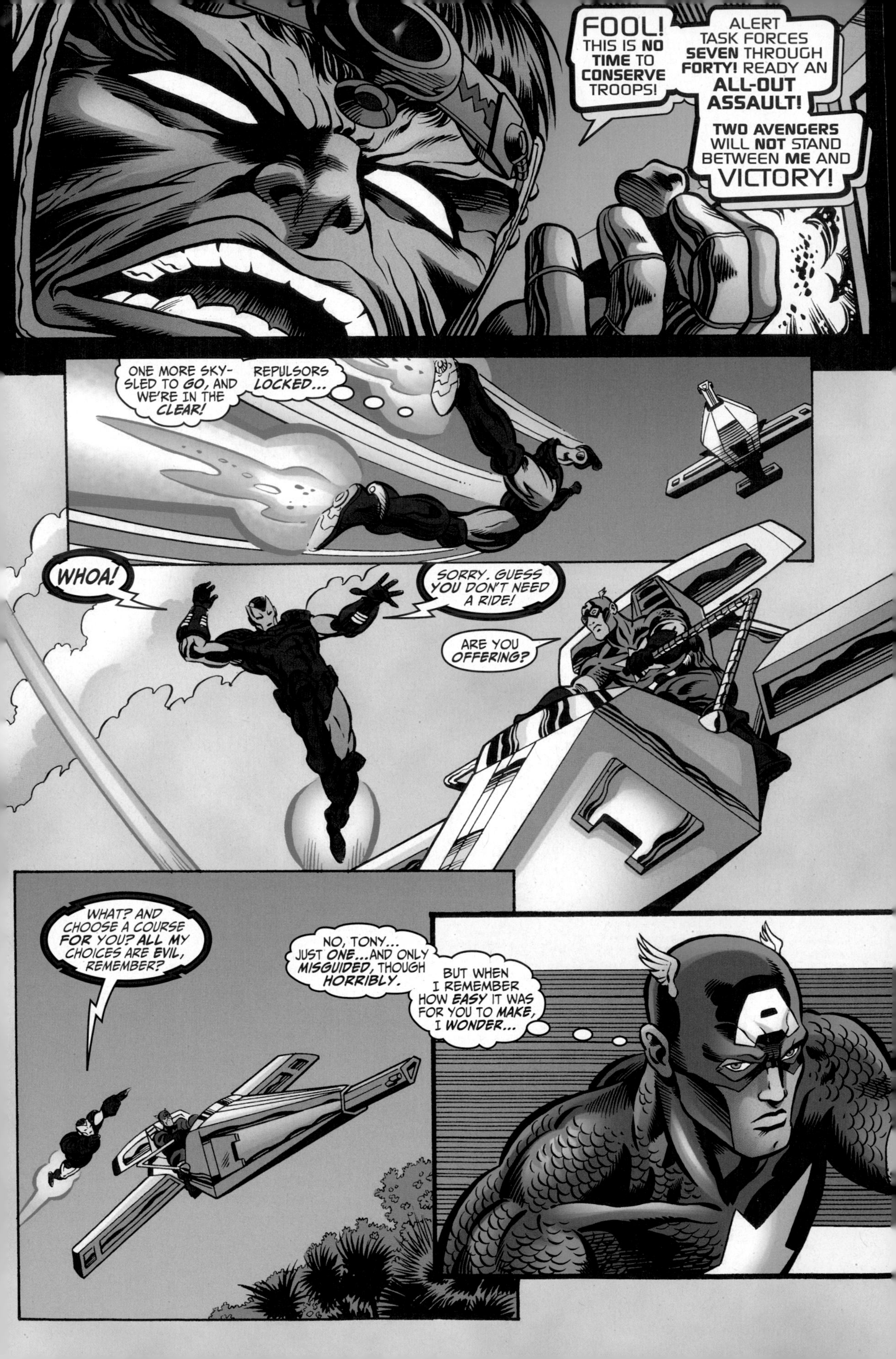
FOOL! THIS IS NO TIME TO CONSERVE TROOPS!
ALERT TASK FORCES SEVEN THROUGH FORTY! READY AN ALL-OUT ASSAULT!
TWO AVENGERS WILL NOT STAND BETWEEN ME AND VICTORY!
ONE MORE SKY-SLED TO GO, AND WE'RE IN THE CLEAR!
REPULSORS LOCKED...
WHOA!
SORRY. GUESS YOU DON'T NEED A RIDE!
ARE YOU OFFERING?
WHAT? AND CHOOSE A COURSE FOR YOU? ALL MY CHOICES ARE EVIL, REMEMBER?
NO, TONY... JUST ONE...AND ONLY MISGUIDED, THOUGH HORRIBLY.
BUT WHEN I REMEMBER HOW EASY IT WAS FOR YOU TO MAKE, I WONDER...

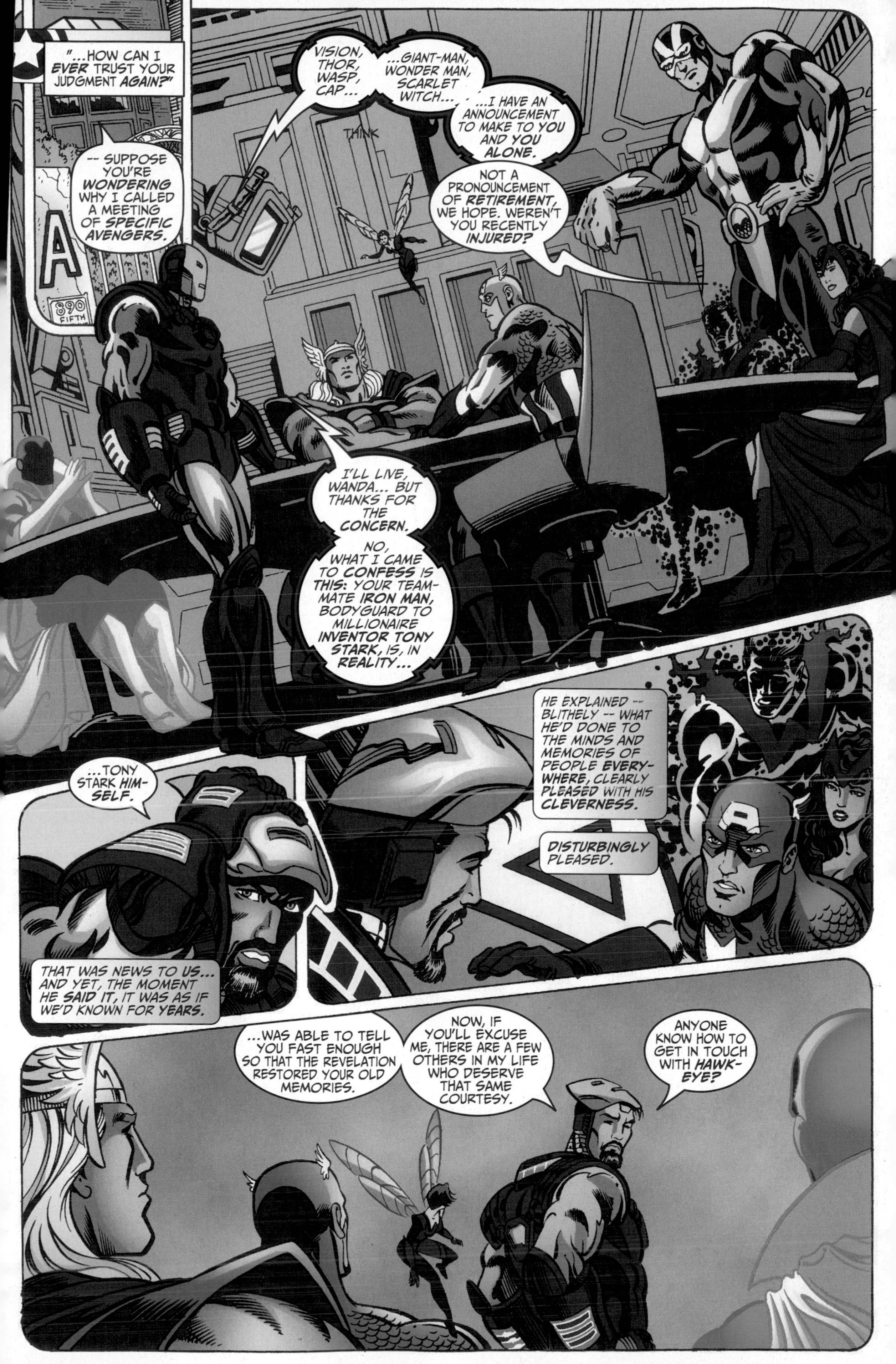
"...HOW CAN I EVER TRUST YOUR JUDGMENT AGAIN?"
-- SUPPOSE YOU'RE WONDERING WHY I CALLED A MEETING OF SPECIFIC AVENGERS.
VISION, THOR, WASP, CAP...
...GIANT-MAN, WONDER MAN, SCARLET WITCH...
...I HAVE AN ANNOUNCEMENT TO MAKE TO YOU AND YOU ALONE.
THINK
NOT A PRONOUNCEMENT OF RETIREMENT, WE HOPE. WEREN'T YOU RECENTLY INJURED?
890 FIFTH
I'LL LIVE, WANDA... BUT THANKS FOR THE CONCERN.
NO, WHAT I CAME TO CONFESS IS THIS: YOUR TEAMMATE IRON MAN, BODYGUARD TO MILLIONAIRE INVENTOR TONY STARK, IS, IN REALITY...
...TONY STARK HIMSELF.
HE EXPLAINED -- BLITHELY -- WHAT HE'D DONE TO THE MINDS AND MEMORIES OF PEOPLE EVERYWHERE, CLEARLY PLEASED WITH HIS CLEVERNESS.
DISTURBINGLY PLEASED.
THAT WAS NEWS TO US... AND YET, THE MOMENT HE SAID IT, IT WAS AS IF WE'D KNOWN FOR YEARS.
...WAS ABLE TO TELL YOU FAST ENOUGH SO THAT THE REVELATION RESTORED YOUR OLD MEMORIES.
NOW, IF YOU'LL EXCUSE ME, THERE ARE A FEW OTHERS IN MY LIFE WHO DESERVE THAT SAME COURTESY.
ANYONE KNOW HOW TO GET IN TOUCH WITH HAWKEYE?

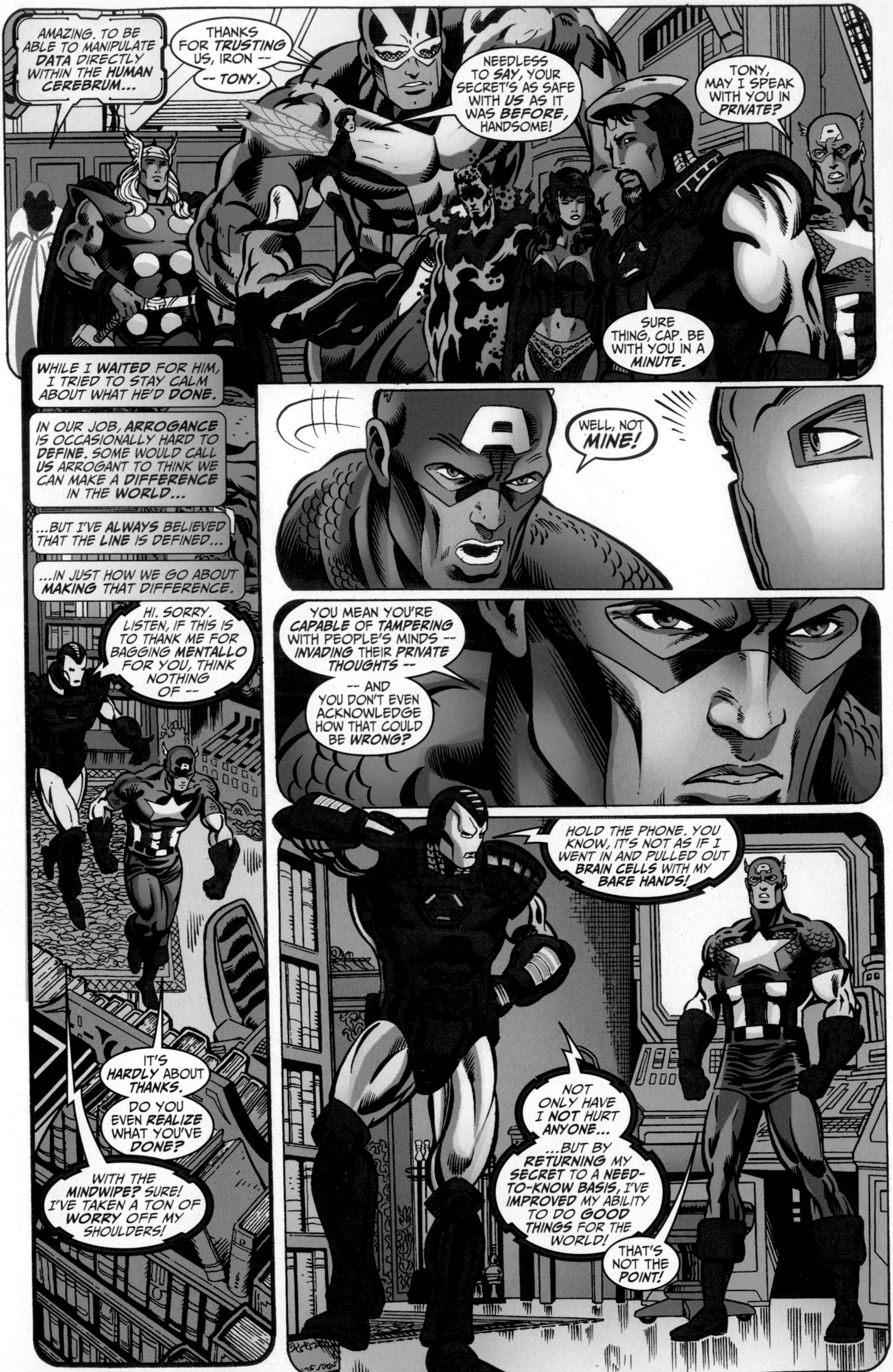

AMAZING. TO BE ABLE TO MANIPULATE DATA DIRECTLY WITHIN THE HUMAN CEREBRUM...
THANKS FOR TRUSTING US, IRON -- -- TONY.
NEEDLESS TO SAY, YOUR SECRET'S AS SAFE WITH US AS IT WAS BEFORE, HANDSOME!
TONY, MAY I SPEAK WITH YOU IN PRIVATE?
SURE THING, CAP. BE WITH YOU IN A MINUTE.
WHILE I WAITED FOR HIM, I TRIED TO STAY CALM ABOUT WHAT HE'D DONE.
IN OUR JOB, ARROGANCE IS OCCASIONALLY HARD TO DEFINE. SOME WOULD CALL US ARROGANT TO THINK WE CAN MAKE A DIFFERENCE IN THE WORLD...
...BUT I'VE ALWAYS BELIEVED THAT THE LINE IS DEFINED...
...IN JUST HOW WE GO ABOUT MAKING THAT DIFFERENCE.
HI. SORRY. LISTEN, IF THIS IS TO THANK ME FOR BAGGING MENTALLO FOR YOU, THINK NOTHING OF --
IT'S HARDLY ABOUT THANKS.
DO YOU EVEN REALIZE WHAT YOU'VE DONE?
WITH THE MINDWIPE? SURE! I'VE TAKEN A TON OF WORRY OFF MY SHOULDERS!
WELL, NOT MINE!
YOU MEAN YOU'RE CAPABLE OF TAMPERING WITH PEOPLE'S MINDS -- INVADING THEIR PRIVATE THOUGHTS --
-- AND YOU DON'T EVEN ACKNOWLEDGE HOW THAT COULD BE WRONG?
HOLD THE PHONE. YOU KNOW, IT'S NOT AS IF I WENT IN AND PULLED OUT BRAIN CELLS WITH MY BARE HANDS!
NOT ONLY HAVE I NOT HURT ANYONE...
...BUT BY RETURNING MY SECRET TO A NEED-TO-KNOW BASIS, I'VE IMPROVED MY ABILITY TO DO GOOD THINGS FOR THE WORLD!
THAT'S NOT THE POINT!

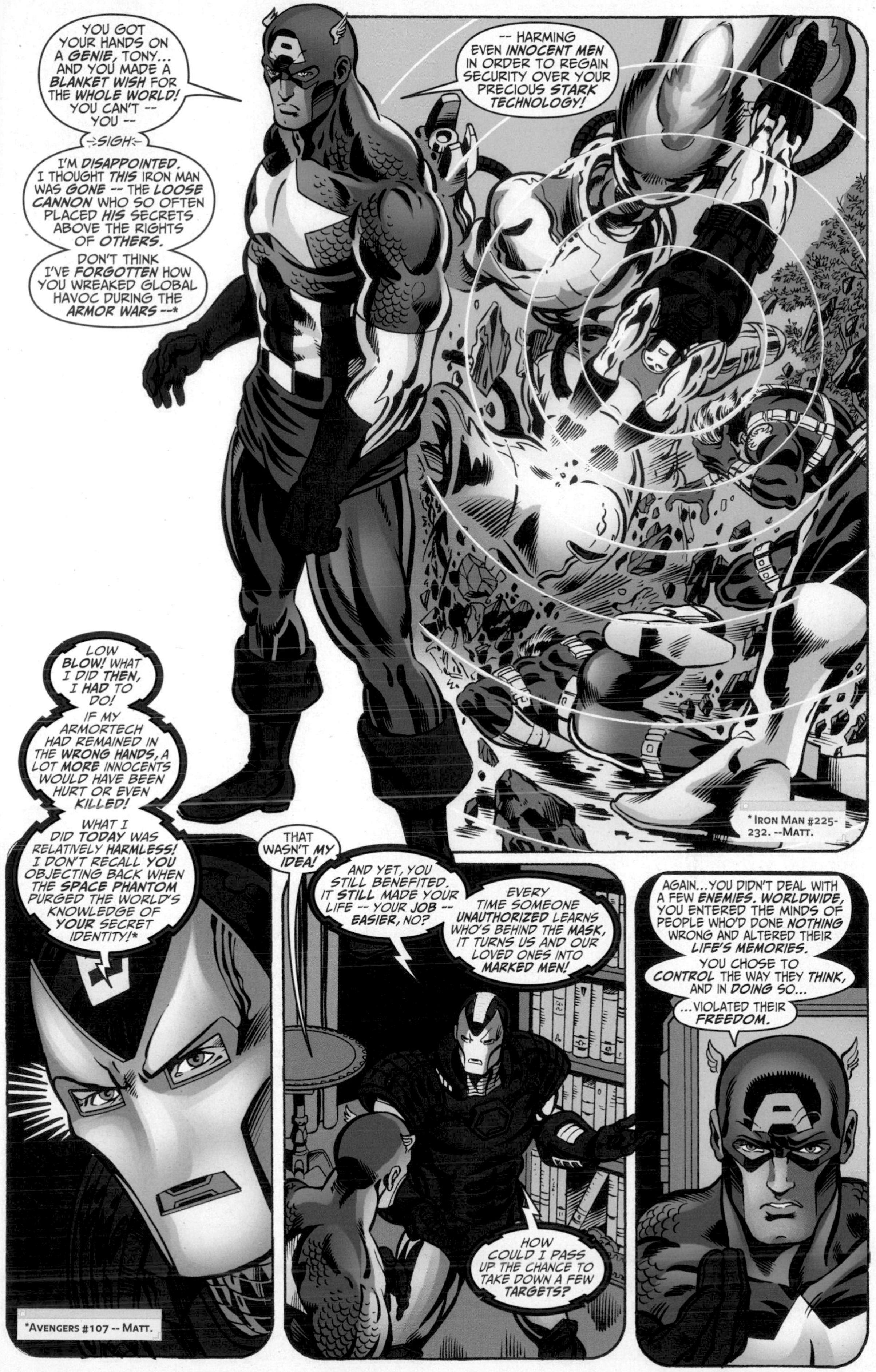
YOU GOT YOUR HANDS ON A GENIE, TONY... AND YOU MADE A BLANKET WISH FOR THE WHOLE WORLD! YOU CAN'T -- YOU --
SIGH
I'M DISAPPOINTED. I THOUGHT THIS IRON MAN WAS GONE -- THE LOOSE CANNON WHO SO OFTEN PLACED HIS SECRETS ABOVE THE RIGHTS OF OTHERS.
DON'T THINK I'VE FORGOTTEN HOW YOU WREAKED GLOBAL HAVOC DURING THE ARMOR WARS --*
-- HARMING EVEN INNOCENT MEN IN ORDER TO REGAIN SECURITY OVER YOUR PRECIOUS STARK TECHNOLOGY!
* IRON MAN #225-232. --MATT.
LOW BLOW! WHAT I DID THEN, I HAD TO DO!
IF MY ARMORTECH HAD REMAINED IN THE WRONG HANDS, A LOT MORE INNOCENTS WOULD HAVE BEEN HURT OR EVEN KILLED!
WHAT I DID TODAY WAS RELATIVELY HARMLESS! I DON'T RECALL YOU OBJECTING BACK WHEN THE SPACE PHANTOM PURGED THE WORLD'S KNOWLEDGE OF YOUR SECRET IDENTITY!*
*AVENGERS #107 -- MATT.
THAT WASN'T MY IDEA!
AND YET, YOU STILL BENEFITED. IT STILL MADE YOUR LIFE -- YOUR JOB -- EASIER, NO?
EVERY TIME SOMEONE UNAUTHORIZED LEARNS WHO'S BEHIND THE MASK, IT TURNS US AND OUR LOVED ONES INTO MARKED MEN!
HOW COULD I PASS UP THE CHANCE TO TAKE DOWN A FEW TARGETS?
AGAIN...YOU DIDN'T DEAL WITH A FEW ENEMIES. WORLDWIDE, YOU ENTERED THE MINDS OF PEOPLE WHO'D DONE NOTHING WRONG AND ALTERED THEIR LIFE'S MEMORIES.
YOU CHOSE TO CONTROL THE WAY THEY THINK, AND IN DOING SO...
...VIOLATED THEIR FREEDOM.

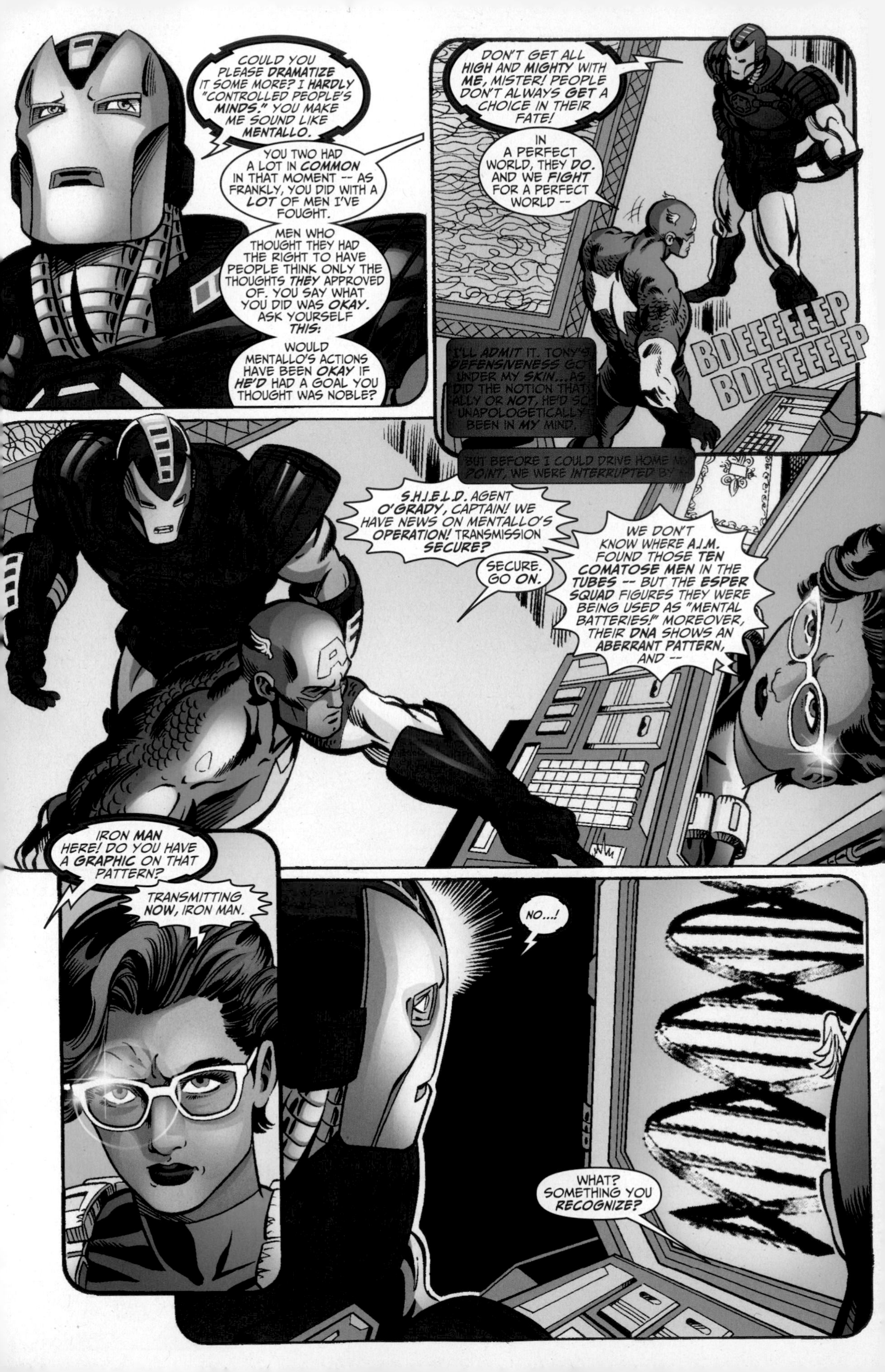
COULD YOU PLEASE DRAMATIZE IT SOME MORE? I HARDLY "CONTROLLED PEOPLE'S MINDS." YOU MAKE ME SOUND LIKE MENTALLO.
YOU TWO HAD A LOT IN COMMON IN THAT MOMENT -- AS FRANKLY, YOU DID WITH A LOT OF MEN I'VE FOUGHT.
MEN WHO THOUGHT THEY HAD THE RIGHT TO HAVE PEOPLE THINK ONLY THE THOUGHTS THEY APPROVED OF. YOU SAY WHAT YOU DID WAS OKAY. ASK YOURSELF THIS:
WOULD MENTALLO'S ACTIONS HAVE BEEN OKAY IF HE'D HAD A GOAL YOU THOUGHT WAS NOBLE?
DON'T GET ALL HIGH AND MIGHTY WITH ME, MISTER! PEOPLE DON'T ALWAYS GET A CHOICE IN THEIR FATE!
IN A PERFECT WORLD, THEY DO. AND WE FIGHT FOR A PERFECT WORLD --
I'LL ADMIT IT. TONY'S DEFENSIVENESS GO UNDER MY SKIN...AS DID THE NOTION THAT ALLY OR NOT, HE'D SC UNAPOLOGETICALLY BEEN IN MY MIND.
BDEEEEEEP
BDEEEEEEP
BUT BEFORE I COULD DRIVE HOME POINT, WE WERE INTERRUPTED B
S.H.I.E.L.D. AGENT O'GRADY, CAPTAIN! WE HAVE NEWS ON MENTALLO'S OPERATION! TRANSMISSION SECURE?
SECURE. GO ON.
WE DON'T KNOW WHERE A.I.M. FOUND THOSE TEN COMATOSE MEN IN THE TUBES -- BUT THE ESPER SQUAD FIGURES THEY WERE BEING USED AS "MENTAL BATTERIES!" MOREOVER, THEIR DNA SHOWS AN ABERRANT PATTERN, AND --
IRON MAN HERE! DO YOU HAVE A GRAPHIC ON THAT PATTERN?
TRANSMITTING NOW, IRON MAN.
NO...!
WHAT? SOMETHING YOU RECOGNIZE?

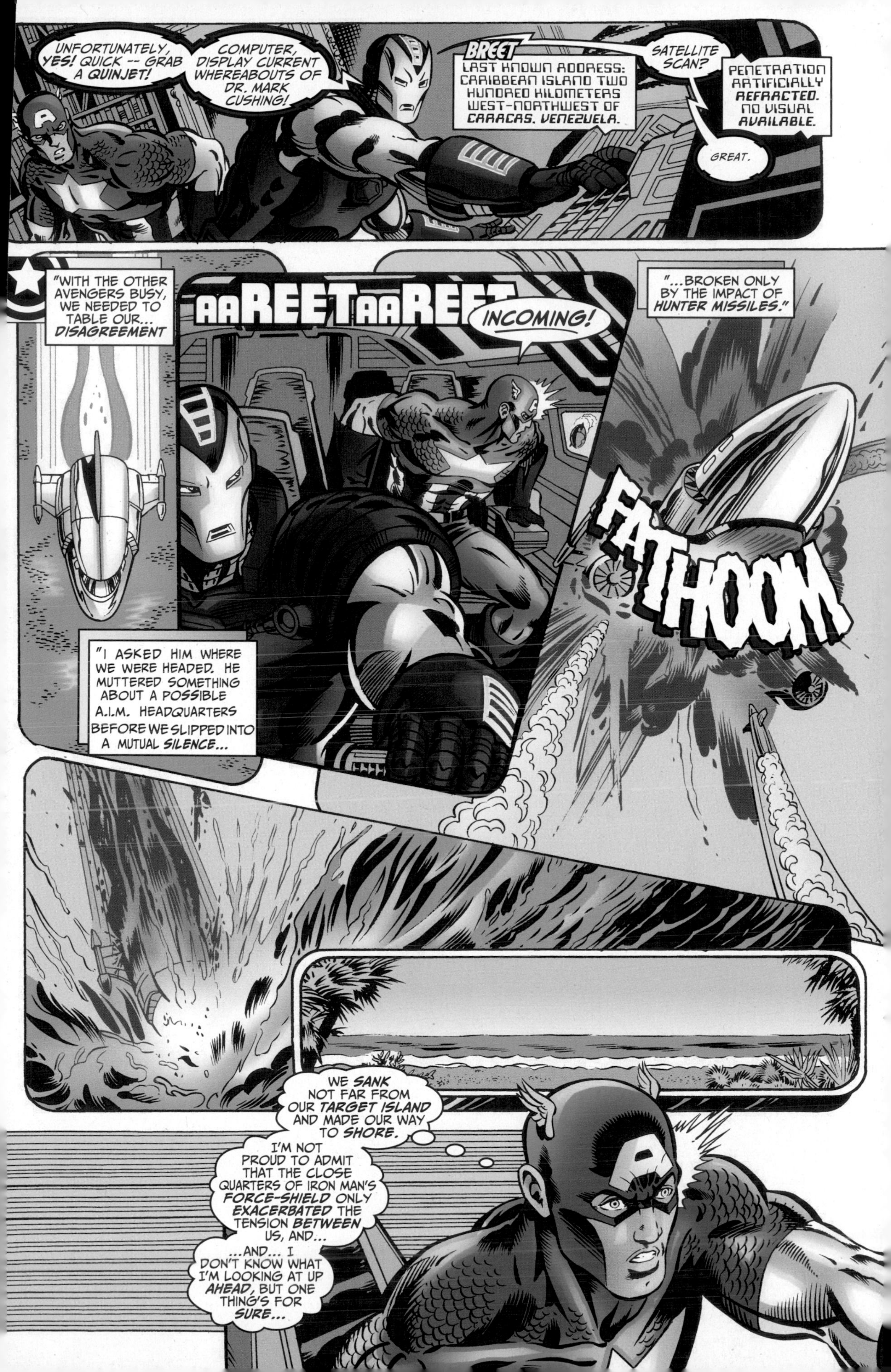
UNFORTUNATELY, YES! QUICK -- GRAB A QUINJET!
COMPUTER, DISPLAY CURRENT WHEREABOUTS OF DR. MARK CUSHING!
BREET
LAST KNOWN ADDRESS: CARIBBEAN ISLAND TWO HUNDRED KILOMETERS WEST-NORTHWEST OF CARACAS, VENEZUELA.
SATELLITE SCAN?
PENETRATION ARTIFICIALLY REFRACTED. NO VISUAL AVAILABLE.
GREAT.
"WITH THE OTHER AVENGERS BUSY, WE NEEDED TO TABLE OUR... DISAGREEMENT
AAREETAAREET
INCOMING!
"I ASKED HIM WHERE WE WERE HEADED. HE MUTTERED SOMETHING ABOUT A POSSIBLE A.I.M. HEADQUARTERS BEFORE WE SLIPPED INTO A MUTUAL SILENCE...
"...BROKEN ONLY BY THE IMPACT OF HUNTER MISSILES."
FATHOOM
WE SANK NOT FAR FROM OUR TARGET ISLAND AND MADE OUR WAY TO SHORE.
I'M NOT PROUD TO ADMIT THAT THE CLOSE QUARTERS OF IRON MAN'S FORCE-SHIELD ONLY EXACERBATED THE TENSION BETWEEN US, AND...
...AND... I DON'T KNOW WHAT I'M LOOKING AT UP AHEAD, BUT ONE THING'S FOR SURE...

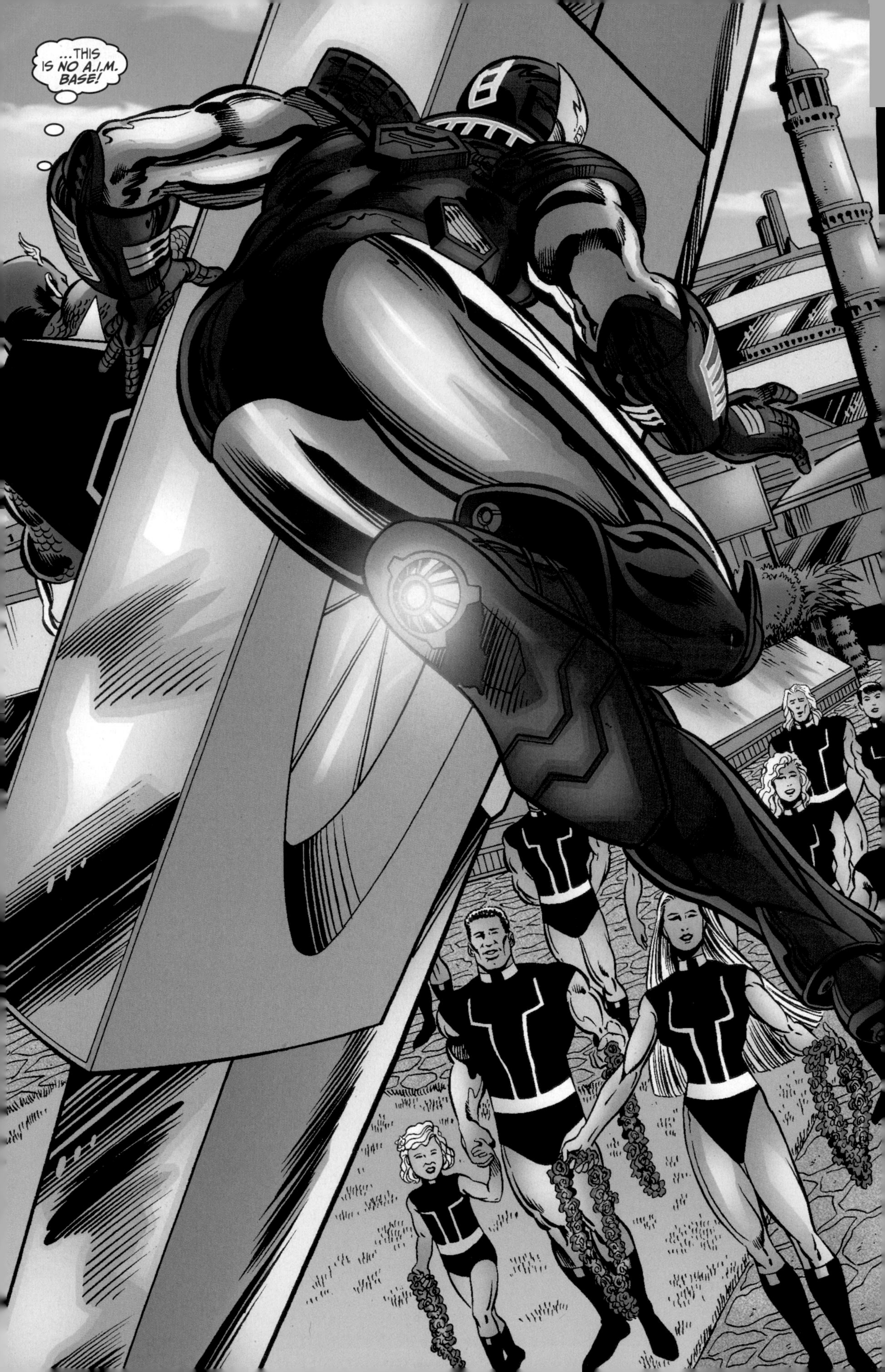
...THIS IS NO A.I.M. BASE!

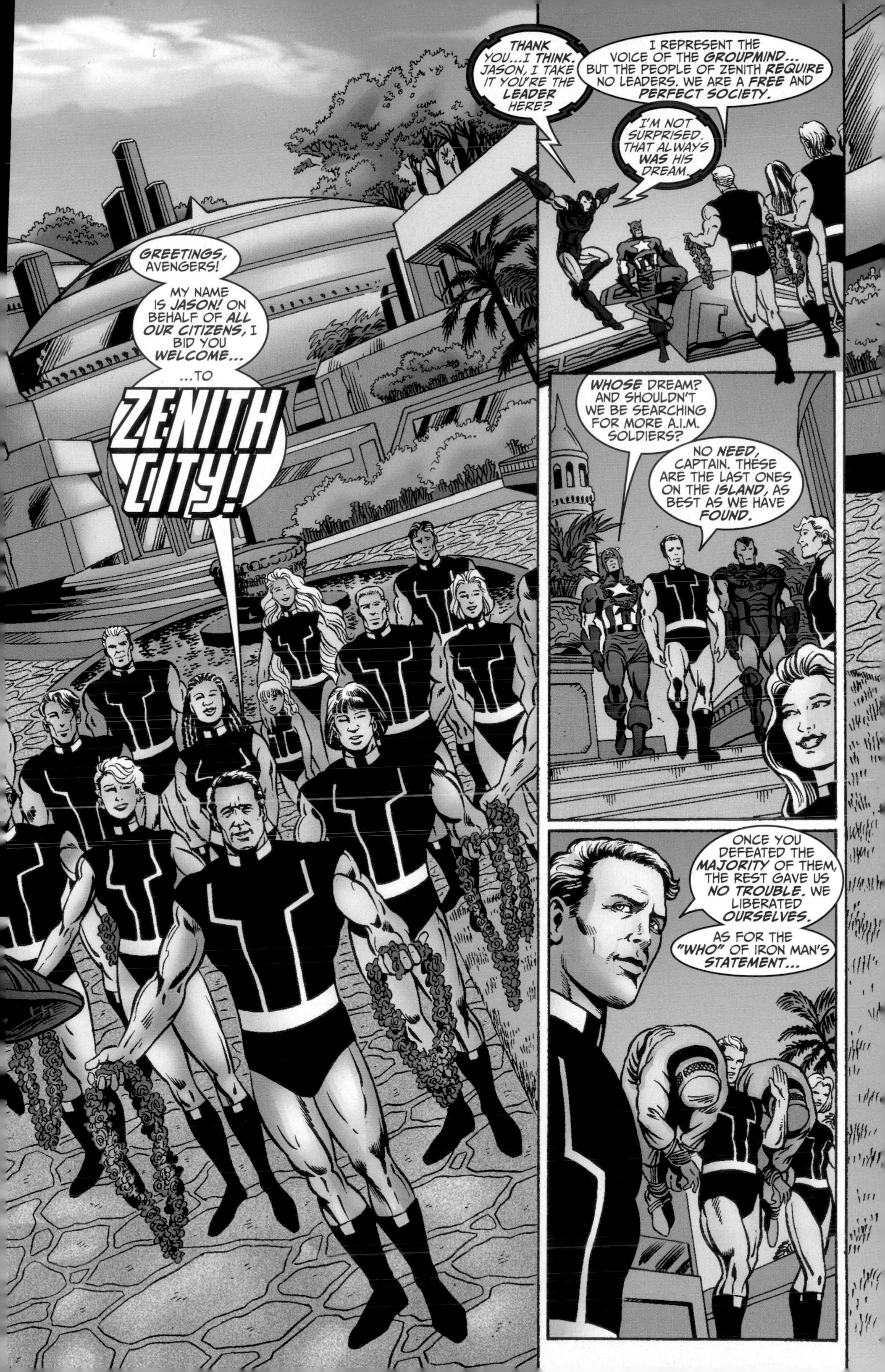

GREETINGS, AVENGERS!
MY NAME IS JASON! ON BEHALF OF ALL OUR CITIZENS, I BID YOU WELCOME...
...TO
ZENITH CITY!
THANK YOU...I THINK. JASON, I TAKE IT YOU'RE THE LEADER HERE?
I REPRESENT THE VOICE OF THE GROUPMIND... BUT THE PEOPLE OF ZENITH REQUIRE NO LEADERS. WE ARE A FREE AND PERFECT SOCIETY.
I'M NOT SURPRISED. THAT ALWAYS WAS HIS DREAM.
WHOSE DREAM? AND SHOULDN'T WE BE SEARCHING FOR MORE A.I.M. SOLDIERS?
NO NEED, CAPTAIN. THESE ARE THE LAST ONES ON THE ISLAND, AS BEST AS WE HAVE FOUND.
ONCE YOU DEFEATED THE MAJORITY OF THEM, THE REST GAVE US NO TROUBLE. WE LIBERATED OURSELVES.
AS FOR THE "WHO" OF IRON MAN'S STATEMENT...

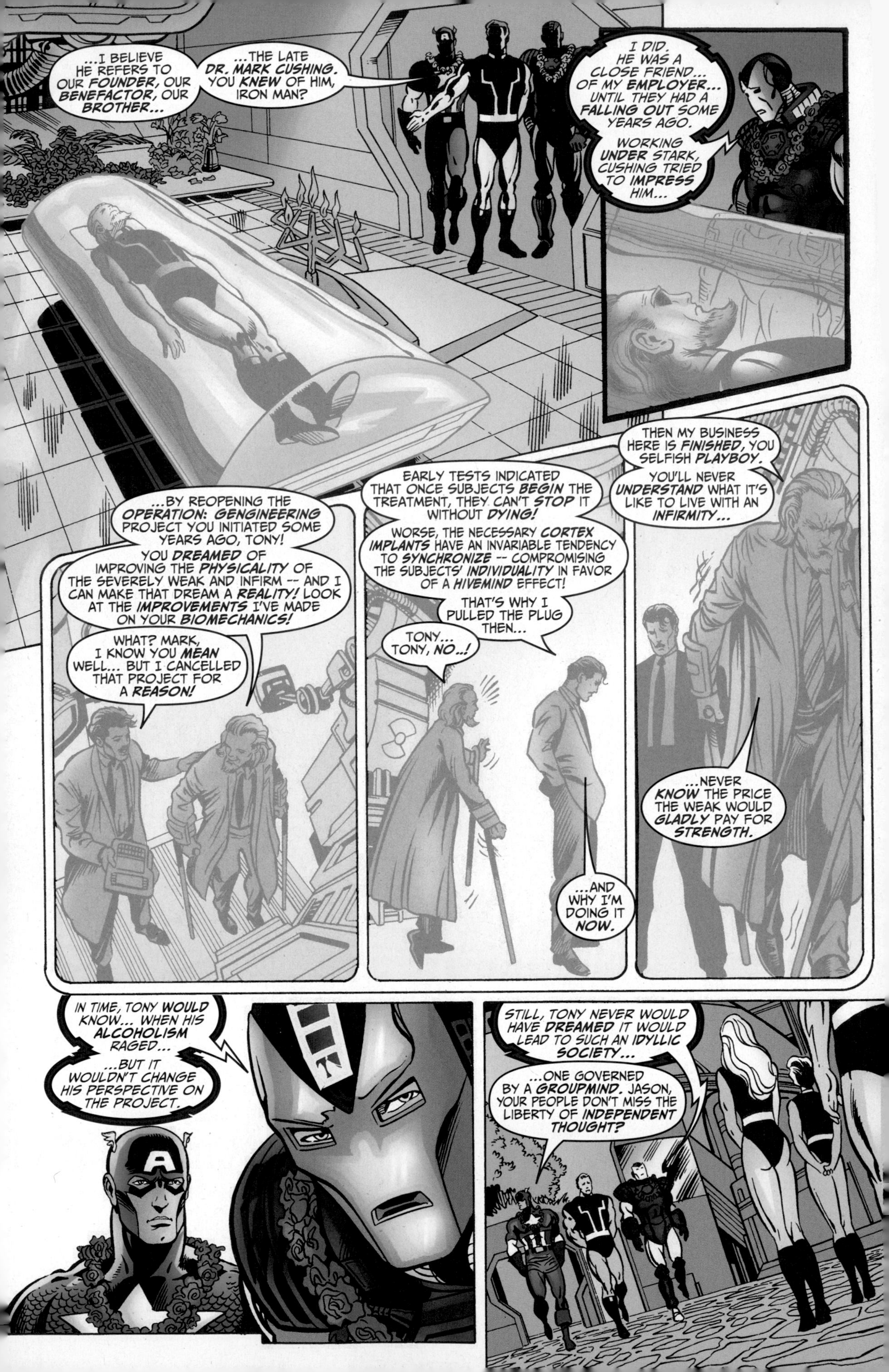
...I BELIEVE HE REFERS TO OUR FOUNDER, OUR BENEFACTOR, OUR BROTHER...
...THE LATE DR. MARK CUSHING. YOU KNEW OF HIM, IRON MAN?
I DID. HE WAS A CLOSE FRIEND... OF MY EMPLOYER... UNTIL THEY HAD A FALLING OUT SOME YEARS AGO.
WORKING UNDER STARK, CUSHING TRIED TO IMPRESS HIM...
...BY REOPENING THE OPERATION: GENGINEERING PROJECT YOU INITIATED SOME YEARS AGO, TONY!
YOU DREAMED OF IMPROVING THE PHYSICALITY OF THE SEVERELY WEAK AND INFIRM -- AND I CAN MAKE THAT DREAM A REALITY! LOOK AT THE IMPROVEMENTS I'VE MADE ON YOUR BIOMECHANICS!
WHAT? MARK, I KNOW YOU MEAN WELL... BUT I CANCELLED THAT PROJECT FOR A REASON!
EARLY TESTS INDICATED THAT ONCE SUBJECTS BEGIN THE TREATMENT, THEY CAN'T STOP IT WITHOUT DYING!
WORSE, THE NECESSARY CORTEX IMPLANTS HAVE AN INVARIABLE TENDENCY TO SYNCHRONIZE -- COMPROMISING THE SUBJECTS' INDIVIDUALITY IN FAVOR OF A HIVEMIND EFFECT!
THAT'S WHY I PULLED THE PLUG THEN...
TONY... TONY, NO..!
...AND WHY I'M DOING IT NOW.
THEN MY BUSINESS HERE IS FINISHED, YOU SELFISH PLAYBOY.
YOU'LL NEVER UNDERSTAND WHAT IT'S LIKE TO LIVE WITH AN INFIRMITY...
...NEVER KNOW THE PRICE THE WEAK WOULD GLADLY PAY FOR STRENGTH.
IN TIME, TONY WOULD KNOW... WHEN HIS ALCOHOLISM RAGED...
...BUT IT WOULDN'T CHANGE HIS PERSPECTIVE ON THE PROJECT.
STILL, TONY NEVER WOULD HAVE DREAMED IT WOULD LEAD TO SUCH AN IDYLLIC SOCIETY...
...ONE GOVERNED BY A GROUPMIND. JASON, YOUR PEOPLE DON'T MISS THE LIBERTY OF INDEPENDENT THOUGHT?

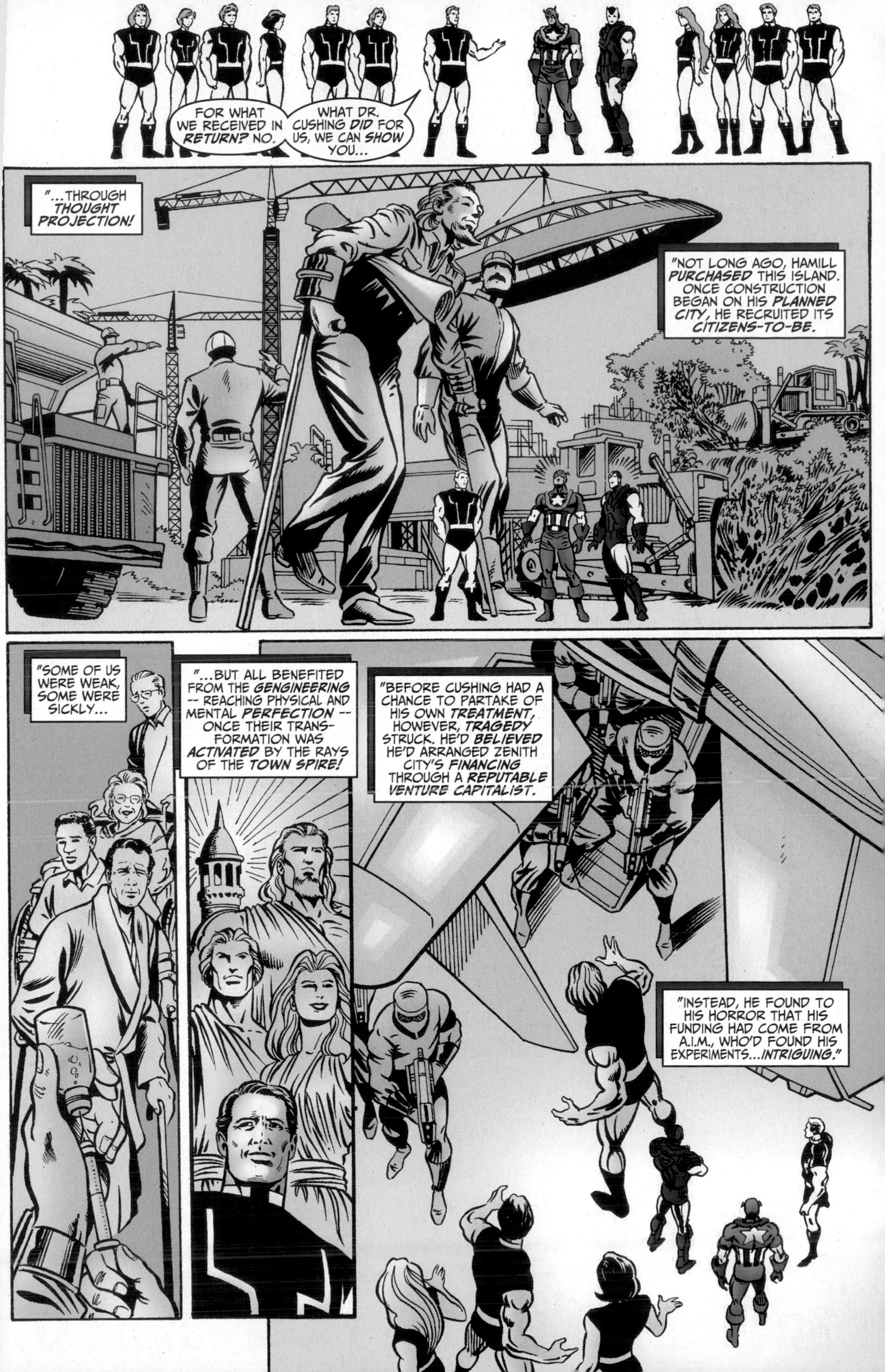
FOR WHAT WE RECEIVED IN RETURN? NO.
WHAT DR. CUSHING DID FOR US, WE CAN SHOW YOU...
"...THROUGH THOUGHT PROJECTION!
"NOT LONG AGO, HAMILL PURCHASED THIS ISLAND. ONCE CONSTRUCTION BEGAN ON HIS PLANNED CITY, HE RECRUITED ITS CITIZENS-TO-BE.
"SOME OF US WERE WEAK, SOME WERE SICKLY...
"...BUT ALL BENEFITED FROM THE GENGINEERING -- REACHING PHYSICAL AND MENTAL PERFECTION -- ONCE THEIR TRANSFORMATION WAS ACTIVATED BY THE RAYS OF THE TOWN SPIRE!
"BEFORE CUSHING HAD A CHANCE TO PARTAKE OF HIS OWN TREATMENT, HOWEVER, TRAGEDY STRUCK. HE'D BELIEVED HE'D ARRANGED ZENITH CITY'S FINANCING THROUGH A REPUTABLE VENTURE CAPITALIST.
"INSTEAD, HE FOUND TO HIS HORROR THAT HIS FUNDING HAD COME FROM A.I.M., WHO'D FOUND HIS EXPERIMENTS...INTRIGUING."

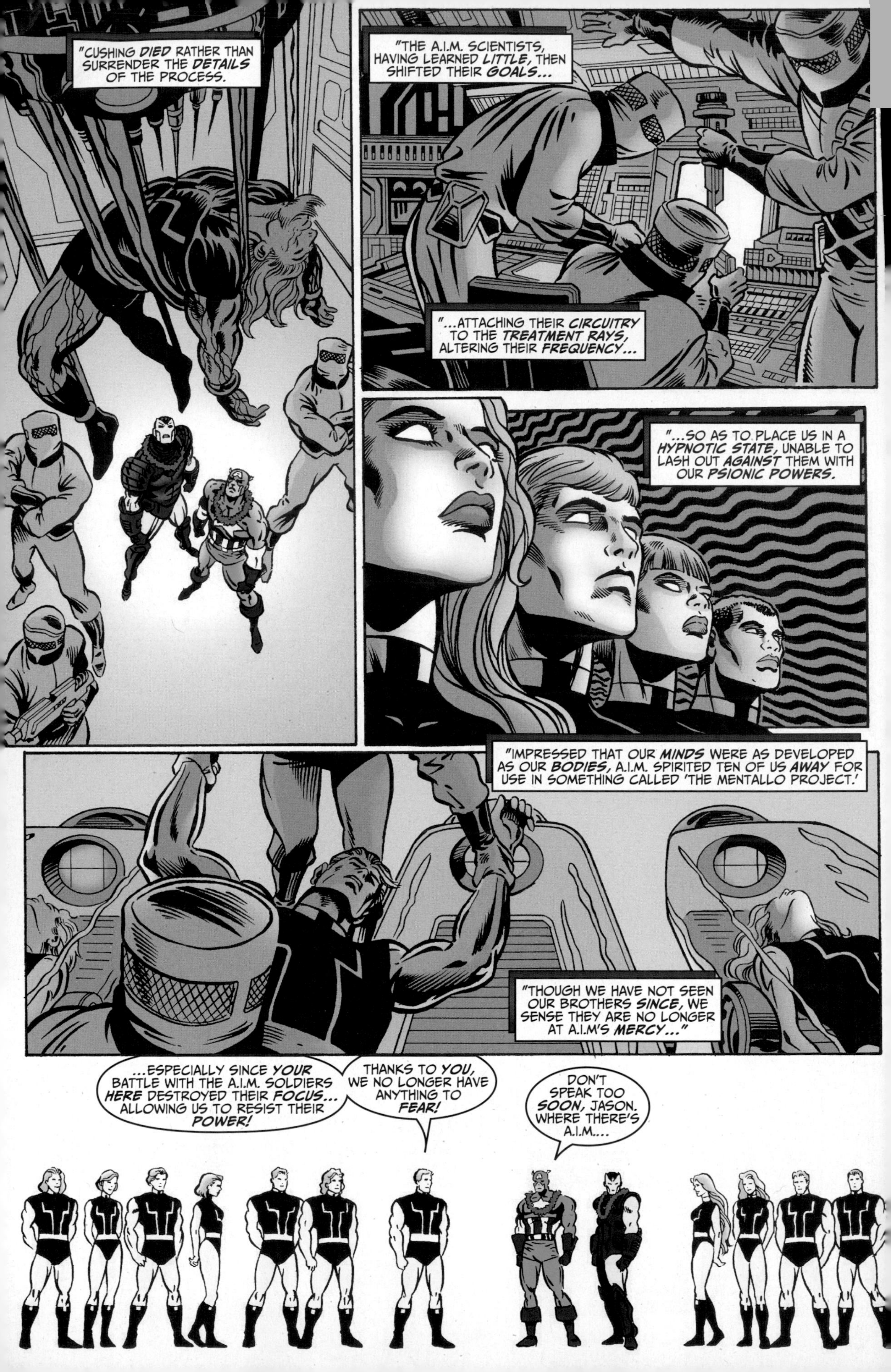
"CUSHING DIED RATHER THAN SURRENDER THE DETAILS OF THE PROCESS.
"THE A.I.M. SCIENTISTS, HAVING LEARNED LITTLE, THEN SHIFTED THEIR GOALS...
"...ATTACHING THEIR CIRCUITRY TO THE TREATMENT RAYS, ALTERING THEIR FREQUENCY...
"...SO AS TO PLACE US IN A HYPNOTIC STATE, UNABLE TO LASH OUT AGAINST THEM WITH OUR PSIONIC POWERS.
"IMPRESSED THAT OUR MINDS WERE AS DEVELOPED AS OUR BODIES, A.I.M. SPIRITED TEN OF US AWAY FOR USE IN SOMETHING CALLED 'THE MENTALLO PROJECT.'
"THOUGH WE HAVE NOT SEEN OUR BROTHERS SINCE, WE SENSE THEY ARE NO LONGER AT A.I.M'S MERCY..."
...ESPECIALLY SINCE YOUR BATTLE WITH THE A.I.M. SOLDIERS HERE DESTROYED THEIR FOCUS... ALLOWING US TO RESIST THEIR POWER!
THANKS TO YOU, WE NO LONGER HAVE ANYTHING TO FEAR!
DON'T SPEAK TOO SOON, JASON. WHERE THERE'S A.I.M....

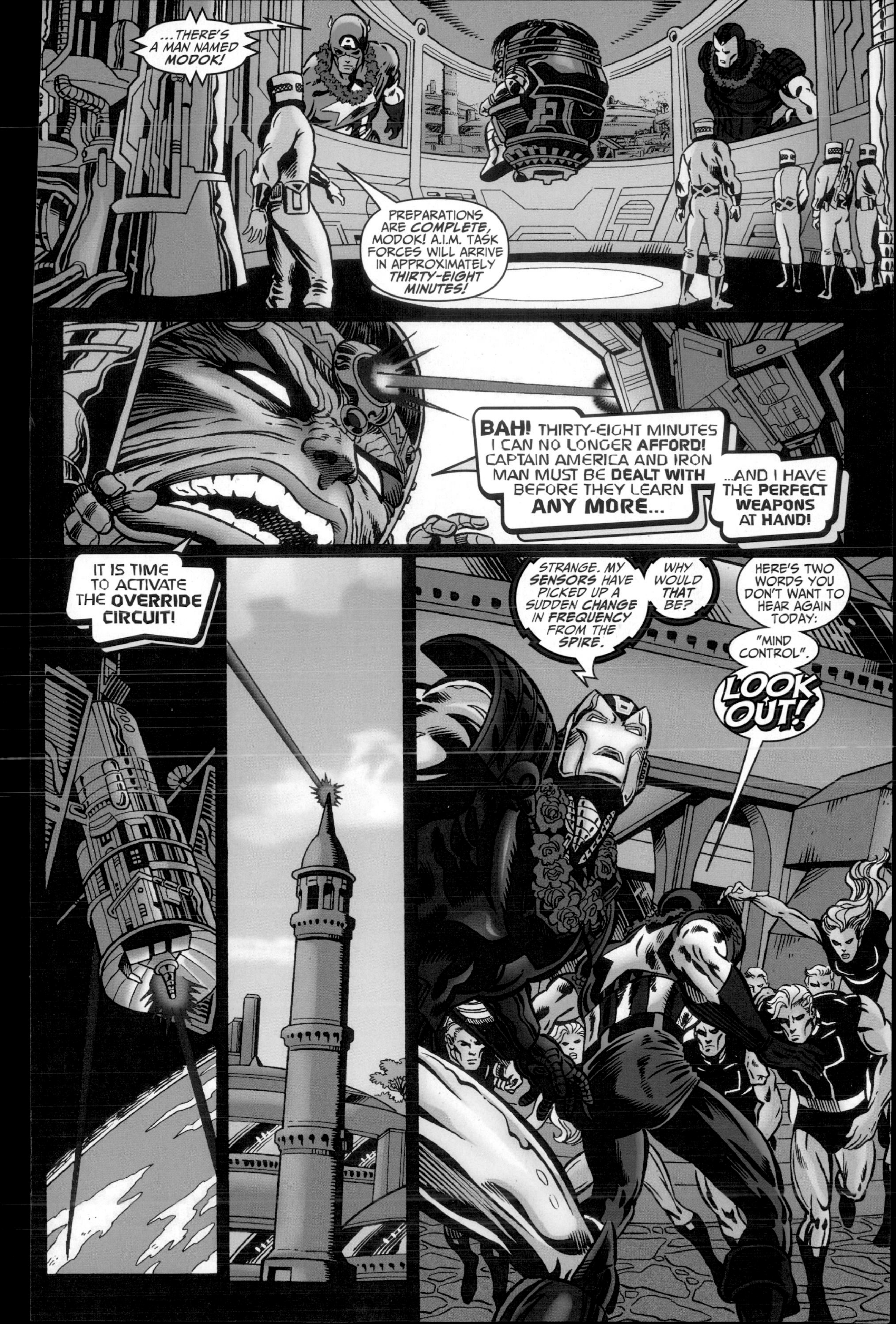
...THERE'S A MAN NAMED MODOK!
PREPARATIONS ARE COMPLETE, MODOK! A.I.M. TASK FORCES WILL ARRIVE IN APPROXIMATELY THIRTY-EIGHT MINUTES!
BAH! THIRTY-EIGHT MINUTES I CAN NO LONGER AFFORD! CAPTAIN AMERICA AND IRON MAN MUST BE DEALT WITH BEFORE THEY LEARN ANY MORE...
...AND I HAVE THE PERFECT WEAPONS AT HAND!
IT IS TIME TO ACTIVATE THE OVERRIDE CIRCUIT!
STRANGE. MY SENSORS HAVE PICKED UP A SUDDEN CHANGE IN FREQUENCY FROM THE SPIRE.
WHY WOULD THAT BE?
HERE'S TWO WORDS YOU DON'T WANT TO HEAR AGAIN TODAY:
"MIND CONTROL".
LOOK OUT!

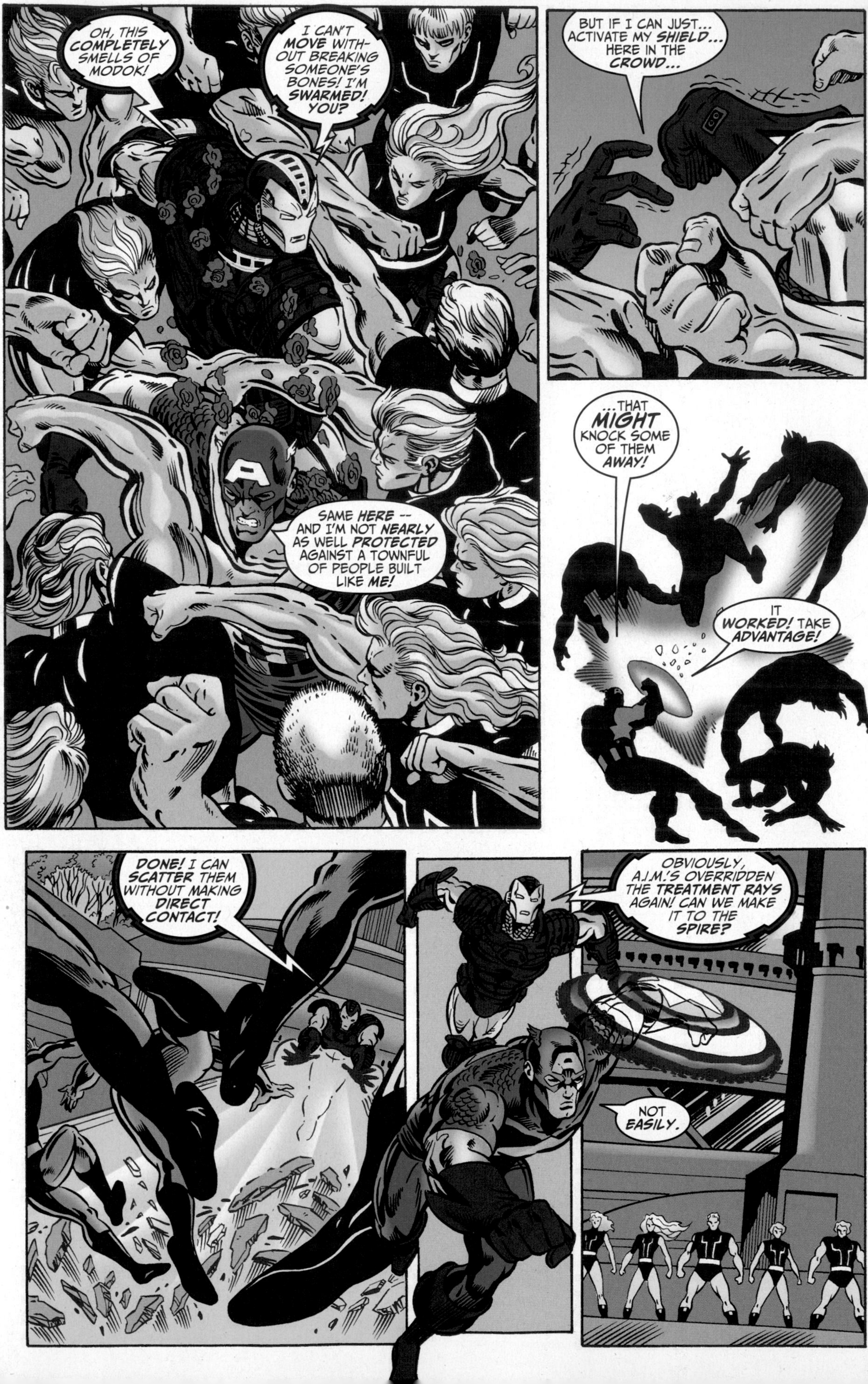
OH, THIS COMPLETELY SMELLS OF MODOK!
I CAN'T MOVE WITHOUT BREAKING SOMEONE'S BONES! I'M SWARMED! YOU?
SAME HERE -- AND I'M NOT NEARLY AS WELL PROTECTED AGAINST A TOWNFUL OF PEOPLE BUILT LIKE ME!
BUT IF I CAN JUST... ACTIVATE MY SHIELD... HERE IN THE CROWD...
...THAT MIGHT KNOCK SOME OF THEM AWAY!
IT WORKED! TAKE ADVANTAGE!
DONE! I CAN SCATTER THEM WITHOUT MAKING DIRECT CONTACT!
OBVIOUSLY, A.I.M.'S OVERRIDDEN THE TREATMENT RAYS AGAIN! CAN WE MAKE IT TO THE SPIRE?
NOT EASILY.

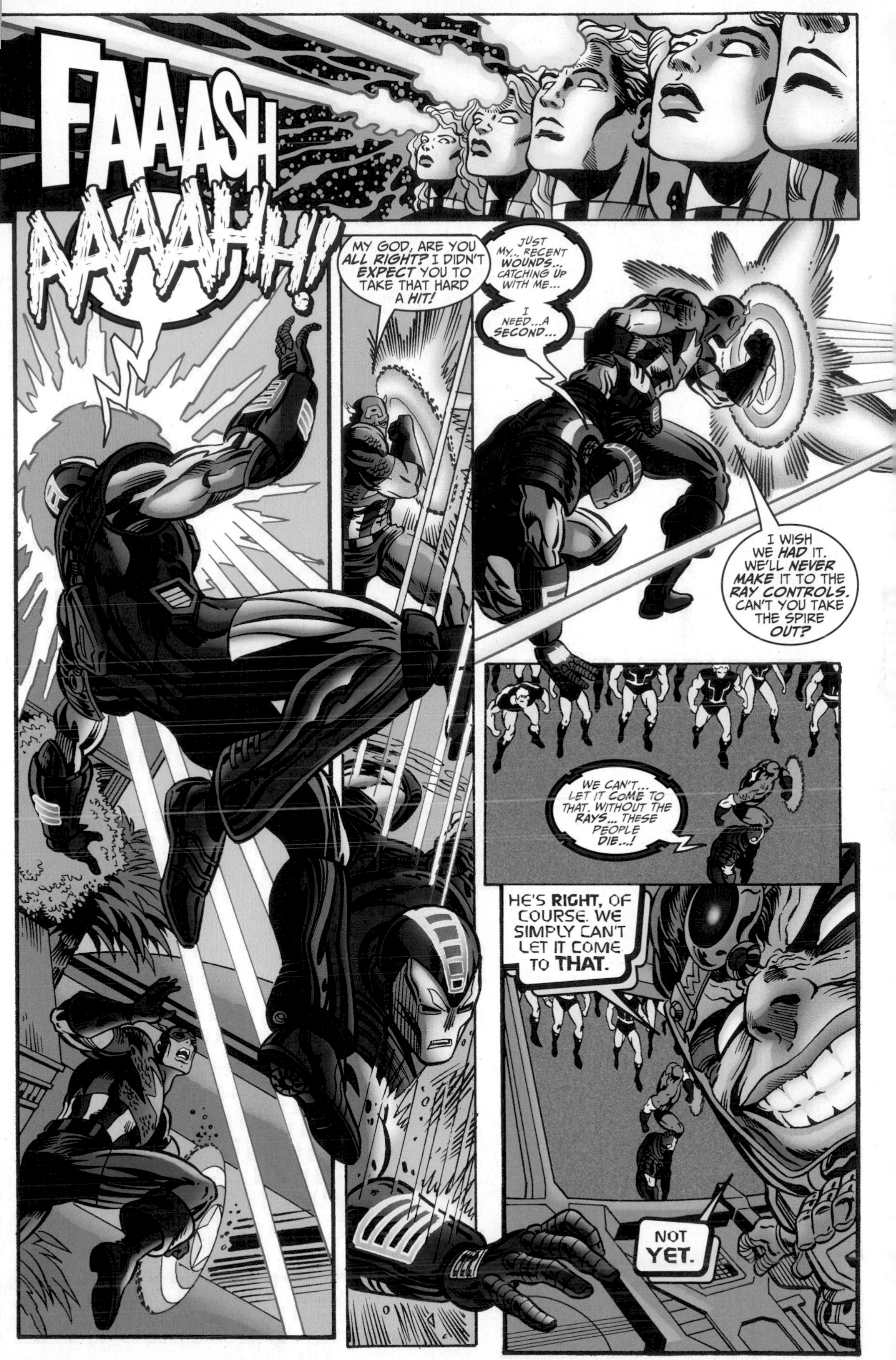

FAAASH
AAAAHH!
MY GOD, ARE YOU ALL RIGHT? I DIDN'T EXPECT YOU TO TAKE THAT HARD A HIT!
JUST MY... RECENT WOUNDS... CATCHING UP WITH ME...
I NEED... A SECOND...
I WISH WE HAD IT. WE'LL NEVER MAKE IT TO THE RAY CONTROLS. CAN'T YOU TAKE THE SPIRE OUT?
WE CAN'T... LET IT COME TO THAT. WITHOUT THE RAYS... THESE PEOPLE DIE...!
HE'S RIGHT, OF COURSE. WE SIMPLY CAN'T LET IT COME TO THAT.
NOT YET.

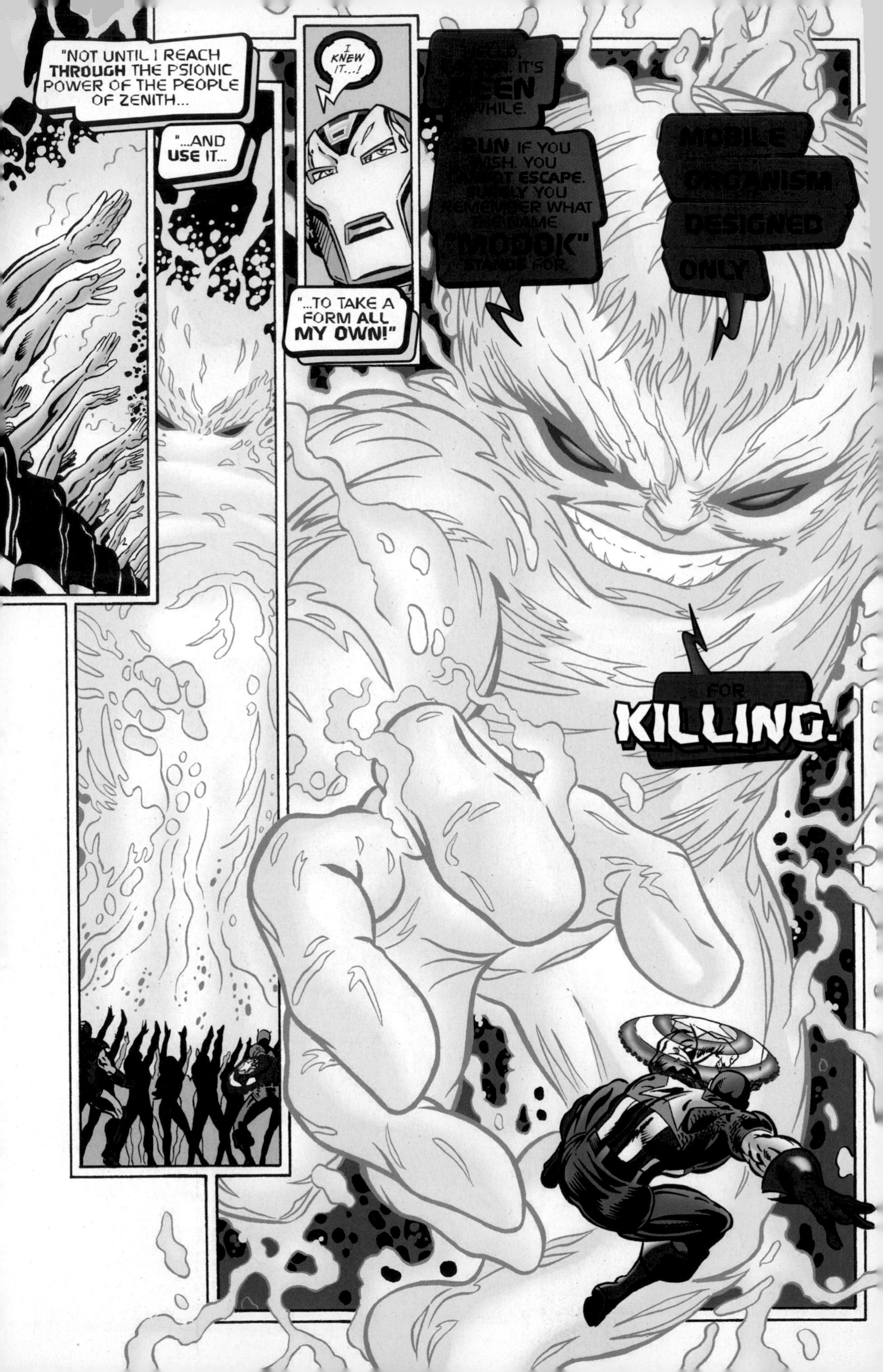
"NOT UNTIL I REACH THROUGH THE PSIONIC POWER OF THE PEOPLE OF ZENITH...
"...AND USE IT...
I KNEW IT...!
"...TO TAKE A FORM ALL MY OWN!"
IT'S ...EEN ...WHILE.
RUN IF YOU ...WISH. YOU ...ESCAPE. ...YOU ...WHAT ...NAME "MODOK" ...FOR.
MOBILE
ORGANISM
DESIGNED
ONLY
FOR
KILLING.

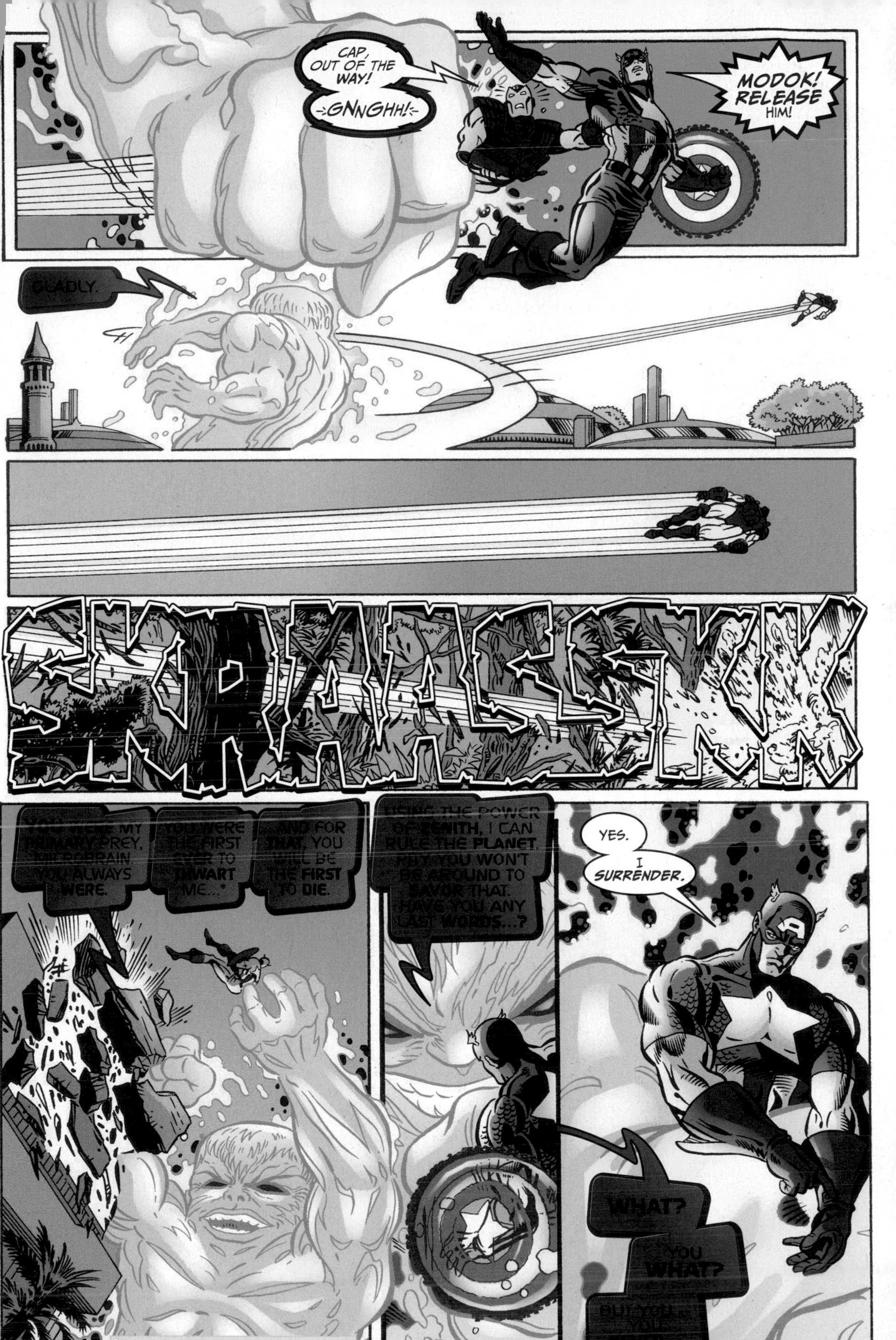
CAP, OUT OF THE WAY!
-GNNGHH!-
MODOK! RELEASE HIM!
GLADLY.
YOU WERE THE FIRST EVER TO THWART ME...*
AND FOR THAT, YOU WILL BE THE FIRST TO DIE.
USING THE POWER OF ZENITH, I CAN RULE THE PLANET. PITY YOU WON'T BE AROUND TO SAVOR THAT. HAVE YOU ANY LAST WORDS...?
YES. I SURRENDER.
WHAT?
YOU WHAT?

*Way back in Tales of Suspense #94. -- Matt.

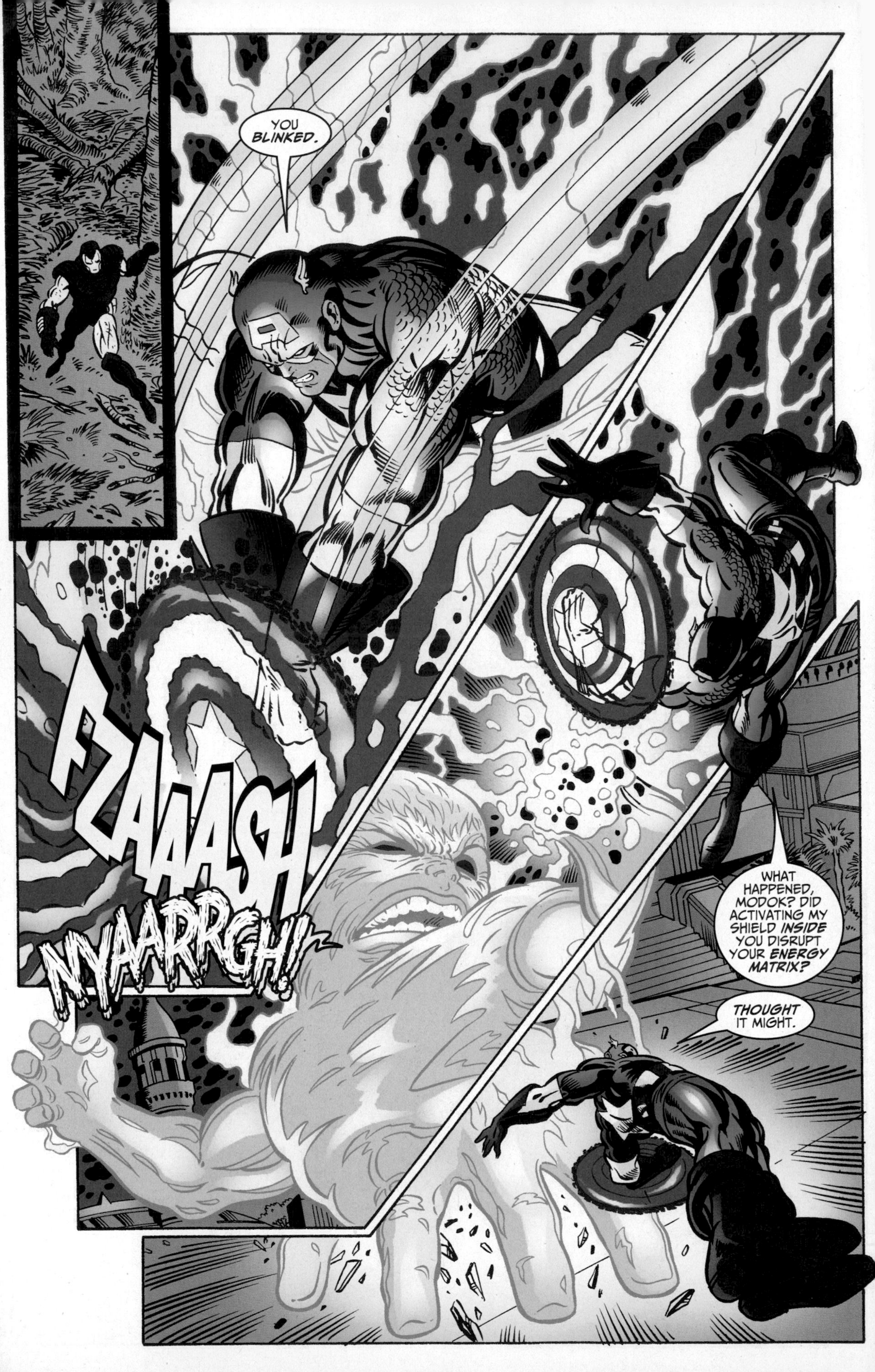
YOU BLINKED.
FZAAASH
NYAARRGH!
WHAT HAPPENED, MODOK? DID ACTIVATING MY SHIELD INSIDE YOU DISRUPT YOUR ENERGY MATRIX?
THOUGHT IT MIGHT.

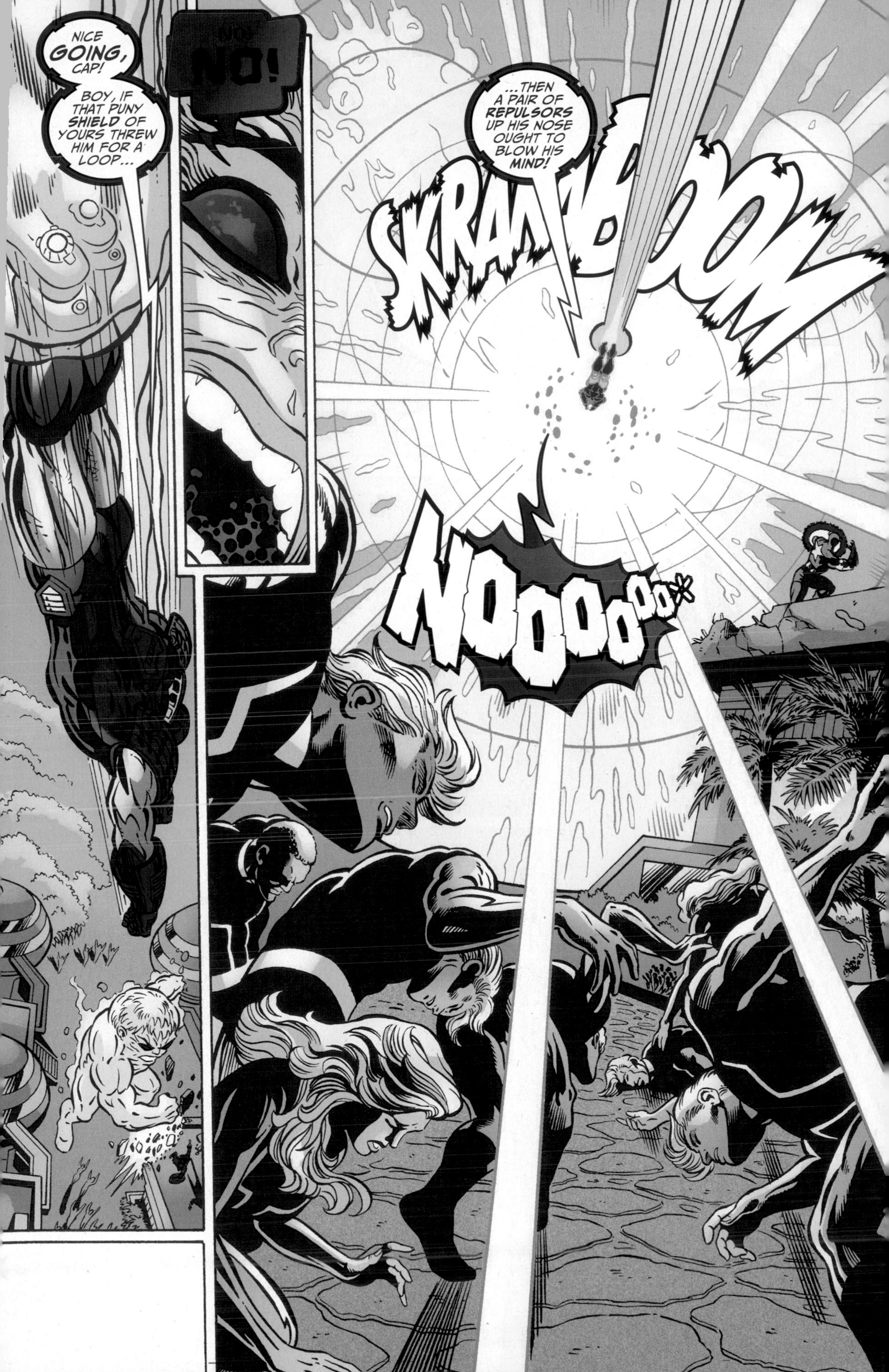

NICE GOING, CAP!
BOY, IF THAT PUNY SHIELD OF YOURS THREW HIM FOR A LOOP...
NO! NO!
...THEN A PAIR OF REPULSORS UP HIS NOSE OUGHT TO BLOW HIS MIND!
SKRAKABOOM
NOOOOOOO*

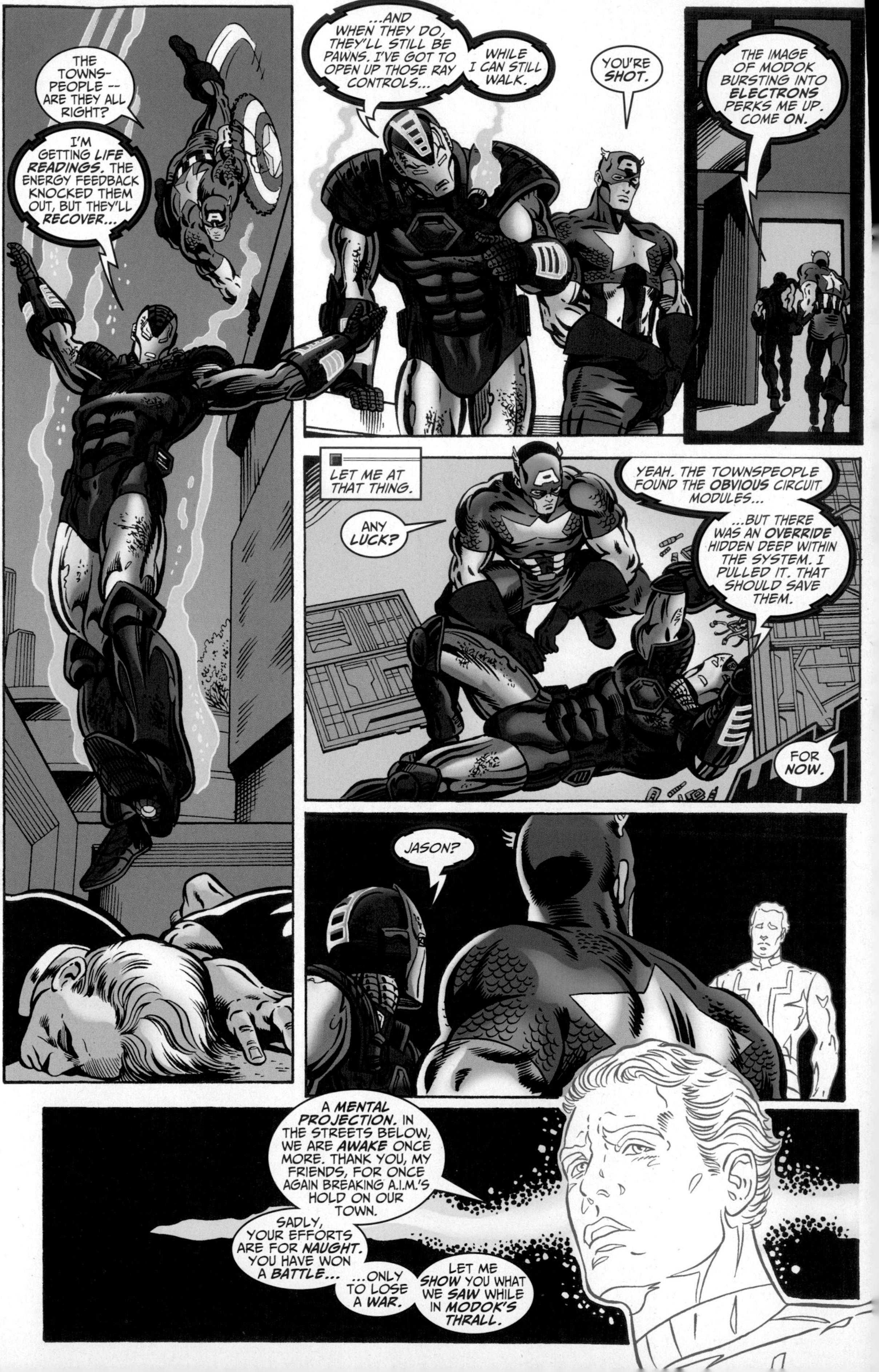
THE TOWNS-PEOPLE -- ARE THEY ALL RIGHT?
I'M GETTING LIFE READINGS. THE ENERGY FEEDBACK KNOCKED THEM OUT, BUT THEY'LL RECOVER...
...AND WHEN THEY DO, THEY'LL STILL BE PAWNS. I'VE GOT TO OPEN UP THOSE RAY CONTROLS...
WHILE I CAN STILL WALK.
YOU'RE SHOT.
THE IMAGE OF MODOK BURSTING INTO ELECTRONS PERKS ME UP. COME ON.
LET ME AT THAT THING.
ANY LUCK?
YEAH. THE TOWNSPEOPLE FOUND THE OBVIOUS CIRCUIT MODULES...
...BUT THERE WAS AN OVERRIDE HIDDEN DEEP WITHIN THE SYSTEM. I PULLED IT. THAT SHOULD SAVE THEM.
FOR NOW.
JASON?
A MENTAL PROJECTION. IN THE STREETS BELOW, WE ARE AWAKE ONCE MORE. THANK YOU, MY FRIENDS, FOR ONCE AGAIN BREAKING A.I.M.'S HOLD ON OUR TOWN.
SADLY, YOUR EFFORTS ARE FOR NAUGHT. YOU HAVE WON A BATTLE...
...ONLY TO LOSE A WAR.
LET ME SHOW YOU WHAT WE SAW WHILE IN MODOK'S THRALL.

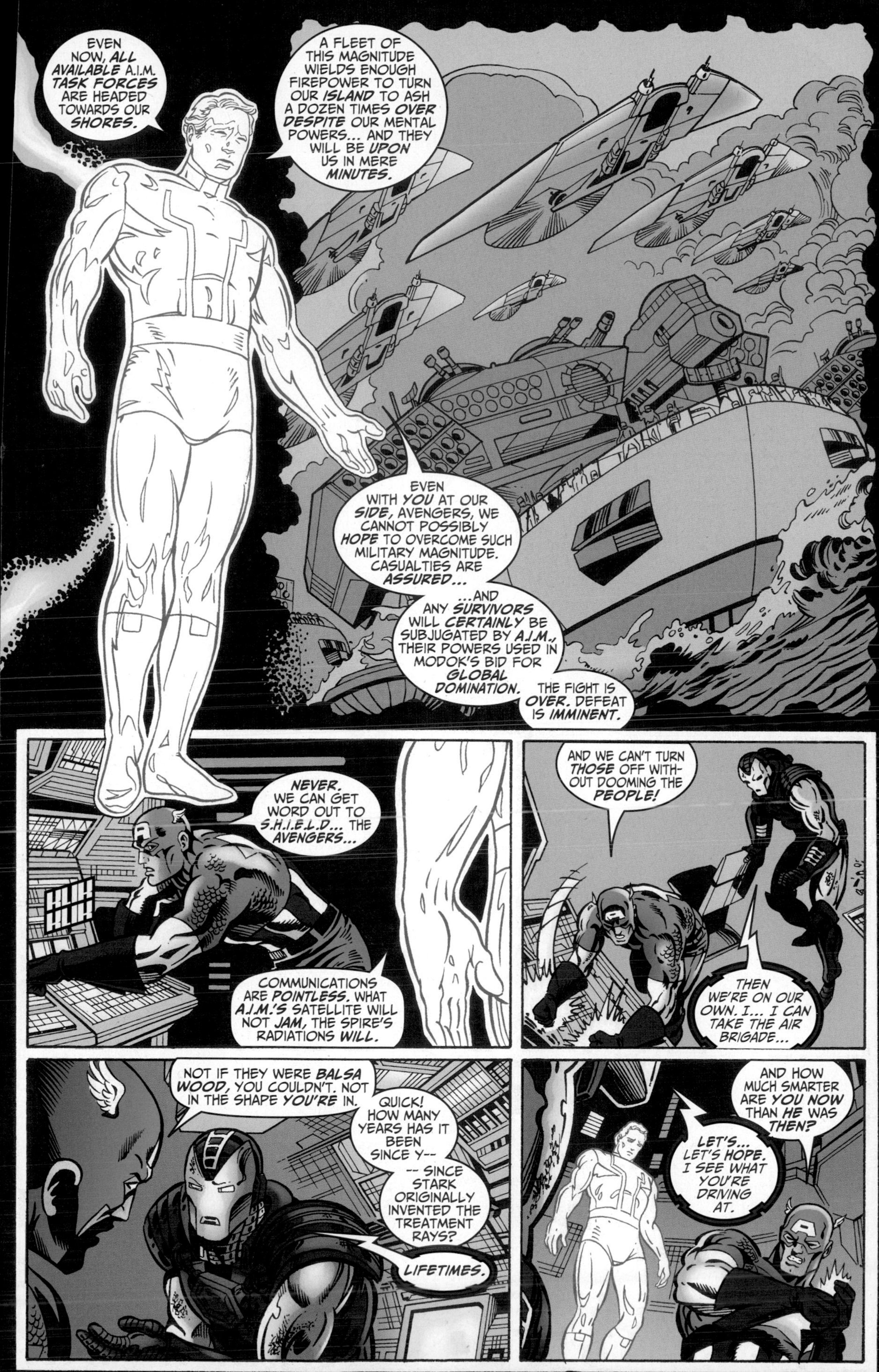

EVEN NOW, ALL AVAILABLE A.I.M. TASK FORCES ARE HEADED TOWARDS OUR SHORES.
A FLEET OF THIS MAGNITUDE WIELDS ENOUGH FIREPOWER TO TURN OUR ISLAND TO ASH A DOZEN TIMES OVER DESPITE OUR MENTAL POWERS... AND THEY WILL BE UPON US IN MERE MINUTES.
EVEN WITH YOU AT OUR SIDE, AVENGERS, WE CANNOT POSSIBLY HOPE TO OVERCOME SUCH MILITARY MAGNITUDE. CASUALTIES ARE ASSURED...
...AND ANY SURVIVORS WILL CERTAINLY BE SUBJUGATED BY A.I.M., THEIR POWERS USED IN MODOK'S BID FOR GLOBAL DOMINATION.
THE FIGHT IS OVER. DEFEAT IS IMMINENT.
NEVER. WE CAN GET WORD OUT TO S.H.I.E.L.D... THE AVENGERS...
KLIK KLIK
COMMUNICATIONS ARE POINTLESS. WHAT A.I.M.'S SATELLITE WILL NOT JAM, THE SPIRE'S RADIATIONS WILL.
AND WE CAN'T TURN THOSE OFF WITHOUT DOOMING THE PEOPLE!
THEN WE'RE ON OUR OWN. I... I CAN TAKE THE AIR BRIGADE...
NOT IF THEY WERE BALSA WOOD, YOU COULDN'T. NOT IN THE SHAPE YOU'RE IN.
QUICK! HOW MANY YEARS HAS IT BEEN SINCE Y--
-- SINCE STARK ORIGINALLY INVENTED THE TREATMENT RAYS?
LIFETIMES.
AND HOW MUCH SMARTER ARE YOU NOW THAN HE WAS THEN?
LET'S... LET'S HOPE. I SEE WHAT YOU'RE DRIVING AT.

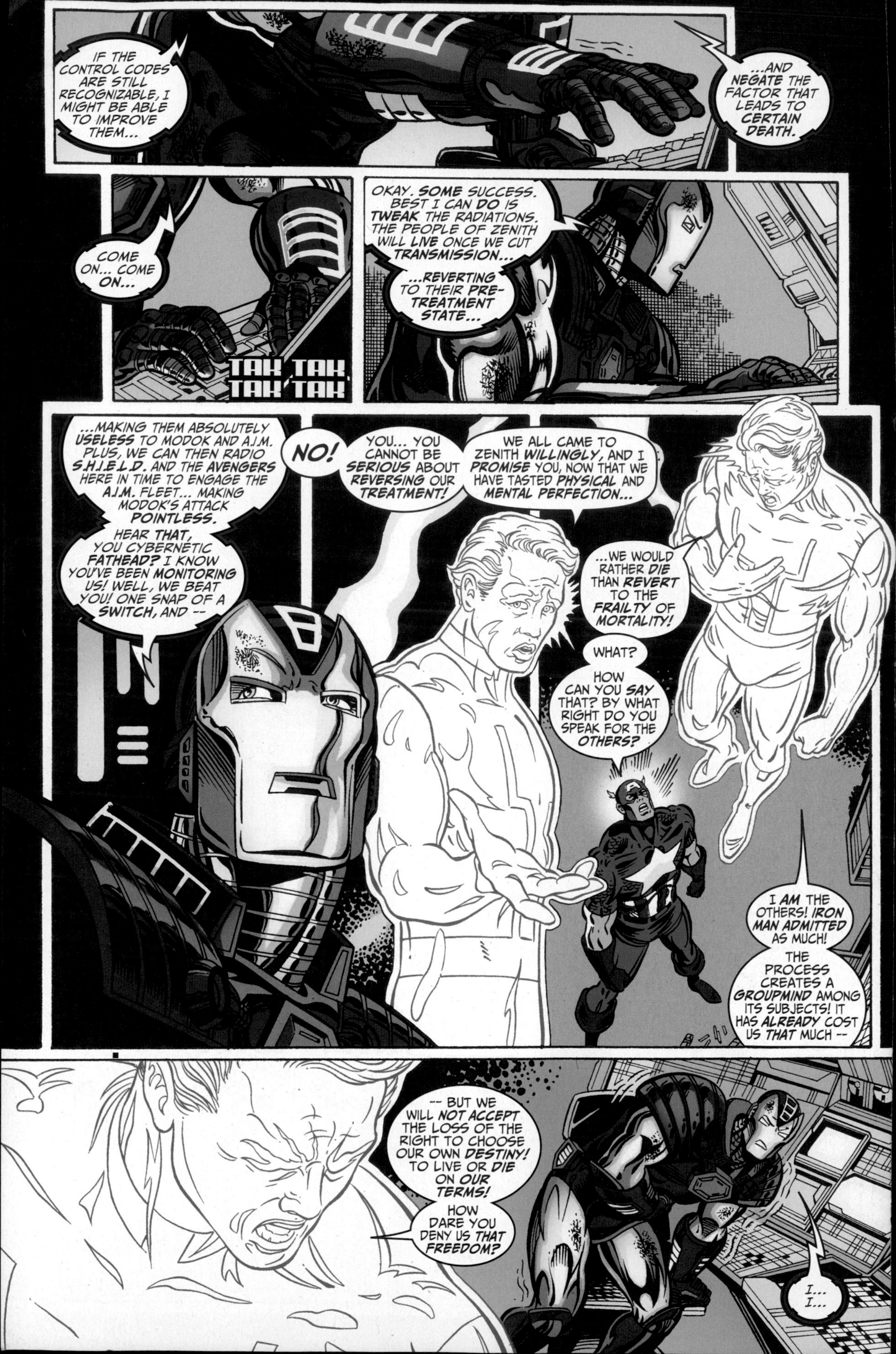
IF THE CONTROL CODES ARE STILL RECOGNIZABLE, I MIGHT BE ABLE TO IMPROVE THEM...
...AND NEGATE THE FACTOR THAT LEADS TO CERTAIN DEATH.
COME ON... COME ON...
TAK TAK TAK TAK
OKAY. SOME SUCCESS. BEST I CAN DO IS TWEAK THE RADIATIONS. THE PEOPLE OF ZENITH WILL LIVE ONCE WE CUT TRANSMISSION...
...REVERTING TO THEIR PRE-TREATMENT STATE...
...MAKING THEM ABSOLUTELY USELESS TO MODOK AND A.I.M. PLUS, WE CAN THEN RADIO S.H.I.E.L.D. AND THE AVENGERS HERE IN TIME TO ENGAGE THE A.I.M. FLEET... MAKING MODOK'S ATTACK POINTLESS.
HEAR THAT, YOU CYBERNETIC FATHEAD? I KNOW YOU'VE BEEN MONITORING US! WELL, WE BEAT YOU! ONE SNAP OF A SWITCH, AND --
NO!
YOU... YOU CANNOT BE SERIOUS ABOUT REVERSING OUR TREATMENT!
WE ALL CAME TO ZENITH WILLINGLY, AND I PROMISE YOU, NOW THAT WE HAVE TASTED PHYSICAL AND MENTAL PERFECTION...
...WE WOULD RATHER DIE THAN REVERT TO THE FRAILTY OF MORTALITY!
WHAT?
HOW CAN YOU SAY THAT? BY WHAT RIGHT DO YOU SPEAK FOR THE OTHERS?
I AM THE OTHERS! IRON MAN ADMITTED AS MUCH!
THE PROCESS CREATES A GROUPMIND AMONG ITS SUBJECTS! IT HAS ALREADY COST US THAT MUCH --
-- BUT WE WILL NOT ACCEPT THE LOSS OF THE RIGHT TO CHOOSE OUR OWN DESTINY! TO LIVE OR DIE ON OUR TERMS!
HOW DARE YOU DENY US THAT FREEDOM?
I... I...

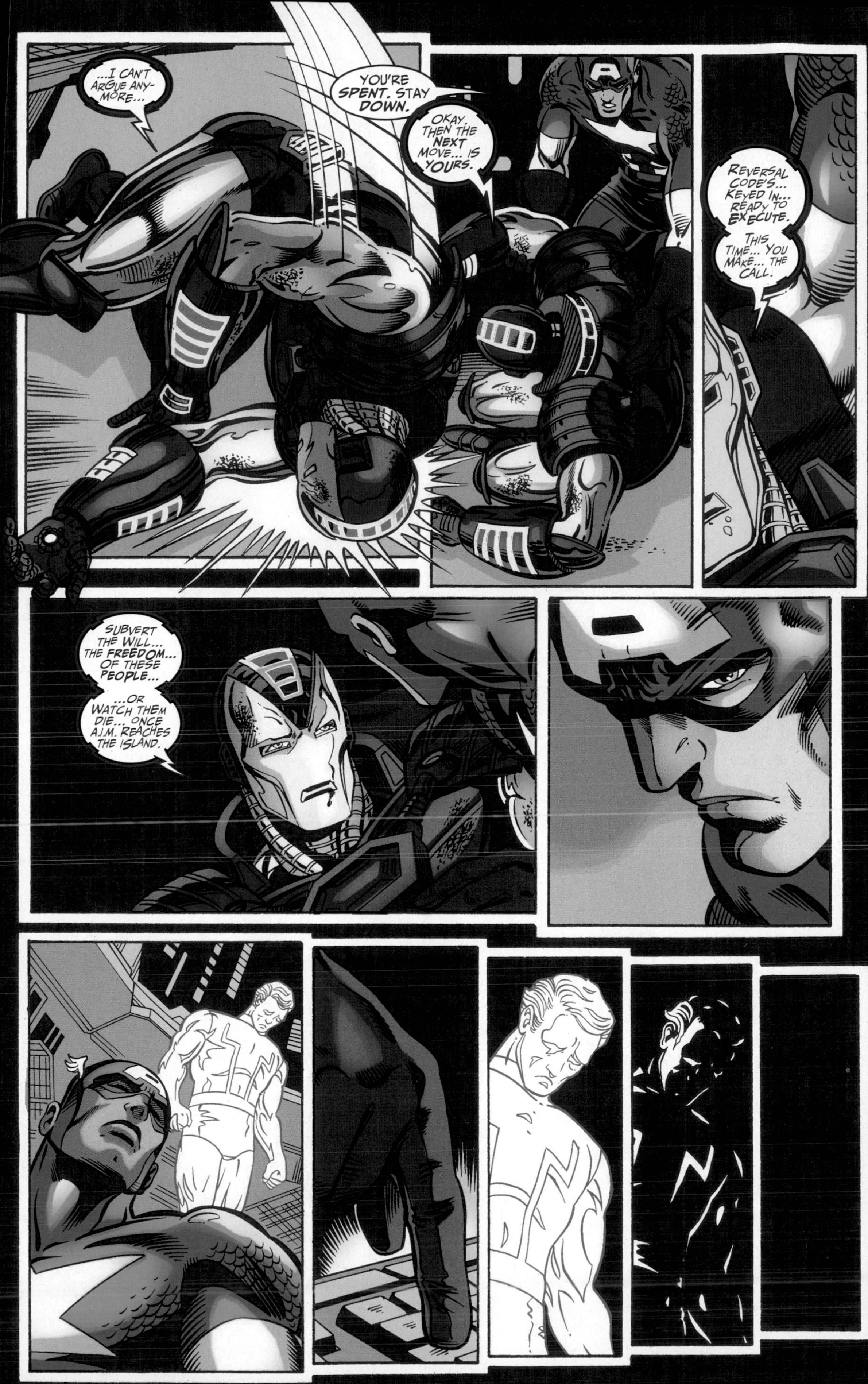

...I CAN'T ARGUE ANYMORE...
YOU'RE SPENT. STAY DOWN.
OKAY. THEN THE NEXT MOVE... IS YOURS.
REVERSAL CODE'S... KEYED IN... READY TO EXECUTE.
THIS TIME... YOU MAKE... THE CALL.
SUBVERT THE WILL... THE FREEDOM... OF THESE PEOPLE...
...OR WATCH THEM DIE... ONCE A.I.M. REACHES THE ISLAND.

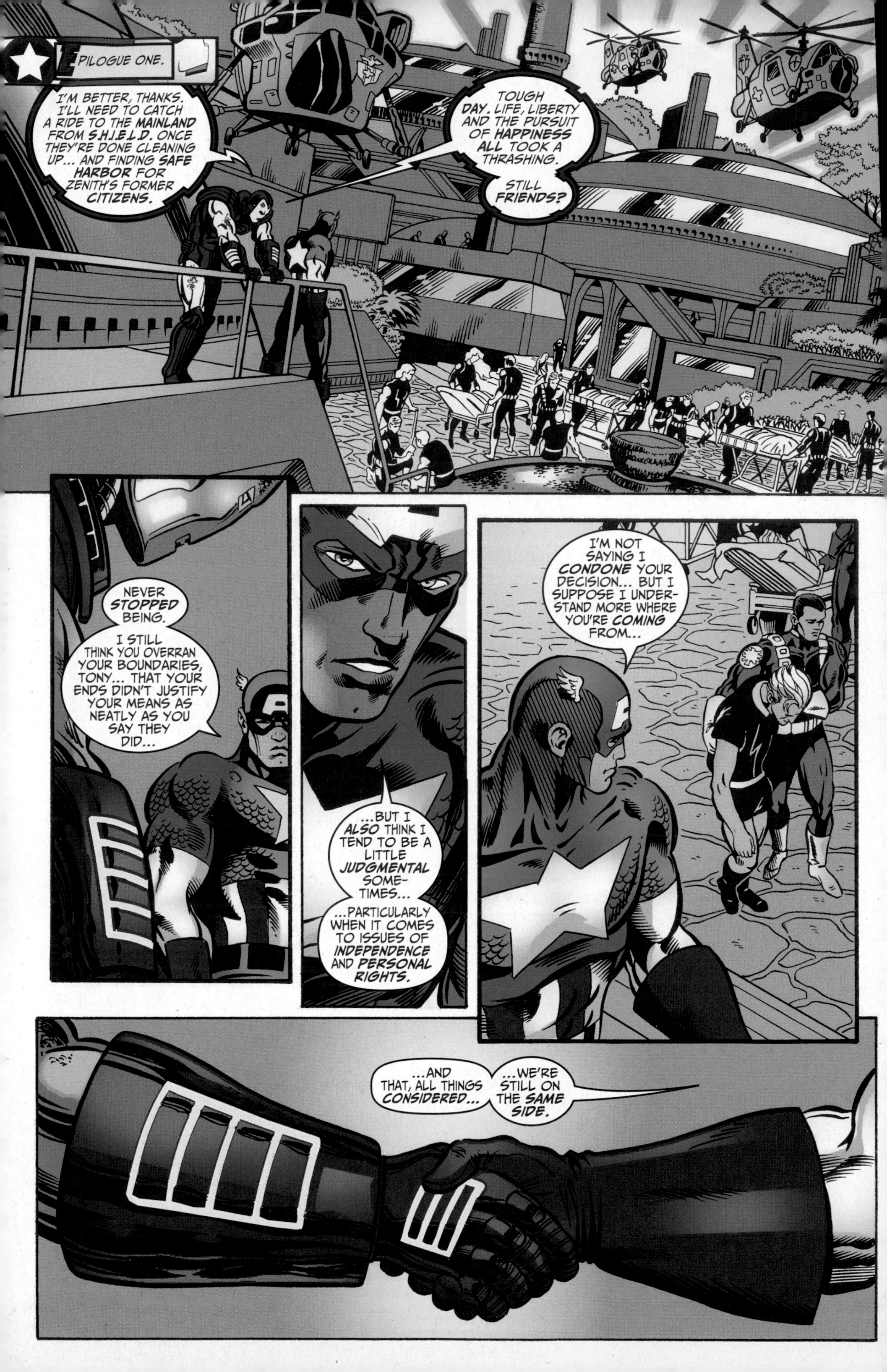
EPILOGUE ONE.
I'M BETTER, THANKS. I'LL NEED TO CATCH A RIDE TO THE MAINLAND FROM S.H.I.E.L.D. ONCE THEY'RE DONE CLEANING UP... AND FINDING SAFE HARBOR FOR ZENITH'S FORMER CITIZENS.
TOUGH DAY. LIFE, LIBERTY AND THE PURSUIT OF HAPPINESS ALL TOOK A THRASHING.
STILL FRIENDS?
NEVER STOPPED BEING.
I STILL THINK YOU OVERRAN YOUR BOUNDARIES, TONY... THAT YOUR ENDS DIDN'T JUSTIFY YOUR MEANS AS NEATLY AS YOU SAY THEY DID...
...BUT I ALSO THINK I TEND TO BE A LITTLE JUDGMENTAL SOME-TIMES...
...PARTICULARLY WHEN IT COMES TO ISSUES OF INDEPENDENCE AND PERSONAL RIGHTS.
I'M NOT SAYING I CONDONE YOUR DECISION... BUT I SUPPOSE I UNDER-STAND MORE WHERE YOU'RE COMING FROM...
...AND THAT, ALL THINGS CONSIDERED...
...WE'RE STILL ON THE SAME SIDE.

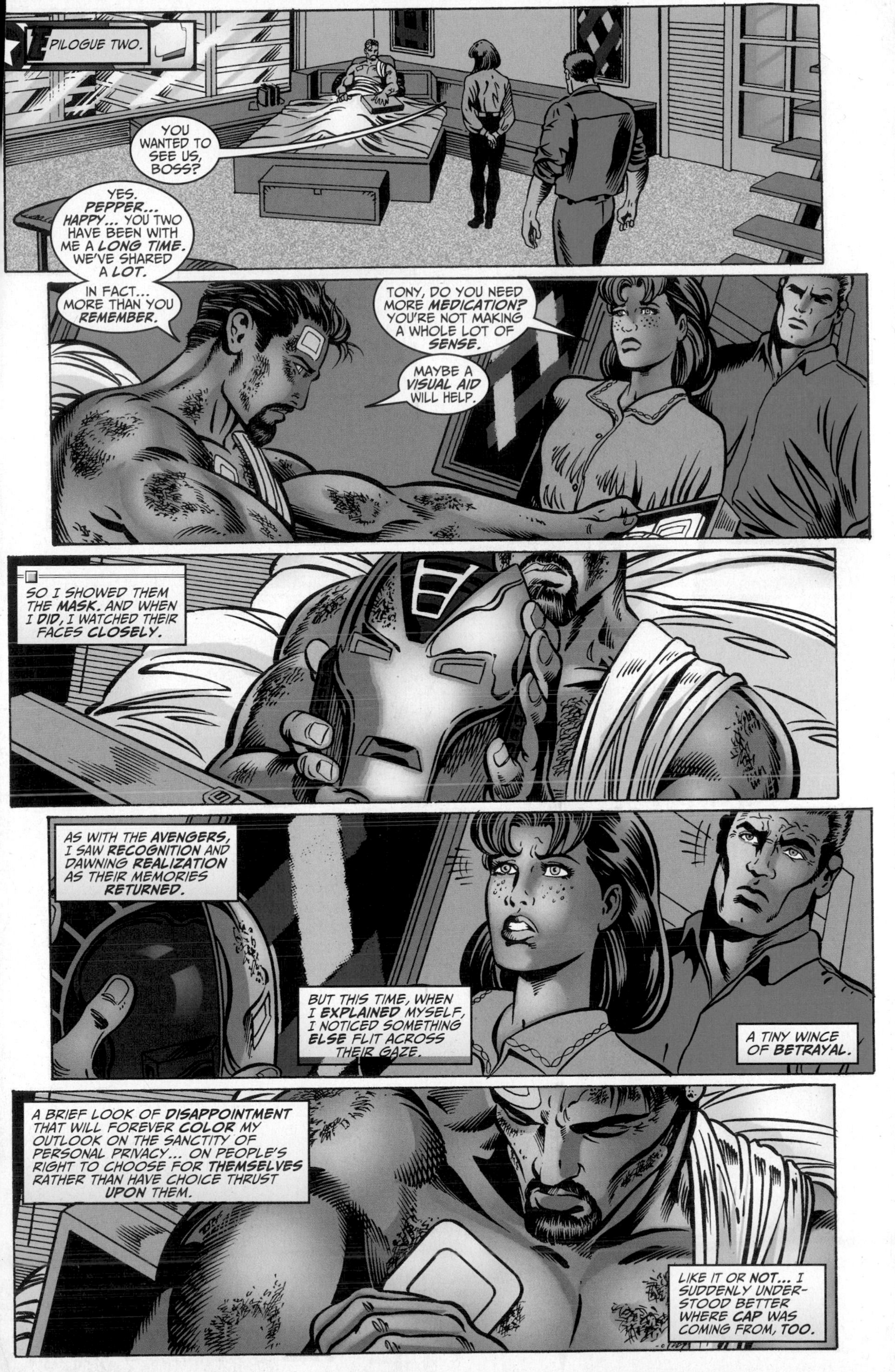
EPILOGUE TWO.
YOU WANTED TO SEE US, BOSS?
YES. PEPPER... HAPPY... YOU TWO HAVE BEEN WITH ME A LONG TIME. WE'VE SHARED A LOT.
IN FACT... MORE THAN YOU REMEMBER.
TONY, DO YOU NEED MORE MEDICATION? YOU'RE NOT MAKING A WHOLE LOT OF SENSE.
MAYBE A VISUAL AID WILL HELP.
SO I SHOWED THEM THE MASK. AND WHEN I DID, I WATCHED THEIR FACES CLOSELY.
AS WITH THE AVENGERS, I SAW RECOGNITION AND DAWNING REALIZATION AS THEIR MEMORIES RETURNED.
BUT THIS TIME, WHEN I EXPLAINED MYSELF, I NOTICED SOMETHING ELSE FLIT ACROSS THEIR GAZE.
A TINY WINCE OF BETRAYAL.
A BRIEF LOOK OF DISAPPOINTMENT THAT WILL FOREVER COLOR MY OUTLOOK ON THE SANCTITY OF PERSONAL PRIVACY... ON PEOPLE'S RIGHT TO CHOOSE FOR THEMSELVES RATHER THAN HAVE CHOICE THRUST UPON THEM.
LIKE IT OR NOT... I SUDDENLY UNDER-STOOD BETTER WHERE CAP WAS COMING FROM, TOO.

SOMETIMES WE
DO HAVE TO MAKE
COMPLICATED
CHOICES...

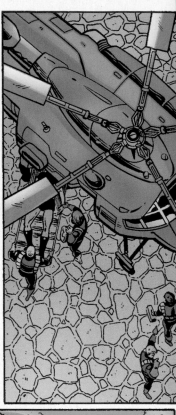

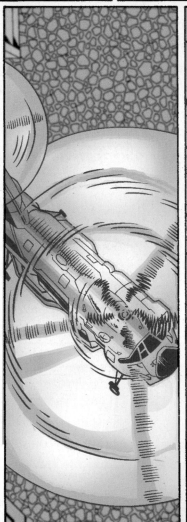

...BUT WE DON'T
HAVE TO LIKE THEM.

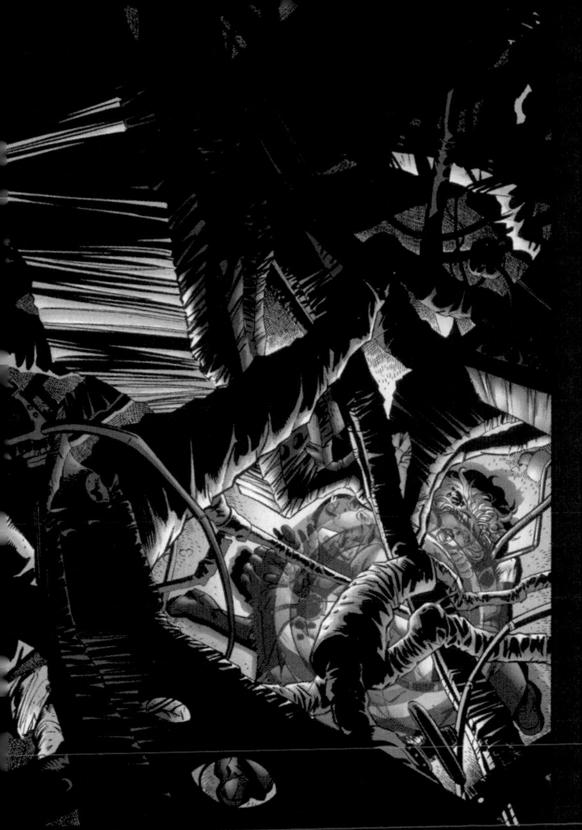

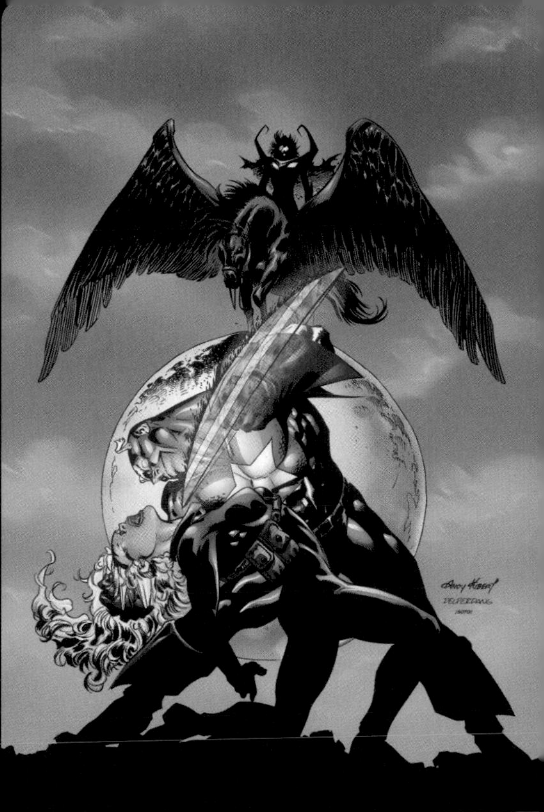

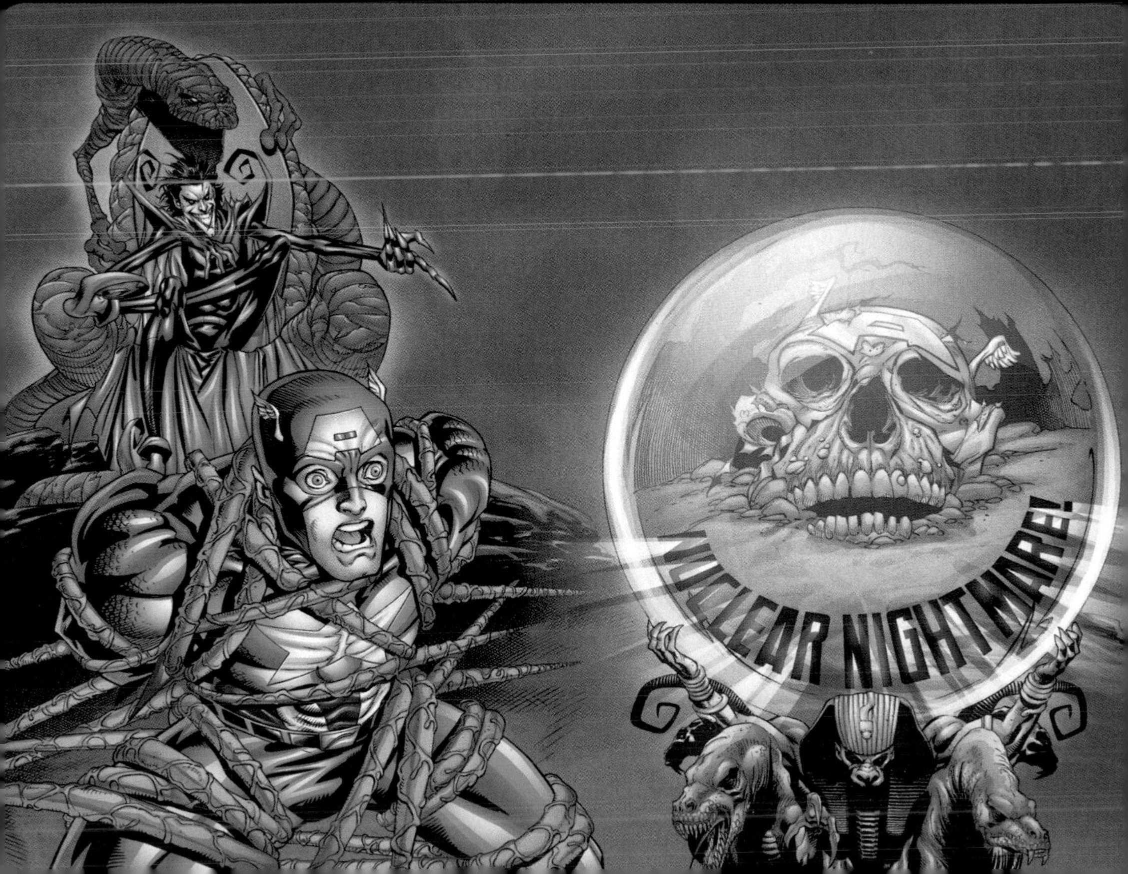
NUCLEAR NIGHTMARE!

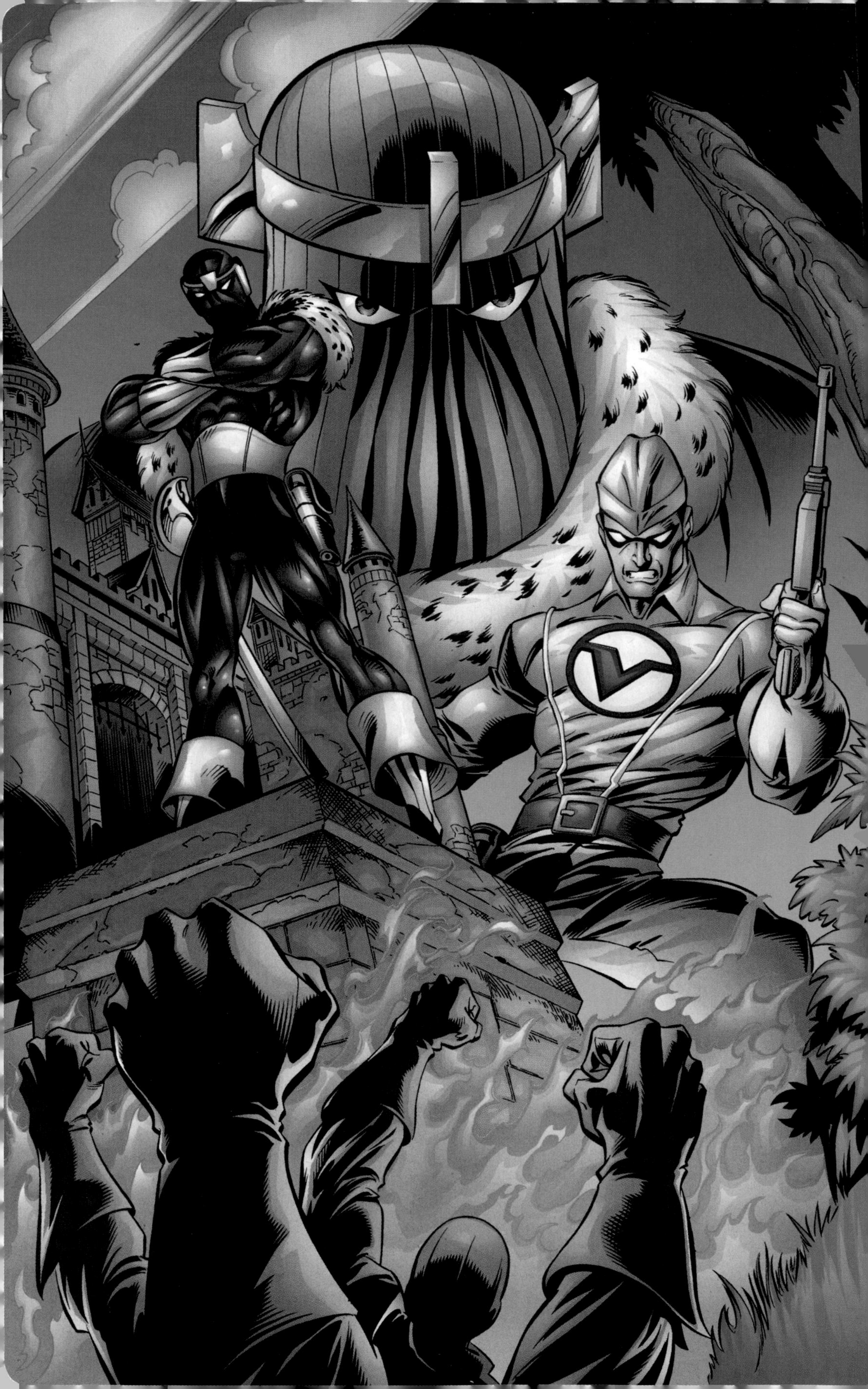

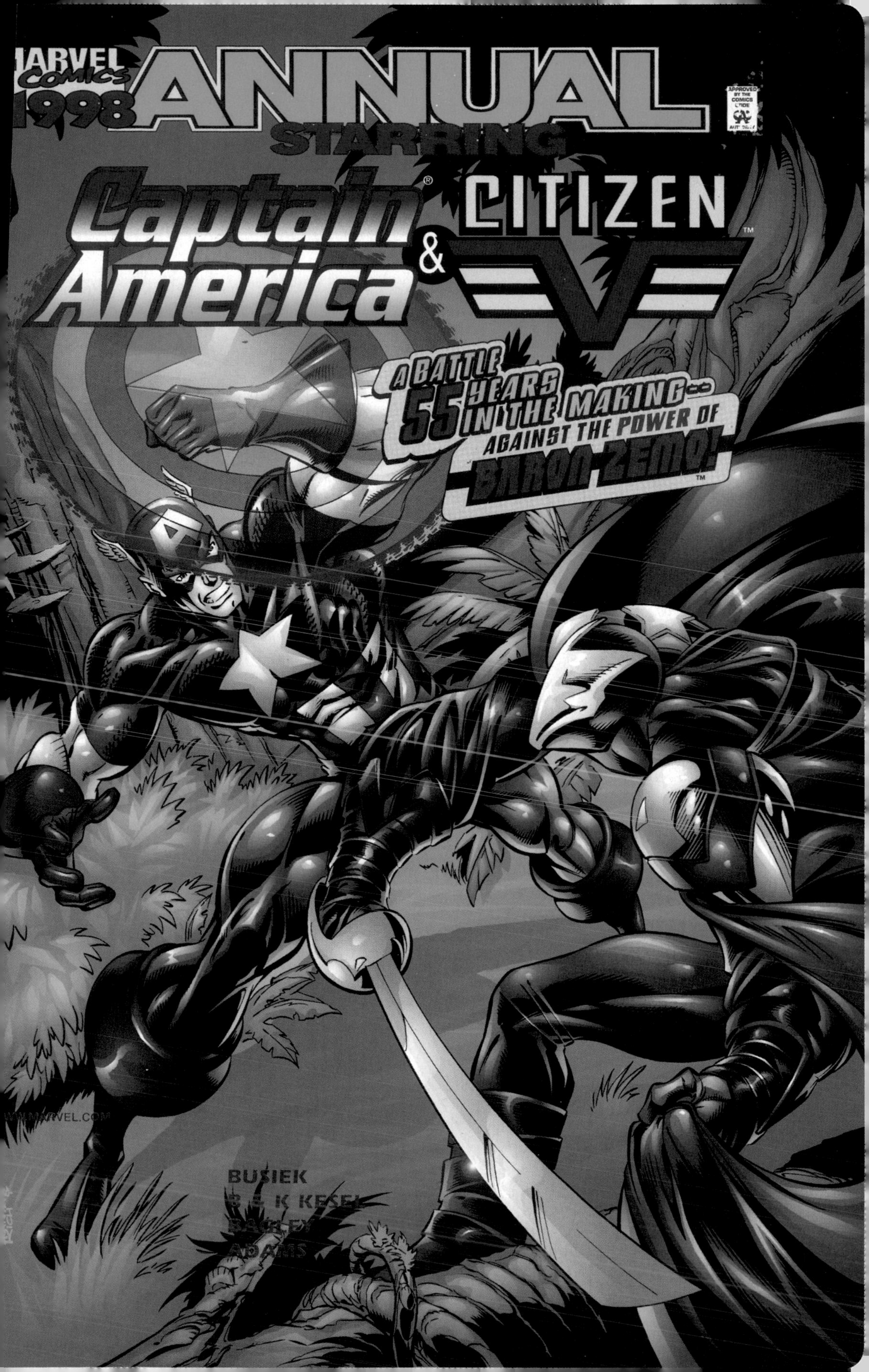
MARVEL COMICS
1998
ANNUAL
STARRING
Captain America
& CITIZEN V
A BATTLE 55 YEARS IN THE MAKING--
AGAINST THE POWER OF BARON ZEMO!
APPROVED BY THE COMICS CODE AUTHORITY
WWW.MARVEL.COM
BUSIEK

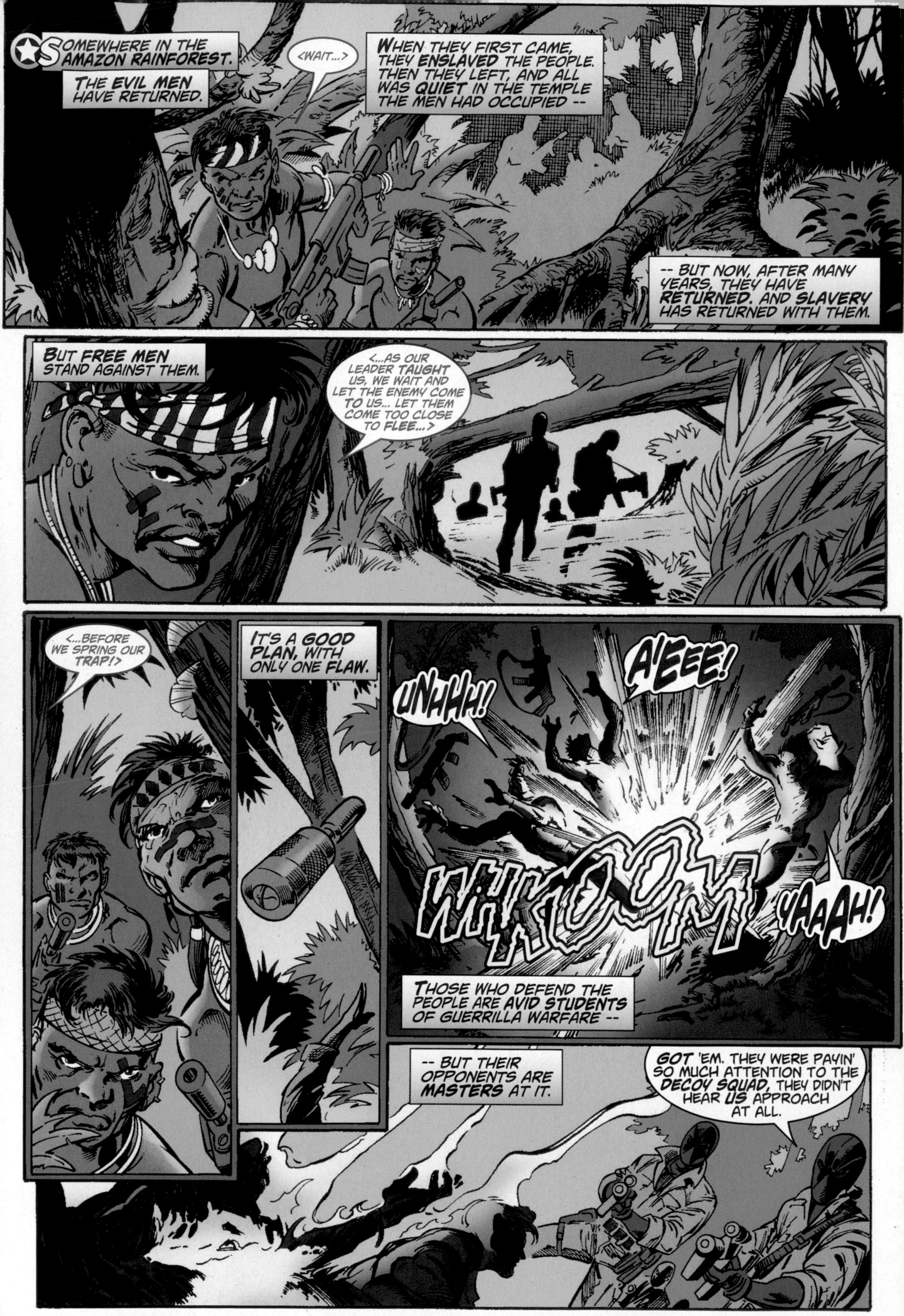

SOMEWHERE IN THE AMAZON RAINFOREST.
THE EVIL MEN HAVE RETURNED.
<WAIT...>
WHEN THEY FIRST CAME, THEY ENSLAVED THE PEOPLE. THEN THEY LEFT, AND ALL WAS QUIET IN THE TEMPLE THE MEN HAD OCCUPIED --
-- BUT NOW, AFTER MANY YEARS, THEY HAVE RETURNED. AND SLAVERY HAS RETURNED WITH THEM.
BUT FREE MEN STAND AGAINST THEM.
<...AS OUR LEADER TAUGHT US, WE WAIT AND LET THE ENEMY COME TO US... LET THEM COME TOO CLOSE TO FLEE...>
<...BEFORE WE SPRING OUR TRAP!>
IT'S A GOOD PLAN, WITH ONLY ONE FLAW.
A'EEE!
UNHHH!
WHKOOOM
YAAAH!
THOSE WHO DEFEND THE PEOPLE ARE AVID STUDENTS OF GUERRILLA WARFARE --
-- BUT THEIR OPPONENTS ARE MASTERS AT IT.
GOT 'EM. THEY WERE PAYIN' SO MUCH ATTENTION TO THE DECOY SQUAD, THEY DIDN'T HEAR US APPROACH AT ALL.

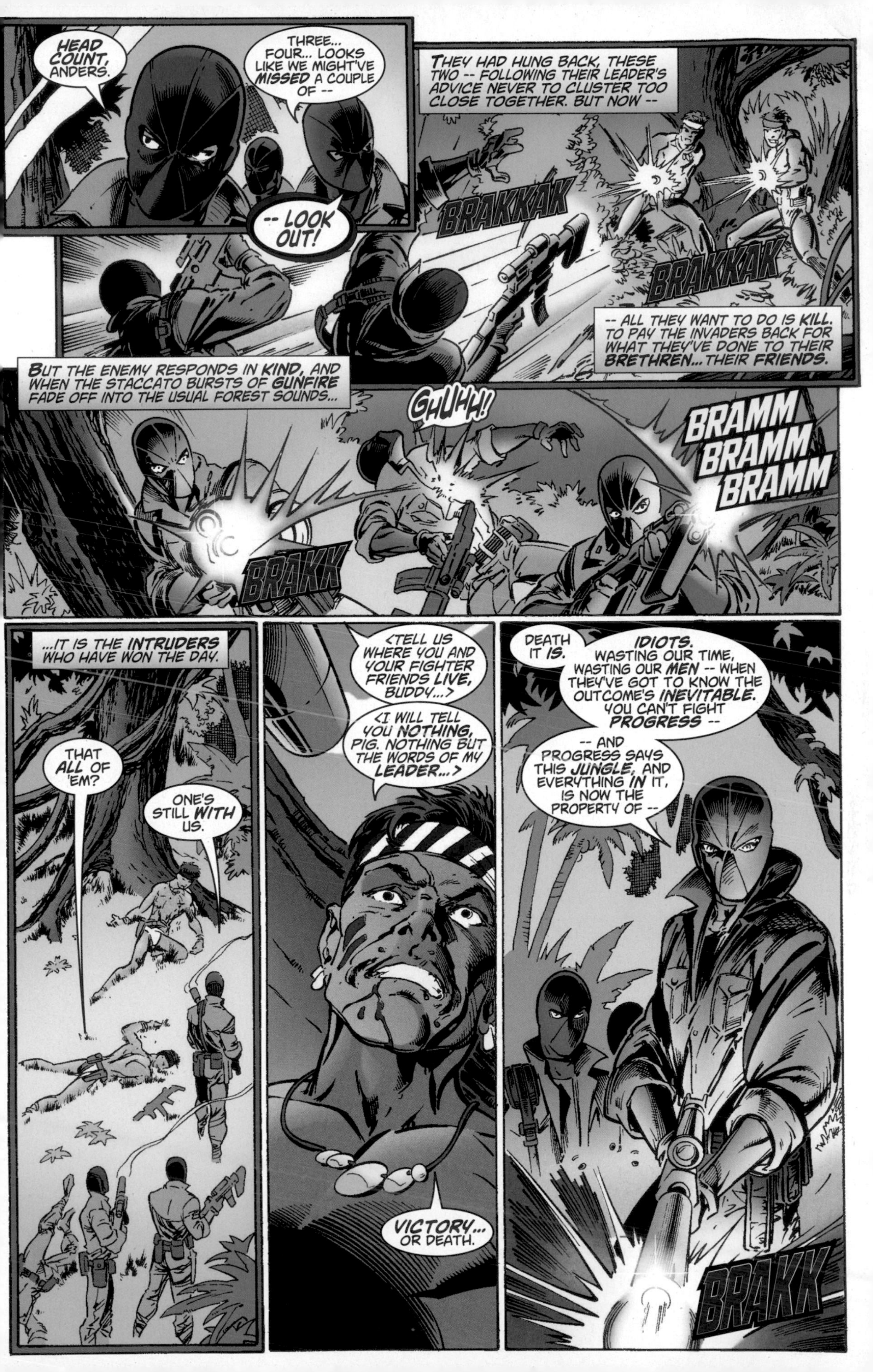
HEAD COUNT, ANDERS.
THREE... FOUR... LOOKS LIKE WE MIGHT'VE MISSED A COUPLE OF --
-- LOOK OUT!
THEY HAD HUNG BACK, THESE TWO -- FOLLOWING THEIR LEADER'S ADVICE NEVER TO CLUSTER TOO CLOSE TOGETHER. BUT NOW --
BRAKKAK
BRAKKAK
-- ALL THEY WANT TO DO IS KILL. TO PAY THE INVADERS BACK FOR WHAT THEY'VE DONE TO THEIR BRETHREN... THEIR FRIENDS.
BUT THE ENEMY RESPONDS IN KIND, AND WHEN THE STACCATO BURSTS OF GUNFIRE FADE OFF INTO THE USUAL FOREST SOUNDS...
GHUHH!
BRAMM BRAMM BRAMM
BRAKK
...IT IS THE INTRUDERS WHO HAVE WON THE DAY.
THAT ALL OF 'EM?
ONE'S STILL WITH US.
<TELL US WHERE YOU AND YOUR FIGHTER FRIENDS LIVE, BUDDY...>
<I WILL TELL YOU NOTHING, PIG. NOTHING BUT THE WORDS OF MY LEADER...>
VICTORY... OR DEATH.
DEATH IT IS.
IDIOTS. WASTING OUR TIME, WASTING OUR MEN -- WHEN THEY'VE GOT TO KNOW THE OUTCOME'S INEVITABLE. YOU CAN'T FIGHT PROGRESS --
-- AND PROGRESS SAYS THIS JUNGLE, AND EVERYTHING IN IT, IS NOW THE PROPERTY OF --
BRAKK

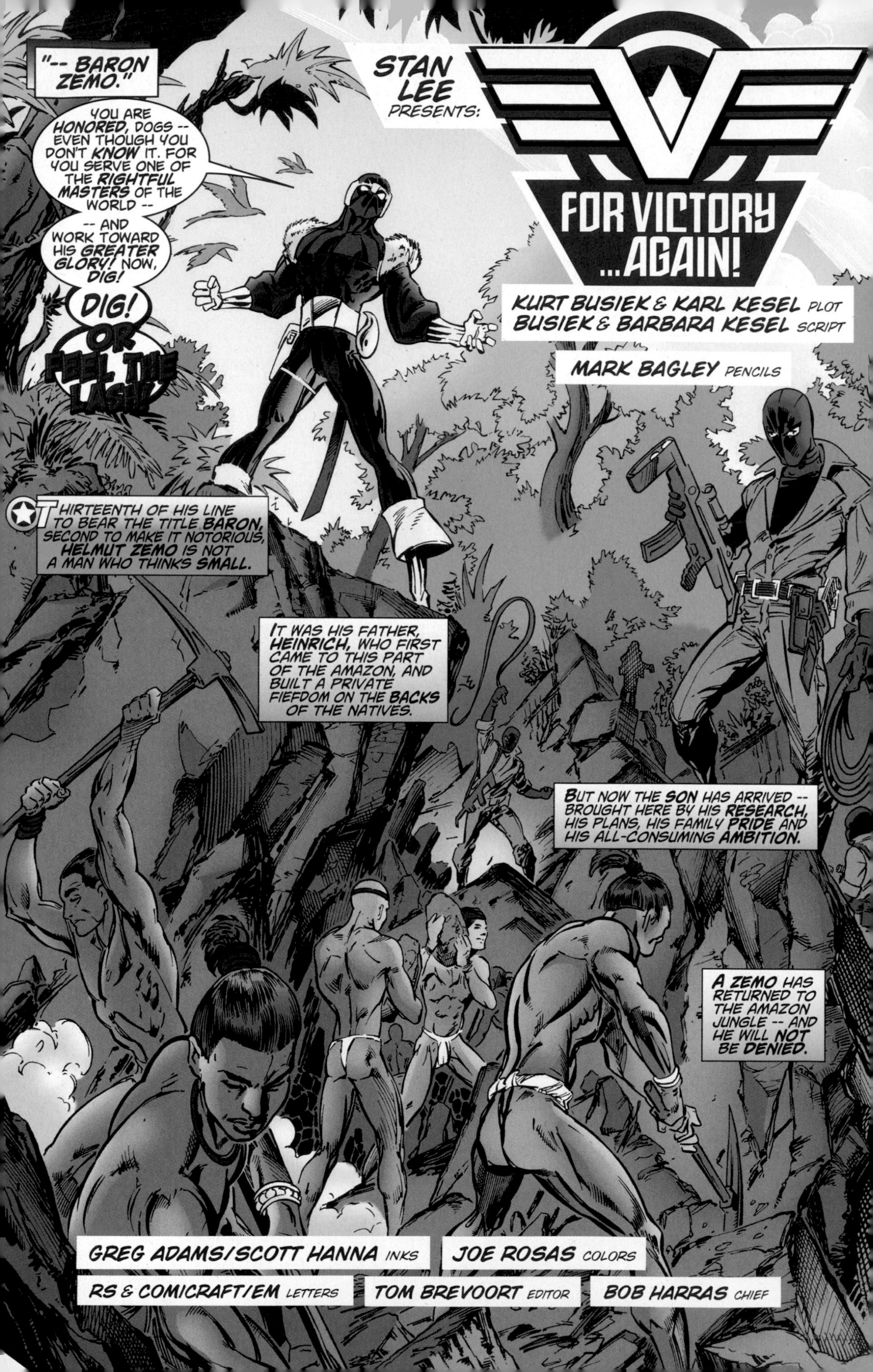

"-- BARON ZEMO."
YOU ARE HONORED, DOGS -- EVEN THOUGH YOU DON'T KNOW IT. FOR YOU SERVE ONE OF THE RIGHTFUL MASTERS OF THE WORLD --
-- AND WORK TOWARD HIS GREATER GLORY! NOW, DIG!
DIG!
OR FEEL THE LASH!
STAN LEE PRESENTS:
FOR VICTORY ...AGAIN!
KURT BUSIEK & KARL KESEL PLOT
BUSIEK & BARBARA KESEL SCRIPT
MARK BAGLEY PENCILS
THIRTEENTH OF HIS LINE TO BEAR THE TITLE BARON, SECOND TO MAKE IT NOTORIOUS, HELMUT ZEMO IS NOT A MAN WHO THINKS SMALL.
IT WAS HIS FATHER, HEINRICH, WHO FIRST CAME TO THIS PART OF THE AMAZON, AND BUILT A PRIVATE FIEFDOM ON THE BACKS OF THE NATIVES.
BUT NOW THE SON HAS ARRIVED -- BROUGHT HERE BY HIS RESEARCH, HIS PLANS, HIS FAMILY PRIDE AND HIS ALL-CONSUMING AMBITION.
A ZEMO HAS RETURNED TO THE AMAZON JUNGLE -- AND HE WILL NOT BE DENIED.
GREG ADAMS/SCOTT HANNA INKS
JOE ROSAS COLORS
RS & COMICRAFT/EM LETTERS
TOM BREVOORT EDITOR
BOB HARRAS CHIEF

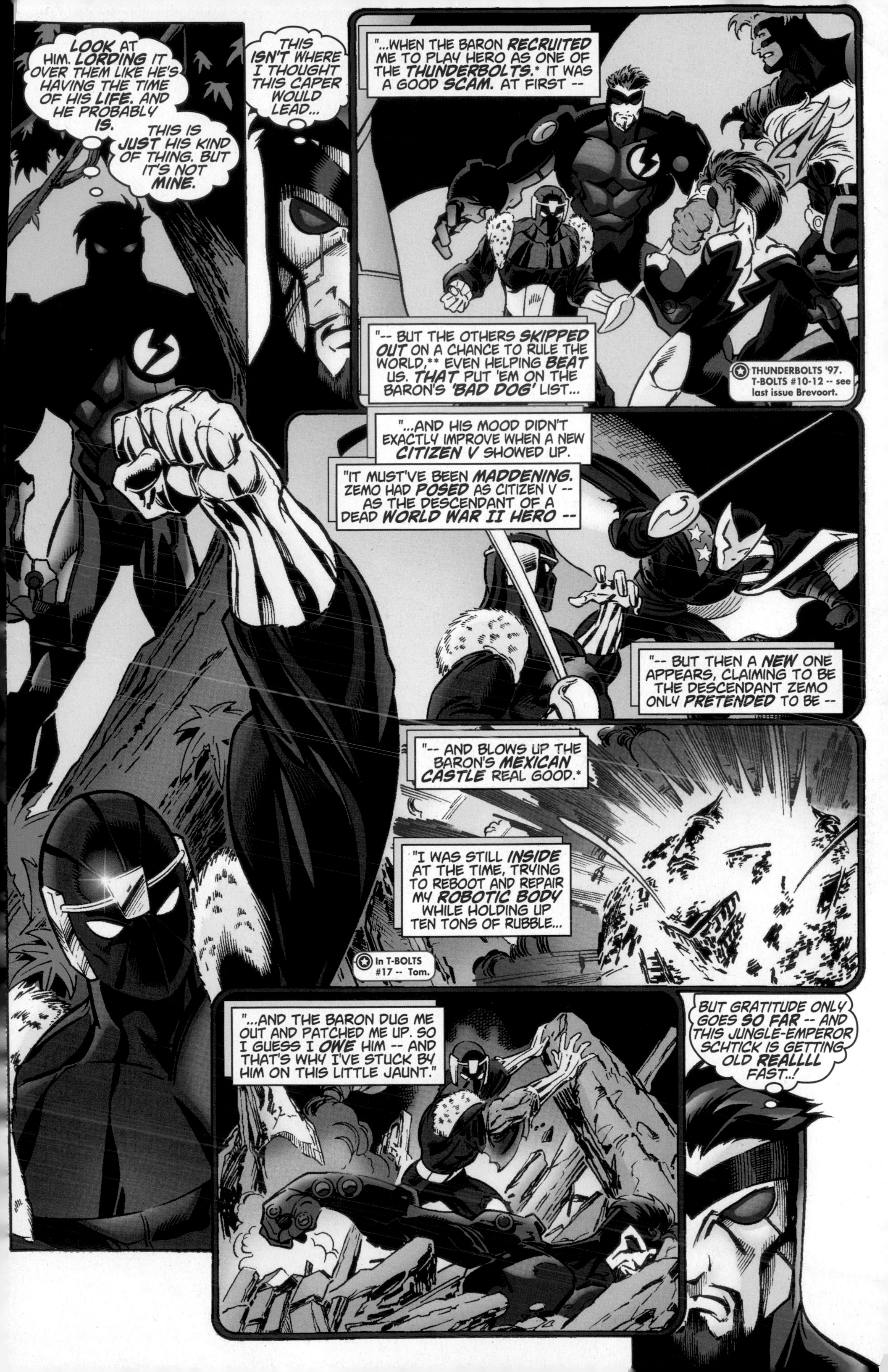

LOOK AT HIM. LORDING IT OVER THEM LIKE HE'S HAVING THE TIME OF HIS LIFE. AND HE PROBABLY IS.
THIS IS JUST HIS KIND OF THING. BUT IT'S NOT MINE.
THIS ISN'T WHERE I THOUGHT THIS CAPER WOULD LEAD...
"...WHEN THE BARON RECRUITED ME TO PLAY HERO AS ONE OF THE THUNDERBOLTS.* IT WAS A GOOD SCAM. AT FIRST --
"-- BUT THE OTHERS SKIPPED OUT ON A CHANCE TO RULE THE WORLD,** EVEN HELPING BEAT US. THAT PUT 'EM ON THE BARON'S 'BAD DOG' LIST...
THUNDERBOLTS '97. T-BOLTS #10-12 -- see last issue Brevoort.
"...AND HIS MOOD DIDN'T EXACTLY IMPROVE WHEN A NEW CITIZEN V SHOWED UP.
"IT MUST'VE BEEN MADDENING. ZEMO HAD POSED AS CITIZEN V -- AS THE DESCENDANT OF A DEAD WORLD WAR II HERO --
"-- BUT THEN A NEW ONE APPEARS, CLAIMING TO BE THE DESCENDANT ZEMO ONLY PRETENDED TO BE --
"-- AND BLOWS UP THE BARON'S MEXICAN CASTLE REAL GOOD.*
"I WAS STILL INSIDE AT THE TIME, TRYING TO REBOOT AND REPAIR MY ROBOTIC BODY WHILE HOLDING UP TEN TONS OF RUBBLE...
In T-BOLTS #17 -- Tom.
"...AND THE BARON DUG ME OUT AND PATCHED ME UP. SO I GUESS I OWE HIM -- AND THAT'S WHY I'VE STUCK BY HIM ON THIS LITTLE JAUNT."
BUT GRATITUDE ONLY GOES SO FAR -- AND THIS JUNGLE-EMPEROR SCHTICK IS GETTING OLD REALLLL FAST...!

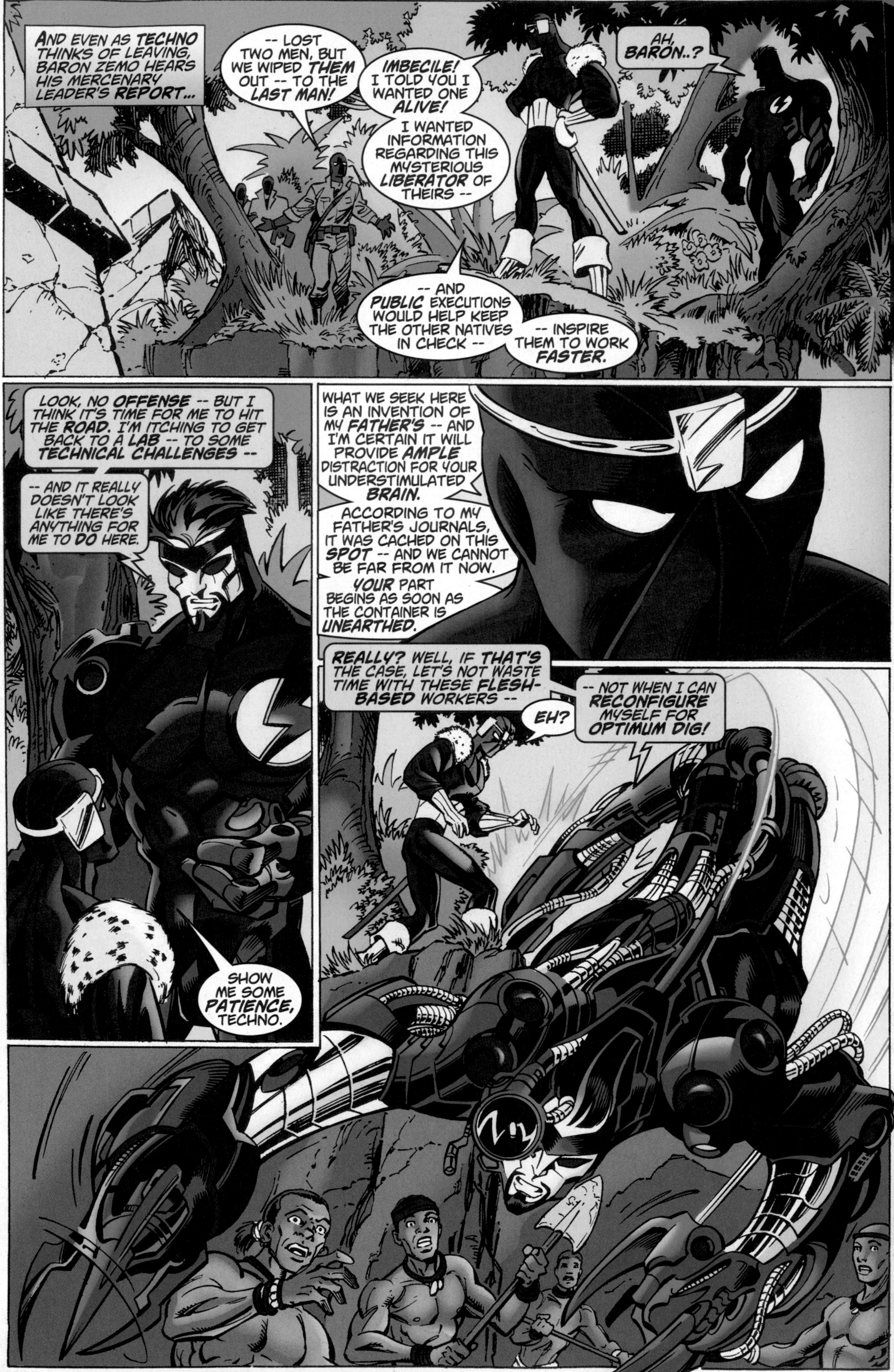
AND EVEN AS TECHNO THINKS OF LEAVING, BARON ZEMO HEARS HIS MERCENARY LEADER'S REPORT...
-- LOST TWO MEN, BUT WE WIPED THEM OUT -- TO THE LAST MAN!
IMBECILE! I TOLD YOU I WANTED ONE ALIVE!
I WANTED INFORMATION REGARDING THIS MYSTERIOUS LIBERATOR OF THEIRS --
-- AND PUBLIC EXECUTIONS WOULD HELP KEEP THE OTHER NATIVES IN CHECK --
-- INSPIRE THEM TO WORK FASTER.
AH, BARON..?
LOOK, NO OFFENSE -- BUT I THINK IT'S TIME FOR ME TO HIT THE ROAD. I'M ITCHING TO GET BACK TO A LAB -- TO SOME TECHNICAL CHALLENGES --
-- AND IT REALLY DOESN'T LOOK LIKE THERE'S ANYTHING FOR ME TO DO HERE.
SHOW ME SOME PATIENCE, TECHNO.
WHAT WE SEEK HERE IS AN INVENTION OF MY FATHER'S -- AND I'M CERTAIN IT WILL PROVIDE AMPLE DISTRACTION FOR YOUR UNDERSTIMULATED BRAIN.
ACCORDING TO MY FATHER'S JOURNALS, IT WAS CACHED ON THIS SPOT -- AND WE CANNOT BE FAR FROM IT NOW.
YOUR PART BEGINS AS SOON AS THE CONTAINER IS UNEARTHED.
REALLY? WELL, IF THAT'S THE CASE, LET'S NOT WASTE TIME WITH THESE FLESH-BASED WORKERS --
EH?
-- NOT WHEN I CAN RECONFIGURE MYSELF FOR OPTIMUM DIG!

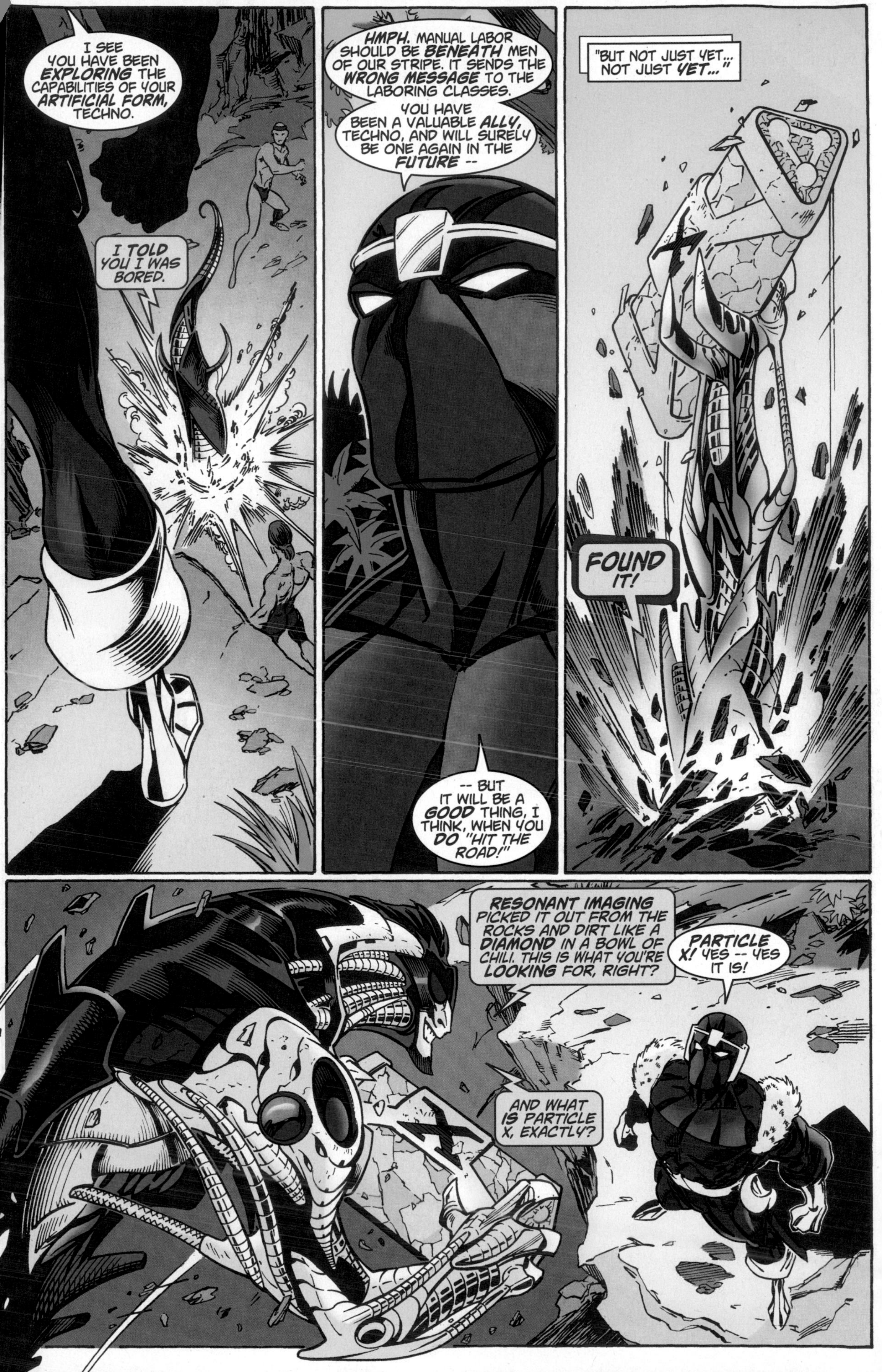
I SEE YOU HAVE BEEN EXPLORING THE CAPABILITIES OF YOUR ARTIFICIAL FORM, TECHNO.
I TOLD YOU I WAS BORED.
HMPH. MANUAL LABOR SHOULD BE BENEATH MEN OF OUR STRIPE. IT SENDS THE WRONG MESSAGE TO THE LABORING CLASSES.
YOU HAVE BEEN A VALUABLE ALLY, TECHNO, AND WILL SURELY BE ONE AGAIN IN THE FUTURE --
-- BUT IT WILL BE A GOOD THING, I THINK, WHEN YOU DO "HIT THE ROAD!"
"BUT NOT JUST YET... NOT JUST YET..."
FOUND IT!
RESONANT IMAGING PICKED IT OUT FROM THE ROCKS AND DIRT LIKE A DIAMOND IN A BOWL OF CHILI. THIS IS WHAT YOU'RE LOOKING FOR, RIGHT?
PARTICLE X! YES -- YES IT IS!
AND WHAT IS PARTICLE X, EXACTLY?

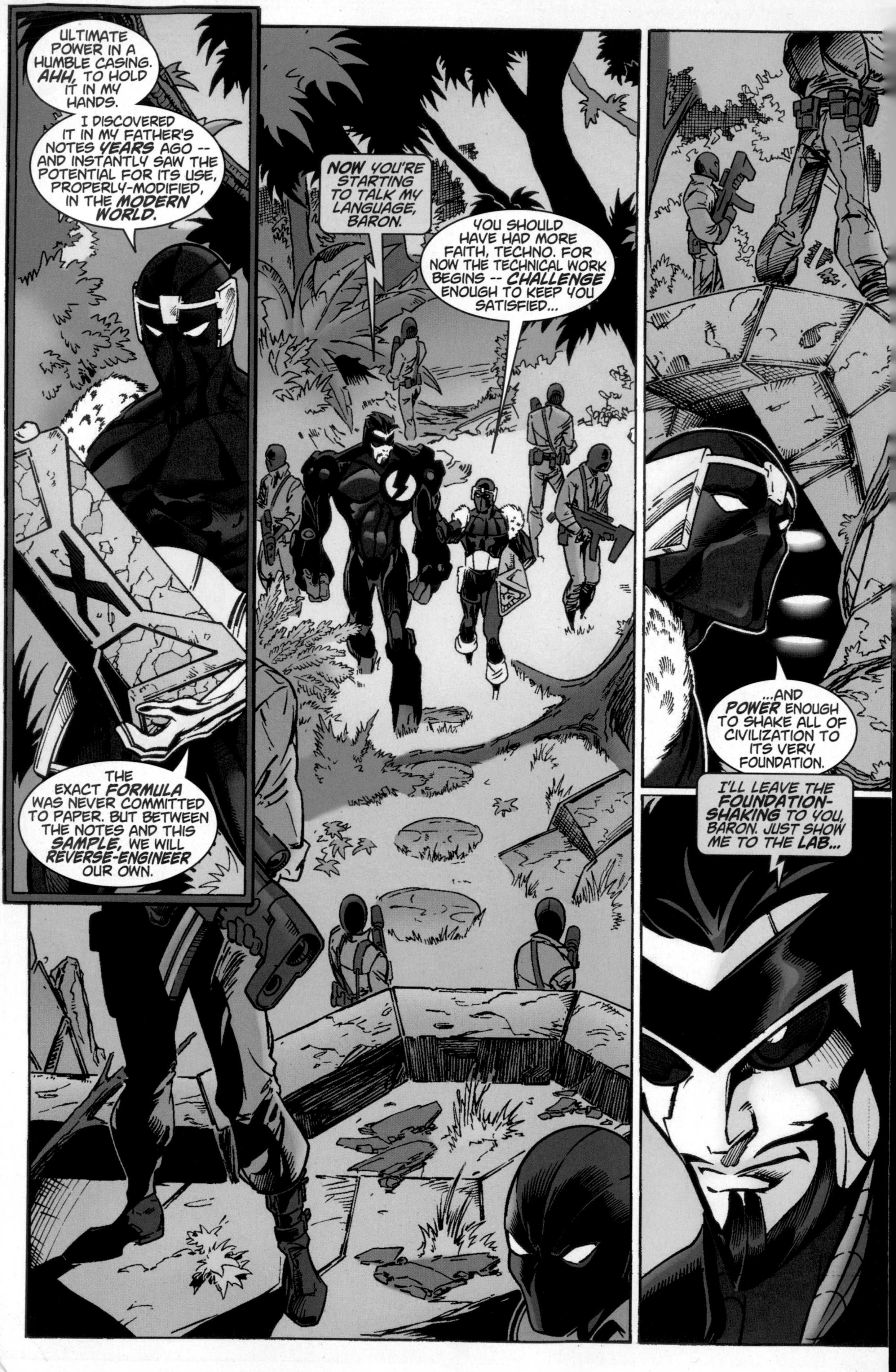
ULTIMATE POWER IN A HUMBLE CASING. AHH, TO HOLD IT IN MY HANDS.
I DISCOVERED IT IN MY FATHER'S NOTES YEARS AGO -- AND INSTANTLY SAW THE POTENTIAL FOR ITS USE, PROPERLY-MODIFIED, IN THE MODERN WORLD.
THE EXACT FORMULA WAS NEVER COMMITTED TO PAPER. BUT BETWEEN THE NOTES AND THIS SAMPLE, WE WILL REVERSE-ENGINEER OUR OWN.
NOW YOU'RE STARTING TO TALK MY LANGUAGE, BARON.
YOU SHOULD HAVE HAD MORE FAITH, TECHNO. FOR NOW THE TECHNICAL WORK BEGINS -- CHALLENGE ENOUGH TO KEEP YOU SATISFIED...
...AND POWER ENOUGH TO SHAKE ALL OF CIVILIZATION TO ITS VERY FOUNDATION.
I'LL LEAVE THE FOUNDATION-SHAKING TO YOU, BARON. JUST SHOW ME TO THE LAB...

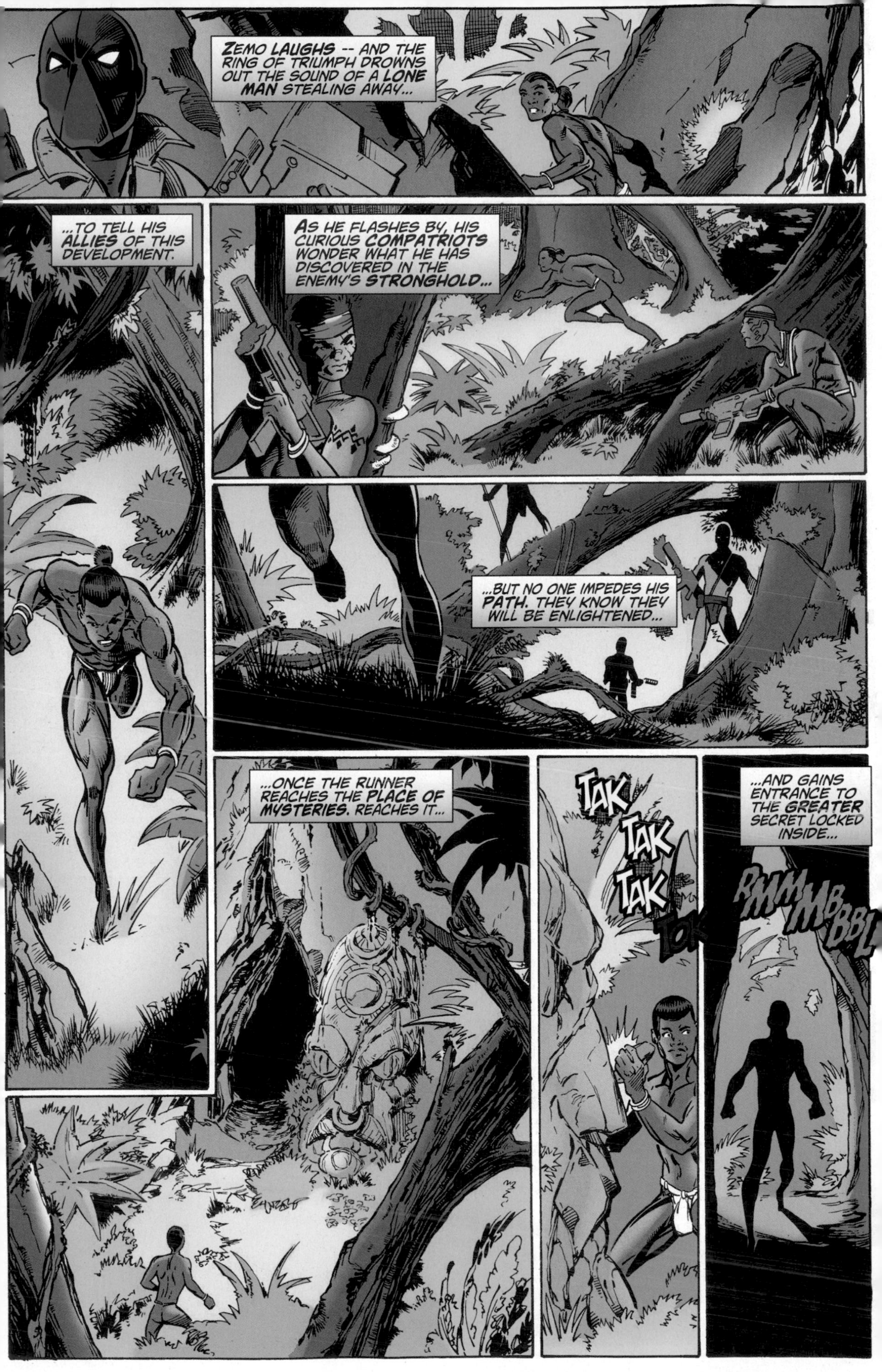
ZEMO LAUGHS -- AND THE RING OF TRIUMPH DROWNS OUT THE SOUND OF A LONE MAN STEALING AWAY...
...TO TELL HIS ALLIES OF THIS DEVELOPMENT.
AS HE FLASHES BY, HIS CURIOUS COMPATRIOTS WONDER WHAT HE HAS DISCOVERED IN THE ENEMY'S STRONGHOLD...
...BUT NO ONE IMPEDES HIS PATH. THEY KNOW THEY WILL BE ENLIGHTENED...
...ONCE THE RUNNER REACHES THE PLACE OF MYSTERIES. REACHES IT...
TAK
TAK
TAK
TOK
...AND GAINS ENTRANCE TO THE GREATER SECRET LOCKED INSIDE...
RMMMMBBBL

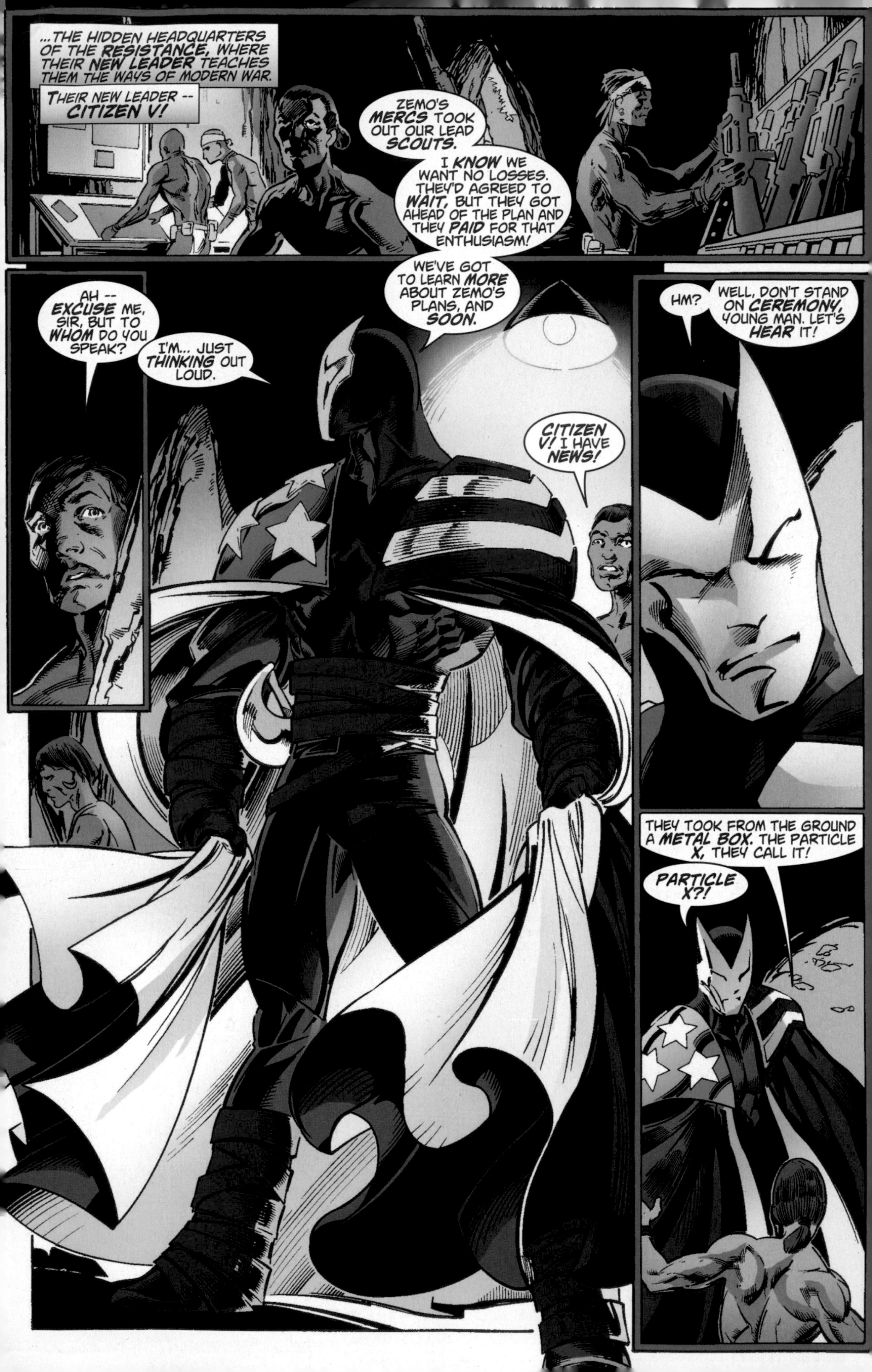
...THE HIDDEN HEADQUARTERS OF THE RESISTANCE, WHERE THEIR NEW LEADER TEACHES THEM THE WAYS OF MODERN WAR.
THEIR NEW LEADER -- CITIZEN V!
ZEMO'S MERCS TOOK OUT OUR LEAD SCOUTS.
I KNOW WE WANT NO LOSSES. THEY'D AGREED TO WAIT, BUT THEY GOT AHEAD OF THE PLAN AND THEY PAID FOR THAT ENTHUSIASM!
WE'VE GOT TO LEARN MORE ABOUT ZEMO'S PLANS, AND SOON.
AH -- EXCUSE ME, SIR, BUT TO WHOM DO YOU SPEAK?
I'M... JUST THINKING OUT LOUD.
CITIZEN V! I HAVE NEWS!
HM?
WELL, DON'T STAND ON CEREMONY, YOUNG MAN. LET'S HEAR IT!
THEY TOOK FROM THE GROUND A METAL BOX. THE PARTICLE X, THEY CALL IT!
PARTICLE X?!

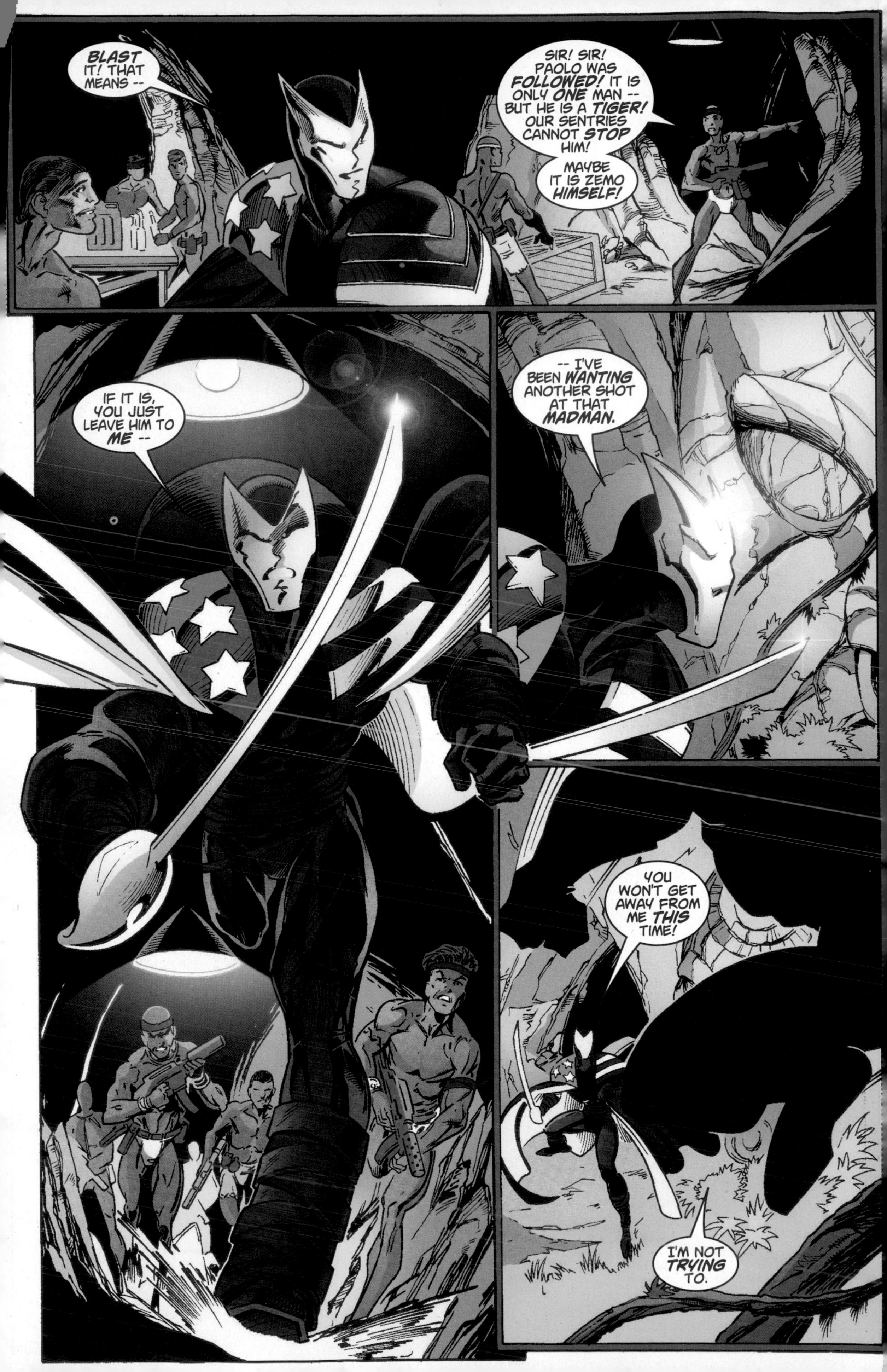
BLAST IT! THAT MEANS --
SIR! SIR! PAOLO WAS FOLLOWED! IT IS ONLY ONE MAN -- BUT HE IS A TIGER! OUR SENTRIES CANNOT STOP HIM!
MAYBE IT IS ZEMO HIMSELF!
IF IT IS, YOU JUST LEAVE HIM TO ME --
-- I'VE BEEN WANTING ANOTHER SHOT AT THAT MADMAN.
YOU WON'T GET AWAY FROM ME THIS TIME!
I'M NOT TRYING TO.

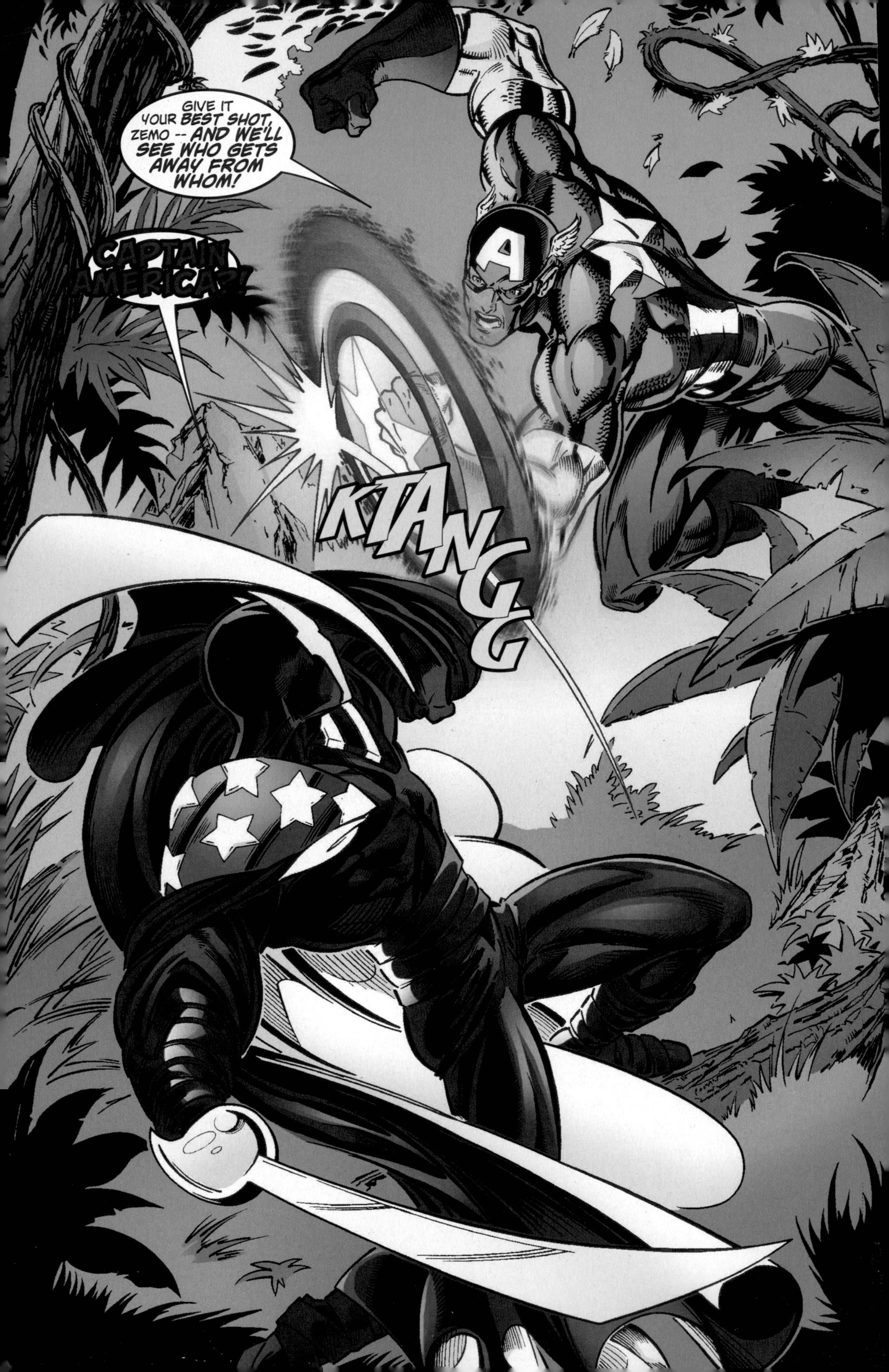

GIVE IT YOUR BEST SHOT, ZEMO -- AND WE'LL SEE WHO GETS AWAY FROM WHOM!
CAPTAIN AMERICA?!
KTANGG

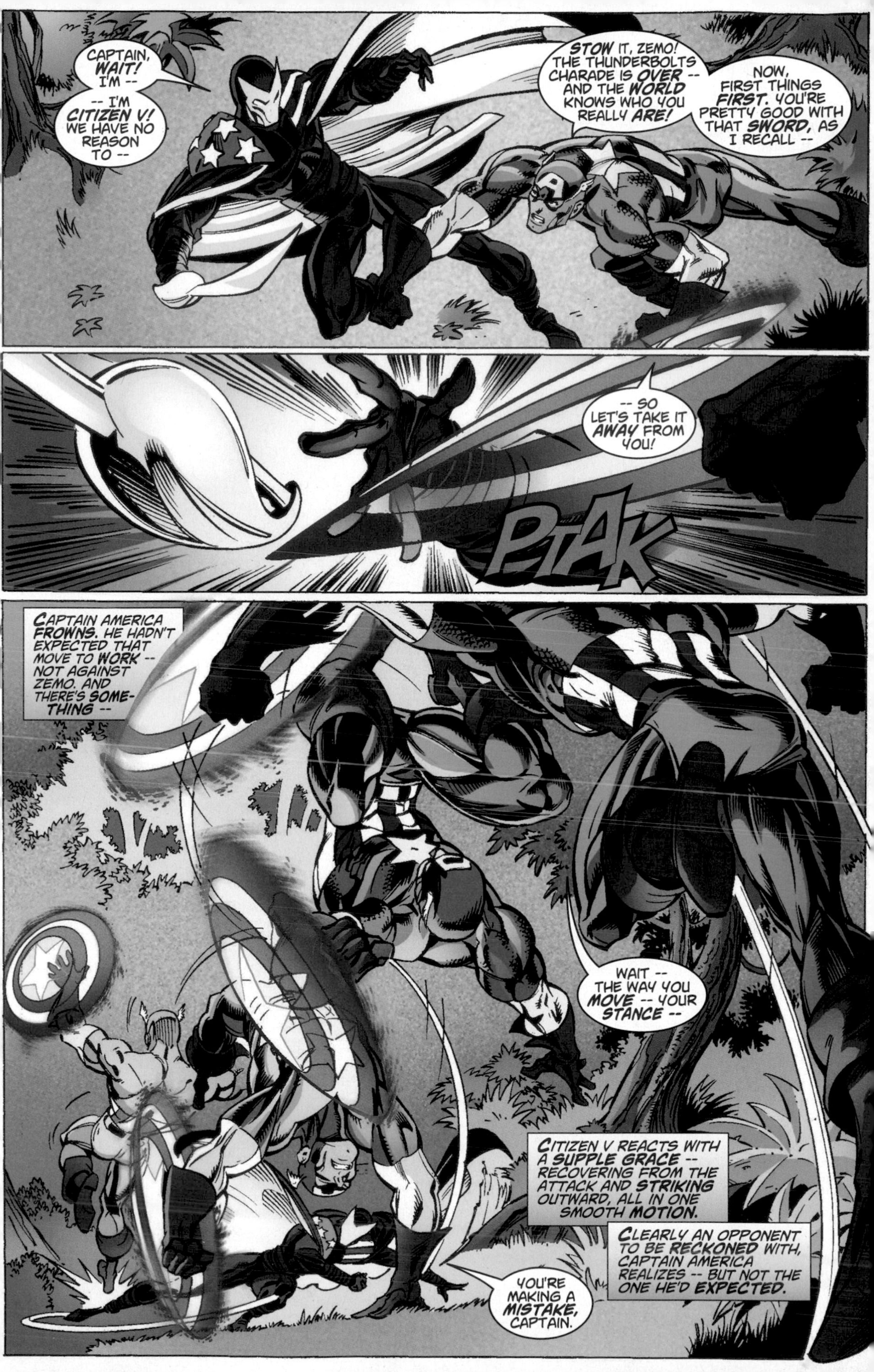
CAPTAIN, WAIT! I'M --
-- I'M CITIZEN V! WE HAVE NO REASON TO --
STOW IT, ZEMO! THE THUNDERBOLTS CHARADE IS OVER -- AND THE WORLD KNOWS WHO YOU REALLY ARE!
NOW, FIRST THINGS FIRST. YOU'RE PRETTY GOOD WITH THAT SWORD, AS I RECALL --
-- SO LET'S TAKE IT AWAY FROM YOU!
PTAK
CAPTAIN AMERICA FROWNS. HE HADN'T EXPECTED THAT MOVE TO WORK -- NOT AGAINST ZEMO. AND THERE'S SOMETHING --
WAIT -- THE WAY YOU MOVE -- YOUR STANCE --
CITIZEN V REACTS WITH A SUPPLE GRACE -- RECOVERING FROM THE ATTACK AND STRIKING OUTWARD, ALL IN ONE SMOOTH MOTION.
CLEARLY AN OPPONENT TO BE RECKONED WITH, CAPTAIN AMERICA REALIZES -- BUT NOT THE ONE HE'D EXPECTED.
YOU'RE MAKING A MISTAKE, CAPTAIN.

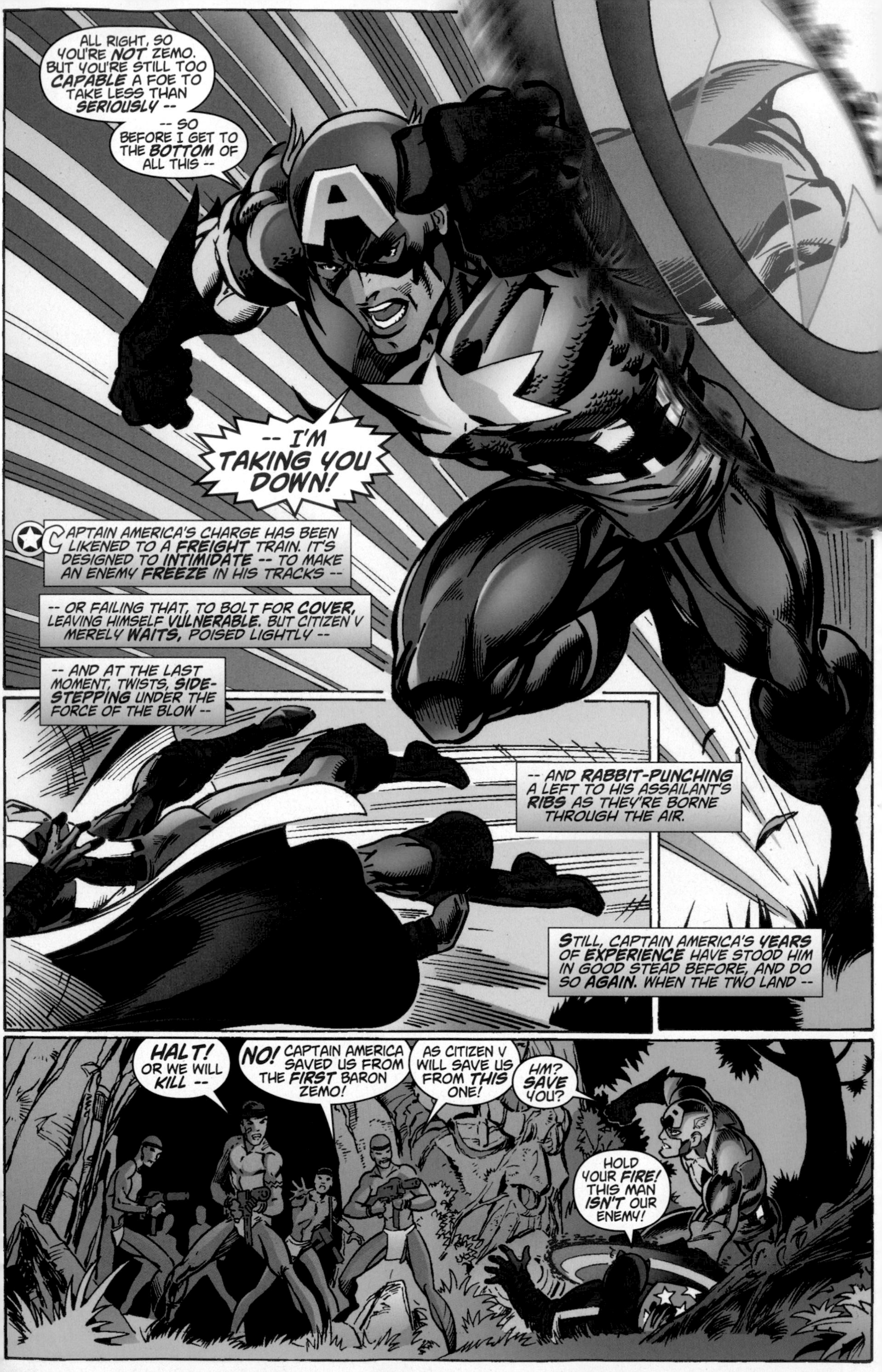
ALL RIGHT, SO YOU'RE NOT ZEMO. BUT YOU'RE STILL TOO CAPABLE A FOE TO TAKE LESS THAN SERIOUSLY --
-- SO BEFORE I GET TO THE BOTTOM OF ALL THIS --
-- I'M TAKING YOU DOWN!
CAPTAIN AMERICA'S CHARGE HAS BEEN LIKENED TO A FREIGHT TRAIN. IT'S DESIGNED TO INTIMIDATE -- TO MAKE AN ENEMY FREEZE IN HIS TRACKS --
-- OR FAILING THAT, TO BOLT FOR COVER, LEAVING HIMSELF VULNERABLE. BUT CITIZEN V MERELY WAITS, POISED LIGHTLY --
-- AND AT THE LAST MOMENT, TWISTS, SIDE-STEPPING UNDER THE FORCE OF THE BLOW --
-- AND RABBIT-PUNCHING A LEFT TO HIS ASSAILANT'S RIBS AS THEY'RE BORNE THROUGH THE AIR.
STILL, CAPTAIN AMERICA'S YEARS OF EXPERIENCE HAVE STOOD HIM IN GOOD STEAD BEFORE, AND DO SO AGAIN. WHEN THE TWO LAND --
HALT! OR WE WILL KILL --
NO! CAPTAIN AMERICA SAVED US FROM THE FIRST BARON ZEMO!
AS CITIZEN V WILL SAVE US FROM THIS ONE!
HM? SAVE YOU?
HOLD YOUR FIRE! THIS MAN ISN'T OUR ENEMY!

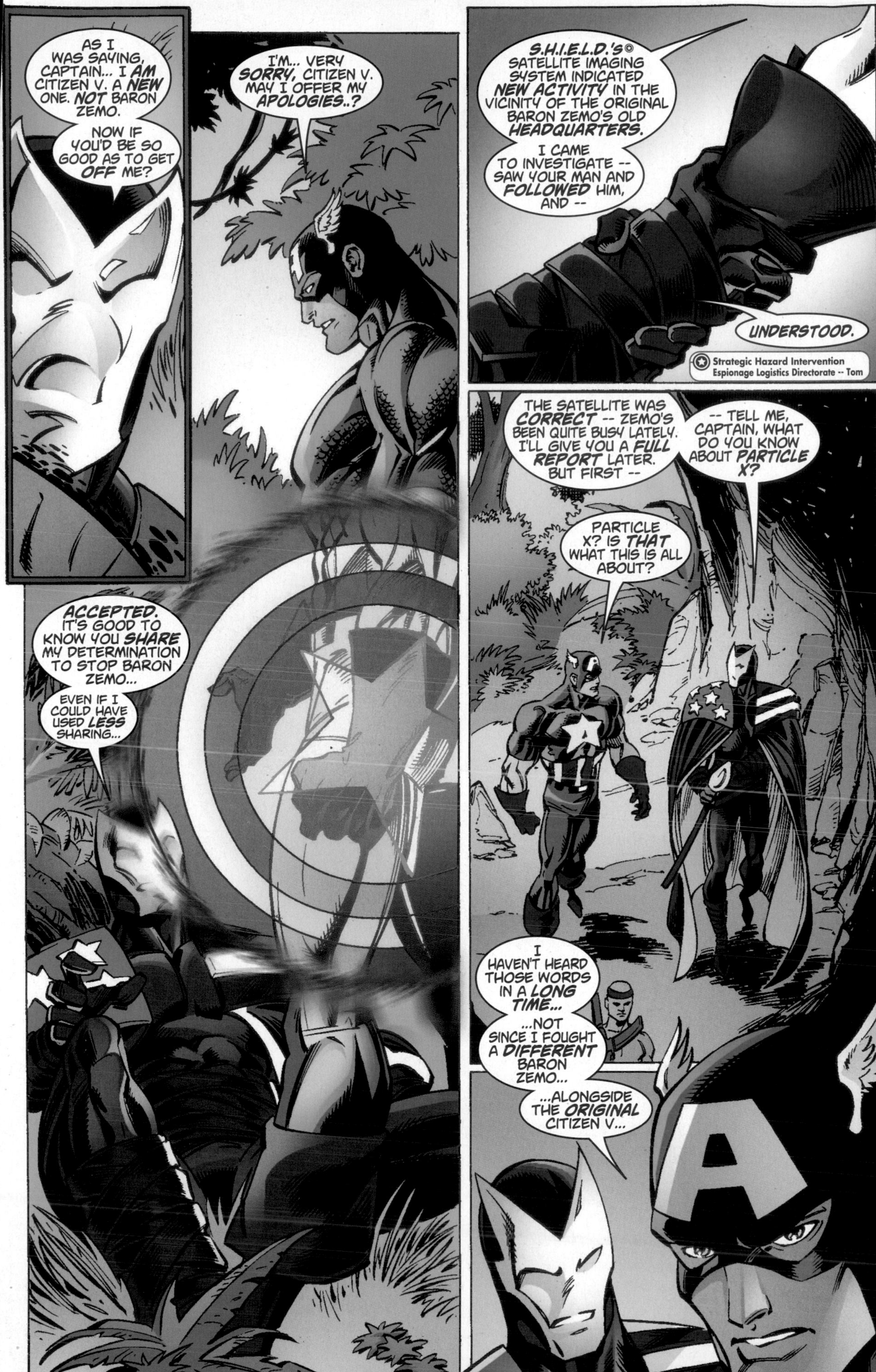
AS I WAS SAYING, CAPTAIN... I AM CITIZEN V. A NEW ONE. NOT BARON ZEMO.
NOW IF YOU'D BE SO GOOD AS TO GET OFF ME?
I'M... VERY SORRY, CITIZEN V. MAY I OFFER MY APOLOGIES..?
ACCEPTED. IT'S GOOD TO KNOW YOU SHARE MY DETERMINATION TO STOP BARON ZEMO...
EVEN IF I COULD HAVE USED LESS SHARING...
S.H.I.E.L.D.'s© SATELLITE IMAGING SYSTEM INDICATED NEW ACTIVITY IN THE VICINITY OF THE ORIGINAL BARON ZEMO'S OLD HEADQUARTERS.
I CAME TO INVESTIGATE -- SAW YOUR MAN AND FOLLOWED HIM, AND --
UNDERSTOOD.
Strategic Hazard Intervention Espionage Logistics Directorate -- Tom
THE SATELLITE WAS CORRECT -- ZEMO'S BEEN QUITE BUSY LATELY. I'LL GIVE YOU A FULL REPORT LATER. BUT FIRST --
-- TELL ME, CAPTAIN, WHAT DO YOU KNOW ABOUT PARTICLE X?
PARTICLE X? IS THAT WHAT THIS IS ALL ABOUT?
I HAVEN'T HEARD THOSE WORDS IN A LONG TIME...
...NOT SINCE I FOUGHT A DIFFERENT BARON ZEMO...
...ALONGSIDE THE ORIGINAL CITIZEN V...

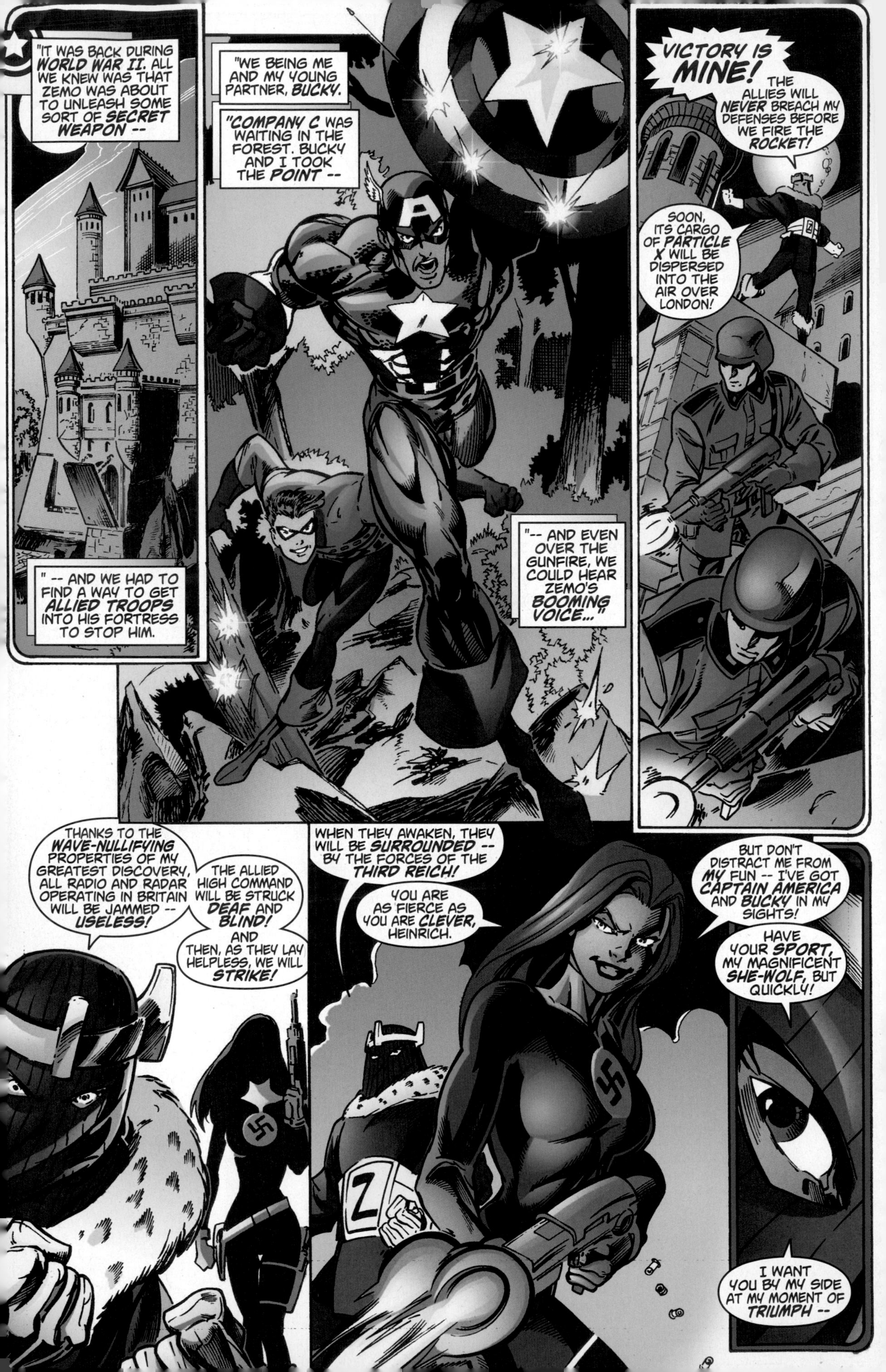
"IT WAS BACK DURING WORLD WAR II. ALL WE KNEW WAS THAT ZEMO WAS ABOUT TO UNLEASH SOME SORT OF SECRET WEAPON --
" -- AND WE HAD TO FIND A WAY TO GET ALLIED TROOPS INTO HIS FORTRESS TO STOP HIM.
"WE BEING ME AND MY YOUNG PARTNER, BUCKY.
"COMPANY C WAS WAITING IN THE FOREST. BUCKY AND I TOOK THE POINT --
"-- AND EVEN OVER THE GUNFIRE, WE COULD HEAR ZEMO'S BOOMING VOICE..."
VICTORY IS MINE!
THE ALLIES WILL NEVER BREACH MY DEFENSES BEFORE WE FIRE THE ROCKET!
SOON, ITS CARGO OF PARTICLE X WILL BE DISPERSED INTO THE AIR OVER LONDON!
THANKS TO THE WAVE-NULLIFYING PROPERTIES OF MY GREATEST DISCOVERY, ALL RADIO AND RADAR OPERATING IN BRITAIN WILL BE JAMMED -- USELESS!
THE ALLIED HIGH COMMAND WILL BE STRUCK DEAF AND BLIND!
AND THEN, AS THEY LAY HELPLESS, WE WILL STRIKE!
WHEN THEY AWAKEN, THEY WILL BE SURROUNDED -- BY THE FORCES OF THE THIRD REICH!
YOU ARE AS FIERCE AS YOU ARE CLEVER, HEINRICH.
BUT DON'T DISTRACT ME FROM MY FUN -- I'VE GOT CAPTAIN AMERICA AND BUCKY IN MY SIGHTS!
HAVE YOUR SPORT, MY MAGNIFICENT SHE-WOLF, BUT QUICKLY!
I WANT YOU BY MY SIDE AT MY MOMENT OF TRIUMPH --

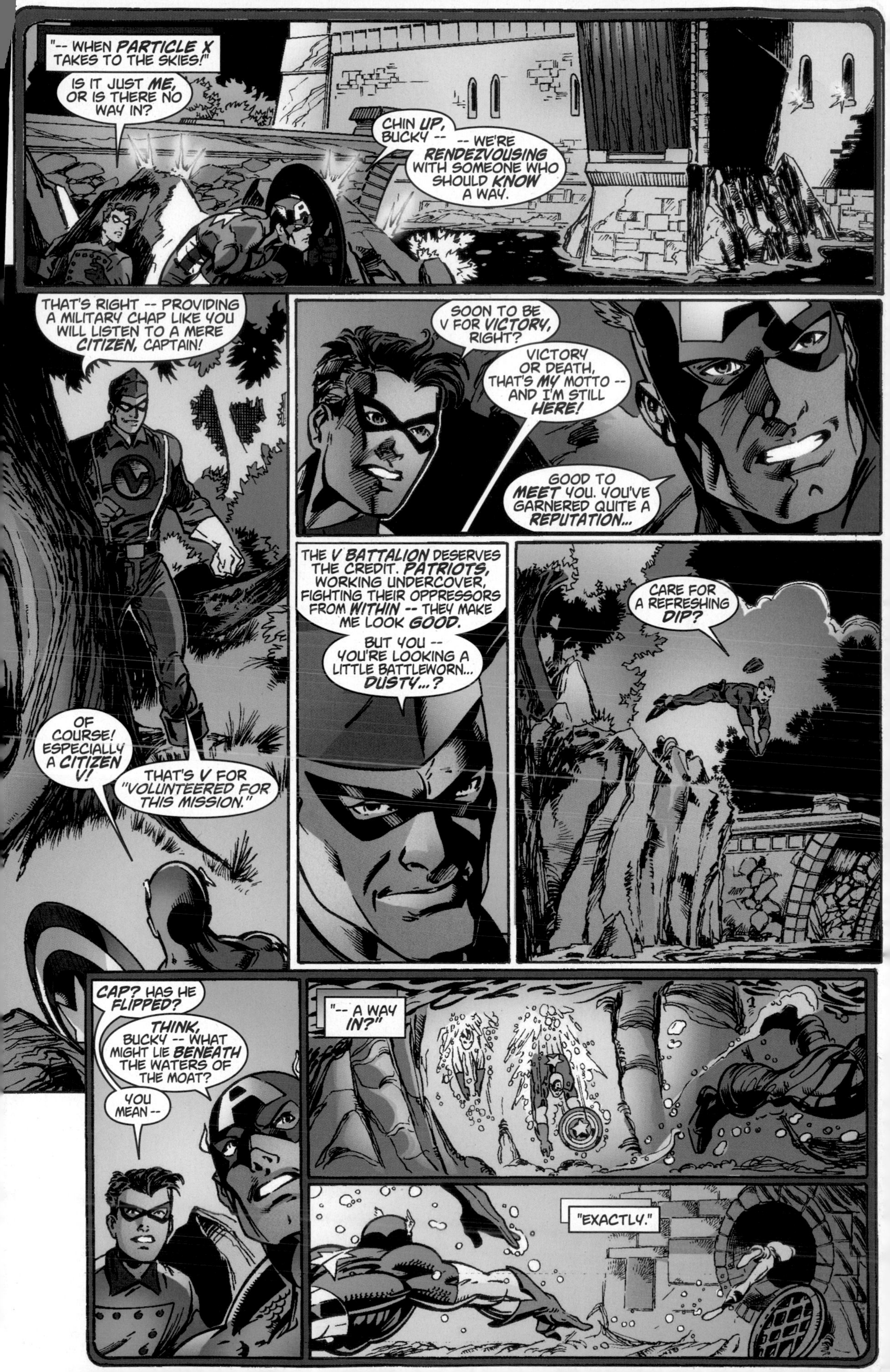
"-- WHEN PARTICLE X TAKES TO THE SKIES!"
IS IT JUST ME, OR IS THERE NO WAY IN?
CHIN UP, BUCKY --
-- WE'RE RENDEZVOUSING WITH SOMEONE WHO SHOULD KNOW A WAY.
THAT'S RIGHT -- PROVIDING A MILITARY CHAP LIKE YOU WILL LISTEN TO A MERE CITIZEN, CAPTAIN!
OF COURSE! ESPECIALLY A CITIZEN V!
THAT'S V FOR "VOLUNTEERED FOR THIS MISSION."
SOON TO BE V FOR VICTORY, RIGHT?
VICTORY OR DEATH, THAT'S MY MOTTO -- AND I'M STILL HERE!
GOOD TO MEET YOU. YOU'VE GARNERED QUITE A REPUTATION...
THE V BATTALION DESERVES THE CREDIT. PATRIOTS, WORKING UNDERCOVER, FIGHTING THEIR OPPRESSORS FROM WITHIN -- THEY MAKE ME LOOK GOOD.
BUT YOU -- YOU'RE LOOKING A LITTLE BATTLEWORN... DUSTY...?
CARE FOR A REFRESHING DIP?
CAP? HAS HE FLIPPED?
THINK, BUCKY -- WHAT MIGHT LIE BENEATH THE WATERS OF THE MOAT?
YOU MEAN --
"-- A WAY IN?"
"EXACTLY."

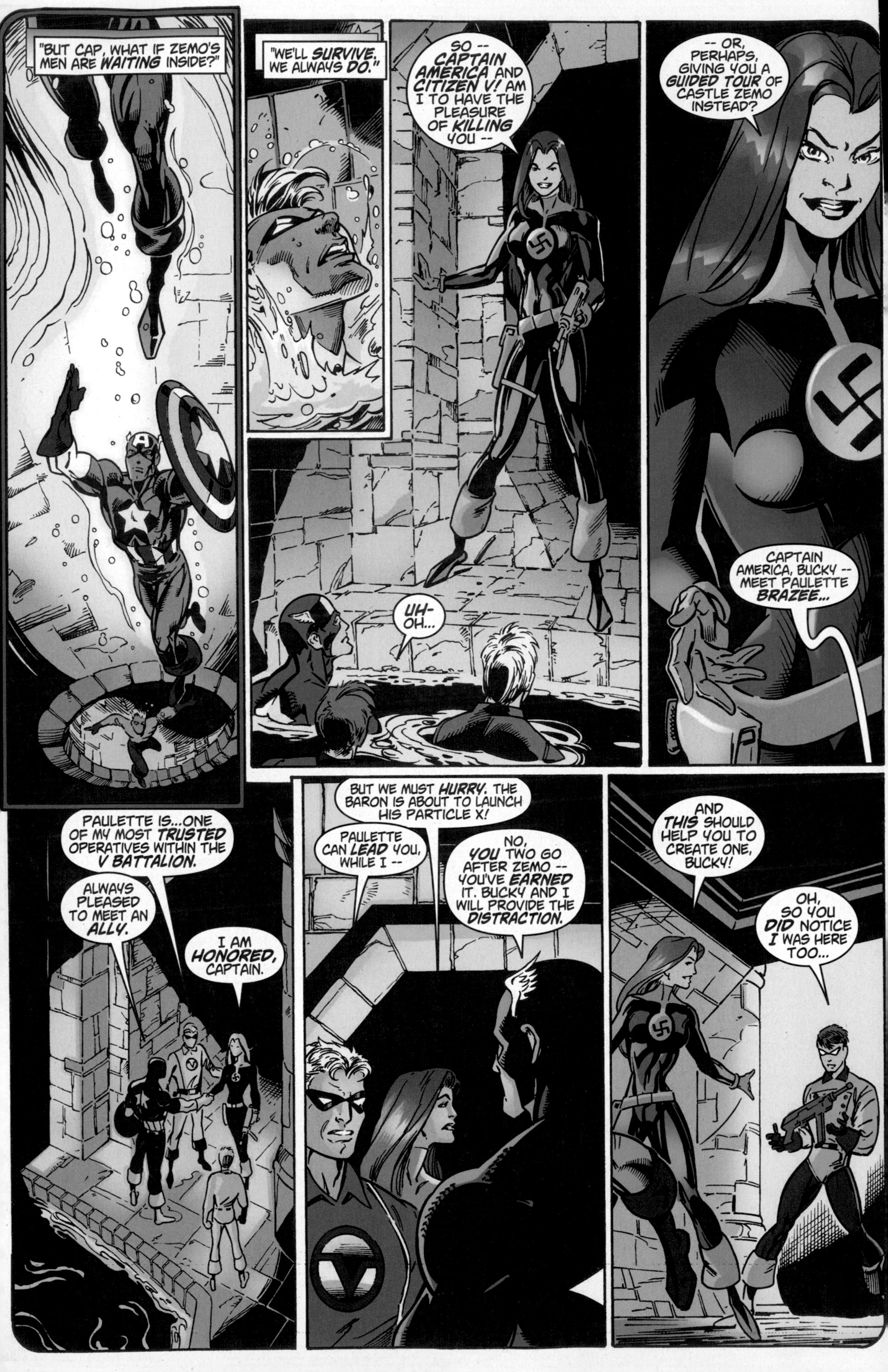
"BUT CAP, WHAT IF ZEMO'S MEN ARE WAITING INSIDE?"
"WE'LL SURVIVE. WE ALWAYS DO."
SO -- CAPTAIN AMERICA AND CITIZEN V! AM I TO HAVE THE PLEASURE OF KILLING YOU --
UH-OH...
-- OR, PERHAPS, GIVING YOU A GUIDED TOUR OF CASTLE ZEMO INSTEAD?
CAPTAIN AMERICA, BUCKY -- MEET PAULETTE BRAZEE...
PAULETTE IS...ONE OF MY MOST TRUSTED OPERATIVES WITHIN THE V BATTALION.
ALWAYS PLEASED TO MEET AN ALLY.
I AM HONORED, CAPTAIN.
BUT WE MUST HURRY. THE BARON IS ABOUT TO LAUNCH HIS PARTICLE X!
PAULETTE CAN LEAD YOU, WHILE I --
NO, YOU TWO GO AFTER ZEMO -- YOU'VE EARNED IT. BUCKY AND I WILL PROVIDE THE DISTRACTION.
AND THIS SHOULD HELP YOU TO CREATE ONE, BUCKY!
OH, SO YOU DID NOTICE I WAS HERE TOO...

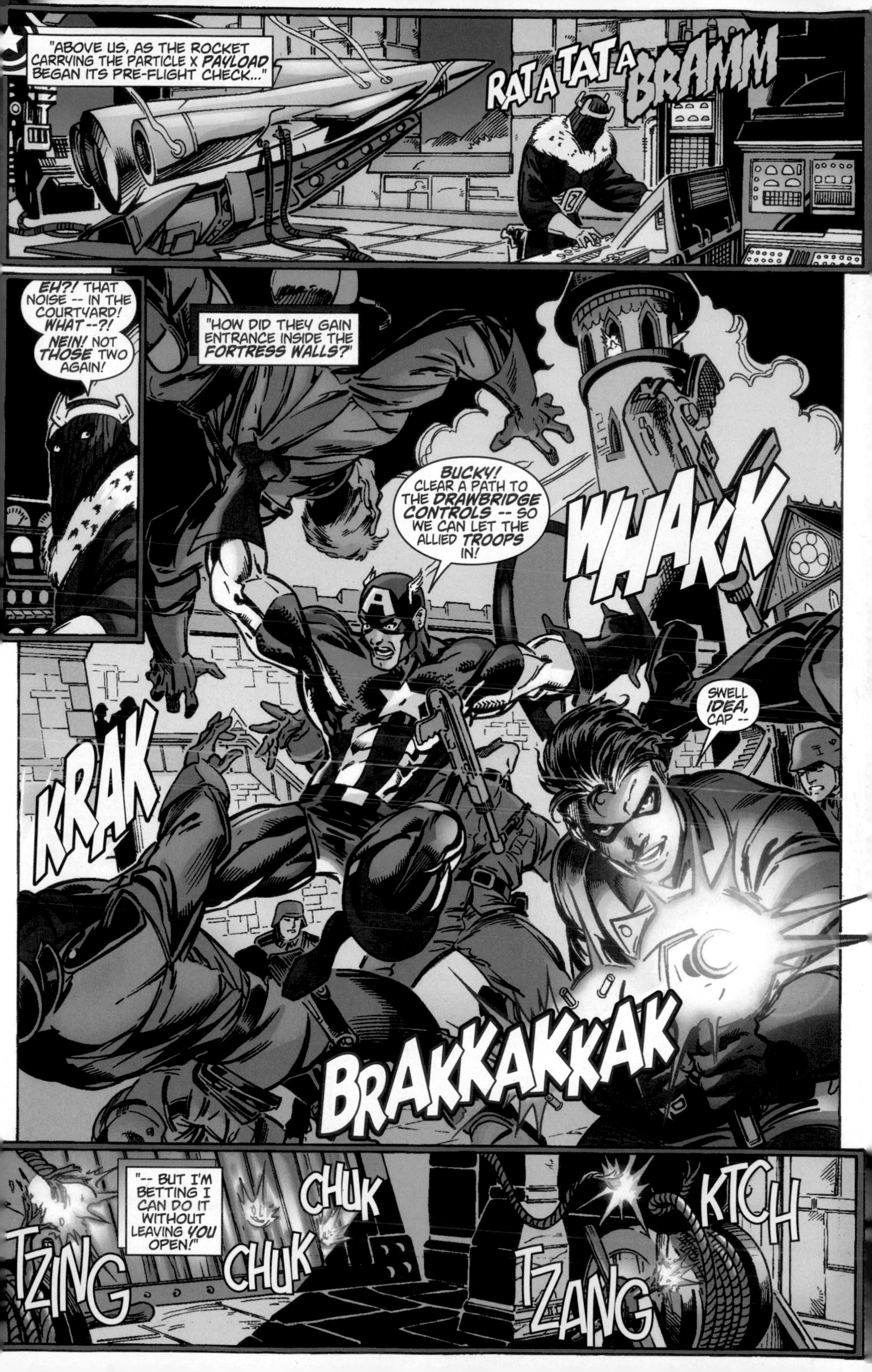
"ABOVE US, AS THE ROCKET CARRYING THE PARTICLE X PAYLOAD BEGAN ITS PRE-FLIGHT CHECK..."
RAT A TAT A BRAMM
EH?! THAT NOISE -- IN THE COURTYARD! WHAT --?! NEIN! NOT THOSE TWO AGAIN!
"HOW DID THEY GAIN ENTRANCE INSIDE THE FORTRESS WALLS?"
BUCKY! CLEAR A PATH TO THE DRAWBRIDGE CONTROLS -- SO WE CAN LET THE ALLIED TROOPS IN!
WHAKK
SWELL IDEA, CAP --
KRAK
BRAKKAKKAK
"-- BUT I'M BETTING I CAN DO IT WITHOUT LEAVING YOU OPEN!"
TZING
CHUK
CHUK
TZANG
KTCH

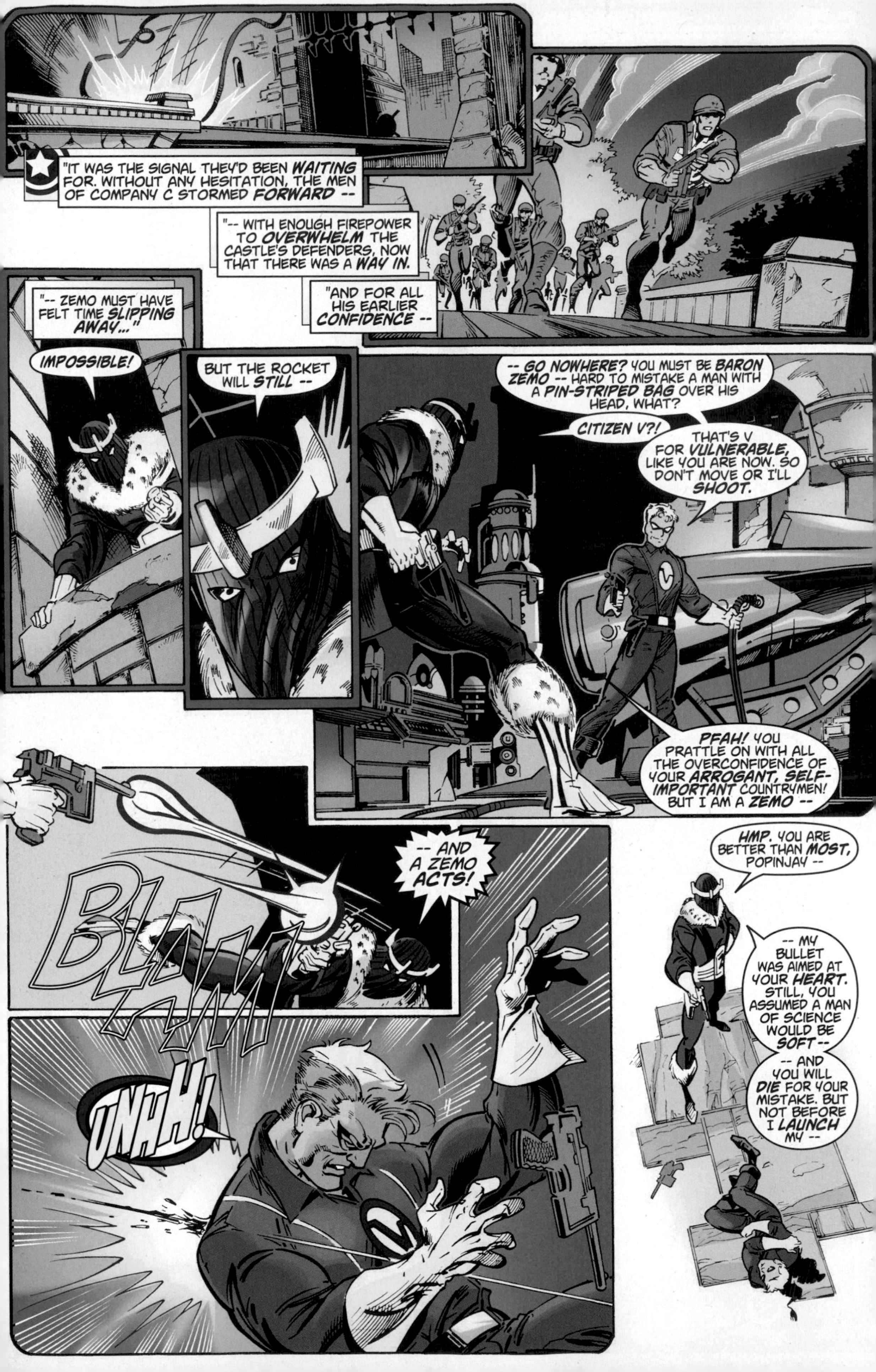
"IT WAS THE SIGNAL THEY'D BEEN WAITING FOR. WITHOUT ANY HESITATION, THE MEN OF COMPANY C STORMED FORWARD --
"-- WITH ENOUGH FIREPOWER TO OVERWHELM THE CASTLE'S DEFENDERS, NOW THAT THERE WAS A WAY IN.
"AND FOR ALL HIS EARLIER CONFIDENCE --
"-- ZEMO MUST HAVE FELT TIME SLIPPING AWAY..."
IMPOSSIBLE!
BUT THE ROCKET WILL STILL --
-- GO NOWHERE? YOU MUST BE BARON ZEMO -- HARD TO MISTAKE A MAN WITH A PIN-STRIPED BAG OVER HIS HEAD, WHAT?
CITIZEN V?!
THAT'S V FOR VULNERABLE, LIKE YOU ARE NOW. SO DON'T MOVE OR I'LL SHOOT.
PFAH! YOU PRATTLE ON WITH ALL THE OVERCONFIDENCE OF YOUR ARROGANT, SELF-IMPORTANT COUNTRYMEN! BUT I AM A ZEMO --
-- AND A ZEMO ACTS!
BLAM
UNHH!
HMP. YOU ARE BETTER THAN MOST, POPINJAY --
-- MY BULLET WAS AIMED AT YOUR HEART. STILL, YOU ASSUMED A MAN OF SCIENCE WOULD BE SOFT --
-- AND YOU WILL DIE FOR YOUR MISTAKE. BUT NOT BEFORE I LAUNCH MY --

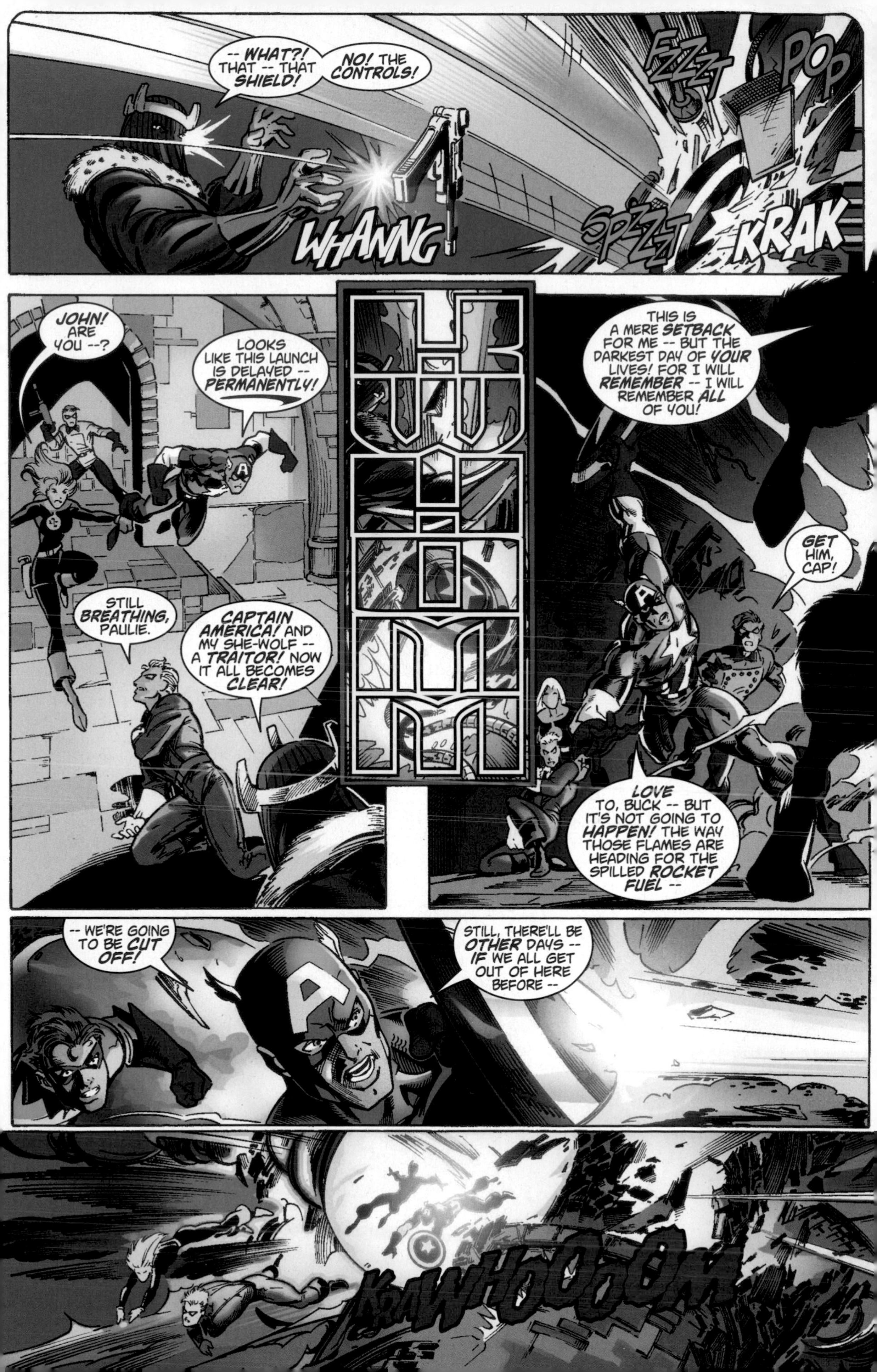
-- WHAT?! THAT -- THAT SHIELD!
NO! THE CONTROLS!
FZZZT
POP
WHANNG
SPZZZT
KRAK
JOHN! ARE YOU --?
LOOKS LIKE THIS LAUNCH IS DELAYED -- PERMANENTLY!
STILL BREATHING, PAULIE.
CAPTAIN AMERICA! AND MY SHE-WOLF -- A TRAITOR! NOW IT ALL BECOMES CLEAR!
THIS IS A MERE SETBACK FOR ME -- BUT THE DARKEST DAY OF YOUR LIVES! FOR I WILL REMEMBER -- I WILL REMEMBER ALL OF YOU!
GET HIM, CAP!
LOVE TO, BUCK -- BUT IT'S NOT GOING TO HAPPEN! THE WAY THOSE FLAMES ARE HEADING FOR THE SPILLED ROCKET FUEL --
-- WE'RE GOING TO BE CUT OFF!
STILL, THERE'LL BE OTHER DAYS -- IF WE ALL GET OUT OF HERE BEFORE --
KRAWHOOOOM

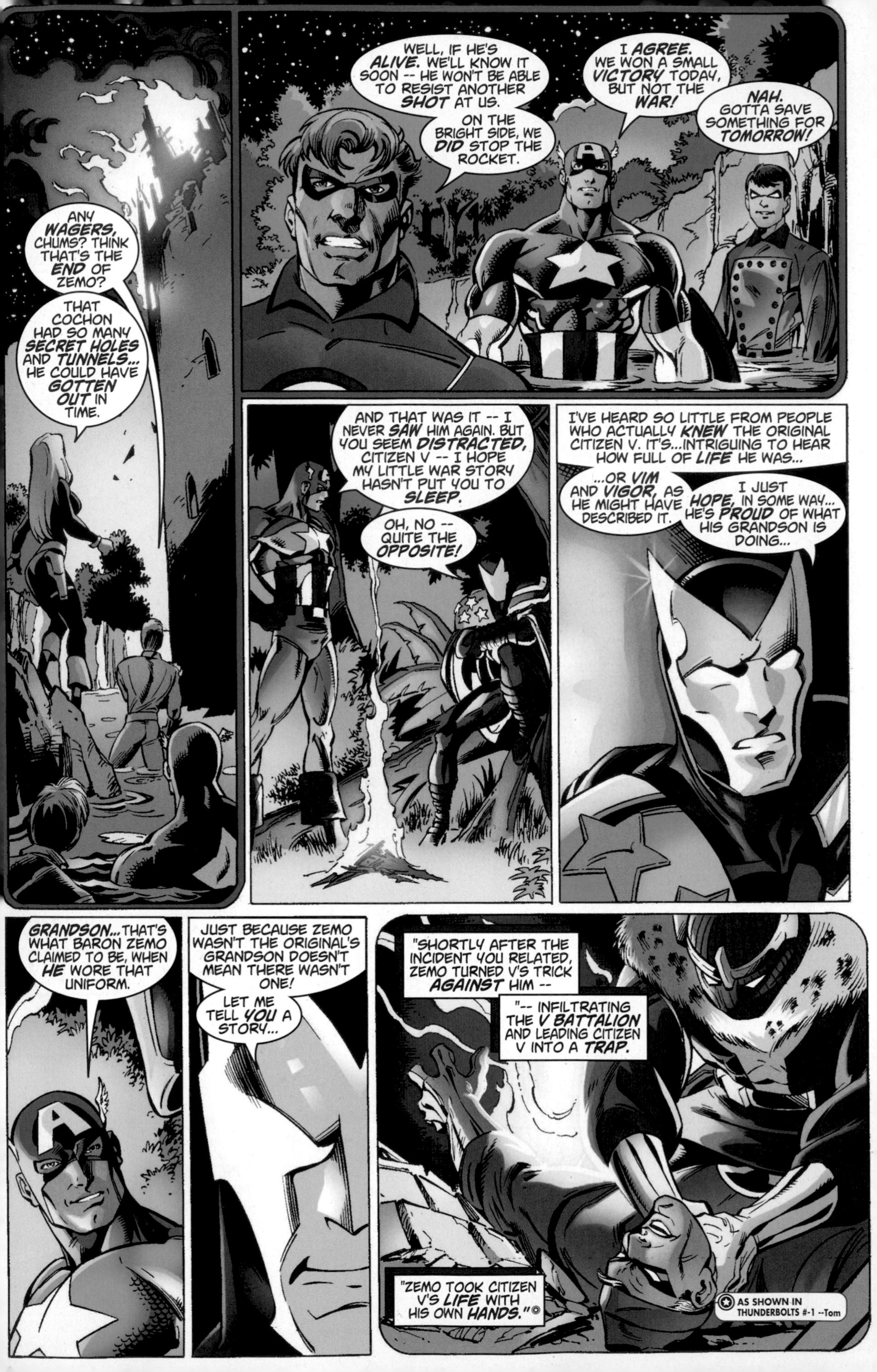
ANY WAGERS, CHUMS? THINK THAT'S THE END OF ZEMO?
THAT COCHON HAD SO MANY SECRET HOLES AND TUNNELS... HE COULD HAVE GOTTEN OUT IN TIME.
WELL, IF HE'S ALIVE, WE'LL KNOW IT SOON -- HE WON'T BE ABLE TO RESIST ANOTHER SHOT AT US.
ON THE BRIGHT SIDE, WE DID STOP THE ROCKET.
I AGREE. WE WON A SMALL VICTORY TODAY, BUT NOT THE WAR!
NAH. GOTTA SAVE SOMETHING FOR TOMORROW!
AND THAT WAS IT -- I NEVER SAW HIM AGAIN. BUT YOU SEEM DISTRACTED, CITIZEN V -- I HOPE MY LITTLE WAR STORY HASN'T PUT YOU TO SLEEP.
OH, NO -- QUITE THE OPPOSITE!
I'VE HEARD SO LITTLE FROM PEOPLE WHO ACTUALLY KNEW THE ORIGINAL CITIZEN V. IT'S...INTRIGUING TO HEAR HOW FULL OF LIFE HE WAS...
...OR VIM AND VIGOR, AS HE MIGHT HAVE DESCRIBED IT.
I JUST HOPE, IN SOME WAY... HE'S PROUD OF WHAT HIS GRANDSON IS DOING...
GRANDSON... THAT'S WHAT BARON ZEMO CLAIMED TO BE, WHEN HE WORE THAT UNIFORM.
JUST BECAUSE ZEMO WASN'T THE ORIGINAL'S GRANDSON DOESN'T MEAN THERE WASN'T ONE!
LET ME TELL YOU A STORY...
"SHORTLY AFTER THE INCIDENT YOU RELATED, ZEMO TURNED V'S TRICK AGAINST HIM --
"-- INFILTRATING THE V BATTALION AND LEADING CITIZEN V INTO A TRAP.
"ZEMO TOOK CITIZEN V'S LIFE WITH HIS OWN HANDS."
AS SHOWN IN THUNDERBOLTS #-1 --Tom

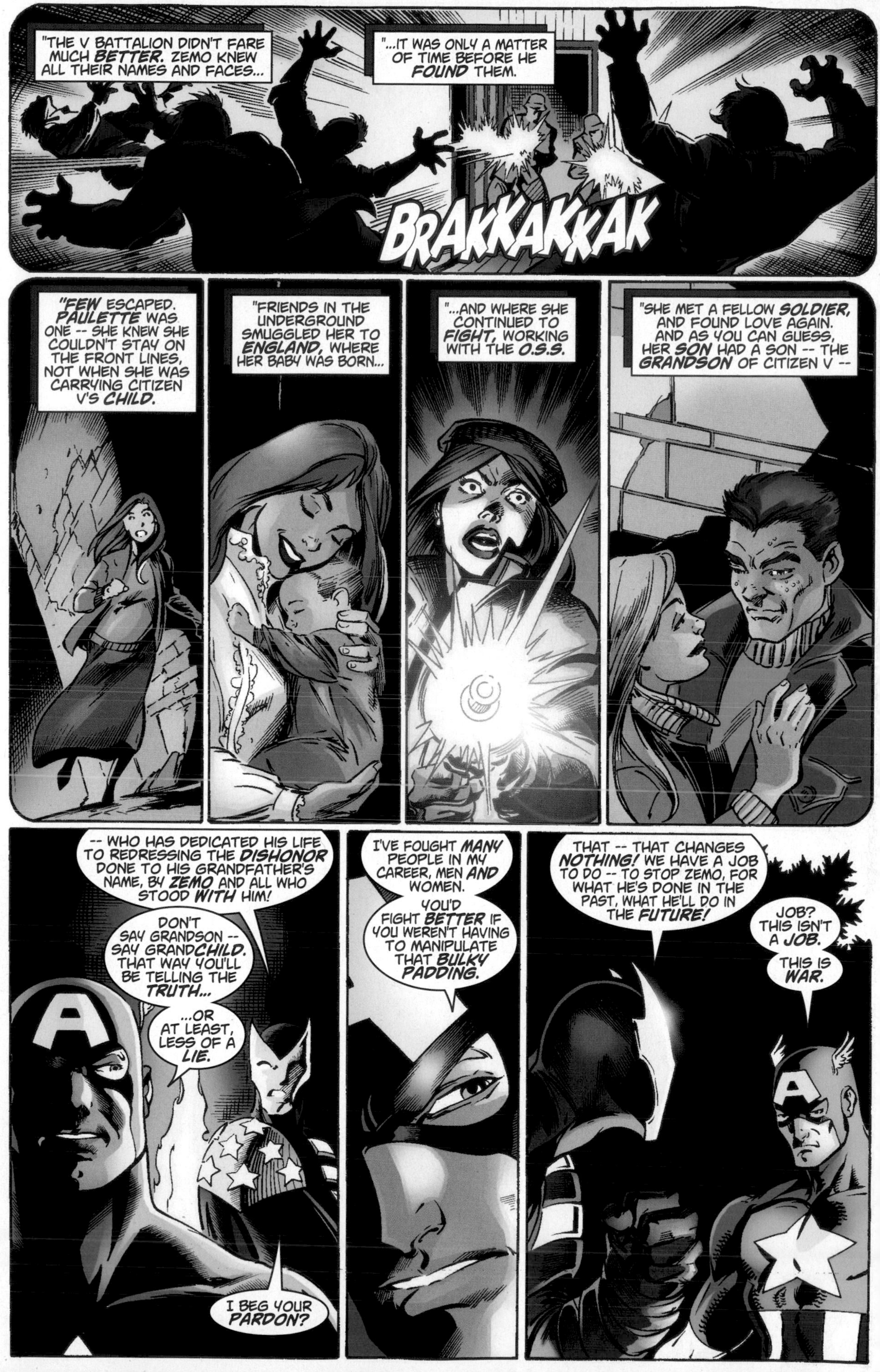
"THE V BATTALION DIDN'T FARE MUCH BETTER. ZEMO KNEW ALL THEIR NAMES AND FACES...
"...IT WAS ONLY A MATTER OF TIME BEFORE HE FOUND THEM.
BRAKKAKKAK
"FEW ESCAPED. PAULETTE WAS ONE -- SHE KNEW SHE COULDN'T STAY ON THE FRONT LINES, NOT WHEN SHE WAS CARRYING CITIZEN V'S CHILD.
"FRIENDS IN THE UNDERGROUND SMUGGLED HER TO ENGLAND, WHERE HER BABY WAS BORN...
"...AND WHERE SHE CONTINUED TO FIGHT, WORKING WITH THE O.S.S.
"SHE MET A FELLOW SOLDIER, AND FOUND LOVE AGAIN. AND AS YOU CAN GUESS, HER SON HAD A SON -- THE GRANDSON OF CITIZEN V --
-- WHO HAS DEDICATED HIS LIFE TO REDRESSING THE DISHONOR DONE TO HIS GRANDFATHER'S NAME, BY ZEMO AND ALL WHO STOOD WITH HIM!
DON'T SAY GRANDSON -- SAY GRANDCHILD. THAT WAY YOU'LL BE TELLING THE TRUTH...
...OR AT LEAST, LESS OF A LIE.
I BEG YOUR PARDON?
I'VE FOUGHT MANY PEOPLE IN MY CAREER, MEN AND WOMEN.
YOU'D FIGHT BETTER IF YOU WEREN'T HAVING TO MANIPULATE THAT BULKY PADDING.
THAT -- THAT CHANGES NOTHING! WE HAVE A JOB TO DO -- TO STOP ZEMO, FOR WHAT HE'S DONE IN THE PAST, WHAT HE'LL DO IN THE FUTURE!
JOB? THIS ISN'T A JOB.
THIS IS WAR.

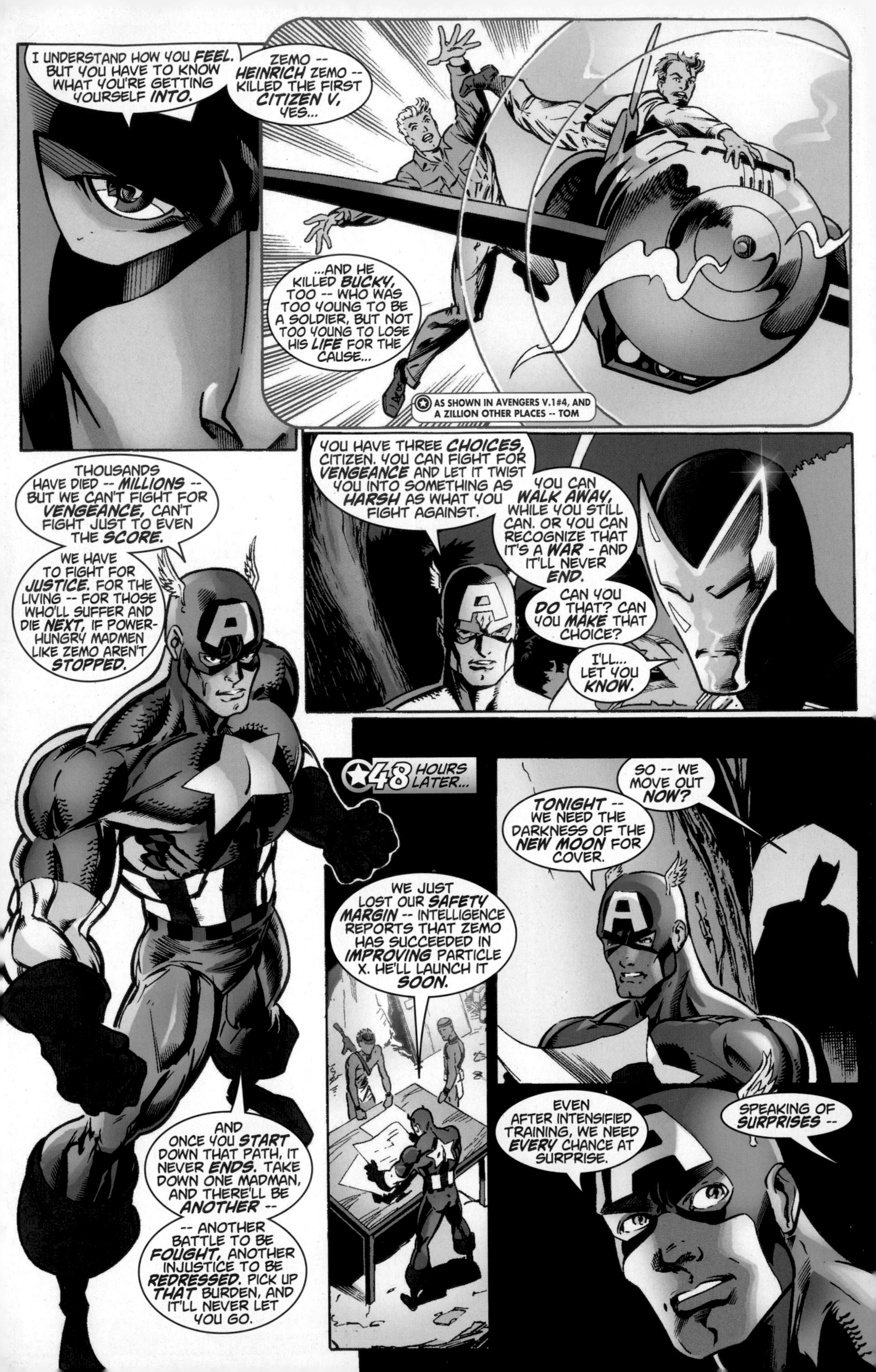
I UNDERSTAND HOW YOU FEEL. BUT YOU HAVE TO KNOW WHAT YOU'RE GETTING YOURSELF INTO.
ZEMO -- HEINRICH ZEMO -- KILLED THE FIRST CITIZEN V, YES...
...AND HE KILLED BUCKY, TOO -- WHO WAS TOO YOUNG TO BE A SOLDIER, BUT NOT TOO YOUNG TO LOSE HIS LIFE FOR THE CAUSE...
AS SHOWN IN AVENGERS V.1#4, AND A ZILLION OTHER PLACES -- TOM
THOUSANDS HAVE DIED -- MILLIONS -- BUT WE CAN'T FIGHT FOR VENGEANCE, CAN'T FIGHT JUST TO EVEN THE SCORE.
WE HAVE TO FIGHT FOR JUSTICE. FOR THE LIVING -- FOR THOSE WHO'LL SUFFER AND DIE NEXT, IF POWER-HUNGRY MADMEN LIKE ZEMO AREN'T STOPPED.
AND ONCE YOU START DOWN THAT PATH, IT NEVER ENDS. TAKE DOWN ONE MADMAN, AND THERE'LL BE ANOTHER --
-- ANOTHER BATTLE TO BE FOUGHT, ANOTHER INJUSTICE TO BE REDRESSED. PICK UP THAT BURDEN, AND IT'LL NEVER LET YOU GO.
YOU HAVE THREE CHOICES, CITIZEN. YOU CAN FIGHT FOR VENGEANCE AND LET IT TWIST YOU INTO SOMETHING AS HARSH AS WHAT YOU FIGHT AGAINST.
YOU CAN WALK AWAY, WHILE YOU STILL CAN. OR YOU CAN RECOGNIZE THAT IT'S A WAR - AND IT'LL NEVER END.
CAN YOU DO THAT? CAN YOU MAKE THAT CHOICE?
I'LL... LET YOU KNOW.
48 HOURS LATER...
WE JUST LOST OUR SAFETY MARGIN -- INTELLIGENCE REPORTS THAT ZEMO HAS SUCCEEDED IN IMPROVING PARTICLE X. HE'LL LAUNCH IT SOON.
SO -- WE MOVE OUT NOW?
TONIGHT -- WE NEED THE DARKNESS OF THE NEW MOON FOR COVER.
EVEN AFTER INTENSIFIED TRAINING, WE NEED EVERY CHANCE AT SURPRISE.
SPEAKING OF SURPRISES --

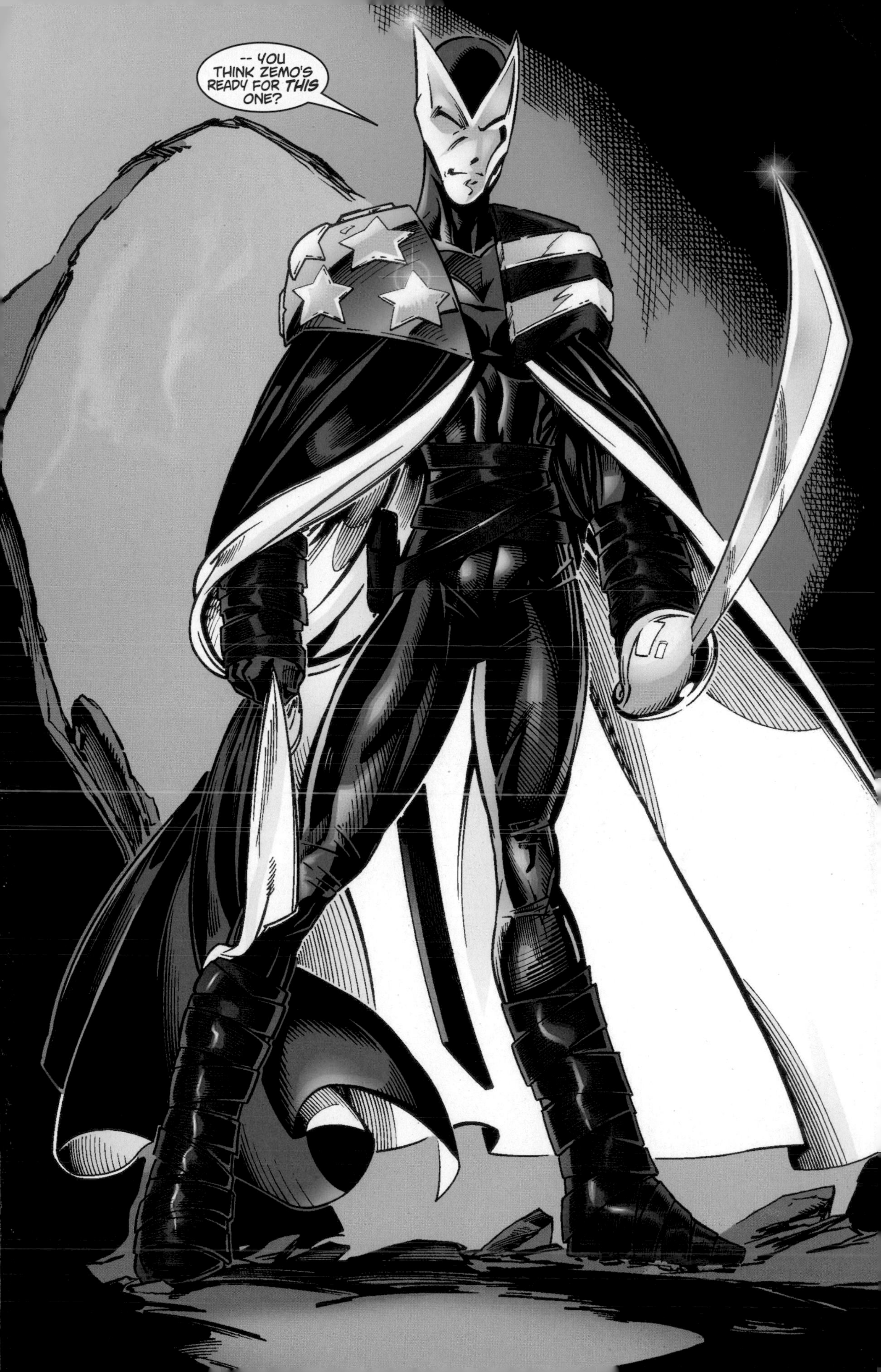
-- YOU THINK ZEMO'S READY FOR THIS ONE?

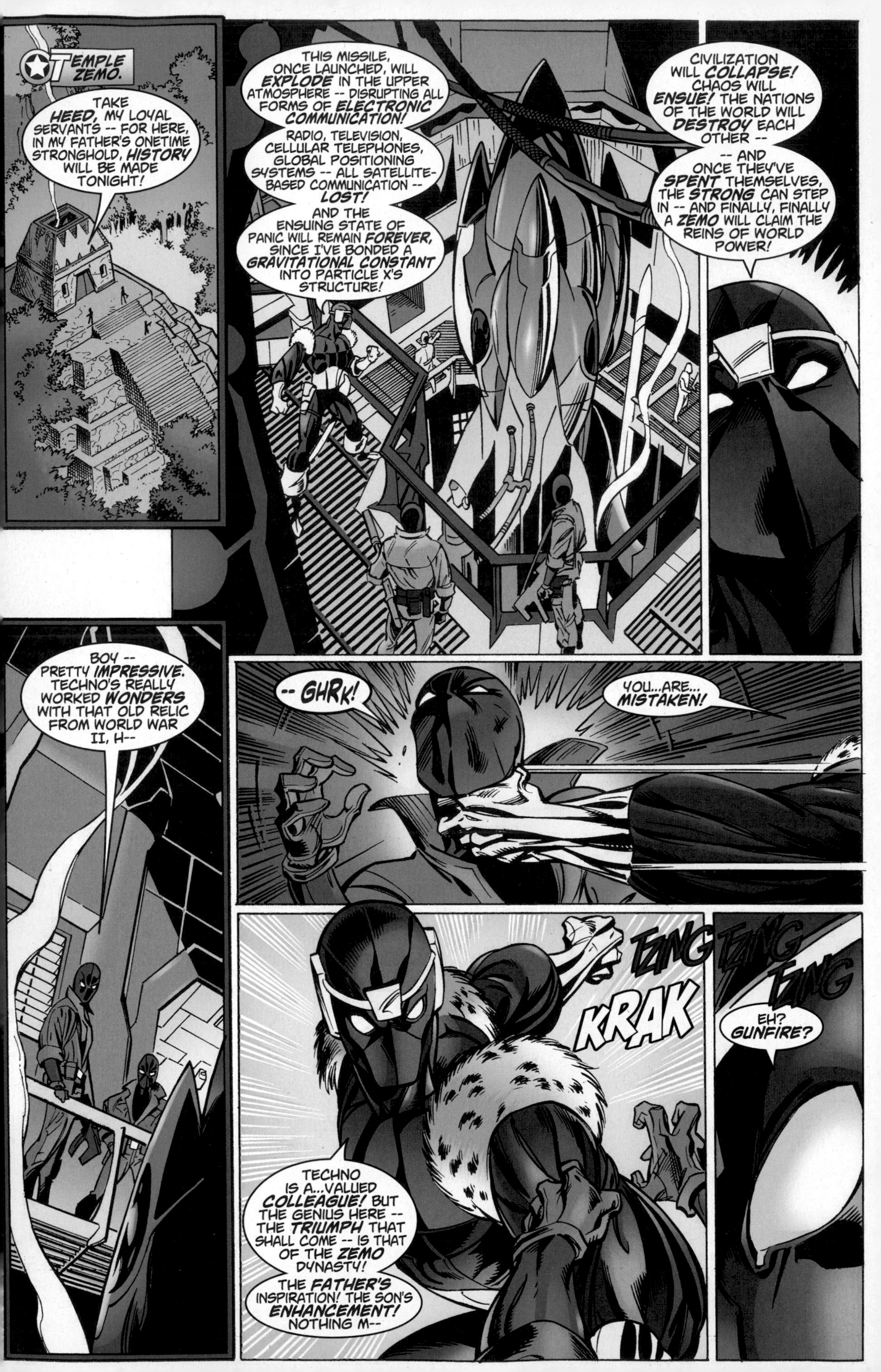
TEMPLE ZEMO.
TAKE HEED, MY LOYAL SERVANTS -- FOR HERE, IN MY FATHER'S ONETIME STRONGHOLD, HISTORY WILL BE MADE TONIGHT!
THIS MISSILE, ONCE LAUNCHED, WILL EXPLODE IN THE UPPER ATMOSPHERE -- DISRUPTING ALL FORMS OF ELECTRONIC COMMUNICATION!
RADIO, TELEVISION, CELLULAR TELEPHONES, GLOBAL POSITIONING SYSTEMS -- ALL SATELLITE-BASED COMMUNICATION -- LOST!
AND THE ENSUING STATE OF PANIC WILL REMAIN FOREVER, SINCE I'VE BONDED A GRAVITATIONAL CONSTANT INTO PARTICLE X'S STRUCTURE!
CIVILIZATION WILL COLLAPSE! CHAOS WILL ENSUE! THE NATIONS OF THE WORLD WILL DESTROY EACH OTHER --
-- AND ONCE THEY'VE SPENT THEMSELVES, THE STRONG CAN STEP IN -- AND FINALLY, FINALLY A ZEMO WILL CLAIM THE REINS OF WORLD POWER!
BOY -- PRETTY IMPRESSIVE. TECHNO'S REALLY WORKED WONDERS WITH THAT OLD RELIC FROM WORLD WAR II, H--
-- GHRK!
YOU...ARE... MISTAKEN!
TZING TZING TZING
KRAK
EH? GUNFIRE?
TECHNO IS A...VALUED COLLEAGUE! BUT THE GENIUS HERE -- THE TRIUMPH THAT SHALL COME -- IS THAT OF THE ZEMO DYNASTY!
THE FATHER'S INSPIRATION! THE SON'S ENHANCEMENT! NOTHING M--

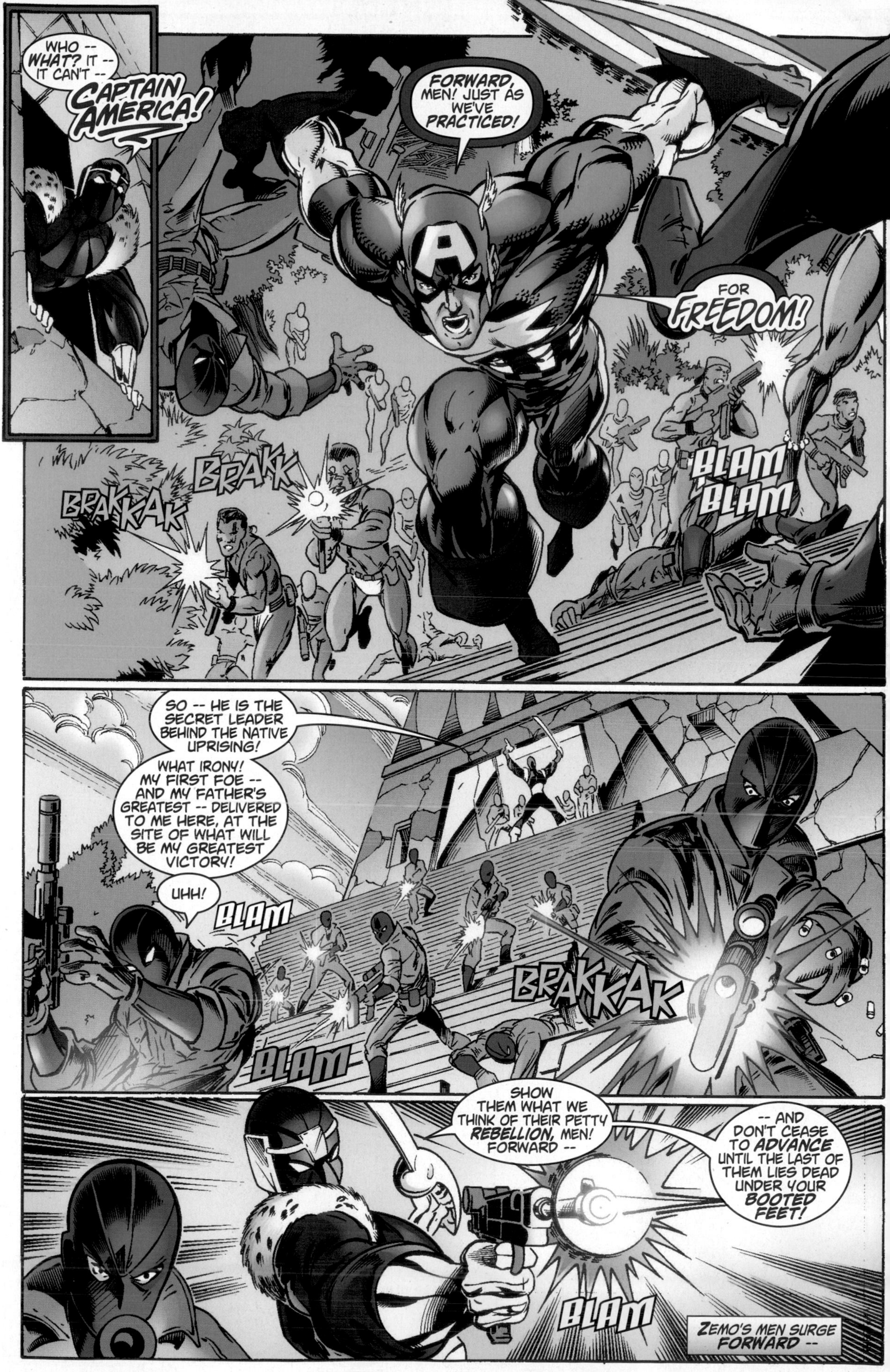
WHO -- WHAT? IT -- IT CAN'T --
CAPTAIN AMERICA!
FORWARD, MEN! JUST AS WE'VE PRACTICED!
FOR FREEDOM!
BRAKKAK
BRAKK
BLAM BLAM
SO -- HE IS THE SECRET LEADER BEHIND THE NATIVE UPRISING!
WHAT IRONY! MY FIRST FOE -- AND MY FATHER'S GREATEST -- DELIVERED TO ME HERE, AT THE SITE OF WHAT WILL BE MY GREATEST VICTORY!
UHH!
BLAM
BRAKKAK
BLAM
SHOW THEM WHAT WE THINK OF THEIR PETTY REBELLION, MEN! FORWARD --
-- AND DON'T CEASE TO ADVANCE UNTIL THE LAST OF THEM LIES DEAD UNDER YOUR BOOTED FEET!
BLAM
ZEMO'S MEN SURGE FORWARD --

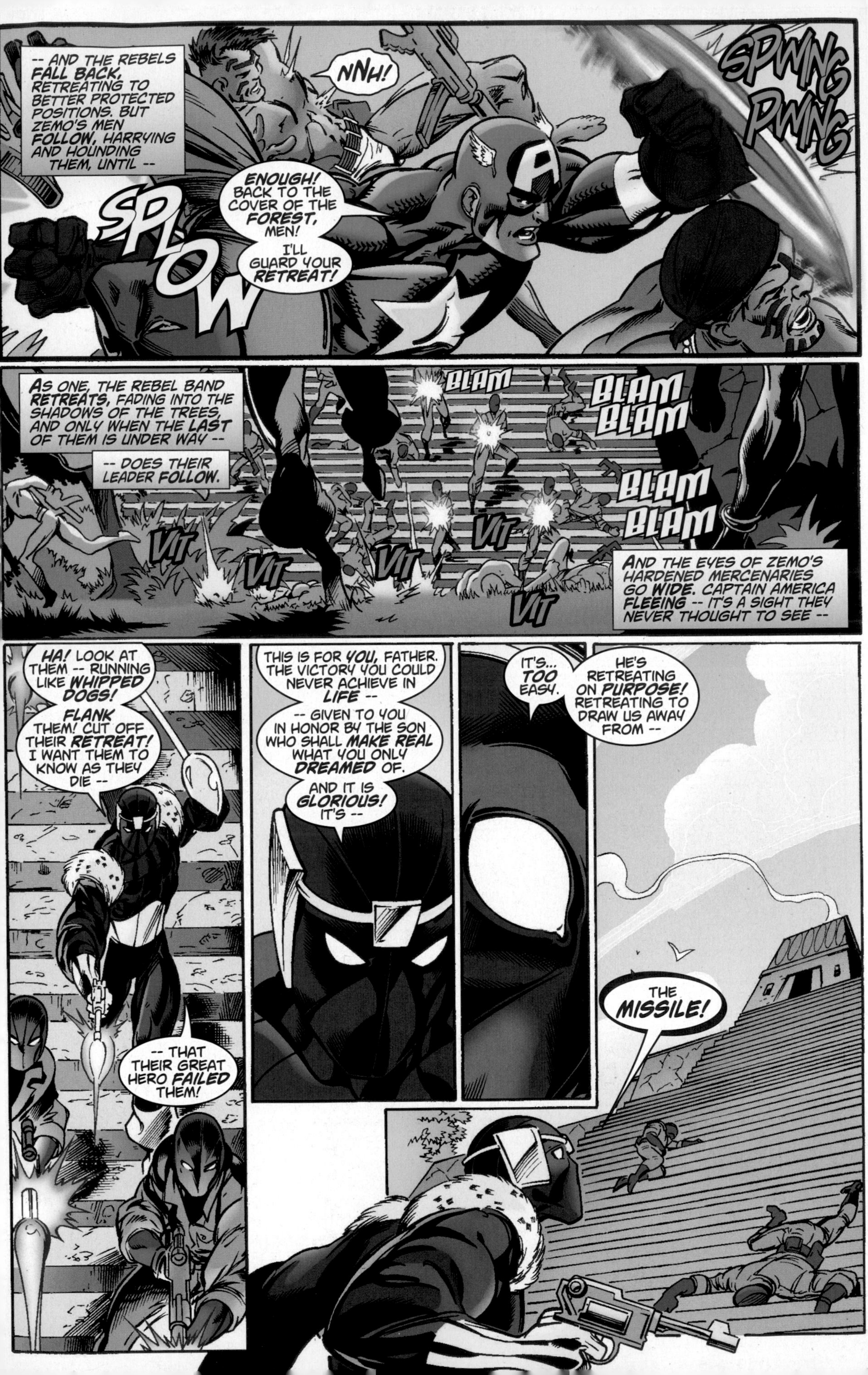

-- AND THE REBELS FALL BACK, RETREATING TO BETTER PROTECTED POSITIONS. BUT ZEMO'S MEN FOLLOW, HARRYING AND HOUNDING THEM, UNTIL --
NNH!
SPWNG PWNG
ENOUGH! BACK TO THE COVER OF THE FOREST, MEN!
I'LL GUARD YOUR RETREAT!
SPLOW
AS ONE, THE REBEL BAND RETREATS, FADING INTO THE SHADOWS OF THE TREES, AND ONLY WHEN THE LAST OF THEM IS UNDER WAY --
-- DOES THEIR LEADER FOLLOW.
BLAM
BLAM BLAM
BLAM BLAM
VIT
VIT
VIT
VIT
VIT
AND THE EYES OF ZEMO'S HARDENED MERCENARIES GO WIDE. CAPTAIN AMERICA FLEEING -- IT'S A SIGHT THEY NEVER THOUGHT TO SEE --
HA! LOOK AT THEM -- RUNNING LIKE WHIPPED DOGS!
FLANK THEM! CUT OFF THEIR RETREAT! I WANT THEM TO KNOW AS THEY DIE --
-- THAT THEIR GREAT HERO FAILED THEM!
THIS IS FOR YOU, FATHER. THE VICTORY YOU COULD NEVER ACHIEVE IN LIFE --
-- GIVEN TO YOU IN HONOR BY THE SON WHO SHALL MAKE REAL WHAT YOU ONLY DREAMED OF.
AND IT IS GLORIOUS! IT'S --
IT'S... TOO EASY.
HE'S RETREATING ON PURPOSE! RETREATING TO DRAW US AWAY FROM --
THE MISSILE!

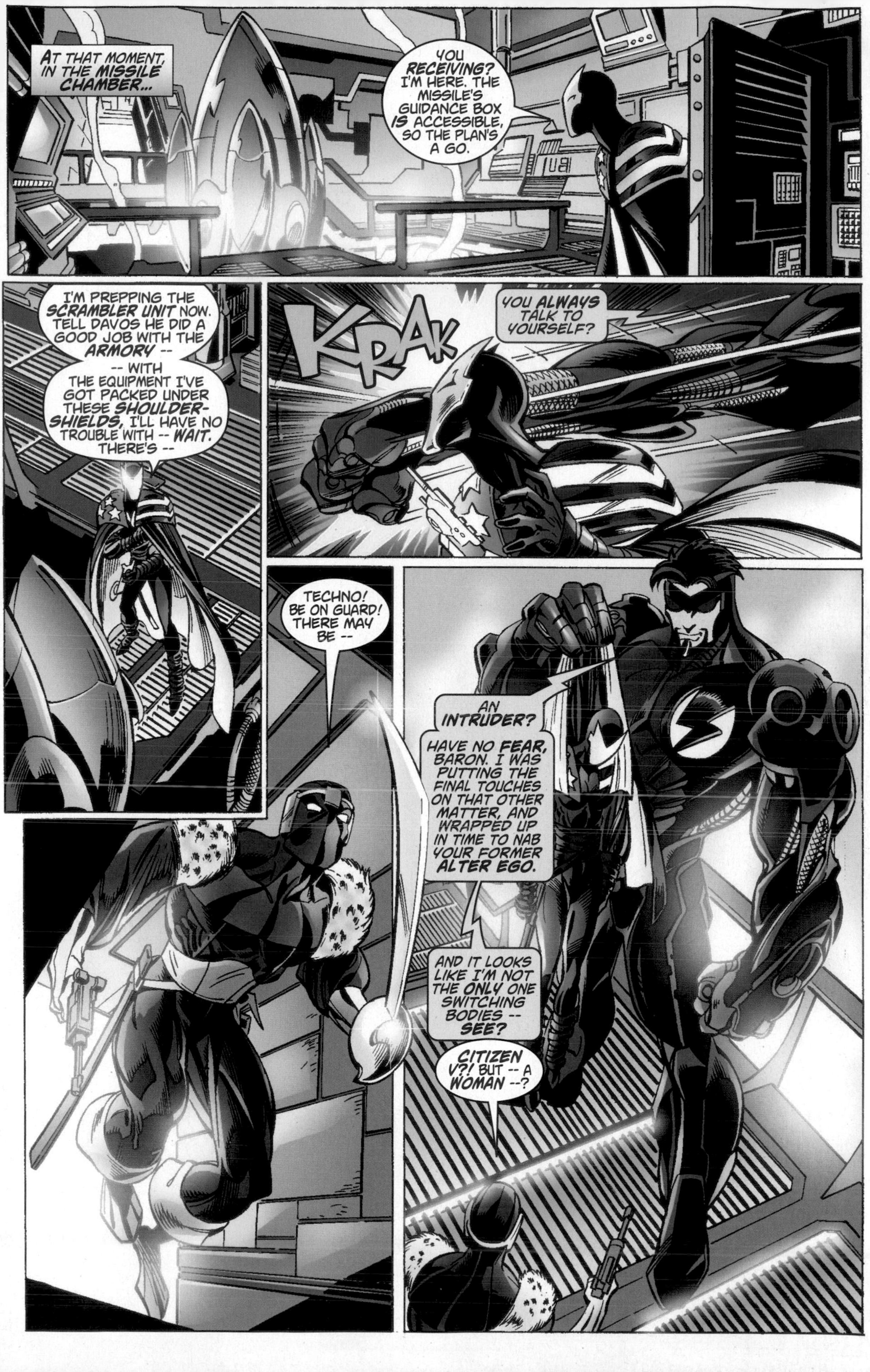
AT THAT MOMENT, IN THE MISSILE CHAMBER...
YOU RECEIVING? I'M HERE. THE MISSILE'S GUIDANCE BOX IS ACCESSIBLE, SO THE PLAN'S A GO.
I'M PREPPING THE SCRAMBLER UNIT NOW. TELL DAVOS HE DID A GOOD JOB WITH THE ARMORY --
-- WITH THE EQUIPMENT I'VE GOT PACKED UNDER THESE SHOULDER-SHIELDS, I'LL HAVE NO TROUBLE WITH -- WAIT. THERE'S --
KRAK
YOU ALWAYS TALK TO YOURSELF?
TECHNO! BE ON GUARD! THERE MAY BE --
AN INTRUDER?
HAVE NO FEAR, BARON. I WAS PUTTING THE FINAL TOUCHES ON THAT OTHER MATTER, AND WRAPPED UP IN TIME TO NAB YOUR FORMER ALTER EGO.
AND IT LOOKS LIKE I'M NOT THE ONLY ONE SWITCHING BODIES -- SEE?
CITIZEN V?! BUT -- A WOMAN --?

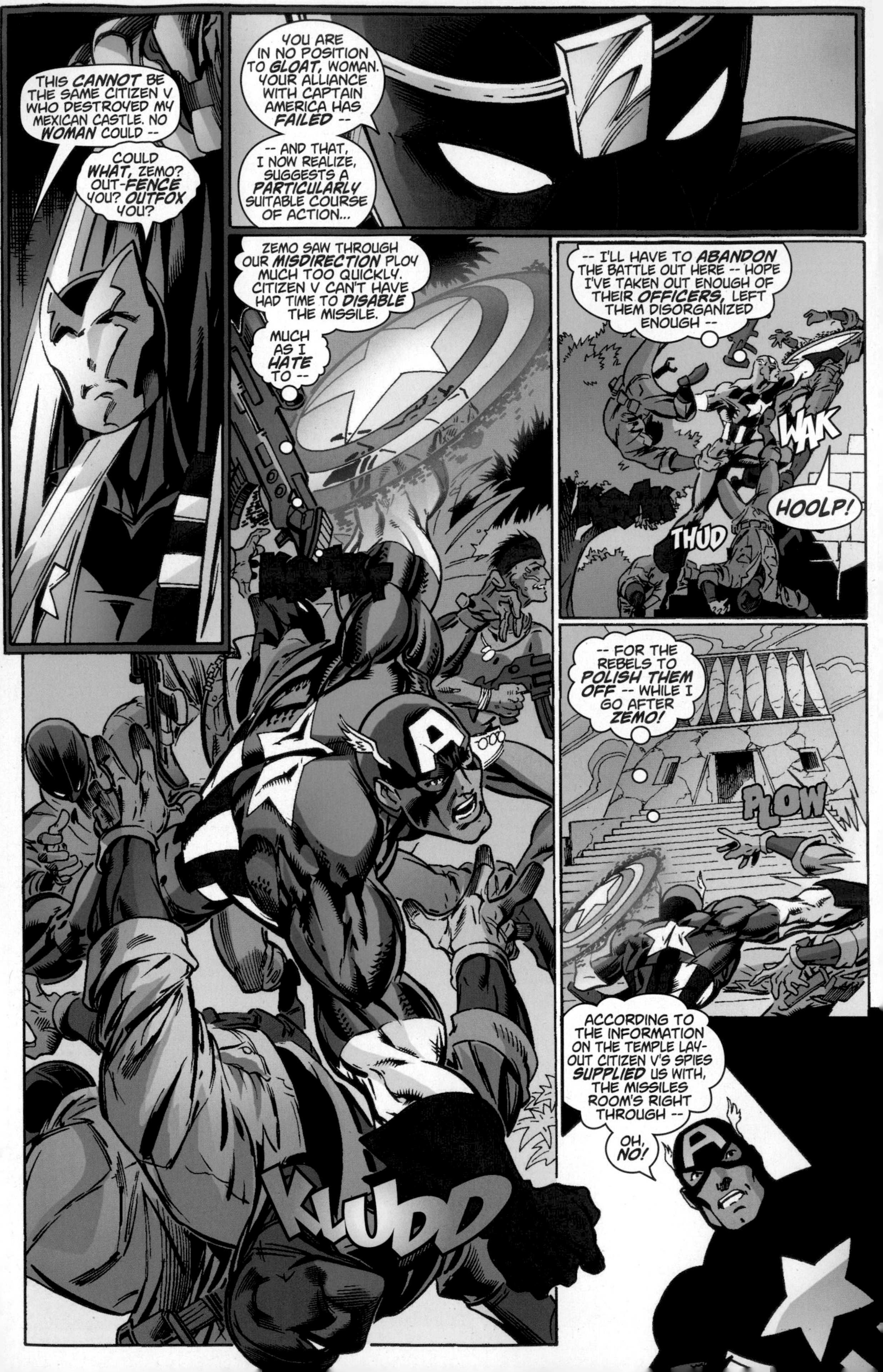
THIS CANNOT BE THE SAME CITIZEN V WHO DESTROYED MY MEXICAN CASTLE. NO WOMAN COULD --
COULD WHAT, ZEMO? OUT-FENCE YOU? OUTFOX YOU?
YOU ARE IN NO POSITION TO GLOAT, WOMAN. YOUR ALLIANCE WITH CAPTAIN AMERICA HAS FAILED --
-- AND THAT, I NOW REALIZE, SUGGESTS A PARTICULARLY SUITABLE COURSE OF ACTION...
ZEMO SAW THROUGH OUR MISDIRECTION PLOY MUCH TOO QUICKLY. CITIZEN V CAN'T HAVE HAD TIME TO DISABLE THE MISSILE.
MUCH AS I HATE TO --
-- I'LL HAVE TO ABANDON THE BATTLE OUT HERE -- HOPE I'VE TAKEN OUT ENOUGH OF THEIR OFFICERS, LEFT THEM DISORGANIZED ENOUGH --
WAK
HOOLP!
THUD
-- FOR THE REBELS TO POLISH THEM OFF -- WHILE I GO AFTER ZEMO!
PLOW
KLUDD
ACCORDING TO THE INFORMATION ON THE TEMPLE LAY-OUT CITIZEN V'S SPIES SUPPLIED US WITH, THE MISSILES ROOM'S RIGHT THROUGH --
OH, NO!

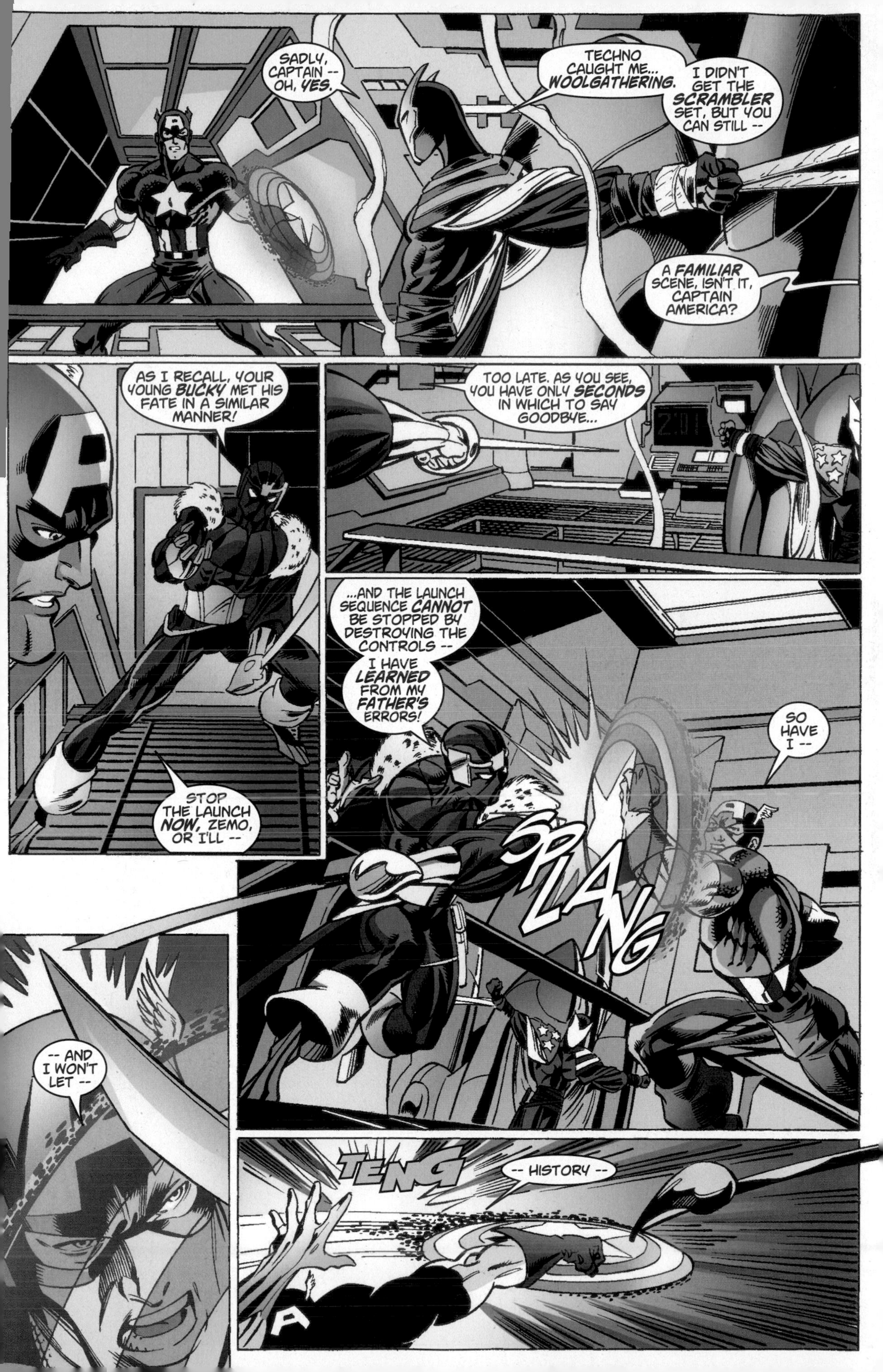
SADLY, CAPTAIN -- OH, YES.
TECHNO CAUGHT ME... WOOLGATHERING.
I DIDN'T GET THE SCRAMBLER SET, BUT YOU CAN STILL --
A FAMILIAR SCENE, ISN'T IT, CAPTAIN AMERICA?
AS I RECALL, YOUR YOUNG BUCKY MET HIS FATE IN A SIMILAR MANNER!
STOP THE LAUNCH NOW, ZEMO, OR I'LL --
TOO LATE. AS YOU SEE, YOU HAVE ONLY SECONDS IN WHICH TO SAY GOODBYE...
...AND THE LAUNCH SEQUENCE CANNOT BE STOPPED BY DESTROYING THE CONTROLS --
I HAVE LEARNED FROM MY FATHER'S ERRORS!
SO HAVE I --
SPLANG
-- AND I WON'T LET --
TENG
-- HISTORY --

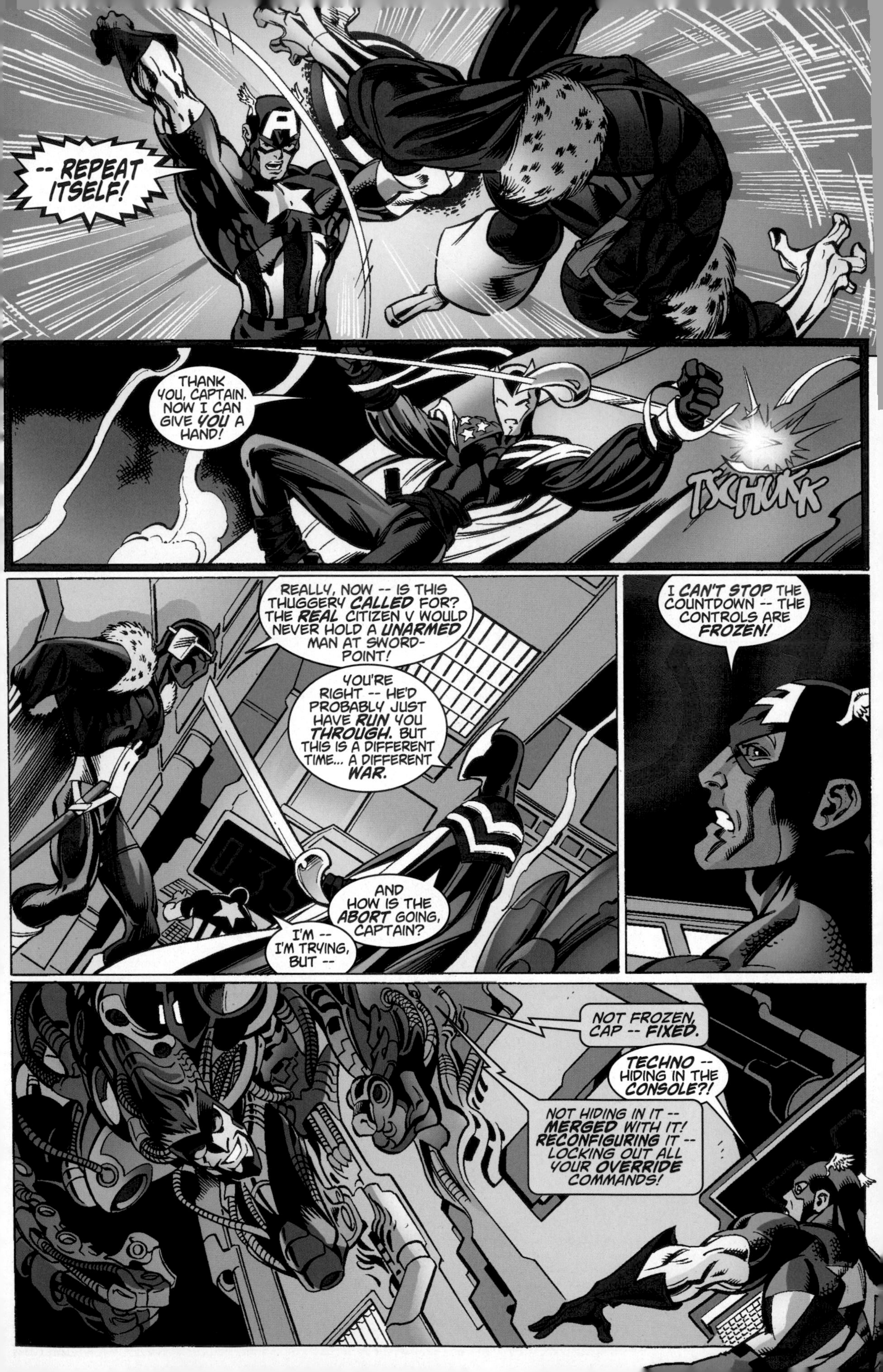

-- REPEAT ITSELF!
THANK YOU, CAPTAIN. NOW I CAN GIVE YOU A HAND!
TSCHUKK
REALLY, NOW -- IS THIS THUGGERY CALLED FOR? THE REAL CITIZEN V WOULD NEVER HOLD A UNARMED MAN AT SWORD-POINT!
YOU'RE RIGHT -- HE'D PROBABLY JUST HAVE RUN YOU THROUGH. BUT THIS IS A DIFFERENT TIME... A DIFFERENT WAR.
AND HOW IS THE ABORT GOING, CAPTAIN?
I'M -- I'M TRYING, BUT --
I CAN'T STOP THE COUNTDOWN -- THE CONTROLS ARE FROZEN!
NOT FROZEN, CAP -- FIXED.
TECHNO -- HIDING IN THE CONSOLE?!
NOT HIDING IN IT -- MERGED WITH IT! RECONFIGURING IT -- LOCKING OUT ALL YOUR OVERRIDE COMMANDS!

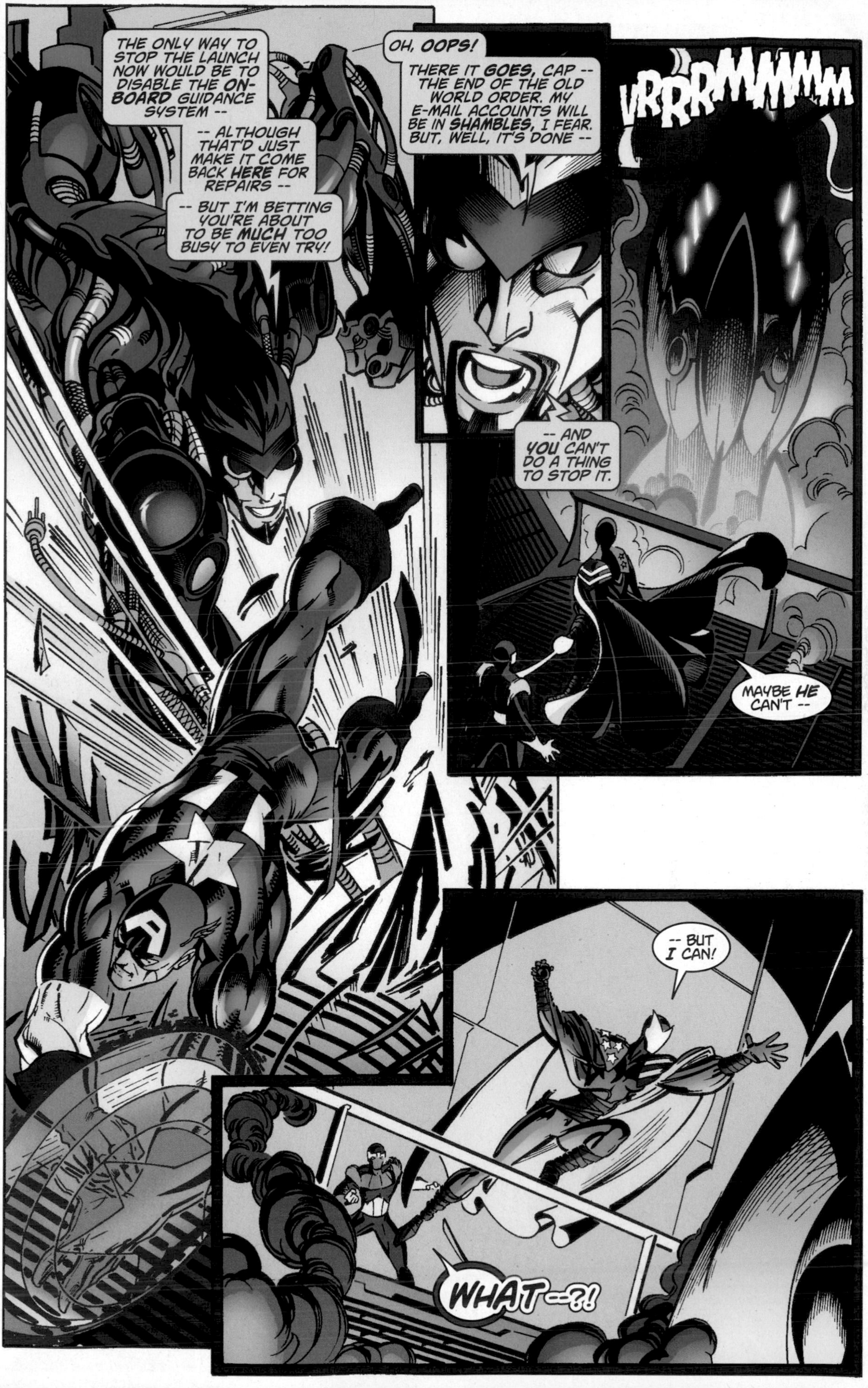
THE ONLY WAY TO STOP THE LAUNCH NOW WOULD BE TO DISABLE THE ON-BOARD GUIDANCE SYSTEM --
-- ALTHOUGH THAT'D JUST MAKE IT COME BACK HERE FOR REPAIRS --
-- BUT I'M BETTING YOU'RE ABOUT TO BE MUCH TOO BUSY TO EVEN TRY!
OH, OOPS!
THERE IT GOES, CAP -- THE END OF THE OLD WORLD ORDER. MY E-MAIL ACCOUNTS WILL BE IN SHAMBLES, I FEAR. BUT, WELL, IT'S DONE --
VRRRMMMMM
-- AND YOU CAN'T DO A THING TO STOP IT.
MAYBE HE CAN'T --
-- BUT I CAN!
WHAT --?!

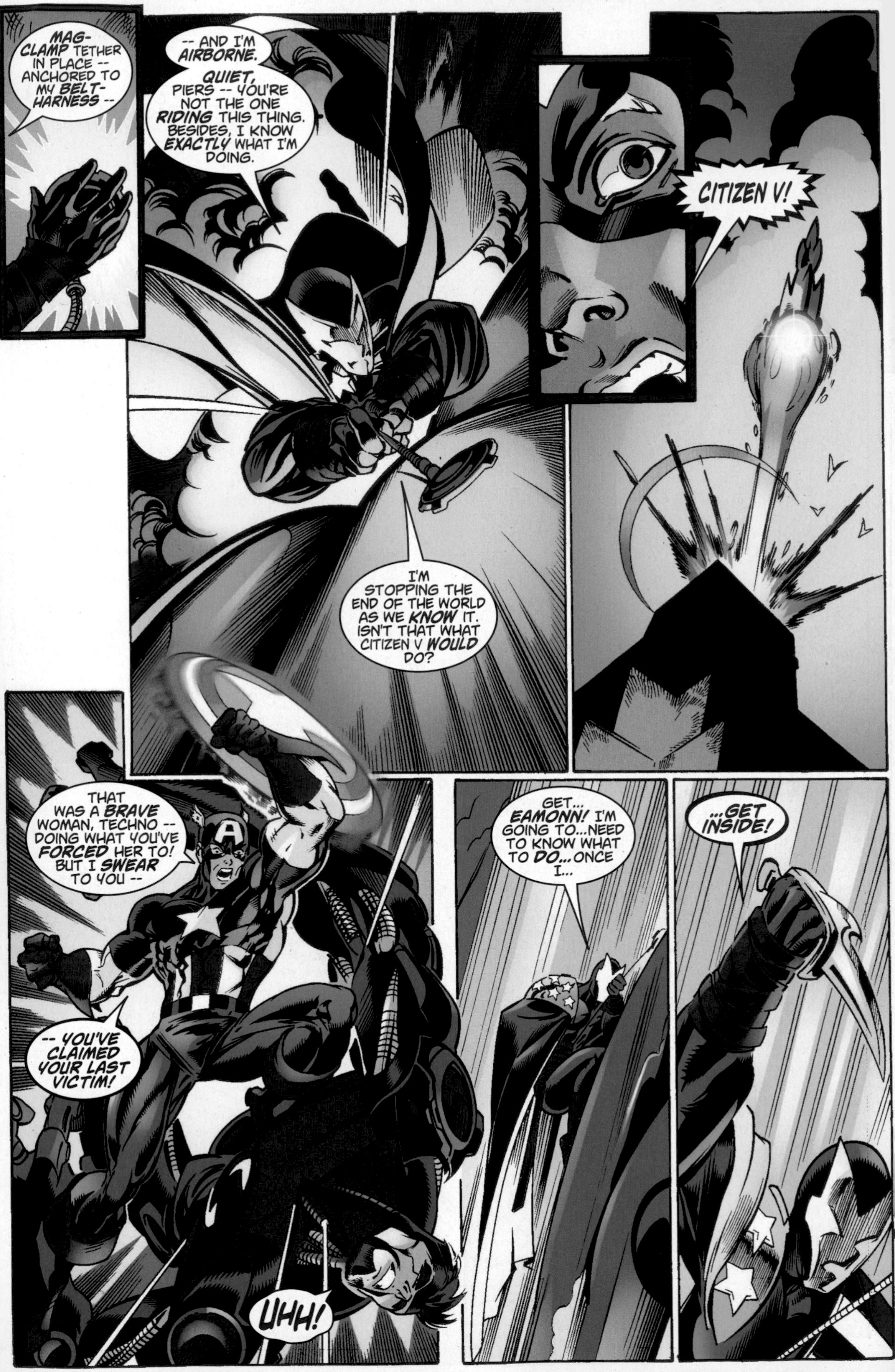
MAG-CLAMP TETHER IN PLACE -- ANCHORED TO MY BELT-HARNESS --
-- AND I'M AIRBORNE.
QUIET, PIERS -- YOU'RE NOT THE ONE RIDING THIS THING. BESIDES, I KNOW EXACTLY WHAT I'M DOING.
I'M STOPPING THE END OF THE WORLD AS WE KNOW IT. ISN'T THAT WHAT CITIZEN V WOULD DO?
CITIZEN V!
THAT WAS A BRAVE WOMAN, TECHNO -- DOING WHAT YOU'VE FORCED HER TO! BUT I SWEAR TO YOU --
-- YOU'VE CLAIMED YOUR LAST VICTIM!
UHH!
GET... EAMONN! I'M GOING TO...NEED TO KNOW WHAT TO DO...ONCE I...
...GET INSIDE!

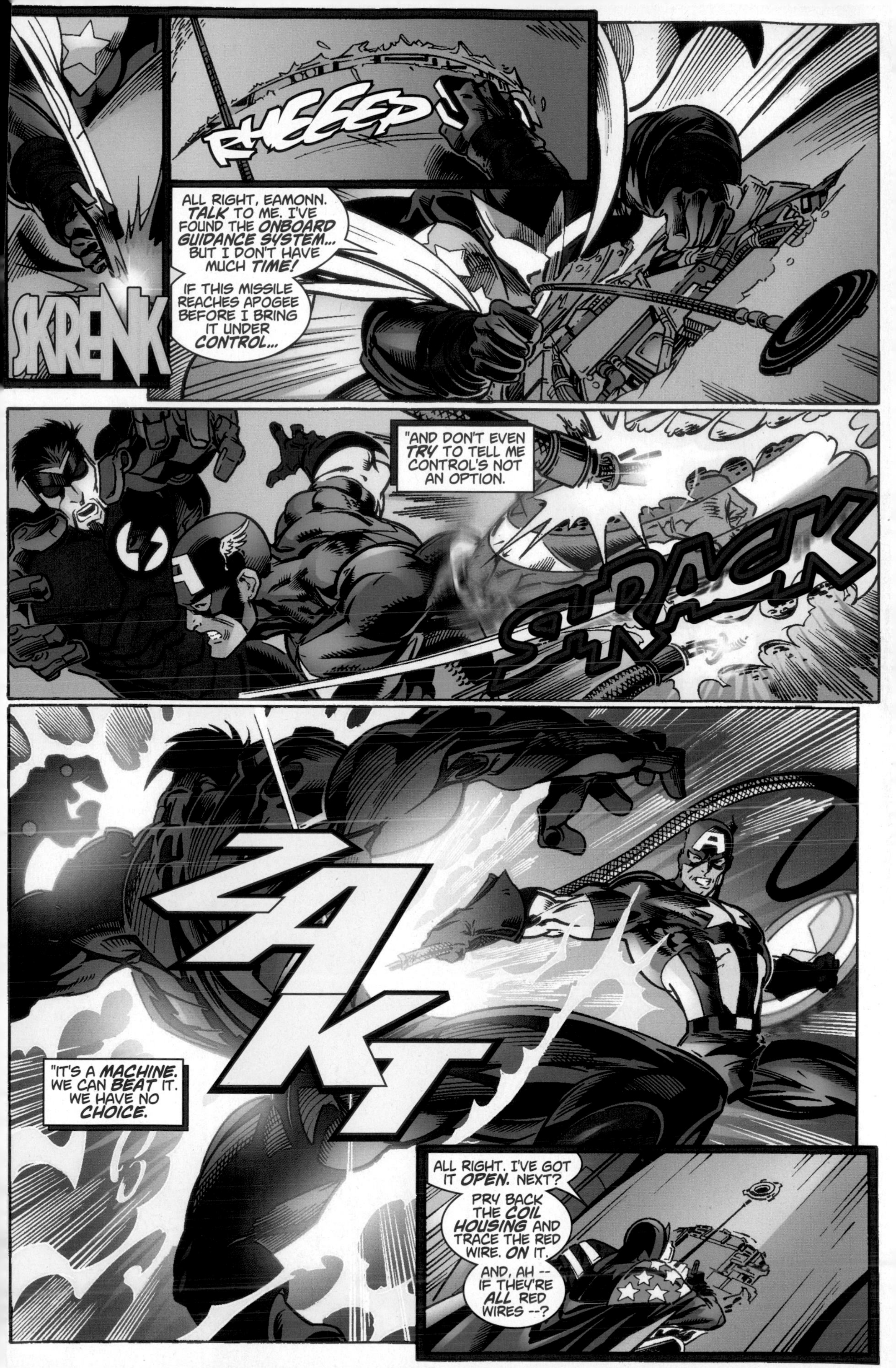
RHEEEP
SKRENK
ALL RIGHT, EAMONN. TALK TO ME. I'VE FOUND THE ONBOARD GUIDANCE SYSTEM... BUT I DON'T HAVE MUCH TIME!
IF THIS MISSILE REACHES APOGEE BEFORE I BRING IT UNDER CONTROL...
"AND DON'T EVEN TRY TO TELL ME CONTROL'S NOT AN OPTION.
SHRACK
ZAKT
"IT'S A MACHINE. WE CAN BEAT IT. WE HAVE NO CHOICE.
ALL RIGHT. I'VE GOT IT OPEN. NEXT?
PRY BACK THE COIL HOUSING AND TRACE THE RED WIRE. ON IT.
AND, AH -- IF THEY'RE ALL RED WIRES --?

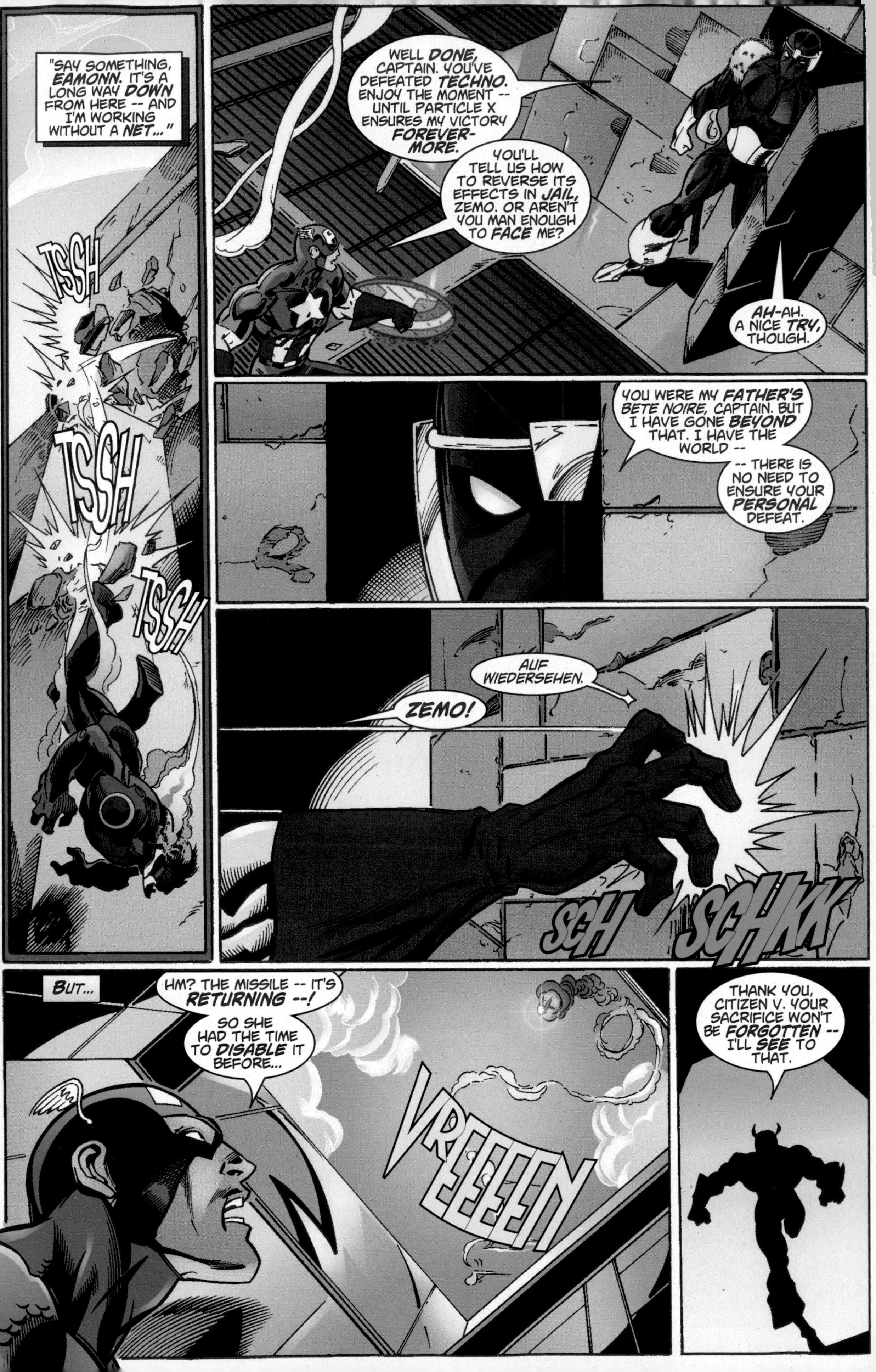
"SAY SOMETHING, EAMONN. IT'S A LONG WAY DOWN FROM HERE -- AND I'M WORKING WITHOUT A NET..."
TSSH
TSSH
TSSH
WELL DONE, CAPTAIN. YOU'VE DEFEATED TECHNO. ENJOY THE MOMENT -- UNTIL PARTICLE X ENSURES MY VICTORY FOREVER-MORE.
YOU'LL TELL US HOW TO REVERSE ITS EFFECTS IN JAIL, ZEMO. OR AREN'T YOU MAN ENOUGH TO FACE ME?
AH-AH. A NICE TRY, THOUGH.
YOU WERE MY FATHER'S BETE NOIRE, CAPTAIN. BUT I HAVE GONE BEYOND THAT. I HAVE THE WORLD --
-- THERE IS NO NEED TO ENSURE YOUR PERSONAL DEFEAT.
AUF WIEDERSEHEN.
ZEMO!
SCH
SCHKK
BUT...
HM? THE MISSILE -- IT'S RETURNING --!
SO SHE HAD THE TIME TO DISABLE IT BEFORE...
VREEEEEN
THANK YOU, CITIZEN V. YOUR SACRIFICE WON'T BE FORGOTTEN -- I'LL SEE TO THAT.

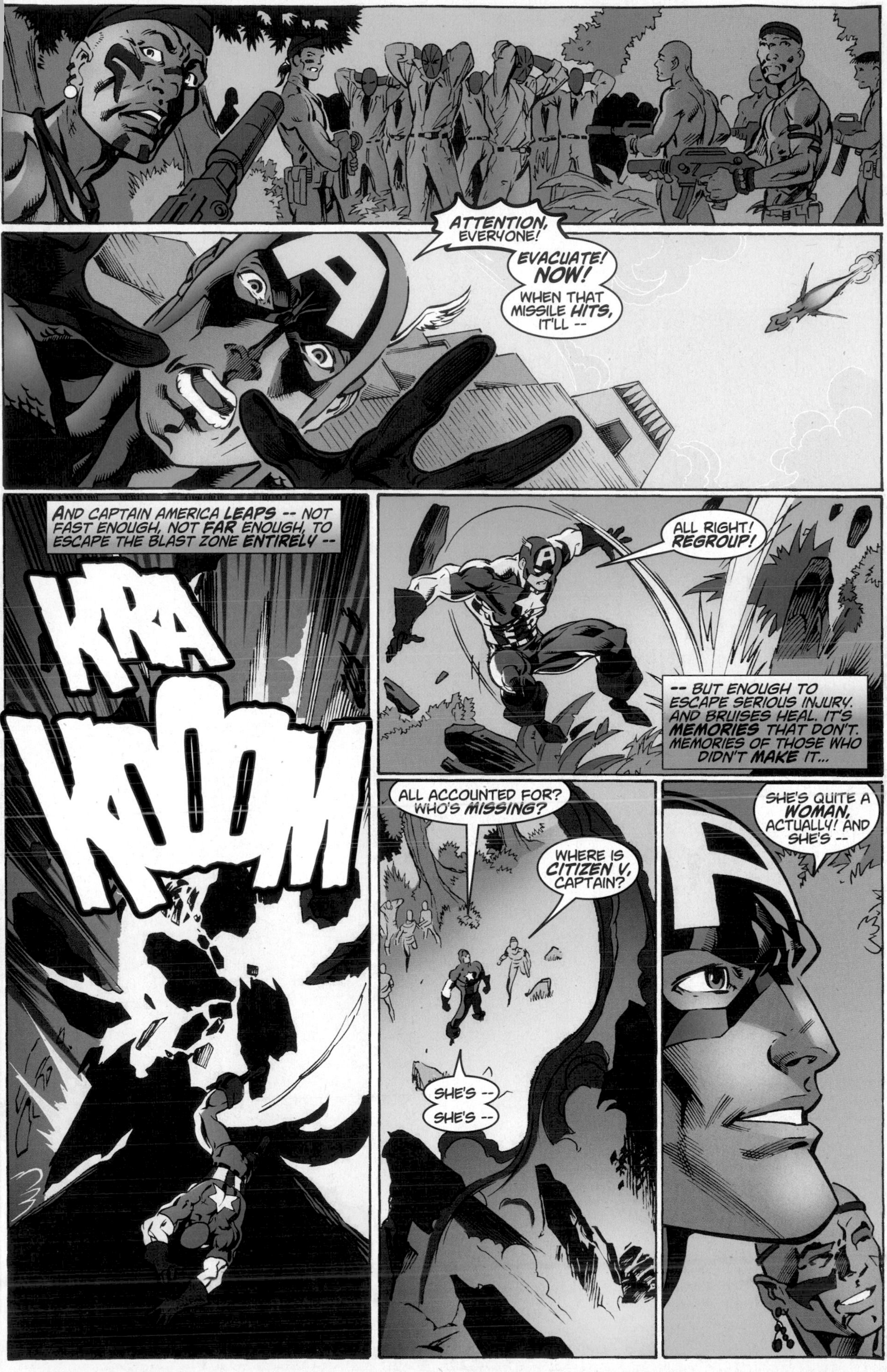
ATTENTION, EVERYONE!
EVACUATE! NOW! WHEN THAT MISSILE HITS, IT'LL --
AND CAPTAIN AMERICA LEAPS -- NOT FAST ENOUGH, NOT FAR ENOUGH, TO ESCAPE THE BLAST ZONE ENTIRELY --
KRA KOOM
ALL RIGHT! REGROUP!
-- BUT ENOUGH TO ESCAPE SERIOUS INJURY. AND BRUISES HEAL. IT'S MEMORIES THAT DON'T. MEMORIES OF THOSE WHO DIDN'T MAKE IT...
ALL ACCOUNTED FOR? WHO'S MISSING?
WHERE IS CITIZEN V, CAPTAIN?
SHE'S --
SHE'S --
SHE'S QUITE A WOMAN, ACTUALLY! AND SHE'S --

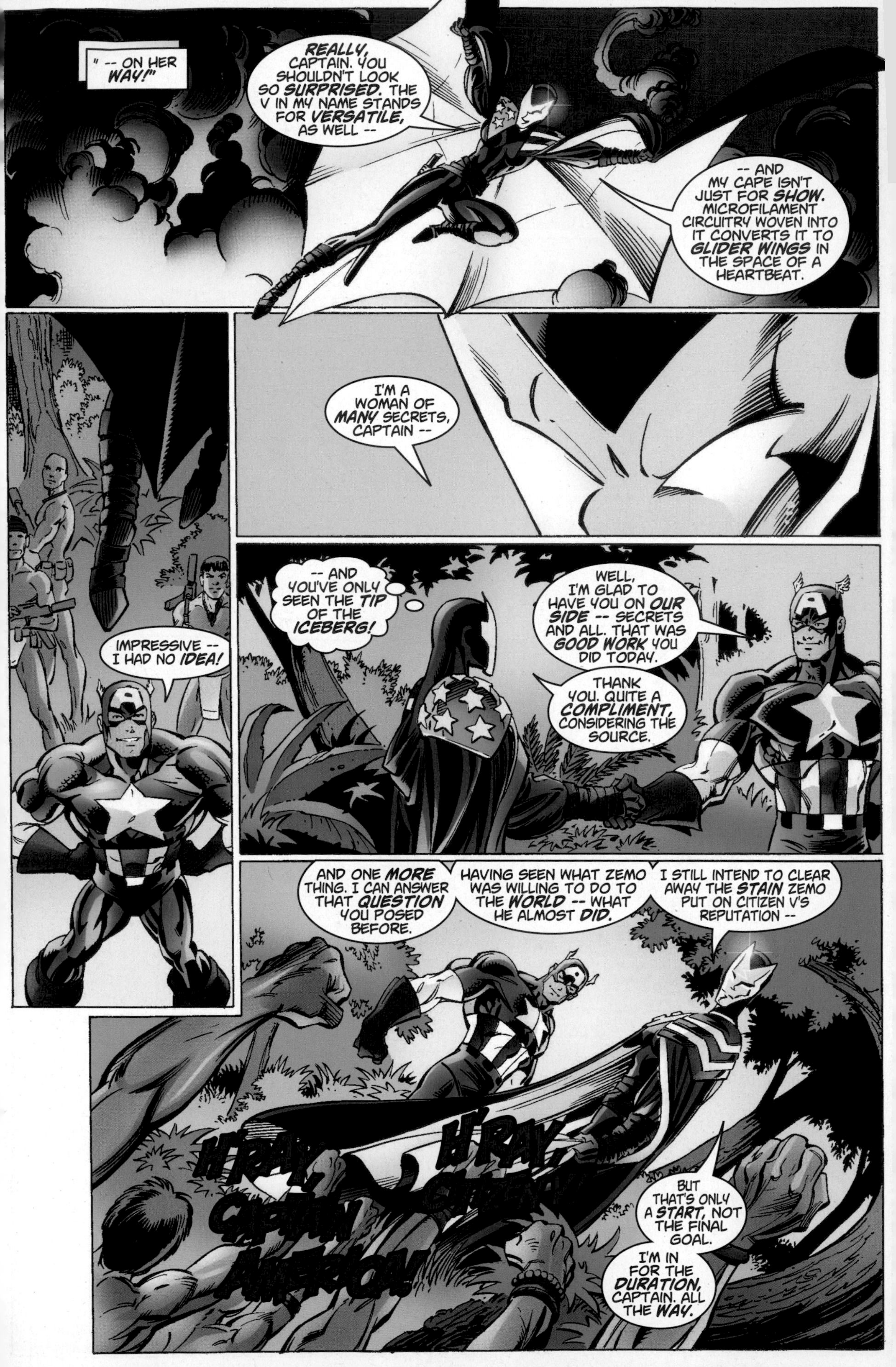

" -- ON HER WAY!"
REALLY, CAPTAIN. YOU SHOULDN'T LOOK SO SURPRISED. THE V IN MY NAME STANDS FOR VERSATILE, AS WELL --
-- AND MY CAPE ISN'T JUST FOR SHOW. MICROFILAMENT CIRCUITRY WOVEN INTO IT CONVERTS IT TO GLIDER WINGS IN THE SPACE OF A HEARTBEAT.
I'M A WOMAN OF MANY SECRETS, CAPTAIN --
IMPRESSIVE -- I HAD NO IDEA!
-- AND YOU'VE ONLY SEEN THE TIP OF THE ICEBERG!
WELL, I'M GLAD TO HAVE YOU ON OUR SIDE -- SECRETS AND ALL. THAT WAS GOOD WORK YOU DID TODAY.
THANK YOU. QUITE A COMPLIMENT, CONSIDERING THE SOURCE.
AND ONE MORE THING. I CAN ANSWER THAT QUESTION YOU POSED BEFORE.
HAVING SEEN WHAT ZEMO WAS WILLING TO DO TO THE WORLD -- WHAT HE ALMOST DID.
I STILL INTEND TO CLEAR AWAY THE STAIN ZEMO PUT ON CITIZEN V'S REPUTATION --
H'RAY, CAPTAIN AMERICA!
H'RAY, CITIZEN V!
BUT THAT'S ONLY A START, NOT THE FINAL GOAL.
I'M IN FOR THE DURATION, CAPTAIN. ALL THE WAY.

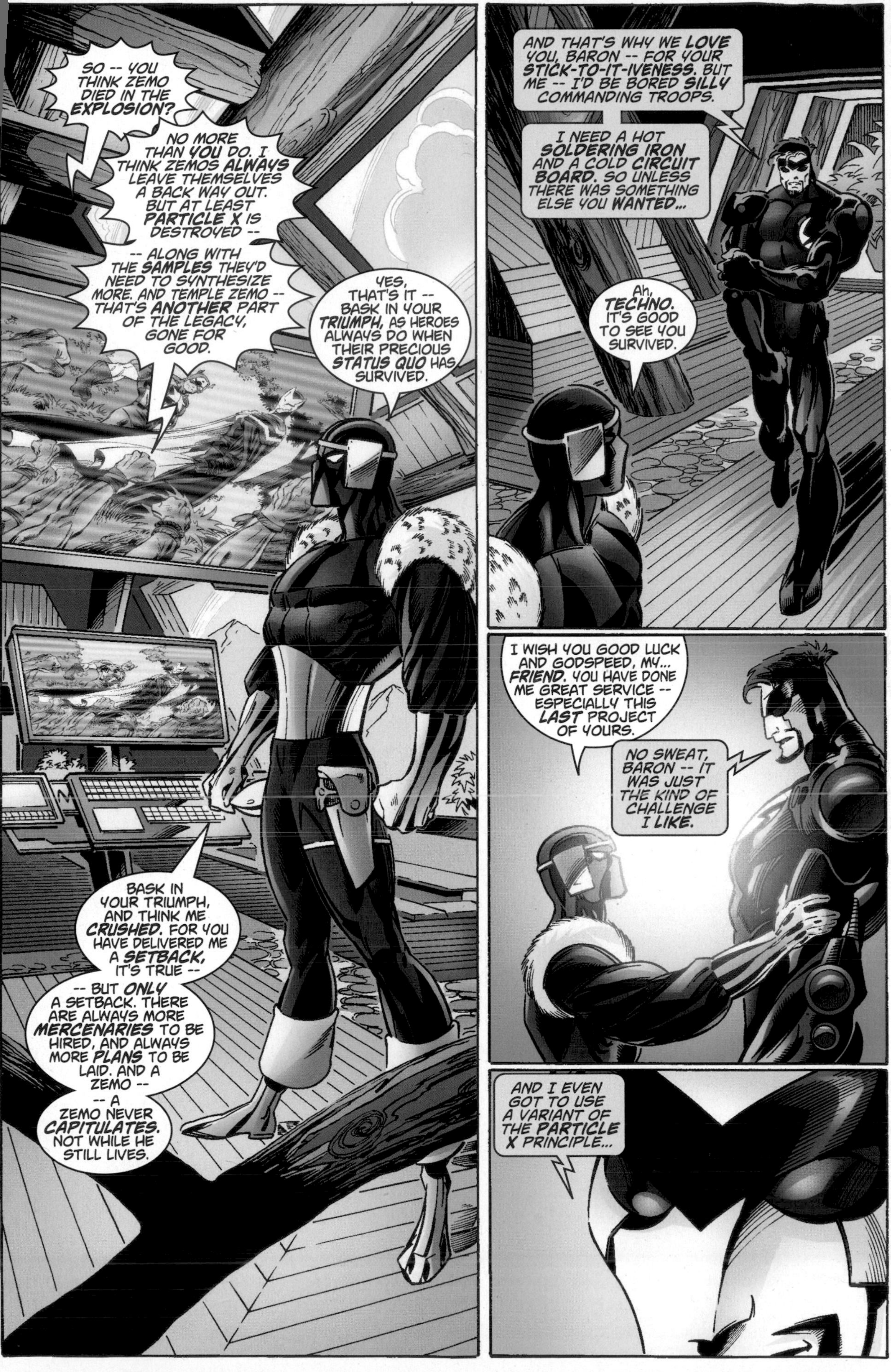
SO -- YOU THINK ZEMO DIED IN THE EXPLOSION?
NO MORE THAN YOU DO. I THINK ZEMOS ALWAYS LEAVE THEMSELVES A BACK WAY OUT. BUT AT LEAST PARTICLE X IS DESTROYED --
-- ALONG WITH THE SAMPLES THEY'D NEED TO SYNTHESIZE MORE. AND TEMPLE ZEMO -- THAT'S ANOTHER PART OF THE LEGACY, GONE FOR GOOD.
YES, THAT'S IT -- BASK IN YOUR TRIUMPH, AS HEROES ALWAYS DO WHEN THEIR PRECIOUS STATUS QUO HAS SURVIVED.
BASK IN YOUR TRIUMPH, AND THINK ME CRUSHED. FOR YOU HAVE DELIVERED ME A SETBACK, IT'S TRUE --
-- BUT ONLY A SETBACK. THERE ARE ALWAYS MORE MERCENARIES TO BE HIRED, AND ALWAYS MORE PLANS TO BE LAID. AND A ZEMO --
-- A ZEMO NEVER CAPITULATES. NOT WHILE HE STILL LIVES.
AND THAT'S WHY WE LOVE YOU, BARON -- FOR YOUR STICK-TO-IT-IVENESS. BUT ME -- I'D BE BORED SILLY COMMANDING TROOPS.
I NEED A HOT SOLDERING IRON AND A COLD CIRCUIT BOARD. SO UNLESS THERE WAS SOMETHING ELSE YOU WANTED...
Ah, TECHNO. IT'S GOOD TO SEE YOU SURVIVED.
I WISH YOU GOOD LUCK AND GODSPEED, MY... FRIEND. YOU HAVE DONE ME GREAT SERVICE -- ESPECIALLY THIS LAST PROJECT OF YOURS.
NO SWEAT, BARON -- IT WAS JUST THE KIND OF CHALLENGE I LIKE.
AND I EVEN GOT TO USE A VARIANT OF THE PARTICLE X PRINCIPLE...

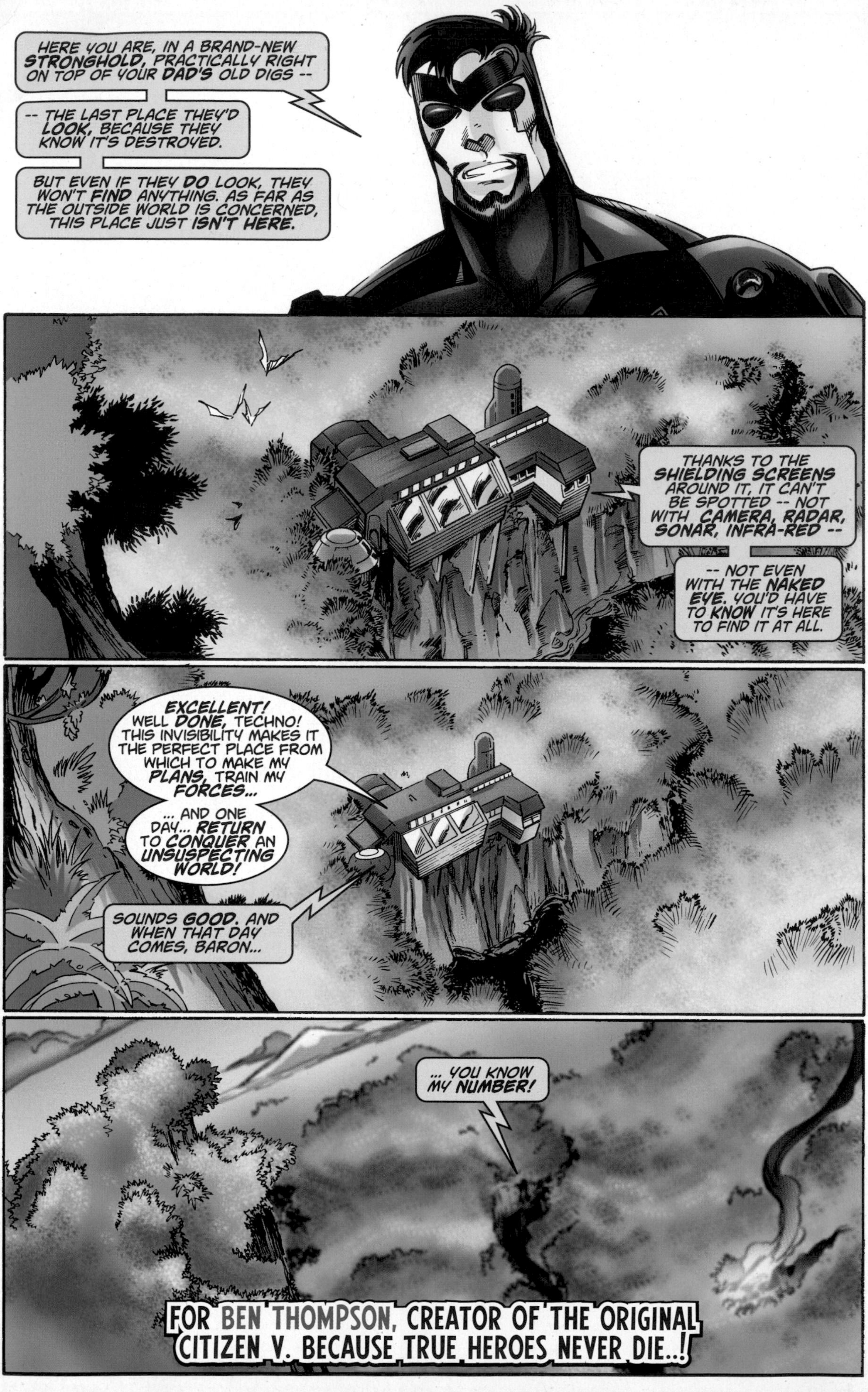
HERE YOU ARE, IN A BRAND-NEW STRONGHOLD, PRACTICALLY RIGHT ON TOP OF YOUR DAD'S OLD DIGS --
-- THE LAST PLACE THEY'D LOOK, BECAUSE THEY KNOW IT'S DESTROYED.
BUT EVEN IF THEY DO LOOK, THEY WON'T FIND ANYTHING. AS FAR AS THE OUTSIDE WORLD IS CONCERNED, THIS PLACE JUST ISN'T HERE.
THANKS TO THE SHIELDING SCREENS AROUND IT, IT CAN'T BE SPOTTED -- NOT WITH CAMERA, RADAR, SONAR, INFRA-RED --
-- NOT EVEN WITH THE NAKED EYE. YOU'D HAVE TO KNOW IT'S HERE TO FIND IT AT ALL.
EXCELLENT! WELL DONE, TECHNO! THIS INVISIBILITY MAKES IT THE PERFECT PLACE FROM WHICH TO MAKE MY PLANS, TRAIN MY FORCES...
... AND ONE DAY... RETURN TO CONQUER AN UNSUSPECTING WORLD!
SOUNDS GOOD. AND WHEN THAT DAY COMES, BARON...
... YOU KNOW MY NUMBER!
FOR BEN THOMPSON, CREATOR OF THE ORIGINAL CITIZEN V. BECAUSE TRUE HEROES NEVER DIE..!

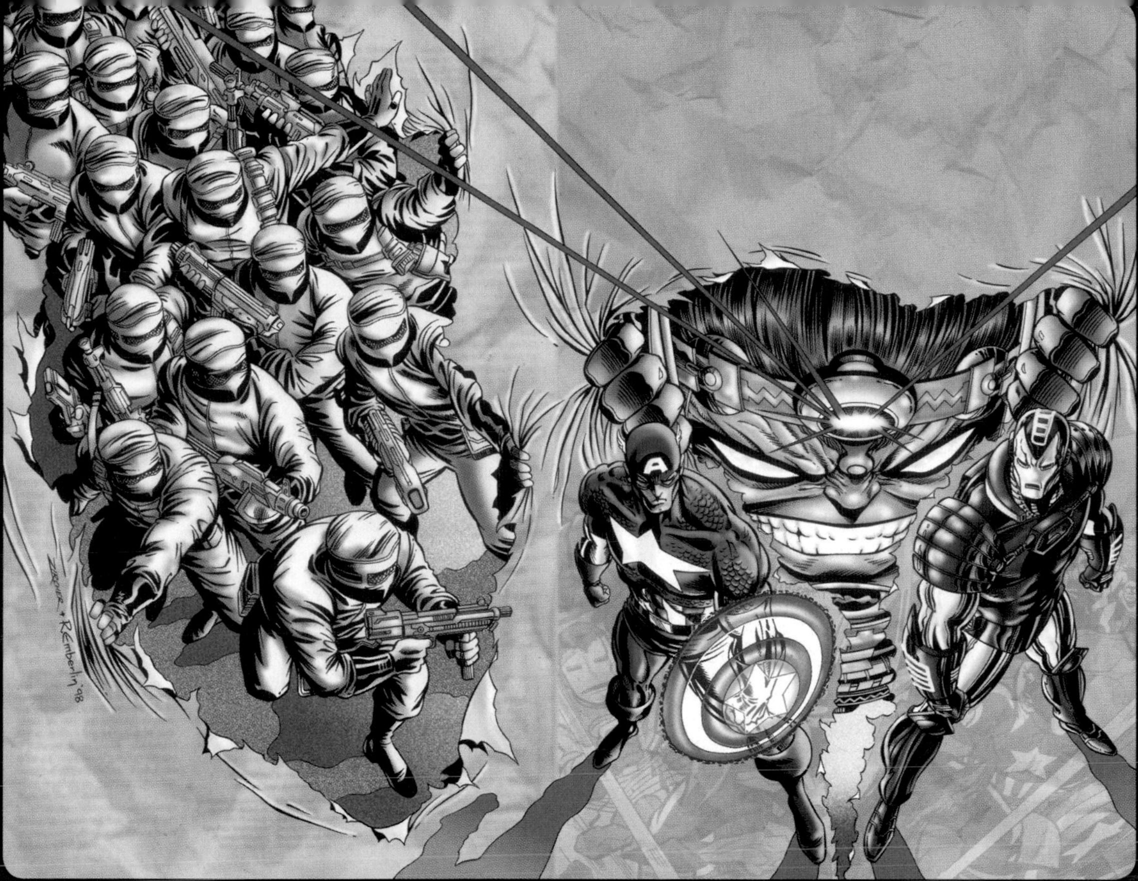

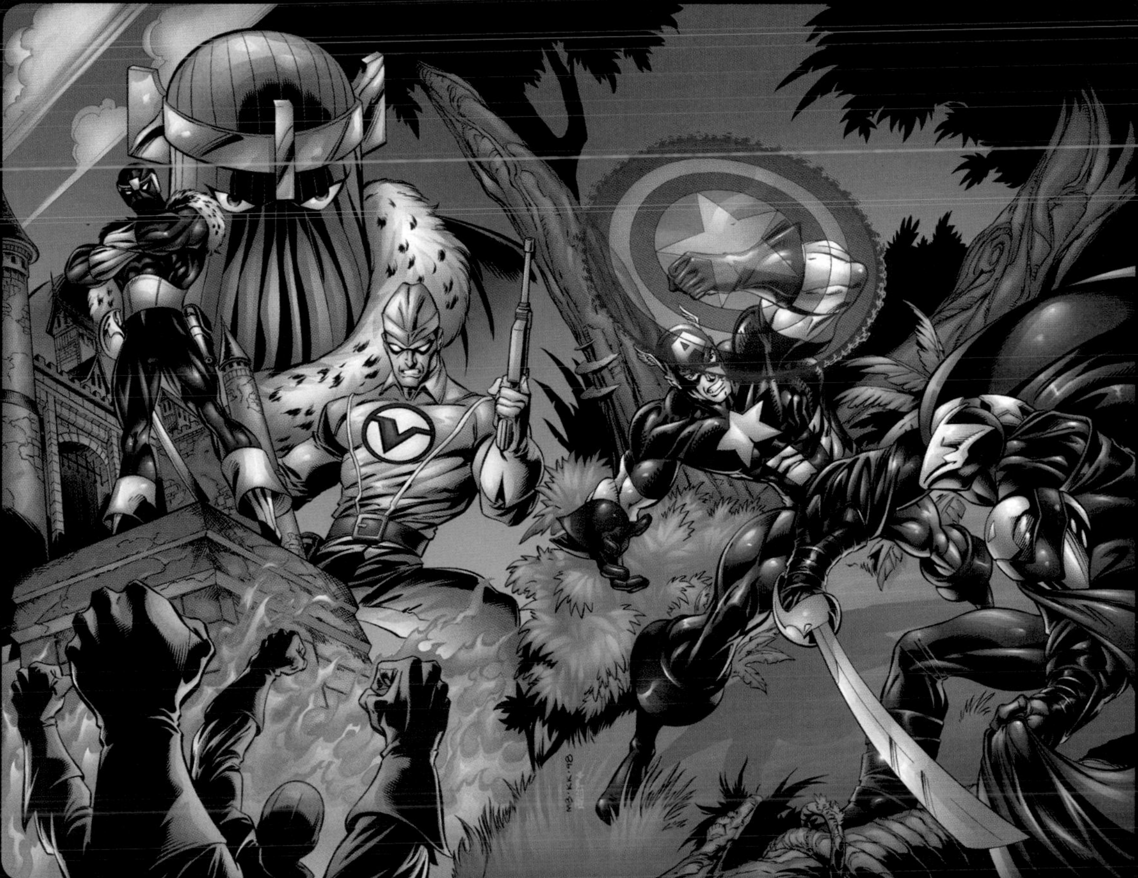

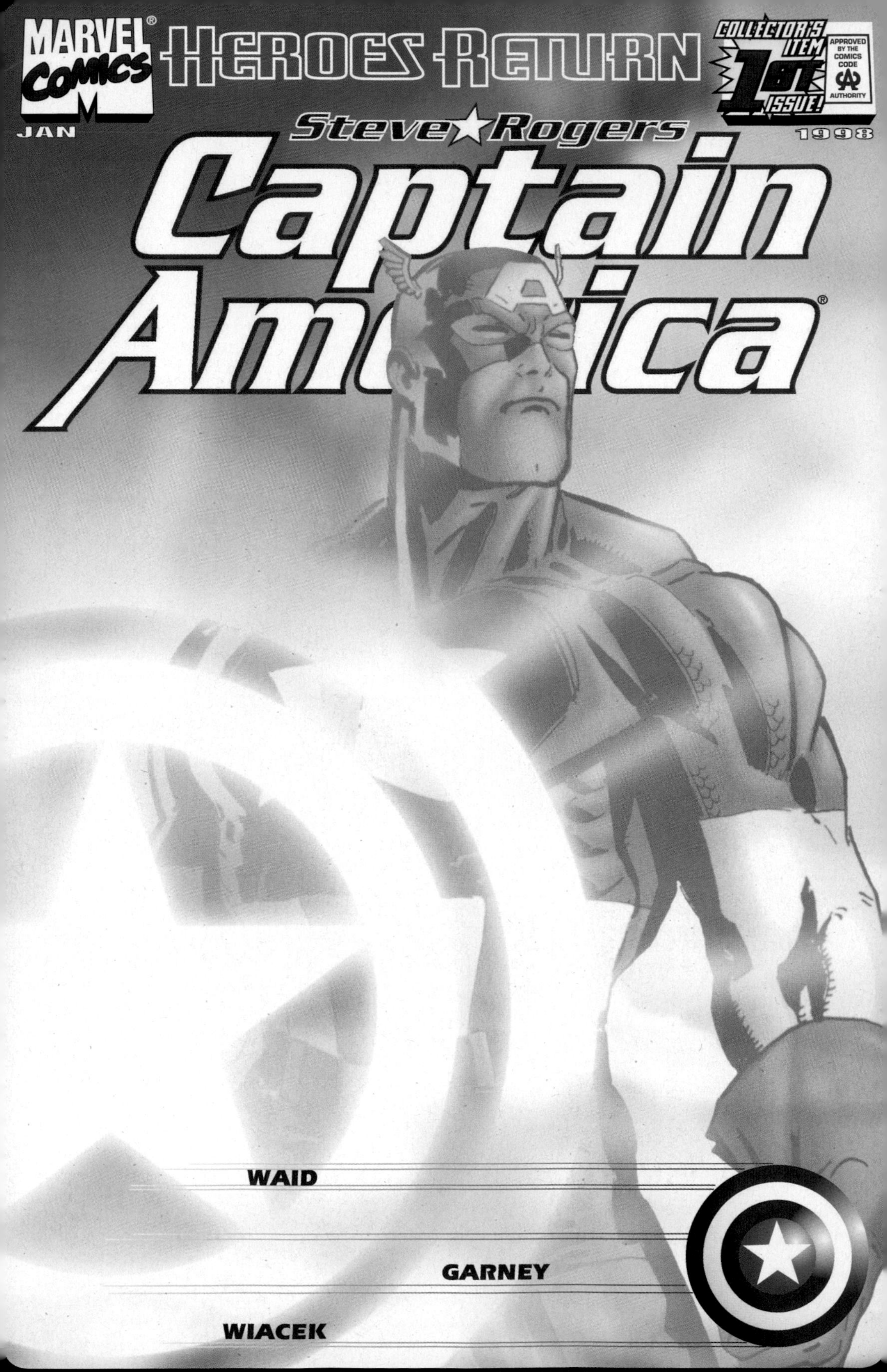
MARVEL COMICS
HEROES RETURN
COLLECTOR'S ITEM 1st ISSUE!
APPROVED BY THE COMICS CODE AUTHORITY
JAN
1998
Steve★Rogers
Captain America
WAID
GARNEY
WIACEK

CAPTAIN AMERICA #1 RETAILER INCENTIVE VARIANT COVER BY RON GARNEY

CAPTAIN AMERICA #2 "2-FOR-2" VARIANT COVER BY RON GARNEY & BOB WIACEK

AMERICAN GRAFFITI

Where did the time go? It seems like eons have passed since Mark Waid and Ron Garney brought their collective talents to the pages of CAPTAIN AMERICA, and yet, upon seeing their new work, it's like they never left. Freaky, huh? Every now and then, a creative team comes along and this incredible magic occurs. It's like they were just born to do the project. You know what we mean. Like Claremont/ Byrne on X-MEN... Byrne on FANTASTIC FOUR... Miller on DAREDEVIL... Simonson on THOR... Hembeck on BROTHER VOODOO (whatever happened to that project, anyway?)... you get the drift. That's the way it was on CAPTAIN AMERICA #444-454. Pure magic.

As is often the case when a crack creative team like this one leaves a title, their exploits and accomplishments sort of drift from the "really cool" realm to that legendary status where the stuff becomes ridiculously flawless and you use the issues to try and convert non-comics readers. From everyone we've ever talked to, that seems to be the case here. Great! In instances like this, said creative team rarely returns to the scene of the crime, raising that dang legendary status a notch higher. Joy. As much as anything else, it was the challenge of meeting those near-impossible expectations that lured Mark and Ron back to CAP (at least that's what they tell us). That, and the fact that Cap is just the coolest character *ever*.

With all that motivation, you can expect these guys (not to mention Bob, Joe, and John—top-notch talents in their own right) will be giving it their all, but don't expect an extension of the previous CAP run. That was then, and this is now. Sure, we saw a couple of familiar faces this issue (or whatever it is the Red Skull is substituting for a face), but the arrival of Kang on the last page should serve as a signal to you all: don't expect the expected. Certainly, old friends and foes alike will be drifting in and out of the book (who in their right mind wouldn't want to do a Batroc story?), but those that came before will be returning with a slight twist, if not an all-out makeover. You'll see what we mean in the next couple of months when a new/old threat pops its many-headed head into the mix. No, change is the name of the game, and we've got changes galore. All in all, it looks like it's going to be a great year for Cap!

At any rate, the letters page will probably be taking the day off next issue (even the speed of e-mail can't compete with the grind of a monthly schedule), but don't let that stop you from sending us your thoughts. As is always the case, we welcome and value not just your nice thoughts, but your concerns and criticisms as well. Lord knows we need it!

Okay, our work here is done.

—*Matt and Paul*

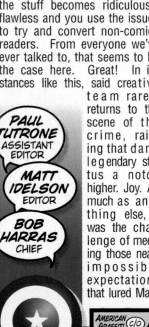

PAUL TUTRONE
ASSISTANT EDITOR

MATT IDELSON
EDITOR

BOB HARRAS
CHIEF

AMERICAN GRAFFITI c/o MARVEL COMICS
387 PARK AVENUE SOUTH • NEW YORK, NY 10016
IF YOU DON'T WANT YOUR NAME AND ADDRESS PRINTED, PLEASE LET US KNOW. LETTERS MAY BE EDITED FOR CONTENT AND LENGTH.

E-MAIL:
MAIL@ MARVEL.COM
MARK E-MAIL "OKAY TO PRINT"

NEXT ISSUE:

CAP FINALLY RUNS INTO SOME AMERICANS, BUT IT'S ALL BUSINESS AND NO PLAY FOR THE STAR-SPANGLED AVENGER-- SOME FAMILIAR BADDIES HAVE TAKEN COMMAND OF A NAVY SUB, AND THE NATION'S SECURITY IS AT STAKE. WE WOULDN'T HAVE IT ANY OTHER WAY!

DESIGN BY COMICRAFT

AMERICAN GRAFFITI

Almost from the dawn of time, there's been a running debate on how Cap should be treated by the characters around him (ultimately meaning: how should Cap be handled by his creative team?). We've seen this guy revered as if he were the president, deferentially being called "sir" and given the best seat in front of the TV. Then there have been the folks that have tried to "humanize" the character, giving him a day job, insecurity about his clothes; that sort of thing. So which is the "right" way to go? Cap the icon or Cap the "gosh-shucks, I'm just happy to be here" fellow? Maybe a little of both.

More than any other character, Steve Rogers very much is the essence of Captain America. Take away that union suit and the ideals, beliefs, and personal motivations of Steve Rogers would remain unchanged. As Mark Gruenwald so effectively pointed out during his run, you can put the suit on anybody, but it's the man that makes the clothes (how's that for a mixed metaphor). And what is it about this guy that makes that so? Steve Rogers represents the very best in all of us, the full potential that you, the mailman and the Fuller Brush Man all have to help others the way we help ourselves, not lie, and basically take that moment to make the world around us a better place. He believes that in helping others he is ultimately helping himself. If he could just get Dr. Doom and the rest of the gang to see that, then the world would certainly be a lot better off and they, too, would be much less tortured. In effect, Steve Rogers is the epitome of selflessness and the model of a person without the self-destructive tendencies that do us in every day.

Of course,

people like that are few and far between, both in the real world and in that next best thing, the Marvel Universe. The other Avengers have always seemed to look up to him, world leaders appear in awe of him--heck, even leaders of alien worlds seem to think he's A-OK (what's up with that?). And how does Cap feel about all this adoration? Does he develop a god-complex? Have his costume refitted for a bigger head? Make Jarvis polish his shield for him (not that that's an issue anymore--hee!)? No way! Sure, Steve's the kind of guy who was born modest, but his humility stems not just from his humble beginnings, but the fact that he honestly can't wrap his brain around this whole hero-worship thing in the first place. To him, the concept of Captain America isn't about expert combat training or having a flashy costume--it's about doing the right thing. In fact, if everyone stopped cheering him on long enough to start doing the right thing themselves, we'd all be better off for it. Of course, the world doesn't work that way, and Cap still hasn't figured out how to deal with being a celebrity. At least, that's our take.

So that's gonna be the theme of the series, at least for a while. As you saw last month, Steve's return from "the grave" has only raised his celebrity status almost to the point of religious stature. He thought he had issues with praise before? He ain't seen nothin' yet! How Cap learns to deal with all this (or fails to--don't want to give the whole thing away yet) will be a fairly constant undercurrent in the book. It should be a fun and enlightening exploration. Certainly you, the proud and in many cases long-standing readership of CAPTAIN AMERICA must have a few choice thoughts on the matter. So, hey, put those pens to paper (or fingers to keyboard if you're gonna e-mail us) and let us know what you think! Ongoing discourses can be fun, and we wanna have fun! So until next time, buy American!

--The Management

PAUL TUTRONE
ASSISTANT EDITOR

MATT IDELSON
EDITOR

BOB HARRAS
CHIEF

U.S. POSTAL SERVICE STATEMENT OF OWNERSHIP, MANAGE-MENT AND CIRCULATION
(REQUIRED BY 39 U.S.C. 3685)
1. Publication Title: CAPTAIN AMERICA
2. Publication No.: 540-010
3. Filing Date: October 1, 1997
4. Issue Frequency: MONTHLY
5. No. of issues published annually: 12
6. Annual subscription price: $23.88/12 issues
7. Complete mailing address of known office of publication: 387 Park Avenue South, New York, N.Y. 10016. Contact Person: Thomas Mathew: (212) 576-4088
8. Complete mailing address of headquarters of general business office of Publisher: Same.
9. Full names and complete mailing addresses of Publisher, Editor, and Managing Editor: Stan Lee, 387 Park Avenue South, New York, N.Y. Editor: Matt Idelson, 387 Park Avenue South, New York, N.Y. 10016. Managing Editor: N/A.
10. Owner (If owned by a corporation, give the name and address of the corporation immediately followed by the names and addresses of all stockholders owning or holding 1 percent or more of the total amount of stock. If not owned by a corporation, give the names and addresses of the individual owners. If owned by a partnership or other unincorporated firm, give its name and address as well as those of each individual owner. If the publication is published by a nonprofit organization, give its name and address.) Approximately 79% of the Common Stock of Marvel Entertainment Group, Inc. is owned indirectly through wholly-owned subsidiaries by Marvel Parent Holdings Inc., and the balance of Marvel's Common Stock is publicly owned. The shares of Marvel's Common Stock are listed for trading on the New York Stock Exchange. Complete Mailing Address: Marvel Parent Holdings, Inc. 5900 North Andrews Ave., Ft. Lauderdale, FL 33309.
11. Known bondholders, mortgages, and other security holders owning or holding 1 percent or more of total amount of bonds, mortgages or other securities. If none, check box ❏ None.
12. Tax Status For completion by nonprofit organizations authorized to mail at special rates. (Check one.) The purpose, function, and nonprofit status of this organization and the exempt status for Federal income tax purposes.: ❏Has not changed during preceding 12 months. ❏Has changed during preceding 12 months. (Publisher must submit explanation of change with this statement)
13. Publication Title: CAPTAIN AMERICA
14. Issue date for circulation data below: SEPTEMBER
15. Extent and Nature of Circulation
A. Total No. Copies Printed (net press run): Average no. copies each issue during preceding 12 months: 217,181. Actual no. copies of single issue published nearest to filing date: 178,100.
B. Paid and/or requested Circulation: 1) Sales through dealers and carriers, street vendors and counter sales: Average no. copies each issue during preceding 12 months: 127,974. Actual no. copies of single issue published nearest to filing date: 127,650. 2) Paid or requested mail subscriptions: Average no. copies each issue during preceding 12 months: 3,240. Actual no. copies of single issue published nearest to filing date: 3,026.
C. Total Paid and/or requested Circulation (sum of 15B(1) and 15B(2)): Average no. copies each issue during preceding 12 months: 131,214. Actual no. copies of single issue published nearest to filing date: 130,676.
D. Free Distribution by mail (samples, complimentary, and other free): Average no. copies each issue during preceding 12 months: 324. Actual no. copies of single issue published nearest to filing date: 303.
E. Free Distribution outside the mail: Average no. copies each issue during preceding 12 months: 0. Actual no. copies of single issue published nearest to filing date: 0.
F. Total Free Distribution (Sum of 15D and 15E): Average no. copies each issue during preceding 12 months: 324. Actual no. copies of single issue published nearest to filing date: 303.
G. Total Distribution (Sum of 15C, 15F): Average no. copies each issue during preceding 12 months: 131,538. Actual no. copies of single issue published nearest to filing date: 130,979.
H. Copies not distributed (1) Office use, leftovers, Spoiled: Average no. copies each issue during preceding 12 months: 125. Actual no. copies of single issue published nearest to filing date: 125. (2) Returns from News Agents: Average no. copies each issue during preceding 12 months: 85,518. Actual no. copies of single issue published nearest to filing date: 46,996.
I. Total (Sum of 15G, 15H(1), and 15H(2)): Average no. copies each issue during preceding 12 months: 217,181. Actual no. copies of single issue published nearest to filing date: 178,100.
Percent Paid and/or Requested Circulation (15C / 15G x 100): Average no. copies each issue during preceding 12 months: 99. Actual no. copies of single issue published nearest to filing date: 99.
16. Publication of Statement of Ownership: ❏Publication required. Will be printed in the January issue of this publication. ❏Publication not required.
17. Signature and Title of Editor, Publisher, Business Manager, or Owner: Armida Fuentes, Marketing Coordinator 10/1/97
I certify that all information furnished on this form is true and complete. I understand that anyone who furnishes false misleading information on this form or who omits material or information requested on the form may be subject to criminal sanctions (including fines and imprisonment) and/or civil sanctions (including multiple damages and civil penalties).

NEXT ISSUE:

Hydra has a new leader (and its not who you expect it to be!). Mayhem at Avengers Mansion. The return of Sharon Carter. And Cap takes a bullet for the cause! (No really!)

DESIGN BY COMICRAFT

AMERICAN GRAFFITI c/o MARVEL COMICS
387 PARK AVENUE SOUTH · NEW YORK, NY 10016
IF YOU DON'T WANT YOUR NAME AND ADDRESS PRINTED, PLEASE LET US KNOW. LETTERS MAY BE EDITED FOR CONTENT AND LENGTH.
E-MAIL: MAIL@MARVEL.COM
MARK E-MAIL "OKAY TO PRINT"

MARVEL VISION #23-24 (1997) ARTICLE EXCERPTS

WHEN THE HEROES RETURN

BY PETER SANDERSON

One of the "new" creative teams of the *Heroes Return* books is actually a familiar one. Writer Mark Waid and penciler Ron Garney collaborated on an acclaimed run of *Captain America* issues that led up to the start of *Heroes Reborn*, and now they are returning to the series. How does it feel to be back? "It feels terrific," answers Mark Waid. "It feels like we were never gone, except, of course, we were. Ron and I are both very much looking forward to the chance to tell the 150 stories that we had worked out that we didn't get the chance to tell on our last round."

When Captain America returns from the "Heroes Reborn" universe, he finds himself not in the United States but in Japan, where he runs up against a band of Japanese terrorists. "The Americanization of Japanese culture is what they're fighting against," Waid says, "and now suddenly they've got this guy in a red, white and blue flag knocking their heads together and just adding insult to injury, so he's really just exacerbating the problem." But, Waid continues, this encounter sets Captain America to thinking about "how he is viewed, and how America is viewed, by other cultures, by other nations."

As a result, Waid, says, Cap will have to begin "to deal with the reality that Captain America is this worldwide icon. He has never really seen himself as an icon. He's not comfortable with it. I think he thinks of himself as just a regular Joe, that anybody with the heart and the super-soldier serum and the suit could do the job, that there's nothing special about him." But now he begins to realize just how much the concept of Captain America means to the world.

And that leads to an important decision. "Heroes Reborn" was not the first instance in which Captain America seemingly vanished, and, Waid says, "he begins to realize it may not be the last. He knows the world can get along without Steve Rogers, but he's not as sure the world can get along without a Captain America, so perhaps it's time to start grooming somebody to replace him should he be unable to fulfill his duties." This would not be a sidekick or a partner, Waid explains, "but essentially a vice Cap, if you will," somebody who could become the new Captain America if need be. "We're not going to say for sure whether or not we'll be dealing with a new character or not," cautions Waid, but Cap will be talking to a number of established Marvel characters, notably the Falcon and Hawkeye, about taking on the role. Some of them, Waid notes, will decline the offer, "but in doing so they will probably say 'If I were Captain America, here's what I would do.' And that could give Cap a whole new perspective on his role as well."

If something happens to Cap or Iron Man in their own books, it might be referred to in *The Avengers* and vice versa. However, Waid states, "We're going to shy away from crossovers for the time being because we want to reinforce to readers they don't *have* to buy all four books. If they're going to buy them it'll be because they enjoy them, not because they feel they've got a gun to their heads."

Waid has high praise for *Cap* artist Ron Garney. "He always serves the story perfectly. He always adds to it and picks up the particular dynamic that is in my head. I think it's astounding that in eleven issues he created a version of Cap that is for a lot of people definitive."

What draws Waid to the character of Captain America? "He's bright and shiny and positive and full of hope, and in a comic book world full of grim and gritty heroes he shines like a beacon. I am really just sick to death of grim and gritty and dark and ugly and urban, and what attracts me to Captain America is he's none of these things." In fact, Waid sees Captain America as being like the classic DC characters. "The thing that always distinguished the Marvel characters is their human foibles. Much like the DC characters [with the exception of Batman], Captain America didn't have a tragic event as his motivation (like Spider-Man). It doesn't mean he's not an interesting character. But he doesn't have that typical Marvel inspiration, which is interesting for the Marvel characters, but I'm looking for somebody a little more classic."

But no hero or heroes can support a series all by themselves. Where would they be without the villains they fight, their romantic interests or their friends and confidantes? In [Waid's] first run on the series he brought back Cap's longtime girlfriend, S.H.I.E.L.D. agent Sharon Carter, who had long been thought dead. She was very different on her return, her outlook on life having grown harsher as a result of her terrible experiences during her long absence.

Now that Waid is back on *Captain America*, he says Sharon will definitely return, although she will not appear in every story as she did before. Waid comments that "she's a great counterpoint to Cap because she's the cynic and he's the idealist."

As for villains, "We've talked about taking Batroc and actually giving him a shave and getting him out of the clown suit and making him into someone formidable." And, of course, "Clearly the Red Skull can't stay gone forever." Mind you, Waid notes, "The last time we saw the Skull he was a Hiroshima shadow on the side of a building." One might think that would defy even the Red Skull's talent for survival. But, Waid points out, "he was infused with a cataclysmic explosion of Cosmic Cube energy at the time," so chances are he is somewhere out there plotting away

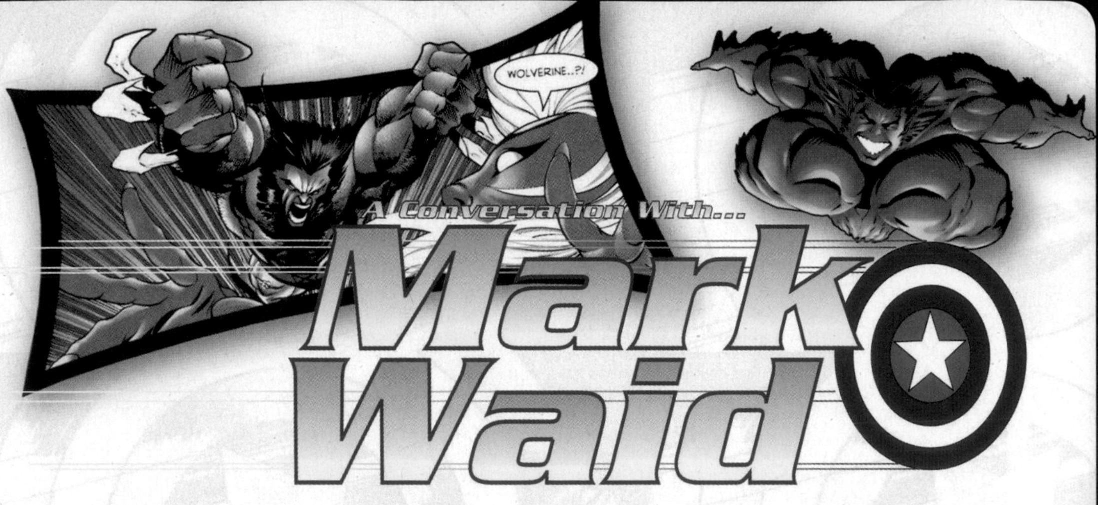
WOLVERINE...?!

A Conversation With... Mark Waid

In thirty years or so when we look back on comics history there're a few writers who will have their stories respected for what they are...well written, pivotal, ground-breaking classics. Mark Waid will definitely be one of those names on that short list. Mark's previous and current work on Captain America has redefined the character as a true American icon. Recently, Marvel VISION reporter-at-large Dean Davis spoke with him about his ideals of the noble hero, his writing style, and his efforts on throwing a vibranium shield with pinpoint accuracy.

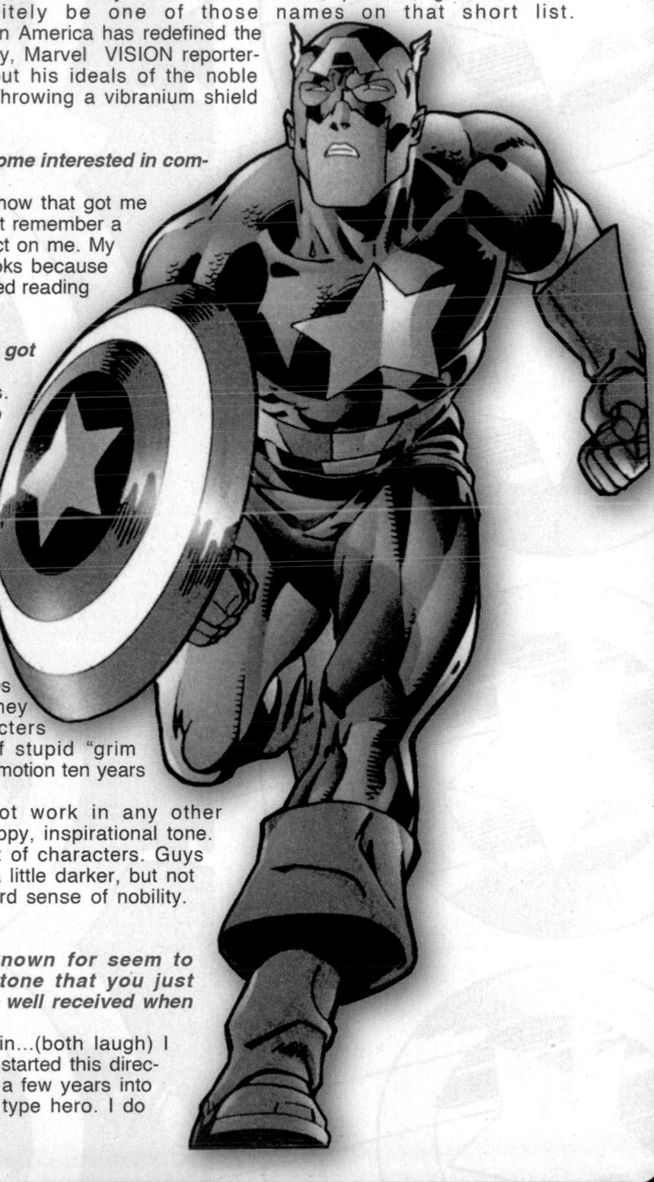

Dean: Here's an easy one. How did you become interested in comics?
Mark: It was really the 1960's Batman TV show that got me interested. I was three years old. I really don't remember a lot about it, but I do know that it had an effect on me. My father also brought home Batman comic books because of my love for the TV show and I never stopped reading comics, not even after I discovered girls.

Dean: What was it about these stories that got you hooked?
Mark: It was the nobility of the characters. Here are guys who put their life on the line to do the right thing because it's the right thing to do. That always appealed to me.

Dean: Maybe it's just me, but when you say "noble" I think of a knight on a white horse. There are some characters who seem "dark" in their sense of nobility. It works for some heroes while it's a joke for others.
Mark: You're right. They don't all have to be shiny and bright. Guys like Punisher and Wolverine shouldn't change. What I want is for the characters to be true to themselves and to how they were envisioned when they were originally created. Brighter characters shouldn't be morphing into some sort of stupid "grim and gritty" identity just to follow a trend set in motion ten years ago with 'Dark Knight'.

To me, Captain America cannot work in any other environment other than a bright, shiny, happy, inspirational tone. That's the same with Superman and a lot of characters. Guys like Wolverine and Batman deserve to be a little darker, but not hideously so. Even the Punisher has a weird sense of nobility. I don't salute it, but it's there.

Dean: The characters you're mainly known for seem to survive best in the bright and happy tone that you just spoke of. Did you find that this style was well received when you started writing?
Mark: No, and actually I had to sneak it in...(both laugh) I absolutely had to come in under the radar. I started this direction in about 1989 or '90 and we were only a few years into the era of the Watchmen and Dark Knight type hero. I do

like both those series, don't get me wrong. They were grim, realistic, magnificent pieces of work in their approach. Frank Miller and Alan Moore knew what they were doing...that stuff was original. The problem is that so many creators came after them following that vision instead of creating their own...they just imitated the style. There was an integrity to Moore and Miller's work that isn't in the work of most people who came after them. Those who followed were just doing "grim and gritty" because it sold.

With Flash I chose to do my thing and not pay attention to the dark stuff that was going on around me. I got flak up and down the halls of DC comics. I had one editor tell me point blank, "I don't know why we even publish your book." Luckily the sales started to rise and people started to pay attention...I knew then that we were on to something."

Certainly Kurt Busiek and Grant Morrison, among others, are all influential to this wave right now. It's not simply a matter of having smiling super heroes. It's a matter of returning some integrity to comic characters. Long answer, but there you go.

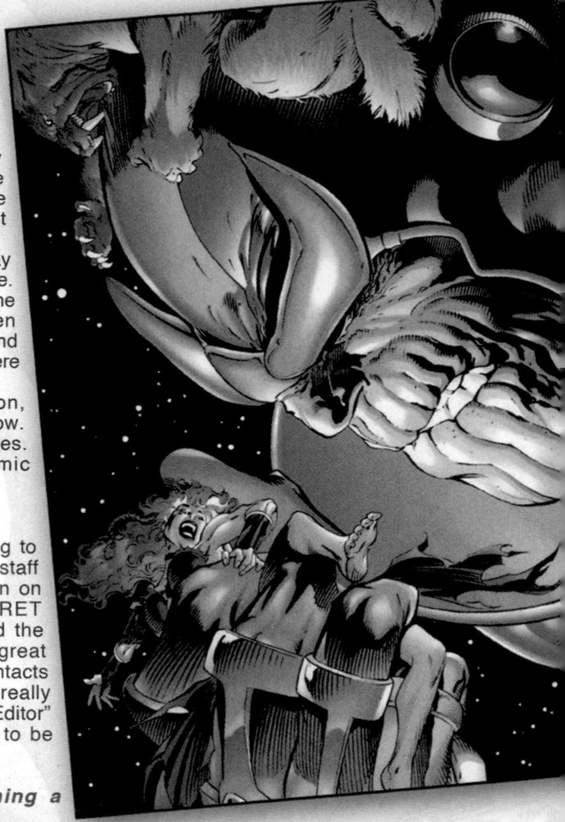

Dean: How did you finally break into the business?
Mark: I did a bit of freelance in the early '80s, nothing to speak of...a couple of Superman stories. I went on staff as a DC editor in 1987. I was editing Grant Morrison on DOOM PATROL. I was also working on SECRET ORIGINS as well LEGION of SUPERHEROES, and the first Elseworlds project, Gotham by Gaslight. The great thing about the job was that I was able to make contacts while at the same time learning what a good story really was by working with a multitude of writers. Frankly "Editor" was the job I always wanted...I never really set out to be a writer, I wanted to be an editor.

Dean: You did change your mind on becoming a freelance writer though.
Mark: Yeah, that was in early 1990. I left staff at DC, but didn't have much going on there, so I went to Archie Comics as a freelance editor. Slowly the writing started to catch on. Brian Augustyn, who was an editor at DC, was the only guy there who would hire me. Everybody else thought that I was an old fanboy who would tell old-fashioned stories that nobody would read. I've said many times that I owe my career to Brian. I did Impact Comics for DC and then the FLASH after that.

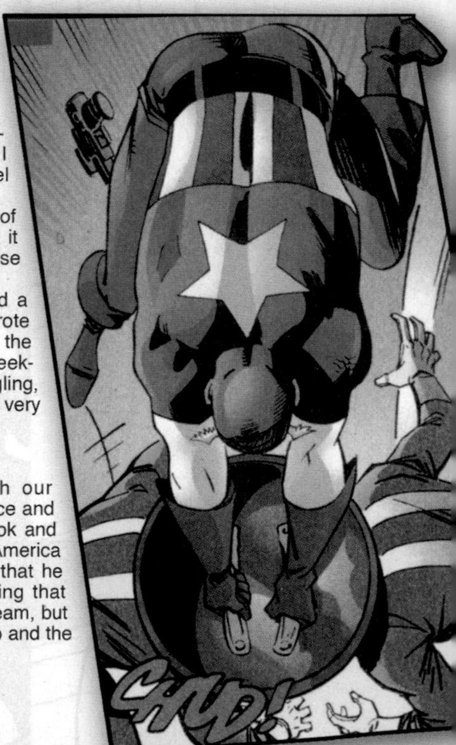
CHUD!

Dean: Let's talk about your writing on CAPTAIN AMERICA. Is that a job you sent in submissions for or did Marvel pursue you?
Mark: Ralph Macchio called me out of the blue. I had done a little bit of work for Marvel...DEADPOOL and some X-MEN work. I had always wanted to do Captain America, he's my favorite Marvel character. Next to Superman he's one of my all-time favorites.

We all knew that Mark Gruenwald had no real intention of leaving the book, so when Ralph called I had no assumption that it was about Cap, but I was hoping for it. Much to my stunned surprise that's what he offered me and it worked out great.

I really wanted to revamp Cap a bit. Mark Gruenwald did a spectacular job with him, and I say this with no disrespect, but he wrote more from the head whereas I write more from the heart...that was the difference in our approach. I wanted stories that were a little more sleeker and simpler—James Bond crossed with John LeCarre...spine-tingling, cliffhanger-type stories. Not to knock what Mark did, though...he was very helpful in making the transition smooth.

Dean: What's in Captain America's future?
Mark: By the time this sees print we should be done with our three-parter, "Power and Glory." This is the story arc where Cap once and for all decides that his future is not sitting around waiting for Modok and the Serpent Society to attack. He now feels it's his job to make America a better place; although he promises to do this, he admits freely that he doesn't know quite what "a better place" means.... We keep saying that Captain America stands for the American way and the American dream, but what does that mean? I'm not sure, but my attitude is, let's have Cap and the readers—and me—figure it out together.

Dean: Would you like to see a sidekick in Cap's life?

Mark: Actually...yeah, I would. I found out much to my surprise while writing CAPTAIN AMERICA #1 that it is impossible for me to write a story showing him risking his life with daring stunts without someone nearby to scream, "Are you nuts?" I'll probably spend more time having Sharon around in the future...I feel she's already a sidekick to him, and her cynicism plays so well off his idealism.

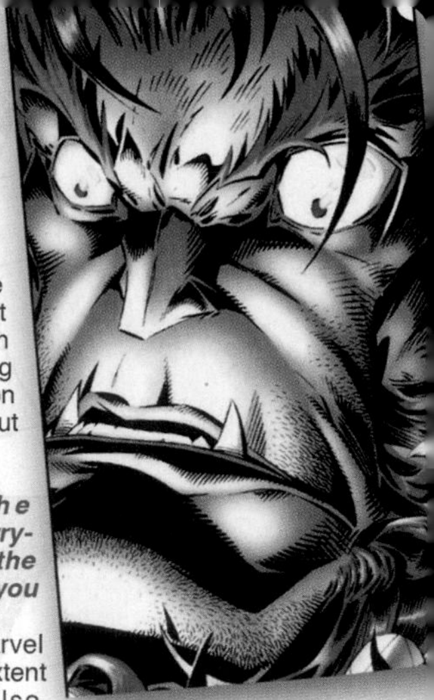

Dean: What type of political leanings would Captain America have?
Mark: Now this is all strictly my interpretation of him, but I see Cap as a liberal. He grew up a Roosevelt era Democrat. He's very much a student of the Constitution, but realizes it for what it is—a set of guidelines that were made up by some great men many years ago who didn't face the obstacles that we do today, and that's something that must be considered when interpreting the Bill of Rights. When Thomas Jefferson and Ben Franklin roughed out the rules on gun control, they lived in a world without automatic weapons.

Dean: Many comic book fans would like to see the industry go back to the readers. Provide good, solid stories and art while worrying less about the packaging for the collector market. Is this a trend you see happening now?

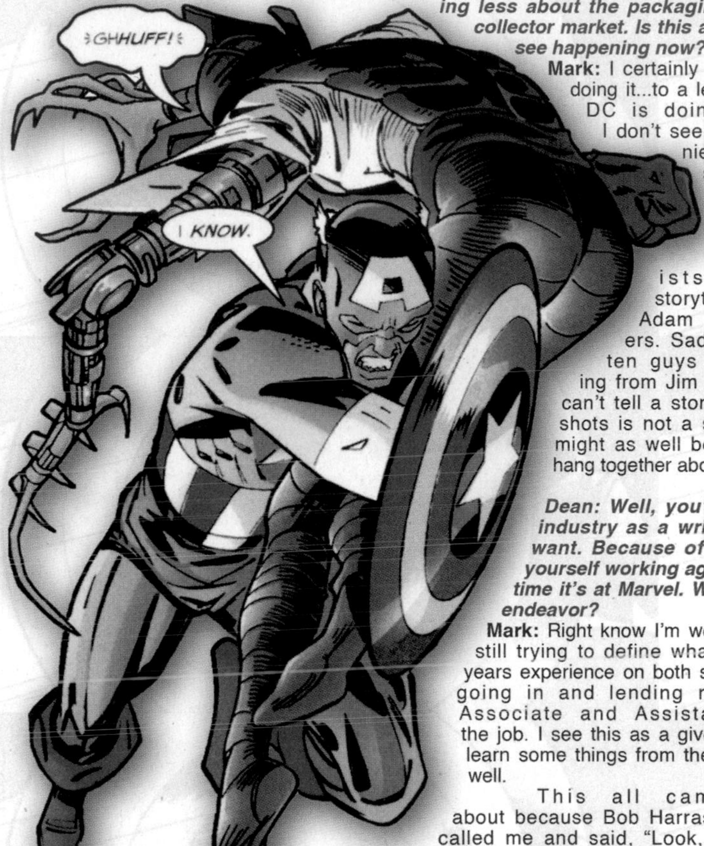

GHHUFF!
I KNOW.

Mark: I certainly see Marvel doing it...to a lesser extent DC is doing it also. I don't see a lot of the other younger companies following this path though. They seem to be satisfied with making money on comics that have no story to them and they see no reason to change that.

There are artists who are consummate storytellers like Ron Garney, Andy and Adam Kubert, Mike Wieringo, and others. Sadly, for every one of them there's ten guys who learned to draw by swiping from Jim Lee and Rob Liefeld comics...they can't tell a story. A series of unconnected pin-up shots is not a story. "Artists" who produce those might as well be drawing postcards...their comics hang together about as well.

Dean: Well, you've surely proven yourself to the industry as a writer who knows what the readers want. Because of this unique talent you now find yourself working again in an editorial position, but this time it's at Marvel. What can you tell us about this new endeavor?
Mark: Right know I'm working as a Consulting Editor. We're still trying to define what that really means. With thirteen years experience on both sides of the desk it's a matter of me going in and lending my assistance to some of the Associate and Assistant Editors who are new at the job. I see this as a give-and-take situation, since I hope to learn some things from them, as well.

This all came about because Bob Harras called me and said, "Look, you probably won't be interested in coming back to editorial, but I thought I'd ask anyway." He was ready to hang up and I was like, "Whoa, hold up...I'd love to come back as an editor in some capacity!" Frankly I can foresee a day, not this year or next year, but sometime in the next few years when writing takes a backseat for me and my duties are far more editorial.

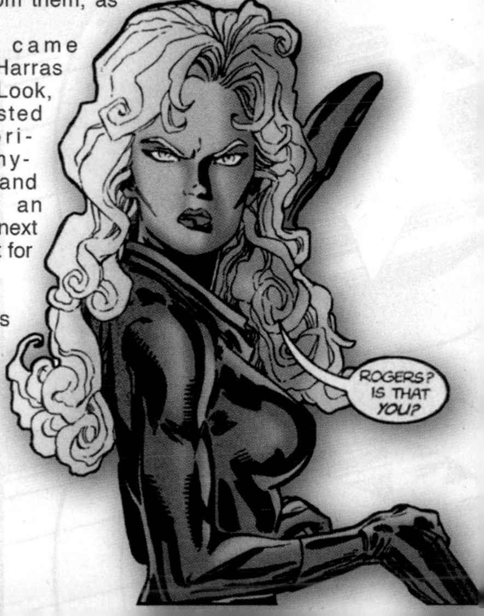

ROGERS? IS THAT YOU?

Dean: Mark, good luck with your new editorial gig. I also want to pass along best wishes on helping Captain America pursue the American Dream.
Mark: Hey, thanks. Once we find it, we'll be sure to let everyone know.

—DEAN DAVIS

BEHIND THE SC

WITH RON GA

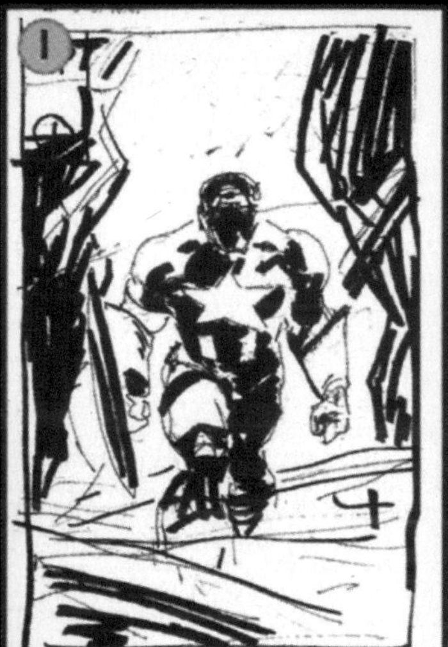
1

Hey, folks! Just to give you some insight into my twisted psyche, I thought I'd use this little forum to illustrate the steps it takes to get a cover I like. And so, let the games begin!

We decided very quickly to have a cover featuring Cap sort of walking out of the wreckage of his crash-landing after HEROES REBORN, since it isn't shown there or in our story. That was the easy part, getting a shot of Cap that we were happy with.

#1--This initial thumbnail sketch was no good. He's walking into darkness instead of out into the light. He's also a little too hunched over--it's more of a mysterious cover instead of some kind of rebirth. Which leads us to...

#2--This puppy. There's more light coming from behind Cap, which is a good thing. While I like the framing on the first thumbnail, I think framing the figure with light is more complimentary to Captain America's character in general. So far, so good.

#3--With the second thumbnail done, it was time to do a finished sketch of the whole cover. I knew I needed some kind of volcanic background with light from the crevasses, and we needed, on some

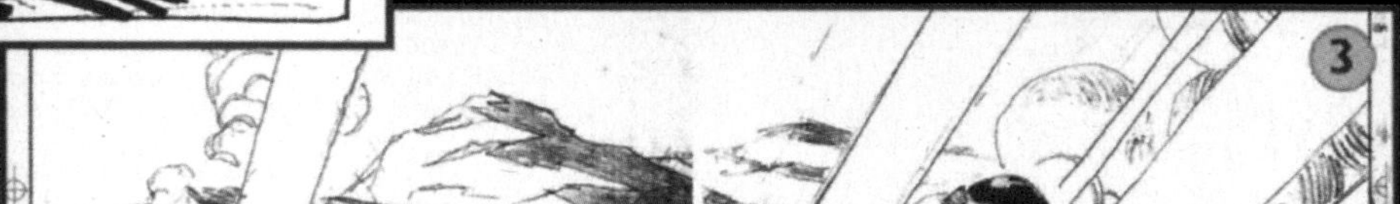
3

level, to illustrate something of Japan, with a Mount Fuji type mountain the background. As I said before, that's the easy part. Then I slave-labored over the figure. The biggest problems I had with this shot were with the leg and the twist of Cap's body. This final version of the cover was done, but it didn't quite work right, either. It didn't hit me until I went back and looked at it later how stiff I had drawn the figure. This particular figure looked too robotic. It didn't capture the presence of Captain America I was looking for. It's too moody, and it focuses too much on the debris itself instead of his relationship to the debris. So, back to the drawing board.

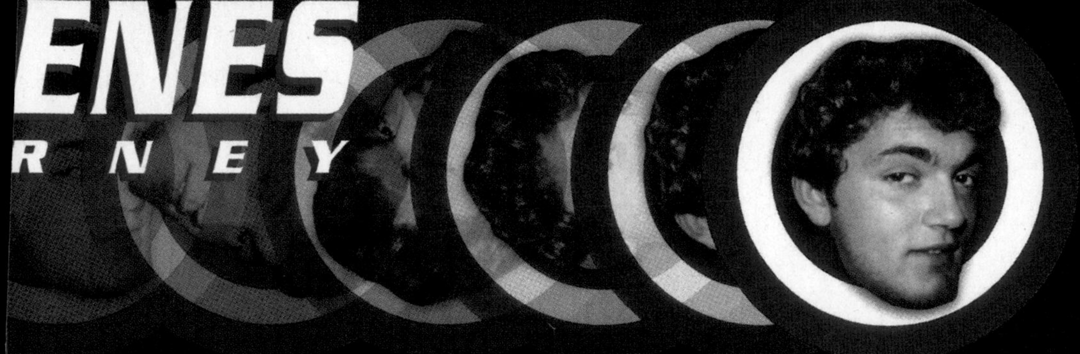

#4--After several discarded attempts, this one started to look like what I was going for. Again, having problems with the right leg coming forward--it was throwing him a little off balance. Plus getting him right with the lighting. The light coming over his trunks was creating a real problem. Not to mention the background--the smoke coming up over Captain America's right shoulder created too much of a tangent problem and didn't frame him well enough. The cover needed some kind of framing device with the debris to get the right point of focus.

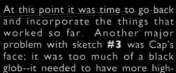

COMING OUT OF VOLCATO LIKE BACKDROP

At this point it was time to go back and incorporate the things that worked so far. Another major problem with sketch **#3** was Cap's face; it was too much of a black glob--it needed to have more highlights underneath to suggest his features. Using the background of **#3** as a point of contrast, sketch **#1** didn't work, and **#2** had Cap going in the same direction as the debris. The lack of chaos around the figure created too much of a static feel, so I needed to rearrange the beams in more of a disorganized manner. This also worked well in helping me create the framing device I was looking for. Applying all these particular problems together led me to sketch **#5**.

There you go. Now you know why I'm insane, but at least the end result was worth the agony. After studying the final thumbnail **#5**, I think I really nailed it with all the principles I was trying to apply in the previous four sketches. Now excuse me while I cut off my left ear, and happy reading!

-- Ron Garney

THE SKULL IS DEAD. LONG LIVE THE SKULL.

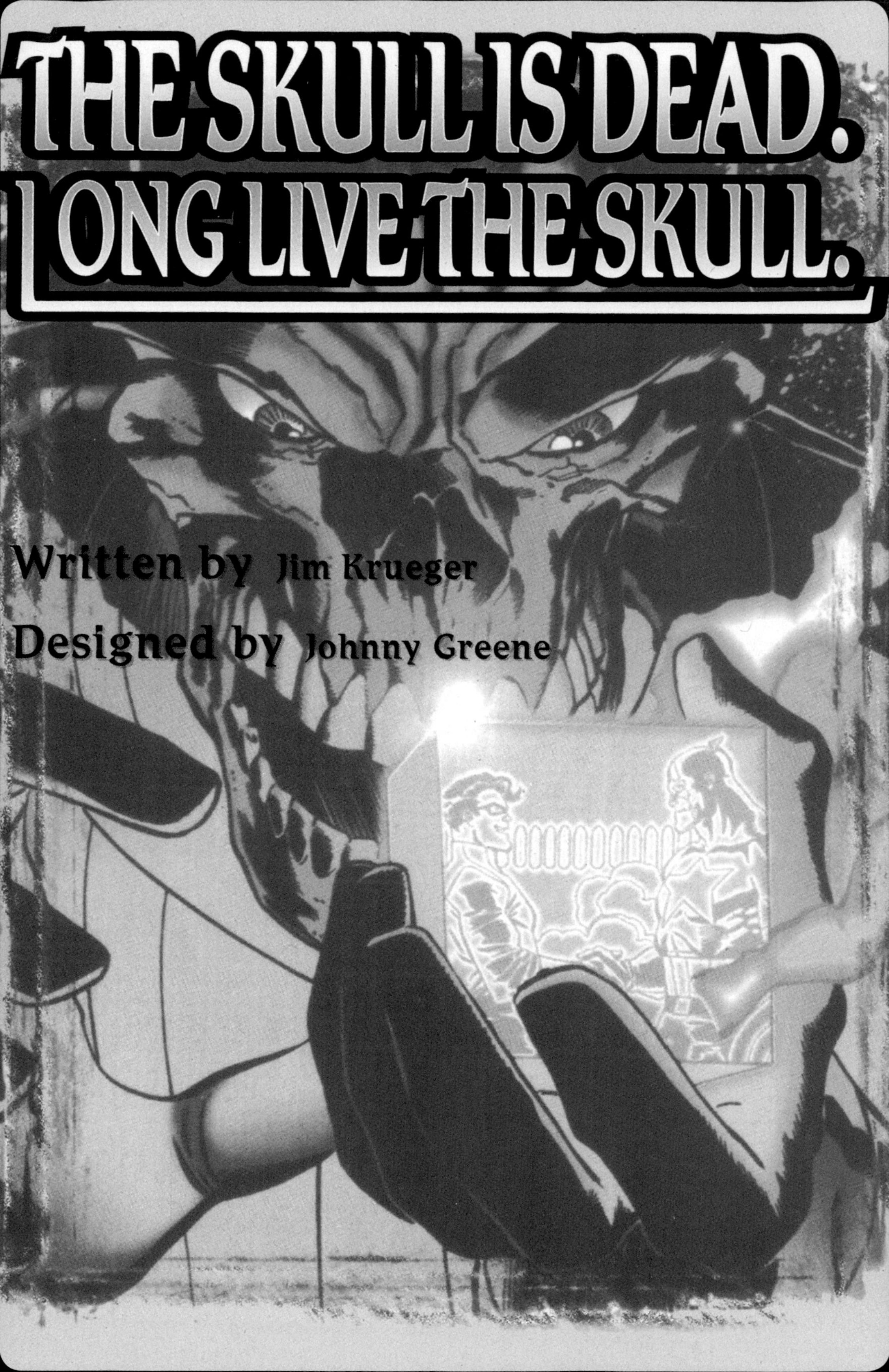

Written by Jim Krueger

Designed by Johnny Greene

CAPTAIN AMERICA #12 **BACKUP FEATURE**

For the last several months, a mysterious black shadow has wafted in and out of these pages. For newer readers, this is a mystery to plunder. For those of you who enjoyed the adventures of Captain America before Heroes Reborn, you know that this shadow is the last remnant of Captain America's archenemy. As we prepare to bring this fellow back in a big, big way, we thought it might be helpful to present to you the life history of Cap's greatest foe... the Red Skull.

He has been called the most evil man who ever lived. The symbol of hate. The incarnation of torture. A bane to all those who would live free from tyranny. And therefore, it should come as no surprise that he is the sworn enemy of the land of the free's protector of liberty, Captain America.

But who is the Red Skull and why is he the archetype of villainy? Why is "evil" the word chosen to most define him? And why won't this specter of the past ever resist the urge to torment humanity?

The Red Skull was born Johann Schmidt. Ironically, Steve Rogers and Johann Schmidt could have been brothers. Both came from poverty. Both suffered rejection for their lack of strength and power. And both were chosen to become more than average men.

But unlike the man who would become Captain America, Johann was born into hatred as much as poverty. Were it not for the doctor who delivered him, Johann would have been murdered, only minutes after being born, by his own father. Johann's father, a man whose senses had long been dulled by the siren call of alcohol, blamed the child for the death of its mother. Martha was the wife Hermann Schmidt repeatedly beat and abused yet claimed to love.

Hermann killed himself the next day. The doctor took Johann to an orphanage where the child remained until the age of seven. Seven years is the age of reason, some say. To Johann, it was the age of madness.

Johann took to the streets. What his begging failed to provide, he stole. The nights not spent under the blanket of the cold German skies were spent in prison for various petty crimes.

As a young man, Johann went to work for a shopkeeper, a Jewish businessman whose daughter was perhaps the only person who ever showed Johann any kindness at all. When she rebuffed his affections, he rewarded her kindness by killing her.

This was Johann's first murder. More, it was his first moment of... joy.

As a bellboy in an era pregnant with the hint and rumor of war, Johann was given the "honor" of serving refreshments to certain members of the growing ranks of the Third Reich, including Adolf Hitler.

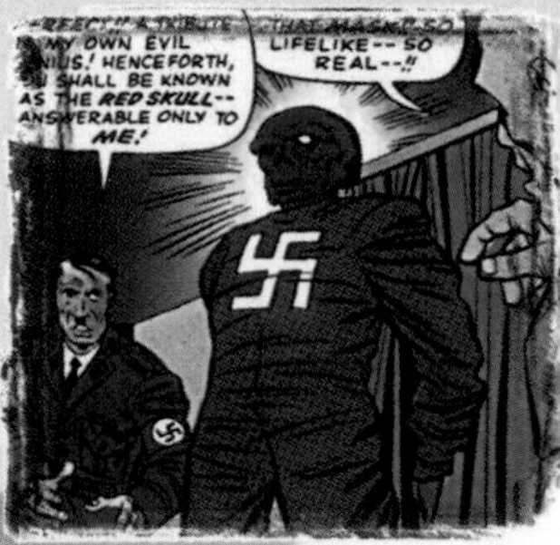
MY OWN EVIL
HENCEFORTH,
SHALL BE KNOWN
AS THE RED SKULL--
ANSWERABLE ONLY TO
ME!
LIFELIKE-- SO
REAL--!!

Hitler saw something of himself in the young man and decided to mentor the bellhop in all things murderous. He gave the boy a mask, a mask the color of blood.

And so... the Red Skull was born.

The Skull commanded many covert operations for Hitler, anything that required the absence of mercy and the vindictive joy of killing. Secret bases all over the world were funded by the Reich for the Skull's purposes. The Skull's subversive missions in the United States were so costly that the United States created a soldier to stop him... Captain America.

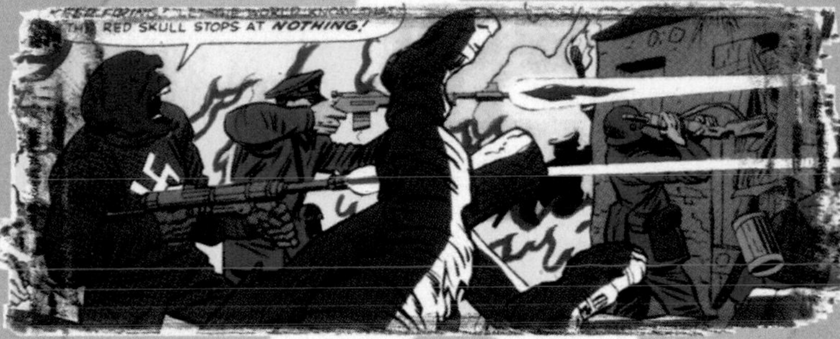
RED SKULL STOPS AT NOTHING!

Hitler's pride in creating the Skull, in time, turned to jealous fear. Hitler had believed he had seen something of himself in that bellboy's eyes years before. But he was wrong. The Red Skull by this point had risen within the ranks to become Hitler's second-in-command. And Hitler knew this man who once served him would not rest until he himself was Uberman. Until he himself was the master of the Master Race.

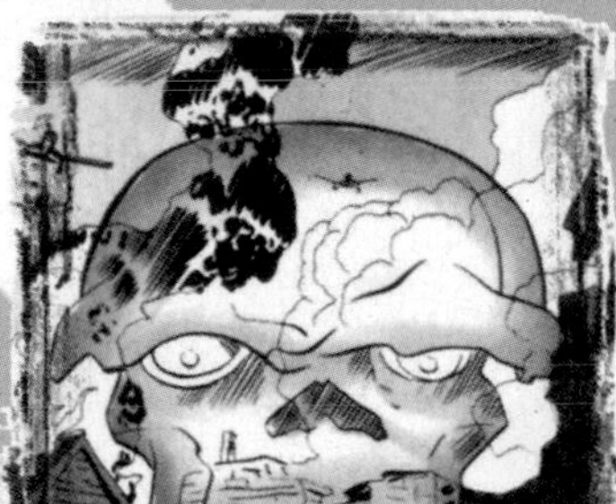

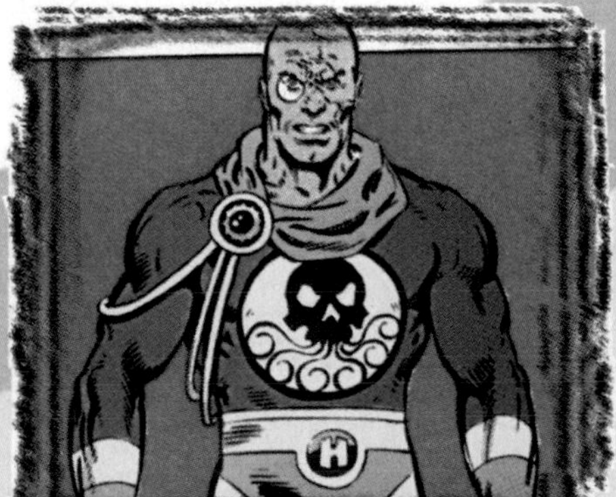

Baron Wolfgang Von Strucker, one of Hitler's greatest officers in the Reich, had fallen from Hitler's grace. But not from the Skull's. The Skull sent him to Japan to create a subversive organization that would one day be known as HYDRA.

Hitler's paranoia regarding the Skull and his own limitations led to the decision that should he not win the world, he would destroy it.

This resulted in the creation of a number of weapons that were buried only to resurface years later. These were robots of mass destruction known as Sleepers.

These doomsday weapons were "lost" when Captain America tracked the Skull down to his hidden bunker and defeated him. The Skull, spitting his vengeance through blood and broken bone, was caught in a cave-in. He was believed lost forever.

This was the first death of The Red Skull.

The Red Skull, unknowingly, had become a Sleeper himself. For the cave-in released an experimental gas that so slowed the Skull's aging process that he virtually became an immortal. It was during this state of suspended animation that his wounds slowly healed.

Then, a number of years later, a research team found the body of the Skull, and revived him. The war was long over, and with the Fuhrer dead, the Skull now had no one to bow to. He would rule the world.

Ironically, Captain America had also fallen into suspended animation towards the end of World War Two only to be revived years later. So when the Skull attempted to conquer the world through the Sleepers, exiled remnants from the past war, and HYDRA, his attempts at world domination were thwarted by the revived Captain America.

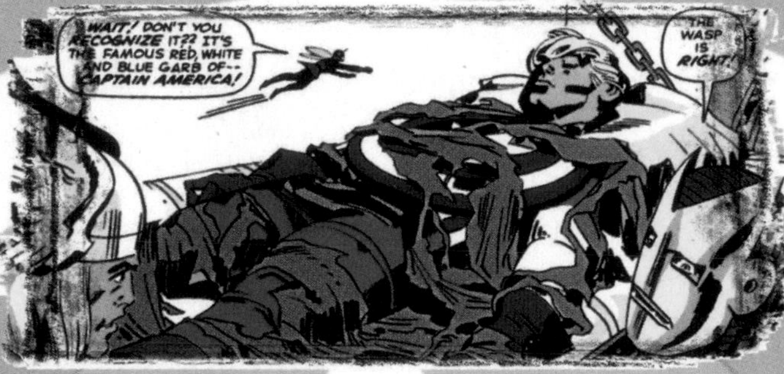

WAIT! DON'T YOU RECOGNIZE IT?? IT'S THE FAMOUS RED, WHITE AND BLUE GARB OF-- CAPTAIN AMERICA!
THE WASP IS RIGHT!

He failed. And so his hatred grew again.

His hatred at last found the vehicle for which he had yearned in the Cosmic Cube. This creation of another secret organization known as AIM had the power to make its holder's imagination become reality. It made ideas happen. If the Skull thought it, it was.

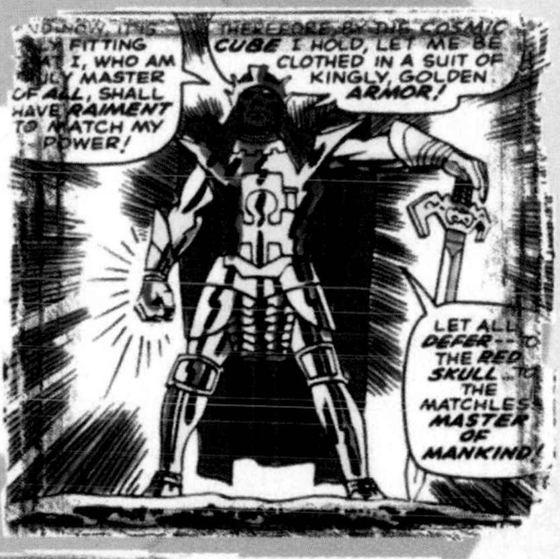

FITTING I, WHO AM MASTER OF ALL, SHALL HAVE RAIMENT TO MATCH MY POWER!
CUBE I HOLD, LET ME BE CLOTHED IN A SUIT OF KINGLY, GOLDEN ARMOR!
LET ALL DEFER--TO THE RED SKULL--THE MATCHLESS MASTER OF MANKIND!

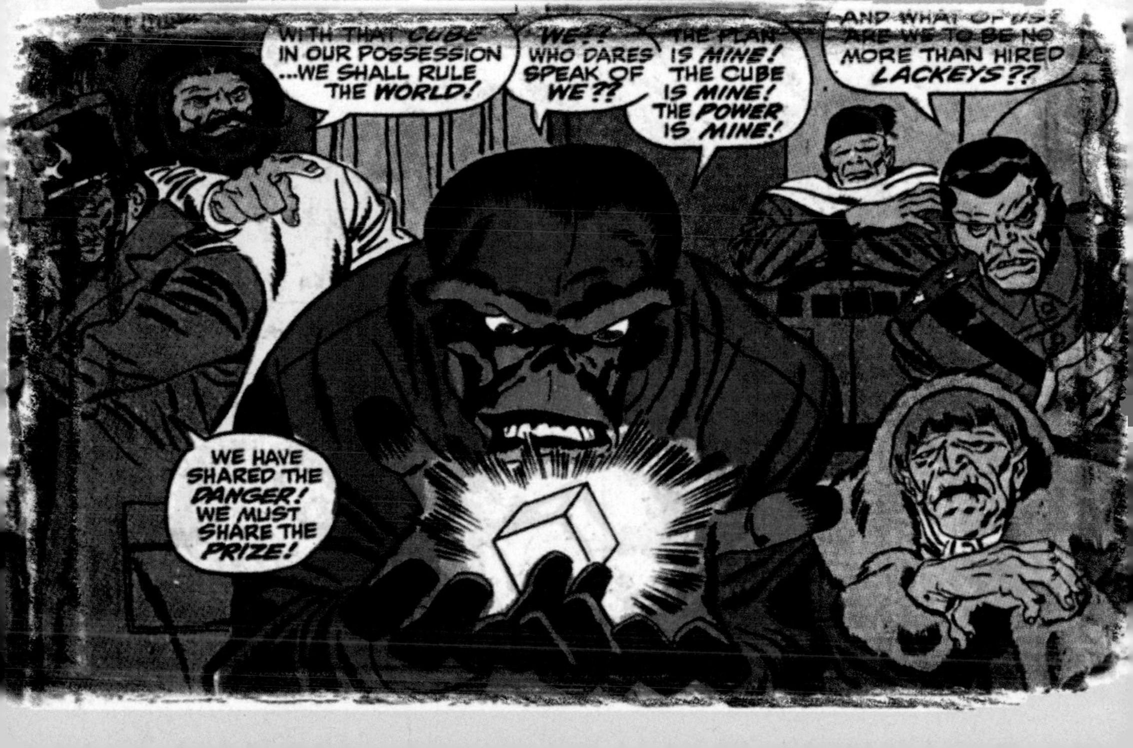

WITH THAT CUBE IN OUR POSSESSION ...WE SHALL RULE THE WORLD!
WE?? WHO DARES SPEAK OF WE??
THE PLAN IS MINE! THE CUBE IS MINE! THE POWER IS MINE!
AND WHAT OF US? ARE WE TO BE NO MORE THAN HIRED LACKEYS??
WE HAVE SHARED THE DANGER! WE MUST SHARE THE PRIZE!

But hate is a consuming blindness. Twice, the Cosmic Cube was lost by the Skull. During his second possession of the Cube, its power was used for purposes other than world domination. Soon the Skull used it to try to discredit Captain America, by having his own mind switched with that of the Captain. This plan failed as a result of Cap's new ally, the Falcon.

Over the years, the Skull's obsession with Captain America so overshadowed his desires for conquest that Cap's demise became the Red Skull's sole aim in life. And death.

The Skull discovered that the gas that had kept him from aging was now failing to sustain him. He had little time left. But time enough for hate. The Skull over the years had struck at Captain America through many of Cap's friends, believing that friendship and love were the weaknesses inherent in Captain America's indomitable spirit.

Using brainwashing techniques, he tricked one of Captain America's allies into dousing Cap's food and drink with an aging formula that would inflict upon Captain America the same dread destiny that refused to let go of the Skull.

But even as the two age-old enemies fought what both believed to be their final battle, a fight that spanned over 50 years of conflict, Captain America refused to give in to the hatred the Skull had so long ago given himself to. Cap chose mercy, while hate remained the Skull's only god.

Captain America was miraculously saved and rejuvenated. And the Skull was cremated. But miracles were not reserved only for Steve Rogers. The Skull awoke in a different body than the one in which he died. He awoke in a body cloned from Captain America himself. He awoke with the hated face of his own enemy and the superhuman strength of a super soldier.

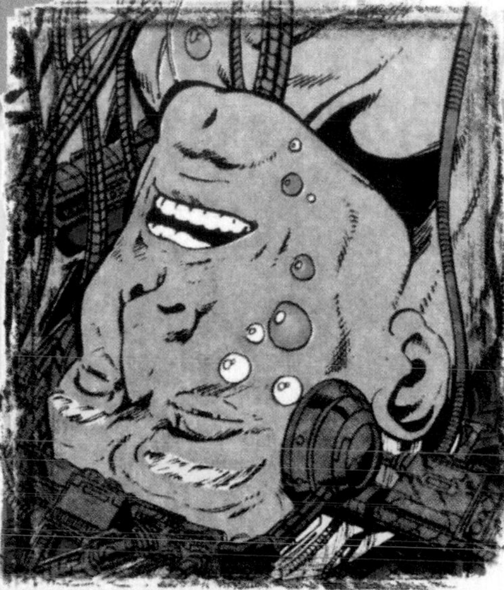

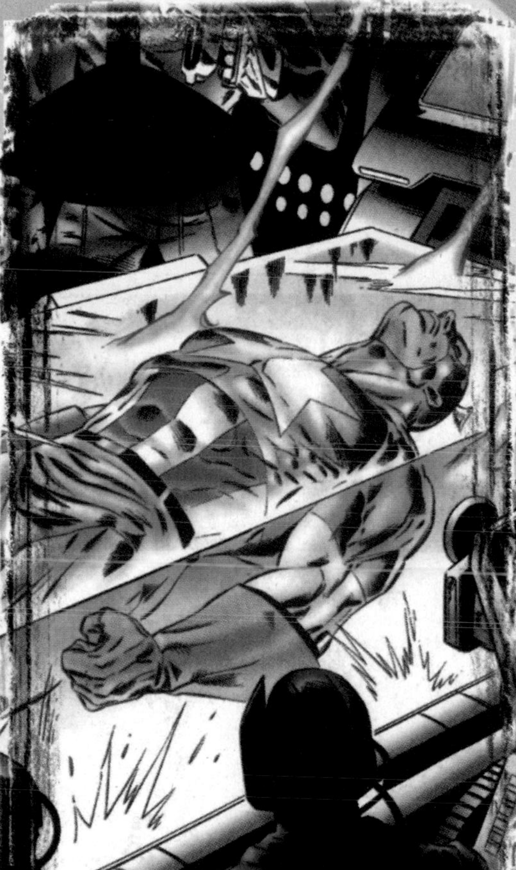

This face, though, would be denied to the Red Skull as the Skull's own "Death Dust" burned the flesh of his face, a loss that ended in the Red Skull's appearance becoming truly that of a red skull. There would be no more masks.

In time, the Super Soldier formula which gave Captain America his powers became like a cancer and began to eat away at Liberty's greatest protector. Cap would have died... were it not for a mysterious blood transfusion from the only blood in existence that also coursed with the Super Soldier Formula — his own. The very cloned blood that coursed through the Red Skull.

Why had the Red Skull saved his enemy, the very man he hated more than life itself?

Perhaps the answer was that the Skull, at last, had found a way to defeat his enemy. There was now something inside Captain America that was also the Skull's. And though the Skull was defeated again, seemingly atomized by the power of the Cosmic Cube, his hatred still flows today in the veins of Captain America.

What effects this will have in the future are unknown.

What is known, though, is the fact that hate still exists in the world. And so, the Red Skull may yet still live.

And so, the final fate of the Skull was written, until his "return" in our very first issue. Since peeling himself off the wall, the shadow of the Skull has searched in vain for a way to reconstitute his body, to make himself whole. To begin once again his private war against Captain America — a war which will continue this December!